Reader's Digest

ILLUSTRATED GUIDE
TO SOUTHERN AFRICA

Reader's Digest

ILLUSTRATED GUIDE
TO SOUTHERN AFRICA

Published by The Reader's Digest Association South Africa (Pty) Limited,
Reader's Digest House, 130 Strand Street, Cape Town 8001,
in association with T. V. Bulpin

Front cover: *The familiar outline of Devil's Peak and Table Mountain forms a backdrop to Cape Town's Victoria and Alfred Waterfront — a colourful combination of refurbished Victorian warehouses, hotels, shops, theatres, strolling musicians, hooting ships and barking seals. Photograph: Walter Knirr.*

Back cover: *An early morning stroller is silhouetted against the surf as the sun rises over the Tongaland coast in Natal. Warm seas and a sub-tropical climate have made Natal one of the prime holiday destinations in southern Africa. Photograph: Anthony Bannister.*

Introductory page: *A sight distinctive of Transkei. Tradition allows a married woman the right to smoke a pipe. An unmarried woman may not. Photograph: Alice Mertens.*

Title page: *Pretoria, administrative capital of the Republic of South Africa — a modern city with a rich history, set in a fertile sub-tropical valley. Photograph: Satour.*

Opposite page: *The colour and excitement of the mine dance. These traditional and newly-invented dances, held on Sundays at mine compounds on the Witwatersrand, offer visitors a spectacle that few will forget. Photograph: Satour.*

ISBN 0-947008-99-3

ORIGINAL TEXT: T. V. Bulpin

EDITOR: Vic Mayhew   DESIGNER: John Meek

ASSOCIATE EDITORS: Tony Duncan, Rosemund Handler

EDITORIAL AND PRODUCTION CO-ORDINATOR: Fay Bentley

RESEARCHERS: Monique Bulpin, Edna Colyer, Hilary Mauve, Hilary Rennie, Arthur Rich

CONTENTS

Cape Province

Transvaal

Orange Free State

KwaZulu / Natal

Transkei

Botswana

Lesotho

Swaziland

Namibia

Zimbabwe

How to use
this book

THERE ARE TWO ways in which *The Illustrated Guide To Southern Africa* can be used to help you plan a holiday — through the index and through the maps.

If you wish to read about a particular town, look up the name of the town in the index. This will refer you to the page on which an entry about that town appears, and the chapter containing the entry will provide a great deal of further information relating to neighbouring places of interest and the history of the region.

If you wish to look up a particular touring region, refer to the numbered list of maps in the left-hand column on the page opposite. This list shows the pages on which regional touring maps appear. For example, the Cape Peninsula map, number 2, can be found on page 27.

If you plan to move from one touring region to another, you will find it useful to look at the small inset map that accompanies each regional touring map. Numbers on the inset map indicate neighbouring touring regions. For example, on the Cape Peninsula map there are the numbers 1, 3, 4, 5 and 6. A glance at the list opposite will show that these refer respectively to Cape Town, Cape Flats, Four Passes, Coast of Flowers and Berg River Valley.

The regional touring map show roads, various features of tourist and historical interest, accommodation and garage services available, and population figures. A detailed list of these features appears on the page opposite, in the right-hand column.

Street plans of major cities show historical monuments and other places of interest.

For convenience, the total area of southern Africa has been divided into ten major touring zones — indicated in capital letters on the map below.

These zones have been demarcated so as to be of most use to the tourist and the holiday-maker, and they differ in places from the provincial boundaries. For example, although the Transkei region is politically a part of the Eastern Cape, it has been treated as a separate touring zone. Similarly, in the province of KwaZulu/Natal, KwaZulu – 'the place of the Zulu' – refers to the Zulu Kingdom, and Natal to the remainder of the province.

Copyright in the map opposite, and in the zone-introduction maps, is held by The Reader's Digest Association South Africa (Pty) Limited.

MAP REFERENCES
North pointer

INDEX MAPS
Map coverage and index to adjoining sheets

BAR SCALE

Dual carriageway
National road with route number
Trunk road
Main road
Main road untarred
Secondary and minor road
Mountain pass, height and gradient
Railway
International boundary
Provincial boundary
National park, game or nature reserve
River with waterfall
Dam, pan or lake
Forest reserve
Rest camp
Place of interest
Lighthouse
Spot height in metres
Custom or border control post
Airport
Shark net
Shipwreck
Battlefield
Wild flower area

CITY OR TOWN FACILITIES
Hotel and garage
Hotel only
Garage only
No facilities

CITY OR TOWN POPULATIONS
More than 200 000
5 000—50 000
Fewer than 5 000

TOWN PLANS
Through-route
Other street
Place of interest
National monument
AA office

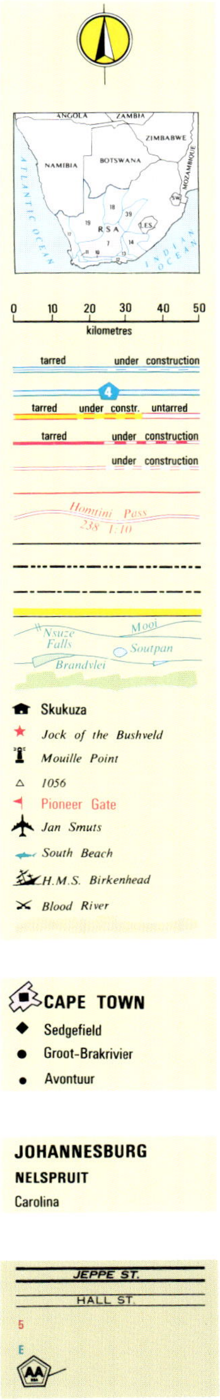

Skukuza
Jock of the Bushveld
Mouille Point
△ 1056
Pioneer Gate
Jan Smuts
South Beach
H.M.S. Birkenhead
Blood River

CAPE TOWN
◆ Sedgefield
● Groot-Brakrivier
● Avontuur

JOHANNESBURG
NELSPRUIT
Carolina

JEPPE ST.
HALL ST.

ACKNOWLEDGMENT
Touring maps and town plans in this book, and the maps shown on pages 10 and 11, were compiled and drawn by The Automobile Association of South Africa which organization holds the sole copyright authority.

Maps reproduced under Government Printer's copyright authority 5908 of 13/5/77.

Land of sunshine and scenic majesty

The world's strangest and most dramatic landscapes...nature's richest treasure chest of gold and diamonds...a unique wealth of animal and plant life...a kaleidoscope of exotic, sun-blessed peoples...can there be a land anywhere else on earth more enticing for the traveller than southern Africa?

Nature's tools of creation — the wind, sun, ice and rain — have worked a special magic. Controlled by the cold Benguela Current on the west and the warm Mocambique Current on the east, the climate has sculptured extremes of deserts, savannas, snow-covered mountains, grasslands, high forests and tropical mangrove swamps.

Within these climatic zones earth's most diverse plant population flourishes. In the deserts are drought-resistant plants and in the swamplands are mangroves with their roots deep in mud and water. There are baobabs,

Bird's-eye view of southern Africa — scenic magnificence beneath a beneficent sun. This is an exhilarating land of fertile plains, towering mountains and tropical splendour lying wedged between the foaming shores of two oceans.

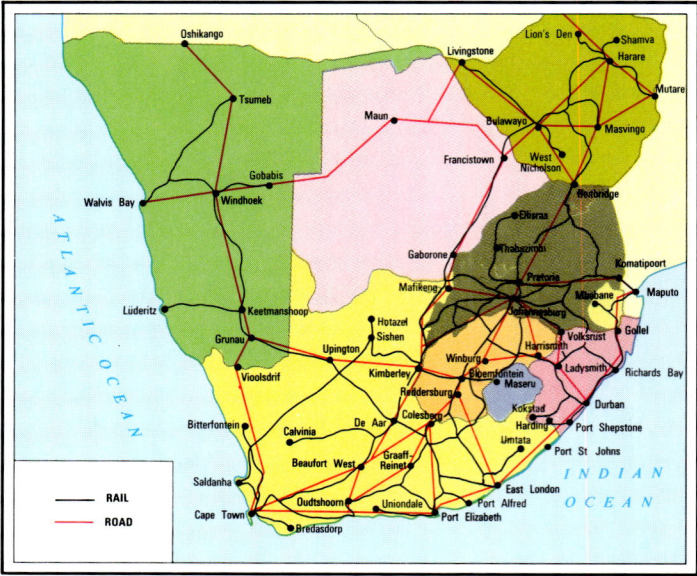

South Africa, Namibia, Zimbabwe, Botswana, Swaziland and Lesotho make up an excitingly varied tourist area, all in one fairly compact region. Most attractions are accessible by road and rail.

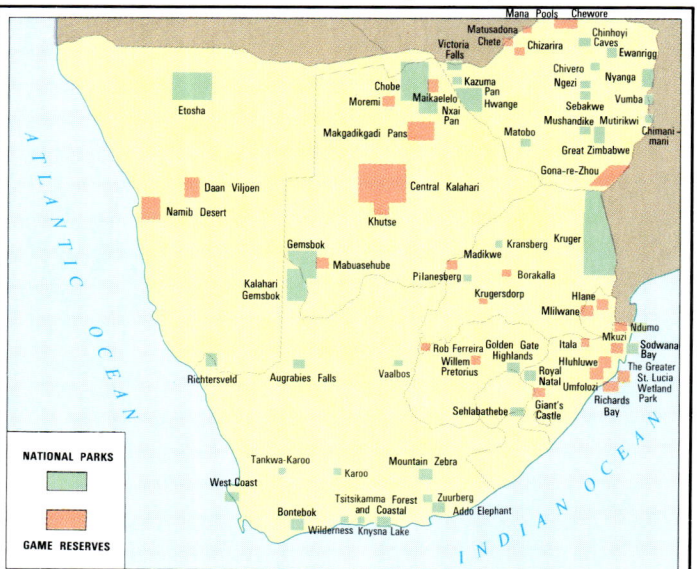

Here are the largest and most varied game sanctuaries in the world — protected and untamed areas where animals of every kind and description roam free, as savage and beautiful as they were in the beginning of time.

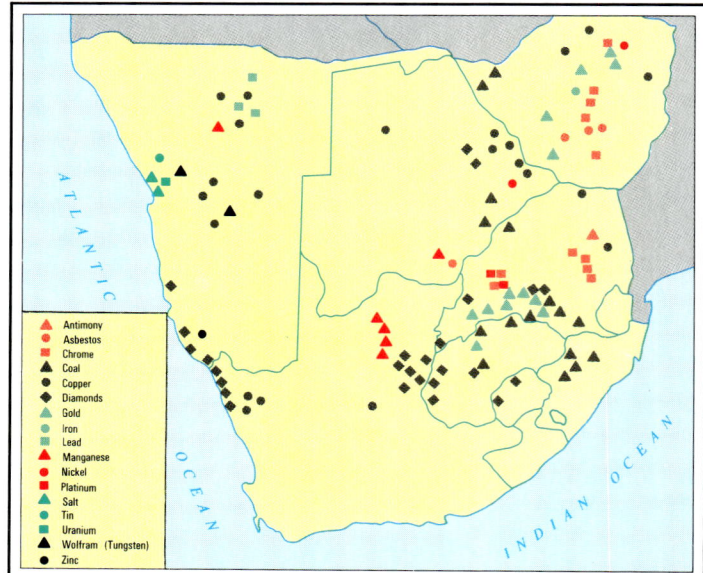

Gold, diamonds, copper, chrome, lead, tin, coal — only some of the abundant riches mined from the vast treasure houses of the continent. Minerals of every kind to meet the insatiable demands of the world all abound here.

acacia trees, brilliant seasonal spectacles such as the musasa trees in the spring and the barlinka vines of autumn.

This land, too, is the home of big game, and hosts of birds as varied as the vast range of habitats and foods that nature has prepared for them.

Southern Africa is still home to the mysterious San, whose legends seem to go back to the beginning of life itself, and to the descendants of the Iron Age peoples who wandered down from the far north during the last thousand years. Here too are peoples whose ancestors journeyed from East and West bringing with them influences good and bad, innumerable subtleties of thought and ideas, and a complex range of life-styles, foods and customs.

Their legacy is one of the most scenically dramatic, healthiest and challenging regions of the world.

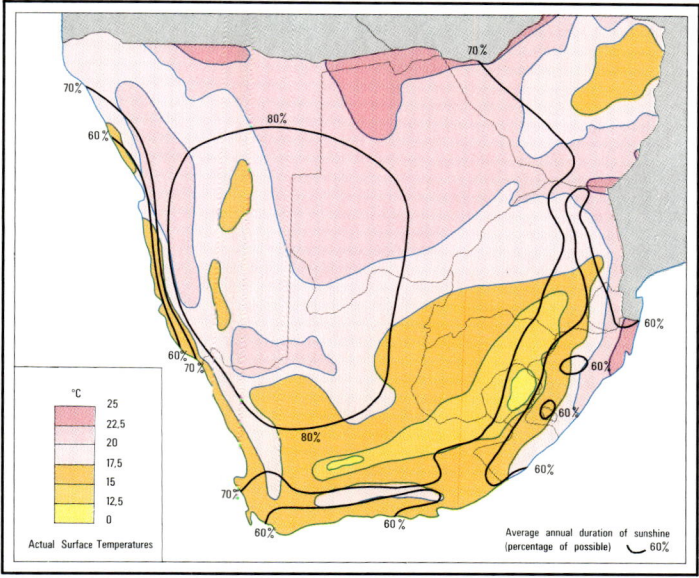

Land of sunshine — places for all seasons — a year-round playground in which to enjoy the great outdoors. Southern Africa has thousands of kilometres of unspoilt countryside, deserts, mountains and rivers — all blessed by the sun.

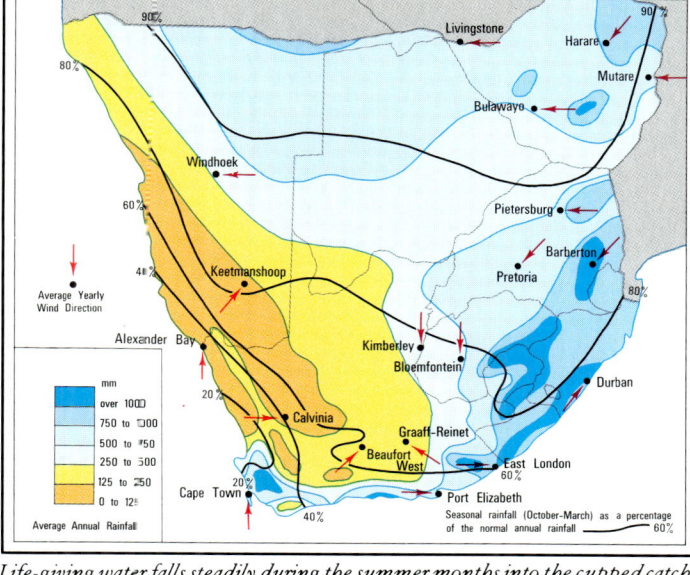

Life-giving water falls steadily during the summer months into the cupped catchment areas. Hail is not uncommon in certain regions. Winter rainfall is soft and steady. Winds are generally mild except along the Cape coasts.

Journey from the present into the past. In southern Africa are people emerging from another age, still observing ancient customs and traditions. The clans, languages, cultures and customs all form a kaleidoscope of colourful contrast.

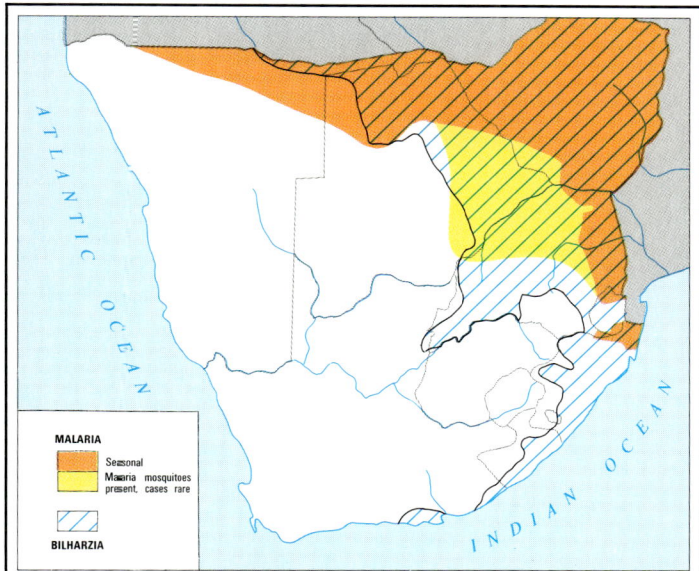

Bilharzia and malaria have taken their terrible toll of human life. Suitable precautionary measures such as avoidance of contact with bilharzia-infected water and the taking of prophylactic drugs for malaria will obviate these dangers.

CAPE PROVINCE

CAPE PROVINCE

Contents:

SIR FRANCIS DRAKE, in the *Golden Hind,* rounded the Cape in 1580. In the ship's log appears this sentence: 'This Cape is the most stately thing and the fairest Cape we saw in the whole circumference of the earth.' Yet from the deck of the *Golden Hind* Drake was able to see only a very small fraction of the splendours of what we now know as the Cape Province. This is by far the largest province of South Africa, has the longest coastline, and also the greatest variety of magnificent scenery.

From the deserts in the west to the beautiful high forest of the east, it is an area of great contrasts in climate, geography, and animal and plant life. Groves of date palms grow in the west; in the east, grassy hills roll down to meet the forests that fringe the coast.

On the central plateau lies the semi-arid Karoo, with its vast sheep runs, wind-pumps and flat-topped hillocks — the famous koppies that provide South Africa with its most characteristic scenic emblem. In the far south-west of the province, the continent of Africa ends almost exactly as it begins thousands of kilometres to the north, with a Mediterranean climate of winter rain and dry summers, and folded snow-tipped mountains strangely reminiscent of the Atlas range in the north.

The Cape Province offers excellent roads, and freedom from the widespread African blights of malarial mosquitoes, tsetse flies and bilharzia. There are superlative beaches, ranging from the sweeping shores of Muizenberg, Plettenberg Bay, St. Francis Bay and Algoa Bay, to the beautiful intimate coast around East London, with its warm, safe water, lazy lagoons, rivers, and green forests crowding close to the edge of the sea.

The whole province is a happy hunting ground for the naturalist — the collector of shells or semi-precious stones, the observer of wildlife, the botanist. For the historian there are the artifacts and rock art of the original San inhabitants. For the gourmet there are wines, fruits, and intriguing local dishes.

For the climber and the walker there are the mountains — the wilderness trails, the crystal pools, the caves and the balancing rocks of the richly coloured Cedarberg range; the dramatic views over Cape Town and Table Bay from Table Mountain and Devil's Peak; the wild-flower paradise of the Hottentots-Holland Mountains and the grandeur of the Groot Drakenstein range.

The Hex River Mountains, Du Toit's Kloof, Jonkershoek, Langeberg, Tsitsikama, Baviaanskloof and the massive, little-visited southern extension of the Drakensberg — all offer endless possibilities for adventure and exploration.

Anglers can fish for big game off the Cape of Good Hope or for the teeming yellowtail in False Bay. Surfers will find majestic breakers at Cape St. Francis and Supertubes in Jeffreys Bay.

For many people, the Cape Province is a special heaven, a place of spectacular beauty and excitement.

Preceding page: The Hex River Valley in autumn, with the barlinka grapevines turning red. On the right are the Hex River Mountains; on the left, the Kwadousberg.

The Cape Province has been divided into 17 touring regions, each marked on this map with a purple border. Turn to the page indicated (large purple numbers) for a detailed map of each region, plus extensive touring information.

NAMIBIA

BOTSWANA

Nossob

Molopo

Mmabatho
282

TRANSVAAL

Molopo

282

282
Harts

171

Upington

ORANGE FREE STATE

Orange

Vaal

Kimberley

181

Springbok

LESOTHO

ATLANTIC OCEAN

163
7

1

CAPE PROVINCE

153

TRANSKEI

Olifants

Clanwilliam

79

Cradock

Beaufort West

143

Kei

Bisho

Saldanha

41 73
123

Fish

East London
156

Worcester

112
Oudtshoorn

Grahamstown

Paarl

Sundays

Cape Town
18

Stellenbosch
48

Swellendam

George 102
Knysna

132

2

27
Strand

94
2

Mossel Bay

Port Elizabeth
136

Simon's Town

61
Bredasdorp

INDIAN OCEAN

THE TAVERN OF THE SEAS

CAPE TOWN, THE mother city of South Africa, nestles in one of the most dramatic scenic settings of any city on earth. Cradled by the imposing bulk of Table Mountain, Devil's Peak and Lion's Head, this is the famed Tavern of the Seas — a vital haven for the world's seafarers.

The city was born on 6 April 1652. On that day, Jan van Riebeeck dropped anchor in Table Bay and gazed in wonder at Table Mountain. On the following day he hoisted the Dutch flag. Soon he had built an earthen-walled fort and had planted a garden of fruit and vegetables. The settlement had begun to grow. Table Mountain, often visible far out to sea, now beckoned like the gigantic sign of an inn. Here was shelter from the stormy seas. Meat, vegetables, fruit and wine could be bought, ships could be repaired, and the sick could be cared for in a large hospital.

Before Van Riebeeck landed, others had long lived in the blue shadow of the mountain. They were Khoikhoi pastoralists, with flocks of fat-tailed sheep; San hunters, who lived off game animals; and primitive beachcombers, who searched the shores for seafood. Of their origin only a few tantalizing clues remained — bones, fragments of ancient tools, and myths that had somehow survived the graveyard of the past.

Legends of earlier visitors also lingered. Phoenicians and Arabs from the days of Sindbad the Sailor are reputed to have been among the many who foundered in storms off the Cape Peninsula. Others are said to have found the eggs of giant birds on the shores of Table Bay.

Today Cape Town remains the great tavern of the seas. Countless ships have used its valuable docks. The mammoth tankers that round the Cape of Good Hope each day, too huge for easy docking, continue on their course while supplies are delivered from helicopters.

The city is one of the world's primary export ports for fruit. It is a major base for fishing, and a principal container port of southern Africa. In its cosmopolitan population and atmosphere the cultures, foods and colours of East and West are blended. And its past, present and promising future create an air of romance, vitality and excitement.

THINGS TO DO AND SEE

Angling Maasbanker and mackerel are numerous in the warmer waters in Table Bay in summer.

Climbing Cape Town is the home of the Mountain Club of South Africa. It advises on climbs in the area.

Music, ballet The Cape Town Symphony Orchestra performs in the Old City Hall. Concerts are also held at the Baxter Theatre on the University of Cape Town campus in Rosebank and in Muizenberg pavilion. The Nico Malan complex offers opera, ballet, theatre and music.

Sailing The Royal Cape Yacht Club has its headquarters in Table Bay. One of the main events in the yachting calendar is the South Atlantic Race, run every third January.

Sports Green Point is the scene of most of the sporting activity closest to the city centre. Tennis, soccer, bowls, hockey, squash, rugby, cricket and golf are played here. The Atlantic Underwater Club is based on Green Point Common.

Soccer is played at Hartleyvale, in the suburb of Observatory, and in the Green Point Stadium. Newlands is the home of international rugby, cricket and swimming.

Walking There are paths on the slopes of Table Mountain, Devil's Peak, Lion's Head and Signal Hill.

The heart of the 300-year-old city, with the Atlantic Ocean visible beyond Kloof Nek.

Like a display of diamonds, the lights of Cape Town shimmer around the bay in the hazy pink glow of a clear winter's evening.

Adderley Street

The principal street and the centre of Cape Town, Adderley Street is named after Sir Charles Adderley, a British parliamentarian who, in 1850, led the successful opposition against a British plan to establish a penal settlement at the Cape.

Notable buildings in Adderley Street include the Groote Kerk (great church), the parent of the Dutch Reformed Church in southern Africa and the oldest church in the Republic of South Africa. It was completed in 1704 and has twice been enlarged. The church contains a wooden pulpit elaborately carved by Anton Anreith.

At the south-western end of Adderley Street is the lodge that housed slaves who worked in the garden of the Dutch East India Company. The lodge is now the South African Cultural History Museum. Among its exhibits is a unique display of furniture and household items of early Cape Town. Also displayed are arms, maritime exhibits, coins and silver, costumes, and Malay arts and crafts.

Other buildings of interest in Adderley Street include the Heerengracht Hotel and the imposing modern Golden Acre, with its weather-protected shopping area. The Woolworth's store in Adderley Street marks the site of Cape Town's first trading centre.

Here too is the modern railway station, southern terminus of the rail-

The growing city: an engraving of Cape Town printed in 1867.

FATHER OF THE MOTHER CITY

Jan van Riebeeck is a great father figure in South African history. He was born at Culemborg, Holland, in 1619 and at 21 joined the Dutch East India Company as an assistant surgeon. He was sent to Batavia (now Djakarta), where he changed his occupation to assistant clerk.

Van Riebeeck and his wife, Maria.

He was recalled to Holland in 1647 after trouble about his involvement in private trading. He left the company, married Maria de la Queillerie, and embarked on several private trading voyages to Greenland and the West Indies. His relationship with the Dutch East India Company had remained cordial, and in 1651 he accepted the leadership of a proposed settlement at the Cape.

With his wife and infant son he boarded the flagship *Drommedaris* and sailed from Holland on 24 December 1651, accompanied by the *Reyger* and the *Goede Hoop*.

On 5 April 1652 Table Mountain loomed into view over the horizon. Usually it took at least 120 days to reach the Cape from Europe, but the three ships had completed the voyage in 104 days with the deaths of only two people, and little serious sickness.

Just before sunset of the next day the three ships entered Table Bay. It was empty and calm. The next day Van Riebeeck went ashore to select the sites of a fort and vegetable garden. He worked diligently, and soon passing seamen were able to replenish supplies in plenty. Cape Town was established as 'the Tavern of the Seas'.

He was promoted to commander in 1654 and remained as the head of the settlement until 7 May 1662, when he was again transferred to Batavia. His wife died there and he remarried. He eventually became secretary of the Council of India and died in 1677.

Always hoping for higher rank, he had never realized that his place in history was assured as the founder of the settlement at the Cape, and that it was to be in South Africa where he would be most honoured.

The castle whose guns have never been fired in anger

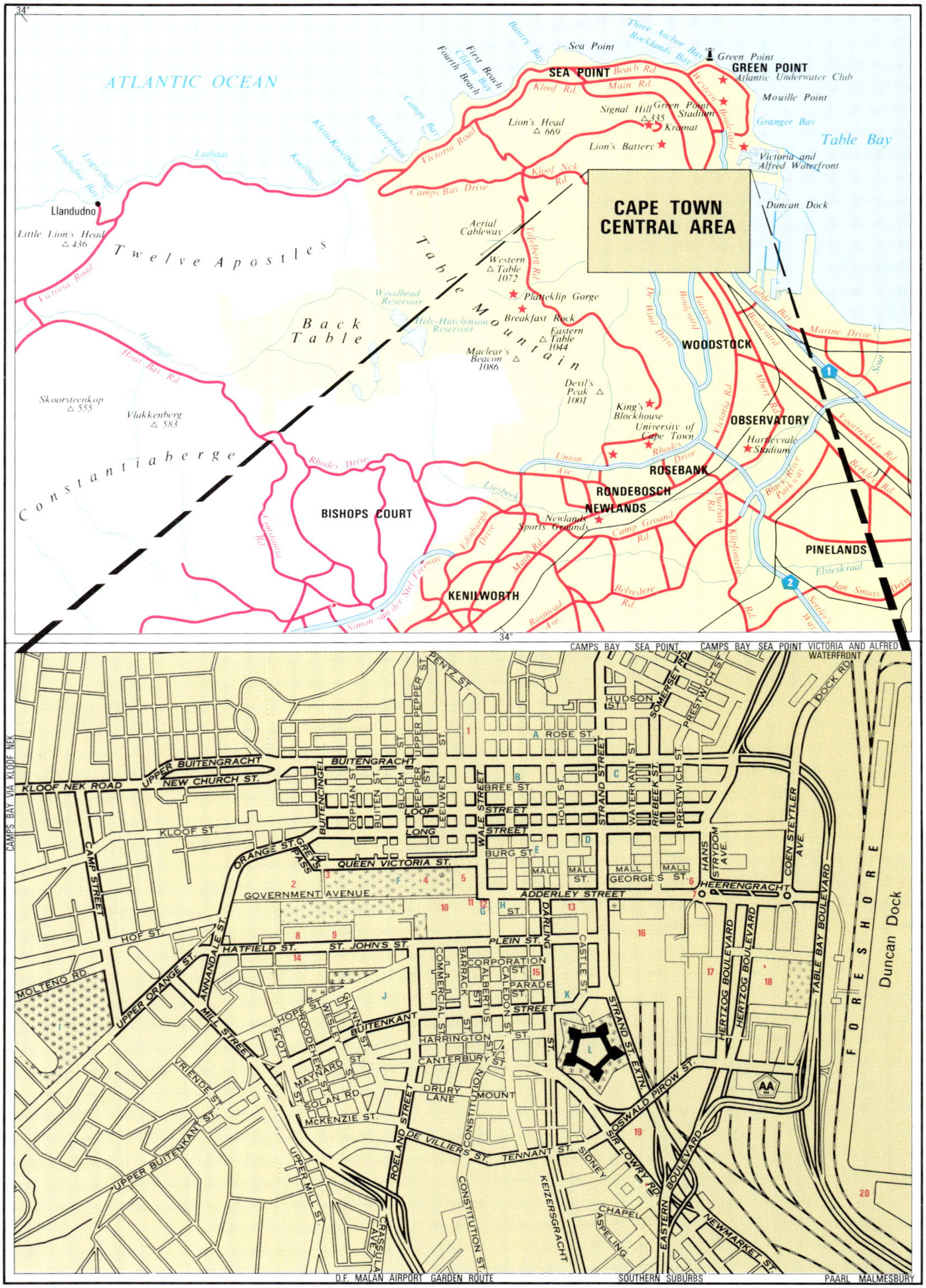

National Monuments
A Malay Quarter
B St. Stephen's Church and Riebeeck Square
C Lutheran Church, Martin Melck House and Sexton's House
D Koopmans De Wet House
E Old Town House and Greenmarket Square
F Company's Garden
G Old Supreme Court
H Groote Kerk (Dutch Reformed Church)
I De Waal Park
J Rust en Vreugd
K Grand Parade
L Castle

Places of interest
1 Bo-Kaap Museum
2 South African Museum
3 Conservatory
4 Cecil John Rhodes Statue
5 St. George's Cathedral
6 Medical Centre
7 Jan van Riebeeck Statue
8 Jewish Museum
9 South African National Gallery
10 Houses of Parliament
11 Queen Victoria Statue
12 South African Cultural History Museum
13 Golden Acre
14 Mountain Club of South Africa
15 Old City Hall
16 Railway Station
17 Civic Centre
18 Nico Malan Theatre Complex
19 Good Hope Centre
20 Royal Cape Yacht Club

City and surroundings map scale

0   1   2   3   4   5
kilometres

City central area map scale

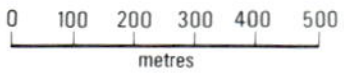

0 100 200 300 400 500
metres

way network of southern Africa. On the concourse of the station stands South Africa's first locomotive, a handsome 'puffing billy' built in Scotland in 1859 and shipped out in pieces to Cape Town.

In front of the Medical Centre, where Adderley Street runs into the Heerengracht, is a small bronze ship dedicated to Robert Falcon Scott — the famed Scott of the Antarctic — who stopped in Cape Town before sailing to his death in the icy wastes far to the south.

Castle of Good Hope

The Castle, near the site of Van Riebeeck's fort, was built between 1666 and 1679 in the shape of a five-pointed star, with walls of stone and earth more than 10 metres high.

Five bastions were built, one at each point of the star, and named after the titles of the Prince of Orange, the Dutch ruler at the time of the settlement. The bastions are named Buren,

Leerdam, Oranje, Nassau and Katzenellenbogen. Each bastion contained living quarters or storerooms. Dungeons were built below sea level.

No attack has ever been launched against the Castle.

Today the Castle is the headquarters of the Western Cape Military Command. It also houses a military and a maritime museum.

Facing the gateway to the Castle is the governor's house, known as the Kat. Its decorous balcony has a wrought-iron balustrade and is flanked by curved steps. From the balcony proclamations and criminal sentences were read. The Kat is now the home of a superb collection of paintings and antiques.

Company's Garden

Situated in the heart of the city, this delightful botanical garden occupies less than 6 hectares of the 18 hectare vegetable garden originally laid out by the Dutch East India Company,

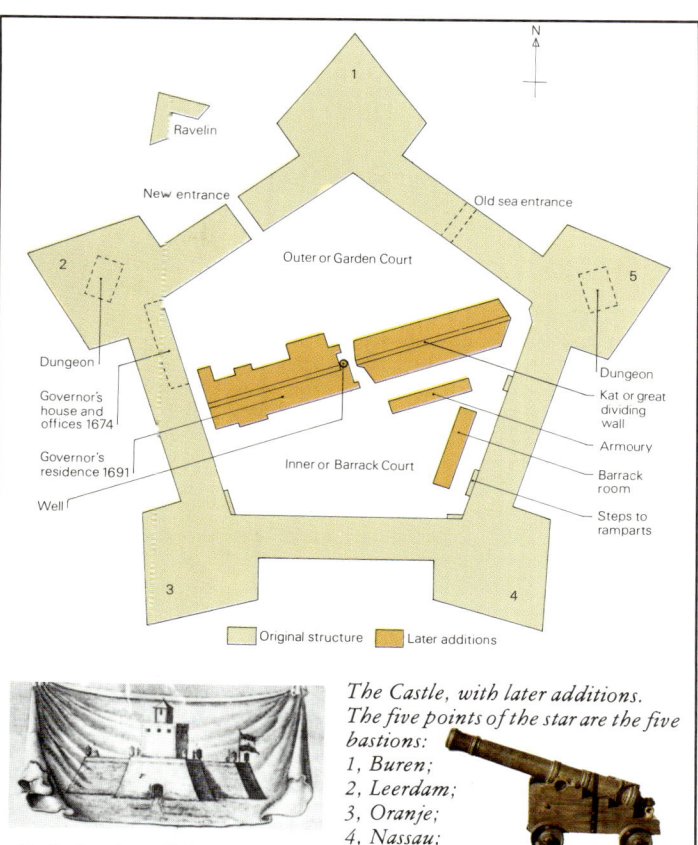

The Castle, with later additions. The five points of the star are the five bastions:
1, Buren;
2, Leerdam;
3, Oranje;
4, Nassau;
5, Katzenellenbogen.

Early drawing of the Fort.

A view of Adderley Street, Cape Town's principal street, as it was in 1870.

South Africa's first locomotive, a 'puffing billy' which now stands on the concourse of Cape Town's railway station. The loco was shipped in pieces from Scotland and assembled in South Africa. The large roof was fitted to give protection from the sun.

The Old Town House, home of the Michaelis collection of paintings.

The garden from which bloomed one of earth's loveliest cities

and developed as a source of fresh produce for the crews of passing ships.

The change from an agricultural to a pleasure and botanical garden occurred gradually as produce became available from newly settled farmers. Trees, flowers, ponds and lawns were added. Governor Simon van der Stel directed the planting of oaks. Now more than 8 000 varieties of trees and plants from all over the world are collected here. The large conservatory at the upper end of the grounds contains many fine orchids and palms. The avenue of oaks that leads through the garden is a favourite walk for Capetonians. Grey squirrels, introduced to South Africa from America by Cecil Rhodes, are abundant and many are so tame that they will accept food from the hands of passersby.

Willem van der Stel, son of Simon and also a governor, built a pleasure lodge in the garden which became the residence of several of his successors, who preferred it to the official quarters at the Kat. The lodge is now the town house of the President of the Republic of South Africa.

Among several statues is one of Cecil Rhodes pointing north. It bears the famous inscription: 'Your hinterland is there'. It was while walking in the garden on 27 December 1889 that Rhodes persuaded Frank Johnson to organize the Pioneer Column that occupied what is now Zimbabwe, Rhodes's most beloved hinterland.

Near the statue is an aviary and an oak tree in which is embedded a water pump high above ground. The pump was slowly wrenched from the ground as the tree grew.

At the southern end of the garden are the South African Museum and the South African National Gallery.

The museum has a unique display of life-sized models of the early San people. Other exhibits include Stone Age implements, a cave tomb and San paintings, and objects recovered from the Zimbabwe Ruins. There are also many displays of traditional African village life. The museum includes a planetarium.

The National Gallery displays a comprehensive collection of South African art of the 19th and 20th centuries and several gift collections, one of which includes work by Romney, Reynolds and Gainsborough.

At the opposite end of the garden are St. George's Cathedral, similar in design to St. Pancras Church in London, and the South African Library, which contains a priceless collection of rare books, among them the oldest book in South Africa, *The Four Gospels*, a manuscript authentically dated about 900.

Devil's Peak

This peak, 1 001 metres high, flanks the eastern side of Table Mountain. It was originally known as the Wind Mountain, but takes its present name from a local legend. Van Hunks, a retired pirate, was said to spend his days sitting beneath a clump of trees at Breakfast Rock, a large boulder on the saddle of land connecting Devil's Peak to Table Mountain. Van Hunks would smoke a mixture of rum-soaked tobacco. One day, so the legend goes, the devil confronted Van Hunks at Breakfast Rock and challenged him to a smoking contest. The contest is said to continue throughout the sum-

The Company's Garden statue of General Smuts.

Before the modern harbour of Table Bay was built this pier reached into the sea across Roggebaai. It was dismantled before the Second World War.

This cast of a postal stone, left by seamen over a parcel of letters in 1635, is displayed in the Strand Concourse where it was found during excavations in 1974.

mer months — in winter Van Hunks suffers from rheumatism and is unable to climb the mountain — and to cause the 'tablecloth' of cloud which sometimes lies on Table Mountain.

On the slopes of Devil's Peak the British, during the first occupation of the Cape, built a trio of small forts. They also dragged an armament of cannon up the slopes and although these were never fired in conflict they remain today, symbolically standing guard over the city, Table Bay and the mountains of the interior.

Foreshore

Few cities have had so generous a gift of a new expanse of open land as Cape Town received in its Foreshore. Before the Second World War, work started on the construction of a new harbour, known as Duncan Dock. The vast quantities of sand dredged up during the building of the dock helped to create 145 hectares of level ground — part of the present Foreshore.

Today it is almost completely built up. Across it runs Table Bay Boulevard, the start of one of the world's most romantic highways — the Cape to Cairo road. On its journey it crosses 7 500 kilometres of Africa.

Notable buildings on the Foreshore include the Nico Malan complex, consisting of the opera house and theatre, and the civic centre.

The Heerengracht is the main thoroughfare through the Foreshore. Where this road leads into Adderley Street are a series of ornamental ponds, much visited by seabirds. The ponds roughly mark the original shoreline of Table Bay. The palm

Cape Town's new Waterfront development is among the world's best.

A disused blockhouse maintains its lonely vigil on Devil's Peak.

Half-way point of the cable-car journey up Table Mountain. In the background is Devil's Peak. Van Hunks, according to legend, met the devil on the saddle between the two peaks, from where the famed 'tablecloth' usually begins to form.

Was the last lion of the Cape shot on these slopes?

The ride in the cable car affords stunning views of Cape Town.

trees growing here are transplanted survivors from the old Marine Parade which once ran along the shore.

Statues of Jan van Riebeeck and his wife stand on what used to be called Roggebaai ('rocky bay'), the old landing place where a stream of fresh mountain water once reached the sea.

Golden Acre
In 1975, during excavations for the ultra-modern Golden Acre shopping and office complex fronting Adderley Street, workers uncovered the ruins of a stone-and-brick reservoir, built in 1663 during the tenureship of Zacharias Wagenaer, second Commander at the Cape. Architects quickly redesigned that portion of the complex to ensure preservation of part of the ruins. This was done in such a way that they can be viewed from different angles and levels.

When first built, the reservoir had a metre-high safety wall and four flights of steps to enable sailors, from visiting ships in need of replenishment, to reach the water.

Grand Parade
This was originally a military parade ground in front of the Castle of Good Hope. It is still used by the military for formal occasions, but is better noted as the site of a twice-weekly open-air market. There are also fruit stalls, and these provide a colourful spectacle, especially on summer nights when, in the midst of the season, they are stocked high with fruit and are brilliantly illuminated. Overlooking the Grand Parade is the old city hall, built of sandstone in the Italian style and completed in 1905. The Cape Town Symphony Orchestra gives regular concerts in the hall.

Lion's Head
The strikingly beautiful sugar-loaf peak, 669 metres high, connected to Table Mountain by a saddle of land known as Kloof Nek. The reason for the name of the peak is obscure. Some say the last lion of the Cape Peninsula was shot on its slopes; others fancy the mountain resembles a lion's head, with Signal Hill as the rump and the connecting ridge forming the body.

In former years, a man stationed on

Stolid amid its surroundings is the old city hall, beyond the Grand Parade.

The Houses of Parliament. Sessions start early in January each year and usually last until July. A statue of Queen Victoria stands in the garden.

the summit of Lion's Head signalled the approach of ships by firing a small cannon, and this warning was relayed to the interior by other cannons mounted at various vantage points.

Distant farmers were thus summoned with provisions for trade with friendly visitors, or to defend the harbour against attack.

A path spirals to the top of Lion's Head, with chains to help climbers up the steep sections. From the summit there is a superb panorama of the city, the sea and the towering bulk of Table Mountain with the buttresses of the Twelve Apostles behind it. Silver trees and wild flowers grow prolifically on the slopes.

Malay Quarter

A surviving residential area of old Cape Town, on the slopes of Signal Hill. It is criss-crossed with narrow streets and contains a large number of the curious, flat-roofed houses of the 18th century, many of them recently restored.

The name 'Malay' is a label given by the people of Cape Town to the city's Muslims, and the Malay Quarter has several mosques.

To the Muslims, Cape Town is a holy place. In 1694, a renowned Muslim leader, Sheik Joseph, was banished to the Cape by the Dutch after the conquest of Java and Sumatra. He founded a Muslim community in the new land.

His grave is one of six Muslim tombs that form a sacred circle around the city. Muslims make frequent pilgrimages to the tombs.

Parliament Street

In the vestibule of the General Post

A mosque in the Malay Quarter.

and Telegraph Offices there is a superbly preserved postal stone. Seamen left letters under such inscribed stones to be delivered by other travellers to appropriate destinations. In the main hall of the post office are murals by South African artists.

In the upper part of Parliament Street are the Houses of Parliament and many government offices.

Robben Island

Lying 9 kilometres off the shore of Table Bay, tiny Robben Island — 3 kilometres long and 1,5 kilometres wide, rising only 35 metres above sea level — has played an extraordinary part in the history of the Cape.

When the first European navigators entered Table Bay they found the island covered with birds and seals. It became a source of abundant food — especially relished were pen-

The historic Wagenaer's Dam (at centre of picture) in the Golden Acre.

23

Like a gigantic inn sign, Table Mountain beckons the world's seamen

The stately Koopmans De Wet House, now preserved as a national monument.

The famous tablecloth, neatly laid, drapes smoothly over Table Mountain.

guins' eggs. The seals were hunted for their pelts. A great asset of the island was its security. Visitors could rest here without disturbance from the Khoikhoi, who appear never to have constructed any form of boat.

Several names were given to the island. The most enduring proved to be the Dutch Robben ('seals') Island.

In 1575 the Portuguese landed a party of convicts on the island, built a storehouse, and left the men to plant vegetables and barter for livestock from the inhabitants of the mainland. What happened to the settlement is unknown. Similar convict settlements were attempted by the British in 1614, but both projects failed.

When Jan van Riebeeck founded Cape Town in 1652 he found the island 'covered with small bushes and grass, with sweet smelling herbs and flowers and streamlets of fresh water'. Above all, there were no predatory beasts or cattle thieves. He decided to use the island for his livestock. A small garrison was stationed here and sheep and cattle were landed and left to fatten.

Also at this time, eight rabbits which Van Riebeeck had brought from Holland were released on the

Inside the elegantly furnished and maintained Koopmans De Wet home.

island. They increased their numbers to such an extent that the vegetation was destroyed. Although greyhounds were put on the island to keep the rabbits in check, the sheep and cattle had to be taken back to the mainland.

The isolation of the island suggested another use to Van Riebeeck. In 1658 he sent convicts here and persons banished to the Cape from the East. The island has had a maximum-security prison ever since.

The first lighthouse on the coast of South Africa — pitch rings burning on the top of a pole — was set up on the island at the same time. It has been replaced by a modern beacon.

The crowning glory of Table Mountain is the strangely neat cap of cloud which, in the summer months, unrolls across the flat summit and drapes itself over the edges in a tidy, almost straight line. The famous tablecloth.

It is just one of the more spectacular manifestations of a quirk of Cape Town's weather that is only too well-known to all who live here — the wind they call the 'Cape Doctor'.

This is the howling south-easter which, among other things, makes the city's atmosphere one of the healthiest in the world by blowing away insects, dust and other forms of pollution.

For those not used to it, this wind, blowing from November to March and sometimes sustaining speeds of 120 kilometres an hour for considerable periods, can be something of a shock. It usually has its lulls in the mornings and its peaks of fury in the afternoons.

But the story of how the Cape Doctor lays the tablecloth on Table Mountain really begins over the sea far to the south. Whirling belts of high pressure which girdle the earth at certain latitudes throw off tongues of air that reach up to the tip of Africa.

On hitting the mountains just along the coast, this air is forced to change direction. Picking up speed, it searches for a way through the mountain barricade. At Cape Hangklip, it finds a gap. It rushes around this Cape, and swirls across the waters of False Bay, collecting moisture on the way.

Reaching the shores of False Bay, the wind collides with the mountains of the Cape Peninsula and is forced to rise. As soon as it reaches the cooler altitudes of the mountain tops it condenses into thick white clouds.

Table Mountain is just the right shape and in just the right place to arrange these clouds in a most unusual way. Being the highest point of the range, it catches the bulk of the clouds, which roll over the flat summit and pour over the edges to be abruptly dissolved in the warmer air of a lower altitude. The tablecloth is laid.

The south-easter can be tiresome to live with. During the summer months, Cape Town is one of the three windiest cities on earth.

But the south-easter also leaves the air invigoratingly clean and clear; it drives warm water into False Bay from the Mocambique-Agulhas Current off the east coast; and, perhaps best of all, it creates the scenic wonder of Table Mountain's tablecloth.

Truly one of the world's scenic wonders. This is the most photographed view of Table Mountain — from Bloubergstrand.

Mountains and the African interior.

More than 290 000 passengers use the cableway each year. At the upper cableway station is a tea-room, a post office where outgoing mail is franked 'Table Mountain', and a radio and television station. The summit is marked by Maclear's Beacon, which forms one of a triangle of survey points originally used as a reference for the mapping of southern Africa.

The animal life on Table Mountain includes baboons, dassies and Himalayan mountain goats. The goats are descended from animals that escaped from Groote Schuur Zoo.

A dazzling variety of wild flowers bloom on the mountain, including *Disa uniflora*, a species of orchid known as the Pride of Table Mountain. Here too is the natural home of the famous shimmering silver trees.

No one who has seen Table Mountain with its famous tablecloth of cloud neatly laid and spilling over its towering cliffs and crags can doubt that he has witnessed one of the most awesome splendours on earth.

Victoria and Alfred Waterfront
The revitalisation of the old Victoria Basin and Alfred Dock has transformed a run-down — and largely disused — area of Cape Town's waterfront into a thriving hub of shops, hotels, restaurants, cinemas, theatres, markets and marinas.

The original harbour was constructed during the 1860s in the most sheltered portion of the bay and eventually included the Robinson Dry Dock, diverse offices, warehouses and other buildings.

The opening of the Duncan Dock after the war, followed by the newer Ben Schoeman container basin, sent the old Victoria and Alfred area into decline, and a committee was formed in the late 1980s to decide on its fate. Its decision was to revitalise it as a tourist attraction.

In November 1988 the Victoria and Alfred Development Company was formed by the Transnet harbour administration, and construction started on the first hotel, shops and restaurants.

Since then, the area has become one of the major tourist attractions in southern Africa.

Stone quarried by convicts on the island has been used for the construction of several of Cape Town's buildings, including the Old Town House.

Among the island's exiles have been lunatics, lepers and even a king — the ex-monarch of Madura.

Captain Cook visited the island and found the 'pretty rabbits' delightful. He took several to Australia — and earned the enduring displeasure of that country's farmers.

Robben Island is noted for its arum lilies. The view across to the mainland is superb, especially at dawn, when the dark bulk of Table Mountain looms over a glowing, purple sea.

Signal Hill
On the slopes of this 335-metre hill overlooking Table Bay is the famous Lion's Battery, used to fire salutes for visiting ships and on ceremonial occasions. One signal gun is fired electrically at noon every day except Sundays, and the boom reverberating around the city scatters multitudes of pigeons from their perches.

A road leads to the summit and views are dramatic, especially at night when the lights of the city sparkle like jewels in the surrounding darkness.

Strand Street
The Koopmans De Wet House in Strand Street is a prime example of late 18th century Cape domestic architecture.

Now a national monument, it was the home of Maria Koopmans De Wet (1838 – 1906), cultural leader and benefactress. It contains many pieces of Cape and European furniture, Cape silver, copper and brass, some very fine glass and Delft.

Adjoining the Lutheran Church in Strand Street is Martin Melck House, built by the German immigrant of that name who built the church.

Table Mountain
Unquestionably one of the world's most famous landmarks, Table Mountain provides the city of Cape Town with a dramatic setting of unrivalled beauty. It has been fittingly described as the 'Old Grey Father' of Cape Town, for without Table Mountain the city would probably not exist.

Visible at times as far as 200 kilometres out to sea, the mountain made the anchorage of Table Bay easy to find and, like a gigantic inn sign, attracted seafarers to 'the Tavern of the Seas' with the offer of shelter, pure drinking water, and produce from the gardens, farms and pastures nestling at its feet.

Table Mountain is a vast block of sandstone, originally deposited on the floor of a shallow sea between 400 and 500 million years ago. It is 1 086 metres high, rising on its northern face as a sheer precipice more than 3 kilometres long. From a distance this great cliff appears to be unbroken, but closer inspection reveals a deep cleft, Platteklip Gorge, splitting the mass from base to summit.

The first recorded ascent of the mountain was in 1503 by Antonio de Saldanha. Mountaineers have now found more than 350 routes to the summit, ranging from easy scrambles to dangerous climbs. Many climbers have been killed on the mountain, and a climb should never be attempted in uncertain weather.

The aerial cableway, built in 1929, takes visitors to the summit in about six minutes. The level but rocky summit provides breathtaking views. The city and Table Bay are spread out below. To the south is the Cape of Good Hope, where the peninsula thrusts between two great currents. To the north lie the Hottentots-Holland

THE UNSURPASSED SEASCAPE

THE PENINSULA OF the Cape of Good Hope — a 75-kilometre finger of rock curving out into the sea — seems as though it might have been added to the main body of Africa as an afterthought. But it is justly ranked as one of the most beautiful places on earth, its ruggedness subtly softened by changing patterns of light and colour.

The peninsula was once an island. About sixty million years ago, the water receded, perhaps as a result of an upheaval of the land mass. A sandy, low-lying arm of land reached from the continent and, like a parent fearful of a child straying too far, grasped the island to the mainland. This linking arm is now known as the Cape Flats. Even today, some intangible atmosphere of the island it once was lingers around the peninsula.

During spring, from August to October, the peninsula is arrayed in all its colourful glory. The renowned Kirstenbosch Botanic Garden is at its most luxuriant. The Cape of Good Hope Nature Reserve provides a wilder display. A walk along the paths that meander through the mountains between Muizenberg and Kalk Bay leads into a wonderland of flowers, caves, strange rock formations and dreamy little forests.

The summers, from November to March, are clear, bright and dry. And although the famous south-east wind frequently blows, mornings are often quiet and there are many still days. The surf on the western shores runs strong and high and the beaches of Clifton and The Boulders offer shelter for sunbathers and picnickers. Anglers crowd vantage points around the shores of False Bay and beneath the clear waters divers explore reefs and wrecks in a strange, silent, turquoise world.

From March to May the Cape is considered by many to be at its most seductive. The south-easter has died, the sea is still warm and the fruit is at its best. Though flowers are few, the leaves are a vivid tapestry of autumn hues and the atmosphere is languorous and caressing.

Winter on the peninsula is green and fresh. Plants of the protea family burst forth in profusion. Rain falls and the north-west wind blows, but the weather follows a pattern of a few cloudy, rainy days, and then some days of delightful, mellow tranquillity when the air seems to have the quality of sparkling wine. The land glistens with waterfalls and swiftly flowing streams. The sea, though cold for swimming, has a good surf on the eastern shores. Warm clothing is necessary, especially at night. The snow that falls on Table Mountain does not remain for long, but the higher mountains on the opposite side of False Bay are often capped with white. Blue waters caress the feet of these jagged, snowy mountains, and at dawn the sky behind them is aflame with the glow of the rising sun.

The Cape Peninsula thrusts southward toward the icy wastes beyond — the view from near Maclear's Beacon at the top of Table Mountain.

Bakoven

A small residential area around a rugged, rocky bay on the southern borders of Cape Town, Bakoven ('baking oven') is named after a rock shaped like a baker's oven.

Bantry Bay

The coastline here is rocky and precipitous. Apartment buildings are clustered along steep roads on the slopes of Lion's Head and overlook the often-turbulent bay.

It was originally called Botany Bay after a botanical garden planted for the cultivation of medicinal herbs. The name Bantry Bay came into use in the mid-19th century when the botanical garden began to be overwhelmed by buildings. Traces of the garden terraces are still to be seen between Kloof Road and Victoria Road.

Bishopscourt

One of the finest of the Cape Town suburbs. Bishopscourt was laid out on the grounds of the farm Boschheuwel ('bushy hill'), originally owned by Jan van Riebeeck. Part of the original hedge of wild almond trees which he

The False Bay coast from The Boulders.

Camps Bay, a favourite for sunbathers though the water is cold for swimming.

planted in 1660 along the top boundary of the farm still flourishes near the Hen and Chickens Rocks on Wynberg Hill. The hedge has been proclaimed a national monument.

Among the handsome residences in the suburb is that of the Anglican Bishop of Cape Town, hence the modern name Bishopscourt.

Boulders

One of the most charming of the swimming resorts of the Cape Peninsula, The Boulders is a jumble of large granite rocks breaking the coastline and providing numerous sheltered inlets and reefs. The water is clear and the undersea world, adorned with seaweed, is populated by shoals of extremely tame fish. Along the walk up the shore to Seaforth beach are small secluded beaches and inlets which cannot be reached by car. There are no facilities along the shore, but it is ideal for a picnic or a lazy summer day far from the sounds of traffic.

Camps Bay

A favourite with sunbathers and picnickers, Camps Bay has a wide, sandy beach, a tidal pool, and is overlooked by Lion's Head and the Twelve Apostles. Though sunny, the area is exposed to the south-east wind. The ocean here is cold for swimming and the backwash occasionally dangerous.

From Camps Bay shore Geneva Drive leads up to Kloof Nek, the saddle of land connecting Table Mountain to Lion's Head. Kloof Road climbs through the trees on the slopes of Lion's Head. There are wind-protected picnic sites along the route and a restaurant in what was once the shooting box of the British governors, known as the Round House. From Kloof Road many fine views can be seen through the trees.

The slopes of Lion's Head above this road are the principal natural home of silver trees, and many hundreds of them can be seen, their leaves glistening in the sunshine like swords of medieval knights in combat, especially when the south-east wind agitates them into a flurry.

Camps Bay was named after an invalid sailor, Ernst Friedrich von Kamptz, who landed in the Cape in 1778. He married the widow of the

THINGS TO DO AND SEE

Angling Throughout the year there is a varied influx of fish into False Bay. There are excellent fishing spots along the shore. Pleasure and fishing craft find shelter at the small harbours of Kalk Bay and Simon's Town. Launching ramps exist at many other convenient spots, such as popular Miller's Point and Buffels Bay. Simon's Town is the principal harbour for tunny boats. There is a club for tunny fishermen and boats can be chartered.

Boating Power-boats can be hired in False Bay. Water-skiing and yachting are popular at Zeekoevlei, light yachting and canoeing at Sandvlei, and surf-boating at Sunrise Beach, near Muizenberg.

Caravanning Miller's Point (Divisional Council), Oatland Point (private), Sandvlei (Cape Town Municipal), Fish Hoek (Municipal), Kommetjie (private), Soetwater (Divisional Council).

Caving Between Kalk Bay and Muizenberg more than 80 caves have been explored, named and mapped. Among the most popular is the Boomslang Cave, which is 146 metres long, with several high chambers and an underground pool.

Picnicking The road around the peninsula has barbecue sites scattered all along its verges. There are many sheltered picnic spots at places such as Perdekloof, Silvermine, the Cape of Good Hope Nature Reserve, on the verges of Sandvlei and Zeekoevlei, on the roadside between Hout Bay and Chapman's Peak, at Kommetjie, Soetwater and Miller's Point.

Swimming Muizenberg, Strandfontein, St. James and Fish Hoek are all on the warm side of the peninsula and fine for swimming. Numerous seals and dolphins often play with the surfers, and whales come into the bay to calve.

There are also smaller, sheltered swimming areas at The Boulders and Seaforth. Miller's Point has a tidal pool and an open swimming area among the rocks.

On the west coast the water is cool for swimming, even in summer — about 15°C. At Sea Point, however, there is a large seawater swimming pool where the water is pleasantly warmed by the sun. Kommetjie has a large tidal pool.

The unspoiled coastline that bewitched Sir Francis Drake

founder of the farm Ravensteyn, which adjoined the bay, and made his home in the farmhouse, which stood on the site of the Rotunda Hotel.

Cape of Good Hope Nature Reserve
Much of what was described in Sir Francis Drake's log as 'the fairest Cape . . . in the whole circumference of the earth' is now the Cape of Good Hope Nature Reserve. It covers 7 750 unspoiled hectares of the southernmost part of the Cape Peninsula and stretches from Schuster's Bay in the west to Smitswinkel Bay on the False Bay coast in the east.

The coastline stretches for almost 40 kilometres of southern Africa's most dramatic scenery, including the famous promontory of the Cape of Good Hope.

The peninsula divides at the tip into three points. The Cape of Good Hope is the most southerly point; east of this is Cape Maclear, named after Sir Thomas Maclear, the 19th century astronomer; and still further east is Cape Point.

On this point a lighthouse and radio beacon have been built.

A favourite scenic drive runs from Simonstown through the reserve to Cape Point. Many small streams, the largest of them the Klaasjagers River, cross the reserve. Several picnic spots, such as those at Buffels Bay and Olifantsbos, have fireplaces, shade and drinking water. At Buffels Bay there

is an enclosed tidal swimming pool and a launching ramp for boats. Near the Buffels River a 19th century farmhouse, with its original walls intact, now serves as a restaurant.

Open to visitors from dawn to dusk throughout the year, the reserve is particularly lovely in spring, when the countryside is covered with a patchwork of wild flowers. Though there are few days in the year when it is not windy at the Cape, the winds vary in strength and venom. Summer brings the full force of the south-easter. During winter, the north-westerly prevails. Autumn, like spring, is relatively tranquil.

Under such generally turbulent conditions there are few trees that flourish. A few milkwoods grow, but their awkward angles of growth suggest that they would like nothing better than to get away from the place. However, although trees are few, everlastings and a profusion of other flowering plants thrive in the decomposed-sandstone soils.

Tortoises and many other small creatures live among the shrubbery, and it is probable that many larger animals once inhabited the area. Attempts to reintroduce zebra and antelope such as eland and bontebok have proved successful, and these species are now doing well. Baboons have always roamed the area and they are often seen combing the beaches for shells, which they break open in order to eat the molluscs inside. Among the

150 species of birds that can be seen are the ostrich, white-fronted plover, black-backed gull, cormorant, sugarbird, Cape francolin, yellow-billed

duck and Cape weaver.

Fishing is particularly good from many rocky vantage points on both sides of the peninsula. The ledges of

---

ETERNAL VOYAGE OF THE FLYING DUTCHMAN

When the wind howls and the waves of the Atlantic crash against the rocks, the world's most famous ghost is reputed to haunt the waters off the Cape of Good Hope — the Flying Dutchman.

Tales have filtered down through the generations of a phantom ship, her masts broken and her canvas in shreds, flying before the gale, doomed to battle forever to round the Cape.

Some say the legend goes back to Bartholomew Dias, the Portuguese navigator, who drowned when his ship sank off the Cape two years after he had become the first European to round the tip of Africa in 1488. But the most often-told version of the tale claims that the ship is captained by a Dutchman, Captain Van der Decken, who ran into a storm while homeward bound in 1641. It is said that while his ship was sinking, he swore that he would round the Cape if he had to keep sailing until doomsday.

In olden times, seafarers believed that all who caught a glimpse of the Flying Dutchman would perish, just as Van der Decken had done. But it was not only superstitious old-timers

who believed that the phantom existed. Keepers of the lighthouse at the tip of the Cape Peninsula have often reported seeing a sailing ship at the height of a storm.

During World War II, German U-boat crews hunting merchant ships off the Cape logged inexplicable sightings of sailing ships, and in 1939 a group of holiday-makers at Glencairn claimed to have seen a battered old sailing ship suddenly materialize.

Perhaps the most famous sighting was on 11 July 1881 when a young midshipman on the Royal Navy ship *Bacchante* recorded in his diary: 'At 4 a.m. the Flying Dutchman crossed our bows. The lookout man on the forecastle reported her as close to the port bow, where also the officer of the watch clearly saw her . . . a strange red light as of a phantom ship all aglow, in the midst of which light the mast, spars and sails of a brig 200 yards distant stood out in strong relief.'

Soon afterwards the lookout man fell from a mast to his death, but the curse of the Flying Dutchman left the midshipman unscathed. He later became King George V.

The Twelve Apostles, Camps Bay. In the foreground are silver trees.

The breathtaking view of the Cape Peninsula from the air, looking north.

Cape Point, its lighthouse overlooking the pinnacle known as Dias Rock.

the steep Rooikrans ('red cliff') enable anglers to fish directly into deep water, and many great catches have been made from here, especially of yellowtail and even tunny.

Plans to establish the reserve originated in 1928, when the area was threatened by the growth of seaside resorts. It was only in 1939 that the reserve was proclaimed by the Cape Divisional Council, the land having been acquired at a cost of R127 000.

Chapman's Bay

A sandy shore borders the bay that lies between Chapman's Peak and Kommetjie. The beach is well worth exploring, though the water is cold and dangerous for swimming.

The wreck of the 1 500-ton *Kakapo* lies half-buried on the beach. The ship ran aground in a north-westerly gale on 15 May 1900 on its delivery voyage from a British shipyard to the Union Steamship Company of New Zealand. The crew of 24 walked ashore. All attempts to refloat the ship failed and eventually parts of its steel plating were used to flank the railway line at Fish Hoek to prevent sand drift. Local residents used the coal from the ship's bunkers. The wreck was used as a set in the film *Ryan's Daughter*.

The bay is believed to have been named after a seaman, John Chapman, who was sent ashore at Hout Bay in 1607 from the English vessel, *Consent* . . . 'to see whether it weare a harboure or not'. Because of unfavourable weather Chapman was

almost abandoned. The bay became known as Chapman's Chance and the peak above it as Chapman's Peak. When Hout Bay was given its present name the bay immediately to the south became known as Chapman's Bay. It is the earliest English place name that has survived in South Africa.

Chapman's Peak Drive

Cut into the cliffs around the 592-metre Chapman's Peak is one of the world's most spectacular scenic drives. The road, marking the line at which the sedimentary Table Mountain sandstone has been laid on a base of Cape granite, slices its way through brilliantly coloured layers of red, orange and yellow silt, and dark lines of manganese.

Picnic spots and numerous lookout points offer incomparable views over the great beach of Chapman's Bay, and across the sweep of Hout Bay to the 331-metre Sentinel, which looms alongside the busy little harbour.

The road, 10 kilometres long, was built between 1915 and 1922. A stone quarried from Chapman's Peak marks the grave in the Woltemade Cemetery of the chief engineer of the project, Robert Glenday.

Claremont

A residential suburb in the municipality of Cape Town, Claremont was once a separate municipality and is still wistfully referred to as 'the village' — its rugby team is known as the 'Villagers'. It has a major shopping centre

and a superb public park, known as Arderne Gardens. The gardens were once part of the estate known as The Hill, which was acquired in 1840 by an English immigrant, Ralph Arderne. On the site he planted one of the finest collections of trees in southern Africa, including Norfolk Island pines, Indian rubber trees, Atlas mountain cedars and North American swamp cypresses.

A spring in the gardens, the source of the Black River, was converted by Arderne into a Japanese garden with bridges, ferns and water-fowl. The gardens are also renowned for azaleas and rhododendrons.

Claremont was the home of the

19th century astronomer, Sir John Herschel, of the Royal Observatory.

Clifton

A residential suburb with four sandy beaches — ideal for sunbathing and surfing though cold for swimming — sheltered from the south-easter by Lion's Head. The beaches are separated by rocky projections of the mountain and can only be reached from the road by steep flights of steps. Many of the beachside bungalows and apartment buildings are supported against the steep mountainside by concrete stilts.

Between the sea and Victoria Road, extending from Fourth Beach to Camps

The Cape of Good Hope, one of earth's stormiest corners.

Where ancient mariners were lured to grief

Winter is a time of rest for Clifton's popular beaches.

Bay, is a small nature reserve, formerly named Schoenmaker's Gat, after an old shoemaker who lived in a nearby cave.

Clovelly

A picturesque seaside resort where the sea washes against the railway station buildings and a sign — surely unique — cautions travellers: 'No fishing from the platform'. Originally the station was known as Trappies ('little steps'), because of the steep flight of stairs leading to the houses.

Clovelly was once known as the Klein Tuin ('little garden') — also the name of a farm owned by the De Kock family, whose original homestead still stands. The name Clovelly is reputed to have been given by an Englishwoman, a guest of the De Kocks, who fancied that the place closely resembled the village of that name in her native Devon.

The Silvermine River reaches the sea here. A road leads up the riverbanks to the Clovelly Country Club and then crosses the Ou Kaapse Weg and continues to Noordhoek.

False Bay

The name of False Bay was given because ships coming from the east often confused Cape Hangklip with the Cape of Good Hope. This vast bay of sparkling blue water is contained between the mountains of the Cape Peninsula and the Hottentots-Holland range, which projects into the sea at Cape Hangklip. By turning into False Bay instead of doubling the Cape of Good Hope, ships not only suffered great inconvenience but sometimes had difficulty extricating themselves from the currents around the opening of the bay.

During the summer, when the prevailing wind is the south-easter, the warm Mocambique-Agulhas Current from the Indian Ocean is deflected into False Bay. This is the gloriously blue water of summer holidays, at its best from November to April, with a temperature of around 22°C.

In winter, the north-west wind takes over. The warm water in False Bay is displaced by the greenish, plankton-rich flow of the Benguela Current from the Atlantic Ocean. The water temperature drops to around 15°C. Surfing conditions are now at their best, with a heavy swell and an offshore wind.

False Bay is one of the world's principal angling areas and of great value and significance to marine biologists. It is bordered by many delightful seaside resorts and a 35-kilometre stretch of beach.

Fish Hoek

This thriving seaside resort is almost unique in southern Africa — the sale of liquor here is prohibited.

The site of Fish Hoek was originally a farm which lay across the road connecting the naval base at Simonstown with Cape Town. Fearful that the area would become a den of iniquity, the British governor, Lord Charles Somerset, prohibited the sale of liquor on the property. This restriction still prevails. There are no bars or bottle stores.

Until recently another of Lord Somerset's rulings still applied — his order that the right of fishing should be free.

The name Fish Hoek is the anglicised version of Vishoek ('fish glen'). The valley in which the resort lies runs directly east to west across the Cape Peninsula. The town lies on the eastern side with a fine beach verging on a bay which provides safe swimming and excellent boating.

In comparatively recent geological times, the valley floor was beneath the sea and the southern end of the peninsula was an island south of it. The full length of the valley floor consists of sand. The valley ends on its western side at Chapman's Bay.

Half way through there is an isolated, rocky ridge containing a rock shelter much used by prehistoric man. The shelter is known as Schildersgat

---

HOW THE SEA CONTROLS LIFE ON THE LAND

Two great currents, one from the Equator and one from the Antarctic, merge off the south-western tip of Africa like water from the hot and cold taps of a bath. Nothing more typifies the Cape's position as the half-way point between different worlds than the collision of these two mighty ocean streams.

The Mocambique-Agulhas Current, born in the equatorial waters of the Indian Ocean, swirls around Madagascar and down the eastern coast of southern Africa. On reaching the submerged Agulhas Bank, most of the current is deflected to the east, while the remainder continues around southern Africa.

Off the Cape of Good Hope the Agulhas meets broadside on with the second current, the Benguela, surging up toward the south-western coast of Africa from its source far south among the icebergs of the Antarctic.

The difference between these two currents means that while bathers can frolic happily in the water at resorts on one side of the Cape Peninsula, only 10 kilometres away on the other side the water is too cold for any but the hardiest swimmers.

But the effects are much more far-reaching than this. For the influence of the Agulhas and Benguela Currents creates stark contrasts in the geographical conditions and the plant and animal life down each side of southern Africa.

The Agulhas, travelling at a speed of 90 to 230 kilometres a day, has a temperature of around 20°C. It evaporates comparatively easily, generating rain and bringing green and fertile conditions to the eastern coast. The Benguela Current, with a speed of between 16 and 40 kilometres a day, is about 5°C. colder. Evaporation is slower, little rain falls on the western coast, and desert conditions prevail.

The differences are marked in the marine life of the waters down each side of southern Africa. The nutrient-rich flow from the Antarctic promotes the growth of plank-

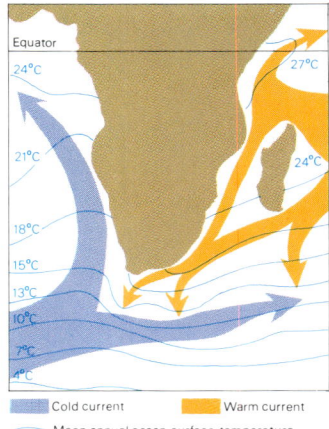

Cold current ■ Warm current ■
Mean annual ocean surface temperature

ton, the start of a food chain which attracts fish, seals and sea-birds to the western coast, and it is here that the bulk of South Africa's fishing industry is concentrated. The eastern coast, where the water of the Agulhas Current is not so rich in nutrients, has its characteristic marine species, but the fish tend to be far less abundant.

A drawing of 1865 showing the old lighthouse at Green Point.

('painters' cave') because of the prehistoric paintings on its walls. In this shelter were found the three fossilized skeletons of Fish Hoek Man, who lived 10 000 years ago.

More recently the cave has come to be known as 'Peers Cave', after Victor Peers, the man who discovered the first of the ancient skeletons in 1927. The cave is now a national monument.

Glencairn
A Scot from the original Glen Cairn is reputed to have named this tiny resort. He was famed for wandering about the valley, playing his bagpipes.

It is a windy area, whose houses are sprinkled on the slopes of the surrounding mountains. The beach is pleasant when the wind is not blowing, and there is a tidal pool. A road leads through the glen up to Da Gama Park, which houses naval personnel.

Among the breakers between Glencairn and Simonstown the tops of a steamship's engine cylinders can be seen. These mark the grave of *Clan Stuart*, a naval collier which was blown ashore there on 20 November 1914. The ship, though anchored, had been carried gently ashore by the south-easter. The crew ended the day playing billiards and drinking beer in the Glencairn Hotel. The ship settled in the sand and refused to budge.

Green Point
A residential area adjoining Cape Town city centre, Green Point nestles on the slopes of Signal Hill and looks down on Green Point Common. This common has many sportsfields and includes a soccer and athletics stadium, tennis courts, cricket grounds and a golf course.

Groot Constantia
The grandest of the Cape Dutch homesteads, Groot Constantia was the private home of one of the most effective governors of the Dutch colonial period, Simon van der Stel. He was a man of taste, intelligence and culture, and his home was built to be lived in — commodious, as befitted a governor's country home, but without ostentation.

He loved the homestead so much that at the end of his term of office in 1699 he retired here and stayed until his death in 1712.

Van der Stel designed the original homestead with his builders, and every corner, curve, angle and gable had to meet with his approval. The home is a fascinating blend of the West, East and Africa, incorporating European ideas, Asian craftsmanship and African materials.

The property was granted to Van der Stel by the Commissioner of the Dutch East India Company, Baron van Reede, whose young daughter was named Constantia. It is thought that Van der Stel named the homestead and estate after her. He laid out the farm and planted oak trees and grape vines. Before he died his estate was producing fine wine.

Van der Stel left no descendants in South Africa. The estate was eventually acquired — in 1778 — by Hendrik Cloete, and he developed the making of wine until the name of the estate was renowned throughout the civilized world. Red Constantia wine and, to a lesser degree, white, became sought-after prizes for the cellars of even French monarchs. The virtues of the wine were sung by poets, praised by writers, extolled by connoisseurs. Orders for Constantia wines had to be placed well in advance, and the estate was never able to meet the demand.

The two Constantia wines had a subtle piquancy in aroma and flavour. A few bottles of these renowned wines have been found in the cellars of such great collectors as the Duke of Northumberland.

Scientific analysis of the contents of the two wines reveals that both had a sugar content of about 128 grams per litre. The red wine had an alcoholic content of 13,42 per cent, with 15,01 per cent in the white.

They were the product of two well-known master winemakers, Hendrik Cloete and a relative, Johannes Colyn, who acquired the estate of De Hoop op Constantia which adjoined Groot Constantia.

On these two estates the cultivar, Muscat de Frontignan, flourished to a

Fish Hoek, where ancient statute granted free fishing rights to all.

particular perfection. This was the principal grape source of the delicate nectar blended to their personal taste by the two men. Neither man ever revealed explicit details of the secret of these two luscious wines.

Groot Constantia's famed and spacious cellars, the home of superb wine.

Along an avenue of oaks stalks the governor's ghost

The imposing main gable entrance of the Groot Constantia homestead.

Hout Bay fort and blockhouse, built by the British in 1796.

Winter at Kalk Bay, headquarters of the snoek fishing industry.

A board of control runs the estate.

The homestead is in excellent condition and houses furniture and ornaments of the period. Behind the house is a superb wine cellar built by Hendrik Cloete from a design by the renowned French architect, Louis Thibault. Anton Anreith sculpted onto it a handsome pediment of plump cherubs drinking wine. Inside the cellars the rich smell of wine has saturated the whole building and, in their various seasons, all the processes of wine-making may be seen. In spring, the vines are fresh, adorned with new leaves; in early summer the berries are beginning to ripen; in February the harvest of wine grapes is being brought in for pressing. Winter is the season of sleep for the vines and oaks, and of maturation for the wines stored in rows of vats, barrels, casks and bottles.

An avenue of oaks leads from the homestead to an ornamental pool where the owners of the estate once bathed. Along the shadowy green tunnel formed by the closely packed trees, visitors have occasionally reported having seen a kindly, distinguished-looking old man, wrapped in towels, walking back from the bath. This is reputedly the ghost of Simon van der Stel. In the dim light he smiles and wishes passers-by a friendly good day. If this is indeed Van der Stel, his attachment to his home is understandable.

Groote Schuur

Cecil Rhodes acquired the Groote Schuur ('great barn') estate in 1893 and bequeathed it to the South African nation on his death in 1902. A delightful estate on the slopes of Devil's Peak, it includes the Cape Town residences of the President of the Republic, the Prime Minister and Deputy Prime Minister, a small game reserve, the Rhodes Memorial, the University of Cape Town and its medical school, and the Groote Schuur Hospital.

Groote Schuur estate shares its name with that of the former residence of the Prime Minister. In its present handsome form, the house was the creation of Cecil Rhodes and famous architect, Sir Herbert Baker. The building was originally a storage barn built by Jan van Riebeeck. It had been converted into a house in later years by English owners, then acquired by Rhodes, partly burned down by fire, and then rebuilt. Adjoining the grounds of Groote Schuur Rhodes built a second house. This was named Woolsack and was used as a summer residence by Rudyard Kipling, a great friend of Rhodes. This house is now used as a residence by the University of Cape Town.

The official residence of the President of South Africa, Westbrooke, is close to Groote Schuur. The three houses stand in a fine setting of trees and gardens.

Large paddocks on the eastern slopes of Devil's Peak and Table Mountain provide grazing grounds for herds of antelope, which include gnu, eland, zebra and bontebok. Until recently there was also a small zoo on the estate. In founding the zoo, Rhodes bestowed a mixed blessing on Cape Town. Among the animals he imported were thars (Himalayan mountain goats). Some escaped and fled up Table Mountain where they rapidly increased in numbers. The descendants of the thars remained on the mountain until quite recently. Chinese deer and American grey squirrels were other imports by Rhodes whose numbers now cause concern.

The Rhodes Memorial was built in 1912 on a site particularly beloved by him. It is an impressive monument, designed by Francis Masey and Sir Herbert Baker. The powerful equestrian bronze by G. F. Watts, Energy, dominates the memorial, with eight lions guarding a flight of stairs leading to a granite building sheltering a bronze head of Rhodes. Underneath the bust are the words Kipling wrote on Rhodes's death:

'The immense and brooding spirit still shall quicken and control.

Living he was the land and dead his soul shall be her soul.'

The memorial stands in a setting of stone pines, and the view out across the Cape Flats is splendid.

The University of Cape Town, founded in 1829 as the South African College, moved to its present site on the Groote Schuur estate in 1925. It is one of the oldest universities in the southern hemisphere.

The vast white building complex of the Groote Schuur Hospital, where the world's first human heart transplant was performed by Professor Christiaan Barnard in 1967, borders the estate on the west. It is a major research centre.

Patients from many parts of the world come to Groote Schuur and the most complex heart surgery is performed here by teams of specialists.

Fishing boats bob gently at their moorings in the mountainous setting of Hout Bay, a centre of the snoek industry.

Hout Bay

The name Hout Bay is the anglicized version of Houtbaai ('wood bay'). In its mountainous setting, its entrance guarded by the peak known as the Sentinel, it makes a beautiful, often-photographed picture. There is a fishing harbour in the bay, and factories processing rock lobsters for export.

The harbour is the home port for a fleet of fishing vessels, and it is the scene of considerable activity, especially in winter when snoek are in season. Smoked snoek and other seafood are sold in the area.

The Hout Bay beach is attractive, but the water is cold. It is often the scene of trek fishing, and nets heavy with fish are hauled onto the beach.

The village has some atmospheric streets. In former years, wood was cut here for use in Cape Town — hence the name of the place.

At one time the area was also the scene of mining for manganese, and this was shipped from the harbour. The old mining jetty still partly survives the battering of the sea, although mining has long since ceased.

The ruins of several strongpoints which guarded Hout Bay also remain. They include the Gordon Battery, above the old manganese jetty, and

The memorial to Cecil Rhodes erected on the slopes of Devil's Peak.

The orange-breasted sunbird, a colourful resident of the Cape Peninsula.

Groote Schuur, designed by Sir Herbert Baker for Cecil Rhodes.

the West Battery, close to the crayfish processing factories. Both were built by the British during the Napoleonic wars.

On a rock overlooking the beach is a bronze leopard, 1,4 metres high and weighing 295 kilograms, the work of the late sculptor Ivan Mitford-Barberton, who had his studio in the village.

Kalk Bay

The fishing harbour at Kalk Bay is always busy, particulary at the peak of the snoek season, around June and July.

In the past, catches of 40 000 snoek have been landed in one day.

The bay was named Kalk ('lime') because of lime kilns set up here in the 17th century to produce lime for painting buildings. Many of the white-walled homes of the Cape owed there appearance to the lime from these kilns. The harbour is a favourite resort for the Coloured community of the Cape Peninsula.

Kenilworth

The Kenilworth Racecourse is the scene of the principal horse race of the Cape, the Metropolitan Handicap, run in January each year. The racecourse is situated in the lower part of the suburb, adjoining the military base of Youngsfield.

The suburb grew into a residential area around the orginal homestead of Stellenberg farm. The Dutch governors are said to have kept the kennels of their hunting hounds here. The name Kenilworth was applied first to the estate, and then to the railway station.

Kirstenbosch

The National Botanic Gardens of South Africa at Kirstenbosch were a gift from Cecil Rhodes to the nation. In 1895, he purchased a largely unspoilt area of flowering plants, shrubs and trees on the eastern slopes of Table Mountain. It was a well-watered area — this is the wet side of the mountain — known as Kirstenbosch, apparently after J. F. Kirsten, an official of the former Dutch government of the Cape. The property covered the eastern slopes of the mountain from the bottom of the slope to the highest

Mystery of the whales that beached themselves to die

Surfing near Kommetjie off Long Beach in Chapman's Bay, where the rollers are at their best in summer.

point, Maclear's Beacon, and provided a varied habitat suited to a wide variety of plants. After the death of Rhodes in 1902, the slopes remained untouched until 1911, when they were selected as the site for a national botanical garden.

This was proclaimed in 1913, and under its first director, Professor Harold Pearson, Kirstenbosch was planned as a garden where the indigenous flora of southern Africa would be collected, propagated, studied and preserved. Several rare plant species have been saved from extinction through the efforts of the trained garden staff, and the use of proteas as cut flowers is a direct result of research carried out at Kirstenbosch.

At present about 9 000 of the 21 000 southern African flowering plants are cultivated in the garden, which covers 560 hectares.

Kirstenbosch is a garden for all seasons, but spring is especially beautiful, with a brilliant display of flowers.

In the garden is a lecture and exhibition hall, the offices of the Botanical Society of South Africa, hot houses, the Compton Herbarium — housing more than 250 000 specimens — and a restaurant.

At one of the springs of the Liesbeek River there is an attractive sunken bath, popularly known as Lady Anne Barnard's bath, but which was actually built by a Colonel Christopher Bird sometime early in the 19th century.

Kirstenbosch is open daily from morning to evening. Botanical literature is sold in the office of the society.

Kommetjie
A pleasant village and seaside resort built around a natural inlet in the rocks. The inlet is basin-shaped, hence the name of the village, meaning 'little basin'.

Surfing is good in summer, when the south-easter brings a powerful swell shorewards. The water is cold for swimming.

Some years ago a school of whales died after beaching themselves in the inlet. No satisfactory explanation for their behaviour has been advanced.

Llandudno
A small residential area in a dramatic

The Green Point lighthouse built in 1824. It is one of the beacons guiding navigators into Table Bay.

setting among the granite boulders at the foot of the peak known as Little Lion's Head — because of its resemblance to Lion's Head at Camps Bay. The water is cold for swimming.

Miller's Point

Originally a whaling base, Miller's Point is now owned by the Cape Divisional Council, which maintains a tidal swimming pool, numerous picnic and barbecue sites, and a caravan park.

Miller's Point has a restaurant, spacious lawns, pleasant walks, safe swimming and a rich underwater life.

The steel tower of Slangkop lighthouse, a vital beacon for shipping.

Mostert's Mill

One of the best-known historical monuments of southern Africa. It was built in 1796 and named after Sybrandt Mostert, who ground wheat here. His farm was bought by Cecil Rhodes in 1891, but the windmill was no longer in operation. It was restored in 1936 and is maintained in working order. The original threshing floor is next to the windmill.

Mouille Point

The site of the construction of a mole in the 18th century as part of the development of Table Bay as a harbour. The mole has long since vanished. A line of apartments faces the sea over an expanse of lawn. The principal features of the area are the Green Point lighthouse, the foghorn, children's playgrounds, and the spectacle of tremendous surf during winter storms.

Muizenberg

'White as the sands of Muizenberg, spun before the gale.'

So wrote Rudyard Kipling. He was a lover of the Cape and, during his long summer visits here, swam in the sea and walked along the beach, which stretches in a gentle curve for

A spectacular underwater world beckons divers at Miller's Point.

The inviting resort of Kommetjie basks lazily in golden twilight.

HOW A WINDMILL WORKS

Wheat-milling was one of South Africa's first industries. One of the country's first windmills, Mostert's Mill, on Cape Town's Groote Schuur estate, is maintained in working order and has been proclaimed a historical monument.

Such a mill has a rigid tower housing the grinding machinery. On top of the tower is a movable cap to which the sails are fixed. A winch enables the sails to be turned into the prevailing wind. The sails are attached to an axle, gears and vertical shaft, which together turn two mill stones, one on top of the other. Wheat is fed between the stones and the turning action grinds it into flour. Other gears and governors control the speed of the mill.

Mostert's Mill, built in 1796.

Windmills have a limited output, but their leisurely action generates little heat in grinding and millers have always claimed that such mills produce the best flour.

Mostert's Mill still produces flour on special festive occasions.

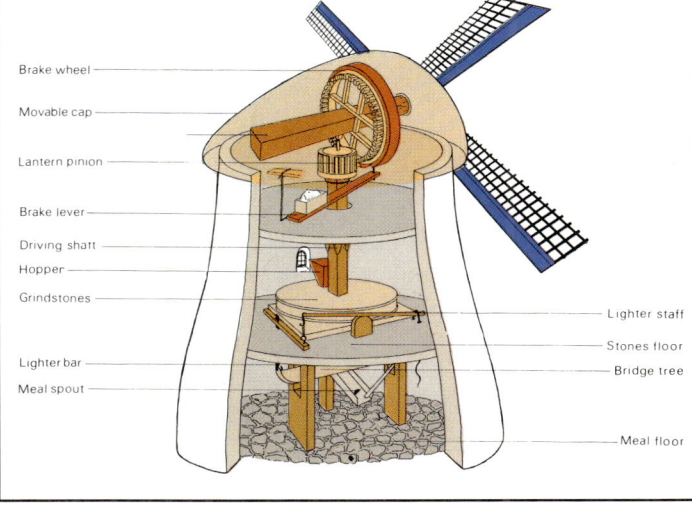

Brake wheel
Movable cap
Lantern pinion
Brake lever
Driving shaft
Hopper
Grindstones
Lighter staff
Stones floor
Lighter bar
Bridge tree
Meal spout
Meal floor

Enchanting playground shared by man and the creatures of the sea

35 kilometres from the suburb of Muizenberg to Gordon's Bay, below the slopes of the Hottentots-Holland Mountains.

The Baden-Powell Drive follows the shoreline and provides a panorama of glorious beaches, restless surf, and serene mountain ranges on both sides of False Bay.

This is one of the world's great playgrounds, and people flock here to swim, surf and fish. The beach is big and safe, with no backwash and few currents. The sand slopes very gradually into the sea and the bed is completely free of rocks and pebbles. Accidents are rare.

Several species of shark, including the fearsome great white, are found in this area, but they remain in general subdued, and keep their distance. This is due to the shallowness of the water near the shore, the plentiful supply of seals and fish for food, and the fact that the water temperature seldom exceeds the danger level of 25°C. beyond which sharks seems to become particularly aggressive.

The water around Muizenberg is warmed by currents circulating in False Bay, and in summer hovers around 22°C. A hot, windless day between November and April is likely to attract vast crowds to the beaches. In winter, the water cools to around 15°C. and the swimmers make way for the enthusiasts of Surfers' Corner. The prevailing north-westerly winds build up waves that are powerful, if a little slow, and even beginners in the sport of surfing find it an ideal nursery confident that a tumble into the sea will not spill them onto the sharp edge of a reef or into the jaws of a shark.

Muizenberg takes its name from Sergeant Wynand Willem Muijs who, in 1743, was in charge of a small outpost here. He became commander of the garrison that was eventually established.

The original posthouse, the oldest building in the Cape, has recently been restored, and is now open to visitors. It is said to have been built in 1673, a year before the castle in Cape Town was first occupied.

As new roads and the construc-

Rudyard Kipling, a frequent visitor to his beloved Muizenberg beach.

tion of the suburban railway made the area readily accessible, the beaches of Muizenberg began to attract more visitors. Fishermen's cottages were bought as holiday homes. Boarding houses and hotels were built. In 1899, Cecil Rhodes, then at the height of his fame, bought Barkly Cottage on the outskirts of the village and Muizenberg suddenly became fashionable. Wealthy families moved in, mainly from Johannesburg, and a millionaires' row of elaborate villas sprang up.

The resort of Muizenberg is full of atmosphere, with back streets filled with odd little cottages of the Victorian and Edwardian era and a sea front in the process of re-development. There is a bright new pavilion, fresh water swimming baths, and wind-free recreation areas. The grassy verges of Sandvlei are much

used by picnickers and the whole area is the principal seaside recreational area for the people of the Cape Peninsula as well as for many visitors from the inland areas.

A unique visitor from the sea often arrives after a south-westerly wind has blown and the tide has been high — the rare nautilus shell. Gulls relish the small sea creatures inside and they search the beaches at first light, tearing the fragile shells to pieces and gulping down the contents. So hunters of these highly-prized marine specimens must begin their search before the first glimmer of dawn.

This is also the best time for those who would follow in Kipling's footsteps, when the sun rises over the Hottentots-Holland Mountains and the beach of Muizenberg stretches away, glowing silver and gold.

Newlands

The choice suburb of Newlands is one of the Cape's most fashionable areas. Imposing houses stand among beautiful woodlands and the gardens are especially lush and green because more rain falls here, in the shadow of Table Mountain, than in any other district around Cape Town.

The suburb began as a logging area and farm, Nieuwland ('new land'), on the upper reaches of the Liesbeek River. It became popular after Governor Willem van der Stel built a country house here in 1700.

Today, many of the wealthy citizens of Cape Town have their homes along the shallow valley of the river. The traces of a cottage named Paradise, where the famous 19th century letter-writer, Lady Anne Barnard, once lived, can still be seen among the trees on the right-hand side of the double carriageway just before it reaches the intersection with Newlands Avenue. Pleasant pathways wind past the ruins and into the cool shadows of the woods. A second home of Lady Anne, The Vineyard, now a hotel, stands further down the course of the Liesbeek.

In its lower reaches the river passes the splendid Newlands swimming baths, gurgles merrily under the Main Road at Westerford and passes the picturesque Josephine Watermill, standing at the entrance to Newlands rugby ground, which is the home of the Western Province Rugby Club. The Liesbeek river then flows close to one of South Africa's finest cricket grounds before meandering off towards the sea.

Union Avenue, which is the section of Rhodes Drive from the Groote Schuur gateway to the intersection of Newlands Avenue, is a scenic gem, with forest-covered mountain slopes and masses of wild flowers growing on the verges.

Noordhoek

A well-sheltered and wooded glen in the folds of Chapman's Peak. There are many agricultural smallholdings and a manor house, formerly the home of politician Sir Drummond Chaplin.

Observatory

The Cape Town suburb where the British Admiralty established South Africa's first observatory in 1821. It sets standard time for the whole republic, and each day at noon sends an electric impulse which fires a gun on Signal Hill. Seamen once corrected their chronometers at the instant of the first smoke emerging from the barrel — not by the sound of the explosion that followed.

Retreat

The suburb of Retreat takes its name from its connections with the British Army. The camps of Pollsmoor and Westlake were used as marshalling

The white sands of Muizenberg stretch far beyond the horizon.

THE MAN WHO CAME TO SOW COTTON AND REAPED MILLIONS

In 1870 a pale, sickly youth of 17 landed in Durban, weary after the sea voyage from England but with a strength of spirit that was to change the face of Africa. The youth was Cecil Rhodes.

He was born on 5 July 1853, the fifth son of an Anglican clergyman who lived in Bishop's Stortford. Cecil developed tuberculosis and emigrated to South Africa to build up his health on a farm run by his brother, Herbert, in Natal.

A year after Cecil's arrival came

the diamond rush to Griqualand West. The Rhodes brothers abandoned their farm and joined the rush. They established three claims and soon prospered, but tragedy was to follow. Herbert was burned to death on a camping trip.

In 1880, Cecil formed the De Beers Mining Company. In a struggle for supremacy against his great rival, Barney Barnato, the frail Cecil emerged as the victor in 1888, when he was able to buy out his competitor with a cheque for £5 338 650.

Meanwhile, he had found time to study at Oxford. He had also surmounted a health crisis, his heart and lungs being badly weakened. Nevertheless, in 1887 he had expanded his empire by forming the Gold Fields of South Africa Company. By 1893 his British South Africa Company was a major force in the economy of Rhodesia (now Zimbabwe). Rhodes's energy as a parliamentarian was equally marked. In 1881, he became Member of Parliament for Barkly West. He became Prime Minister of the

Cape Colony in 1890.

Rhodes dreamed of a South African federation within the British Empire of the then four states (the Cape, Natal, Orange Free State and Transvaal). In an attempt to overthrow President Paul Kruger and gain supreme power, Rhodes supported the ill-fated Jameson Raid from Zimbabwe into the Transvaal. The raiders, led by Sir Leander Starr Jameson, were routed. Rhodes was forced to resign the premiership in 1896. In the same year he had to cope with an uprising of the Ndebele peoples in Zimbabwe, but he continued his innumerable activities, building the railway across the Zambezi at Victoria Falls, launching the Rhodes Fruit Farms in the western Cape, and drawing up a will which ploughed back into southern Africa the seeds of future prosperity.

Rhodes died in his holiday cottage in St James on 26 March 1902. His body was taken by train to what then was still Rhodesia and was buried in a grave he had chosen on top of a granite dome in the Matobo Hills.

stocked with impressive exhibits, and hippos have recently been reintroduced to the area.

St. James
Named after the first church built here, this suburb is well sheltered from the wind and has a pleasant beach and tidal swimming pool. South Africa's first marine biological station was opened here in 1903 but this is no longer in existence.

Among the attractions is the cottage formerly owned by Cecil Rhodes, where he died on 26 March 1902. It is now a museum housing many of his possessions and photographs.

Sandvlei
The shallow lake formed by several streamlets that reach the sea at Muizenberg, Sandvlei ('sand marsh') is a pleasant stretch of water reserved for light yachts, wind surfers and canoes. The edges of the lake, well-grassed and shady, are used by picnickers, walkers and fishermen. The lower reaches have beds of prawns; the upper reaches contain large carp. Pelicans are common here.

On the eastern side of Sandvlei an interesting residential area has been created, known as Marina da Gama. Canal extensions of the lake have been built and houses erected on waterside plots.

A large recreational island known as Park Island has also been built, and this is linked to the mainland only by a bridge.

Scarborough
This small village consists of a cluster of seaside cottages close to the oddly shaped roadside landmark known as Camel Rock. The beach at Scarborough is flanked by picnic sites and camping grounds.

The surrounding countryside is wild and bush-covered.

Old cottages at Newlands have recently been restored to their former splendour.

The serene and sheltered Long Beach surfing paradise at Noordhoek.

and resting places for troops in transit to Asia and Europe during both world wars.

Rondebosch
A fashionable suburb, Rondebosch ('the round bush') is noted for its trees, gardens and schools. The Rustenburg Junior School for Girls has on its grounds the original summer residence of later Dutch governors of the Cape.

Rondevlei
The renowned bird sanctuary at Rondevlei ('round marsh') is one of South Africa's leading ornithological field research stations.

215 bird species have been recorded within its 120 hectares — consisting of a large lake surrounded by shallow, reedy marshes and indigenous bush. The birds are particularly abundant here between January and April, and can be observed from a number of observation towers and waterside hides.

A museum on the site is well

Chalets border St. James beach, where Cecil Rhodes often walked.

The cottage at St. James where Cecil Rhodes died. It is now a museum and contains many of his possessions.

Home of the navy and the intrepid seadogs of old

View from the old prospecting shaft of Silvermine. Beyond is Fish Hoek.

A nautilus shell, or argonaut. The animal is a member of the octopus family.

Zeekoevlei is a playground for yachtsmen, power-boat enthusiasts and windsurfers.

Seaforth
Some of the great pots used for melting whale blubber in the days when Seaforth was a whaling station still remain. It is a sheltered spot for swimming, and has a restaurant and a picnic ground.

A walk along the shore from Seaforth to The Boulders leads past secluded bathing areas which can be reached only on foot.

Seal Island
This is a small, rocky island, lying almost in the centre of False Bay. The island is densely populated with seals.

Sea Point
Cape Town's liveliest and most densely populated suburb — a congested, cosmopolitan area noted for its restaurants and delicatessens.

Along the promenade is the largest sea water swimming pool in the southern hemisphere.

Silvermine Nature Reserve
The reserve is named after a shaft sunk here in 1687 by prospectors searching for silver. No silver was discovered, although manganese is present.

The reserve is notable for its walks and wild flowers, especially around the old reservoir. A forest track leads to the mountain summit above the reservoir and at the top is a superb view down to Hout Bay. There are many picnic and barbecue sites in the reserve, a favourite place for Capetonians on a Sunday outing.

Simon's Town
The principal base of the South African Navy, Simon's Town is steeped in naval history. In 1671, the Dutch East India vessel *Isselsteijn* found the bay to be so excellent a harbour that the governor, Simon van der Stel, founded the port, which was named in his honour. The British developed Simon's Town as a base for their South Atlantic squadron.

The town that grew around the harbour was distinctly nautical in atmosphere. Many celebrated naval personalities visited or were based in Simon's Town, and the epitaphs on tombstones in the churchyard record a colourful history of sea fights and other misadventures.

Compressed between mountain range and sea, the town has attractive, winding streets. Among its notable buildings are Admiralty House, St. Francis's Church, and a Martello tower built by the British in 1796 as a defence against the French. The tower is now a maritime museum. Among its exhibits is a copy of *The Times* of London of 7 November 1805, which records the the death of Nelson and the victory of Trafalgar.

Simon's Town is also the home port for many deep-sea pleasure craft.

Smitswinkel Bay
The name Smitswinkel ('the blacksmith's shop') was given to this pretty bay nestling at the foot of steep cliffs because of two rocks in the sea which resemble an anvil and bellows. The bay is reached by a steep footpath. The mountain slopes above the road are populated by numerous baboons.

Swartklip
Fishermen congregate at Swartklip and it is renowned for the great white sharks that lurk offshore. There is a gull sanctuary in the cliffs.

Pleasure craft now shelter in the historic harbour of Simon's Town.

In the cliffs of Constantiaberg, overlooking the forest, the entrance to a cave known as Elephant's Eye can be seen. Legend claims it to have been the retreat of a princess of an early Khoikhoi people, and its former name was Prinseskasteel ('castle of the princess').

Twelve Apostles

The coastal drive between Hout Bay and Camps Bay runs along the foot of the mountain ridge known as the Twelve Apostles. Formerly known as the Gable Mountains, these buttresses were given the name of the Twelve Apostles by the British governor, Sir Rufane Donkin, who fancied that he could identify the various apostles in their shapes. The buttresses are impressive in their steepness.

Victoria Road provides a popular scenic route. To the west is the Atlantic Ocean, its rocky shore littered with huge granite boulders; to the east is the high sandstone ridge of the Twelve Apostles; to the north is a superb view of Lion's Head, dominating Camps Bay.

Wynberg

Cape Town's largest suburb, Wynberg ('wine mountain') has a magnificent park known as Maynardville after James Maynard, a member of the old Cape legislative assembly, who had his home here. In 1949 the Cape Town municipality bought the property. It is now a public park with a well-used open-air theatre.

Old cottages on the upper slopes of the suburb have been restored.

Zeekoevlei

The largest of the natural lakes of the Peninsula, Zeekoevlei ('hippopotamus marsh') is popular with powerboat enthusiasts, water-skiers, windsurfers and yachtsmen.

Three Anchor Bay

A small bay used for launching boats. In former years three anchors held a defensive chain across the inlet. The Sea Point lawns continue past the bay. The area is noted for the size of its waves during the north-westerly storms in winter.

Tokai

Originally Tokai was a farm graced with a superb Cape-Dutch farmhouse. The land has been cut into housing developments. The homestead remains, however, complete with tales of hauntings by the ghosts of a horse and rider. The son of a former owner is said to have ridden his horse up the steep steps into the manor and around the guests seated at dinner, for a wager. On the way down the horse stumbled and the youth was killed. His ghost is said to ride again on certain nights.

The name of the estate originated from the Tokai hills of Hungary.

The Tokai Forest, which extends up the slopes of the Constantiaberg range, was established in 1883 as the pioneer re-afforestation plantation in South Africa. A large experimental nursery was set up. During the winter rainy season, permits may be obtained from the forester to visit the area.

Tokai Manor House, named after the hills in Hungary where the delicate wine, Tokai Essence, is produced.

PLAIN OF PLENTY WON FROM THE SEA

BETWEEN THE MOUNTAINS of the western Cape and the sea is a sandy, low-lying plain, scattered with farms, booming fish factories and growing townships. This plain was once the bed of the sea. The waters receded about 60 million years ago, leaving the former bed to become what is known today as the Cape Flats and the Sandveld. But for the hand of man, this would have remained an arid desert of dunes and salty sand.

In the days of the early settlers it was known as De Groote Woeste Vlakte — the Great Desolate Plain. Its drifting dunes made it a serious obstacle to farmers wishing to travel between the coast and the Hottentots-Holland, Stellenbosch and beyond. In the early 19th century, convicts were brought in to construct a wagon road across the Flats, and the task of reclaiming the area had begun. The next stage came in 1845 when the secretary to the Cape government, John Montagu, imported hardy shrubs and trees from Australia, particularly the Port Jackson wattle and hakea. Soon these began to overwhelm the sand, binding it together so successfully that today the debt to them has been forgotten, and in fact some are now regarded as a threat to natural vegetation.

When the sand had finally been settled, farmers moved in and began to cultivate the region. Canals were built to drain away the lakes, or 'vleis', which formed in the hollows between the dunes during the winter rains.

Today, strawberries, wheat and vegetables grow where once the Atlantic breakers rolled in. Flowers bloom, and towns have grown up on the reclaimed sands.

The essentially sandy nature of the soil and its salinity make it an unlikely setting for rich vegetation, but flowering plants grow in abundance. Hundreds of species of wild flowers have the Sandveld as their home. The Port Jackson wattle, one of the original Australian imports, with its fragrant golden blossom, also serves as a reminder of how the wilderness of the Cape Flats was tamed.

The south-western coast has been discovered in recent years as a holiday playground. Saldanha Bay has been transformed into an ore-exporting harbour and a centre for marine farming. Seafood restaurants flourish; marinas for pleasure boats have been created; and what is called the Rock Lobster Coast is an area of fun and industry.

Bellville

The expanding city of Bellville grew up around a village called Twelve Mile Stone — the exact distance from the centre of Cape Town. It was renamed in 1861 after Charles Bell, surveyor-general of the Cape.

Leisure facilities include one of the best cycle tracks in the country and an Olympic-standard swimming pool. The handsome civic centre and theatre were opened in 1957. The Elsies River meanders through the town and a pleasant park has been created in its valley.

Bellville is built on the slopes of the 415-metre Tygerberg, so named because of the pattern of the soil and vegetation resembling the spots of a leopard — formerly the leopard was known as a 'tyger'. A fairly easy 4-kilometre walk along a tarred track from the suburb of Welgemoed leads to the summit of the Tygerberg, with magnificent views over the Cape Flats and mountains of the interior.

Bloubergstrand

A village and holiday resort with one of the finest views in the whole of South Africa — an unforgettable panorama of Table Mountain on the other side of the bay with the mother city nestling in its lap.

Some of the older houses are built of timber washed up on the beach.

Memorial near Darling to C. P. Hildebrand, killed in the Anglo-Boer War.

The fishing is good, and great rollers make it a popular spot for surfing, but the water is cold for swimming.

The village lies at the foot of the 231-metre Blouberg ('blue mountain') which, from a distance, has a pronounced bluish tinge.

Cape Columbine

The area around Cape Columbine is noted for its wild flowers, and the numerous promontories and bays attract many anglers. This rocky coast is marked by a lighthouse and radio beacon and it is a major navigation point for shipping approaching South Africa from the west.

Churchhaven

A small fishing village on the western shore of Langebaan Lagoon. The cemetery has several headstones bearing the names of seafarers from all over Europe.

Darling

The area around Darling is famous for its flowers. A wild flower show is held in the town in the third week of September and the Tienie Versfeld Wild Flower Reserve lies 12,5 kilometres away on the road to Ysterfontein. Chincherinchees and lupins are grown for export.

THINGS TO DO AND SEE

Angling Good fishing at many points along the coast, especially Cape Columbine and Tieties Bay. Rock lobsters can be caught around Melkbosstrand.

Camping and caravanning Holiday camp, with caravan and camping sites, at Saldanha. Caravan parks at Langebaan, Ysterfontein, Oupos, Melkbosstrand, Churchhaven, Velddrif-Laaiplek, Bellville, Parow and Kuilsrivier.

Sailing Saldanha Bay and Langebaan Lagoon offer yachting, boating and water-skiing. The three-day canoe race to the mouth of the Berg River in August attracts competitors from all over the world.

Sightseeing The view from Bloubergstrand across the bay to Table Mountain is world-famous. Other attractions: the wild flower show at Darling in the third week of September; the sailors' graveyard at Salamander Bay; fossil deposits at Elandsfontein; the old mission station at Mamre; antelope and other wild life on the isthmus at Langebaan.

Surfing Elands Bay is South Africa's second-best surfing beach. Waves are also good at Ysterfontein and Bloubergstrand.

The town is named after a lieutenant-governor of the Cape, Charles Darling, and is the centre of a prosperous dairy farming district. A few kilometres outside the town is a monument to C. B. Hildebrand. Of all Boer fighters killed in the war of 1899 – 1902, his grave is the closest to Cape Town.

Donkergat

The old whaling station of Donkergat lies at the tip of the isthmus separating Langebaan Lagoon from the sea. A road runs along the isthmus, passing through wild country inhabited by steenbok, grysbok, hares, bat-eared foxes and ostriches.

On reaching the southern end of the lagoon, the road branches up the eastern and western shores. The western road passes the villages of Churchhaven and Skrywershoek. There is a beautiful, sheltered bay called Kraalbaai and, beyond it, Oupos, which

A crèche of jackass penguins huddles together at Saldanha Bay, a haven for vast colonies of sea birds.

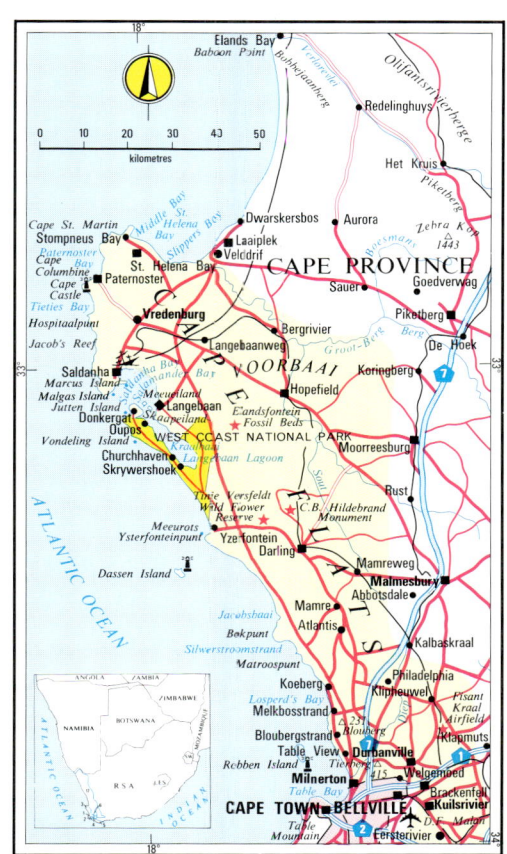

One of the finest views in the Cape — the soaring bulk of Table Mountain from Bloubergstrand.

The 30-million-ton graveyard of the oyster

Langebaan Lagoon. Under its still waters lie 30 million tons of oyster shells.

A vivid spring display of arum lilies and blue heliophila near Darling.

was named after the establishment there in 1666 of a small military post.

There was a spring of fresh water at Oupos and for some years the French and Dutch squabbled over its ownership. The area around the spring is now the Postberg Nature Reserve.

The road up the isthmus ends at Donkergat, which is now a military area and closed to the public. All that remains of the disused whaling station is a picturesque jumble of dilapidated buildings, wharves and a few abandoned whalecatchers. Just offshore lie the small islands of Skaap ('sheep') and Meeu ('gull').

Durbanville

The town of Durbanville grew up around a settlement with the homely name of Pampoenkraal ('pumpkin corral'). No industrial development is allowed within the municipal area, and this has helped to preserve the rural atmosphere. Attractions include horse-racing, gliding from Fisantekraal airfield, and some good local wine. The Meerendal estate has a beautiful Cape Dutch style homestead, and many of the homes have magnificent views of the Stellenbosch and Hottentots Holland mountains.

Elands Bay

The rollers at Elands Bay are one of the reasons why South Africa is rated second only to Hawaii for surfing. The left-breaking waves are big, fast and powerful, particularly in summer when the south-easter blows.

Elandsfontein

One of the world's most important prehistoric sites. The finds include remains of early humans, stone implements and the fossilized bones of many extinct animal species.

The site lies amid a series of high dunes which have had bays scoured into them by the wind, exposing the underlying layers of chalk. It is thought that it was once a water-hole used by animals and Stone Age men. The remains that have been found date from about 75 000 to 150 000 years ago.

The first discoveries were made in 1951 by a Cape Town professor. Since then, more than 20 000 animal fossils and around 5 000 human artefacts have been collected. Most of them are now in the South African Museum in Cape Town.

The most significant find was the skull of a Neanderthal-type of human, dug up in 1953. This is now known as Saldanha Man.

Goodwood

A residential centre named after the famous British racetrack because horse races were once held here. The Western Cape Province Agricultural Society's show is held here at the end of February and the showground is also used for exhibitions and circuses.

Hopefield

Built on the banks of the Soutrivier ('salt river'), Hopefield is the centre of the Voorbaai, a wheat and sheep-farming area in the midst of the Sandveld.

This is a flat and rather drought-prone land, but the spring flowers can be beautiful. The famous fossil deposits on the Elandsfontein farm lie 15 kilometres to the west.

Kraalbaai

The warm clear waters of Langebaan Lagoon lap the sand of this beautiful bay. It is sheltered from the wind by high cliffs and is an excellent spot for swimming, boating and water-skiing. Its calm waters make a permanent anchorage for several houseboats and yachts.

Kuilsrivier

A rapidly growing residential centre on the banks of the Kuilsrivier, which takes its name from its succession of small pools ('kuils'). South Africa's first school for epileptic children was opened here.

Langebaan

The village of Langebaan lies at the point where Saldanha Bay joins Langebaan Lagoon. Out in the channel, the islands of Skaap and Meeu stand like two stepping stones. There is a good beach and in summer the water is warm enough for swimming.

Yachtsmen and aquaplaners use Langebaan as a base and the South African Navy has a crash boat station here. A yacht club was founded in 1982 and provides facilities for small

A beautifully preserved watermill, typical of the mission buildings at Mamre.

and ocean-going yachts. There is a caravan and camping park, and holiday cottages can be hired.

Langebaan Lagoon

The lagoon is 16 kilometres long and 4,5 kilometres wide, and is connected to Saldanha Bay by a narrow channel.

It is a magnificent stretch of sheltered water, only 6 metres deep at its maximum and about 10°C. warmer than the bay itself.

Many different species of fish find their way into the lagoon, and the mudbanks, which are exposed at low tide, make this a favourite feeding ground for birds, including large numbers of migrant waders from Europe, and flamingoes.

On the eastern shores are several farms with Cape Dutch homesteads. To the west, the narrow isthmus separating the lagoon from the sea shelters picturesque fishing villages.

The lagoon was the home of huge colonies of oysters, but changes in the water temperature killed them off. Today there are no live oysters, but the bed of the lagoon is covered with shells — more than 30 million tons of them piled to a depth of 7 metres in places — making it one of the largest oyster graveyards in the world.

Losperd's Bay

The bay where the British landed in 1806 and, after a brief battle around the slopes of Blouberg Hill, went on to occupy Cape Town. The village in the bay, Melkbosstrand, is a popular spot, with a wide sandy beach littered with the shells of Atlantic marine creatures.

Maitland

A suburb on the northern boundary of Cape Town. Voortrekker Road leads through it, with Wingfield military base on the west side and, to the east, Cape Town's principal cemetery, known as Woltemade in memory of Wolraad Woltemade, a South African folk hero.

In 1773, Woltemade repeatedly rode his horse into the waves of Table Bay to save 14 men from the wreck of the *Jonge Thomas*, before he was drowned, along with 138 men from the ship.

Mamre

The mission station at Mamre was established in 1808 by the German Moravian Society at the invitation of the governor of the Cape. The area had long been regarded as a sanctuary for the few remaining Khoikhoi peoples.

The missionaries took over abandoned military buildings and built a church, a school and a watermill, and laid out the present picturesque settlement of white-walled, black-thatched cottages.

Today it has a large population of Coloured people, many of whom work in Cape Town and return to Mamre at weekends.

The original church and parsonage were listed as national monuments in 1967. The watermill has been restored and is now a museum.

Melkbosstrand

Northwards from Bloubergstrand, the wide sandy beach takes the name of Melkbosstrand from the milkwood trees that grow here. It is a popular resort for inland farmers who hold sports on the beach during the Christmas holidays, with tug-of-war competitions and other trials of strength.

The water is cold for swimming, but the fishing is excellent, and delicious rock lobsters abound among the reefs. They are protected south of Melkbosstrand, but north of the resort divers are entitled to recover five lobsters a day during the season. The season runs roughly from November to May, but exact dates vary from year to year.

Milnerton

This is a rapidly developing town on the banks of a lagoon on the Dieprivier, just before it flows into Table Bay. The lagoon offers boating and water-skiing, and other attractions include a golf course and race course, and beautiful walks along the beach.

Paardeneiland

Little of the original flavour of Paardeneiland ('island of horses'), in the delta of the Salt River, remains today. The land has been levelled, the river channelled, and now the area is completely built over with factories. It has a good view of Table Bay harbour and is a popular spot for surfing.

Parow

In 1865, Johann Parow, a Prussian sea captain, was wrecked in Table Bay. Unceremoniously dumped on the shores of South Africa, he made the best of things, became a farmer, and left his name to this town which has now grown up on his lands. Stellenbosch University has a big teaching hospital, the Tygerberg, in Parow.

Paternoster

One of the most attractive fishing villages on the shores of Paternoster Bay. The name probably comes from a particular kind of fishing tackle, though there is a local legend that survivors of a shipwreck gave thanks for their deliverance by means of the paternoster prayer.

It is a great centre for the catching, processing and export of rock lobsters.

Mamre church, built in 1817, is now a national monument.

The vicarage at Mamre in a tranquil setting of trees.

A perfect harbour that missed the boat

Perlemoen and other seafoods are also found in considerable quantities.

Port Owen

Port Owen, named after the developer, Owen Wiggins, is a marina created for pleasure boats. It lies at Velddrif, where the Berg River reaches the Atlantic Ocean in St Helena Bay. Yachts, power boats and canoes find shelter and sporting pleasure here.

St. Helena Bay

Vasco da Gama discovered this great bay while on his pioneer voyage to the east. He sailed into it on 7 November 1497 — St. Helena's Day. The explorers anchored their four ships and relaxed in the bay for four weeks. It was at this time that a brawl developed between one of Da Gama's men and a group of Khoikhoi. This was the first clash on the shores of southern Africa between Europeans and Africans.

St. Helena Bay is the most important centre of the fishing industry in the whole of South Africa. The cold Benguela Current surges along this coast, bringing to the surface large concentrations of nutrient salts and providing food for huge shoals of pilchards and anchovies.

The shores of the bay are lined with processing factories. There are also fine beaches, although the water is too cold for swimming.

Salamander Bay

Ruined buildings and the wrecks of old whale-catchers and other boats give Salamander Bay a rather melancholy atmosphere. So, too, does the cemetery, with its headstones bearing the names of sailors from many lands who came to grief on these shores.

The bay was named after the Dutch ship, *Salamander*, which found shelter here when its crew were stricken with scurvy. There is a splendid view over the entrance to Saldanha Bay with its islands and, on the opposite shore, the new harbour developments.

Saldanha

The days when Saldanha was a peaceful little fishing village, with weather-beaten men drying their catches on the beach, have gone forever. The shortage of fresh water which held up development of the town was solved by the construction of a pipeline to the Berg River during the Second World War. After that, Saldanha began to grow rapidly.

Fishing is now a big industry, with factories for the processing of lobster, mullet and tunny for export. In the last few years, massive harbour works have been undertaken to cater for ore carriers. They are loaded from trains, 2 kilometres long and hauled by up to seven locomotives, which bring iron, manganese and other ores from the mines of the northern Cape.

Despite these developments, Saldanha still retains some of its earlier atmosphere, and is scattered with well-preserved old cottages. The municipality hires out holiday bungalows and runs an attractive caravan park.

Saldanha Bay

This is one of the great natural harbours of the world. Apart from a narrow entrance, it is completely landlocked and the water is deep enough for large ships. Its one disadvantage in the past was its shortage of drinking water. But for this, Saldanha Bay would almost certainly have been the main port of the Cape rather than Cape Town.

In fact, the name Saldanha really belongs to Table Bay after the visit there, in 1503, of the Portuguese admiral, Antonio de Saldanha. It was nearly a hundred years later that the Dutch transferred his name to the present Saldanha Bay, which he had never visited.

The French seem to have been the first to appreciate the possibilities of Saldanha Bay, with its sheltered water and its prodigious population of fish, seals and sea-birds. French sealers made a fortune from pelt hunts on the islands of Vondeling, Jutten, Malgas and Marcus around the entrance to the bay.

The same four islands were also found to be rich in guano. Ships began to crowd into the bay, and there were outbreaks of fighting as crews jostled for the best positions for excavating the deposits. One grisly reminder of these violent days was the body of a French sailor, perfectly preserved by the chemicals in the guano, which was dug up and shipped to Europe where it was exhibited in sideshows.

Pirates, too, came to Saldanha Bay and the sea bed is littered with wrecks. In modern times, treasure hunters have made some rich finds. From the wreck of the *Meresteijn*, sunk in 1702, silver and coins worth more than R500 000 were recovered by divers, one of whom used a wooden barrel as a diving bell. Another interesting wreck is that of the Dutch warship *Middelburg*, set on fire and sunk by the British Navy in 1781.

There are still many seals on the islands in the bay, as well as gannets, cormorants and jackass penguins.

Sea farming

Sea farming, also known as aquaculture, is an industry concerned with the artificial cultivation and harvesting of marine flora and fauna. Saldanha Bay is very suitable for such an industry, particularly in the cultivation of what are known as filter feeders, those animals such as mussels, clams and oysters which feed by filtering from the sea the minute creatures known as plankton. The water of Saldanha Bay, constantly replenished by the Benguela Current flowing up the coast, supports some 30 million minute life forms (plankton) in every cubic centimetre. The filter feeders fatten on this rich food supply.

The first sea farm was created in Saldanha Bay in 1982 by a civil engineer, Philip Steyn, who had observed the possibilities of the area while working on harbour construction. He leased rights to 42 ha of water in the bay and started cultivating the blue Mediterranean mussel, the South African clam and the Japanese oyster. In 1984 his first harvest found an eager market.

Skrywershoek

A small community of Coloured fisherfolk on the western shore of Langebaan Lagoon. The village is named after Ensign Izaak Schryver, who was in charge of a Dutch garrison established in the area in the 17th century.

Stompneus Bay

One of the centres of the vast fishing industry of St. Helena Bay. Twelve fish processing factories lie along the 21-kilometre curve between Stompneus Bay and the mouth of the Berg River.

Table View

As the name suggests, this fast-developing township on the northern shores of Table Bay is noted for its magnificent view of Table Mountain. It is a popular spot for horse-riding, fishing, and for walking along its 5-kilometre beach. Although it is rather windy there are pleasant picnic sites among the trees.

Tieties Bay

A beautiful but dangerous little bay, named after a fisherman who was drowned here. There are fine camping sites along this coast, but few facilities. It is a place of wild flowers, bracing air and rugged seascapes.

Velddrif

A busy fishing centre at the mouth of the Berg River, with boats constantly sailing up the wide river, their holds filled with pilchards, anchovies, mackerel and rock lobsters.

Velddrif was originally a fording place across the river for the road across the Sandveld from Cape Town. It has

A thriving sea farm at Saldanha Bay, one of several along the coast.

now become a combined municipality with Laaiplek ('the loading place'), which once served as a shipping point for wheat.

In 1871 a Cape Town merchant, Johann Carel Stephan, patched up an old ship, the *Nerie*, which had been wrecked in Table Bay, and sailed it to Laaiplek where his family had already started a business. He became known as the Koring Koning ('corn king') and for 30 years was the trading baron of the coast. He built stores, started fisheries, and employed an entire community of Italian and Portuguese fishermen, whose descendants still work in the area.

The first factory of the Berg River mouth was opened in 1944. Its development took another step in 1966 when a deeper, artificial harbour entrance was constructed to bypass the silting estuary.

The fording place has now become the site of a graceful bridge. The shallows above the bridge are frequented by flamingoes, avocets, spoonbills, and even the rare glossy ibis. Velddrif is the finishing point for the annual three-day canoe race down the river from Paarl in August.

Vredenburg
An important centre for a prosperous sheep- and wheat-farming area, Vredenburg was founded on the site of a spring of drinking water. Rights to the spring led to so many quarrels that it was originally known as Twisfontein — the 'fountain of strife'.

The West Coast National Park
The West Coast National Park was proclaimed on 30 August 1985. It encompasses 5 700 ha of the Langebaan Lagoon and its marshlands, 40 ha of the precincts, four islets (Jutten, Malgas, Marcus and Skaap) and two sections of what is known as Sixteen-Mile Beach.

Five privately owned farms and the sand-dune area of De Hoek were later added to the conservation area, as well as the private nature reserve of Oude Post in August 1987.

The park is an extremely important conservation area for many different life forms. Living in the area, either permanently or seasonally, are, for example, 50 per cent of the world's

population of swift terns, 25 per cent of the world's population of Cape gannets, 15 per cent of the world's population of crowned cormorants, and 12 per cent of the world's population of African black oyster-catchers. A substantial percentage of the remaining jackass penguins also have a last sanctuary on the islets in the park.

Ysterfontein
The great rollers sweeping into the bay at Ysterfontein make it one of the finest surfing spots in the area. Nearby are the ruins of an ill-fated fish canning factory built just after the Second World War. Its 150-metre jetty provides a lee for surfers and a vantage point for anglers. The rock promontories along the coast are also excellent for fishing.

Out in the bay is the rocky islet known as Meeurots (gull-rock), because of its large colony of gulls. Dassen Island lies to the south-west.

The road to Ysterfontein is lined with wild flowers, and kilns used to burn shells for lime-making are passed along the route.

The islands of Saldanha Bay teem with wildlife. Here, jackass penguins strut along the shore of Marcus Island.

The Langebaan Lagoon in the West Coast National Park.

The fabulous sea-birds of the southern coasts

The southern and south-western coasts of Africa provide sea-birds with an almost ideal home. The Benguela Current supports a prolific population of fish of the kind which sea-birds find to their liking. Sardines, herrings, mullet, anchovies and mackerel abound in these waters, while the Agulhas area is also richly populated with fish, although of larger species not quite so susceptible to the predations of birds. The bird life, therefore, dwindles northwards up the east side of Africa but remains considerable up the west side until the Benguela Current eventually loses itself in the warmer waters of the tropical areas, which have a sparser fish population.

The most numerous of the sea-birds of the southern coast are the cormorants, particularly of the Cape, Bank, and Whitebreasted species. About 1 250 000 of these birds live around the southern and south-western coasts and they are therefore easily seen. They are noted for flying in great 'V' formations.

Cormorants are often seen perching on rocks, apparently drying their feathers by holding their wings open to the sunshine.

They swim underwater to catch fish, but are quite capable of normal flight even after successive spells of diving — which has led to some debate amongst ornithologists as to whether drying their feathers really is the purpose of this spread-wing posture.

When a big shoal of fish is discovered, cormorants gather from a considerable distance, forming huge 'V'-shaped flocks. The leader of the flock is periodically relieved by some other pace-setter. As they settle on the water above the shoal, any semblance of the orderly control apparent during their flight disappears. It is each-bird-for-itself, diving, darting underwater and gorging to the point of discomfort.

Cormorants breed during the summer on rocky islands off the coast or on the artificial platforms made for them by collectors of the guano they deposit. Their droppings, gathered each year from the islands and the platforms, provide rich fertilizer for South African agriculture.

The second most numerous of the sea-birds is the Hartlaub's Gull, a

A Cape Gannet, a beautifully marked bird with a notorious appetite.

noisy, garrulous bird, found along the western and south-western coasts. Eastwards it is replaced by the Grey-headed Gull. Both species are tame and audacious in obtaining food. The Hartlaub's Gull has the amusing trick of 'puddling' in wet sand or in shallow water, treading up and down, disturbing mud-dwelling creatures which panic, rise to the surface and are eaten.

The Kelp, or Southern Black-backed Gull, is a much larger bird which can often be seen scavenging the shoreline in search of food.

These birds swoop down on shell creatures exposed by the waves, fly high with the shells in their beaks and drop them in order to force open the shells and feed on the animals inside.

The great eater among the seabirds of the southern coast is the gannet. Its luxuriant plumage is delicately coloured, creamy on the body, shading to yellow on the head, with black tips to the wing feathers, decorative black markings on the face, and pale-blue rims to the eyes.

Gannets hunt from the air, and their eyes are so placed that they can see downwards without bending the head from a level flight. On sighting a fish they dive with great speed into the water, paralysing their prey by the suddenness of onslaught.

A nesting colony of gannets is a magnificent and animated sight. On islets such as Malgas in Saldanha Bay they gather in vast communities.

Like cormorants, gannets breed during summer and deposit vast amounts of guano.

Terns are also common along the southern coast. The Swift Tern is a permanent inhabitant while the Sandwich, Common, and Arctic terns are summer visitors. The colloquial name 'comic' tern is applied to both the Common and Arctic terns because they are difficult to distinguish when not decked out in breeding plumage.

The Arctic Tern migrates from the

A Whitebreasted Cormorant guards its nest from a nearby Kelp Gull.

Common, Arctic and Sandwich terns in flight over Dassen Island.

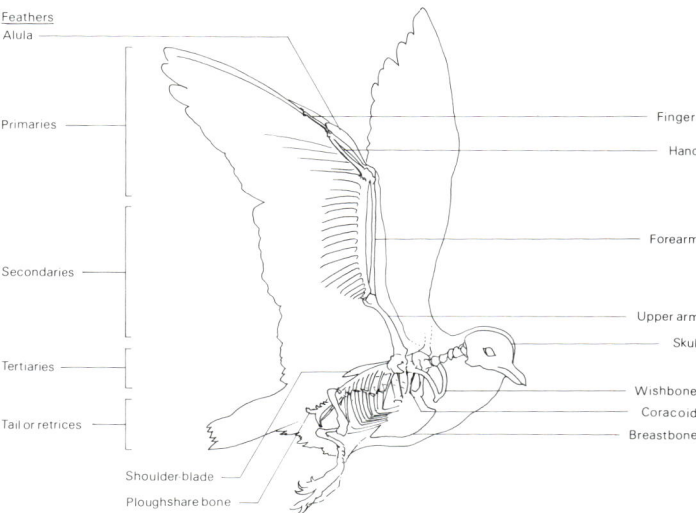

Feathers
Alula
Primaries
Secondaries
Tertiaries
Tail or retrices
Shoulder blade
Ploughshare bone
Fingers
Hand
Forearm
Upper arm
Skull
Wishbone
Coracoid
Breastbone

The skeleton of a gull, revealing the basic uniformity of the bone structure of all birds. A bird needs a generous supply of food to maintain the high energy level required for flight. The demand for instant energy is so great that a bird's heart can reach several hundred beats a minute.

The ingenious design of a bird's bone. To save weight but retain strength, the bones are honeycombed with air spaces and strengthened by struts.

Arctic to the Antarctic each year, using the coast of South Africa only as a staging post. Other terns stay longer.

All terns are notable for their long, swallowlike tails, and they are called 'Sea Swallows' in most other languages, including Afrikaans.

A delightfully perky bird of the southern coast is the Oystercatcher. It has jet-black plumage, red legs, beak and eye-rims. This is a bird of the tidal zone, a forager for mussels and other molluscs. It makes its nest by scooping a slight hollow into the sand, generally among kelp lying on the beach.

The Whitefronted Plover and the Sanderling are common along the shores. They are both small birds and they run at high speed. their legs almost a blur, following the waves as they recede, and then running inshore again as the water turns.

The Sanderling is a migrant from the Arctic; the Whitefronted Plover is a permanent inhabitant of the southern coast.

Petrels, such as Cape Hens and Sooty Shearwaters, and albatrosses visit the coast, as well as Sabine's Gull and the Grey Phalarope.

Most delightful of the permanent residents is probably the Jackass Penguin. They breed on the coastal islands off southern Africa.

The Cape Gannet, Morus capensis. *These birds live in great colonies on islands such as Malgas, Bird Island, and Ichaboe.*

A whitefronted plover, an alert and agile little bird, always foraging the tidal zone, snatching up invertebrates.

Cape Cormorants, popularly known as Duikers, nesting on Bird Island in Lamberts Bay. They are prodigious eaters.

The pelican, whose bill, says the rhyme, holds more than his belly can.

The Kelp (or Southern Blackbacked) Gull, a common sight all along the southern African coastline.

The Black Oystercatcher, a perky, active bird, often seen scavenging along the shore for odd morsels.

47

THE WONDERLAND OF THE FOUR PASSES

THE MOUNTAINS OF the western Cape, with their spectacular peaks, fertile valleys, farms and vineyards, are made accessible by means of a stunningly beautiful scenic route known as the Four Passes.

A tarred road describes a great circle more than 200 kilometres long through some of the most rugged mountain regions in the Cape. On its way, the road snakes over Sir Lowry's Pass, Viljoen's Pass, Franschhoek Pass and Helshoogte Pass. Some of the dizzy trails were originally blazed by wild animals, whose tracks laid out the route for the road-makers.

The road leads through valleys full of lovely homesteads, fruit farms, historic towns and villages, and breathtaking mountain landscapes. It passes through the Eerste and upper Berg river valleys, and the towns of Stellenbosch, Franschhoek and Grabouw. In spring, the region is ablaze with wild flowers; in summer and autumn the orchards are laden with apricots, peaches, grapes and apples.

There are diverting little side roads, rivers in which to fish or swim, areas for walking and climbing, picnic and camping grounds, wayside stalls from which fresh fruit can be bought, wine cellars to be inspected — and sampled.

The Four Passes Route can be completed by car in a day, or a most beguiling holiday can be spent, covering the area one section at a time. Every month there is something special along the route: the flowers of spring, the fruit of summer, the leaves of autumn, the greenery and freshness of the rainy winter. This part of the world is a delight.

THINGS TO DO AND SEE

Angling Many rivers in the region are well stocked with trout.

Climbing Among the mountains favoured by climbers are The Twins (near Jonkershoek), the Groot Drakenstein (especially Duiwelskloof) and Simonsberg. The view from the summit of the latter is spectacular.

Game parks There are two private game parks near the Four Passes Route, Safariland and Wiesenhof. Each has wild animals, picnic grounds and restaurants.

Gardens Flowers bloom throughout the year in this rich botanical region, though the months of September, October and November are the most spectacular. The University of Stellenbosch Botanical Garden and Protea Heights are two of the most luxuriantly stocked gardens in Africa.

Picnicking On the banks of the Eerste River, just before the entrance gates to the Department of Nature Conservation, is a large picnic ground beneath the oaks. Just after the road to Franschhoek crosses the Berg River there is another spacious picnic ground. Still another favourite picnic site is below the wall of the Wemmershoek Dam — a permit must be obtained to visit it from Cape Town or Stellenbosch Municipalities.

Walking The Hottentots-Holland Wilderness Trail starts from the top of Sir Lowry's Pass and leads through stunning scenery to Stellenbosch. The walk up the Jonkershoek Valley as far as the upper waterfall attracts many visitors. The 24 km Vineyard Trail leads from Stellenbosch Railway Station to Kuilsrivier Station.

Devon Valley
Renowned for its wine, fruit and flowers, Devon Valley is also the home of the Protea Heights Nature Reserve (see page 51).

Drakenstein Valley
The name Drakenstein ('dragon rock') was given to this portion of the Berg River Valley by Governor Simon van der Stel in 1687.

The soil is deep and consists of decomposed sandstone, granite and shale. A variety of crops grow here and different parts of a vineyard will produce wines of notable difference in flavour and bouquet.

For 200 years farmers in the Drakenstein Valley produced mainly wheat, meat and wine. Although pears, plums, peaches and apricots grew in abundance, they were of little profit to the farmers because of marketing difficulties. Surplus fruit was left to rot where it fell until, in 1886, several boxes of grapes were successfully transported to London with the

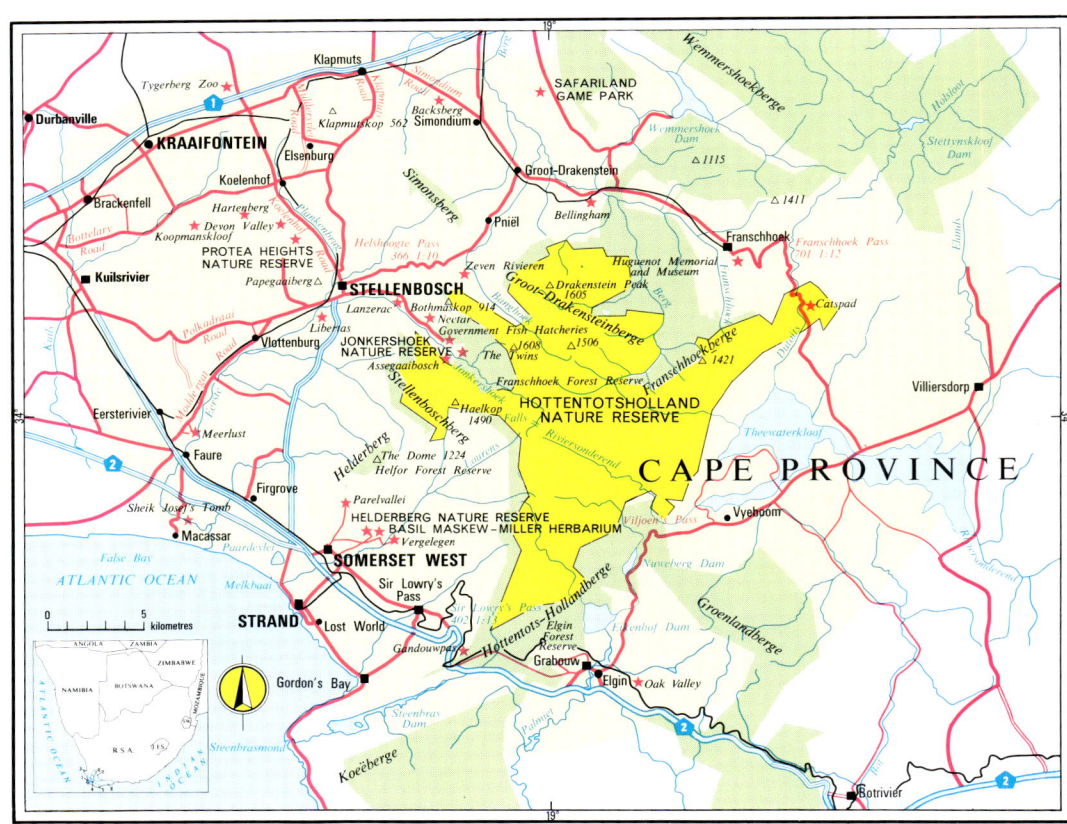

In winter the orchards of Elgin are lulled to sleep by the cold air.

stems of the bunches sealed with wax. These grapes were sold for 15 shillings a pound, when the average price on the Cape Town market was only a penny a pound. The shipment was the birth of southern Africa's now well-established fruit export industry.

Eerste River Valley
The Eerste ('first') was the first river encountered by explorers from the Cape settlement. Sixty kilometres long, it flows through a shallow, fertile valley. Here more than half of southern Africa's wines and a considerable amount of fruit are produced.

The river has its source in the Jonkershoek Valley, sweeps through Stellenbosch and lush fruit farms and vineyards, then the sand dunes of the coastal belt before reaching the sea in False Bay.

Elgin
Although Elgin is little more than a railway station, its name is known in many parts of the world. From here is sent much of the fruit grown in the western Cape. Long trains of refrigerated trucks take apples, pears and peaches to Table Bay, to be loaded into the insulated and refrigerated holds of waiting ships.

During the apple-picking season (January-May) the two great packhouses near the railway station are scenes of frantic activity and the sweet smell of millions of apples fills the warm Cape air. A continual stream of trucks brings bulk containers of apples to be graded, washed, polished, packed, cooled and loaded, then sent on the first stage of their journey. Tourists can visit the packhouses, though tours are not arranged during busy periods.

Franschhoek
A lovely vale in the mountains through which flows the Berg River. The name Franschhoek ('French glen') was given when the Huguenots settled here in 1688 after leaving France to escape persecution. The homesteads they built are serenely beautiful.

The small town of Franschhoek is a straggling little commercial centre for surrounding farms. It has the Huguenot Memorial and Museum and the Franschhoek Wine Cellars Co-operative. (See next page.)

Franschhoek Pass
One of the 'four' of the Four Passes, Franschhoek Pass takes the main road from Franschhoek over the mountains into the basin at the headwaters of the Riviersonderend. From its summit (701 metres) are superb views over the upper valley of the Berg River to the west, and a dramatic and difficult descent to the east, winding through a narrow gorge before emerging into a wide basin surrounded by mountains. Snowfalls and landslides often block the pass in winter and it always demands careful driving.

The history of the pass goes back to before the first European settlers, who discovered that migrating wild animals had found the most practical way over the mountains. For more than a hundred years the settlers used what they called the Oliphantspad ('elephants' path') when they crossed the mountains. In 1819 some simple improvements were made by a local farmer, S. J. Cats. Then the military were called in and the Catspad ('road of Cats') became a rough wagon trail.

Today the pass is crossed by a tarred road. Its sinuous bends take the traveller above the Franschhoek

Valley. The view is magnificent. In winter the landscape is a snow-covered wonderland. In spring, wild flowers bloom in abundance. Many pathways lead off from the road and wind deep into the mountains.

Grabouw
In 1856, the pioneer Wilhelm Langschmidt settled at the ford across the Palmiet River and built a small trading station. He named it Grabow, ultimately to be corrupted to Grabouw, after his birthplace in Germany. The trading station had an instant population — Langschmidt was the father of 23 children. A constant stream of wagons travelling along the main road linking Cape Town with the south-eastern Cape brought prosperity, and today Grabouw is the commercial centre for the fruit- and timber-producing areas of Elgin and the Hottentots-Holland.

There is a small museum in the town featuring the apple industry.

From Grabouw there are several pleasant drives into a district of great scenic beauty and much agricultural activity.

Helderberg
The great dome summit of the Helderberg ('clear mountain'), 1 224 metres high, is noted for its relative freedom from the clouds which gather around the rest of the peaks of the Hottentots-Holland Mountains. The Helderberg is a spur of the main range and from its summit there is a 360° view of the surrounding mountains and farmlands. Its dome has long been a stronghold for black eagles and peregrine falcons.

From eyries on the great rock precipices, these birds soar and float on air currents while hunting for food.

A nature reserve comprising 245 hectares of the south-east slopes of the Helderberg was proclaimed in 1960.

It is one of the showpieces of the western Cape. Paths provide access to

Franschhoek, with the valley of the Berg River covered in vineyards.

The mission church of Pniel, with Simonsberg in the background.

49

Orchids grace a summit where only the brave dare to venture

most parts of the reserve. One leads to the summit of the Helderberg. This is for the sturdy and the courageous and their reward is a superlative view and the sight of countless orchids growing on the faces of the high crevices.

The Basil Maskew-Miller Herbarium at the entrance to the reserve has displays of plants and animals.

Helshoogte Pass

This pass between Stellenbosch and the Drakenstein Valley is one of the Four Passes. Helshoogte means 'precipitous heights', and the pass (366 metres) is noted for fine views of Simonsberg, the Drakenstein Valley and the Wemmershoek Mountains.

The small valley at the eastern end of the pass became known as Banghoek ('fearful glen'), supposedly because of the wild animals lurking in the area. The name has become corrupted to Banhoek.

The descent of the pass at its eastern end leads eventually through the great fruit and wine estates of the Rhodes' Fruit Farms and the old German mission of Pniel.

Among the many handsome farms in this region, Zeven Rivieren ('seven rivers') is notable for its Cape Dutch homestead. One of the best known is Boschendal, built in 1812 by Paul de Villiers. Cecil Rhodes bought the Boschendal estate in 1896 and it became one of the magnificent block of Rhodes Fruit Farms. The homestead was proclaimed a national monument in 1976 and, carefully restored, it is today a showpiece of Cape-Dutch architecture, and a museum. The outbuildings include a handsome poultry house with tiers of built-in nests.

The farmyard buildings at Boschendal now house a fine restaurant and a shop where the wine of the estate is sold. In addition, picnic packs are provided so that visitors may enjoy them at the tables on the tree-covered slopes at the side of the main drive.

Huguenot Memorial and Museum

The graceful Huguenot Memorial was built in 1938 at the foot of the Franschhoek Pass to mark the 250th anniversary of the arrival of Huguenot settlers in the Franschhoek Valley. The female figure, the work of the sculptor Coert Steynberg, symbolizes freedom from religious persecution. In her hands are a Bible and broken chain. The calm pool below her represents tranquility of spirit, the globe at her feet lifts her to the regions of the spirit and the three arches behind her represent the Trinity.

Close to the memorial stands the Huguenot Memorial Museum, opened in 1965. The building housing the museum is a reconstruction of a famed old building in Cape Town, Saasveld, the former home of Baron Pieter van Rheede van Oudtshoorn, which was demolished to make way for development. It is a fine example of Cape Dutch architecture.

The interior contains many relics of the Huguenots, including furniture, letters, deeds of properties, glassware, a copper still and a four-wheeled cart which was hauled by goats to carry provisions to the British soldiers who made the Franschhoek Pass.

Jonkershoek

This spectacular glen, named after Jan de Jonker, an early settler in the area, is one of the great scenic features of the western Cape. Here are the headwaters of the Eerste River, with a superb waterfall, masses of flowering plants and an exciting panorama of mountains on all sides of the valley. To the north are the dominant peaks of The Twins (1 608 metres), a favourite with climbers, while on the south side the Stellenboschberg is overlooked by the 1 490-metre

---

RHODES AND PICKSTONE, THE BEGINNING OF EXPORT FRUIT CULTIVATION IN SOUTH AFRICA

If ever there was a man of destiny in southern Africa, it was Harry Ernest Pickstone, who arrived in Cape Town in 1892. He was 27 years old, and although he had no money, he had a dream of starting a nursery in South Africa. He had one asset, a letter of introduction to another great dreamer, Cecil John Rhodes.

Pickstone had been to South Africa on military service in 1889, returned to England, and then gone to California where he worked as a nurseryman. South Africa had captured his heart, however, and he was intent on coming back to fulfil his dream. He would transform the economy of fruit farming by introducing the finest cultivars, and try to find a way of exporting the crops to the markets of the world.

Pickstone found a receptive listener in Rhodes. The depressed state of fruit and wine farming in the Cape had been of concern to Rhodes for some time, but he had found no solution. Pickstone provided the answer to the problem.

Rhodes financed Pickstone in the establishment of a fruit nursery at Groot Drakenstein. As Pickstone searched to find the ideal cultivars for the Cape, Rhodes stimulated technicians and shippers to solve the problems of cold storage and the transport of fruit to overseas markets.

By 1896 Pickstone's fruit trees were flourishing, and Rhodes took a dramatic leap forward. He summoned Pickstone to a meeting at Groote Schuur and completely flabbergasted the nurseryman by instructing him to buy every farm in the Groot Drakenstein Valley. Within the year, 29 of the farms had been acquired, and on this block of so-called Rhodes Fruit Farms, peach, pear, plum and apple trees were planted as fast as Pickstone's nursery could provide them.

The whole concept worked brilliantly. A new era of prosperity came to the farmers of the Cape. The fruit and wine farms of the Groot Drakenstein Valley and the Berg River Valley are today a pastoral symphony of orchards and vineyards graced with the restored and lovingly maintained original Cape-Dutch style homesteads such as Boschendal, La Rhône, and Harry Pickstone's manor-house of Lekkerwijn (sweet wine). He died in 1939.

The Rhodes fruit farms are great producers of top-quality apples. Here farm labourers unload a freshly picked consignment.

Haelkop ('hail summit'). The eastern, closed end of the valley has a high divide separating it from the head of the Riviersonderend Valley. By following the path that leads up Jonkershoek glen, the enthusiastic walker can visit the waterfall on the route, climb over the divide and continue on a three-day hike through unspoilt mountains and valleys to the top of Sir Lowry's Pass in the Hottentots-Holland Mountains.

In the Jonkershoek Valley are the historical farms Lanzerac and Nectar, and the Jonkershoek Nature Reserve, which contains the hatcheries of the Fisheries Research Station, the principal trout hatchery on the African continent. Here trout, lake bream and bass are bred for mountain streams, dams and rivers all over the country.

Assegaaibosch is a nearby reserve for plants, birds and animals and has a huge variety of proteas. In the upper region of Jonkershoek the forestry reserve borders on the Nuweberg and Franschhoek reserves.

Meerlust

One of the best-preserved of the old farms of the Eerste River Valley is Meerlust ('sea longing'), so named because from the homestead there is a view of the distant sea. The interior and exterior have been maintained much as they were in 1776, when the house which originally stood on the site was enlarged.

The house has been the property of the Myburghs since the middle of the 18th century. British authorities at the time of the occupation of the Cape suspected the Myburghs of harbouring seditious sentiments, so in the early days dragoons were quartered at the homestead. To the surprise of the British, farmer Johannes Myburgh welcomed the dragoons. He invited the commanding officer to bring his family to the farm and also opened his cellars and pantry to the dragoons.

The dragoons worked willingly in the vineyards, labouring harder than any of the slaves, and became so devoted to Meerlust that they were reluctant to leave.

There is rumoured to be a ghost at Meerlust — a beautiful, daintily dressed woman who wanders about,

usually in early morning, as though attending to the freshly-cut flowers. Occasionally she is said to have been seen peeping through the curtained windows toward the sea.

Neethlingshof

Originally known as Wolwedans (dance of the wolves), the estate, in 1844, was acquired through marriage by Johannes Neethling and received its present name. After Neethling's death in 1870, the estate was passed to his daughter Jeanne who had married

The elegant Boschendal wine estate in the Franschhoek valley.

Jakobus Louw. It stayed in the possession of the Louw family until 1963 when it was purchased by Jannie Momberg. It is a superb estate with 273 ha of hill slopes which provide the master winemaker, Gunther Brözel, with infinite possibilities for the subtle art of his profession. The modern owner of the estate is Hans-Joachim Schreiber of Singapore, who realised the great potential of Neethlingshof, and developed it accordingly. The original homestead now contains a restaurant of considerable charm,

Neethlingshof, originally known as Wolwedans.

specialising in Singaporean cookery of very high standard. A notable feature of the estate is the avenue of pine trees which is illustrated on the labels of Neethlingshof wines.

Protea Heights

Amid the pleasant farmlands of the Devon Valley lies the 25-hectare haven of the Protea Heights Nature Reserve. The land was bought by Frank Batchelor in 1944 and presented by him to the South African Nature Foundation in 1976. In the reserve are rare flowers such as painted ladies (*Gladiolus blandus*), pincushions (*Leucospermum sp.*), the famous blushing brides (*Serruria florida*) and a host of proteas, ericas and other indigenous plants.

Sir Lowry's Pass

Wild animals were the trail-blazers of Sir Lowry's Pass, the busiest of the Four Passes.

Herds of migrating game, confronted by the Hottentots-Holland Mountains, found the easiest way over the heights. San hunters and Khoikhoi pastoralists followed and the route became known as the Gandoupas ('pass of the eland').

With the settlement of the Cape, the first Europeans also used the Gandoupas as the route east to what was known as the Overberg ('over the mountain'). One can still follow this early route, but only on foot. Deep ruts worn into the rock by the wheels of the wagons of pioneers are a memento of the days when oxen and horses laboured up these fearsome gradients.

It took long public agitation before a modern road was made over the Hottentots-Holland Mountains.

The graceful Huguenot Memorial, against the Franschhoek mountains.

Cape Governor Sir Lowry Cole, the builder of Sir Lowry's Pass.

For a few goods the Khoikhoi sold a new Holland

Money was scarce in the Cape and the wealth of the interior still had to be discovered. Ambitious road-building programmes were invariably vetoed by financial controllers in London. As a result, an entire farming district was being hopelessly retarded because of one impossible bottleneck.

Eventually the governor, Sir Lowry Cole, braved the wrath of his superiors and, on his own initiative, allowed the pass to be built. It was opened in 1830.

Sir Lowry's Pass today carries the major roadway over the Hottentots-Holland Mountains from Cape Town through the Garden Route to Port Elizabeth and Durban. The railway line connecting Cape Town to Elgin and Caledon keeps company with the road and is the delight of rail enthusiasts with its tunnels, gradients, cuttings and superb scenery. The view from the summit of the pass (402 metres) embraces the whole of False Bay, the Cape Peninsula from Table Mountain to the lighthouse on the tip, and the fertile farming areas of Somerset West, the Eerste River Valley and the Cape Flats.

Somerset West

The town of Somerset West is a popular residential area for people working in Cape Town who are prepared to commute the 48 kilometres from the city. The environment of Somerset West is superb. In a basin at the foot of a range of mountains a number of streams find their source and converge to form the bustling Lourens River. A quarter of the way along the river's journey to the sea lies Somerset West.

The region was first visited by Europeans in 1657. They encountered a small clan of Khoikhoi people, whom the Europeans then referred to as Hottentots. These original inhabitants grazed their livestock in the basin, and they so praised their homeland to the pioneer Europeans that the visitors, half jocularly, half nostalgically for their own homeland, named the area the Hottentots-Holland. The mountain range still bears this name although the Khoikhoi have long vanished from the scene. For about R1 500 worth of trade goods they sold their 'Holland' to the Europeans and wandered off with their flocks and herds.

Beautiful farms were created in the basin. Parelvallei ('pearl'valley') and Vergelegen ('far away') were the homes of two of the sons of Governor Simon van der Stel. One of the sons, Wilhelm, succeeded his father as governor, but devoted so much time to his farm and the making of his private fortune that he was accused of neglecting his duties. The Van der Stel brothers were ordered away from the Cape in disgrace and their farms were broken up.

A community of farmers replaced the Van der Stels and the basin is today covered with vineyards, orchards, timber plantations, vegetable fields and meadows. In 1817 a church was built and the town established. In 1820 the town was named in honour of the governor, Lord Charles Somerset. With another town carrying the same name in the eastern Cape, the name Somerset West came into use.

Today the town is notable for its gardens and pleasant residential areas. On the outskirts is the Helderberg Nature Reserve.

Broadlands stud farm, near Somerset West, with the south-east clouds pouring over the Hottentots-Holland Mountains.

Nestling among the oaks, the Dutch Reformed Moeder Church in Stellenbosh.

La Gratitude, from which the 'all-seeing eye of God' looks down on townsfolk.

The Rhenish Parsonage in its colourful setting of flowers and trees.

Stellenbosch's distinctive Grosvenor House, now part of the Village Museum.

Stellenbosch

Of all the towns founded in the Cape during the period of control by the Dutch East India Company, Stellenbosch is one of the best preserved. It is the second oldest town in South Africa after Cape Town and is situated 111 metres above sea level on the banks of the upper reaches of the Eerste River. Here the river flows out of the mountains and into a shallow, alluvial and fertile valley.

Stellenbosch has become known as 'the town of oaks', these trees being abundant. Some of the oaks have been proclaimed national monuments.

When Governor Simon van der Stel first visited the area in November 1679 he was much taken by its beauty.

The name Stellenbosch ('Van der Stel's bush') was given to the site of the governor's camp, and by the following year the first settlers had arrived from Cape Town. There was ample water from the river and the streets were lined with furrows, which brought the water to every house. Oak trees were planted and houses built of locally available material, with thick walls, doors and windows made of local woods such as yellow-wood and stinkwood, and roofing of black thatch. The houses were finished with white-lime wash. The handmade furniture of these early settlers has become much sought after by collectors.

Stellenbosch was established not simply as a centre of agriculture. With the authorities in Cape Town distracted by the problems of the development of the Cape Peninsula, it became a romantic frontier town. The mountain ranges overlooking Stellenbosch from the north marked the limits of the little-known world of southern Africa, and beyond lay a great expanse of unexplored land. To control the hunters, explorers and

The Kruithuis, or powder magazine, now a military museum, in Stellenbosch.

At the gateway to the unknown, the idyllic 'town of oaks'

Isie Smuts, wife of General Jan Smuts, was born in this house in Dorp Street, Stellenbosch. It is a street of oaks, water furrows and venerable buildings.

Interior of the Stellenryck Wine Museum containing wine-industry antiques.

pioneers intent on penetrating the interior, a magistracy was established in 1685, and for the next century the incumbent of this post wielded authority over an interior without geographical limit. Though in Stellenbosch there was law, order and the tax collector, north of the town was nothing but wilderness.

Each year on his birthday Simon van der Stel visited Stellenbosch and presided over a fair with shooting competitions, feasting and games. There he would meet the hunters, adventurers, traders and others attracted to this gateway to the unknown.

Today's Stellenbosch is perhaps even more beautiful than when the governor first founded it. He never saw the oak trees in their maturity, or the main thoroughfare, Dorp Street, lined with houses, cottages and shops, or the town square, the Braak, with its arsenal, parades, quaint houses, inns and churches.

The University of Stellenbosch — the original Victoria College founded in 1881 — was established in 1918. The University Botanical Garden in Van Riebeeck Street has many odd-looking plants, including the *Welwitschia mirabilis* from the Namib Desert. Bonsai trees, ferns and orchids can also be seen here.

The recently created Village Museum comprises a number of original houses which have been restored. These have been furnished in the styles characteristic of several historical periods. The Schreuderhuis forms part of this group, and is the oldest restored townhouse in South Africa. No. 18 Ryneveld Street serves as the entrance to this collection of restored buildings.

In Dorp Street is one of the longest rows of old buildings surviving in any major town in southern Africa. Most of the buildings date from the 19th century. Among these is No. 116,

The view from the summit of the Franschhoek Pass, with the town of Franschhoek nestling in its emerald-green valley.

Voorgelegen, which contains some of its original Batavian tiles in the parlour. Also in Dorp Street, the old Lutheran church, built in 1851 by Carl Otto Hager, is used by the university as an art gallery.

Nearby is the old home of the Reverend Meent Borcherds, La Gratitude, on the gable of which the original owner modelled the 'all-seeing eye of God' to look down on townsfolk. Lower down the street there is the immaculately restored homestead of Libertas Parva, now the Rembrandt van Rijn Art Gallery.

A military museum is housed in the Kruithuis ('powder house') on the west side of the town square. This was built in 1777.

A perfect example of an H-shaped Cape Dutch dwelling is the Burgher House, a national monument. Built in 1797, it has been restored and is now an office building, furnished with 18th century antiques.

Viljoen's Pass

Another of the Four Passes, Viljoen's Pass was named after Sir Antonie Viljoen, one of the leaders of farming and political life in the Elgin fruit-producing area following the Anglo-Boer War. From its summit (525 metres) there is a fine panoramic view of the basin in the mountains where the Riviersonderend has its

headwaters, the great dam of Theewaterskloof and the fruit farms clustered around the small rural centre of Vyeboom ('fig tree').

The pass is an important communications link. During the harvest season many heavily laden trucks make their way through the pass taking fruit to the packhouses at Elgin.

Villiersdorp

A small rural centre in a handsome mountain setting, Villiersdorp is named after Pieter de Villiers, a farmer who established the village in 1843. Fruit is farmed in the district and there is a local industry in the making of comfits — fruit preserved with sugar and dried.

Villiersdorp is a convenient refreshment centre for visitors exploring the Four Passes.

Wemmershoek

The western Cape takes much of its water from the 307,5-hectare dam completed at Wemmershoek in 1958. The original valley occupied by the Wemmer family has been submerged. The earthen wall of the dam, 565 metres long, overlooks a picnic site, and the spectacle of the water overflowing during the winter rainy season attracts many visitors. Permits to visit the dam must be obtained from the Civic Centre, Cape Town.

Wine Route

Over mountains and through valleys, pausing to discover a fresh taste here, a tantalizing new bouquet there — these are the delights of a journey along the Wine Route.

Here, in the fertile valleys of the Berg, Eerste and Breë rivers, are the great estates and cellars which form the heart of southern Africa's wine industry.

Biggest of all the producers is the Stellenbosch Farmers' Winery, founded in 1924 by an American doctor, William Charles Winshaw. The company has its cellars on the Libertas farm, 1 kilometre from Stellenbosch on the road to Cape Town.

The original farm cellar is still in use for maturing certain red wines, and it makes an interesting comparison with the vast modern complex of cellars around it.

Nearby are the headquarters of the Distillers' Corporation, whose Bergkelder ('mountain cellar') stands on the lower slopes of the Papegaaiberg. There are regular guided tours of the cellar.

Still another wine industry giant, Gilbey Distillers and Vintners, has its headquarters alongside the Plankenbrug stream below Papegaaiberg.

The Bellingham estate in the Groot Drakenstein Valley, with its

immaculate Cape Dutch homestead, is another of the best-known wine producers of the western Cape. Visits to the cellars can be arranged.

The roads down the east and west sides of the Eerste River Valley pass several estates whose cellars offer some notable wines. Amongst these are several estates which offer lunch beneath the trees.

The Bottelary road from Stellenbosch to Kuilsrivier takes the Wine Route to the cellars of Simonsig.

Still another interesting road that is part of the Wine Route leads for 12 kilometres from Stellenbosch to Klapmuts.

This road finds a curving way through the foothills of the Simonsberg massif and reveals to the traveller a serene stretch of farmland, with fresh fruit to be bought from roadside kiosks during the season (December-April) and several fine wine estates such as Muratie, Delheim and Kanonkop.

The road rises over the saddle of land connecting the Simonsberg massif with the outlying peak known as Klapmutskop from its resemblance to a Dutch sailor's cap, then descends smoothly through vineyards until it reaches Klapmuts rural centre.

Nearby is the Backsberg estate, which produces some of the finest wines of southern Africa.

The wines for which Van Riebeeck wrote 'praise be the Lord'

The original home of the grape is believed to have been in ancient Persia. It was there, we assume, that man first tasted the naturally fermented juice of some berry crushed by accident and found it even more to his liking than the fresh fruit.

At least 6 000 years ago wine was being made in Egypt. Today vineyards have been cultivated in every suitable part of the world.

Jan van Riebeeck planted the first vines at the Cape soon after he arrived from Holland to establish the settlement in 1652. On 2 February 1659 he wrote in his diary: 'Today, praise be the Lord, wine was made for the first time from Cape grapes.' Wine was soon in demand by the crews of every ship calling at Table Bay.

After Van Riebeeck's first experimental plantings, in the Company's Garden in Cape Town, vines were introduced into the valleys in the mountains as soon as they were settled by pioneer farmers.

Several varieties of grape cultivated by these pioneers have survived.

The soil and climate of the western Cape were particularly suited to grape growing. Even the notorious south-east wind of summer was beneficial, for it prevented grape diseases from becoming established.

With skilled wine-makers settling in the Cape, particularly the Huguenot refugees of 1688, the industry expanded. Production was limited only by the extent of areas of suitable winter rainfall. This factor has held back South Africa to the position of eleventh largest wine producer in the world (700 million litres in 1980 — a tenth of the output of Italy or France).

The principal historic grapes of southern Africa were the Muscat varieties, which produce the sweet musk-flavoured red and white muscadel wines; Green Grape (or Semillon) from which are derived sweet white wines; and the Cinsaut (or Hermitage) which produces red wines.

About 100 other varieties are established today. The principal white-wine varieties are the Chenin Blanc (or Steen), Riesling, Colombar, Clairette Blanche and Semillon (Green Grape). The red wines are produced from Cabernet Sauvignon, Shiraz, Pinotage (a South African hybrid from Pinot Noir and Cinsaut) and Cinsaut (or Hermitage).

The historic Constantia wines were fortified wines thought to have been produced mainly from grapes of the Muscat family. Though these recipes have been lost to antiquity, the Groot Constantia estate of today remains renowned for its wines.

Imported vines — influenced by the soils, winds, temperature and moisture of different regions — have produced a unique variety of wines. One of the fascinations of wine lies in these variations. The same grape on different parts of a farm can produce wine notably different in nature.

Winelands of Stellenbosch, with Table Mountain and Lion's Head in the distance.

When, to these variations, are added the effects of different techniques and skills of the winemaker, the results are wines of intangible character — delicate, dainty, charming, capricious and, above all, stimulating.

How wine is made

Man facilitates and influences the making of wine, but basically it is a natural process.

Having chosen his grape varieties, influenced their development by fertilization, irrigation and chemical protection from parasites, the vintner judges their readiness for wine-making by testing the sugar content and assessing the final possible consequences of weather. The timing of the harvest is crucial.

In the western Cape, February and March are the months of harvest of wine grapes. All the picking is done by hand, because experimental harvesting machines proved unsatisfactory. The scene in most vineyards, therefore, is still a painting from the past.

Tractors, trucks and trailers take the grapes in bulk containers to the presses. Long queues of vehicles form at the weighing-in scales. Eventually, the grapes are tipped into the hoppers. The heavy loads are devoured and masticated by stainless steel presses, gears and mechanical worms. The stems are discarded, the grapes crushed to a thick 'must' — a mixture of the skin, juice and flesh of the grape.

The next steps are determined by which basic type of wine is required — white or red. The juice of all grapes would produce white wines. The hues of red wines come from the skin.

If white wine is to be produced the skins are separated almost immediately — the time they remain influences the flavour of the wine. The skins are pressed again to extract all the juice and are then used to make compost. The must is now carefully clarified to remove most of the solids. Fermentation would now take place spontaneously, but not necessarily with a result desired by man. The wine-master accordingly adds a selected yeast artificially cultured and known to produce the result he wants. Under refrigeration, at between 15°C. and 18°C., fermentation proceeds, the sugar being converted to alcohol and the carbon dioxide escaping into the atmosphere.

Left to itself, fermentation would proceed until all the sugar was converted into alcohol. But not all wines are required completely 'dry' — lacking in sweetness. The wine-master, therefore, judges when fermentation has proceeded far enough and ends it by drastically lowering the temperature, and clarifying the wine. This paralyses the yeast and leaves the desired amount of sugar — the law permits a maximum of 3 per cent.

The presence of carbon dioxide determines whether the wine is still (normal wine), perlé (slightly effervescent) or sparkling. Full sparkling wines, or champagnes, are selected still wines which are subjected to a second fermentation. This is gener-

The task of harvesting the grapes begins.

Grapes being fed into the crushers.

Spring in the vineyards. It is early morning, but already the labour starts as horse-drawn ploughs furrow the soil.

Maturation proceeds at its leisurely pace in a cool, silent cellar.

The wine is bottled. This process is highly automated and utterly hygienic.

ally done in large sealed containers, but sometimes in the bottles in which they are to be sold.

Some wines are fortified by the addition of pure wine spirit to the fermenting must. This kills the yeast, stops fermentation and leaves some sugar and the additional spirit in the wine, giving to it a high alcohol content — up to 20 per cent, compared to the maximum of 14 per cent of natural, unfortified wines. Among fortified wines are jerepigos, sherries, ports, marsalas and muscadels.

If red wines are to be produced the skins of the grapes are left with the must during fermentation, the wine-master removing them only when he judges the colour to be right. From the skins also come the flavour and tannins of red wines. When fermentation has reduced the sugar content to between 10 per cent and 4 per cent, the red wine is usually transferred to wooden vats. The wood of the vats allows natural gases of the atmosphere to penetrate into the wine.

These gases are said to flirt with the wine, reacting on the tannin and minerals, mellowing the wine in the almost mystical process of maturation.

Traditionally, three years at least were considered necessary to mature red wine, but some wines today can be drunk after twelve months. Some red wines are not matured in wood at all, but in stainless steel containers.

Rosé wines, delicate and light, are made at their best by the wine-master leaving the skins of red to light black grapes in the must only long enough to impart the rosé tint and the delicate flavour. They can also be made by blending red and white wines.

Sherries are fortified wines which undergo ageing in wooden casks in the presence of a yeast known as flor.

This yeast is responsible for the nutty taste of sherry. Flor is found in the bloom of grapes in the western Cape and Spain, and without it sherry could not be made. Sherries range from very sweet to dry, and traditionally mature for up to ten years to reach perfection. Modern production processes have not shortened this period. Port wine is even more leisurely in its natural maturation — one hundred years is not considered excessive.

Despite the unquenchable thirst of the wine market and mass production methods, the traditional mystique and romance of wine-making remain.

The special grapes that produce special wines

Muscat d'Alexandrie, or hanepoot, which produces white wines.

A cluster of Cinsaut grapes, from which red wines are produced.

Cabernet Sauvignon — a noble red.   Colombar — a white variety.   Clairette Blanche — a delicate white.   Tinta Barroca — a port variety.

A CONCISE DICTIONARY OF WINE TERMS

The following is a mini-dictionary of terms used by wine experts:

Acidity Sharpness, or tartness.

Alcoholic strength The ethyl alcohol in wine is measured by percentage of volume. Pure alcohol is said to have an alcoholic strength of 100 per cent, natural wine 12 per cent, sherry 20 per cent and brandy 43 per cent.

Aperitif A wine stimulating the appetite.

Aroma That part of the smell of wine derived from the grape.

Astringency The amount of tannin in a wine — the quality that makes the mouth pucker.

Body The apparent weight of the wine in the mouth due to alcoholic content and extract matter.

Bouquet That part of the smell of wine originating during fermentation and maturation.

Brut Exceptionally dry — a wine, generally sparkling.

Burgundy Dark red, dry, full-bodied wine with an alcoholic strength of around 13 per cent. The term is correctly used only for wines from the Burgundy district of France.

Claret Popular English name for light-bodied red wines, particularly those originating from Bordeaux, with an alcoholic strength of 12,6 per cent.

Corked Having the taste of a decayed cork.

Cuvée A special blend.

Dessert wine A fortified wine.

Doux Sweet.

Dry A dry wine has little or nothing of the original grape sugar.

Fortification The addition of wine spirit to a dry wine or a fermenting must. This results in an increase in alcohol content and stops fermentation.

Full-bodied High in alcohol content and extract matter.

Hock White table wine from the Rhine Valley.

Jerepigo Fortified, dessert wine with almost maximum sugar.

Mellow Well-matured, soft and ripe.

Muscadel (or **Muscatel**) Derived from an aromatic grape, which yields a sweet dessert wine of fine aroma.

Natural wine Unfortified. Free of any additions.

Nose The bouquet of wine; its fragrance.

Perlé Slightly effervescent.

Ripe A wine fully matured.

Sec Dry.

Sour A wine spoiled by acetic acid.

Tart Of a fruity-acid taste.

Vintage The grape-gathering season.

Woody A taste imparted by the wooden cask.

THE ART OF THE WINEMAKER

South Africa has been fortunate in its winemakers, in a profession which requires not only a high degree of dedication and skill for its success, but also something of the intangible magic of the artist.

In the photograph above, 'Spatz' Sperling is working in the cellar on the Delheim estate. He has created several outstanding wines. There is an amusing story about one of them, which relates to one of his wine's labels: 'Sperling' means 'sparrow', and 'Spatz' is the colloquial name for the perky little bird. Amongst 'Spatz' Sperling's wine creations was a late harvest, of which he felt justifiably proud. But when he gave samples to some friends to taste, they were disdainful.

'Just some more crap from Spatz,' one of them remarked. 'Spatz' put the wine on the market with a label showing a sparrow from the rear, relieving itself and looking backwards very cheekily. The wine, named Spatzendreck (sparrow droppings), was a great success.

The great estate of Bellingham, a name considerably distorted from the original name of Bellegam (beautiful sounds), was much run down when it was acquired in 1943 by Captain J. Bernard Podlashuk and his wife Fredagh. They restored the homestead, replanted the vineyards and created some of the most successful wines produced in the

Cape. They liked their wines dry. South Africans tended to prefer their wines sweet, but the Podlashuks changed popular taste. They introduced the first dry Rosé and a Premier Grand Cru, which contained no fermentable sugar whatsoever. Both wines were regarded as amongst the most delectable produced in southern Africa.

Then came one of the most popular of all the Cape wines, Bellingham Johannisberger, made from grapes of an unusual German cultivar grown in Schloss Johannisberg on the Rhine. Dirk Schwenke, foreman of Bellingham, managed to obtain a few cuttings of the vine from Germany. They flourished in their new home in the Cape. To contain this wine, a little sweet with a gentle aroma, Mrs Podlashuk designed a special bottle similar in shape to a mountain of the Groot Drakenstein range.

The famous estate of Nederburg, for 33 years, had as its winemaker, Gunther Brözel. He created many fine wines, including the first Edelkeur or Noble Late Harvest wine produced in southern Africa. Such a wine demands the most stringent discipline in the cultivation of the vines and their pruning, and constant checks on the vagaries of climate. The cultivation techniques were devised by the Benedictine abbey of Fulda in Germany, where

the rare spore known as Botrytis cinerea is found in the soil. This same spore was found in the soil in parts of the western Cape, including Nederburg. It is essential in the production of Edelkeur.

To produce this wine in South Africa, the wine law of the country had to be changed in 1969 to allow the marketing of what is known as a 'royal wine'. To produce it, Gunther Brözel devoted years to research in his laboratory and experiments in the fields. After several false starts, he achieved his dream, with a wine of rich, golden colour and a sweet velvety smoothness to the palate.

On the estate of Klein Constantia a dedicated team of winemakers: Douglas Jooste, his son Lowell, Professor Christopher Orffes, Ernst le Roux the viticulturist, and a master winemaker, Ross Gower, have spent over 10 years in experimentation to revive the classic two wines of Constantia. The story of this work is an ongoing saga of human endeavour aided by the presence of the migratory Steppe buzzard, which guards the special vines from the predation of such birds as starlings.

The first of the classic wines to be resurrected, the white, called Vin de Constance, in very special bottles similar to those used by the historic makers, was declared to be 'exquisite' at its first tasting.

EARTH'S LOVELIEST COASTAL GARDEN

IN WONDERMENT, MAN named the coast from Muizenberg, around Cape Hangklip to Danger Point, Cape Agulhas and Arniston, the Coast of Flowers. Nowhere in the world do splendid flowers so vividly paint such a stunning landscape. Here are spacious beaches with sweeping bays, precipitous cliffs, caves and secluded coves.

This is a coast of great beauty, and great danger. Snug holiday cottages and camps nestle along the shore. And wrecks and graves serve as mute reminders of wild nights and prodigious storms. For it is here, around the southern end of the continent of Africa, that the sea one afternoon can be a mirror reflecting the face of heaven, and by the following dawn a ruthless, murderous chaos of turbulent water. Countless ships have succumbed to what Rudyard Kipling called 'the dread Agulhas roll' and modern seamen call 'the killer wave' — a sudden monstrous surge of water by which even the strongest vessel is likely to be torn asunder.

In many of the farmhouses in this part of the world are figureheads of ships and other fragments of wrecks. Beyond Arniston, a gravel road takes a circuitous route to Ryspunt, an atmospheric little coastal resort where a wrecked ship spilled its cargo of rice along the beach — hence the name of Ryspunt ('rice point'). The remnants of another wrecked ship, the *Clan McGregor*, still thrust above the sands here, 75 years after it ran ashore.

Except for the tantrums of periodic storms, the climate is mild. Rain falls mainly in the winter; spring and autumn are generally tranquil; summer can be warm to hot.

Numerous aquatic birds are attracted by the wealth of marine life along the coast. Penguins, gulls, cormorants and gannets thrive. Flamingoes occasionally breed in the shallow lakelets south of Bredasdorp and blue cranes, bustards and white storks are common. The white storks sometimes winter in the area instead of returning to Europe. Seals are also common.

On the beaches are many Stone Age fish traps, still in use. Fish are stranded in these traps at low tide.

For the botanist, ornithologist, fisherman, climber and walker, this is a unique and fascinating region to explore.

Arniston (*Waenhuiskrans*)

The fishing village of Arniston, with its many restored cottages, has retained its romantic character and atmosphere of the 19th century. The name comes from the shipwreck of a British troopship, the *Arniston*. The village is also known as Waenhuiskrans ('wagon house cliff'), from a nearby cavern, and this has recently become the official name.

The coastline here shows many spectacular results of sea erosion — huge caverns, arches and all manner of odd shapes.

Prehistoric fish traps can be seen along the coast. These are low, stone-built enclosures, submerged at high tide. Fish are trapped as the tide recedes. Huge piles of fish bones and shells on the beach are memorials to the feasts of a vanished people known as strandlopers ('beach walkers'), who foraged along the sea-shore for food.

Betty's Bay

The wealth of flowering plants that abounds in Betty's Bay is probably the most varied in southern Africa. This coastal area is the home of the 188-hectare Harold Porter Botanic Reserve, bequeathed to the National Botanic Gardens of South Africa in 1959 by one of the partners in Cape Hangklip Estates, Harold Nixon Porter. The beautiful red disa (*disa uniflora*) is found in the reserve.

The mountains, valleys and caves of the region were once hideaways for runaway slaves.

Betty's Bay was named after Betty Youlden, daughter of a property developer. The resort is beloved by fishermen and nature lovers.

Bredasdorp

On the north slopes of the 400-metre hill known as Preekstoel ('pulpit') lies the town of Bredasdorp, terminus of a railway line from Cape Town and a wheat and wool centre. The town was named after Michiel van Breda, a member of the Legislative Assembly in the 1830s.

The Waenhuiskrans cottages have large baking ovens.

Fishermen's cottages at Waenhuiskrans (Arniston).

Crudely sculpted tombstones in the fishermen's graveyard at Waenhuiskrans village.

THINGS TO DO AND SEE

Angling For the angler this is an enticing but dangerous coast. Many spectacular catches have been made, but many fishermen have been toppled by unexpected waves.

No other part of the coast of southern Africa, however, offers a greater variety or quantity of fish. The sea is full of game fish at all seasons of the year.

Yellowtail and bonito, leervis, tunny, huge kob, elf in shoals of thousands and red steenbras are all taken from the rocks around Cape Hangklip.

Hermanus is renowned for geelbek, kob and red stumpnose. Galjoen and white stumpnose are also present around Hermanus, and in Walker Bay. Whales also like Walker Bay and often calve there.

Boating Gordon's Bay, Strand, Hermanus, Gansbaai, Struisbaai and Arniston have harbours for small boats and there are many launching ramps along the coast. The lagoons at Hermanus, Bot River, Kleinmond and Palmiet River are favoured for yachting and canoeing.

Botanical and nature reserves Betty's Bay (the Harold Porter Botanic Reserve) and Hermanus (Fernkloof Nature Reserve) have collections of indigenous plants. In the mountains above these reserves one of the rarest of flowers, the marsh rose, has its home. Everlasting flowers are numerous in this area. The red species grows at Betty's Bay. Elim is also an area for these flowers.

Camping and caravanning The caravanner and camper are particularly well catered for. Site fees and standards vary to suit most pockets and requirements. There are clusters of caravan and camping grounds around such resorts as Kleinmond, Onrus, Hermanus, Cape Agulhas, Strand, Gordon's Bay, Struisbaai and Arniston. Other camping grounds are at Uilenskraal, Pearly Beach, Hawston and Gansbaai.

Hiking Start from any resort and walk to the next one, and you will find many secluded bays and promontories. Hermanus has a pleasant footpath winding for 12 kilometres along the rocky shore. The coast on either side of the great cave of Waenhuiskrans is wild and unspoiled, with many unusual rock formations and examples of natural erosion.

Swimming Apart from the beaches at such places as Strand, Gordon's Bay and Hermanus, there is fine fresh water swimming in rivers such as the Palmiet. Water in sea and rivers is generally around 21°C. in summer. An unusual place in which to swim is the underground stream at Die Kelders. The pools in the cave are filled with crystal clear water.

Spring in the Harold Porter Botanic Reserve at Betty's Bay. Daisies are in full bloom. In the distance is the blue sea.

Two of the town's earliest buildings survive as the Shipwreck Museum, which contains figureheads and wreckage from some of the many ships that have foundered on the southern coast.

Wild flowers, particularly the giant proteas, grow prolifically on the slopes of Preekstoel. A flower show is held in the town each August.

Cape Agulhas

According to De Castro's *Roteiro* the Portuguese gave the name Agulhas ('needles') to this cape because it is here, at the southernmost tip of Africa, that the needle of a compass points due north, without magnetic deviation.

At Cape Agulhas the African mainland peters out into a vast plain, with a last sigh in the form of a low range of hills. The plain slips beneath the waves, continues under the sea as the shallow Agulhas Bank — only 60 fathoms deep for 250 kilometres — and then abruptly plunges to 1 800 fathoms.

The Agulhas Bank is one of the world's most prolific commercial fishing grounds. Huge waves pound

Paradise for swimmers in underground pools

AMAZING JOURNEY OF THE SEA BEAN

The warm, powerful Agulhas-Mocambique Current brings a strange visitor to the coast of southern Africa — the sea bean.

Along riverbanks in tropical Africa grows a creeper, *Entada pursaetha*, which produces a bean pod about 1 metre long. The pod splits to release seeds which are dropped into the rivers, carried downstream, find, if they are fortunate, a place on which to grow on some mud bank or mangrove island, or are carried out to sea. The current then carries the seeds to Cape Agulhas, or even beyond as far as False Bay. Then the waves deposit the seeds on a beach, or in such an unlikely place as the great cavern of Waenhuiskrans.

African herbalists and Europeans have always prized these seeds. Their tough outer cases polish well and they can be seen in many display cabinets among collections of shells.

Horticulturists have successfully germinated such sea beans.

South of Cape Agulhas the sea remains shallow for 250 kilometres — then deep water stretches all the way to the Antarctic.

Flowers bloom on the thatched roof of a fisherman's cottage at Cape Agulhas.

in upon the cape's rocky coast. An 18 000 000-candlepower lighthouse guides shipping around the cape. Nearby are holiday cottages, a camp site, hotel and swimming pool.

Cape Hangklip

The Hottentots-Holland Mountains tumble into the sea at Cape Hangklip ('overhanging rock'), the most easterly point of False Bay. At the foot of the mountains is a lighthouse, a cluster of bungalows and a hotel.

This isolated territory once offered sanctuary to runaway slaves. In the late 18th century the Hangklip Drosters ('deserters') sheltered in a cave and stole the cattle of farmers who sent their livestock across Gandoupas ('pass of the eland'), the present Sir Lowry's Pass, to Cape Town. One group of herdsmen was murdered and two children kidnapped by the deserters. Their hideout was subsequently discovered, the children rescued and the band of 43 deserters massacred.

Danger Point

A lighthouse guards the rocky promontory of Danger Point, scene of the *Birkenhead* ship disaster. Near the lighthouse is a blow-hole which, in rough weather, sends a jet of water more than 10 metres into the air. (The blow-hole is the opening of a chasm leading to the sea.)

Die Kelders

An underground stream flows to the sea through the series of caves known as Die Kelders ('the cellars'). Crystal pools in the caverns are safe for swimming.

On the cliffs above the caves are a hotel and a cluster of bungalows.

Elim

The streets of the Moravian Mission station of Elim, established in 1824, are lined with water furrows, fruit trees and white-walled thatched cottages — Elim's roof-thatchers are renowned throughout southern Africa.

The lighthouse of Cape Agulhas and its keeper's quarters.

The Hottentots-Holland Mountains across Koeëlbaai.

THE SHIPWRECK THAT BEGAN THE HEROIC TRADITION OF 'WOMEN AND CHILDREN FIRST'

The captain of the sinking troopship gave the order: 'Every man for himself'. But the soldiers lined up on deck did not move. They knew that if one man broke ranks, it would lead to a rush that might overwhelm the lifeboats carrying women and children to safety.

This moment, when the troops stood on the doomed ship calmly awaiting their fate, was a milestone in the annals of heroism at sea. And it ensured a place in history for *HMS Birkenhead*, which went down off the coast of southern Africa in the early hours of 26 February 1852 with the loss of 445 lives.

The 1 900-ton *Birkenhead* was surrounded by controversy from the day she was launched, for she was one of the first warships with a hull of iron rather than wood. She had steam-driven paddle wheels as well as sails and was originally intended to be a frigate. But it was in the role of troop transport that she sailed from Cork for South Africa on 7 January 1852.

At Simon's Town, she took on coal and provisions and sailed again on 25 February with 638 people on board. They included 476 British soldiers bound for the Eighth Frontier War being fought in the eastern Cape, and 20 women and children.

The weather was calm and a course was set well clear of a coast notorious for its rocks.

But either through compass error, or currents taking the ship inshore, the *Birkenhead* went off course, and the following morning she ran on to

Thomas Hemy's classic painting of the troops awaiting their fate on the Birkenhead.

a pinnacle of rock off Danger Point, between Cape Hangklip and Cape Agulhas.

The metal hull was torn open and about 100 of the soldiers sleeping on the lower deck were drowned in their bunks. The rest of the troops were marshalled on deck and began helping the crew to man the pumps and free the lifeboats. The ship was grinding and shuddering on the rock and it was then that the master, Captain Robert Salmond, made what turned out to be a disastrous mistake. He tried to get the ship off the rock by ordering the crew to reverse engines. All this achieved was to rip out the bottom. The *Birkenhead*, and most of those on board, were now doomed.

The ship had eight boats, but some were awkwardly lashed to the paddle boxes and most had been so little used that their rigging was clogged with paint and the davits were jammed. Eventually, three boats were lowered into the water and the women and children scrambled into them.

The captain, realizing the end had come, cried out: 'Save yourselves. All those who can swim jump overboard and make for the boats.' At these words, the soldiers' commanding officer, Lieutenant-Colonel Alexander Seton, leaped in front of his men and told them: 'Stand fast. I beg you, do not rush the boats carrying the women and children. You will swamp them.' Colonel Seton drew his sword, ready to cut down the first man who panicked. But he had no need to use it. The soldiers remained in their ranks — even when the ship split in two and the

funnel and main mast crashed on to the deck.

A number of horses which had been in stalls on the deck were blindfolded so they could be driven over the side to take their chance in the water. A few moments later, the *Birkenhead* tilted and all on deck were hurled into the sea.

Some were picked up by the lifeboats. Others clung to floating wreckage. Those who could swim struck out for the shore.

For many, there awaited an even worse fate than drowning — the water was infested with sharks.

Of the 638 people who sailed from Simon's Town, only 193 survived. The captain and Colonel Seton were among those who perished.

Gold reputed to be worth almost £300 000 also went down with the *Birkenhead*. Admiralty attempts to salvage the gold were made in 1854, 1893 and 1958, but without success. The remains of the wreck lie in about 30 metres of water and are fairly easy to reach. Scuba divers still periodically explore the area, but if any of the gold has been found it has not been reported to the authorities.

Echoes of the tragedy survive to this day, for the behaviour of the troops became known as the Birkenhead Drill and established the standard of manly courage summed up in the cry: 'Women and children first.'

The rock on which the ship came to grief is known as Birkenhead Rock and a memorial to those who died can be seen at Danger Point.

Sea creatures great and small find a special haven

The town's watermill is one of the oldest of its kind in southern Africa.

Figs grow particularly well here and in mid-summer masses of everlasting flowers cover the countryside. These strange and beautiful flowers are exported in large numbers and are placed on graves all over the world.

Gans Baai
The harbour of Gans Baai ('goose bay') shelters a fleet of boats which fish in Walker Bay and on the Agulhas Bank.

Gordon's Bay
A famed marine drive is cut into the mountains that crowd along the shoreline overlooking the fishing harbour at Gordon's Bay, named after Captain Robert Gordon, of the Dutch East India Company, who explored the area in 1778. Gordon's Bay has camping and caravanning facilities, and many holiday houses. Fishing is the major pastime.

Hermanus
An itinerant teacher and shepherd,

THE SPORTING FEAST THAT AWAITS THE ANGLER IN THE WATERS OF SOUTHERN AFRICA

Anglers can find tremendous sport and many an excellent meal among the 1 300 or so species of fish frequenting the waters around the coast of southern Africa. About 43 per cent of the species live exclusively on the east side in the warm Mocambique Current, while the rest live either on the cold west side or are cosmopolitan, moving from one coast to the other and adapting to great changes in temperature.

Many of the warm-water fish make

A gleaming haul of silverfish.

fine eating and since most of them are shallow-water species they can be caught by line fishermen from the shore.

The yellowtail is the great game fish of this coast. It weights 5-20 kilograms and is a courageous fighter. Bonitos go up to 10 kilograms and will put up stiff resistance.

Garrick, or leervis, and geelbek are abundant. The kabeljou is plentiful and makes fine eating grilled or fried. The shad, or elf, feeds along the coast in huge shoals.

Weighing up to 8 kilograms, it is a lively and very tasty fish and is caught in considerable numbers.

Grunter, bronze bream and hottentot are all plentiful and excellent to eat. Steenbras and stumpnose are numerous too. Of the others, the galjoen is arguably the tastiest of all South African table fish, and the red roman is also popular.

Apart from game fish, commercial species such as kingklip, sole and hake are caught by trawler fleets in the deeper waters of the Agulhas Bank.

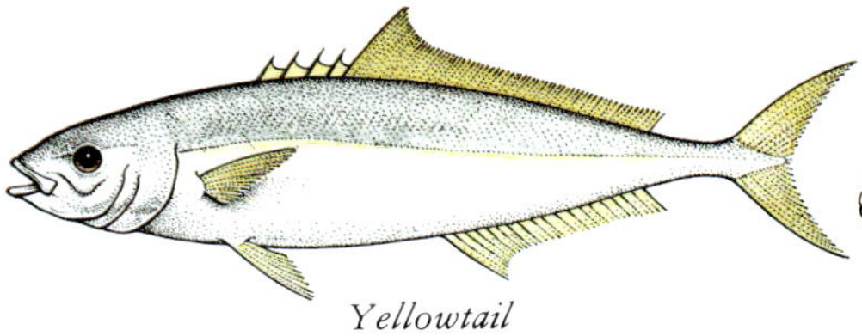

Yellowtail

Red stumpnose

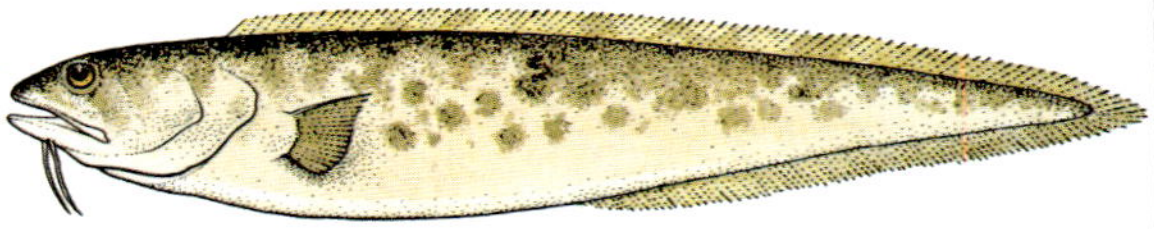

Kingklip

Leervis

Geelbek

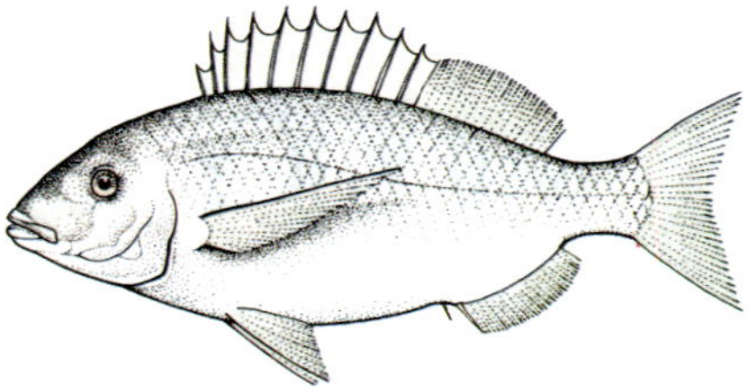

White steenbras

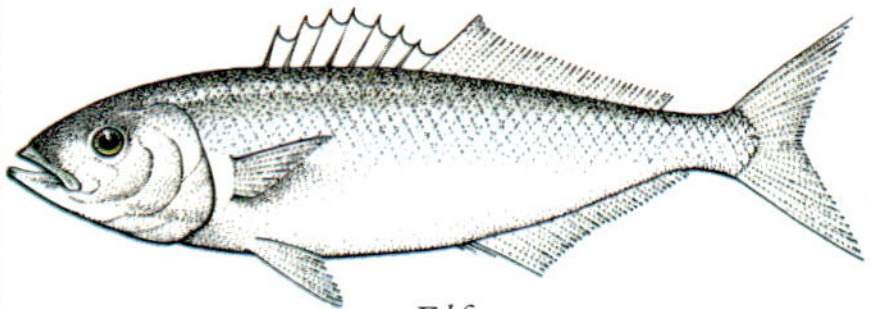

Elf

Silverfish

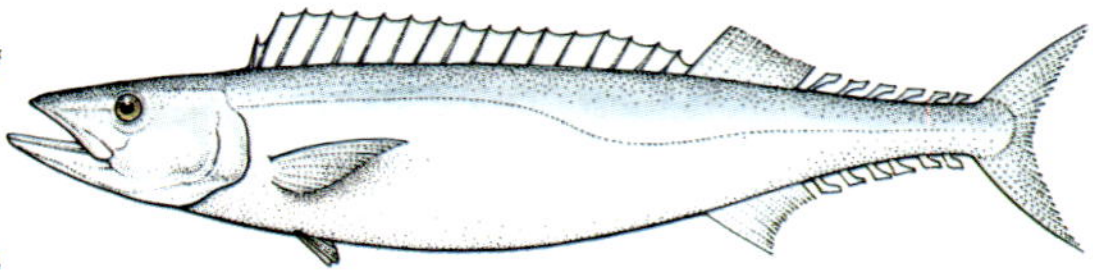

Snoek

Galjoen

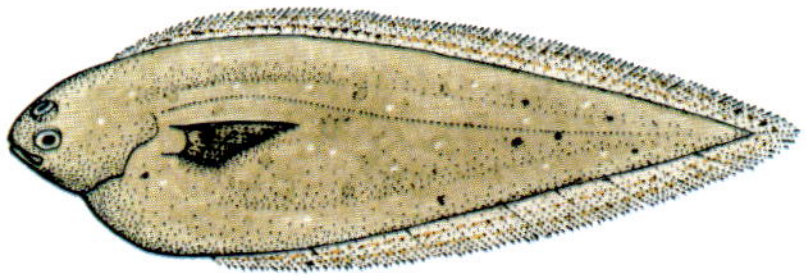

Sole

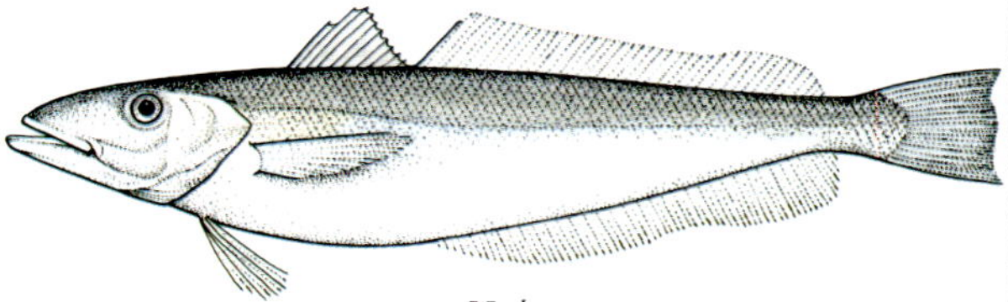

Hake

The watermill at Elim, now restored and a national monument.

The mission church of Elim. Its clock, built in 1764, was imported from Germany.

Hermanus Pieters, was the father of Hermanus. He crossed the mountains and, in the 1830s, camped near a fountain on the shore. Each summer he fished here and grazed sheep.

Others joined Pieters at his fountain. Fishermen and lime-makers were attracted by the shoals of fish and the deposits of shells along the coast.

There was a small natural harbour for fishing boats tricky to enter but snug inside. Fish were caught in vast quantities and shipped to Kalk Bay.

Anglers and holidaymakers were eventually attracted to the area, and a village grew, with hotels and stores. Most buildings were white-walled (the lime was obtained by burning sea-shells) and black-thatched (reeds at the lagoon provided the roofing).

The whole of the old harbour has been restored and converted into an open-air museum. Old-fashioned fishing boats have been placed on the ramp leading down to the water. Old buildings have been reconstructed, and now house a small museum.

The village is famous as a fishing resort. Many large sharks and kabel-jou have been caught. Fishing craft shelter in the new harbour. There are several hotels and caravan parks, and the lagoon is popular for water-sports.

A scenic drive has been cut into the mountain slopes and provides panoramic views of the town and the sea.

The fishing harbour of Gordon's Bay at sunset. The Hottentots-Holland Mountains loom in the background, their peaks covered for the night in a blanket of cloud.

The pine-bordered dam that is a scenic wonderland

The Fernkloof Nature Reserve at Hermanus has 30 kilometres of footpaths giving access to areas rich in birds, game and wildflowers.

There is also a picturesque 18-hole golf course, and 12 kilometres of beautiful 'cliff paths' that lead along the shore.

Kleinmond

A resort at a minor mouth of the Bot River, Kleinmond ('small mouth') has camping, picnic and caravan sites. The Palmiet River reaches the sea through a lagoon nearby, and there is a 650 hectare reserve noted for its unique indigenous flora. Lagoons here are safe for swimming but the shelved beach is dangerous.

Koeëlbaai (Kogelbaai)

A handsome bay below the Hottentots-Holland Mountains. The beach at Koeëlbaai ('bullet bay') is spacious but dangerous for swimming because of a powerful backwash. Fishing is good. The resort has a large camping ground and caravan park.

Onrus

The name Onrus ('restless') refers to the pounding of the surf on the rocky coast.

Onrus has a small beach, lagoon, natural swimming pool in the rocks, and a large camping ground.

Orothamnus Reserve

A conservation area for the marsh rose, *Orothamnus zeyheri*, was established in 1969 in a 12-hectare area of the mountains above Hermanus. Recent experiments have shown that by grafting the marsh rose onto *Leucosper-*

Fishermen's vantage points on the coast towards Cape Hangklip.

The calm waters of the lagoon at Hermanus are ideal for water sports.

The old fishing harbour at Hermanus, now a national monument.

The view west from Cape Hangklip across False Bay to the Cape Peninsula. False Bay is one of the great angling waters of the world.

Waenhuiskrans coast in tranquil mood.

The gaping cavern of Waenhuiskrans.

Fisherman's cottage at Waenhuiskrans, well insulated by thick walls and thatch.

mum conocarpodendron root stock, it may be propagated in nurseries. Such grafted plants therefore will become reasonably common in protea nurseries and botanical gardens.

Pearly Beach
Great sand dunes border the shore at Pearly Beach where swimming and walking are popular.

Salmonsdam Nature Reserve
The 856-hectare Salmonsdam Nature Reserve, controlled by the Caledon Divisional Council, provides a sanctuary for plants and animals of the area. The reserve, at the head of a deep valley, has a network of paths, a dramatic mountain drive for cars, and camping facilities.

Steenbras Dam
The dam at Steenbras, developed as a recreational area, is one of the scenic show-pieces of southern Africa.

Twelve hundred hectares of pines have been planted around the dam, the wall of which rises 24 metres above its foundations. The riverbanks below have been terraced and laid with rock gardens.

Beyond the dam the river bed drops rapidly 300 metres to the Steenbras River mouth, 3 kilometres away.

Permits to visit the dam are available at the municipal offices in Cape Town and most of the towns nearby. Rondavels can be rented.

Strand
Once a seaside suburb of Somerset West, Strand has grown into a considerable town.

Its spacious beach is considered to be one of the safest beaches along the South African coast.

Struisbaai
Originally known as Vogel Struis (ostrich) Baai, this resort is popular with fishermen and swimmers.

Uilenskraal
Off the shore at Uilenskraal ('owl corral') lie two small islands, Dyer and Geyser, the homes of penguins and seals.

The resort has a large camping ground and caravan park, and is a favourite spot for swimming and fishing.

Waenhuiskrans
The giant sea cave of Waenhuiskrans ('wagon house cliff'), 1,5 kilometres south of Arniston, takes its name because of its resemblance to a waenhuis — the structure in which ox-wagons were sheltered. The cave can be visited at low tide. Sea beans (see box, page 62) are often found on the floor of the cave.

Where the king of flowers reigns supreme

The name of the Coast of Flowers was not given without excellent reason. It is the heart of the spectacular natural garden of the western Cape — a garden which yields a profusion of wild flowers, a number of which are shown here and overleaf.

The mountains overlooking the coast are rich in proteas. Carolus Linnaeus, the Swedish botanist, named these spectacular flowering plants after the Greek god Proteus, who was gifted with the power of infinitely changing his appearance. The protea family are noted for their varied appearances and extraordinary individuality. They grow mainly in South Africa and Australia. In South Africa there are 14 genera and nearly 400 species.

Protea cynaroides, the king protea or giant protea, is the national flower of South Africa. With a flowerhead about 30 centimetres across, brilliantly coloured a deep pink, and an imposing presence, this protea is regarded by many as the king of all flowers.

P. repens is the sugarbush. It is light yellow or red and noted for the unusually large amount of nectar it produces. This flower was particularly prized by early settlers, who derived from it sugarbush syrup.

P. compacta is deep pink and *P. nerifolia* is a bearded protea, with black hairs at the tips of the bracts. It ranges from white to red.

P. stokoei has a brown beard on

Serruria florida, *the 'blushing bride', which was once almost extinct.*

red bracts. It grows high on mountain slopes, liking mists and coolness.

P. grandiceps, coral red in colour, and *P. magnifica*, red to yellow, have fluffy flowerheads often likened to a Father Christmas with red cloak, ermine trims and white beard.

P. aristata is a rare, red protea, protected in Seweweekspoort in the Swartberg. *P. lorea*, a brilliant golden species, grows in the southern Cape, especially near Heidelberg.

P. cryophila is the pure white so-called snow protea, which grows above the snow line in the Cedarberg. This is a gorgeous flower. If it was not so resistant to cultivation it would be the pride of florists' shops for its snowball-like appearance.

The beetle daisy, a Gorteria *species.*

A Leucospermum *pincushion.*

The Dimorphotheca pluvialis *daisy.*

Protea cynaroides, *national emblem.*

The Kolkol, Berzelia abrotanoides.

Red hairy erica, Erica cerinthoides.

Orothamnus zeyheri, *the marsh rose.*

The March Lily, Brunsvigia bosmaniae.

The Euryops speciosissimus, *daisy bush, a native of the south-western Cape.*

The water oxalis, Oxalis disticha, *which grows on the surface of calm ponds.*

Fragrant, long-lasting Chincherinchees (Ornithogalum thyrsoides).

Gold clusters of the mealie heath, Erica patersonia, *grow in the southern Cape.*

How the marsh rose defied extinction

Arctotis fastuosa *can stand extremes of weather, but prefers arid areas.*

The rare *Orothamnus zeyheri*, the marsh rose, is also a member of the protea family. The wax-like, red flowers are so seldom seen that at times they have been feared to be extinct. Their home is in the high mountains above Betty's Bay and Hermanus.

They defied cultivation until recently, when a means was discovered of grafting them onto a root stock of the *Leucospermum* genus — popularly known as the pincushions.

There are many varieties of pincushions in most parts of the southern and western Cape. *L. cordifolium* grows in the Caledon area; *L. cuneiforme* is to be seen from Swellendam to Mossel Bay; *L. reflexum* and *L. spathulatum* have their homes in the Cedarberg, and throughout the Cape the visitor is constantly delighted by the sight of these shrubs covered in hundreds of vividly coloured flowers.

The genus *Mimetes* has 12 species in the southern Cape. They resist cultivation, but have the most exotic-looking flowers imaginable.

The lovely *Serruria* genus is yet another family division of the *Proteaceae* with flowers of great delicacy. *S. florida* is the blushing bride, now cultivated, while *S. barbigera* and *S. elongata*, with their coral-coloured flowers, grow in the Caledon area.

There are 80 species of *Leucadendrons*, the second largest genus of the *Proteaceae*, and they are found throughout the Coast of Flowers. The delight of exploring the area for such flowers provides many people with their most memorable holidays.

A species of Gladiolus.

A rocket-like Leucospermum.

A species of Trachyandra.

Drosanthemum *growing in mats.*

Leucospermum conocarpodendron, *Kreupelboom, used as firewood by colonists.*

The flowers of Grielum humifusum *are a delicate blend* of cream and yellow.

The colours of the bearded Protea magnifica *range from yellow to red.*

Dainty Dorotheanthus bellidiformis.

Lovely Helichrysum, *or everlasting.*

Arum lilies, a rare prize in Europe, grow like weeds in the western Cape, especially in damp or marshy soil.

THE VALLEY OF PEARLS

IN 1657 AN EXPLORER named Abraham Gabbema was sent from the settlement at the Cape to search for additional supplies of fresh meat. He was the first European to find a way into the Berg River Valley.

The cluster of granite domes that dominates the valley's middle reaches was glistening after rain, and looked to Gabbema like giant pearls and diamonds. He named the valley Pêrelvallei ('valley of pearls'). The valley's original name still clings to the town of Paarl, the principal centre and most convenient base from which to explore this green, fertile part of southern Africa.

As the name Berg ('mountain') suggests, this is a valley set amid mountain ranges. The source of the river is located high above Franschhoek. It then flows north, veering to west, to the Atlantic Ocean 200 kilometres away. The river runs through one of the richest farming areas of the western Cape and the vineyards, orchards and estates are well worth seeing. Many Cape-Dutch style homesteads are visible from the main roads, and their proud owners have maintained them in their original splendour.

Throughout the year the valley is graced with scenic beauty: in autumn the deciduous trees are brilliantly coloured; winter brings snow to the high peaks and a multitude of waterfalls to the lower slopes; spring is gay with the hues of myriad flowers; and in summer, warm and sultry, the orchards and vineyards are heavy with fruit.

For wine lovers, March is a particularly exciting month in the Berg River Valley. Fruit is being harvested, and the packing houses are all working to capacity. The aroma of grapes and new wine pervades the air. It is in this month, too, that South Africa's annual wine auction is held on the Nederburg estate. This auction has an international standing, comparable to the great auctions of Europe, and attracts connoisseurs and buyers from all over the world.

Backsberg

In 1916 Charles Back acquired the wine estate of Klein Babylonstoren ('little tower of Babylon'), the vineyards of which lie on the lower slopes of Simonsberg.

Differences in soil and climate favour the production of delicate white wines and full-bodied reds. Visitors are able to tour the cellars, and there is a small museum containing wine-making implements.

Bain's Kloof Pass

The 30-kilometre Bain's Kloof Pass, completed in 1853, is one of the most picturesque roads in the Cape. It was built, using convict labour, by Andrew Geddes Bain, the most famous of southern Africa's road engineers.

At the summit (595 metres) are a plantation of trees and a picnic ground.

Here the road joins the valley of the Witrivier (or Witte Rivier), which descends the northern side of the mountains through a precipitous cleft to a stretch of rapids, waterfalls and natural swimming pools.

Half way down the pass is an attractive camping ground, with an especially beautiful river pool set amid smooth boulders. Here begins a popular circular walk through what is known as Wolvenkloof ('cleft of the hyenas'), which has many interesting rock formations and wild flowers.

Du Toit's Kloof Pass

The Cape to Cairo road finds its way from the Berg River Valley to the Breë River Valley over high mountains by means of Du Toit's Kloof Pass.

Francois du Toit, who gave his name to the pass, was a 17th century Huguenot pioneer who settled in the foothills of the mountains below the pass, then little more than an animal track. A road was not built along the pass until World War II.

A tranquil stretch of the Witrivier flowing through Paradise Valley.

Sunlight sparkles on the Berg River as it meanders among lush vegetation.

The romantic Cape-Cairo road threads its way through the dramatic Du Toit's Kloof Pass. These craggy heights were once known as 'the mountains of Africa'.

The original pass was 48 km long and climbed to an altitude of 820 m. In 1988 the Huguenot Tunnel, 3 913 m long, was opened. With an approach viaduct, the largest curved structure in South Africa, the tunnel shortens the mountain passage by 11 km and is operated as a toll road.

The surrounding peaks, often snow-covered, offer some exhilarating climbs. The Cape Town and Paarl sections of the Mountain Club of South Africa have huts in the area.

The highest mountain overlooking the pass is Dutoitspiek, 1 995 metres high.

K.W.V.

Founded in 1918, the Co-operative Wine Farmers' Association of South Africa, the K.W.V., has its offices at La Concorde on Main Street in Paarl. In Kohler Street are the K.W.V. cellars, among the largest cellar complexes in the world. From here 70 per cent of South Africa's wine exports are transported.

The cellars contain superbly hand-carved vats. Tours are arranged.

Nederburg

With a tradition dating back to 1792, the Nederburg estate is famous for its fine wines.

The original H-shaped dwelling house, with its elaborate gables, has been magnificently preserved, and nestles amidst the beautiful vineyards that blanket the valley floor. Tours of the homestead and the cellars can be arranged.

Paarl

The 'pearl' of the Berg River Valley,

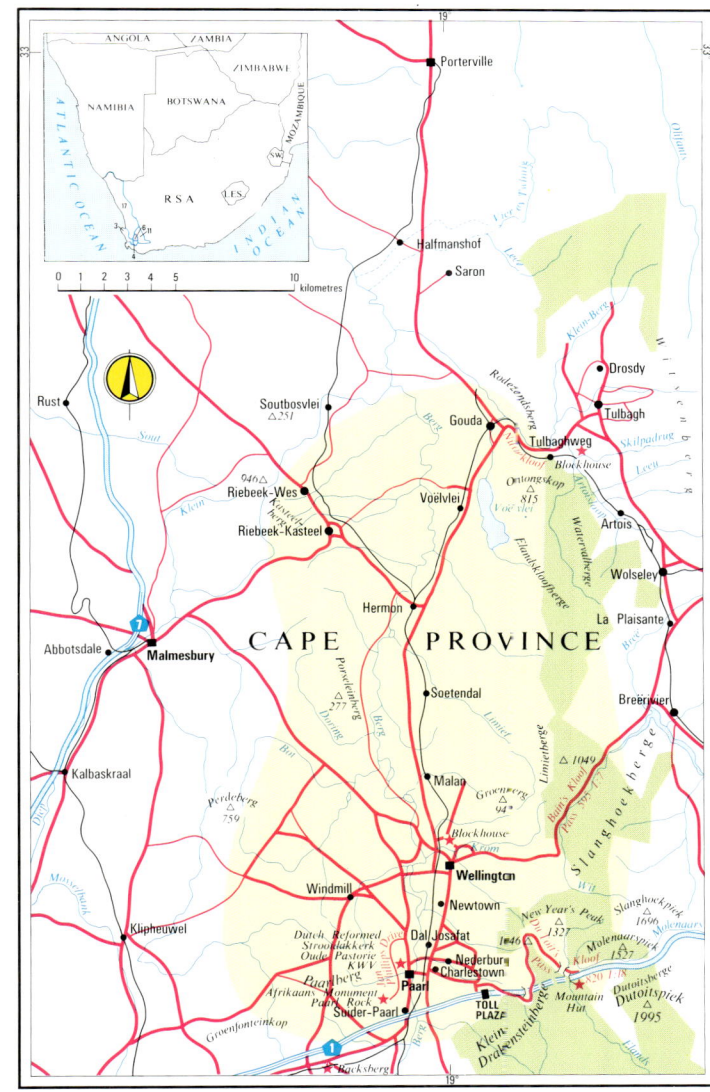

THINGS TO DO AND SEE

Angling The Berg River and the Witrivier are good for trout fishing.

Camping and caravanning The Paarl Municipal Caravan Park at Wateruintjiesvlei is pleasantly situated in a pine forest. Wellington Municipality has a popular camp. At the north-eastern end of Bain's Kloof Pass there is a camping ground managed by the forestry department, opposite a swimming pool in the Witrivier. Campers' Paradise is on the banks of the Berg River above Paarl. Oude Molen, with its bungalows, flats, caravan and camping sites, is higher up the valley.

Canoeing The Berg River is the scene of the annual four-day canoe race staged during the July flood season.

Climbing The Paarl and Cape Town sections of the Mountain Club of South Africa have huts in the Du Toit's Kloof area.

Sailing The great dam of Voëlvlei is used by yachtsmen. It has slipways and a clubhouse.

Swimming The Witrivier, a raging torrent of white water in the rainy season (hence its name, 'wit', or 'white'), contains waterfalls, rapids and many deep pools.

Tours The huge cellars of the K.W.V. in Paarl provide a fascinating tour. Lectures and films are given in the exhibition hall, and there is a wine house and restaurant, Laborie. The famous wine estates of Backsberg, Bellingham, Landskroon and Nederburg also welcome visitors.

Walking Paths lead to the tops of all the granite domes overlooking Paarl. A permit from the Bainsberg forestry station allows access to many paths in the Bain's Kloof area.

A romantic old town standing in the shade of stately oaks

Paarl is a romantic town built on both sides of a 10-kilometre Main Street, shaded by oaks and jacarandas.

Although Europeans settled in the valley in 1687, Paarl did not begin to take shape until 1720, when a church was built and a street laid out and planted with the oaks for which the town is famous.

Paarl became the principal centre in southern Africa for the manufacture of wagons. The local granite provided ample raw material for the manufacture of tombstones and prepared building stone. Other industries include fruit-growing, wine-making, the manufacture of eau de cologne, cigarettes and jam, and the canning of fruit and vegetables.

Many of Paarl's ancient buildings remain. Among these is the Dutch Reformed Strooidakkerk ('thatched church'). Built in 1805, it is one of the oldest churches still in use in southern Africa. The graveyard contains several famed gabled vaults.

Another of the older buildings in the town — the Oude Pastorie ('old parsonage') — is a museum. Its displays include Cape Dutch furniture, silver, brass and copper.

The Gideon Malherbe House in

FRUIT FROM ALL OVER THE WORLD FLOURISHES IN THE ORCHARDS OF THE CAPE

The Berg River Valley is the birthplace of South Africa's fruit export industry. With rich soil, warm climate, ample water, easy access to Cape Town harbour and the markets of the interior, the valley is ideally endowed and situated for such an industry.

The types of fruit produced, the so-called cultivars — cultivated varieties — originate from many countries.

Nurserymen and researchers imported and bred them, always searching for improved varieties that were more prolific, more resistant to disease, and more suited to handling, packing and shipping.

The Government Fruit Technology Research Institute's farm of Bien Donne is the scene of many experiments in the breeding of new varieties, and the testing of imported cultivars.

A few kilometres down river lies the celebrated commercial nursery founded in the late 19th century by the indefatigable Harry Pickstone and his brother Horace. The Pickstones introduced fruits from many countries to South Africa.

After the apple and grape, the peach is the most important of the deciduous fruits grown in the western Cape. From its origin in China the peach reached Europe through Persia — its name means 'Persian apple'.

The Portuguese carried peach stones to many of their overseas possessions and planted trees in suitable areas.

One of their orchards was on St. Helena Island and it was from there that the first seeds were obtained by Jan van Riebeeck for his garden in Cape Town.

The pioneer peaches were the hardy yellow variety and they took to South Africa so well that many escaped the fetters of cultivation and the veld became their home. The yellow peach trees growing alongside the railway lines in many parts of South Africa are the result of train travellers throwing peach stones out of their windows.

Harry Pickstone imported several peach cultivars, such as the once widely grown Peregrine. Other varieties, such as the early-season Rhodes and the late-season Boland, have been bred in the research nurseries. The standard canning peach, the Kaka-

One of the most succulent of South Africa's peaches is the Rhodes peach.

The Santa Rosa plum, from America, is a standard dessert variety.

mas, was found in 1933 by chance, growing wild on the banks of the Orange River at Kakamas. A teacher of agriculture, A. D. Collins, sent samples down to the fruit research scientists in the western Cape. The peach proved to be a prolific bearer, perfectly adapted to South Africa, with large golden fruit, flesh of fine but firm texture and delicious in flavour. It was propagated as quickly

The Bon Chrétien pear (or Bartlett), bred in Britain in the 18th century.

The Golden King plum is beautiful in colour and piquant in flavour.

as possible and in the first year of bearing — 1943 — increased by two-and-a-half times the volume of canning in South Africa.

The pear is another major fruit crop of the western Cape. Its natural home is Europe. The most widely grown pear cultivar in the world is a variety bred in England in the 1760s and perfected by a nurseryman named Williams who named it the Bon Chrétien ('good Christian'). Enoch Bartlett introduced this succulent pear to America in 1799 and his name is attached to it by many producers. In the western Cape it is a standard cultivar and forms the bulk of the 119 000 tons of pears produced each year.

Plums originated from Japan and the East. As a commercial crop they have been perfected largely by American nurserymen and scientists. South Africa imported most of its cultivars from America, the most popular in the western Cape being the Santa Rosa, the Kelsey and the Gaviota.

The home of apricots seems to have been southern Europe and their name comes from the Latin *praecox* ('early ripe'). In their short season about 33 000 tons of such cultivars as the old French Royal are produced, mainly for jam, canning and drying. Dried, cooked apricots, with pumpkin, rice and succulent lamb, have been a favourite dinner for South African farmers since the early days.

In recent years a growing number of fruit farmers have begun producing nectarines in considerable quantities, and many have been experimenting successfully with Kiwi fruit, also known as Chinese gooseberry.

Much of the western Cape's fruit is exported. With modern handling and refrigeration methods, it can be on sale in perfect condition at markets overseas two weeks after being picked.

The homestead of the Nancy estate nestling amid lush vineyards.

End of the production line . . . the bottling plant at Nederburg.

Casks of wine maturing in the spacious cellars of the KWV in Paarl.

The Oude Pastorie in Paarl is a museum famed for its Cape Dutch furniture.

Parsonage Lane was the home of Gideon Jozua Malherbe, one of the eight founders of the Genootskap van Regte Afrikaners, which was formed in 1875 and laid the foundations of the Afrikaans language. In the house, among many of its former owner's possessions, is the printing press on which *Die Patriot*, the first Afrikaans newspaper, was printed.

Nearby, on the southern slope of Paarl mountain, stands the Afrikaans Language Monument.

Originally part of a farm, the Huis Vergenoegd in Main Street is owned by the Historical Houses of South Africa and administered by the Dutch Reformed Church as a home for the aged. It retains its old windows and yellow-wood and stinkwood doors.

The original well is in the backyard.

Many of Paarl's gardens have spectacular displays of roses, hydrangeas and indigenous flowers.

Paarl Mountain (*Paarlberg*)

The Khoikhoi called this granite cluster Tortoise Mountain — its domed, oval summit (728 metres) is indeed like a tortoise shell. The mountain is one of the few to have been proclaimed a national monument.

On the slopes tower the three largest granite outcrops in South Africa — Paarl Rock, Britannia Rock (Bretagneklip) and Gordon's Rock. From their summits are fine views of the Berg River Valley, with Table Mountain in the distance.

The 11-kilometre Jan Phillips Drive,

THE GHOST WITH THE RED-HOT HANDSHAKE

The old homesteads of the Cape are rich in folk-lore and tales of phantoms, ghosts and other supernatural squatters. One of the most colourful is the story of the apparition said to haunt the Brakfontein farm near Wellington — the ghost with the red-hot handshake.

About 1880, the legend goes, a former owner died and the farm was taken over by his brother-in-law, an unpleasant character who began to make life difficult for the dead man's widow and daughter.

The girl was being courted by a young man from Wellington. One night, after spending a few hours with his sweetheart, he was untethering his horse in the dark beyond the verandah when he became aware of a figure looking at him. Feeling an eerie chill, the young man asked the stranger to identify himself. The shadow answered that he was the former owner.

'But he's been dead for a year,' the youth gasped. The ghost chuckled and moved into the light. There was no doubt who it was.

'I want you to give a message to my brother-in-law,' said the ghost. 'Tell him to treat my wife better or it will be the worse for him. To prove that I mean it, here is my hand — but first, wrap your saddle blanket around your own hand.'

The young man was puzzled, but did as he was told. The ghost then firmly shook his hand and, as it did so, there was a puff of smoke and a strong smell of burning.

The next instant the ghost had vanished, but it had left behind a distinctive calling card — the imprint of a hand burned into the blanket. This was enough to send the brother-in-law packing, and the family was left to live in peace.

Another strange story is told about the original house of Paarl Diamant on the west side of Paarl Mountain. The owner of this farm in the 1920s was visited in a dream by a ghost which told him of a treasure of old coins hidden in the walls of the house.

When he awoke, the owner explored and found the coins. But he ignored the ghost's plea that the money should be returned to the previous owner from whom the ghost had stolen it.

The ghost kept returning to repeat its plea, so the man moved house. But by this time the age of the telephone had caught up with him, and he became plagued with phantom calls about the money.

At last, his nerves shattered, he sent what was left of the money to the rightful owner and the persistent ghost ceased its haunting.

The place they called 'the limit of civilization'

built in 1928 and largely financed by Jan Phillips, a wagon builder, leads to the foot of Gordon's and Britannia rocks. The drive branches off Paarl's main street, climbs the mountain, crosses the massif and then loops down into the town. Along the drive are a picnic ground and paths leading to the Mill Stream Wild Flower Garden, notable for its pincushions and blushing brides. Close to the garden a road branches off and climbs to Britannia Rock and Gordon's Rock.

Porterville
A farming centre, founded in 1863 and named after William Porter, the attorney-general at that time.

The old naval gun that stands outside the court was formerly used as a signal gun by the Dutch East India Company.

Van Riebeeck's Kasteel
Two small villages, Riebeek-Kasteel and Riebeek-Wes, lie on the slopes of the rugged Van Riebeeck's Kasteel (Kasteelberg), a solitary mountain dominating this section of the Berg River Valley.

Voëlvlei
The dam at Voëlvlei ('bird marsh') supplies water to the western Cape.

During the dry summer months it also feeds the Berg River.

The dam was originally a marsh containing more mud than water. In 1952 the marsh was converted into a dam 8 kilometres by 1,5 kilometres, fed by water deflected from the Klein-Bergrivier by a canal.

Voëlvlei Dam is the headquarters of the Voëlvlei Yacht Club. The dam is well stocked with bass.

The granite dome known as Britannia Rock at Paarl. Behind it, to the left, lies the Groot Drakenstein Valley. To the right, its head in the clouds, is the Simonsberg.

The Strooidakkerk in Paarl . . . one of the oldest churches in use in South Africa.

The imposing facade of La Concorde, KWV administrative headquarters.

Racks of apricots drying in the sun at Groenvlei Farm, in the Bovlei area of Wellington. Fruit harvesting time brings the countryside colourfully alive.

FROM THE MELTING POT OF MANY CULTURES, A VITAL NEW LANGUAGE IS BORN

Arnoldus Pannevis championed the first study of Afrikaans.

Part of Pannevis's Afrikaans poem, Ideaal.

DIE
Afrikaanse Patriot.

"Eert uwen vader en uwe moeder, opdat uwen dagen verlengd worden in het land dat u de Heere uw God geeft."
—Het vijfde Gebod.

DEEL I.] SATURDAG, 15 JANUARY, 1876. [No. I.

"DIE AFRIKAANSE PATRIOT."

Een Afrikaanse koerant! Wie het dit ooit gedroom! Ja, Afrikaanders! een koerant in ons ei'e taal! Dit het baiang moeite gekos om so vêr te kom; dit kan ek julle verseker, want die meeste Afrikaanders is nes steeks pêrde, hulle wil mos nie glo dat ons een ei'e taal het nie. Die ou'e Patriotte hou vas, en klou vas, an die *Hollans* taal;

The historic first issue of Die Afrikaanse Patriot.

It can be said of Afrikaans that, like the celebrated Topsy, 'it just growed' from the soil of South Africa. In the human melting pot of the Cape it was inevitable that, from the original Dutch spoken by the first settlers, a colloquial form would be evolved by people such as the Khoikhoi and slaves from Malaya, Indonesia, Madagascar and West Africa.

These diverse peoples all needed to talk to one another and basic Dutch, littered with additional words of Malaysian and African origin, became the vehicle of communication common to them all. Huguenot settlers added new words and altered the sound of old ones, and a multi-national community of seafarers introduced other novelties of speech. Then the occupation of the Cape by the British brought English words and influences to the local 'lingua Cape'.

While Dutch remained the official language, more and more words of the new tongue began to appear in the books of travellers describing the speech and life of the peoples of the Cape. By the mid-19th century, the world had an expressive and solidly entrenched new language — Afrikaans.

At Paarl Gymnasium High School, a Dutch teacher of classical languages, Arnoldus Pannevis, was fascinated by this language. In 1875 he and some colleagues formed the Genootskap van Regte Afrikaners ('Institute of True Afrikaners').

Meetings were held in the Paarl home of one of the members, Gideon Malherbe, and a grammar and vocabulary were prepared. A small press was obtained and, on 15 January 1876, the first issue of the first Afrikaans newspaper, *Die Afrikaanse Patriot*, was published. The little press, set up in a spare room in Malherbe's house, turned out many pioneer books in Afrikaans. The house is a museum today, displaying books and other items from the childhood of the Afrikaans language.

In 1896 a congress to discuss the usage of the language was held in Paarl and a campaign was launched which led to the substitution, in 1925, of Afrikaans for Dutch as one of the two official languages of South Africa.

Today Afrikaans is the home language of 20 per cent of the people of southern Africa. In its short life it has adapted to great changes in the world. It is an expressive language, rich in similes and metaphors.

'You can't squeeze blood from a stone,' says the Englishman.

The Afrikaner agrees with a nonchalant shrug, 'You can't pluck feathers from a frog'.

Born in the Cape — the tavern of the seas — with its wines, seafarers and happy drinkers, Afrikaans has many terms of value to the drinking man. What could be more descriptive of a sailor rolling back to the docks than:

'His hold's full and some's on deck, too.'

Or, of a drunken farmer:

'He's doing the ostrich trot behind the fence.'

Or:

'He's riding home back to front on the horse.'

In 1975 a monument to Afrikaans was unveiled on a site overlooking Paarl and the Berg River Valley.

Designed by Jan van Wijk, it consists of three linked columns symbolizing the contribution of the Western world to Afrikaans, three rounded shapes representing the contribution of Africa, and a wall standing for the contribution of the Malaysian people.

A fountain symbolizes new ideas and a pillar soaring 57 metres above the fountain represents the growth of the language. The pillar is hollow, and light from above pours down it, illuminating the fountain.

A second pillar represents the political development of the Republic of South Africa and its close associations with the growth of Afrikaans.

Wellington

The valley in which Wellington lies was regarded by the early settlers as the farthest limit of civilization. When they settled here, in 1688, they named it Limiet Vallei. Later it was renamed Wagenmakers Vallei — a wagon-building industry developed when the Kimberley diamond fields were discovered.

The town of Wellington, named after the Duke of Wellington by the governor, Sir George Napier, was established in 1840.

Among Wellington's most prominent citizens have been the Voortrekker leader, Piet Retief, the Reverend Andrew Murray and the Reverend M. L. de Villiers, composer of the national anthem.

The region is famous for its fruit, particularly apricots, and wine. Among the historic farms here are Champagne — on which the town was founded, Hexenberg, De Fortuin and Leewen Vallei.

Wellington is also a major educational centre, home of the Huguenot College, founded in 1873 by the Reverend Andrew Murray, and South Africa's oldest teacher-training college, established in 1896.

Here too is the Republic's largest piano factory.

The most southerly of a chain of blockhouses that were built by the British during the Anglo-Boer War still stands alongside the railway line just north of Wellington. This blockhouse has now been proclaimed a national monument.

The Rev. De Villiers composed South Africa's national anthem.

MOODY, MYSTERIOUS KAROO

KAROO ... ONE'S first impression of this arid landscape is its endlessness. It stretches from one far horizon to the other, and there is an atmosphere of ancient mystery brooding over it like some intangible spirit ceaselessly mourning the primeval past.

The Khoikhoi named this wilderness the Karoo, meaning 'land of thirst'. The name was used to describe the high-lying central plateau of southern Africa, which projects down over much of the interior of the Cape Province. The area is drought-stricken and bare of surface water. Scientists, however, use the name Karoo to describe a vast system of sediments laid down between 150 and 250 million years ago. This system covers two-thirds of the surface of southern Africa. In the north the Karoo System is better watered, and the land there is covered with grass and trees; but beneath this green mantle, the soil and rocks are exactly the same as in the south.

The thickness of this sedimentary deposit is so great (many thousands of metres) that the source of the material which comprises it is a mystery. Perhaps an earlier landscape totally disintegrated, or vast eruptions of volcanic matter reached the surface only to be eroded by heavy rains and dispersed in complex layers of sedimentary rocks, mud-stones and shales.

What the scientists know as the Karoo (or Karroo) System was laid down in three main layers, all abundant in fossils.

At the bottom of the Karoo lies the Dwyka Series, a layer 900 metres thick and consisting of pebbles, boulders and rocks which have engraved on their surfaces the typical scars and grooves of glacial activity. This material is surrounded by mud-stone and moraine, and appears to be the debris left behind by an ice age. A profound change had obviously taken place in the climate of the southern hemisphere. A period of warmer weather was beginning, and in the upper levels of these rocks fossils of small reptiles, fish, molluscs and plant leaves can be found. At that time, the surface of the centre of southern Africa must have been a slimy mixture of melted ice, mud and scarred rocks, with the sun slowly warming the whole quagmire, creating a steamy swamp.

From this mess, a 3 000-metre-thick layer of shales and sandstones was formed. Known as the Ecca Series, this layer contains the great bulk of South Africa's coal and carbonaceous shale deposits. Tantalizingly, the deposits must once have contained vast quantities of oil, but with no adequate rock strata underneath to act as a reservoir, this oil simply soaked into the depths of the earth. In the Ecca Series enormous fossil plants and trees are to be found. Many fossil tree stumps have been discovered, still preserved in their original growing positions, and it seems that what is now the arid Karoo must at that time have been a tropical forest densely covered with trees.

The third deposit of the Karoo System lies above the Ecca Series. Known as the Beaufort Series, this is 5 600 metres thick and is rich in fossil reptiles, including dinosaurs and amphibious creatures with mammalian features. The Beaufort Series is the surface of the arid expanse of the Karoo as it is in the Cape today. A more recent series, the Stormberg Series, forms the 1 500-metre-thick upper deposit of the highlands of Lesotho and the Drakensberg.

Since the days of the mighty freshwater swamps, times have changed in the interior of the Cape, and the basin-shaped surface of the Karoo is now in the grip of drought. The little rain that does fall is highly erratic and tends to come in violent thunderstorms; these are short and powerful, causing flash floods to pour down normally dry watercourses and create havoc.

The surface of the Karoo is protected by only scanty vegetation. The periodic floods cause considerable erosion, and this gives the area its distinctive appearance. Strangely shaped rocks and hillocks cover the plains, watercourses gash the surface with complex, erratic, sharply eroded miniature ravines which, from the air, appear similar to the rocks scarred by an ice age.

A remarkable feature of the Karoo landscape is the intrusion of hard, dolerite rocks into the sedimentary materials. At some stage after the great thicknesses of the Karoo sediments had been laid down under fresh water, a mass of molten rock was forced to the surface from the underground melting pot. In attempting to penetrate the different layers of sediments, this molten matter found lines of weakness and spread vertically and horizontally. On the surface the vertical exposures of dolerite resemble the Great Wall of China; from the air, these long, natural walls of dark, hard rock, known as dykes, meander over the Karoo, appearing and vanishing unexpectedly.

The horizontal layers, known as sills, have had an even stranger effect on the landscape. In places where sections of these sills remain, they form a hard roof over the soft sediments beneath them. Rainstorms steadily erode the unprotected soil around the dolerite 'umbrellas'. A hillock emerges with its summit capped with dolerite. This is the famous koppie, a scenic emblem of South Africa. Eventually, these dolerite caps are themselves eroded away. The entire koppie then disappears, borne away in a few seasons of rainstorms.

In the early mornings or late afternoons, when the sun is oblique and the air cool, one sees the Karoo in its most enigmatic mood. The dawns and sunsets are like vast volcanic eruptions of red, orange and golden light. The air is clear as crystal, and the nights are brilliant with many more stars than are normally visible to the human eye.

Spring . . . and a green mantle transforms this land of thirst.

Beaufort West

More than 150 millimetres of rain fall annually in Beaufort West, a relative abundance that has earned it the title of 'the oasis town'. It is the only town in Africa with streets shaded by pear trees. It was established in 1818 on the banks of the intermittently flowing Gamka River at the foot of the Nuweveld Mountains and was named after the fifth Duke of Beaufort, father of the Cape governor, Lord Charles Somerset. In 1837 Beaufort West became the first municipality in South Africa. It is now the Karoo's largest town.

The town became prosperous with the introduction of merino sheep to the area. One of its early citizens, Sir John Charles Molteno, a wool trader

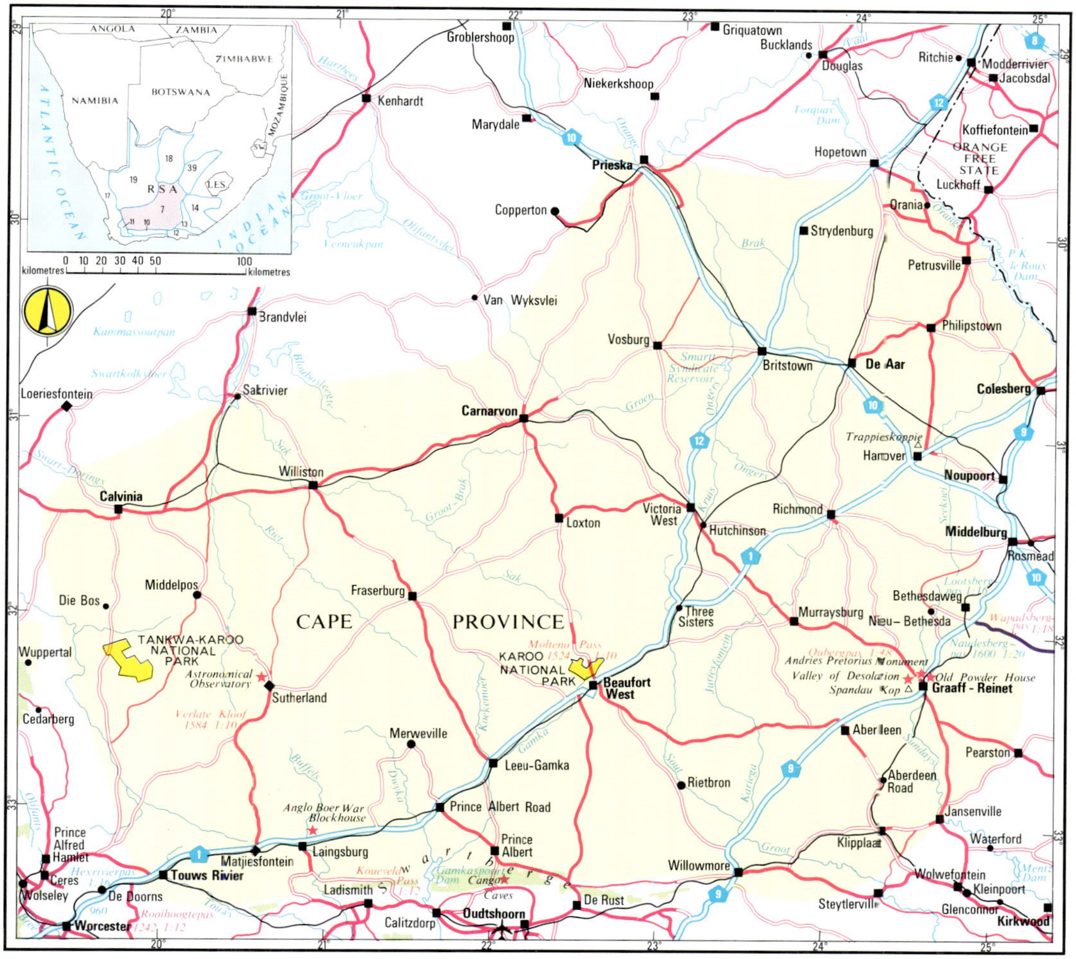

THINGS TO DO AND SEE

Astronomy The unusually clear air and absence of clouds makes the Karoo an ideal place for the amateur astronomer. A good pair of binoculars and a light telescope will open up the night sky, while a peep through one of the great telescopes in the observatory at Sutherland is an awesome introduction to the immensity of space.

Bird-watching Despite its aridity, the Karoo has a surprising variety of birds. They are often seen at the watercourses, even when there is no water. During the summer immense numbers of European storks migrate to the Karoo, where they feed on locusts.

Camping and caravanning Caravans and tents are accommodated at Graaff-Reinet, Beaufort West, Victoria West, De Aar, Britstown, Touws River, Laingsburg, Prince Albert, Richmond and Hanover.

Hunting The Karoo is the home of such antelope as the springbok, herds of which, as well as other species of plains game, are to be found on many of the sheep farms. Some farmers permit shooting by arrangement.

Game birds are also common.

Museums Graaff-Reinet has a beautiful museum in Reinet House. The cultural museum at Victoria West has a display of vintage cars. An assortment of Victoriana can be seen at Matjiesfontein.

Rocks and gems The eroded landscape, unprotected by any dense vegetation, makes the Karoo a haven for geologists. It is a region of flat-topped koppies, balancing boulders, tiger's eye and other semi-precious stones.

Sightseeing The Valley of Desolation is dramatic. On a more human scale, there are the streets of beautifully restored period houses in Graaff-Reinet, and the relics of Victorian days in Matjiesfontein.

Sport There are golf courses at Graaff-Reinet, Beaufort West, Richmond and Laingsburg. Beaufort West has bowling clubs and tennis courts.

Wildlife The Karoo is the home not only of the springbok, but of many other animals, including tortoises, jackals, bat-eared foxes, hares, meerkats and antbears.

Wild town that became the 'gem of the Karoo'

Beaufort West, famous for mutton and the pear trees lining the main street.

and champion of responsible government nicknamed 'the Lion of Beaufort', founded the town's first bank in 1854. He was to become the first Prime Minister of the Cape.

The first edition of Beaufort West's local newspaper, *The Courier*, was printed in 1869. When the railway reached the town, in 1880, Beaufort West became a marshalling yard and locomotive depot.

The town hall, which has been proclaimed a national monument, houses a museum. Among its exhibits are the Chris Barnard collection of trophies and awards, and items belonging to the late Dr Eric Louw, M.P.

The town is a staging post on the road from Cape Town to Johannesburg. It has several hotels, two caravan parks and a motel.

The Karoo National Park is 11 km from the town.

Britstown

Sheep, wool, mutton and karakul skins are the chief products of the Karoo, and Britstown is one of the principal centres of these industries. It is also a staging post on the Diamond Way — the trunk road between Three Sisters and Johannesburg through Kimberley — and a junction where this road crosses the major route to South West Africa.

The town was named after Hans Brits, who owned the farm on which it was laid out in 1877.

Colesberg

One of the landmarks along N1, the Cape-to-Cairo road, is the table-topped mountain, 1 707 metres high, known as *Tooverberg* (towering mountain) or Coleskop. From all directions the shape of this mountain is extraordinarily symmetrical and it became an important landmark for early travellers venturing into the interior of southern Africa.

Vast herds of game watered in a marsh at the foot of the mountain. In 1814 a mission station was established here and in 1830 a town was founded, named Colesberg in honour of the Cape Governor, Sir Lowry Cole. It grew as a frontier town and staging post on the main road to the north. Many travellers still regard it as the halfway point between Cape Town and Johannesburg. Several hotels and caravan parks provide accommodation. The local mutton, claimed to be the most succulent in the world, makes excellent eating.

The architecture of the town, especially in the side streets, dates from the period when Colesberg was founded. The Dutch Reformed church dominates the main street while the Anglican church contains several interesting features such as a stained glass east window and a carved oak lectern.

In 1867 a trader, John O'Reilly,

The symmetrical Tooverberg, once an important landmark.

EARTH'S MOST ASTONISHING LANDSCAPE

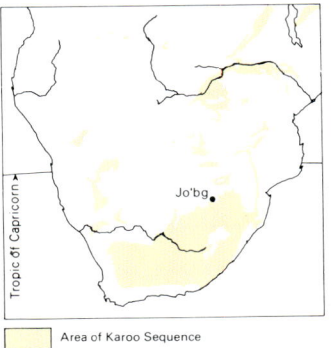

Area of Karoo Sequence

The Karoo Sequence is a thick, extensive deposit of sedimentary and volcanic rocks that covers two thirds of southern Africa.

Between 150 and 250 million years ago this deposit was laid in a variety of environments — glacial, shallow sea and lake, riverine, desert and volcanic.

This sequence was laid down in three major layers, and one of its fascinations for geologists is its immense richness in fossils.

Near the bottom of the sequence lies the Ecca Series, rich in plant fossils and coal. Above this lies the Beaufort Series, rich in vertebrate fossils.

The uppermost layer is the Drakensberg Group, with lavas, wind-deposited sandstone, and water-deposited sandstones and shales rich in plant, reptile, fish and amphibian fossils.

A particularly notable feature of the Karoo is caused by the intrusion of hard, dark, dolerite rock. This dolerite intruded in a molten form from the underground melting pot, spreading out vertically and horizontally. At the surface, these intrusives form long natural walls of dark, hard rock occurring at random over the Karoo for many kilometres. They are known as dykes.

The horizontal layers, or sills, have had a dramatic effect on the landscape.

Where sections of these sills remain they provide a hard roof to the softer rocks supporting them. Weathering steadily erodes away the softer rock that is unprotected by the hard dolerite cover. Eventually a hillock is left, the summit, dependent on the extent of the sill, being either table-topped, stool-topped or pointed with only a small cap of dolerite to protect it. These are the famous koppies — rocky hillocks — which provide South Africa with its most characteristic scenery.

The dolerite tops eventually are eroded themselves. The whole hillock then soon disappears, but hundreds of others are in various stages of formation.

Approximate age			Geological term	Maximum thickness
170 million years		Volcanic basalt lavas	Stormberg Series	1 500 m
		Aeolian sandstones	Cave Sandstone	300 m
		Red mud-stones and sandstones	Red Beds	500 m
		River-laid sandstones	Molteno Series	600 m
		Sandstones and shales with fossil vertebrates	Beaufort Series	5 600 m
		Sandstones and shales with coal in north-east	Ecca Series	3 000 m
280 million years		Shales and glacial tillite	Dwyka Series	900 m

The groups of rocks that form the Karoo Sequence.

came into the little town with the first diamond found in South Africa. The Civil Commissioner tested it by scratching the letters 'D.P.' into the windowpane of his office. This memento of the start of South African mineral prosperity may still be seen.

De Aar

After Germiston, De Aar is the second largest railway junction in the Republic. The lines from the western and eastern Cape, the Transvaal and Namibia meet here, and within the precincts of the town are 110 kilometres of track. Trains pass through at the rate of 92 a day – increasing considerably during peak periods. The main line between De Aar and Kimberley is still worked by steam. For the railway enthusiast, De Aar is a delight, with its varied rolling stock and locomotives.

The ore trains from the iron and manganese mines of the northern Cape also use this route.

Crack passenger trains, such as the Blue Train, Trans-Karoo and Orange Express, stop here to change crews.

De Aar ('the vein') takes its name from an underground watercourse. Among the town's prominent citizens was authoress Olive Schreiner, who lived here from 1907 to 1913, and a visit to her house is worthwhile.

In the Damfontein district many San paintings can be seen.

A caravan park and hotels accommodate visitors. Nearby at Vanderkloof is an inland holiday resort.

Fraserburg

A principal sheep-farming centre, this isolated little town is surrounded by vast sheep runs.

The famous six-sided 'Pepperbox' in the centre of the town has been used as offices for the municipality, magistrate and church. Built in 1861, it was originally the office of the market master. The powder magazine above the town was an ammunition depot for British forces during the Anglo-Boer War.

Graaff-Reinet

The 'gem of the Karoo', as it is sometimes called, Graaff-Reinet is one of the most intriguing of the small towns of South Africa. The town was

With a wind-pump and a few trees for company, this is a typical Karoo farm beneath a stormy sky.

THE SIMPLE INVENTION THAT BROUGHT WATER TO THE THIRSTLAND

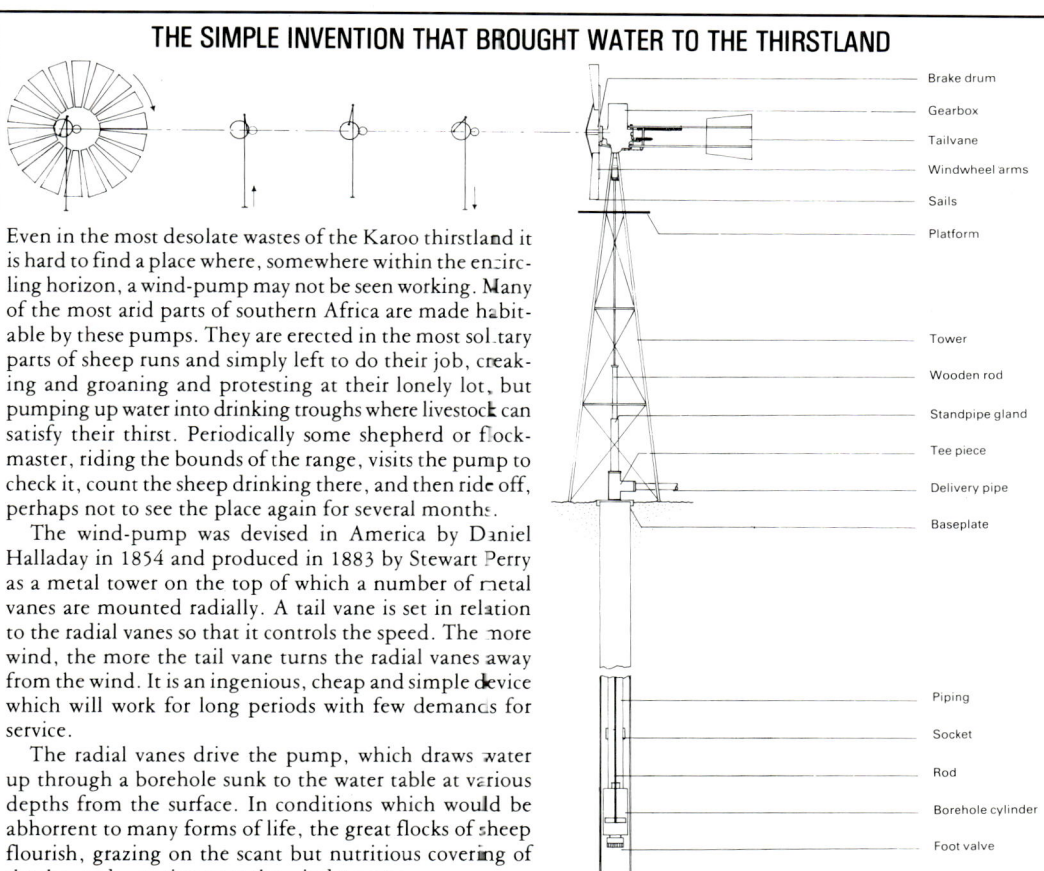

Even in the most desolate wastes of the Karoo thirstland it is hard to find a place where, somewhere within the encircling horizon, a wind-pump may not be seen working. Many of the most arid parts of southern Africa are made habitable by these pumps. They are erected in the most solitary parts of sheep runs and simply left to do their job, creaking and groaning and protesting at their lonely lot, but pumping up water into drinking troughs where livestock can satisfy their thirst. Periodically some shepherd or flockmaster, riding the bounds of the range, visits the pump to check it, count the sheep drinking there, and then ride off, perhaps not to see the place again for several months.

The wind-pump was devised in America by Daniel Halladay in 1854 and produced in 1883 by Stewart Perry as a metal tower on the top of which a number of metal vanes are mounted radially. A tail vane is set in relation to the radial vanes so that it controls the speed. The more wind, the more the tail vane turns the radial vanes away from the wind. It is an ingenious, cheap and simple device which will work for long periods with few demands for service.

The radial vanes drive the pump, which draws water up through a borehole sunk to the water table at various depths from the surface. In conditions which would be abhorrent to many forms of life, the great flocks of sheep flourish, grazing on the scant but nutritious covering of shrubs, and watering near the wind-pumps.

Brake drum
Gearbox
Tailvane
Windwheel arms
Sails
Platform

Tower
Wooden rod
Standpipe gland
Tee piece
Delivery pipe
Baseplate

Piping
Socket
Rod
Borehole cylinder
Foot valve

Graceful legacy of the old master-builders

Reinet House, now a museum, is a classic example of the Cape-Dutch architecture.

Dutch Reformed Church, Graaff-Reinet.

founded in 1786 by the governor, Cornelius Jacob van de Graaff, whose wife's maiden name was Cornelia Reinet. The first settlers were a rugged crowd and there were scandals of wild outrages, shootings and rustlings. The government hoped that by establishing a town — with a minister and tax-gatherer — order would be maintained. Accordingly, a church, revenue office and gaol were built on a site in a huge 'U' bend of the Sundays River. The hopes were to be only partly fulfilled. In 1795 the inhabitants of Graaff-Reinet drove out the representatives of government and declared an independent republic, with Graaff-Reinet its capital. The 'republic' was overthrown by the British a year later.

The town lies in a setting of rocky hills, with the Valley of Desolation to the west and, overlooking the town like a sentry, the prominent landmark of Spandau Kop.

More than 200 buildings in the town are national monuments. An entire street — Stretch's Court — has been restored, its slave cottages having been renovated by Historical Homes of South Africa. The Simon van der Stel Foundation has done much restoration in Parsonage Street.

Reinet House, built in 1805, was the home of a noted churchman and author, the Reverend Andrew Murray. In April 1980 the building was partly destroyed by fire, but was restored, and is now a museum.

In the garden grows the largest living grape vine in the world. Planted in 1870, it covers 124 square metres, has a girth of 2,38 metres at a height of 1,5 metres and still bears fruit.

Built in 1821, the Dutch Reformed Missionary Church was bought and restored by the Rembrandt Tobacco Company, who donated it to the Municipality. Now called the Hester Rupert Art Museum after the mother of the firm's chairman, it has a large collection of contemporary South African art.

To the north of Graaff-Reinet, on Magazine Hill, is an old powder magazine built in 1831 by a firm of merchants to contain gunpowder for blasting, and firearms for the protection of its workers against wild animals. The magazine has been restored and is now a national monument, contain-

The graceful simplicity of the old buildings is seen to good effect in the stairway and rear entrance of Reinet House.

Sunlight on stone . . . the imposing town hall of Graaff-Reinet.

The world's largest grape vine spreads over the garden of Reinet House.

Graaff-Reinet, 'the gem of the Karoo', enclosed by a bend of the Sundays River.

Stretch's Court — an example of restoration work done in Graaff-Reinet.

A tuishuis ('town house') built in Graaff-Reinet.

The spirit of the Voortrekkers is symbolized by this sturdy monument in the form of a wagon wheel surmounted by the figure of Andries Pretorius.

A powder magazine built in the hills above Graaff-Reinet.

83

Streets echo the days of Victorian grandeur

The town of Hanover is an oasis in the great dry plains of the Karoo.

ing arms, ammunition and explosive devices.

The statue of Andries Pretorius on the Middelburg Road recalls the days of the Great Trek of the 1830s, when he and Gert Maritz led hundreds of families from the district.

Wool, angora hair and furniture are local products. The town has a caravan park and several hotels, one of which is the restored Drostdy, built in 1806.

Hanover

In 1854 Gert Gous agreed to the setting-up of a township on his farm provided that it was to be called Hanover, after the birthplace of his German ancestors. Adequate water was available from a spring at the foot of a group of hillocks, and the town steadily expanded, becoming the centre of a world-famous merino sheep-raising area.

The nucleus of the town was the

The solid outlines of an Anglo-Boer War blockhouse near Laingsburg.

Dutch Reformed Church. Hanover's first magistrate, C. R. Beere, directed the laying-out of the streets and the planting of peppercorn trees. His work is commemorated in the stone pyramid on the summit of the Trappieskoppie ('hillock of little steps').

A footpath which he made leads to the memorial.

HARDY HERBS AND SHRUBS OF AN INHOSPITABLE LAND PRODUCE THE WORLD'S MOST MOUTH-WATERING MUTTON

The South African Mutton Merino.

The South African merino rams.

Spanish merinos, wool producers.

The Dormer — a cross-breed.

The Dorper, another cross.

Mutton from the Karoo is renowned for its flavour and tenderness. The pasturage of herbs, succulents and shrubs, helps to produce this special flavour.

About 34 million sheep are kept in southern Africa and the Karoo is their great home. Most of the woolled sheep are of the merino breed. Their wool is clipped and sold in auctions at the coastal ports, with much of it exported to Britain, France and West Germany. The annual yield generally exceeds 100 million kilograms. South Africa is the second largest producer in the world, after Australia.

The principal non-woolled (mutton) sheep are of the Dorper breed — a mixture of the Dorset Horn and the Persian breeds. The Dormer is also kept, and is a mixture of the Dorset Horn and the South African Mutton Merino (German Merino). Karakul sheep are kept in the north-western areas of the Cape, these handsome black animals yielding valuable skins.

The merino breed originated in Spain. In the 1780s the King of Spain presented some of these animals to the ruling family of Holland. The merinos did not flourish in the climate of Holland and in 1789 two rams and four ewes were shipped to the Cape.

There was an indigenous fat-tailed, non-woollen sheep in South Africa. These animals were kept by the Khoikhoi pastoralists for mutton and the remarkable amount of fat they stored in their tails. They had been introduced to southern Africa several thousand years ago when their flockmasters had migrated from the north.

The merinos sent to the Cape were placed in the care of Colonel Robert Gordon, military commander at that time.

He kept the little flock pure by sending it to the outpost at Groenkloof, where the mission station of Mamre is situated today. The merinos flourished and yielded superb wool.

Two years later, however, Gordon was ordered to return the sheep to Holland as the Spaniards had never intended that their gift would be sent out of Europe.

Colonel Gordon neatly sidestepped his orders by returning to Holland the original number of sheep and keeping their offspring. These became the forebears of the South African woolled sheep.

The ornate frontage of the Lord Milner Hotel at Matjiesfontein, a survivor of Victorian times. Its fashionable guests once included the Sultan of Zanzibar.

Laingsburg

Where the main railway and road to the north cross the Buffels (Buffalo) River, the town of Laingsburg grew from its origins as a trading post. The centre of the sheep and wheat districts in this region, it was named after John Laing, a senior civil servant in the lands department of the Cape, and was laid out in 1881.

Because so many of its buildings date back to the last century, the town is an excellent example of a South African dorp ('country town') of the Victorian period, when much use was made of corrugated iron, wrought-iron decorative work and heavy, imported building materials.

In January 1981 a disastrous flood struck the town, destroying many buildings. A number of people lost their lives.

North of the town stands a well-preserved three-storey Anglo-Boer War blockhouse. This building is a national monument.

Matjiesfontein

In the 1890s an official on the Cape Government Railways, James Logan, found health and fortune in the Karoo. Suffering from a chest complaint, he found a transfer to the Karoo so beneficial that he settled there. He bought a farm, named it Tweedside, planted trees and wheat, and built a fine house, sank boreholes and steadily acquired a vast land holding.

Among Logan's properties was the area around the railway station of Matjiesfontein ('bulrush spring'). There was nothing much here when he acquired it — just some corrugated iron railway sheds. It was a most improbable site for any development, but Logan saw virtues to Matjiesfontein not apparent to others. Locomotives hauling trains across the Karoo were thirsty, and so were the passengers. Logan piped water to Matjiesfontein from his farm boreholes and sold it to the railways. He opened a restaurant on the station and, while the locomotives replenished water, served meals and drinks to the passengers. He even started an aerated water plant. His venture proved to be big business. A steam locomotive consumed about 250 000 litres of water between Touws River and De Aar and there were few sources of supply. Logan, a Scot who had arrived in South Africa penniless in 1877, built a grand, Victorian-style hotel at Matjiesfontein. It was eventually named after Lord Milner and from its opening it became highly fashionable. Fountains played in its garden; the air was crisp, unpolluted, dry and clear, and attracted sufferers of lung complaints.

Matjiesfontein was accessible by train, the food was splendid, the Karoo lamb was delicious and so was the local springbok venison.

Logan ornamented his village with lamp posts from London. He brought out two teams of British cricketers to play at Matjiesfontein. George Lohmann, one of the English greats of cricket, settled here.

The Anglo-Boer War changed Matjiesfontein. It became a military headquarters and a marshalling

Stairway of the Lord Milner Hotel.

The snow-capped Swartberg provide an impressive backdrop to Matjiesfontein.

Cloudless skies that are made for stargazing

Blue asbestos, source of tiger's eye.

Crocidolite, or 'blue' asbestos, is found in considerable quantities in the northern Cape.

One form of this mineral is the gem-stone known as tiger's eye.

This beautiful stone, golden in colour, is much favoured by jewellers, who use it in the manufacture of brooches, rings, necklaces, bracelets and earrings.

There is a blue variety popularly known as bull's eye, the yellow cat's eye variety, the green hawk's eye and the red devil's eye.

Tiger's eye and its variants are commonly found in beds of banded ironstone, of which a component can be red jasper — itself a valuable stone.

Such gem-stones of commercial quality are found only in South Africa and even then are limited to the Prieska-Griquatown area.

The 'blue' asbestos found in other parts of South Africa seldom yields stones of gem quality.

ground for troops. Famous regiments were quartered here. The hotel became a hospital and war correspondents such as Edgar Wallace used the little post office's brass telegraph key to send urgent despatches. At the end of the war, Matjiesfontein was restored to its owner, who died in 1920.

Today Matjiesfontein remains perfectly preserved, and in 1975 it was declared a national monument. All the original buildings, the London lamp posts, the hotel, fountain, post office, are still here. It is a favoured weekend retreat from Cape Town and a unique stopover for travellers along the Cape-to-Johannesburg road.

Prieska

The first trail blazed across the Karoo reached the Orange River at a ford known to the Khoikhoi as Prieskap ('the place where the goat was lost'). When the number of travellers to the interior increased, a handful of traders and a missionary settled at the ford and, in 1878, the town of Prieska was born.

Today the town is noted for copper mining, livestock breeding and farming. Very hot in summer, the town is shaded by trees and there is no shortage of water. The sheep runs produce wool, mutton and karakul pelts.

Prieska is famed for semi-precious stones, especially tiger's eye which is exported all over the world.

It was north of Prieska, where the

Spring in the Karoo sees a great stirring of life — such as this blister beetle.

Brak River flows into the Orange, that General Christiaan de Wet, the famous Anglo-Boer War leader, outwitted the British forces. When his greatly outnumbered commando was cornered in the area where the rivers meet, General de Wet escaped through the British lines back to the Orange Free State.

Prince Albert

A 42-kilometre road runs from the railway station of Prince Albert Road to the southern end of the Karoo. This road is a major scenic route, with its dramatic approach to, and eventual passage of, the Swartberg range. Prince Albert is noted for fruit, especially peaches and apricots. Its watermill is still in working condition

and has been declared a national monument.

Richmond

The sheep-farming town of Richmond, founded in 1845, was named after the Duke of Richmond by his son-in-law, the British governor, Sir Peregrine Maitland.

This was the birthplace of the South African medical pioneer, Dr. Emil Hoffa, who founded the science of orthopaedics.

Richmond was also the scene of several skirmishes during the Anglo-Boer War.

The area is now noted for cattle- and horse-breeding, and the town serves as a welcome halfway house for travellers between the Cape and the

After long service on a Karoo farm, this tractor lies abandoned near Prieska.

A sun-baked old fort stands out like a gigantic oven on the plain around Prieska.

Transvaal. The town has two hotels and a caravan park.

Strydenburg

The little town of Strydenburg ('town of strife') takes its name not from any great battle fought here, but because of squabbling by its founders over the siting and naming of the town. It is a staging post between Britstown and the diamond fields.

A large shallow pan outside the town attracts flocks of greater flamingoes during rainy seasons.

Local inhabitants claim that the world's best mutton is produced around Strydenburg. There is a garden of succulents and a caravan park.

Weeds straggle over the wooden wheel of an old watermill at Prince Albert.

Sutherland

The unenviable record of being the coldest town in South Africa belongs to Sutherland, 1 456 metres above sea level. The mean minimum temperature is $-6{,}1\,°\mathrm{C}$.

Founded in 1857, the town was named after a prominent minister, the Reverend H. Sutherland. It is the principal astronomical centre in Africa. Because pollution and glare had made observation difficult in cities, the main telescopes mounted in the observatories in Cape Town, Johannesburg and Pretoria were removed in 1972 to the South African Astronomical Observatory in Sutherland, where the skies are usually clear.

A thunderstorm looms in the late afternoon. Before the rain comes, an atmosphere of brooding expectancy seems to hover over the wilderness near Richmond.

Nature's bizarre masterpiece – the Valley of Desolation

Three Sisters

One of the landmarks of the trunk road through the Karoo is the cluster of three stool-shaped hillocks known as the Three Sisters. Like most of the Karoo's table-topped hillocks, the Three Sisters are capped with dolerite which protects the soft sediments underneath from erosion.

Touws River

When the railway line was built from Cape Town to the north, the first major staging post, locomotive depot and marshalling yard after Cape Town was built on the banks of the Touws River ('river of the pass') at the summit of the Hex River mountain pass. A town of railwaymen and their families settled here. Although electrification of the line has eliminated the need for coaling and servicing of locomotives in Touws River, train crews are still changed and freight trains marshalled here. A great many old steam locomotives have been 'retired' here, to the fascination of railway enthusiasts.

One of the Three Sisters, with its protective cap of dolerite. In the foreground, an acacia tree is in flower.

THE LOVABLE MEERKAT

An inquisitive family of meerkats.

One of the most delightful of the wild animals of the Karoo and the grassveld is the suricate, or meerkat. These little creatures were often kept as pets in farmhouses, but their numbers have been reduced by rabies and the spread of farming.

They are intelligent animals with tawny-grey coats and belong to the mongoose family. At dawn they emerge from their burrows, sit on their haunches to soak up the sun, and talk to each other in low, excited voices. They are carnivorous, but harmless to man.

The Valley of Desolation — an awesome example of natural erosion. Beyond stretches the thirsty wilderness of the Karoo.

THE HUMBLE, HARMLESS TORTOISE – ONE OF NATURE'S GREAT SURVIVORS

The Cape Province has the greatest variety of land tortoises on earth. Of the world's 39 known species, nine live in the Cape and three are found nowhere else.

The largest of the Cape species is the leopard, or mountain, tortoise, 600 millimetres long and weighing up to 45 kilograms. At the other extreme is what is probably the world's smallest tortoise, *Homopus signatus*, only 100 millimetres long and 150 grams in weight. Its shell, speckled black, may be fawn or a handsome salmon-red. This creature inhabits semi-desert areas.

The rarest tortoise in Africa is the suurpootjies, or 'sour foot', found on the coastal terrace of the south-western Cape. It is also known as the geometric tortoise *(Psammobates geometricus)* because of the curious pattern of yellow stripes on its dark shell.

The rare Psammobates geometricus.

Fewer than 2 000 of these tortoises survive, mostly in nature reserves.

Tortoises may appear to be awkward, helpless, primitive creatures, but they are well equipped for survival. Man is their worst enemy. Agriculture has destroyed much of their natural habitat, bush fires take a big toll of their numbers and millions have been picked up and carried away as pets. In South Africa they are totally protected. It is illegal to export them and they may only be kept in captivity by permit from the regional conservation authorities.

Living mainly on succulent plants, grasses, toadstools and occasionally old bones, tortoises eat virtually nothing of value to man. They mate in early spring and the females, depending on the species to which they belong, lay between one and 20 eggs in a hole scooped out of the soil. They cover the eggs, tread the soil down tightly and then leave the rest to nature. Between six and 18 months later the eggs hatch and the little tortoises work their way to the surface to begin the struggle for survival on their own.

Like knights in armour, different species have different shells. Some have an ingenious hinged flap in the back of the shell which they can close completely when danger threatens.

*The leopard or mountain tortoise (*Geochelone pardalis*).*

The tiny Homopus signatus.

An adult H. signatus, *100 mm long.*

Behind the Douglas Hotel are two concrete pillars on which, in 1882, were mounted astronomical instruments used to observe the transit of Venus. The sightings enabled a measurement of the distance between the sun and the earth to be made. The pillars have been proclaimed a national monument.

Valley of Desolation

The entire Valley of Desolation, one of southern Africa's most remarkable phenomena, has been proclaimed a national monument. The dolerite-capped shale heights towering above Graaff-Reinet have been eroded in the course of millions of years into a variety of bizarre shapes. There are crumbling cliffs, massive piles of boulders, and views of Spandau Kop, Graaff-Reinet, the great bend in the Sundays River, and over the Karoo.

A tarred road leads from Graaff-Reinet to the region. In the valley is the Karoo Nature Park.

Victoria West

In her glorious empire, Queen Victoria had many places named in her honour. A few of them might have

Victoria West, a sunny little town that has changed little in 140 years.

inspired her famous comment: 'We are not amused'.

If she had ventured as far afield as the Karoo, however, Victoria West might have given her cause for a nod and a smile. It is a sun-baked little oasis in the thirstland, a meandering street of commercial buildings, many built in the last century when fortune-seekers streamed through on their way to the diamond fields.

Victoria West has changed little since its beginning in 1843. When diamonds were discovered in Hope-town in 1867, a highway, cutting at right angles across the main street, was made to the north. Hotels, stores and a newspaper were founded. The railway missed the town by 12 kilometres. Victoria West had to be satisfied with a siding, incongruously named Victoria West Road, and a bumpy gravel track to the town.

At a nature reserve near the town are springbok, eland, black wildebeest, blesbok, gemsbok and other game.

On a nearby farm is a considerable private collection of old cars, including steamers and one of Adolf Hitler's bullet-proof vehicles.

The springbok — antelope and emblem

The Karoo has always been the favoured home of the springbok, the lithe and beautiful little antelope that served as the national emblem of South Africa. Before man settled in the area and claimed the watering places, springbok wandered the thirstlands in herds of many thousands. One of the great natural spectacles of the world was the sight of springbok migrating from drought-stricken areas to better grazing.

On these occasions the animals congregated in hundreds of thousands.

The crossing of hollows or rivers always caused the death of many animals. The surging pressure from the rear simply overwhelmed any hesitant antelope in front. The rear-guard would clamber over the backs of the vanguard, crushing them into water or mud and filling up hollows with corpses.

The springbok, *Antidorcas marsupialis*, is the southern African representative of the gazelle group of animals and is only found in southern Africa on the central plains, where it flourishes on the grassveld despite the considerable aridity. Male and female springboks have horns, are handsomely marked, and are particularly distinguished by a dorsal fan.

The fawn upper parts are separated from the white underparts by a dark-brown lateral stripe. The front parts of the head, inside of the legs and back of the thighs are white. A reddish-brown stripe stretches along the side of the face from the base of the horn to the corner of the mouth.

The dorsal fan consists of long, white, bristly hairs which are erected when the gazelle starts its astonishing 'pronking'.

The motivations of this springing into the air are not fully understood. It seems to be partly a nervous reaction. If the animal is startled, it erects its fan and draws its lithe body into a position similar to that of a bucking horse. The head is lowered almost to the feet, the legs are fully extended with hoofs almost bunched together. Then the animal takes off, shooting straight up into the air for some three metres, seeming to hang in space as though defying gravity, then dropping to earth and shooting up again as though mounted on coiled springs.

To see a herd of these delightful little creatures pronking about on the central plains is an unforgettable sight. They hardly seem to touch the earth, bounding up and down sometimes at an angle, always full of an intense excitement.

Writers of the 19th century have described the springbok as swarming over the plains in countless millions, and this was probably not a great exaggeration. Often the springbok were accompanied by other antelope such as wildebeest, blesbok, quagga and eland.

These creatures either joined the springbok host voluntarily or were simply swept along by the tide. The animals fed as they moved, the vegetation being denuded — either eaten or trampled by the millions of hoofs.

*The springbok (*Antidorcas marsupialis*), the South African representative of the gazelle group and an animal emblem of South Africa.*

Springbok 'pronking' — the strange, excitable habit of bounding into the air.

If they decide to bolt to avoid a predator they extend their necks, lay their horns and ears back and seem to take off like the wind. The dorsal fan is not erected during flight.

Black springboks and albinos are fairly common.

Many farmers protect springbok and there are large herds in game reserves such as the Kalahari National Park and the Etosha National Park. They are common in Botswana.

The use of the springbok as the national sporting emblem of South Africa originated in 1906. The first South African rugby team to tour Britain had just reached London.

Sports journalists enquired about the team's nickname — the New Zealand team had recently been named the 'All Blacks' on account of their black togs. The South Africans had no nickname, but the next day the players visited London Zoo. They were amused to see a small herd of springbok irrepressibly pronking about to the delight of the spectators. Some members of the team suggested that they adopt the springbok as their nickname.

The idea was received with approval and team captain Paul Roos suggested to the accompanying newspapermen that they call the South African team 'De Springbokken'. This was shortened to 'Springbokke' and eventually to 'Springboks'.

On 12 September 1906 the South African Rugby Board approved the springbok as the team's official emblem.

A springbok first appeared in heraldry on 10 December 1904, when a royal warrant granted to the Orange River Colony a coat of arms. On this coat of arms appeared the imperial crown and a springbok.

In 1910, when the four colonies (the Cape, Natal, Orange River and Transvaal) joined to form the Union of South Africa, Arthur Holland, of

Badge of the Amateur Swimming Union.

South African Airways, created in 1934, has as its emblem the flying springbok, one version of which is shown here.

A 'merbok' — the emblem of the South African Ocean Racing Trust.

A 'royal springbok' — emblem of the Orange River Colony, granted in 1904.

The springbok in family heraldry — the crest of the Michael Hoyer family.

The springbok and the gnu supporting the Bloemspruit coat of arms.

The sporting springbok, emblem of South African international rugby.

The emblem of the South African Society of Otorhinolaryngology.

The double springbok of the Association for Injured Workmen.

The badge and emblem of the Boy Scouts of South Africa.

How South Africa got its coat of arms

The unembellished coat of arms of South Africa, taken into use in 1933.

the Government Printing Works in Pretoria, designed a coat of arms which was granted to the new state by royal warrant of 17 September 1910.

In this coat of arms, in a quartered shield, appeared symbols taken from the arms of the four former colonies which were now joined as provinces of the Union of South Africa. Supporting this shield were a gemsbok and a springbok.

This coat of arms remained in use until 1933. Doubts had been expressed about technical aspects of the original drawing and a new drawing was then obtained from the College of Arms. This new drawing,

known as the unembellished coat of arms, is still in use.

At the same time, Sir Herbert Baker, the renowned architect, was working on the design of South Africa House in London. Sir Herbert, with Sir Arthur Cochrane and the artist Kruger Gray, designed a more elaborate version intended for use in the new buildings, for formal occasions and on the South African Railways.

This coat of arms is known as the embellished coat of arms. Both the unembellished and embellished coats of arms are in general use today, although the latter is usually used on ceremonial occasions.

The coat of arms granted to South Africa by the earl marshal in 1910. This was replaced by the unembellished coat of arms and the embellished form.

The embellished coat of arms redrawn by the artist Kruger Gray. It was taken into use in 1933 and originally designed for use in South Africa House in London.

The Kruger Rand, first struck in 1967. It contains one ounce of gold.

The All-South African and Rhodesian Women's Hockey Association emblem.

The springbok watermark contained in the South African R2-banknote.

The springbok badge was worn by South Africans in two world wars.

The gilded springbok ornamenting South Africa House, Trafalgar Square.

The engraving of a springbok on an old South African R10-banknote.

The coat of arms of the municipality of Bedford, founded in 1854.

Coat of arms of Sandringham High School, worn on blazers.

The air mail sign used by the postal authorities from 1949 to 1994.

Coat of arms of Leslie, which now forms part of the municipality of Leandra.

The badge of the South African Lawn Tennis Union formed in 1903.

The South African R1-coin. It is 80 per cent silver with a milled edge.

The small, nickel R1-coin of the third decimal series was first minted in 1990.

The coat of arms of the South African Broadcasting Corporation.

THE TIMELESS SOUTHERN CAPE

THE SOUTHERN CAPE, the coastal terrace between the Langeberg ('the long mountains') and the sea, is a sandy, gently undulating plain with an occasional rocky outcrop. Its economy is based on wheat and sheep and it has seen few changes since Europeans first settled in the area in the 18th century. Before then, a few Khoikhoi clans wandered about the area with their livestock, San lived in the mountains and hunted game on the plains, and primitive groups of uncertain origin, known simply as strandlopers ('beachcombers'), foraged along the beaches.

The southern Cape is airy and spacious with an odd, old-world touch about its ambience. Much of the area is pleasantly insulated from the outside world. There are still places that are difficult to reach — solitary stretches of coast where only a walker can make his way, remote farms and rural centres with black-thatched, white-walled buildings where strangers are not often seen and the clothes of tourists are inspected with polite amusement. Except when the south-east wind blows, the climate is mild; dry and warm in summer, with a moderate rainfall in winter. The equable weather makes the area an ideal holiday place for those who like to roam footloose and free.

The mountain ranges of Langeberg and Riviersonderend are so seldom explored that there is always a chance of finding a new gallery of San art on the walls of an as yet undiscovered rock shelter. These ranges are gashed by ravines, some of which have deep pools. No paths lead to the heights — climbers and hikers who wish to explore these peaks must find their own way. And for the outdoor lover, one of the great delights in the mountains is the sense of potential discovery — he may be the first to enjoy a view, stumble on a rare plant in flower, surprise a family of klipspringers and watch, awed, as they leap nimbly along the very edge of a precipice.

Albertinia

The bulk of South Africa's ochre — a natural earth used for colouring paint, cement and linoleum — is mined in Albertinia, much of it for export. Xhosa women use ochre to stain their costumes a golden colour. The opencast pits from which it is extracted are a colourful feature of the landscape.

Kaolin, a porcelain and medicinal clay, is also mined here. Albertinia was founded in 1900 and named in memory of the Reverend J. R. Albertyn, a Dutch Reformed minister.

Bontebok National Park

Bontebok — varicoloured, medium-sized antelopes of sturdy build — were for many years an endangered species. By the 1920s their numbers had dwindled to only 22.

In 1931 the National Parks Board established a small sanctuary for them at Bredasdorp but this proved unsuitable. In 1960 the Bontebok National Park at Swellendam was proclaimed. The park, 18 square kilometres of rolling country, had been the home of bontebok in former years. Now they are thriving once again. Surplus bontebok have been sent to private farms and other nature reserves.

Duiker, grey rhebok, grysbok and steenbok have long been common here. The reserve offers panoramic views of the Langeberg mountain range.

A restcamp has been laid out along

THINGS TO DO AND SEE

Angling Fish are abundant in this area. Kabeljou feed on the mullet in the estuaries. Leervis, white steenbras, grunter, kob and elf are also found. To fish this coast the angler must be prepared for long walks to reach a likely spot.

Boating The coast is well provided with launching ramps for powerboats. The estuaries offer good sailing water and small boats can penetrate many kilometres upstream.

Botany Wild flowers may be seen everywhere.

Of particular interest are the aloes which can be seen in the gardens at Caledon and Riversdale.

Camping and caravanning Camping grounds abound along the coast. Well-equipped caravan parks are at Caledon, Swellendam, Heidelberg, Riversdale and Stilbaai.

Climbing and walking Much of the Langeberg range is seldom, if ever, explored. It is a long range with 300 kilometres of peaks, precipices, and spectacular river passes.

A walk along almost any part of the coastline reveals prehistoric mounds of shells or stone fish traps.

Diving So many ships have been sunk along this coast that it is not difficult for a diver to locate some relic of disaster.

Swimming Stilbaai, Witsand and Puntjie have safe swimming. The water averages 20°C. in summer.

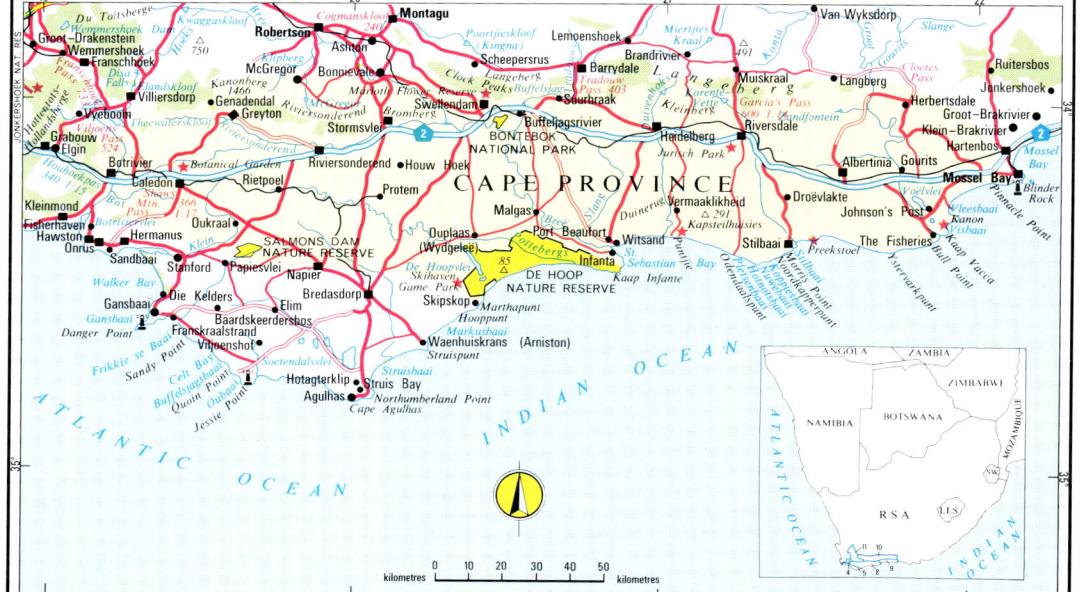

the tree-lined banks of the Breë River, which borders the reserve.

Botrivier

The name of Botrivier ('butter river') was given to this river because the Khoikhoi people resident here sold butter to European pioneers. The town is now the centre of an onion-growing industry.

Caledon

The town of Caledon originated as a result of the famous hot springs here. Seven springs reach the surface in a cluster. Six have a temperature of 50°C.; the other is cold. The springs produce 900 000 litres of water daily. The water carries iron and other minerals in solution and is reputed to have curative qualities.

In 1709 the first white settler here, Ferdinand Appel, built a small house for sick visitors. This was the start of the town, which was eventually named in honour of the governor, the Earl of Caledon.

In 1946 a sanatorium and recreational complex which had been established at the springs was destroyed by fire. It was not rebuilt, but in recent times a luxurious hotel has been erected on the site.

Caledon is also famous for its botanical garden. Founded in 1927, it covers more than 10 hectares of valley and hill slopes. Its flowers are renowned throughout the world. A flower show is held each September.

Caledon has an interesting museum, covering the years 1840 to 1900. The building is divided into two — one half a town house, the other a farmhouse.

Cloete's Pass

The Langeberg range, which separates the southern Cape coast from the Little Karoo, is penetrated by several spectacular road passes, among which is the little-known Cloete's Pass. This pass is named after the Cloete family, who formerly owned a farm at its southern end. The road through the pass is gravel, but well maintained. Flowering plants are numerous, and along the route there are ruins of the original toll houses and of blockhouses built by the British at the time of the Anglo-Boer War.

Sheep and wheat flourish side by side in the Caledon district — an area of rolling hills and carpets of wild flowers.

Garcia's Pass

Maurice Garcia was civil commissioner of Riversdale in 1868 when he made a bridle path along the banks of the Kafferkuils River through the Langeberg range. Later this path was converted into a road by the famed engineer, Thomas Bain. The pass was reconstructed in 1963.

Garcia's Pass is a scenic gateway to the Little Karoo. Wild flowers in the region are numerous. Once in the Little Karoo, a return journey can be made through Cloete's Pass. These routes pass mountains, ravines, red-orange sandstone cliffs, innumerable waterfalls in the rainy season and many farmhouses.

The toll house at the summit of Garcia's Pass has been declared a national monument.

Genadendal

The 'Apostle of the Hottentots', George Schmidt, founded South Africa's first mission station at what was to become Genadendal in 1737. After six years he returned to Europe and the station fell into disuse until 1792, when it was re-established by the Moravian Missionary Society. Then known as Baviaanskloof ('ravine of the baboons'), the village took its present name of Genadendal ('valley of grace') in 1806.

Streets of neat black-thatched white-walled cottages, the church and manse, watermill and groves of oak trees have survived from the beginning of the last century.

An old bell, formerly used to summon people to church, children to school, and to signal the beginning and end of shifts for workers in the fields, has been proclaimed a historical monument.

Genadendal has a caravan park and picnic ground.

Gourits River

This is the principal river in the southern Cape. The trunk road and the main railway line from Cape Town to Port Elizabeth cross it over a gorge 65 metres deep and 75 metres wide. The sides of this ravine are covered with flowering aloes.

The river is named after the Gouri-qua Khoikhoi people who lived in the area. At the mouth of the river are a caravan park and a hotel. Fishing and swimming are good.

THE COLOURFUL VISITORS OF WINTER

Aloes in a Caledon garden.

The southern Cape is great aloe country. In many species and in countless thousands they cover the coastal belt, blanketing the hillsides with an astonishing blaze of colour in June and July.

The area between Albertinia and Mossel Bay is particularly rich in aloes and the winter months see a fine spectacle of orange, red and yellow flowers. *Aloe ferox* is especially numerous in this area and is the basis for an unusual industry.

The aloe contains an extremely bitter sap which is used internationally in the making of several medicines.

The sap is collected from the leaves and by means of a process of evaporation is reduced to solid masses of concentrated bitterness. This is exported to many countries.

The river of doves flows peacefully down to Heidelberg

Greyton

The village of Greyton lies in the shadow of the peaks of the Riviersonderend range. From here can be explored the Noupoort ('narrow pass') gorge, which passes near the 1 466-metre summit of the Kanonberg. There is a 2 220-hectare nature reserve nearby, and an attractive 4-hour hiking trail leads over the mountains to the town of McGregor.

In a wood on the banks of the Riviersonderend is a municipal camping site with facilities for swimming and canoeing.

The mountains near Greyton.

Cosy old kapsteilhuisies at Puntjie.

Heidelberg

The river known from the number of doves living there as the Duivenhoks ('dovecote') flows from the Langeberg range through undulating foothills. Wheat covers most of the farmlands. The small town of Heidelberg was founded on the riverbanks in 1855. It is a trading, railway and administrative centre for a prosperous farming community.

Houw Hoek

After the trunk road climbs the Hottentots-Holland Mountains and passes through the fruit orchards of Elgin, it descends to the wheatlands of the Overberg ('over the mountain') by means of the Houw Hoek ('pass of the glen'). The railway through the pass provides a delightful train journey. The Houw Hoek Inn, established in 1834, is the oldest surviving coaching inn in the country.

Kanon

Cannons salvaged from the 1763 wreck of the French ship *La Fortune* stand at the small resort known as Kanon. The burial site of some of the shipwrecked sailors is nearby.

Puntjie

A unique resort, Puntjie ('the little point') is a real museum piece. Every cottage here is of the type known as a kapsteilhuisie — literally, a 'roof-house'. These queer little structures are simply thatched roofs which reach the ground. They have only two walls. One, at the front, has a door; the other, at the rear, has a window. Each structure has about 8 metres by 6 metres of floor space. Such homes were built by primitive peoples in ancient times in Europe.

Puntjie stands on a small point projecting into St. Sebastian Bay, where the Duivenhoks River reaches the sea. There is a sandy beach with eroded cliffs and caves.

Puntjie is privately owned and cannot normally be visited without prior arrangement.

Riversdale

The air of Riversdale is saturated with the distinctive odour of the various species of aromatic *Agathosma* shrubs that grow here. These plants have a

---

HOW THE EARTH'S BOILER KEEPS THE HOT SPRINGS HOT

All hot springs begin as cold rain. On reaching the ground the water soaks through the soil and rocks until it reaches a barrier of non-porous rock. Held by this barrier the water spreads out, with its upper level forming what is known as the water table.

Depending on how far it sinks before reaching this rock bed, the water is warmed by the heat of the earth, which increases by about 1°C. for every 50 metres of descent. Hot springs vary from tepid to almost boiling. The hottest in southern Africa, the Zongola geyser at the confluence of the Gwai and Zambezi rivers in Zimbabwe, reaches the surface at 90°C.

As the rainwater that creates hot springs accumulates underground and spreads out through fissures and cracks, its level may be intersected by a valley.

The water then flows out in the

A warm spring oozing to the surface.

form of a spring. If the main source of the water is on much higher ground, the spring will emerge under pressure and may take the form of a geyser. Such a geyser can have an impressive jet, rising many metres into the air.

Occasionally the rock formation underground is in the shape of a saucer. Water soaks down to the centre of this natural basin where it is heated and then, forced by the pressure from behind, finds a weak spot and rises to the surface as a hot spring.

There are 73 major hot springs in southern Africa.

Most contain chemicals from contact with underground deposits of minerals such as iron or sulphur. Some are slightly radio-active.

Hot springs have attracted man since the Stone Age. Many springs are believed to have medicinal value. People drink or bathe in their waters, or even lie in special mud baths, as a treatment for such complaints as rheumatism, arthritis and various skin ailments. Addicts claim that the effect is like a gentle, soothing massage. Certainly, the warmth of hot springs is refreshing and relaxing.

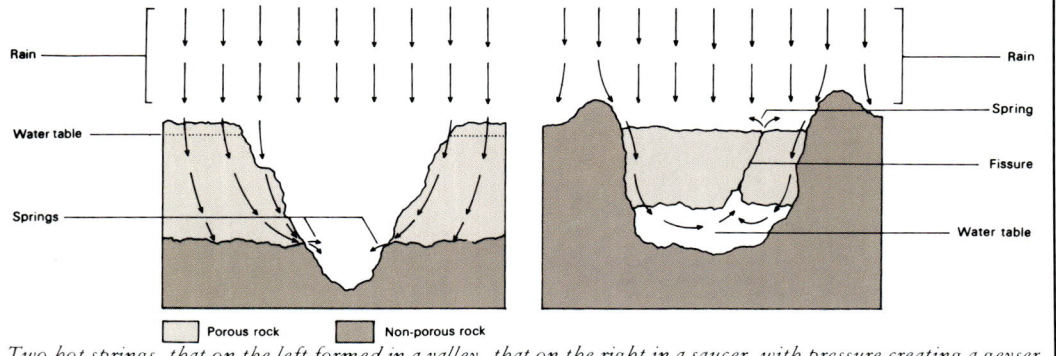

Rain — Water table — Springs

Rain — Spring — Fissure — Water table

☐ Porous rock   ■ Non-porous rock

Two hot springs, that on the left formed in a valley, that on the right in a saucer, with pressure creating a geyser.

The Riviersonderend flows at the foot of the mountains in the Vyeboom Valley.

perfume that is antiseptic-like, but not unpleasant.

In the Jurisch Park are mesembryanthemums and flowering aloes and a dam which is the haunt of several species of wild water-birds.

Near the town is the Werner Frehse Nature Reserve, containing bontebok, gemsbok, eland, and many other species.

Riversdale was founded in 1838 and named after Harry Rivers, a local government official.

It was the home of the artist J. E. A. Volschenk, the first native-born South African landscape painter. Several of Volschenk's paintings, and a number of works by other South African artists, can be viewed in the Julius Gordon Africana Collection located in Versfeld House.

The town has several hotels and a caravan park with fully equipped chalets.

Riviersonderend
To the first explorers, the river flowing eastwards from its source in the Hottentots-Holland Mountains seemed to meander on 'without end', hence its name. It flows through a fertile valley where fruit, wheat and wool are the principal products.

The small town of Riviersonderend is a convenient centre from which to explore the neighbouring countryside. The town itself offers a caravan park and a public swimming pool.

St. Sebastian Bay
The Breë River reaches the sea in a windy bay named by the Portuguese after Saint Sebastian. The estuary is a popular fishing area and is notable for shell fish, including oysters. The river is navigable for small ships for 35 kilometres — as far as Malgas. Before the railway was built from Cape Town to Mossel Bay, a coaster service connected the river mouth and Malgas to Cape Town. Wool, ostrich feathers from the Little Karoo, wheat and other local products were shipped out.

Today the river and the bay are pleasure grounds, favoured by boatmen and anglers. Sudden winds here can be dangerous, but higher up the river the water is calm and ideal for small craft.

Most fishing in the estuary is done from power-boats and some spectacular catches are made. Fish such as grunter, which are big and powerful, are capable of putting up tremendous resistance and have been known to

A typical southern Cape scene . . . a eucalyptus-shaded homestead.

Fields of new wheat start to sprout as winter begins in the Caledon district.

A shore scattered with the remains of prehistoric feasts

pull boats for some distance in their efforts to escape.

The resort at the mouth of the river is known as Port Beaufort.

Stilbaai

A wide estuary divides the settlement of Stilbaai ('still' or 'quiet' bay) into a western and an eastern section. Swimming, fishing, boating and collecting shells are the pastimes here. There is a small fishing harbour and numerous holiday cottages.

In many ways, Stilbaai is regarded as almost the classic prototype of the seasonal South African holiday resort. For nine months of the year, the place is practically deserted. When the school holidays arrive, however, there is an overnight influx and the resort becomes a bustling centre for such competitive pastimes as jukskei (a form of skittles) and tug-of-war.

The holiday homes of Stilbaai are interesting examples of local folk architecture. Many of them are built

Stilbaai, with its sheltered, sandy beaches, is a favourite holiday spot.

on stilts to keep them clear of the high spring tides. Many of the older cottages have freshwater wells under them.

The social centre of the community is a wooden hall where dances and

various other festivities are held.

The shores of Stilbaai have always attracted beachcombers. Prehistoric man found the area to be a prolific source of seafood. The huge dumps of shells which he left along the shore

remain as mute evidence of a great deal of feasting. The shallow water off the shore was ideal for the making of stone fish traps, in which fish are trapped at low tide — often thousands of mullet are caught in a single trap. Many of these traps are still in use. Their walls are regularly repaired and the bottoms kept clear of debris.

It was on this coast that evidence was found of what is called the Still Bay Culture and the shore is a rich hunting ground for collectors of ancient relics of these people.

Shells and drift seeds washed down from the tropics by the Mocambique-Agulhas Current are often found. Many museums have exhibits from this area. Shells are used locally to decorate graves.

The streams and rivers of this area are the homes of a vast population of edible eels, many weighing around 7,5 kilograms. On some farms in the locality eels in the rivers are tame enough to take food from the hand.

The farming community of the southern Cape regard Stilbaai as their particular holiday resort. At Christmas they gather here to play games and hold open-air dances.

Around the region are several strange rock formations such as Preekstoel (Pulpit Rock), 3 kilometres east of Stilbaai.

There is a considerable variety of accommodation available — caravans, camping sites, bungalows, boarding houses and hotels.

Swellendam

For a memorable three months in 1795, Swellendam was one of the capitals of the world. Its citizens, enraged at misrule by the Dutch East India Company, dismissed their magistrate, declared an independent republic and appointed a president.

Soon, however, the British occupied the Cape and the rebel republic — it consisted of only twenty houses scattered along the valley of the Korenlands River — faded away.

After Cape Town and Stellenbosch, Swellendam was the third settlement to be established by the Dutch East India Company. Founded in 1747 and named after the governor, Hendrik Swellengrebel, and his wife, Helena ten Damme, the town lies in a hand-

The high mountain wall of the Langeberg near Swellendam.

A snug homestead built in the Swellendam district in 1798.

The drostdy built for Swellendam's first magistrate.

A farm mill with its waterwheel in the Swellendam district.

The Dutch Reformed Church in Swellendam, dating from 1910, stands on the site of an older church that was built in 1802.

some setting below the Clock Peaks of the Langeberg range. From some of these peaks, known east to west as Seven o'clock, Eight o'clock, Nine o'clock, Ten o'clock, Eleven o'clock, Twelve o'clock and One o'clock, the time can be told by the way the shadows fall from their summits.

Swellendam is entered from the east through a stately avenue of oaks along Swellengrebel Street. The original drostdy ('residence') built for the first magistrate of the district is now a museum. It houses period furniture and household oddments.

Opposite the Drostdy is a unique craft museum, housed in a complex of restored buildings.

The thatched house next to it, the Old Post Office, was the home of the gaoler, who was also the postmaster.

The Marloth Flower Reserve is accessible from the scenic mountain drive.

Swellendam has several hotels and a municipal caravan park.

Tradouw Pass

One of the principal passes through the Langeberg range is the Tradouw ('women's pass'), so named by Khoikhoi people. Noted for its waterfalls in winter and wild flowers in spring, the pass follows the precipitous sides of the Tradouws River.

San paintings in caves along the way are evidence of its use by prehistoric man.

Near the San caves a track leads to a swimming pool in the river.

A new road through the pass was built in 1873 by the engineer, Thomas Bain. The camp used by convicts who comprised his labour force can be seen half way up the pass.

Vleesbaai

The coastal resort of Vleesbaai ('flesh bay') is a popular holiday place for fishermen. Its name comes from visits made to this bay by early Portuguese and Dutch sailors who traded with the Khoikhoi inhabitants for meat and cattle.

The beach is a haunt of shell collectors.

There are many heaps of shells left by prehistoric people, who obviously found the fishing as good in their distant times as it is today.

The serene, silent fairyland that shimmers beneath the sea

Beneath the sea lies a fairyland — a dream world of which man had little knowledge until the invention of the simple goggle, scuba gear (self-contained underwater breathing apparatus), flippers and the wet suit. Even the sprouting of wings could not have given man a more sensational entrance to another element than did the invention of the first free-diving apparatus in 1872 by a French naval officer, Auguste Denayrouze. With such equipment, man could glide down into the silent realm of fish and coral. Later developments enabled him to wander virtually at will through the undersea forests of plants, the gardens of anemones, the lovely shoals of fish — and swim freely with them in a cool world of crystal purity.

The coastline of southern Africa, from the mouth of the Zambezi to the mouth of the Kunene, is more than 5 500 kilometres long. Few coastlines in the world can surpass it for variety. With cold water to the west and warm water to the east there is a prodigious variety of marine life.

In the far south and on the cold west coast, the diver finds great forests of kelp, rock lobsters and pools and gullies crowded with brilliantly coloured anemones and sea urchins. Perlemoen shells live on the rocks together with a rich variety of marine plants and molluscs.

Up the east coast, as the water gets warmer, corals start to grow, turtles and dugongs feed on meadows of underwater weeds while shoals of tropical fish swim like butterflies fluttering in an enchanted garden.

About 1 500 different species of fish live around the shores of southern Africa, most of them immediately offshore, in what is known as the littoral. In such shallow waters around all continents, four-fifths of the earth's plants and animals have their homes. They feed on the foodstuffs washed into the sea, or, in the case of southern Africa, they consume food carried to them by the Benguela and Mocambique currents.

This littoral portion of the continental shelf is the domain of the diver, his special underwater wonderland — filled with surprises, and with countless delightful scenes and strangely beautiful creatures.

Low tide along the southern Cape, where life teems beneath the surface.

A basket star on the sea bed.

An anemone and sea urchins.

China coral and delicate sea sponges.

Anemones find their home on a reef.

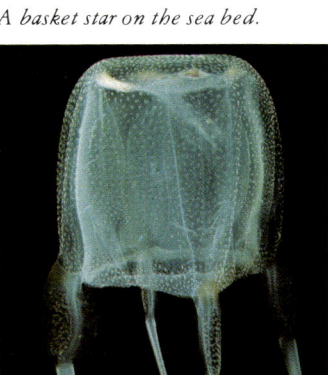

A sea wasp, almost transparent.

A gas flame nudibranch, waving in the current.

Exotic-blooming anemones.

A sea star on the lower tidal bed of Tsitsikama coastal park.

Complex jewellery made by nature — a multi-tentacled Gorgon's Head.

Zoanthids, related to the sea anemone.

Two chitons, a webbed sea star and a limpet from a rock pool in the park.

THE MAGIC OF THE GARDEN ROUTE

FROM MOSSEL BAY to the Storms River is a necklace of bays, beaches, cliffs and rocky capes strung together along a line of pounding white surf. The mountain ranges crowd close to the shoreline and, with a rainfall of around 2 500 millimetres on the peaks, bring a plentiful water supply to the narrow coastal terrace. This terrace is covered so densely in trees and flowering plants that a cultivated garden would pale into insignificance in comparison.

The 227 kilometres of this coastline is the Garden Route, a region of eternal freshness and greenery.

The climate is mild and equable. Rainfall is scattered throughout the year, most of it falling at night. A blight of most of the African continent is thus avoided – rainfall concentrated into a short season of floods followed by months so dry that rivers become sand and the vegetation so dead that it is simply a fire waiting to be started.

The French explorer, Francois le Vaillant, passed this way in the 1780s and the description he has left might apply today. 'The land bears the name of Outeniqua, which in the Khoikhoi tongue means "a man laden with honey". The flowers grow there in millions, the mixture of pleasant scents which arises from them, their colour, their variety, the pure and fresh air which one breathes there, all make one stop and think nature has made an enchanted abode of this beautiful place.' The enchantment and the beauty are here still, for the modern traveller to enjoy.

Seldom cooler than 20°C, the coastal waters teem with game fish. Divers find a magic world of brilliantly coloured sea plants, molluscs and vast shoals of little fish. Suddenly a rocky shoreline will give way to a secluded, sandy beach. Victoria Bay is renowned as one of the world's best surfing beaches. The rivers, deeply stained with the amber colour of the soil, have lovely stretches navigable by small boats; the chain of lakes and the great lagoon at Knysna cheerfully lend themselves to swimming, boating and fishing; the wild flowers and the high forests offer long, charming drives beneath the trees; there is a mining ghost town to explore, and gold still to be panned.

Along the Garden Route is little to harm man other than his own folly. For the continent of Africa this is indeed a rare pleasure. There are no malarial mosquitoes, no bilharzia snails in the rivers, no crocodiles or other predatory animals save leopards, which keep to themselves in the mountains. A few elephants still survive in the depths of the Knysna Forest, but are seldom seen.

At some time or other, nearly every South African with the means to go on holiday spends some time on this coast. For visitors to the country it is one of the highlights of a complete tour. The region is excellently served by roads and has a delightful branch railway from George to Knysna still worked by steam locomotives. It has many hotels, caravan parks and camping grounds.

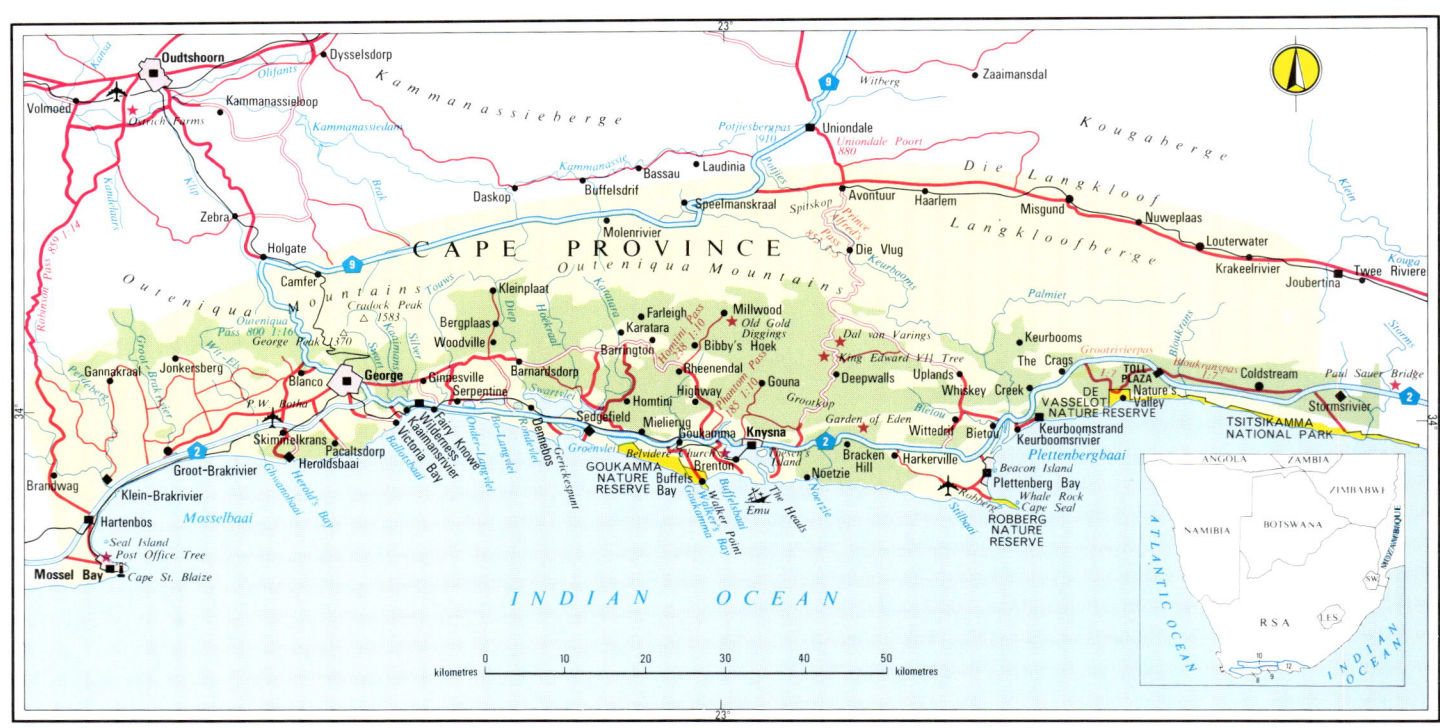

Belvidere church, a delightful piece of architecture close to Knysna lagoon.

Belvidere

The famed Norman-style church at Belvidere was built by Captain Thomas Duthie, husband of Caroline, daughter of the 19th century pioneer George Rex (see box, page 107).

When consecrating the church in 1855, Bishop Robert Gray described it as 'the most perfect church yet in the diocese'.

Thomas and Caroline Duthie are buried in the church graveyard. The farm of Belvidere, around which the settlement was founded, was their homestead.

Brenton-on-Sea

From the road to the seaside resort of Brenton-on-Sea are spectacular views of the Knysna lagoon and hill slopes rich in wild flowers. The resort is noted for its fishing. On the beach are a caravan park and hotel.

Buffelsbaai

The buffaloes that gave Buffelsbaai its name have long vanished. It is now a resort favoured for swimming, surfing and angling. The bay has a caravan park and a number of holiday houses.

Elephant Walk

A permit to explore the Elephant Walk can be obtained from the forestry station at Deepwalls. The walk, a circular trail of 18,2 kilometres, leads through luxuriant high forest. Elephants are often in the area.

Bushbuck, wild pigs and duikers can also be seen along the route, and giant yellow-woods are found here, among them a specimen named after King Edward VII. It is 46 metres high, 9,5 metres in circumference, and is believed to be some 700 years old.

Two shorter walks provide alternatives to the Elephant Walk.

George

The English novelist Anthony Trollope praised George in 1877 as 'the prettiest village on the face of the earth'. Overlooked by the George Peak (1 370 metres) and Cradock Peak (1 583 metres) of the Outeniqua Mountains, George nestles on a coastal plateau in a setting of parkland and garden. Flowers grow profusely in every garden, and trees grow wherever man has failed to cut them down. Only 8 kilometres from the sea and with an adequate rainfall, balmy climate and altitude of 226 metres, George has the best of several worlds. It is the principal town of the Garden Route.

Founded in 1811, it was named after George III. It grew as an administrative, communications and timber centre. One of the oak trees which were planted along the streets during these early years has been proclaimed a national monument. A chain, to which slaves are said to have been fastened and sold at auction, is embedded in the trunk of the tree.

Because of the widespread destruction of the wealth of indigenous forest, in 1936 the government prohibited the felling of indigenous trees for 200 years. The decision has ensured the preservation of stinkwood and yellow-wood trees.

George became a municipality in 1837 and in 1850 Bishop Robert Gray, founder of the Diocesan College for

A tidal pool at Buffelsbaai. The Indian Ocean is warm, full of fish, and provides marvellous fun for holiday-makers.

One of the world's great rail journeys starts here

One of the old steam locomotives climbing over the Outeniqua Mountains between George and Oudtshoorn.

Boys in Cape Town, consecrated the town's St. Mark's Church, which became a cathedral in 1911. George's Dutch Reformed Church, built in 1842, is the town's oldest Church. The church of St. Peter and St. Paul, built the following year, is the oldest Roman Catholic church in South Africa. Among other old buildings is the Town House, built in 1847 at a cost of £478.

The George Museum has South Africa's largest collection of old gramophones, all in working order. The theme of the museum is indigenous timber and its use in South Africa.

This is the only region of South Africa which produces hops — imported varieties have been successfully transplanted in recent years.

George has a flying club, 18-hole championship golf course, several hotels and caravan parks.

From the town two dramatic train journeys can be taken. The main railway line from Cape Town to Port Elizabeth crosses the Outeniqua Mountains through what is widely regarded as one of the world's most beautiful railway passes. In 25 kilometres the railway climbs by means of zigzags, tunnels and cuttings to an altitude of 715 metres before descending into the Little Karoo. The second railway journey from George is by steam train, along the branch line to Knysna, through tunnels and forests, across lakes and cliffs overlooking the sea. The climax of the arrival in Knysna, with a long approach by bridge over the lagoon, is unforgettable.

Goukamma Nature Reserve
The coastal dunes and the estuary of the Goukamma River are the resort of many water-birds, including ducks, geese, plovers, gulls, kingfishers and dikkops. Trails lead to most parts of the reserve established here. A permit to enter the reserve must be obtained from the ranger's office.

Great Brak River
Two 'brak' ('brackish') rivers, the Little Brak and the Great Brak, reach the sea between George and Mossel Bay, and both have holiday resorts on their lower reaches. The Great Brak River has a lagoon at its mouth.

Dutch Reformed Church, George.

The railway pass and the old road pass over the Outeniqua Mountains.

The Goukamma River, bathed in sunshine as it flows through the verdant landscape of the hills near Knysna.

MYSTERY OF THE HIDEAWAY ELEPHANTS OF THE KNYSNA FOREST

The elephants of the Knysna forests are the remnants of a famous, once numerous population. They are large specimens of their kind. It has been suggested that living in a high forest area stimulated their growth, while the elephant community of the Addo bush, further east. were slightly stunted because they lived in an area of low shrub.

The Knysna elephants. unfortunately for themselves, carried excellent ivory and were systematically hunted. Sportsmen, too, were attracted to the forest by the size of the elephants, and, using the local inhabitants as guides, they hunted the big bulls and carried away their heads, tusks and tails as trophies.

Today, the last of these animals live in the depths of the forest and are seldom seen.

They are silent, elusive creatures, occasionally looming out of the shadows and surprising foresters, hikers and campers. Motorists sometimes see them crossing the roads and relate exciting tales of charges and narrow escapes.

With the habits of these elephants confining them to deep forests, they are difficult to photograph and little is known about their numbers, or whether they have, in their isolation, developed different characteristics

The elephants of Knysna, living deep in the high forest, are shy and seldom seen.

from those of savanna elephants in the rest of Africa.

In former years elephants were found as far south as the Cape Peninsula, and also up the west coast as far as the Olifants River and the verges of Namaqualand.

These elephants of the far south of Africa were blood-brothers of the elephants of the Knysna forests.

Elephants could not have crossed the more arid Karoo areas or Namaqualand — they could only have migrated down the watercourses to the Orange River or the well-watered Garden Route, or retreated up it when pressed by hunters from the settlement at the Cape.

The elephants of Knysna are therefore the last of a most interesting branch of their kind. They belong to the same species, *Loxodonta africana*, as all the bush or savanna elephants of Africa, but their life-style has modified their habits, causing them to resemble those of one of the two sub-species of African elephant —

the forest elephant, *Loxodonta africana cyclotis*, whose habitat is the equatorial forests of West and Central Africa.

In appearance, however, the Knysna elephants are identical to the bush elephants. Both have curved tusks of excellent soft ivory, easily carved, unlike the brittle ivory of the forest elephants.

Left to themselves, these Knysna elephants will stay in their forest home for an indefinite period. They have a rich food supply.

Excessive dampness is thought to be their greatest enemy, inflicting them with rheumatism.

They breed quite regularly, but elephants are not fast breeders. Breeding starts when they are about 12 years old, and their prime is between 40 and 50 years. The gestation period is 22 months.

Life in the high forest also has special hazards for calves. They can be trapped in mud, catch cold or be pinned by falling trees.

The town was founded by the Searle family in 1859 and the footwear and timber industry they established here still thrives. The font in the Spanish-style church was made from the post of a turnpike built by the first Searle to settle here.

Hartenbos
During the Christmas holiday season, the camping ground near the mouth of the Hartenbos River is a city of tents and caravans.

An open-air stadium, seating 10 000, is used for folk festivals, church services and athletics.

A Voortrekker museum exhibits two wagons which took part in the 1938 symbolic trek to Pretoria.

Herold's Bay
The cliffs along the Garden Route occasionally pull back to form a sandy, sheltered bay. Herold's Bay is an example of such bays. The cliffs on both sides fall steeply into the sea. The sandy beach has a sea-water swimming pool. A ridge overlooking the bay is the site of the village. There are many trees.

The resort is named after the Rev. Tobias Herold, the first minister of George's Dutch Reformed Church.

Keurboomstrand
Boating and fishing are major pastimes at Keurboomstrand, the resort at the mouth of the Keurbooms River. Here the river, named from the sweetly scented flowering trees which grow on its banks, joins the Bietou River to form a lagoon. On the beach are mounds of shells thousands of years old. Nearby is the Matjies River Cave, where Late Stone Age relics have been found.

The upper reaches of the Keurbooms River are roofed with trees, notably at Whiskey Creek.

Knysna
'This fair land is the gift of God'. So reads the motto on the Divisional Council's coat of arms. It bears testimony to the pride local people have in this resort of great scenic beauty.

A name sounding like Knysna to Europeans was given to the river by the Khoikhoi. Scholars offer several translations of the Khoikhoi term — 'place

The fair land that was 'the gift of God'

The beautiful valley of the Knysna River, below Phantom Pass.

of wood', 'fern leaves' or, simply, 'straight down', which would presumably refer to the two steep sandstone cliffs, known as The Heads, which guard the harbour. The naval brig *Emu* foundered between The Heads in 1817. The rescue ship *Podargus* succeeded in negotiating the gap and during the next hundred years many freighters followed to ship timber. Today the mouth to the sea is deep enough to allow the passage of medium-sized ships.

More than 200 species of fish are found in the lagoon. Oysters, of which Knysna is a major supplier, exist in considerable numbers. The lagoon is also the home of a rare sea-horse, *Hippocampus capensis*. Knysna is beloved by anglers. Divers encounter innumerable forms of marine life, and the lagoon has recently become a very popular place for windsurfing.

The town's most distinguished resident was George Rex, reputed son of George III (see box). George Bernard Shaw lived here during 1932 while writing *The Black Girl in Search of God*.

Knysna has several hotels and caravan parks. A museum contains many items connected with the Rex family.

This narrow channel, providing an entrance to Knysna lagoon, leads between two high sandstone cliffs known as The Heads.

Looking west towards the Outeniqua Mountains, the spacious Knysna lagoon.

Craft shops sell furniture and curios made from local trees. An old steam train offers holiday makers an attractive way of travelling between Knysna and George.

Millwood

In 1886 gold was found in several of the streams in the forestry area known as Goudveld ('gold field'). The town of Millwood grew up during the inevitable rush, only to be abandoned when none of the discoveries proved to be payable. Today Millwood is a ghost town of overgrown foundations, shafts and trenches. A permit to visit the town can be obtained from the Goudveld forestry station. A little gold can still be panned in the region. The forest has several picnic sites.

HOW GEORGE REX BECAME THE UNCROWNED KING OF KNYSNA

The romantic, enigmatic and forceful personality of George Rex is part of the folk-lore of southern Africa. He arrived in the Cape in 1797, at the time of the first British occupation. A man of distinguished bearing, he was well-educated and obviously well-connected.

In Cape Town he was appointed marshal of the vice-admiralty court, notary public to the governor, and advocate for the Crown. He met Johanna, a beautiful and wealthy young widow, and settled down with her and her four children.

When the British occupation ended he remained in the Cape and in 1804, at the age of 39, he purchased the farm Melkhoutkraal, on the shores of Knysna lagoon.

To reach this farm, Rex made a coach journey on a grand scale. His family rode with him in a coach bearing a coat of arms and drawn by six horses. Riding alongside the coach was a retinue of friends.

To the awed locals the journey resembled a royal procession — and the name of the man, George Rex, conjured up images of royalty travelling incognito.

Stories spread that Rex was the son of George III of England and Hannah Lightfoot, daughter of a Wapping shoemaker. Modern research does not confirm this, and there is no record of Rex ever having made such a claim. But his life-style and grand manner convinced the residents of the Cape, and especially of Knysna, that the man in their midst was indeed of royal descent.

Rex rebuilt the homestead of Melkhoutkraal, which had been destroyed in a Xhosa raid, and created a beautiful, rambling home for his family — now there were eight children. The farm was expanded. There was a watermill, blacksmith's shop and spinnery producing silk from silkworms fed on the leaves of groves of mulberries. The lagoon occupied the full attention of Rex. He started a fishery, built boats from the timber of the forest and persuaded the British admiralty to develop Knysna as a port.

On 11 February 1817, the first vessel to enter the lagoon, the naval brig *Emu*, came to grief on a sunken rock and had to be run ashore to save it from sinking. For Rex and the people of Knysna watching from the shore, this was a sad spectacle, but it was not the end of the venture. The navy sent up a second vessel to salvage the first and this, the *Podargus*, had no difficulty in entering and leaving the lagoon in May 1817.

From then on Knysna was established as a port for medium-sized vessels.

Rex built his own 127-ton vessel, the *Knysna*, on the shores of the lagoon, and used the ship for trading along the coast.

Rex never returned to Britain. He died on 3 April 1839, after a full and rewarding life.

One of the best-known of his descendants was the late celebrated circus clown known as Stompie.

The grave of George Rex, the legendary character who lived at Knysna for 35 years.

For centuries this tree served as a postal clearing house. Seamen would leave letters in packets on the tree to be delivered by other seamen travelling to appropriate destinations. A letter-box has been erected nearby in the shape of a seaman's boot, and letters posted there are franked 'Old Post Office Tree'.

During his stay, Da Nova built South Africa's first church. Seeing the Khoikhoi with their herds of cattle near the bay, he named it Golfo dos Vaqueiros ('bay of the herdsmen').

In 1601, the Dutch navigator Paulus van Caerden gave Mossel Bay its present name — he was said to have been able to replenish his ship's provisions only with mussels.

Mossel Bay has seen the comings and goings of many ships. In 1787, a storehouse was built to facilitate the export of such local products as wheat. Around this building the town grew and port facilities were expanded over the years. Wheat, canned fruit, jams, ochre and bitter aloe juice are shipped out through Mossel Bay, but it is as a holiday resort that the town is best known.

Over the Christmas holidays, large numbers of visitors travel to Mossel Bay's camping sites, caravan parks, bungalows and hotels.

The warm summer air becomes heavy with the smell of barbecues. Open-air dances, sports, parties and public meetings are held. Swimming, surfing, fishing and boating are other pastimes.

A considerable development in Mossel Bay in recent times (and one which has boosted commercial interest in the Mossel Bay area) is known as Mossgas. It is concerned with the refining of natural gas recovered from boreholes in the seabed. An information bureau close to the beach depicts the search for oil in South Africa.

The town has a maritime museum, and one of the best shell museums in the country.

Noetzie

Holiday homes designed like odd-shaped castles overlook the beach at Noetzie and give the resort a unique character. The Noetzie ('black') River runs into a picturesque lagoon here, bordered by a small beach.

Mossel Bay

The Garden Route starts at Mossel Bay and this is certainly a handsome beginning to so fine a scenic route. The bay is overlooked by the Langeberg and Outeniqua mountain ranges. It has sandy beaches, safe for swimming; a rocky islet used as a rookery by seals; and a commanding cape, Cape St. Blaize, with a lighthouse on the summit and caves in its face.

Prehistoric man discovered the rich stores of seafood along the shore. Mussels and oysters flourish here and it was from these molluscs that the Dutch name of Mossel ('mussel') was given to the bay. For passing ships it was a pleasant anchorage. In 1488, Bartholomew Dias, attempting to find a sea route to the East, became the first European to sail into the bay. For Dias and other early Portuguese navigators, the perennial spring near the shore provided fresh water. When Vasco da Gama visited the bay on his way to India in 1497 he called it Aguada de Sao Bras ('watering place of St. Blaize'). He obtained cattle by bartering with the Khoikhoi — the first known commercial transaction between Europeans and the natives.

In 1500, with what little remained of his fleet after confronting a fierce storm, Pedro d'Ataide ran for shelter into the bay and left an account of the disaster in an old shoe which was hung on a milkwood tree. João da Nova visited Mossel Bay in 1501 and found d'Ataide's report in the shoe. The tree on which it hung still stands and has been declared a historical monument.

Fern Creek, on the old gold fields.

The site of the spring on the shores of Mossel Bay. Many of the early Portuguese navigators drew their fresh water at this spot.

Mossel Bay — rocks and blue water.

Trees a thousand years old still reach toward the sun

The Langeberg range, from Robinson Pass; wild flowers and majestic views.

The Anglican Church of St Andrews, built in 1850 in Plettenberg Bay.

The beach of Plettenberg Bay, bordered by the lagoon of the Bietou River.

Beacon Island, once a whaling station, now a holiday centre.

Outeniqua Hiking Trail

Much of the Garden Route is overlooked by the Outeniqua Mountains, named after the Khoikhoi people of that name. 'Outeniqua' was said to mean 'a man laden with honey' — the profuse wild flowers here attract swarms of bees. A hiking trail, maintained by the forestry department, covers 150 kilometres of the range. Along the route are numerous huts. The path links the Witfontein and Deepwalls forestry stations.

Passes Route

The first proper road connecting George to Knysna was built in the late 1860s, thus converting an appalling wagon trail into a more acceptable road. This route, subsequently improved by means of bridges, cuttings, easier gradients and a firmer gravel surface, remained the principal road until the modern national road (N2) was built after the Second World War. The modern road, however, follows the coast, while the old road, known as the Passes Route, keeps inland. This old road is still in use, providing a link to several forestry stations and settlements, and it offers a very beautiful 82-kilometre drive, best done in dry weather and with enough time allowed for taking things slowly, admiring the scenery, turning aside to see the big trees, picnicking by the wayside and enjoying at leisure a very pleasant scenic experience. By allocating a full day to this trip, there will be time for the tourist to visit an area such as the Goudveld ('goldfield') Forestry Station and to see the old gold rush area of Millwood. The passes that give this route its name are those of the Swart ('black') River; the Kaaimans ('alligator') River; the Touw ('river of the ford or pass'); the Diep ('deep') River; the Homtini ('place of the passage'); and Phantom (named after the phantom moths found there).

Between the Swart and Kaaimans rivers stands Saasveld, the college for the Department of Forestry. The college receives its name from the ancient castle in Holland, the seat of the Van Rheede van Oudtshoorn family. A baroness of this family married E. Bergh, Civil Commissioner of George, who owned part of the ground on which the college stands. One yellow-wood tree, reached by a signposted turnoff from the main road, is 31 metres high, with a girth of 9 metres. It is estimated to be 600 years old.

Plettenberg Bay

The Portuguese, with some restraint, named this bay Formosa ('beautiful'). Three spacious, safe beaches, a lagoon and a river mouth are backed by

The sandstone cliffs of the Robberg, a resting place for countless gulls.

mountain ranges and a prominent cape, Cape Seal, at the end of a promontory known as Robberg ('mountain of seals').

This popular holiday resort's present name was given in 1778 by Governor Joachim van Plettenberg, who erected a beacon claiming the bay as the possession of the Dutch East India Company. The beacon was removed by the Historical Monuments Commission in 1964 and placed in the South African Cultural History Museum in Cape Town, and a replica was erected on the original spot.

The Dutch tried to develop the bay into a port for the shipment of timber, but only the ruins of the storehouse they built in 1788 remain. The ruins have been proclaimed a national monument.

Norwegian settlers built a whaling base on what is known as Beacon Island from a beacon erected there. When the Norwegians left in 1920, holiday-makers started to move in, and nowadays Plettenberg Bay is devoted almost entirely to their enjoyment.

The suspension foot-bridge across the mouth of the Storms River in the Tsitsikama Coastal National Park.

Prince Alfred's Pass

The road from Knysna to Avontuur in the Langkloof finds a spectacular way over the Outeniqua Mountains by means of the pass named after Prince Alfred, second son of Queen Victoria. He hunted elephants here in 1867. The journey leads through dense forest, pine and gum plantations, the forestry station of Deepwalls, through the Dal van Varings ('dale of ferns'), climbs steeply to a 1 045-metre summit and descends into the fruit-producing valley of the Langkloof.

Robberg Nature Reserve

Fishermen consider Robberg to be only slightly inferior as a vantage point to the famous Rooikrans on the Cape Peninsula. Robberg ('the mountain of seals') is a peninsula of red standstone and conglomerate projecting into the sea and terminating in Cape Seal. The 243 hectares of the peninsula are a nature reserve, administered by the Department of Nature and Environmental Conservation. Sea-birds are numerous and intertidal life is rich. Among caves and rock shelters are kitchen middens and ancient tools, revealing that prehistoric man found the area productive of seafoods. The Plettenberg Bay Angling Club hires out fishing huts on Robberg.

Storms River

The formidable gorge of the Storms River is spanned by the spectacular Paul Sauer Bridge, which was officially opened in 1964. It is 191 metres long and 130 metres above the river. This concrete bridge, designed by Ricardo Morandi of Rome, is built on the principle of a castle drawbridge. Two sections were hinged onto a platform on each side of the river and lowered to meet in the centre. There is a restaurant near the bridge.

The original pass, built by Thomas Bain in the 1870s, is still open.

Tsitsikama Forest and Coastal National Parks

The name Tsitsikama derives from a Khoikhoi word meaning clear or sparkling water. The Tsitsikama Forest and Coastal national parks cover a 73-kilometre coastal strip of high rainfall, with many rivers and streams. It is a wild and unspoiled stretch of rocky coast, with steep, forested cliffs. In the centre, near the mouth of the Storms River, is a camp with a restaurant, bungalows and caravan park. Swimming, fishing and walking are the chief pastimes here. In the coastal pools is an abundance of marine life.

The Otter Trail hiking path runs along the southern length of the park. There are huts for overnight stops and the coastal scenery is a delight. The walk takes five days.

A field museum at the mouth of the Storms River displays relics of the prehistoric beachcombers who lived on the coast.

In the forest there are several massive trees — the tallest is 36 metres — some of which are reputedly 1 000 years old. There are more than 30 species of indigenous trees, ferns and climbers, and such rare birds as the Knysna loerie and the Narina trogon may also be seen in the forest.

Victoria Bay

Getting in and out of Victoria Bay took some doing for the road engineers. It is a small bay set in steep cliffs. The road winds down to a small beach with a cluster of holiday homes. Surfing is popular here.

Wilderness

Honeymooners have long favoured Wilderness, a romantic seaside resort of international repute. The road passes over a unique curved bridge across the Kaaimans River and provides stunning views. The forest-covered hills of the region tumble down to a sandy beach more than 8 kilometres long. It has a dangerous backwash, but is fine for sunbathing, angling and walking. There is just room between beach and hills for a line of hotels, holiday homes, and a chain of lakes and lagoons.

George Bennet, who bought the area in 1877, called it Wilderness, for that was exactly what it was. It has developed into one of the most fashionable resorts in southern Africa.

THE TSITSIKAMA TOLL ROAD

The original road from Plettenberg Bay to Storms River was built between 1879 and 1885 by Thomas Bain. It was a difficult road to construct, rising and falling over three river valleys which provided travellers with fine scenery but seriously slowed through-traffic along the coast.

To solve this problem, between 1980 and 1984 a major new toll road was constructed, involving the erection of three spectacular bridges — all great feats of engineering. The Bobbejaans River bridge has a deck 286 m long which is situated 170 m above the river bed.

The Groot River bridge has a deck 301 m long. It is 172 m above the river bed.

The Bloukrans River bridge has a deck 451 metres long, 216 metres above the river bed. It is the largest — and probably the most scenic — concrete bridge in Africa and the fourth largest in the world.

Exploring the enchanted depths of the high forest

Stretching for 177 kilometres between the mountains and the sea, the high forest of the Garden Route is one of southern Africa's richest botanical treasures. Slanting shafts of sunlight pierce magic glades where trunks of ancient hardwoods rise like cathedral columns. More than 80 kinds of tree grow here, from venerable giants soaring towards the sky to exquisite small shrubs with dazzling blossoms and haunting perfumes. Many of the trees produce valuable timber used in building, the making of furniture and craft work. Elephants, leopards, monkeys and many birds have their homes in the forest's enchanted depths. It is a place of beauty, mystery, and for those who wish to delve deeply into its secrets, a place to learn.

The high forest of the Garden Route is the largest indigenous forest in southern Africa. Originally it covered more than 100 000 hectares, but fires and the predations of man have reduced this to around 40 500 hectares. This area of naturally growing trees is greatly enlarged by softwood plantations of pine and gum trees.

The name 'high forest' refers to the height of the trees rather than the altitude at which they grow. The giant among them is the common yellow-wood, which can reach up to 50 metres and live for 1 000 years. In several areas, the forestry department has constructed special paths which take visitors to particularly impressive specimens. One of the most famous is a yellow-wood known as King Edward's Tree, which is 46 metres high with a girth of 9,5 metres and thought to be about 700 years old.

The handsomely coloured timber of the common yellow-wood is much in demand for furniture. Selected trees are auctioned after being felled and are then carted away by the buyers. The pale timber of a slightly smaller species, the real yellow-wood, is also highly prized.

Many a pioneering railway has been laid on the hard, durable sleepers produced from another forest giant, the black ironwood tree. Today, railway sleepers are usually made of concrete, but ironwood is often used for flooring and veneers. In March, the blossoms of the ironwood spread a creamy canopy over the forest.

South Africa's history also owes much to the stinkwood tree. Its timber was used to build the trek wagons, surely among the toughest vehicles ever built. This tree takes its name from the characteristic pungent odour of the wood when it is first cut.

Some of the smaller trees, while not so highly valued for their timber, nonetheless enhance the beauty of the forest, displaying attractively coloured foliage and sweetly scented flowers. Among these are the keurboom, with

Lichens and gazania daisies growing along the sea front of the Tsitsikama coast.

its fragrant pink blossom, the wild pomegranate, with its clusters of red flowers, and the mauve-flowering Cape chestnut.

One of the best places for exploring the forest is an area known as the Garden of Eden, 16 kilometres from Knysna along the trunk road on the way to Plettenberg Bay. There is a picnic site with paths branching into the deeper parts of the forest, and many typical tree species are identified by numbers. The Garden of Eden is also a favourite haunt of elephants.

Wild pigs and small forest antelope such as the blue duiker can also be seen.

Because of the almost permanent dampness of the forest floor, however, most of the wild life consists of tree-dwelling species, including monkeys, leopards, tree hyraxes, snakes and birds.

Many varieties of ferns and creepers decorate the forest, and the Dal van Varings, or Dale of Ferns, is a happy hunting ground for specialists in this field.

For all its marvels, southern Africa has always been short of rain and the regions where forests flourish are comparatively few. This makes the great forest of the Garden Route all the more precious — a place of rare wonder.

A tangle of high forest trees, yellow-wood and stinkwood, in the Tsitsikama Forest National Park near Storms River.

Deep in the high forest a brilliant jewel, a spider's web, with the spinner lurking patiently nearby.

HOW TO IDENTIFY THE TREES OF THE FOREST

Telling one tree from another can be a baffling task for the amateur in an area with as many different species as the high forest of the Garden Route. But identification has been simplified by a system of numbering devised by the Botanical Research Institute in Pretoria.

The institute has allocated numbers to more than 700 species throughout South Africa, and in many large forests typical specimens bear their particular number.

These are the numbers of 61 trees that are common in the high forest of the Garden Route:

Tree number	Name
2	Forest tree fern
16	Outeniqua yellow-wood
18	Real yellow-wood
20	Mountain cypress
39	White stinkwood
50	Cape fig
74	Terblans beech
118	Stinkwood
139	Cheesewood
140	Red alder
141	White alder
142	Black witch-hazel
221	Keurboom
254	Knobwood
256	Cape chestnut
261	White ironwood
265	Horsewood
298	Cape ash
307	Coalwood
388.1	Glossy currant
394	Wild currant
395	Kuni-bush
397	Cape holly
398	Silky bark
399.3	White forest spike-thorn
401	Cape blackwood
408	Red candlewood
409	Candlewood
411.1	Climbing saffron
414	Bastard saffron
415	Common saffron
418	Spoonwood
420	Lemon thorn
422	White pear
452	Dogwood
457	Cape stock-rose
479	Cape plane
494	Wild peach
496	Red pear
498	Thorn pear
503	Wild mulberry
513	Hard pear
570	Assegai
578	Cape beech
579	White milkwood
603	Poison peach
611	Bladder-nut
618	Bastard ironwood
618.2	Ironwood
634	Forest nuxia
636	Bastard olive
637	Sagewood
641	Kamassi
670	Tree fuchsia
688	Wild pomegranate
693	Wild gardenia
708	Turkey berry
710	Rock alder
711	Quar
729	Waterwitels
733	Camphor bush

The unique bladder grasshopper. Its abdomen produces a loud call.

Ancient giant yellow-woods, near Knysna in the main forest.

In the shadows of the high forest, Polystictus sanguineus fungus.

A forest stream, sweet to the taste, near the otter trail of the Tsitsikama Coastal National Park. Here leopards and wild boars drink in the moonlight.

The pattern of colours and designs made by lichens growing on tree trunks in the dark depths of the high forest.

Fungi growing on a dead tree in the high forest. Moisture, warmth, shade and decomposing wood suit this plant.

111

THE CURIOUS KINGDOM OF THE OSTRICH

EVEN IN A PART of the world as full of contrasts as southern Africa, the area known as the Little Karoo is unique. This is the country of the ostriches. There are ostriches in many parts of Africa, but this is their idea of perfect heaven, a paradise for a feathered community of strange characters. Even a Gulliver used to the unusual would have considered the area completely novel and the habits of its ostrich population to be singular and remarkable, with their struttings, preenings and courtship displays.

This is a place abounding with wild flowers, leopards and strange, highly coloured rock formations, where every horizon is filled with mountains. Little rain falls, but the soil is irrigated by a network of sparkling streams flowing down from the highlands.

The San name for the Swartberg Mountains was Kango, meaning a place rich in water. This is a different world from the endless, hot expanse of the Great Karoo, the 'great thirstland', to the north. The plain of the Little Karoo is about 60 kilometres wide and stretches for 250 kilometres from east to west. It is sandwiched between the Swartberg to the north and the continuous range of the Langeberg and Outeniqua mountains to the south, which separates the Little Karoo from the coastal terrace.

The Swartberg massif is gashed by road and rail passes which are among the most spectacular in Africa. Here lies the strange valley of Die Hel, a deep, wild gorge, embraced by two great arms of rock, where leopards hunt baboons, antelope and, if they get the chance, sheep, goats and donkeys. It is a world of ravines, or kloofs, cut deep into the mountains by streams choked with vegetation and teeming with wildlife. Some of these kloofs are so deep that it can take days or even weeks to explore them thoroughly. Wild flowers lay a blanket of colour over the wilderness of the mountain heights. Even where mountain fires have raged, the blackened trail is quickly soothed by glorious masses of fire lilies and painted ladies.

In the foothills of the Swartberg range are intricate networks of caves, decorated with San art and fascinating dripstone formations. The climate is warm — a comfortable compromise between the rainy weather of the coast and the thirsty heat of the Great Karoo. For the ostriches, the blend of climate, vegetation and terrain is close to perfection. Even the pebbles scattered over the plain are of the size and shape they need to aid digestion. And the ostriches themselves are merely one of the many attractions that this unique region offers the tourist.

Camping and caravanning There are first-class parks with caravan, camping and bungalow facilities at Montagu, Barrydale, Ladismith, Oudtshoorn and the hot springs at Calitzdorp. There are also camping sites at the foot of the Huisrivier Pass, at Aristata in Sweweekspoort, and near the entrance to the Cango Caves.

Climbing and walking The sheer size of the Swartberg range makes it ideal for the adventurous. Gorges, secret valleys and sheer rock faces abound. The valley of Die Hel, also known as Gamkaskloof, is in this region. The highest peak, Seweeekspoort Mountain, and the heights of Toorkop provide demanding climbs. The Outeniqua and Langeberg mountains are cooler than the Swartberg.

Plants and flowers A marvellous variety of plants flourishes in the Little Karoo. In winter and spring, the mountains are ablaze with proteas, watsonias and other flowering plant species. The rare *Protea aristata* grows in Seweeekspoort.

Sightseeing The mountain passes of the Little Karoo are spectacular. Many of them lead through regions characterized by strange, brilliantly coloured rock formations.

On the plain of the ostrich country are show farms which are open to the public, offering conducted tours of the paddocks and incubator houses, and ostrich races and rides. Shops on the farms sell ostrich souvenirs, including feathers and boas and bags and shoes made from handsome ostrich leather. Ostrich biltong may be sampled, and ostrich eggs can be bought. One of these makes an excellent omelette for a dozen people. Around Oudtshoorn are several of the great mansions, or ostrich palaces, with their elaborate decorations and furnishings. The museum at Oudtshoorn has a section devoted to the history of the domesticated ostrich of the Little Karoo. The mission station at Zoar is an attractive spot, with black-thatched, white-walled houses, straggling streets and gardens full of fig trees.

Swimming The hot springs near Calitzdorp and at Warmwaterberg and Montagu all have swimming baths. It is a novel delight to take a dip in the warm waters on a crisp winter evening. There is a pool fed by a mountain stream at Aristata in Seweeekspoort.

A cottage in the mission station of Amalienstein.

Barrydale, with the Langeberg range in the distance.

Amalienstein

In 1833 the Berlin Missionary Society established the mission of Amalienstein next to that of Zoar, which had been founded in 1817 by the London Missionary Society. The gardens, irrigated by a stream flowing out of Seweeekspoort, produce apples, figs and pears.

Amalienstein is now managed by the Lutheran Church.

Barrydale

John Joseph Barry established a great commercial empire in the Swellendam district and parts of the Little Karoo midway through the last century. Whenever a new settlement grew, a shop built by Barry would often be among its first buildings. In 1882 his family created Barrydale. It is a small, tranquil village of neat, comfortable houses with large gardens.

Barrydale is renowned for its mesembryanthemums, apples, peaches, apricots and brandy. On the outskirts of the village is the Anna Roux Wild Flower Garden.

Calitzdorp

The sienna-red stone church of Calitzdorp, with its quaintly capped tower, can be seen for some kilometres along the road from Oudtshoorn. In crossing the plain of the Little Karoo the road passes many ostrich farms, where the birds can be seen wandering around, feeding on the lucerne fields, sitting on their eggs or watching the passing traffic, their chickens huddled together in compact little groups.

Calitzdorp is the terminus of the railway branch line from Oudtshoorn and the centre of an irrigated farming industry. The site was originally a farm owned by the Calitz family and called Buffelsvlei ('buffalo marsh').

Cango (Kango) Caves

These are one of the great wonders of the world. Within this cave system is a fabulous collection of speleothems — all manner of bizarre dripstone formations.

The caves were discovered by man in prehistoric times. The entrance was used as a home by San and the walls were painted by them with pictures of game animals. But without portable light, the San would have been unable to explore far into the caves. For centuries most of the secret treasures of the caves were known only to hoards of bats. The petrified skeletons of such bats, sheathed in transparent calcite, are to be found in the 'bats' graveyard' of the caves.

In 1780 a herdsman stumbled into the entrance to the caves while following a wounded buck. He told his master, Barend Appel, who was employed as a tutor and farm manager by a local landowner named Van Zyl, of the mysterious opening. Appel visited the caves and reported to Van Zyl. Soon Van Zyl led the first expedition deep into the caves. With their flickering torches, Van Zyl and his men found their way to the first great chamber — to be named Van Zyl's Hall — 98 metres long, 49 metres wide and 15 metres high. This remains one of the greatest treasure chests of nature. From every nook and cranny glimmer stalactites (hanging columns), stalagmites (which grow upwards) and helictites (which grow in all directions).

Van Zyl was lowered to the floor of this mammoth chamber and gazed in awe at what was to become known as Cleopatra's Needle, 9 metres high and at least 150 000 years old.

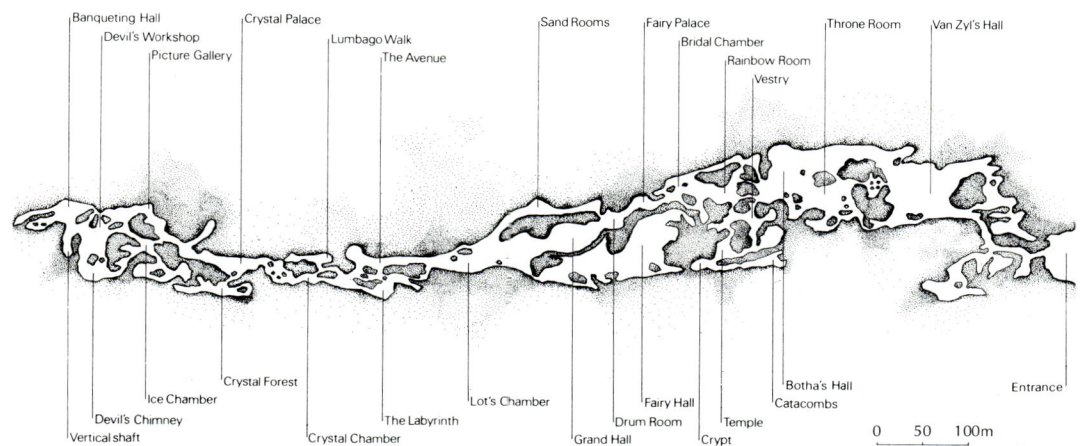

The areas of the Cango Caves open to the public. The areas beyond the Devil's Workshop are closed to visitors.

A glittering wonderland
of fantastic shapes

How much further Van Zyl continued is unknown. But over the years each of a vast sequence of chambers was given a fanciful name until, at 762 metres from the entrance, there seemed to be a dead end. Cave experts were certain that the sequence continued, for there was a draught of fresh air, but dripstone formations and rock falls had blocked the passage.

It was this first sequence of caves — Cango One — that was developed and opened for tourists. There are innumerable dripstone formations in the main chambers and antechambers. The largest of the chambers is Grand Hall, 107 metres across and 16 metres high. The highest dripstone formation, a 12,5-metre column, is in Botha's Hall.

The mystery of the unexpected dead end of Cango One was cleared up in modern times. In 1956 the Spelaeological Society surveyed the

The subterranean wonder world of the Cango Caves, decorated by nature with the bizarre sculptures of countless dripstone formations.

caves and noted that when the atmospheric pressure outside dropped, air flowed out of the caves. When pressure outside mounted, air flowed into the caves. This proved that there was a continuation of the cave sequence.

The Whale's Tooth formation.

Two of the professional cave guides, James Craig-Smith and Luther Terblanche, assisted by Dart Ruiters, devoted their spare time to further exploration. In the last chamber of the known sequence, the Devil's Work-shop, they followed a draught to a small crevice. For months they painstakingly expanded the crevice. At last, on 17 September 1972, they broke through into a breathtaking fairyland, a 270-metre extension of the sequence

Glass-blowers' fantasy in Cango Two.

The Bridal Couple in Cango Two.

The Coral Chamber in Cango Two.

Throne Room made of gold.

A formation like a hanging shawl.

All the delicacy of Venetian glass.

The weird Cango Candle.

An enchanted fairy fountain.

The entrance to Cango Two.

Jack Frost in the Wonder Cave.

'Attainment', a miracle of dripstone.

The exquisite Angel's Wing.

115

Paradise of a lost valley called Die Hel

never before seen by man.

This extension is Cango Two, or the Wonder Cave. Spelaeological Society experts were called in to investigate further. At the end of Cango Two they found a stream flowing back towards the entrance and disappearing into a course about 20 metres below the level of the cave. Two members of the society, Dave Land and Peter Breedt, went down the stream until they reached an obstruction.

In 1975 a pump was brought into the caves and the water level of the stream lowered enough to allow a party led by Floris Koper, on 2 August 1975, to continue through the stream and find their way into what is known as Cango Three, a sequence of chambers 1 600 metres long (twice the length of Cango One and Cango Two combined), and with one chamber more than 300 metres long. This is probably still not the end of the cave sequence and exploration continues.

Cango Two and Cango Three are not open to the public. The pure, crystalline beauty of the dripstone formations in these two sequences is thus preserved, for man carries destruction into such caves. Cigarette smoke deposits nicotine over the white lime, and litter invites bacterial invasions which can also dull the colours of the rocks. Stalactites and stalagmites have been snapped off by souvenir-hunters. Limited oxygen is replaced by carbon dioxide.

The whole cave sequence originated as a fault, up to 91 metres wide, in the limestone rock here. Nature sealed this fault with calcite. Water soaked in and slowly eroded the huge chambers. The water drained away. Rainwater dripping down through the roof picked up carbon dioxide from the plant roots and humus in the upper soil. Passing through calcite, the carbon-rich water came to contain calcium carbonate, which is soluble in a mixture of carbon dioxide and water.

Dripping through the ceiling of the caves, the water encountered air far less rich in carbon dioxide. In the balancing action of nature, carbon dioxide was then transferred from water to air. The calcium carbonate could not be transferred with the carbon dioxide. It was now unwanted, and so

The tunnel through the colourful rock strata of Cogmanskloof.

it solidified, a minute amount from each drop of water, and over hundreds of thousands of years this process has decorated the caves with dripstone formations of astonishing beauty and variety of shapes. Occasionally, stalactites and stalagmites joined, forming columns.

In this wonderful way nature worked in the dark for so many forgotten years, and then gave man the privilege of seeing a work which is still in the process of change and growth.

Cogmanskloof

The Koekemans Khoikhoi people, with their fat-tailed sheep, wandered through this pass between the Little Karoo and the Breë River Valley. Europeans developed their path into a trail and named it Cogman's, a corruption of the Khoikhoi name. In 1877 a road through the pass, built by the engineer Thomas Bain, was opened.

Bain must have enjoyed making the pass. Though only 6 kilometres long, it traverses glorious scenery and tunnels through a rocky ridge known as

Kalkoen Krans ('turkey cliff'). The ruins of a fort built by the British during the Anglo-Boer War stand on top of the pass.

In the shade of the trees in Keurkloof, half way through the pass, is a camping ground.

Gamkaskloof

Deep in the Swartberg, the mountains suddenly bulge into two great arms. These arms embrace a 20-kilometre gorge. Its only links with the outside world were along the precipitous course of the Gamka River, which flows at right angles directly across the valley, forcing a way in through the northern mountain wall and rushing out again through the southern range.

The valley is extremely fertile, with two tributary streams of the Gamka flowing down its length, from the east and west. Aloes grow in profusion and their flowers — orange and scarlet — turn the whole valley aflame in the winter months.

The old name for the valley was Die Hel, but more recently the name Gamkaskloof has come into fashion. It is beautiful in its solitude; its air and water are completely unpolluted.

For centuries Gamkaskloof was a refuge of the San and Khoikhoi peo-

An old Anglo-Boer War fort looks out over the Cogmanskloof Pass.

The Gamka River flowing through the Swartberg and entering the brooding and isolated valley of Die Hel.

The waterfall in Meiringspoort.

The town of Ladismith, overlooked by the towering Swartberg range.

ple until, about 175 years ago, nomadic European farmers discovered the valley when their cattle, smelling water and grazing, fled from their corrals and followed the Gamka River. The farmers tracked them down the next day, and in this lush paradise they eventually made their home. They had sufficient food, made their own clothes, and paid no taxes.

For more than a hundred years the valley was left to itself. Then the taxman, the churchman and the schoolmarm arrived.

In 1921 a school was built. In 1962 a tortuous road was built into the valley from the top of the Swartberg Pass.

The inhabitants were a self-reliant, hard-working and amiable people. They produced wheat, vegetables, figs and magnificent Muscadel grapes, used in the making of raisins. Goats and cattle were kept. These picturesque inhabitants of Die Hel have all been removed in recent times, and it is intended to convert the valley into a national park.

Huisrivier Pass

The Gamka River is crossed at the eastern end of the Huisrivier Pass, which climbs over a spur of the Swartberg in a series of curves. The Huisrivier Pass is scenically spectacular. The sandstone rock cliffs are coloured orange and red.

Ladismith

Lady Juana Smith, wife of Governor Sir Harry Smith, was one of the great beauties of southern Africa. Two towns were named after her, and to distinguish between them the one in Natal is spelled Ladysmith, while the one in the Little Karoo is Ladismith. Overlooking Ladismith is the Swartberg's 2 203-metre Toorkop ('bewitched peak'), said to have been cleft in two by a witch.

The district produces ostrich feathers, lucerne, fine cheeses and fruit.

The town has many Victorian houses, with wide stone steps and elaborate exterior wrought-iron work.

Meiringspoort

Of the three road passes through the Swartberg Mountains, Meiringspoort is the most used. It takes the trunk road through the mountains from the Karoo to the Little Karoo.

The 12,9-kilometre highway finds a complex way through the mountains by following the course of the Grootrivier, which penetrates the range through the spectacular cleft of Meiringspoort.

The pass is named after Petrus Meiring, a local farmer. It crosses the river 26 times. Sandstone precipices, eroded into odd shapes and richly coloured by iron oxides, tower on both sides of the road.

Flowering plants surround a 55-metre-high waterfall 3 kilometres from the road's northern end.

A memorial tablet has been placed on a rock face where the renowned Afrikaans writer, C. J. Langenhoven, carved the name Herrie, referring to an elephant that figures in his stories.

The ostrich-feather capital of the world

A Cape-Georgian house in Montagu.

Montagu

A town named after John Montagu, the colonial secretary, was founded in 1851 at the western end of the Little Karoo. Nearby is a 35,5 °C hot spring.

Montagu is a fruit and wine centre. Muscadel grapes and apricots are particularly favoured.

Among the town's attractive old buildings is the Montagu Museum, which exhibits antique furniture made from yellow-wood and stinkwood.

The oldest street in the town, Long Street, is considered by experts to be architecturally one of the most important in South Africa. At least 14 of the houses in the street have been declared National Monuments.

Montagu's nature garden is reputed to have southern Africa's finest displays of mesembryanthemums.

The nearby mountain valleys offer innumerable walks. Montagu is a convenient base from which to explore

The winding Montagu Pass, climbing over the Outeniqua Mountains near George to reach the Little Karoo.

A Cape-Dutch house in Montagu with an old-fashioned outside stairway.

Burgers Pass, winding through the farmlands of the Montagu district.

THE TEMPERAMENTAL BIRD WITH A FORTUNE ON ITS BACK

An ostrich hen peers inquisitively at the photographer and seems every bit as curious as he is

In the Little Karoo man found treasure as alluring as the diamonds of Kimberley and the gold of the Transvaal — ostrich feathers. The men who supplied these feathers, obligatory items of high fashion just before World War I, to the fine ladies of London, Paris and New York became the feather barons of the Little Karoo. They built the elaborate mansions, or ostrich palaces, which can be seen in the Oudtshoorn area today.

The ostrich is the world's biggest bird. It is unable to fly and, though it has many strange habits, burying its head in sand is not one of them. This myth probably arose from its practice, when threatened, of flopping to the ground and stretching its neck flat so that it merges into the landscape.

The ostriches of the Little Karoo are of the *Struthio camelus* variety. A well-built male will reach a height of about 2,4 metres and weigh up to 135 kilograms.

They possess a formidable kick, though for defence they rely chiefly on speed — over short distances they can reach up to 50 kilometres an hour. An ostrich lives for about 40 years. Although the birds are generally docile, the male is temperamental during the breeding season. When agitated it makes roaring noises rather like a lion, displays its feathers, dances and bows before the hens, and its skin turns bright pink.

Pairs of birds often remain together for life. Hens lay clutches of up to 20 eggs in hollows scooped out of the ground and the chicks hatch after about six weeks. Parents are protective, constantly on the alert for jackals, hyenas and wild cats.

The great feather boom began around 1870. At its height, there were more than 750 000 domesticated ostriches in the Little Karoo and feathers were being exported at the rate of around 450 000 kilograms a year. Breeding pairs could fetch what was for those days the princely sum of R2 000. The finest feathers came from the cocks, which were clipped every nine months. A good-sized bird would yield up to 9,9 kilograms of feathers and the top quality 'super plumes' fetched R420 a kilogram.

Then came World War I and things were never the same again for the feather barons. Austerity became fashionable as a mark of patriotic support of the war effort. Many farmers went bankrupt.

In later years the industry revived with a demand for ostrich leather, biltong, eggs and feathers. At present, there are about 90 000 birds in the Little Karoo. A central co-operative was created to promote the industry and an abattoir built capable of processing 40 000 birds a month.

Koo, in the apple- and apricot-growing area, and the western end of the Little Karoo. The town has two hotels and a caravan park.

Oudtshoorn

The principal centre of the Little Karoo and capital of the southern Cape, Oudtshoorn is also the ostrich-feather capital of the world. The town is named after Baron Pieter van Rheede van Oudtshoorn, who died in 1773 on his way to the Cape to become governor. It was founded in 1847 and became a municipality in 1887.

On a site 300 metres above sea level, the town spreads itself along both banks of the Grobbelaars River. It is sheltered by the Swartberg range to the north and the Outeniqua range to the south. The region is warm in summer, with little humidity, and has plenty of sunshine in winter.

Oudtshoorn's C. P. Nel Museum owes its origin to a local businessman who collected historical objects. In 1953 he bequeathed the museum to the town. It is housed in what was formerly the Boys' High School, a green-domed building of sandstone blocks. Its facade is regarded as southern Africa's finest example of stone-masonry. The museum's exhibits include firearms, a chain-drive car of 1898, and an ox-wagon made in 1837. The Ostrich Room has a series of exhibits depicting every aspect of the evolution and commercial use of ostriches. Part of the Museum is the town house at 146 High Street. It is the only ostrich feather palace open to the public. Furnished in Edwardian style, it was designed by Charles Bullock, who was also the architect of the main museum.

An albino ostrich hen with her mate and her chicks.

The ostrich derby; a bird and jockey race for the winning post.

C. J. Langenhoven, author and champion of the Afrikaans language.

A majestic pass slices through towering peaks

A second museum is housed in Arbeidsgenot, the home of Senator Cornelius Jacob Langenhoven (1873-1932), champion of the Afrikaans language, writer, and author of the national anthem of South Africa, *Die Stem van Suid-Afrika*. The museum contains many of his personal belongings, including carvings of Herrie the elephant, one of his literary creations so beloved by readers that many nt him gifts of figures of the elephant.

The sundial in the garden at Arbeidsgenot was designed by Langenhoven and installed in 1926.

Among Oudtshoorn's 'ostrich palaces' — elaborate homes built during the boom years of the ostrich industry — Pinehurst (no longer open to the public) is the most renowned.

The town has a municipal tourist camp and several hotels.

Outeniqua Pass

One of the major road passes of southern Africa, it carries the highway known as the Road of South Africa over the Outeniqua Mountains from George into the Little Karoo. Opened in 1951, the pass took ten years to build and is a fine example of road engineering. It is 16 kilometres long and climbs from George, at 210 metres above sea level, to 800 metres above sea level. The summit offers a fine panoramic view.

One particular view site, about 6 kilometres up the seaward slope, has a plaque identifying the historic passes in the range.

Robinson Pass

This modern pass is a reconstruction

The road to Rus en Vrede.

of one built in 1869 by Thomas Bain. It is named after the commissioner for roads, M. R. Robinson. From its 859-metre summit there are sweeping views. Along the roadsides, heath, proteas and other veld flowers add a profusion of beauty and colour to the scene. The pass is the most direct route from Mossel Bay over the Langeberg Mountains into the Little Karoo.

Rus en Vrede

The main road to Rus en Vrede ('rest and peace') from Oudtshoorn leads through the spectacular scenery of the Oude Muratie Valley, a wild kloof formed by the Le Roux River. There are camping grounds and picnic places along the way and impressive views of the Swartberg.

The old farm of Rus en Vrede is a

water catchment area for the region. Nearby is a 61-metre-high twin waterfall.

Seweweekspoort

Overlooked by the 2 326-metre Seweweekspoort Mountain, the highest in the Swartberg, this great pass ranks among the scenic wonders of the world. The pass is a classic example of

THE OSTRICH PALACES THAT STAND AS MONUMENTS TO THE FEATHER BOOM

A feather baron's palace on Greylands farm.

A mansion from the days of the ostrich boom.

The homestead of Welgeluk farm, built in 1910.

Pinehurst, built in 1911 for E. J. Edmeades.

Life was very good in the Little Karoo during the years of the feather boom. With fashion so fickle it is remarkable how long feathers remained in vogue. For more than 20 years, no woman of style would appear in public without a feather cape, fan or boa.

The money resulting from this

world-wide demand financed an affluent society in the Little Karoo, made up of successful farmers and dealers and their wives.

The houses they built reflect these habits. The architects designed them to please clients who had simple, rural backgrounds. Each ostrich palace seemed to have

more rooms than its predecessor, and was stuffed with sumptuous furnishings. When the feather boom collapsed, there was insufficient money to maintain the great houses. The palaces, though many have been restored, became cold, dark, neglected monuments to their owners' ostentation.

The Koos Raubenheimer Dam, with the Swartberg range reflected on its calm surface. The dam supplies Oudtshoorn with water.

a South African kloof ('cleft'), impressive in its sheer size.

The origin of the name of Seweweekspoort, also known as Seven Weeks Port, is uncertain. There are many stories, some romantic, such as the tale that brandy smugglers used the pass to evade revenue collectors who patrolled the highway from Cape Town to the Karoo. The long way round, through this pass, is said to have taken seven weeks by ox-wagon.

On the pass are the original toll-house and the ruins of an old water-mill. A camping ground here is called Aristata, after the rare species of protea.

This majestic pass also has a resident ghost. The spectre of a toll keeper is still said to be seen, swinging his lantern to stop passing traffic in the night. The cliffs are full of echoes . . . the calls of birds, the rush of the wind and the subdued chatter of the stream talking to itself as it flows to the sea. Even the noise of wagons rumbling through the place seems to be part of the sound.

Swartberg Pass
This magnificent pass is another work of Thomas Bain. It was built between 1881 and 1888 by convict labourers housed in stone buildings whose ruins still stand beside the road. The pass is 24 kilometres long and reaches a height of 1 436 metres above the level of its beginning in the Little Karoo. The road winds under overhanging rocks in steep, zigzag curves.

Proteas, watsonias and other indigenous wild flowers bloom on the mountain slopes, and in winter there is usually heavy snow, often closing the pass. On the summit a turn-off leads to Gamkaskloof.

Toorwaterpoort
The railway line from Cape Town to Port Elizabeth penetrates the Swartberg by means of the Toorwater ('bewitched water') gorge.

The rather curious name comes from a peculiar local phenomenon. Nearby is a hot spring, and at different times and places, marsh gas escapes. The gas sometimes ignites and ghostly-looking flames then flicker about like will-o'-the-wisps.

The springs are 45°C and are reputed to have medicinal qualities. The resort has a swimming bath.

Uniondale
This farming town had its beginning in 1865 when two townships, Lyon and Hopedale, were amalgamated and given the name of Uniondale. It was formerly a major ostrich-farming and wagon-building centre.

Warmwaterberg
The Warmwaterberg range takes its name from the 39,25°C mineral spring at its foot. The spa baths here attract many visitors.

Zoar
The mission of Zoar was established in 1817 by the South African Missionary Society. It is named after the place mentioned in the Bible, ' Like the Garden of the Lord, as thou comest into Zoar.' The mission is well-known for its irrigated gardens.

The mission church of Zoar, near the entrance to Seweweekspoort.

BOUNTIFUL WATERS OF THE BREË

OF THE THREE fruit and wine producing valleys of the western Cape, the Breë, meaning 'broad', is the largest. With the valleys of its tributaries, such as the Hex River, it is an intensely farmed area, warm to hot during summer, and well-watered by rains in winter.

The Breë River has its headwaters in a superb basin in the mountains. The principal centre here is fittingly named after Ceres, the goddess of agriculture. The mountains surrounding this basin, the Hex River, Witsenberg and Skurweberg, receive some of the heaviest snowfalls in the Cape and the winter scene is often a vast, white playground. The snow still lingers on the tops of the highest peaks when the floor of the basin is covered with the blossoms of thousands of fruit trees.

In this Ceres basin, the headwater streams of the Breë River gather and with their rushing flow, force a way through the mountains by means of the narrow, precipitous and beautiful Michell's Pass. This is an exciting area for mountaineers, trout fishermen and those who like to explore mountain rivers with their succession of pools, rapids and waterfalls. The Witels ('white alder') River is a classic for this type of adventure.

Between the Witsenberg and the Elandskloofberg, the Breë swings south-eastwards and flows through kilometres of vineyards and fruit orchards. Many tributaries join it. By the time it reaches Robertson, the river is substantial, but well harnessed to the needs of irrigation, and much used for recreation in places such as the Silverstrand resort, and Brandvleidam with its yacht club.

The Hex River in its own right ranks as a major feature on the continent of Africa. Only 40 kilometres long before it joins the Breë, it flows through a valley extraordinary in its concentrated agricultural wealth. From this valley, through two dramatic passes, the road and railway to the north penetrate the mountains. In autumn, the valley, with its blood-red barlinka grape vines, is a superb spectacle.

Ashton
The town of Ashton serves as the residential area for employees of the Langeberg Koöperasie, the largest producer in southern Africa of canned fruit, jams and vegetables. Their principal factory, the largest of its kind in the southern hemisphere, is on the southern slopes of the Langeberg range near the entrance to Cogmanskloof.

Ashton is also noted for its rose nurseries and horse breeding.

Ceres
Man has wisely exploited the generous gifts nature has bestowed on Ceres. The town lies on the western side of a fertile basin surrounded by mountains. The Dwars River bustles through the town, its course shaded by willow and oak trees. The river forms pools and rapids in which rainbow trout can be seen darting like glints of light from one hiding place to another. And all around are gardens full of flowers.

The basin is warm for most of the year and well supplied with water. Even in winter, when the mountains are well-covered in snow, the town has a fine, crisp, sunny climate with frosty winter mornings. Everything seems to grow well, even the occasional tropical specimen. During winter there is generally sufficient snow for skiing on the higher mountains. Ceres is known as 'the Switzerland of South Africa'.

The town was established in 1854 as a centre for the rich fruit-growing area of the Warmbokkeveld and was named after the Roman goddess of agriculture. It has a fine hotel, a nature reserve, and a municipal recreation area built around a swimming pool. Campers are accommodated in the shade of a pine plantation. There are also bungalows and picnic sites.

De Doorns
The principal centre of the Hex River Valley, De Doorns is spectacularly situated but sun-baked, without shade. The name means 'The Thorns' — many thorn bushes formerly grew here. In the old days the town was a railway base where a second 'pusher' locomotive was attached to trains to enable them to make the steep climb up the Hex River Mountain pass. Nowadays the electric units take the trains unaided. De Doorns is a busy loading point for table grapes being transported to Cape Town docks or the inland markets of southern Africa.

Goudini
The site of a 40°C thermal spring. The resort and spa of Goudini has been developed around the spring, which is near Goudiniweg railway station.

Hex River Pass
The difficulty of taking a railway through the barrier of folded coastal mountains of the western Cape, and up the escarpment of the central South African plateau, provided engineers with a problem. The engineer who first solved it, Wells Hood, given the technical limitations of construction in the early days, did a magnificent job.

From De Doorns, 477 m above sea-level, in the Hex River Valley, the railway climbed up the face of the escarp-

An apple orchard waiting for the spring.

The Breë River near its source in the Ceres basin.

The fertile floor of the Ceres basin, hemmed in by mountains and covered with orchards, vineyards and irrigation dams.

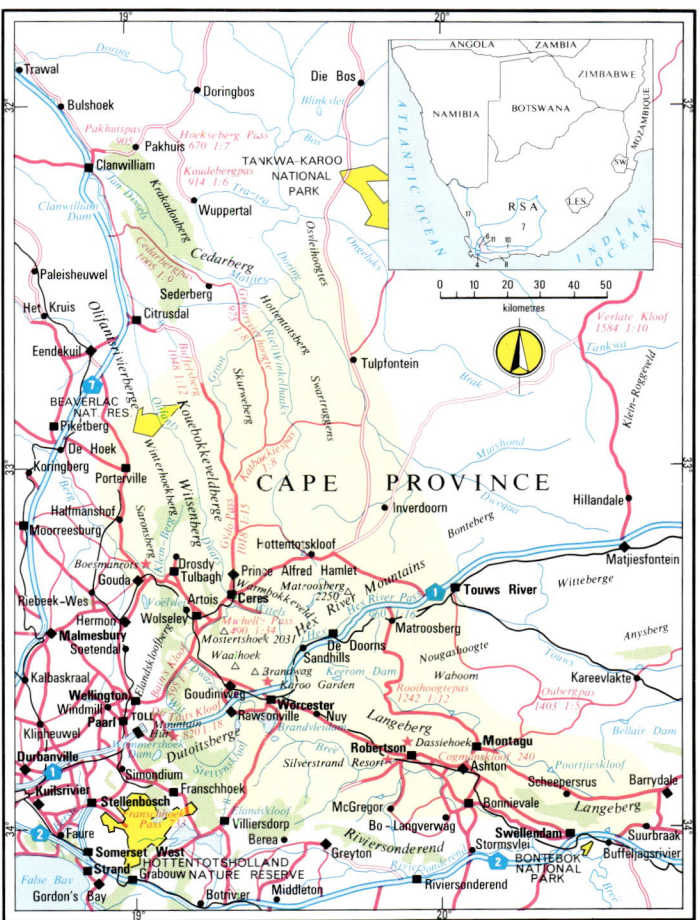

ment in sweeping curves which, if put together, would have taken a train through 16 complete circuits in 25 km before it reached the top of the pass 959 m above sea-level.

This pass gave spectacular views to passengers, but it was an economic problem. The ruling gradient was 1-in-40, uncompensated at curves. Only limited loads could be hauled up the pass, and at least two steam locomotives were required.

The first Hex River railway pass, however, carried traffic to the interior from its opening in 1876 until 27 November 1989 when a new pass came into use. This pass was located by W.H. Evans. It involved four tunnels, two of 0,8 km each, one of 2,4 km and one of 13,5 km. There was a saving of 8 km over the length of the old pass. A single line goes up the pass, but in the centre of the longest tunnel there is a crossing-point where trains can pass each other.

Hex River Valley

A folk story is often told of a beautiful girl named Eliza Meiring, who is said to have once lived on one of the farms, Buffelskraal, in the Hex River Valley. Much courted, she told local young men she would consider marriage only to a man who would bring her a disa of a kind which grew only on the most treacherous heights of the mountains. One of her suitors, so the

THINGS TO DO AND SEE

Angling The tributary streams of the Breë River include some of the finest trout waters in the Cape, among them the Dwars River, flowing through the town of Ceres and yielding excellent rainbow trout. The Witels is also fine for trout fishing. The Hex River is noted for rainbow trout, and smallmouth bass can be caught in the upper Breë River.

Camping and caravanning Ceres and Robertson have bungalows, camping and caravan areas. Worcester has a caravan park, and there are camping grounds in Michell's Pass.

Climbing and Hiking The Hex River Mountains are the highest in the western Cape. Their tallest peak is Matroosberg (2 250 metres). Climbing is rugged and there are many deep gorges in the range. One of the most famous is Jan du Toit's Kloof (not the road pass). This and the Witels provide strenuous hikes and climbs, with complex sections only to be crossed by swimming. Both require several days to explore. The Langeberg range is seldom explored by climbers. The Stettynskloof area, where Worcester gets its water supply, offers fine walking and many tough climbs.

Sightseeing The buildings of Tulbagh, restored after the damage of the 1969 earthquake, make a most attractive scene. The Hex River Valley is spectacular, especially in autumn and early winter. There is generally snow on the mountains, and the leaves of the barlinka grapes widely grown in the area turn bloodred just before they fall.

There are museums in Ceres, Tulbagh and Worcester, including an open-air farm museum in Worcester. The Robertson area is famous for its muscadel grapes and wines.

Skiing Southern Africa is not usually considered for a winter sports holiday, but many of the mountain ranges offer ski runs during the winter months. In the Hex River range, on the Matroosberg, the Cape Town Ski Club has a hut, while there are ski runs, huts and lifts on the Brandwagberg and the Waaihoek peak, where the University of Cape Town Ski Club has its snow fields.

Swimming The pools of the mountain streams offer superb swimming. The amber-coloured water is absolutely pure, with none of the hazards of tropical waters.

Summer glories of the valley of vines

story goes, was killed on the mountains and Eliza, guilt-stricken, had a nervous breakdown. She was locked in an upstairs room. One night she carved the date 1768 and her initials into the wooden window sill, then committed suicide. Whatever the truth of the story, the initials and date said to have been carved by Eliza Meiring could still be seen in the old homestead until they were removed by modern rebuilding.

From the story comes the legend about the hex ('witch') said to haunt the Hex River Mountains in search of her lover.

When the moonlight glistens on the high snows of winter, and the mists swirl around the summits, the people of the valley say that the witch is on the mountain that night, and many make sure that the doors of their houses are bolted.

The climate of the valley is ideal for grapes and it is here that more than 6 000 000 vines produce most of South Africa's export grape harvest. Grapes like plenty of moisture, but not on their leaves and bunches of fruit. They prefer a hot dry summer and rain in winter. They like decomposed sandstone and shales, deep and well-drained, irrigated by cool water from passing streams. Such conditions exist in the Hex River Valley.

Once covered in thorn bush, the home of lions and antelopes, the valley has been farmed since the early 18th century. From the mountains come the streams that form the river. Dams hold back the water and supply it for irrigation. Every possible part of the valley is planted with grapes, most of which are of the barlinka variety, which was imported from Algeria in 1909. It is a large, luscious, sweet, round, black grape, a generous bearer, and with a strong skin which allows it to survive handling, refrigeration and all the jolts of long-distance marketing. The barlinka never grew quite so well in Algeria as it did when introduced into the Hex River Valley.

The main railway to the north and the Great North Road of Africa run the length of the valley and then, in two passes at the north-eastern end, climb the escarpment of the central plateau and emerge onto the Karoo. The railway and road provide the 175

The Hex River Valley — snug homesteads and vineyards of barlinka grapes.

A grape picker at work amid the vineyards of the Breë River valley.

The Pines, one of the Cape Dutch homesteads of the Hex River Valley.

Heralds of autumn in the Hex River Valley — red-tinted barlinka vines.

grape-producing farms in the valley with a ready outlet to markets. The valley is a glorious spectacle in summer when the trellised vines are heavy with green leaves, and with the huge bunches of black grapes waiting for harvest in April and May. In June, before they fall, the leaves turn a deep red.

Michell's Pass
In any listing of the road and railway passes of southern Africa, Michell's Pass would rank high for scenic beauty. The infant Breë River was responsible for finding, if not creating, this pass. After its various headwater streams in the Ceres basin unite to form the river, its first task is to find an escape route from the mountains. Where the Witsenberg and the Hex River Mountains join there is a line of weakness in an otherwise implacable wall of rock.

The Breë River shoulders its way through this gorge. Migrating wild animals and man found their way along the banks of the river and in the 1760s a farmer, Jan Mostert, who lived at the south-western entrance, made a rough wagon track through the pass. His name was given to the 2 031-metre double peak near the entrance to the pass, the Mostertshoek Twins.

In 1846 Andrew Geddes Bain, with 240 convicts as labourers, started work on the first modern road through the pass. It was named after Charles Michell, surveyor-general of the Cape, and its opening in 1848 was a great boon to inland farmers. Until the building of the Hex River Pass in 1875, Michell's Pass carried the Great North Road of Africa through the mountains and thence on to the summit of the central plateau of South Africa.

The Witels tributary reaches the Breë in the midst of this pass and the adventurous climber and hiker find many challenges in the gorges and precipices of the surrounding mountains.

Prince Alfred Hamlet
The branch railway from Wolseley, through Michell's Pass to the Ceres basin, has its terminus at Prince Alfred Hamlet. This village is a centre for

The Sheilam Garden flourishes in Robertson's perfect cactus climate.

deciduous fruit and potato growing, with substantial packhouses and railway facilites. Pears, peaches and plums are sent from here to many parts of the world. A trip through the hamlet to the top of the Gydo Pass gives a memorable view of the Hex River Mountains.

Robertson

The Breë River at Robertson is banked by deep, rich alluvial soils. Fruit trees thrive here, watered by the river and basking in sunshine. Further away from the river, shales of the Karoo System provide the foothills of the mountains with excellent soils for vineyards. Muscadel grapes are common. The red muscadel and the Muscat d'Alexandre, or hanepoot, reach perfection here and superb dessert wines are produced. Communion wine for the Dutch Reformed Church originates from the area. White table wines, sherry and liqueurs are also produced. The largest brandy distillery in southern Africa is at Robertson.

Nature endowed Robertson with its own 'riviera' — a generous stretch of sandy beach alongside the river.

The old toll gate house at the entrance to the spectacular Michell's Pass.

A FEAST OF FISHING FOR THE ANGLERS OF THE WESTERN CAPE

The rivers of the western Cape contain a considerable population of indigenous fish, mainly members of the *cyprinid* family, of which the witvis *(Barbus andrewi)*, reaching 3,5 kilograms, is perhaps the best eating.

A somewhat smaller but very pretty member of the same family is the redfin minnow *(Barbus burchelli)*.

The Olifants River is particularly rich in indigenous fish. Largest is the Clanwilliam yellowfish *(Barbus capensis)* which can reach a mass of over 9 kilograms. Mudfish *(Labeo seeberi)* are also present.

Largemouth bass were introduced to the Olifants River in 1933 and specimens of 1-2 kilograms are common, but smallmouth bass, introduced from America in 1938, have tended to replace them. All bass are excellent sporting fish and are now very common in most of the river systems of the western Cape.

Trout are looked upon as the princes of fresh-water fish, with a delicious flavour. They display great fighting courage when caught. Trout are not indigenous to any of the waters of southern Africa; the first were brought to the Cape in 1875.

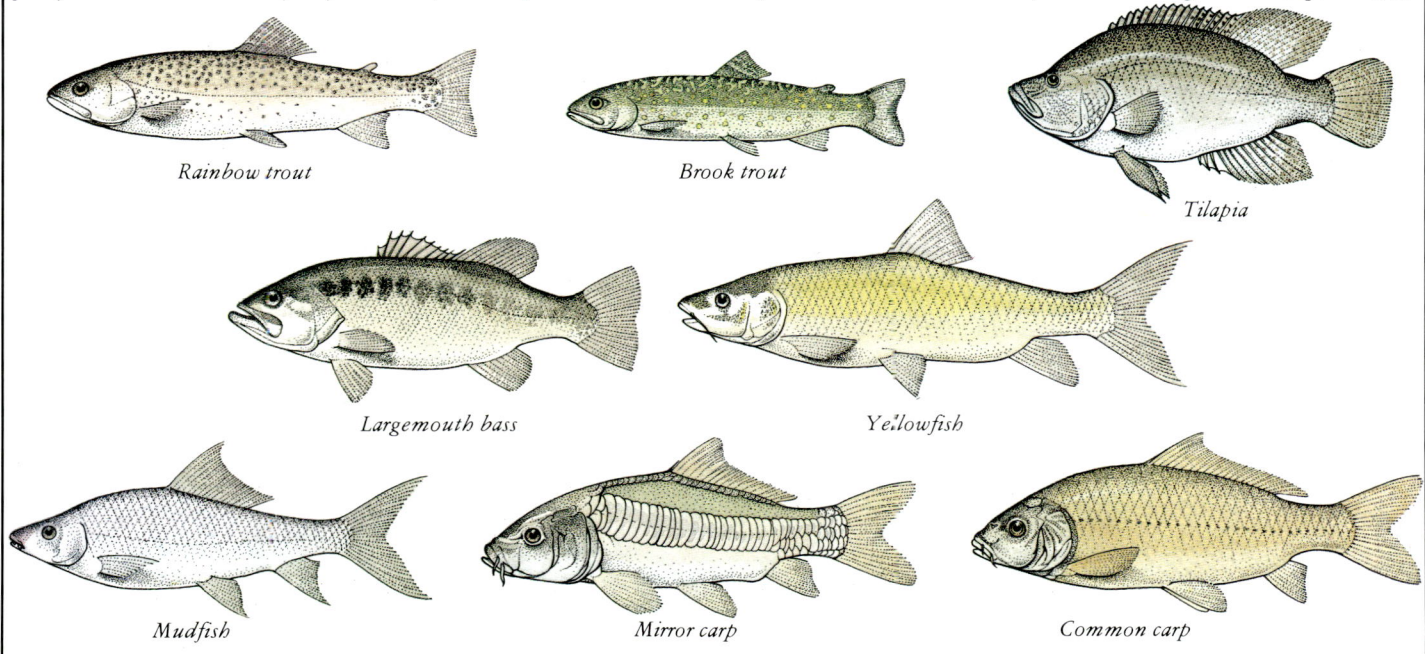

Rainbow trout

Brook trout

Tilapia

Largemouth bass

Yellowfish

Mudfish

Mirror carp

Common carp

Lovely town reborn on the ruins of an earthquake

High on the slopes overlooking Stettynskloof — a breathtaking view of precipices rising on both sides of a narrow valley.

This area has been developed for the holiday maker and offers rondavels, a caravan park and a camping site.

The town is popular as a base for climbs into the Langeberg range, to Dassieshoek and De Hoek. It is warm in summer, its streets shaded by flowering jacaranda trees.

The Sheilam Cactus Garden is 8 kilometres from the town. Here the visitor can see one of the world's finest collections of cactus species. Although the plants have originated in north and central America, they thrive in the climate and soil conditions of the Robertson district.

Tulbagh

Southern Africa is fortunate in that it is geologically relatively stable. Volcanic eruptions do not occur, and earthquakes have seldom been serious. Tulbagh, however, lies directly on top of a dislocation of the subterranean rock systems. This fault occasionally moves, and tremors are felt in the Tulbagh area. On 29 September 1969 the tremors amounted to an earthquake in which nine people were killed and a large part of the town destroyed. A second earthquake shook the town on 14 April 1970.

Many of the town's loveliest buildings have since been restored. The 32 rebuilt dwellings in Kerk Street form the largest concentration of national monuments in the country.

Tulbagh was first settled in 1699, and was then known as the Land of Waveren, in honour of a family in Holland with whom Governor W. A. van der Stel was connected. The origins of the present town are to be found in the village of Roodezand, which grew up around the Old Church, built in 1743 and damaged in the 1969 earthquake. Modern Tulbagh started to emerge in 1795, and was named in 1804 after the Dutch governor, Ryk Tulbagh.

A museum is housed in the old Dutch Reformed Church. It has antique furniture, eight prints of Cape Town by the 19th century artist, Thomas Bowler, and six paintings of Victoria Falls by Thomas Baines. The Old Drostdy is also open to the public.

Tulbagh is overlooked by the Witsenberg, Winterhoekberg and Saronsberg ranges. Mountain streams provide ample water, the soil is good decomposed sandstone, and the climate excellent for fruit. Table grapes and a considerable amount of wine, mainly white table varieties and sherries, are produced. At least one company offers daily tours of its cellars.

Tulbagh Pass

The Klein-Berg River, principal tributary of the Berg River, has its source in the Tulbagh basin. It tumbles through the Tulbagh (or Nuwe Kloof) Pass to reach the Berg River Valley. Through this pass the main railway line to the north makes its way. On the western side of the pass is a detached rock known as Bushman's Rock (Boesmanrok), believed to have been used by the San as a look-out for game.

Witsenberg

The north-eastern wall of the Breë River Valley and the Tulbagh basin is the Witsenberg (sometimes spelt Witzenberg), named after Nicolas Witsen, a director of the Dutch East India Company. The slopes are covered in vineyards.

Wolseley

Sir Garnet Wolseley was a British general of considerable dash and character. He inspired the expression 'It's all Sir Garnet', meaning that everything is in meticulous order. The little town named in his honour at the south-western entrance to Michell's Pass is a sun-baked place, a centre for fruit canning and packing. Fruit farmlands surround the town and dessert grapes

A street lined with Cape-Dutch houses in the delightful town of Tulbagh.

Tulbagh's mountain backdrop.

A Tulbagh church, now a museum.

The Breë River near Worcester. Many of the fertile farmlands in this part of the valley are irrigated by water from the Breë River.

Waaihoek — one of the rugged peaks overlooking Worcester.

are a tasty speciality of the district.

West of the town are two block-houses, built by the British during the Anglo-Boer War.

Worcester

The largest town in the Breë River Valley is Worcester, founded in 1818 and named after the Marquis of Worcester, brother of the governor, Lord Charles Somerset. The town lies at the entrance to the Hex River Valley.

Worcester is a busy commercial, communications and industrial area. Grapes are grown in vast quantities. There are seventeen co-operative wine cellars in the district and several brandy distilleries.

Worcester has a spacious central square dominated by the tall tower of the Dutch Reformed Church. An Afrikaner museum is housed in an attractive cottage. The World War I Garden of Remembrance was designed by the landscape artist, Hugo

Naudé, who made his home in the town. His house has been converted into the Hugo Naudé Art Centre. The War Memorial stands in the Garden of Remembrance together with a stone cairn commemorating the symbolic Ossewa Trek of 1938, which honoured the pioneers of the Great Trek of 1838. Other cairns record the 150th anniversary of the Huguenots' arrival and Worcester's centenary.

On the outskirts of Worcester lies the Karoo Garden, which covers 115 hectares of the foothills of the Brand-wag mountains. This garden, opened in 1948, is devoted to the succulent plants of the Karoo, many of which bloom profusely in spring.

There are hotels and a caravan park in the town. A sports stadium has been built at Boland Park. The bowling greens are floodlit and there is an 18-hole golf course. Mountain streams and rivers in the vicinity are well stocked with trout and black bass.

The last stronghold of 'the puffing Billy'

Southern Africa was for long one of the last strongholds of steam locomotives and there are many who regret the passing of these spectacular engines.

There are a few steam locomotives still in use on branch lines and shunting duties, but all the main lines are now either electrified or operated by diesel units.

One of the last stretches where steam locos did main-line work was between De Aar and Kimberley. There were some demands for the section to be left for steam, but this line too is now operated by diesel units. Even the narrow-gauge lines are now having their steam locomotives replaced by diesel, although there is some prospect that at least one of these lines will be left for steam. The 'name' trains of South Africa work between the country's major centres.

They travel the main line from Cape Town over the Hex River Mountain pass, and across the Karoo to Johannesburg, Pretoria and Durban.

The most celebrated of these luxury expresses is the Blue Train, the pride of the South African Railways and in 1969 ranked among the most famous trains in the world. Since then it has been further improved, and today it is one of the most luxurious trains in the world.

The Blue Train originates from the 1920s, when two express trains were introduced: the Union Limited, which ran from Johannesburg to Cape Town, and the Union Express, which made the return journey. Ordinary coaches were used initially, but in 1927 special articulated saloons were imported from Britain, each saloon consisting of two coach bodies with bogies at the outer ends and a bogie in the middle, joining both coaches. In 1939, twelve all-steel air-conditioned coaches arrived from Britain. Despite the outbreak of war, these were followed later by lounge, dining and kitchen cars until there were two complete train sets painted blue.

It was not a suitable time to introduce luxury trains, however, and after a few runs the two sets of coaches were stored for the duration of the war. When the dust covers were removed in 1946, the minister of transport at that time, Frederick C. Sturrock, officially named the coaches the Blue Train, and they commenced a service which soon became very popular.

In 1972 the Blue Train became even more luxurious. Two new sets of saloons, dining cars and vans were built in South Africa at a cost of over R5 000 000. One of the coaches in each train set contains a complete three-roomed suite — lounge, bedroom, and bathroom with toilet. The trains are air-conditioned. There is a valet service, electrically operated venetian blinds over the windows, four channels of music, and hot, cold and iced water in each compartment.

The lounge and dining car are superbly appointed, the food is genuine cordon bleu, and the cellar excellent.

The Blue Train consists of 16 coaches with accommodation for 107 passengers. It travels from Cape Town to Pretoria, a distance of 1 608 kilometres. Electric locomotives haul the train most of the way, with diesel units taking over between Beaufort West and Kimberley. The journey takes 26 hours. The most spectacular section, through the Cape mountains and over the Hex River Pass, is traversed during daylight by both the up and down trains.

When the Blue Train's new luxury coaches were introduced, the original sets were painted green and, as the Drakensberg Express, put on a new route from Johannesburg to Durban.

Another of the 'name' trains is the Orange Express, or Trans-Oranje, which runs for 2 091 kilometres from Cape Town to Durban, taking 37 hours to complete the journey. The train originates from the British royal family's tour of South Africa in 1947. A special set of luxury coaches was used as a pilot train for the royal train. In the pilot train travelled the press cor-

Steam on the veld. Two 15ARs hauling freight between Stormberg and Rosmead.

A British-built 15F — once a standard main line locomotive, but now largely replaced by electrification.

The class 12AR was widely used on freight and light passenger trains. Diesel and electric locos have now made these nostalgic steamers redundant.

A 15AR hauling a passenger train from Port Elizabeth to Uitenhage.

North-bound freighter between Cape Town and Bitterfontein. The loco is 19C.

A South African Railways' luxury train on the Johannesburg-Durban route.

A BRIDGE BETWEEN TWO WORLDS

THE COAST OF the eastern Cape Province, from Storms River to Algoa Bay, is a botanical and scenic meeting ground of several distinct formations. The winter rainfall area of the western Cape merges with the area of summer rainfall. The zone of transition receives some rain throughout the year but this is inclined to be erratic. The vegetation is equally capricious. In the south of this region, there is an overlap of the characteristic plant life of the western Cape. This is gradually phased out with erratic and contrary patches, and is replaced by the most southerly stretch of the great botanical division of savanna, which dominates so much of the eastern side of the continent of Africa, extending as far as the frontiers of Ethiopia.

With the Garden Route behind him, the traveller along the trunk road crosses the Storms River and enters a landscape covered in familiar western Cape plants such as watsonias and many species of erica. Awareness of approaching change comes as the mountains, which have been so inseparable a companion to the coast all the way up from Cape Town, disappear. The weather becomes warmer, and at the crossing of the Gamtoos River the traveller first sees a dense, stunted type of bush ahead, consisting principally of acacia species of thorn trees with, among them, a rich growth of aloes, spectacularly flowering in many colours, and gorgeous and exotic-looking plants such as crane flowers, the area's true floral emblem.

With this first stretch of savanna, wild life also changes, and the scene becomes more familiarly 'African' rather than that of the Mediterranean-like world of the western Cape. The diverse scenes, odours, and experiences are stimulating. There is the excitement of something new to enjoy with every kilometre travelled.

Addo Elephant National Park

The Addo elephant, of which just over 130 remain, has its home in the Addo Elephant National Park. Although it belongs to the same species as the African elephant (*Loxodonta africana africana*), the reddish Addo elephant is smaller, with more rounded ears, and the females generally have no tusks.

The park covers 8 600 hectares of the dense Addo bush. Europeans named it Addo after the Khoikhoi name Kadouw, meaning a river passage, which they gave to a fording place over the nearby Sundays River.

The bush is a tangle of acacia, spekboom, ghwarrie, boerboom, and numerous other trees and shrubs. Beard-like strands of moss and lichen hang from the branches and give the bush an atmosphere of enchantment.

Elephants always liked this bush. Spekboom is one of their favourite foods (its English name is 'Elephant's food') and the thorny bush discouraged hunters. Buffaloes, hippos and black rhinos also roamed here. But when settlers arrived during the 1820s the area was too small for man and beast to co-exist peacefully. The elephants raided farmlands; man hunted the elephants.

In 1919 the professional hunter, Major Jan Pretorius, was hired by the administrator of Cape Province, Sir Frederic de Waal, to destroy the entire elephant herd. It took him a year to kill 120, then he abandoned the slaughter because of public outcry. Only 16 Addo elephants remained,

many of them peppered with bullets, panic-stricken, vengeful and cunning. They declared war on man. Any person venturing into the Addo bush did so at his peril.

In 1931 the National Park was proclaimed, and a fence of tram rails and lift cables was erected in 1952. This created an elephant-proof barricade and prevented elephants from marauding into the orange groves of the Sundays River Valley.

In return for the farmers' immunity from damage, the Citrus Corporation delivered huge piles of waste oranges to the park. The oranges did much to tame the once irascible elephants. The fruit was dumped near observation areas so that the elephants could be viewed. This practice has now been stopped.

The herd has now increased to over a hundred and thirty, and the elephants are clearly visible to visitors without special feeding.

Watering places have also been created at view areas and attract buffalo, black rhino and other game, as well as elephants. The black rhino were re-introduced in 1961 — the first in the Cape for a hundred years.

The bush in the antelope park has been cleared and eland, red hartebeest, grysbok, kudu, and bushbuck — all native to the eastern Cape — roam freely.

THINGS TO DO AND SEE

Angling Yellowtail are abundant at Cape St. Francis in late summer and autumn. Although not as numerous as in False Bay, many are far larger, weighing around 22 kilograms. Kob, leervis and rock-feeders are numerous in late autumn. Winter is the season for elf. Galjoen, hottentot and dassies frequent the coastal water throughout winter and spring. The mouth of the Gamtoos River, with grunter, silvi and kob, offers good estuary fishing.

Fish life here is distinctly different from that of the southern Cape area as water temperatures throughout the year are a few degrees warmer. Katonkel or barracuda appear. Algoa Bay, while not as abundant with fish as St. Francis Bay, still offers good sport.

Camping and caravanning There are excellent caravan and camping grounds all along this coast, and a good range of hotels, boarding houses, bungalows and other accommodation. Port Elizabeth has a beautifully situated caravan park, while along the coast of Algoa Bay there are resorts such as those at the mouth of Van Stadens River and The Willows, where caravans and campers stand on the beach front.

Sea-shells The shores of St. Francis Bay, especially the resort of Jeffreys Bay, are famous for their shells. There are many treasures for the keen shell-hunter to discover.

Sightseeing Fort Frederick in Port Elizabeth attracts many visitors. The Port Elizabeth museum has a fine marine hall, and the historical hall exhibits include a kakebeenwa, a wagon of the pioneer and Great Trek period. There is also a botanical hall containing tropical plants.

An international community of surfers enjoy riding the waves at St. Francis Bay and Jeffreys Bay.

Baviaanskloof is scenically overwhelming, but it is for experienced drivers only. Port Elizabeth has a renowned oceanarium, museum and snake park. A walk up Happy Valley, with its lights, models, flowers and ornamental ponds, is very pleasant.

The Van Stadens Gorge Wild Flower Reserve and Bird Sanctuary has many indigenous plants. The Addo Elephant National Park has a variety of flora and fauna. Take a ride on the Apple Express — during the holiday season there are special sightseeing excursions along this line. The Seaview Game Park is also well worth a visit.

Swimming The beaches of St. Francis Bay and Algoa Bay are safe and spacious. The summer water temperature is around 25°C. In winter the temperature drops to about 21°C.

A peaceful family gathering at a water-hole deep in the Addo bush.

Twisting road through Baviaanskloof.

Algoa Bay

The Portuguese named this bay Bahia de Lagoa ('bay of the lagoon') because of the small lagoon at the mouth of the Swartkops River, which enters the sea here. The Portuguese name became corrupted to Algoa Bay. The western arm of the bay is Cape Receife ('cape of the reef') and the eastern arm is Cape Padrone ('cape of the pedestal').

In the bay are bird-covered rocky islets. The bay has fine beaches but offers little protection from the weather and was considered a death trap by the masters of sailing ships. In one storm in 1902 nineteen ships were wrecked within a few hours.

The harbour of Port Elizabeth has been created on the shores of the bay by the building of breakwaters and the dredging-out of deep-water berths.

Baviaanskloof

The actual Baviaanskloof ('cleft of the baboons') is a 150-kilometre long ravine through which runs a remarkable scenic road. From Patensie the road climbs a succession of three mountain passes, penetrates a mass of mountains, forested hills and deep valleys, and emerges onto the Karoo. This is an unforgettable drive. It requires a full day to complete the journey.

There is no accommodation along the route, and there are no garages.

A rendezvous of elephants. This congregation is assembled at the watering point in front of the main Addo camp.

Each tide brings a fresh harvest of beautiful shells

Petrol is available only at the occasional small farming centre, such as Studtis or Coleskeplaas.

Hankey
The London Missionary Society founded a mission station in the valley of the Gamtoos River in 1822. The station was named after William Hankey, treasurer of the society. The intention of the society was to settle Khoikhoi converts on irrigable land. The project was not a success. The land was sold and today the village is the administrative centre for an area producing citrus fruits, tobacco and vegetables.

Humansdorp
The principal commercial centre for the Cape St. Francis area is the town of Humansdorp. It is also one of the major stations on the narrow-gauge Apple Express railway from Port Elizabeth to the Langkloof and a popular stop-over for travellers along the Garden Route.

Humansdorp was named after Matthys Human, on whose farm the town was founded in 1849. The town has a park laid out in the form of a Union Jack, with a fountain in the centre. It also has a caravan park with bungalows.

Jeffreys Bay
Surfers have made Jeffreys Bay internationally famous. Within easy walking distance of the town are many renowned surfing beaches.

Long before surfers discovered the area, shell-collectors had found it to be one of the most prolific sources of sea-shells on the coast of Africa. Found here are shells of the temperate southern Cape and tropical Indo-Pacific species. Commercial collectors have removed the original thick carpets of shells, but each high tide brings fresh specimens. Collectors search the sand as the tide recedes. Curios made from the shells are sold in the town. A museum displays rare and exquisite specimens.

The beach offers safe swimming.

The bay is named after J. A. Jeffrey, who had a trading station on the shores here during the first half of the last century. The resort that has grown up is an attractive assort-

The pyramid and lighthouse in the Donkin Reserve. The pyramid commemorates Lady Elizabeth Donkin, after whom Port Elizabeth is named.

ment of residences, hotels, caravan parks and bungalows.

Paradise Beach
The resort of Paradise Beach is on the western side of the lagoon formed at the mouth of the Seekoei and Swart rivers. The lagoon is a bird sanctuary. Flamingoes, swans and some 55 other species can be seen here. The swans are said to be descendants of two birds being transported on a ship which was wrecked on Cape St. Francis in 1929. Before abandoning the ship, one of the crew released the swans. They flew to the lagoon and settled. Today there are about 400 swans in the area.

Patensie
The name Patensie, said to be from a Khoikhoi word meaning a resting place for cattle, has been given to a village that serves as the trading centre for the farms of the broad valley of the Gamtoos River. Citrus fruit, tobacco and vegetables grow here.

A branch of the Apple Express, the narrow-gauge railway from Port Elizabeth, ends at Patensie.

Port Elizabeth
The third largest port and the fifth largest city in southern Africa, Port Elizabeth was founded in 1799 when Fort Frederick was built by the British on a site overlooking Algoa Bay. The garrison made up the first population

'Who is watching whom?' is the question at the Port Elizabeth Oceanarium.

of the future city. The fort, named after Frederick, Duke of York, has been proclaimed a historical monument.

It was under the protection of the fort that the 1820 Settlers from Britain were landed, and it was in that year that Sir Rufane Donkin, acting governor of the Cape, named the settlement Port Elizabeth after his wife, who had died of fever in India two years previously. On what is known as the Donkin Reserve, the acting governor erected a stone pyramid in memory of his wife. The pyramid is a national monument. The lighthouse beside the pyramid was built in 1861.

The ocean front is bordered by a miniature railway, children's playgrounds and the Happy Valley park, reached by walking from the beach up the valley of a stream. The fairyland figures, trees and flowering plants here are illuminated at night. Near Humewood Beach there is the renowned snake park, where more than 1 000 snakes are exhibited. Lectures are given at intervals daily. Next to the snake park is the museum, the oceanarium, and a tropical house where visitors can wander through a tropical jungle. The museum has exhibits of natural history, early vehicles and shipwrecks. The oceanarium's performing dolphins, caught in Algoa Bay, are a favourite of the crowds.

The city hall was seriously damaged by fire in 1977, resulting in an involved restoration programme. The old Mayor's Garden in front of it was rebuilt as an ornamental area. In front of the city hall stands a replica of the

Port Elizabeth's busy harbour complex. In the background is the city's industrial area.

This row of houses is characteristic of Port Elizabeth's Victorian architecture.

The elegant old building housing the public library in the centre of Port Elizabeth.

A 23-bell carillon rings out across the old city

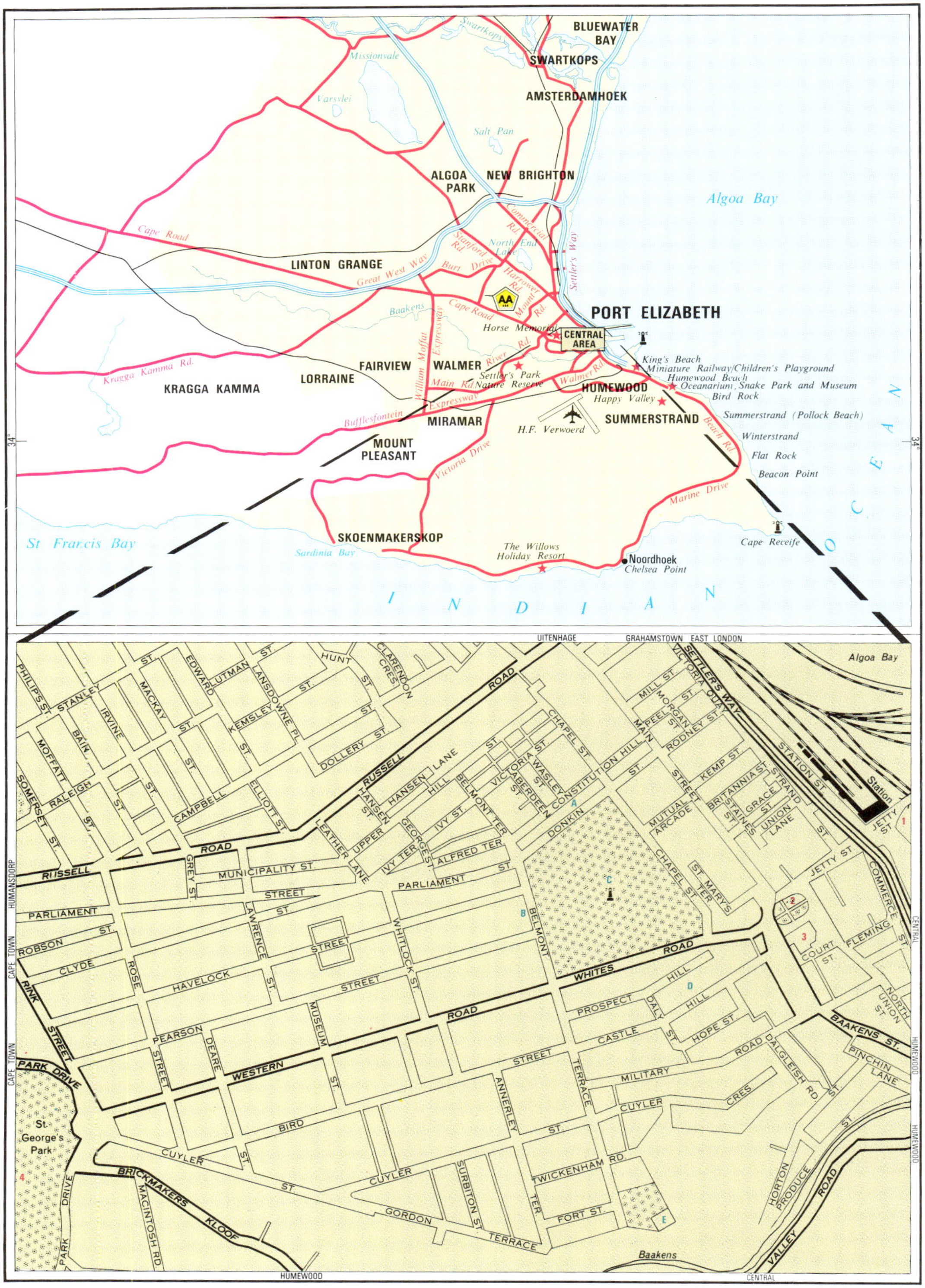

PORT ELIZABETH

National Monuments
A Donkin Street Houses
B Old Grey Institute
C Donkin Memorial and Reserve
D Rectory, Castle Hill
E Fort Frederick

Places of interest
1 Campanile
2 Market Square and Dias Cross
3 City Hall
4 King George VI Art Gallery

City and surroundings map scale

0 1 2 3 4 5   kilometres

City central area map scale

0   100   200   300   metres

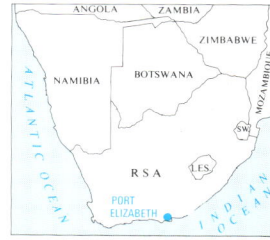

The Memorial Campanile, now partly hidden by highways.

Typical houses of the last century.

Port Elizabeth's old Rectory.

dunes that the region resembles the Namib Desert.

The Seaview Game Park is open every day of the week except Monday, and on Monday too during school holidays. Here one can see cheetah, lion, zebra, rhino, giraffe, ostrich, and a variety of buck. A walkway on stilts takes visitors from the hilltop restaurant over the cheetah camp. There are picnic and camping facilities.

St. Francis Bay
The Portuguse navigator, Manuel Perestrello, named St. Francis Bay in 1575 in honour of the patron saint of sailors. From Cape St. Francis in the

Dias Cross erected at Kwaaihoek in 1488 where Bartholomew Dias and his men first landed.

The city's famed Horse Memorial, dedicated to horses that perished in the Anglo-Boer War of 1899 – 1902, is in Cape Road, near Rink Street.

The oldest private dwelling in Port Elizabeth is The Rectory, 7 Castle Hill. Built in 1827 for the Reverend Francis McCleland, it is now a museum containing antique furniture and household appliances.

Other attractions of the city are the King George VI Art Gallery and the Settlers' Park Nature Reserve. The reserve, on the banks of the Baakens River, preserves a piece of the landscape and some of the wild life as it was at the time the city was founded.

The 52-metre high Memorial Campanile, built in 1923 in memory of the 1820 Settlers, stands on the site where the settlers landed — in Jetty Street at the exit from the docks. It has a flight of 204 steps leading to a view platform at the top. The campanile contains a carillon of 23 bells which ring changes three times a day.

Humewood and King's beaches offer safe swimming. The Swartkops River has a spacious yachting area. Along the coast on both sides of Port Elizabeth are resorts such as The Willows, Swartkops, Skoenmakerskop, Sardinia Bay, Sea View, and Maitland River Mouth. These resorts have fine beaches.

The Sundays River reaches the coast of Algoa Bay in a setting of such vast

In the service of man . . . a famous Port Elizabeth memorial that pays tribute to the horses that died in the Anglo-Boer War.

A JOURNEY TO ADVENTURE ABOARD THE APPLE EXPRESS

The harbour at Port Elizabeth is the terminus of a fascinating little train called the Apple Express. It runs on a narrow-gauge line that begins 285 kilometres away at Avontuur ('adventure').

The trains are mainly used to transport fruit from the Long Kloof orchards, but on Saturdays from 1 June to 31 January special sightseeing trains run as far as Loerie, offering day-long return excursions along some of the most spectacular parts of the line.

The train leaves Port Elizabeth hauled by a chunky little steam locomotive with shining brasswork and shrill whistle, bustles past the Walmer residential area and through thick bush on the plain between the mountains and the sea.

After crossing a high bridge over Van Stadens Gorge, the line leads westward into rugged country covered with bush and noted for its flowering aloes. The massive Elandsberge and Groot Winterhoek mountains dominate the landscape. There is a steep pass into the valley of the Gamtoos before the train reaches Loerie.

From Loerie, the Apple Express

The Apple Express in Long Kloof.

reaches a small junction where one branch swings north to Patensie and the other continues west, crosses the Gamtoos River and, after a stop for water at Humansdorp, reaches the mouth of the Long Kloof.

In spring and summer the kloof is ablaze with wild flowers and is covered with kilometre after kilometre of orchards. The smell of blossom, or the fragrance of ripe fruit during the picking season, fills the air. Mountains and hillocks crowd close on the north and south sides of the valley.

The Apple Express then chugs on to its final destination, to be loaded up with the harvest of the Long Kloof before turning back for Port Elizabeth.

Great orchards that fill the night air with their fragrance

west to Cape Receife in the east, the bay is 100 kilometres across with sandy beaches curving smoothly between the capes. The Gamtoos River reaches the sea in the centre of the bay.

Several resorts have been created along the shores of the bay, including Jeffreys Bay, Paradise Beach and Aston Bay. A resort at the mouth of the Krom River, formerly called Sea Vista, has a marina and elegant black-thatched holiday homes.

The 3-kilometre beach is popular with swimmers, surfers and collectors of exotic sea-shells.

Wild flowers and birds flourish in the area.

Sundays River Valley

The name 'Sundays' is believed to be a corruption of that of the Zondagh family, who were among the early settlers here. The Sundays River rises in the Sneeuberg Range, flows through Graaff-Reinet and Jansenville, then breaks through the Suurberg Range to Lake Mentz. In its middle reaches the river flows through

---

THE BIG, THE BAD AND THE BEAUTIFUL IN THE DEADLY WORLD OF SOUTHERN AFRICA'S SNAKES

Despite their sinister reputation, few snakes are really aggressive. The big constrictors — pythons, boa-constrictors and others — may eat medium-sized mammals, including the occasional human being, but most snakes have nothing to gain from a confrontation with man.

Of the world population of about 3 000 species of snake, some 300 live in Africa. About 75 per cent of these are non-venomous. The remainder give the entire snake population its repellent reputation.

The best known of the poisonous snakes of southern Africa is the black mamba Growing to a length of three to four metres, it is widespread in warm areas. It is a fast-moving snake with rigid fangs. The venom is a powerful nerve poison and is fatal unless action is taken quickly by the injection of anti-snake-bite serum or other medical emergency measures.

The tubular fangs of the mamba are surprisingly small. A victim may escape the full dose of venom if the snake bites through clothing.

The green mamba is shorter than the black, usually about two metres fully grown. It lives in the tree tops and feeds on birds and small reptiles. It is a shy snake, and less poisonous than the black mamba.

There are about ten species of cobra in South Africa. They include the Cape cobra, which is golden or brown, the Egyptian cobra, which has bands of yellowish brown or black, the Angolan and forest cobras, and several species of spitting cobras. Most cobras grow to a length of roughly two metres.

Like the mambas (which also possess a rudimentary hood) the cobras have short, fixed fangs, with the venom flowing down through tubes in the fangs.

The rinkals, or South African spitting cobra, is a short, squat snake

Skull and fangs of a puff-adder.

with white bands over its throat. It differs from the true cobras in that it produces live young rather than eggs. This snake can expel its venom with considerable force. The spray can carry up to four metres. Its effect on eyes and open wounds is disastrous unless promptly treated with serum, or by washing, preferably with some anti-acid such as milk.

Most cases of snake-bite in southern Africa result from people accidentally treading on some member of the adder family. These snakes — short, fat and lethargic — are unaggressive but bite if trampled on. They have hinged fangs, larger than those of the mambas or cobras, and the venom flows down a duct in each fang.

Adders are thus more efficient biters, but their venom is slow-acting and allows time for treatment.

The largest of the poisonous adders in southern Africa is the Gaboon viper, which inhabits hot and humid regions. It grows to about 2 metres with an especially fat, vividly coloured body. It has hinged fangs, about 50 millimetres long. A deep bite from a Gaboon viper is invariably fatal.

Puff-adders are common. These fat, indolent snakes, growing to about 1,5 metres long, rely on camouflage, lying about waiting for food to approach within easy reach.

Their curved, hinged fangs, 25 millimetres long, are like hypodermic needles; each fang has a duct to convey the venom to a hole in the tip. The poison can be fatal, but slow-acting and allows time for treatment.

The puff-adder has a habit of drawing itself up into an 'S' shape, like a spring. It hisses loudly and launches itself with great force.

Several snakes spend most of their lives in trees. One of these is the boomslang, considered by many experts to be the deadliest of African snakes. It grows up to 2 metres long and varies from dark green to brown or black. The boomslang is agile but not aggressive. Its poison acts on the blood. The fangs, however, are small and far back in its mouth. It must chew to inject its venom.

During the breeding season, in spring, boomslangs congregate in large numbers and professional snake catchers have found as many as 400 in one tree. All end in medical institutes to be used in the production of anti-snake-bite serum.

The mole snake constricts its prey.

Angry boomslang with throat puffed.

Black mamba — graceful and deadly.

The handsome banded cobra.

A puff-adder ready to bite.

The non-venomous slug-eater.

a broad alluvial valley. The agricultural possibilities here were apparent to the first European settlers.

In the early 19th century, however, the valley was the scene of battles between Xhosas and Europeans, and there was little opportunity for development. In 1887 James Kirkwood, a Port Elizabeth auctioneer, bought 30 000 hectares of land in the valley and formed the Sundays River Land and Irrigation Company.

This was South Africa's first private land development company, but times were depressed. Ostriches were the big money-makers and Kirkwood's schemes for irrigation remained unfinanced. Not until 1913 was the first large irrigation weir completed. Several companies were then formed to work here and citrus orchards flourished.

During World War I the valley became the home of Sir Percy Fitz-Patrick, author of *Jock of the Bushveld* and a major figure in the financial and mining worlds. Sir Percy formed the Sundays River Settlements Company and bought up a substantial part of the valley.

The government was persuaded to build a dam, known as Lake Mentz, and a considerable number of settlers were attracted to the area. There was a long wait, however, before the irrigation schemes could be completed. A railway from Port Elizabeth had to be built and Sir Percy's company became involved in much litigation.

In 1924, 69 farmers formed the Sundays River Citrus Co-operative. With the railway completed, Lake Mentz filling to capacity in 1928, and fruit of superlative quality being produced, the valley was on the verge of becoming one of the world's major producers of citrus fruits. By the beginning of World War II, 220 000 cases of oranges were being exported each year. In 1947 the figure exceeded a million and today it is about 29 million — approximately two thirds of South Africa's citrus fruit production. (Each case contains 15 kilograms of fruit.) The valley also produces vast amounts of fruit juices.

The road up the valley from Port Elizabeth takes the traveller into a world of citrus trees. In October the trees are in full blossom and the warm

Van Stadens Gorge, with the concrete-arch road bridge making a spectacular crossing 125 metres above the river.

Neat ranks of orange trees flourish in the warm climate and deep alluvial soil of the Sundays River Valley.

The Cape St. Francis lighthouse looks out on the great swells that roll in from the vast expanse of the Southern Ocean.

air of the valley is heavy with perfume. Winter is picking season.

Tropical flowers such as bougainvillaea, hibiscus, poinsettia, poinciana and frangipani ornament the valley.

On the promontory that forms the east bank of the Sundays River is the Look Out, burial place of Sir Percy FitzPatrick and members of his family. The site is a historical monument.

Uitenhage
In 1804 General Jacob Abraham Uitenhage de Mist, representative of the Batavian Government which had occupied the Cape in 1802, toured the eastern frontier, an area much troubled by Xhosa raids. His task was to establish a new Drostdy for the protection of the settlers. He chose a site,

watered by perennial artesian springs, beside the Zwartkops River at the foot of the Winterhoek Mountains.

Today Uitenhage has a population of more than 100 000 and is an important industrial centre, encompassing car component and tyre manufacturing, motor assembly and textile processing. An ultra-modern R200-million railway workshops complex is currently under construction.

Well worth a visit are The Old Drostdy Africana Museum, the Cuyler Manor Cultural Museum with its unique water mill, and the Old Railway Museum, which attracts steam enthusiasts from all over the world.

The nature reserve at Uitenhage Springs contains a number of rare botanical specimens.

Van Stadens Pass
The Van Stadens River has scoured a deep gorge as it passes on its way towards the sea. The gorge, reached by the beautiful Van Stadens Pass, is crossed by one of the longest concrete arch bridges in southern Africa. The bridge, 350 metres long, rests on a concrete arch 25 metres wide, which was built from opposite banks simultaneously.

The four-lane road across the bridge is 125 metres above the floor of the gorge.

An old road, which crosses the gorge by descending to the bottom, is still in use.

On the east side of the gorge a 373-hectare wild flower reserve and bird sanctuary has been created.

Riding high and wild on Bruce's Beauties

To the surfing enthusiasts of the world, southern Africa is second only to Hawaii for the blend of size, speed and power of the waves that roll onto its shores. The breakers that surfers seek are born far out in the ocean and generated by tides and winds. They begin as a swell which can travel vast distances, concentrating its energy as it moves up the slopes of the continental shelf. Wildly irregular in the open sea, the swell is steadily disciplined by the shelving beach until, in the ideal surfing spots, it is drilled into long crests, all moving at the same speed and at the same angle to the shore. As the seabed rises, the base of the wave is braked, and the crest begins to curl over, forming the stupendous curved wall of water known to surfers as a 'tube'. Visually alone these waves are stunning, but the surfer is not content simply to stand and stare. He seeks a total experience, riding the raw power of the ocean, caught up in a kaleidoscopic pattern of sea and sky that reaches a peak of perfection and then shatters into fragments.

Southern Africa has several beaches where conditions are almost ideal for surfing. These are places where the waves begin to break sufficiently far from shore to give a long run, so that various manoeuvres and skills can be tried out. A big wave breaking too near the shore is spectacular to see but useless for surfing.

Variations in tide, weather and undersea topography all affect waves, making surfing conditions at any particular place and time notoriously difficult to predict. To the surfer, this unpredictability is a source both of joy and of frustration. One enthusiast's account of an exhilarating day's sport can draw others to the same spot and they find only disappointment. The ultimate is to discover some deserted beach with big waves rolling up in majestic succession where, for a few gloriously uncrowded hours, surfing is life and each moment is a new climax.

The speed of a good surfing wave varies from 25 to 32 kilometres an hour. It must have 'muscle' — strength — and weight, be at least 3 metres high, and have the capacity to 'wipe out', or dump, the surfer, thus adding spice and adventure, making the ride high and wild, taxing stamina, skill and experience.

The major international surfing centre on the South African coast is St. Francis Bay, on the southern coast of Cape Province. The water is never too cold for comfort and at Cape St. Francis itself, at the western end of the bay, there appear in winter the waves celebrated in surfers' lore as Bruce's Beauties.

These reputedly perfect surfing waves are named after the American film producer and surfing enthusiast Bruce Brown, who was the first to draw attention to their sporting potential.

The only imperfection of Bruce's Beauties is that they are elusive requiring special weather and tide conditions and appearing on perhaps only 25 days a year.

These waves begin as huge swells in the Southern Ocean which surge in over deep water. With an incoming tide and an offshore westerly wind, they are caught up by the tip of Cape St. Francis and form long, elegant, stunningly beautiful tubes which sweep the surfer a good kilometre, giving time for a tremendous variety of manoeuvres.

Further north-east lies the resort of Jeffreys Bay and the superb surfing spot known as Supertubes.

The waves here, second only to Bruce's Beauties for the sport they provide, are about 5 metres high and close to a kilometre long, forming fine tubes that move with power and speed. They are right-point breaking — they break on the surfer's right side — and are not for beginners. These waves appear far more frequently than Bruce's Beauties. Further up the coast at East London, there is a fine reef wave at Nahoon.

Also among the foremost of southern Africa's surfing beaches is Elands Bay, on the south-west coast, and some of the fastest and largest waves in southern Africa appear at The Hoek, in Chapman's Bay, and at Sunset Reef. Surfers speak in awe of waves here large enough for a bus to drive through the tube.

Professional surfer Mike Tomson, hanging under the lip at Cape St. Francis.

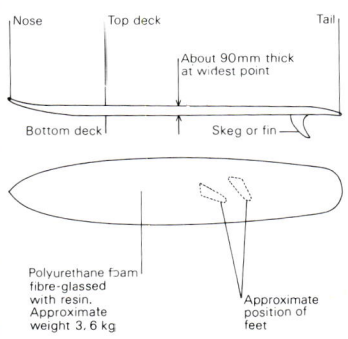

Nose   Top deck   Tail

About 90mm thick at widest point

Bottom deck   Skeg or fin

Polyurethane foam fibre-glassed with resin. Approximate weight 3.6 kg

Approximate position of feet

Surfboards have changed through the years. This diagram shows a modern board with foot positions.

Neatly tubed-in at The Hoek: human skill and sea power in perfect harmony.

Cutting back at Cape St. Francis, which is considered to have some of the best surfing waves in the world.

The last of a big wave — and a long day. Sunset solo at Elands Bay.

The exhilaration of a high-speed run along a clean roller at St. Francis Bay.

COUNTRY OF THE BRAVE

THE COUNTRY OF THE 1820 Settlers extends along the coast from Algoa Bay to the mouth of the Great Fish River, and inland for 300 kilometres up the wild and vast valley of that river. This was the old frontier of Kaffraria, the line of bitter contention between white settlers moving northwards from the Cape and black settlers moving southwards — the whites from homelands far away in Europe, the blacks from homelands in the north, somewhere in the region of the great lakes and a place they venerated as eMbo, the legendary birthplace of their kind.

Many influences contributed to the history of this frontier area. Sadness, tragedy, heroism, treachery, stubborn courage — all these and many more are the ingredients of the unique atmosphere that lingers over this land of bush-covered hills and valleys.

It is a hard land, beautiful in rainy seasons, but heart-breaking during droughts. A chain of good seasons is inevitably broken by one or two years during which the sky forgets how to rain and the hopes of man wither with the vegetation. Only the strong have survived in such a setting.

In 1820 the British government, wrestling with a depression and the problem of absorbing soldiers returning from the Napoleonic wars, seized on the idea of settling people in the frontier districts of the Cape. More than 4 000 British people landed on the beach in Algoa Bay and were guided inland to their allocated farms. There they came into bitter conflict with the Bantu peoples moving south. The British who survived sank their emotional roots deep into the soil of this frontier land. They paid for their land with blood and tears, and their descendants became some of the bravest and most patriotic of all the people of southern Africa.

Alexandria
The centre of the chicory-growing industry of South Africa. Pineapples also grow in abundance.

The town is named after the Reverend Alexander Smith. It has a hotel and a caravan park, and serves as the terminus of a branch railroad from Port Elizabeth.

Bathurst
On the road from Grahamstown to Port Alfred lies Bathurst, founded in 1820, named after the colonial secretary, Lord Bathurst, and intended to be the administrative centre of the Settler Country. The town lost its status to Grahamstown and is today one of the smallest municipalities in southern Africa. It is memorable for its many trees, huge wild figs and brilliantly flowering coral trees.

The Anglican St. John's Church, built in 1832, is a historical monument. It was used as a refuge before it was completed and in 1834 came under determined attack. Women and children sheltering in the church loaded guns while their men held off an army of warriors until relief arrived from Grahamstown. The church was fortified with outer earthen works and was the strong-point of a countryside reduced to ruin. Again, in 1846, the church was besieged. It also provided protection for local inhabitants during the war of 1850-53.

One of the first settlers in Bathurst, Thomas Hartley, built a forge and inn in 1821. Burned down, looted,

re-stocked, this inn, The Pig and Whistle, still survives.

The Methodist Church in Bathurst, also a historical monument, withstood the siege of 1846 and an attack in 1836.

Bathurst is a convenient starting place for a drive to the horseshoe bend of the Kowie River — an astonishing example of a meandering river. The banks are densely covered with trees and flowering plants. Crane flowers, tecoma, plumbago, aloes and numerous succulents grow in profusion. Cycads, sneezewood, colodendron and coral trees are common. Flowers seen in so many gardens — the pelargonium, gazania, Cape honeysuckle and many others — have their natural home in this area. Phoenix palm trees grow on the flats.

Two kilometres from Bathurst is a vantage point known as Thornridge. From here, Colonel Jacob Cuyler, the man in charge of allocating farms to

Lombard's Post, near Bathurst, a settlers' stronghold during the frontier wars.

St. John's Church, Bathurst, a refuge as well as a place of worship.

The bronze bell of St. John's Church.

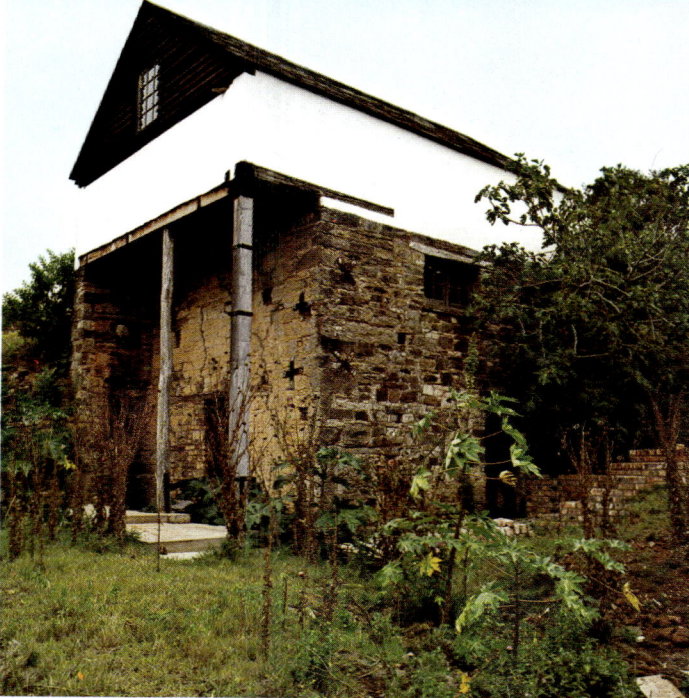

The pioneer wool mill in Bathurst, as it was prior to its restoration in 1976.

the settlers, directec them to their future homes. In 1968 a toposcope was built here around a beacon erected in 1859. This toposcope has 57 bronze plates around it indicating where parties of settlers were allocated farms. From here the whole coastline of the Settler Country is visible.

Bathurst is one of the main centres in the pineapple growing region of southern Africa. It was here that the first pineapples of the eastern Cape were cultivated.

Cradock

The upper reaches of the valley of the Great Fish River were not as exposed to frontier disturbances as the lower reaches, but, at the end of the

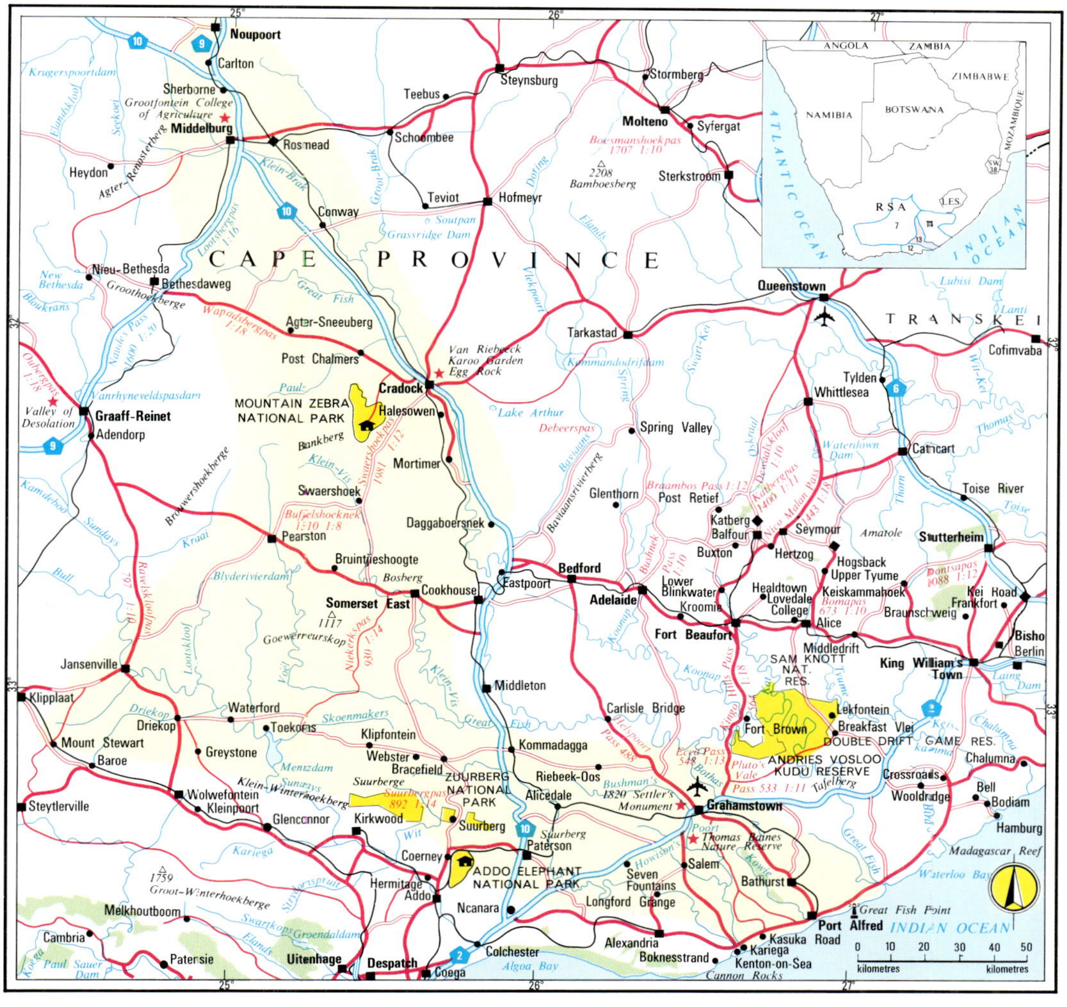

THINGS TO DO AND SEE

Angling The coast of the Settler Country does not offer any exceptional fishing but among the fish species found here is a most delicious fish, the John Brown, known as the hottentot further south and the bronze bream in the north. A good specimen weighs around 3 kilograms. They are taken throughout the year. Galjoen, blacktail (or dassies) and musselcrackers are found in winter and spring.

Antiquities Grahamstown has the first-class Albany Museum, the splendidly situated 1820 Settlers' Monument on Gunfire Hill, and Fort Selwyn. There is a perfectly restored old trading post — Piet Retief's Trading Store — and Church Square contains the oldest examples of early Victorian architecture in the southern hemisphere.

Boating The Kowie is navigable by small boats for 24 kilometres from Port Alfred. Other good rivers for boating are the Sundays, the Bushman's and the Kariega.

Botany The flora of the eastern Cape is very varied, with gorgeous flowering aloes and other plants. There is a wild flower garden in Grahamstown.

Camping and caravanning Grahamstown, Port Alfred and Cradock have caravan and camping grounds. Alexandria and Somerset East both have caravan parks. The Mountain Zebra National Park offers accommodation. There are several hotels and motels throughout the area.

Sightseeing The view of the Great Fish River Valley from the trunk road between Grahamstown and Peddie is one of the grandest in Africa. An old military watchtower stands guard close to this point and is a reminder of early wars. There is a mountain drive through the hills overlooking Grahamstown. The coast road from Port Alfred to Alexandria leads along a superb coastline and offers a fine circular 340-kilometre drive: Port Elizabeth — Grahamstown — Port Alfred — Alexandria — Port Elizabeth. Signposts along the way direct the traveller to many places famous in settler history.

Swimming The coast of the Settler Country is known as the sunshine coast. There are delightful beaches at Port Alfred, and at the mouths of the Bushman's and the Kariega rivers.

The 'City of Saints' with more than 40 churches

Frontier War of 1812, Sir John Cradock ordered that two strongholds should be created to secure the eastern area. One was Grahamstown and the other was Cradock, now sometimes known as the 'capital of the Midlands'.

Cradock lies in a broad part of the upper valley. It has rich soil, plentiful water and the climate is warm. This is a lucerne, fruit and dairy farming region. Of the three large irrigation dams, the largest, Lake Arthur, is much used for recreation. Supplementary water is also fed to the river valley from the Orange River by means of a tunnel 82 kilometres long, one of the longest irrigation tunnels in the world.

A tepid sulphur spring outside the town has been directed into a swimming bath. The spacious town park also has a swimming bath among its facilities.

The town's Dutch Reformed Church, completed in 1867, is a replica of St. Martin's-in-the-Fields, London. Other attractions are the Van Riebeeck Karoo Garden and the Egg Rock, a large egg-shaped dolerite rock.

There is a museum in the Old Parsonage building, and the Mountain Zebra National Park is only 24 kilometres outside the town.

Cradock is an important railway centre on the main line from Port Elizabeth to the north.

Grahamstown
The city of Grahamstown has been given many picturesque names: the 'City of Saints', because there are

Fort Brown, in the Fish River Valley.

Trompetter's Drift — one of the forts built on the Great Fish River.

THE BRAVE, THE BRILLIANT AND THE BARMY OF SOUTH AFRICA'S EARLY SETTLERS

It took enterprise and courage for anyone, no matter how poor, to abandon his home in Britain in 1820 and migrate to a far and unknown part of the world such as southern Africa. The difficulties, delays and expenses of transport were such that once leaving his native soil, the emigrant knew that it was unlikely that he would ever see his old home again. Hard work and frontier dangers kept most immigrants to their lands. It was for their children to have the leisure to follow less arduous pursuits, and several became celebrated for their eccentricities.

Joshua Norton became world-famous as Emperor Norton I of the United States of America. His father, John Norton, was an 1820 Settler who brought Joshua to South Africa when he was two years of age. He grew up on the frontier, then went to California during the gold rush of the forty-niners, became an eccentric and set himself up in San Francisco as an emperor. From 1859 until his death in 1880 he and his court were tolerated with affection.

Sir Harry Smith escapes from Fort Cox. Illustrated London News, 1851.

Nineteen medical doctors emigrated with the 1820 Settlers. Two died soon after landing in Algoa Bay, but the remaining 17 were a blessing to South Africa. Medical services on the frontier, until they arrived, consisted of little more than 'sick-comforters' — untrained people who had some home-made ointments or so-called inherited skills — and an occasional visit from an army doctor.

William Guybon Atherstone, the son of one of the settler doctors, Dr. John Atherstone, also became a doctor and was instrumental in the founding of Grahamstown's library, botanical gardens and the Albany Museum. He successfully conducted the first operation in South Africa using ether as an anaesthetic, and positively identified the first diamond found in Hopetown in 1867. He was a member of the legislative assembly, a co-founder of the ostrich-feather industry in the eastern Cape, did valuable research into horse-sickness and tick-fever and concerned himself with astronomy, music and art.

The settlers produced books, poems, articles and lampoons on the colonial administration, sympathized with the Dutch frontiersmen who moved away from British control in the Great Trek to the interior, and pleaded incessantly for a better understanding of extremely difficult local conditions.

Thomas Pringle also an 1820 Settler, became a renowned South African poet. He was a friend of Sir Walter Scott and Samuel Taylor Coleridge, and his works have always been highly regarded.

Andrew Geddes Bain arrived in Cape Town in 1816 and was also to give South Africa some worthwhile writing. He was a pioneer in the study of geology, the discoverer of many fossils, a great road builder, and a tireless explorer and observer of the wonders of nature.

Settler women also played a major role in the early cultural life of southern Africa. Mrs. Mary Barber was a poet, botanist, entomologist and zoologist, and contributed papers to several learned societies in Britain. She supplied Charles Darwin, Dr. W. H. Harvey, Sir William and Sir Joseph Hooker and other great scientists with information and specimens. Her private herbarium, paintings of plants and animals, and her series of pictures of life during the Kimberley diamond rush are now housed in the Albany Museum.

A tombstone from the frontier wars.

more than 40 places of worship here; 'Sleepy Hollow', because it lies in a warm hollow in the hills; 'City of Schools', because of the large concentration of schools and the Rhodes University; the 'Settler City', because its history is so much part of the settler story.

Grahamstown was created out of anguish. In 1806, when the British occupied the Cape for the second time, they were immediately confronted by disturbances on the eastern frontier. Cattle rustling, murders, kidnappings, raids and counter-raids hampered the country's development; there were even threats of a major invasion by the warlike Xhosas.

The British tried to persuade the warrior groups to respect the Great Fish River as their southern boundary. The principal British negotiator was murdered, and the raids increased. Full-scale war broke out in 1811 and the government had to drive more than 20 000 warriors back across the Great Fish River.

To stop further invasion, the governor, Sir John Cradock, decided to create a line of forts along the Great Fish River Valley, with two central strong-points as military headquarters. Colonel John Graham was given the task of selecting the sites for these points. In a setting of hills where the Kowie ('rushing') River has its headwaters, Graham found a deserted farmhouse that had been looted and partly destroyed. It was patched-up and became the officers' mess for the garrison. Tents and primitive houses were erected and the place was named Grahamstown, after the colonel. Every effort was made to establish the outpost before further trouble developed.

Grahamstown's first great trial came on 22 April 1819. About 9 000 Xhosa warriors, led by a renowned diviner named Makana, came down like a thunderstorm on the little town. The garrison's 350 soldiers held fast. The Xhosas withdrew, leaving about 1 000 corpses behind and the name, Makana's Kop, on the hill where they mustered for attack.

Grahamstown again was reinforced. In the following year the 1820 Settlers were hastily lured to the frontier area to provide a settled

The Provost building in Grahamstown, built as a military prison in 1836. Some very tough characters were held in this gaol.

population and manpower for defence, and Grahamstown became their centre. Within five years it grew into a town as well as a military stronghold, and a colourful scene it must have been, its trading stores and streets bustling with red-coated soldiers, hunters, settlers looking very sunburned, and a wild-looking selection of the region's inhabitants visiting Grahamstown to trade, suspiciously eyeing its people and fortifications.

One of the trading stores of the period, Piet Retief's Trading Store, opened in 1819, has been restored. The builder-owner was destined to become one of the great leaders of the Voortrekkers.

The town market place was a busy trading centre. Ivory and skins, ostrich feathers, aromatic gums and cattle were all bartered for beads, blankets, copper and European produce. It was the one place where warriors and soldiers encountered each other without reaching for weapons. As many as 2 000 wagons lumbered into the town on market days. Many of the settlers, disillusioned by their land allocations in poor farming situations, moved to the town and resumed their original trades as millers, wheelwrights, wagon-makers and gunsmiths.

The signal tower and stronghold built in 1843 near Fraser's Camp.

Streets where once every window bristled with guns

The house occupied by Advocate Randell, built in Grahamstown about 1820.

An elegant old office block.

Verandah of a Grahamstown home.

Grahamstown at this time was the second largest town in southern Africa. Wandering through its streets today reveals to the visitor many buildings surviving from the city's earliest days. Among these are the old gaol. The drostdy (residence of the magistrate) has unfortunately disappeared but the gateway is now the entrance to Rhodes University. There is also the Provost House built by the Royal Engineers, and several little cottages, houses and shops.

The first school was opened in 1814. The children of the garrison and their master sat in the shade of the wall of the barracks. Today Grahamstown's schools are among the biggest and best of South Africa. School and university life in the town so dominates modern Grahamstown that during the vacation periods the streets are often empty and the stillness of the air is disturbed only, it is said, by the subdued weeping of commercial travellers.

Grahamstown suffered a severe setback in 1834 when the Xhosas launched a new invasion of the frontier area. Seven thousand refugees fled into the town. The streets were barricaded and every window bristled with guns at the slightest sound or rumour of attack. On hearing of the invasion Colonel (later Sir) Harry Smith, the British military commander, rode on horseback from Cape Town to Grahamstown across more than 900 kilometres of rugged mountains, bush and rivers — in six days of real hell-for-leather riding.

On reaching Grahamstown the colonel took command. St. George's

Sir Harry Smith, a settlers' hero.

114 High Street in Grahamstown, the premises of the Albany Club.

PINEAPPLE PARADISE

The great crop of the Settler Country is pineapples, vast fields of which cover the hill slopes.

The industry had its beginnings in the unlikely setting of a Grahamstown barber's shop in 1865. A customer, Charles Purdon, a farmer from the Bathurst district, noticed that the barber had pineapple tops growing in jars of water in his shop as a curiosity for his customers. Purdon took some home, planted them and found that the soil and climate suited them perfectly.

There are two main varieties of pineapple — the Queen and the Cayenne. They are grown for home and export markets.

The ornate tower of Galpin's Tower House, actually an observatory ingeniously combined with a camera obscura.

Church became the central shelter for women and children and a depot for the distribution of arms. The men were rallied, patrols and attacks launched and by September of 1835 the Xhosa chief Hintza was dead, other leaders were captured, and the frontier fires stamped down for a few more years. It was during these disturbances that Fort Selwyn was built and the Provost House became a military prison.

In contrast to this resolution and bustle, the war was followed by political confusion, with the British government, deciding matters from the other side of the globe, so befuddled by conflicting advice that the frontier people felt themselves betrayed.

Dutch settlers abandoned the area. This was the start of the Great Trek into the interior of southern Africa.

The English, though demoralized, remained. They had been persuaded to emigrate to this wild part of the world by being offered fine farms and the lasting support of their government. Now they were being accused of land-grabbing and oppression, and were even being criticised for taking up arms against unprovoked attack. Nevertheless, Grahamstown remained the main frontier garrison. It

was in 1842 that Dick King made his famous 1 000-kilometre ride to Grahamstown from Port Natal in ten days on one horse. He forded some 122 rivers to bring news of the siege of the British garrison at Durban.

The year 1846 saw another vicious clash with the Xhosas. Grahamstown was jammed with refugees while the warriors looted the countryside. Once again the fires were stamped out, but in 1850 war broke out again, the largest and most brutal of the frontier disturbances. At its end the British

government was forced to annex the area as far north as the Kei River. The Settler Country was no longer the battle-torn frontier of the Cape and peace came to the farmlands, Grahamstown and its outposts and forts.

More schools were built, the botanical garden laid out, the Albany Museum founded, the Eastern Districts' Supreme Court established, and, in 1864, a full parliamentary session was held in Grahamstown instead of Cape Town. There was talk of making Grahamstown the capital of the Cape Col-

ony because of its central position.

Grahamstown became a city with the establishment here in 1853 of an Anglican bishop and the Cathedral of St. Michael and St. George. This cathedral, with a handsome spire 45,75 metres high, dominates the centre of Grahamstown. The town square in which it stands contains many shops whose facades have not changed since Victorian days. Of Grahamstown's other surviving churches, the Baptist Chapel, the first in South Africa, was built in 1823; the Wes-

The gateway to the Grahamstown drostdy, which now forms the entrance to Rhodes University.

Mountain refuge of one of the world's rarest animals

leyans built their chapel in 1832; the convent, also the first in South Africa, was founded in 1849; and St. Patrick's Catholic Church was built in 1839.

The Albany Museum exhibits items of settler history, natural history and African peoples. Here are paintings of scenes of frontier life, wars, and the people of the period.

In the J. L. B. Smith Institute of Ichthyology is a specimen of a coelacanth, the prehistoric fish thought to have become extinct 80 million years ago until a live specimen was found in 1938. Grahamstown's coelacanth was the second to be found. It was caught in 1952 off the Comoro Islands.

The South African Library for the Blind in Grahamstown supplies braille books, discs, tapes and cassettes to members all over South Africa.

The Grahamstown Botanical Garden was founded in the 1850s. Covering 60 hectares, it is maintained as a wild flower reserve as well as a general botanical garden. It has an old English garden of the type found in Britain at the time of the departure of the settlers.

The gardens have a romantic ghost. The wife of the dashing colonel, Harry Smith, later knighted and made governor of the Cape, was a renowned Spanish beauty, the Lady Juana. She is said still to wander through this lovely garden, leaving behind her, in the warm night air, a trace of a Spanish perfume.

On Gunfire Hill, overlooking the city, stands the 1820 Settlers' National Monument, and Fort Selwyn.

The Thomas Baines Nature Reserve covers 1 000 hectares and provides a

Part of the Grahamstown monument to the 1820 settlers

The 1820 Settlers National Monument on Gunfire Hill, overlooking Grahamstown.

Mountain zebras, once all but extinct, in their sanctuary near Cradock.

protected home for wild animals indigenous to the area, including white rhinoceros, buffalo, zebra, eland and gnu. This reserve is at Howison's Poort, 13 kilometres along the trunk road to Port Elizabeth.

The Mountain Drive should not be missed. There is also a kudu reserve, sanctuary for the magnificently horned kudu, one of the largest of the antelopes of Africa. Among smaller animals in the area are porcupines, antbears, various wild cats, large monitor lizards and numerous birds, including hoopoes and hadedas.

Middelburg
In 1852 it was decided to establish a town midway between Cradock and Colesberg on the road to the north. The town lies in a circle formed by Graaff-Reinet, Cradock, Steynsburg, Colesberg and Richmond, and so was named Middelburg. The town has a generous supply of underground water, is the centre of a sheep farming area, and has the Grootfontein College of Agriculture on its outskirts.

The original gabled Grootfontein homestead, built in 1857, is now a museum. Visiting hours are limited, so enquire first.

Mountain Zebra National Park
The mountain zebra, *Equus zebra zebra*, is still on the endangered list as one of the rarest mammals in the world. It is the smallest of the zebras,

standing only a little more than a metre high. It is brilliantly striped — one of the reasons it was so much hunted, for its skin makes a handsome trophy.

Once found in many of the mountain ranges of the Cape, its numbers were steadily reduced until there were fewer than a hundred. At this stage, in 1937, the Mountain Zebra National Park was created to provide them with a permanent sanctuary. The park comprises 6 536 hectares on the high slopes of the Bankberg Range, 24 kilometres from Cradock. There are panoramic views from the heights to the north, east and west, the landscape being dominated by flat-topped hillocks, classic examples of the koppies of southern Africa.

The mountain zebras now number more than 200. Living with them are several other species of wild animals indigenous to the Karoo, including springbok, mountain reedbuck, blesbok, kudu, grey rhebuck, klipspringer, steinbuck, duiker, eland, gnu and red hartebeest. There are 190 bird species, including ostrich.

The vegetation is typical of the Karoo, with such trees as the karee, acacia, wild olive, kiepersol, and white stinkwood growing in the valleys. Aloes and mesembryanthemums provide beautiful displays.

Gravel roads lead to various parts of the park. There are no dangerous predators and walking is allowed.

Noupoort
The railway junction of Noupoort is a bleak place, bitterly cold in winter and blazing hot in summer. The main railway line from Port Elizabeth to the north tunnels its way deep below the old 'narrow pass' which gives Noupoort its name. Some hundred trains a day pass through the town. Despite its two hotels, this is no holiday resort. Day and night the trains rumble through here, including the heavy ore trains, each more than a kilometre long and hauled by five linked diesel electric locomotives.

Port Alfred
One of the many problems faced by the 1820 Settlers was poor accessibility to the outside world.

The mouth of the river known to

The Methodist Church built in Salem in 1832. The Sephton party of settlers used the church as a stronghold from which they fought off several attacks.

Europeans as the Kowie seemed to be an answer. It was wide and deep enough to allow the entrance of fair-sized sailing ships.

In 1821 the first coasters entered the river and this was the start of Port Alfred, first known as Port Frances, after the daughter-in-law of the governor Lord Charles Somerset, but in 1860 renamed in honour of Prince Alfred, who was then visiting South Africa.

For years attempts continued to develop the port. Many ships visited the place but the river mouth was difficult to enter and several ships were wrecked. In 1881 a railway was built connecting Grahamstown to Port Elizabeth. The construction of the railway put Port Alfred into decline as a harbour.

Today the mouth of the Kowie is a holiday resort. Small craft meander inland through a spectacular wooded valley. The beaches at the mouth are safe for swimming.

Among remnants of settler times is the Settler Church built by the Methodists in 1826 and used as a place of refuge in troubled times as well as a place of worship. Alongside it is a settler cemetery. The churchbell comes from the wreck of some forgotten ship.

The town's Cock's Castle was built in 1840 by William Cock, a man involved in the early attempt to develop a port. He built his home in romantic Gothic style, with strong crenellated walls and a flat roof reinforced to support a cannon.

Over 1 800 different types of seashells, including rarities, have been collected on the beaches. Such shells as the perlemoen, phasignella, nautilus and turbonilla are often found.

The Port Alfred golf course is reputed to be one of the best in South Africa. Tennis and bowls are also played. The pier and beaches provide good vantage points for fishing.

Salem

Hesekiah Sephton and his party of 344 settlers founded the village of Salem in 1820.

It is a well-preserved village of the period. The houses were stoutly constructed and double-storied for security and for economy of roofing material. The church served as a central fort and place of worship. There is a village green, where cricket is played, and farmlands with great pineapple plantations and sheep runs.

The name Salem, taken from Psalm 76, means peace, and the inhabitants were people who feared only God. During one Xhosa raid on the village the church was packed with refugees. One of them, Richard Gush, was a man of peace and heartily tired of his farmlands being ruined and his stock rustled. He put his gun aside and walked out alone to confront the warriors. They were nonplussed at his boldness. Their commander, who knew Gush, strode forward, bristling with skins, feathers and weapons. The two men greeted each other. The chief explained that his warriors were hungry.

Gush watched his livestock being rounded up by the warriors. He returned to the church, and despite the protests of his comrades, took back to the warriors fifteen huge loaves, an armful of tobacco rolls and a dozen pocket knives. He handed over these presents to the chief, then protested about Xhosa thefts of the settlers' cattle. The warriors looked at him in wonder and patiently listened to a sermon about the wrath of God. Then, one by one, they shook hands with Gush, took up his presents and went back into the wilderness, leaving the cattle to run loose in the bush.

Somerset East

In 1815 Lord Charles Somerset, governor of the Cape, founded a farm below the handsome range of the Bosberg ('bush mountain'). The principal purpose was to produce horse fodder for the cavalry garrisoning the frontier areas. The site had deep soil, plenty of water from a tributary of the Great Fish River, and so many streams flowing down from the mountains that 16 waterfalls can be seen from the town.

A village was laid out on the site of the farm in 1825 and today, grown into a town, it is a pleasant little place. The original Wesleyan Church is a museum of local history.

There is a 10-kilometre mountain drive and attractive walks to beauty spots in ravines and forest. A caravan park has recently been established in one of the nearby valleys.

The magic and mysterious world of the sea-shell creatures

The magic world of sea-shells still tantalizes man with many mysteries. About 1 500 different species of shell have so far been found on the coast of southern Africa, but the collector, especially if he is also fortunate enough to be a diver, has the certainty that there are many more species still to be found on the sea bed, and a vast amount still to be learned about the habits and life cycles of the marine molluscs that live inside them. In the past the study of these creatures could only be carried out under the artificial conditions of an aquarium. The invention of the aqualung has made it possible in modern times to observe shells in their natural environment, and many mysteries that previously puzzled scientists are now being solved.

Probably the best known of all the shells are the cowries. There are so many different cowries, each with its own colour and pattern, that they make collections in themselves.

One of the cowries, *Cypraea leucodon*, is regarded by collectors as the rarest of all. Until fairly recently there were only two known specimens — one kept at the British Museum, the other at the Museum of Comparative Zoology at Harvard University. There are now about a dozen, most of them found in the South Seas and along the shores of the Philippines.

Another only slightly less rare cowrie is the prince cowrie (*Cypraea valentia*), of which there are something over 100 known specimens. The orange cowrie (*Cypraea aurantium*), is often described as the most beautiful of all shells, while the tiger cowries (*Cypraea tigris*) are probably the best known and are cherished by collectors.

The 'money' cowrie, *Cypraea moneta*, has been used in trade for many centuries, especially in West Africa and India. A young wife could be bought in West Africa for 60 000 to 100 000 of these cowries.

Totally different from the cowries, but rivalling them for beauty, are the *Haliotis* shells, popularly known as sea ears, Venus ears, ear shells, abalones, or perlemoen. The largest of the family, *Haliotis midae*, approaches 200 millimetres in diameter and the inside of the shell is beautifully coloured. *H. midae* is much hunted for the edible flesh of the animals. Small species such as *H. spadicea* and *H. parvum* have a richly coloured outside as well as the typical mother-of-pearl interior.

Cone shells, of the family Conidae, are beautifully shaped and coloured but have to be handled with considerable care. All of the family are capable of inflicting a poisonous sting which can in some cases be fatal. *Conus geographus* has killed at least one would-be collector. *Conus gloriamaris* (the 'glory of the sea' shell) is also one of

A typical gastropod, of the mollusc class. The name 'gastropod' means 'stomach foot', from the fact that the stomach lies directly on top of the muscular foot.

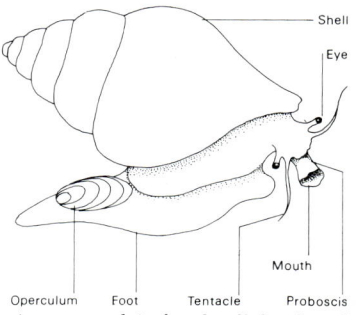

A gastropod, its head well developed with eyes, proboscis and tentacle.

The Bivalves *make good eating but can become poisonous after a red tide.*

Shells of the Conidae family, popularly known as cones. They are common along the eastern seaboard, with a few different species being found on the west coast.

the rarest of shells, with only a few hundred known to be in various collections all over the world.

'Slit-lip' shells of the *Pleurotomaria* genus are also rare collectors' pieces. They are deep-water shells known to live along the eastern shores of southern Africa. They were considered to be extinct, for the only specimens found were fossils. In 1855 a living specimen was found and since then several more have been collected. They have been recovered at depths of 200 fathoms off the Natal coast but remain rare pieces in any collection.

Only a few hundred of the South African species, *Pleurotomaria africana*, have been found. This shell is yellow, with streaks of orange. The name 'slit-lip' comes from a slit in the outer edge of the lip of the shell.

A shell of considerable interest along the Wild Coast is *Nerita texti-*

lis. These shells are rare and taboo. Worn as an ornament, they are a sign of wealth. If two are found on a beach, one is immediately thrown back into the sea in the belief that it will return, bringing another shell. If both shells are taken then the collector will be cursed with bad luck.

The fragile paper nautilus shell is another great treasure for collectors. Large specimens are difficult to find because they are so often damaged while being washed ashore. The shell is so thin that it takes very little to break it, and sea-birds pounce upon the shells, tear them to pieces and feed on the animal inside. The shell, which serves as an egg case, encloses only the female of the species. The paper nautilus is a small octopus which makes excellent eating although few people are ever fortunate enough to find so exotic a banquet.

The goose barnacle is classed as a crustacean because of its jointed legs.

Shells of the beautiful Haliotidae (perlemoen) family with their gorgeous mother-of-pearl interiors. The largest species is Haliotis midae, *growing to over 100 millimetres in diameter.* Haliotis queketti *has a lovely scarlet colour.*

Shapes, colours of extraordinary variety, patterns. These shells, mostly of the Patellidae family, are found all around the coast in both warm and cold water.

Most of these shells are of the Cypraeidae family, the famous cowries found in the Indian and Pacific oceans. There is an infinite variety in sizes and colours.

FRONTIER LAND OF MYTH AND MAJESTY

FOR MANY SEASONS of war and turmoil the Great Fish River marked the frontier between black and white, the civilisations of Africa and of Europe, paganism and Christianity. The river valley is deep, but not nearly as abysmal as was the ignorance of people living on both sides about one another. A host of legends could be compiled of stories told by the frontier people, black and white, about those who lived on the other side of the enigmatic river.

The original home of most of the modern people of southern Africa was either Africa or Europe. Europeans immigrated to southern Africa by sea; Negroid people immigrated overland. Earlier people had lived in the area for many thousands of years before the advent of the newcomers, but their origin is uncertain. There were never many of them and they offered little resistance to the advent of the newcomers. They eithers wandered away or were wiped out or absorbed by the newcomers.

When Europeans came to the Cape, they found living there several families and small clans of these early people. One group lived as hunter-gatherers. Europeans called them Bushmen. The second and larger group were pastoralists. The larger group referred to themselves as *Kho* (an individual) or *KhoiKhoi* (people). Europeans called them Hottentots, apparently from the odd sounds in their language. They referred to the hunter-gatherers as *San* (pronounced *Saan* or *Son*).

The hunter-gatherers were the older people. It is unknown whether they had migrated from the north or were the end-product of an evolutionary chain stretching back to the Australopithecus man-apes whose skeletons were discovered in southern Africa. Their past is a mystery, but at least 2 000 years ago their ancient hunting grounds were intruded on by the pastoralists. Behind these people came the more warlike migrants who called themselves after their chiefs and knew no generic name other than that collectively they were *baNtu* (people) or *muNtu* (an individual).

The main migrating mass always had a few groups wandering ahead, often far in the vanguard. Tradition tells of one such group, a section of the Hlubi people, that was engaged in hunting. In a brawl over the division of ivory, the leader was killed. The culprits fled south, led by a woman named Nomagwayi. As they moved southwards the group encountered *KhoiKhoi*, who named them *amaXhosa* ('the people of the woman'). From these refugees the Xhosa people grew, and it was this group that met the European settlers south of the Great Fish River.

The Xhosas built strong, weather-proof huts of mud and thatch. A bold, medium-sized people, lighter in complexion than their fellows in the north, they were brave fighters and hunters. The women did most of the work, tilling the fields and cooking; the boys tended the cattle; the men drank, talked and fought.

Both sexes wore skins, but they acquired blankets, beads and copper wire for bangles from Europeans, and used these materials to create their costume. Their favourite colour was a brilliant orange-red, which they derived from ochre found in clay pits. They did not manufacture anything other than items of war and a number of crude agricultural implements.

Early European settlers considered the indigenous peoples of Africa to be primitive, and they named the Xhosa homeland 'Kaffraria', derived from the Arab term for non-Muslims, or unbelievers. To Africans, the Europeans seemed aggressive and insatiably hungry for land in this strip that became known also as 'the Border'. A later name was 'Ciskei' — or the land 'this side of the Kei River' — to distinguish the area from 'Transkei', the area to the north and west of the Kei. Ciskei existed as an independent state under the former 'homelands' policy of the South African Government from 1981 to 1994, when it was reincorporated into the Republic of South Africa. This land was the superb scenic stage for the tragic succession of nine frontier wars that ended in 1878.

In the centre of open, undulating, grass-covered downland looms a mass of forest-clad mountains — Winterberg, Amatole, Hogsback and Katberg. Natural strongholds of old invite peaceful exploration, where natural assets include magnificent scenery, a pleasant climate and an atmosphere rich in history and legend.

Adelaide

During the frontier wars a military post was created on the banks of the Koonap River and named Adelaide, after the wife of England's King William IV. A town has grown up on the site of the fort.

The town's museum exhibits settler relics, including mid-19th century English and Dutch furniture, glass, silverware and ceramics.

Alice

The Lovedale mission for the people living in the valley of the Tyume River was established in November 1824 by the Glasgow Missionary Society. It was twice abandoned and re-established, and eventually the town of Alice grew as a commercial and farming centre close to the mission. The town was named after Princess Alice, daughter of Queen Victoria. The University College of Fort Hare was established here in 1916. The town has an attractive central square and is a busy trading centre. The district produces wool, mohair, citrus fruit, tobacco, timber and livestock.

Aliwal North

On the south side of the Orange River, close to an ancient fording place, two thermal springs surface at 34,4°C. The daily flow is consistent: more than 2 million litres from one spring and 1 million litres from the other. From early times these springs were credited with curative properties and were visited by sufferers from ailments such as rheumatism, arthritis, lumbago and neuralgia.

The combination of ford and springs attracted people to the area and in 1848, when the governor of the

Superb pasture amid groves of citrus trees and flowering aloes near Alice, in the valley of the Tyume River.

Post Retief, a stronghold in the days of the frontier wars.

Fine old furniture in the Adelaide museum.

Cape, Sir Harry Smith, passed this way, he was asked by the settlers to found a town.

The town was established the following year and named in commemoration of Sir Harry's victory over the Sikhs at Aliwal in India in 1846. 'North' was added to the name because it was intended that Mossel Bay would be renamed Aliwal.

The town is pleasantly situated

on the south bank of the Orange. A large watermill was built here, trees planted to shade the streets, and the Juana Square Garden was created in honour of Sir Harry's wife.

The hot springs have been extensively developed. A park and an attractive garden surrounds them, and the water is piped into two large outdoor swimming pools and two children's pools. The main spring is enclosed. There are private baths and a restaurant. A treatment block houses amenities for invalids.

Fort Hare, near Alice, built in 1847 at the end of the Xhosa War of the Axe.

THINGS TO DO AND SEE

Angling Several rivers in the Ciskei are stocked with trout. The Pirie hatchery is one of the principal hatcheries in southern Africa. The Tyume, the rivers in Keiskammahoek, numerous dams, and the Klipplaat River are noted for freshwater fishing. Salt-water fishing is not exceptional, but musselcracker and kob are caught at Hamburg. The harbour walls of East London are also popular sites.

Antiquities The East London Museum has exhibits of natural history, traditional African costumes and beadwork. The Kaffrarian Museum in King William's Town has a fine collection of African mammals.

Camping and caravanning Noteworthy caravan parks in this region are those at King William's Town, East London, Queenstown, Gonubie and Gulu River. The coastal resorts are ideal for camping.

Rural life The Xhosas make superb subjects for photographers and artists. Always ask permission before taking a photograph. Presents are expected.

Walking The Katberg and thickly forested Hogsback are a must for enthusiastic explorers.

Where you can see the only dodo's egg in the world

One of the large open-air baths at the hot springs at Aliwal North.

Burgersdorp nestling in a valley in the foothills of the Stormberg.

Beacon Bay
Two rivers, the Quenera and the Nahoon, reach the sea immediately north-east of East London. Both have lagoons and sandy beaches. Swimming is safe, and the reef at Nahoon produces some of the most consistently good surfing waves on the South African coast. It is the venue for many surfing competitions. The whole area, a residential and holiday resort, combines what used to be Bonza Bay and Beaconhurst farm into a municipality called Beacon Bay.

Bedford
The thickly wooded Kagaberg overlooks a rich cattle, sheep and horse-breeding district. The centre for the area is the town of Bedford, founded in 1854 and named after the Duke of Bedford, a friend of Sir Andries Stockenström, who owned the farm on which it was laid out. The area was occupied by a party of Scots led by Thomas Pringle, the poet, writer and philanthropist. The site of his rough little cabin is marked with a plaque.

Each year Bedford is the scene of a large gymkhana. This is one of the major events for South African horse-riding enthusiasts.

Berlin
In 1857 soldiers disbanded from the British German Legion founded and named this quiet little rural centre, lying in a setting of grass-covered hills. They fought for the British during the Seventh Frontier War and remained in the country with the coming of peace.

Burgersdorp
This historic town, the oldest in the north-eastern Cape, was founded in 1846. It is the administrative and trading centre for a wool and livestock farming area, and also has an interesting cultural heritage. The regional museum complex includes two national monuments, namely the first theological school of the Reformed Church and the parsonage of Jan Lion Cachet, one of the first professors of the school. Other national monuments are the Language Monument, the Centinel (a British blockhouse erected in 1901), the old gaol, and Christ Church, built in 1861.

Cathcart
This rural centre was named after Sir George Cathcart, governor of the Cape from 1852 to 1854. Originally a military stronghold, it is now popular for gliding — the hill slopes provide excellent launching sites and the thermal air currents permit extensive soaring.

Several dams in the area are stocked with bass.

Dordrecht
Founded in 1856 and named after Dordrecht in Holland, this town is a centre for sheep farming. Nearby is a beauty spot, Dordrecht Kloof, which has rock shelters containing San paintings. Dordrecht is cold in winter and has heavy snowfalls.

East London
The river known to the Khoikhoi as Igaab! ab ('place of buffaloes') provides South Africa with its only river port of any significant size. The first vessel known to have visited it was the *Centaurus*, in 1688. This ship was sent

The City Hall at East London overlooks the equestrian memorial to the men of the Colonial Division who fell during the Anglo-Boer War.

up from the Cape to search for survivors of shipwrecks. On 7 February that year the *Centaurus* picked up 18 survivors from one of the frequent wrecks along this 'Wild Coast'. A year later a second rescue ship found two more shipwreck survivors.

The captains of both rescue ships reported favourably on the prospects of establishing a river port, but at the time there was no trade in the area. In 1835, when the British annexed the coastal region after the Sixth Frontier War, Colonel Harry Smith rode to the river mouth and, subsequently, recommended that it be used for the landing of military supplies. As a result, the brig *Knysna*, owned by the pioneer George Rex, sailed to the river with stores. The sand bar across its mouth prevented access, but stores were landed on the beach and the Union Jack hoisted on what is now called Signal Hill. The name of Port Rex was given to the area. No development took place until 1846, when the War of the Axe broke out. Fort Glamorgan was built as one of a chain of

fortresses to protect the supply route from the river mouth to King William's Town.

In 1848 a proclamation annexed the area to the Cape Colony, and the name of East London was given to the river harbour. German soldiers, disbanded from the British German Legion, were settled here. Most of these men were bachelors, so the British government shipped out 157 Irish girls — probably the most welcome cargo ever landed here.

Today East London is a harbour for the export of citrus fruit, mineral ores and wool, while considerable imports are handled here, particularly for the Orange Free State. The harbour has been dredged and the river is navigable by small craft.

Of three beaches within the city limits, Orient Beach is closest to the city centre. It is separated from the harbour by a long pier built over the wreck of the Russian vessel *Orient*, which was grounded here in 1907. The beach is popular for bathing and surfing. It has a children's playground and

Orient Beach, close to the city centre, is considered one of the safest beaches in South Africa.

Period pieces . . . the museum at Gately House.

The first coelacanth, caught by a trawler off East London.

Nahoon beach stretches south from the mouth of the Nahoon River, offering excellent surfing and fishing.

The Guild Theatre, a centre for the dramatic arts.

paddling pool, and the Orient Bath, a sea-water swimming pool. The near-by Eastern Beach also has fine surfing waves. Nahoon Beach, on the south bank of the Nahoon River, offers good fishing and surfing.

The East London Museum has probably the most comprehensive natural history exhibits in South Africa. Among them is the first coelacanth, *Latimeria chalumnae*, to be caught in the world. This primitive fish has fins resembling stumpy legs. Until this specimen was caught off the Chalumna River near East London in 1938, the coelacanth had only been known from fossil remains and was believed to have been extinct for some 80 million years. There is a hall that contains a collection of southern African shells. The museum also houses collections of moths, butterflies and insects, as well as geological and archaeological sections, and a skeleton of an extinct Karoo reptile, *Kannemeyria wilsonii* Broom. Another section is devoted to the Xhosa and Fingo peoples and usually there are women of these same population groups outside the museum making necklaces and other handicrafts. A unique item in the museum is the only known dodo's egg.

At Gately House there is a second museum. John Gately was an Irishman who came to East London in 1860 and was mayor of the town in 1875. This house was his home, continuously occupied by members of his family until 1963. In 1966 it was bequeathed to the municipality.

East London Museum, home of the first coelacanth.

Breathtaking views from the peaks of the Hogsback mountains

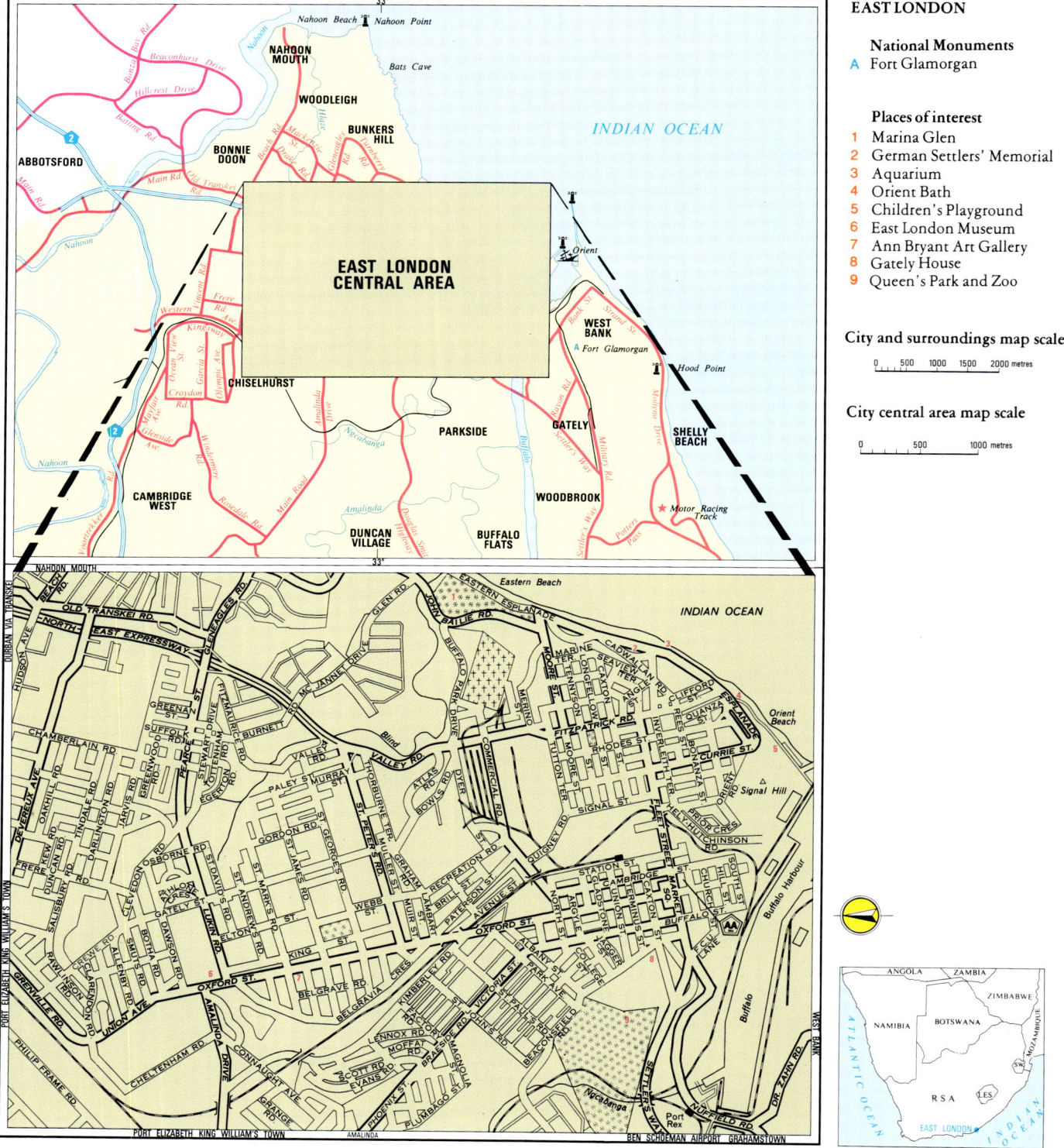

EAST LONDON

National Monuments

A Fort Glamorgan

Places of interest

1 Marina Glen
2 German Settlers' Memorial
3 Aquarium
4 Orient Bath
5 Children's Playground
6 East London Museum
7 Ann Bryant Art Gallery
8 Gately House
9 Queen's Park and Zoo

City and surroundings map scale

0 500 1000 1500 2000 metres

City central area map scale

0 500 1000 metres

The coast north of East London is a pleasant succession of river mouths and bays.

The Ann Bryant Art Gallery is housed in a building bequeathed to the city in 1947 by the late Ann Bryant, together with a collection of paintings originally consisting mainly of works by British artists but now also by South African artists.

The arrival of more than 2 000 German men, women and children at the port during 1858-59 helped to expand the settlement and this is commemorated in the German Settlers' Memorial, which stands near the aquarium. In a natural bowl between the city centre and the river is Queen's Park and Zoo, with its attractive gardens of trees and shrubs.

East London has a motor-racing track. Rowing, yachting and powerboat regattas are also held here.

Marina Glen is a picnic area of grass shaded by trees, with a children's playground and a tea garden.

Elliot
This pleasant country town was founded in 1885 and named after Sir Henry Elliot, whose negotiating skills prevented many a border dispute from developing into a major uprising.

There is a hotel in the town, fishing and water-skiing at nearby Thompson Dam, and attractive mountain walks close by. The mountains are often covered in snow during winter.

Fort Beaufort
On the banks of the Kat River is Fort Beaufort, the centre of a citrus farming area.

The town originated in 1822 as a military stronghold and was named after the Duke of Beaufort, the father of Lord Charles Somerset, governor of the Cape. The fort still stands. On 7 January 1851 it withstood a full-scale assault by Xhosa warriors.

The mess house of the officers of the garrison is used as a museum, packed with guns, military uniforms and badges.

From Fort Beaufort the military road, known as the Queen's Road, crosses the Great Fish River Valley to Grahamstown. This was completed in 1842 and provided the British with quick access to the troubled frontier.

Gonubie
The Gonubie River reaches the sea in a fine lagoon at the holiday resort of Gonubie. The beach is safe for swimming and is backed by gigantic sand dunes. The river is navigable for small boats. Gonubie has an attractively situated caravan park.

The name of the town is derived from the Xhosa word qunube, meaning wild bramble berries.

Hamburg
The coastal resort of Hamburg is much visited by fishermen. Cob, spotted grunter and pignose grunter are caught in the river. Sea anglers frequently catch silver and black steenbras, blackfish, bluefish and blacktail.

The beaches are safe for swimming.

Hogsback
This resort in the heart of the Amatole Mountains is near Fort Mitchell, a border outpost dating from around 1850. Close by is Gaika's Kop, where San diviners once lived. The name Gaika's Kop comes from the renowned Xhosa chief, Ngqika.

The Hogsback Mountain, 1 937 metres high, overlooks a handsome indigenous forest.

There are three hotels here and a caravan park, and a beautiful camping site set in the forest.

Paths have been laid out through the forest, and breathtaking views greet the climber after an easy hike to the top of the peaks.

A rough road leads from Hogsback to the Amatole Basin, where there are many sites connected with the frontier wars, including Fort Cox.

Indwe
At the southern end of the Drakensberg range are the great sandstone cliffs known as Xalanga ('the place of vultures'). Beneath these cliffs lies the small town of Indwe, named from the Xhosa word for the blue crane, the bird emblem of South Africa. The town was founded in 1896 as a coalmining centre, but the mine is no longer worked.

Katberg
The Katberg ('cat mountain'), with its crisp climate and grass-covered hills, is an inland holiday resort popular with walkers and riders. The road from Balfour to the Katberg (1 800 metres) climbs steeply, and there are glorious views. Several of the bridges on the road were built by the British during the Anglo-Boer War.

Kidd's Beach
The small coastal resort of Kidd's Beach lies south-west of East London. The town was named after Charles Kidd, who was mayor of nearby King William's Town in the 1860s. There is a tidal pool and a beach at the mouth of the river. A great variety of fish can be caught along the rocks. Kidd's Beach is safe for bathing. Holiday shacks can be hired at nearby Palm Springs.

King William's Town
In 1835 Sir Benjamin D'Urban, governor of the Cape, founded King William's Town as the military centre for the recently annexed area named after Queen Adelaide, between the Keiskamma and Groot-Kei rivers. After the annexation King William's Town eventually became the capital of British Kaffraria. The old mission station used as Government House at that time is in Reserve Road.

The town was laid out on the site of the mission station, which had been built in 1826. The military reserve, containing barracks, arsenal, parade ground and government offices, was the centre of all activity. From 1850 to 1853 King William's Town was the headquarters for eight regiments of troops, and it was 1861 before the town was given a civil administration. Many troops settled in and around King William's Town after demobilization, including about 2 000 German Legionnaires who had served

The gun on the Martello tower, Fort Beaufort, could be rotated in a full circle.

Roadside tribute to the major who won South Africa's first VC

The hospital at King William's Town dates from the time of the British garrison.

Relics from the Xhosa trade days — a herbalist's shop in King William's Town.

The ruins of Fort Murray, a stronghold on the outskirts of King William's Town.

The imposing building of the original town hall in King William's Town.

with the British in the Crimea, and a further 2 000 families who left Germany in 1858-59.

The town, named in honour of the British king, William IV, remained a British garrison headquarters until 1914.

The Kaffrarian Museum, founded in 1884, contains what is probably the most comprehensive collection of African mammals in the world — more than 30 000 specimens, among which stands Huberta, the famous hippo whose wanderings down the east coast of South Africa in the 1930s made world news (see box), and fascinating displays of birds and lower vertebrates.

An annex to the main building of the museum contains a reconstruction of a trading store. Here are displayed a variety of oddments sold to the Xhosa in the past.

Also in the town is the South Afri-can Missionary Museum, housed in a renovated church. It exhibits pictures, photographs and documents concerned with the history of missions in southern Africa.

A botanical garden lies on the north bank of the Buffalo River.

Bisho, built as the capital for the period of 'independent statehood' of Ciskei, is a modern town to the east of King William's Town, and its amenities include a hotel and casino.

Komga
The name Komga means 'place of clay'. The town lies in a setting of rolling green grassland. It was near Komga, during the Ninth Frontier War of 1877, that Major Hans Garret Moore of the 88th Connaught Rangers won the First Victoria Cross to be awarded on South African soil.

A memorial next to the road, at Draaibosch, marks the site where, on 29 December 1877, he led a patrol against the Gaikas. One of his scouts was surrounded by the enemy. Major Moore rode to his rescue, but the scout was killed. The major escaped with a wounded arm.

Maclear

The town of Maclear, named after Sir Thomas Maclear, official astronomer at the Cape of Good Hope from 1833 to 1879, lies beneath the cliffs of the Drakensberg. This is primarily a sheep farming district, but cheese and other dairy goods are also produced.

From Maclear a gravel road climbs directly over the Drakensberg by means of the highest road pass in South Africa — Naudé's Nek. This pass reaches an altitude of 2 623 metres and is often blocked by snow in winter. Skiing is good on the high slopes. Close to Maclear there is an oddly shaped mountain known as Gatberg ('hole mountain'), so named

Naudé's Nek snakes its tortuous way over the Drakensberg range.

HOW HUBERTA THE WANDERING HIPPO AMBLED INTO THE HEART OF A NATION

No one will ever know just what strange impulse made Huberta the Hippo suddenly leave her muddy lagoon in Zululand and begin the great trek southwards. But the journey she began that day in November 1928 was the start of one of the most delightfully dotty animal adventures of all time.

For the next three years Huberta ambled for 1 600 kilometres through South Africa. She crossed roads and railways, trampled over golf courses, munched her way through fields and gardens, popped up in cities and towns. At every twist and turn of her route she attracted an ever-growing following of pressmen, photographers and big game hunters, and the interest of thousands of ordinary people.

Within a few days of the start of her travels, rumours spread that there was a hippo wandering down the Natal coast. On 22 November a party of sugar estate workers found Huberta having a snack in sugar cane fields. The story appeared in papers all over South Africa the next day and this was when Huberta first got her name. In fact the papers got it wrong: they called her Hubert the Hippo, because at that time no one realized Huberta was really a lady. Meanwhile, she had taken refuge in a pool close to the north coast railway. Bus operators began offering trips to view her. Passing trains slowed down, the drivers giving Huberta a whistle and passengers throwing fruit.

Huberta seemed to have wandered into the good life and she began to grow fat.

But she was being lulled into a false sense of security. Johannesburg Zoo had a female hippo pining for a companion. An expedition, accompanied by a newsreel camera crew, was mounted to catch Huberta.

She made a run for it, barging southwards from one river to another with the zoo men, camera crew and press corps in hot pursuit. Reports came in of hunters falling into mud holes and intrepid cameramen being chased up trees.

The public began to love the adventurous hippo and Huberta became a national heroine. The Natal Provincial Council proclaimed her royal game and the zoo men were ordered to leave her alone.

One night a truck driver found her fast asleep in the middle of a bridge 7 kilometres from Durban. He gently nudged her with his bumper and Huberta charged off down the road.

She spent the night in the bush, but next day the citizens of Durban were all agog. It was the holiday season. Was Huberta coming to join in the fun?

The hippo reached the lagoon at the mouth of the Mlanga River and remained there throughout the season, feeding on sugar cane and the gifts of visitors, frolicking in the waves, wandering along the beach and delighting vast crowds.

Early in March Huberta was on the move again. One morning her gigantic footprints were found on the greens of the Beechwood golf course.

A few days later, hippo tracks were seen on a new housing estate. Rumour spread that Huberta was looking for a house but was unable to find one with a sufficiently large bathroom.

After a brief stop in the reservoir at Pinetown, Huberta pulled off her most sensational exploit to date — she gate-crashed a party at the Durban Country Club. In the early hours of April Fool's Day 1929 she crept unnoticed past the cars of courting couples in the grounds and suddenly appeared amid the revellers on the verandah of the club. In the ensuing confusion she charged off across the golf course, pushed down a few fences and walked into the city.

A policeman found her in the doorway of a chemist's shop in West Street. By dawn a big crowd had gathered to watch as Huberta lumbered through the centre of the city on her way back to the comparative peace of the Mgeni River.

Huberta now travelled down the holiday coast of Natal and was feted and pampered wherever she appeared. At Anerley, the Indian population deified her. Drums were beaten, incense burned, and a goat was sacrificed in her honour.

The Zulus were convinced she had some connection with their chief Shaka, because she spent so much time in sacred Zulu pools. When she reached the Wild Coast the Pondo people overlooked the fact that she was devouring their crops because they believed she was a reincarnation of a legendary diviner.

In March 1931 Huberta had reached East London and was spotted sleeping on the main railway line. An engine driver, failing to wake her with his whistle, edged the train forward and gently shoved her off the track.

But while South Africans were still applauding her sheer audacity, Huberta's luck finally ran out. In April 1931 three hunters shot her as she was bathing in the Keiskamma River. She ended her marathon journey floating lifelessly downstream. There was a national outcry and her killers were tracked down. They pleaded ignorance about the animal and were fined R25 each for destroying royal game. Experts from the Kaffrarian Museum, King William's Town, recovered Huberta from the river. The body of the hippo who walked into the hearts of countless South Africans today occupies pride of place in the museum.

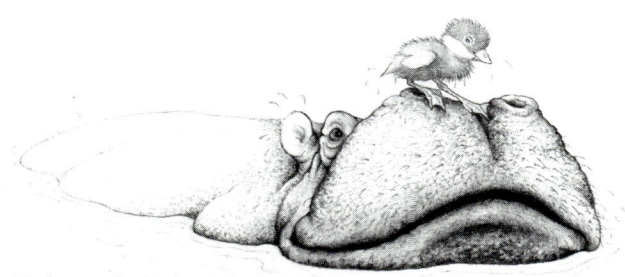

Huberta, the hippo that went on a three-year ramble, and friend.

The old fort that withstood a siege by 9000 warriors

because of a large hole through the centre of the peak.

Morgan's Bay
This is one of the most charming of the attractive coastal resorts north of East London. It lies on the south bank of the Ntshala River, and has a pretty lagoon and a fine beach.

Morgan's Bay is named after A. F. Morgan, master of the Royal Navy survey ship *Barracouta*, which surveyed the area in 1822. It is a favourite haunt of shell-collectors.

Peddie
In 1835 a star-shaped fort was built to protect the 1 600 members of the Fingo people, refugees from the area now comprising the Transkei who were allies of the Europeans in the wars with the Xhosa. The fort was named after Colonel John Peddie of the Seaforth Highlanders. In 1846 it withstood a siege by 9 000 warriors.

A town grew around the fort. Peddie today is a trading and administrative centre and serves an area which is famous for its pineapples.

In 1836 the Reverend John Ayliff was responsible for the resettlement of the Fingo into the colony from 'the country beyond the Kei', and a bronze plaque has been erected under a large

milkwood tree in Peddie by the Monuments Commission recording the Fingo's declaration of loyalty to 'God and the King'. Fingo people congregate around the old milkwood tree on 14 May every year for a remembrance service.

Queenstown
The principal town in the eastern Cape midlands, Queenstown was founded in 1853 and named in honour of Queen Victoria. A condition of its establishment was that its inhabitants had to be responsible for its defence against the hostile peoples in the area.

The town was laid out around a hexagonal centre. From this point the defenders could direct fire down the six radiating thoroughfares. It was not necessary to use the fort, and nowadays the Hexagon, with its coloured fountain and lovely gardens, is an unusual town centre.

Queenstown, built on the banks of the Komani River, is a busy communications, railway, farming and educational centre. It has a dry and bracing climate.

The trunk road from East London enters the town through a sunken garden, named after Walter Everitt, a former park superintendent who was mainly responsible for the development of the Queenstown municipal gardens. Numerous birds frequent these gardens. Queenstown is famed for its beautiful roses.

A nature reserve on the slopes of Madeira Mountain has a scenic drive yielding superb views of the area. Many game animals have free range in this reserve, and it is also noted for its aloes, cycads and various acacia species. The tamboekie thorn, *Erythrina acanthocarpa*, is found only in this district. It grows in dense patches, giving masses of bright red and yellow flowers in October and November before the leaves are produced.

The Queenstown and Frontier Museum in Shepstone Street and the Art Gallery in Ebden Street are both well worth a visit.

Seymour
Beneath the slopes of the Katberg and Elandsberg ranges, a military stronghold was built in 1853 known

Circular homes of the Xhosa people dot the rolling Border hills.

THE SOLUTION TO A PRICKLY PROBLEM

The prickly pear was introduced into South Africa from central America in the early 18th century — and found its new country much to its liking.

With no natural enemies, it rapidly covered vast areas of grazing land and threatened man with an ever-encroaching jungle of thorns.

Mechanical attempts to tackle the problem proved ineffective. The prickly pear is so prolific that if even a fragment of leaf is left in the ground during a clearing operation it will quickly take root and sprout anew. Clearly some kind of biological warfare was needed to fight the prickly pear's advance.

The spread of some cactus plants had been restricted in the early 1900s by encouraging their infestation by various insects, but none of these insects found the prickly pear sufficiently appetizing. In 1932 the prickly pear moth, *Cactoblastis cactorum*, was introduced from Argentina. Although it held back the spread of prickly pears in Australia, it was unable to cope with the larger plants of South Africa.

The successful weapon, intro-

A cochineal-infected prickly pear.

duced six years later, was the humble cochineal, *Dactylopius opuntiae*, an insect related to the *Dactylopius coccus*, the vivid red body fluid of which was used for colouring foods and textiles before the discovery of artificial dyes. The female cochineal inserts her proboscis into the cactus, feeds on the plant, and over a period of months, weakens it. If the weakened cactus is felled at this stage it dies.

Of the 725 000 hectares of land in the Karoo and the eastern Cape once infested by prickly pears, only a small area, around Uitenhage, remains so today.

Simple lines of the Lutheran Evangelical Church, Stutterheim.

Fort Peddie, built in 1841 on the site of an earlier earth stronghold.

as Elands Post. In this handsome setting a village grew. In due course the village was renamed Seymour, after Col. Charles Seymour, military secretary to Governor Cathcart. The village lies close to the Kat River Dam and is an agricultural centre and terminus of a branch railway from Fort Beaufort.

Stutterheim

In 1837 soldiers disbanded from the British German Legion which had fought during the Sixth Frontier War (1835) settled on the forest-covered slopes of the Kologha Mountains. They founded a town which they named after their commander, General Richard von Stutterheim. Today the town is a prosperous and busy centre for forestry, citrus fruit, sheep, dairy and beef production.

The Kabousie River is popular for boating, fishing and swimming. Wild flowers are numerous.

Six kilometres to the south of the town is a turn-off to the grave of San-dile, warrior chief of the Gaikas, who was killed in June 1878 in the Ninth Frontier War. North of the town is the Bethel Mission, built in 1865 on the site of the first Berlin mission station in the eastern Cape.

Tarkastad

A centre for sheep farming, and the terminus of the branch railway to Queenstown, Tarkastad lies to the north of the Winterberge range. The name Tarkastad comes from the Xhosa language, and means an area of many birds.

Ugie

Beneath the cliffs of the southern Drakensberg, on the banks of the Inxu River, lies Ugie, founded in 1863 by the Reverend William Murray and named after the Ugie River in Scotland. The town is a centre for sheep and cattle farming. Here too is the M. T. R. Smit Children's Haven, the largest children's home in the Cape.

Morgan's Bay on the coast north of East London offers all the ingredients for a pleasant seaside holiday — a fine beach, warm water and a good river for boating.

NAMAQUALAND'S SPRING GLORY

NAMAQUALAND, ON FIRST impressions, is a harsh, relentless, arid wilderness. Surface water is almost non-existent and subterranean water is brackish and hard to find. Namaqualand's few inhabitants are burned and dehydrated by sun and scorching winds. But far from loathing this territory, they have an intense affection for it. The poverty of the surface is richly compensated for by many mineral treasures. Copper, diamonds, gem stones, gypsum and sillimanite are all mined in the area. The rocky, salty, sun-baked soil, which a human gardener would scorn or lavish fortunes on in the course of fertilizing, has been casually gifted by nature with the greatest and most prolific flower garden in the world.

The contradictions of Namaqualand are part of its fascination. The trunk-road route offers many scenes and novelties. The tarred road has the finest of departures from Cape Town. The classic frontal view of Table Mountain, with the city and Table Bay at its foot, dominates the beginning of the highway and is visible from 75 kilometres away. At night the sparkling lights of the city and the shipping in the harbour provide a glorious scene.

For the first 160 kilometres of the journey, the road leads through the principal wheatlands of South Africa, the country's breadbasket. In the winter months this area (known as the Swartland, or black land, from the colour of the soil) is a green sea of wheat; in spring it turns golden.

Beyond the wheatlands there is a profound scenic change. The road climbs the Olifants River mountains and then descends into the magnificent river valley. The alluvial floor is covered with groves of citrus trees. Along the road are wayside stalls where some of the finest and sweetest of all oranges can be bought. The road leads down the valley to the west of the river. To the east is the Cedarberg range, the first wilderness area proclaimed in South Africa.

Passing the great dam of the Olifants River and the irrigated farms of Klawer and Vredendal, the road enters Namaqualand proper. Here the spring flowers make a most beautiful botanical spectacle, provided that just enough rain has fallen in the winter, and the searing desert winds do not blow until after the flowers bloom.

The road continues northwards across a seemingly endless plain. Then it enters an area of granite, richly mineralized and covered with vast domes and whalebacks of rock. The hot and arid landscape is prodigious in its expanse and strength. Such a granite landscape, flooded with sunshine, less than half-tamed by man, is awesome in the age and mystery of its primitive geological origin.

Beyond the granite mountains, the legendary copper mountains of the Nama people, the road crosses a great plain. To the west, the Namib Desert lies along the coast, the Skeleton Coast of diamonds and shipwrecks, where the cold water of the Benguela Current washes an oven-hot shore and clammy mists blanket the land. Rain seldom falls. From the plain, the road descends through a wilderness where date palms grow and gem-stones lie on the ground. At the bottom of this valley the Orange River flows, a moody, enigmatic river of the wilderness, its banks lined with strips of irrigated farmlands. Palm trees, oranges, dates, figs and pomegranates flourish in a setting of scorched, vividly coloured cliffs.

Spring in Namaqualand . . . the arid landscape, through some whim of nature, is transformed into a vast garden. Within weeks all will again be wilderness.

Namaqualand daisies, with a blister beetle hunting for food in a setting of gold.

THINGS TO DO AND SEE

Angling The Olifants River, below the dam wall at Clanwilliam, is probably the best water in southern Africa for smallmouth bass. There are also many yellowfish. Largemouth bass are caught in the Clanwilliam Dam.

Boating The Clanwilliam Dam offers splendid opportunities for boating. The dam is used by yachts and power-boats, while the river has stretches for canoeists.

Camping and caravanning The Cedarberg has a caravan park at the forestry station of Algeria. Citrusdal has a caravan park on the banks of the Olifants River. There are camping grounds, rooms and bungalows at Sanddrif and Krom River.

Flowers Each spring thousands of people travel to Namaqualand to see the flowers. There is no way of predicting whether a season will be good or bad. In a bad year there are few flowers; a good year sees hundreds of kilometres completely covered in flowers. Everything depends on a delicate balance of winter rain and absence of hot winds.

Hiking and climbing The Cedarberg is a wilderness area. Permits to explore the range must be obtained from the forestry station at Algeria. There are no roads, but footpaths lead to all parts of the range.

Swimming In the Cedarberg most of the streams have pools ideal for swimming. There are large natural pools in the camps at Algeria and Sanddrif. The Olifants River offers swimming throughout its course.

Alexander Bay

The world's richest deposits of alluvial diamonds are in the area around Alexander Bay, and part of it is closed to the public to prevent unofficial prospecting. But it was copper, not diamonds, that first put the bay on the map. James Alexander, the man who founded the copper industry of Namaqualand, floated ore down the Orange River in barges and transferred it to ships in the bay at the mouth of the river. This system was used until the narrow-gauge railway to Port Nolloth was opened in 1876. Alexander Bay fell into disuse until 1926, when diamonds were discovered here.

The finds were so rich that within a year the government had taken over the diggings and closed off the whole stretch of the coast to Port Nolloth to prevent the market being flooded. In 1928 diamond-hungry prospectors threatened an armed uprising, but strong police forces guarding the area persuaded the mob to break up.

The diamond mining town of Oranjemund has now grown up on the northern bank of the Orange River, just over the border in Namibia. The town, which is in an area closed to the public because of the diamond workings, is a marvel of self-sufficiency, growing its own fruit and vegetables and also producing it's own fresh water by evaporation from the sea.

Bitterfontein

The railway from Cape Town to Namaqualand comes to a sudden

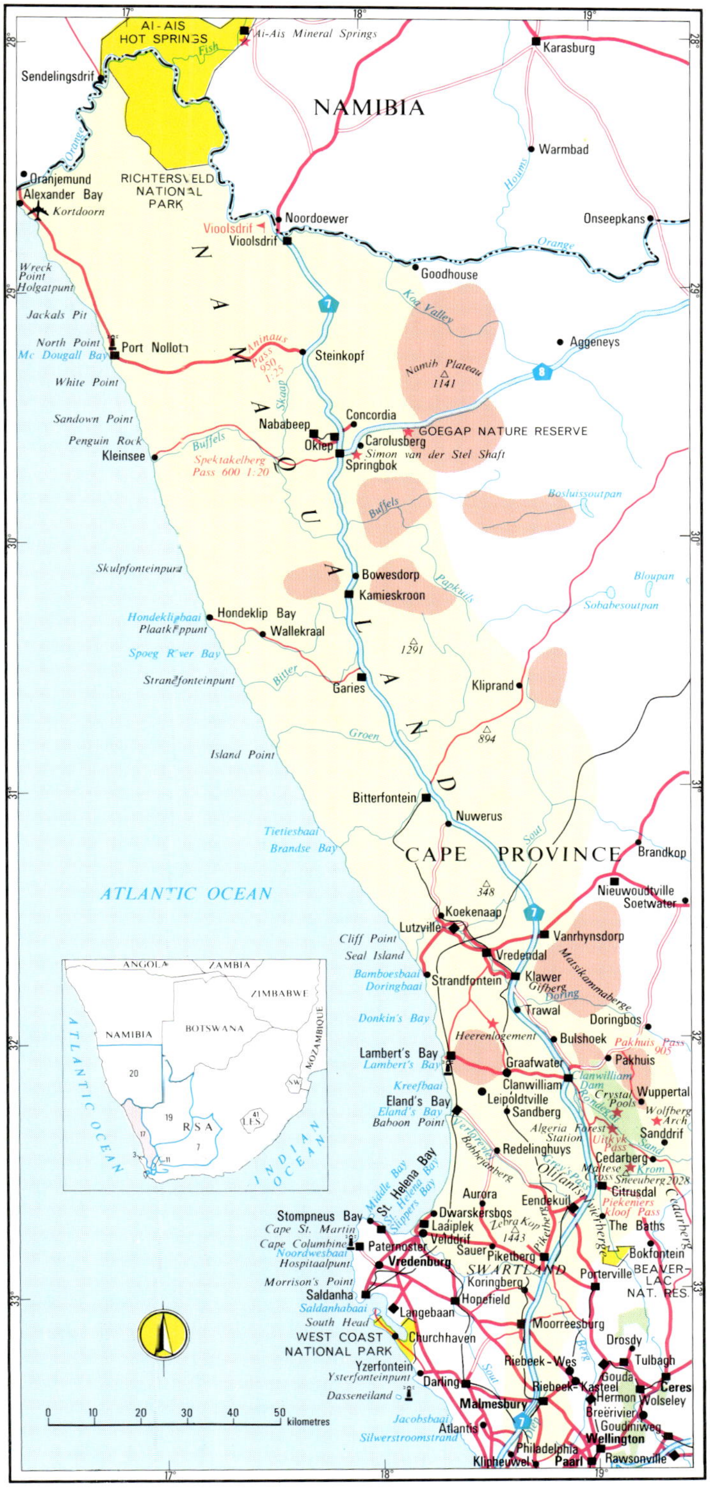

The forlorn little ghost town that had no room to grow

An orange tree in full bearing in the fertile valley of the Olifants River.

and rather disconcerting end at a bleak little railhead called Bitterfontein, from the taste of the water in a nearby spring.

In 1931 Bitterfontein was the scene of one of the world's great diamond robberies, when R140 000 worth of diamonds vanished without trace from a mailbag.

Bowesdorp

Looking at the forlorn little ghost town of Bowesdorp today it is hard to believe that it was once a thriving community. The first church in Namaqualand was built here by the Dutch Reformed Church in 1864 and a hamlet grew up around it. But the valley in which it stands is so narrow that further expansion was impossible, so in 1924 the church, school, police station, traders and residents were all moved to the new town of Kamieskroon. Bowesdorp was left to fall into ruins.

Citrusdal

From May to July, the air in Citrusdal is heavy with the perfume of freshly picked oranges and other fruit making their way down the conveyor belts of the packing stations. This warm, pleasant town is the main handling and despatch centre for the vast citrus farms of the Olifants River Valley.

About two million cases of fruit leave the packing stations of Citrusdal each year. The packing is done by hand and the faster the girls work the more they earn.

The record is 204 000 oranges packed by one girl in a 46-hour week.

There is a hotel and a caravan park among the trees on the banks of the river. Good local wine can be bought in the town, particularly the red and white jeripigos and the sweet muscadels. The surrounding countryside has been cultivated for a long time, with at least one farm dating back to 1725.

Clanwilliam

A delicately flavoured herbal brew known as rooibos tea is exported from Clanwilliam to all parts of the world. The town stands in a warm, well-watered and very fertile valley where the rooibos, or red bush, grows wild. The tea is free of tannin and rich in vitamin C. Its health-giving properties were first popularized by local resident, Dr. P. le Fras Nortier. The local library, which includes paintings by Hugo Naudé and other artists among its collection, is named after Dr. Nortier and his great friend, the poet Dr. Louis Leipoldt.

The valley produces a wide variety of sub-tropical and other fruits, as well as vegetables, wheat and tobacco.

Clanwilliam has two hotels and a caravan park. There is a wild flower reserve at Ramskop on the outskirts of the town and a recreation area nearby on the shores of the Clanwilliam Dam.

Eland's Bay

For surfing enthusiasts, Eland's Bay is a place of pilgrimage. The majestic, fast-moving waves that roll into the bay in summer when the south-easter blows are world-famous. Surfers can work into the sea from a headland to catch the waves early and enjoy long rides.

The high cliffs of the Bobbejaanberg project into the sea at Baboon Point on the south side of the bay. In these cliffs is a large rock shelter with walls decorated with primitive San paintings, mostly crude outlines of hands and various strange shapes. The floor is a vast midden of prehistoric litter.

Garies

Rugged granite mountains frame the odd, lonely little village of Garies, with its one straggling street lined with

---

HARD-WON TREASURE OF THE COPPER MOUNTAIN

The first settlers at the Cape were lured northwards by tales of a mountain where pure copper lay on the ground. In 1681 a party of Nama people visited Cape Town Castle to trade. With them they brought pure copper, and Governor Simon van der Stel saw this as proof of the tales that had been carried to the Dutch by other Khoikhoi informants.

Several expeditions had already been sent out, each one penetrating further northwards. In 1685 Van der Stel led a major expedition and reached the fabled mountains. There was no copper on the surface, but the rocks were stained with the green-blue of malachite and three shafts sunk by Van der Stel's miners revealed a vast lode of rich copper ore.

For nearly 200 years nothing was done about the discovery. The 'copper mountain' was in the centre of Namaqualand, remote and difficult to reach. Mining operations had to wait until the 19th century.

The Scottish explorer James (later Sir James) Alexander was the first to investigate Van der Stel's discovery. In 1852 he re-tested the old prospecting shafts, found several other copper outcrops and started mining. Fortune-hunters rushed to the area. Many newly formed mining companies collapsed because of transport difficulties, but one of the two that survived, at Okiep, was ranked as the richest copper mine in the world.

The first miners were mostly Cornishmen. The ruins of their buildings, the stone work of the culverts and bridges of the narrow-gauge railway built to convey the ore to the sea at Port Nolloth remain as examples of their workmanship.

The narrow-gauge railway was opened in 1876 and worked for 68 years carrying copper to Port Nolloth and bringing back stores. In the beginning mules and horses pulled the carriages, then steam locomotives were introduced and the last of these, the *Clara*, today stands on a pedestal at Nababeep. Nowadays the blister copper is transported in trucks to the railhead at Bitterfontein.

There are major mines at Carolusberg and Spektakel, together capable of producing 7 000 tons of ore a day, and several smaller workings. At night white-hot waste slag pours down the sides of the dumps like a stream of lava.

Van der Stel's original shafts can still be seen. There are also remnants of the early mining days — smokestacks, pumps and abandoned railway stations. A collection of mining memorabilia is housed in the Peter Philip Museum at Nababeep.

The disused ore-handling plant at the Okiep mine and relics of early mining.

FANTASY-WORLD OF TOWERING ROCKS ON THE WILD TRAILS OF THE CEDARBERG RANGE

The Cedarberg range, some 100 kilometres long, is a gigantic mass of sandstone, richly coloured by iron oxides and eroded into a variety of strange shapes.

These weird rock formations give the range its most remarkable distinction, but added to this is a rich plant life, including such rarities as the snow protea, which flowers only above the snow line, and the Cedarberg, or rocket, pincushion.

The cedar trees which give the range its name are of the *Widdringtonia cedarbergensis* species. They grow at an altitude of 1 000 metres to 1 500 metres and some specimens are believed to live for 1 000 years.

The centre of the Cedarberg is the forestry station of Algeria, superbly situated in the deep valley of the Rondegat River. Above it looms the 1 513-metre Middelberg ridge.

From the forestry station a path climbs to the top of the ridge, passing close to a fine waterfall and reaching the summit through a forest of cedar trees. On the summit there are two huts. From here paths lead into the heart of the mountains, to such places as Crystal Pools, Sneeuberg, Langberg, Tafelberg and many other beautiful spots.

There are huts and caves throughout the range.

A reasonably detailed tour of the Cedarberg takes about two weeks. Pack donkeys and guides may be

A cedar tree, safe from bush fire, gnarled and weather-beaten.

The Cedarberg's Maltese Cross.

hired through the forester at Algeria, but there is scope for shorter walks and climbs.

Apart from Algeria, with its caravan park, camping ground and swimming pool in the river, there are privately run camps on the banks of the Sand River — at Sanddrif — and the Krom River. A path leads to the summit ridge, penetrating on the way the extraordinary Wolfberg cracks and eventually reaching the Wolfberg Arch. This is a strenuous day-long outing.

Another fine walk from Sanddrif is to the remarkable 10-metre-tall rock formation known as the Maltese Cross. This is also a day trip and it can be extended as far as the hut on the slopes of the Sneeuberg (2 028 metres), the highest peak in the range.

Near the southern end of the range is the extraordinary Stadsaal, or 'town hall' — a mass of rock honeycombed with chambers, caves,

crevices and passages. There are San paintings in some of the shelters.

Every month the Cedarberg puts on a new face and hikers walk its trails throughout the year.

Winter has its rain and snow but the crisp air is ideal for climbing; spring brings a mass of flowers of phenomenal variety; summer is warm for climbing but fine for walking; autumn is warm by day and cool at night, with the pools still comfortable for swimming.

The trail to Crystal Pools is an enchanting walk through the Cedarberg.

High on the route to the Wolfberg Arch . . . a distant view to the south-east.

The road to Stadsaal . . . a drive to a weirdly beautiful world of rocks and caves.

The twisting course of the Jan Dissels River, near its source in the Cedarberg.

The health spring around which a town bubbled to life

trading stations, two hotels and a few houses. The name derives from the Khoikhoi word 'xharies', the name of a grass which grows in the valley.

Graafwater
The railway at Graafwater is a despatch point for the agriculture of Clanwilliam and the seafood products of Lambert's Bay.

A road leads north to Vredendal and after 23 kilometres reaches a remarkable rock shelter known as the Heerenlogement, or 'gentleman's lodging'. Scores of travellers who in former times broke their journey at the shelter have used the walls as a kind of visitors' book. Kaje Jesse Slotsbo inscribed his name here in 1712 while en route with an expedition against the Namaqua Khoikhoi.

Cape Governor Hendrik Swellengrebel, who passed this way on an expedition in 1737, later wrote an account of the shelter, in which he mentioned the wild fig tree growing from a cleft at the back of the cave. This ancient tree is still here today and the cave is now a historical monument.

Hondeklip Bay
In former years Hondeklip Bay was used for the shipment of copper ore. Today it is a fishing centre with a factory for processing the catches, which include large numbers of rock lobster. A rock shaped like a dog gives Hondeklip ('dog stone') its name.

Kamieskroon
A huge complex of granite mountains, known to the Nama Khoikhoi as the Thamies, meaning 'a jumble', surrounds the little village of Kamieskroon. It is overlooked by a peak with a cleft in its summit known as the 'crown' of the Thamies Mountains and from which, with a little juggling, the village gets its name.

Koringberg
Looming up out of an ocean of wheat is the high hill known as Koringberg, or 'mountain of wheat', and the name is also applied to the little railway town at its foot from which the golden harvest is despatched.

Lambert's Bay
A large fishing fleet has its base in Lambert's Bay. Rock lobsters are caught here and there are two fish processing plants. The harbour is sheltered by a rocky islet known as Bird Island, which yields more than 300 tons of guano a year. In winter, gannets, cormorants and penguins nest on the island, which is linked to the mainland by a causeway.

Malmesbury
The largest town in the wheat country of the Swartland, Malmesbury began as a small collection of houses built around a tepid sulphur-chlorine spring in the middle of the 18th century. For some time there was a vogue for the waters and a small sanatorium was built. The British governor, Sir Lowry Cole, visited the spa in 1829 and named it Malmesbury after his father-in-law, the Earl of Malmesbury. Today the spring runs to waste, but Malmesbury has become a very important grain distributing centre and is known for its wine.

It lies in the valley of the Diep River and is so awkwardly situated that trains have to back out before being switched on to the northern continuation of the railway.

The early pioneers called this area the Swartland ('black country') because of the rich deep colour of the soil. The local Afrikaans dialect has a characteristic guttural 'r' not found elsewhere. General Jan Smuts, who was born in the district, spoke with a distinct Malmesbury accent.

Moorreesburg
Much of South Africa's bread comes from the wheat fields surrounding Moorreesburg. It is worth paying a visit to the museum, devoted to the history of the cultivation of wheat. On the outskirts is the Langgewens experimental farm, where the government sponsors research into wheat farming. It may be visited by appointment.

Nababeep
The largest of Namaqualand's copper mining towns. It was established on the site of a spring known to the original Nama people as Nababeep, meaning 'the water behind the little hill'.

Visitors can be taken on a guided tour through the mine's mill and smelter. *Clara,* a locomotive once used on the railway to Port Nolloth, now stands in front of the town's museum. The museum houses a photographic display of the old mining days.

A visit to one of the copper-smelting plants at night provides some spectacular sights. The waste slag, molten and tremendously hot, is trammed to the top of dumps and poured down the slopes like a river of fire. This is simply the end of a complex process of milling and smelting. In the mills the ore is finely ground and is subsequently converted into a damp concentrate. This is taken to the smelter plant where it is reduced to a molten matte.

THE GOLDEN OCEAN OF THE WHEAT LANDS

The wheat lands near Malmesbury, where the dark soil produces luxuriant crops.

The cereal plant that provides western man with his staple food derives its modern English name from the old Teutonic word, hwait, meaning white.

Wherever western man has gone, there he has taken wheat, and it was certainly the first crop to be planted by Jan van Riebeeck when he landed at the Cape.

The winter rainfall areas of the western and southern Cape were well suited to wheat cultivation, and Moorreesburg became the centre for great golden harvests. The town has a museum devoted to the history of wheat cultivation.

The principal wheat cultivars, or strains, in South Africa are the varieties known as T4, Inia and Zambezi II and their derivatives. They were introduced to South Africa in the 1960s when the Rockefeller Foundation wheat research programme, based in Mexico, released different varieties of the revolutionary short-straw breeds.

The new breeds transformed wheat production all over the world.

They were easier to cultivate, hardy, with shorter stalks and more responsive to fertilizers.

The South African Department of Agricultural Technical Services and various private breeders have produced additional cultivars.

Although wheat is basically a winter-rainfall crop, new techniques of moisture conservation have allowed large-scale production in the summer-rainfall area of the Orange Free State, helping to make South Africa self-sufficient in wheat, with a substantial surplus for export.

Wheat is planted in late autumn and spring. Soon the fields are vast green seas, swaying in the wind as though a heavy ocean swell were sweeping across the countryside.

During the spring they turn to gold and soon the combine-harvesters are busy working backwards and forwards, reaping the crop.

The tall grain elevators at the railway despatch centres seem to swell visibly as long queues of heavy trucks and tractor-trailers bring in the harvest from the fields.

After treatment to remove unwanted sulphur and iron, the molten copper, which is 99 per cent pure, is poured into moulds and then cooled into the bars which are the finished product of the mine.

Olifants River

The river where, in 1660, the first European explorers from the Cape, led by Jan Danckert, came across a great herd of elephants, is today of major importance to the economy of South Africa. From its source in the mountains near Ceres, the Olifants ('elephants') River flows through a narrow, rocky ravine, then enters a broad alluvial valley where fine farms produce citrus fruit.

Above the town of Clanwilliam, the Olifants is harnessed by a dam, built in 1935 and expanded in 1968, which irrigates 12 140 hectares of farmland. The dam also provides an excellent stretch of water for boating, water-skiing, swimming and fishing. Below the dam the river continues northwards, with fine rapids for canoeists. Then it curves west and, where it reaches the sea, helps to hold back the sands of the Namib Desert.

Okiep

The spring known to the Nama people as U-gieb, or 'the great brackish fountain', became the site of a large copper mine. Europeans have corrupted the original name to Okiep. There are several relics of early Cornish-style buildings, including a smokestack and an ancient pump.

Pakhuis Pass

The direct road from Clanwilliam to Calvinia climbs over the mountains by means of the Pakhuis Pass (905 metres). This is a region of strange rock formations and near the summit is a rock shelter with walls decorated by San paintings. The poet Dr. Louis Leipoldt, who often visited this spot before his death in 1947, has his grave here. There is a picnic ground, with scenic walks into the rock wilderness on either side of the road.

Piekenierskloof Pass

The trunk road climbs the Olifants River mountains by means of the

Piekenierskloof Pass, whose summit, 518 metres above sea level, looks out over the wheat country and the Piketberg range in the west.

This was the route used by the first Europeans to explore the area. It was also the way that Governor Simon van der Stel came in 1685 with a large party of soldiers and wagons in search

In Lambert's Bay, the fishing trawlers are at rest.

of Namaqualand's copper.

The name of the pass comes from a squad of pikemen who pursued Khoikhoi rustlers through the cleft in the mountains in 1675. The present road was completed in 1978.

Piketberg

The mountains piled up behind the

Nababeep, largest of Namaqualand's copper towns.

wheat centre of Piketberg were a great stronghold of the San people, and many of the caves contain examples of their art. Khoikhoi herdsmen also used the mountains as hideaways for rustled cattle and it was because of this that a small military outpost, or picket, was established at the foot of the range in the 1670s.

A grasshopper of Namaqualand, perfectly camouflaged.

The mission station of Goedverwag, in the Piketberg.

Where diamond hunters brave desert winds to reap a fortune

Hondeklip Bay, with crayfish boats beached for overhaul during the off-season. A rock shaped like a dog gives Hondeklip ('dog stone') its name.

Kokerbooms among the copper mountains of the Hester Malan reserve.

From Piketberg a 22-kilometre road leads to the summit via the spectacular Versveld Pass. It was privately built by a farmer, who included three great loops in the route to provide easier gradients for ox-wagons, and these give the road a curious corkscrew effect. Excellent apples are grown in the mountains, as well as a herb known as buchu, which is exported for the making of medicines. The range is dominated by the 1 443-metre Zebra Kop.

Port Nolloth

Sea mists and occasional desert winds sometimes make Port Nolloth an inhospitable place, but it is a centre for the alluvial diamond mining operations along the coast.

In 1854 Captain M. S. Nolloth, a surveyor of the Royal Navy, picked on this place, then known as Robbebaai ('seal bay'), for development as a port for the Namaqualand copper mines. A harbour for small vessels was established behind the reef and a narrow-gauge railway was built to the mines in the interior. The whole transport operation was difficult. Only small coasters could work their way in behind the reef; rainfall is practically non-existent so there was an acute shortage of water both for drinking and for the locomotives; and shipping in coal to fuel the ore trains was expensive.

But for 68 years Port Nolloth re-mained the principal outlet for copper ore, until 1942, when a road was built from the mines to the main railhead at Bitterfontein. By then, however, Port Nolloth had already branched out and as well as being a hub of the diamond industry it is now a major fishing centre.

There are chalets to rent and also a caravan park at nearby McDougall Bay.

Richtersveld

Named after a German missionary, the Reverend W. Richter, this is the only true mountain desert in South Africa.

With a rainfall of 5 mm to 200 mm a year and a temperature ranging from 0 °C to 52 °C, it is the home for only the hardiest of life forms. Such life forms have a very special interest.

The isolation and extremely harsh conditions create an environment in which there are numerous opportunities for research into adaptation techniques, with flora (notably succulents), fauna, and especially insects and reptiles, harmonising their lifestyles with different habitats — each with slight variations in conditions.

The Richtersveld National Park, 162 445 ha in extent, was proclaimed on 16 August 1991.

Springbok

Baked by a relentless sun and surrounded by high, granite mountains,

RIDDLE OF THE DIAMONDS OF THE DESERT COAST

One of the great mysteries of southern Africa is the presence of a huge deposit of alluvial diamonds on the coast of Namaqualand and Namibia. The deposit was discovered in June 1926 by Captain Jack Carstens, an officer in the Indian Army who was spending his leave visiting his father, a trader in the fishing village of Port Nolloth.

His finds started a tremendous diamond rush, but the prospectors faced great hardships. This part of the coast is not exactly considered to be a holiday area. Sand, scorching heat and the complete absence of surface water except where the Orange River reaches the sea, made prospecting an arduous venture.

In spite of the difficulties, fantastic finds were made. The renowned geologist Hans Merensky picked up 487 diamonds from under one flat stone and recovered 2 762 diamonds in the single month of September 1926 in the Alexander Bay area.

Merensky and other geologists soon observed a baffling fact. The diamonds were invariably found in beds of gravel mixed with the fossilized shells of an extinct warm-water oyster known as *Ostrea prismatica*. Diamonds and oysters have no connection, but some geological change must have occurred that killed the oysters — possibly by altering the temperature of the sea — and produced diamonds.

Where the diamonds came from remains a mystery. For long it was thought they had been washed down the Orange River, but prospectors who searched the bed of the river

Captain Jack Carstens, who discovered Namaqualand's diamonds.

for the mother lode found nothing.

On 22 February 1927, only a few months after the first discovery, the government was forced to step in. They secured vast areas where the public is forbidden and mining operations are controlled so as not to flood the market.

Port Nolloth was jammed with prospectors who threatened to seize the field by storm. Massive police reinforcements were sent in to quell the rebellion.

Today diamonds worth between R6 million and R10 million are recovered from the area each year.

Springbok is a nostalgic little place, rather like a setting for a Western film. Herds of springbok once drank at a spring here, but that was before the copper mines were opened up. Today Springbok is the commercial and administrative centre for the mining area and is regarded as the capital of Namaqualand.

Nearby is the Hester Malan Nature Reserve, with springbok, gemsbok and other desert creatures. Despite the aridity here, many wild flowers grow in the spring, transforming the veld into a blaze of colour.

There are several reminders of the early days of the copper boom in the area, including Governor Simon van der Stel's original prospecting shaft, sunk in 1685, and an old smokestack, built by Cornish miners, where copper was first smelted in 1886.

The Baths

People suffering from rheumatism and similar ailments have long been recommended to try the supposedly radioactive waters of a hot spring that bubbles to the surface in a thickly wooded valley of a tributary of the Olifants River near Citrusdal. Testimonials to the benefits of the water, some dating back to the 18th century, are inscribed on the rocks.

Within easy reach are a swimming pool, private baths, sleeping accommodation and a restaurant.

Vanrhynsdorp

A convenient centre for trips to see the wild flowers of Namaqualand is the sun-baked town of Vanrhynsdorp. Roads lead to the Matsikamma Mountains, the Gifberg, and Vredendal, all famous for their flowers.

Vioolsdrif

The trunk road reaches the border of Namibia at a fording place on the Orange River called Vioolsdrif. There is a bridge over the river and a line of tall cliffs with brilliantly coloured rock, called Vioolsdrif Stone, which is often used in building. The valley is extremely hot, but irrigation from the Orange River allows lucerne, citrus fruit, dates and other crops to be cultivated.

Vredendal

Vineyards and orchards surround the thoroughly modern little town of Vredendal — the name means 'valley of peace'. The area is famous for its spring flowers.

Wuppertal

The Rhenish mission station of Wuppertal is an attractive cluster of black-thatched cottages, with a church and a parsonage. Tobacco and rooibos are grown in the area and a specialized local industry is the manufacture of the tough, comfortable walking shoes known as 'velskoene'.

A Nama hut, made of sacking, near Steinkopf. No rain to worry about, only heat.

A clay oven at Komaggas, used by the Nama people for cooking and baking.

THE SUN-DRENCHED DIAMOND WAY

THE CAPE TO CAIRO road, the great north road of Africa, has an interesting division in the centre of the Karoo, at the landmark of the Three Sisters. Here the road forks. To the north-east, the road continues on the Golden Way, across the Orange Free State with its maize lands and gold fields, and on to the Witwatersrand and across the Transvaal. The other branch of the fork is known as the Diamond Way. This leads north on a romantic journey through Hopetown, Kimberley, Bloemhof and Christiana, and sends branches off to such famous diamond fields as Lichtenburg. At Johannesburg, this road rejoins the Cape to Cairo road.

It is not only places such as Kimberley that are accessible by this road, but from it many explorations are possible into the wide spaces of the northern Cape, to Mafikeng, Kuruman, Vryburg, the asbestos mountains, or the diamond diggings in the gravels of the Vaal at Barkly West. Such places were the scenes of many old battles and adventures, a part of southern Africa where flaming sunsets are a reminder of the thirstland to the west and where odd little towns and villages are rich in memories of strange characters, outlaws, rustlers, diamond thieves, and personalities quite as colourful as the sunsets.

The landscape is a prodigious, sun-drenched plain, covered in grass and acacia thorn trees. The very spaciousness of the land is exhilarating. It is the prairie country of southern Africa, not a soft, gentle landscape, but a world akin to the Wild West of America, and with a story every bit as special. In the towns are odd little bars and saloons where thirsty men have washed down vast quantities of dust, and old gaols that have housed many tough customers.

To the geologist and the collector of rocks and gem-stones, the whole area is a bewildering delight. Diamonds have been found, or can be found, everywhere. Iron, manganese, blue asbestos, limestone, tiger's eye and a dozen other precious and valuable things all tantalize the prospector with traces of their presence, suddenly revealed in huge deposits, but more often deluding some eager searcher, luring him on with tempting traces and then, when he is sure of the treasure at rainbow's end, vanishing into the empty sky.

All mining areas are littered with stories of hard luck and success. The glitter of diamonds brought to South Africa many fortune-seekers. The story of each of the great diamond fields is a romance. Visiting an abandoned diamond field is a memorable experience. They look like old battlefields, pock-marked with countless holes, trenches, piles of rubble, rusted machinery, collapsed shacks, broken fragments of carts and ancient automobiles.

The thirst of Kimberley made it a dream town for sellers of any type of liquid. To the women of the world, Kimberley might be a name dear to their hearts as the source of the stones in their rings, but to the brewers, vintners and distillers mere mention of the name was like the sound of a river of liquor flowing through a rapid where the rocks were made of solid gold. Today, things are easier along the Diamond Way. Water is piped in from the rivers, the dust has settled, but it is still fun to visit the diggers' pubs at places such as Barkly West or Windsorton, to hear the talk when the diggers are in town to sell their stones, or to share the excitement if somebody has been lucky; to see the sorters at De Beers, studying the piles of rough diamonds, evaluating, testing, sorting them into parcels for the diamond market in London; to go out to one of the working fields and watch a hopeful digger searching each load of gravel, never knowing when his fingers will touch some gem large enough to bring him fortune.

The urge to join the fortune-seekers is strong. The traveller along the Diamond Way has to be singularly unimaginative not to feel the temptation. The past seems so glamorous, the present so full of possibilities and challenge, it is with a sigh that many visitors return to some less exciting home, carrying with them memories of the diamond country.

Barkly West

The old diamond town of Barkly West has many reminders of the days when the diggers declared it a republic and even elected their own president. The town stands on the Vaal River close to the fording place called Klip Drift. It is over-looked by Canteen Koppie, a hillock that has signs of occupation going back to prehistoric times. Numerous artefacts left by various early inhabitants have been found here.

It was also the site of the first diamond diggings in Africa and is now a national monument.

In 1849 the Berlin Missionary Society established a station nearby on the left bank of the river and named it Pniel ('the face of God'). It was a tranquil scene, with the broad waters of the Vaal sweeping steadily past the mission buildings, and parties of San, Khoikhoi and Tswana people fording the river, resting in the shade of the trees, or hunting the game animals that came to the water to drink.

But the peace was soon shattered. In January 1870 Captain Loftus Rolleston, with a party of prospectors from Natal, found diamonds in the gravels of the Vaal. There was a rush of diggers, first to the mission station and then across the river where they set up a camp at Klip Drift.

Nobody knew who owned the area. It was first-come-first-served and many greedy hands reached out to claim possession. First Khoikhoi and Tswana chieftains claimed ownership and demanded taxes, but the diggers banded together and drove them away. Then the republics of the Orange Free State and the Transvaal claimed the land. The Transvaal president, M. W. Pretorius, made a personal trip to the region with a magistrate. The magistrate was thrown into a boat and told that if he returned to Klip Drift he would be tarred and feathered.

The diggers then formed their own Klip Drift Republic and elected Stafford Parker as president. Parker took his office seriously. He was a dignified-looking man. Dressed in dark suit and top hat, he held court, settling involved squabbles about water rights, claim jumping and theft, and administering rough justice by having troublesome characters run out of town, pegged out in the sun, or dragged across the river on a rope.

This intriguing experiment in frontier democracy did not last. In

The old bridge and toll house across the Vaal River at Barkly West, built in 1886 from steelwork made in London.

sionaries and adventurous traders.

In the days when Tickey the clown was running a mini-circus he performed in Campbell on a rickety stage in a ramshackle hall, with two wrought-iron lamps and a spotlight made of a paraffin tin with a candle inside. The place still seems to echo with whispers of old sermons, and the fervent singing of hymns.

It is worth wandering down Campbell's one street and looking into some of the old buildings. The surroundings are wild and lonely and signs on the road constantly warn motorists against kudu jumping across the way. Some of these huge antelope have been known to jump through the windshields of motor vehicles.

December 1870 the British stepped in and, after arbitration, the area was awarded to the Griquas. The British promptly bought it from them and the diggers' republic came to an end. Many left to join the rush to Kimberley. Klip Drift, renamed after the governor of the Cape, Sir Henry Barkly, became more law abiding.

The river diggings still attract many prospectors. For 150 kilometres the Vaal gravels are rich in diamonds, gem-stones and decorative pebbles. During the dry season (June to November), when the river is at its lowest, diggers build breakwaters to deflect the current and then excavate the gravels, recovering many valuable stones. Each Saturday the diggers come to town with their diamonds and haggle in the offices of the diamond buyers. The local pubs do a roaring trade and the stores are busy with diggers getting supplies for the coming week.

There is a small mining museum with stones, artefacts, fossils and geological specimens on display. St. Mary's Anglican Church, the first to be built on the diamond fields, stands on the site of the old diggers' camp.

There is a municipal holiday park on the banks of the Vaal. The original bridge with its toll house, built across the river in 1886, now serves as the entrance to the park. Along the river are atmospheric places such as Gong-Gong, Waldeck's Plant, Beaumont's Folly and Bosman's Fortune.

Campbell

The village of Campbell lies in an unspoilt gorge known to the Griquas as Knovel Vallei ('valley of wild garlic'). Up this gorge ran the old road to the interior which was followed by so many of the early explorers, mis-

THINGS TO DO AND SEE

Antiquities The museum at Kimberley's Big Hole has reconstructions of the pubs, shops and offices of the days of the diamond rush. The Magersfontein Battle Museum is 31,5 kilometres from Kimberley. It covers 428 hectares of battlefield and has 7 memorials, picnic sites and a tea-room. At Driekops Island, in the bed of the Riet River, there are remarkable rock engravings of unknown origin. There are engravings of game animals behind the original site of the old Halfway Hotel on the road to Barkly West.

Camping and caravanning Kimberley, Riverton, Warrenton, Kuruman and Mafikeng all have caravan parks. Riverton has a resort on the Vaal River with swimming and boating. The park at Kuruman is next to the remarkable 'eye' of the Kuruman river, which has vast numbers of fish. There are hotels throughout the area, and many camping grounds.

Diamonds and gem-stones A prospector's licence is needed for diamond hunting, and this is difficult to get, but diamonds, tiger's eye, jasper, rose quartz, agates and other gem-stones can be bought in Kimberley.

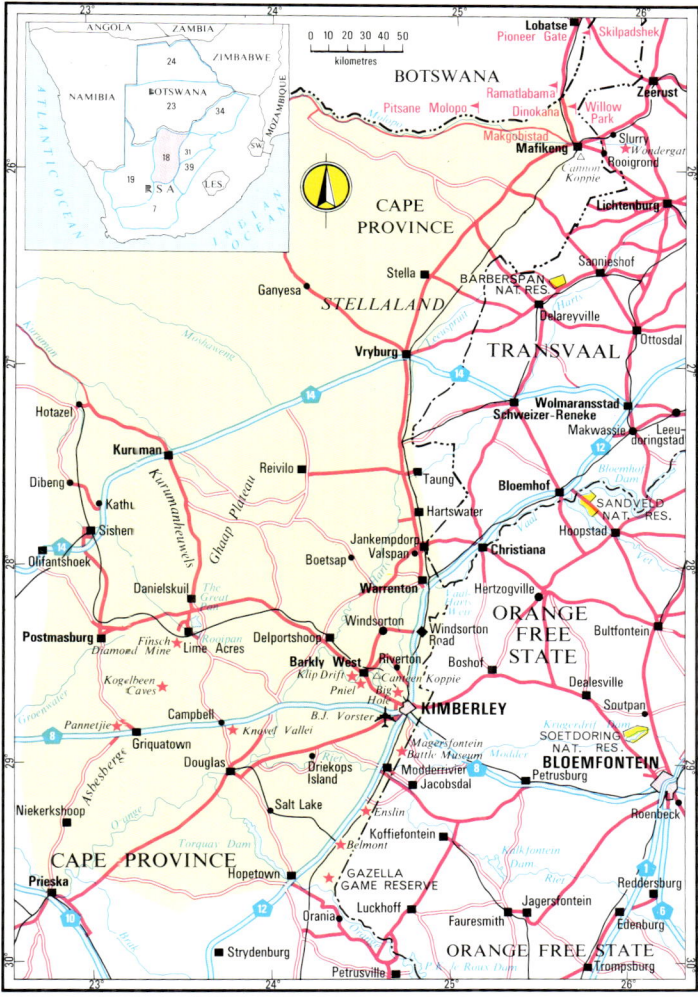

171

The city that grew around a giant hole

The mission church at Campbell. Here many pioneer missionaries held services.

Danielskuil

In the dolomite of the Ghaap Plateau there are many sinkholes, and one of these deep pools was used by the Griquas as a place of trial by ordeal. It was infested by snakes and accused persons lowered into it were considered to have proved their innocence if they survived the night.

The tradition reminded the early pioneers of Daniel in the lions' den and they named the village which has grown up here Danielskuil.

It has now become a bustling centre for the mining of asbestos, diamonds, limestone and marble.

Douglas

Near its meeting point with the Orange River, the Vaal is broad and beautiful, irrigating farms that produce lucerne, potatoes, cotton, and vegetable seeds. The town of Douglas grew up at a fording place across the river, and what is today the main shopping complex was, in 1775, the scene of a bloody battle, which ended in the annihilation of the Korana by the San at a place named Go-Koo-Lume ('where no mercy was shown').

Many San skeletons and artefacts have been recovered in the area, while some prehistoric people of unknown identity covered the rocks on Driekops Island in the nearby Riet River with several hundred rock engravings of an unusual style.

Douglas is a pleasant place, with fine gardens and good boating, fishing and swimming in the river. Nearby is Salt Lake, a large, dried-up lake which is South Africa's greatest source of salt.

Finsch Diamond Mine

In November 1961 a prospector named Allister Fincham was searching for asbestos when he noticed variations in the vegetation that made him suspect the presence of diamond-bearing formations. The find was so rich that two years later he was able to sell his claim to De Beers Consolidated Mines for R4 500 000. The Finsch Diamond Mine is now one of the biggest in Africa.

Griquatown

In former years Griquatown was the capital of an independent state, and a sanctuary for all kinds of adventurers, thieves and liquor traders. The wide streets are much emptier now, but it is easy to imagine the old days when the town was half full of horsemen, wagons, and rugged-looking characters. A tree where law-breakers were hanged still grows in the town.

The Griquas were a Khoikhoi people who lived near Piketberg in the western Cape. Led by a freed slave known as Adam the Cook, or Adam Kok, they wandered northwards and in 1800 settled in the foothills of the Asbesberge (Asbestos Mountains) at a place called Klaarwater ('clear water'). Here they led a colourful existence, rustling, farming, fighting, and drinking strong liquor brought by traders from the Cape.

In 1803 the London Missionary Society established a station around which grew Griquatown — the first town north of the Orange River. The Griquas became a people of some consequence on the frontier and their country, Griqualand West, had its own flag and coinage.

Missionaries notwithstanding, Griquatown was a wild and woolly place. It was a staging post on the route to the interior, and many travellers and explorers passed through it on their way north. Among them was David Livingstone, whose wife, Mary Moffat, was born in the Griquatown mission. The mission house is now the Mary Moffat Museum, displaying many relics of the old days. The bell outside the mission was a ship's bell brought up from Cape Town.

The Griquas eventually split into two sections. One section under the Kok family wandered eastwards, first to Philippolis, and then across the Drakensberg to Griqualand East. The rest of the Griquas remained around Griquatown and were absorbed into the British Empire when diamonds were discovered in their country.

The grave of their great chief, Andries Waterboer, is guarded by two little cannons named Hans and Griet. The cannons were a gift from Queen Victoria and saw action in the rebellion of 1878.

Griquatown is a centre for the production of wool, karakul pelts, cattle

Cotton growing on the north bank of the Orange River. Pickers are harvesting the crop to be taken to packing sheds.

The volcanic pipe of the Finsch Mine. In the foreground are the buildings where the diamond-bearing ore is processed.

and asbestos. Tiger's eye and several other gem-stones are found in the area. There are San engravings 5 kilometres away at Pannetjie, and 40 kilometres along the road to Danielskuil are the Kogelbeen caves.

Hopetown
It was the hard, shiny pebble found by young Erasmus Jacobs on the banks of the Orange River near Hopetown in 1866 that led to the great South African diamond rush.

Erasmus showed the pebble to a neighbour, Schalk van Niekerk, and he had it taken to Colesberg to be examined by the local magistrate, Lorenzo Boyes. In his office Boyes carried out a simple, but momentous experiment. He thought the stone might be a diamond and knew that a sure proof was whether it would cut glass. He went to the window and, with a flourish, cut into the pane two letters.

An expert confirmed that the stone was a yellow diamond of 21,25 carats. It became known as the 'Eureka' and was later bought for £500 by the governor of the Cape, Sir Philip Wodehouse. It is now kept in the Houses of Parliament, Cape Town.

The origin of the stone was a mystery. There were no experienced prospectors in South Africa at that time, and the few farmers and traders who began searching around the farms near Hopetown found nothing.

Then, in 1869, came the second discovery. A Griqua known as Booi picked up a magnificent diamond of 83,5 carats. He took it to Schalk van Niekerk in Hopetown and traded it for a span of oxen, 500 sheep and a horse — all his possessions. Van Niekerk sold the gem to traders for £11 000. It was eventually bought by the Earl of Dudley for £30 000, and later became known as the famous 'Star of South Africa'. Its present ownership is unknown.

There was a rush to the Hopetown district, but diamonds proved maddeningly elusive. Over the years some alluvial deposits were found along the banks of the Orange River but no major find was ever again made in the area. However, Hopetown succeeded in attracting hordes of prospectors to South Africa, and inspired the search

that led to the discovery of the great diamond deposits of Barkly West and Kimberley.

Hopetown today is a centre for sheep, cattle and fruit farms on the banks of the Orange River. The nearby P. K. le Roux dam diverts water into an otherwise arid area. There is a pioneer cemetery about 14 kilometres from the town. The Gazella Game Reserve on the banks of the Orange River contains gemsbok, eland, kudu and springbok.

Hotazel
Manganese, iron and asbestos are found in great quantity in the northern Cape. Hotazel is one of the principal manganese mining centres. Its odd name was given to it in 1917 by the surveyors Dirk Roos and J. W. Waldeck. At the end of a scorching hot day they marked the name on the map without realising that they were sitting on top of one of the world's richest deposits of manganese.

Kimberley
Some cities grow up in fertile valleys. Others sprawl around natural harbours. Kimberley is the city that grew up around a great big hole in the ground. The Big Hole, as it became known, grew and grew until it was deep enough to accommodate more than two buildings each the height of Johannesburg's J. G. Strijdom Tower.

Diamond rushes in South Africa were like tropical storms — they struck unpredictably and were ruthless in their effect on the surroundings. The

The monument in Kimberley to the workers in the great diamond mines.

The Honoured Dead Memorial to the men who fell in the siege of Kimberley.

A fabulous collection of diamonds recovered from the mines around Kimberley. The large stones in the middle would be worth a king's ransom.

When the diamond-diggers lit cigars with bank-notes

first rush into the Kimberley area was in 1869 when diamonds were found in the walls of the farmhouse on Bultfontein. Enthusiastic diggers eventually pulled the house down, and pegged out the area of the homestead. All that is left now is a hole in the ground. But that is not the Big Hole.

Some 22 months after the Bultfontein finds, diamonds were discovered on a nearby hillock subsequently named Colesberg Koppie. There was a frantic rush, and soon the entire hillock had vanished to be replaced by a hole which rapidly reached colossal proportions. Around the verges of this vast hole, buildings sprang up. The mushrooming town was named after the Earl of Kimberley, the secretary of state for colonies. The twin town of Beaconsfield grew up as a centre for the diggings of Bultfontein and Dutoitspan and later Wesselton. Kimberley and Beaconsfield eventually combined in 1913 and became a city.

At the time of the finds there was some understanding of where diamonds occurred, but no one knew how. Even today knowledge about diamond formation is incomplete. What is known is that about 60 million years ago there was a spasm of volcanic activity in the region which left a number of volcanic pipes, or throats, reaching to the surface from very deep levels. Through these the earth, as though suffering from indigestion, burped up a strange, blue, waxy-looking material known as kimberlite. Mixed in this kimberlite is a variety of substances, including diamonds. Exactly how the diamonds come to be in the kimberlite remains a matter for speculation. Diamonds are made of carbon under tremendous pressure. Kimberlite contains no carbon. Not all volcanic pipes contain diamonds in the kimberlite. Of 150 pipes so far found, 25 bear diamonds, the others nothing of any significant value.

On the surface, the pipes produce low volcanic cones made of such soft material that they are soon eroded by the weather. The material contained in the cones is then scattered over the surrounding surface and carried away into the gravels of rivers. The Vaal River at Klip Drift probably received

its diamonds in this way. In other areas, such as Lichtenburg, the diamonds were carried down a river which subsequently disappeared, leaving diamonds scattered over the veld.

In the early days prospecting a pipe was often a frustrating business. Claims could be highly profitable right up to the outer edge of the pipe, and then it would end so abruptly that a claim pegged immediately beyond its confines would be completely sterile.

When the diggers got to work, a diamond pipe often resembled the inside of an ant heap. Up to 30 000 men were labouring all day and most of the night clearing the choked-up throat of the Kimberley Mine.

In the beginning nobody knew how deep a pipe would go, or whether the diamonds would peter out. The deeper the workings the more complicated life became for the diggers. Fights and riots over rights of way to claims became commonplace. A cat's-cradle of cables and ropeways linked the central claims to the rim. With no safety regulations or control there were many accidents when loads of rubble being hauled over the heads of workers suddenly collapsed.

In those early days no one could possibly have dreamed that the original hillock would become the mighty pit of the Kimberley Mine. There was just no end to the diamonds and world demand increased with the supply. The glamour of Kimberley spread throughout the world as the diamond became the great symbol of romance.

Successful diggers went on mammoth sprees, lighting cigars with bank-notes while their women bathed in champagne. Merry-go-rounds which headed for the boom town did a roaring trade as prospectors, delirious with their good fortune, just rode round and round on the wooden horses, drinking as they went and shouting ribald comments to the spectators.

The complex workings made the Big Hole increasingly chaotic as men dug deeper. Some kind of order had to be introduced. Diggers were forced to combine into syndicates, which were then steadily absorbed into companies.

From this welter of wheeling and

The Big Hole at Kimberley. Much of the hole is now filled with water.

A hazardous descent by ropeway into the ever-deepening Big Hole in 1903.

A diamond crystal embedded in blue ground, as excavated in Kimberley.

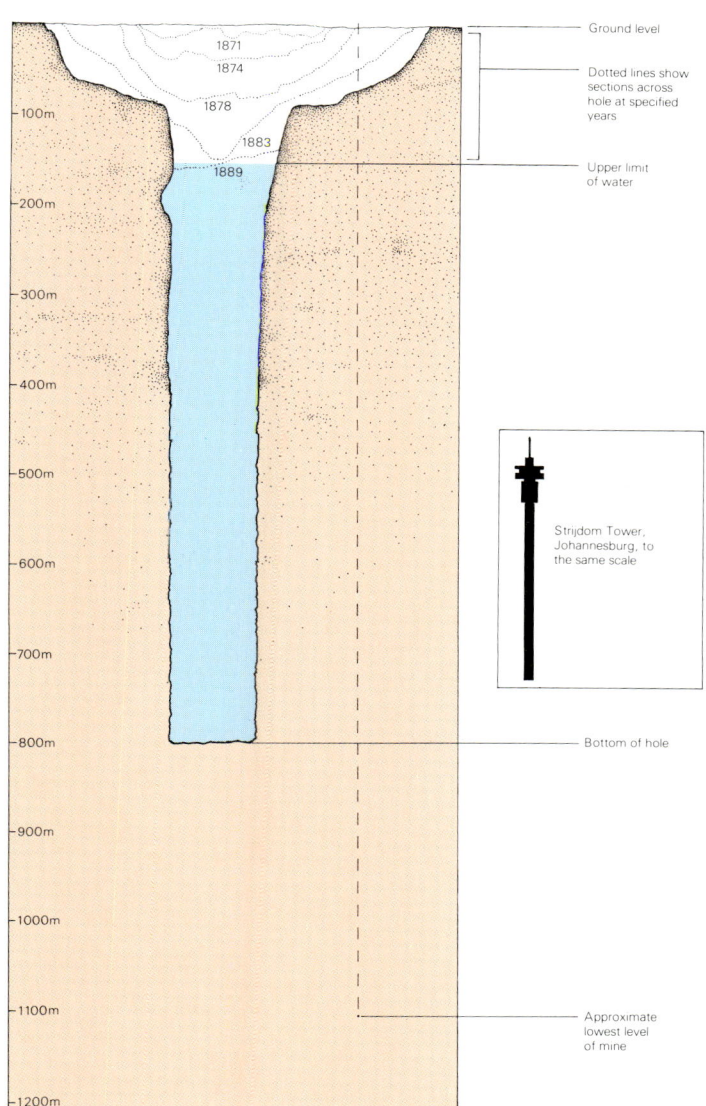

Ground level

Dotted lines show sections across hole at specified years

1871
1874
1878
1883
1889

Upper limit of water

Strijdom Tower, Johannesburg, to the same scale

Bottom of hole

Approximate lowest level of mine

The Big Hole — more than twice as deep as the 269-metre J. G. Strijdom Tower. Digging began in 1871 and produced more than 14 million carats of diamonds.

Ready for blasting — the explosives are placed and the fuses connected.

An underground tramway, one of many in Kimberley diamond mines.

The Big Hole in 1875 with each claim connected with its own aerial ropeway to the rim of the pipe. The deeper the mine the greater the chaos in working.

The Big Hole during the 1870s. Some diggers struck it rich, others found only despair. At times 30 000 diggers joined the mad scramble for diamonds.

The mercurial, audacious, flamboyant Barney Barnato, and the cheque given to him by Cecil Rhodes to buy out his interests in the Big Hole, made out for £5 338 650. The deal gave Rhodes sole control of the greatest diamond mine in the world.

175

The city that boasts the world's only drive-in pubs

Dunluce, in Kimberley's Lodge Road, is a fine example of late-Victorian domestic architecture. Built in 1897, it was the home of the Orr family for over 70 years.

The clock tower on the Kimberley Mine Museum.

dealing two giants emerged, Cecil Rhodes and Barney Barnato. To elbow their way to the top of the pile in Kimberley, these two had to be very precocious.

Barney Barnato started life as Barnett Isaacs. He worked as a barman in London before going on the music hall stage with his brother, Harry. The diamonds of Kimberley lured the brothers to South Africa and from a small start as a diamond buyer at the age of 20, Barney was a multi-millionaire within five years.

Cecil Rhodes was even more remarkable, for his background seemed to make him quite unsuitable for the uproar of a diamond rush. He was the son of an English country parson and in his youth was seriously ill with tuberculosis. To recuperate he journeyed to South Africa to join his brother Herbert, who ran a farm in Natal. The two young men rushed to Kimberley on hearing news of the discoveries and Rhodes started his fortune by going into partnership with C. D. Rudd, making ice. Rhodes was a genius at getting people to work for him and wily when it came to negotiation, amalgamation and control. With a squeaky voice and a pudgy, unhealthy

appearance, his personality was still such that he could achieve miracles.

Rhodes ended up running Kimberley, and his company De Beers Consolidated Mines Ltd., monopolized the diamond market of the world. In 1888 when Barney Barnato sold out to Rhodes, the former music hall hoofer received a cheque for £5 338 650, and so great were Rhodes's achievements by then that any teller in any bank would have cashed the cheque without demur, providing only that his bank could find the ready money. Rhodes was then only 35 years of age.

The cheque now hangs in the De Beers' boardroom in Kimberley.

The corrugated-iron and brick office where Rhodes planned his projects and from where he controlled his financial empire still stands in Warren Street. The boardroom is worth seeing. The visitor may well feel a need to pause awhile and think of the talk, the negotiations, the commercial coups, the great schemes that originated in this quiet little room. The ambitions of Rhodes were vast, and dedicated not simply to enriching himself but to expanding the British Empire and consolidating the Anglo-Saxon race as what he considered the

God-appointed leaders of the world.

From the Big Hole of Kimberley, and neighbouring mines, Rhodes obtained the finance for his ambitions. The hole got deeper and deeper each day — there was no end to the diamonds. It became impossible to go on working it as an opencast pit. In 1889 the first major shaft was sunk and mining continued through shafts and adits. The opencast working was by then 400 metres deep, with a circumference to the hole of 1,5 kilometres. Underground workings continued for another 900 metres, with 25 million tons of kimberlite removed and 14 504 566 carats of diamonds recovered.

The outbreak of World War I and the attendant slump in diamond prices caused the abandonment of the Kimberley Mine in 1914. Strangely enough, quite a number of diamonds from the Big Hole are still being recovered. In the early years, before the nature of kimberlite was properly understood, a fair amount of it was spread out to level building sites and roads. Now, whenever a building is demolished, diggers rush to the site, wash and search the ground beneath the foundations, and often find good diamonds.

Kimberley in its heyday was a very bright place indeed. Races, lotteries, pubs, dance halls, boxing booths, ballrooms, all flourished. It was the first city in Africa to have its streets illuminated by electric light. Five years later, in 1887, a tramway company started operating.

Apart from financing the ambitions of Rhodes, the diamonds of Kimberley also provided money for numerous other developments, including religion. In 1891 the De Beers company paid £451 438 for the property of the Wessels family where the Wesselton Mine was being developed. Pieter Wessels used this money to fund the Seventh Day Adventists in South Africa. He had been excommunicated from the Dutch Reformed Church for fomenting great contention over the fourth commandment ordaining the seventh day as the Sabbath. From an American digger he learned that there were people who shared his views in the United States and he financed the establishment

of churches in Kimberley and Cape Town for the Seventh Day Adventists. Missions were started for the African people, and branches of the church established in Australia.

It was in Kimberley's market square that F. W. Alexander, a travelling produce dealer, created a sensation on 16 July 1886 by publicly panning samples of gold-bearing ore from the Witwatersrand. A stampede began. Barney Barnato rode up to the new gold fields in a coach so elaborate that it was popularly supposed that he had bought the vehicle from a bankrupt Cinderella pantomime company. The sub-social strata of characters who fancied themselves to be the aristocracy of Kimberley — swindlers, rogues, madames, adventurers — provided Johannesburg with some of its most lurid inhabitants.

It was from Kimberley that Rhodes sent 'Matabele' Thompson to negotiate his famous mining concession with Lobengula, chief of the Ndebele (Matebele) (see box, page 503). It was also here in the diamond city that the notorious Jameson Raid was organized, throwing the Transvaal into uproar (see Rhodes box, page 37). The Boers felt particularly antagonistic

The reconstructed bar in the mine museum at the Big Hole. This was a haunt of thirsty men and flashy ladies.

The original headgear of the Big Hole, after many years of working, now pensioned off to the mining museum.

The entrance to the reconstructed bar at the mining museum at the Big Hole.

A street from the old-time Kimberley, reconstructed at the Big Hole museum.

The transport section of the mining museum with many weird vehicles.

towards Kimberley because of their dislike for Cecil Rhodes.

When the Anglo-Boer War broke out they besieged the place from 14 October 1899 for 124 days, lobbing shells into it and being counter-shelled by a locally made piece of artillery named Long Cecil, built in the mine workshops and firing 28-pound shells. Rhodes was in Kimberley throughout the siege, with the Boer gunners frequently trying to bag him with a well-placed round from Long Tom, their rival to Long Cecil. About 3 000 women and children were sheltered in underground mine workings during the last few days of the siege.

Some of the most notable battles of the war took place on the outskirts of the town. Under the command of Lord Methuen, a British army with the task of relieving Kimberley set out to fight its way up the line of railway from the Cape. A series of battles took place, first at Belmont, then at Enslin, Modderrivier and Magersfontein, where the famous Boer general, De la Rey, developed defences consisting of trenches, later used with such hideous effect in World War I. The first trenches are well preserved on the battlefield and make an interest-

ing if melancholy scene.

The battlefields around Kimberley are all marked by memorials. In Kimberley there is the Honoured Dead Memorial, designed by Sir Herbert Baker and built of granite from the Matobo Hills in Zimbabwe. The home-made Long Cecil gun stands guard in front of the monument.

Rhodes died in Cape Town on 26 March 1902. His body was conveyed through Kimberley to what was then Rhodesia for burial.

Kimberley is fortunate in its museums. The Big Hole is in itself a most extraordinary sight. Original buildings of Rhodes's time still line the streets around it and at the Big Hole a fascinating museum preserves such buildings as Barney Barnato's Boxing Academy, a pub, the De Beers' homestead, a pawnbroker's shop, blacksmith's shop, the tobacconist shop where Perilly produced his famous hand-made cigarettes, the diamond buyers' office and various shops stocked with articles, fashions and groceries from the diamond-rush days. There is also a collection of transport vehicles, including a large, heavy, windblown tricycle used to convey John Derbyshire from Knysna to

Kimberley, and a dazzling display of real diamonds

The town's McGregor Museum was built in 1907 in memory of a former mayor of Kimberley, Alexander McGregor. This museum displays a collection of natural history specimens and San relics. The museum is now housed in what used to be the Kimberley Sanatorium, where Rhodes stayed during the siege.

This magnificent building was erected in 1897 as a convalescent home, was then developed as the luxury Belgrave Hotel, and was then converted to a convent school. Now it is restored and preserved in its original state. Recreated in the drawing room is the scene of Rhodes's meeting with General French after the raising of the siege.

During his stay in Kimberley, Rhodes sometimes visited the Halfway Hotel which had what was possibly the world's only ride-in bar. Horsemen could order a drink without even dismounting. This hotel and the West End Hotel, also in Kimberley, are now believed to be the only drive-in pubs in the world.

Next to the McGregor Museum is the Duggan-Cronin Bantu Gallery,

housing 8 000 photographs assembled by Alfred Martin Duggan-Cronin, and many other exhibits of ethnological interest, including collections of beadwork. The Duggan-Cronin photographs are unique. He came to South Africa in 1897 and became a mine official. He was also an expert photographer. African labourers were recruited from most of the peoples of southern Africa to work on the mines. These individuals were still in a very primitive state and provided Cronin with superb photographic models, with their traditional hairstyles, face markings, clothes and decorations. No comparable collection of photographs could ever be gathered again for customs have changed and many of the beautiful decorations, beadwork and elegant traditional costumes have been forgotten. His collection was offered to the Kimberley Municipality in 1935 and in 1937 the De Beers company provided a fine old building as a home.

The Humphreys Art Gallery has many exhibits from Europe and South Africa. It was founded in 1952 when William Benbrow Humphreys, Member of Parliament for Kimberley for 25 years, donated his collection of paintings. The Kimberley public library has a notable collection of Africana and material on the history of the diamond rush.

Kimberley was the nursery for flying in southern Africa. The continent's first flying school was established here in 1912. This was the birthplace of the South African Air Force. There was only one aircraft in the beginning, a weird, homemade affair brought out from England. This crashed with the future Major-general K. van der Spuy, then a pupil pilot, aboard, but he was uninjured. The aircraft was rebuilt but the second version also crashed. During World War II a vast number of pilots were

A puffer in retirement at the mining museum at the Big Hole in Kimberley.

The pool that 'boils' with countless fish

Robert Moffat's church in Kuruman, a stepping-stone of Christianity.

trained in Kimberley under the Empire Air Training scheme.

An outdoor display of photographs of the early days of aviation is on the site of South Africa's first flying school.

The treatment and recovery plants of De Beers are open to visitors. Permits, issued on weekdays, must be obtained. On the first and third Sundays of each month Alsatian dogs from De Beers Kennels put on a special display. This is one of the great dog-training schools of the world, where Alsatians are bred and trained for security purposes in mines and diamond store-rooms, as well as for other police work.

There are several hotels and also a caravan park in Kimberley, while 25 kilometres from the city the municipality operates a pleasure resort at Riverton, on the Vaal River. The resort has a large swimming bath, boating and fishing on the river, a spacious caravan and camping area, and holiday bungalows.

Kuruman

One of the natural wonders of southern Africa is the 'eye', or source, of the Kuruman River. At the foot of a range of low hills, a spring of crystal-clear water gushes out from the dolomite, 20 million litres each day, with little variance between wet and dry seasons. The presence of so powerful, pure and dependable a supply of water in an otherwise arid area made human settlement inevitable. In 1801 a mission was established here but after eight years the missionary, Johan Kok, was murdered. Then, in 1824, Robert Moffat of the London Missionary Society arrived, and established what became probably the most famous mission station in Africa. The source

of the Kuruman River was often described as the fountain of Christianity in Africa, and this station was a jumping-off ground for many ventures into the interior by people such as David Livingstone.

The original mission buildings still stand, surrounded by irrigated fields and shaded by magnificent trees, including giant syringa trees, pear trees, figs, pomegranates and almond trees. The trunk of the almond tree under which David Livingstone proposed to Mary Moffat still stands in an overgrown garden. It is a lovely and gentle place, full of memories. The mission church is still in use and is the scene of many gatherings, especially at New Year when church members have a reunion, with many ceremonies and services. The Tlapin section of the Tswana people hold this mission in great reverence. The mission buildings are in excellent condition.

The modern town of Kuruman is a small, neat place, the centre for a great cattle and mining area.

The town draws drinking water from the source of the Kuruman River, and the surroundings of the 'eye' have been developed as a park. At the spring there is a pool inhabited by countless thousands of fish. A handful of bread crumbs or mincemeat thrown into the pool creates such an upheaval of fish that the water seems to boil.

Mafikeng

The frontier history of southern Africa was a brawling, boisterous, violent chapter in human history. It was contemporary with the Wild West of America and much the same type of man was involved. In southern Africa, however, women were far more numerous. They journeyed with their men into the most remote regions, produced infants in quite impossible situations, backed up their men with a stubborn resolve, and by their presence moderated much of the bad behaviour that was so conspicuous on the American frontier. There were still plenty of wild men in southern Africa, but the presence of women tended to subdue them, and there was less gun play and violence.

Mafikeng's beginning was during a period of considerable frontier insta-

bility. The Rolong people who lived in the area were divided into two factions. Both sides recruited European mercenaries, and some wild individuals, known as freebooters, joined the fray. Rewards from the local chiefs for services rendered consisted of farms, and the result was the creation of a miniature republic named Goshen, with Rooigrond, 20 kilometres from Mafikeng (known then as Mafeking) as its capital.

There was considerable uproar. The British government sent a force to occupy the area and the commander, Sir Charles Warren, annexed what became known as British Bechuanaland. An administrative centre was established at the place known to the Tswana as maFikeng ('place of boulders'). This was the foundation in 1885 of Mafeking, as it was known to Europeans until recent years.

The great glory of the town came with the outbreak of the Anglo-Boer War. Mafeking was besieged by the Boer forces from 14 October 1899 until 17 May 1900.

Colonel R. S. S. Baden-Powell was the British commander, and it was during the siege that he conceived the idea of the Boy Scouts. The small boys of Mafeking were almost as tough as their fathers. To keep them usefully employed and out of mischief during the months of the siege, the ingenious colonel gave them non-combatant tasks. They proved so useful at carrying out the town's essential services that the idea of the Boy Scout movement became firmly established.

The siege of Mafeking captivated the British public. It was not particularly violent. The Boer forces completely outnumbered the defenders of the town but they were content simply to besiege Mafeking, with an occasional shelling, and no attempt at a massed onslaught was made. There was seldom any fighting on Sundays and apart from monotony, short rations, shell dodging, sniping, periodic patrols, raids and minor clashes, the whole siege was a singularly civilized example of warfare, with polite notes exchanged between the opposing commanders on such matters as the status of non-combatants.

The relief of Mafeking was a great delight to the British people. London

enjoyed a wild night of celebration. So many odd little stories had reached the outside world about the siege — escapes and tragedies of individuals, tales of heroism and cowardice, and of the personalities of the besiegers and the besieged — that the siege of Mafeking will always be remembered and discussed.

In the modern town there are numerous mementoes of the siege. Cannon Koppie with its fort is maintained as a historical monument. Guns and cannons are preserved in several of the original buildings.

Mafikeng has reverted to its original Tswana name and forms part of the sprawling urban complex that includes Mmabatho and Montsiwa.

Thirty-one kilometres away is a vast sinkhole in the dolomite. Known as the Wondergat ('wonder hole'), it is nearly 100 metres deep and 70 metres at its widest point.

It is filled with clear water and legends still linger of its use as an execution place by Mzilikazi and his Ndebele raiders before they were driven across the Limpopo by the Voortrekkers.

Postmasburg

In the midst of the vast dolomite plain of the northern Cape the little town of Postmasburg, founded in 1892, was simply an isolated ranching centre. After 26 years of quiet, diamonds were found near the town. Then in 1922 manganese was discovered, followed in 1940 by the colossal iron deposits at Sishen.

An electrified railway was built in 1930 to convey ore to the main line north of Kimberley, and another electrified line was built in 1974 to link the mines directly to the sea at Saldanha.

Postmasburg is no holiday resort, but as a marshalling yard for the trains, and a commercial and administrative centre for the mines, it now plays a major part in the economy of South Africa.

Reivilo

The cheese factory at Reivilo is one of the largest in South Africa, with an annual output of more than 2 000 tonnes of cheese and large quantities of whey powder. The name of the vil-

THE SIEGE THAT GAVE A NEW WORD TO THE ENGLISH LANGUAGE

A new word was born to the English language out of the siege of Mafeking. The word is maffick — to maffick is to celebrate with riotous rejoicing, and the rejoicing was indeed riotous after the siege.

Among items of memorabilia prized by historians in southern Africa are copies of the newspaper published during the siege, *The Mafeking Mail*; treasury notes and postage stamps printed in the town; pieces of literature, private letters and reports, as well as some manuscripts, including a diary written by Solomon Tshekisho Plaatjie, a Tswana who lived and worked in Mafeking as a secretary-typist throughout the siege. His opinions of events and personalities provide a revealing picture of the siege.

Mafikeng is a place of pilgrimage for Boy Scouts. It was during the siege that Colonel R. S. S. Baden-Powell, the British commander — impressed by the roles played by young boys of the locality — conceived the idea of the Boy Scouts movement.

The site of the siege fort of Mafeking during the Anglo-Boer War. It is now a national monument rich in memories of Baden-Powell and his men.

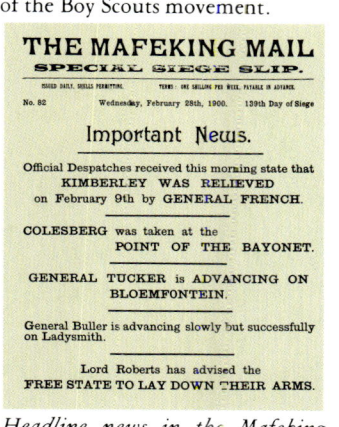

Headline news in the Mafeking Mail on the 139th day of the siege.

Left: Colonel Baden-Powell. Top: A ten-shilling note issued during the siege. Above: Inscription on the fort.

comet that had been visible while the fighting was in progress.

Vryburg, the 'town of freedom', was laid out as a capital for this roughneck republic. A flag was designed, postage stamps issued (great collectors' pieces), a gaol built, and the state was launched. Its life was short. The Transvaal Republic and the British government in the Cape refused to tolerate continuous frontier disturbances. An expeditionary force under Sir Charles Warren was sent from the Cape with orders to 'remove filibusters from Bechuanaland and restore order in the country'. Stellaland was occupied in 1885, and the flag was sent to Queen Victoria and hung in Windsor Castle until 1934, when King George V returned it to Vryburg. It remains in the town hall. King George was the proud possessor of a full set of Stellaland stamps.

Vryburg is today a ranching centre. In the stockyards many thousands of head of cattle are auctioned each week.

For visitors there is a museum and the ruins of the original gaol. In its heyday the area was a roaming ground for rustlers and horse thieves, including the renowned Scotty Smith (see box, page 184).

Warrenton

In 1880 a syndicate purchased the farm on which Warrenton stands today to produce vegetables to supply the Kimberley diamond diggings. Vegetables were in great demand by the diggers.

Diamonds were found in the gravels on the farm in 1888 and there was a rush of prospectors to the place. Digging continues today.

Windsorton

The diggers' town of Windsorton lies on the banks of the Vaal River. It started life as the Hebron Mission. Then, when diamonds were discovered in the river gravels and the place went to drink and brawls, it was renamed after the Windsor family, who owned the land.

The surroundings are typical of a diamond-rush area, resembling a battlefield with thousands of holes and gravel dumps. A few diamond-diggers are still working here.

lage comes from the Reverend A. J. Olivier, who was a local minister in the early 1900s. Olivier spelt backwards is Reivilo.

Taung

This is the centre for the quarries of the Northern Lime Company. In one of the quarries in 1924 was found the skull of the Taung Child — the first fossil to be discovered of the African ape-man, *Australopithecinae*. Taung was the home of the small Tau people, hence the name, which means 'the place of the lion' — the totem of these people.

Vaalharts

The Harts River, one of the tributaries of the Vaal, flows to join it through a valley much lower than that of the Vaal. The broad Harts valley has an excellent climate and deep alluvial soil. The irrigation possibilities of the two valleys, separated by a high ridge, were apparent to the first settlers in the area. In 1881 Cecil Rhodes sent surveyors to plan an irrigation scheme on his usual vast scale, but nothing developed until 1933. In that year of the depression, the South African government decided to launch the scheme to provide much-needed employment.

The Vaal-Harts irrigation scheme became the second largest in the world and the largest in the southern hemisphere. A storage dam was built in the Vaal River and this feeds water into

a grand canal that carries it 120 kilometres into the Harts valley, where it irrigates 1 250 farms and 1 550 small plots. Two towns have been created as centres for this area — Hartswater and Jankempdorp.

Vryburg

In the wars between the Tlapin people and the Korana Khoikhoi a large number of European adventurers served as mercenaries with the two sides. At the end of the fighting, in July 1882, 416 of the mercenaries who had fought for the Korana received payment in the form of farms.

These mercenaries then proclaimed their block of ranch land a republic and named it Stellaland because of a

MOTHER OF ALL RIVERS

LIFE IN THE NORTHERN Cape is dominated by the Orange River, one of the most erratic of the world's first-class rivers. It is a true river of the wilderness — moody, sullen and enigmatic. To the San and Khoikhoi who first discovered it in its lower reaches, it was the mother of all rivers, the !Garib ('the great river'). It brought life to the desert areas, but the source of the vast flow of water was a mystery. The course of the Orange is some 2 000 kilometres long. The great bulk of its water, from its own source and that of its principal tributary, the Vaal, comes from the mountains of Lesotho. To the people living in the arid northern and north-western Cape, this flow of water came from another world. The river rises and falls, sometimes scarcely flowing, sometimes a raging flood eight kilometres wide, across a sun-baked landscape bare of trees or grass. Only along the verges of the river is there a splash of greenery.

Modern irrigation has transformed this landscape. Lucerne, cotton, fruit, dates, and great quantities of sultanas and raisins are produced on the banks and islands of the river. Karakul sheep browse on the succulents of the surrounding thirstlands. Occasionally, in a freak season, the normally dry watercourses that enter into the Orange in its lower reaches, and which on a map have the appearance of tributaries, do carry a rare flash flood. For most of the time, however, they are simply rivers of sand, with only a little water below the surface.

Like the Nile, the Orange is therefore the alchemist, transmuting drab yellow to a glowing green. It is broad and full of islands. The banks and islands have deep soil and are extensively irrigated. Waterwheels lift the water from the river to the irrigation canals. Almost anything seems to grow well here. The atmosphere is warm and the river, divided into numerous channels, flows steadily through a world of floating gardens.

In the 1880s these islands were used as strongholds by number of freebooters and bandits. River pirates such as Captain Afrikaner, his lieutenant (a condemned Polish forger named Stephanus who had escaped from a gaol in Cape Town where he was being held for execution), Captain Stuurman, and several other tough characters, with their following of rustlers and renegades, made the region notorious. An odd little 'war' had to be fought by the Cape government in order to subdue the river pirates. The last of them were only dispersed in 1884, about 100 years after the river was first explored by Europeans and named in honour of the Prince of Orange. The defeat of the river pirates allowed settlers to make their homes on the Orange and transform the river into a great producer of food. Sultanas were introduced in 1900 and these grow to such perfection that the farms of the Orange provide the bulk of the country's crop. Thousands of vines grow and nearly every farm has a concrete-floored sultana drying yard.

The Orange is interrupted by one of the six largest waterfalls of the world, where the river tumbles into one of the greatest of all gorges cut through granite. This waterfall and its gorge, at Augrabies, just below Kakamas, is one of the natural wonders of Africa and a gigantic spectacle.

Apart from the river, this part of the Cape contains the Kalahari Gemsbok National Park, such strange features as the roaring sand dunes, and several little towns, villages and isolated mission stations like the one at Pella, a perfect example of an oasis in a wilderness made splendid by the colours of the earth and the semi-precious stones — rose quartz, amethyst, amazonite, garnet, beryl, tourmaline, agate, onyx, jasper and tiger's eye — which are found throughout this spacious part of the country.

Augrabies Falls National Park

In 1775 a Swedish mercenary soldier, Hendrik Wikar, deserted from the garrison at the Cape and wandered off into the wilderness of the north. On 6 October 1778, after three years of wandering, he became the first European to see the great waterfall on the Orange River at what the Khoikhoi called Aukoerebis ('the place of the great noise'). In that month the waterfall would not have been in full spate. At a peak flood, 405 million litres of water go over the falls every minute in a direct drop of 85 metres, with a cataract fall below the direct plunge of 54 metres. In such a flood there are 19 separate waterfalls tumbling nearly 92 metres into the upper end of a prodigious gorge eroded into a massive granite barrier. The circular

The deep granite gorge of Augrabies, the largest in Africa. At flood-time there are 19 waterfalls into the gorge and the scene is awesome and thunderous.

crater-like pool below the falls is 92 metres in diameter and 130 metres deep.

The contrast and clash between immovable granite, 3 000 million years old, and the surging flood of new season water, irresistibly forcing a way through the ancient rock, is breathtaking. At peak flood the scene is obscured by heavy mist. At medium flood, with the river concentrated into one fall at the head of the gorge, the area is more approachable, and more easily seen. As the flood increases so additional waterfalls appear over the lip of the gorge until, at full spate, the 19 falls send such a mass of water crashing its way down the gorge that the granite trembles, a vast column of spray rises into the air, and the roar of the river is strangely brutal.

A cameraman, suspended alongside Augrabies Falls, can barely be pinpointed.

The face of the wilderness, arid, hot and dusty, near Renosterkop.

The gorge is 9 kilometres long and 260 metres deep. It is full of rapids and minor falls. In the 130 metre hole at the foot of the main fall, legend has it, there is a treasure in diamonds which have been washed down the river, over the waterfall and trapped in the gravel at the bottom of the pool. Reports of the sighting of a river monster in the gorge have frequently been made, but are probably a fanciful account of shoals of giant barbel, which reach about 2 metres in length.

In 1967 the Augrabies Falls National Park was opened. This preserves 9 000 hectares of river landscape. There is a rich variety of plant life, including kokerboom (tree aloe), lithops, haworthia, Karoo thornbush, Cape willow and wild olive, as well as numerous birds, monkeys, steenbok, wild cats and otters. The bird life in the park includes water plovers, swifts, siskins, warblers and wagtails.

The national park is centred on Klaas Island, which has a restaurant, caravan park, huts, and a curio shop built of decorative stonework with an attractive thatched roof. There are observation points along the verge of the gorge. In earlier days the locality of the island and the waterfall was the resort of Khoikhoi and San. The last of the Khoikhoi leaders to rule here was Klaas Lucas, from whom the island takes its name.

In former years it was impossible to reach the gorge during peak floods because the river spreads out, overwhelming all approaches. With the

THINGS TO DO AND SEE

Angling The Orange River is the home for large yellowfish and barbel. The granite gorge below the Augrabies waterfall is noted for giant mud barbel reaching 2 metres in length. Even larger specimens are said to lurk in the deep hole at the foot of the waterfall and these are probably the origin of local legends of river monsters.

Boating The Orange has splendid stretches for boating and canoeing, especially at Upington.

Camping and caravanning There are caravan and camping grounds at the Augrabies Falls National Park, the Kalahari Gemsbok National Park and Upington. There are hotels in all the towns, and rest camps in the Kalahari Gemsbok National Park.

Gem-stones One of the great fascinations of this area is the variety and number of gem-stones to be found almost anywhere on the surface.

Sightseeing The Augrabies Falls and the Kalahari Gemsbok National Park provide tourists with vastly different scenes, but both are novel and exciting. Augrabies during the flood season of late summer is awe-inspiring. The Kalahari Gemsbok National Park is dramatic at all times of the year. It is very hot in summer but particularly beautiful, for thunderstorms bring magnificent cloud formations and red sand dunes provide superb photographic studies against deep blue skies and banked clouds.

The Roaring Sands are said to roar during the months with an 'r' in them.

Old pirate haunts where wild peaches grow

The river boils and storms its way through the great gorge of Augrabies, reputedly haunted by a giant serpent and containing a treasure of diamonds.

development of the national park a tarred road was built with a series of bridges to link the main bank with the island. The waterfall can now be reached at all seasons and provides visitors with one of the most dramatic scenes in Africa. The barren surroundings, the enormously powerful river, the ominous roar of the waterfall, the chaos of contending rocks and water in the gorge, the eerie atmosphere and the ceaseless, darting flight of numbers of swifts that live in the gorge, all contribute to a moving spectacle.

Boegoeberg Dam
The concrete dam across the Orange River at Boegoeberg, built in 1931, has a wall 610 metres long. It diverts water from the Orange into the Boegoeberg Canal which eventually irrigates 6 700 hectares of farmland. The dam offers fishing and boating. Alongside it is a camping ground.

Kakamas

The Khoikhoi Chieftain Klaas Lucas, who gave his first name to the island in the Orange River that is now the centre of the Augrabies Falls National Park, started life as a river pirate and then became devoutly religious. In 1870 he asked for a missionary to be sent to his people, and this was the beginning of great change in this part of the Orange River.

The missionary who answered the call of Klaas Lucas was Christiaan Schroder. He established a mission in the area known to the Khoikhoi as Kakamas, meaning a place of poor pasture. This was abandoned when war was declared against the river pirates, but Schroder never forgot his venture to the Orange River. In 1895 he recommended that a settlement of poor people should be made at Kakamas, and this was founded in 1898. Led by Schroder and the Dutch Reformed Church, settlers arrived at Kakamas. Canals were dug, farms were laid out, and the town of Kakamas was established as the centre for what became a highly successful community producing fruit, sultanas, cotton and lucerne. In recent years a substantial wine industry has developed.

The water and the rich mud brought down by the Orange River ensure the fertility of an area where rainfall is sparse and erratic. With irrigation, crops flourish in the warmth. Dates grow excellently and yellow peaches, long escaped from cultivation, grow wild.

In 1933 on the banks of the river near Kakamas, A. D. Collins, a teacher of agriculture, found the remarkable peach known as the Kakamas, or Collins, peach. The fruit of this peach was large, with a beautiful golden colour, firm flesh and a delicious flavour. It was ideal for canning. The tree was also a prolific bearer and very hardy. Within five years of its discovery at Kakamas, this peach transformed the South African canned-fruit industry, increasing the total volume of canning two-and-a-half times.

A variety of semi-precious stones can be found in the river near Kakamas. The umbrella-like kameeldoring grows in this locality. Waterwheels can still be seen in the irrigation channels.

In a cemetery outside the town is a memorial to German soldiers killed in a battle with South African troops in February 1915.

Kalahari Gemsbok National Park

From the administrative centre, Twee Rivieren, the warden of the Kalahari Gemsbok National Park controls a

A pride of lions laze in the Kalahari Gemsbok National Park.

A remarkable stone and timber homestead of the corbel type, built about 1850, on Stuurmansfontein farm in Carnarvon.

THE MYSTERY OF THE ROARING SAND DUNES

If you disturb the surface of the sand on the western side of the Langeberg Dunes in the northern Cape you will hear a sound that varies from a hum to a roar.

The roaring sands are part of a group of white dunes 12 kilometres long and 3 kilometres wide contrasting sharply with the usual red dunes of the northern Cape that surround them. It is thought that the white dunes were formed over springs of fresh water which leached out the red iron oxides.

Stroking the fingers through the sand produces a sound like snoring or the grunting of a pig. A booming noise is created by scooping a hand through the sand. Walking through the sand produces a roaring sound. The same effect is achieved by sliding down the dunes.

A strong, dry night wind produces an eerie moaning. The sound is loudest on the southern face of the dunes. Extreme cold or rain mutes the sound. The locals say the dunes normally roar during any month with an 'r' in it — particu-

The great dunes of the Roaring Sands.

lary during a dry December and January. The exact cause of the sounds made by the dunes is unknown.

As a memento, a sample of the roaring sands can be put in a pair of fruit-preserving jars which have been attached lid to lid with a finger-sized hole bored between them, so that the device resembles an egg-timer. If the jars are upturned the sand runs through the hole and makes its roaring noise. However, if the jars are not tightly sealed before leaving the dry atmosphere of the region, the sand will absorb moisture from the air and be muted.

Perfect oasis within a sub-tropical walled garden

park of almost 1 000 000 hectares, with an area of similar size immediately adjoining it across the Botswana border. In this huge landscape of red-coloured sand dunes and bush-covered watercourses live more than 10 000 springbok, as well as gemsbok, cheetah, hyena, tawny-maned lion, red hartebeest, eland, kudu, wildebeest, ostrich and bat-eared fox. The animals wander at will into the park from the surrounding wilderness of the Kalahari.

Two rivers have their courses through the park — the rivers that give Twee Rivieren its name. They are the Nossob and its tributary the Auob. Only rarely does any water flow down these watercourses, but beneath the surface there is sufficient water to provide drinking holes and to keep alive a covering of grass and trees. It is this water and grazing that attract the various species of antelope. Roads lead up the two watercourses, with a dune road linking the two at the upper end of the park.

A journey up either of the watercourses, then along the dune road and back down the second watercourse, provides the tourist with a unique experience in wilderness travel. There are two rest camps besides Twee Rivieren: Mata Mata, on the south-west border, and Nossob, 160 kilometres north of Twee-rivieren in the Nossob River bed.

Plants in the park include the superb kameeldoring and other species of acacia. Their umbrella-shaped canopies provide shade, while their seed pods, and the tsamma melons, are staple items of food for the local fauna.

The park is open throughout the year and accommodation is available in family cottages and huts. There are sites for tents and caravans.

Kenhardt

This solitary little town on the Hartebees River is a true orphan of the frontier, unaware even of the origin of its name. It started life as a rustlers' lair. In 1868 a party of 50 policemen were sent to capture the rustlers and occupy their lair. The police found only a few ramshackle hovels around a waterhole. For some unknown reason the rustlers called the place Kenhardt.

The dry bed of the Auob in the Kalahari's red sand dune country.

Today Kenhardt, a centre for karakul sheep and mutton production, is a very solitary town of the wilderness, having few visitors, but it is a sunny, pleasant place with a nostalgic atmosphere.

The salt pan country around Kenhardt is noted for its extremes of hot and cold weather. Village settlements in the neighbourhood are Brandvlei, Sakrivier and Vanwyksvlei.

Marydale

The small agricultural centre of Marydale was named after Mrs. Mary Snyman, wife of the farmer on whose lands the village was laid out in 1909. The countryside here is famous for the minerals and semi-precious stones that can be found lying on the surface.

Pella

The London Missionary Society established a station in 1814 for Christian Khoikhoi who had been driven south of the Orange River by disturbances in their home at Warmbad. The station was named Pella, after the biblical town which was a refuge for Christians in Macedonia.

In 1872 the London Missionary Society was forced to abandon Pella when drought conditions became too harsh. The Roman Catholic Church took over the station in 1878 and developed this small oasis.

Pella is the perfect picture of an oasis. In a sandy plain backed by high, sun-baked hills, denuded of vegetation but vividly coloured by the minerals in the soil, a spring of water reaches the surface. Around this source of life there is a walled garden and a grove of date palms. Figs, grapes, pomegranates, and vegetables flourish. The dates have a special flavour and are sold in wooden boxes to mail-order customers all over South Africa.

Next to the garden is the church, which was hand-built by the first two Catholic missionaries, Father Simon, who became first Bishop of Namaqualand, and Father Wolf. Beautifully decorated inside, the church is a cool haven in a climate that often seems to be a blast from the infernal regions.

The area around the mission is

rich in gem-stones and the rocks are vividly coloured — malachite green from the presence of copper, red oxide from iron, silver from mica-schists, and white and rose from quartz.

What scanty vegetation manages to exist in the area is singularly aromatic, and the warm air, especially during the evenings, is perfumed with subtle odours.

Camels, introduced for police patrols, were released when four-wheel-drive vehicles replaced them. They now run wild.

Pofadder

Klaas Pofadder was a cattle rustler whose headquarters were at a lonely, inaccessible little spring of fresh water. In 1875 he and his band were pursued to their hideaway and killed in a gun fight. A mission station was then established at the spring and the present town developed as a centre for karakul and woolly sheep.

The area is harsh in the extreme. In a good season perhaps 75 millimetres of rain will fall. But most seasons are bad, without any rain at all, and livestock have to be transported to other districts to be fed.

A lonely but cheerful little place, Pofadder somehow or other survives its hardships, always hoping that sometime just a little rain will fall, no more in a year than many cities in Europe receive in a day, but enough to keep the wilderness just slightly better than a total desert.

Upington

Sir Thomas Upington, attorney-general of the Cape, was the man principally responsible for liquidating the business activites of the Orange River pirates and capturing their leader, Klaas Lucas. When the desperadoes were finally driven away in 1884, a town was founded in the area on the banks of the Orange River, and named

The broad Orange River, with the town of Upington on its banks in the distance.

Dates, sweet and luscious, ripening near Kakamas on the Orange River.

in honour of the pacifier of a very tumultuous part of the country.

Among the first pioneers were Oom Japie Lutz and the missionary Christiaan Schroder who, in 1890, dug the first irrigation canal, erected a pump on the banks of the river, and started a pontoon ferry here.

Upington is the principal town of the northern Cape and lies on the north bank of the Orange River. The railway reaches the town by means of a bridge 1 067 metres long, the second longest bridge in southern Africa. The town is the centre for a considerable industry in the production of lucerne, sultanas, raisins, dried fruits, cotton, peas, karakul sheep, goats and cattle. Scheelite and tungsten are mined in the area. Salt is produced from natural salt pans such as Loch

Maree, and many tourists use the town as a transit point on the way to the Augrabies Falls or the Kalahari Gemsbok National Park.

The river is ideal for boating, swimming and fishing. One of the islands in the river, Olyvenhoutsdrift, has been developed into a park, with a caravan and camping ground, bungalows and sports fields. It is connected to the riverbanks by a bridge.

Dates grow well at Upington. The first palms are said to have originated during the Anglo-Boer War, when British soldiers received dates as part of their rations. The men pushed the date stones into the mud on the riverbanks and many thousands of palm trees grew. On Olyvenhout Island there is an avenue of date palms 1 065 metres long.

Upington has several hotels as well as its tourist resort on the island. It is a pleasant, modern town, with an international airport. Roads lead to all parts of the district, known as Gordonia, after Sir Gordon Sprigg, prime minister of the Cape at the time the river pirates were defeated.

The Spitskop Nature Reserve outside the town is open daily. In it the plants indigenous to the area can be seen.

In the local cemetery there is the grave of the famous Scotty Smith, highwayman, horse thief, rustler, bank robber, adventurer — one of the most celebrated of South African desperadoes (see box, page 184).

Verneuk Pan

This vast, dry salt pan was used by Sir Malcolm Campbell in his efforts to break the world land-speed record in his car, the famous *Bluebird*, in 1929. The name means 'deception' and the pan is famous for its mirages.

Such pans are a feature of the northern Cape. In an area of low relief and poor rainfall, any water that does fall tends to find its way into shallow depressions. There it evaporates, leaving salts picked up in its run-off concentrated in the pan. The white surface of these salts is a dazzling reflector of heat and light. Mirages linger over the pans all through the hot hours, and dust devils run riot, caused by hot air spiralling violently as it rises to cooler levels.

TRANSVAAL

TRANSVAAL

Contents:

THE TRANSVAAL HAS been a land of extraordinary adventures and equally extraordinary characters. The landscape is endowed with such scenic splendour and mineral treasures that it inevitably became the stage for great human dramas.

In the south, high-lying grassveld projects across the Vaal from the Orange Free State. This rocky and treeless highveld ends abruptly in a steep escarpment. In the north, 1 000 metres below this escarpment, lies the bushveld — the savanna country that covers much of the African continent. This area is the haunt of big game.

The entire territory of the Transvaal is a treasure chest of valuable rocks, minerals, metals and precious stones. Exposed in parts of the lowveld are the granite domes of the Primitive System, earth's oldest known rock system. For at least 3 000 million years these huge domed and whalebacked rocks have withstood the ravages of weather and time. They remain as memorials to the earth's beginning, when a fragile outer surface floated on an inner core of molten matter.

Through this surface, as though from a mighty storm of fire and molten rock, surged masses of granite and other molten minerals. For 1 000 million years the earth was permeated by strange odours, multi-coloured vapours, the glow of fires, rivers of molten metal sluggishly flowing through lines of weakness and filling depressions with lakes of white-hot matter.

Then, as water vapour formed, the rains came. The surface of the Transvaal was further cooled, and the water eroded and dissolved the higher masses of original material into sludge, depositing it as mineralized sediments, forming such rock systems as the gold-bearing series of reefs known now as the Witwatersrand.

Nature was indeed generous in the creation of the Transvaal. Beneath the ground she bestowed vast wealth; on the surface the soil is deep and fertile.

Man desired the area on sight. He came to the Transvaal in a bewildering, complex assortment of peoples.

When the Voortrekkers arrived in the 1830s they found a war-torn shambles. From this inauspicious beginning they created the South African Republic, which had its capital first at Potchefstroom, and later at Pretoria.

In 1886, George Harrison stumbled on an outcrop of gold on the main reef of the Witwatersrand. From all parts of the earth the gold prospectors poured in. There were political upheavals, petty wars with the earlier inhabitants, and eventually the grim Anglo-Boer War of 1899-1902.

The British then annexed the Transvaal, but soon afterwards they gave it a substantial degree of self-rule, and in 1910 it became part of the Union of South Africa. Today the Transvaal remains one of the most desirable, varied and beautiful parts of the world.

Preceding page: A baobab tree in its summer leaves at sunset in the northern Transvaal — a giant of a tree, dominating the savanna.

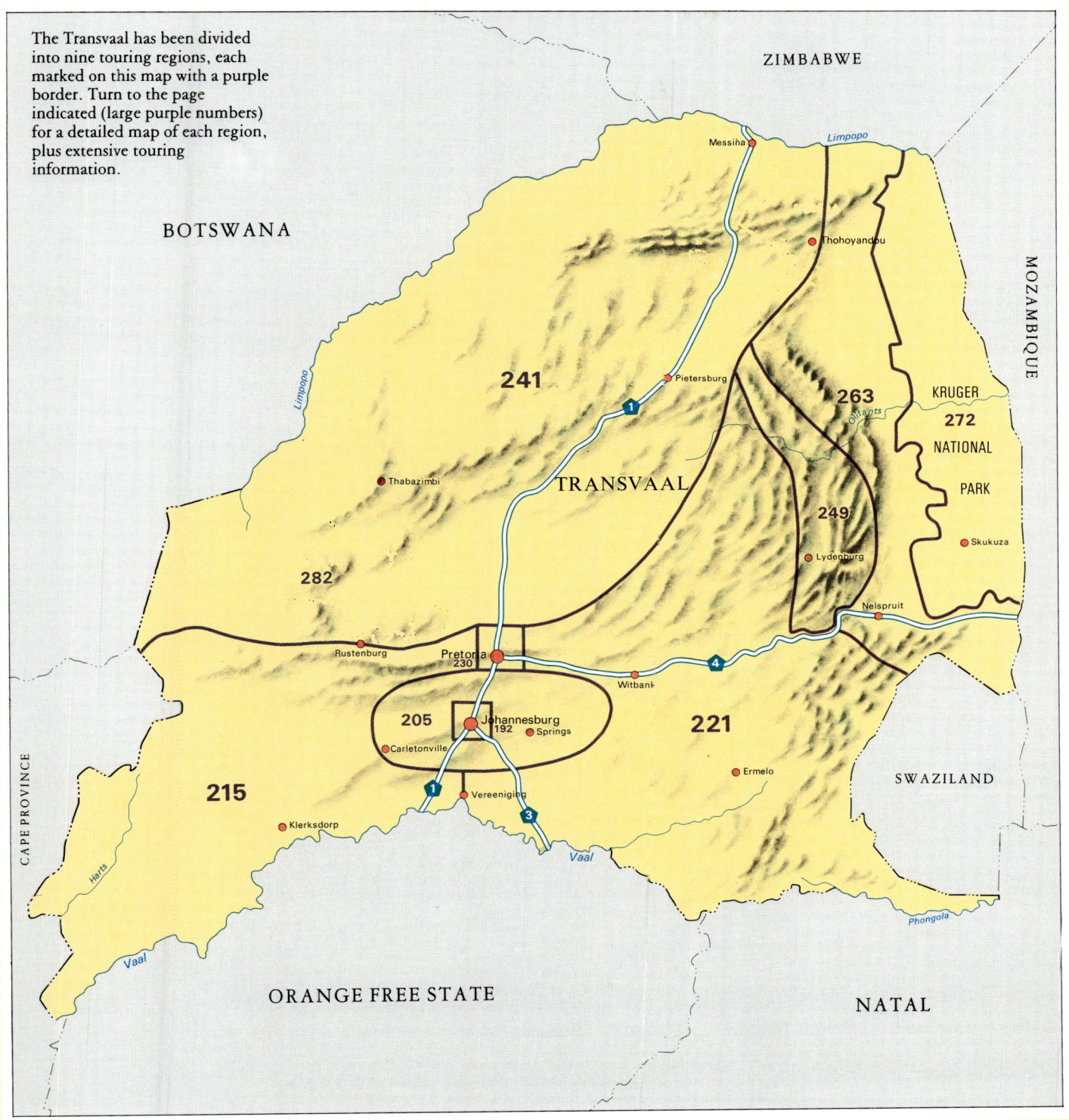

The Transvaal has been divided into nine touring regions, each marked on this map with a purple border. Turn to the page indicated (large purple numbers) for a detailed map of each region, plus extensive touring information.

ZIMBABWE

BOTSWANA

MOZAMBIQUE

Limpopo

Messina

Thohoyandou

241

Pietersburg

263

KRUGER

272

Olifants

NATIONAL

TRANSVAAL

Thabazimbi

249

PARK

282

Lydenburg

Skukuza

Nelspruit

Rustenburg

Pretoria
230

Witbank

4

205

Johannesburg
192

Springs

221

Carletonville

Ermelo

SWAZILAND

215

Vereeniging

Klerksdorp

3

Vaal

Harts

Vaal

Phongola

ORANGE FREE STATE

NATAL

CAPE PROVINCE

THE CITY THAT GOLD BUILT

JOHANNESBURG IS THE gold-mining shanty town that just kept on growing — an ugly duckling that became, if not beautiful, at least dramatically big and bustling.

Everything about Johannesburg was improbable. Its setting was a bleak patch of windswept veld. It owes its existence to the discovery of gold by a penniless prospector. Brashly, the town sprouted through grubby infancy, ragamuffin adolescence and brawling youth until, in a strange about-turn, it settled down to sober, middle-aged respectability. Today, a mere hundred years after its unpromising beginnings, it is the largest mining, manufacturing and engineering centre in Africa.

The city seems to change every year. In Europe, buildings may stand for 1 000 years or more; in Johannesburg, any building that is 20 years old has avoided demolition largely owing to an oversight by a property developer. Architecture has tended to be judged by height rather than beauty. It is a city of straight streets, towering office blocks, air-conditioned, well-stocked shops, smartly dressed women and preoccupied, career-orientated men.

Though Johannesburg has many thriving industries, there is no forgetting the origin of its prosperity. The city is dominated by the man-made mountains of tailings and rocks from the now disused mines of the central Witwatersrand gold field.

A convenient point at which to begin an exploration of Johannesburg is the George Harrison Park, five kilometres west of the city. This is the spot where, on an unrecorded day in March 1886, a prospector named George Harrison casually panned a sample of strange-looking rock. He left no description of his emotions as he washed away the mud and revealed the most fabulous tail of gold ever seen in any prospectors' pan.

He had stumbled across the only surface outcrop of the main gold-bearing reef of the Witwatersrand.

Harrison pegged the first claim on the reef, later sold it for £10, and vanished without trace — nothing is known of what became of him. But his report to the government on his discovery led to the greatest rush of fortune-seekers the world has known.

The mighty gold-mining industry of the Witwatersrand and the complex city of Johannesburg mushroomed around the site of this first discovery, but Harrison is commemorated only by this park and one street named after him. The city itself is named after two civil service officials who happened to be called Johannes.

A few kilometres east of the city centre, in Bezuidenhout Park, stands one of the original farmhouses of the Witwatersrand. The surrounding landscape is as it was in Harrison's time. To stand in this spot where so little has changed and gaze back to the concrete towers of modern Johannesburg is to feel the awesome processes of history.

Bedfordview
A municipality on the eastern side of Johannesburg, Bedfordview contains Gillooly's Farm, a 44-hectare picnic area frequently used for dog shows.

Bezuidenhout Park
Among the eastern suburbs, at Dewetshof, Bezuidenhout Park is refreshingly unspoilt. It was originally the heart of the farm of Doornfontein, owned by F. J. Bezuidenhout at the time of the rush to the Witwatersrand. The farm was off the gold-bearing reef and although it was prospected, gold was not found. The

The site where George Harrison discovered the Witwatersrand reef.

One of the headgears of the Village Main Reef gold mine looms up against a background of tall buildings.

Johannesburg photographed in 1898. Tall buildings had still to come and corrugated iron was a principal building material.

Modern Johannesburg reaches skywards.

THINGS TO DO AND SEE

Art The art gallery in Joubert Park houses works by English, French and Dutch masters, and many pieces of sculpture.

Bird watching The Melrose Bird Sanctuary is the home of 120 species of indigenous birds.

Boating Several artificial lakes in the parks offer boating. Water pumped out of the mines, together with rainwater, forms substantial lakes such as Wemmer Pan, where rowing and other boating takes place.

Camping and caravanning The municipal caravan park in Bezuidenhout Park is within easy reach of Johannesburg city centre.

Diamonds Johannesburg is the principal centre for the South African diamond-cutting industry. At the Adamant Research Laboratory, the only one of its kind in the world, artificial diamonds are made. Visits can be arranged only by special permission from the De Beers Corporation. Visits to the diamond-cutting factories can be arranged through the Master Diamond Cutters' Association, Diamond Exchange Building, De Villiers Street.

Gardens The Wilds, in Houghton, is a garden of indigenous plants. The rose garden at Emmarentia has more than 12 000 rose plants.

Gold mines The public relations department of the Chamber of Mines arranges visits to mines.

The Gold Reef City mine museum south of the city recreates the pioneering days of early Johannesburg with a mining village, restaurants, rides to be had on old steam locomotives, and opportunities to go underground. Traditional African dancing may be seen at the museum on Sundays. To make enquiries telephone 835 1027.

Museums Johannesburg is noted for its museums. These include the Africana Museum (Market Street), Africana Museum In Progress (cnr Bree and Wolhuter Streets), Railway Museum (Eloff Street), South African National Museum of Military History (Erswold Way), Geological Museum (Market Street), Archaeological Museum (Market Street), Pharmacy Museum (Market Street), Jewish Museum (Main Street), Transport Museum (Rosettenville Road), Bernberg Museum of Costume (cnr Duncombe Road and Jan Smuts Avenue) and the Bensusan Museum of Photography (Empire Road).

Planetarium The planetarium, in the grounds of the University of the Witwatersrand, is the largest in South Africa. Demonstrations are given from Wednesdays to Sundays.

Rand Show The largest agricultural and industrial exhibition in Africa, the Rand Show, is held each year in Johannesburg. Organized by the Witwatersrand Agricultural Society, the venue is at the old Crown Mines, the site of one of the richest gold ore deposits ever worked. Smaller shows are also held here periodically.

Sports Ellis Park is the home of swimming, tennis and rugby. Horse racing is held at Turffontein, cricket at the Wanderers' ground, and soccer at the Rand Stadium and other venues. Carlton Skyrink is an Olympic-size skating rink.

Theatre, music and ballet Johannesburg is the home of the National Symphony Orchestra of the South African Broadcasting Corporation.

The civic theatre stages opera and ballet by the Performing Arts Council of the Transvaal. There are several theatres and many cinemas.

Zoo The Johannesburg Zoo, one of the largest in Africa, is housed in the Hermann Eckstein Park.

Bezuidenhouts, however, made a fortune by selling land for townships. Suburbs such as Bezuidenhout Valley, Doornfontein and Judiths Paarl were laid out on their property.

The nucleus of the farm, with the homestead and graveyard, remain intact.

Old Bezuidenhout died in 1900 and his son, Barend, in the 1920s. The Johannesburg city council bought what was left of the farm. The deed of sale contained the condition that 40 hectares encompassing the homestead, garden and dam, cemetery and the original trees, mainly *Acacia karoo*, be preserved intact.

Bezuidenhout Park is therefore a historical monument and recreational area. It has a children's playground and swimming pool, restaurant, sports grounds, picnic spots and caravan park.

Braamfontein

West of Hospital Hill is the heavily built-up suburb of Braamfontein. It contains the campus of the University of the Witwatersrand, which originated in Kimberley in 1896 as a training institute for the mining industry. An offshoot of the institute was established in Johannesburg after the Anglo-Boer War. In 1906 it became the Transvaal University College.

A branch of the college, opened in Pretoria in 1907, later became the University of Pretoria.

Johannesburg at night — a glittering view from the J. G. Strijdom Tower.

Bird's-eye view of where the gold comes from

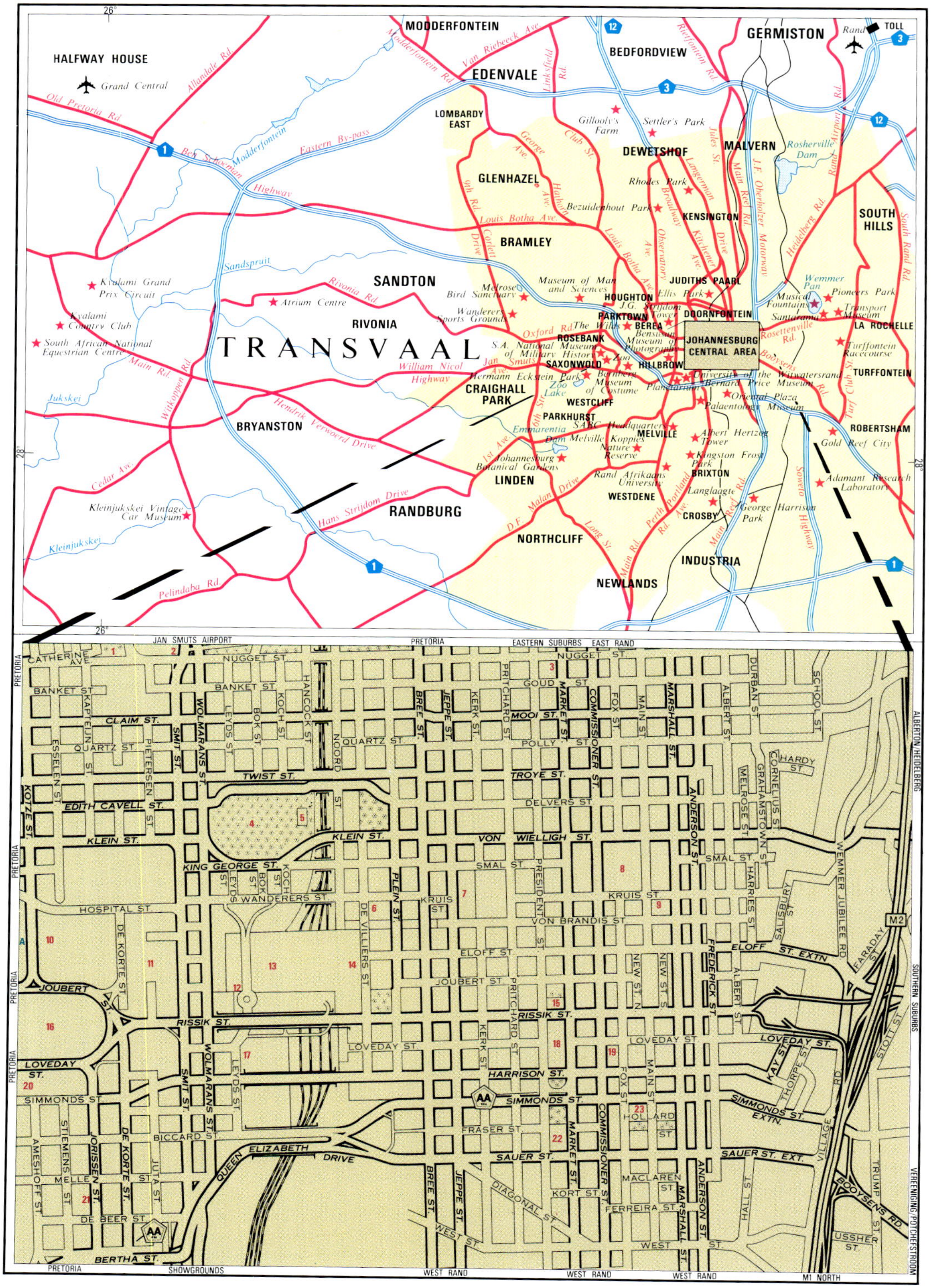

JOHANNESBURG

National Monuments

A Old Fort

Places of interest

1 Pullinger Kop
2 Roman Catholic Cathedral
3 Islam Mosque
4 Joubert Park
5 Art Gallery
6 St. Mary's Cathedral
7 Post Office
8 Carlton Centre
9 Jewish Museum
10 Medical Research Institute
11 Witwatersrand Technikon
    Hotel School
12 Locomotive
13 Station
14 Railway Museum
15 Post Office
16 Civic Centre
17 Airways Terminal
18 City Hall
19 Rand Club
20 Civic Theatre
21 Pharmacy Museum (old site)
22 Library, Africana Museum,
    Geological Museum, Pharmacy
    Museum, Archaeological Museum
23 Chamber of Mines

City and surroundings map scale

kilometres 0 1 2 3 4 5 kilometres

City central area map scale

metres 0 500 metres

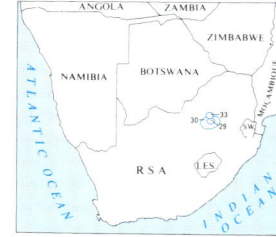

Night falls on the Golden City and the evening traffic turns Rissik Street into a river of light.

During its early years the Johannesburg College taught only mining and technology, but other departments were gradually added and in 1922 it became the University of the Witwatersrand. The Johannesburg city council had already presented a 32-hectare site at Milner Park to the college, and from the handful of buildings built here in 1922 the present massive complex has arisen, housing 16 000 students.

Included in the campus are the planetarium and the Bernard Price Institute of Palaeontology. This is the premier museum in South Africa devoted wholly to the study of extinct plants and animals. It is part of the University of the Witwatersrand, but is housed in a separate building off Showground Road.

The museum displays the geological periods of the earth, and has a vast collection of fossils, including a treasure trove of ancient animal bones recovered from Makapansgat in the northern Transvaal. The deposits in this cave are so enormous and scientifically valuable that teams of excavators will be kept busy there for years to come. The museum also has detailed collections of the bones and tools of a type of early man, *Australopithecus*.

The Rand Afrikaans University was established west of the campus of the Witwatersrand University in 1966.

On the ridge of nearby Brixton stands one of the two tall towers in Johannesburg. It was built in 1961 for the South African Broadcasting Corporation, which has its main studios in the vicinity. The tower, 239 metres high, graceful, and flood-lit at night, has a restaurant at its base. It was named after the former minister of posts and telegraphs, Albert Hertzog, but is increasingly called the SABC, or Brixton, Tower.

The 3,39-hectare Kingston Frost Park in Brixton has aloes collected from throughout southern Africa.

Commissioner Street

One of the principal streets of Johannesburg, Commissioner Street, runs east to west through the centre of the city. It was named in honour of the government commissioners involved in the proclamation of the gold-fields

Looming against an old mine dump, the Brixton radio and television tower.

Heat and hurry and tired feet — but also a sense of big city excitement.

The ape-man, Australopithecus, who lived in southern Africa about three and a half million years ago. Early forms of this man were little more than one metre tall, but probably walked erect.

MINI-QUAKES

Several times a year the buildings of Johannesburg give a slight shudder. These periodic tremors are mildly alarming to visitors, but 'Joburgers' regard them with indifference for they bear no relation to genuine earthquakes.

They are caused by rockfalls and subterranean adjustments in the deep gold workings of the Witwatersrand reef which send tremors through the rocks under the city.

Contrary to the belief of many people, however, the city is not built on top of the mine workings.

It has grown up to the north and south of the long band of mining operations.

Seen from an elevated position, such as the observation platform of the Carlton Centre, the mine workings and dumps stretch east and west, dividing the city in half.

The deepest mine in the central area is the Crown Mines. Before operations in this mine were discontinued, a depth of more than 3 000 metres had been reached.

Although such workings often make their presence felt, the tremors are not strong enough to do significant damage.

The bustle of Africa's biggest railway station

and the establishment of the city.

Among its buildings is the Carlton Centre, claimed to be one of the largest all-concrete buildings in the world. It is 50 storeys high and contains a shopping complex, ice-skating rink and hotel.

Ellis Park

In the suburb of Doornfontein, 3 kilometres east of the city hall, lies Ellis Park, named after a former mayor, J. Dowel Ellis. It is the principal venue in the city for rugby, tennis and swimming. In the park are the headquarters of the Transvaal Rugby Football Union. The famed old Ellis Park ground was recently replaced by a sophisticated new stadium.

The Southern Transvaal Lawn Tennis Association has its headquarters at Ellis Park. Johannesburg's major tennis tournaments are played here. And the largest swimming bath in Jo-hannesburg is also to be found here. Built to Olympic standards, the bath is the scene of international competitive swimming.

Open-air boxing matches are staged at the park.

Eloff Street

Named after Jan Eloff, private secretary to President Paul Kruger when Johannesburg was laid out, Eloff Street is one of the principal streets of Johannesburg.

It is lined with commercial buildings and at its northern end is the entrance to Johannesburg railway station, said to be the largest railway station in Africa.

The old station concourse, built in the 1930s on the site of an earlier station, contains the first locomotive to serve the Witwatersrand. This little 'puffing Billy' was carted in pieces from Durban to Johannesburg by ox-

Curved roof lights, escalators and passageways in the Carlton Centre.

An arcade of old Johannesburg, just off Commissioner Street.

wagon in 1890. Murals by the South African artist J. H. Pierneef are displayed in a special gallery in the concourse.

Behind this building is the modern station, completed in 1966 and covering a full 22 hectares of platform and track.

More than 250 000 passengers use this station daily.

The new main concourse is 168 metres long, 43 metres wide and 18 metres high; it contains shops, restaurants and snack bars.

Adjoining the station are the railway offices and airways terminal in a garden setting.

The railway museum is housed in a part of the station building. In the museum is a wall decorated with models of locomotives and rolling stock from the early days to modern times. Several cases display old tickets, signalling systems, uniforms, badges, lamps, dining car menus, a lighthouse, road transport, harbour equipment and aircraft.

There are dozens of working models.

In the Railway Museum, a steam locomotive of 1889 with its oil head-lamp.

A chocolate bar vending machine, a reminder of days of penny bargains.

THE CITY WHERE SUMMER AFTERNOONS ARE SHATTERED BY DRAMATIC ELECTRIC STORMS

Johannesburg is pleasantly mild in summer, with the days warm to hot and nights cool and refreshing. Most of the rain falls in summer, usually in the form of afternoon thunderstorms which are sudden, brief, and often spectacular.

In the early morning the sky is usually clear blue. Before noon the first clouds appear — white cumulus which build up steadily until they resemble gigantic cloud castles or great dollops of whipped cream floating lazily through the warm air.

If a thunderstorm threatens the clouds turn black in the afternoon. Tremendous electrical charges build up. Then come the lightning flashes. Most of the flashes are hidden in the cloud, but about one in every six strikes the earth, releasing energy for one thousandth of a second.

Modern buildings are normally unaffected by lightning. The two high telecommunication towers in Johannesburg are sometimes struck several times in the course of a single storm. Conductors take the discharge safely to earth.

Motor vehicles are not affected. Aircraft are occasionally struck but survive with minor damage. Power lines and telecommunication networks suffer the greatest disruption.

Much research on lightning has been done in South Africa. Dr. (later Sir) Basil Schonland began work on the subject at Somerset East in the late 1920s. When the Bernard Price Institute for Geophysical Research was founded in Johannesburg, Dr. Schonland became the first director.

Between 1933 and 1935 Dr. Schonland's team took many high-speed photographs of lightning flashes and were able to time them to a few millionths of a second.

Research continued with the establishment in 1945 of the Council for Scientific and Industrial Research. With Dr. Schonland as its first president, the council has devised many protective systems against lightning with the aid of instruments known as lightning flash counters.

Since the ground flashes are the only kinds of lightning that cause damage, the council has developed a counter that differentiates between inter-cloud flashes and cloud-to-ground flashes to a degree that had not been possible before.

While the summer lightning is an integral part of life in Johannesburg, the high-lying areas of Lesotho, Zimbabwe and Madagascar have even more frequent electrical storms.

In winter Johannesburg is left in peace from the storms. There is little rain, the days may be cold and the nights bitter. Snow is rare, however, and when it does fall it melts quickly. Most vegetation becomes dormant and it takes a hardy tree or plant to retain its greenness when touched by the highveld frosts.

A cathedral flooded with multi-coloured light

Taking it easy . . . a brown bear in the Johannesburg Zoo.

Summer afternoon siesta time for a lion in the zoo.

In the military museum of the Hermann Eckstein Park, artillery of the late 19th and 20th centuries is displayed.

Hermann Eckstein Park

Situated in Saxonwold and covering an area of more than 100 hectares, the Hermann Eckstein Park was presented to Johannesburg in 1903 by a mining house, the Wernher Beit company.

They asked that the area be named after a late senior partner in the firm who had started a private zoo on the estate before his death.

These animals became the nucleus for the Johannesburg Zoological Garden, which today covers 55 hectares of the area and exhibits 140 species of mammals, 160 species of birds and 20 species of reptiles from all over the world.

Also in the park is the South African National Museum of Military History, which exhibits weapons and uniforms.

More people visit the museum than any other in Johannesburg. It displays tanks, armoured cars, and military air craft, including a Hawker Hurricane, a De Havilland Mosquito and Spitfire, and planes from World War I.

There are battle flags, medals, decorations, insignia, war photographs, steel helmets, rifles, handguns, swords, daggers, knives and bayonets. There are many paintings of battle scenes, portraits and a German one-man submarine.

In another part of the park there is the 45,32-hectare Zoo Lake, popular for boating. There are also extensive picnic grounds, an illuminated fountain and a restaurant.

Hillbrow

The suburb of Hillbrow, the most densely populated residential area in southern Africa, lies on top of the Hospital Hill ridge, and is dominated by the J. G. Strijdom Tower (269 metres).

Hillbrow is also reputed to be the home of the most cosmopolitan community in Johannesburg — many immigrants gravitate to this area despite its congestion. Restaurants offering a wide variety of foods and flavours flourish here.

Hollard Street

Named after Emil Hollard, lawyer and financier, Hollard Street is the financial heart of Johannesburg. Most of the big mining houses, and the

Emmarentia

One of the northern suburbs, Emmarentia is the home of the 79,41-hectare Johannesburg Botanic Garden. In the garden are a variety of herbs, more than 12 000 rose trees, and many other plants.

End Street

Originally the eastern end of the Municipality of Johannesburg, End Street now leads through the busy centre of a heavily built-up residential and light-industrial area.

At its northern end, just before it climbs the slopes of Hillbrow, stands the Roman Catholic cathedral of Christ the King. Built in 1960, the cathedral has an unusual design: a variety of materials were used to produce a finish of mellow brick, red granite and stained glass — which floods the interior with crimson, emerald-green and gold light.

The Emmarentia Dam. Johannesburg's botanic garden is on its shores.

FOUNTAINS BRING A TOUCH OF SPARKLE TO THE CITY

The Rissik Street fountain, a memorial to Sir Ernest Oppenheimer.

One of Johannesburg's crowning glories is its fountains.

The sculptor Ernest Ullmann designed the delightful fountain depicting two antelope drinking

Mining monument on Hospital Hill.

Musical fountain in Pioneers Park.

near the entrance to the University of the Witwatersrand.

The same artist created the fountain in front of the civic theatre, which consists of three bronze figures dancing, with water playing at their feet.

In a small garden behind the Rissik Street Post Office, the sculptor Herman Wald created a fountain of 18 bronze impala leaping over fine jets of water.

In Hollard Street there is a fountain flowing from a pile of dolerite boulders into a series of pools, and another near the civic centre, on Hospital Hill, depicts a group of miners working a drill.

On Pullinger Kop in Berea there is a series of artificial waterfalls while in Settlers Park, at the main entrance to the city from Jan Smuts Airport, are three gold-lit fountains. Another illuminated fountain can be seen in the Zoo Lake gardens.

At Pioneers Park in La Rochelle, on the banks of Wemmer Pan, there is a spectacular fountain with changing colours and patterns synchronized by computer to music.

Chamber of Mines, have their administrative headquarters in the vicinity.

The Johannesburg Stock Exchange, formerly in Hollard Street but now in Diagonal Street, has a visitors' gallery, open to the public on weekdays.

Hospital Hill

Overlooking the city area of Johannesburg from the north is a high ridge, densely covered with flats and office blocks. Part of this ridge, Hospital Hill, takes its name from the old General Hospital.

On the summit of the ridge stands the Johannesburg Fort, a grim old stronghold built in the 1890s and designed by Colonel A. H. Schiel, a German soldier in the employ of the South African Republic. A garrison of the state artillery was maintained at the fort together with armaments of cannons and machine-guns, all intended to keep the boisterous digger community in order.

The fort was never the scene of violent action. After the Anglo-Boer War it was converted into a prison and is now a museum.

Above the fort's main entrance is the former Republic's coat of arms, reputedly carved by the well-known sculptor Anton van Wouw.

Close by the fort, built on the original parade ground of the garrison, is the medical research institute, and to the west are the civic centre, an administrative office block for the city council, and the civic theatre — the home of Johannesburg's ballet, opera, drama and music

The tallest building in Africa is the 269-metre J. G. Strijdom Tower on Hospital Hill. This tower, resembling from a distance a ramrod used by old-time artillery men, was completed in 1971. The tower was named after a former prime minister of South Africa and is used as a transmitting centre for the South African Post Office. There is a dramatic view of the city area from the observation room at the top, but for the time being, for security reasons, the tower remains closed to the public.

Houghton

In the suburb of Houghton, a 17,45-hectare expanse of ground covering part of the foothills of the Witwaters-

rand was presented to Johannesburg in 1937 by one of the major mining houses, the Johannesburg Consolidated Investment Company. It was to be a permanent home for the spectacular collection of South African wild flowers exhibited at the 1936 Empire Exhibition held in the city.

Since then these foothills, known as The Wilds, have been converted into a garden dedicated to the memory of General Jan Smuts, an enthusiastic naturalist as well as a major statesman.

The garden was originally part of the grounds of Hohenheim, the home of Sir Percy FitzPatrick, author of *Jock of the Bushveld* (see box, page 281) and a director of the mining company which presented the property to the city.

In a corner house on Jan Smuts Avenue is the Bernberg Museum of Costume. The house has been reconstructed to enable visitors to make a complete circuit through two displays. In the first, costumes are worn by dummy models standing in beautifully designed period interiors. In the second are wall cases with collections of accessories. On the walls a range of fashion plates is exhibited.

There are complete wedding groups, a reconstructed dress salon

The 269-metre J. G. Strijdom Tower, with Brixton Tower in the distance.

The oldest park — and still a welcome oasis

of the 1920s, an art gallery from 1810, a kitchen, children's costumes and all the bric-a-brac of high fashion, including underclothing, smoking hats, buttons, gloves, shoes, shawls, bags, purses, cigarette holders and jewellery.

Jan Smuts International Airport

The Jan Smuts International Airport is the principal gateway of South Africa for world travel. It was opened in 1953, but has since been substantially enlarged. The present terminal buildings were opened in December 1971, when wide-bodied jets were brought into service in the country.

About 4 million passengers use the airport every year.

The spacious, two-level terminal building has restaurants, shops, banks and a post office. The airport is also the base for South African Airways, the largest airline in Africa.

The airport is used for scheduled services by most of the world's principal airlines, and it handles over 90 million metric tons of freight a year.

Joubert Park

The best-known and oldest park in Johannesburg, Joubert Park was laid out in 1887 on 6,43 hectares of vacant ground close to the city centre.

Named after Christian Johannes Joubert, first chief of the mining department, the park is a green oasis in a setting of asphalt streets and concrete buildings.

In the park are a giant open-air chess board with figures 1 metre high, a conservatory of tropical plants, restaurant, fountain, illuminations, art gallery, and an art market where artists sell direct to the public.

Kensington

One of the eastern suburbs of Johannesburg, Kensington contains Rhodes Park. This 24,90-hectare park has a small lake and restaurant.

In the overlooking heights there is a cave, really an old mining shaft, which was the scene in September 1914 of a renowned gun fight when the Foster Gang — a much-wanted gang of professional hold-up men — were finally cornered by the police. William Foster, leader of the gang, had with him two henchmen, Carl Mezar and John Maxim.

They decided to kill themselves rather than surrender.

Foster, who wanted to make a final farewell to his wife, baby daughter, and his parents and two sisters, shouted to police that he would surrender if they were allowed to see him.

After some official deliberation the police allowed the visits. Foster's parents and sisters left the cave with his daughter.

Shots were heard. Police entered the cave and found the three men and Mrs. Foster dead.

Kyalami

The 1 000-hectare farm Kyalami takes its name from the Zulu 'kaya lami', meaning 'my home'. In 1961 the farm was converted into a racing track for cars and motor-cycles. From 1 January 1968 Kyalami became the scene of

MINE DANCING BRINGS BACK THE JOY OF LIFE BACK HOME

Men from about fifty different African groups are employed in the mines of the Witwatersrand. Their work is arduous and they live in hostels for the duration of their contract period, usually about one year.

Their women are far away. Only in their traditional dances can they participate in their rural lifestyle, exchanging miners' clothes for the skins and adornments of their own people back home.

The men organize themselves into teams, each with its own manager and music director. Costumes are designed and rehearsals are held in preparation for Sunday mornings — the big day for traditional dancing.

One of the most amusing dances is the isicathulo ('gumboot dance') of the Bhaca. It is said that a missionary once forbade the Bhaca from performing their traditional dances as he considered them to be pagan.

The people were taught a more 'genteel' Austrian folk dance, which they performed in cumbersome Wellington boots as a humorous gesture of protest.

Men from the Shangane-Tsonga group in Mocambique also have a modern dance, known as the Makwaya. It is a source of great amusement because the participants poke fun at the modern world and the ways of the white man, their bosses on the mines, the missionaries back home, the tax collectors and other government officials.

Dances are held every Sunday (weather permitting) at the Gold Mines Museum.

An open-air chess game played with giant pieces in Joubert Park.

A 19th century steam engine in the transport museum.

A horse-drawn steam fire engine of the last century.

A British-built, steam-powered corn thrashing machine.

the annual world championship Grand Prix of South Africa.

Most of the road races of South Africa are staged at Kyalami. Crowds of 100 000 are common.

La Rochelle

The southern suburb of La Rochelle includes the Rand Stadium, used for soccer matches and boxing, and Wemmer Pan, much used for boating.

On the shores of this pan is Pioneers Park, covering 88,87-hectares with a restaurant, picnic grounds, and a musical illuminated fountain which plays for an hour and a half every evening in summer. There is a miniature town on the northern shores. Boat trips on the lake are provided.

In this park is the James Hall Museum of Transport. The exhibits include agricultural machines, steam rollers, steam engines, trams, buses, fire engines, ancient automobiles, bicycles and early roller-skates. There is also a collection of photographs of old vehicles.

Market Street

The handsome library building, housing the Johannesburg Public Library and the Africana and Geological museums, dominates Market Street.

The building, completed in 1935, was designed by John Perry.

The Africana Museum occupies the upper floor. It is divided into two parts: one on the way of life and his-

tory of South Africa; the other providing a portrait of Johannesburg.

The first division exhibits Cape-made furniture which survived the long ox-wagon journeys into the interior by the pioneers.

Cape silver, glass, china and other domestic items of former years are displayed.

The Johannesburg division includes a Zeederberg mail coach, which was used on the wild stretch from Pretoria to Bulawayo. Once the coach was drawn by zebras because so many oxen fell victim to nagana, the livestock disease inflicted by the tsetse

fly. The zebras were immune to the bite of the fly but had little stamina and slowed the coach considerably.

Throughout the museum the walls are used to display the paintings of artists such as Thomas Baines, Samuel Daniell, Barbara Tyrrell, and others whose works are accepted as classic representations of the life of southern African peoples.

The Geological Museum, started by the Chamber of Mines in 1890 but now maintained by the Johannesburg Geological Society, explains the geological history of the earth with diagrams, specimens, and a spectacular

collection of minerals and gem-stones of southern Africa.

There is also a showcase with gold exhibits, and many specimens of gold-bearing ore.

On the corner of Market and Nugget streets stands the Madressa Himayatil Islam mosque. It has a tower 30 metres high, equipped with a public address system in order to save the muezzin from climbing for the five daily obligatory calls to prayer.

The floor is electrically heated for the comfort of the devout while praying. The mosque was built in 1916 and has since been enlarged.

Grand Prix racing for the world championship series on the Kyalami track.

A curiosity in the Africana Museum — an early print showing a giraffe.

199

A place untouched by the march of progress

A cast-iron drinking fountain with brass cups, in the Africana Museum.

Rissik Street in the late 1890s. On the left is the famous Grand National Hotel.

Melville

A 45-hectare nature reserve at Melville — Melville Koppies — has been left entirely in its natural condition. The principal attraction is the original flora which flourishes around the remains of an iron-age furnace. The reserve is a national monument and a sanctuary for more than 150 species of birds, including spotted eagle owls.

Oriental Plaza

West of the Johannesburg City Hall, off Bree Street, stands the Oriental Plaza, a lively shopping centre with about 300 shops in an area of 9 hectares. Opened in 1974, this shopping centre replaces the hotch-potch of shops, under Indian management, which lined Fourteenth Street, Pageview, and have since been demolished.

The new centre is a joint project in urban renewal by the Department of Community Development and the Johannesburg City Council.

Parktown

The Bensusan Museum of Photography, in Parktown's Empire Road, displays the history of photography with many examples of early photographs and equipment.

There are magic lanterns, cinematographic cameras, a reproduction of a turn-of-the-century dark room and photographer's studio, and an extensive library.

Parktown is notable for its jacaranda trees.

Plein Street

An open square ('plein'), now used as a parking ground and bus terminal, probably gives Plein Street its name. Another possibility is that the street was named after J. J. Plein, a prominent Transvaal businessman at the turn of the century. The principal building on Plein Street is the Anglican St. Mary's Cathedral, which was built in 1926 and designed by Sir Herbert Baker, an architect whose creative genius gave South Africa many of her finest buildings (see box, page 237).

The cathedral was constructed of hammer-dressed sandstone.

Randburg

Thirteen of the northern suburbs of Johannesburg combined in 1959 to form the municipality of Randburg, a rapidly growing town with its own light industrial area, civic centre and shopping centres. Randburg is being developed as a garden city. It has 37 parks and the first fully fledged pedestrian mall in South Africa.

An open-air fresh produce market is held on Saturdays between the municipal buildings and the law courts.

On the Witkoppen road, on the banks of the Kleinjukskei River, is the Kleinjukskei Vintage Car Museum, with a large collection of veteran cars.

This is a private collection, open to the public on weekends only. There is a picnic ground on the banks of the river.

Rissik Street

One of the few buildings linking Johannesburg with its boom-town past is the Rissik Street Post Office, designed by Sytse Wierda, head of the public works department of the Transvaal during the 19th century.

The laying of the foundation stone of this building in 1897 was a great occasion for the people of Johannesburg.

For the government to erect so substantial a building was reassurance that authority at last considered the town to be permanent, and it would not become a dilapidated, abandoned place of ghosts, with exhausted mines.

The building, attractively designed and faced with red bricks, had three floors. There were two cupolas and a central bell tower.

Acacia trees in flower during spring in the Melville Koppies Nature Reserve.

Trust Bank building, a modern skyscraper in the centre of Johannesburg.

The Rissik Street Post Office shortly after its completion in 1897. An additional storey and clock tower were added in 1906.

After the Anglo-Boer War, the British refurbished the building by adding a fourth storey and a clock tower. The cupolas and the central bell tower were removed, but, to commemorate the coronation of King Edward VII in 1902, a clock was later installed.

It was made in England by the same firm that had manufactured the clock of Big Ben, and its chimes make a similar sound to those of that famous London landmark.

A modern, new main Johannesburg Post Office of the inevitable concrete type was opened in Jeppe Street in 1935, but the Rissik Street Post Office in its charming old building is still functioning.

Though dwarfed by the towering modern glass and concrete skyscrapers, the old building has a subtle charm and a mellowness of design and colour.

Facing the Rissik Street Post Office is the city hall, designed in the Italian renaissance style. It was built between 1910 and 1915 and is still in use today, although most of its functions have now been taken over by the new civic centre and the civic theatre.

The old building, solid and imposing, resembles a mausoleum, with high ceilings and cold, echoing corridors and stairwells. It contains a sumptuous mayoral parlour that has been carefully maintained in virtually mint condition.

Rissik Street was named after Johann Rissik, one of the government officials after whom the city itself is named.

Sandton

The dormitory town of Sandton was created in 1969 by the blending of three urban areas — Sandown, Bryanston and north-eastern Johannesburg.

Sandton is one of the most parklike and spacious of Johannesburg's dormitory towns, with well-planned shopping centres and recreation areas. Dominating the central business area is the Sandton City complex which is probably the largest suburban shopping centre in the southern hemisphere. It has nine major stores, over 200 smaller shops, a number of cinemas, banks and building societies, office towers and a luxury hotel.

In the Atrium Centre there is an African handicrafts market.

The South African National Equestrian Centre is situated on the outskirts of Sandton, next to the Kyalami Country Club.

On Sunday mornings the equestrian centre stages magnificent displays by white Lipizzaner stallions, which are known throughout the world for their manificent dressage performances.

These remarkable horses were originally bred from the Andalusian horses of Spain, which were brought to the Imperial Austro-Hungarian court in Vienna in the 16th century.

A stud was established in Lipizza, near Trieste, by Crown Prince Karl, who was a great horse-lover, and from here the Lipizzaners spread to private studs, owned by noblemen of the Austro-Hungarian empire.

The Spanish Riding School in Vienna became world famous for training its Lipizzaner stallions.

The ancestors of the South African Lipizzaner horses were kept in Hungary by Count Jankovich Besan. In 1944, with the approach of the Red army, the count fled, telling his staff they could do what they pleased with his horses. His accountant and stud manager succeeded in getting about a dozen out of the war zone and these eventually reached Bavaria, where the count reclaimed them.

In 1946 they were taken to Lord Digby's estate in England where they were looked after until 1948, when they were brought to South Africa by Count Besan. In 1964 the stud was sold to National Chemical Products, now part of the Sentrachem group of companies.

Outside Vienna, the South African equestrian centre is the only school with Lipizzaners performing to the classical standard of the Spanish Riding School.

The soft pink glow of a highveld sunset signals the end of a hot and busy day.

When the randlords ruled the roost in Johannesburg

Traces of gold had been found in streams flowing off the Witwatersrand as early as 1853, and in 1884 a small mine was worked, without much success, on a farm named Wilgespruit, close to the present site of Johannesburg. It was this little mine that attracted two men, George Walker and George Harrison, who had journeyed from the Cape in search of fortune in the eastern Transvaal. Walker took a temporary job in the mine, while Harrison was employed to build a new homestead on the farm Langlaagte.

Harrison spent his spare time prospecting and, in March 1886, found an outcrop of the gold-bearing reef of the Witwatersrand. His discovery was the start of the greatest gold rush the world has ever known.

All along the Witwatersrand tents and shelters went up at such speed that parked wagons were frequently hemmed in by newly built shacks, and their owners had to dismantle their vehicles to extricate them.

Two commissioners, Johannes Rissik and Christian Johannes Joubert, were hastily appointed to inspect the discovery and its implications. They declared the farms along the line of reef to be public diggings, and a representative of the State President, F. C. Eloff, was sent to find a suitable site for a town. Eloff rode over the area, gazing in wonder at the hodge-podge of humanity. Every day more people arrived on the scene.

The site eventually chosen was a vacant piece of ground — a government-owned farm named Randjeslaagte ('dale of little ridges') — which was well off the lie of the gold reef and unlikely to be undermined by any workings. Randjeslaagte was surveyed as quickly as possible, and the first 980 stands were auctioned on 8 December 1886.

The site was named Johannesburg, after the two commissioners who had confirmed Harrison's discovery.

Life in Johannesburg in those days was far from comfortable. On every side holes were being dug and buildings being erected or demolished. A cloud of dust covered everything. Wagons rumbled in day and night bringing foodstuffs, mining equipment, and more and more people.

The diamond diggings of Kimberley provided the men in the first rush; as soon as the Witwatersrand discovery was confirmed, all the diamond magnates raced for concessions.

Johannesburg automatically became the centre for their activities. Shacks fetched premium prices and offices and rough hotels charged small fortunes for accommodation.

In some ways Johannesburg was a ready-made town. It was the age of corrugated iron, and traders moving to Johannesburg from other areas had brought their stock and their premises

Commissioner Street during Queen Victoria's Jubilee in June 1897.

with them, the latter carried in pieces on wagons. In other South African towns gaps began to appear in the commercial streets as buildings were dismantled to accompany their owners in the rush to the golden city.

Liquor shops, canteens and bars sprang up like weeds, and in an effort to counter the influence of these establishments the government offered free stands for churches in the new town.

Anglicans, Roman Catholics, Baptists, Presbyterians and the Salvation Army all hastened to the scene.

The first post office in the town had a delivery service consisting of a clerk shouting out the names on the letters to an expectant crowd milling around the building. It was at this time that Joubert Park was laid out as a recreation area. There was also a morning market, a hospital, clubs — the Johannesburg Club and the Rand Club — and many entertainers, prize-fighters, card-sharps and confidence-tricksters to distract the public.

By 1889 Johannesburg was the largest town in southern Africa. Each day nearly a thousand ox-wagons carrying supplies made their way to the gold fields.

By the end of 1889 a total of 630 499 ounces of gold, worth over R200 million at today's value, had been recovered from the reef. Johannesburg was without doubt the new El Dorado. Businesses were booming, a stock exchange had been founded, the Chamber of Mines had been organized in 1887 as the representative body for the mining industry, and workers were forming unions. The first strike took place on 7 September 1889 with the aim of obtaining a 48-hour week and pay increases. The citizens began agitating for a municipality and direct representation in the Transvaal government.

To supply such a rapidly growing city with services would have taxed any government. In 1890 limited drinking water was still supplied by a private company, and the demand was so great that taps released little more than a trickle of liquid mud.

Vast numbers of draught animals which were used to transport goods into the city, consumed all grazing, and the area around Johannesburg began to resemble a desert littered with the skeletons of oxen and horses that had died of starvation.

Plans for railway to Johannesburg encountered much opposition. Transport riding had become a major industry and for those working this service a railway would have been ruinous. They had a powerful anti-train lobby in the Transvaal parliament.

The first railway service into the town was surreptitiously introduced under the guise of being a 'tram'. This line ran from Johannesburg to Springs, where coal was being mined. The rolling stock and rails were brought by wagon from the coast and the service began before the opposition realized what was happening. However, the transport men soon took action. The service was opened on 17 March 1890. On 8 May the 'puffing Billy' hauling the train collided violently with an ox-wagon loaded with coal which had been deliberately outspanned across the line.

Despite all opposition, however, the railway from the Cape reached Johannesburg on 15 September 1892.

Mr. H. W. Prior, in the bowler, with customers outside his old Criterion Bar.

St. Mary's Choir on a picnic near Johannesburg in 1895.

The last stage-coach to carry mail departed the next day.

The opening of the railway ushered in a new epoch to Johannesburg. The town began to grow more quickly. While miners laboured in primitive conditions and slept in bleak, company accommodation, the financiers, gamblers, swindlers, thieves and prostitutes lived in style and gave the town an ostentatious facade.

Pritchard Street was the main trading thoroughfare, but the hub of the town was a portion of Simmonds Street in front of the stock exchange. This area — known as 'Between the Chains' because all vehicles were kept out by chain fences — contained rows of brokers' offices.

It was here that the cosmopolitan nature of Johannesburg was most obvious. In a variety of languages and accents shares were bought and sold, and rumours, gossip and tips exchanged.

By the middle of the 1890s there were 200 mining companies with head offices in Johannesburg. A gold mine was often cynically described during those times as a hole in the ground with a fool at the bottom, a liar on top and a crook in an office in Johannesburg. There were 75 000 men working in the mines. The accident rate was high. Every 11 858 tons of ore mined produced gold worth £23 702 — and cost one man his life. Many others were seriously injured.

Dominating Johannesburg at this time were the so-called 'randlords' — the heads of the principal mining houses. Chief among these were Julius Wernher and Alfred Beit, whose company ran many of the most profitable mines, including the fabulously rich Crown Mines and Rand Mines.

The second largest company was Consolidated Gold Fields of South Africa, run by Cecil Rhodes and Charles Rudd. From this company Rhodes drew a personal income of £300 000 a year.

Next came the Johannesburg Consolidated Investment Company, run by Barney Barnato, who revelled in the money-making scramble of Johannesburg. He built himself a huge mansion complete with imported English butlers, chambermaids and footmen.

Early in the second half of the 1890s

Park Station, photographed about 1898.

'Between-the-Chains' — a chained-off share market.

A Johannesburg family outside their wood and iron house in the 1900s.

the randlords clashed with the Transvaal government, whom they considered to be inept and standing in the way of still bigger profits. The clash resulted in the Jameson Raid, a futile effort supported by Cecil Rhodes and his financial allies to dislodge the government by means of an invasion of armed men from what were then Rhodesia and Bechuana-

land, led by Dr. Starr Jameson, Rhodes's principal assistant (see Rhodes box, page 37).

The mass of the population of Johannesburg, with nothing to gain, kept out of the squabble. The government rewarded them for their neutrality by making Johannesburg a municipality. The first burgermeester, Johannes de Villiers was appointed in September 1897.

The town continued to grow. The suburbs of Hillbrow, Mayfair and Rosebank sprang up. Burgermeester de Villiers found himself mayor of a town of more than 100 000 inhabitants. Of these half were European. The men outnumbered the women by three to one — a statistic reflected in the fact that there were 591 hotels and bars within the municipal limits and almost the same number of brothels.

The first motor car was brought to Johannesburg in January 1897 by J. P. Hess, and within two years the streets were thronged with an assortment of animal-drawn and motorized vehicles. Streets and shops were electrically lit and entertainments ranged

Tivoli Music Hall girls lead an 1898 procession.

Frank Connock, pioneer car dealer and his 1902 Gladiator.

from flashy music halls and circuses to horse racing at Turffontein.

Over the heads of this boisterous community the political storm continued and, on 11 October 1899, the Anglo-Boer War broke out. Johannesburg was almost deserted as train-loads of refugees fled. The rumbling of gold ore being ground day and night was stilled.

For two years the town remained quiet. Then, with the British now in control, the citizens came back, together with a mass of newcomers. The mills began operating again and their roar once more became a familiar sound. They continued without pause for the next 70 years until the mines of the central Rand started to close down owing to technical complications at deep levels. The mining industry then began to spread east and west of the city.

Johannesburg became a city in 1928. By 1960 it had more than one million inhabitants, and today it is the centre of the most densely populated region in southern Africa — a vast built-up area spreading almost 100 kilometres from east to west.

THE GREAT TREASURE CHEST

THE WITWATERSRAND IS the richest treasure chest ever opened by man. To geologists the name, which means 'ridge of white waters', describes a massive gold reef, most of which is buried far below the surface. The name is commonly applied, however, to an 80-kilometre rocky ridge, 1 748 metres above sea level at its highest point and running east to west, acting as a major watershed in the southern Transvaal. North of this ridge, streams drain into the Limpopo River, which flows to the Indian Ocean. To the south, streams feed the Vaal River, flowing to the Atlantic.

In summer the Witwatersrand is lushly covered with grass. The air is generally clear and warm to hot, and the skies form a vivid blue backdrop for bizarre cloud formations. Often there are short but violent thunderstorms in the afternoons. In winter, the dry air can be keen on the lips and the knuckles and there may be frost or even light snow at night.

Many theories have been formed to explain the origin of the Witwatersrand but all are controversial. Almost certainly, a lake was once formed in this part of South Africa; water drained into the lake and carried with it a thick sediment eroded from the ancient, mineral-rich soil. In this sediment, gold, carbon, uranium, iron pyrites, chromite, silver and platinum were all mixed together with pebbles, sand and silt like the ingredients of a fruit cake. Over the years, this mixture settled on the floor of the lake. Gradually the lake dried and its floor solidified.

For a while this material remained on the surface as the floor of an elongated basin about 250 kilometres by 160 kilometres. In the centre of this basin was an island-like intrusion of granite known to geologists today as the Vredefort Dome. The basin was steadily buried under later geological systems, and the bed of the lost lake was tilted and warped by pressure and heat. The fruit cake was baked, and became a hard reef of rock, so laden with assorted ingredients that it resembled the sweetmeat known to the Dutch as banket, now the name for this type of rock.

When man arrived the only visible part of the old lake bed was its northern rim, which forms the line of the Witwatersrand. The rest of the bed is tilted downwards and southwards, buried more than 2 000 metres deep in parts.

The exposed section of the Witwatersrand is about seven kilometres wide and consists of sloping layers. Several layers are composed merely of shales, which have no commercial value. The upper levels, however, are mainly quartzite with bands of conglomerate rock. Three of these bands carry gold — the icing on the cake. These gold-bearing layers are the Main Reef, the Main Reef Leader and the South Reef. They occur close together and are called the Main Reef Group of Conglomerates. For the past 90 years the bulk of the world's gold has come from these reefs. They are also the world's primary source of uranium.

The appearance of the Witwatersrand is unique. From the air a range of mining dumps stretches like strangely shaped, multi-coloured mountains for the entire length of the Rand. Their contents vary from grey rock and rubble to the vivid yellow and orange of 'tailings' — the waste matter, chemically stained, that is drained off during gold-extraction processes. The tailings, pumped to these dumps, are poured onto them in successive layers, and they harden to form striking shapes and hues.

At the foot of the dumps lies a chain of lakes, created with water pumped from the mines. The area has been beautified by countless trees. Cities and towns, factories, housing complexes and the headgear of mines all cluster along the Rand, forming a unique man-made landscape.

Benoni

The city of Benoni had an uneasy birth. In 1881 the government of the Transvaal republic decided to assign title deeds to unclaimed State property lying between occupied farms.

Bunny Park, Rynfield, is a sanctuary for rabbits and other small animals.

The task fell to Johann Rissik, later to become surveyor-general and administrator of the Transvaal. One region was particularly irregularly shaped and difficult to survey. Rissik gave it the mournful name of Benoni ('son of my sorrows') — the name Rachel gave to her son Benjamin (Genesis 35:18).

In September 1887 gold was discovered at Benoni. The Chimes Mine was established here and staffed by Cornishmen, who were particularly intolerant of 'foreigners'. The mining village became a 'little Cornwall', with whippet racing, gambling and organized dog fights.

Benoni owes much of its beauty to Sir George Farrar, chairman of the mining company which first owned the area. During the early 1900s he had thousands of trees planted in the town. Water was pumped from the mines to a natural marsh, and a chain of reservoirs was created and stocked with fish. These reservoirs are large enough for yachting and boating, and there are many picnic sites on the banks.

The town became a municipality in 1907 and, apart from gold, it produces iron, steel and brass. In the town is the 44,2-hectare Korsman Bird Sanctuary, the home of waterfowl such as flamingo, ibis and egret as well as antelope, particularly duiker, blesbok and springbok.

The Rynfield Children's Park is a 17,5-hectare playground, inhabited by hundreds of rabbits, tame sheep and birds which somehow survive repeated overfeeding and affectionate handling.

Benoni is the headquarters of the Eastern Transvaal Football Association and the Cricket Union. The town has a motor-racing track, bowling greens, two golf-courses and a notable bird sanctuary.

Boksburg

Several of the richest and deepest gold mines in the world are clustered on the land of what once was a farm, Leeuwport. To serve these mines a town was laid out in 1887 and named in honour of Eduard Bok, State Secretary of the South African Republic.

Boksburg's first government administrative officer, the mining com-

Sunset over the Witwatersrand . . . the gold dumps, drenched in unreal colours, might well be mountains on a remote planet.

missioner Montague White, set out to beautify the countryside. He planted trees and by building a wall across the Vogelfontein stream he created a dam of such size that President Paul Kruger, who owned the nearby farm of Geduld, jokingly asked White whether he was trying to create an inland sea. The dam, however, remained empty for more than a year and became known as White's Folly until, during a particularly violent storm in 1889, it filled to the brim. Now known as Boksburg Lake, it covers 15 hectares and is surrounded by terraces, lawns, gardens and trees.

The Cinderella Dam offers an alternative resort. Field sports are staged at Prince George Park.

The so-called 'Rand Tram', the first railway service of the Transvaal, built in 1890, links Boksburg and Johannesburg.

Boksburg has a children's farmyard, known as 'Bokkie Park', a rollerskating rink, an ice-skating rink, and other sports facilities.

Brakpan

Near Brakpan is a pan of brackish water from which the town is said to have taken its name. Proclaimed a municipality in 1919, Brakpan flourished as a gold and coal centre for the first half of the century.

Today it is on the brink of another industrial boom. Modern technology has been enlisted to reclaim gold and uranium from the mine dumps created in earlier years when refining processes were less sophisticated.

Witwatersrand wind-surfers on Benoni's attractive Homestead Lake.

THINGS TO DO AND SEE

Angling Most of the lakes along the Witwatersrand are stocked with trout, carp and other fish.

Boating and water sports The lakes at Germiston, Florida, Benoni, Boksburg, Brakpan, Randfontein and Springs offer all water sports.

Camping and caravanning Notable among the many camping and caravan grounds here are the municipal caravan parks at Florida, Springs and Germiston.

Caves The Sterkfontein Caves are fascinating. There is a museum here.

Parks The Rynfield Children's Park, otherwise known as Bunny Park, at Benoni is stocked with rabbits, sheep and birds. The Martiens Kotze Park is laid out with statues, windmills and gardens. Many of the parks around the lakes have picnic areas.

Sightseeing Germiston's Simmer and Jack Mine offers visitors a fascinating glimpse of how the old gold mines operated, and a demonstration of how to pan for gold.

Sky-diving There are clubs at the Carltonville, Klerksdorp and Vanderbijlpark airfields which are open on weekends. Competitions are held regularly, and spectators are welcome.

Wildlife There is a municipal game reserve at Krugersdorp and the rest camp here is a pleasant stopover for visitors to the Witwatersrand. The South African Lion Park is on the Muldersdrift road.

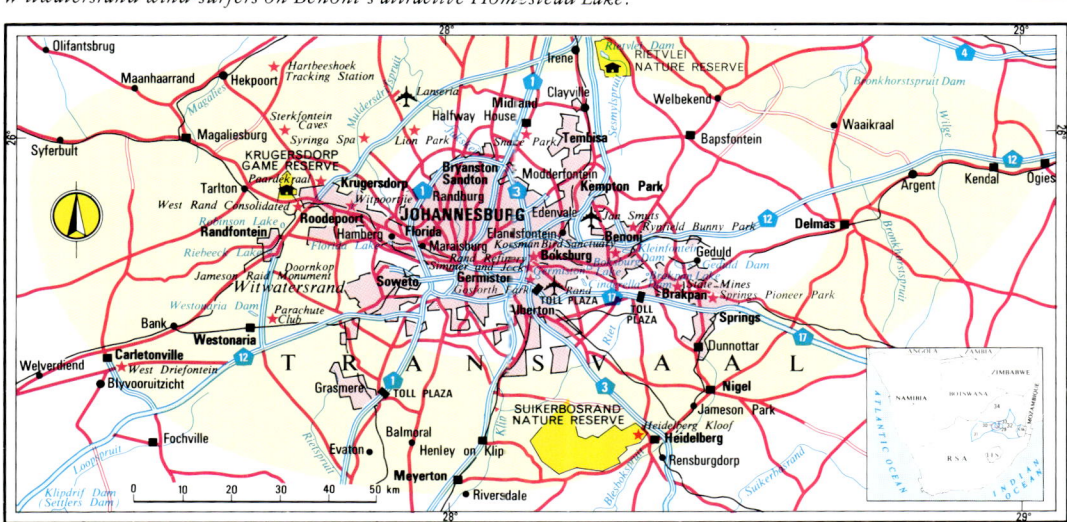

Where three giants of history led a fight for independence

Germiston

During the rush to the Witwatersrand gold fields a Scot named John Jack, an itinerant trader, decided to try his hand at prospecting. He was passing the farm Elandsfontein when he made his decision, and immediately began scraping around in the ground. He found traces of gold almost at his first attempt.

With his partner, August Simmer, Jack bought the farm — which at one time had been exchanged for an ox-wagon — and floated a mining company, Simmer and Jack. Both men made fortunes.

The town that grew next to the mine was named Germiston by Jack, after the farm near Glasgow where he was born. The original Elandsfontein homestead still stands near the city centre. The colossal dumps of waste rock from the mines have enclosed the city within great man-made mountains.

Germiston became a municipality in 1903 and a city in 1950. The Simmer and Jack mine closed down in 1964, by which time it had produced 15 802 469 ounces of gold. Germiston is today a major industrial centre with over 2 000 factories. The busiest civil airport in South Africa, the Rand Airport, is close to what has

The huge tailings wheel on the disused Balmoral Mine near Germiston.

grown from a mining camp into the sixth-largest city in South Africa.

There are many relics of the mining industry around Germiston, and at one time the Simmer and Jack Mine was converted into a museum.

In 1921 the world's largest gold refinery, the Rand Refinery, was established at Germiston. More than 70 per cent of the gold produced in the western world passes through this refinery. The city is also the largest railway junction in South Africa.

Germiston has few pretensions to beauty. The towering dumps form a man-made scenic backdrop to the city, and water pumped from the mines, added to the natural run-off of rain water, has been used to create the 65-hectare Germiston Lake, which has a park on its banks.

At the entrance to Germiston, on the western side, is a fountain in the shape of a mine headgear; the play of the water and brilliant illumination at night contribute to a spectacular effect.

Germiston Sporting Club and Benoni Turf Club hold race meetings at nearby Gosforth Park. A special attraction for nature-lovers is the Rondebult Bird Sanctuary, famous for its rich variety of water birds.

Krugersdorp

Between 8 and 18 December 1880 more than 6 000 men gathered on the farm Paardekraal, which forms part of what is now the municipal area of Krugersdorp, and swore to stand together until they had secured the independence of the Transvaal. To pledge his faith, each man placed a stone on a cairn and three men were appointed to lead the struggle for independence — Paul Kruger, Piet Joubert and Marthinus Wessels Pretorius.

After the short war with the British in 1881, and the subsequent declaration of independence, the men of the Transvaal resolved that once every five years, on 16 December, there would be a celebration at the site of the cairn during which thanks would be given for independence and for the victory of the Voortrekkers over the Zulus at the Battle of Blood River, which had taken place on that date in 1838.

The cairn mysteriously disappeared during the 1899-1902 war. A sandstone monument, 18 metres high, was built on the site and dedicated in 1891

HOW THEY TURN AN UNGLAMOROUS 'RUBBLE' INTO 99 PER CENT PURE GOLD

Pouring gold into bars at the Rand Refinery.

Bars of gleaming gold ready for the banks.

The gold that is extracted from the South African gold fields is hidden in an unglamorous-looking grey rock. Once on the surface the rock is crushed to a fine powder and water is added to form a fine slime.

Cyanide is added to dissolve the gold and the waste solids are then separated by means of rotary filters. The gold is precipitated from the solution left after filtration by further chemical processes, smelted in a furnace and poured into bullion bars, each weighing about 31 kilograms and containing about 90 per cent gold, 10 per cent silver and

traces of copper, lead, osmiridium and zinc.

The bullion bars produced by the various Witwatersrand mines are sent to the Rand Refinery at Germiston — the world's biggest — for further purifying.

This technique, invented in Australia in 1868, involves passing chlorine gas through the molten gold. Impurities form metallic chlorides which rise to the surface, where they are skimmed off. The gold that remains is cast into bars weighing about 12,5 kilograms.

These bars are either of a purity

of 996 parts in 1 000, which is acceptable for monetary purposes, or 999 parts in 1 000. The latter are produced in an electrolytic plant to meet the demand for gold of this purity from industry and the arts.

The purer gold is used for plating contacts and circuits where high conductive reliability and corrosion resistance are essential.

A thin layer of gold is sometimes used as an outer case for space satellites because it is an efficient radiation barrier. Astronauts' visors are plated with pure gold for the same reason.

by President Kruger. This monument still stands today.

After gold was discovered in the vicinity and the creation of a town became necessary, the government bought a portion of Paardekraal farm on 26 April 1887. This was laid out as a town and named Krugersdorp in honour of the president. The town has wide, tree-lined streets, and several attractive old buildings, including its original courthouse.

It was near Krugersdorp, at Doornkop, that the Jameson Raid came to a violent end on 2 January 1896. Dr. Starr 'Jim' Jameson and his rebels had intended to capture Johannesburg. They were routed, and survivors were marched into Krugersdorp as prisoners, and the wounded of both sides treated in the local hospital.

The rout marked the end of the hopes held for high political office by Cecil Rhodes, who had supported the raid.

Krugersdorp became the principal town of the West Rand. The West Rand Consolidated Mine was the first in the world to produce uranium as a by-product of the gold-refining process and a uranium recovery plant was opened here in 1952. Manganese, iron, asbestos, dyes, lime and dolomite are also mined.

Hill-climbing races for motor vehicles, cyclists and athletes are often held along the main road from Pretoria to Krugersdorp, where it ascends the northern slopes of the Witwatersrand at Muldersdrift Hill. The Wanderers' Sports Ground, where football, cricket, hockey, athletics, cycling, bowls, swimming and gymnastics are staged, lies alongside the 37-hectare Coronation Park.

The Krugersdorp Game Reserve is 7 kilometres from the town centre, on the north-western slopes of the Witwatersrand. Its 1 400-hectare area is stocked with 1 300 wild animals, including lion, rhino, giraffe, several species of antelope, and ostrich. There is a rest camp here with bungalows, a tea-room and swimming pool, and near the reserve is a privately run bird sanctuary.

Also in the district is the Kromdraai Palaeontological Reserve, which contains a display of models of extinct animals and birds.

Krugersdorp town hall dates from the time of the Transvaal republic.

The Krugersdorp Game Reserve.

The arrest of Dr. Jameson as depicted in the Petit Parisien magazine in 1896.

Randfontein

The mining financier J. B. Robinson bought the farm Randfontein ('spring of the ridge') during the scramble for properties immediately after the 1886 discovery of gold on the Witwatersrand.

The purchase paid off handsomely, and in 1889 he floated the Randfontein Estates Gold Mining Company.

The town of Randfontein was created in 1890 to serve the mine. Originally the town was administered as part of Krugersdorp, but it became a municipality in 1929.

There are recreational areas at Riebeeck and Robinson Lakes, and a wide range of sports are catered for. There is a caravan park on the banks of Riebeeck Lake.

Roodepoort

The first gold mine on the edge of the Witwatersrand was established on the farm Wilgespruit in 1884. The prospector Fred Struben found a vein of rock which he claimed contained payable gold. Fred and his brother Harry showed some specimens to President Kruger and started to mine ore from the foot of what they called the Mont d'Or ('mountain of gold'). The little mine, however, proved uneconomic. Its so-called Confidence Reef was unpredictable, but while it was being worked its noisy mill attracted many other prospectors to the area of Roodepoort ('the red pass').

After George Harrison's fabulous gold discovery in 1886 there was a wild scramble all along the Witwatersrand to identify the same gold-bearing formation. Several mines came to life in the Roodepoort area and a wild mining camp grew, with the usual grog shops and bawdy houses. In 1904 this untidy collection of shacks became, to its surprise, a municipality. It became a city in 1977 and incorporates within its boundaries the once separate townships of Hamberg, Florida and Maraisburg.

THE ELUSIVE GOLD REEF

As gold mining developed along the Witwatersrand the question of how far the reef would extend became a matter of great debate.

West of Randfontein, in the long, shallow valley of the Mooi River, there were no superficial indications of gold, but geologists believed the gold-bearing reef extended under the dolomite rocks of the valley.

A series of boreholes struck gold at deep levels, but the great problem for prospectors was water.

There was no technique to deal with this until the introduction towards the end of the 1920s of the cementation process, which forces cement into fissures and helps to seal off excavations.

Another major development was the use of the magnetometer by the German geophysicist, Dr. Rudolf Krahmann.

This instrument, which traces certain magnetic shales associated with gold-bearing rock, enabled Dr. Krahmann to show that the reef extended under the dolomite.

Farms were hastily bought up and mining began on a huge scale. The technical difficulties were daunting.

The Blyvooruitzicht Mine — one of the richest gold mines in the world — and other famous mines, such as the nearby West Driefontein and East Driefontein, together with the bustling modern towns of Carletonville and Westonaria which have grown up around them, are evidence of the success of the great search for the western extension of the gold reef.

An underground lake touched with magic

The underground lake in the Sterkfontein Caves. Reflected in its still waters are many lovely dripstone formations.

This Dutch windmill is one of many novelties in Martiens Kotze Park.

Florida is built around an artificial lake which was filled with water pumped from the mines.

This lake is the home of numerous waterfowl, and is bordered by picnic sites. Boating, fishing and swimming are popular here.

The city's local history museum has exhibits of the several different types of gold-bearing ore found in the area. The original mine workings at Wilgespruit can be visited by arrangement with the museum.

Springs

Coal was discovered around Springs in 1888 and six collieries were opened to supply fuel for the gold-mining industry of the Witwatersrand. The railway service known as the 'Rand Tram' carried the coal to Johannes-

burg. Most of the miners were Welsh and the Springs Male Voice Choir became famous in the Transvaal.

For various technical reasons the coal mines were not a success. The coal was of a type that tended to catch fire spontaneously, the ground was prone to subsidence, and the collieries were gradually abandoned. Later discoveries of gold brought rapid expansion and at one time, with eight important gold mines surrounding it, Springs was the largest single gold-producing area in the world. Apart from gold, there are now substantial local industries producing paper, glass, bicycles and foodstuffs.

There is a lake and a leisure resort at Murray Park, a nature reserve within the municipal area, and the unique Springs Pioneer Park which is

built on an old mine dump and laid out with a windmill, aloe gardens, attractive walks and fountains.

Springs is the headquarters of the Eastern Transvaal Rugby Union and international matches are played at the P. A. M. Brink Stadium.

Sterkfontein Caves

In 1896 an Italian gold prospector named Guigimo Martinaglia found the entrance to a complex series of caves on Sterkfontein farm. The caves are now regarded as one of the world's most important prehistoric sites.

They consist of a series of chambers connected by passages. The largest is the Hall of Elephants, 23 metres high and 91 metres long. Other chambers are called Milner Hall, Fairy Chamber, Bridal Arch, Lumbago Alley, Fossil

Chamber and The Graveyard.

At a depth of 40 metres is a perfectly calm underground lake. Local African peoples regard it with awe, believing that the water has medicinal properties and can even cure blindness. They hold ceremonies at the edge of the lake, during which water is carried away for treatment of the sick.

Dr. Robert Broom, of the Transvaal Museum in Pretoria, began excavations in the cave in 1936 and made several discoveries of bones and other fossils. His great find came in 1947 — the exceptionally well-preserved skull of a species of early man-ape which he called *Plesianthropus trans-vaalensis*, who lived about two million years ago. The skull was that of a female and became known as 'Mrs. Ples'. A bust depicting Dr. Broom examining 'Mrs. Ples' stands at the entrance to the caves. The species has subsequently been reclassified as *Australopithecus africanus*.

Excavations in the caves for bat guano have unfortunately destroyed or damaged many dripstone formations. There is a museum containing fossils found in the caves, a restaurant and picnic grounds, and regular guided tours of the chambers.

Westonaria

Westonaria consists of ten separate townships, and is noted for its extensive holiday resort on the shores of Westonaria Dam. There is also a large caravan park.

This is a popular spot for sky-divers. The sport is most spectacular here, especially during summer when the wide, open valley is intensely green,

The headgear of one of the shafts of a Westonaria gold mine. Despite complex flooding problems, rich deposits are worked at tremendous depths.

FAIRYTALE SETTING FOR THE GIDDY DRAMATICS OF THE SKY-DIVERS

The clear air, blue sky and towering whipped-cream cloud formations of summer provide a fairytale setting for the Witwatersrand's most spectacular sport — skydiving.

Leo Valentin, the famous birdman of France, invented skydiving in the early 1950s when he experimented with controlled freefalling.

Skydiving in South Africa began in 1952 in Pietermaritzburg. Ten years later the first South African skydiver to be sent overseas took part in the world championships in West Germany.

Competitions include "relative work" events which are perhaps the most spectacular to watch, 4- and 8-man teams of skydivers compete to make various perfect formations within time limits. Formations include a box, diamond, springbok, wedge, snowflake, jewel, caterpillar and accordian. The largest formation built to date is one linking 34 jumpers.

Other competitions for skydivers include canopy relative work in which skydivers build parachute "stacks"; and accuracy, in which the jumper has to strike a 10 cm disc.

Skydiving has revolutionised parachuting. The modern high-performance parachute is square, not round like the early models. It is highly steerable and slow in its descent, with a high, but controllable, forward speed. It can cut into and out of the wind line, almost like a fabric glider.

The exhilarating leap into space.

Free-fall over the Witwatersrand.

Sky-divers in a tricky group formation — the ultimate in skill and timing.

and the blue sky crowded with cotton-wool clusters of cumulus.

Witpoortjie

A number of streams feeding the Limpopo River pour down the northern side of the Witwatersrand. One of these tributaries takes a spectacular 80-metre tumble into the ravine known as Witpoortjie ('little white pass').

This is a popular picnic area, and it offers visitors a pleasant walk through the ravine to the summit of the Witwatersrand and the city of Roodepoort.

The small wayside hotel was the scene of a famous fight in 1889. John McKeone and Joseph Terpend were fleeing through the area with £4 500 stolen in an armed hold-up at the Standard Bank in Krugersdorp.

A member of the posse pursuing them suddenly remembered that a racehorse named Atlas was stabled behind the hotel at Witpoortjie. He jumped on the horse and raced after the outlaws, who suddenly found themselves being overtaken by what seemed like a whirlwind.

To lighten their load they tossed £1 500-worth of gold nuggets into a passing wagon belonging to a poor woodcutter.

But they still were not fast enough to outrun Atlas. Eventually the chase came to an end with a blazing showdown and the surrender of the two bandits.

It is said that when the woodcutter unloaded his wagon and found the bags of gold, he gave thanks to the Lord for this gift from heaven and bought a farm on the bushveld.

South Africa's gold – the real El Dorado

Gold is beauty. Gold is power. Gold is mystery and romance. For almost 10 000 years gold has been the supreme symbol of earthly riches. Its weight, its lustre, its almost mystical purity have, throughout history, driven men to pursue gold and prize it above all other things. And nowhere has this quest been rewarded with more staggering abundance than in South Africa.

Today, about half of the new gold found in the world each year comes from the seven great mining districts of South Africa. They stretch in a 500-kilometre arc from Evander in the eastern Transvaal, through the Witwatersrand and Johannesburg, to the 'West Wits Line' in the Klerksdorp area, and south to the Welkom gold field in the Orange Free State.

Within this arc some 37 mines produce between them approximately 700 tons of gold worth more than R10 000 million each year.

The story of South Africa's gold began millions of years ago when much of the Transvaal and the Orange Free State lay beneath the waters of a vast inland sea, fringed with mountains. Rivers rushed down these mountains, carrying particles of gold to the sea.

The particles sank on the shores nearest the river mouths. As time passed the grains of gold mixed with pebbles and mud into something like concrete.

Over the ages this conglomerate was covered with molten rock and the sea was filled in as the surface of the ancient volcanic world flamed and crumpled.

The pebbles and gold from the ancient sea shore, packed into hard rock, now lie in hard layers deep below the surface. The 'golden arc' of gold mines spreads along the rim of the basin that once held the sea.

From the very earliest days, the belief was widely held in Europe that gold was to be found in most parts of Africa, and this was undoubtedly one of the main reasons for the earliest expeditions to South Africa. Portuguese voyagers noted that some of the indigenous people sold gold to Muslim traders on the coast. Some of

A bar of gold fresh from the refinery being weighed before despatch to the Reserve Bank.

this gold was found in streams and some was recovered by mining quartz reefs, the ore being crushed, then treated with fire and washed. Joao dos Santos, a 17th century Dominican writer, records that the Makalanga people in present-day Zimbabwe, had a special word, ukubura ('people who collected'), for these gold-seekers. These early prospectors evidently penetrated to Zimbabwe and the northern Transvaal, where the gold ornaments found at Mapungubwe testify to their success.

Ancient workings in Zimbabwe and many parts of the Transvaal represent the removal of an enormous quantity of ore, and the value of the gold that must have been recovered has been estimated at up to R100 million.

The richest part of this great gold store was found in 1886 by George Harrison, a digger from Australia. He was working as a handyman on a farm called Langlaagte, a few kilometres from the future site of Johannesburg, when he stumbled upon a part of the ancient shoreline at a place where the gold-bearing conglomerate happened to show above ground. His prospector's eye told him these rocks might bear gold. He broke off a piece and crushed and panned it in a kitchen basin at the farmhouse.

The gleaming gold tail that came up in the basin prompted George Harrison to stake a discoverer's claim. 'I think it is a payable gold field', said his official statement. It was the understatement of the century. He inexplicably sold his claim for ten pounds and moved on. Harrison's discovery started the rush to the goldfields which appear to be inexhaustible.

Gold is found in two main forms — alluvial gold, where grains or nuggets are washed down streams and rivers, and reef gold, also known as lode gold, where the deposit is mixed with its parent rock.

There never was a happier man than the prospector who found a good alluvial deposit in a stream and could set up a simple recovery plant and extract his gold from the mud or gravel with little investment other than hard work.

Gold crushing of the most primitive kind on the field at Eersteling as seen by the artist Thomas Baines.

The beginning of a mine on the golden Witwatersrand in the early 1880s — a bucket of ore being winched to the surface.

A golden rhinoceros and other fragments found at Mapungubwe.

A modern gold mine of the West Witwatersrand with its headgear built over a shaft 3 770 metres deep.

The headgear of a gold mine standing above its shaft.

Visible gold contained in quartz from a reef in the Transvaal. Gold is seldom seen as clearly as this.

Reef deposits, such as the Witwatersrand, however, require the investment of an enormous amount of money and technical expertise.

The early diggers worked the Witwatersrand by open trenches dug along its length.

The reef was narrow — less than a metre wide in most places — and it dipped below the surface at an angle of about 20°.

The trenches were made as deep as possible but there were limits to such surface workings.

The average yield of gold in the Witwatersrand reef was 15 grams per ton of rock. Because the reef was so narrow, highly specialized mining techniques were needed to keep the amount of waste rock extracted to a minimum.

As the operations went deeper it be-came even more essential to mine as little waste as possible, for every rock has to be hoisted to the surface and the deeper the mine the more costly the hoisting. The more non-productive rock that was fed into the mill the more expensive the whole process of gold recovery would become, with the danger of the whole process becoming uneconomic.

In modern mining a shaft is sunk to the lowest level planned for current working. On the Rand, the deepest level so far is 3 777 metres. From the vertical shaft, horizontal drives are sent out at various levels to intersect the sloping gold reef. From these drives other excavations, known as stopes, are worked up the reef, the ore being pulled by mechanical scrapers to the drives where it is hauled by electric or diesel locomotives, which tip it

A mule emerges from a tunnel at a Pilgrim's Rest gold mine.

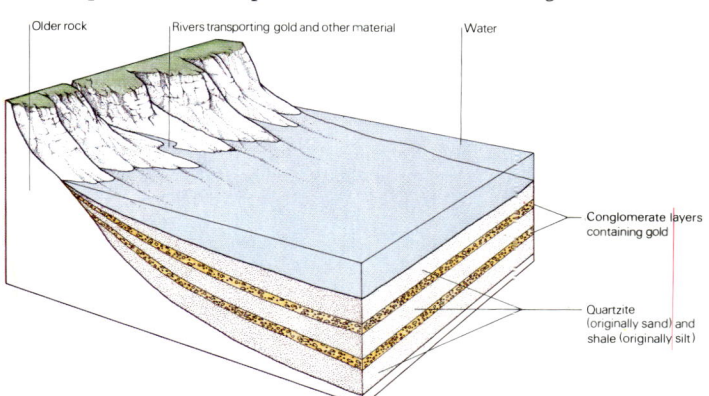

Older rock   Rivers transporting gold and other material   Water

Conglomerate layers containing gold

Quartzite (originally sand) and shale (originally silt)

The Witwatersrand when it was formed as the bed of a freshwater lake.

A prospector's pan with a tail of gold revealed in the bottom ring.

Gleaming bullion bars for Zürich and London

Panning for gold in a stream on the Transvaal highveld. Note the formal dress — including bowler hats.

Sluicing for gold at the Duiwel's Kantoor in the hills above Barberton. The photograph dates from January 1888.

Drilling into the gold-bearing reef on the Witwatersrand. The drill-holes will be charged with explosives.

Pit-props supporting the ceiling of mine workings deep below the surface where the pressures are enormous.

out into the bottom of the hoisting shaft. The stopes are kept as narrow as possible, covering the width of the gold reef with just enough space on either side to allow the men to work.

Ventilation and cooling have to be provided on a massive scale to make conditions tolerable for the miners. The deeper the mine, the greater the heat and humidity, the temperature rising by more than 1°C. for every 100 metres of descent.

Opening a new gold mine is an expensive business. The bill, before the first ton of gold-bearing rock goes into the processing plant, will be not less than R400 million and may be R700 million or even more. From the first million tons of reef will come about 7,3 tons of gold, all of which would — surprisingly — fit into the boot of a car.

The rock from the mine is crushed, treated with chemicals, filtered and smelted. At last the gold is poured as a glistening molten liquid into a mould little bigger than a brick. This bar from the mine smelt house contains about 9 per cent silver, about 88 per cent gold and 3 per cent of other metals and impurities. The bars are further refined at a central refinery which produces near-pure gold and silver bars. These gold bars, weighing 12,5 kilograms, are sold mainly on the gold markets of London and Zürich.

Much of the newly mined gold is used to make jewellery or for industrial purposes, particularly in the electronics industry and, more recently, in space programmes. The visors of

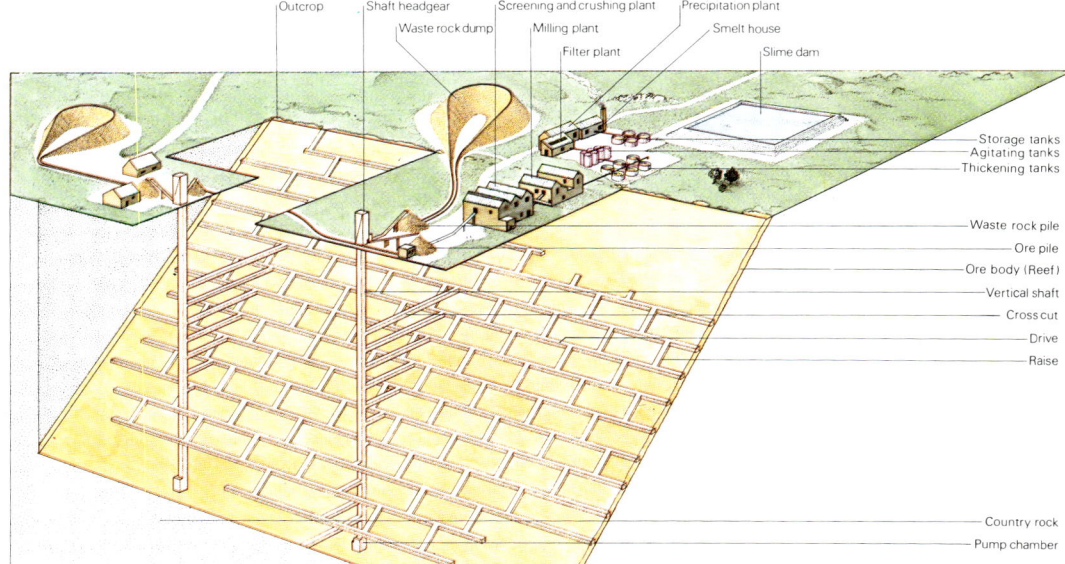

Outcrop · Shaft headgear · Screening and crushing plant · Precipitation plant
Waste rock dump · Milling plant · Smelt house
Filter plant · Slime dam
Storage tanks
Agitating tanks
Thickening tanks
Waste rock pile
Ore pile
Ore body (Reef)
Vertical shaft
Cross cut
Drive
Raise
Country rock
Pump chamber

The surface buildings and underground workings of a gold mine, typical of those on the Witwatersrand.

Tramming gold-bearing ore to a shaft where it will be raised to the surface.

TALKING GOLD

From the men who mine it to the dealers on the world's money markets and the craftsmen who fashion it into exquisite works of art, gold has a language all its own. Here are some of the more commonly used expressions:

Alluvial gold Gold that has been picked up by rivers and streams and carried far from its original source. Also known as placer gold, it exists in many forms, from fine particles to nuggets, and ranges in colour from yellow to black.

Carat A measure of the purity of gold. Pure gold is 24 carats. The term derives from the Greek word *keration*, meaning 'carob bean'. Such beans were once used as weights.

Dyke An intrusion of igneous rock interrupting the line of a gold reef.

Fanakalo A simple language taught to miners so that gold workers from different language groups can communicate with one another.

Fool's gold The name for iron pyrites — a gold-coloured ore.

Lash A miners' expression meaning to shovel. It is derived from the Xhosa *layisha* ('to load').

Pay limit The lowest grade of gold ore that can be mined economically.

Raise A tunnel driven upwards to connect different levels in a gold mine.

Reef Rock stratum containing gold.

Rolled gold Also known as gold plate, this is a thin covering of liquid gold poured over inferior metals or wood and allowed to harden, thus giving an object the appearance of pure gold. Gold can also be hammered into fine sheets, called gold leaf, used to decorate wood or books.

Skip An open-topped elevator used to hoist gold ore out of the mine.

Stope A working place in the mine from which gold-bearing ore is extracted.

Troy ounce The standard measure by which gold is weighed, equivalent to 31,103 grams. The common ounce is 28,349 grams.

Winze A tunnel driven downwards to connect different levels.

Gold-bearing ore being milled to a fine powder before recovery of the gold.

Pouring gold on the Geduld Mine of the Orange Free State. This raw gold will be sent to the Rand Refinery.

Weighing and assaying gold at the Rand Refinery, where all gold mined in South Africa is treated.

astronauts, for example, are coated with gold to protect them from harmful rays.

Uranium is also found in many of the gold-bearing reefs and South Africa is one of the world's largest producers of uranium.

Today there are some 470 000 men from ten independent countries of southern Africa working in South Africa's gold mines. They bring with them many languages and at least 50 dialects. To overcome this problem they attend mine schools where they learn to speak a simple common language — a kind of lingua franca of mining called 'Fanakalo'.

Since the first discovery in the Transvaal, more than 36 000 tons of gold worth more than a staggering R50 000 million have been recovered.

Two large mines, the Vaal Reefs and the Harmony, mill 9,5 and 7,5 million tons of ore respectively each year. The world's richest mine, West Driefontein, produces about 44 tons of gold every year.

In recent years computers have helped to take some of the chance out of new gold-mining projects. The computers give information on the best shape and position for underground workings and in what sequence the reefs should be mined to cause the lowest level of energy release in the rock, thus cutting down the possibility of rockbursts — the violent explosions caused by the build-up of geological stresses.

Other advances are being made in devising ways of extracting ore without the use of explosives which inevitably leave much unproductive debris — often twice as much barren rock as gold reef is blasted out. Among the latest developments are rockcutters which gorge out the reef and special powered hammers.

Gold bullion at the South African Reserve Bank, most of which will be sold on the world's bullion markets.

THE LAND OF SARIE MARAIS

IN MANY WAYS the western Transvaal epitomizes the whole Transvaal. That popular Afrikaans song of Anglo-Boer War days, *Sarie Marais*, adapted by some unknown writer from an American civil war song, wistfully describes the area:

'O bring my terug na die ou Transvaal
Daar waar my Sarie woon,
Daar onder in die mielies by die groen doringboom,
Daar woon my Sarie Marais.'

('O take me back to the old Transvaal,
That's where my Sarie dwells,
Down there in the maize lands by the green thorn tree,
That's where my Sarie dwells.')

This is a region of vast plains covered with maize fields; of thorn trees with boughs heavy with birds' nests; of dusty roads; isolated farmhouses; dazzling summer sunshine; crisp, frosty winters; hazy little towns and hamlets all dominated by tall, well-filled maize silos; branch railway lines carrying trains loaded with corn, groundnuts, sunflower seeds, salt, cattle, dairy produce; and suntanned men and pretty, cheerful girls — the Sarie Marais of South Africa.

In summer the western Transvaal is a green sea of maize. The endless fields are comparable to the great wheatlands of America and Canada. Only in the far east of the region is there a change of scenery, when the countryside climbs to the high, sub-tropical Magaliesberg range, with its many holiday resorts and beauty spots.

The soil of the plains is deep and fertile. Great herds of game once roamed here, pursued by San hunters. The land was farmed by Tswana people, who lived in complex cities of huts surrounded by low stone walls, the remains of which can still be seen in some areas.

In 1832, two French missionaries, Prosper Lemue and Samuel Rollard, opened a mission west of Zeerust in the Mosega Valley. It was the first European building in the Transvaal. But within a few months the area was invaded by the Ndebele people of Mzilikazi. The missionaries fled and the Tswana were driven away. Chaos reigned in the western Transvaal until 1837 when Mzilikazi was chased north by the Voortrekkers and the area was permanently settled by Europeans.

For years the western Transvaal remained a farming region, ideal for maize, groundnuts and sunflowers, and with excellent grazing for cattle. Few dreamed that beneath the rich soil lay a fortune in diamonds.

The discovery of diamonds in the gravels of the Vaal River at Barkly West, in the Cape, caused excitement all along the river — if there were diamonds in one stretch, why not in others? In 1872 diamonds were found in the gravels of a former course of the river at Christiana, and the first diamond rush in the western Transvaal began. Other discoveries followed, always in the gravels of dried-up river courses, never in the gravels of a flowing river. In 1926 diamonds were found at Lichtenburg and the greatest rush of all began. Once again, the gravels containing the diamonds lay in the shallow valley of a vanished river.

A tantalizing mystery remains: how many other dried-up rivers, with a gleaming harvest, lie beneath these rolling plains? One day, perhaps, a farmer digging out an old maize stump will find a diamond in its roots and a new flood of fortune-hunters will pour across the veld, fingers stretched to reach a glittering star . . .

Bloemhof

The town of Bloemhof possibly owes its existence to the luck of John Barclay, who survived the famous *Birkenhead* shipwreck of 1852 (see box, page 63) to buy a farm on the veld. The place became known for the flower garden, or bloemhof, laid out by his daughter, which made a colourful contrast to the bleak surroundings.

For some years Barclay ferried animals and vehicles across the Vaal River on a pontoon known as the *North Star*. Diamonds were discovered in the area in the 1870s — remains of the old diggings can still be seen — and Barclay's farm became the centre of a town.

Bloemhof is now an agricultural centre with tall maize silos, a creamery, and factories producing salt and malt. Bloemhof Dam, upstream from the town, has created a lake popular for fishing, boating and swimming. On the shore is a caravan park. A short distance from the town is the Lombard Nature Reserve.

Christiana

Diamonds discovered in the gravels of the Vaal River in 1870 led to the hurried establishment of a town by the Transvaal government to settle ownership of the diggings. It was named Christiana after the daughter of President Marthinus Pretorius.

The rush of diggers turned it into a boom town, with a rowdy community of prospectors, diamond dealers and liquor sellers. The flat countryside became scarred with mine workings and rubble. Diggers still work in the area, but only a few diamonds remain.

Christiana is an agricultural centre, with tall grain silos, orchards and vegetable gardens. Tree-covered islets dot the river, and on the willow-shaded banks there is a caravan park and a picnic spot — a favourite haunt for boating and swimming.

The prehistoric rock engravings at Stowlands are a national monument. Six kilometres out of the town are the Rob Ferreira Mineral Baths, a resort developed around a sulphur spring with private baths for invalids, an open-air swimming pool, a caravan park, bungalows and a restaurant.

Coligny

The maize-farming centre that grew up alongside the Kimberley-to-Johannesburg railway was originally named Treurfontein ('spring of sadness'). The inhabitants objected to this depressing title and in 1923 it was renamed after the Huguenot leader, Admiral Gaspard de Coligny.

Delareyville

Maize and groundnuts are produced in vast quantities around Delareyville, a town founded in 1914 and named in honour of General Jacobus de la Rey. A small quantity of salt is extracted from two shallow pans nearby. More than 2 million sacks of mealies are harvested here every year, and townspeople are proud of the fleet of 4 000 tractors registered in the district.

The town has a golf course, as well as tennis courts, football fields and a swimming pool. There is a hotel and a caravan park.

Fochville

A 'golden horseshoe' of mines, including the great Western Deep Mine, almost surrounds Fochville. There are numerous ruins of Sotho or Tswana kraals in the surrounding hills. A monument to the Boer hero Danie Theron stands close to the road, 5 kilometres north of the town (see box, page 216).

H. C. Bosman, the renowned author, who once taught in Groot-Marico.

C. Claasen, who found many fine stones on the Christiana diamond fields.

Fochville was established in 1920 as an agricultural centre and named in honour of Marshal Ferdinand Foch, commander-in-chief of the Allied forces in France during World War I.

Groot-Marico

The fertile valley of the Groot-Marico River is densely cultivated with maize, citrus fruit and tobacco. This valley is the setting for many of the tales of Herman Charles Bosman, the South African author who evolved a unique style of Afrikaans-flavoured English in books such as *Mafeking Road*.

The town of Groot-Marico has an intriguing Wild West atmosphere. Many of the inhabitants are descended from Voortrekkers. Marble, slate and andalusite are mined in the district, which is also famous for some remarkable dolomite caves containing animal fossils.

Klerksdorp

The discovery of gold in 1886 ended the rural tranquillity in which Klerksdorp had basked for some 50 years since becoming the first white settlement in the Transvaal. More than 4 000 would-be diggers drew lots for rights to mine the area. A town of corrugated iron shanties sprang up almost overnight. Within a year there were nearly 200 stores, 70 bars and a stock exchange.

Twelve months later the boom was over. There was still a great quantity of gold in the ground, but, as in the Witwatersrand, it demanded complex recovery techniques and most diggers abandoned the field.

Today, with modern extraction methods, Klerksdorp is a major producer of gold and uranium. It is also an important farming centre. The second largest grain co-operative in the world, the Central Western Co-operative Company, has its headquarters in the town.

The prehistoric rock engravings at Bosworth, 18 kilometres north of Klerksdorp, are a national monument. Their origins are a mystery.

Near the town is the Faan Meintjies Nature Reserve, containing rhino, giraffe, and a variety of antelope species. A rest camp is in the process of being developed in the reserve, and the town has four hotels.

THINGS TO DO AND SEE

Angling Yellowfish and barbel are numerous in the Vaal River and lakes such as Barberspan. The record large-mouth yellowfish caught in the Vaal River, in 1972, weighed 21,4 kilogrammes.

Camping and caravanning The Magaliesberg range has many camping and caravan grounds. There are sites at Potchefstroom, Lichtenburg and Rustenburg. The Rob Ferreira Mineral Baths, near Christiana, has a park with chalets and a restaurant. The Wentzel Dam resort near Schweizer-Reneke has a camping site.

Gliding The thermals (rising currents of warm air) along the Magaliesberg range provide some of the best gliding in South Africa. The vultures that frequent the range will often soar up from the crags to join a glider, apparently regarding the strange giant 'bird' as a leader.

Sightseeing The Magaliesberg is a delight to explore. At Parrots' Paradise thousands of exotic birds can be seen. The Lichtenburg diamond fields are fascinating. The Potchefstroom museum contains a great assortment of historical bric-à-brac.

Swimming The Rob Ferreira Mineral Baths, fed by a sulphur spring, has a large outdoor pool and private baths. There are deep natural pools at Castle Gorge, at other resorts in the Magaliesberg, and at the source of the Molopo River near Lichtenburg. At Potchefstroom swimming and boating are permitted at the Mooi River Dam.

Treasure hunting You cannot look for diamonds without a prospector's licence, but the old gravel dumps at exhausted diamond fields often yield beautiful semi-precious stones.

Wildlife Lichtenburg has a nature reserve and animal breeding farm run by the National Zoological Gardens.

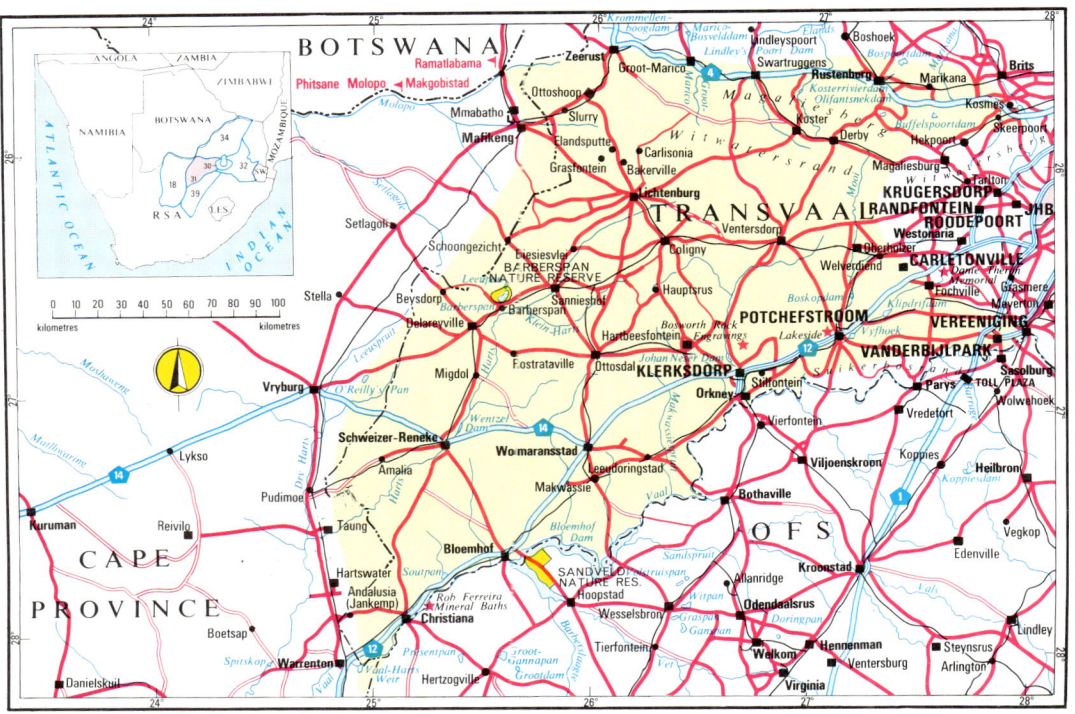

The town they believed was a new El Dorado

The equestrian statue in Lichtenburg of General Jacobus de la Rey.

Koster

The last diamond rush in South Africa took place at Koster on 11 November 1970 when 167 diggers lined up and raced one another to stake their claims. There is a recreational area and caravan park on the shores of the Kosterrivier Dam. There are several large caves in the surrounding hills.

Leeudoringstad

On 17 July 1932, the railway town of Leeudoringstad literally exploded into the headlines. A train carrying 1 200 tons of dynamite from the De Beers factory at Somerset West to the Witwatersrand gold fields blew up 2 kilometres from Leeudoringstad. The guard and four people living near the line were killed and almost every building in the town was damaged.

Maize, sunflower seeds and groundnuts are grown in the district. The town has a small hotel.

Lichtenburg

When President Thomas Burgers named Lichtenburg ('town of light') in 1873 he said he hoped that it would be a beacon of progress. More progress than he had dreamed of hit this remote, rural community 33 years later when it became the scene of the greatest diamond rush of all (see box).

Lichtenburg is a handsome, modern town. In the spacious central square, shaded by elegant karee trees, there stands a superb equestrian statue of General Jacobus de la Rey, the Anglo-Boer War leader. Among the public buildings is a museum displaying relics from the time of the diamond rush.

A caravan park and two hotels offer accommodation, and there is a nature reserve on the outskirts of the town.

THE SINGLE SPARKLE THAT LED TO THE GREATEST DIAMOND RUSH OF ALL

At the height of the Lichtenburg diamond rush it is said that the frenzied crowd of diggers created so much dust that cars had to keep their headlights on throughout the day.

It all started on 13 March 1926 when Jacobus Voorendyk, son of the postmaster of Lichtenburg, found a single diamond on the family farm Elandsputte. Within 12 months there were 108 000 fortune-hunters on the scene. It was the biggest diamond rush of all.

Claim-pegging races organized by the police sometimes had more than 31 000 participants — a frenzied human flood pouring over the veld to stake their claims.

The Voorendyks made a fortune by claiming 15 per cent on all diamond finds on their farm, taking 50 per cent of claim fees, and selling water at 6d. a barrel. In the first three months they made £45 000.

The diamonds of Lichtenburg were excellent gem-stones. Long ago, a river meandered across the plains in this area and at some point along its course had picked up diamonds, possibly from a hidden diamond pipe. The river twisted in its course and eventually, with the passing of time, it disappeared, leaving the gravels to be buried beneath a shallow mantle of top soil and grass. So the diamond field was formed. Though abundant, the diamonds were widely scattered, and when the rush came, it quickly spread to neighbouring farms.

So tantalizing and elusive were the deposits that one digger could be throwing a frenzied party celebrating a lucky find, while his neighbour on the next plot was starving in complete despair. Some fortunate diggers found that their claims lay over former potholes in the bed of the river. These were filled with gravel, and there seemed to be almost as many diamonds as stones. Others, less fortunate, worked hard, excavating considerable areas — and found nothing.

The Lichtenburg rush lasted for ten years. The original shallow river valley was excavated.

Remnants from the past include odd little diggers' pubs, trading stations and administrative buildings. Over all, there still lingers a romantic atmosphere of a world where men lived on dreams of the magic moment when a diamond would blaze into their lives.

Magaliesburg

The village of Magaliesburg lies in a fertile, sub-tropical valley below the southern slopes of the Magaliesberg range. The mountain, village and the river flowing through the valley are all named after Magali (or Mohale), chief of the Po people during the 19th century. Fruit and tobacco are grown in the valley and there are several holiday resorts near the village.

Makwassie

The small town of Makwassie is named

DANIE BOY – SCOURGE OF THE BRITISH

The Danie Theron memorial.

Danie Theron was a renowned figure in the Anglo-Boer War — a scourge of the British Army. He first achieved fame in 1899 when he gave W. F. Monypenny, editor of the Johannesburg *Star*, a thrashing for writing an insulting article about the Boers.

At the start of the Anglo-Boer War, Theron formed the Wielrijders Rapportgangers, a corps of cyclists, and later became the leader of a special group of scouts. His most famous exploit was in February 1900, when he crawled through the British lines at Paardeberg with a message for a Boer general.

Seven months later, he was killed fighting single-handed against a British detachment.

A memorial stands on the spot where he fell — on a hill near the trunk road half way between Johannesburg and Potchefstroom. This 24-metre high structure of concrete, steel and stone is topped by a symbolic 'flame of freedom' in copper. A path leads to the top of the hill, where there are ruins of defensive stone walls built in prehistoric times. The settlements they protected were largely abandoned when the Ndebele overran the area during the early 19th century.

after the Makwasi River (Makwassiespruit), which flows nearby. The town is a centre for maize, groundnuts and milk production. There is a caravan park at the nearby dam, and a hotel in the town.

Makwassie claims three distinctions in Transvaal history — the first white birth (in July 1823), the first printed matter (a Tswana spelling book and religious tracts) and the oldest town hall (built in 1910).

Orkney

The town is named after the Orkney Isles off the north coast of Scotland, birthplace of Simon Fraser, one of the gold-mining pioneers of the 1880s. His mine is now used as a ventilation shaft by the giant Vaal Reefs Mine. There is an attractive resort here on the banks of the Vaal, with many chalets and caravan sites.

Potchefstroom

A tangible atmosphere of the pioneer days of the Voortrekkers still survives in Potchefstroom, the oldest European town in the Transvaal and former capital of the South African Republic.

It was founded in 1838 by the Voortrekker leader Andries Hendrik Potgieter after his victory in the Nine

On the Lichtenburg diamond fields. The alluvial gravel is washed in the tank and the mud removed with larger rocks.

The fine gravel left in the centrifugal washer is sorted to trap diamonds.

Days Battle with the Ndebele (see box, page 219). The new town was well planned, with broad streets aligned along the points of the compass.

As well as being the new republic's headquarters, it was also a trading centre and a base for exploration of the interior. Adventurers, hunters, traders and prospectors streamed through Potchefstroom. Among them was Pieter Jacob Marais, a former 'forty-niner' from the California gold rush, who in 1853 brought to the town a few specks of gold he had found in a stream flowing off the Witwatersrand. Although no more gold was found at the time it was a hint of things to come.

In 1854 the capital was shifted to Pretoria, but Potchefstroom retained its commercial and cultural importance. The first newspaper in the Transvaal, the *Transvaal Argus*, was printed here on 8 May 1866.

The following year, the newly-formed Transvaal Agricultural Society offered a £5 prize at its annual show for the best display of Transvaal minerals. It was won by Karl Gottlieb Mauch, the German geologist who was destined to be the great prophet of South Africa's golden future.

Mauch had collected his minerals during a trip with the renowned hunter Henry Hartley, who showed him the remains of ancient mines in the Transvaal and Zimbabwe.

In 1867 Mauch returned to Potchefstroom after a second trip into the wilds and claimed that he had discovered the legendary golden Ophir of Solomon and Sheba, a vast, ancient gold field scarred with abandoned mine workings.

His tales, though never proved, started a rush. Fortune-hunters poured in from all over the world, and Potchefstroom came to be regarded as the gateway to a new El Dorado.

Mauch won another £5 for his mineral specimens at the next agricultural show, but these two prizes were all the profit he ever made from his prospecting. He correctly believed

A Victorian farmhouse in the western Transvaal, with a typical water pump.

A fearsome, but harmless, giant zonure lizard of the western Transvaal.

A fruit stall by the roadside near Rustenburg. A range of fruits are sold.

Where the first shot of the Anglo-Boer War was fired

that what he had found was the tip of an immense iceberg of mineral treasure and predicted that great fortunes would be made, but he discovered no payable deposits.

In 1872 Mauch returned to Germany, penniless and despondent. One night, as he was sitting at the open window of his bedroom, reflecting on his luckless adventures in Africa, he dozed off, fell to the ground and was killed. This was in 1875, just a few years before the great discoveries of the Witwatersrand con-

firmed all his predictions.

The first shot in the Anglo-Transvaal War was fired at Potchefstroom on 16 December 1881, when 500 Republicans rode into the town and occupied the printing works. British soldiers who tried to throw them out were driven off in a gun battle and had to retreat into the Old Fort, where they were besieged for three months.

Though 25 soldiers and six Republicans died in the siege, it ended amicably on 23 March 1882, with the Republican leader Piet Cronje inviting

Water-skiing on the lake in the Mooirivier at Potchefstroom.

SOARING VULTURES OF THE MAGALIESBERG

The dam at Olifantsnek, reflecting the red colours of the sedimentary rocks.

A coral tree in spring bloom on the Magaliesberg range.

The Magaliesberg cable-car station near the 1 852-metre summit.

The high ridge of the Magaliesberg is about 120 kilometres long and its summit rises 1 852 metres above sea level. The slopes are densely covered with trees and many streams tumble from the heights.

Citrus fruit, tobacco, vegetables and various sub-tropical fruits are grown on the slopes, and there are nurseries where flowers such as cyclamen are cultivated.

In the past, elephants and other wild animals roamed the ridge. Today it is the home of Cape vultures. There are about 250 breeding pairs. Often these great birds can be seen circling in the thermals. Vultures are slow breeders, laying only one egg a year, and the mortality rate for fledglings is high. Ornithologists climb to the rocky ledges to ring the chicks, and ringed vultures have been found as far afield as Etosha Pan, 1 200 kilometres away in South West Africa.

It is interesting to see the reaction of vultures to gliders. In their pecking order, a glider is apparently classed as a very big boss bird, and they follow closely, banking, wheeling, diving and spiralling as it does, manoeuvring in complete harmony and at exactly the same speed.

A particularly beautiful part of the Magaliesberg is Retief's Kloof, which has been used as a setting for several motion pictures.

Many hotels and holiday resorts have been developed on the slopes, and there is a Hiking Trail along the summit of the range, with several overnight huts for use by hikers.

the British officers to dinner at the Royal Hotel. The next day the British marched out of the fort with drums beating and flags flying. The remains of the fort and the adjoining cemetery are a national monument.

Potchefstroom is the centre of an agricultural area producing maize, vegetables, fruit and poultry.

A theological school opened by the Dutch Reformed Church in 1905 has grown into the Potchefstroom University for Christian Higher Education.

There is a music conservatory, a library, and a remarkable museum, whose exhibits include original Voortrekker wagons, old weapons, and 75 paintings by the celebrated German artist Otto Landsberg.

Potchefstroom has a leisure resort at Lakeside, on the Mooi River, with swimming, boating, fishing, and a caravan park with chalets. The town itself has several hotels.

Rustenburg

In a green, well-wooded setting, overlooked by the red-tinted heights of the Magaliesberg, a church and township was established in September 1851.

Rustenburg ('a place of rest') grew as the church and administrative centre for a rich farming area producing citrus and other fruit, cattle, Virginia tobacco, groundnuts, sunflower seeds, maize and wheat.

Boekenhoutfontein farm, northwest of Rustenburg, was a home of President Paul Kruger. Of its original 500 hectares, 32 are maintained as a museum. On the grounds are a cottage of 1841 (the Transvaal's oldest pioneer house), a house built by Kruger when he moved here in 1863,

Boekenhoutfontein homestead. At left are a house built by President Kruger in 1863 and a later home of his son Pieter.

THE OXEN CAVALRY

The Voortrekkers were expecting a fresh attack, but it was still a shock when it came. For thundering towards them through the bush came the Ndebele secret weapon — a cavalry charge of warriors mounted on oxen. The oxen had been specially trained and their horns sharpened to rip the flanks of the Voortrekkers' horses.

It was November 1837 and near the end of what came to be known as the Nine Days Battle — the final showdown between the Voortrekkers and the Ndebele chief, Mzilikazi.

Andries Hendrik Potgieter had mustered a force of 330 and set out to defeat the troublesome Mzilikazi once and for all. There was a series of bitter clashes in which the Ndebele suffered heavy losses and their villages were in flames.

On the sixth day of the battle, Mzilikazi made his last desperate bid for victory by sending in the oxen cavalry. There was a wild battle, but the clamour and the smell of blood overwhelmed the oxen. They stampeded through the bush, goring and trampling their own masters. For three days the Voortrekkers chased the shattered Ndebele army northwards. Mzilikazi's power in the Transvaal was completely broken. He fled across the Limpopo and, on the high central ridge of the future Zimbabwe, he re-established his people in what came to be known as Matabeleland.

The 1841 Boekenhoutfontein cottage — the Transvaal's oldest pioneer house.

The old game-viewing tower in the Quaggapan Park near Rustenburg.

the Kruger homestead (built by the President in the 1870s), and a house built for his son Pieter in 1892.

On 10 February 1859 the Gereformeerde Kerk was founded under a syringa tree in Rustenburg and a memorial marks the spot. Outside the town are the two largest platinum mines in the world.

There are several hotels, caravan parks and camping grounds in and near the town. In a nearby ravine in the Magaliesberg is a municipal holiday resort with chalets, caravan park and a restaurant.

About four kilometres south-west of the town there is the Rustenburg Nature Reserve, and the town serves as the jumping-off point for the two-day Rustenburg Hiking Trail.

Schweizer-Reneke

In 1885 the Transvaal government attacked a rustlers' hideout on Massouskop on the banks of the Harts River. Ten government men were killed, but the hill was captured and the rustlers, a mixed crowd of Europeans, Khoi-

khoi and Tswana, were driven away.

A town that later grew up at the foot of the hill was named after two of the soldiers who died in the skirmish — Captain G. A. Schweizer and Field-cornet G. N. Reneke.

There is a hotel in the town and a holiday resort with many facilities at the nearby Wentzel Dam.

Stilfontein

Between Klerksdorp and Potchefstroom are the workings of three of the largest gold mines in South Africa — the Hartebeesfontein, Buffelsfontein and Stilfontein mines. Stilfontein ('quiet spring') was created in 1949 as the residential centre for the mines. It has grown rapidly, with tree-shaded streets and a spacious pedestrian shopping centre built around a fountain. There are two hotels.

Wolmaransstad

The stream known as the Makwasi ('wild spearmint') from the bushes growing on its banks flows through a shallow valley to join the Vaal. At the point where the main road from Kimberley to Johannesburg bridges the river, a town was laid out in 1891 and named after J. M. A. Wolmarans, a member of the volksraad ('people's council'). It is a centre for maize production, and there are old alluvial diamond diggings in the area. There is a hotel and a caravan park, and a small game reserve nearby.

Zeerust

A thorn-bush wilderness dotted with large sheep and cattle farms surrounds Zeerust, and the town is often thronged with ranchers.

Lead is mined in the area, which also produces wheat, tobacco and citrus fruit. There is a museum with relics of the town's early days.

Zeerust originated in 1864 when Casper Coetzee employed a builder, Walter Seymore, to build a church and fort on his farm. Coetzee died before the buildings were completed and the town which grew around them was named Coetzee's Rest, or Zeerust, in his memory.

The town has two hotels and there are caravan sites at the Marico Bushveld Nature Reserve, 30 kilometres north-east of the town.

Schweizer-Reneke, with its maize silo and the stone fortifications on Massouskop.

LAND OF THE VAAL

THE SOUTH-EASTERN TRANSVAAL is dominated by the Vaal — the great river system that has its beginnings in the highveld plains bordering the mountains of Swaziland away to the east. Shallow hollows and low hillocks form a natural sponge where water collects in hundreds of pans and lakelets which glitter like the fragments of a mirror dropped on a carpet of emerald grass.

Streams trickle across this landscape, collecting water here and there, dallying in deeper lakes, and losing themselves for a while in bogs and vleis. But, one by one, the streams link up and the Vaal River is born, flowing westward on a long, lazy course, without rapids or waterfalls, broadening into a good-natured giant, dotted with tree-covered islets and lined by willows.

To the San, the river was known as Gij'Gariep ('tawny') from its muddy colour. The European name, Vaal, also means tawny. The Sotho called it iliGwa ('erratic') because of the unpredictable variations in its flow. The river has exerted a decisive influence on all the people of the south-eastern Transvaal. It has quenched the thirst of wild animals and men, and watered the crops along its banks.

In earlier times, many little dams were built to deflect the water over the level plains and irrigate farms. These dams were the forerunners of the great barrages that today control the river on which the gold fields of the Witwatersrand and the surrounding industrial complex depend so heavily.

The Loch Vaal reservoir, created by a dam built in 1923, is 64 kilometres long and supplies 1 045 million litres of water a day to a densely inhabited area embracing the Witwatersrand, Pretoria, the southern Transvaal and the northern Orange Free State. The Vaal Dam was built further upstream in 1936, and there are large barrages at Bloemhof, and at Christiana, where a complex series of canals takes water to 1 200 farms in the largest irrigation scheme in the southern hemisphere.

Despite being harnessed to man and his industries, the river is relatively unpolluted. Holiday resorts have grown up on its banks and people swim, fish and boat on its waters. The Vaal has brought life and leisure to this region.

THINGS TO DO AND SEE

Angling Yellowfish, barbel and bream abound in the Vaal River. Large fish are often caught in the Vaal Dam. Fishing competitions are held at many resorts on the river.

Boating and canoeing Many stretches of the Vaal are suitable for power-boats. Water-skiing is also popular. The lakes behind the dam attract many yachts.

Canoeists can negotiate the Vaal all the way to its junction with the Orange River.

Camping and caravanning There are many caravan parks and camping grounds along the Vaal. Sites can be found at Vereeniging and at the Vesco Caravan Park on the shores of the Vaal Dam. The hot spring at Badplaas has a caravan park, camping ground and chalet complex. Standerton and Volksrust both have caravan parks.

Hot springs The thermal spring at Badplaas has been developed into a resort, with several open-air swimming pools and private baths for invalids. There are shops, a restaurant and a hotel.

Sightseeing On the eastern side of the region the land rises to the mountains on the Swaziland border. The road from Badplaas to Diepgezet and Steynsdorp is dramatic, but demands careful driving.

Amsterdam

If the ambitious dreams of a Scot named Alexander McCorkindale had come to fruition, the out-of-the-way little town of Amsterdam would today be the thriving capital city of a 'tartan republic' called New Scotland.

In 1864 McCorkindale arrived in South Africa with a bold plan for bringing new life to the Transvaal. He wanted to bring 300 Scots into the area, establish farms, build towns, and develop a sea route to a new port he planned to create at the mouth of the Usutu River.

The Transvaal government was delighted at the prospect of an economic revival in the moribund state. They offered to sell McCorkindale 200 farms in one huge block on the Swaziland border for £8 000 cash.

McCorkindale formed the Glasgow and South Africa Company in Britain and in 1866 he returned to the Transvaal and toured the area with President Pretorius. He envisaged that New Scotland would be divided into three sections: Industria in the north, near Lake Chrissie, Londina in the south, centred on the present town of Derby; and between them the capital, Roburnia, named after the Scottish poet, Robert Burns.

The first 50 Scots arrived in 1867. They brought with them flocks of sheep, and established some superb farms, such as Lochiel, Waverley and Bonnie Braes. But McCorkindale failed to raise the essential capital and died of fever on Inyack Island in 1871 while surveying the site of his proposed new seaport at the mouth of the Usutu River.

His efforts were not entirely wasted, however, for the Scots who did arrive proved to be hardworking settlers. Roburnia did actually exist for about a year, but in 1882 the township was renamed Amsterdam, and today only the town square commemorates the name of McCorkindale.

There are large plantations of gum, pine and wattle in the district, and the Usutu Forest, just across the border in Swaziland, is the largest man-made forest in the world.

Badplaas

The hot sulphur spring that bubbles out of the ground at Badplaas at a rate of 30 000 litres an hour used to be known to the local people as Emanzana ('the healing waters'). The spring is said to have been presented as a gift to a white trader, Jacob de Clercq, by the chief of the Swazis in 1876.

De Clercq built a store near the spring and its medicinal properties became widely known, particularly when gold was discovered in the De Kaap Valley.

In modern times the spa has been greatly developed, with swimming pools and private baths for invalids.

The backdrop to Badplaas is a range of hills called Ndlumudlumu ('place of much thunder') by the Swazis.

Torbanite — a classic whistle-stop on the plains of the highveld.

A relaxing dip in the crystal-clear waters of the hot springs at Badplaas.

Belfast

The main railway to the eastern Transvaal rises to 2 025 metres at Belfast. This is a centre for sheep and dairy farming, maize, potatoes and timber. Coal is mined, and also a fine black granite. Trout and bass can be caught in the local streams. There are two caravan parks.

Bergendal

The last pitched battle of the Anglo-Boer War was fought at Bergendal on 27 August 1900 when the British sent more than 20 000 men against the Boer positions. A memorial marks the spot where 25 British officers and men were killed.

Dullstroom

The highest railway station in southern Africa is Dullstroom, 2 077 metres above sea level. Dullstroom was founded in 1883 as the centre for an irrigation settlement directed by Wolterus Dull, of Holland.

The first small irrigation settlement became a town in 1893, named after Dull and the 'stroom' — the Crocodile River — that flows through the district.

During the Anglo-Boer War the settlement was destroyed and most of the original Dutch settlers returned to Holland. Elm and beech trees planted by the Dutch pioneers remain. There is a small memorial erected by the Dutch settlers in 1887.

The town is dominated by the highest point in the Transvaal, the bulky 2 332-metre-high mountain known simply as Die Berg ('the mountain').

The district is renowned for its trout fishing.

Ermelo

In 1871 the Reverend Frans Lion Cachet founded a parish in the eastern Transvaal and named it after Ermelo, the town in Holland, in honour of a friend who lived there. The parish developed as a centre for farming and communications in the fertile area at the headwaters of the Vaal River.

Maize, cattle, potatoes, beans, wool, pigs, sunflower seeds, lucerne and sorghum are major industries in this high-rainfall area. There is also much afforestation. Seven coal mines

The highveld — a blend of rolling plains, maize lands, blue skies and white clouds.

work huge deposits, and South Africa's principal sources of anthracite and torbanite are found in the area.

This is an attractive town, its streets planted with trees. There are recreational areas on the shores of irrigation dams.

Greylingstad

The small fort on a ridge of hills overlooking Greylingstad was built during the Anglo-Boer War by the Scottish Rifles. The initials of the regiment — S. R. — can be seen on the rocks.

Heidelberg

In the quiet days before the gold rush

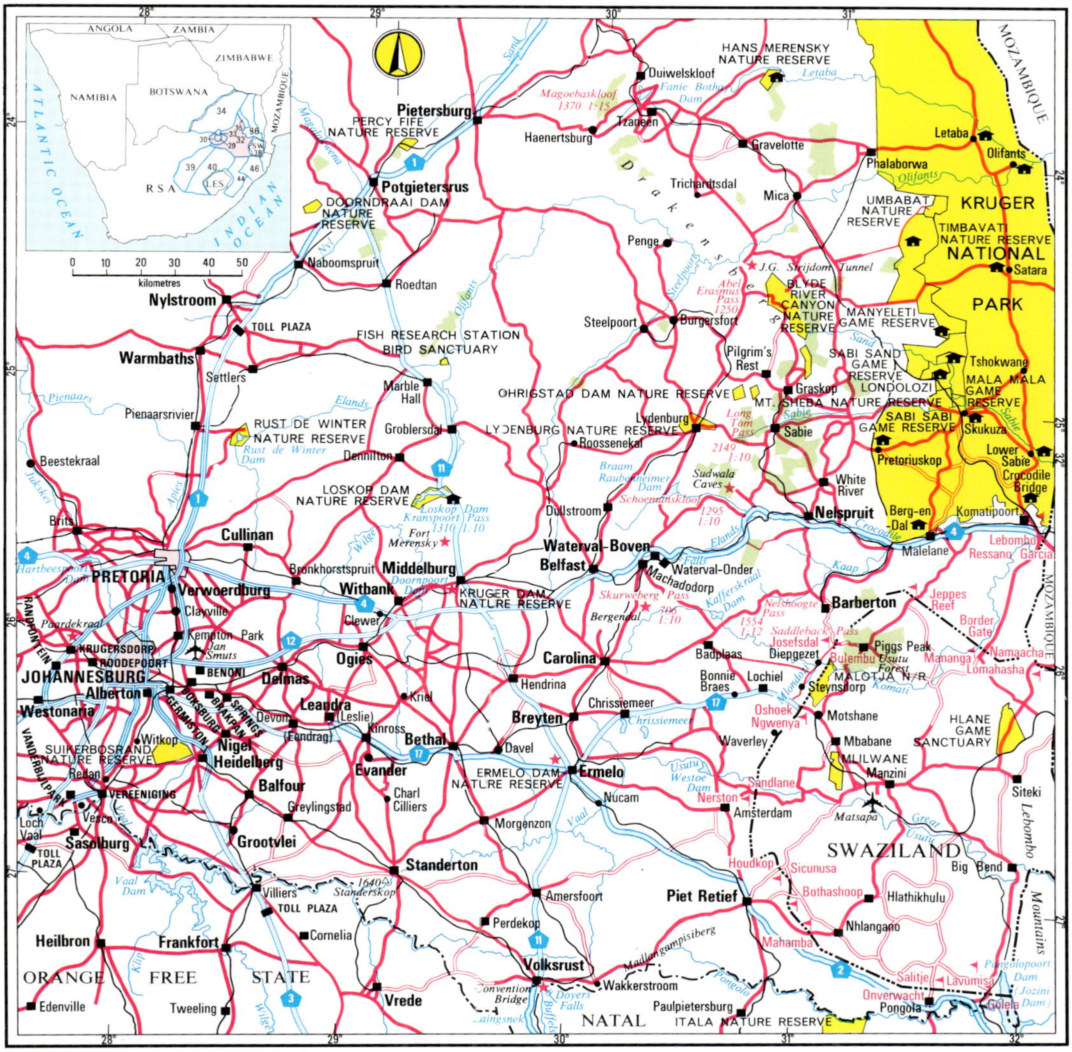

The store that grew into a boom town

to the Witwatersrand, a German, H. J. Uekermann, built a trading station in 1862 at the foot of the rocky Suikerbosrand ('ridge of sugar bushes'). The store stood at the junction of the main wagon trails entering the Transvaal from Natal and the Orange Free State. In 1865 Uekermann laid out a town around his store and named the place after his old university in Germany.

At the height of the Witwatersrand gold rush there were 18 hotels in Heidelberg. Though those boom days have passed, the town remains a busy point on the modern road and main railway line to the Witwatersrand and the north. The old railway station has been restored and is now a transport museum.

In the Suikerbosrand there is a kloof that is a nature reserve, with chalets, a caravan park and a picnic area.

On the hills bordering the town are many ruins of stone kraals built by early Sotho people.

For three months during the Anglo-Transvaal War, Heidelberg was the seat of the Boer provisional government. A monument commemorates Paul Kruger, Marthinus Pretorius and Petrus Joubert, who headed the struggle for independence.

Lake Chrissie
The largest natural body of fresh water in South Africa, Lake Chrissie (Chrissiemeer) lies in a hollow in the highveld plains surrounded by grassland. It is 9 kilometres long and 3 kilometres wide, with a maximum depth of about 3 metres. Large herds of blesbok roam the area and the lake is the home of a great variety of birds.

Machadodorp
A radioactive spring reputed to have powerful healing qualities surfaces at Machadodorp and baths have been built around it.

The town was the seat of the Republican government for a few months in 1900 after the evacuation of Pretoria during the Anglo-Boer War. Its brief moment of glory ended when it was shelled by the British. A bronze plaque marks the house near

Blaauboschkraal Ruins, near Machadodorp, a long-abandoned settlement.

Waterval Onder where President Paul Kruger stayed.

Trout are abundant in the Elands River that flows through the town.

Middelburg
The town that was established in 1864 in mountainous country on the banks of the Klein Olifants River was eventually named Middelburg because it lies half way along the route between Pretoria and Lydenburg. It is a busy point on the trunk road and railway from Pretoria to the eastern Transvaal.

Meijer's Bridge, one of the sturdy old stone bridges built by the Trans-

vaal Republic, dates from 1896 and is a national monument.

On the road to Groblersdal, 13 kilometres out of Middelburg, is the perfectly preserved little stronghold of Fort Merensky, built in 1865 by Sotho inhabitants and their missionary, the Rev. Alexander Merensky. It was intended as a defence against raiding warriors of the Pedi and the Swazi peoples.

A game park is being established around the Fort and accommodation is available.

The Kruger Dam on the outskirts of Middelburg is popular for swim-

THE POWER-HOUSE OF SOUTH AFRICA

The south-eastern Transvaal, with its plentiful water and coal, is the power-house of South Africa.

The national grid system begins in the generating plant built in 1962 at Camden, near Ermelo. Twenty-three other power stations contribute to a grid that criss-crosses the country with 80 000 kilometres of transmission line.

A traveller cannot fail to notice these thermal power stations, with water-cooling towers projecting from the surrounding maize lands.

The Electricity Supply Commission (Escom), which manages the entire undertaking, supplies South Africa with 90 per cent of its electric power. Escom was formed by the government in 1923 as a non-profit public corporation. In 1948 it absorbed the Victoria Falls and Transvaal Power Company, and became the sole bulk supplier of electric power in South Africa.

The Zambezi is also a vital source of power. The Portuguese govern-

The vast Camden power station.

ment, before granting independence to Mocambique in 1975, dammed the Zambezi at Cabora Bassa and created a hydro-electric station with a power potential of 4 000 000 kilowatts — South Africa buys 1 500 000 kilowatts of this output. From Cabora Bassa the power is transmitted across wild country for 1 200 kilometres to the Apollo station near Pretoria.

South Africa's first nuclear power station, at Koeberg in the western Cape, will also feed power into the grid, which is expected eventually to link virtually every city, town and village in South Africa. Many remote areas have hope of receiving electricity within the next decade.

An African homestead basks in winter sun on the highveld near Middelburg.

HOW THE TRANSVAAL WON BACK ITS INDEPENDENCE

During the 1870s the Transvaal was in serious economic and political difficulties.

On 12 April 1877 the British authorities in Natal annexed the Transvaal. British rule, though mild and economically beneficial, united Transvalers under the common cause of regaining independence.

Paul Kruger emerged from rural obscurity as a farmer in the Rustenburg area, went to England and pleaded with Queen Victoria for the restoration of the Transvaal to its people. Her refusal heightened the sense of grievance of the people of the Transvaal.

The armed struggle against the British started at Paardekraal — the site of Krugersdorp. A large gathering there swore to achieve independence. Each man deposited a stone on a pile as a pledge of his support. Three commandos were organized, and war began in December 1880.

One commando occupied Heidelberg, and this became the seat of government, with Paul Kruger as leader. A second commando occupied Potchefstroom and pinned down the British there by laying siege to the fort. The third commando was sent to Pretoria. Before they reached the capital they clashed at Bronkhorstspruit with a British column. Eighty-seven of the British force of 246 men were killed.

After further reverses the British set out to outflank the Transvaal force holding Laings Nek, near Volksrust.

The British commander, Major-general Sir George Colley, led 554

The battle memorials of Majuba.

of his 4 000 men to the summit of the 2 146-metre-high mountain Majuba ('place of rock pigeons') which dominates Laings Nek.

There were about 3 500 Transvaal men holding the top of Laings Nek. At dawn on 27 February 1881, they discovered that the British were on the mountain top above them. They immediately set out to change the situation. They were all expert shots, and Colley had overlooked the fact that his men would be exposed on the sky-line when they defended the summit.

There was a ferocious struggle, which ended at nightfall. By that time, 92 British soldiers had been killed and 134 wounded. Among the dead was Major-general Colley. The Transvalers lost one man and five were wounded.

The battle ended the Anglo-Transvaal War. A meeting was arranged between British and Transvalers in the homestead of Mount Prospect farm on the southern slopes of Majuba. On 23 March 1881, an agreement was signed in the little farmhouse, now a national monument, and independence was restored to the Transvaal.

---

ming and fishing and has a restaurant, rondavels and a caravan park.

Piet Retief

Trees flourish in the belt of misty rain along the edge of the highveld, and the busy town of Piet Retief, named after the Voortrekker leader who was murdered by the Zulus in 1838, is a centre for large timber estates and a paper-making industry.

Perfectly preserved, Fort Merensky has never experienced an attack.

The town was almost completely destroyed during the Anglo-Boer War.

Standerton

Lying on the banks of the Vaal, and often flooded by it, is Standerton. The town is overlooked by Standerskop (1 640 metres).

During the Anglo-Transvaal War a garrison of 350 British soldiers was besieged in the town.

A Transvaal force occupied Standerskop and peppered the town with bullets each day for the three months of the siege until the war ended and the garrison marched away with colours flying.

The British published a newspaper, *The Standerton News*, throughout the siege, and copies are now collectors' pieces.

Standerton today is a railway and agricultural centre for a region pro-

The mountainous border between Swaziland and the Transvaal near Steynsdorp.

ducing maize, wool, sunflower seeds and groundnuts.

Two weirs have been built across the Vaal River here, providing an 8-kilometre stretch of water popular for fishing, boating and other aquatic sports. Alongside the river is a municipal caravan park.

Steynsdorp

Long grass creeps over the crumbling remains of buildings that bustled with life when Steynsdorp was a booming gold town.

In July 1885 two prospectors, Frank Austin and Jim Painter, found gold in the Mlondozi stream running through a deep valley close to the Swaziland border. It was difficult, mountainous country, but thousands of fortune-hunters rushed to Painter's Camp to peg claims.

Dozens of bars, boarding houses and liquor stores sprang up along a straggling main street. By 1887, when it was officially recognised as a town and named Steynsdorp, it had an unruly population of 3 000 people governed by lynch law; summary trials led to men being strung up, flogged or run out of town.

At its height, Steynsdorp had seven hotels, a gaol, and two newspapers, *The Observer* and *The Phoenix*, which were filled with rumours and gossip about finds, fights, murders and assorted local outrages. Newsprint was hard to come by and some issues appeared on paper of various colours

and even on sheets of blotting paper.

But the boom did not last. The gold was difficult to extract and while some diggers found rich pockets and made their fortunes, most lived on hope. Finally, men began to drift away to the new gold fields of the Witwatersrand, and Steynsdorp was deserted. In an area of high rainfall, with abundant termites, the mud-brick, wood and corrugated iron buildings soon decayed and crumbled into ruins.

Today it is still possible to follow the course of the streets and the foundations of buildings amid the grass,

The raucous toad, whose voice is heard all over South Africa.

Old-time 'El Dorado' where gold is still panned

Easter near Volksrust, with the cosmos in flower and the crops being reaped.

CHURCHILL'S ESCAPE

On the night of 13 December 1899 the manager of the Transvaal and Delagoa Bay Colliery answered a knock on the door of his house near Witbank. Standing before him was a bedraggled character who pleaded for something to eat.

The visitor introduced himself as Winston Churchill, and said he was a British war correspondent who had been captured by the Boers and imprisoned in Pretoria. The night before, he had escaped, had jumped a freight train and had been transported in a coal truck to Clewer siding, near Witbank.

The mine manager, John Howard, hid his visitor in the underground stables of the mine. After six days, Howard slipped Churchill into a goods truck destined for Lourenco Marques.

After two days, Churchill cabled Howard — 'Goods arrived safely'. Churchill sailed to Durban, where he enjoyed a rousing welcome as a hero.

The site of the mine shaft in which he hid, named the Churchill Shaft, has been marked with a plaque.

but only the walls of the gaol, which were built of stone, still stand.

An occasional prospector may be seen foraging among the abandoned shafts and trenches — for traces of gold are still found and small nuggets are quite common in the river. But the days when Steynsdorp seemed to be the new El Dorado are gone forever.

Vanderbijlpark

In 1941 the South African Iron and Steel Industrial Corporation began building a steel works close to the Vaal River, downstream from the Vaal Dam. A place to house the workers was essential. A 118-hectare site with a river frontage was selected, and here a town was laid out, named after Dr. H. J. van der Bijl, then chairman of the corporation. The town became a municipality in 1952.

Though primarily an industrial centre, more than half a million trees have been planted to shade the streets, and Vanderbijlpark is generously provided with parks. A caravan park is attractively situated on the banks of the river.

Vereeniging

The Vaal River provides many sites for anglers at Vereeniging and is also used for rowing and aquatic sports.

A large number of Stone Age rock engravings can be seen at Redan, on the outskirts of the town. At nearby Witkop there is an Anglo-Boer War block-house.

It was in Vereeniging that the Boer and British generals met in May 1902 to end the Anglo-Boer War. The terms of peace were negotiated here. The town's museum contains photographs and relics of the war and fossil plants found in the surrounding area.

Today Vereeniging is a flourishing industrial centre. Giant thermal power stations in the Vaal Triangle convert local coal and the water of the river into electricity for transmission through the national grid.

The town became known as Vereeniging ('company') in 1882, after the company which first mined the area's rich coal deposits.

Volksrust

A historic Transvaal frontier town, founded in 1888, Volksrust ('people's rest') is linked with Natal by the ruins of Convention Bridge. It was at the bridge that President Paul Kruger and Sir Henry Loch, the British high commissioner, signed the Third Swaziland Convention in 1894 — a short-lived agreement that brought Swaziland under the administration of the Transvaal. Both men refused to negotiate on foreign soil, so the bridge, spanning the Grenspruit ('border stream'), was chosen for their meeting. A railway coach was hauled to the middle of the bridge. The statesmen sat at opposite ends of a conference table in the coach, each on his own soil — the president in the Transvaal and the high commissioner in Natal, then under British control. The bridge is a historical monument.

During the Anglo-Boer War,

A foam-nest frog waits for the developing tadpoles to drop into the water.

The muddy waters of the Vaal at flood-time are a formidably destructive force.

The Vaal in repose where it is joined by the Klip River near Vereeniging.

The old tunnel between Waterval-Onder and Waterval-Boven.

Volksrust was a marshalling yard for the Transvaal army. From here Transvaal troops rallied to drive the British off Majuba (see box, page 223).

The Slang River Falls are 13 kilometres from the town.

Wakkerstroom

The Wakkerstroom ('lively stream') which flows through the south-eastern Transvaal gave its name to the town established in 1859 on its banks.

The district owes its prosperity to sheep, cattle and coalfields.

During the Anglo-Transvaal War a small British garrison was besieged

for three months in a fort in the town. When peace came they marched out with colours flying.

Waterval-Boven

At Waterval-Boven ('above the water-fall') the Transvaal highveld comes to an abrupt and spectacular end as the escarpment falls away to the lowveld. In 1894 a railway marshalling yard and locomotive depot was created here.

From Waterval-Boven the railway line drops 228 metres at a gradient of up to 1:20 into the valley of the Elands River. On the station of Waterval-Boven there is a monument to the

men who built the Eastern line. It consists of one of the countless boulders they moved, and a section of the original rack line used on the pass. It is said that in the construction of the railway as many men died from fever as there are sleepers in the track.

The original route of the line, through a tunnel 213 metres long and past the magnificent waterfall of the Elands River from which the town gets its name, is a national monument.

Witbank

Coal simply bursts out of the ground in the Witbank area. The first Euro-

peans to pass this way noticed coal in the beds of streams. Coal was used for camp-fires, and wagons carried away as much of it as possible to burn in the stoves of nearby farmhouses. A staging post for wagons was established close to a large outcrop of whitish stones which gave Witbank ('white ridge') its name.

When the railway from Pretoria to Lourenco Marques was built in 1894 it passed close to Witbank, and a full-scale coal industry developed. Today there are 22 coal mines in the vicinity.

A dam on the Olifants River, on the outskirts of Witbank, is a pleasant recreational area.

COAL TREASURE-CHEST

South Africa's coal deposits are widespread throughout the Karoo System in the north-eastern Cape, Orange Free State, Natal and the Transvaal. The largest deposits so far found are around Witbank, where 45 per cent of South Africa's coal is produced.

The Witbank coal seams have an average width of 6 metres. They are practically horizontal, and lie not deeper than 300 metres below the surface. Mining is carried out mainly by the method known as pillar mining — an underground checkerboard pattern of roads up to 7 metres wide is driven into the coal, removing it and leaving the roof supported by pillars of coal between the roads. With this technique, about 30 per cent of the available coal is left in the supporting pillars, but these can be removed one by one as the mine approaches exhaustion. As they are removed the ceiling collapses, and the mine is abandoned.

Prospecting constantly reveals new coal deposits in South Africa. Reserves are enormous, and the country is a considerable exporter of coal.

The 228-metre high Elands River Falls, from which Waterval-Boven and Waterval-Onder take their names.

The fleeting, fragile, fairyland reign of the butterfly

The butterfly has such fragile beauty that it might well be a creature of a fairyland. Its real world, alas, is one of danger from a host of predators and the reign of the butterfly is all too fleeting. Few survive for more than four weeks, and many live only for a matter of hours.

In southern Africa there are nine families of butterflies divided into some 800 different species. The most popular of the families are those containing the most colourful species, such as the *Acraeidae*, *Danaidae*, *Nymphalidae*, *Papilionidae* and *Pieridae*.

To the collector, however, every family is worthy of study and contains at least one species considered a prize in any display.

Butterflies and moths are both insects. There are thousands of species of moths in southern Africa, however. It could be said that butterflies merely comprise a small group of families within the order of moths, distinguished by differences of features. Butterflies also are mainly diurnal, and moths mainly nocturnal.

The simplest way of distinguishing between them is to see them at rest. Butterflies in general close their wings together above the body; moths usually spread their wings out flat or roof them down the body.

The life cycle of the butterfly is similar to that of some other insects. The females, after mating, lay their eggs on the leaves of trees or shrubs suited to the tastes of their species.

When the eggs hatch, the larvae feed on the leaves, although some of them have more varied diets. Many of the blue butterfly larvae exude droplets of a sweet fluid. This attracts ants.

In a forest in the Pungwe Valley, Zimbabwe, a Charaxes violetta *at rest.*

The ants feed on the droplets, like what they taste, and laboriously carry the larvae back to the safety of their nests. Once in this sanctuary, the larvae feed on the ant grubs. The larvae still reward the ants with sweet liquid, but obtain more nourishment from the grubs than they give. Such larvae can devour 20 000 times their own weight in food before they mature.

Eventually, pampered, protected and well fed, the larvae turn into pupae, from which they eventually emerge as butterflies.

Their predators include birds, other insects, reptiles and mammals.

The *Acraeidae* family are small to medium in size, with orange and red as their most common colours. They have a defence mechanism of exuding unpleasant-tasting liquid which repels predators. Some live in the warm forest and bush country along the eastern seaboard and elsewhere, but others in open tracts of country.

A mother-of-pearl butterfly, *its wings patterned, coloured and sheened with all the glow of a mother-of-pearl shell. This is a butterfly of the Magoebaskloof forests.*

A joker butterfly *sunning itself in the high forest country of the north-eastern Transvaal, wings outstretched and colours all aglow in a ray of light.*

A citrus swallowtail butterfly resting on the surface of a road.

The *Nymphalidae* family is a large group including several of the most beautiful of all the butterflies, such as the *Charaxes* sub-family. Reds, blues, yellows and violets are their most common colours, often blended in complex patterns and shades. They live in forest and thick bush country.

The *Papilionidae* family are the popular swallowtails and swordtails, which include the largest butterflies in the world. Not all of them have the tails on their hind wings that give their family its name. They are commonly yellow, black and white.

The *Pieridae* family are generally white or yellow. They are medium-sized and numerous in southern Africa. The remaining five butterfly families in southern Africa are the *Satyridae*, or browns; one species of *Libytheidae*; the *Lycaeridae*, or blues and coppers; the *Hesperiidae*, or skippers; and the *Danaidae*, or monarchs, of which there are six southern African species.

Migratory butterflies resting on the branch of a shrub on the Transvaal high-veld. During these migrations, butterflies are in great peril from predators.

An African monarch butterfly feeding on the nectar from spring flowers.

A leaf-mimicking butterfly sunning itself in the Magoebaskloof forests.

A forest swordtail butterfly in the Woodbush Forest Reserve.

A migratory butterfly replenishing energy with a good feed.

A Charaxes butterfly in the friendly but unusual company of a paper wasp, both feeding on sap oozing from a tree in a high forest of the north-eastern Transvaal.

227

THE JACARANDA CITY

MAN FIRST SETTLED on the site of Pretoria about 350 years ago. These pioneers were Nguni-speaking people of the same migratory group as the Zulus and Swazis. The Sotho already living in the Transvaal called them maTebele ('refugees', or 'people who hide') and this name in the Nguni language became Ndebele. To Europeans these people came to be known as the Matabele.

The site consists of two well-sheltered, warm and fertile valleys, bordered by ridges parallel to the edge of the highveld. The newcomers built their huts along the banks of the river that became known as the Tswane ('little ape', or 'Apies' — as it is known today) after one of their chiefs. The descendants of these people are noted for the colourful patterns painted on their homes by the womenfolk, and for their spectacular costumes, made with beads, ornaments and distinctively patterned blankets.

The early settlers were peaceful, but in about 1825 a second group of runaways appeared here. Though also called maTebele by the Sotho, these were renegade Zulu warriors, led by a young commander named Mzilikazi. They had broken away from the Zulu army and had set out to loot the people living on the highveld.

Mzilikazi made his stronghold in the valley of the Apies. The first European traders and the missionary Robert Moffat visited him there. Other Zulus also came to call. Those whom Mzilikazi had deserted learned of his whereabouts as stories of his newfound prosperity spread, and eventually regiments sent by Shaka drove him into the western Transvaal.

The site of the present Pretoria was abandoned until 1837, when the Voortrekkers discovered the pleasant valley of the Apies and created a number of farms here. Remnants of the first Ndebele people built new homes close to the farms.

One of the Voortrekkers was Andries Pretorius, who established a farm, Grootplaats, in the valley where the Apies joins the Crocodile River. Shortly after Pretorius died of pneumonia at the age of 55 in 1853, the valley of the Apies was chosen as the home for the capital of the South African Republic. Marthinus Pretorius, son of Andries, selected a site on the farm Elandspoort, and on 16 November 1855 the new town was named Pretoria in honour of his father. A self-trained surveyor, Andries du Toit, mapped out the town with the aid of a wagon chain, which he used to measure building plots.

Quiet and remote, Pretoria's only excitements were the regular three-monthly nachtmaals ('communions') when the country people came on their wagons, outspanned in the central square and crowded the little church for a day. Business was conducted on the days before and after the service. On these occasions there was great rivalry between town and country boys. During one celebrated nachtmaal the town boys diverted the irrigation canals leading water down the sides of the streets, so that in the early hours of the morning practically the full flow of the Apies River was directed into Church Square. The country people found themselves flooded, and there was great confusion as they swam about in the dark.

Pretoria was the scene of fighting during the Boer Civil War of 1863-69. During the British annexation, between 1877 and 1881, it was the home of novelist Sir Henry Rider Haggard, then a junior civil servant.

The town was besieged by Republican forces between December 1880 and March 1881 during the Anglo-Transvaal War. At the end of this war Paul Kruger became President of the restored South African Republic, and he held this office for 19 years. Pretoria will always retain rich memories of this remarkable character, and today his house is a museum and national monument.

Fortunately, Pretoria suffered no damage during the Anglo-Boer War. It was occupied by the main British force under Lord Roberts on 5 June 1900 and it was here that the Peace of Vereeniging, which ended the war, was finally signed on 31 May 1902. Pretoria remained as the capital of the Transvaal until 1910, when it became the administrative capital of the Union of South Africa. It became a city on 14 October 1931 and the administrative capital of the Republic of South Africa in 1961.

It is a sunny, spacious city, notable for its beautiful gardens, flowering trees (especially jacarandas), its concentration of government and provincial offices, and of various official organizations with their many civil servants.

Austin Roberts Bird Sanctuary
This sanctuary, with an observation hide, is situated in Boshoff Street in the suburb of New Muckleneuk. It was named in honour of Dr. Austin Roberts, an authority on the birds of South Africa. The hides are open during weekends and public holidays.

Burgers Park
Thomas Francois Burgers was president of the South African Republic from 1872 to 1877. During his term of office he founded several public amenities in Pretoria, including a library, a museum, and the first botanical garden in the Transvaal. The garden — Burgers Park — was created on a site used by early settlers as a camp when they first reached the valley of the Apies River.

Although Burgers Park was

Burgers Park with its jacarandas, palm trees, green lawns and pigeons.

planned as a botanical garden, it was eventually developed as a recreational park. A statue of President Burgers was erected here in 1955, and there is a memorial commemorating South Africans of Scottish origin who died in World War I — President Burgers's wife, Mary Bryson, was a Scotswoman.

Church Square
Pretoria became a city in 1931. Occu-

Church Square, the centre of Pretoria. Anton von Wouw's statue of Paul Kruger looks towards the Palace of Justice.

Andries Pretorius, namesake of Pretoria.

The founder of Pretoria, Marthinus Pretorius.

THINGS TO DO AND SEE

Angling Rietvlei Dam contains trout, carp and yellowfish. Hartbeespoort Dam is stocked with tilapia (or kurper) which are good sporting fish and make excellent eating. There are also large silverfish and carp in most of the dams and rivers of the region.

Antiquities Pretoria has many museums including the Transvaal Museum, Kruger House Museum, Fort Klapperkop Military Museum, National Cultural and Open Air Museum, the Museum of Geological Survey, the William Prinsloo Agricultural Museum, Melrose House, Premier Diamond Mine, and the Voortrekker Memorial Museum.

Bird watching The Austin Roberts Bird Sanctuary hides are open on weekends and public holidays. A variety of birds use this sanctuary in the course of their migratory flights. The main entrance is in Boshoff Street.

Boating Hartbeespoort Dam is much used by sailing boats and power-boats. Sudden squalls can make the lake hazardous for the unwary visitor. There is also boating at Bon Accord, Rietvlei and Roodeplaat.

Camping and caravanning The municipal caravan and camping grounds at Pretoria North (the Joos Becker Caravan Park) and Fountains are in attractive settings. There are also caravan parks at Hartbeespoort Dam and Roodeplaat.

Paintings The Pretoria Art Museum, a treasure-house filled with many of southern Africa's finest paintings, is open daily, except on Mondays and religious holidays.

Picnics There are excellent picnic sites at Fountains and Wonderboom Nature Reserve.

Sightseeing The Johann Rissik scenic drive offers superb views of Pretoria, as well as a visit to the Klapperkop fort and war museum. The grounds of the Union Buildings also have fine viewing sites.

Voortrekker Monument This vast monument dominates the southern approaches to Pretoria. There is an amphitheatre where gatherings and folk-dancing take place, and also an interesting museum. On December 16 each year there is a gathering at the monument to commemorate the 1838 Battle of the Blood River.

pying 570 square kilometres, it has the largest municipal area in South Africa, and is the fourth largest city after Johannesburg, Cape Town and Durban. When the town was laid out it was centred around Church Square, with Church Street leading through it from east to west and Paul Kruger Street from north to south. These two remain the principal streets of Pretoria today.

Church Square is dominated by a statue of Paul Kruger by the sculptor Anton von Wouw. The southern side of the square is styled after Trafalgar Square in London, and the northern side after the Place de la Concorde in Paris.

Among the buildings overlooking the square are two official edifices from the time of Paul Kruger: the raadzaal ('council chamber'); and the palace of justice, completed after the Anglo-Boer War. During the war the incomplete building was used by British troops as a hospital. The old Netherlands Bank building and the Reserve Bank building also date from the days of the South African Republic.

The raadzaal is open to the public on weekdays by prior appointment. It is full of atmosphere and well worth a visit.

Church Street

Claimed to be the longest street in southern Africa, Church Street runs for 43 kilometres across the municipal area of Pretoria from east to west. The street widens into Church Square in the centre of the city. West of the square, Church Street passes to the south of the modern provincial administration building. Three blocks west of the square, on the north side of Church Street, is President Paul Kruger's house, now a national monument and museum. Kruger made his home in this unpretentious little house from 1883 until 1900, when he went into exile in Europe. He died in Switzerland in 1904.

As well as many of Kruger's belongings, such as his pipes, the house con-

Pretoria, administrative capital of the Republic of South Africa, in the valley of the Apies River.

A mining tycoon's gift to the president

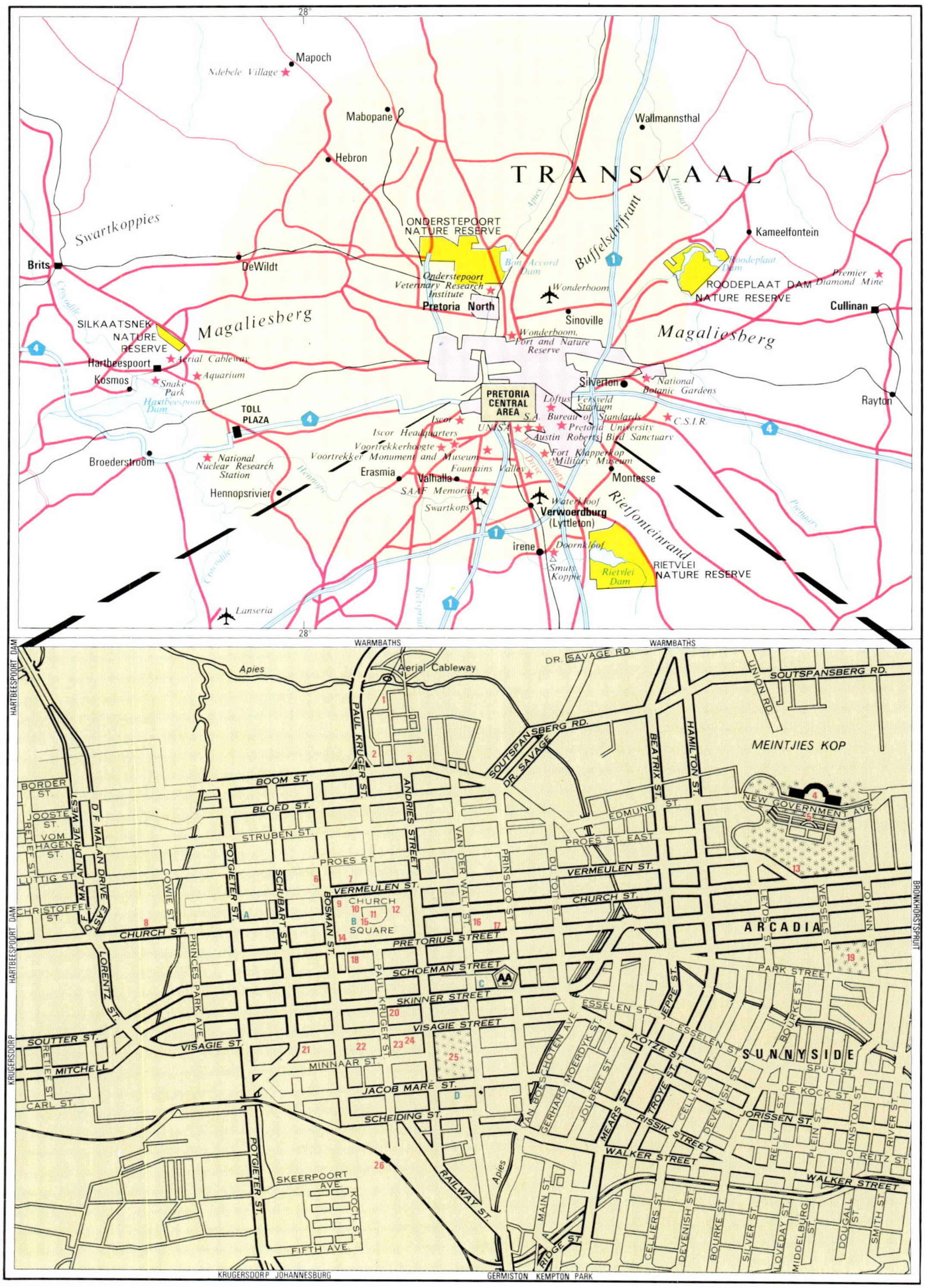

National Monuments
A Kruger House Museum
B Old Government Building
C Staats Model School
D Melrose House

Places of interest
1 National Zoological Gardens
2 Aquarium and Reptile Park
3 National Cultural and Open Air Museum
4 Union Buildings
5 Delville Wood Memorial
6 Government Printer
7 Post Office Museum
8 Heroes Acre
9 General Post Office
10 Palace of Justice
11 Statue of Paul Kruger
12 Netherlands and Reserve Bank Building
13 Statue of General Louis Botha
14 Transvaal Provincial Administration
15 Raadzaal
16 Strijdom Monument
17 State Theatre Pretoria
18 Police Museum
19 Art Museum
20 South African Museum of Science and Technology
21 South African Mint
22 City Hall
23 Transvaal Museum and Austin Roberts Bird Hall
24 Museum of Geological Survey
25 Burgers Park
26 Pretoria Railway Station

City and surroundings map scale
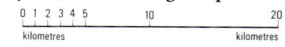

City central area map scale
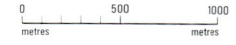

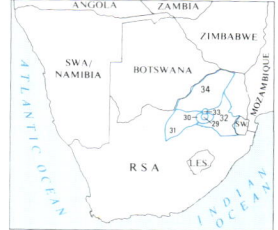

The official residence of Paul Kruger, President of the old South African Republic. He often sat on the shady verandah acknowledging the bows of passersby.

tains a host of other exhibits. These include the Vierkleur (Republican flag) that flew for the last time in 1900 when Kruger left for Europe, unaware that he was leaving his home for ever; the desk before which he must have spent many anxious hours; the chair, bearing the arms of the South African Republic, in which he was often photographed; and one of the first telephones to be installed in Pretoria.

Kruger obviously had little regard for personal comfort, and none at all for pomp and show. There is, however, a handsome official dinner service decorated with the arms of the Republic, porcelain cups with his portrait, and beautifully draped curtaining.

At the back of the house is the president's state coach and his private railway coach. The rail coach was built in the Netherlands and is made up of two coaches which were joined together on arrival in the Transvaal.

West of Kruger's house, Church Street continues through suburbs such as Westpark, with the Pretoria industrial area on the southern side of the street. Dominating this area are the steelworks of Iscor.

West of the industrial area, Church Street leads into the country, to the Hartbeespoort Dam and the atomic energy plant at Pelindaba.

On the east side of Church Square, Church Street passes through the city's commercial centre. Three blocks east of the square, on the south side of the street, is a square named after Advocate Johannes Strijdom, prime minister of South Africa from 1954 to 1958. Here too is a giant bronze bust of Strijdom by the sculptor Coert Steynberg, and a group of sculpted charging horses.

In the same block as this memorial to Strijdom is Republic Square, which contains the new opera house. East of the square, Church Street crosses the Apies River by means of a bridge adorned with carved lions, presented to President Kruger by the mining magnate Barney Barnato. The street then enters the suburb of Arcadia, dominated on the north side by the rocky ridge known as Meintjeskop.

On the east side of the grounds of the Union Buildings lies the ministerial residential area of Bryntirion. Here are the homes of the State President and the Administrator of the Transvaal, as well as many other lovely residences. The streets are lined with jacaranda trees.

Church Street continues to the east. To its south stands the international rugby stadium named after Robert Loftus Versfeld, the South African rugby administrator. The stadium seats 66 000.

The campus of the University of Pretoria also lies in this suburban area, to the south of Church Street. This is the largest residential university in South Africa and has more than 17 000 students. It was originally the Pretoria section of the Transvaal University College, established in Johannesburg in 1903. In 1908 the Pretoria section was detached from the Johannesburg section and became the Pretoria centre of the Transvaal University College. On 10 October 1930 this college became an independent university.

As it leaves the eastern suburban area, passing through Hatfield (south)

The vast administrative headquarters of the Transvaal Provincial Council.

The Loftus Versfeld Rugby Stadium, with a test in progress.

The Groote Kerk of the Dutch Reformed Church in Bosman Street.

The memorial to J. G. Strijdom, Prime Minister from 1954 to 1958.

Where the world's biggest diamond was found

and Colbyn (north), Church Street reaches Silverton, planned in 1890 as a rural recreational area for the citizens of Pretoria.

At this point, 8 kilometres from Church Square, Church Street leads into the trunk road to the eastern Transvaal. On the north side of the merging point of the two roads is the entrance to the national botanical garden, which contains a large collection of plants grouped according to the various climatic regions of the country. The gardens are open to the public daily.

On the opposite side of the road stands the complex of buildings housing the major departments of the Council for Scientific and Industrial Research (CSIR).

Council for Scientific and Industrial Research

Some 8 kilometres east of Pretoria is the complex of buildings housing the Council for Scientific and Industrial Research (CSIR). Established in 1945, this research organization employs more than 5 000 people in 21 national research laboratories and numerous separate, specialized units. Its interests embrace practically the full field of

---

THE WANDERING HERDBOY WHO BECAME THE 'OLD LION' OF THE TRANSVAAL

Stephanus Johannes Paul Kruger was born on 10 October 1825 on the farm Bulhoek, near Cradock in the Cape Province. He was the son of Casper Kruger, descendant of a Prussian immigrant who had arrived in the Cape in 1713. The family worked as nomadic stock men, wandering about with their herds in search of grazing and water.

Young Kruger received very little formal schooling, beyond learning to read and write. In 1835 the family trekked across the Orange River and while their livestock were grazing on the banks of the Caledon, Hendrik Potgieter, one of the leaders of the Greak Trek, passed them on his way to the north. The Kruger family joined Potgieter's party and accompanied him first to Natal and then to the Transvaal, where they fought the Ndebele and established the town of Potchefstroom.

Kruger was 16 when he took over his first farm, Waterkloof, near Rustenburg. A year later he married Maria du Plessis, who had been his sweetheart during the Greak Trek. For four years his young wife accompanied him on hunting trips and travels with Potgieter in the eastern Transvaal. In 1846 his wife and baby died of malaria. The following year he married Maria's cousin, Gezina du Plessis, who was to bear him 16 children.

Kruger took part in most of the stormy political events of the early years of the Transvaal Republic. By 1854 he was commandant of Rustenburg and in 1862 he became commandant-general of the Transvaal army.

After the British annexation of the Transvaal in 1877 Kruger visited London twice in an attempt to persuade the British government that annexation was wrong. In December

President Paul Kruger, the 'Old Lion' of the Transvaal.

Gezina Suzanna Frederika Kruger, second wife of President Kruger.

1880, at a gathering at Paardekraal, Kruger joined Piet Joubert and M. W. Pretorius in a triumvirate pledged to lead an armed struggle for independence.

The war was won and Kruger was elected State President in 1883. He began a programme of railway construction and expansion of trade. The gold rushes gave the republic a spectacular economic boost, but also created serious problems. The influx of uitlanders ('foreigners') to the Transvaal threatened the dominance of Kruger's own people; the provision of services to the new communities of miners strained the state's resources, and the expanding British Empire was a constant threat to the independence of the Transvaal.

In 1888 Kruger was re-elected to a second term as president, but now his handling of affairs, especially his favouring of various individuals with commercial concessions, caused widespread dissatisfaction.

The presidential election of 1893 saw Kruger returned for a third five-year term of office, but his majority was so narrow that there were rumours that the vote had been rigged, and there were dire predictions that the 'Old Lion' would lead the state to war and ruin.

Vast political difficulties faced the Transvaal government but Kruger's basic wisdom saw him through many crises, including the abortive Jameson Raid of 1896 (see Rhodes box, page 37). Kruger's position was actually strengthened as, realizing the dangers confronting their state, the people forgave him his autocracy, and he won the 1898 presidential elections with a considerable majority.

Throughout the Anglo-Boer War President Kruger was the inspiration and guiding hand behind the Boer forces. When the British approached Pretoria he left the city and, using a train as his seat of government, gradually retreated down the Eastern Line until, on 11 September 1900, he crossed the border into Mocambique. Six weeks later he sailed for Europe.

For some time he travelled about, endeavouring to enlist support for the Boer cause. During the war he stayed in Holland, where the Dutch held him in great esteem. He then moved to the French Riviera, and eventually to Clarens, in Switzerland, where he died on 14 July 1904.

Kruger's embalmed body was brought by ship to Cape Town and then by train to Pretoria where, on 16 December 1904, he was buried in what is now called Heroes Acre.

Boekenhoutfontein, the farm of Paul Kruger in the Rustenburg district. The original farmhouse is on the right. Left is the house built for Kruger's son Pieter.

Krugerhof, at Waterval-Onder, from where Kruger governed in 1900.

human development and understanding of the environment.

Visitors are permitted by special arrangement.

Cullinan

In 1902 Thomas Cullinan discovered the immense diamond pipe in the area now known as Cullinan. The Premier Mine was established to work this pipe and ever since it has been a seemingly inexhaustible source of diamonds. In 1905 the largest diamond ever found in the world, the famed Cullinan, was discovered here. The stone, which had a mass of 3 106 carats, was bought by the Transvaal government and presented to King Edward VII. It was then cut into the 530-carat Star of Africa, which is set in the sceptre of the Crown Jewels; the 317-carat Lesser Star of Africa, which is set in the Imperial State Crown of the Crown Jewels; seven other gems worn by the Royal Family; and 96 lesser gems, also known as brilliants.

Fountains

The Apies River has its source in a fountain of crystal clear water in a tree-covered valley on the southern side of Pretoria. The Fountains Valley is a nature reserve and recreation area, with picnic sites beneath the trees, a swimming pool, restaurant, miniature lakes with swans and other aquatic birds, a miniature railway worked by a steam locomotive, a large caravan park and many beautiful flowering plants.

Hartbeespoort Dam

Several boating and angling clubs are based at Hartbeespoort Dam. The shores are dotted with hotels, cottages and caravan parks. The cottages of the township of Kosmos, on the northern shores, are almost buried under flowering trees and creepers.

Among the area's attractions are tea-rooms, wayside kiosks, amusement parks, a snake park, a freshwater aquarium, and a two-kilometre cableway taking visitors to a viewing site on the Magaliesberg.

Iscor

A familiar sight at night in Pretoria is the flare from the blast furnaces of the Iscor steelworks. The Iron and Steel

The elaborate home of the University of South Africa.

Paul Kruger's Dutch Reformed Church, Church Street.

Corporation (Iscor) was created by the South African government in 1928 to promote the development of iron, steel and allied industries.

Johann Rissik Drive

Johann Rissik was one of the two government commissioners who gave their names to Johannesburg. The

scenic drive named after him in Pretoria runs along the summit of the ridge overlooking the city from the south. The views are superb and the ridge is covered in jacarandas, including the rare white variety.

On this ridge in 1896 — after the Jameson Raid (see Rhodes box, page 37) — the Transvaal government erected Fort Klapperkop, one of a chain of four military strongholds defending Pretoria. The fort is well preserved and surrounded by landscaped grounds with spacious, panoramic views to the north.

Fort Klapperkop is maintained as a military museum. In the grounds are several World War II military aircraft. The fort is entered by a drawbridge.

In the courtyard stands one of South Africa's most remarkable curiosities — a nine-seater military bicycle, apparently constructed from bits and pieces of other bicycles, and equipped with flanged wheels for railway lines. Devised by the British during the Anglo-Boer War, it was apparently used for locating booby traps,

---

GLOWING TRIBUTE TO JACARANDA JIM

During October and November Pretoria seems to shimmer with a mauve haze of blossoming jacarandas.

Millions of flowers fall to the ground, forming pools of colour beneath each tree.

About 70 000 of these beautiful trees line the streets of the city — a glowing tribute to the work of James Clark, the nurseryman who came to be known as Jacaranda Jim.

In its early years Pretoria was known as the city of roses. Ramblers grew everywhere and today they still tumble over fences and walls in almost every garden.

But in 1888 a citizen of Pretoria, J. A. Celliers, imported two *Jacaranda mimosifolia* trees from Rio de Janeiro (they are actually native to north-west Argentina).

He planted the trees in the garden of Myrtle Lodge, his home in the suburb of Sunnyside. They still stand in the garden of what is now Sunnyside School. Bronze plaques identify them as the pioneers of their kind in Pretoria.

It was in 1898 that James Clark arrived. He obtained a contract to grow trees for the government. He ordered seed from Australia and included in the selection was a packet of seeds of the same species of jacaranda as Celliers had imported.

Clark planted the seeds in the state nurseries at Groenkloof and they flourished. In 1906 he presented a number of jacarandas to the city of Pretoria. They were planted in Bosman Street and blossomed so profusely that it was decided to plant jacarandas throughout Pretoria.

In 1961 H. Bruinslich, the director of parks, saw the white species of jacaranda in South America and introduced it to Pretoria, where it grows in several streets today.

Jacarandas grow easily in well-watered areas with a warm climate. The seeds are winged, and when they are released from the mussel-shaped seed pods, are distributed by the wind. The trees grow to a height of roughly 15 metres and have a wide, shady spread.

One of the first two jacarandas in Pretoria, still blooming at Sunnyside.

The Crocodile River as it leaves Hartbeespoort Dam.

The hill that was once sold for a pony

for despatch riding, the transport of wounded, and for scouting along railway lines. Eight men, seated on saddles, pedalled the bicycle. In the centre was another saddle for the commanding officer.

In the fort is a series of small rooms with displays illustrating the military history of the old South African Republic. There is a stable room dedicated to military horses. The museum also exhibits uniforms, badges, decorations, a reconstruction of a general's office, weapons, transport vehicles, signalling devices, the 'red duster' flag flown at Mafeking during the siege, coins and the field mint which made them at Pilgrim's Rest during the Anglo-Boer War, a rebuilt field hospital with an amputation in progress, and various types of ammunition. The museum is open throughout the week, including weekends.

Meintjeskop

The hill that dominates the centre of Pretoria, now the site of the Union Buildings, was once exchanged for a pony.

The pony was given in 1856 by Andries du Toit, the first surveyor of Pretoria, to Marthinus Pretorius, the city's founder, who later became the first president of the Transvaal Republic.

In 1870 Du Toit's farm on the hill was bought by Stephanus Meintjes, who named the land Meintjeskop.

In 1910, when Herbert Baker, the renowned architect, was commissioned to design a central government building for the newly created Union of South Africa, he selected this hill as the ideal site. The Union Buildings were constructed from delicately coloured sandstone. A large garden surrounds the buildings and sweeps down the hill slopes to an expanse of green lawn.

In the clock tower on the west side of the building is Oom Paul, the clock whose chimes are heard over the South African radio network. In the grounds is an equestrian statue of General Louis Botha and a memorial to soldiers killed in the Delville Wood battle of World War I, where 2 683 South African soldiers lost their lives.

Melrose House

Built in 1886, Melrose House, at 275 Jacob Maré Street, Pretoria, was the home of George Heys, who ran one of the principal stage-coach and transport vehicle lines serving the Transvaal. It is a handsome and well-maintained Victorian house, lavishly furnished. The stained glass, including a window representing Sir Walter Scott's *The Lay of the Last Minstrel*, is exquisite. The billiard room, the elaborate drawing room, the dining room (in which the Treaty of Vereeniging, ending the Anglo-Boer War, was signed on 31 May 1902), the bedrooms, kitchen and conservatory — all retain an atmosphere of the building's historic past.

Museum of Geological Survey

Adjoining the Transvaal Museum in Paul Kruger Street is the Museum of Geological Survey. This houses a display of the geology and mineralogy of the earth, focussing on South Africa.

Many precious and semi-precious stones are exhibited, with reproductions of the world's largest diamonds. There is a fossil display which includes a skeleton, in excellent condition, of a Jonkeria reptile, which lived about 250 million years ago.

An exquisite Italian mosaic table set with semi-precious stones — an artistic masterpiece — is also displayed. Here too is a large, oval stone used as a crusher on the Eersteling gold fields. The museum is open throughout the week.

National Cultural and Open Air Museum

A wide variety of items can be seen at

Fort Klapperkop, now a historical monument, overlooking Pretoria.

An extraordinary piece of military hardware — a bicycle built for nine.

THE MIGRANTS WHO BROUGHT A SPECIAL BEAUTY

Many a European fashion model would envy the elegance, colour and sheer presentation of the well-dressed women of the Ndebele people.

The dresses and beautifully decorated homes of these people are unique. So elaborate is the beadwork of the women that many of their garments and trinkets can be removed only by being destroyed, and the heavy rings around the feet and neck remain there for most of the wearer's life.

The Ndebele history begins about 350 years ago, when a section of the Nguni, then migrating down the south-east coast of Africa, diverged under the leadership of a man named Musi. They wandered into the Transvaal, eventually settling on the site of modern Pretoria.

In their new home the migrant people developed new styles of dress and art. The Sotho of the highveld named them *maTebele* ('refugees') and this became, in their own Nguni language, Ndebele. The original

An Ndebele girl in full dress.

Sotho term has been corrupted to 'Matabele' by Europeans.

The Ndebele survived the troubles of the early 19th century by discreetly hiding in the bush. They never possessed enough wealth to arouse the murderous attentions of raiding Zulu bands. In the process of trying to remain alive however, they divided. One section remained immediately north of Pretoria; a second section moved east to the Olifants River, where they became known to Europeans as the Mapochs, from their chief Mabogo; a third section wandered northwards into the area of modern Potgietersrus. A few other minor sections of the Ndebele are found in different parts of the Transvaal. Some sections disappeared entirely in the tribal wars of the last century.

Though surrounded by the Sotho, the Ndebele have developed a distinctive identity. As with most African peoples, the women do the work, and they also create the traditional costume and decorative art. Wall decorations are done by finger painting. The Ndebele are familiar figures to tourists; brilliantly photogenic, they are often beside the main highways, offering curios for sale.

The courtyard of an Ndebele home.

Ndebele beadwork laid out for sale.

Melrose House in Jacob Maré Street, home of George Heys, a transport magnate at the end of the last century. In this home the Treaty of Vereeniging was signed.

the National Cultural and Open Air Museum. Among them is the country's largest collection of rock art, particularly engravings, of many ancient cultures, not exclusively South African.

Other exhibits include an Egyptian mummy, Inca articles, furniture and objets d'art, silver and glass, a replica of the room in which General Jan Smuts died, and a replica of General Louis Botha's study.

Also of interest is a collection of all the coins used at the Cape, pottery, arts and crafts of the indigenous Transvaal peoples, costume displays, and examples of the domestic architecture of various peoples of South Africa. The museum, in Boom Street, is open throughout the week.

Onderstepoort

The Veterinary Research Institute at Onderstepoort is the principal institution of its kind in Africa. It was founded in 1908 on the farm Onderstepoort, on the northern outskirts of Pretoria. The first director, Dr. Arnold Theiler, was knighted for his achievements in finding vaccine controls for livestock diseases such as rinderpest, distemper, blue tongue and horse sickness.

Onderstepoort is the foremost training school for veterinary surgeons and has the only faculty of veterinary science in the country.

Among the achievements of Onderstepoort was the discovery of widespread phosphorus deficiency in South Africa, and its connection with the disease of botulism, or lamsiekte. This discovery radically changed livestock-rearing techniques in South Africa. It was the first mineral deficiency found to be a cause of livestock disease and it stimulated similar work throughout the world.

Onderstepoort occupies 200 hectares, with a farm of 7 000 hectares where approximately 1 500 farm animals are kept. There is a breeding station for small animals and more than 270 000 mice, rabbits, guinea pigs and other creatures are supplied every year to various laboratories for

Inside Melrose House, where the Treaty of Vereeniging was signed.

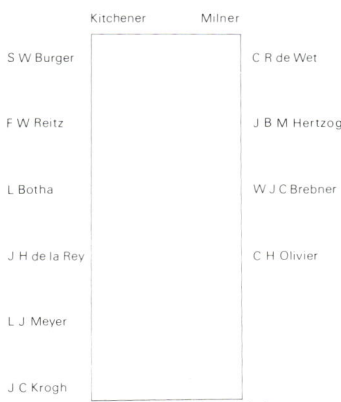

Kitchener		Milner
S W Burger		C R de Wet
F W Reitz		J B M Hertzog
L Botha		W J C Brebner
J H de la Rey		C H Olivier
L J Meyer		
J C Krogh		

The seating arrangement of the signatories to the Treaty of Vereeniging.

The Union Buildings on Meintjeskop, and the statue to General Louis Botha.

Cable-car ride across the country's foremost zoo

A replica of the Delville Wood Memorial looks out over Pretoria's increasingly modern skyline.

use in research. The institute's poultry plant supplies more than 1 000 fertile eggs each day.

Paul Kruger Street

One of the major streets of the central city area of Pretória is named in honour of Paul Kruger. The street begins at the imposing railway station buildings and leads north through the densely built-up commercial area. It reaches Church Square in the centre of Pretoria and continues past the zoological gardens to the northern suburbs. Here, at Wonderboom, it joins the trunk road to the northern Transvaal.

The large railway station at the southern end of Paul Kruger Street had its foundation laid in 1910. This impressive building was designed by the famous architect, Sir Herbert Baker (see box). Mounted in the concourse is one of the first locomotives to operate in the Transvaal — a 'puffing Billy' numbered 1283.

Three blocks north of the station,

Paul Kruger Street passes the city hall. The garden in front of it is graced by jacaranda trees, and contains statues of Andries Pretorius, the namesake of the city, and his son Marthinus, who founded the city. The pediment in front of the building, and the statues, are the work of the South African sculptor, Coert Steynberg.

Opposite the city hall, on the east side of Paul Kruger Street, stands the Transvaal Museum, housing many fascinating exhibits of natural history. The Austin Roberts Bird Hall is the most comprehensive in southern Africa. Dr. Austin Roberts compiled *Birds of South Africa*, in which every bird of South Africa has been given a number, and these numbers now serve as a standard reference in books about birds. In the bird hall every bird is displayed in this numerical order. A coin-operated case displays many birds and reproduces the sounds they make.

There is a skeleton of the extinct dodo from Mauritius, and a collection of skeletons of prehistoric animals. Shells are exhibited and there are galleries devoted to mammals and reptiles. The museum is open throughout the week.

On the northern side of Church Square, Paul Kruger Street continues, its pavements shaded by jacaranda trees. After four blocks it passes on its eastern side the National Zoological

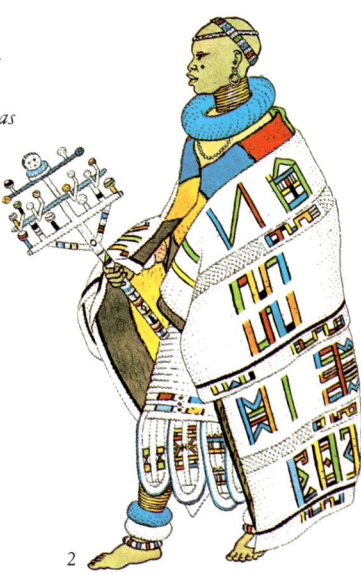

The costume devised by the Ndebele women is unique. They use large quantities of beads, and many of their items of clothing cannot be removed. The wearer has to sleep in them.

1. An unmarried girl emerges from puberty into her 'coming out'.
2. A young married woman, elaborately dressed for a dancing party. Her stick is decorated to resemble a telegraph post.
3. A bride, completely shrouded, being guided on her ceremonial journey to her groom's kraal.
4. A small girl in characteristic double-layer cloth skirt.
5. A small girl loaded with heavy bead hoops and bangles.
6. A married woman wearing a heavy bead apron and blanket.

1 2 3

In Pretoria Zoo stands this fountain built by financier Samuel Marks.

ARCHITECT SUPREME

No architect of southern Africa is responsible for more artistic or satisfying buildings than Sir Herbert Baker (*above*).

Herbert Baker was born in Cobham, Kent, on 9 June 1862. He studied architecture in London and was articled to his cousin, Arthur Baker. In 1892 he travelled to the Cape to see his younger brother, Lionel, who was buying a farm. Herbert Baker decided to investigate the possibilities of starting an architectural practice. Fortunately for him and South Africa, he met Cecil Rhodes, who had a genius for recognizing talent and employing it on large-scale, ambitious projects.

Rhodes gave Baker an exciting commission: to remodel Groote Schuur in Cape Town. The result was the magnificent house that became the official residence of the Prime Minister.

Baker went on to restore many of the neglected Cape-Dutch homesteads, which were then little appreciated and were slowly collapsing into ruin.

Working for Rhodes and for others, Baker produced one fine building after another, including many of the principal buildings of southern Africa.

In Pretoria, Baker designed the railway station and the Union Buildings.

The latter is regarded as his greatest achievement. He also designed the Anglican Cathedral, Cape Town.

In 1912, Baker went to India to work with Sir Edwin Lutyens on the designs of the new legislative buildings in New Delhi. For this work he was knighted. He ended his life in practice in England. He died on 4 February 1946 and is buried in Westminster Abbey.

The view from the Pretoria City Hall towards the Transvaal Museum.

ing 'the end', and ndaba, meaning 'the affair'. The reason for this name — 'the end of the affair' — was that the Hartbeespoort Dam was planned and, when completed, would submerge most of the farm beneath its waters.

The Atomic Energy Board, formed in 1949, purchased 1 195 hectares of the higher ground of this farm for the creation of an atomic research centre. Here, an advanced programme in the development of nuclear fuels is under way. Radio isotopes are made in the reactor and supplied to industry, medicine and agriculture.

Police Museum
The South African Police Museum, in the Compol Building, Pretorius Street, has an interesting, if melancholy, display of weapons and other exhibits connected with crimes. The museum is open from Mondays to Saturdays.

South African Bureau of Standards
The South African Bureau of Standards has the duty of maintaining nation-wide vigilance on standards of manufacture in South Africa. It was established in 1945. Its laboratories may be visited by arrangement through the visitors' bureau.

The Mint
The offices of the South African Mint and the Post Office Museum in Pretoria may be visited by arrangement through the visitors' bureau. All the coinage used in South Africa is produced in the Mint.

Verwoerdburg
On the south side of Pretoria lies the Municipality of Verwoerdburg, named in honour of Dr. Hendrik Verwoerd, Prime Minister of South Africa from 1958 to 1966. Verwoerdburg embraces

Gardens of South Africa, which has an aquarium and reptile park. This is the foremost zoo of southern Africa, containing an extensive collection of the animals of the world. Its setting is park-like, with shady trees, flowers, picnic places, a refreshment kiosk, and an aerial cableway which provides visitors with a spectacular ride over many of the enclosures where animals live in simulated natural settings.

The zoo is open daily and attracts many visitors every year.

Pelindaba
The farm originally owned by artist and author Gustav Preller was named from two Zulu words — phela, mean-

4   5   6

The modest charm of a great statesman's home

several townships such as Lyttelton, Irene and Doornkloof. It was created in 1964 and covers 20 000 hectares. The air-force station of Waterkloof adjoins the municipality to the east.

Irene, named after Irene Nellmapius, daughter of a Hungarian financier well known before the Anglo-Boer War, is the centre of the South African film industry. Adjoining it is the Doornkloof farm where General Jan Smuts had his home until his death in 1950. The Doornkloof homestead is a surprise to most visitors. It is a modest galvanized iron and wood house, simply furnished with the original furnishings and many reminders of Smuts. Two of his motor-cars are also on display. The ashes of Smuts and his wife, Isie, are scattered on the nearby Smuts Koppie.

The house is open daily.

The wonderboom, a remarkable specimen of the wild fig tree, Ficus pretoriae.

Fording the Orange River — part of a tapestry in the Voortrekker Museum.

Voortrekker Museum

Near the impressive Voortrekker Monument is the Voortrekker Monument Museum, which depicts scenes from the pioneer days. An accurate reconstruction of a Voortrekker homestead occupies three rooms.

There are exhibits of weapons, bullet moulds, clothing (including a case displaying 22 different styles of women's bonnets), photographs, lamps, two trek wagons, and a series of 15 tapestries designed by W. H. Coetzer and stitched by nine women from the Railways' Vrou en Moederbeweging.

The tapestries, which contain 130 differently coloured wools and 3 353 600 stitches, took eight years to complete.

Wonderboom

The wonderboom ('wonderful tree') that gives its name to the most northerly suburb of Pretoria is a colossal specimen of a *Ficus pretoriae* tree, estimated by experts to be approximately 1'000 years old.

It was discovered in August 1836 by Hendrik Potgieter while he was travelling north to join Louis Trichardt in the Soutpansberg. The tree is 23 metres high, with a spread of 50 metres. Many travellers have camped in its shade and it became customary for people to congregate here on the Day of the Covenant (16 December) to hold a church service.

The tree grows on the sheltered approaches to the Wonderboom ridge, on which stand the ruins of a small fort built for the defence of Pretoria after the Jameson Raid in 1896 (see Rhodes box, page 37).

In 1949 the Pretoria City Council proclaimed a 450-hectare nature reserve around the tree. Several small antelope species live in the reserve, together with a variety of birds and other small wild creatures. There is a picnic site in the shade of the tree.

The Airforce Memorial overlooking the runway of the pioneer flying school base at Swartkops, originally Roberts' Heights.

AN AWESOME LANDMARK WHERE THE SPIRIT OF THE VOORTREKKERS LIVES ON

The awe-inspiring Voortrekker Monument, 40 metres high and towering above a base 40 metres by 40, dominates the Pretoria skyline.

In 1936 the Sentrale Volks Monumente Kommittee invited architects from all over the world to submit designs for the monument. It was to symbolize the fortitude, courage and indomitable spirit of the Voortrekkers, and had to harmonize with the vastness, solitude and mystery of the African landscape.

The design that was accepted was that of Gerard Moerdijk, a South African architect who specialized in public buildings. His concept of the monument was bold. He sought a uniquely African design, uninfluenced by the outside world. He regarded the Cape-Dutch style, though characteristically African, as unsuited to the severe setting of the highveld plains, and too soft and tranquil to depict the uproar, adventure and dynamic expansion of the Voortrekker period. Moerdijk felt that the essential cultural influence on the Voortrekkers was the Bible, and that they would have built a simple altar of thanksgiving.

He turned to the strange medieval ruins of the northern Transvaal and what was then Rhodesia for his inspiration. These vast constructions of granite, known as maDzimbabwe ('great stone buildings'), are walls that once enclosed villages built from the traditional mud and thatch. The walls, though primitive, blend with the vastness of southern Africa without being overwhelmed by it.

Moerdijk adopted the maDzimbabwe technique of piling small stones on top of one another. The African builders had used flakes that had been fractured from granite outcrops by heat, cold and water. The walls were severely functional but, occasionally, especially to mark the residence of a chief, they were decorated with chevron, herringbone or other patterns made of darker rock. The zigzag chevron line represented water and was associated with fertility.

In preparing his design, Moerdijk elaborated on the basic structures of the maDzimbabwe. He visited the one known as Great Zimbabwe, near Masvingo (formerly Fort Victoria), where he carefully measured the stones and studied the decorations and design. On his drawing board he projected the full power of a primeval structure built of the oldest rock known to man.

The Voortrekker Monument surrounded by its laager of wagons.

The Voortrekker Monument was opened on 16 December 1949. Built from granite quarried and cut to size from a site in the northern Transvaal, where prehistoric peoples had also obtained building materials, it forms a huge altar. Guarding three of its four corners are busts of Great Trek leaders — Piet Retief, Andries Pretorius and Hendrik Potgieter. A symbolic, nameless leader guards the fourth corner. At the entrance to the monument stands a bronze of a Voortrekker woman with two children clutching her skirts.

Looming above this group, in bronze, are representations of wildebeest, symbolizing the dangers confronting civilization. Their presence was suggested by an episode during Retief's visit to the Zulu king, Dingane. As the two were talking there was a thunderous stamping outside the royal enclosure.

'What is that?' asked Retief.

Dingane smiled. 'My regiment of wildebeest dancing', he answered with a disarming shrug.

Above the main entrance is the head of a buffalo, regarded as the most dangerous and determined of all animals when wounded. The entrance leads into the lower hall. In this hall lies a cenotaph of polished granite on which are the words, Ons vir jou, Suid-Afrika ('We for thee, South Africa').

The cenotaph is so positioned that at precisely noon on 16 December — the anniversary of the 1838 Battle of Blood River — a shaft of light penetrates a hole in the roof and sweeps across the inscription.

Also in the lower hall is an eternal flame lit from a torch carried in relays by members of the Voortrekker youth movement from Cape Town during the 1938 centenary of the Great Trek and kept burning in Pretoria until it could be placed in its present position in the monument.

From this lower hall a staircase leads to the Hall of Heroes, 30 metres square and with the domed ceiling 30 metres above. Along the walls of this hall is a frieze, 92 metres long and 2 metres high, of 27 marble panels on which events of the Great Trek are depicted in bas-relief. On 16 December at 11 a.m. — the time of the beginning of the Battle of Blood River — the shaft of light through the roof illuminates a tableau showing Voortrekkers making their vow to God to build a church if He would grant them victory over the Zulus.

To reach the cenotaph below, the shaft of light passes through a circular opening in the floor of the Hall of Heroes.

In the domed roof is a bas-relief of a segment of the globe, including southern Africa. The aperture in the domed ceiling through which the sunlight shines marks the site on the map of the battlefield of Blood River.

The frieze was modelled in clay in South Africa, sent to Italy, and sculpted in the same marble from the Apennines as was used by Michelangelo. Direct descendants of the Voortrekkers concerned in the events depicted posed for the modelling of the frieze. Original items of furniture and dress were meticulously copied. When a dog was required, one was bred from a female greyhound and a Dobermann pinscher. The cross was suggested by two casual sentences in Voortrekker chronicles: 'The bitch caught a rietbok this morning', which indicated that the bitch ran as fast as the wind; and, 'The people awoke to the barking of the dogs', from the Voortrekker records of the Bloukrans massacre, suggesting alert and resolute watchdogs, which had to brave a full-blooded charge from the Zulu army without turning tail.

A staircase with 260 steps leads from the lower hall to the roof, where a panorama of Pretoria and its surroundings is revealed.

The monument is surrounded by a wall of 64 stone ox-wagons. The wall symbolizes the laager of wagons that Voortrekkers formed when in fear of attack. Next to the monument is the Voortrekker Museum and a large amphitheatre where open-air religious services, public meetings and exhibitions of folk-dancing are held.

On the eastern hillsides near the monument is a giant-scale relief map reconstructing the five main routes taken by the Voortrekkers.

The monument's bronze figure of a Voortrekker mother and children.

THE VANISHING LANDSCAPE

ON THE ROAD that leaves Pretoria for the north, to Kipling's 'great, grey-green, greasy Limpopo River', to the land of baobab trees, to Zimbabwe and the enigmatic heart of central Africa, the traveller is confronted by an unexpected scene — a vast plain, covered in thorn trees, with deep, reddish soil, and only the merest hint of a mountain 100 kilometres away on the northern horizon.

What happened to all the scenery? Solving this mystery took the combined labours of many geologists and prospectors. Finally the guilty force was established: a massive geological intrusion into an ancient terrain.

About 600 million years ago the whole continent of Africa was almost torn in half. An imprisoned giant beneath the surface had heaved convulsively, and the Great Rift Valley appeared in East Africa. The crack in the continent spread southwards across Zimbabwe, where it is called the Great Dyke. Through this a river of fire flowed southwards — a mass of molten rock rich in chrome, platinum, nickel, iron, tin, tungsten and other minerals.

On entering what is now the northern Transvaal, the great crack vanished underground, with the river of fire still flowing along it. Just north of Pretoria, the tear reached its most southerly point, and the river of fire was trapped in a cul-de-sac. With colossal pressure behind it, the flow of molten material was forced to intrude into the sedimentary layers of the Transvaal System.

The entire base of the established landscape was undermined by this molten lake, insidiously, irresistibly spreading into every deep crevice, crack and fault. And eventually the surface collapsed into the lake — mountains, valleys and hills tumbling like houses of cards.

The result is comparable to the top of a witch's cauldron once filled with lumps of lead. The fire below never reached the surface; the lead subsided into it, and the once-rough crust became a smooth floor surrounded by a ridge — all that is left of the original surface. Beneath the floor the river of fire has cooled. Where it once flowed, it has left a deposit of minerals so rich that this geological area, known as the Bushveld Igneous Complex, is one of the most productive parts of the world for raw materials.

This is the largest flat-bottomed basin, or lopolith, in the world. In the basin, at Hammanskraal, 42 kilometres from Pretoria, there is a well-preserved volcanic crater, its throat choked with a shallow lake on top of a plug of mud permeated with chloride and carbonate of soda.

To the west, dimly visible from the southern side, is another strange volcanic relic — the Pilanesberg, a circular mountainous mass rising abruptly 300 metres above the floor of the plain and containing the largest known outcrops of syenite, a rock similar to granite.

To the east, the basin ends in a landscape of gaunt peaks looming upwards from a bushy, rocky plain. Asbestos, chrome and platinum are recovered from many isolated mines. Here the Pedi live in the area named after one of their great leaders, Sekhukhuneland.

To the north, the Bushveld Igneous Complex ends in the ridge of the Strydpoortberg and Waterberg ranges. Here the land is densely covered with trees and shrubs, and is tropical in appearance. There are tin mines in the hills, hot springs at many places, and orange groves and orchards of sub-tropical fruits.

The road to the north climbs easily to the level, grassy summit of the northern heights, passes through Pietersburg, and gently descends to the savanna bushveld. The road's crossing of the Tropic of Capricorn is marked by a sign. Ahead looms the giant natural wall of the Soutpansberg, running from east to west. This range, for many people in the south, was once a barricade between civilization and slave raiders, ivory hunters, adventurers and barbaric peoples in the north.

From the town of Louis Trichardt, on the southern side of the range, the road penetrates the Soutpansberg through Wyllie's Poort.

North of the range an immense scenic change is immediately apparent: a vast tropical parkland, dominated by mopani and baobab trees, stretches away to the north. Intensely hot, it gradually descends past the hot springs of Tshipise and the copper mining centre of Messina, and eventually reaches the Limpopo River, which serves as the frontier between South Africa and Zimbabwe.

Brits
Orange blossom perfumes the warm air in the green and fertile countryside around Brits. The waters of the Hartbeespoort Dam irrigate this rich farmland, which produces tobacco, wheat, vegetables, flowers and citrus fruits.

South of the town is an old karee tree beneath which the peace treaty that ended the Boer civil war was signed on 15 January 1864. Also nearby is De Wildt Station where, in 1912, General James Hertzog made a famous speech which led to the formation of the National Party.

Eersteling
The first gold mine in the Transvaal was opened up by a prospector named Edward Button on the farm Eersteling, 30 kilometres north-east of Potgietersrus, in 1871. His operations led to a minor rush and several other small mines were started. The boom ended with the discovery of richer gold fields in the eastern Transvaal.

A primitive piece of mining 'machinery' used by the Eersteling prospectors — a half-ton granite boulder which was see-sawed back and forth to crush the ore — is now in the Transvaal Museum in Pretoria.

Among the relics of the old mining days to be seen at Eersteling is the smoke stack of the Transvaal's first gold-smelting plant. Built of specially imported Aberdeen granite, it was the tallest building in the district and was regarded with awe by the Boer farmers who thought it symbolized the British Empire. If it could be pulled down, the Empire would collapse. Many young bloods pitted their strength against the stack, and there was even an attempt to demolish it with a team of 16 oxen, but it is still standing.

Groblersdal
A vast irrigation scheme has dramatically boosted the fertility of the area around Groblersdal. It is sometimes

referred to as the 'Canaan of the Transvaal' — a land exceptionally rich in sunflowers, groundnuts, maize, tobacco, rice and other crops.

Groblersdal has a caravan park, and facilities for most sports.

Hammanskraal

A cattleman named Hamman built a stockade to protect his livestock from the lions that formerly roamed the Springbok Flats, and the town named

A Virginia tobacco farm near Brits. The leaf-curing sheds are in the background.

The smoke stack of the Eersteling mine, the Transvaal's first gold-smelting plant.

after him now serves a large rural population. From Hammanskraal a road leads to the Pretoria Salt Pan, where mineral salts are extracted from the crater of an extinct volcano.

Loskop Dam

Water from the Olifants River was harnessed for a complex irrigation scheme by the construction of the Loskop Dam in 1938. The area around the dam is a popular holiday resort, with bungalows, a caravan park and a restaurant. The dam is popular with anglers.

The Loskop Dam nature reserve, covering 12 755 hectares, is stocked with antelope, giraffes, hippos and os-

triches. History was made here in April 1964 with the birth of the first white rhino calf since the species became extinct in the Transvaal in 1896.

Louis Trichardt

After a war with the Venda in 1898 the Transvaal government established a town from which to control the area of the Soutpansberg. It was named after Louis Trichardt, the Voortrekker who camped here in 1836 before leaving on his fateful expedition to what was then Lourenco Marques (see box, page 242).

The town, its streets and gardens gay with flowering trees, is a handy base for exploring the Soutpansberg

---

THINGS TO DO AND SEE

Angling Anglers should take care in the tropical parts of the region because this is crocodile country. Tigerfish are caught in the Limpopo. Bream, tilapia, barbel and yellowfish abound in the Loskop Dam.

Archaeology Makapansgat and Maphungubwe are two of the most important sites for palaeontological research in South Africa. Visitors to the caves must obtain permits from the Bernard Price Institute of Palaeontological Research in Johannesburg (for Makapansgat) and the University of Pretoria (for Maphungubwe).

Boating The Loskop Dam is popular for speed-boats and yachts. Canoeing down the Limpopo is a great adventure but the water is infected with bilharzia and the hazards include crocodiles and hippos.

Camping and caravanning The hot spring holiday resorts of Warmbaths and Tshipise have caravan and camping grounds, and there are caravan parks at Nylstroom, Potgietersrus, Pietersburg, Louis Trichardt, Messina and Lydenburg.

West of Naboomspruit there are hot springs with chalets, camping sites and caravan sites.

Hiking and climbing The Soutpansberg Hiking Trail, running for 75 kilometres along the top of the range from Hanglip to the Entabeni State Forest, is a particularly beautiful walk. Many detours from the main trail provide opportunities for climbing and sightseeing.

Mineral Baths Holiday resorts have grown up around the springs at Warmbaths and Tshipise, with accommodation, swimming pools and private baths for invalids. There is also a hot-springs resort west of Naboomspruit.

Sightseeing The scenery in Sekhukhuneland is dramatic, but the roads demand careful driving. The route along the northern side of the Olifants River from Chuniespoort is unforgettable.

Wildlife The Trans-Oranje Bird Sanctuary at Naboomspruit and the Rust der Winter Reserve have a large variety of local and exotic birds. The Soutpansberg range is perfect for bird-watching. Big game can be seen at the Loskop Dam Nature Reserve and the Percy Fife Reserve.

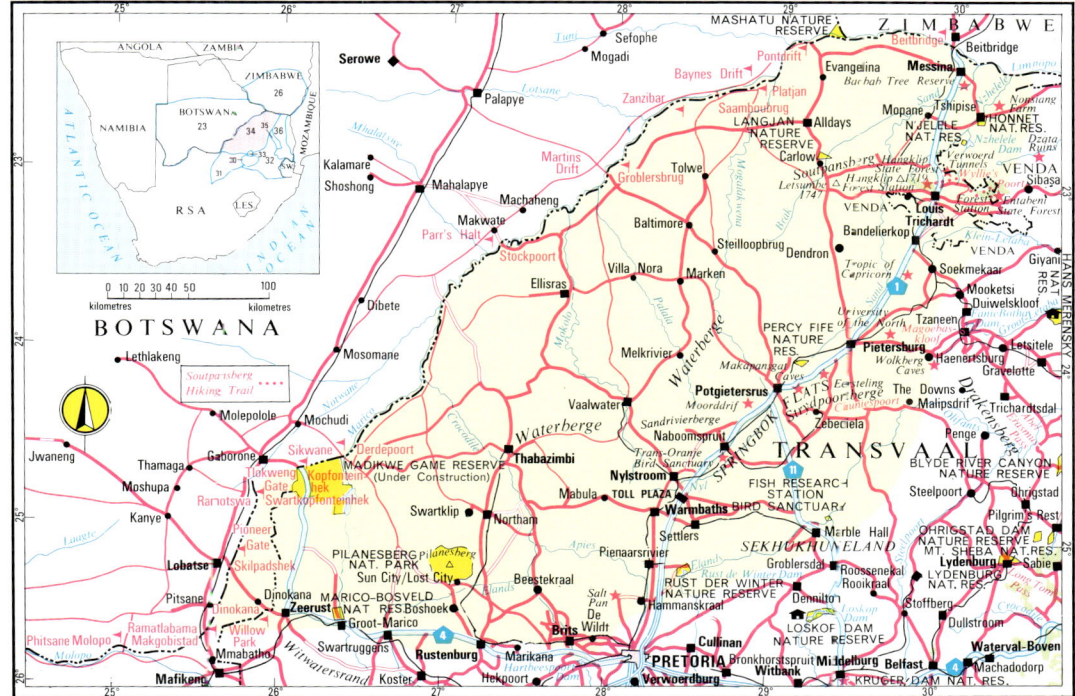

Caves still pervaded by sombre memories

Fort Hendrina, at Louis Trichardt, built of iron sheeting.

The summit of the Soutpansberg. Hanglip mountain is in the distance.

and Venda. There are several hotels on the heights overlooking Louis Trichardt. The Soutpansberg Hiking Trail starts at the nearby Hanglip Forest Station. There is a fairly easy climb to the summit of Hanglip (1 719 metres).

East of the town a road runs through impressive scenery to Punda Maria, the northernmost entrance to the Kruger National Park.

Makapansgat

In a wild, overgrown valley hemmed in by high hills, the gigantic limestone caves of Makapansgat still seem to be pervaded by the sombre atmosphere of one of the most macabre episodes in South Africa's history.

The two main entrances, one below the other, lead into a series of huge

A giant grasshopper. They swarm periodically in the northern Transvaal.

HEROIC WIVES OF LOUIS TRICHARDT'S TREK

The history of the Transvaal echoes to the exploits of brave men, but one epic journey at least is a tribute to the courage and resourcefulness of the frontier women.

In September 1837 Louis Trichardt and a party of eight families set out from the southern slopes of the Soutpansberg to reach the Portuguese coastal port of Lourenco Marques (Maputo).

For reasons unknown, Trichardt led his party south instead of southeast and they ended up in some of the wildest country in the Transvaal.

First, they had to penetrate the Strydpoortberg and reach the Olifants River. This was tough going, but once they reached the banks of the river their troubles really started: elephants, lions, mosquitoes, crocodiles and formidably difficult mountain terrain made their journey a terrible ordeal.

The Pedi people in the area warned the trekkkers that there was no wagon route through the mountains, but the journey continued. A rough footpath climbed the mountains and this the trekkers followed.

The route, though dangerously steep, was at least a change from the river, which they had been compelled to ford no fewer than 13 times in five days, each crossing seeming-

ly more hazardous than the last.

The path led them to the cloudy summit of the Transvaal Drakensberg. At a little spring they eventually outspanned and began to scout a way down the escarpment to the country lying about 1 000 metres below them. The footpath that had led them to the summit had petered out, and wind, rain, cold and mist on the mountain made life unpleasant.

It was the women who found a route down the mountains. They then joined their men in making a passable track, and on 9 December 1837 they began to lower the first wagon down the slopes.

They removed the hind wheels from each wagon and tied treetrunks below the axle to protect the rivets and provide friction on the slopes. It took two months and ten days of incessant labour to manoeuvre the nine wagons to the bottom of the mountains. Miraculously, despite tumbles and minor accidents, there were no serious injuries or damage.

On 13 April 1838 the trekkers reached Lourenco Marques. But the mosquitoes had done their work. One by one the trekkers succumbed to fever, and 27 of the party of 53 died — including Trichardt.

chambers, each darker and more remote from the surface. It was here, in 1854, that 2 000 members of the Tlou people fled after the gruesome massacre of 28 Voortrekkers at Moorddrif, Pruizen and Mapela.

A government force under Piet Potgieter, son of Andries Potgieter, the Voortrekker leader, put the cave under siege. It lasted 30 days, with the soldiers shouting demands for surrender into the caves and the fugitives replying with shots from the darkness. One of these shots killed Potgieter.

As the days passed, resistance from within the cave gradually petered out and the government forces decided to storm the entrance. The scene illuminated by their flickering torches as they advanced into the chambers was horrific: the caves were strewn with more than 1 500 bodies, most of whom had died from thirst or starvation. In fact, not a single person was found alive, the remainder of the original 2 000 having presumably escaped under cover of darkness earlier in the siege.

The decorative costumes of the Venda:
1. The figure of Muwhira, an important character in Venda magic.
2. An initiate makes low obeisance.
3. An initiate in the Domba school dances in a typical attitude.
4. A marimba drum and drummer in the Domba school.
5. A post-initiate of the Domba wears a feather as a sign of maturity.
6. The thong around this young mother's waist is said to prevent a baby crying while she is away working.

The entrance to the vast limestone cave of Makapansgat, a place of tragic memories. The inside floor is still littered with defensive walls and relics of war.

Remains of a man-like ape, *Australopithecus africanus*, believed to have mastered the use of fire, have been discovered near the caves, as well as many animal fossils. Extensive palaeontological research is still being carried out.

Visitors are allowed on the sites only if they have a permit from the Bernard Price Institute at the University of the Witwatersrand.

Marble Hall

The limestone and marble mine of Marble Hall was once a peculiar depression known as Marmerhol, or Marble Hole. Animals trying to reach the water at the bottom of the depression were often trapped here and many died. Marble was clearly exposed in the depression.

In 1913 Christoffel Visagie contracted a fever while he and his wife were hunting in the area. His wife set out with him in their wagon on the journey home to Pretoria. On the way she stopped to examine some prominent white rocks. One of her children

4   5   6

THE PLACE OF THE VENDA

At the beginning of the 18th century people belonging to the Karanga-Rozvi group from what is now Zimbabwe migrated south of the Limpopo River, led by a chief named Dimbanyika. They wandered up the valley of the Nzhelele River, a tributary of the Limpopo, and eventually reached its headwaters in the mountain range they named Venda ('the pleasant place').

It was an exciting new homeland. The soil was fertile and there was also a lake, formed by an ancient landslide which had blocked the exit from a valley of the Mutale River. In this lake, known as Fundudzi, was said to dwell the giant python god of fertility, which demanded the sacrifice of a maiden each year.

This annual sacrifice became an integral part of their life, together with a remarkable ceremony known as the Domba, performed every night somewhere in Vendaland as part of the complex puberty rites of young women. The Domba dance, with long files of girls imitating the sinuous movements of a python, is a singularly beautiful spectacle, with drums thudding out a symphony in praise of sexual love and the ancient mysteries of the people.

The Venda built extensive stone walls. Lacking the granite flakes used by their people in Zimbabwe, they had to make do with cruder materials and, as a result, their structures were far smaller. Many ruins remain, the largest being at Dzata, a place which has great significance for the Venda — the faces of their chiefs are always turned towards it when they die.

Living with the Venda is a rather mysterious group known as the Lemba, descendants of Arab safari traders. These people are expert potters, metal workers and miners. Their ancestors tramped thousands of kilometres carrying trade goods. The beads they brought with them are still treasured by the Venda: the pale blue uhulungu hamadi ('beads of the sea') and the long, white, opaque limanda ('powerful ones') are used in divination and magical ceremonies.

The great hero-chief of the Venda was Makhato, who led them in the battle against the ivory hunters of Schoemansdal. When Europeans abandoned the town in 1867 Makhato reigned supreme over the area of the Soutpansberg, and it was not until 1898 that the Transvaal government regained control of it.

The former independent state of Venda is 6 500 km² in extent and the principal town is Thohoyandou.

The river they thought was the source of the Nile

had recently died, and she loaded enough of the rock onto the wagon to make two gravestones — one for the child and the second for her husband, whom she did not expect to live.

In Pretoria, Mrs Visagie took the stone to a tombstone maker, Tom Taylor. He identified the rock as first-class marble.

Visagie recovered from his fever, and he and his wife took Taylor to see the white rocks, and the depression at Marmerhol. Visagie and Taylor mined marble from the depression, but transport difficulties made the venture uneconomic, and they abandoned it.

In 1929 the Marble Lime Company was formed to work Marmerhol. A railway was built to the mine in 1936.

Messina

The copper-mining centre of Messina is the northernmost town in South Africa — 2 003 kilometres from Cape Town and 16 kilometres from the Zimbabwean border.

Copper was first discovered here in prehistoric times. The discoverers called it musina ('the spoiler') because it adulterated the metal they were really looking for — iron. But they learned to use the copper and, as well as making cooking utensils, fashioned it into ingots which became standard items of barter with neighbouring peoples and Arab safari traders.

The copper was re-discovered shortly before the Anglo-Boer War when a prospector, John Pasco Grenfell, met a hermit known as Wild Lotrie who told him about the old mines. Grenfell was amazed to find rich lodes of high-grade copper. The town that grew up to serve the new copper mines was called Messina, from the old African word.

The climate is hot and the town is gay with tropical flowering trees and creepers. There are several exceptionally large baobab trees in and around Messina. One, on the road to Malala Drift, is known as the Elephant's Trunk from the shape of one of its boughs. It stands in a little park named in memory of Eric Mayer, a well-known painter of baobab trees. Another larger baobab, on Nonsiang farm, has a girth of 19 metres and is 26 metres tall.

Moorddrif

A stone monument where the road crosses the Nylstroom at Moorddrif ('murder ford') marks the spot where 12 Voortrekker men, women and children were massacred by 2 000 followers of the Tlou chief Makapan in September 1854.

The Voortrekkers, led by Hermanus Potgieter (brother of the famous Voortrekker Andries Potgieter), had been hunting in the district, and it is

thought they may unwittingly have broken some Tlou taboo. Potgieter was skinned alive, and six children in the party had their skulls smashed against the trunks of the two acacia trees that flank the memorial.

Naboomspruit

A prospector named Adolph Erasmus found tin on the Waterberg in 1910 and miners streamed into the district. The canteens and trading stores that sprang up on the banks of the Naboomspruit were the start of the present town. Many flowering trees and creepers adorn its streets and gardens.

Several hot springs that surface around the Waterberg have been developed as health resorts. There are many beauty spots and the Trans-Oranje Bird Sanctuary is nearby.

Nylstroom

The first Voortrekkers in the northern Transvaal found a river flowing northwards and on consulting the maps on the back of their family Bibles concluded that it must be the legendary source of the Nile. They called it Nylstroom and their theories about it seemed to be strengthened by the discovery of what resembled a ruined pyramid near the river. In fact this was a natural hillock, known to the local people as Modimollo ('place of

spirits') and revered as a burial ground of ancient chiefs.

The town of Nylstroom, with its streets shaded by poinciana and jacaranda trees, is now the centre of a large groundnut and cattle farming district.

Pietersburg

The principal town of the northern Transvaal, Pietersburg is a bustling, modern centre, with wide streets, many shops and several hotels, making it a popular stopping-off place for tourists heading for the Kruger National Park and Magoebaskloof.

It also serves as the commercial and administrative centre for some of the finest cattle ranches in South Africa. Despite the town's location on the Tropic of Capricorn, the climate is invigorating, because it stands on a plateau 1 280 metres above sea level.

Some of the buildings of the University of the North at Turfloop, on the eastern approach to the town, are decorated with African motifs. Just to the south, there is a 2 000-hectare nature reserve and recreation park.

Potgietersrus

The name of Piet Potgieter, the Voortrekker killed in the siege of the Makapansgat Caves in 1854, is commemorated in the warm, sheltered town of Potgietersrus. The subtropical gardens here are a glorious sight.

The town's cultural history museum, named after Arend Dieperink, its founder and first director, contains many items of local interest, including letters written by President Thomas Francois Burgers; a Bible once owned by the family of the Voortrekker leader, Andries Potgieter; an organ built in Canada in 1860 and previously used in the St. Albans Cathedral in Pretoria; tools used during the building of the council chamber in Pretoria; and an extensive collection of wagonbuilders' tools.

Dr. David Livingstone is said to have camped beneath the prominent cluster of ana trees 16 kilometres out of the town.

To the north-east is the Percy Fife Nature Reserve. Visitors to the reserve must contact the Officer-in-Charge beforehand.

The Pedi people live in one of the most rugged parts of the central Transvaal. Their costumes are mainly of cloth and beadwork. Their life-style is essentially that of the Sotho-Tswana to whom they are related, although their legends describe how they originally displaced people of Karanga origin, who influenced them in several of their customs.

1. A young girl in short smock and skirt, carrying a typical Pedi earthenware pot.
2. A Pedi mother in full smock and apron, the modern dress for womanhood.
3. A small Pedi girl, her hair ochred, wearing the characteristic short smock.
4. A Pedi bride in a smock of a pale shade, her hair modelled into a matted cap and decorated with beads.

1   2   3   4

Schoemansdal

Piles of rubble and a few fruit trees still struggling to stay alive in the encroaching bush are all that remain of the rumbustious old frontier town of Schoemansdal.

Founded in 1847, it soon became the haunt of ivory hunters, cattle rustlers, and an unruly host of other adventurers and renegades seeking their fortunes in the Soutpansberg.

In its heyday Schoemansdal had a population of about 1 800 people. There were constant fights and feuds, and at one time the town's trade was said to include more than 30 tons of lead a year for making bullets. An annual fair was held, where vast quanti-

Basket makers and orange sellers offer their wares near Warmbaths.

The great north road from Cape Town reaches the Limpopo at Beitbridge.

The holiday resort at the hot springs of Tshipise, a pride of the northern Transvaal.

A massive mature baobab.

LORD OF THE SAVANNA

The baobab (Adansonia digitata) is the undisputed monarch of all the savanna trees of Africa. Even a single, isolated baobab dominates its surroundings with its bulky form. In winter, without their leaves, baobabs resemble petrified octupuses with tentacles groping towards the sky.

Almost every part of the tree is useful to man. The leaves can be boiled and eaten as a vegetable. The pollen of the flowers yields an excellent glue, and the seeds are pleasant to suck, or can be ground and roasted to make a palatable coffee. The fruit pod contains tartaric acid (used in sherbet) and the baobab is often called the cream of tartar tree. The spongy wood can be used to make ropes or paper.

Young trees are so unlike mature specimens that Africans say baobabs are dumped whole from Heaven.

---

ties of ivory and animal skins were bought and sold.

The feuding factions in the town eventually presented a united front in a major battle against the Venda in 1867. The Europeans lost, and left the town to be looted and reduced to rubble by the victors. There was little regret in official circles over the demise of this unruly place.

Thabazimbi

The Iscor steelworks of Pretoria draw much of their raw materials from Thabazimbi, which literally means 'mountain of iron'. Rugged mountains looming from a bush-covered plain are the spectacular setting for the mine and the town that has grown around it. The red soil bears witness to the enormous treasure of iron, and the ore trains are on the move day and night. The surrounding area is ranching country, and game farming has also developed into an important local industry.

Tshipise

The hot spring at Tshipise has been developed into a popular holiday resort, with outdoor swimming pools, private baths, a hotel, hundreds of rondavels and a caravan site set amid natural parkland.

In 1969 it was claimed that the waters of Tshipise cure diabetes, and the spring enjoyed a boom. Medical tests subsequently threw doubt on the claim, but the resort still attracts thousands of visitors every year, especially during the winter months.

Warmbaths

Long before man came on the scene the water of the mineral spring at Warmbaths was relished by animals, and elephants and buffalo wallowed in the warm, mineralized mud.

Various African peoples used the spring in the Iron Age, and Europeans discovered it soon after settling in the Transvaal. They could hardly miss it, for in winter a cloud of steam, visible for many kilometres, rises over the veld. Settlers soon began scooping out bathing hollows in the mud.

The spring was bought by the Transvaal government in 1873 and it has since grown into a health and holi-

Virginia tobacco leaves hanging in a curing shed and soon to be marketed.

The civic centre of Pietersburg, largest town of the northern Transvaal.

The hunter who stumbled into a miracle of nature

day resort, with more than 250 000 visitors each year.

A hospital housing a special section dealing with rheumatic complaints has been established at the spring. The water, which flows out of the ground at about 23 000 litres an hour, is rich in sodium chloride, calcium carbonate and other minerals. It is also mildly radio-active.

Wolkberg Cave

In 1927 young Jan Hendrik Meintjies, son of the owner of Mizpah farm on the slopes of the Wolkberg ('cloudy mountain'), was hunting with his dog

Aloes, granite boulders and euphorbia trees on the savanna plains.

and encountered a mountain reedbuck. Meintjies shot and wounded the reedbuck, and the dog leapt off in pursuit. The hunter followed the blood trail, but both animals had disappeared. The trail led Meintjies to a vertical shaft with a wild fig tree growing over the entrance. Both animals had fallen into the hole and lay dead at the bottom of a 20-metre drop. Meintjies climbed down, using the roots of the fig tree, which were exposed on the surface of the rock.

Having found the animals dead, Meintjies, lacking a torch, explored no further. However, later that day he returned with his elder brother John, bringing torches and ropes. They hauled the animals to the surface and began exploring deeper into the cave.

They were the first people to venture into the huge chamber at the beginning of one of the world's most spectacular sequences of underground caves.

All around them was a shimmering whiteness — the floor looked as though it was covered with a thick hoar frost.

Over the next few months the cave was explored but never penetrated to the end. One chamber after another was discovered, all decorated with complex dripstone formations.

During World War II bat guano was removed from the first chamber and considerable damage was done to the formations. Inside the cave sequence, fortunately, there is an extensive lake which prevented easy access.

Today the farm containing the Wolkberg Cave is owned by the Transvaal Provincial Administration. It is being explored and studied by members of the Cave Research Organisation and the South African Underwater Diving Union. The sequence of underground lakes, streams, chambers and passages is being mapped and photographed.

The hazardous entrance to the caves at present makes them accessible only to experienced cavers. The reward for those who do venture in is a scenic dreamland of mirror-like lakes reflecting complex dripstone formations, and to glide over these waters in a canoe is to journey into a world of fantasy.

Wyllie's Poort

The road from Louis Trichardt climbs spectacularly through the Soutpansberg and then begins a complex descent down the northern side of the range. The climax of this pass is a narrow gorge known as Wyllie's Poort.

The original road was subject to flooding and in 1961 two tunnels, one 274 metres long and the other 457 metres, were driven through the solid rock of the gorge.

The tunnels, named after Hendrik Verwoerd, the former Prime Minister, now carry the main road through the mountains.

Ndebele girls with their elaborate, heavy, and extremely hot costume of blankets and beadwork.

The brilliantly coloured sap-feeding bug, Callidea sp.

Harvest time for tobacco in the northern Transvaal. The Soutpansberg range provides a backing to the savanna plains north of the Tropic of Capricorn.

THE ANCIENT OASIS OF THE 'SALT PAN MOUNTAINS'

The Soutpansberg ('salt pan mountains') take their name from a powerful brine spring which surfaces on the western end of the range. This spring has been a source of salt to inhabitants of the region since ancient times.

Though not a large range — just over 130 kilometres from west to east — it is richly forested and extremely impressive. Its highest point is Letsumbe (1 747 metres).

The mountains consist of reddish sediments, sandstones, grits and conglomerates laid down by water about 400 million years ago. Though the surrounding region receives little rain, the mountains themselves have an annual rainfall of nearly 2 000 millimetres in places, making the range perfect for afforestation. There are large government-owned plantations of exotics. A wide variety of indigenous trees also grow here, including the tree fern, yellow-wood, stinkwood, wild fig, Cape chestnut, waterberry, ironwood, fever tree and many others.

Oribi, klipspringer, bushbuck, grey and red duiker live in the mountains and bird life includes the crowned eagle, black eagle, crested guinea fowl, Narina trogon, crowned hornbill, forest canary, Cape glossy starling, yellow-billed hornbill, black-headed oriole and the collared sunbird.

Traces of the presence of man in the Soutpansberg go back to the

Fundudzi, the Soutpansberg lake.

Stone Age. San people of the Later Stone Age painted on the walls of rock shelters, and the Khoikhoi made their homes here. Later, Iron Age people replaced them — a section of the Rozvi-Karanga people of Zimbabwe, who reached the Soutpansberg about the beginning of the 18th century, discovered its fertility and named it Venda ('the pleasant place'). These people settled along the summit ridge of the range, especially towards the east, and they are the ancestors of the Venda people of today (see box, page 243).

The southern face of the Soutpansberg has the appearance of a great wall, thickly forested and with no visible natural passes. Paths find their way up these steep slopes and the great trunk road of Africa, the famous old Cape to Cairo road, climbs steeply to the heights above the town of Louis Trichardt and then, in a succession of snaking curves and gradients, crosses the plateau summit and descends into the hot savanna plains where baobab trees grow and the wilderness of Africa stretches northwards, seemingly without end.

Zebediela

Nearly 400 million oranges are harvested each year from the groves of Zebediela — the world's biggest citrus estate. The output is sufficient to provide one orange for every eight people on earth.

At the height of the season about 15 000 cases of oranges leave Zebediela every day. The fruit comes from more than 600 000 trees irrigated by enough water to supply a city. The main harvesting periods are from April to June, when the navel oranges are ripe, and August to October, when the Valencias are ready.

The whole estate is highly mechanized and many of the most advanced handling techniques in world citrus production have originated from Zebediela.

The extraordinary irrigation possibilities of the region were first realized in the 1890s by W H Gilfillan,

surveyor-general of the Transvaal government. The Anglo-Boer War postponed his plans for the development of the area, but when peace came Gilfillan returned and bought two farms, Uitkyk and Schaapplaats.

There were more troubles ahead for Gilfillan. He tried to farm ostriches, but the ostrich-feather boom collapsed.

Then came World War I, which created an escalation in the demand for fresh fruit. Gilfillan convinced Isidore Schlesinger, the financier, that the area had great potential for producing fruit. Schlesinger bought Gilfillan's farms and divided them into 1 200 plots each of 2 hectares.

A handsome brochure was produced offering the plots at £67 each, to be farmed as a profit-sharing co-operative.

The scheme proved particularly attractive to retired army officers, and by 1921 most had been sold. Houses sprung up in the new Zebediela township, the great citrus groves were planted, and the first fruit was picked in 1926.

Two years later the branch railway to Naboomspruit was opened to carry the ever-growing harvest on the first stage of its journey to all parts of the world.

In 1974 the government bought the Zebediela estate for fuller development and operation in conjunction with the local authority.

The estate is named after an Ndebele chief of the area, nicknamed Sibitiela.

One of the two Verwoerd tunnels which burrow through the Soutpansberg.

THE HAUNTING EDGE OF THE BERG

THE EDGE OF THE BERG — no more hauntingly beautiful landscape exists in all Africa than the eastern escarpment of the Transvaal. Here the lowveld savanna sweeps in to meet the highveld like a sea of adventure breaking in on cliffs of mystery and romance. The scene is incomparable, breathtaking in its vast scale. Hunters, slave raiders, safari traders, elephants and big game, prospectors, raiding warrior bands, transport riders, and countless characters who wandered here in search of fortune — all have vanished, but have left behind a wistful legacy of pure enchantment that colours this part of the world.

The highveld is about 1 000 metres above the lowveld. The escarpment runs south to north for more than 300 kilometres before dwindling to the level of the savanna. All along this length are spectacular gorges, isolated buttresses, unusual geological features, and passes taking roads from one world to another.

Wherever rivers penetrate the escarpment they have eroded the slopes and created majestic scenery. The Olifants River makes its way down to the low country through a vast and lovely gorge, with cliff faces dyed red, yellow and orange by lichens and by iron oxides in the rock. The Blyde River, a tributary of the Olifants, has a gorge so spectacular that it ranks as one of the scenic wonders of Africa. The Crocodile River penetrates the escarpment through a valley that is gloriously warm and fertile. Numerous streams and lesser rivers tumble from the heights in waterfalls, rapids and cascades.

Many of the footpaths have been here as long as man himself and most of the passes are scenically spectacular, among them Long Tom Pass, Abel Erasmus Pass and Magoebaskloof. Swartbooi's Path, descending from Graskop to Bosbokrand, is a 1 000-metre staircase of moss-covered boulders, winding through a tunnel of trees whose roots cross the path like pythons waiting for victims.

An ancient safari path followed the banks of the Sabie River into the interior of the Transvaal. Several stories are told of this path, at least one of which has inspired searches for lost treasure. According to this old tale, one of the Portuguese safari traders who used this path decided on a final expedition before retiring. He had a successful trip, trading with communities living along the edge of the Berg near the headwaters of the Sabie River. On his return to Lourenco Marques (now Maputo) he employed extra porters to carry the proceeds of his trade — ivory, copper ingots, gold dust and skins. Once at the port, the trader, having no intention of returning to the interior, sold his porters as slaves and set sail for home.

In Portugal, the trader sold his business to a young man who followed the same path and also did good trade. When he tried to hire porters for the return journey, however, he was called to account for his predecessor's action of selling his porters as slaves. There was a struggle, some killings, and the bulk of the trading party was forced to take refuge in a cave. There they were starved to death and the cave was blocked up. However, one man had escaped and returned to Lourenco Marques, where he died of fever. He left a garbled account of his misadventure, and a leather crucifix bag with a rough message scraped on it, giving some details of the location of the cave. The treasure of ivory and gold has never been recovered and the lost cave has never been traced.

Legend tells of many other strange events that occurred in this scenic dreamland: there are lost mines, the curious mystery of Swan's Race (see box, page 257), tales of prospectors who found gold and kept it hidden, paying debts with glittering nuggets, then dying of fever, being murdered or vanishing, leaving their finds forever lost — and all this is but a small part of the indefinable, elusive nature of the edge of the Berg.

Abel Erasmus Pass
The Zederberg stage-coaches originally used this pass on their way to the lowveld. The modern tarred road snakes down beneath rust-coloured cliffs, daubed with the brilliant yellow of lichen growing on the rocks.

The modern pass was opened on 8 May 1959 and named after Abel Erasmus, a 19th century pioneer of the lowveld. It descends 800 metres in its 24-kilometre length and includes a 133,5-metre-long tunnel named after J. G. Strijdom, the former prime minister (1955-58). The pass reveals panoramic views of the Olifants River Valley and the eastern lowveld. There are picnic sites by the roadside, and at

The Abel Erasmus Pass, finding a complex way through the Drakensberg.

the foot of the pass a caravan park, restaurant and bungalow complex.

Blyde River Canyon
When Voortrekker leader Hendrik Potgieter led an exploratory party to the Portuguese port of Lourenco Marques in the winter of 1840, the womenfolk were left on the malaria-free summit of the Drakensberg near Graskop. They waited far beyond the time at which the men were due to return, then, thinking that their menfolk must have died, named the stream on whose banks they were camped the Treur ('sorrow'), and set off for home. On the way they were overtaken by Potgieter and his party.

Bourke's Potholes in the Blyde River, an extraordinary example of river erosion.

The Treur River waterfall near Bourke's Potholes . . . white water in the bright sun.

The reunion took place as the women were about to ford a river which was promptly named the Blyde ('joy').

The Blyde has a spectacular course. From its source on the Berg it flows to meet the Treur. At this meeting point, near the site of a once profitable gold mine known as Bourke's Luck after its owner, Tom Bourke, there are extraordinary potholes — Bourke's Potholes — and rock formations. Paths and footbridges take visitors to viewing sites overlooking these formations.

The river then plunges headlong into a gigantic gorge. Viewing sites have been created at several points along the edge of the gorge and the scenery is sensational, with the river some 800 metres below the summit of the escarpment. Dominating the gorge are the triplet peaks known as the Three Rondavels, and the great, flat-topped summit of Mariepskop (1 944 metres).

The Transvaal Board of Public Resorts has created the Overvaal Blydepoort Resort on the edge of the gorge, with chalets, a caravan park, restaurant, swimming bath, sporting facilities, nature trails and horses for hire.

The Blyderivierspoort Hiking Trail stretches from God's Window (see Panorama Route, page 256) northwards along the edge of the Berg, through the Blyderivierspoort Nature Reserve to the Sybrand van Niekerk Public Resort at Swadini, in the lowveld. There are huts at Watervalspruit, Clearstream and Old Mine. The entire walk is 56 kilometres.

THINGS TO DO AND SEE

Angling Trout are common in many of the streams in this area.

Antiquities Pilgrim's Rest is a superbly preserved old-time gold-rush town. The Royal Hotel is a treasure, the odd little shops a delight.

Camping and caravanning There is a large, luxurious caravan park at the Overvaal Blydepoort Resort. There are also caravan parks at Graskop, Lydenburg, Pilgrim's Rest, Sabie, and the Sybrand van Niekerk Resort.

Hiking There are two magnificent hiking trails along the escarpment — the Blyderivierspoort Hiking Trail and the Fanie Botha Hiking Trail.

Prospecting There is still gold in the hills and streams of the escarpment. Potential prospectors must either be accompanied by a licensed prospector, or they must obtain a licence and a permit to possess unwrought gold.

Sightseeing The Panorama Route is a circular drive taking in Graskop, Pilgrim's Rest, the Lisbon and Berlin waterfalls, and other spectacular features of the area.

The road along the edge of the Blyde River Canyon is breathtaking. Magoebaskloof, the Woodbush Forest drives, the incredible roads up and over The Downs and Long Tom Pass, and the first sight of Pilgrim's Rest from the top of the divide — all are unforgettable.

An ancient battlefield rich in memories

Through a dream landscape of silver mist, the Blyde River sweeps along the floor of its deep gorge. The mountains known as the Three Rondavels loom in the distance.

The plant life of the area is rich; there are ferns, cycads, creepers, cabbage trees, wild figs, mobola plums, proteas, orchids, ericas, and many other trees and flowering plants.

Baboons, leopards, lynxes, porcupines, grey and red rhebuck, klipspringers and grey duikers are common. Bird life includes a breeding colony of the rare bald ibis, all three South African loeries, and many owls.

Relics from the Middle Stone Age have been found, as well as the bones of victims of tribal wars. Mariepskop was once a scene of great strife. In the days when the Swazis raided the lowveld communities, the local residents,

Pedi and Pulana people, used this flat-topped massif as a natural fortress. In one battle, known as Moholoholo ('the great, great one'), the Swazis were heavily defeated by a combined force of local peoples led by Mohlala of the Pedi and Maripi Mashile and Tshilwane of the Pulana. Large numbers of Swazi skeletons littered the slopes after the battle and the peak is named in honour of Maripi, who conducted himself with great valour in the conflict.

The Blyde River is dammed in the gorge by a 72-metre-high wall, creating a lake that serves as a picturesque home for many hippos and crocodiles.

Echo Caves

The Echo Caves lie in a ridge of dolomite hills at the head of the Molapong Valley. Tools and implements dating from the Middle and Late Stone Ages have been found here.

In 1924 Dr. J. A. Classen bought the farm containing the valley. He created a museum of early man in a San rock shelter, displaying skeletons and relics from the area.

Classen also opened one of the caves to the public in 1960. The sequence of chambers is known as the Echo Caves, owing to a dripstone formation which, when tapped, makes echoes. The largest chamber in the caves is 100 metres

long and 40 metres high.

Cannibal Cave is a sanctuary for bats and is not open to the public. Access to it is through a vertical shaft connected to a complex series of passages and chambers inhabited by millions of bats.

There is a motel and caravan park at the caves.

Fanie Botha Hiking Trail

This hiking trail, named after Stephanus Botha, minister of forestry and water affairs (1968-76), leads for 80 kilometres along the escarpment from the Ceylon State Forest, six kilometres west of Sabie, to God's Window,

where it links up with the Blyderivierspoort Hiking Trail. There are five huts for overnight shelter and several pools suitable for swimming.

The trail takes hikers around the eastern slopes of the 2 114-metre Mauchsberg (named after Karl Mauch, the renowned German geologist) and the 2 284-metre Mount Anderson (named after an early surveyor), the second highest mountain in the Transvaal after Die Berg (2 331-metres).

The surroundings are diverse, with many tree ferns, flowering plants and indigenous trees, numerous butterflies and abundant bird life, including the bush loerie, crowned eagle, hoo-

The Blyde River gorge, overlooked by the Three Rondavels.

poe, white stork (in season), spotted owl and hadeda.

Also common are monkeys, baboons, bush pigs, grysbok, grey rhebuck, red and grey duiker, and even the occasional leopard.

Along the trail is the largest man-made forest in the world. South Africa has a meagre 0,24 per cent of natural high forest area — Canada has 25 per cent and Finland 65 per cent. But in 1903 some 140 hectares were planted with eucalyptus and black wattle on the farm Driekop (near Graskop), owned by the Transvaal Gold Mining Estates, and now the afforested areas of South Africa cover more than a million hectares.

SWEET HARVEST FROM THE SUB-TROPICAL GARDEN OF THE TRANSVAAL

The north-eastern Transvaal has soil and a climate ideal for the cultivation of sub-tropical fruits, and man has made the most of the opportunity. The area produces abundant crops of pawpaws, avocados, mangoes, passion fruit, bananas, litchis and tomatoes, as well as citrus fruit, sugar cane and a small amount of coffee.

The avocado was introduced into South Africa from its native home in Central America. The fruit varies considerably in size, shape, colour and flavour.

Bananas are among the world's most important fruit crops. The trees — actually gigantic herbs with false trunks composed of leaf sheaths — are cultivated in more than 100 varieties. Banana trees come from southern Asia, where sages were so fond of musing in their shade that the family name of the banana became musa.

Guavas are another import from tropical America, the name being derived from the Spanish guayaba. They are canned, and used to make drinks, jams and jellies.

Litchis, of which there are at least 50 varieties, originate from southern China. They were introduced into South Africa from Mauritius. The trees are handsome, but bear fruit erratically.

Mangoes come from India, where they have been cultivated for more than 4 000 years. To the Asian, the mango is the king of all tropical fruits — Buddha himself rested in the shade of a mango tree.

The Arabs were so fond of this fruit that they carried its seeds wherever they traded. As a result, mango trees grow in many strange places. The safari paths from the coast of East Africa to the great lakes are lined with mango trees, and their shade and fruit provided rest and

refreshment for many a weary slave.

The name 'mango', first used by the Portuguese, is the corrupted form of the Tamil name 'mankay'. The maison rouge species and the peach mango are two of the most delicious of cultivated fruits. They originated from varieties cultivated by the Portuguese in Goa.

The passion fruit belongs to the family *Passiflorum*. The flower is said to symbolize the Passion of Christ: the corona depicts the crown of thorns; the five petals and five sepals represent ten of the twelve apostles (Peter, who denied Christ, and Judas, who betrayed Him, are left out); and the other parts of the flower are symbolic of the nails and wounds.

There are more than 400 species of passion fruit in their natural home, tropical South America, with several of them cultivated in southern Africa

The pawpaw is indigenous to North America and the Caribbean, where the trees grow to a height of more than 15 metres.

Only one species is recognized, although the colour and flavour of the fruit varies: pawpaws with orange-coloured flesh are sweet, and those with white flesh are bitter. They are cultivated in large numbers in South Africa, and used in salads or as a breakfast dish.

Tomatoes come from Peru and Ecuador. A yellow variety was introduced into Europe in the middle of the 16th century and named the pom d'ora ('apple of gold'). The red variety was prized for its reputed aphrodisiac properties and cultivated as the pomme d'amour ('apple of love').

Tomatoes are grown mostly in the north-eastern Transvaal and marketed for use in salads and cooking, or for the production of tomato juice.

Avocado

Pawpaw

Litchis

Mango

Mountains that echoed to Long Tom's thunder

The Transvaal colonial government also planted a forest of pines on their Graskop farm in 1906.

The hiking trail passes through both forests. About R200 million worth of timber is produced in the area annually.

Graskop

In the 1850s a renowned eastern Transvaal character, Abel Erasmus, known to the Africans as Dubula Duzé ('he who shoots at close range'), had a farm called Graskop ('grassy hill'). From here he exercised rough justice as the Native Commissioner of the lowveld. Today, Graskop is the terminus of the branch railway from Nelspruit and a centre of a substantial timber industry.

From Graskop the scenic Panorama Route leads northwards along the edge of the escarpment to the Blyde River Canyon.

A dramatic sky frames the Lydenburg Voortrekker School, built in 1851.

Long Tom Pass

The helter-skelter gradients of the Long Tom Pass carry the tarred road from Lydenburg over the top of the Transvaal Drakensberg to Sabie. The pass, 57 kilometres long, with its summit 2 149 metres above sea level, is one of southern Africa's scenic treasures.

The origin of the pass goes back to 1871 when a wagon road was built to connect Lydenburg with the lowveld, and from there to Lourenco Marques (Maputo). This old trail runs close to the modern tarred road. Its gradients were formidable, and the Devil's Knuckles (four consecutive steep summits) were a graveyard for many transport vehicles. At the stage of the pass known as The Staircase, wagon wheel tracks are visible in the slate surface.

The pass is named after the Anglo-Boer War 15-centimetre gun used by the Boers and nicknamed Long Tom

---

THE KRUGER MILLIONS

In *Silver Blaze* by Sir Arthur Conan Doyle there are four celebrated lines. Inspector Gregory asks Sherlock Holmes:

"'Is there any other point to which you would wish to draw my attention?'
'To the curious incident of the dog in the night-time.'
'The dog did nothing in the night-time.'
'That was the curious incident', remarked Sherlock Holmes.'"

At the end of the Anglo-Boer War rumours spread that President Paul Kruger had a fortune in gold with him on his retreat from Pretoria to Lourenco Marques (Maputo).

There was in fact no such treasure. Like the silent dog in the Holmes story, Kruger had attracted an unexpected kind of attention. More than 50 different expeditions searched in vain for what became known as the Kruger millions.

The frenzy subsided, but there are still rumours, and would-be guides lurk around the pubs in the lowveld, available to lead hopefuls on yet another search for the solution to the mystery of the dog that never barked.

The Long Tom Pass snakes its way over the thickly afforested Drakensberg by means of finely graded curves.

by British soldiers. On 7 September 1900 General Redvers Buller and his army captured Lydenburg. The Boer forces withdrew to the summit of the Drakensberg. The Boers set up Long Tom and no sooner were the British comfortably settled in Lydenburg than they were bombarded with shells.

Next day the British set out up the pass to dislodge the Boers. A succession of battles took place and the Boers gradually retreated, fighting every inch of the way. After a tough day and a cold, misty night, the British reached the summit soon after dawn on 9 September. (Eastwards from this summit is the stupendous view over the plateau of the Sabie River and the distant lowveld.) Long Tom was already well down the pass and greeted the British on the summit with more shells. All day the Boers stubbornly shelled the British and the sound of firing echoed through the mountains like a long-drawn-out thunderstorm.

That night the British managed to haul some of their own artillery to the summit, and at dawn on 10 September they opened fire. The Gordon Highlanders were given the task of clearing the road. The Boers withdrew, tumbling 13 of their transport wagons over the Devil's Knuckles, but safely dragging the cumbersome Long Tom with them.

The last position of Long Tom in action is marked by a sign, and craters made by its shells can still be seen.

There is a camping site at Whisky Spruit.

Lydenburg

Survivors of the malaria-stricken town of Ohrigstad (see page 255) established Lydenburg in 1849 in an area known to the Africans as Masising ('place of the long grass'). The new town was named Lydenburg ('town of suffering') in memory of the hardships of its founders.

Although it was the main seat of the 'Republic of Lydenburg in South Africa' from 1857 to 1860, the town grew slowly. Despite the fertile surroundings the place was remote, and few people wanted to live here, surrounded by the truculent Pedi and threatened by the presence of fever. During the Transvaal War (1880-81) a small British garrison was

The twin waterfalls of the Mac-Mac River tumble into a gorge, where ferns cling to the rocks and strange echoes sound.

besieged in the town, occupying a stronghold named Fort Mary after the wife of the commanding officer, Second-Lieutenant W. H. Long. For artillery the British built a gun from the barrel of a water pump, and this threw 1,5-kilogram cannon balls. The garrison held out for 84 days. From Lydenburg, a British relief force was sent to Pretoria, and was severely defeated at Bronkhorstspruit.

The oldest building in the town is the Voortrekker School, completed in 1851 and the oldest remaining school building in the Transvaal. The building also served as a church until the

Voortrekker Church was completed in 1853. Adjoining it is the later Dutch Reformed Church, built in 1894, and still in use. These three buildings are proclaimed national monuments.

Stones of the demolished Fort Mary were used to build the gunpowder house in 1890.

The Transvaal Provincial Administration has its fish hatchery in Lydenburg. From here trout and other fish are supplied to rivers and dams all over the Transvaal. Near the hatchery is a freshwater aquarium, which contains more than 60 species of fish.

East of the town lies a 685-hectare

nature reserve, conserving local plant and animal life.

Soya beans, tobacco, fruit (notably yellow peaches), wool, cattle, dairy produce, wheat, barley, maize and lucerne are all produced in the district. The local rivers, such as the Spekboom and the Sterkspruit, are powerful, clear, and offer excellent fishing, as does the P. T. C. du Plessis Dam.

Mac-Mac

In 1873 Johannes Muller discovered gold in a stream that plunges 56 metres over the lip of a precipice into a deep gorge covered by ferns and

Where two warrior chiefs duelled to the death

The forest of Magoebaskloof, a place of memories of old fights and wars.

TREES OF THE WOODBUSH FOREST

One of the most beautiful trees to be seen in any high forest is the redwood (*Ochna arborea*). Its budding spring leaves are bronze; as they grow, they slowly turn green. Showy masses of golden flowers then appear, and as a climax to the cycle, these flowers later produce blood-red seeds.

Other trees found here include the cabbage, or kiepersol, trees (*Cussonia spicata*), with their curious cabbage-like leaf heads; the giant ironwoods (*Olea capensis*), which reach a height of 40 metres with trunks 5,5 metres in circumference; the forest fever trees (*Anthocleista grandiflora*); and the Natal mahogany (*Trichilia emertica*).

The deep, rich, granite soil and heavy rainfall make the Woodbush area ideal for yellow-woods, red stinkwoods, ironwoods and many other species.

Permits for camping in this area may be obtained from the forest station, which is close to the source of the Broederstroom River.

A walk through the Woodbush Forest is a delightful adventure. There are views into dark green valleys; gloomy shadows suddenly give way to open glades flooded with sunshine; and there is always the chance of surprising an interesting bird or animal.

The samango monkeys of the Woodbush Forest are particularly handsome; their thick fur has always been in great demand as part of the costume of African dancers.

The road through the Woodbush Forest at De Hoek, near Debegeni.

forest. There was good gold, but the stream was too small to support many diggers. There was the usual rush to the place, however, and its odd name is reputed to have originated in 1874 when the Reverend Thomas Burgers, President of the South African Republic, visited the scene and found so many Scotsmen working here that every second man seemed to be called 'Mac'.

The waterfall — the Mac-Mac Falls — can be seen from a site just off the main road from Sabie on the way to Graskop. Roughly two kilometres from the Falls are the Mac-Mac Pools, a favourite haunt of swimmers, with changing rooms and picnic sites. The pools can be reached by an untarred track leading off the road from Sabie.

Mining in the stream has long been abandoned.

Magoebaskloof

The 97-kilometre road down the escarpment from Pietersburg to Tzaneen is one of the most popular tourist drives in southern Africa. It passes through a superb variety of scenery, with side roads and circular routes to scenic viewing sites. At one stage it drops 600 metres through 6 kilometres of dense forest.

Magoebaskloof takes its name from Makgoba, chief of the Tlou people who lived at its foot. In 1894 Makgoba and his people refused to pay taxes to the Transvaal government. A punitive force was sent to discipline the community. Makgoba and about 500 of his followers fled into the deep forest of the kloof and defied all efforts to prize them out.

After several months and many skirmishes, the Transvaal government secured the help of Swazi warriors. They were expert trackers, and captured two Tlou women. They killed one and tortured the other, and she told them where to find the chief.

The Swazis surrounded the Tlou stronghold. Catcalling, whistling and hissing their peculiar war cry, they challenged Makgoba to personal combat with their own commander. In a glade in the forest, the two men fought with spears and clubs. Makgoba was battered to his knees, and the Swazis cut off his head and carried it back to claim bounty money from

the government. The Tlou people were dispersed, but Makgoba's name will always linger in this beautiful part of the edge of the Berg, with its high forest full of shadows and memories.

The lower portion of Magoebaskloof and the adjacent slopes of the escarpment are tea-producing areas. Two large estates, Grenshoek and Middelkop, belonging to the Industrial Development Corporation, cover the escarpment with dense green blankets of tea plants. Cultivation of tea began here in 1963, when experts such as Douglas Penhill, from Kenya, settled in the area and, with government backing, started the production of what was named Sapekoe, or South African tea (from the Chinese word pekoe, meaning tea). During the long picking season — September to May — the air is heavy with the smell of tea. Tours of the curing and packing plant can be arranged.

Higher up the valley the Directorate of Forestry has plantations, but there are also lovely patches of indigenous forest, noted for their yellow-woods, red stinkwoods, ironwoods, cabbage trees, and the spectacularly beautiful rooi hout, whose Latin name, *Ochna o'connorii*, derives from Alexander O'Connor, who, as director of forestry after the Anglo-Boer War, was responsible for much of the afforestation of the area.

There is a cascade, swimming pool, natural slide and picnic ground in the midst of the forest at Debegeni ('place of the big pot'), which is named from the pool at the foot of the waterfall believed by some of the local people to be inhabited by water spirits.

At the top of Magoebaskloof is a turn-off to the Woodbush Forestry Station, 11,5 kilometres along the edge of the escarpment. This drive provides views over the lowveld, and scenes of forest and wild flowers. Beyond the forestry station, the gravel road leads on to Broederstroom, where there is a camping ground beneath the trees, below the walls of the dam that supplies Pietersburg with drinking water. A tangle of side roads meanders on through the trees, taking the traveller either back via detours to the main Pietersburg-Magoebaskloof road, or past the travelling station of Houtbosdorp to Duiwelskloof.

The Debegeni Waterfall, a place of sacrifices to the spirits by the Tlou people.

South of the main road, after it reaches the summit of Magoebaskloof (1 280 metres), two roads branch off and lead past the Ebenezer Dam in the Letaba River, amid glorious scenery overlooked by the Wolkberg range, and then down to Tzaneen through George's Valley.

The Valley was named after a roadmaker, George Deneys, who carefully routed the roads to reveal attractive scenes and, by creating detours, laybys and picnic spots, to tempt travellers to pause and appreciate the scenery — waterfalls, cascades, wild flowers, forests — and the bracing fresh air of this unspoilt landscape.

Ohrigstad

The town of Ohrigstad died in 1849, to be reborn almost a century later.

In 1843 Andries Hendrik Potgieter rode from Potchefstroom to Lourenco Marques (Maputo), where the cargo ship *Brazilia* had arrived from Holland with gifts for the Voortrekkers, sent by a merchant named George Ohrig. On the ship Potgieter was told of a new British law, the Cape of Good Hope Punishment Bill, which extended British authority northwards to latitude 25 degrees south. This was a great blow to the Voortrekkers, because it included Potchefstroom and a good part of the Transvaal. Potgieter immediately decided to move north of the 25th parallel to establish a new town which would be closer to Lourenco Marques. The site of the settlement was a well-watered valley he had discovered in 1840 on the western side of the Berg.

In June 1845 Potgieter led his followers to this area and a town was laid out with a fort, water furrows and broad streets. It was named Andries-Ohrigstad — a combination of the first name of Potgieter and the surname of Ohrig — and eventually abbreviated to Ohrigstad.

Unfortunately, the choice of the site was a disaster. In summer came floods, mosquitoes and relentless heat. After much unrest, Potgieter led some of the townsfolk north to the Soutpansberg. Others remained in Ohrigstad, but finally abandoned the town in 1848-49 after many inhabitants had died of malaria. The survivors estab-

Picking tea in Magoebaskloof. The estates cover many hectares and the air is rich with the perfume of the curing sheds.

In the Magoebaskloof, a patient labourer in an ocean of tea leaves

The stunning view through God's Window

The main street of Pilgrim's Rest, unchanged since gold mining days.

lished the town of Lydenburg on a higher-lying site to the south.

Ohrigstad fell into ruin. Nowadays, however, with the conquest of malaria, the valley has been resettled. The modern town of Ohrigstad was established in 1923 south-west of the site of the old town, whose ruins can still be seen. The valley is covered with tobacco, sunflowers, maize, vegetables, and orchards of yellow peaches.

Panorama Route

The Panorama Route is a circular drive with several detours; it leads from Graskop to the Blyde River Canyon, Pilgrim's Rest, and back over the divide to Graskop. The round trip, just on 70 kilometres, is a scenic gem. The visitor may well spend a day on this route. It is well signposted, with several turn-offs leading to waterfalls, swimming pools and other natural beauty spots.

Highlights of the route include The Pinnacle and Driekop Gorge (1,5 kilometres from Graskop); the Lisbon Falls (6,5 kilometres from Graskop); and God's Window (8 kilometres from Graskop) with its stunning view across the lowveld to Mocambique. Near God's Window is the Lowveld Panorama and Nature Reserve, with paths leading among flowering plants and trees.

Less than a kilometre beyond the turn-off to God's Window is a road to swimming pools in the Blyde River. One kilometre further along the Panorama Route is a turn-off to the Berlin Falls, an 80-metre waterfall plummeting into a deep pool. Another 5 kilometres on is a turn-off to the pic-

nic and swimming site known as Watervalspruit, set amid tree ferns and wild flowers.

For the next 21 kilometres the route leads through dense plantations of trees and then reaches a crossroads at Vaalhoek, where there is a tea-room, shop and garage. At this crossroads the traveller has a choice: northwards, the road leads to the spectacular potholes of Bourke's Luck in the Blyde River, where Tom Bourke had his gold mine, and on to the Overvaal Blydepoort Resort; the Panorama Route proper swings south-west at the Vaalhoek junction and makes its way up the western side of the valley of Pilgrim's Creek. After 21 kilometres it reaches Pilgrim's Rest. From there the road climbs over the mountain-divide back to Graskop.

This drive is a must for every tourist with time to appreciate superb scenery and delightful picnic places.

Penge

Johannes Rissik was given the task in 1888 of surveying the jumble of mountains in the area where the Olifants River shoulders its way through the Drakensberg. On the south bank of the river he surveyed a number of farms, among them Penge and Streatham, named by him after two London suburbs. The farms were in rugged country, with summer temperatures of more than 40°C.

Prospectors made their way into the area and found a strange type of asbestos — quite different from any other known kind. This asbestos had exceptionally long, springy fibres. It had an obvious value for insulation —

it was resistant to heat, acid and salt water corrosion — but manufacturers were suspicious of it. The deposit was so isolated, and possibly restricted in quantity, that to adapt existing manufacturing processes in order to exploit it involved a considerable financial risk.

Prospectors persisted in exploring the area, however, and in 1907 the geologists A. L. Hall and J. H. B. Wayne travelled here to investigate the extent of the deposit. It proved to be vast. To work it, Asbestos Mines of South Africa was formed and the asbestos variety became known as amosite, from the initials of the company. This material is now used all over the world for the lining of ships' boilers and many other insulation purposes, and in the manufacturing of cement products.

Penge remains the only mine in the world producing amosite, but it is a large-scale operation with large reserves and an output of more than

Mining operations in Pilgrim's Rest about 20 years ago.

40 000 tons a year. Connected to the outside world by a tarred road, the mine is unexpected in such a wild and beautiful setting.

A small town houses the workers and every possible comfort and sporting facility is provided. The mine is managed today by a company called EGNEP — Penge spelt backwards.

Pilgrim's Rest

Alec Patterson, known as Wheelbarrow Alec because he carried his belongings in a wheelbarrow, trundled into a deep valley on the western side of the edge of the Berg in 1873. He prospected the stream, and found gold in the middle reaches. Another prospector, William Trafford, joined him and named the place Pilgrim's Rest, because to him it seemed he had found his El Dorado.

There was a frantic rush to the area as soon as news spread of the discovery. Various earlier discoveries along

Gold ore being trammed away by mule power in the Pilgrim's Rest area.

Pilgrim's Rest country . . . grassy hills, distant mountains, rocks rich in gold.

In a rugged land of waterfalls, Berlin Falls is one of the loveliest.

STREAM OF GOLD

In 1878 John Swan found gold. It was no secret, for he began paying for his stores and drinks with nuggets. But he refused to tell where his mine lay. The only certainty was that it was in a dry area, for Swan began to dig a watercourse, or 'race', to direct a stream to his find.

Swan's Race became one of the unnatural wonders of southern Africa. For five years he worked on it, employing other men and paying them with gold dust or nuggets. There was tremendous speculation as to where the race would end, for that would be the site of Swan's discovery.

Then a company suddenly secured rights to land across the line of Swan's Race. With his labours blocked, Swan was offered a deal; if he revealed the site of his find, the company would work it and give him a 20 per cent interest.

Angrily, Swan went off to prospect in the De Kaap Valley, where he died of fever.

His mine has never been found. The course of the race may still be followed for many kilometres; it ends abruptly, and from this point many fortune-seekers have attempted to trace Swan's route — but to no avail.

Swan's last words as he lay dying are reputed to have been: 'It's good, but it's deep and well hid. They'll never find it.'

They never have.

the escarpment, such as at Mac-Mac and Spitskop, had caused minor rushes, but the gold from Pilgrim's Creek was the richest alluvial deposit found at the time in southern Africa, and it lured fortune-seekers from all over the world. Many renowned characters came to Pilgrim's Rest from the Australian and Californian gold fields.

The diggers liked Pilgrim's Rest; it was healthy, cool and pleasant, and although the middle reaches of the stream produced the richest finds, there was gold all along its course. Many fine nuggets were recovered, and the men worked hard, rooting up the entire length of the stream. Claims were about 50 metres square. To work them, a digger had to clear away the topsoil, which in some places was as much as 6 metres deep and littered with large boulders. All this had to be carried away in buckets and wheelbarrows before the underlying gravel was exposed, beneath which, against the bedrock, was the gold.

Running water was essential for the recovery of this gold. The entire flow of the stream was soon used up by diggers in the upper reaches, and only a turgid flow of mud reached the lower portion of the valley. To overcome this problem a number of speculators devised ingenious irrigation schemes.

They located streams higher up on the mountain slopes and built watercourses (known as 'races') to direct this water, sometimes for several kilometres, to any claim whose owner had the means to pay.

Once water was available the digger would construct a sluice box from 3 to 7 metres long and slightly less than a metre wide. Slats of wood or slivers of rock were fixed across the floor of this box to make what was called a Venetian Ripple. The gravel from the claim was then steadily fed into the water directed into the sluice box. The heavy gold would sink to the bottom and be trapped by the ripples. To trap very fine gold, coarse blankets would be laid in the sluice box and the fibres would retain the specks of gold. A proportion of gold would escape the trap and was borne on with the water, which then entered a small dam. The last of the gold would be deposited in the mud at the bottom of this dam.

From time to time the claim-holder panned the mud and recovered the residual gold.

During 1874 the rush to Pilgrim's Rest was at its peak. Traders and bar keepers arrived; an Irishman, M. V. Phelan, started a newspaper, the *Gold News*, later renamed *The Gold Fields Mercury*; and a hard-drinking Anglican clergyman, the Reverend St. Charles Frederick Cawkill Barker, set up a school and church in a tent, and later in a shack. Women also arrived, most of them hard-working wives who joined their men on the fields. Some women worked their own claims.

Several other discoveries were made in the vicinity of Pilgrim's Rest. Waterfall Gully and Peach Tree Creek were the scenes of rushes and every tributary stream of Pilgrim's Creek was prospected and worked. Early in July 1975 G. Russell and his partner S. Lilley found a nugget 6 038 grams in mass. The largest found in the creek up to that time, it was called the Reward Nugget. About £200 000 of gold was recovered from Pilgrim's Creek in 1875 — at current gold values this would amount to much more than R1 million.

The old Joubert Bridge over the Blyde River, now a national monument.

In 1876 productivity began to decline. The gravels were steadily worked out. Several companies were formed to mine deeper levels and explore the leaders and reefs from which the gold had originally been eroded. The idea of working for a company did not appeal to the diggers — they wanted the freedom of owning their own claims. There was an exodus from Pilgrim's Rest, especially when news came of gold discoveries elsewhere.

The companies that remained in Pilgrim's Rest produced good gold.

The Sheba Hotel, near Pilgrim's Rest, in a setting of forested hills.

257

The stray pistol shot that struck gold

From Sabie, looking east, far away over the lowveld, with the sun rising from the warm waters of the Indian Ocean.

Long Tom Pass, looking east with the road twisting off towards the town of Sabie.

Mount Anderson — and the 2 114-metre Mauchsberg. On this plateau the Sabie River gathers its upper tributaries, tumbles down in a waterfall, and then, through a succession of spectacular cascades, finds its way down to the lowveld. The name of the river is said to come from the Shangane word, uluSaba, meaning a fearful river — presumably because of the crocodiles and floods in its lower reaches.

The town of Sabie originated in 1895. The well-known hunter H. T. Glynn, who had bought a farm on the upper reaches of the river, was entertaining friends on a picnic at the waterfall. During a target match after the picnic, bullets chipped the rock and revealed indications of gold. Some of the guests immediately became eager prospectors, and one of them, Captain J. C. Ingle, who knew something of mining, proved over the next few days the existence of a substantial gold reef.

The Glynns-Lydenburg Gold Mining Company was formed to work the discovery, and by the time the mine closed, in July 1950, they had recovered 1 240 646 ounces of gold worth well over R500 million at today's prices.

The town of Sabie was the child of the mine. It became a municipality in 1924, and today is the centre for large-scale afforestation and sawmilling enterprises. The timber industry came about owing to the demand for pit props in the mine, but it soon became apparent that soil, climate and water supply made the escarpment an ideal area for trees. The government forestry department followed the lead of the mining companies and also established huge plantations of pine and gum trees after the Anglo-Boer War.

In the Sabie district today there are several sawmills, including the Mondi Timber Mill, the largest in the southern hemisphere. East of the town is the government tree-breeding station, where cross pollination and experimental breeding take place in a constant effort to improve timber quality and yields.

Patches of indigenous forest survive in some of the valleys, and the banks of streams are covered with wild flowers and ferns. The Bridal Veil Falls, the Lone Creek Waterfall and the Horse-

Eventually they amalgamated into the Transvaal Gold Exploration and Land Company, which successfully mined gold for some 50 years. When the mines approached exhaustion, the company switched to afforestation.

A handful of prospectors still work the streams of the area and it is difficult to imagine Pilgrim's Rest without a whisper of hope of a new discovery somewhere in the hills.

A museum is housed in the old post office building. The entire town in fact is one glorious living museum, and a walk through the surrounding hills is a fascinating excursion into a world of old mines and memories of gold-rush days. There is a hotel in the town and two fine caravan parks nearby.

Sabie

On the edge of the escarpment is a plateau, 1 109 metres above sea level and overlooked to the west by the highest peak of the Transvaal Drakensberg — the 2 284-metre

The forest country near Sabie. Eucalyptus and pine trees cover hills and valleys.

shoe Falls can all be reached from the scenic forest track along the south bank of the Sabie River.

There is fishing and swimming in the river, and on its banks are a hotel and a caravan park. The Sabie Village Council maintains South Africa's only Forestry Museum, which caters for many thousands of visitors each year.

Spitskop
The first payable alluvial gold deposit in the eastern Transvaal was discovered on the slopes of Spitskop in March 1871 by the well-known prospectors Tom McLachlan, James Sutherland and Edward Button. It was not a large deposit in area, but McLachlan and his partners found good gold and this attracted many other prospectors to the site. Other finds were then made at Mac-Mac and Pilgrim's Rest.

In its day, Spitskop was a busy mining area with a rough camp consisting of a handful of stores and canteens. Nothing is left of the field today other than a few piles of rubble, and a number of old shafts and adits.

Sybrand van Niekerk Resort
This resort has been established inside the Swadini section of the Blyde-rivierspoort Nature Reserve. It includes a caravan park and chalets, tennis courts, and a heated swimming pool. All around are nature trails and scenic view sites.

The Downs
Many who have taken the stunning road to The Downs have remarked that it should have been called 'The Ups', because the route leads to the top of the Transvaal Drakensberg. The views are magnificent, revealing, on the western side, one of the wildest river valleys in southern Africa.

In 1905 Orlando Baragwanath, one of the great prospectors whose names are part of the history of southern Africa, was prospecting along the escarpment. He came across another prospector, Haffenden Meintjes, who told him of a valley in the mountains where the Mohlapitse River flows down from the Wolkberg to join the Olifants.

The two set out to explore the valley. It was completely wild. They had to ford the river 45 times in the course

of a day's travelling from their base at Haenertsburg. A deep forest grew in the valley, and the water was crystal clear. Towards the bottom of the valley they found a footpath which led along the riverbanks and then climbed directly up the Drakensberg. The two men followed the path. When they reached the summit they were astounded to find, nearly 1 500 metres above the valley, a lovely, undulating area of rich soil and grass. Nobody lived there; the path simply continued, descending the eastern side of the escarpment where, precariously situated on the slopes there was a small mine run by an eccentric character named Ebenezer Gurr-Reed. He had called his mine The Crags and he named the plateau summit above him The Downs because it reminded him of the Surrey Downs in England.

Baragwanath took an immediate liking to The Downs. With his partner, Frank Lewis, who had been with him prospecting the copper deposits of Zambia, he bought the area from the government, began farming sheep and seed potatoes, and built the road down the eastern escarpment to Leydsdorp.

Later, General Jan Smuts came to study the botany of the area. He loved the wildness of the place and used his political influence to convert the old pathway descending into the Mohlapitse Valley into what is known as the Smuts Road. This road continues past several asbestos mines, following the north bank of the Olifants River, the route of Louis Trichardt's trek to Lourenco Marques (Maputo), and then leads through the Strydpoort mountains to Pietersburg.

The Downs, together with a number of adjoining farms, was declared a Nature Reserve in 1984.

Cut pines in the Sabie forest.

Lone Creek Waterfall tumbles down to a cool pool in the high forest near Sabie.

The lore and the language of lions

The elephant might be the true king of the beasts in Africa, but the lion is the warlord. His rumbling roar is the voice of the wilderness. In East Africa they say that the roar of the lion proclaims: 'Hi ni intshi ya nani? Yangu! Yangu! Yangu!' ('Whose country is this? Mine! Mine! Mine!').

In former years lions were the most widely distributed of all the animals of Africa. They ranged from the Cape of Good Hope in the south to Algeria in the north, from the horn of Africa in the east to Morocco in the far west.

In southern Africa today lions survive in the lowveld of the eastern Transvaal, the Gordonia district of the Cape, northern Kwazulu, Botswana, Namibia, and Zimbabwe.

They vary little in appearance from place to place. Differences are confined mainly to slight variations in the mane of the males, and in colour.

The Barbary lion of North Africa, now extinct, was reputedly a particularly large animal with a heavy mane. The lions of the southern Cape, also extinct, were similarly large and powerful, with massive manes. The few mounted specimens remaining in museums have broader heads than the lions of central Africa, and the manes are heavy, suited to the temperate areas of the Cape where the extra coat of matted hair was necessary to keep the animals warm.

The lions of the south tended to be very dark in colour, with black manes, while the lions of drier areas, such as Namibia and the verges of the Sahara, were more golden, with tawny, yellow manes.

The lions of the lowveld, the Kruger National Park and the savanna country of the eastern side of Africa are powerfully built and silvery grey to dark ochre-brown in colour, lighter in the belly. The males usually have well-developed black manes, but these vary with the individual in thickness and shade.

Cubs are marked with brindlings along the body and light, ochre-coloured, rosette-like spots and bars along flanks and limbs. These markings tend to fade as the lion matures, but in some individuals they do not disappear.

The Shanganes of the lowveld talk of a distinctive, spotted breed of lion, small and vicious, known as mong-wawane, but these are probably just immature animals.

White lions also occur. In the central area of the Kruger National Park, around Tshokwane and in the south and west of the lowveld, a strain of white lions has periodically appeared.

There was a frequently photographed white lioness at Tshokwane in 1962, and a trio of white lions was reported in 1976 in a private nature

A black-maned lion and lionesses laze on a hot afternoon in the Kalahari park.

reserve, Timbavati, immediately to the west of Orpen, just across the border of the Kruger National Park.

A big male lion weighs about 180 kilograms; a female 135 kilograms. They live for about 20 years. Their strength, audacity, courage and opportunism make them very formidable.

The language of lions is being se-riously studied. They seem to have a vocabulary of about 50 distinct sounds.

Recordings of these sounds have a particular effect when played back to other lions, apparently influencing their behaviour.

Some experts, like S. P. Kruger, former warden of the Manyeleti Game Reserve, are adept at speaking this lion language and can communicate with lions.

The relationships of wild lions with human beings have led to many strange episodes. Lions can be extremely tolerant; the Shanganes have many accounts of lions that allowed men to share their kills.

On one of his poaching forays from the Transvaal lowveld into Mocambique, a professional ivory hunter, S. C. Barnard, was visited at his camp by an agitated village headman named Mawasa, who lived near the Lundi River. The man had heard that Barnard intended to hunt in the area and he begged a favour. There was a lion living in the vicinity which was accustomed to sharing its kills with Mawasa and he did not want it harmed. Barnard sought elephant, not lion, and he assured Mawasa that his pet was safe.

During his stay in the area, Barnard observed this curious relationship. The lion would kill and Mawasa or his wife would walk up to the lion, beating an empty paraffin tin. The lion would give them a somewhat disgusted look, but obligingly move away and watch from the shade of a tree while the two cut away their chosen portion of the carcass.

A lioness of the Kruger National Park, her ear tabbed with identification marks.

A banquet in the Hwange park. Vultures in the tree await left-overs.

A young lioness, still marked with the spots of cubhood, but now about ready for her first mating.

They would then salute the lion and return home, leaving the beast to continue with its dinner.

Lions do not often regard human beings as prey, but unfortunately they occasionally discover that man is made of meat beneath his clothes, and serious trouble arises. In Tanzania the man-eating lions of the Njombe district killed a record of 1 500 people between 1932 and 1947.

In areas such as the Singida district there is still a widespread belief in lycanthropy — men who change into beasts, in this case, lions.

In southern Africa people have been killed by lions as far south as the Cape Peninsula. A particularly famous man-eater lived during the 1870s in the dense bush of the valley of the Pongolo River in northern Zululand. It was said to have been responsible for the deaths of several hundred people.

The professional hunter, W. H. Drummond, wrote an account of this lion in his book, *Large Game Of South Africa*. The lion was so cunning that the local Zulus were certain that witchcraft was involved. Nobody knew the secret of the man-eater's lair and he never killed twice in the same area. His mistake was to attack a village during a period of rains, when the earth was soft and tracking easy.

The lion killed a young woman, a relative of the chief. Drummond happened to be sheltering from the rains in the village and he and his Zulu hunters were awakened by the screaming of the woman.

In the pitch dark of the overcast, drizzly night they could do nothing. A big lion is capable of carrying an ox over a coral fence and dragging it off into the bush.

This man-eater had scratched and clawed its way into the woman's hut and, with her in its jaws, melted into the night.

At dawn every man in the village was mustered to pursue the lion. The hunters followed the tracks in the soft earth and found the remains of the woman about 200 metres from the village. After its meal, the lion had walked another kilometre to a stream. From here the tracks led to a dense patch of bush known as the mbeka.

More than 500 men beat the bush, each terrified of the lion and expecting a horrible manifestation of witchcraft.

Drummond and his men urged the beaters to sing war songs and shout encouragement to one another. Suddenly, the lion appeared. It regarded the beaters with a malevolent stare. To one side were Drummond and his hunters, silently praying that the noise from the beaters would make the lion retreat in their direction.

After some indecision the lion turned towards the hunters. As it came within range, one of the hunters fired. The bullet appeared to strike home, for the lion did a complete somersault before struggling to its feet. The exultant beaters rushed forward to cheer the hunters — and found to their dismay, that the lion had been little more than stunned. It charged like a thunderbolt. The hunters poured bullets into it, but still it came.

The beaters stood in a petrified line. But their numbers seemed to overawe the lion. Ten metres from them it halted its charge and glared. One of the beaters threw a spear into the animal's chest and it sprang, killing a beater and mauling the spear-thrower. The remaining beaters swiftly overwhelmed the beast.

When Drummond examined the carcass he counted six bullets and more than 500 spear wounds.

Two of the famed young white lions of Timbavati.

A young lioness of the Kalahari with two black-maned admirers.

THE LOWVELD — THE TRUE AFRICA

THE SAVANNA COUNTRY of the lowveld is, for the great majority of people, the true Africa. The continent has areas of desert, tropical forest, swamps, snow-covered mountains, gentle and temperate landscapes — but it is the savanna that is the haunt of big game and where memories linger of old-time slave raiders, ivory hunters, warriors, safari traders, of Livingstone and Stanley and innumerable restless wanderers.

The savanna sweeps southwards down the eastern side of Africa, from the great lakes, across Zimbabwe, and through the lowveld of the eastern Transvaal, Swaziland and Zululand. As the climate changes from tropical to temperate, the bush thins, until nothing is left save a few probing fingers reaching down to the shores of Algoa Bay.

The average altitude of the lowveld of the eastern Transvaal is approximately 350 metres. It is generally an area of summer rainfall. Rivers that are simply successions of pools in the dry season swell with rainwater in the summer and become surging floods. The grass is long and the trees are heavy with creepers, moss and lianas. Cicada beetles and mosquitoes sing all night.

In former years, before Sir Ronald Ross, working in India, isolated the mosquito as the carrier of malaria, the lowveld was a death trap for man during the summer. Weird potions were tried and suspicion was cast on all manner of things thought to cause the disease, such as night mists and the spectral *Acacia xanthophloea*, which was called the fever tree. The inhabitants of the area considered malaria to be a blight inflicted by evil spirits, and the local doctors flourished by divining so-called causes and prescribing strange, useless remedies.

Winter was the time for forays into the lowveld. Mosquitoes were banished by the cool nights. From May to October the climate is healthy, with warm, dry days and crisp nights when a camp fire is a comforting, romantic companion. In these months the professional hunters raided the bush to search out the big tuskers among the elephants, and saleable skins and meat. There were few permanent inhabitants here. As spring approached and the coral trees bloomed blood red, man noted this early warning of approaching summer and prepared to leave the area. By the time the air became heavy with the freshly-cut-potato smell of the prolific *Phyllanthus reticulatus* shrubs, most men were safe on the high escarpment, and the lowveld was left to its fevers.

The discovery of gold on the escarpment brought a great change to the lowveld. Men could not wait for winter. Transport riders from the coast faced the risk of fever as well as the all-year-round threat to their draught animals of nagana disease from the bite of the tsetse fly. Low mounds of stones marked the wayside graves of many men who died while trying to cross the lowveld during the danger months, and the early trails became littered with skeletons of countless oxen.

The conquest of malaria and the disappearance of the tsetse fly opened the lowveld to human settlement. In 1896, when the livestock disease of rinderpest swept through the area, so many game animals were killed off that the tsetse fly which fed on them was also eliminated. Even when the population of animals was restored the tsetse, mysteriously, did not return. Gone for ever from the region was the threat of fever and nagana.

Today the lowveld is densely populated. Farmers, ranchers, miners and industrialists live and work here. There are holiday resorts, residential areas, nature reserves, game-viewing lodges, and controlled hunting areas. The production of mica, antimony, copper, phosphates, gold, emeralds, vermiculite, iron, sub-tropical fruits, winter vegetables and nuts — all these contribute greatly to the economy of South Africa.

Times have certainly changed in the lowveld. But its fundamental nature is eternal — an enigmatic, elusive, challenging spirit, luring men on to unique adventures in the solitude of the bush.

Barberton

The valley in which Barberton lies was known to early prospectors as the Valley of Death. Thick clouds of mosquitoes haunted the area, and man penetrated their domain at his peril. Many died exploring the valley, but traces of gold in rivers and reefs constantly attracted newcomers.

The first payable gold found in the valley was the Pioneer Reef, discovered by French Bob (Auguste Robert) on 3 June 1883. This discovery was the lure for the largest onslaught of fortune-seekers to reach South Africa up to that date. Among those who came to the valley were Graham Barber, from Natal, and his cousins Fred and Henry Barber. In June 1884 they found what they named Barber's Reef — a reef so rich that it glittered with gold.

This discovery led to the founding of Barberton. A flood of diggers arrived on the scene and a hotch-potch of shacks, stores and canteens sprang up. On 24 June 1884 David Wilson, mining commissioner of the De Kaap Valley, broke a bottle of gin over a lump of rock to christen the town, thus launching it on a lively career.

The name of Barberton was said to have been written large in the hearts of British investors. From its birth it was a centre for wild speculation, gambling and fraudulent company promotion. Gold there was in plenty, but scoundrels substantially outnumbered honest producers.

During 1886 Barberton was at the height of its boom. Two stock exchanges traded night and day. Dozens of canteens, liquor shops and music halls competed with the mines to make the greatest profits in town.

Flashy beauties such as Florrie the Golden Dane and Cockney Liz reigned over a frenetic night life. Cockney Liz was a particular favourite

Cockney Liz, celebrated Barberton beauty, toast and pin-up of prospectors.

Pilgrims Hill, marked with old excavations, as seen from Mount Sheba. Gold is still to be found in these hills.

and would parade on a billiard table before her clientele and impishly snap her garters.

It was all a bubble that had to burst. So much money had poured into Barberton that it was hopelessly over-capitalized, with too many investors chasing limited profits. From a few mines, shareholders and owners were making fortunes, but others had put money into bogus companies whose principal assets were elaborately printed pamphlets and names which implied that they were connected with King Solomon or El Dorado.

The gold of the Witwatersrand was also discovered at this time, and there was an exodus from Barberton. Stock exchanges, newspapers, bars and gambling halls closed down. Some mining activity saw Barberton through this crisis, but it had to undergo transformation. From being one of the infamous glamour towns of the mining world, it turned sober and honest.

Today it is a charming little place, with many of its old buildings still standing. Mining, agriculture and afforestation have given the town a lasting prosperity. It is the terminal point for the great 20-kilometre aerial cableway that carries materials across the mountains to and from the Havelock Asbestos Mine in Swaziland.

In the Barberton Park is a statue of Jock of the Bushveld, South Africa's most famous dog (see box, page 281). Outside the town is a large acacia tree

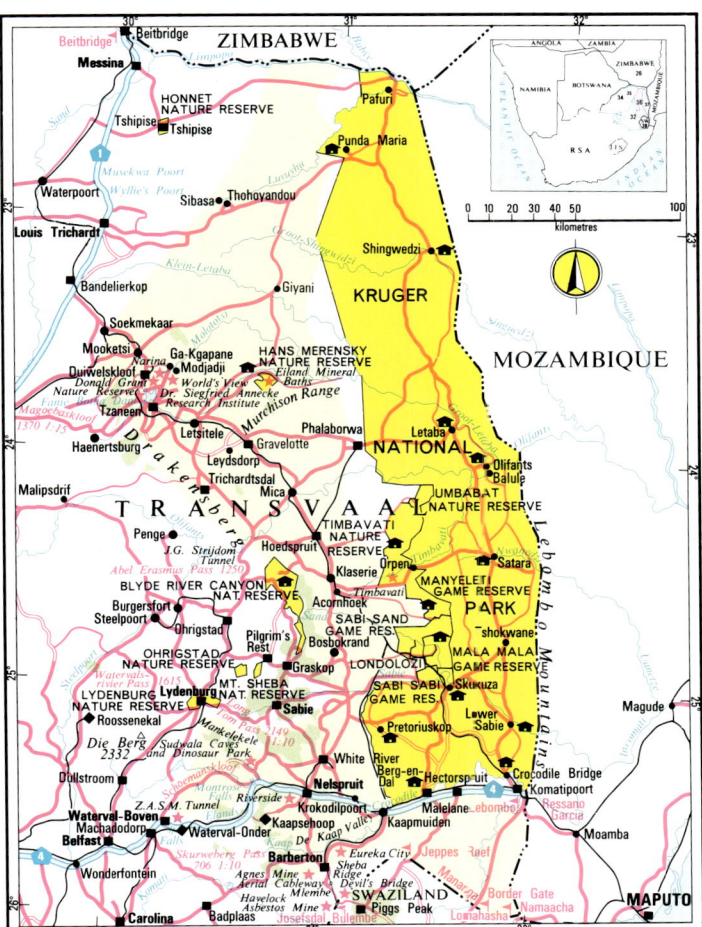

THINGS TO DO AND SEE

Antiquities The museum at Barberton displays exhibits relating to the gold-rush days.

Camping and caravanning There are caravan and camping sites at Duiwelskloof, Tzaneen, the Eiland mineral bath resort, Phalaborwa, Hippo Pools, White River, Nelspruit, Barberton, Komatipoort, Sudwala Caves, Montrose Falls, Kaapsehoop, and several sites on the north-south road.

Caving The Sudwala Caves are visited by thousands of people every month. There is a restaurant here, a swimming pool, and a variety of accommodation.

Game viewing There are several privately run game reserves along the western borders of the Kruger National Park. These places offer luxury accommodation, viewing platforms and conducted tours.

Hunting Trophy hunting, with professional hunters as guides, is carried out on several private estates in the lowveld. The would-be hunter should select his area with the help of a professional travel or safari agency.

Rock collecting Gem-stones and ornamental rocks can be found here. The area around the Murchison Range produces emeralds and mica. The De Kaap Valley, apart from gold, has buddstone, serpentine and other minerals. The streams around Barberton often produce a tail of gold in a prospector's pan.

Sightseeing To visit the capital of Modjadji, the rain queen, a permit must be obtained from the Balobedu regional authority at Ga-Kgapane.

Swimming The lowveld rivers abound with crocodiles, hippos and bilharzia, but there are swimming baths at most hotels, and at Eiland the Transvaal Board of Public Resorts has a spa around the mineral springs, with an open-air pool.

Walking The hills around the De Kaap Valley are criss-crossed with footpaths tramped by prospectors. It is still possible to follow the bridle path that used to be the only route from Barberton into Swaziland over the Devil's Bridge, high on the slopes of the mountain known as Bulembu ('place of the spider'). A walk from the village to World's View is particularly rewarding.

The enchanted valley of the Crocodile River

Barberton in its sub-tropical setting, on the floor of the De Kaap Valley.

wards and reaches the edge of the highveld. It flows through a valley known as Schoemanskloof, after a certain P. S. Schoeman, who settled there in 1848. The old roadway from Machadodorp to Nelspruit follows the same route. Gradually the grasslands of the highveld give way to the bush of the lowveld. Within 50 kilometres the road has dropped 800 metres.

At the foot of the Schoemanskloof, the Crocodile tumbles over the 12-metre Montrose Falls and is joined by its principal tributary, the Elands. From here the Crocodile River Valley is at its most enchanting. The mountains open wide and the valley floor is broad and deeply covered with rich soil; the air is warm, and the vegetation lush. Tobacco, maize, citrus fruit, mangoes, avocados, litchis and pecan nuts are grown. Roadside stalls offer fresh fruit for sale, as well as flowers, plants, honey, jams and other delicacies.

The Sudwala Caves lie northwards, up the valley of the Houtbosloop tributary. Midway down the valley lies Nelspruit, in a setting of estates such as Riverside and the Crocodile Valley Estate, whose managements have planted palms, golden cypress trees and the blood-red Pride of De Kaap along the road-sides.

At 14 kilometres from Nelspruit the Crocodile River encounters a massive barrier of granite hills. For the next 11 kilometres the river forces its way through the barrier by means of a narrow gorge filled with rapids and boulder-choked pools. Then it emerges onto a bush-covered plain, with the Kruger National Park on its northern side and a series of sugar estates on the southern side, irrigated by the water of the river.

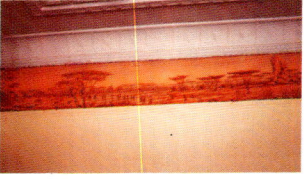
under which Jock and his master, Sir Percy FitzPatrick, often camped.

Inside the Impala Hotel is a mural frieze of scenes from the Jock of the Bushveld story, painted by a wandering artist, Conrad Genal (see box). The Noord Kaap Hotel also has walls decorated by Genal, depicting hunting scenes and the Zeederberg stage-coaches travelling through the bush.

Flowering trees shade the streets of Barberton and many scenic roads lead to such places as the ghost town of Eureka City, the Pioneer Reef, Havelock Mine in Swaziland, Badplaas, Kaapsehoop and the Agnes Mine. Next to the Agnes Mine entrance is a waterfall.

All these drives offer magnificent views. There is a forest of the paperbark thorn tree (*Acacia siebeviana*) on the road from Nelspruit, and the De Kaap Valley is the natural home of the blood-red flowering Pride of De Kaap (*Bauhinia galpinii*) and the Barberton Daisy (*Gerbera jamesonii*).

Crocodile River Valley

The highest mountain in the Transvaal is rather unimaginatively named Die Berg ('the mountain'). It is 2 332 metres high and the source of the Crocodile River is on its slopes.

The river flows across high grasslands and past the rural centre of Dullstroom.

The Crocodile River then veers east-

The Sheba Reef, still in operation, proved a prolific producer of gold.

Old lime kilns at Ngodwana, in the Elands River Valley.

The Olifants River with acacia trees in blossom.

For 65 kilometres the river runs across this plain, its waters inhabited by crocodiles and hippos. The river sweeps on until, at Komatipoort, it joins the Komati River and with it flows through the Lebombo Mountains and on to the sea.

Duiwelskloof

The thick, red soil of Duiwelskloof ('ravine of the devil') becomes a sea of mud during the rainy season — a curse to early transport drivers, who gave the valley its name. But the soil and high summer rainfall (1 500 millimetres) are a blessing to a host of plant life.

Trees cover the sides and floor of the valley. There are dense plantations of eucalyptus, and the air is rich with the fragrance from the sawmills. Pawpaws, bananas, avocados, mangoes and other tropical fruits grow well, and vast amounts of tomatoes are

The Crocodile River below Montrose Falls, a powerful flow of water which irrigates vast estates of sub-tropical fruit and nuts.

THE LAND AND PEOPLES THAT INSPIRED A GENIUS

The myths, legends and history of southern Africa were the inspiration for some of the most exciting adventure stories ever written — the novels of Sir Henry Rider Haggard (*right*).

Rider Haggard was born at Bradenham, Norfolk, on 22 June 1856 and he travelled to South Africa when he was 19. He became a civil servant and took part in the annexation of the Transvaal, personally hoisting the British flag in Pretoria. He then became registrar of the high court and travelled widely in the Transvaal. In this capacity he heard many strange cases in a setting abounding with pioneers, treasure-seekers, prospectors and primitive inhabitants.

He built a cottage near the railway station in Pretoria and here his imagination was further fired by stories he heard of real people and events which he was to translate into unforgettable fiction.

Back in Britain in 1884 Rider Haggard was called to the bar, but he found time to produce a rather bitter novel, *Jess*, dealing with the siege of Pretoria, with most of the action centred around the cottage where he had lived. The cottage became known as Jess's Cottage.

His first big success was in 1885 with the publication of *King Solomon's Mines*. In 1887 came *She* and in the same year *Allan Quartermain*, followed by nearly 60 other novels.

Rider Haggard's most famous literary characters were based on real people. The mysterious She was the rain queen of the Lobedu people in the Transvaal (see box, page 266). Allan Quartermain and the Zulu warrior, Umslopogaas, were also derived from actual people. Many features of the landscape of southern Africa also appeared in his books — caves, ruins, rivers and forests.

Rider Haggard was knighted in 1912. He died in London on 14 May 1925.

The Montrose Falls tumbling through Schoemanskloof.

Where they found the reef of solid gold

produced, especially at Mooketsi. Bougainvilleas, poinsettias, frangipani, cassias, acacias, bauhinia creepers, poincianas, potato trees, jacarandas and many other species of flowering trees and plants make the valley a glorious sight, especially in spring and summer (October to January).

There are several forest drives and walks from Duiwelskloof, and it is the administrative centre for the rain queen's country (see box). The town's park has a swimming pool, rondavels, and caravan and camping ground.

The naturalist, artist and writer, Charles Astley Maberly — 'the man who could talk to animals' — lived for many years in the forests of Duiwelskloof (see box, page 267).

A cassia tree near Duiwelskloof, noted for its flowering plants.

Eiland

There are several islands in the Letaba River, and a nearby farm, Eiland, owes its name to them. This property was bought in October 1950 by the Transvaal Provincial Administration, and expanded by the purchase of other properties.

The main attraction of Eiland was a thermal spring, which has been a source of salt for the local inhabitants, as well as a medicinal bath that is reputedly beneficial to sufferers from rheumatism.

The Transvaal Board of Public Resorts has developed a spa around the spring, with rondavels, a restaurant, shop, open-air swimming bath, and a caravan and camping ground with 500 sites shaded by trees.

Eureka City

Ghost towns are the waifs of the mining industry — relics of boom years, abandoned foundlings of fickle prospectors and diggers who used them wantonly, and then left them to the wind and the wilderness.

On the heights of the Sheba Ridge, overlooking Barberton, lie the ruins of one of these towns, Eureka City. The town was born in the great boom year of 1885. A Yorkshireman, Edwin Bray, was prospecting the ridge when he discovered what became known as the Sheba Reef.

Bray started a mine called the Golden Quarry which, in its day, was the richest and most famous gold mine in the world. It was said to contain not gold in the rock, but rather just a little rock in solid gold. Eureka City was the town created to house the workers of this mine and the men who rushed to the area hoping to find another reef of equal value. The town was founded by J. Sherwood, who erected a butcher's shop and a hotel.

His wife, who was notoriously ugly, was jocularly known as the Queen of Sheba, and the hotel was named the Queen of Sheba Hotel.

At its peak, Eureka City had a population of 650 men and a handful of women. It had three hotels, about a dozen canteens, a race track, music hall and, reputedly, some of the flashiest barmaids in the De Kaap Valley.

Social life was rowdy and during

STRANGE SPELLS AND SECRETS OF MODJADJI THE 'IMMORTAL' RAIN QUEEN

During disturbances in the 16th century a princess of the Karanga people of Zimbabwe fled southwards with a few follwers, carrying with her the rain-making secrets of the ruling family.

They eventually reached the warm and fertile valley of the Molototsi River, east of Duiwelskloof. Here the refugees founded the Lobedu settlement. The princess became the most famous rain-maker in Africa.

She called herself Modjadji and withdrew from public view. People came to believe that she was immortal — the 'She' who must be obeyed. It was on this strange personality that Sir Henry Rider Haggard based his famous novel, *She*. Even the savage warriors — the Swazis and the distant Zulus — regarded her with awe. Her small group was inviolate. She was sent presents and offerings, and from her secret den she wove strange spells to bring or withhold rain.

The mystique of Modjadji remains to this day. The capital of the present successor to the original rain queen is perched on a hill slope, below a weird forest of trees known as Modjadji cycads. These trees flourish under her protective mantle, and are taboo to other humans.

Gifts are still sent to Modjadji as inducements to make rain. Her methods are a secret. At times of drought, even the European popula-

Modjadji, the celebrated rain queen.

The forest above Modjadji's capital.

tion of the Duiwelskloof area have persuaded her to join them in their prayers to bring rain.

Modjadji's capital has a large central courtyard surrounded by a palisade of wooden staves, many of which have been carved into weird shapes and faces. The queen's quarters are secluded and she can be seen only by favoured visitors.

The courtyard in Modjadji's capital. In it are held gatherings of the inhabitants.

Merensky Dam, on the Westphalia estate. A lovely setting of the forested slopes of the Transvaal escarpment.

THE MAN WHO 'TALKED' TO THE ANIMALS

A Maberly painting of a duiker.

1887 the notorious Irish Brigade, a gang of construction workers from the Eastern Line, took over the town for a wild week of fights, gambling and drinking. They were forced to leave by a posse of police.

Bray's Golden Quarry yielded 519 565 ounces of gold in ten years. It produced 50 000 ounces of gold from the first 13 000 tons of ore crushed — one of the highest yields in the history of gold-mining.

When the mine was exhausted, Eureka City went into decline. Its ruins lie high in the hills on the north-eastern side of the De Kaap Valley. A track from Barberton takes visitors to the site. Only piles of rubble remain of the old buildings, and not a single inhabitant.

Hans Merensky Nature Reserve

Adjoining the Eiland resort is the Hans Merensky Nature Reserve which was established in 1950. It provides sanctuary for impala, zebra, blue wildebeest, sable, waterbuck, warthog, duiker, steenbuck, klipspringer, bushbuck, reedbuck, eland, giraffe, tsessebe, Sharpe's grysbok and other animals. There is also a reconstructed Tsonga kraal in the reserve.

Dr. Hans Merensky, who gave the reserve its name, was the geologist and mining magnate who prospected the diamond deposits of Alexander Bay, the platinum of Rustenburg and the mineral riches of Phalaborwa.

Kaapsehoop

In 1882 Bernard Chomse claimed to have found gold in the bed of a stream on a high, narrow plateau which projects like a finger between the valleys of the Elands and the Little Crocodile rivers, with the tip of the finger ending in the Crocodile River Valley. A rush took place to the area. The setting was scenically stunning, and slightly weird: a cluster of giant rocks, many with odd shapes like faces or

Near the junction of the Duiwelskloof road and the Tzaneen-Modjadji forest drive there is a turn-off to the farm Narina, former home of one of South Africa's most celebrated naturalists, Charles Thomas Astley Maberly — known as 'the man who could talk to animals'.

Maberly was murdered in 1972, but during his life he maintained his farm as a game reserve. A black mamba lived near his kitchen, and vervet monkeys gambolled around the house, chattering at him while he painted.

Other members of this happy family included bushbuck, leopards, two crocodiles named Whisky and Soda (they lived in a nearby stream) and about 60 wild boars which emerged every sunset from the forest to spend the evenings on Maberly's lawn.

The farm is preserved as a nature reserve.

Charles Thomas Astley Maberly, artist, writer, naturalist.

Panning for gold near Duiwelskantoor. The pebbles behind are rejects.

The ghost town of Eureka City, high in the hills near Barberton. This was the gold-rush town built at the time of the finding of the Sheba Reef.

The hollowed-out baobab which became a bar

figures, stands on the summit as though some prehistoric meeting had been turned to stone.

The diggers called this strange place Duiwelskantoor ('devil's office'). An early record says: 'No description could convey anything approaching an adequate idea of the difficulties of a journey through this region. The mountains are so rugged that only the devil could live here.'

On the eastern side of the plateau the ground falls away abruptly nearly 1 000 metres into the De Kaap Valley, where the Little Crocodile River has its headwaters.

The valley is often covered in mist, and the plateau then resembles a cape in a sea of clouds. It became known as De Kaap ('the cape'), and the centre of the gold rush was named Kaapsehoop ('hope of the cape').

Along the drives to Kaapsehoop from Nelspruit and the Elands River Valley the views of the De Kaap Valley are unforgettable. The village of Kaapsehoop has a lingering atmosphere of the gold-rush days, and prospectors still work in the area.

Around the village are many natural camping sites.

Komatipoort

The principal gateway between South Africa and Moçambique is the gorge taking the Komati River through the Lebombo Mountains. The border runs along the summit ridge of this bush-covered range. The town of Komatipoort lies at the western edge of the gorge.

Komatipoort became the depot and construction camp of the Dutch company, the Nederlandsche Zuid-Afrikaansche Spoorweg Maatschappy, during the building of the Eastern Line. A boisterous crowd of railway workers was recruited for the construction.

During the Anglo-Boer War, Komatipoort was the base for the celebrated Colonel Ludwig Von Steinacker and his Forty Thieves (see box). Today the town is much more sedate, with streets shaded by flowering trees, and formidable summer temperatures often reaching 40°C.

The town is 11 kilometres from the Crocodile Bridge entrance to the Kruger National Park.

Leydsdorp

In 1870 Edward Button and James Sutherland found gold in the mountain range they named after Sir Roderick Murchison, the British geologist.

The hollowed-out baobab tree near Leydsdorp, once used as a bar.

The discovery did not prove payable, but in 1888 the renowned prospector French Bob, who had discovered the Pioneer Reef near Barberton, found more gold in the range and this started a rush. Several mines were opened, thousands of claims were pegged, and about 600 prospectors were active in the area.

The centre of excitement was the camp of French Bob. In 1890 this camp was selected by the government as the site for a town from which to administer the Murchison Range goldmining fields. The town was named Leydsdorp, after Dr. W. Leyds, the state secretary. It grew rapidly into a conglomeration of shacks, pubs, hotels, stores and a printing works which published a newspaper, *The Leydsdorp Leader*.

About 90 metres off the road linking Leydsdorp to Gravelotte is South Africa's only 'bar tree' — a hollowed-out baobab containing a makeshift counter over which drinks were served to thirsty gold-seekers. A dozen or so men could gather at a time inside the tree.

The mining area was called the Selati Gold Fields, after Shalati, the female chief of the Tebula people who lived in the bush around the Murchison Range.

For transport to the gold fields a railway called the Selati Line was planned. It is said that the railway was as crooked as its promoters, a pair of continental confidence tricksters, Baron Eugene Oppenheim and his elder brother, Robert.

After much wheeling and dealing, construction of the Selati Line began in 1892 from Komatipoort on the

The De Kaap Valley, once a prospector's paradise but a death trap because of fever. Every hill and valley contained gold.

LUDWIG'S FORTY THIEVES

One of the strangest regiments in the history of warfare was surely the band of desperadoes known as Steinacker's Horse.

Ludwig Von Steinacker (*above*) claimed to be a Silesian baron. He emigrated to South West Africa in the 1890s and, at the outbreak of the Anglo-Boer War, persuaded the British to allow him to organize a force of 40 men assigned to disrupt Boer communications.

With the rank of sergeant, Von Steinacker soon recruited his men. Their pay was ten shillings a day. Von Steinacker insisted that he and his men should eat pickles at each meal, supposedly to prevent fever.

The Forty Thieves, as they were nicknamed, had their first success near Malelane — they blew up a bridge and a train.

Von Steinacker was soon promoted to major, and then to lieutenant-colonel. His command was increased to 600 men and named Steinacker's Horse. They were stationed at Komatipoort, and these 'Wild West' characters held the border while the guerilla war was fought in the Transvaal.

After the war, Von Steinacker became a handyman on Champagne farm, near Bosbokrand.

At the outbreak of World War I he became truculent and police came to arrest him. While he was supposedly packing, Von Steinacker fell dying from a dose of strychnine. Today a pile of stones in the bush on Champagne farm is all that marks his grave.

A lilac-breasted roller of the lowveld.

Eastern Line. By that time the Selati Gold Fields had petered out, but in fact it was doubtful that the railway promoters ever intended the line to reach the area. They simply set out to sell shares and make money. When the scandal was exposed in 1895 it was found that more than 40 kilometres of unnecessary bends and loops had been added to the line. Baron Oppenheim and his brother ended up in gaol and the 120-kilometre length of line already built was left to rust.

Only in 1912 was the Selati Line relocated and completed — 330 kilometres of line were laid from Komatipoort to Tzaneen and, later, to Duiwelskloof and up the escarpment to join the Pietersburg-Messina line. Leydsdorp by that time was almost a place of ghosts, and even today the cemetery is often described as the liveliest part of the town.

Mining still flourishes in the Murchison Range, however, although not much gold is produced. Antimony, cinnabar, emeralds, feldspar, mica and silica are the main products of the area. Its principal centre is Gravelotte, named after the battle in the 1870 Franco-German war, and created as a railway centre when the completed Selati Line missed Leydsdorp by 11 kilometres.

The Consolidated Murchison Mine, near Gravelotte, is the world's largest producer of antimony. The station of Mica, at the southern end of the range, is the despatch centre for several mica mines, and glittering fragments of this mineral litter the ground.

Manyeleti Game Reserve

The name of Manyeleti ('place of

Death in the afternoon in the Manyeleti Game Reserve. A lioness guards the kill.

stars') derives from a small lake noted for its reflections of the stars. The entrance to the Manyeleti Game Reserve lies about 45 kilometres to the east of Acornhoek.

Originally there were five large ranches in the area, used mainly for hunting. These farms were bought by the South African Government and in 1967 were opened as a game reserve for blacks. It is the first game park and holiday resort to be established for the exclusive use of blacks. The reserve has a camp with bungalows, dormitories and a restaurant.

The 20 000-hectare reserve is densely bushed and provides a sanctuary for impala, wildebeest, zebra, giraffe, waterbuck, lion, rhino, cheetah, buffalo, sable, nyala, steenbuck, reedbuck, bushbuck, duiker, elephant, leopard, and the occasional elephant.

Visitors to the reserve may enter the Kruger National Park through a border gate.

Nelspruit

When the Eastern Line was constructed up the Crocodile River Valley in 1892, a station was built on a farm owned by the Nel family. Known as Nelspruit ('Nels' stream'), the station was the natural centre for the fertile middle reaches of the valley. Traders built stores, and farmers recognized the potential for irrigation — rich soil, a level valley floor and ample water from the river.

Men such as Hugh Hall settled in the area. Hall's farm, Riverside, became a model of successful development. He combined the name of two of his major crops — tomatoes and

mangoes — to make the trade name Tomango for his food products.

Nelspruit became the second largest grower of citrus fruits in South Africa after Zebediela. Tobacco, nuts, litchis, mangoes, avocados, pawpaws, vegetables, cattle and timber are also produced on a large scale.

In its early years Nelspruit was cursed with malaria, but control of the disease in the 1930s enabled the Crocodile River Valley community to surge ahead. Today Nelspruit is a substantial town, situated amid orange groves and dominated by a cluster of granite domes. The streets are shaded by flowering trees. In December and January the town seems to be aflame with the brilliant scarlet of poinciana flowers.

Nelspruit is the home of the Government Research Institute for Citrus and Subtropical Fruits and of the Lowveld Botanical Garden.

Among the attractive buildings is the town hall. The sundial on the island outside this hall is in the shape of a wagon wheel and serves as a memorial to Louis Trichardt and his 1837 trek to Lourenco Marques.

The town is a stopover on the tourist route to the Kruger National Park.

Phalaborwa

About 2 000 million years ago a volcanic eruption occurred in the lowveld. The cone of the eruption has vanished, but the pipe, or throat — an astonishing geological feature — remains. The pipe is 19 square kilometres in area, and it is stuffed to an unknown depth with minerals such as phosphates, copper, zirconium, vermiculite, iron, mica and gold.

269

Weird figures in nature's underground art gallery

About 150 years ago a small party of African prospectors, said to have come from Messina, found the pipe and began mining copper and iron. They named the place Phalaborwa ('better than the south'), meaning that it was healthier than the fever-ridden areas in the south. At the beginning of this century European prospectors also discovered the extraordinary variety and richness of the mineral content of the pipe. Dr. Hans Merensky, the famed geologist, started mining vermiculite from this pipe in 1938.

Phosphate production began in 1952, when Foskor (Phosphate Development Corporation) was created by the government in order to make South Africa independent of phosphate imports.

The phosphate deposits in the pipe are thought to be large enough to supply South Africa's requirements for many hundreds of years.

Copper and iron are also extracted from the pipe. Much of the copper is exported to West Germany and the iron to Japan, for the output far exceeds the needs of South Africa.

The town of Phalaborwa was created in 1957 as a centre for this assortment of mines. There is an entrance gate to the Kruger National Park on the eastern outskirts of the town.

Sabi-Sand Game Reserve

The largest private game reserve in South Africa is a block of farms covering 65 000 hectares of densely bushed country on the western boundary of the Kruger National Park. The Sabie and the Sand rivers flow through the reserve hence its name, Sabi-Sand Game Reserve.

The owners of the individual farms have separate homesteads, but there are no fences other than the boundary fence — all of the farms form a sanctuary for game. A professional warden manages the area.

The game population includes impala, wildebeest, zebra, giraffe, kudu, elephant, lion, cheetah and leopard. Bird life and vegetation are abundant.

Some of the farms, such as Mala Mala ('sable antelope'), have luxurious lodges from which guests are taken on game-viewing drives in the early morning and by spotlight at night.

Sudwala Caves

These are one of the major tourist attractions of the Crocodile River Valley. The caves occur in the Mankelekele ('crag on crag') mountain, overlooking the valley of the Houtbosloop.

The mountain is composed of dolomite. Rainwater percolated into deep cracks and steadily eroded them into a system of caves, decorating the succession of chambers with a great variety of stalagmites and stalactites. On the ceilings are the peculiar saucer-like shapes of the fossils of ancient algae known as stromatolites.

Stromatolites played an important role in the development of life. When the atmosphere of the earth was still mainly nitrogen and carbon dioxide, this type of alga was a vital producer of oxygen. Vast colonies of stromatolites floated on the waters of the earth, and in the Sudwala Caves some of them became embedded in the ceilings. Converted into fossils by silica, they are clearly visible.

Prehistoric people discovered the caves and used the entrance as a shelter. Swazi people used the caves as a retreat during the years of friction at the beginning of the 19th century when they were being harassed by raids from Zululand. One Swazi grandee, Somcuba, established a village close to the caves. He was a renegade who had once been a regent during the reign of the Swazi king, Mswazi. During his regency Somcuba had accumulated large herds of cattle.

Mswazi came of age in 1841, and Somcuba retired to the village at the caves, and refused to return the cattle to the Swazi king.

Time after time the Swazis raided Somcuba, but he always evaded them by retreating into the caves. Eventually, his luck ran out. He was caught in a surprise attack and killed. Only a portion of his followers, led by an officer named Sudwala reached their hiding place in the caves. They survived, and when the first European reached the area it was Sudwala who showed them the wonders of the caves, and after whom the caves were named.

The caves have still not been completely explored. Rich deposits of bat guano were removed from the first few chambers in the early years of this century, but fortunately not much damage was done to the caves' peculiar dripstone formations.

A banana plantation near Tzaneen.

Tourists are now conducted into the caves through an entrance in a forest half-way up the cliff face of the mountain. A 12-metre corridor leads to the P. R. Owen Hall, named after a previous owner of the caves. The hall, roughly circular, is 18 metres high and has a diameter of 66 metres. Concerts have been held here.

Visitors can explore a 600-metre route through passages and small halls with a total floor area of 14 000 square metres. Guides provide tours lasting an hour and a half, though a five-hour tour can be made by special arrangement.

In one passage hangs the tongue-like formation known as Somcuba's Gong — when struck, it resounds through the caves.

Many chambers display weird sculptures — there is the so-called 'Screaming Monster'; the 'Weeping Woman'; Biblical characters such as the Madonna and child, Samson and Lot's wife; and fairy-tale characters including Little Red Riding Hood, the Cunning Fox and others. The tallest stalagmite in the caves, 11 metres high and with a girth of 7 metres is named the Space Rocket.

The formations are mainly creamy yellow, though some are tinted red and brown by iron and manganese oxides.

Local rumour has it that the caves extend for at least 30 kilometres. There is a constant flow of fresh air, but where it comes from is unknown.

In July 1967 two young men from Pretoria penetrated through narrow passages for 2 500 metres and discovered a hall 90 metres long and 45

A long view of the lowveld from the summit of the escarpment near Sabie.

The 'Screaming Monster', a dripstone formation in the Sudwala Caves.

metres wide with stalagmites and stalactites of pure white, emerald green and blue. From this hall a passage leads still deeper into the mountain.

Beyond the tourist area the going becomes more difficult, and there are many gloriously unspoilt chambers — such as the Arctic, Penguin and Crystal Chambers, discovered in 1968 by Harold Jackson. A master spelaeologist, Jackson has explored and mapped much of the cave sequence, but has not yet reached the end — the mysteri-ous source of the flow of fresh air.

A resort has been built in the warm valley below the cave entrance. There is a swimming pool, restaurant, bungalows and a curio shop. Life-sized models of prehistoric animals, startling to see in a setting that has changed very little since they were alive, have been placed in a quiet park near the caves.

Tzaneen

The river known to Europeans as the Letaba (from the African Lehlaba, meaning 'sandy river') cascades down from the highveld and flows eastwards across the lowveld through a fertile valley. Tea, sub-tropical fruits, nuts, flowers, winter vegetables, potatoes and timber are grown in the valley.

The town of Tzaneen was established in 1912 as a centre for this agricultural area.

The origin of the name of the town is uncertain. One theory is that the name comes from the Tzaneng people who lived here. The elimination of malaria in the eastern Transvaal, largely the result of the advice of Professor N. H. Swellengrebel, of the League of Nations, and the work of Dr. Siegfried Annecke, made the valley as healthy as any other part of the sub-tropics, and Tzaneen prospered.

The Dr. Siegfried Annecke Research Institute is situated here. With its work on malaria largely completed, it is now involved in research on bilharzia.

A circular 40-kilometre drive around Tzaneen passes woodlands, streams and farming landscapes.

White River

At the end of the Anglo-Boer War a settlement for demobilized soldiers was established on fertile land on the farm Witrivier ('white river'). A canal 26 kilometres long was built to channel water from the Manzemhlope ('white water') River, and smallholdings of 40 hectares were offered on easy terms. The holdings proved to be too small to be economic, and in 1914 a syndicate purchased the area, planted 60 000 citrus trees, and soon had a viable agricultural industry.

Today more than 2 500 farmers live on smallholdings within 8 kilometres of the town of White River, which developed to serve this densely cultivated area.

Vegetables, sub-tropical and tropical fruits, flowers and timber are produced.

The town's streets are shaded by flowering trees.

Among beauty spots in the vicinity are three irrigation dams, a number of forests, and sites offering impressive views of the Crocodile River Valley.

The ceiling of the Sudwala Caves. Petrified into the rock are relics, left by water, of the algae known as stromatolites, the earliest identifiable forms of life.

KINGDOM OF THE KRUGER PARK

ON 26 MARCH 1898 President Paul Kruger signed a proclamation establishing a sanctuary for wildlife between the Sabie and Crocodile rivers. It was an auspicious day for conservation. The first national park in the world had been created by the Americans at Yellowstone in 1872 — but the Sabie Game Reserve (the original name of the Kruger National Park) was the first large wildlife reserve in Africa.

In a continent where man and wild animal had been fighting a war of extermination since prehistoric times, this was man's first offer of the hand of friendship.

The Kruger National Park will therefore always be regarded as the prototype of wildlife sanctuaries in Africa. Comparisons with other reserves are inevitable, and some reserves will be acclaimed as better, bigger, wilder, more varied in their animal populations, but the Kruger National Park sets a formidable standard. Other parks may indeed have natural assets which the Kruger Park lacks; but its scenery, plants and animals, as well as its singularly romantic history, will always ensure that it has a unique place among the world's wildlife reserves.

The park occupies 1 948 528 hectares of the eastern Transvaal. This area contains over 450 species of birds, more than 200 species of trees, 138 mammal species, 50 fish varieties, 33 types of frog, 115 reptile species, and countless different insects.

The park has five main botanical divisions. The environment and natural food of each division determine the variety and density of wildlife within its boundaries.

The largest division is also the hottest and most arid. This is the area north of the Olifants River, extending as far as the valley of the Luvuvhu River, a tributary of the Limpopo.

The vegetation is dominated by the medium-sized mopane tree, *Colophospermum mopane*, which seems to be untroubled by the poor, alkaline soil and erratic rainfall of the region.

Nature has ingeniously adapted the mopane for such conditions; when the heat becomes unbearable, the leaves fold along the mid-rib. This allows rays of the sun to pass directly to the ground, and moisture in the tree is thus conserved. The tree, therefore, casts a poor shadow, but absorbs a minimum of heat.

Its leaves taste and smell like turpentine, but they are nutritious and relished by antelope and elephants. A fat, spotted caterpillar, the mopane worm, feeds on the leaves and is itself eaten by man. With a high protein content and a piquant, nutty flavour, the worms can be dried and stored, or roasted and eaten immediately. To the local inhabitants they are a delicacy.

The second largest division lies south of the Olifants River, on the eastern side of the park as far as the

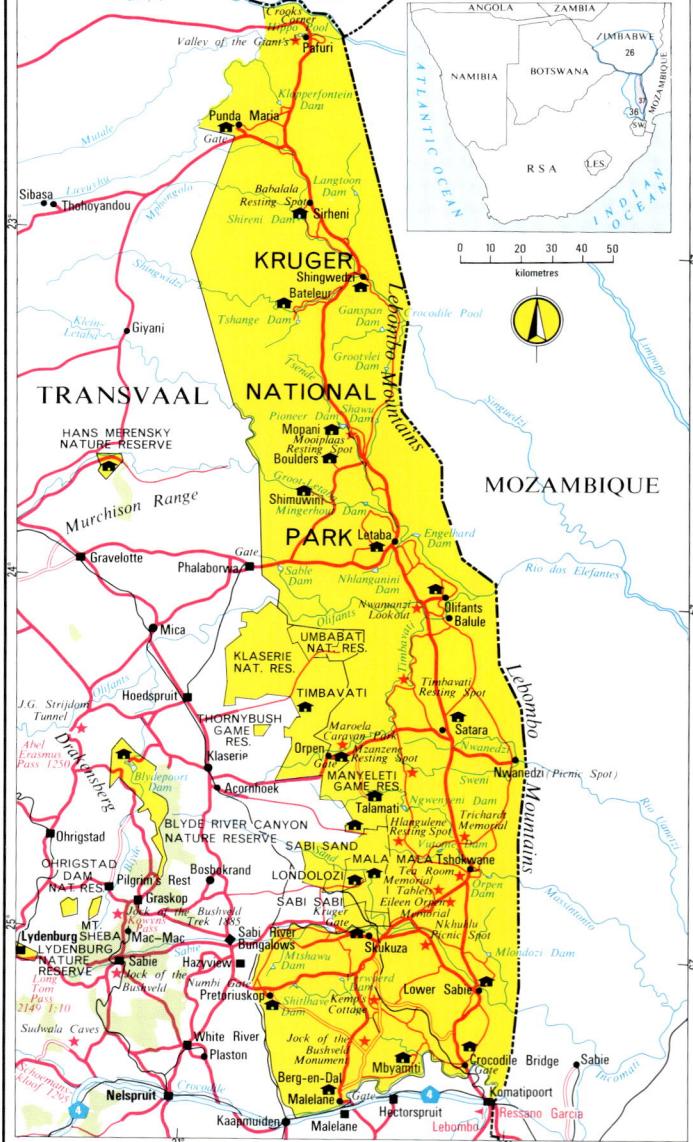

The perennially flowing Shingwedzi River, a watering place for many game animals.

A Cape hunting dog resting by the roadside, alert and always eager to be up and away on a relentless pursuit of some antelope.

CAMPS IN THE PARK

Berg-en-dal A new rest camp in a picturesque montane setting 12 kilometres from the Malelane entrance gate. It has 360 beds, caravan sites, a restaurant and other facilities.

Letaba The camp stands on the south bank of the Letaba River, and is noted for its trees, flowering plants and fine views.

Lower Sabie This camp lies in some of the best lion country of the park. Many antelope are also found here.

Mopani Situated between Letaba and Shingwedzi, this camp has self-contained cottages, a swimming-pool, shop and restaurant.

Olifants A modern camp, it lies on a cliff overlooking the Olifants River, with panoramic views over a vast expanse of game country.

Pretoriuskop This camp lies in parkland noted for its flowering trees. It has a swimming pool.

Satara Another modern camp, Satara has a large restaurant and supermarket block.

Shingwedzi An old favourite brought up to date, this camp is situated in a forest on the banks of the Shingwedzi River.

Skukuza The largest camp in the park, it is also the administrative centre, with stores, workshops, offices, staff residences and recreational areas. It has an open-air cinema, wildlife library and a museum.

Other camps Boulders, Crocodile Bridge, Malelane, Punda Maria, Orpen, Balule, Nwanetsi, Roodewal, Jock of the Bushveld. There are also Bushveld camps at Mbyamiti, Talamati, Shimuwini, Bateleur, Sirheni, and Jakkalsbessie.

southern boundary on the Crocodile River. This division is dominated by acacia thorn trees. It has a higher rainfall and more fertile soil than the area north of the Olifants. Its sweet-tasting grasses offer excellent grazing and support a higher population of animals. It is the home of great herds of impala, zebra and wildebeest, as well as buffalo, giraffe and many other species of game.

The acacia trees of this division belong to a family of 700 species, mainly native to Africa and Australia. The name acacia derives from the Greek word, akakia, meaning thorny. All the species are valuable to man and animal: they have nutritious leaves and seed pods; the gum of certain species provides gum arabic, used in the manufacture of adhesives; the wood is excellent for kindling and has a pleasant aroma. Even the thorns have been used — as gramophone needles. They were used as an alternative to

The Kruger monument at the Kruger entrance gate to the park.

Rondavel accommodation for tourists at Satara Camp, north of Sabie.

steel needles before the diamond stylus was perfected. The thorns caused less wear to records.

Each spring, the delightfully fragrant white and yellow acacia blossoms provide a superb show. The umbrella-shaped canopy of many acacias offers shady camping sites for man, and cool areas in which wild animals doze away the hot hours.

The third largest division of the park — between the Olifants and Crocodile rivers, west of the acacia division — also has sweet grazing, and is a parkland populated by many antelope. The red bush-willow tree, *Combretum apiculatum*, flourishes here.

West of this area is the fourth largest division of the park. Lying between the Sabie and Crocodile rivers up to the park's western boundary,

this natural parkland is well-watered — about 760 millimetres of rain falls a year — thickly wooded, but with sour-tasting grass, less favoured by antelope. Here is a great variety of trees. Acacias do well, and there are many elegantly canopied species. Combretums also grow in large numbers, and there are giant sycamore figs, mkuhlus, marulas, kiaats, and spectacular flowering trees such as the wild pears and the red and orange coral trees.

The smallest division of the park lies along the northern boundary, in the valleys of the Luvuvhu and Limpopo rivers. This is an area of tropical, riverine forest — huge wild figs, spectral fever trees, ebony, mahogany, ironwood, wild syringa, and many baobabs (especially in the Valley of the Giants, where they grow in an enchanted forest of their own).

A total of more than 250 000 mammals inhabit the five divisions of the park. The most numerous is the impala, with a population of about 120 000, mostly concentrated in the sweet-grazing areas, particularly along the Sabie River. This graceful creature is the record jumper of all the antelope, surpassing even the springbok (a species not found in the Kruger National Park). Impala have been seen to clear 3 metres in height and 9 metres in length.

The second most common animal species is the buffalo. More than 30 000 roam the sweet-grass plains along the eastern borders between the Sabie and Crocodile rivers.

Some 26 000 Burchell's zebra are scattered throughout the park, but they prefer the sweet grazing on the eastern side.

There are 11 500 blue wildebeest spread throughout the park but also concentrated in the sweet-grass areas.

Elephants wander all over the park; about 7 500 live here permanently.

Among other game are 7 500 kudu, 4 700 giraffe, over 3 000 warthog, 3 500 waterbuck, 2 200 hippo, 1 200 lion, 2 100 sable antelope, over 1 000 reedbuck, 900 leopard, 950 tsessebe, 700 eland, 350 wild dog, 350 roan antelope, 250 cheetah, over 100 black and 750 white rhino, and nocturnal creatures and forest dwellers whose numbers are impossible to assess from the aerial surveys conducted every year. These smaller animals include hyena (spotted and brown), the aardwolf, black-backed and side-striped jackal, various species of mongoose, badger, civet, genet, caracal, serval, otter, porcupine, bush squirrel, pangolin, cane rat, wild hare and spring hare, vervet and samango monkey, baboon, night ape, bushbaby, bush pig, nyala antelope, bushbuck, grey and red duiker, oribi, steenbuck, Sharpe's grysbok and klipspringer.

Few humans have attempted to settle permanently in the area of the park. The conservationists of the past were the mosquito and the tsetse fly. Their presence made vast areas of bush inhospitable to man, and thus provided game with sanctuary from their most dangerous enemy.

From paintings on the walls of rock shelters, it is evident that the San hunted in the area of the park. They came from the highveld each winter, when the mosquitoes were less active, and retreated to the safety of the heights as soon as summer came. The tsetse fly did not worry the San as they kept no cattle. Although the fly had a vicious bite, the species in the park did not carry sleeping sickness. But it did spread nagana, which was lethal to horses and draught animals. Even dogs died of nagana.

Most men entering the area found

Wonderland created from a wilderness

it so hostile that they soon fled, though a handful of refugees from tribal disturbances, who had already lost their livestock, eked out an existence in the bush until they were killed or driven away by malaria.

The first non-Africans to explore the area of the park were safari traders and slave raiders, who trekked from the coastal trading ports through the bush to reach the groups of people settled on the highveld. This trade was handicapped by malaria at the ports. In 1725 the Dutch, who had taken over Delagoa Bay from the original Portuguese occupants in 1721, abandoned their settlement because of fever and attacks by pirates. The Portuguese then re-established the trading base of Lourenco Marques, now known as Maputo, and their safari

FATHER OF THE PARK

When the area between the Sabie River and the Crocodile River was proclaimed a game sanctuary in 1902 the post of chief game warden was given to a major James Stevenson-Hamilton (*above*). Stevenson-Hamilton was destined to become known as the 'father' of the Kruger National Park.

Stevenson-Hamilton was given vague instructions to prevent poaching within the reserve, but had no staff to enforce his authority. Yet by 1903, with only two game wardens, he had so sternly enforced the poaching laws that he was nicknamed siKhukhuza ('he who sweeps clean'). The European form of this name — Skukuza — was later given to the park's headquarters.

Stevenson-Hamilton devoted most of the rest of his working life to keeping the boundaries of the Kruger National Park intact. He retired in 1946.

parties blazed well-trodden paths through the bush to the interior of the Transvaal.

Settlement of the highveld by the Voortrekkers in the 1830s, and the subsequent discovery of gold in places such as Spitskop, Mac-Mac, Pilgrim's Rest and Barberton, gave impetus to exploration of the lowveld. Traders built depots in the bush where their porters could rest and loads could be marshalled.

The Voortrekkers developed some of these paths into wagon trails which were improved and used by professional transport men, who carried supplies from the coast to the sites of the eastern Transvaal gold rushes.

The entire period from 1870 to 1890 was a restless, adventurous time, peopled by hunters and prospectors, and highlighted by stories of fortunes found and lost by many unusual characters. The Kruger National Park contains many simple piles of stones marking the graves of such men.

Among these were many of the transport men, who resorted to ingenious schemes to defeat the tsetse fly. They travelled through the worst areas at night, when the fly was less active. They smeared their draught animals with grease and potent mixtures thought to repel the tsetse fly, and used exotic creatures such as camels in the vain hope that they would prove resistant to nagana. The modern tourist roads in the park which follow old transport trails have in their foundations the bones of countless oxen which died from the disease.

In 1896 the livestock disease of rinderpest swept down from central Africa and killed great numbers of cloven-hoofed animals, which were particularly susceptible to it. These animals, such as buffalo, were favoured hosts of the tsetse fly, and it died with them, never to return. By then, however, the day of the transport wagons was over — trains of the Eastern Line had superseded them.

With the fly gone, wild animals were ruthlessly hunted for ivory, skins, horns and biltong. Professional hunters were joined by crowds of construction workers from the Eastern and Selati lines, and the contractors who supplied them with food. The entire game population of the lowveld might

A vervet monkey, one of a large population of this particularly agile species.

Warthogs are among the most amusing of the wild creatures of the savanna country. When alarmed they make a stately retreat, their tails held erect.

The steenbok is one of the daintiest of antelope. Nimble, agile, quick to dart off into the undergrowth, it has no defence against predators other than speed.

A spotted hyena, principal scavenger of the Kruger National Park and undertaker for most animals.

The greater kudu bull is one of the largest of the antelope family and noted for the magnificence of its proudly displayed horns.

The baboon, inquisitive, mischievous, and a favourite dinner for leopards.

A young bull elephant of good size but with typical medium-weight tusks.

The slaughter that had to be stopped

have been wiped out had it not been for the intervention of several members of the Transvaal government, supported by President Kruger.

The Sabie Game Reserve of 1898 covered only 350 000 hectares but this was the area which was most plagued by the hunters, and therefore an ideal nucleus for the future national park. Unfortunately there was little opportunity for the Transvaal government to enforce the ban on hunting. Political problems were mounting, and in October 1899 the Anglo-Boer War broke out.

Komatipoort, the railway centre on the southern boundary of the reserve, was occupied by the British. In order to hold the border with Mocambique, a force of 600 bushrangers and adventurers was raised. It was named Steinacker's Horse, after its commanding officer, Lieutenant-colonel Ludwig Von Steinacker (see box, page 269).

Von Steinacker and his men shot game for the pot, but at least their presence, together with the war, kept out the biltong hunters, whose wholesale slaughtering of animals was a major threat to wildlife in many wilderness areas of southern Africa.

At the end of the Anglo-Boer War, in 1902, the British administration set out to restore the processes of government in the shattered Transvaal, and they supported the original conservation ideals of President Kruger. A warden was appointed to care for the Sabie Game Reserve.

It was a most fortunate appointment. The man selected was Major J. Stevenson-Hamilton, short in stature and temper, but packed with resolution, courage, energy, and a deep understanding of wild animals.

With severely limited resources, he had to establish control over a wild area, keep out poachers, and cope with numerous adventurers and treasure-seekers looking for what was popularly known as the Kruger millions (see box, page 252). He also had to fend off so-called land developers, and others who were constantly asking him — and members of parliament — when the reserve was to be 'thrown open for shooting'.

For the administrative centre of the reserve, Stevenson-Hamilton selected the site where the rusty, unused Selati railway line reached the Sabie River. During the Anglo-Boer War a small blockhouse had been built there, and this became the warden's home and office. At first it was known simply as Reserve, but to the Africans it was the home of the man they knew as siKhu-khuza ('he who sweeps clean'), because of Stevenson-Hamilton's bustling reorganization of the area. Today, Skukuza — the European form of the name — is the administration centre and principal tourist camp in the park.

Stevenson-Hamilton recruited his first two rangers from the disbanding ranks of Steinacker's Horse. Gaza Grey was stationed on the lower Sabie River, and Harry Wolhuter was stationed in the western section near the old transport trail landmark known as Pretoriuskop. This hillock, according to some historians, was named after President Marthinus Pretorius. Others say that it was named after a certain Willem Pretorius who was buried near the koppie.

Apart from the old transport trail and the Selati line, there were no roads in the reserve and no facilities. A ganger's trolley was the only vehicle on the abandoned railway line.

The Shingwedzi, flowing through the hot northern portion of the Kruger Park, supports countless game.

Of the 900 bird species found in South Africa, more than 450 may be seen in the Kruger National Park. The casual visitor is captivated by their beauty and their antics, while the ornithologist is in a paradise.

Every visitor will notice birds such as the glossy, metallic blue starlings, with their yellow button eyes. Cheeky and hopelessly spoilt by visitors, they frequent the camps and picnic places, thriving on hand-outs.

Equally noticeable at such places are the hornbills. Comical to watch, inquisitive and tame, they are the clowns of the bird world.

Vultures, of various species, are repellent but fascinating when they gather at a kill.

Secretary birds and ground hornbills, grave of demeanour, promenade through the bush in search of food.

At the rivers and pools hadeda ibis, along with the hamerkop, sandpiper and numerous aquatic birds such as the knob-billed duck, hunt for frogs and fish. Ox-pecker tick birds cluster on the game animals, relieving them of parasites; egrets, herons and storks follow the grazing herds in search of grasshoppers and other insects; at night several species of owl fly out to hunt as the sun sets.

Ostriches are common here, while in the trees a mass of song birds cluster.

A white-bellied sunbird hen. The flowering aloe that provides her perch is one of many species in the park.

A bee-eater watching for prey from a sunny perch in the savanna country of the Kruger National Park.

White storks spend summer in southern Africa, feeding on insects and reptiles.

Barred owlets, decorous and wide-eyed. They hunt during the night and maintain the balance of nature by preying on rodents and small reptiles.

Among the most amusing of the park's birds — the perky, cheeky hornbills.

The hamerkop, waiting patiently for an unwary frog or fish.

A saddle-billed stork, surveying the park from a dead tree.

The Cape glossy starling, easily tamed by hand feeding.

The gorgeously coloured blue waxbill, a photographer's delight.

A sanctuary for all time is proclaimed

A giraffe nibbling the leaves of the wag-'n-bietjie thorn tree.

The game rangers had to patrol on foot or horseback. In 1903 the Shingwedzi Game Reserve was proclaimed, covering 500 000 hectares in the north, between the Letaba and the Luvuvhu rivers. This was separated from the Sabie Game Reserve by a block of privately owned ranches and mining concessions. This wild ranching area was also placed under the control of Stevenson-Hamilton, together with the Shingwedzi Game Reserve.

Taken together, these three areas covered substantially the area of the Kruger National Park today. To control them efficiently with his existing means was impossible for Stevenson-Hamilton. He appointed as ranger of the Shingwedzi Reserve an eccentric character named Major A. A. 'Manjoro' Fraser, who made his home in a rondavel on the Shangololo river. Here Fraser was content with his isolated existence; when unwelcome visitors called, Fraser would jump through the back window and hide in the bush until they had departed.

The extreme north of the Shingwedzi Reserve, on the banks of the Luvuvhu, adjoined what was known as Crooks' Corner, the haunt of ivory hunters, smugglers, illicit labour-recruiters known as blackbirders, and renegades. These men were out of Stevenson-Hamilton's area, and thus free of his authority.

Controversy developed over the future of the three separate areas. To Stevenson-Hamilton the protection of wild animals was of prime importance, but he soon realized that the area could never be retained as a pure wilderness. It was threatened by too many private interests, and there was a mounting clamour about good ground going to waste — it was thought that it should all be de-proclaimed and disposed of as farms.

With the revival of the Selati railway and its completion as far as Tzaneen in 1912 there was further controversy, for the line made the area accessible and set many people thinking of ways to make money through commercial activities in the lowveld.

World War I broke out with the future of the three areas still undecided. Stevenson-Hamilton and several rangers went off to war, and the animals were left to the care of Major Fraser and a skeleton staff. During the war, however, a commission was appointed by the government to inquire into the whole concept of game reserves, and when Stevenson-Hamilton returned with the rank of lieutenant-colonel in 1918 he was delighted to find that the commission had recommended that government policy be directed towards 'the creation of the area ultimately as a great national park where the natural and prehistoric conditions of our country can be preserved for all time'.

Stevenson-Hamilton busied himself with essential post-war administrative changes. Old hands had retired, and new men had to be found. New posts were established at such places as Punda Maria, and on the Letaba River. The first visitors arrived in 1923, brought in by train on a package tour service organized by the South African Railways and known as the 'round in nine', because it lasted nine days. The tourists slept on the train, parked at Skukuza, were escorted on a walk through the bush, and had a camp-fire party. Clearly, there was little doubt that if the area was opened up by roads there would be a flood of visitors.

The government, public, tourist industry, and bodies such as the Wild Life Protection Society were all increasingly enthusiastic about the concept of a national park. In order to consolidate the area, 70 privately owned farms between the Sabie and Letaba rivers were expropriated. Others, lying between the Sabie and Sand rivers, were excluded but belonged to people who were sympathetic to conservation, and many of these farms are now included in the Sabi-Sand Game Reserve, the largest private game reserve in Africa.

It was Stevenson-Hamilton and Stratford Caldecott, an artist appointed by the railways to publicize the park, and the Afrikaans newspaper 'Die Burger', who conceived the name of Kruger National Park. On 31 May 1926 the South African Parliament unanimously passed the second reading of the National Parks Act, and the Kruger National Park came into full legal existence. Stevenson-Hamilton was appointed its first warden under a board of control made up of members selected by the government, Transvaal Provincial Council and the Wild Life Protection Society.

The immediate intention was to open the park to the public. It was felt that the best way of winning general support for the concept of conservation was to allow people to see the beauty of the wilderness and its wealth of wildlife. Road-building began.

The first road was from Skukuza to the Olifants River, the second from Skukuza to Pretoriuskop, and the third from Skukuza to Crocodile Bridge. In that year — 1927 — the first three cars were allowed through the Pretoriuskop gate, and the Kruger National Park was launched on a career destined to make it one of the great tourist attractions of the world.

An enormous amount had to be done to make the park hospitable to visitors. Roads had to be extended and improved, camps had to be built, services had to be provided for food, petrol, breakdowns and other emergencies. The park authorities had to learn many things by experience.

The southern area was opened to visitors and at first they were free to come at any time of the year. In 1929 a large party of round-the-world American tourists arrived in the midst of the rainy season. Their vehicles became bogged down and they were

---

THE MASTER POACHER OF THE PERILOUS IVORY TRAIL

The professional ivory hunters were a very special breed of adventurer. Heat, humidity, fever, the constant menace of wild animals, reptiles, insects, and primitive human inhabitants, combined to make life very precarious.

Stephanus Barnard (*right*), known to the Africans as BveKenya ('the swaggerer'), was the king of these hunters. He was born in Knysna on 19 September 1886 and grew up in the western Transvaal. After some years as a policeman he turned ivory hunter and in 1910 he made his way to the strange part of the north-eastern Transvaal known as Crooks' Corner — isthmus of bush-covered land between the Limpopo and the Luvuvhu rivers used as a hideaway by poachers, smugglers and renegades.

The attraction of the area was its remoteness and the fact that the borders of the Transvaal, Mocambique and what was then Rhodesia all met here. Any punitive force could easily be avoided by simply crossing into another territory.

From this base, Barnard ran a poaching industry.

Elephants were his speciality. His

knowledge of them was profound and he was one of the very few hunters to witness the strange periodic gatherings of elephants when herds meet to mix their young and stage an almost ritualistic 'communion' of their kind.

Barnard left the bush in November 1929. In his own words he 'turned honest', married, and settled down to farm in the western Transvaal near Geysdorp.

He died on 2 June 1962, but the peoples of the wilderness where he hunted still speak wistfully of the day when BveKenya will return to the old ivory trail.

A nimble and elusive duiker, one of the smaller antelopes.

The stately and massively built eland, largest of the antelopes.

A kudu surveys his territory. Despite its long horns, this creature moves with ease beneath the trees, holding its head low.

A lion cub. The spots fade as it approaches maturity.

A young zebra happily provides a pair of ox-pecker birds with a meal of ticks.

For the first tourists, the going was rough

forced to spend the night perched in thorn trees to avoid lions. In their exposed positions they could not escape the mosquitoes, and several tourists went down with malaria.

This caused considerable bad publicity. After this incident the park was closed during the rainy season, except for Pretoriuskop, where a permanent camp was built, with comfortable accommodation for tourists throughout the year. Pretoriuskop has ever since been a favoured camp from which to tour the park.

In 1931 a road was built providing access to the far northern areas of the park, all the way up to Crooks' Corner, where the last of the renegades and adventurers, including the renowned ivory poacher, BveKenya (S. C. Barnard), found civilization fast encroaching on their hide-out and began leaving for other parts (see box, page 278).

This was a period in the history of the park which is fondly remembered by many of the early visitors. The simplicity of the camps, the rough roads and the absence of strict regulations made a tour a great adventure.

Charles Astley Maberly, the naturalist and artist, known as the man who could talk to animals, spent months each year travelling about on a bicycle. Whenever he saw a suitable subject to draw he would jump off his cycle without the least fear of danger and set to work (see box, page 267).

An African game ranger, who also travelled about on a bicycle, perhaps summed up these times when a tourist stopped to warn him that he was pedalling straight towards a large pride of lions on a hill next to the road. The ranger simply shrugged.

'Eat you,' he said without a smile, 'but not me. Me government.'

Unconcerned, he continued on his way.

World War II delayed further development in the park. In 1946, Stevenson-Hamilton retired after 44 years of service.

He left with a plea that his beloved park should not be turned into a glorified zoo and botanical garden dotted with scientific experimental stations, hotels and recreational facilities.

To him a national park was essentially a wilderness area. Excessive

A waterbuck bull with a fine pair of horns. Powerfully built, this species is a good swimmer and a resolute fighter.

The fastest of all animals: two cheetahs on the hunt in long grass.

development and over-management would only destroy its unique atmosphere. His philosophy was: the game ranger's rifle and the veld manager's box of matches might be important tools of control, but indiscriminate or careless use of them could have drastic results, and regrets could not revive the corpse of an animal or a tree.

He was succeeded as warden by Colonel J. A. B. Sandenbergh, but the days of the paternal game warden figure were over. Changes were inevitable in the post-war Kruger National Park. Sandenbergh saw the beginning of them when the British Royal Family visited the park in 1947 and brought world-wide publicity. Suddenly it seemed that everybody wanted to visit the famous park — foreign politicians, touring sports teams, celebrities by the score, and tourists by the thousand. Pressures on services and management became immense.

Control of the park was substantially changed with the appointment of an overall director of national parks, under whom were specialists in charge of tourism, works and engineering, and biological control. The post of warden vanished after Sandenbergh resigned in 1953, and his successor, L. B. Steyn, retired in 1961. The post was re-instated in 1978.

In 1955 more than 100 000 tourists visited the park. Ten years later the number exceeded 200 000, and in 1983 there were more than 450 000 visitors.

Human pressure on the wilderness was relentless. The Kruger National Park had become a tourist wonder of the world and its management had to confront the reality that it was going to become more difficult to control people in the park than wild animals.

Roads were extended and the principal routes tarred. New camps were built and old ones were enlarged, modernized, and provided with shops, restaurants and other facilities. Boreholes and dams were built to supply drinking water.

The park was divided into 400 veld-burning blocks, each block with its vegetation and wildlife carefully studied by scientists. They use computerized aids to assess trends and the maximum carrying capacity of the blocks for particular plants and animals.

Surplus animals have to be culled, and a by-products factory at Skukuza produces biltong, skins and curios.

The entire area of the park is now open throughout the year. Modern hygiene and medication have reduced the menace of mosquitoes, and the lush green growth of the rainy season in the park is revealed to visitors in all its splendour.

Each month has its own character, with innumerable fascinating things to do and see, to discuss in the camps at night, or to remember long afterwards, perhaps in the setting of some distant city.

THE MAN WHO GAVE THE WORLD ONE OF THE GREATEST DOG STORIES EVER TOLD

Jock of the Bushveld, by Sir Percy FitzPatrick, ranks as a literary classic of South Africa. It is ranked as one of the greatest dog stories written. From the date of its first publication in September 1907, it has never been out of print.

Sir Percy was born on 24 July 1862 in King William's Town, in the Cape Province, where his father was a judge. He grew up in Cape Town, and on the death of his father he became, at the age of 16, a clerk in the Standard Bank. The life proved intolerable to him and after five years he resigned. He then made his way to the eastern Transvaal, where he became a transport rider and enjoyed six glorious years of adventure in the lowveld. During these years he acquired his dog, Jock.

Jock of the Bushveld is, therefore, essentially a true story, rich in episodes of hunting, real-life characters and adventures in the haunts of big game. The book covers Sir Percy's years as a transport rider and ends in 1889 when tsetse fly infected all his oxen with nagana and he was ruined. He walked penniless into Barberton, found a job and also a wife, Lilian Cubitt, whom he married on 16 February 1889.

Sir Percy's job was with the Johannesburg mining group, the Corner House. He gave Jock to a friend of his, who eventually gave the dog to a trader who had a store in Mocambique at a place known as Old Pessene, 25 kilometres north-west of Maputo. There Jock was killed one night when he rushed out to attack a stray dog who was raiding the fowl run. Jock killed the thief but was then shot when his master mistook him in the darkness for the other dog.

In Johannesburg, Sir Percy rose rapidly in the mining world. He eventually became a senior partner, entered politics and wrote *Transvaal from Within*.

After the Anglo-Boer War, Sir Percy became even more active in politics. He was knighted in 1902, and was one of the founders of the Union of South Africa. He wrote a collection of short stories entitled *Outspan*, and then, persuaded by Rudyard Kipling and his own children, he wrote *Jock of the Bushveld*.

By now Sir Percy was wealthy, and he was determined that the book should be well illustrated. In London, chance led him to an exhibition of paintings, and among them he saw a water-colour of a kudu bull which he particularly admired. The artist was Edmund Caldwell, and Sir Percy offered him a commission to travel to the eastern Transvaal and illustrate the book. Caldwell accepted with delight.

On his return to London, Caldwell continued his career, but never made much money — his share of *Jock of the Bushveld* was paltry. He died on 28 March 1930, aged 78.

Sir Percy retired from the mining world some years before this. He had built himself a home, *Amanzi*, near Uitenhage in the eastern Cape.

He died on 24 January 1931 and is buried at the Outlook overlooking the Sundays River Valley.

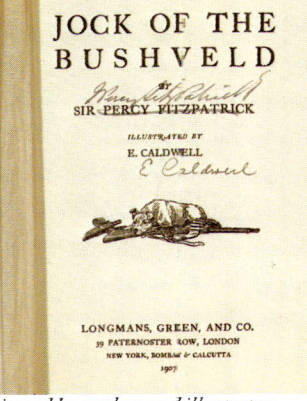

A first edition Jock of the Bushveld, *signed by author and illustrator.*

The patchwork country of Bophuthatswana

Bophuthatswana, which means 'that which binds the Tswana', comprises seven fragments of land scattered through the Transvaal, the Cape and the Orange Free State. These fragments are the independent homeland of the Tswana people. The total area is 3 820 142 hectares, and the population is 865 000. The homeland received its independence on 6 December 1977. Its capital, Mmabatho ('mother of the people'), is near the Anglo-Boer War town of Mafikeng. The Tswana homeland includes 410 000 hectares of arable soil, part of it being 100 000 hectares of black turf in the northern sections ideal for the production of wheat, maize, sorghum, sunflowers, groundnuts and cotton. A large part of the remaining area is magnificent ranching country.

The Tswanas migrated into central southern Africa in the 14th century. As hunters, herders and cultivators they found the high plains to their liking.

Game animals abounded, the grass was excellent for cattle, there were no serious endemic livestock diseases and the soil was deep and easy to cultivate.

Sorghum, beans, pumpkins, sweet melons and gourds were planted, and the Tswana found that maize, introduced by the Portuguese into the country, was also highly productive.

The origin of the name 'Tswana' is a mystery. It is applied to a number of groups who all speak the same language, have similar customs, but separate names. None of them ever knew themselves as the Tswana. As with several other people in southern Africa — including Europeans, who are called abeLungu ('ship people') by Africans — their name was given by foreigners. The meaning is unknown.

There are 59 different groups in South Africa who now accept the overall name of Tswana. The total number of these people is 1,7 million; another 600 000 live in the neighbouring country of Botswana.

The first Tswana consisted of two main groups, probably divisions of a parent group split between brothers. One division adopted the dew ('fokeng') as their totem symbol and called themselves Bafokeng ('people of the dew'); the other group were metal workers, led by a chief named Morolong ('the blacksmith'), and they called themselves the Rolong people.

The Rolong people wandered into what is now the Transvaal and settled in the valley of the Mosega River.

These people were peaceful and gregarious. They lived in large communal groups and on the slopes of the mountain known as Enzelberg they erected a labyrinthine hut-city named Tshwenyane, with a second city nearby named Kaditshwene, corrupted by Europeans to Kurrechane.

Elements of the Tswana people who

A Tswana homestead on the Bophuthatswana plains — a characteristic scene.

encountered the Nguni people in Swaziland and Zululand became known as the Suthu, or Basotho, and today these are the people of Lesotho — identical in language and life-style to the Tswanas.

Perhaps because the Tswanas were not warlike, sons of chiefs tended to break away and form groups of their own rather than fight one another over succession to the main group. In this way the 59 different groups came about in the Transvaal, all acknowledging a blood relationship but living independently of one another.

The first Europeans to enter the Transvaal found the Tswana people in great distress. They were being looted and harried by raiders from Zululand and elsewhere.

Two traders, Robert Schoon and William McLuckie, who travelled through the country in 1829, found most of the Tswana cities in ruin.

In some areas the people had taken to living in trees, building huts in the branches, reached by ladders which they hauled after them when they retired at night.

The Tswana people, like the Karanga of Zimbabwe, used stone in

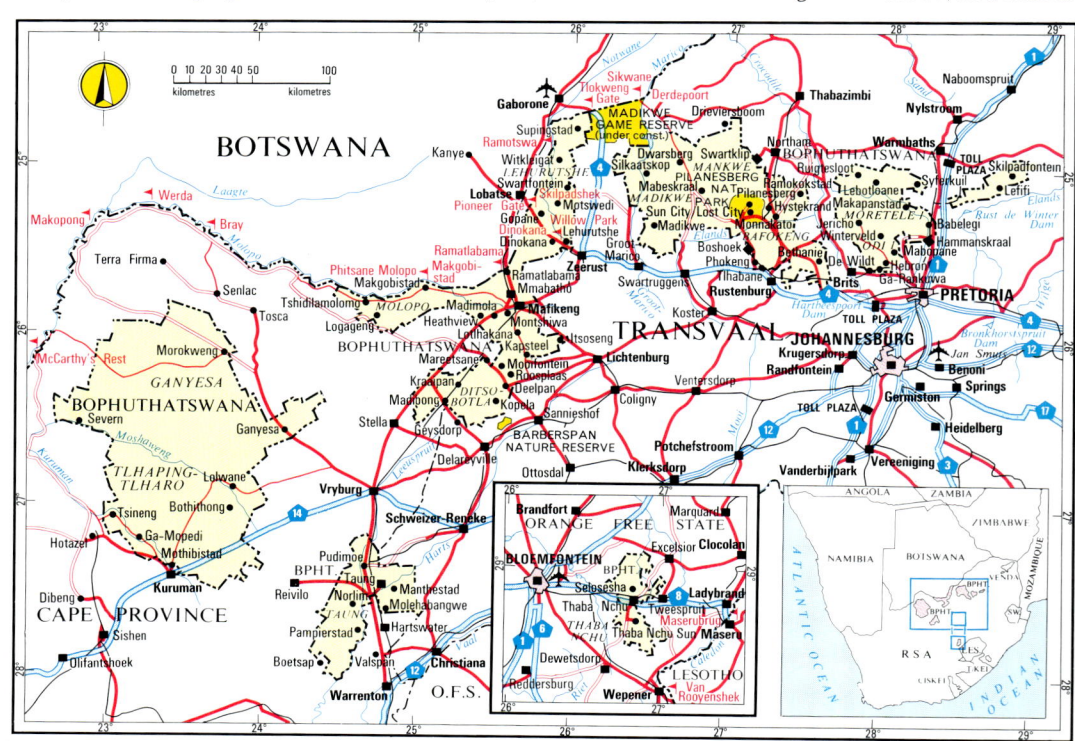

An aerial view of part of Sun City, an international tourist resort set amid the dramatic and unspoilt scenery of the Pilanesberg range.

building defensive enclosures around their residences and cattle kraals.

Complex examples of such stone walls may still be seen in many parts of the Transvaal.

The Tswana people accepted European political control in return for protection against the predatory bands, and they fought with the Voortrekkers against the Ndebele. The European protectors enabled the Tswanas to continue their traditional way of life in various parts of the Transvaal and the Orange Free State — the areas that form the autonomous republic of Bophuthatswana.

The land is well endowed with minerals. Its platinum deposits are colossal, and limestone, fluorspar, iron, and several types of gem-stones are also present.

The platinum metals are divided into two groups. One group — palladium, ruthenium and rhodium — is lighter than gold. The second group — platinum, iridium and osmium — is heavier than gold.

Platinum and palladium are commercially the most important of the two groups. They are used in the manufacture of jewellery and for many specialized applications in electronics, precision instruments, dentistry and laboratory ware.

Osmium and iridium are used in petrol refineries.

Platinum in small quantities was found in the reef of the Witwatersrand in 1892, but in the hey-days of the great gold rush it was not considered important. Then in 1924 a prospector, A. F. Lombard, panned rich platinum in a dry watercourse on the farm Maandagshoek in the Lydenburg district of the Transvaal. Lombard took the discovery to the geologist, Hans Merensky, and under his control the reef that became known as the

Merensky Reef was located. It proved to be the largest platinum deposit found anywhere in the world at that time.

The principal platinum workings are near Rustenburg and in the Lydenburg district, as well as in several other parts of the Transvaal.

The workings of Rustenburg Platinum Mines are the world's largest underground mining operation.

Scenically, the most spectacular feature of this region is the volcanic complex of six mountain rings form-

A portion of the highly ornate and imaginative Lost City.

ing the 1 682-metre-high Pilanesberg. Pilane is said to mean 'impala'.

This mass of rock, stretching 27 km across, consists of concentric rings of granular red stone, enclosing volcanic intrusions of syenite and other material. In the setting of this extraordinary exposure of alkaline rock, the Pilanesberg National Park has been created, providing a sanctuary for many of the species of wild animals which once roamed this part of the Transvaal.

As a complete contrast to this area of wilderness, the gigantic recreational and gambling resort of Sun City has been built in the Pilanesberg from the imaginative concepts of hotel magnate Sol Kerzner.

The son of Russian immigrants to South Africa and born in Johannesburg on 23 August 1935, he has been responsible for many spectacular resort developments in many parts of the world.

Sun City consists of three luxurious hotels, gambling, sporting and theatrical facilities, and a cluster of cabanas.

The most recent of the hotels, opened in December 1992, is known as the Palace of the Lost City, not far from Rustenburg, an elaborate fantasy of odd shapes, enchanted gardens and waterways.

ORANGE FREE STATE

ORANGE FREE STATE

BETWEEN THE ORANGE River and its principal tributary, the Vaal, lies a rolling prairie, about 1 400 metres above sea level, flooded with sunshine, green and warm in summer, brown and crisply cold in winter. From one horizon to another, north, south, east and west, this prairieland stretches away with the winds like a whispering siren's voice tempting the traveller ever onwards with only a distant hillock to act as a beacon on a journey seemingly without end.

This prairieland is the summit of the central plateau of South Africa. Geologically it forms part of the Karoo Sequence, the great series of sedimentary deposits that were laid down in successive epochs between 250 and 125 million years ago.

The soil is deep and rich, and the surface only gently undulating. In the portion drained by the Vaal River grow huge fields of wheat, maize, sorghum, groundnuts, sunflowers, oats, potatoes, onions, barley, peas, beans, lucerne and buckwheat. The towns are small inhabited islands scattered at random in this ocean of cultivation.

In the dryer southern portion, drained by the Orange, sheep graze — the flocks wandering over the land like white shadows of ghost clouds, while wind-pumps murmur and creak as they fill the drinking troughs and reservoirs with the characteristic alkaline water of the Karoo Sequence.

Nearly 30 000 farms cover these central plains. The area has always been regarded as one of the principal pantries of the continent of Africa. In former years, the San hunted the plains game — springbok, blesbok, hartebeest, gnu and qwagga — which lived here in herds so large that their numbers were beyond count. European hunters were also lured into the area and the sound of their guns was an incessant voice of doom until the game animals were almost completely eliminated.

The hunters told the farmers in the south of the fertility of the central plains, and at the time of the Great Trek of the 1830s many hopeful families moved up from the Cape Colony to occupy what was then a no-man's land — for the San and the few other resident groups who had lived in the area for many years had been driven away by raiding bands of Zulu warriors, and by the various renegades who had fled from the general bloodbath that occurred in Natal at the time of the rise of Shaka.

The farmers created on the central plains a republic of the veld which they named the Orange Free State.

For roughly a century this quiet little rural community had an economy concerned only with agriculture. Then, in 1947, there came the discovery of gold. Diamonds, uranium and coal have also been found, but the gold fields around Odendaalsrus transformed the simple little country maid into a glamorous princess.

Preceding page: The Clarens sandstone country of the eastern Free State, with a flock of Angora goats grazing the slopes.

CAPE PROVINCE

TRANSVAAL

The Orange Free State has been
divided into two touring regions,
the west and the east, with
the purple line indicating the division
between them. Turn to the page
indicated (large purple numbers)
for a detailed map of each region,
plus extensive touring
information.

Vaal

Sasolburg

1

Kroonstad

Vaal

3

Welkom

289

299

Bethlehem

Harrismith

ORANGE FREE STATE

NATAL

Modder

Caledon

Bloemfontein

282

LESOTHO

1

Orange

Caledon

Zastron

NATAL

Orange

CAPE PROVINCE

THE GLITTERING GOLDEN WAY

THE CENTRAL PLAINS of South Africa are golden in colour and product. Even in midsummer, the green grass carries golden-yellow seeds and straws. The corn on the cobs in the vast maize fields is golden. The sunflowers are a vivid yellowish gold, growing in millions on farms producing oil seeds. Wheat turns quickly from green to golden. Rivers have the tawny-golden colour of the earth. And the mines of the Free State gold fields bring from deep underground the gold, pyrites and uranium that makes this one of the richest parts of South Africa.

The trunk road running across the Free State from south to north is known as the Golden Way, crossing these enormous plains and linking towns with farms and mines. Its route is not greatly different from the first trail blazed by the hunters, traders and missionaries who ventured up from the Cape in earlier centuries. Essentially the same route was also followed by the Voortrekkers.

The frontier between the Cape Province and the Orange Free State is the Orange River, a moody giant of a river. Only in the last few years has man really harnessed its power by building across it irrigation dams such as the Hendrik Verwoerd, the P.K. le Roux and the projected Torquay dams. Even with a modern bridge spanning the river instead of dangerous fords and slowly moving ponts, there is still a sense of change and excitement in crossing the Orange River and reaching on the northern bank a subtly different world, more fertile than that which the traveller has left behind.

In the centre of the plains the spring of Bloemfontein still surfaces in the middle of the city that grew around it. A pillar, a plaque and a caravan park mark the spot today. In the past this little spring was a drinking place for wild animals, early man, San hunters, Sotho farmers, raiding bands of warriors, and for countless oxen drawing the sturdy wagons of the pioneers.

In the extreme north of the region flows the powerful Vaal River, the border with the Transvaal, through a fertile valley lined with willow trees. Here man can find blissful solitude on innumerable islets in the river — one of the major rivers of South Africa.

The headgear of a shaft at Allanridge on the Orange Free State gold fields.

Allanridge

Allan Roberts, geologist and prospector, was one of the pioneers of the Free State gold fields, and Allanridge was named after him. The town is the centre for the Loraine Gold Mines, and is dominated by the tall headgear and complex reduction works that treat 75 000 tons of gold-bearing ore every month. Water pumped from the underground workings fills an extensive lake, where several thousand flamingoes and other birds make their homes.

The town was designed in 1950 on futuristic lines by William O. Backhouse, who also planned the city of Welkom. His plans for Allanridge provided for an eventual population of 25 000, and the town is spacious.

Bethulie

The small old-world town of Bethulie shelters beneath a ridge of hills on the northern bank of the Hendrik Verwoerd Dam. The town was originally a station of the London Missionary Society, which handed it over to the French Missionary Society in 1833. They named it Bethulie ('chosen by God'). In 1863 this quiet God-fearing settlement became a village.

The original mission buildings still stand, including the oldest serviceable European-built house north of the Orange River. Named Pellissier House after the first French missionary, the Reverend Jean Pellissier, it is now a local history museum, where some of Pellissier's personal belongings are on display.

On the banks of the Bethulie Dam are a nature reserve and a holiday resort, with a caravan park and launch-

Monument at the site of the Golden Way's first prospecting borehole.

The railway viaduct and bridge at Bethulie, the longest in southern Africa.

The waters of the Orange River, impounded in the Hendrik Verwoerd Dam.

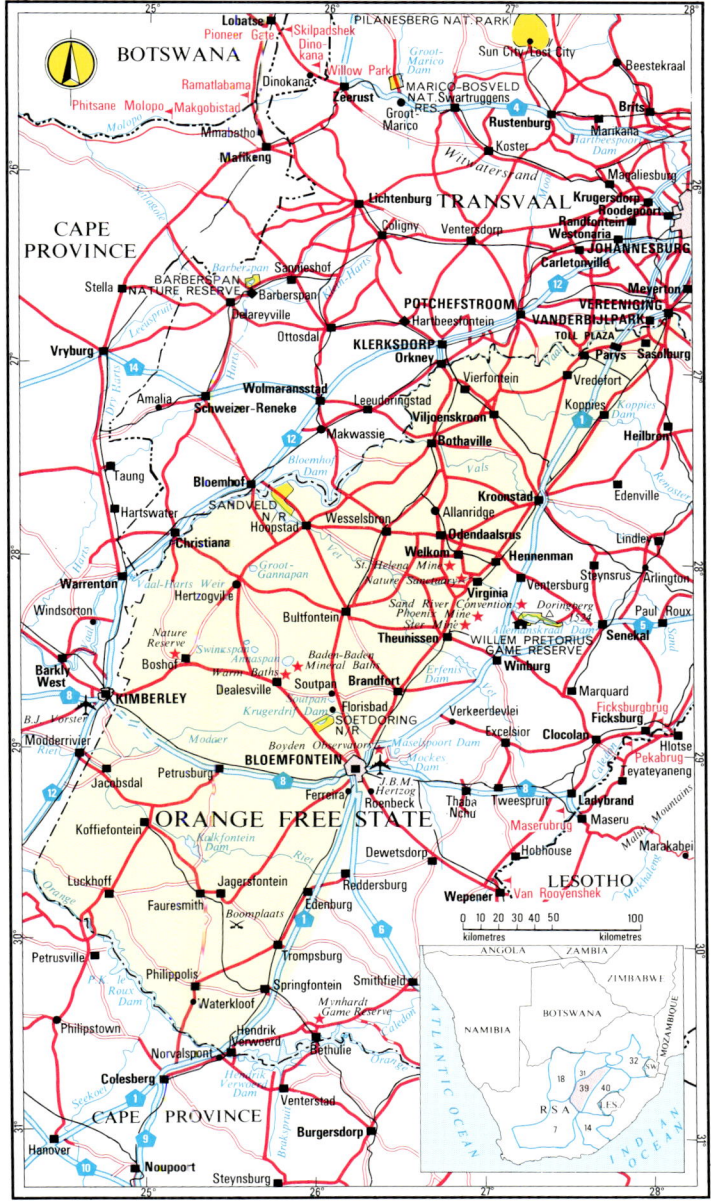

ing ramps for boats. The nature reserve is a sanctuary for various antelope and a few exotics such as spotted deer and American mountain sheep. The Hendrik Verwoerd Dam also offers opportunities for boating and other water sports

The railway line from the north to East London crosses the valley in which Bethulie lies by means of a concrete viaduct, then crosses the Orange River on a bridge 1 152 metres long.

Bloemfontein

The judicial capital of South Africa and provincial capital of the Orange Free State, Bloemfontein is also the most centrally situated city in the country. It is a pivotal point for communications and a popular venue for conventions and sporting events.

The name of the city comes from a spring ('fountain') that surfaces here. This spring was known to the Africans as Manguang ('place of leopards') but the Europeans who stopped here for water on their journeys across the central plains called it Bloemfontein ('flower spring').

Today the site where so many of the pioneer traders, missionaries, hunters, explorers and Voortrekkers camped with their wagons is a caravan park, shaded by tall trees and gay with beds of brightly coloured flowers.

The first European to settle at the spring was Johannes Brits. In 1840 he started to farm, but in March 1846 the British appointed Major H.D. Warden as the official resident on the central plains, and he selected Bloemfontein as the most central and convenient point from which to observe events in the area. After some hard bargaining, Brits sold his farm for £37 10s. Major Warden moved in, but had to pay Brits (who had second thoughts about the deal) another £50. This farm substantially covered the site of the modern city.

Close to the flower spring, Warden built a small fort, but nothing remains of it other than its name — Fort Drury — which has been adopted by a hotel built on the site.

In January 1848, Sir Harry Smith, the volatile governor of the Cape, rode up to Bloemfontein and called a meeting of the pioneer settlers of the central plains.

Most of these people were Voortrekkers who had abandoned the Cape Colony because of dissatisfaction with the government, but such was the charisma of Sir Harry — a bluff, hardriding man after their own hearts — that he won the approval of many of them for his project of proclaiming British rule over what was known as the Orange River Sovereignty.

THINGS TO DO AND SEE

Angling Yellowfish, barbel, black bass and carp are numerous in most of the rivers and dams of the Orange Free State.

Antiquities Ruins of a Leghoya settlement are sited on the summit of Doringberg in the Willem Pretorius Game Reserve.

The national museum in Bloemfontein has a comprehensive archaeological exhibition. The Florisbad skull is exhibited here along with a reconstruction of the man to whom it once belonged. The skull is the earliest find in South Africa of *homo sapiens*. The museum has a meteorite panel, displaying some of the meteorites that have fallen in southern Africa.

Boating Allemanskraal Dam, the Vaal River at Parys, the Vals at Kroonstad, the Sand at Virginia, various irrigation dams and the Orange River — all offer opportunities for boating.

Camping and caravanning Bloemfontein, Kroonstad, Parys, Virginia, the Hendrik Verwoerd Dam and the Willem Pretorius Game Reserve have resorts with all facilities for the camper. Most towns have caravan parks.

Gliding Bloemfontein and the area north of the Hendrik Verwoerd Dam are ideal for gliding, and competitions are held here.

Riding The prairie country of the highveld is superb riding country. Horses can be hired in the larger towns and from some farmers.

Sightseeing The Willem Pretorius Game Reserve, the flamingoes on the gold fields, the fields of yellow sunflowers, the oceans of maize, willowcovered islands on the Vaal at Parys — all are unforgettable scenes.

Swimming Bloemfontein, Maselspoort and the Allemanskraal Dam have open-air swimming baths.

'This prosperous, peaceful, happy place'

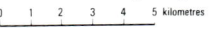

National Monuments

A Dutch Reformed Church with Two Spires
B Queen's or Bloemfontein Fort
C Fourth Raadzaal
D First Raadzaal
E The Fountain
F The Presidency

Places of interest

1 White Horse
2 SAR Workshops
3 Old Lamont Hussey Observatory
4 National Museum
5 Supreme Court
6 City Hall
7 Appeal Court
8 Free State Archives
9 Johan Brits caravan park
10 Free State Stadium
11 National Women's Memorial
12 War Museum of the Boer Republics
13 King's Park
14 Prince's Rose Garden
15 Zoo

City and surroundings map scale

0 1 2 3 4 5 kilometres

City central area map scale

0 500 1000 metres

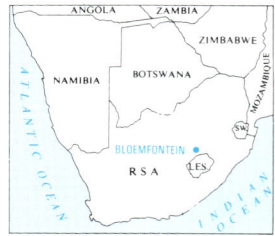

Bloemfontein, as seen from the summit of Naval Hill, a sunny, spacious place, with rich, deep soil, fine gardens and trees.

When Sir Harry left, the pioneers, uneasy about submitting once again to British rule, began — like Brits over the sale of his farm — to have second thoughts. On 17 July 1848 an armed commando appeared before Fort Drury and ordered Major Warden to leave within three days. He had no alternative but to comply. His force consisted of 45 Khoikhoi soldiers and 242 civilians. They all packed their belongings onto wagons and rode back to the Cape Colony.

A month later, Sir Harry was back on the scene, this time at the head of an army. At Boomplaats, south of Bloemfontein, he encountered the Voortrekkers, led by Commandant-general Andries Pretorius, and decisively defeated them. Major Warden was re-established in the fort at Bloemfontein and the British continued to control the Orange River Sovereignty until 1854.

During this period Bloemfontein grew into a small town. The British stationed a garrison of 450 men here and Warden built a stronghold, Queen's Fort, to house them. This fort still stands.

Sir Harry's addition to the Empire was regarded with disfavour by the British government. They judged the territory to be useless, and on 11 March 1854 handed it back to its inhabitants. The Union Jack was replaced by a flag of a new republic, and a volksraad ('people's council') was elected to sit in the simple little raadzaal ('council chamber') which still stands in St. George's Street. A trader, Josias Hoffman, became first president of a state that had a European population of 12 000, few means of support, and was in constant danger of attack by the Sotho who lived to the east.

President Hoffman did his best for the state, but after nine months he was accused of high treason for presenting Moshoeshoe, the paramount chief of the Sotho, with a barrel of gunpowder — the gift had been a token of peace and friendship. He resigned.

Jacobus Boshof, a magistrate from Natal, became the new president, and served the state with notable ability for the next four years.

Bloemfontein in those days was a typical frontier town. The plains around it teemed with antelope, especially springbok, black wildebeest, hartebeest and blesbok. The roaring of lions was a common sound at night, and under the cover of darkness, hyenas and jackals scavenged the streets.

A sun-bronzed, rugged crowd of pioneers came to town to trade or see the taxman, and their wagons and horses provided the traffic along the streets that were dusty during the frosty, dry winters, and buried in mud during the summer rains.

In 1859 President Boshof resigned. For the next four years Marthinus Wessel Pretorius combined the presidencies of both the Orange Free State and the Transvaal, but the joint tasks proved to be particularly arduous. He was in a constant state of official transition and the amount of hard riding he did ran into thousands of kilometres.

On 5 November 1863 Johannes Brand, a lawyer from the Cape, was elected president, and his 25-year term of office saw the republic through an eventful but singularly happy period of its history. Bloemfontein was then the capital of a true Ruritania — a model republic of the sunny veld.

Anthony Trollope, the British author, visited Bloemfontein in the 1870s and left a description of the town: 'There is a hill to the west which I used to mount when the sun was setting because from the top I could look down upon the place and see the whole of it. The town is so quiet and seems to be so happy and contented, removed so far away from strife and want and disorder, that the beholder as he looks down upon it is tempted to think that the peace of such an abode is better than the excitement of Paris, London or New York.'

'There is an atmosphere of general prosperity about Bloemfontein which is apt to make the dweller in busy cities think that though it may not quite suit himself it would be good for everybody else and thus, there comes upon him a question of conscience as he asks himself whether it should not be very good for him also.'

President Brand was a simple, honest, sincere man whose philosophy of life was founded on a conviction that everything would come right providing everybody did his duty. This philosophy saw the state through many of its troubles, including war with the Sotho and the financing of progress from a scanty revenue.

Brand died in 1888 and his successor, Frederick Reitz, found himself at the head of a perfectly sound state. By then Bloemfontein was a large and prosperous town, connected by railway to the Cape (in May 1888) and possessing several substantial buildings. In 1893 an imposing new coun-

British author Anthony Trollope, who was captivated by Bloemfontein.

Bloemfontein's statue of General De Wet, the Anglo-Boer War hero.

How the Orange Free State got an extra orange

The Hendrik Verwoerd Building of the Provincial Administration.

The National Women's Memorial to Boer women and children.

The Appeal Court, Bloemfontein, the highest court in South Africa.

cil chamber was built — an elegant memorial to the days of the Republic.

President Reitz resigned in 1896 and was replaced by M. T. Steyn, who supported a close union with the Transvaal. This political association inevitably drew the Orange Free State into the quarrels that culminated in the Anglo-Boer War.

Bloemfontein was declared an open city and on 15 March 1900 the British Army under Lord Roberts marched in and made the town their base and supply depot, buying from the Sotho hardy mountain ponies to be used by the cavalry and to draw artillary.

Bloemfontein has several reminders of the war years. A naval brigade was included in Lord Robert's force and in Bloemfontein the sailors were quartered on top of a flat-topped koppie which overlooks the centre of the modern city. This hill became known as Naval Hill. The Wiltshire Regiment had their remount camp below the eastern slopes, and in memory of the famous prehistoric white horse on a hill slope in their home country in Britain, they decorated the side of the hill with a similar figure, and the words 'For Remounts', all done with whitewashed rocks. These still remain on the slope.

With the war over, Bloemfontein became the capital of the Orange River Colony. In 1910, with the creation of the Union of South Africa, Bloemfontein, the most central town in the country, aspired to be the capital, and the final meeting of the national convention that devised the basis for the unification of South Africa took place here. In an effort to please as many

people as possible in the new state, the capital was split into three: the legislative capital was Cape Town, the administrative capital was Pretoria, and the judicial capital — the seat of the Appeal Court — was Bloemfontein, which also remained the capital of what was from that date known as the province of the Orange Free State.

Bloemfontein became a city on 17 March 1945. From a rustic beginning it has grown into a busy centre of transport, communications and trade. The largest railway workshops in South Africa are maintained here by the South African Transport Services. It is the home of the University of the Orange Free State and the Glen Agricultural College.

The Free State Stadium, for rugby and athletics, seats about 65 000 spectators. The South African Bisley Association has its headquarters and rifle

range on the outskirts of the city. And at the recreational resort of Maselspoort there is the largest fresh-water swimming bath (135 metres long) in the southern hemisphere.

Naval Hill is now a unique nature reserve named after Stuart Franklin, who was mayor of Bloemfontein at the time of the establishment of the sanctuary in 1928. There is a panoramic view of the city from the road that leads around the summit of the hill. In 1928 the Lamont-Hussey Observatory was built on the top of Naval Hill by the American University of Michigan. Equipped with a 68,5-centimetre telescope, it discovered more than 7 000 binary stars — double-star systems — before it was closed down in 1972. The domed building of the observatory is now a cultural centre.

A second observatory was built at Maselspoort, on the outskirts of

Bloemfontein. This is the Boyden Observatory, built in 1927 by the Harvard University of America, and equipped with a 152,40-centimetre telescope.

Among the noteworthy buildings in Bloemfontein, the original raadzaal — a simple, one-roomed building with a thatched roof and a dung and mud-smeared floor — stands in St. George's Street. Since 1849, when it was built by Major Warden, it has been used successively as a council chamber, church, town hall, school, museum and conference centre.

The fourth and last raadzaal stands in President Brand Street, opposite the Court of Appeal. This building was completed in 1893 from a design by L. Canning. Executed in classical style, it is surrounded by Doric columns and crowned with a domed tower. Today it is the seat of the Provincial Council.

There are busts of the six former presidents of the Free State Republic on the walls, and the original coat of arms of the Republic, carved in wood, hangs behind the seat of the chairman.

The coat of arms is the product of a chapter of accidents. In 1854 the Free State government asked King William of Holland to provide them with a flag and a coat of arms. There was no response, and when J. N. Boshof became president, he asked the governor of the Cape, Sir George Grey, to produce a design for a Great Seal for the republic. Sir George commissioned a design dominated by a wild olive tree, symbolizing liberty; in its shade three sheep rested, indicating patience, and a lion representing courage; an ox-wagon at the bottom of the seal stood for immigration and the Great Trek.

Then, in 1856, the ambassador from Holland arrived to take up his appointment in Bloemfontein, and he surprised everyone by bringing with him the design for a coat of arms and a flag. These designs were accepted, but Sir George Grey's Seal was placed in the central shield.

The coat of arms was hung in the council chamber until the Anglo-Boer War. It was then removed by Lord Roberts and taken to Britain as a souvenir of his capture of Bloemfontein. In 1938 Lord Roberts's family

Dawn over Bloemfontein, with water vapour billowing from the cooling towers.

The rural charm of the Orange Free State: clouds, and the vast space of the veld.

returned the coat of arms to its rightful place in the council chamber. While it had been gone, however, a curious error had been perpetrated. A coat of arms which had been privately made in 1892 had mistakenly replaced the olive tree with an orange tree in full bearing. With the coming of Union in 1910, and in the absence of the correct coat of arms, the new government accepted the authenticity of the faulty coat of arms and in the South African coat of arms an orange tree represents the Orange Free State. The same error occurs in the mosaic coat of arms on the floor of the entrance hall of the raadzaal.

The impressive buildings of the Court of Appeal and the Supreme Court have elaborately designed interiors. Diagonally opposite the Supreme Court is the Presidency — the official residence of the presidents of the Orange Free State, built on the site of the original farmhouse belonging to pioneer settler Rudolph Brits and his son Johan.

Also in President Brand Street is the modern city hall, a sandstone building with two halls used for conventions, municipal offices and a council suite. Designed by Sir Gordon Leith, it exhibits paintings and photographs depicting the historical development of Bloemfontein.

Opposite the city hall is an extensive memorial made up of 33 fountains and a statue dedicated to General J. B. M. Hertzog, Prime Minister of the Union of South Africa.

Queen's Fort, built in 1848, is a historical monument overlooking the city centre. The mother church of the Dutch Reformed Church stands at the top of Church Street in the city, its twin steeples modelled on the cathedral of Bamberg in Bavaria.

Naval Hill provides Bloemfontein with a unique nature sanctuary in the centre of the city and there are several parks. Foremost among these is King's Park, which contains a zoo, the Prince's Rose Garden and the Free State Stadium.

The Johan Brits caravan park stands opposite the stadium, and on the banks of the Modder River at the municipal waterworks of Maselspoort there is a recreational area offering boating, swimming, bungalows, a caravan park and a restaurant.

The National Women's Memorial occupies a commanding site in Monument Road. Designed by Frans Soff, with sculpting by Anton von Wouw, this memorial was built in memory of the 26 370 women and children who died in concentration camps during the Anglo-Boer War. The monument is in the form of an obelisk, 35 metres tall. At its foot President and Mrs M. T. Steyn are buried and also General C. R. de Wet and the Reverend J. D. Kestell, an influential church leader. At the base of the obelisk lie the ashes of the renowned Emily Hobhouse, who did so much to ease the suffering of people in the concentration camps during the Anglo-Boer War.

Below the National Women's Memorial is the War Museum, containing a comprehensive collection of items connected with the Anglo-Boer War and other struggles in South Africa. The museum is a standard source of material on the Anglo-Boer War. It also has photographs, paintings and sculptures, uniforms, books and documents.

The Free State archives in Elizabeth Street also contain a museum room. The National Museum has an outstanding anthropological exhibition and many other treasures.

An interesting feature of the Bloemfontein district is the abundance of smallholdings, numbering about 3 600. Most of these are between 8 hectares and 15 hectares in size, and produce vegetables.

Boshof

The agricultural and salt-producing centre of Boshof, founded in 1858, was named after Jacobus Boshof, president of the Orange Free State. There is a small municipal nature reserve here sheltering springbok, blesbok and other wildlife.

Bothaville

Boating, fishing and swimming are popular on the Vals River at Bothaville. The town also has a racecourse.

Bothaville is the centre of what is known as the sandveld. The district produces maize in large quantities, and the town is a busy shipment point with a grain elevator and a mill.

Brandfort

A landscape of maize fields, sheep farms and gold mines surrounds Brandfort. The town was originally a church centre on the farm Keerom. A small fort on the farm burned down during the wars with the Sotho in the 1850s, hence the name Brandfort ('burned fort'). It is also said that the town was named after President Brand, and both he and the fort are depicted on the town crest.

There is a memorial to the Voortrekkers in front of the Dutch Reformed Church. The house where the first aeroplane was built in Africa is still in the town.

Dealesville

Salt pans and several thermal springs are found in the region around Dealesville. The town was established in 1914 on a farm owned by John Deale.

There are sheep farms in the district and maize is grown. Some 40 kilometres away is the mineral spring of Florisbad, where rich fossil deposits have been found. The skull of Florisbad Man, dating back more than 41 000 years, was discovered here in 1930 by Professor Thomas Frederick Dreyer. Florisbad Man's stone implements are among the most primitive ever found. The relics can be seen at the National Museum in Bloemfontein.

The plains around the town are so level that water drains into shallow depressions, carrying in mineral salts from the surrounding surface. Constant evaporation of water and its replenishment have concentrated salt in these depressions and many of them are dazzling to the eye, owing to the sun's reflection from the white floors. Large quantities of salt are heaped nearby, ready for packing.

Numerous wind-pumps can be seen in the area, providing water for household and agricultural use.

Edenburg

Founded in 1862 as a church centre, the town of Edenburg lies on the main railway line and roadway from the Cape to the north. Cattle and sheep roam the plains around the town.

Fauresmith

On the grassy plains of the southwestern Orange Free State is Fauresmith, a little town where the railway line runs down the main street. It was originally a church centre, named after two men — the Reverend Philip E. Faure and Sir Harry Smith, the well-loved governor of the Cape.

Fishing and boating are popular in the Kalkfontein irrigation dam. Sheep and cattle in great numbers graze on the veld around the town.

Hennenman

Cement and a railway station resulted in the establishment of the town of Hennenman. A railway whistle-stop called Ventersburg Road was first built here to serve the town of Ventersburg, 12 kilometres away. Then lime deposits were discovered near the station and two cement factories were built.

The place became a town in its own right rather than just a road to somewhere else, and in 1927 at a public

Where Al Capone got his favourite diamonds

meeting held at the railway station, the name of the town was changed in honour of Petrus Hennenman, a local farmer.

Jagersfontein

In 1870 diamonds were found on Jagersfontein farm and prospectors rushed to the area. The farmhouse was bought by the government as an office. In front of the office was a unique gaol — a eucalyptus tree trunk to which prisoners were tied.

The mines are now closed, but some magnificent diamonds were found here while they operated, ranging from blue-white to sapphire in colour. The Excelsior Stone, found in 1893, weighed 971 carats, and until the Cullinan Diamond was found near Pretoria in 1905, it was the largest in the world.

Al Capone, the gangster, liked to display a large Jagersfontein diamond, and many famous beauties have dazzled admirers with a flash and a twinkle from this area.

Jagersfontein became a municipality in 1904. It lies in an attractive valley set amid hills.

Koffiefontein

The pleasant name of Koffiefontein ('coffee-spring') is applied to a diamond-mining and farming centre on the Riet River. A dam at Kalkfontein feeds water to farmlands growing lucerne and potatoes.

HARNESSING THE MIGHTY ORANGE RIVER

The Orange River system, with its principal tributaries, the Vaal and the Caledon, is one of southern Africa's most valuable assets. The system carries to the sea 23 per cent of the total water run-off of South Africa — up to 9 million litres per second during floods.

The Vaal is already thoroughly harnessed by man, but the Orange and the Caledon are only now starting to play a major role, irrigating more than 200 000 hectares of dry Karoo land, supplying 455 million litres of water per day, and generating 600 000 kilowatts of hydroelectric power at the two main dams.

The source of the Orange is the rainy roof of southern Africa — the 3 000-metre-high mass of basalt that comprises the highlands of Lesotho. Drenched by heavy rains in summer, this vast block of mountains feeds the river with prodigious volumes of water.

The Orange, in its middle and lower reaches, flows through the most arid country in South Africa. As along the Nile, there is a startling contrast between the green islets and banks of the river, and the desert of the surrounding landscape.

The engineering achievement of harnessing the Orange is impressive. The Hendrik Verwoerd Dam, covering 374 square kilometres, has been completed as a central storage dam. From it a tunnel, 83,8 kilometres long, directs water southwards to the upper valley of the Fish River. This water supplements the flow of the Fish River and then, via another tunnel 13,2 kilometres long, and a canal and pumping system, boosts the flow of the Sundays River and waters citrus estates and other farms in the lower Sundays River Valley.

A second dam, the P. K. le Roux Dam, constructed 130 kilometres below the Hendrik Verwoerd Dam, will eventually irrigate 150 000 hectares of land.

The Hendrik Verwoerd Dam, a vast, life-giving man-made lake.

Water cascades through the flood gates of the Hendrik Verwoerd Dam.

Kroonstad

Kroonstad is named after a horse named Kroon ('crown'), which drowned in a pothole in a stream on the site of the present town. As a result, the stream became known as Kroonspruit. In 1855, when the town was founded, it too was named after the horse.

Kroonstad stands on the banks of the Vals River which is lined with willow trees. On its banks is a holiday resort with bungalows, a caravan park and camping sites much used by anglers and water-sports enthusiasts.

Cattle, sheep, wheat and fruit are farmed in the district.

Odendaalsrus

For many years Odendaalsrus was one of the most isolated towns in the Free State. Founded in 1899 as a church centre, it was named after Jasaja Odendaal, who owned the farm on which it was established. All around the town stretched the flat, featureless sandveld, and there was an almost impassable track meandering off to a railway whistle-stop 34 kilometres away.

Vehicles travelling along this track were frequently bogged down and a common sight was a wagon up to its axles in soft sand. By 1946 Odendaalsrus had grown into a town of only 40 houses, 3 shops and a hotel.

Then came a golden explosion — in that same year a diamond drill probed down and produced from the Geduld borehole a core revealing such a treasure of gold that within days a flood of fortune-seekers descended on Odendaalsrus, and its name featured in newspaper headlines worldwide.

The secretary of the village management board, who eked out a monthly salary of £2 by playing a gramophone in the local pub, was deluged with thousands of letters and telegrams from overseas investors seeking advice. Some of them addressed their letters to the 'Lord Mayor of Odendaalsrus'.

Today Odendaalsrus is a modern gold mining town with a variety of facilities, including a motor-racing circuit and a gliding club.

Parys

On the southern bank of the Vaal River lies the attractive town of Parys. It is said that the surveyor of the town

Statue of Sarel Cilliers in front of the Dutch Reformed Church, Kroonstad.

was a German who had fought in the siege of Paris in 1870 and the situation of the South African town (established in 1876) reminded him of Paris and the Seine.

Parys is a popular holiday resort. Here the Vaal River is more than a kilometre wide, and studded with islands. Boating, swimming and fishing are favourite pastimes and there is a resort on the banks of the river with bungalows, a restaurant and caravan park. The gardens in the town are luxuriant.

Suspension bridges link some of the islands to the riverbanks. On Golf Island there is a nine-hole golf course.

Philippolis

This nostalgic little town was made a station of the London Missionary Society in 1823, and was named after Dr. John Philip, their superintendent in South Africa. In 1826 a section of the Griqua Khoikhoi settled here with their leader, Adam Kok.

The town they created was the capital of their state and had a council chamber, trading store, residences and a gaol and gallows.

The Griquas eventually sold the town for £400 to the government of the Orange Free State. They then trekked over the Drakensberg to settle in Griqualand East.

In the town there is a small museum, which is housed in a typical old Griqua cottage.

Two ships' cannons used by Adam Kok are now in the municipal garden.

Sasolburg

The South African Coal, Oil and Gas

Yellow-coloured Afrikander bulls, with the characteristic zebu hump.

The Orange River, flowing strongly through the rocky area high up its course near its junction with the Caledon.

Corporation (Sasol) established its complex and unique chemical plant on a vast coal field south of the Vaal River. From the raw materials of coal and water the plant produces many chemicals as well as Sasol petrol.

Several other manufacturers, supplied with raw materials by Sasol, have their plants in the vicinity. Fertilizers, plastics, synthetic fibres, detergents and other materials are produced.

The town of Sasolburg, established in 1954, houses the employees of these industries. The glow of the exhaust flames and the distinctive, sweetish odour from Sasol petrol are familiar features of this part of the world.

A holiday resort has been established here on the banks of the Vaal River, and two nature reserves nearby preserve the flora and bird life of the highveld.

Theunissen

In the centre of the Orange Free State, surrounded by rich agricultural lands grazed by horses and Afrikander and Friesland cattle, and producing maize and wheat, lies the town of Theunissen.

The only Estate Winery in the Orange Free State is also situated here.

The Erfenis irrigation dam on the Vet River, 15 kilometres away, provides ample water for farming and recreation, including boating, swimming and fishing.

In the district are two diamond mines, the Phoenix and the Star, and

THE FREE STATE'S FABULOUS GOLD FIELDS

The gold fields of the Orange Free State rival those of the Witwatersrand as the richest in the world. Clues to the vast wealth that lay here were discovered as far back as the 1890s, yet it is only in the last 40 years that these vast treasures have been exploited.

The first major discoveries were made in 1904 when Gustav Furst, who had a trading store on the farm Zoetininval in the northern Free State, guided Archibald Megson, a prospector, to a quartz reef exposed on the farm. Megson and two partners, Donaldson and Haines, prospected here and found gold, but not enough to interest financiers.

The prospectors formed a syndicate with Furst and sent Donaldson and Haines on a mission to London to interest a company promoter. They sailed on the *Drummond Castle*. At midnight on 16 June 1896 the ship was wrecked off Ushant and the two prospectors were among the 250 people drowned.

For the next 28 years nothing was done about the discovery. Then in 1932 Megson met Allan Roberts, a geologist and dental mechanic, and told him about the reef. With a partner, Emmanuel Jacobson, Roberts raised £50 000 and sank a borehole close to the reef, on the farm Aandenk, 5 kilometres north of Oden-

Pouring molten gold on the President Brand Mine at Welkom.

daalsrus. The borehole went down 1 233 metres, encountering two gold reefs, neither of which was payable.

Other prospectors followed, but it was not until April 1939, on the farm St. Helena, near Welkom, that the first really big strike was made. A reef was encountered with a fabulously rich gold content.

The advent of World War II hindered further exploration of the new gold field. Then on 16 April 1946 a drill on the farm Geduld intersected, at 1 195 metres, the Basal Reef — with an even richer gold content. In the midst of the excitement Anglo-American re-opened one of Allan Robert's old boreholes on the farm Aandenk. They went down an additional 120 metres — and reached the gold reef that Roberts had so narrowly missed.

A Sotho house near Theunissen. The houses are decorated by the women.

a new gold mine, the Beatrix mine.

Theunissen was named after Colonel Helgard Theunissen, commandant of the Winburg Commando during the Anglo-Boer War. He founded the town and for many years served as its mayor.

Virginia

Founded in 1954 as one of the centres of the new Free State gold fields, Virginia stands on the banks of the Sand River, and its surroundings differ from those of the other gold towns on the level plains of the sandveld. The town is completely modern — only the name derives from a former whistle-stop on the railway.

It is the centre for the Harmony Gold Mining Company Ltd, Western Holdings Ltd (Saaiplaas Division), and Beatrix Mines (Pty) Ltd. Gold, uranium, pyrite concentrates and sulphuric acid are produced here.

A perfect travellers' rest for the birds

On the Free State gold fields — one of the deep-level mines at Virginia.

A resort has been developed on the southern banks of the Sand River with bungalows and a caravan park. The area is also a nature sanctuary.

Vredefort

In former years herds of blesbok, black wildebeest, springbok and other plains game congregated in the area of Vredefort and hunting was a major occupation of the first settlers. The animals have long since vanished but the area is still a resting place for large flocks of birds during the course of their seasonal flights.

A town was established in 1876 on the farm Vredefort ('peaceful fort') by its owner in thanksgiving for the peaceful end in 1857 of a threatened war between the republics of the Orange Free State and the Transvaal.

The district produces maize, sunflowers, sorghum, groundnuts and cattle. In 1886 gold was found near the town and for some years the Vredefort gold fields attracted considerable attention. However the gold did not prove payable.

A curious geological feature in the district is an exposure of ancient granite emerging through thick layers of Karoo sediments. Known to geologists as the Vredefort Dome, this island-like dome of granite is surrounded by quartzites of the Witwatersrand System.

Welkom

The main centre of the Free State gold fields is Welkom, created in 1947 and since developed into a miniature city with a population of over 150 000. Welkom lies in a rectangle of mining claims 20 kilometres by 10 kilometres in area. Working these claims are the St. Helena Gold Mining Company, whose shaft was the first to produce gold from the Free State gold fields; the Welkom Gold Mining Company;

THE COLOURFUL BIRD POPULATION THAT STALKS THE GRASSLANDS

The central plains of southern Africa are open, almost treeless areas, well grassed but with little bush — the home of many species of ground-dwelling birds.

Among them is the blue or Stanley crane, South Africa's bird emblem. This crane is almost entirely restricted to the central plains and the midlands of Natal. They feed on insects, small reptiles, fish and other titbits.

Secretary birds also roam the central plains. The long feathers at the back of their heads resemble quill pens. A battle between a secretary bird and a snake is a dramatic spectacle. The bird kicks and stamps the reptile, relying on its scaly, bony feet, its feathers and its agility to protect it from bites.

The snow-white cattle egret is another common bird of the central plains. It accompanies grazing herds of domestic and game animals, snatching at insects disturbed in the grass, or riding on the backs of livestock and picking at the ticks that feed on them.

Among the most beautiful birds

The lively Burchell's glossy starling. It feeds on insects and fruit.

of the plains are the red and golden bishop birds. The feathers of the red bird have always been highly prized by Africans — Swazi princesses wear them in their hair to signify royalty.

An extraordinary bird is the long-tailed widow or sakabula. In the breeding season the male changes colour, turning from brown to black, and grows magnificent tail feathers.

The Kori bustard and the smaller bustards, called korhaan, have always been hunted because they make excellent eating. During courtship the

male fans its feathers, inflates its neck pouches, throws back its head and proudly parades in front of the hens.

Plovers and dikkops are also permanent inhabitants of the central plains, and each summer sees vast numbers of migratory white storks flying in to escape the cold of Europe.

Helmeted guineafowl are plentiful in the open, grassy areas and cultivated fields. At watering places they gather in large, chattering groups each evening.

Also numerous are the francolins, often called partridges. They are members of the pheasant family. Like their relatives, the quails, they make excellent eating.

Grass and marsh owls hunt the central plains for food. Cisticolas of several species dart through the grass and scrub looking for insects with a pleasant, tinkling song. Pipits and larks of several species (but not the skylark of Europe), ant-eating chats, speckled rock pigeons, turtle doves and Cape sparrows — all feature in the bird population of the central plains.

The crowned plover, noted for hatching its eggs in exposed situations.

A flock of crowned guineafowl scavenges the grasslands for food.

Le Vaillant's cisticola, a shy bird and expert at camouflaging its nest.

Flamingoes and other aquatic birds feed on algae and insect larvae in one of the shallow pans near Welkom.

Western Holdings; Free State Geduld Mines; President Brand Gold Mining Company; President Steyn Gold Mining Company; Beisa Gold Mining Company; Unisel Gold Mining Company, and the new Erfdeel/Dankbaarheid Gold Mining Company. These Free State gold fields currently produce 21% of the world's gold and 48% of South Africa's output.

Headgear, dumps and reduction works surround Welkom. Gold and uranium are produced in great quantities from considerable depths, and flooding is a problem. Enormous volumes of water have to be pumped from these mines. This water is saline and collects in hollows on the plains, where it forms lakelets, attracting aquatic birds, notably flamingoes. Desalinization techniques produce fresh water from the saline water and this is used for domestic purposes.

Winburg

The first town to be established in the Free State by the Voortrekkers was Winburg. In 1837, in exchange for 42 head of cattle, Andries Hendrik Potgieter purchased rights from a local chief to the area between the Vet and Vaal rivers. A town was necessary as a centre for the area, and after some dispute a site was selected and named Winburg ('victory town') because the owner had won a battle in persuading others to accept the site.

Winburg is a classic example of a South African town from that period. There is a large, central square dominated by a Dutch Reformed Church.

Near the town is a monument to the Voortrekkers, the oldest of the Voortrekker cemeteries, and an Anglo-Boer War cemetery.

WILLEM PRETORIUS GAME RESERVE, PRIDE OF THE ORANGE FREE STATE

One of the foremost recreational areas for the Orange Free State has been developed on the north-western shores of the Allemanskraal irrigation dam, built on the Sand River in 1960. There are rondavels, a restaurant, caravan park, swimming bath, sporting amenities, boating, and excellent angling for fish such as carp, yellowfish and black bass.

On the northern side of the dam there is a range of hillocks, surprisingly bushy for the Free State. On the summit of one of these hillocks, Doringberg, there is a well-preserved ruin of a prehistoric settlement, apparently of the long-vanished Leghoya people.

These people built extremely small huts, cattle kraals and walls — all from stone, without mortar. The size of the huts was possibly dictated by the difficulty of roofing with slabs of stone, but they must have been very uncomfortable homes.

On Doringberg there are several of these ruined buildings, each pervad-

The ruins of an old settlement of the Leghoya people near Winburg.

ed by ghostly reminders of their former owners.

The surroundings of the Allemanskraal dam, including Doringberg and its ruins, are a nature sanctuary, the Willem Pretorius Game Reserve, named in honour of Senator Willem Pretorius of the Orange Free State executive committee.

The reserve is 10 500 hectares in extent and is a sanctuary for many species of highveld game. It has the

world's largest herd of black wildebeest, as well as springbok, blesbok, red hartebeest, eland, zebra, white rhino and giraffe. There are also many smaller creatures and a wealth of bird life.

Notable among the trees in the reserve are white stinkwood, sweet thorn (Acacia karoo), karee, taaibos, buffalo thorn, wild peach, highveld cabbage tree, ghwarrie and wild olive (the tree emblem of the Free State).

Part of the Allemanskraal Dam.

Zebra and blesbok graze contentedly in the Willem Pretorius Game Reserve.

The monument built to the memory of the Voortrekkers near Winburg.

297

CASTLES IN THE AIR

THE EASTERN ORANGE Free State is blessed with a great scenic gift — the massive rock layer known as Clarens sandstone. Vividly coloured, it has been modelled through the ages by wind and water to form a majestic landscape of isolated piles of rock and numerous flat-topped mountains with precipitous cliffs, grassy summits, and pools of water from summer rains.

Many of these heights provided man with natural strongholds. The early San hunters found shelter in the caves. Until the coming of iron-age Bantu groups, the San freely hunted the game that roamed the central plains — black wildebeest, zebra, eland, hartebeest and springbok. But the iron-age people drove away the San and settled in groups around the protective sandstone hills. Each group sought a secure height, preferably one reached only by a single, easily-defended route.

The iron-age settlers came down from the west. They spoke the same language as larger groups who had migrated down from an unknown origin somewhere in central Africa. The newcomers recognized no generic name for themselves, but each group had a totem or emblem, and from these they called themselves such names as the Kwena ('crocodile'), Tlokwa ('wild cat'), Phuti ('duiker') and Rolong ('iron'). It was the Nguni people from the east coast who called them all the Suthu ('dark brown'), not because of their colour but because they were first encountered when they were living in the valley of the Usutu River in Swaziland.

The Suthu people (Basotho in their language today) had a difficult time in the early 19th century. It was the time of the Lifaqane ('migratory') wars. Raiding bands of warriors roamed the plains; destitute people were reduced to eating one another. The sandstone hills were the fortresses that saved many groups from extinction.

These hills dominate the plains of the eastern Free State with a calm strength and a distinctive character. They are the monarchs of a scenically spectacular kingdom of fields of wheat and maize, orchards of yellow peach trees and cherries, willows and poplars, deep valleys overlooked by towering golden cliffs, streams tawny from the soil, colourful homesteads made of sandstone blocks, and Sotho huts skilfully decorated by the women.

The traveller in the eastern Free State has much to discover: superb specimens of rock art; San caves to explore; dramatic natural features such as the great hole in Aasvoëlberg at Zastron; pathways at Witsieshoek that seem to reach the stars; the stately pile of Kerkenberg; and the glorious outlook of Blijdevooruitzicht, where the Voortrekkers descended the escarpment — some destined for happiness, the majority to meet their deaths in battles with the Zulu.

The eastern Free State is rich with all these assets — and many more. It is an area of scenic treasures, a landscape with a unique and colourful character.

The dramatic Clarens sandstone rock system that provides the base for the higher layers of volcanic basalt forming the mountain ranges of Lesotho.

The plains of the central South African plateau reach the Clarens sandstone foothills in the eastern Orange Free State.

black bass, yellowfish and blue-gill sunfish.

The municipality has created a pleasure resort on the shores of Loch Athlone with a restaurant in the shape of a mailship, the *Athlone Castle*, standing in the water. The restaurant contains many items from the ship as it was before it was scrapped through old age. There are bungalows and a caravan park at the resort.

The Pretorius Kloof Bird Sanctuary has been created where the Jordaan River passes through the Pretorius Kloof. There is a museum of local history in the former mission church.

Bethlehem

The sandstone foothills of the Maluti Mountains contain many inviting valleys. In one such valley wheat grew so well that early settlers established the town Bethlehem ('town of bread'). They aptly named the river flowing through the valley the Jordaan.

The Jordaan has been dammed to form Loch Athlone. Regattas are held regularly on the loch. Three dams now provide Bethlehem with water — Gerrand's, Athlone and Saulspoort.

All are used for fishing, boating and swimming and they make the town a popular inland holiday resort. They are stocked with largemouth

Loch Athlone, the great storage and recreational dam at Bethlehem.

The concrete version of the Athlone Castle, *built as a restaurant.*

299

Where a pig was found as big as a donkey

The district has cattle and champion racehorses. Maize, wheat, potatoes, apples and peaches are grown. Local people are proud of their crisp 'champagne' climate.

Clarens

President Paul Kruger died in exile in Clarens in Switzerland on 14 July 1904. The village of Clarens in the eastern Free State, founded in 1912, was named in his memory.

The village lies beneath high sandstone hills and close to the battlefield where five men of Paul Kruger's Transvaal Commando were killed in the Basuto War of 1886. The Kruger Memorial Hall in the village commemorates the president.

Clarens lies close to the entrance of the Golden Gate Highlands National Park. There is a picnic and recreational area in Leibrandt Kloof on the outskirts of the village.

Clocolan

The name Clocolan is a European corruption of the Sotho, Hlohlowane ('ridge of the battle'), the name given to one of the heights overlooking the town of Clocolan.

Originally occupied by the Kwena people, the area was looted by raiding renegade bands during the period of major upheavals at the beginning of the 19th century.

The town was established in 1906 as a centre of the production of maize, wheat, cherries, asparagus, potatoes and cattle.

Cornelia

Cornelia Reitz was the wife of President Francis William Reitz of the Orange Free State. The little rural town of Cornelia was founded in 1918 and named in her honour. It is a centre for livestock and maize farming.

Ten kilometres north of Cornelia, on the banks of the Skoonspruit, lies one of the most significant fossil sites in the Orange Free State. Isaac Hipkin, the owner of the farm Uitzoek on which the site lies, had been aware of the fossils since his boyhood, but only in 1930 was their value appreciated, when Dr. E. C. N. van Hoepen of the National Museum in Bloemfontein was shown the first portions of a horse-like creature's mandible containing only four incisors instead of the usual six. The creature was named *Eurygnathohippus cornelianus*.

Large-scale excavations were undertaken at the site and the National Museum secured its collection of Cornelia fossils.

Among these fossils are the remains of pigs (including one the size of a small donkey), many species of extinct antelope, a giant buffalo, an extinct sub-species of hippo and four new species of horse — together with many stone tools left by ancient men.

Deneysville

On the southern banks of the Vaal Dam the Deneysville Estates Company laid out a recreational township in 1936, named in honour of Colonel Deneys Reitz, who was minister of lands and irrigation.

Deneysville has camping and caravan grounds. Fishing and swimming are popular here, and three boating clubs cater for power-boat and sailing enthusiasts.

The prominent Clarens sandstone cliff known as Face Rock, in the area of the Golden Gate Highlands National Park.

In the Clarens district a solitary wind-pump works at its task of raising water for domestic use in a farmhouse.

Harvesting lucerne in the fertile valley of the Little Caledon River, in the beautiful Clarens sandstone country.

In the winter the vegetation sleeps through the months of frost.

The Sotho decorate their homes with elaborate patterns and colours.

Sotho women are the creators of the attractive decorations on the the walls.

The nocturnal African hedgehog, a bustling and lively highveld creature.

Ficksburg

Beautifully situated on the west bank of the Caledon River, the border between Lesotho and the Orange Free State, Ficksburg was founded in 1867. The Basuto War had just ended and the Orange Free State government decided to establish three towns in what was called the Conquered Territory. The purpose of the towns was to hold the area taken from the Sotho and provide stong-points to prevent the rustling and raids that had preceded the war.

Ficksburg was named after Commandant-General Johan Izak

THE MAIZE TRIANGLE — SOUTH AFRICA'S LARDER

Maize, corn, mealies — whatever the name, the crop is so widely grown in Africa, providing so many people with their staple diet, that it is surprising to realise that it was only relatively recently introduced into the continent.

Maize is indigenous to North America, and Portuguese explorers introduced it into Africa. Missionaries carried it into the interior and the Africans welcomed it.

The crop is hardy, growing in most difficult conditions; it is also resistant to disease, highly productive, and its cultivation demands little skill. The original staple food of the Africans — millet, commonly known as grain sorghum — could not equal maize as a crop, though it is still grown for beer-making.

The Nguni groups along the east coast (Swazi, Tonga, Zulu, Xhosa and others) called the maize they received from the Portuguese either mlungu or mbila. The Afrikaans name for maize, mielie, is a corruption of the Portuguese word, milho, meaning grain.

Today maize is the principal food crop of southern Africa, eaten as mealiemeal porridge, mealie rice, on the cob, or as samp. It is also a basic food for poultry and livestock. Edible oil and starch are made from it. The stalks are used for making silage feed for cattle. From the cobs, alcohol can be extracted — and a fuel can be made which is capable of running a motor vehicle.

The principal maize-producing area in South Africa is the so-called 'maize triangle', which covers the northern and eastern Orange Free State and the southern and western Traansvaal. About 9 million tons of maize are produced annually. Zimbabwe also grows vast quantities of

Maize, mealie and Indian corn are the popular names for this staple crop.

high-quality maize.

Maize production on a commercial scale demands considerable mechanization and 85 per cent of the total crop comes from highly developed farms. The balance is produced by subsistence farmers.

In America the average maize yield is 6,3 metric tons per hectare. The South African maize triangle yields 3,83 to 5,95 metric tons per hectare, depending on regional variations in rainfall.

There are 3,7 million hectares of maize fields in South Africa, but the yield of subsistence farming is low and this reduces the average South African crop to 2,1 metric tons per hectare. Record yields can reach up to 10 metric tons per hectare.

Hybrid seed obtained by carefully controlled cross-pollination is generally used. These hybrids are adapted to suit conditions in specific areas.

Willows brought from the grave of Napoleon

Fick. Settlers in the town were instructed to have in their possession a rifle, 200 bullets, powder and emergency rations. Houses had to be built within six months and each plot had to be protected with walls of sod or stone thick enough to provide security in the event of attack.

To the west, the town is overlooked by the 1 854-metre high Mpharane Mountain. This tree-covered height is now a government forest station. There was originally a Wesleyan Mission Station on its slopes and it is said that the missionaries planted cuttings there from the willows shading the grave of Napoleon on St. Helena Island. Descendants of these willow trees are said to grow in the town. Wild willow trees are common in the area.

Ficksburg, a busy trading centre, is a border gateway to Lesotho. The district produces grain, corn, livestock, dairy products, potatoes, yellow peaches, apricots and plums, and is the largest cherry-producing area in South Africa. The town is noted for its gardens. There are recreational areas at Morgenzon and Meulspruits.

Summer hail-storms are a problem for farmers in the district. Ficksburg is the home for the Farmers' Hail Insurance Co-operative which, with a mem-

A summer thunderstorm casts a brilliant rainbow as the sun emerges.

The Dutch Reformed Church at Ficksburg, with its distinctive clock.

An isolated hillock made of Clarens sandstone, dominating the country near Ficksburg like a giant sentry turned to stone.

Autumn in the eastern Orange Free State. The maize fields and the pasturage are turning golden and soon the trees will lose their leaves.

bership of more that 10 000 farmers, provides compensation for damage caused to farms by these short but destructively violent storms.

Soil conservation and the large-scale production of compost, largely as a result of the pioneer work of J. P. J. van Vuuren of the Department of Agriculture, has made the district of Ficksburg a model farming area despite the ravages of the hailstorms.

There are many examples of San rock art in the caves, and superb views of the Maluti Mountains in Lesotho, which are often covered in snow. On Mpharane Mountain there is a 150-hectare nature reserve. Ficksburg town hall, built in 1895, has in front of it a memorial to Commandant-general Fick. At the foot of this monument lie the remains of the commandant-general and his wife.

Fouriesburg

For a few months during the Anglo-Boer War this little town served as the

Evening near Fouriesburg, with the cloud-covered mountains of Lesotho on the horizon.

The setting sun touches the cliffs with gold

seat of the Orange Free State government. It was founded in 1892 and named after Chistoffel Fourie, who owned the land. The town, surrounded by sandstone hills and with a spectacular view of the mountains of Lesotho, is a centre for farming and trade with Lesotho. The Caledonspoort border post is 9 kilometres to the east.

Frankfort

The Wilge ('willow') River provides boating, swimming and fishing for much of its 250-kilometre length. The town of Frankfort was founded on the banks of the river and had its beginning in the late 1860s. It was apparently named after Frankfurt in Germany by Albert van Gordeon, a member of the first council — but how the 'o'

Sandstone cliffs glow in the afternoon light.

Poplar trees shade a long, lonely rural road.

Autumn comes to the eastern Orange Free State. The long grass, willow trees and poplars change colour from green to gold.

crept in is unknown. This was a church and farming centre, but the recreational potential of the site led to the construction of a large inland holiday resort near the town, with bungalows, caravan and camping sites, and many sporting facilities.

Frankfort is in the heart of the so-called 'maize-triangle' and is surrounded by wide fields of corn (see box, page 301).

Golden Gate Highlands National Park

Water has modelled the Clarens sandstone of the upper valley of the Little Caledon River into spectacular formations — steep cliffs, great caves, rock shelters and many bizarre shapes — and has interacted with iron oxides to produce a brilliant range of yellows, oranges and reds.

A national park was proclaimed in 1963 to conserve 4 792 hectares of this remarkable landscape. In the park is the Golden Gate, a vast cliff face, vividly coloured, which catches the rays of the setting sun. Gladstone's Nose is another unusual cliff formation, and the valley contains many large caves.

Eland, red hartebeest, springbok and black wildebeest live in the valley, as well as many birds, including the huge vultures known as lammergeyers, with wing-spans of nearly 3 metres. There are also black eagles, jackal buzzards, blue cranes, secretary birds, rock pigeons, guineafowl, and many smaller birds and water fowl.

Plant life includes arum lilies, watsonias, fire lilies and red hot pokers. Wild willow trees grow along the banks of the river and provide shady picnic sites.

The National Parks Board has created two rest camps in the park, with chalets, rooms, huts, a caravan park and two restaurants. Walking, climbing, trout fishing and horse riding are favourite pastimes here.

Harrismith

Wool, maize and magnificent scenery make the town of Harrismith a prosperous and attractive centre of the eastern Free State. The town was created in 1849 and named after the British governor, Sir Harry Smith, who rode this way in 1848 to try to persuade

Near Harrismith at night, with a veld fire sweeping through the long dead grass.

Autumn near Harrismith with the poplar trees losing their leaves.

the disgruntled Voortrekkers not to abandon Natal. The town lies at the foot of the 2 396-metre Platberg and has an outlook south towards the mountains of Lesotho and the Drakensberg. The Free State-Natal trunk road and main railway route pass through Harrismith. At Van Reenens Pass, 31 kilometres east of the town, road and railway descend the Drakensberg through two great mountain passes (see Van Reenens Pass, page 387).

Harrismith lies on the Wilge River and a resort area has been created here with a menagerie, bird sanctuary, caravan park and picnic grounds shaded by the many wild willow trees that give the river its name.

The crisp, bracing air of the district is well known. Sheep and horses flourish here. Polo is popular and the district is magnificent riding country.

Every year the Harrismith mountain race is held — one of the foremost cross-country events in southern Africa. The course is rigorous, climbing 609 metres in 5 kilometres to the plateau summit of the Platberg, and from there along the top and down to the town again, following a zigzag bridle path made by the pack animals of the British army during the Anglo-Boer War.

The Platberg is well forested, with

The Elands River near Harrismith surges with flood-water in summer.

The town hall of Harrismith, agricultural and communications centre.

The town that became a capital — for a week

Autumn near Kestell, dominated by mountains.

The historic Dutch Reformed Church at Kestell.

many picnic spots. A road leads to the summit. A blockhouse built on the heights by the British in 1900 is a national monument.

Harrismith is at an important crossroads: a tarred road from the Transvaal joins the trunk road at the town.

The town has a caravan park on the banks of the Wilge river in President Brand Park. Next to the town hall is a petrified tree, 33 metres long and estimated to be 150 million years old. The Sterkfontein Dam, 15 kilometres from the town, is open to anglers and water sport enthusiasts.

Heilbron
A medicinal spring surfaces close to the town of Heilbron ('fountain of blessing'), founded in 1890.

The region produces milk, maize, sorghum, sunflower seeds and wheat. At Uniefees Dam there is a boating, swimming and fishing recreational area with camping and caravan sites.

For one week, in May 1900, Heilbron was the capital of the Orange Free State, when President Marthinus Steyn had his headquarters here.

Hobhouse
Close to the Caledon River border of Lesotho lies the small town of Hobhouse, the centre of a region providing maize, wheat, cheese and livestock. Founded in 1912, Hobhouse was named after the British suffragette, Emily Hobhouse, who worked on behalf of the Boer women and children in British concentration camps during the Anglo-Boer War.

Kestell
Amid the eastern Free State's rolling highland of maize and wheatlands, with its herds of cattle and blesbok, and imposing views of the Maluti and Drakensberg ranges, lies the small town of Kestell.

It was founded in 1905 and named after the Reverend J. D. Kestell, a well-known churchman of this period.

Ladybrand
The situation of Ladybrand is spectacular: the Platberg ('flat mountain') sandstone ridge shelters a basin close to the valley of the Caledon River and the mountains of Lesotho.

Man settled in this basin in ancient times, and it is rich in Stone Age implements and fossils. The sandstone cliffs contain caves and rock shelters renowned for their San rock art. Prehistorians, among them Abbe Breuil, have done much research in this area and the rock paintings have been reproduced in several books. The caves at Rose Cottage, Modderpoort and Tandjiesberg are particularly noted for their rock paintings.

Several gorges provide beauty spots within walking distance of the town. Lilyhoek has been developed into a weekend holiday resort. Nearby is a fissure in the rocks known as The Stables. This great rock shelter was used by the Boers to stable horses during the Basuto War of 1858.

Ladybrand was established in 1867 as one of the towns of the so-called Conquered Territory after the last war with the Sotho. It was named in honour of Lady Catharina Brand, mother of President Johannes Brand of the Orange Free State. Today it is a trading and agricultural centre, and a gateway to Lesotho.

Lindley
The valley of the Vaal River is the setting for the town of Lindley, founded in 1875 and named after an American missionary, Daniel Lindley. A weir had been built across the river and this holds back a 5-kilometre stretch of deep water ideal for fishing, boating and swimming.

Willows line the banks; after the Anglo-Boer War a local resident, John Collister-Oats, led a campaign during which many thousands of trees were planted in the valley.

Lindley is a centre for dairy products and the site of a powdered milk factory. It is also a popular inland holiday resort, with a caravan park beneath trees on the riverbanks.

Marquard
After several abortive attempts to establish a town in this prosperous farming region east of Winburg, the farmers secured the support of the Reverend J. J. Marquard, the Dutch Reformed Church minister of Winburg. His influence led to the establishment of the town in 1905.

The Tandjiesberg ('mountain of teeth') near Harrismith.

General C. R. de Wet, one of the best-known former residents of Memel.

Memel

The north-eastern Free State is a richly grassed landscape of undulating slopes and occasional high koppies. Close to the edge of the central plains is one well-watered basin where grass grows so tall and thick that in 1890 a traveller reported that a span of oxen was invisible from 20 metres away.

Several passes lead down to Natal from this part of the highveld. Botha's Pass and Muller's Pass, both named after farmers, Rudolf Botha and Joel Muller, were regularly used after the Anglo-Boer War, and a small settlement grew around a blacksmith's shop and a store in the grassy basin.

In 1911 the Memel Township Promotion Society was formed, headed by General Christiaan De Wet. A town was established and given the Prussian name of Memel ('surrounded by water'). The town has known some excitement in the past — in 1914 General De Wet, living on his farm Allanvale in the area, planned the abortive rebellion against the British and South African governments.

Paul Roux

The upper valley of the Sand River is noted for the handsome colouring of the sandstone cliffs. The town founded here in 1909, named after the Reverend Paul Roux of the Dutch Reformed Church, has many buildings constructed from this distinctive sandstone.

Dinosaur footprints can be inspected on a farm 10 kilometres from the town. An interesting collection of semi-precious stones from all over the world can be seen in the grounds of the Dutch Reformed Church. Among local products is poplar wood, used to make safety matches.

Reitz

In the 'maize triangle' of the northern Free State (see box, page 301) the town of Reitz is the centre for one of the largest co-operative agricultural societies in South Africa. A grain elevator dominates the place and Reitz is a prosperous example of a 'corn town'.

The town was founded in 1889 and named after Frederick Reitz, who was then president of the Orange Free State. It is noted for its attractive parks and gardens.

Rouxville

Wool, prizewinning cattle and several studs of saddle horses, famous for their five different gaits, are the pride of the Rouxville district. The town was founded in 1863 and named after the Reverend Paul Roux, who for ten years used to ride around the eastern Free State to conduct services.

Smithfield

The rural centre of Smithfield is the fourth oldest town in the Orange Free State (after Winburg, Bloemfontein and Philippolis). It was founded in 1848 and named after the bluff Sir Harry Smith, governor of the Cape. Sheep and cattle are among the products of this prosperous district.

In the vicinity is a farm established in 1828 by French missionaries and named Beersheba. The missionaries left in 1856 and since then the Swanepoel family has owned the property, living in the homestead built by the missionaries. The building has 18 rooms, passages 3 metres wide, linenfold ceilings of wood and walls nearly a metre thick.

An odd relic in the town is a former ship's gun named Ou Grietjie ('Old Margaret'). The origin of the gun is unknown, but it was carried about the plains for many years and used in various wars against the Sotho, and even as a threat against the Transvaal (when two unsuccessful attempts were made to fire the gun). In 1860 the weapon was brought to Smithfield. Prince Al-

The strange rock cavern known as 'The Stables', overlooking Ladybrand.

An odd rock formation on the Orange Free State side of the Caledon River.

Ladybrand, principal town of the so-called Conquered Territory.

A picturesque farm near Ladybrand in the valley of the Caledon River.

The sandstone hill that is 'whiter than white'

bert, son of Queen Victoria, visited the town, and at the official welcome the gun was loaded by two veterans and the wick ignited, but again the gun did not fire. The expectant crowd grew restless, the two gunners peered down the barrel — and promptly had their heads blown off.

The gun was last used in 1868 to bombard Thaba-Bosiu during the final Basuto War.

Thaba Nchu

The landmark known to the Sotho as Thaba Ntsho ('black mountain') looms over the central plains 64 kilometres east of Bloemfontein. Thaba Ntsho was the stronghold of the Morolong, whose chief Moroko was an ally of the Voortrekkers. His grave is a historical monument.

The mountain was called Thaba Nchu by Europeans and a town of the same name was founded at its foot in 1873. It is the trading and administrative centre for a large Tswana population.

Vegkop

On 15 October 1836 an Ndebele army looking for possible plunder on the central plains found a Voortrekker laager of 50 wagons drawn up below the edge of a flat-topped ridge.

There were only 35 men in the laager, but around it was a concentration of livestock.

The Ndebele attacked, throwing 1 137 spears into the laager. They killed two of the defenders and wounded 14, but lost 155 of their own men. Loot, however, was what the raiders were after, and when their commander Mkhaliphi realized that his men could not overrun the laager, he withdrew, taking booty of 50 000

sheep, 5 000 cattle and 100 horses.

Without their horses the Voortrekkers were unable to pursue the raiders.

Although the Ndebele escaped with their loot, success was to prove their undoing. In order to recover their livestock the Voortrekkers organized a strong punitive force, and three months later they raided the Ndebele stronghold of Mosega, decisively defeated the defenders, and recovered many of the stolen animals.

The ridge overlooking the site of the struggle is known as Vegkop ('battle peak'). In former years this ridge was a Sotho stronghold, and its summit is littered with the ruins of stone huts, kraals and walls. The site of the laager is marked by a memorial, a camping ground and a small museum, as well as various buildings used for an annual religious gathering held here in memory of the Voortrekkers.

Villiers

The town of Villiers was established in 1891 at the point where the main road from the Transvaal to Harrismith crosses the Vaal river into the Orange Free State. It was named after Lourens de Villiers, who owned the land. The district produces maize and cattle.

A boating, swimming and fishing recreational area has been created on the southern bank of the Vaal, with bungalows and a caravan park.

To the west of the town, 34,5 kilometres away, lies the J. J. Fouché inland holiday resort maintained on the banks of the Vaal Dam by the Provincial Council of the Orange Free State. Named after President J. J. Fouché of the Republic of South Africa, this resort offers boating, swimming, and fishing for yellowfish, carp and barbel. Horses can be hired, and birdwatchers have a prolific field of study in the countless aquatic birds. There are rondavels, a caravan park and a camping ground.

Wepener

Lying close to the border of Lesotho, the district of Wepener has been the scene of many fights, raids and stock thefts. Numerous graves, mainly without identification, are reminders of stormy events from the past. During the Anglo-Boer War a British garrison of 2 000 men under Colonel

The town of Villiers on the willow-lined banks of the Vaal River.

E. H. Dalgety was attacked by General Christiaan De Wet at Jammerdrif on the Caledon River. British reinforcements which were rushed to the scene brought an end to the struggle.

The town was founded in 1867 and named in honour of Louwrens Wepener, who was killed in 1865 while trying to storm Thaba-Bosiu, in Lesotho. Wepener lies in the valley of the Jammersbergspruit, and it is an attractive little frontier town. Building sand, wool, grain, corn and livestock are produced in the district.

On the farm Welbedacht, 32 kilometres south-west of the town, a

dam has been built, storing 110 million cubic metres of water from the Caledon River. This dam supplies drinking water to Bloemfontein and many other towns.

Witsieshoek

In the 1830s a group of Kglolokwa people under a chief named Whêtse fled from Zulu raiding bands and sought safety in a rugged glen where the Elands River — after tumbling off the summit of Mont-aux-Sources — finds its way through the sandstone foothills of the Maluti Mountains. In this wild glen, after the Zulu raids had

The Caledon River at Jammerdrif, scene of a battle in the Anglo-Boer War.

stopped, Whêtse (or Witsie) and his men set themselves up as cattle rustlers. They were so proficient that in 1856 a commando was mustered by the farmers of the Orange Free State to flush them out.

Whêtse and his band retreated to a cave, where the commando besieged them. The rustlers were defeated but Whêtse escaped through a secret tunnel and fled deep into the mountains of Lesotho. The government of the Orange Free State kept careful control of the glen, which from that time was known as Witsieshoek.

Friendly Kwena and Tlokwa people were settled in the area and in 1874 a mission station of the Dutch Reformed Church was established. Today there is also a theological school and the Elizabeth Ross Hospital, named after a missionary's wife.

From 1969 to 1994 the area of Witsieshoek was self-governing as the homeland of the baSotho ba Borwa ('Sotho people of the south'). The area was named QwaQwa ('whiter than white') from a sandstone hill that dominates it.

Wepener town hall and the monument to Louwrens Wepener, killed by the Sotho.

A road leads up the glen and the scenery is magnificent. In 1972, as part of the economic development of the area, a holiday resort was built high on the Drakensberg close to Sentinel Peak. The resort is at an altitude of 2 680 metres and from it a bridle path leads to climbing routes to the top of the Sentinel, and to a series of chain-aided ascents to the top of Mont-aux-Sources.

There are chalets, luxury rooms and a licensed restaurant.

Zastron

Throughout the south-eastern Orange Free State rocky hillocks and isolated mountains in a variety of shapes loom from the grassy plains. To the east, beyond the Caledon River, lie the mountains of Lesotho. The San people loved this area and there are specimens of their rock paintings and engravings in many of the caves and rock shelters.

In this setting the town of Zastron was founded in 1876, taking the maiden name of the wife of President Johannes Brand, Johanna Sibilla Zastron.

Cattle, maize and wheat make the district prosperous.

On the western side of the town lies Eeufeeskloof, with a road leading to viewing sites, a dam, and a caravan and camping ground.

Zastron was laid out on the farm Verliesfontein, owned by Jan du Wennaar. Living with Du Wennaar was his brother, Renier, one of the drollest characters of the day and a master story-teller (see box, page 308). His grave is in the cemetery at the foot of Eeufeeskloof, and on the tombstone is the date of his birth — 15 September 1781 — and his death 10 September 1883. In his 102 years he spun so many yarns about his adventures and misadventures that he became a legend. His fanciful stories are mainly concerned with his brushes with the devil and other supernatural characters such as the Donderkoppe ('thunderheads'). With his faithful San companion, known as Boesman, Renier invariably got the better of his adversaries by resorting to all manner of ingenious tricks.

The famed 'Eye' of Zastron, a hole 9 metres in diameter, is in a cliff on the slopes of the nearby Aasvoëlberg.

The Sentinel Peak, as seen near Witsieshoek Mountain Resort.

The Aasvoëlberg, with a hole said to have been made by the devil.

The Clarens sandstone foothills of the Drakensberg as seen from Witsieshoek.

309

The heroic adventures of the indomitable Voortrekkers

If everybody in South Africa returned to the country of their ancestors, there would be nobody left at home. The diverse immigrant population is astonishing, and any map depicting the mass movements of people during the first quarter of the 19th century resembles a chart showing the counter movements of ocean currents, or currents of air. At this time, three principal flows of human migration took place in the country: black people moved down the east coast; white settlers travelled north and north-eastwards over the central plains; and Khoikhoi, trapped between the two main streams of immigrants, were either absorbed by them or streamed north-westwards to the sanctuary of the arid areas that nobody else wanted.

The sub-continent was in disarray. In the Cape colony, white immigrants moving north confronted black immigrants moving south.

Only the Great Fish River separated them. The political confusion was vast. Some peoples, such as the Zulu, were aggressively building an empire; other empire-builders were more hesitant. The British were increasing their empire rather reluctantly, and like a mother hen trying to control her unruly chicks, constantly reclaiming wayward members of the brood who defied maternal discipline.

Border friction between black and white was incessant. Successive governors of the Cape floundered in a mire of contradictory instructions sent to them by political leaders in England who were constantly changing their minds, influenced by advice that was confused and frequently out of date by the time it was given.

The ending of slavery had left a guilt complex in people who had only recently been among the principal slave dealers of the world. The cult of the noble savage became fashionable and frontiersmen found themselves regarded as aggressors — even when they defended themselves against attack.

Dutch frontiersmen of the Cape colony had little cause for loyalty to the British and became increasingly restless. There was talk in the farmhouses of moving northwards to the central plains, where there were vast areas of land supposedly wide open for settlement.

In 1835 two parties of Voortrekkers ('pioneers'), led by Louis Trichardt and Johannes van Rensburg, made their way to the far north of the Transvaal. Van Rensburg's group was wiped out by Shanganes on the border of Mocambique; Trichardt's party mostly died of fever at Lourenco Marques (Maputo).

Behind these advance parties, however, many other individuals and groups followed. They found the central plains between the Orange and Vaal rivers to be uninhabited; only in the east were there a few residents —

A Voortrekker wagon crossing a stream in the foothills of the Drakensberg.

Sotho who had been protected by mountains from Zulu and Ndebele raids. Across the Vaal River, however, the Ndebele were based at Gabeni in the valley of the Marico River and posed a threat to settlement in the north.

There were clashes between the Voortrekkers and the Ndebele at several places along the Vaal River, and at Vegkop on the Free State plains. The main body of Voortrekkers was congregating around the great landmark of Thaba Nchu ('black mountain'), where there was a Wesleyan mission station serving the Morolong people of chief Moroka.

This group had welcomed the Voortrekkers as allies against the raiding bands who had created havoc on the central plains.

There was abundant vacant land, and the majority of Voortrekkers had almost decided to settle in the area. They elected a volksraad ('people's council') headed by Gert Maritz, with Andries Hendrik Potgieter as military commander.

Potgieter's first task was to bring retribution to the Ndebele for their attacks on Voortrekker camps and to recapture stolen livestock. He led his men to the attack in January 1837, and caught the Ndebele by surprise. They

scattered in the bush, but the Voortrekkers recovered many of their cattle.

Shortly after the Voortrekkers' attack the Ndebele were raided by a Zulu army and suffered heavy losses. Finally, in May 1842, the Voortrekkers returned and drove the Ndebele out of the Transvaal and across the Limpopo.

The departure of the Ndebele placed the Transvaal in the hands of the Voortrekkers, but they were divided about how to determine their future. Potgieter had set his heart on settling in the Transvaal; others wanted to stay on the central plains. Another renowned Voortrekker leader, Piet Retief, was enthusiastic about Natal, and a majority of Voortrekkers supported him.

A party of Cape farmers led by Piet Uys had explored Natal in 1834 and found that the Zulu had ceded land lying south of the Zulu boundary of the Tugela River to the traders of Port Natal. The traders had assured the visitors that they would be welcome to settle. Shaka had been assassinated and his half-brother, Dingane, seemed to be a peaceful man who did not resent the presence of Europeans.

Some Voortrekkers doubted whether it would be possible to cross the Drakensberg into Natal. This doubt was dispelled when Retief sent five scouts to explore the escarpment. After 24 days they returned, having found five passes used since time immemorial by herds of antelope migrating each winter from the highveld to the warmth of Natal.

Retief led 54 wagons eastwards. On 21 October 1837 they reached an imposing, flat-topped sandstone hill which they named Kerkenberg ('church mountain'). Retief left the bulk of his party encamped at the foot of this great landmark. Then, with fourteen men and four wagons, he continued eastwards on a mission to Dingane, to negotiate land rights for the Voortrekkers.

Sarel Cilliers, one of the dominant spiritual leaders of the Great Trek.

Piet Retief, the ill-fated leader who took the Voortrekkers into Natal.

Fifteen kilometres from Kerkenberg Retief reached a point ever afterwards known as Blijde Vooruitzicht ('joyful prospect'). Below it lay Natal, and Retief noted in his diary: 'From the heights of these mountains I saw this beautiful land, the most beautiful I've ever seen in Africa.'

He made his way down an easy pass known as the Step Pass, and without incident, but with great exhilaration, he and his party reached the settlement of ivory traders at Port Natal. Here they received a hearty welcome. They hunted hippos in the bay, fished, and were shown the crops and wild fruits in the area.

The traders assured the trekkers that both Shaka and Dingane had ceded the land known as Natal to them, and they welcomed the idea of more Europeans. All Retief needed to do was pay a courtesy visit to Dingane and assure him of their peaceful intentions.

Retief sent two of his men posthaste back to the camp at Kerkenberg, carrying samples of the luscious fruit of Natal and a letter telling the Voortrekkers that Natal was open to them. There was wild excitement when this news was received on 11 November 1837.

The next day was Sunday. The Voortrekkers spent it in giving thanks and preparing to descend the escarpment. The day was also the 57th birthday of Retief, and his 22-year-old daughter, Deborah, painted his name in green on the face of a huge boulder. This historical piece of graffiti can still be seen today.

The next day the wagons moved to the edge of the escarpment. The Voortrekkers spent their last night on the Free State plains. At dawn on 14 November one of the greatest events in the history of southern Africa began. One wagon after another made its way down 1 000 metres of escarpment to Natal. It was a surge of joyful movement.

On 27 November Retief rejoined the Voortrekkers at the foot of the escarpment. He had visited Dingane and had told the Zulu king of the Voortrekkers' desire to settle in Natal, and Dingane had asked him to prove his friendly intentions by recovering some livestock stolen by Tlokwa raid-

Dominating the high plains of the eastern Orange Free State, the sandstone pile known as Kerkenberg, or Church Mountain.

ers under chief Sikonyela, who lived in the valley of the Caledon River. These people had masqueraded as Voortrekkers when they stole the cattle, and Dingane wanted Retief to furnish proof that the trekkers were in fact innocent. The king sent some of his advisers with Retief to investigate. When the issue was settled, Retief would be allowed to visit the Zulu king again and discuss settlement in Natal.

Sikonyela was arrested and admitted his guilt, surrendering 700 head of cattle, 63 horses and 11 guns. Retief immediately set out with the recovered loot for the Zulu capital of Mgungundlovu taking 69 of his men,

a few youths and 30 herdsmen to drive the cattle. Behind him, more than 1 000 wagons had already crossed the escarpment to Natal, and the trekkers were happily selecting potential sites for their farms.

Retief's party reached Mgungundlovu on 3 February 1838 and received a hearty welcome. They were told that the full Zulu army had been mustered to stage a dance in their honour.

Dingane and his advisers had argued at great length over the coming of the Voortrekkers. The army commanders judged the Voortrekkers to be dangerous and their settlement on the borders of Zululand undesirable.

On 4 February Dingane gave Retief

a witnessed document ceding to him all the land between the Tugela and Mzimvubu rivers, including territory belonging to independent groups such as the Pondo, and that long ceded to the traders of Port Natal.

Two days later there was a farewell dance. At his seat by the side of Dingane, Retief was disturbed by the brutal power of the drums and thudding on the ground.

'What is that?' he asked Dingane.

The king smiled.

'My regiment of wildebeeste dancing', he replied, handing over another pot of beer.

Suddenly, the pretence was dropped. Dingane leaped to his feet

The rock shelter where Deborah Retief painted her father's initials.

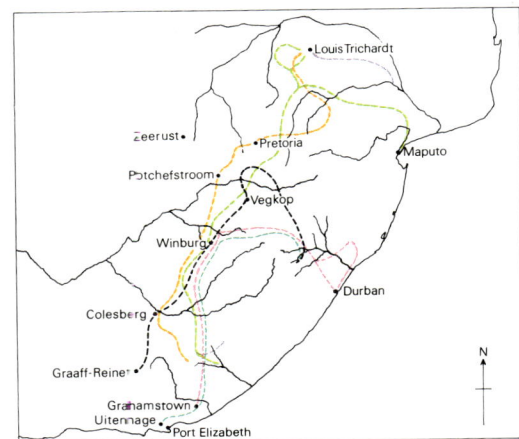

The routes followed by the principal groups of Voortrekkers, who left the frontier areas of the Cape colony in the 1820s and resettled in the interior of southern Africa.

and shouted, 'Bambani aba Thakath' ('Kill the wizards').

The astonished Voortrekkers were powerless. Their weapons had been left at the entrance to the kraal, proving their peaceful intentions. They were overwhelmed and dragged away to be butchered on a hill outside the kraal.

After the massacre the Zulu army prayed at the ancestral graves and then set out to surprise the unsuspecting Voortrekkers descending the escarpment.

At 01h00 on 17 February the Zulu army reached the first encampment of the Voortrekkers on the Bushman's River near Weenen. One Voortrekker camp after another was overwhelmed. Bloukrans, Moordplaas and Rensburgspruit were all scenes of bitter fighting. By dawn 41 Voortrekker men, 56 women, 185 children and 250 servants had died. About 500 Zulus had also perished.

There was total confusion in the rear camps of the Voortrekkers. Only on the following day did they receive news of the fate of Retief and his party. One of the traders of Durban, Dick King, reached them after a hasty journey from the coast (see box, page 323). The traders had had news of the killings and King had come to warn the trekkers — a day too late. The Voortrekkers reorganized themselves as quickly as possible, forming a strong laager and marshalling a punitive force to pursue the Zulus.

The death of Retief had left the trekkers without a dominant leader. Maritz was sickly, Uys and Potgieter were feuding with each other and only agreed to participate in the punitive expedition at the head of their own followers. This split the Voortrekkers in half and resulted in another disaster.

The Voortrekker force of 350 mounted men encountered the Zulu army of about 6 500 warriors on the slopes of the hill known as Itala, a few kilometres west of Umgungundlovu. Attacking in two separate sections, the Voortrekkers killed about 650 Zulus, losing only 10 of their own men, but they were forced to retreat. Among the trekkers killed were Piet Uys and his 14-year-old son, Dirk, who bravely

refused to leave the side of his dying father.

The British traders of Durban had also gathered to attack the Zulus. They raided into the Tugela valley and found the Zulu men absent — fighting the Voortrekkers. The traders seized more than 4 000 head of cattle and about 500 Zulu women and children as hostages, and then returned to Durban.

A party of 17 traders and 800 natives set out on a second attack against the Zulus. They crossed the Tugela and reached a kraal named Ndondakusuka. They destroyed the kraal, but were attacked by a Zulu force of about 7 000 men. Thirteen of the traders and 600 of their followers were killed. The surviving four traders fled to Durban, where they sought refuge on Salisbury Island while a Zulu army ransacked the entire area, burning down all the houses of the infant city of Durban.

The Voortrekkers and the traders were left to review their position. The Voortrekkers organized two large fortified camps — Maritzlaager, on the upper Tugela River, and Gatslaager, on the upper Bushman's River. In these strongholds they concentrated 640 men, 3 200 women and children, 1 260 servants, 300 000 sheep, 40 000 head of cattle and 3 000 horses.

The Zulus made no move until August 1838, when they suddenly appeared at the Gatslaager and killed one of the trekkers. Surrounding the camp, they rounded up a booty of livestock. They spent a night feasting and dancing, collected more livestock the next day, and after hurling spears wrapped in blazing grass at the wagons, withdrew, leaving the trekkers dejected and despondent.

Many thought of returning to the safety of the central plains. To add to their dismay, Maritz died on 23 September, and as Potgieter had already left for the Transvaal, these trekkers in Natal were again without a leader.

At this low point in their fortunes, a big, cheerful, charismatic man, Andries Pretorius, rode to their aid with 60 followers and a bronze cannon. He was from the Graaff-Reinet district of the Cape — a successful farmer who had no desire to trek until he heard of

Louis Trichardt, who led the trek to the Transvaal and Lourenco Marques.

the disaster that had occurred to Retief. He then decided to trek to the aid of his distressed fellows.

Pretorius was a godsend. He plunged into organizing everything and was soon acknowledged as the Commandant-general of the Voortrekkers. By December 1838 he had the Voortrekkers ready for an offensive against the Zulus. Most of the surviving traders from Port Natal, led by Alexander Biggar, came up to join him, and a combined force of 464 men

set out in search of the Zulus.

Pretorius and Sarel Cilliers, the principal spiritual leader of the Voortrekkers, discussed their prospects on many occasions. The trekkers felt that, provided God was on their side, victory was assured.

On 9 December 1838, near the site of the present town of Wasbank, the men rallied around a gun carriage. Cilliers gave an inspiring address, in the course of which he made a promise to God that if He granted them victory, the Voortrekkers and their descendants would hold the day sacred for all time as a time of thanksgiving. This is the origin of the Day of the Covenant.

Pretorius and his men set off. There were few incidents. While crossing a range of high hills, the cart driven by Biggar tipped onto its side in a bog and, half-jocularly, the range was named the Biggarsberg — his name was but a slight corruption of the word he repeatedly used at the mishap.

On 15 December the army reached a river called by the Zulus the *Ncome* ('praiseworthy'), because of its perennial water and green banks. The Voortrekker scouts had reported signs of the presence of a Zulu army nearby, and Pretorius sought a secure camp. He found a site on a tongue of land bordered by the river and a steep-sided watercourse.

Here the trekkers marshalled their

A reconstruction in the Voortrekker Monument Museum of a pioneer-type of kitchen. The floor is made of cow dung strengthened with peach stones. The ceiling is made of reeds bound with thongs. The walls are of dried mud or clods. The roof is thatched. There are cooking utensils and various other items.

wagons in a triangular laager, with wheels linked by skins, ladders and other obstructions.

It seemed too good to be true that the Zulus would attack so formidable a camp, and what made them do so will never be known. But, at dawn on 16 December, about 12 000 warriors tried repeatedly to take the camp by storm.

Ndlela lost 3 000 men before his ranks fell back. The water was red with blood — hence the name Blood River.

Only four trekkers had been wounded, including Pretorius, who was stabbed in the hand. The Voortrekkers were jubilant and the night was spent in thanksgiving, hymn singing and excited discussion.

The next day the Voortrekkers set out for Dingane's capital. They reached it on 20 December and found the city of 2 000 huts deserted and in flames. There was no sign of the defeated Zulu army. The trekkers searched the area, and found the mutilated bodies of their friends. In Retief's shoulder bag they found the treaty ceding the land of Natal to the trekkers.

They buried the corpses, then set off to find Dingane, the Zulus and the stolen livestock. They immediately fell into a trap. They encountered a Zulu, Bongoza, who had been left as a decoy. He offered to guide them to their cattle in the dense bush of the White Mfolozi River. Pretorius was hesitant, but there was no sign of the Zulu army and vast numbers of cattle

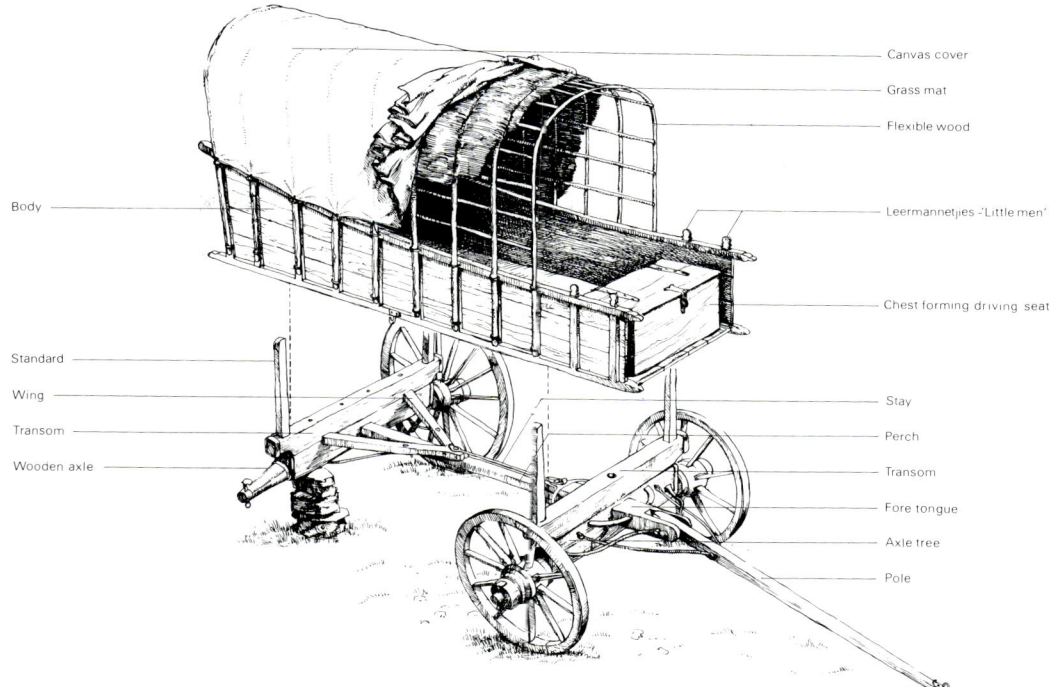

A *Voortrekker wagon, simple in design, extremely tough, easy to repair and maintain in service.*

could be seen in the deep valley.

At dawn on 27 December, 300 Voortrekkers commanded by Carl Landman, and 75 men from Natal led by Alexander Biggar, rode down into the valley. Pretorius and 160 men remained in camp.

The Voortrekkers who were following Bongoza suddenly found themselves alone. Bongoza had vanished, but dense masses of Zulu warriors materialized on all sides, blocking the route back to camp.

The Zulus had expected the Voortrekkers to fight their way back to camp. Instead, they raced down the valley, forded the river, and made their way up the other side of the val-

ley. Six Europeans including Alexander Biggar, and 70 of Biggar's followers, were killed by the Zulus. The remainder returned to camp.

Three days later they set out for home without sighting the Zulus again. They had retrieved 5 000 head of their stolen cattle — the rest had vanished. Nonetheless, the power of the Zulu army had been all but broken, and the Voortrekkers began to establish towns in Natal.

The ultimate reckoning with Dingane came in January 1840. A younger half-brother of Dingane, Mpande, had fled Zululand after a quarrel. He became an ally of the Voortrekkers and the leader of Zulu refugees in Natal.

The trekkers decided to support him in a bid to displace Dingane, who had fled to the north of his kingdom and built a new capital. Pretorius, Mpande and their followers invaded Zululand. On 30 January Mpande's followers clashed with Dingane's men on a high ridge overlooking the Mkuze River. Dingane's men were winning when news spread of the impending arrival of the Voortrekkers. His men fled, and he made his way to the summit of the Lebombo mountain range, hoping to find sanctuary. Instead he was assassinated by the local Nyawo people.

Mpande became king of the Zulus, a friend and ally of the Voortrekkers — and peace returned to Zululand.

The site of the Battle of Blood River is marked by a laager of replica wagons.

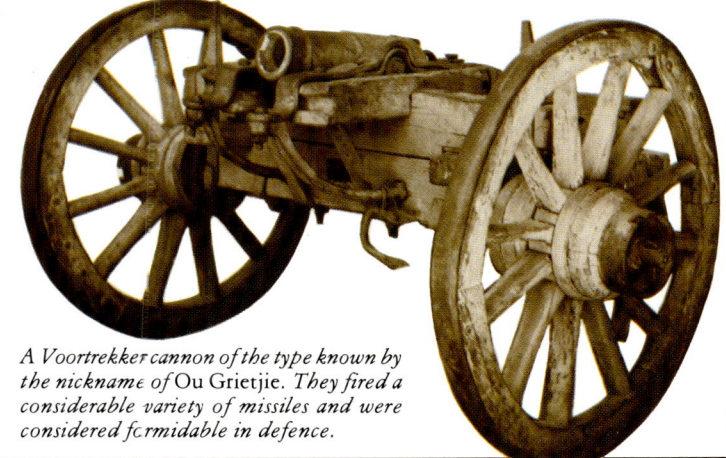

A Voortrekker cannon of the type known by the nickname of Ou Grietjie. They fired a considerable variety of missiles and were considered formidable in defence.

NATAL

NATAL

Contents:

Preceding page: The main wall of the Drakensberg as seen from Basuto Gate. The Amphitheatre is on the right. On the extreme left is Cathedral Peak and The Bell. The higher cliffs are basalt, the lower slopes sandstone.

KWAZULU/NATAL has long been described as the 'garden province' of South Africa. The sub-tropical luxuriance of its coastal vegetation and river valleys, the rich sweet-grass grazing of the midlands, the foothills and heights of the Drakensberg — home of many ferns and flowering plants — provide the province with an extremely varied vegetation.

Well watered over most of its area of 86 967 square kilometres, this was the smallest of the original four provinces of South Africa, but nevertheless supports a dense population of many forms of life. In past years the midlands offered grazing for great herds of gnu, zebra, blesbok, hartebeest, eland and other antelope. Some of these were permanent residents; others migrated from winter frosts on the central plains of the highveld in the Orange Free State and Transvaal, and then returned in the spring to feed on the first shoots of the young green grass. These mass movements of game animals blazed the first paths over the escarpment and opened up the passes through the Drakensberg.

The eastern regions of the province, especially that portion formerly designated KwaZulu, are covered with typical African savannah. This region is warm to hot, and blanketed with tall grass and thorn trees.

Hunters once considered this to be one of the most productive hunting areas in Africa, with its elephant, rhino, lion, cheetah, wild dog and other predators, and antelope herds prolific both in their size and their variety. Four game reserves preserve something of this glamorous world of big game.

The coastline of KwaZulu/Natal is lined with high forest, sandy beaches and lagoons at the mouths of scores of rivers. Down this coast flows the warm water of the Mozambique Current. The atmosphere is languid and humid, the Indian Ocean blue and clear.

San hunters were among the earliest human beings to explore this countryside. In the rolling valleys of the Drakensberg foothills they found caves and rock overhangs in which to shelter. Crystal-clear streams provided drinking water, copses of trees provided firewood, and the antelope and other game animals were fat and numerous.

The black people who migrated here from central Africa during medieval times also found the vegetation and climate ideally suited to their pastoral existence. They settled here, ejected the San, and then started to fight one another for the choicest areas. The undulating ocean of hills and valleys of the northern region, and the downlands of the south and midlands became a paradise buried under a hell of intergroup warfare.

Here the Zulus became the most formidable military power ever to grow from any early African people. Battles and wars stained the rich soil with blood, and many a maize field of today has been fertilized by the charred ruins of destroyed huts and the calcium of human bones.

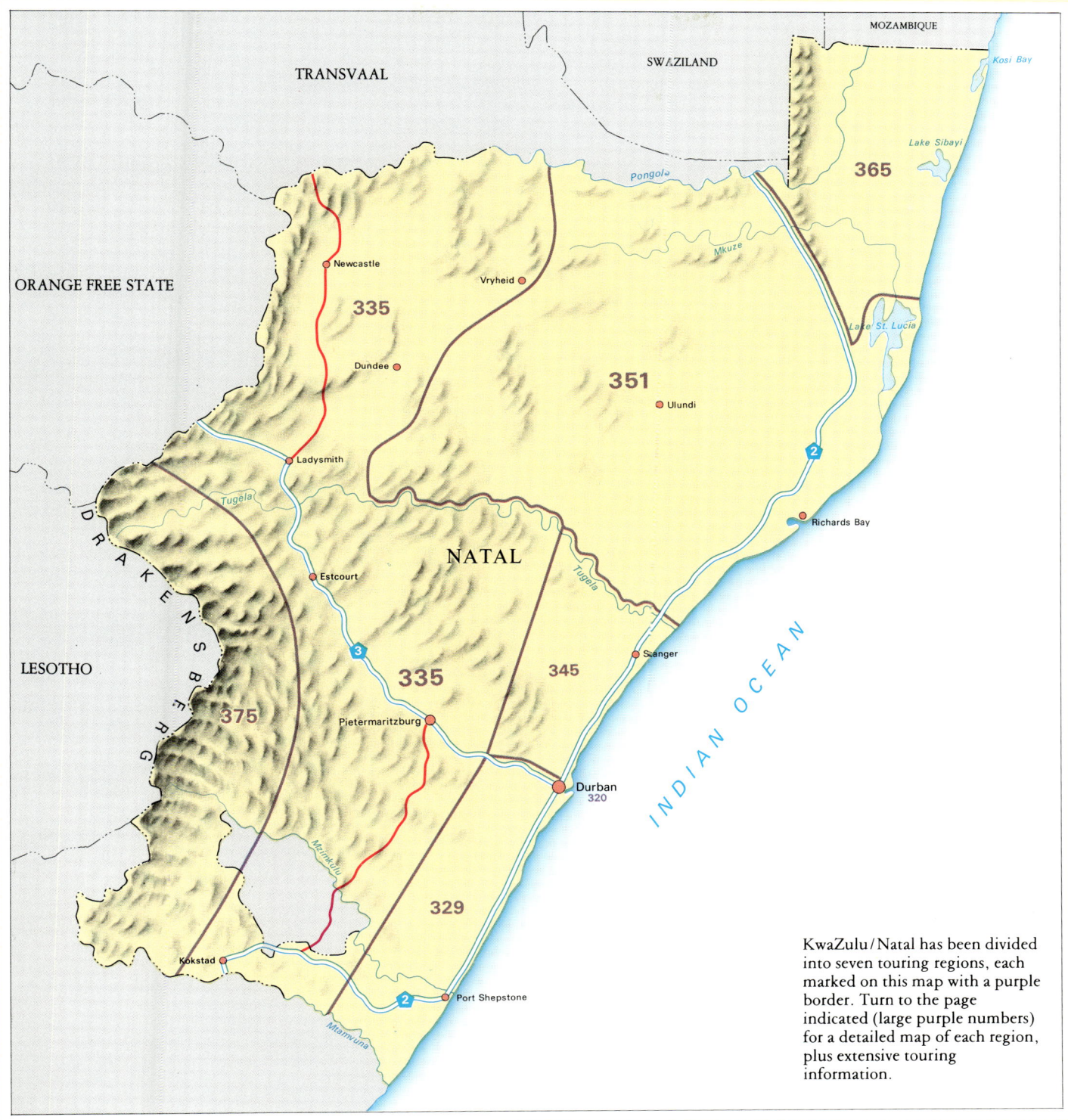

TRANSVAAL

SWAZILAND

MOZAMBIQUE

Kosi Bay

Lake Sibayi

ORANGE FREE STATE

Pongola

365

Mkuze

Newcastle

Vryheid

335

Lake St. Lucia

Dundee

351

Ulundi

Ladysmith

2

Tugela

Richards Bay

LESOTHO

Estcourt

NATAL

Tugela

D R A K E N S B E R G

3

335

345

S. anger

375

Pietermaritzburg

I N D I A N   O C E A N

Mzimkulu

Durban
320

329

Kokstad

2

Port Shepstone

Mtamvuna

KwaZulu/Natal has been divided
into seven touring regions, each
marked on this map with a purple
border. Turn to the page
indicated (large purple numbers)
for a detailed map of each region,
plus extensive touring
information.

THE PLEASURE-SEEKER'S CITY

THE GREAT NATURAL harbour of Port Natal, on whose shores the city of Durban now stands, was presumed by the Portuguese navigators of the 15th century to be a lagoon at the mouth of a large river which flowed down from the interior. They called the harbour Rio de Natal ('Christmas river') for it lay on the coast discovered on Christmas Day 1497 by Vasco da Gama.

The entrance was narrow and shallow but, once inside, a ship could anchor in safety. A number of minor streams flowed into a land-locked bay.

Dense coastal forest surrounded the bay, with mangrove swamps growing on the mud banks and over a small island in its centre. Hippos, pelicans and other birds lived in and on the water, and elephants and other big game wandered through the dark forests along the shore.

Pirates and slave traders, merchants and shipwrecked crews, all landed on the shores of Port Natal in search of food, water, trade or sanctuary. A few stayed. One colourful character, a penitent pirate, lived as a recluse here at the end of the 17th century, and at different times several renegades used the place as a hideaway.

In November 1823 a party of traders from the Cape found their way here and liked it so much that the next year they returned. Led by Henry Francis Fynn, they built a settlement in the bush where the old railway station now stands. It was the beginning of the city which, 11 years afterwards, on 23 June 1835, was named in honour of Sir Benjamin D'Urban, the governor of the Cape.

The settlement in these days was a primitive little place that grew without any support from the British government, which officially disowned it. It lacked planning and administration. Individuals cut clearings in the bush and built rough shacks and store-rooms for their trade goods and ivory. Refugees from wars all over Natal found sanctuary here, attaching themselves to different traders or hunters, until each settler ended up with a considerable band of followers.

Life was always precarious; the boundaries of the Zulu country were less than 100 kilometres to the north and the Zulus regarded all Natal as their raiding ground. The settlement at Port Natal was tolerated by the Zulus simply because they found it convenient to trade there. The land was ceded to the traders but a Zulu garrison was established nearby in a military stronghold pointedly named uKangel' amaNkengana ('watch the vagabonds'). The traders lived with the uneasy feeling of being watched.

The Voortrekkers arrived in 1838. The traders welcomed these people of their own kind, and after the massacres at Mgungundlovu and Weenen (see feature, pages 310-313) the traders took up arms against the Zulus. Sixteen traders and about 600 of their African followers died in a clash with the Zulus on 17 April 1838 at Ndondakusuka. The rest either fled from Durban or took refuge on an islet in the harbour (Salisbury Island), where the Zulus, who had no boats, could not follow them.

News of these disturbances at last brought the British government to Port Natal. On 3 December 1838 a British force landed at the harbour and found about 25 Voortrekkers and a few traders living there; the traders who had not fled had joined the Voortrekkers and had fought against the Zulus in the Battle of Blood River on 16 December 1838 in retribution for the massacres.

When the area had settled down the British withdrew their force, but renewed disturbances brought them back again in May 1842, and this time they built what is known as the Old Fort. It was this fort that the Voortrekkers besieged for 34 days, and from where Dick King set out on his celebrated 1 000-kilometre ride, reaching Grahamstown in ten days with a plea for reinforcements (see box, page 323). The fort was relieved on 26 June 1842.

After some indecision on the part of the British, they eventually annexed Natal to the Cape Colony in 1844. The Voortrekkers withdrew from the area and returned to the Transvaal and Orange Free State. Natal was open to British settlers and free to develop into a separate colony — and ultimately a province of South Africa.

From its romantic beginning Durban grew to become a municipality in 1854 and a city in 1935. It is one of the principal cargo ports on the continent of Africa, a centre of industry, and a major holiday resort. It is a bustling, sub-tropical city, with a warm, sometimes hot and sultry climate, abundant trees and luxuriant gardens.

Beachfront

The beachfront of Durban is a pleasure-seeker's paradise. An imposing line of hotels stands on the western side of the Marine Parade. East of this road is a 3-kilometre strip where the visitor to the city can find amusement parks, an aquarium, a mini-town, an aerial cableway, a snake park, bowling greens, children's pools, a swimming bath, a sunken garden, as well as several tea-rooms and fair-ground rides.

The fun strip is separated from the beach by the Lower Marine Parade. The sands run into the warm waters of the Indian Ocean, and three fishing piers project seawards, seeming never to lack fishermen — night or day, storm or shine.

At the Durban Aquarium and Dolphinarium, turtles, sharks, marine shells, crayfish, octopus, corals, seals and dolphins are displayed in large tanks. Spectators look in through glass observation portholes. At meal times scuba divers in the tanks feed many of the fish by hand.

Minitown is a miniature town with 1/24th-scale reproductions of South African buildings. There is a miniature drive-in cinema with film being projected onto the screen, traffic moving in the streets, lighting, factories at work, and many other aspects of life in a real town.

At the northern end of the beachfront the Fitzsimons Snake Park exhibits about 80 of the 157 species of snake found in South Africa, as well as a variety of other reptiles. Natal snakes, such as black and green mambas, are well represented. The name Fitzsimons is now firmly associated with the study of snakes and the

The beachfront of Durban. An aerial cableway, a swimming pool and fair-ground rides are just some of the attractions.

The city area of Durban, the streets lined with shops. Beyond is the Berea.

production of serum. Frederick Fitzsimons established the Port Elizabeth snake park and throughout his life was involved in research on snakes. His book, *Snakes of South Africa*, was a classic on the subject for years. His son, Dr. Vivian Fitzsimons, former director of the Transvaal Museum in Pretoria, wrote the standard modern work, also called *Snakes of South Africa*. Another son, Desmond, started the Fitzsimons Snake Park in Durban in 1939. The park sells the standard anti-snake-bite kit produced by the South African Medical Institute in Johannesburg.

The Amphitheatre garden is also on the beachfront. This is a sunken garden with pools, fountains, lawns, flower beds, bridges, crazy paving, and thatched summer-houses. Illuminated by night, the garden is a sheltered contrast to the boisterous amusement parks. Concerts and other

THINGS TO DO AND SEE

Angling Durban is a major angling centre, especially in spring and summer.

Grunter, shad, stumpnose, snapper, salmon, mullet, mackerel, barracuda, as well as sharks of up to 450 kilograms, are caught in the harbour and from the three piers.

During the sardine runs in July, many game fish are taken from these piers; in August there is a run of geelbek. Organized deep-sea fishing trips are available.

Boating The Royal Natal Yacht Club has headquarters, anchorage and a club-house in the harbour. There are clubs and associations for most boating enthusiasts. Boats leave the Gardiner Street jetty on trips around the harbour. On calm days deep water yachts cruise along the coast.

Entertainment Durban is like a giant holiday camp, with sideshows, concerts, amusement parks, fun-fair rides and cinemas.

There are colourful African dancing contests at the non-European railway recreation ground in Wellington Road and at the kwaMashu township north of Durban. Hindu fire-walkers can be seen at the Umbilo Temple during Easter. The Durban Military Tattoo is an annual winter attraction which includes pipe bands and demonstrations of military expertise.

Sports Golf competitions are held at the Durban Country Club course and the Royal Durban course. King's Park is the home of the Natal Rugby Union and international matches are played here. Also in the park is a cycling and athletics stadium, and a test cricket ground.

There is an ice-skating rink and ten-pin bowling in Brickhill Road.

Horse races are run at Clairwood and at Greyville, the venue for the annual July Handicap — South Africa's premier horse race.

Swimming North Beach, South Beach and Brighton Beach are all protected by shark nets, but the sidewash and backwash can be dangerous.

There are numerous swimming baths throughout the region.

Surfing The three fishing piers produce right-point breaking waves from any reasonably large swell and these attract large numbers of surfers.

Gardens bloom along the old ivory trails

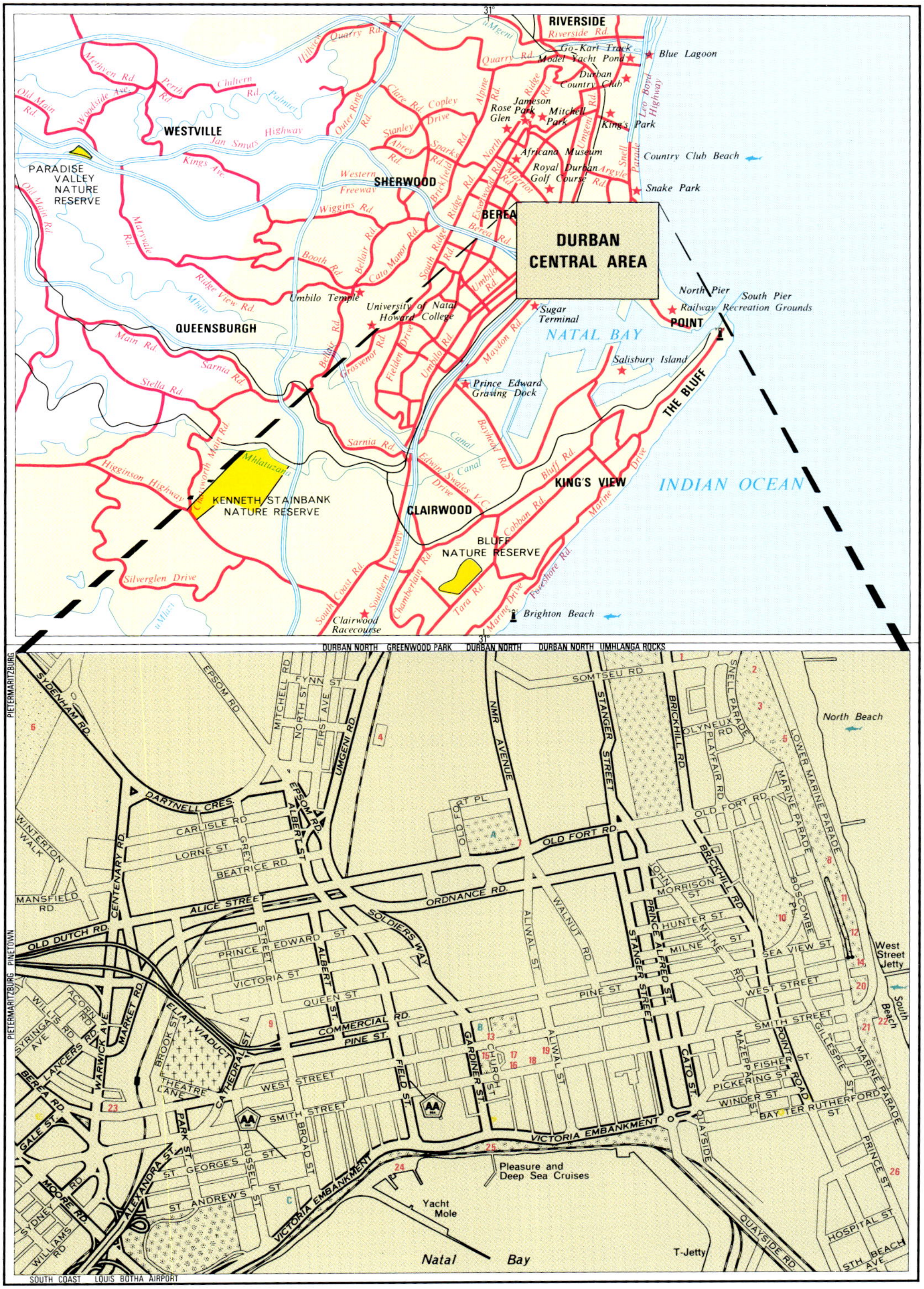

National monuments
A Old Fort and Cemetery
B Post Office
C Old House Museum

Places of interest
1 Ice Rink
2 Minitown
3 Amphitheatre, Sunken Gardens
4 Station
5 Amusement Park
6 Botanic Gardens
7 Warrior's Gate
8 Swimming Bath
9 Mohammedan Mosque
10 Bowling Green
11 Paddling Pools
12 Aerial Cableway
13 Plaque to Winston Churchill
14 Aquarium
15 Francis Farewell Square
16 Art Gallery
17 City Hall
18 Library/Museum
19 Local History Museum
20 Dolphinarium
21 Bowling Green
22 Cineland
23 Indian Market
24 Royal Natal Yacht Club
25 Dick King Statue
26 Addington Hospital

City and surroundings map scale

City central area map scale
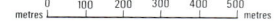

Poinsettias blooming in the warmth.

The botanic gardens on the Berea contain a vast and varied collection of plants. The orchid house is particularly notable.

open-air entertainments are held in the amphitheatre occasionally, and once a month a craft market takes place here.

Berea

The long ridge that overlooks Durban harbour, the city centre and the beach-front is known as Berea. The name originates from 1835 when Captain Allen Gardiner established a mission on the northern end of the ridge and named it after the place mentioned in the Acts of the Apostles.

The ridge was densely covered with coastal forest and bush where elephants and other wild animals roamed. Ivory traders from Port Natal hunted here. The ridge is completely built up today, and all that remains of the forest are the trees that shade the streets and gardens.

The botanic gardens on the eastern slopes of the ridge were created in 1848 on land originally occupied by an ivory hunter, John Cane, and his followers. The gardens cover 20 hectares and contain local and exotic trees and an orchid house.

There is a rose garden in Jameson Park on the summit of the Berea ridge. The municipal aviaries are in Mitchell Park, which also has a collection of tortoises and monkeys.

At the corner of Marriott Road and Essenwood Road is Muckleneuk, originally the home of the sugar magnate Sir Marshall Campbell, and now an Africana museum.

Sir Marshall's daughter, Dr. Margaret Roach (Killie) Campbell, devoted her life to collecting rare books, pictures, maps and unpublished manuscripts about Africa from

Durban in 1907, with plenty of cosy tea-rooms and a safety rope for the nervous.

THE BOLD AND BREATHTAKING BOUGAINVILLEA

The popular Killie Campbell *variety.*

The dramatic Bougainvillea poultonii.

The spectacularly flowering bougainvillea was introduced into Natal from Mauritius and adapted well to its new home. They flourished in the garden of Muckleneuk, the home of the Campbell family on Berea hill in Durban, and here several new colour varieties were bred in the 1930s by William Poulton.

Poulton had worked at the Durban Botanic Gardens and on his retirement the Campbell family allowed him to use their garden to carry out experimental work.

The first new colour variety he bred was a delicate, dusty pink, registered under the name of Natalia.

A multi-coloured variety followed, with blending shades of bronze, cerise and mauve. This lavish and almost continuous

flowerer was named Killie in honour of Killie Campbell, the mistress of Muckleneuk.

Another colour variety was called Gladys Hepburn, after Killie's married sister. Then came a vivid magenta strain, named *Bougainvillea poultonii*, after Poulton himself.

A later variation of this plant, with an even larger flower, is known as Poultonii Special.

A red, twin-flowered variety was named Wac Campbell after Killie's brother William. African Sunset is a two-tone, pinkish red and yellow bougainvillea.

Bougainvillea Rememberance was one of the last of his seedlings, named in memory of a man whose patient work lives on in countless gardens.

The battle to build Africa's greatest port

numerous sources throughout the world. The museum displays Zulu bead-work and more than 400 original paintings by Dr. Barbara Tyrrell, an authority on African costumes. It took Dr. Tyrrell 20 years and much travel to find authentic subjects for these unique paintings.

The garden of the Campbell home contains many species of bougainvillea (see box, page 321).

After Dr. Campbell's death in 1965, the house and grounds and her collection were presented to the University of Natal by her brother, William. The William Campbell Africana Museum is maintained as a research library and study centre and is open to the public.

The campus of the University of Natal dominates the skyline of the western end of Berea ridge. Originally the Howard College, it was built by the father of Howard Davis, an engineering student who was killed in World War I. The university has a second campus in Pietermaritzburg.

Blue Lagoon
The Mgeni (Umgeni) River reaches the sea at the Blue Lagoon. On the south bank of the river are various amusements, including fun-fair rides, go-carts, a putt-putt course, a model yacht pond and a model engineering centre.

Bluff
The 4-kilometre ridge that provides the land-locked harbour of Port Natal with its southern arm is known as the Bluff, or to the Zulus as isiBubulungu ('the long bulky thing').

The ridge is actually a 90-metre-high dune of silt and sand, laid down aeons ago when the sea level was higher.

The bush-covered Bluff protects the harbour from south-easterly winds. In

---

FROM FIRE-WALKERS TO BEAUTY QUEENS — THE MANY FACES OF THE PEOPLE OF DURBAN

Durban is home for a diverse cosmopolitan population. Asians, Africans, Europeans — each ethnic group has contributed to the development of the city, and its character is a combination of many cultural influences.

The Asian population is mainly Hindu and in Umgeni Road there is the largest and oldest Hindu temple in South Africa — the Sri Vaithianatha Easvarar Alayam — elaborately decorated with religious figures. There are smaller temples in and around the city. Various Hindu festivals take place during the year.

At the Kavady festival in February and July, penitents garlanded with marigolds, and with their faces and torsos pierced by needles, hooks and daggers, set out from the temples drawing decorated chariots through the streets. These colourfully adorned vehicles are eventually thrown into the Mgeni (Umgeni) River as a sacrifice to the gods. At Easter the ritual of the fire-walking takes place at the Umbilo temple.

The Muslim community has a fine mosque at the corner of Grey Street and Queen Street. This is said to be the largest mosque in the southern hemisphere. In summer the Muslims stage a procession of floats to mark the tenth day of the first month of the Muslim calendar. This is to remind the faithful of the martyrdom of the Son of Mohammed.

In Warwick Avenue there is an Indian market. Fruit and vegetables, cloth, jewellery, curios, Asian delicacies, spices and curry powders are sold here.

The African population of Durban consists mainly of people from Kwazulu and Natal, all of whom speak the same Nguni language, generally known as Zulu. The women, particularly those in from the country to visit their men working in the city, are usually dressed in decorated cloths and beads. On Sundays the men also dress up, donning furs and feathers. Ngoma dancing contests are held, with rival teams of dancers gathering at various venues.

The Europeans of Durban also contribute to the atmosphere of the city. As well as those who live here, there is a floating population of holiday-makers, stimulating trade and entertainments ranging from ballet and opera to beauty contests and horse races such as the famous July Handicap.

There is no month when Durban is really 'out of season'.

The Grey Street Mosque, largest in southern Africa.

Spices for sale, and curry powders from 'mild' to 'hell fire'.

A Muslim shopkeeper at work.

A Hindu at a religious festival.

The old Indian Market.

Produce in the Indian Market.

The Durban yacht basin, an anchorage for sailors of many nationalities.

former years crews of several wrecked ships found sanctuary on the Bluff, and during the Zulu disturbance of the early 1820s many refugees from shattered clans fled here. Its bush was difficult to penetrate — mangrove swamps, bogs and the waters of the harbour blocked approach from the land, and the sea guarded its eastern side.

Lieutenant James King, one of the pioneer traders and founders of Durban, had his home on the Bluff. He lived here with his following of hunters and dependants until his death on 7 September 1828. A commemorative plaque now marks his grave.

The Bluff is today a largely residential area. Marine Drive runs along the seaward side and leads to a viewing site on the eastern end. From here there is a panoramic view of the harbour and city.

Harbour

The almost completely land-locked bay of Durban harbour was once a lagoon. Today it is one of the principal cargo ports in Africa. The Zulus call the harbour the Thekwini ('lagoon'). Europeans have given it a number of names. The Portuguese called it Parva de Pescaria ('the fisheries') because of the fish traps set in the shallows by African fishermen, or Rio de Natal ('Christmas river'). Most other Europeans called the harbour Port Natal.

The potential of the harbour was apparent from the beginning, but it had one serious handicap — a narrow entrance with a shallow bar of sand, varying unpredictably in its depth from one season to the next.

Once across the bar, a ship could anchor in completely sheltered water, but passing through the entrance was hazardous. Between 1845, when

records were first kept, and 1885, a total of 66 large ocean-going ships were wrecked on Durban beach, caught by storms or sudden winds and unable to cross the sand bar.

There was much discussion as to what to do about the shallow entrance. The bar was made up of sand brought down by rivers which had their mouths in the harbour, and of sand from rivers south of Durban which was borne up the coast by a strong inshore current.

Several engineering schemes were attempted in an effort to deepen the bar.

Moles were built to deflect the sand from the entrance and to scour the channel by enclosing its sides. A large amount of money was spent but by 1855 the bar had a high-water depth of less than 5 metres and no large ships could cross it safely.

The answer to this difficult problem came with the invention of dredgers. In 1895 two cumbersome bucket dredgers somehow managed to reach Durban without turning turtle on the long voyage from Europe. They removed 9 928 348 tons of sand from the harbour entrance and by 1898 the water depth had been increased to slightly more than 6 metres.

Today, as a result of incessant work, the depth of the harbour bar is 12,8 metres at low water, with an additional 2 metres at high water, and the largest vessels can enter the harbour safely.

The harbour handles a large percentage of all cargo shipped through South African ports.

There are 12 kilometres of quayside, pre-cooling stores for perishables, a grain elevator with a capacity of 38 100 tons, and a sugar terminal holding 400 000 tons.

The equestrian monument commemorating Dick King's ride to Grahamstown.

The business of ship and harbour repairs is unending and hazardous.

DICK KING'S EPIC RIDE

It was around midnight when a small boat slipped across Durban Bay towards the shore.

The boat carried two passengers — an Englishman and his African servant, with two horses swimming behind, tethered to the stern.

So, in the early hours of 25 May 1842, began one of history's epic journeys — Dick King's marathon ride to Grahamstown to fetch reinforcements for Durban's besieged British garrison.

Dick was born in England in 1813, and came to South Africa in a group of 1820 Settlers.

He was in Port Natal when the British arrived in 1842, but no sooner had they established a garrison in what is now the Old Fort than they were besieged by the Voortrekkers. Dick was on board the trading vessel *Mazeppa*, anchored in the bay. The British were short of food and completely isolated. Their only hope of survival was relief from the Cape.

Under cover of darkness a small boat landed Dick, his 16-year-old servant, Ndongeni, and their horses on Salisbury Island. Then they set out across the perilous mangrove swamps, following a secret path to avoid Voortrekker posts.

Ahead lay nearly 1 000 kilometres of wild country, with 122 rivers and streams to ford. Ndongeni, without saddle or stirrups, managed about half the distance before giving up.

Dick reached Grahamstown in ten days, and reinforcements were hastily shipped from Port Elizabeth.

On 26 June the siege was broken. Ndongeni was rewarded with a grant of land on the northern bank of the Mzimkulu River, and his grave lies there.

Dick was given land at Isipingo, south of Durban, where he died in 1871. His house has been renovated.

The equestrian monument to Dick King on the Victoria embankment was erected in 1915.

The siege fort that is now a place of prayer

The city hall of Durban, built in 1910. It is an almost exact replica of the city hall of Belfast, in Northern Ireland.

An ocean-going liner berthed in Durban's bustling harbour.

Luxury high-rise hotels look out over the Durban beachfront.

The Prince Edward Graving Dock is 352 metres long and an offshore oil terminal can take tankers of up to 203 000 tons.

These tankers bring crude oil which is processed in two refineries in Durban, or pumped via a pipeline to a third refinery at Sasolburg, in the Orange Free State.

Salisbury Island in the harbour was named after the brig *Salisbury* which, under Lieutenant James King, surveyed the harbour in 1823. The island is now used as a naval base and is part of a large-scale development of 15 berths for deep-draught container ships.

Old Fort

In 1842, when Captain Thomas Smith led a small British force up the coast from Pondoland to occupy Port Natal, he selected a site in Durban for a fortified camp. On 5 May, just as they had completed the defences, the British were besieged by the Voortrekkers. Short of supplies and hopelessly outnumbered by a resolute enemy, the garrison would have been overwhelmed had it not been for Dick King and his marathon ride to fetch help from the Cape (see box, page 323).

Today the Old Fort stands amid gardens planted with many species of cycads. The original ammunition magazine is an inter-denominational chapel.

In one corner of the grounds stands the ornamental Warrior's Gate, the shrine and headquarters of the ex-soldier's organization, the Memorable Order of Tin Hats (M.O.T.H.), and a museum of battle trophies and relics of old Natal.

Old House Museum

Built in 1849 by a settler named John Goodricke, the Old House Museum in St. Andrew's Street later became the home of Sir John Robinson, the first prime minister of Natal. After being restored it was opened in 1954 as a museum. It contains a dining room, bedroom and kitchen furnished with authentic period pieces from the middle of the last century.

There are paintings and engravings of early Durban.

The museum also has an extraordinary French clock with a great number of dials, giving time, date,

Durban, from the air — the city, harbour and Bluff, and Greyville racecourse.

day, phases of the moon. equinoxes, barometric pressure and other information.

Another exhibit is a sundial made in Europe in 1700 and brought to Durban before the owner realized that it would be useless as it was designed for the northern hemisphere.

Point

The spit of sand that forms the northern arm of the harbour was originally named Point Fynn, after Henry Francis Fynn, who led the first settlement of traders at Port Natal. It is now simply known as the Point, and is built up with harbour buildings, warehouses, apartments, the Addington Hospital and staff residences.

The Point ends at the North Pier, one of the two piers built to make the harbour entrance narrower, deeper and easier to dredge. The North Pier is a favourite spot for fishermen and provides a fine view of Durban beachfront.

The Point was the terminus of the first railway in southern Africa. Early in 1859 a company was formed to build a railway from the Point to Durban 3 kilometres away and from there to a quarry on the banks of the Mgeni (Umgeni) River, where stone could be obtained for harbour works.

RICKSHAW-PULLERS BLAZE A COLOURFUL TRAIL

The rickshaws of Durban have been a famous feature of the city for many years.

They were introduced from Japan, where they had been invented in 1853 by an American missionary, the Reverend Jonathan Goble. His wife was an invalid and he had to improvise a form of transport for her.

His vehicle was a single-seater which was popularized by geishas, who liked to be seen in such decorative and novel little carriages.

In 1893 a Natal sugar magnate, Sir Marshall Campbell, saw the rickshaws in Japan and brought a few of them to Durban, where he had them adapted to two-seaters. He employed Zulus to pull them, and they snatched at the idea of dressing in flamboyant costumes and competing for customers.

The most favoured among the rickshaw-pullers were those with the most decorative rickshaws and the greatest ability to prance and bound along the highways.

For a time rickshaws were popular in Pietermaritzburg, on the Rand, and even in Cape Town.

There were more than 1 000 rickshaws in Durban during the 1930s. Annual competitions were held to decide the best-dressed rickshaw-pullers and the most gaily decorated rickshaws. The scene at the parades was delightfully animated.

After World War II the rickshaws went into a decline. Traffic authorities disliked them; there were allegations that it was cruel to use people to draw a carriage; and many rickshaw-pullers found they could earn more in other jobs.

By 1960 there were only 500 rickshaws left, and the companies that made them discontinued operations.

In 1973 rickshaws almost disappeared from the scene when financial losses forced the last major operator out of business. Rickshaw services were eventually revived, with their pullers operating only during the holiday season.

Today there are about 15 licensed rickshaw-pullers in Durban. Lavishly dressed, they operate mainly along the sea-front.

A rickshaw puller in full regalia.

Horns, beads, feathers and oddments — costumes are worth a small fortune.

Where young Winston was given a hero's welcome

The West Street of the 1890s. Only the post office, with its clock tower, remains.

Durban's Post Office, formerly the Town Hall.

A 24-horsepower steam train was imported from Britain in pieces and assembled by its driver, Henry Jacobs.

The maiden journey was on 23 June 1860. The train ran from Durban to the Point with the chairman and directors riding on the footplate, waving at the crowd. From then onwards the train had three scheduled return trips each day, with passengers paying one shilling first class and 6d second class.

If the locomotive broke down, the train was pulled by oxen.

West Street

The principal street of Durban, West Street was named after Lieutenant-governor Martin West, who administered the affairs of Natal from 1845 to 1850.

The street begins on the beachfront and leads westwards through the centre of the city.

The post office in West Street was built in 1885 as the town hall. In 1908 it was the scene of the convention that brought the four colonies of South Africa together to form the Union of South Africa. The present town hall was completed in 1910 and the original building then became the post office. Its clock is the official timekeeper of Durban.

The new city hall is an almost exact replica of the Belfast city hall in Northern Ireland. It faces a square named after Lieutenant Francis Farewell, one of the traders who founded the city in 1824.

The city hall contains the municipal offices, a main hall seating 2 500 people, a library, art gallery, and a natural history museum.

The museum is noted for its realistic displays of South African birds. It also has what is believed to be the most complete skeleton in existence of the extinct dodo of Mauritius. Mammals are also displayed, and there is a room depicting the life, customs and history of the Zulus.

The art gallery in the city hall contains ceramics, silver, ivories, and a general collection of paintings by local and international artists.

Next to the city hall is the local history museum, housed in Durban's first public building which was erected as a court house and post office in 1865.

One room exhibits costumes worn by South African men, women and children between 1750 and modern times. Another room houses relics and information concerning the discovery and colonization of Natal, including

Durban harbour as seen from the Bluff at night, with the reflections of countless lights twinkling merrily.

A few of the amusements that line Durban's beachfront, with the harbour entrance and the Bluff in the background.

shipwrecks and early residents.

There are models of the Zulu chief Dingane's capital, Mgungundlovu, and of Lieutenant Farewell's camp on the site of Durban's present city gardens.

At the intersection of West Street and Church Street is a plaque marking the spot where Winston Churchill addressed the people of Durban, who gave him a hero's welcome when he arrived from Lourenco Marques after his escape from a Boer prisoner-of-war camp in Pretoria in 1899 (see box, page 224).

WORLD OF THE SHARK, THE KING OF THE DEEP

For 300 million years sharks have reigned supreme as the kings of the deep. Man enters their domain at his peril — except where the beaches are protected by nets.

Shark nets have dramatically reduced attacks on bathers in southern Africa. During the 25 years before nets were erected off Durban beaches in 1952 there were 22 attacks on bathers; since 1952 there have been no attacks.

Sharks must move constantly to survive. A continuous current of water, passing into the mouth and out through the gill slits behind the eyes and above the pectoral fins, is essential to their breathing process.

When a shark is about to bite, the upper part of the head is flexed by its back muscles. The jaws are then protruded, with the teeth of the lower jaw pointing forward. At the moment of impact, the upper jaw clams shut and the prey is clenched between razor-sharp teeth.

Sharks are often assumed to have small brains and limited behaviour patterns. Modern research has disproved such theories.

Of 300 species of shark, the smallest is *Squaliolus laticaudus*, which is sexually mature when barely 12 centimetres long, and the largest is the harmless whale shark, a plankton-feeder which reaches 12 metres in length.

The Natal Anti-Shark Measures Board (NASMB) headquarters at Umhlanga Rocks provide guided tours on Wednesday mornings or by special arrangement. The following are among the sharks that can be seen at the headquarters:

The great white, white death, or blue pointer shark (*Carcharodon carcharias*), a hunter of large sea mammals — seals, dolphins and whales (the great white's maximum length is 5-7 metres);

The mako (*Isurus oxyrinchus*), a shiny blue shark of the open seas, growing up to 3 metres, with a pointed snout, large eyes and smooth awl-like teeth;

The tiger shark (*Galeocerdo cuvieri*), blotched with partial banding on its back and a wide blunt head (4-7 metres);

The raggedtooth shark (*Odontaspis taurus*), with teeth protruding from the mouth (2-3 metres);

Servicing shark-protection nets.

The great hammerhead (*Sphyrna mokarran*), the largest of the three Natal hammerheads but with a relatively small mouth and not normally a threat to man (3-4 metres);

Grey sharks (*Carcharhinus*), including the dusky, or ridge-back grey (*C. obscurus*), the longnose blackfin (*C. brevipinna*), the blacktip (*C. limbatus*), and the zambezi (*C. leucas*). Sharks of this family generally grow up to 3 metres long.

The great white shark, hunter of large mammals.

An anti-shark patrol boat heading out across the surf to service the nets.

PLAYGROUND OF THE SOUTH COAST

THE 160-KILOMETRE COASTLINE of Natal south of Durban is a vast holiday playground. The weather ranges from warm to hot and humid. A green ribbon of sub-tropical forest about two kilometres wide runs all the way along the coast, broadening in some places, narrowing in others.

The trees are mainly evergreens such as the ficus (or umthombe), marula, and Natal mahogany (or umkhuhlu). Lala palms and wild bananas also grow in great profusion and mangroves cover the shallows and mud flats of the rivers.

There are 4 800 plant species in Natal, many flourishing in the rich soil, high rainfall and warmth of the coastal belt. Here are ferns, orchids and multi-coloured lilies. On rocky ledges can be found the scarlet flame lily and the ifafa lily, the white arum lily, the blue lily (or agapanthus), the fire lily and the blood lily.

Vervet monkeys in countless chattering groups gambol through the trees, feeding on wild fruits, caterpillars and leaves, and being preyed on themselves by the crowned eagles and pythons who relish young monkeys.

Wild pigs, duikers and bushbuck live in the shadows of the forest floor, but it is in the sunlit canopy that most forms of life find a home. The bird-lover is frustrated as he listens to the constant song and bustle of birds but seldom sees them. The monkeys peep down through the trees and tauntingly drop a shower of peel, pips and other litter.

The coastal forest reaches down to the shoreline, where the Indian Ocean surges onto a beach the colour and consistency of golden-brown sugar. Blue water, green forest, white surf, the rich colour of the sands — all is harmony. To complete the picture there is barely a kilometre of this coast where either a river or a stream does not reach the sea. Invariably each has a lagoon at its mouth, serenely mirroring the surrounding forest by day and the stars by night.

This is a coast of lagoons, lilies and lala palms; wild bananas seemingly always in flower; hibiscus, bougainvillea, frangipani and other exotic flowering plants; legends of mermaids and mermen resting in the sunshine on the sands, or calling and singing as they catch in their hands the phosphorescent jewels sparkling in the waves on warm summer nights.

A highway runs down the coast, and a railway line hugs the shore, its trains — often drenched in spray, clattering across bridges, twisting between shore and forest — linking a necklace of holiday resorts, seaside villages and towns.

Amanzimtoti
When the great Zulu chief Shaka led his army down the south coast on a raid against the Pondos in 1828 he rested on the banks of a river. His servant fetched a calabash of water. Shaka tasted it and said: 'Kanti amanza mtoti'. ('So, the water is sweet'). The river became known as the Amanzimtoti ('sweet waters').

Amanzimtoti is today a residential area for Durban commuters and for workers at a large explosives and chemical factory on the banks of the Umbogintwini River. It is also a holiday resort with a beach and a tidal pool.

Doonside
The resorts of Doonside and Warner Beach lie on opposite sides of the Little Manzimtoti River and share a protected bathing area at its mouth.

The name Doonside originated when a railway siding was built close to a house named Lorna Doone, after the heroine of the famous novel by R. D. Blackmore.

Hibberdene
Fishing, swimming and sunbathing are the main pursuits on the balmy stretch of coast around the village of Hibberdene. The coastal forest fringes the beach. There are picnic sites among the trees and anglers fish from the rocks at Reef End.

Ifafa Beach
The Fafa River has one of the finest lagoons on the south coast of Natal. Ifafa Beach is the resort on this lagoon at the mouth of the river. This is a popular angling area, and there are holiday camps on both sides of the river.

The Zulu word iFafa ('sparkling') describes the light glittering on the surface of the river.

Illovo Beach
The river named by the Zulus iLovo (now corrupted to Lovu), because of the mlovo trees growing on its banks, flows into a spacious lagoon. A ridge covered with tall trees, creepers and flowering plants overlooks the beach. In the shade of the trees lies the village of Illovo.

Isipingo
The resort of Isipingo is built on a high ridge of sand at the mouth of the river called by the Zulus isiPhingo, their name for the cat-thorn (*Scutia myrti-na*) shrubs that grow here. People come to Isipingo to swim and fish. Also here is the renovated farmhouse of Dick King, famed for his historic ride on horseback from Durban to Grahamstown (see box, page 323).

Karridene
During World War I a Rand mining magnate, Walter Karri-Davis, decided to build a sanatorium on the south coast of Natal, among the trees overlooking the Indian Ocean. It was intended for mine workers suffering from phthisis, a respiratory ailment caused by inhalation of rock dust.

The sanatorium has since burned down but the popular holiday resort that has grown up on this scenic spot is named Karridene after Karri-Davis.

The Natal south coast with its rivers, beaches, blue ocean and patches of forest.

Kingsburgh

Several small holiday resorts and residential areas combine to form the municipality of Kingsburgh, named in memory of Dick King, who passed this way on his famous 1 000 kilometre ride to Grahamstown in 1842 (see box, page 323).

Margate

Originally a coastal farm named after the English seaside town, Margate has grown into one of the most popular holiday resorts on the lower south coast of Natal. It has a beach with protected swimming, a tidal pool, a children's paddling pool, an Olympic-size freshwater pool, a fishing pier and a lagoon. The lagoon lies at the mouth of the river called Nkhongweni ('place of entreaty') because the original inhabitants were reputed to be so mean that travellers had to beg for hospitality.

Margate hit the headlines in 1922 when an enormous, white, furry creature was washed up on the beach. Unfortunately the 'Margate monster' was too decomposed to be identified accurately.

Margate's popularity as a tourist resort has grown considerably in recent years.

Mtamvuna

The border between Natal and the Transkei lies along the river known as Mtamvuna ('the reaper of mouthfuls') from the damage its floods do to crops. It is said that any person failing to confess his sins before fording the river will be carried away by the water spirits. It is also supposed to be the home of mermaids, who have often been reported playing in the water on moonlit nights.

The river is wide and unpolluted, with a lagoon and mangrove swamps at its mouth. Inland, boats cruise between high, forested cliffs. A suspension bridge carries the road across the river.

A caravan and camping ground stands on the site of the original pont used in crossing the river before the bridge was built.

Oribi Gorge Nature Reserve

Part of the spectacular gorge of the Mzimkulwana River was proclaimed a nature reserve in 1950. Tall, red-

A wide-sweeping horseshoe bend near the Oribi Gorge on the Natal Coast.

A vervet monkey mother and child, members of a cheerful family.

THINGS TO DO AND SEE

Angling Most fish found in the waters of Natal are migratory and there are periods when there is nothing to be caught. But in winter and spring great shoals arrive. May brings maasbanker, shad, mackerel, kingfish and barracuda. June on the south coast, when the sardine shoals appear, is the high point of South Africa's angling year. July, August and September are good for shad. October offers salmon, garrick (leervis), galjoen and bronze bream. This is also the month for sharks.

Boating The largest rivers — the Mtamvuna, Mzimkulu and Mkomazi — have long stretches suitable for power-boats. The scenery is spectacular with bush-covered hills and cliffs rising steeply on both sides as the rivers twist deep inland. There is canoeing on the upper reaches of the large rivers and on some of the smaller rivers.

Camping and caravanning There are caravan and camping sites all along the coast. Most are in grassy, tree-shaded settings, close to beaches and rivers.

Swimming The sea is warm throughout the year (often 25°C. or above). All the resorts have anti-shark nets or barricades and there are many tidal pools and children's paddling pools. Swimmers in lagoons risk bilharzia. Bathers in the open sea face the danger of shark attacks.

During summer floods the flow of the rivers can be violent.

A paradise of tumbling streams and grassy slopes

orange sandstone cliffs overlook a dense forest of trees, creepers and flowering plants. Baboons and dassies live on the cliffs and are preyed upon by leopards and pythons. Various species of antelope live here — duiker, bushbuck and the oribi that give the gorge its name. Monkeys and birds live in the tree tops and several species of wild cat hunt at night.

The road from Port Shepstone winds through hills until it reaches the summit of the Oribi Flats, the plateau that lies between the converging gorges of the Mzimkulu and its tributary, the Mzimkulwana. From the edge of this plateau there are superb views into the two gorges.

In the reserve is a hutted camp run by the Natal Parks Board, and nearby is a hotel and picnic ground. There are many trees, flowers and shrubs, including the *Brunfelsia* — known as 'yesterday, today and tomorrow' because its flowers change colour from deep mauve to lavender to white.

A turn-off 27 kilometres from Port Shepstone on the road to the reserve leads to the famous Hanging Rock. More than 300 million years old and made of sandstone, this feature juts out 2 metres. The surrounding softer layers of rock have been eroded away by wind and rain.

Park Rynie

Set amid parkland dotted with lala palms, the resort of Park Rynie was established in 1857 and named after Mrs Renetta (Rynie) Hoffman, wife of one of the two landowners who developed the area. There was a whaling station here before World War I and the slipway is still used by fishing boats.

Pennington

The palm-fringed Nkhomba River flows through one of the loveliest stretches of natural parkland on the south coast of Natal. Trees shade a gentle grassy slope and streams tumble down to the river.

The area, known as Pennington, was originally a farm owned by the Pennington family, settlers from Bri-

---

THE BIRD LIFE OF THE COASTAL FOREST

The monarch among the birds of the warm, humid coastal forest is the crowned eagle. A bird of great strength and a skilful hunter, it stages ambushes in the forest by crouching quietly amid the leaves, watching and waiting for an unwary creature. Then, with a wild swoop, it snatches up its victim and carries it off.

Other predators of the forest are the African goshawk and the wood owl.

Buff-spotted fluff-tails skulk among the shadows below the canopy. Here too are cinnamon and tambourine doves. Pigeons of several species live in the canopy, feeding on the seeds and fruits ripening in the sun.

The gorgeous purple-crested loeries, the emerald cuckoo, the forest weaver and the narina trogon — these are among the most brightly coloured and eye-catching of the forest birds.

Perhaps the noisiest are the trumpeter hornbills, which gather in groups and seem to scorn one another with their cries.

High in the trees are red-fronted and golden-rumped barbets, scaly throated honeyguides, cheeky little square-tailed drongos and bulbuls.

The most characteristic calls of the forest are the musical whistle of the sombre bulbul and the endless scolding of the yellowbellied bulbul.

Hanging Rock, high above the gorge of the Mzimkulu River.

The gorgeously coloured paradise flycatcher, noted for its warbling whistle.

The wood owl feeds on insects, frogs, small birds and rodents.

The old jetty, all that is left of the original whaling station at Park Rynie.

Banana palms of the Strelitzia family, namesake of the Strelitzia Coast.

The titanium-tinted sands at Port Edward, eerie in their atmosphere.

A train crosses the lagoon at the mouth of the Umgababa River.

tain. At the beginning of the century Sir Frank Reynolds, the sugar magnate, bought part of the farm and developed a country home which he called Umdoni Park, because of the mdoni (water myrtle) trees.

On the estate Sir Frank built a seaside residence for South African prime ministers as a sign of his admiration for the first premier of the Union, General Louis Botha. King George VI of Britain was offered the use of this lovely, secluded home when his health was failing in 1952, and he was planning to visit it just before he died.

Port Edward

A spacious beach, protected swimming and the unspoilt setting of a forest of lala palms are the attractions of Port Edward. a resort named in honour of the Prince of Wales, later Edward VII.

The beach is overlooked by Tragedy Hill (see box).

Port Shepstone

The Mzimkulu ('the great home of all rivers') is the largest river of the south coast of Natal, and Port Shepstone, at its mouth, is the largest town.

Port Shepstone was founded in 1880 and named after Sir Theophilus Shepstone, an administrator of native affairs in the Natal government. The products of the district are sugar and marble. Coasters sailed into the mouth of the river and provided a transport link with the outside world until the railway was built from Durban.

In 1882 a party of 246 Norwegian immigrants was landed at Port Shepstone and these hard-working farm people played a large part in the development of the area. As well as being the end of the line from Durban, Port Shepstone is also the terminus of a narrow-gauge railway that makes its way inland through beautiful hill country to Harding. There is boating on the river, swimming in a tidal pool, and fishing from the beach and in the estuary. A golf course is laid out on the banks of the river.

Port Shepstone's industries include a sugar mill, a lime works and a marble quarry. Timber, wattle bark and sub-tropical fruit are produced in the district. It is the administrative, educational and commercial centre for southern Natal.

Ramsgate

The name of Ramsgate was given by a surveyor to the coastal farm at the mouth of the river known as Bilanhlolo ('the marvellous boiler') because its pools, through some action of the current, bubble as though on the verge of boiling. Europeans sometimes call the river 'Big Billy' from its African name.

At the mouth of the river there is a

HILL OF DEATH

Tragedy Hill, near Port Edward.

In 1831 there was a crisis between the traders of Port Natal and Dingane, the Zulu king. A discontented Zulu spread a false rumour that the British intended to attack Dingane's country. Dingane marshalled his army.

The traders fled. Some boarded a ship in Durban harbour, others made off down the coast to the Cape. Among the latter were the family and followers of Henry Francis Fynn, who had founded the settlement at Port Natal in 1824.

Driving their cattle ahead of them, the refugees reached the southern side of the mouth of the Mbilanhlola River. There they were attacked by Zulus who thought the Fynns were absconding with cattle owned by Dingane.

Henry Fynn escaped by swimming down the shore from one rocky promontory to another. His son Frank, accompanied by a large number of dependants, was pursued south as far as the hill that looms over the beach at the modern resort of Port Edward.

Here the Zulus massacred the whole party. The place has been known ever since as Tragedy Hill and its slopes are still littered with the bones of the victims.

Dingane subsequently learned that there had been no planned British invasion and ordered the Zulu who had started the rumour to be shot. The sentence was carried out by one of the traders, Henry Ogle, who received a fee of five head of cattle for the execution.

Haunt of a legendary man-eating crocodile

lagoon surrounded by wild banana palms. In 1922 the only person living here was a romantic character called Paul Buck, a painter and violin-maker who called the place 'Blue Lagoon' and built himself a house on the banks of the river.

Today Ramsgate is a holiday resort and retirement centre with boating on the lagoon, a sandy beach, protected swimming and good fishing.

Scottburgh

One of the most popular of the south coast resorts, Scottburgh was founded in 1860 and named after John Scott, the governor of Natal. This resort has a fine beach at the mouth of the river named by the Zulus Mpambanyoni ('the confuser of birds') because of the complex twists of its course.

There is a large sugar mill upstream and for some years the beach was a precarious loading area for ships.

Scottburgh is an attractive town with a protected bathing area in Scott's Bay, tidal pools, a championship golf course, bowling greens, tennis and squash courts, and a famous miniature railway, which runs through one of the largest caravan parks in Natal.

Sezela

Tradition tells of a man-eating crocodile that once terrorized the Malangeni people. The crocodile was called iSezela, meaning 'the one who smells out', for it was said that it hunted like a wild dog following a trail.

In 1828, when Shaka led his Zulu army down the coast, he heard of this reptile and resolved to have its skin. A hunt was organized. Shaka's men went into the river with their spears and killed the crocodile.

Today the legend of iSezela lives on in the name of the river, and in the village at its mouth which grew up around a sugar mill.

Strelitzia Coast

A forest of wild banana trees grows between Umkomaas and Scottburgh, and the botanical name for them, *Strelitzia sps.*, has led to the area being called the Strelitzia Coast.

The small resort of Clansthal, named after a town in Germany, lies in the midst of this forest, while offshore is a notorious shipping hazard — the Aliwal Shoal, a rocky reef first reported in 1849 by the captain of the barque, *Aliwal*, which narrowly avoided being wrecked on it.

Several other ships have been wrecked on the reef.

The shoal is marked by a lighthouse on Green Point.

Umgababa

The Luthuli live in the valley of the river they know as the uMgababa ('the place of jealousy') — a name that comes from an ancient feud.

On the northern bank of the river is a large market place next to the main coastal road and known to Europeans as Umgababa. Stalls display carvings, beadwork, baskets, mats, and subtropical fruit.

Litchis grown in this region are

The open-air market place at Umgababa where tourists buy curios.

reputed to be particularly sweet.

A large plant was built to extract titanium here but it was closed down because the process caused serious sea pollution.

Umkomaas

Large numbers of whales once used the estuary of the great Mkomazi River as a nursery, giving birth in the shallows and lolling around in the warm water. The Zulus named the river after this spectacle (uMkhomazi means 'the place of cow whales').

The town of Umkomaas on the southern bank was originally a harbour for the export of sugar.

The building of the coastal railway made the port redundant, but the town of Umkomaas became a popular holiday resort, with golf course, bowling greens and a tidal pool for swimming.

Umtentweni

The delightful resort of Umtentweni stands at the mouth of the Mtentweni River, named after a species of grass that grows on its banks.

Visitors will find a calm lagoon which is popular for boating, a protected swimming area, a tidal pool and fine fishing sites.

Umzinto

The first public company in Natal was established at Umzinto in 1858 to produce sugar. Javanese labourers — the first to be brought to Natal from Asia — were recruited to work on the sugar estates. The town developed as a centre for the mill, and as a terminus for a branch of the main line from Durban and a narrow gauge railway leading inland to Ixopo and Umzimkulu.

Umzumbe

A band of Hlongwa cannibals, who had their stronghold in the valley of the Mzumbe ('the bad kraal') River, were almost wiped out in 1828 when they were surprised by the Zulu king, Shaka, as he led his army down the coast.

A reminder of these times is one of the most famous vivanes (heaps of lucky stones) in South Africa. As Shaka led his men south they reached the top of a saddle of land from which they could look down into the area occupied by the Hlongwa cannibals. To appease the spirits and ensure good fortune when he led his men down into this new world, Shaka followed an ancient custom. He picked up a peb-

A favourite fisherman's vantage point near Scottburgh. From such a bases fishermen catch barracuda, shad and other fish.

ble with the toes of his left foot, transferred it to his right hand, spat on it, murmured a supplication to his ancestors, and placed the pebble by the side of the path. Each member of his army repeated the ritual until there was a pile of pebbles.

At the mouth of the river is the resort of Umzumbe.

Uvongo
A number of holday resorts lie along the attractive stretch of coast between the Mzimkulu River and the Transkei border.

This area is noted for its lala palms and the fact that summer humidity is lower than on the coast north of the Mzimkulu.

South of Port Shepstone the river known as Ivungu (from a Zulu word describing the sound of the waterfall or the wind in a gorge near its mouth) flows into a lagoon in a sheltered bay. Here among the wild banana and lala palms lies the village of Uvongo.

Uvongo has a tidal swimming pool, as do its sister resorts, St. Michael's-on-Sea and Manaba Beach. There are also protected bathing beaches, good fishing, boating, a golf course and other sports facilities.

The Thure Lilliecrona Park at Uvongo Beach is named after a renowned Natal fisherman who originally owned the area and laid it out as a garden village.

Warner Beach
In 1910 a residential area for government pensioners was laid out on a ridge south of the Little Manzimtoti River. The surveyor was P. A. Warner and the place was named after him. It has a beach, and a protected swimming area.

Winkelspruit
The Schooner *Tonga* was wrecked on 10 May 1875 at the mouth of the Lovu River. The ship carried wares for Durban shops and rather than let the cargo go to waste the salvors set up a store on the river bank and sold water-damaged goods.

The store was known by the Afrikaans name winkel ('a shop') and Winkelspruit became the name of the holiday resort that developed here in later years.

A beautiful camping and caravan park on the banks of the Mtamvuna River, at the site of the old pont.

SPECTACLE OF THE SARDINE RUN, WHEN THE SEA BOILS WITH FISH

The foremost event in the South African angling calendar is the sardine run up the south coast of Natal between June and August.

The migrating sardine shoals are accompanied by large numbers of predatory big-game fish, and these provide marvellous sport.

Sardines normally live in the cool waters of the southern and western Cape, where they provide food for tunny, yellowtail, leervis, kob and other predatory fish.

With the coming of autumn they gather in prodigious shoals and move northwards up the Mocambique Current to find warmer water in which to spawn.

The migration takes six months and is extremely regular. Along most of the Cape coast the sardines keep well out to sea, but off Port St. Johns, on the Wild Coast, counter-currents bring them close to the shore.

Travelling in successive shoals, the sardines hug the coastline for 250 kilometres. They complete their migration just south of Durban, where they swing out to sea again, and the Mocambique Current carries them back to the Cape for the six months of spring and summer.

Each successive shoal of sardines consists of many millions of the little fish, followed by a horde of predators. Cormorants, gannets and other sea-birds dive at them from overhead or rest on the water in over-fed masses, themselves a prey to sharks.

Game fish attack the fringes of the shoals, gorging on the sardines but careful never to venture into the midst of the mass for fear of their gills becoming clogged up. Predators that follow the shoals up from the Cape are joined by voracious local fish such as barracuda, king-fish, prodigal son, queenfish, snoek, sharks, skates and rays.

The spectacle of these passing shoals is remarkable. Anglers crowd every vantage point. If a shoal has been driven far enough inshore by weather or predators even housewives wade into the surf to scoop out the fish in buckets and aprons. Birds circle in thousands overhead and the surface of the sea is churned up as though it was boiling.

It takes about 30 days for the shoals to pass. The size of the catches can be affected by various factors: rough seas or a heavy swell can send the sardines deep below the surface where they will escape their predators; high atmospheric pressure gives them extra energy owing to the increase of oxygen in the water; low barometric pressure makes them sluggish.

It is not known how many of the little fish complete the return journey to the Cape in safety, but hundreds of millions must surely be eaten on the way. Each female, however, lays about 100 000 eggs. Only one or two of these need to survive for the number of sardines to remain stable.

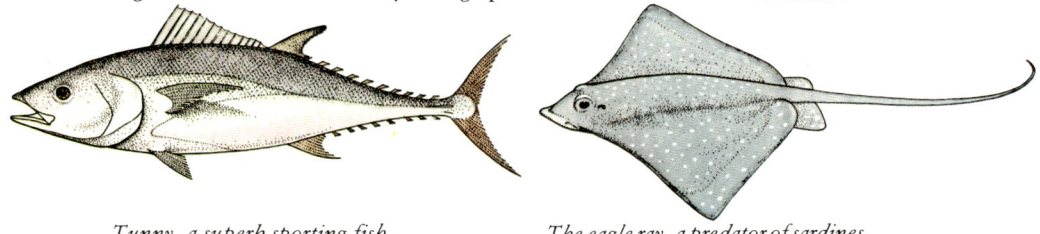

Tunny, a superb sporting fish.

The eagle ray, a predator of sardines.

THE BLOOD-STAINED EDEN

BETWEEN TWO EXTREMES — the warm coastal forest and the gaunt, snow-covered heights of the Drakensberg — lie the 200-kilometre-wide Natal midlands. Through this undulating landscape of hills the ground rises from sea level to 1 200 metres at the foot of the Drakensberg. It is a grassy downland, the lower levels always green, the higher levels changing to reddish-brown during the frosty winters.

Countless hills and deep river valleys are the chief scenic features. All the rivers of Natal have their headwaters in the Drakensberg. They lose considerable altitude within short courses, creating waterfalls, rapids and deep gorges. The Mzimkulu, Mkomazi, Mgeni and Tugela are the principal rivers. Together with their tributaries, these rivers and their valleys provide spectacular scenery, wonderful fishing and canoeing, and vast economic potential in the supply of water for industry, agriculture and the generation of power.

Years ago great herds of plains game migrated each winter from the highveld of the Transvaal and the Orange Free State and grazed on the sweet grass of the midlands. Eland, hartebeest, gnu, zebra and springbok wandered throughout the area, and remnants of these herds survive in the Giant's Castle Game Reserve.

San hunters followed the game, some migrating with the herds to escape the cold of the high central plains, others living permanently in the sheltered valleys in the foothills of the Drakensberg.

The end of the 18th century was almost a fairy-tale period in the story of Natal. Many legends, myths and superstitions originate from this time. Man lived close to nature. Rivers, waterfalls and mountains all had their spirits. Diviners and mediums flourished. The indigenous people had little knowledge of what lay beyond their territory, limited trade, and little curiosity as to what lay over the horizon of a world they were certain was flat, with themselves living in the choicest part.

In 1818 disaster struck. Shaka had started to build the Zulu nation, and in the upheaval groups of refugees fled in all directions. The San were overwhelmed.

At this point the first Europeans reached Natal and found the whole area uninhabited. All had fled south from the Zulus. British ivory traders settled on the coast and founded Durban. When Piet Retief and the Voortrekkers looked down on the midlands of Natal from the escarpment of the central plains, their hearts ached at the sight of the lovely land.

But almost all the people who came to Natal, from the San to the British settlers who replaced the Voortrekkers, paid in blood for the land that had captivated them.

The hills and valleys of Natal are the face of a beautiful woman, destined to watch the deaths of many of her suitors. In her smile is a compassionate understanding of the enigma of man's inhumanity to his fellow creatures in a land large and rich enough to sustain them all.

Charlestown

The main railway line from Natal to the Transvaal climbs 455 metres up the escarpment between Newcastle and the Transvaal border. When the line was opened on 7 April 1891 the route encompassed a series of zigzags, reversing stations and a tunnel. The old steam locomotives had a tough time on this pass, which was named Laing's Nek after Henry Laing, who farmed on the lower slopes.

To provide the exhausted passengers and railway staff with refreshment a town was laid out at the summit of the pass on the Natal side of the border. This was called Charlestown in honour of Sir Charles Mitchell, the governor of Natal, and it was between here and Volksrust, in the Transvaal, that the third Swaziland Convention was signed in a railway carriage in 1894 (see Volksrust, page 224). Charlestown remained the end of the line for four years until political differences with the Transvaal government were settled and the last 280 kilometres of the line to Johannesburg were completed.

Electric locomotives now flow smoothly along the relocated route and Charlestown is a small village, overlooked by the high peaks of the northern Drakensberg.

Colenso

The Tugela River is a source of water and power for many industries. The town of Colenso, named after Bishop J. W. Colenso, was created on the upper reaches of the river in 1855. It is the site of a large power station feeding the national grid, and has recently developed as an industrial area of considerable potential.

There is boating and canoeing on the Tugela river and a caravan park on its banks. Several major battles of the Anglo-Boer War were fought in the vicinity.

Dundee

In many areas of Natal the early settlers found coal exposed on the ground's surface. A geological survey in 1880 proved that there were workable deposits in northern Natal, with especially rich deposits on and around the farm Dundee. A pioneer of the Natal coal mining industry, Peter Smith, laid out a town on Dundee to serve as a centre for several mines. It soon grew to be a substantial trading and railway centre with several smaller towns developing nearby, such as Dannhauser, Glencoe, Wasbank and Elandslaagte. There is a geological and mining museum, and a local history museum featuring relics of the Anglo-Zulu wars.

Estcourt

A fort was built in 1847 to guard the fording place over the Bushman River — a staging point on the road from Pietermaritzburg to the north. Shopkeepers, blacksmiths and innkeepers were attracted to the area and in 1863 the growing town was named after Thomas Estcourt, an English parliamentarian who had promoted immigration to Natal.

With ample water from the Wagendrift Dam, 5 kilometres upstream, Estcourt has flourished, with a farmers' co-operative sausage and meat packing plant, a milk canning and drying plant, a hardboard factory and a coffee factory.

Estcourt is on the main line from the coast to the north.

The town has a caravan park on the banks of the Bushman River.

Greytown

The Umvoti district of Natal produces timber and wattle bark. Cool and high, the district lies along a part of the mist belt where moisture-laden winds from the Indian Ocean form blankets of cloud and drizzle. Greytown was established in 1854 as a centre for this area.

It was named in honour of Sir George Grey, Governor of the Cape, and was in those days a frontier town, separated from the independent country of the Zulus by the deep val-

Sugar cane fields north of Greytown with plantations of wattle covering the hills.

ley of the Tugela River.

There are comfortable rondavels and a caravan park nearby on the shores of Lake Merthley.

General Louis Botha was born on a farm 5 kilometres south of Greytown. The site of the house is marked by a memorial. Botha commanded the Boer forces during the Anglo-Boer War, and became the first Prime Minister of the Union of South Africa in 1910.

A museum is now housed in the old Residency.

Harding

A narrow-gauge railway leads for 87 kilometres from Port Shepstone through a rolling sea of hills to the small town of Harding, founded in 1873 and named after Walter Harding, a supreme court judge. The town is an administrative, agricultural and timber-producing centre. The narrow-gauge railway is a gem of its kind. The miniature steam locomotives are well maintained by their proud drivers.

Hilton

The farm of Upper Hilton lies on the brow of the escarpment above Pietermaritzburg. Misty rains maintain the area in perpetual greenness and Hilton, below the escarpment, is one of the loveliest residential districts of Natal.

In 1872 the Reverend W. O. Newnham opened a school in the original farmhouse and this became known as Hilton College — today one of South Africa's leading private schools.

Howick

A scar in the ground made by wagons and footprints following a line of least resistance over mountains and valleys was the first trail from the coast of

THINGS TO DO AND SEE

Angling Between August and May the trout fishing is excellent in the upper reaches of many rivers of the Natal midlands, where they were introduced in 1889. Indigenous fish include several species of barbus (also known as scalies), eels (often more than 2 metres long) and barbel (or catfish). Carp, large-mouth and small-mouth bass, black bass and bluegills have been introduced into many dams.

Antiquities The Natal Museum and the Voortrekker Museum in Pietermaritzburg are major South African museums. Ladysmith and Dundee have smaller museums. Battlefields of the Anglo-Boer War can be seen in northern Natal. The siege sites around Ladysmith are signposted.

Boating and canoeing There is boating at Midmar and most of the other big irrigation dams such as Chelmsford. The upper Tugela and its main tributary, the Buffalo, have long stretches suitable for canoes. In January each year there is a 3-day canoe race on the Mgeni River through the Valley of a Thousand Hills from Pietermaritzburg to Durban.

Camping and caravanning Pietermaritzburg, Howick, Ladysmith, Newcastle and Estcourt all have large caravan parks. There is a recreational area and camp at Midmar Dam.

Railways There are delightful narrow-gauge railways from Umzinto to Umzimkulu, from Port Shepstone to Harding, and from Cato Ridge to Mid-Illovo. These lines are still worked by steam.

Traditional scenes The costumes of the Bhaca women at Richmond are noted for their elaborate beadwork. The road to the Nagle Dam in the Valley of a Thousand Hills leads through a densely inhabited area.

A steam engine resting in Greytown's historical museum.

Fort Durnford at Estcourt. It is reputed to be haunted by military ghosts.

The high falls — a place of treacherous beauty

The wattle tree in blossom.

Natal is the principal area in South Africa for growing wattle — the versatile tree that produces tannic acid for the leather industry and wood pulp for the making of paper.

The black wattle (*Acacia mearnsii*) was introduced to Natal by an immigrant, John Vanderplank, who brought seeds from Tasmania and planted them on his farm, Camperdown, between Durban and Pietermaritzburg. In Tasmania wattles were grown as windbreaks and hedges, but in Natal they grew into trees, with sweet-smelling flowers in spring.

One farmer, Sir George Sutton, of Howick, noticed a liquid between the surface wood and the bark of the trees and sent a bundle of the bark to London for testing.

For 12 years the bark lay untouched in a Thames warehouse. Then, by chance, an analytical chemist saw the bundle and tested it, discovering the high tannic acid content of the bark.

Sutton was astonished to receive a report on his long-forgotten sample, but in 1889 he published the findings and this was the start of the use of wattle in the tanning industry. Later it was found that wattle makes excellent pulp for paper.

Today paper manufacturers in the Far East take the bulk of South African wattle wood.

Natal to the interior of South Africa. This unplanned route would sometimes lead to awkward situations. So it was with the crossing of the Mgeni River, which was swift and deep. The best natural fording place was immediately above a 95-metre waterfall known to the Africans as kwaNogqaza ('place of the tall one'). It was a beautiful, but treacherous spot, and many travellers and wagons were swept over the falls. A modern bridge has replaced the ford.

At most of the important fording places blacksmiths, traders and innkeepers established businesses to supply travellers. The first inhabitant of the town of Howick — named after the Northumberland home of Earl Grey, the British colonial secretary — was a hotel keeper who also provided a ferry service. His young son was swept over the falls during a flood. A pile of stones marks his grave at the foot of the waterfall.

There is a viewing site, a tea-room and a caravan park on the banks of the river above the waterfall, which is now known as the Howick Falls.

There are several other waterfalls in the vicinity and all of them have claimed human lives. Near Howick are Cascade Falls (25 metres) and Shelter Falls (37 metres), while Karkloof Falls (105 metres) is 16 kilometres to the east.

The Midmar Dam, 3 km from Howick, is a scenic holiday resort.

Ixopo

Few villages in Africa have a lovelier rural setting than Ixopo. Founded in 1878 as an agricultural and timber-producing centre, the village takes its name from a marsh called by the Zulus eXobo, from the sound made by a person squelching through the mud.

The narrow-gauge railway that serves the district passes through beautiful hill scenery on its route from Umzinto on the south coast.

Kloof

The road to Pietermaritzburg climbs 550 metres above sea level in the first 27 kilometres out of Durban. At this point the hills are covered with trees, there are gardens full of flowers, and in the distance the Indian Ocean, blue and hazy, surges restlessly against the

The Karkloof River tumbling over a cascade just above its main waterfall.

shores of Africa.

A deep ravine cuts through the hills with a stream known as the Molweni ('stream of high cliffs') rushing down through rapids, cascades and a waterfall. This ravine is the 447-hectare Krantzkloof Nature Reserve. The town of Kloof ('ravine') surrounds the reserve. Green, park-like and cool, it is one of the most attractive residential areas in the hills above Durban.

Kokstad

One of the most harrowing and difficult mountain journeys in the history of South Africa was accomplished in the early 1860s when a section of the Griqua people, led by their chief, Adam Kok, left their homes at Philippolis in the Orange Free State and trekked eastwards to a reputed

promised land. The route took them through the rugged, mountainous country of Lesotho and over the Drakensberg at a saddle in the mountains which they named Ongeluksnek ('accident saddle'), owing to the death of one of their men during a hunt for eland.

On reaching what later became known as Griqualand East, they found that they had indeed discovered a promised land — a region ideal for agriculture. They established a centre which they called Kokstad after their leader. Every male Griqua was allocated a farm of at least 1 200 hectares, but most of them sold their estates and squandered the money.

In 1874 Griqualand East was annexed to the Cape colony and Kokstad became the administrative centre for

The summit of Kranskop standing like a giant sentry over the Tugela Valley.

Howick Falls, close to the trunk road and a favourite site for tourists.

The Soofie Mosque and Madressa, a beautiful example of Muslim architecture, built in the hot valley of the Klip River.

a district named Mount Currie after the 2 224-metre peak that looms over the town. The mountain was named by the Griquas after Sir Walter Currie, a champion of their interests.

Kokstad today is a centre for cheese and other dairy products. Griqualand East is riding country, where polo matches and gymkhanas are popular. Horses are bred here. The town has a lingering atmosphere of the past when it was temporarily the capital of the independent state of Griqualand East. It has an elegant little civic hall, with a bandstand in the garden, and a memorial to the men of the Cape Mounted Rifles — the tough regiment that garrisoned the frontier in the early days. Adam Kok is buried in the main street of the town.

Kokstad is the railhead for a line

Morning mist covers the rolling hills of Kwazulu in splendour.

from Pietermaritzburg. The surrounding district is green grassland with trout-filled streams, and in winter snow-covered mountains.

Kranskop
Towering over the wide valley of the Tugela River is the 1 175-metre Kranskop ('precipice summit'), called by the Zulus iTshe lika Ntunjambili ('the rock with two holes'). The Zulus have a myth about young girls who, weary of carrying water from the river, asked the mountain to give them sanctuary. It obliged by opening a great cavern and tempting them inside with sounds of revelry. Once in the cavern the entrance closed and they were seen no more.

In 1894 the village of Kranskop was founded on the edge of the valley close to the mountain. It is a centre for the production of timber, a railhead for the line from Pietermaritzburg and a trading place for the great valley.

Ladysmith
The Anglo-Boer War made Ladysmith a household name. The 118-day siege of the town, lasting from 2 November 1899 to 28 February 1900, so captivated people's imaginations that songs were composed, poems written, and every incident of the ordeal reported in the newspapers of the day.

Ladysmith lies in the warm valley of the Klip River ('stone river'). In 1847 a number of Voortrekkers settled here, finding the area to be excellent ranching country. They formed an independent republic — the Klip River Republic — with Andries Spies as their commandant. However, the British government soon intervened in this rural Utopia. They annexed the area in 1850 and established a town as an administrative centre for what they called the Klip River District.

The town was named after Lady Juana Smith, a renowned Spanish beauty who was the wife of the popular governor of the Cape, Sir Harry Smith. A town named Harrismith in his honour, 80 kilometres away, had just been created by the Orange Free State on the top of the highveld escarpment, and it was considered fitting to give the new Natal town the title of his consort.

Ladysmith is a busy junction on the main road and railway from Durban to the Transvaal and to the Orange Free State. Cattle and horses are bred in the district and dairy products, maize, millet, oats, soya beans, fruit and vegetables are produced. It is also the centre for a variety of industries.

The public buildings date from the days of the siege. The town hall clock tower was shelled by the Boers. A museum exhibits many items from the war years.

Matatiele
The southern reaches of the Drakensberg have a particularly forbidding appearance and the very name (meaning 'dragon mountain') is thought to have originated from a myth about a mighty dragon that once lived in this part of the range.

When the Griquas migrated from Philippolis in the early 1860s they settled in this area and the town of Matatiele was founded on the verges of a marsh called Madi-i-Yila ('the ducks have flown').

Until 1874 the area was on the wild side of law and order. Rustlers, smugglers and renegades hid here from the police of Natal and the Cape, and it was a base for horse thieves, who hid the stolen animals in the Drakensberg.

When the Cape government annexed Griqualand East in 1874 they started to 'clean up' the area. The Griqua leader, Adam Kok, had appointed a magistrate at Matatiele but he was drunk most of the time and usually prepared to close his eyes to law-breaking provided he was supplied with whisky. The Cape government sent a more respectable police force but it was driven away in 1880 when the disturbances in Lesotho known as the Gun War — an attempt by the British to disarm various unruly elements — spread over the mountains to Griqualand East.

After 12 months, authority was restored in the district, and Matatiele was garrisoned by a detachment of the Cape Mounted Rifles. However, gun-running to Lesotho, together with rustling, remained profitable for the locals, and some colourful characters made their homes here.

Matatiele is now the centre for a prosperous farming district producing basic food crops such as maize and

A capital worthy of the trekkers' dreamland

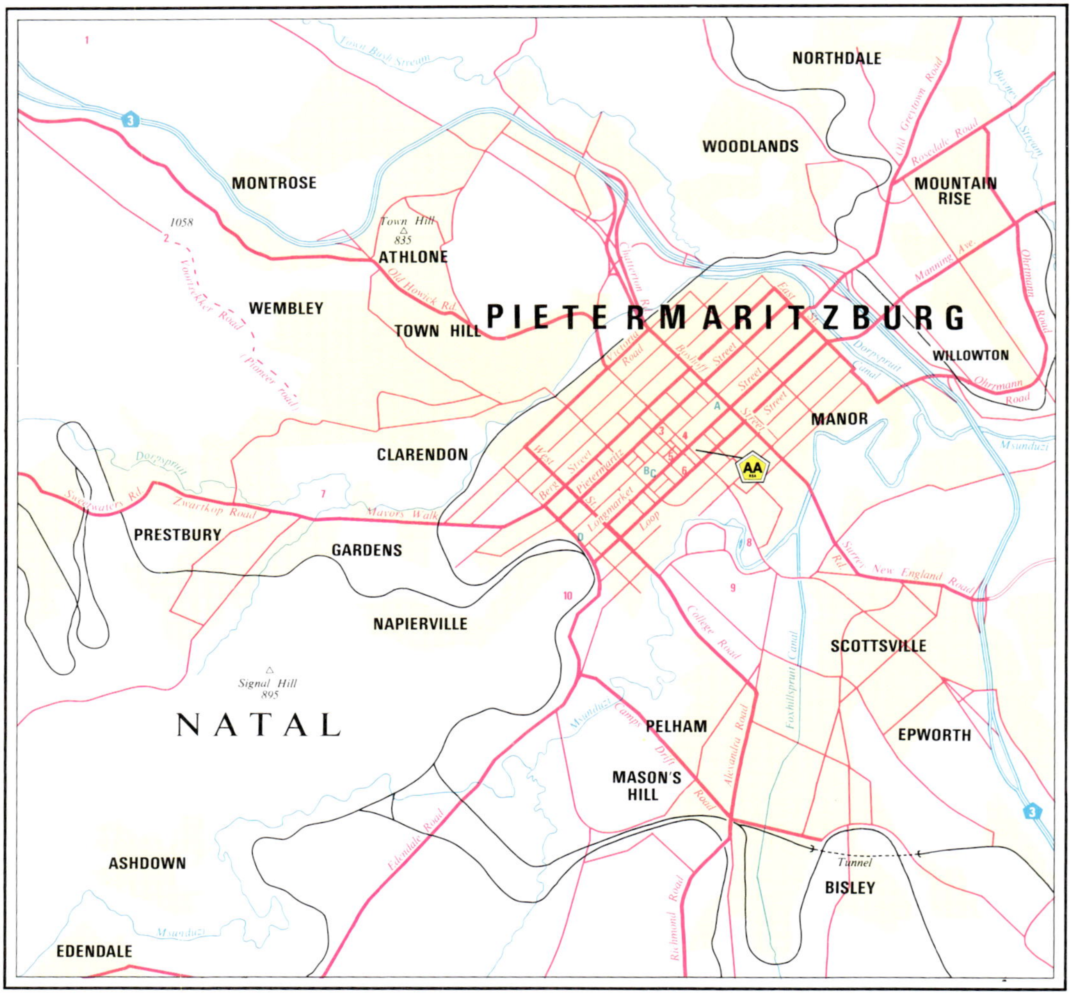

PIETERMARITZBURG

National Monuments

A Voortrekker Museum (Church of the Vow)
B St. Peter's Church
C Natal Legislative Council and Legislative Assembly Buildings
D Old Government House

Places of interest

1 Queen Elizabeth Park
2 World's View
3 Old Supreme Court
4 City Hall
5 Provincial Council Building
6 Natal Museum
7 Botanical Gardens
8 Kershaw Park
9 Alexandra Park
10 Fort Napier and St George Garrison Church

City and surroundings map scale

---

dairy goods.

Horses are bred in the area and polo is a local sport. There are two nature reserves, one of which has a large lake offering excellent trout fishing.

Mooi River

The Mooi River ('beautiful river') flows through a fertile valley. Willow trees droop along the riverbanks and the hillsides are richly grassed.

In 1921 a town was established on the banks of the river. It is a busy agricultural centre and on the first Wednesday of every month the Mooi River Farmers' Association holds what are claimed to be the largest stock sales in southern Africa.

Fish are caught in the river and there is a country club with a golf course and other sporting amenities.

The altitude of the town — 1 389 metres above sea level — gives the area a crisp climate in contrast to the heat and humidity of the coast 160 kilometres to the south-east.

Newcastle

The fourth town established in Natal after Durban, Weenen and Pietermaritzburg, was Newcastle — named after the British colonial secretary, the Duke of Newcastle. It was founded in 1864 as a trade and administrative centre for northern Natal. There was much fighting around Newcastle during the Anglo-Transvaal War of 1881 and the Anglo-Boer War of 1899-1902 when the town was used as a depot by the British Army. The

Cattle and dairy farming are the principal industries of the Natal midlands.

The redbrick city hall of Pietermaritzburg with its elaborate ornamentation.

battlefields of Majuba, Laing's Nek and Ingogo are nearby.

The Chelmsford Dam supplies the largest thermal power station in Natal, the Ingagane power station. The dam has recreation amenities.

The third Iscor steelworks is at Newcastle.

There is a caravan park with a swimming pool near the Amcor dam.

New Germany

Immediately inland from Durban the country rises steadily and within 20 kilometres reaches an altitude of 400 metres. The coastal heat and humidity diminish and in the cool, well-watered, green setting several towns and villages have grown.

New Germany dates from 1848 when a party of 183 German immigrants arrived here to settle on a cotton-growing estate named Westville after the lieutenant-governor of Natal, Martin West. Cotton proved an unsuccessful crop in these parts but the settlers prospered, growing vegetables and flowers.

Paulpietersburg

A hot spring, the Lurula Natal Spa, surfaces on the southern approaches to the 1 536-metre mountain known as Dumbe from the wild dumbe fruit that grows on its slopes. A village was founded here and named after President Paul Kruger and Commandant-general Pieter Joubert of the Transvaal. A resort has grown up around the spa 14 kilometres from the town.

Pietermaritzburg

The Voortrekkers had a good eye for town sites. After their defeat of the Zulus at the end of 1838 the trekkers selected farms and settled down to enjoy life in Natal. To serve as capital of their republic they created the town named Pietermaritzburg after their two leaders, Piet Retief and Gert Maritz. The site was in a fertile hollow at the foot of a tree-covered escarpment where the midlands of Natal rise 400 metres above the surrounding landscape.

The soil was rich and there was ample water for irrigation from the river known as the Msunduzi ('the pusher') from the surging power of its floods. The town was planned with

A typical private residence of the mid-19th century, built of red brick.

Macrorie House in Pietermaritzburg, full of vivid memories.

The gardens and building of the Church of the Vow, built by the Voortrekkers.

wide streets, water furrows along each side, and large gardens for each home. Thatched cottages lined the streets and there was a church and a small hall for the quarterly sittings of the volksraad ('people's council').

The British took over Pietermaritzburg in 1843 and it became the seat of their administration for Natal. The first lieutenant-governor, Martin West, made his home here, and Fort Napier, named after the governor of the Cape, Sir George Napier, was built to house a garrison.

The first newspaper in Natal, the *Natal Witness*, was published in Pietermaritzburg in 1846. This was a lively sheet which, in some of its earlier issues, had as its editorial address the Pietermaritzburg gaol, owing to the imprisonment there of the editor for offending the governor.

The town had shops, inns and a large central square used as a market and as an outspan area for wagons travelling between the coast and the interior of southern Africa. Hunters, explorers and traders passed through the town in vehicles laden with skins, horns and tusks, and often accompanied by tame animals such as zebras and ostriches.

In 1893 Natal received responsible government and a handsome assembly building was created in Pietermaritzburg to house its parliament. In the same year the massive, redbrick city hall was completed, adorned with domes, clock tower and stained-glass windows, and containing, apart from its offices and hall, a small art gallery exhibiting a collection of paintings, china, glassware and clocks.

The building was destroyed by fire in 1895, but was rebuilt in 1901.

The original church built by the Voortrekkers when they established Pietermaritzburg stands on the market square on the eastern side of the city hall.

This is now the Voortrekker Museum, which houses relics of the pioneer days and of the battles with the Zulus. A new addition to the museum is Welverdient, the historic home of the hero of the Battle of Blood River, Andries Pretorius. There are statues of Gert Maritz and Piet Retief in the garden.

The Natal Museum in the centre of

A cool, green retreat for the city workers

the city features items of natural and cultural history. A reconstruction of an early street scene is one display of interest.

The gardens of Pietermaritzburg are luxuriant. The warm, relatively wet climate and deep soil suit flowering plants such as roses and azaleas. The azalea flourishes in this part of Natal so spectacularly that in September Pietermaritzburg has an annual azalea festival.

The city has several public parks. Alexandra Park, named after Queen Alexandra of Britain, covers 44,5 hectares and contains sports fields as well as gardens. There is a 5-hectare rock garden — the Mayor's Garden — with palm trees and roses and a site used for open-air art exhibitions staged annually in May. Next to Alexandra Park is another pleasant open space, Kershaw Park.

Wylie Park was presented to the city by Mrs G. H. Wylie together with a legacy for the development of its 8 hectares into a garden of largely indigenous plants. Azaleas also grow here in profusion and in spring the multi-coloured display of flowering plants is delightful.

The Botanic Gardens were created in 1872 by the Botanic Society of Natal. A collection of trees from many parts of the world grows on this 46-hectare site. The collection includes a fig tree 46 metres high and a magnificent avenue of plane trees that change colour with the seasons. There are ornamental ponds, bird sanctuaries and walks.

Eight kilometres north of the city, on the trunk road to the Transvaal, a 101-hectare nature reserve, the Queen Elizabeth Park, contains many indigenous plants, trees and wild animals.

Pietermaritzburg today is the provincial capital of Natal, and the Provincial Council building next to the old Legislative Council building contains mementos and portraits of Natal's early days. The Supreme Court building, like the City Hall, is built of red brick in the shade characteristic of the natural clay of the district.

Government House, once the official residence of the British governors, is now part of a teachers' training college. The original Fort Napier and the garrison's Church of St. George are maintained as historical monuments and contain relics of the British occupation, including antique artillery pieces and other weapons. There is a military graveyard close to the church and the tombstones carry the names of many who died in service here.

The Anglican Cathedral of St. Peter, consecrated in 1857, is another building intimately linked with the city's past. Bishop J. W. Colenso, a controversial churchman of the last century, is buried in this church.

Pietermaritzburg is the centre for numerous industries. Aluminium is produced here from material mined in Natal. Timber, wattle bark and dairy goods are also produced in the district.

There are many drives and beauty spots around the city. There are picnic places at World's View, 1 139 metres high on the escarpment overlooking Pietermaritzburg, and traces may be seen here of the pioneer road to the interior. Henley Dam, 22 kilometres away on the Bulwer Road, has been developed into a recreational area with boating and fishing. A turn-off 16 kilometres along the highway to Durban leads to the Natal Lion Park. The drive to Durban is magnificent. The road loses altitude from 676 metres above sea level to the coast by means of smooth gradients through an ocean of rolling hills. In May the annual Comrades' Marathon, run since 1921 between Durban and Pietermaritzburg, takes place along this road. The race now attracts thousands of entrants including international runners.

There is an annual canoe race from Pietermaritzburg to Durban — down the Msunduzi to its meeting with the Mgeni, and from there through the Valley of a Thousand Hills to the mouth of the Mgeni at Blue Lagoon in Durban.

The University of Natal grew from the original Pietermaritzburg College. Founded in 1909 as the Natal University College, it was extended to Durban in 1922, when it absorbed the Durban Technical Institute. The dual campus was incorporated into the University of Natal in March 1949.

Pinetown
The old road from Durban winds towards Pietermaritzburg in a series of curves, rises and drops. A number of inns were built along this route. The Wayside Hotel was one of these hostelries, where stage-coaches changed horses and passengers refreshed themselves. The inn was built in 1849 and during the next year a town was laid out around it and named Pinetown after the governor of Natal, Sir Benjamin Pine.

Pinetown has many industries and a large population of commuters who work in Durban but prefer to live here in a garden setting of trees and flowers 350 metres above the humidity and heat of the coast.

Queensburgh
Before finally falling away into the narrow belt of humid coastal forest, the jumble of hills of the midlands of Natal sweeps close to the sea. Many Durban workers build their homes on the inland hills to escape the ener-

Natal Table Mountain, dominating the Valley of a Thousand Hills.

1 2 3

The upper reaches of the Mzimkulu River flowing placidly through the foothills of the Drakensberg.

vating climate of the city. Several residential areas have developed where the air is cool and trees and flowering plants abound.

In 1924 four of these hillside residential townships — Malvern, Escombe, Northdene and Moseley — combined to form the Town Board of Malvern. In 1954 Malvern became a municipality and, it being coronation year, took on the name of Queens-burgh. Within this garden environment are sports grounds, schools, shopping centres and industrial areas.

Richmond

An influx of British settlers to Natal in 1850 brought to the upper valley of the Illovo River a number of former tenants from the Duke of Buccleuch's estate at Beaulieu in England. The village they founded, in a verdant and well-watered part of the valley, was at first named Beaulieu, but later, largely because the Africans found it difficult to pronounce, the name was changed to Richmond, another seat belonging to the duke.

The town is the railhead of a branch line from Pietermaritzburg. Timber, sugar cane, poultry, citrus fruit and dairy goods are produced here. A tangy blackberry jam is a speciality in the district. The surrounding countryside is varied and there are several scenic drives. The road to Eastwolds leads down into the deep valley of the Mkomazi River and up the slopes of the high sandstone cliffs of the Hela Hela ('buttresses'), with a spectacular viewing site at the summit.

The arrival of the English settlers at Richmond coincided with a slow return to the area of remnants of various peoples who had been driven away by raiding Zulu regiments and had fled southwards. The Zulus called these refugees amaBhaca ('people who hide'). These people joined the English settlers and Richmond is today their principal centre.

Although composed of elements of many different groups, the Bhaca have developed their own identity and their women are some of the most beautifully dressed in Natal. On Tuesdays, Bhaca brides can be seen in their best outfits when they come to town to register their marriages.

Utrecht

In 1854 a group of cattle-men obtained from Mpande, the Zulu king, grazing rights in the area of northern Natal between the Buffalo and the Blood rivers. Having been granted grazing rights, however, the ranchers then claimed the land as their own and formed an independent republic which they named Utrecht after the ancient city in Holland.

The republic was only 32 kilometres by 64 kilometres but it covered some choice cattle country. The straggling little capital, also named Utrecht, was like a Wild West town with one long main street. There was a triumvirate government of three elected leaders and law and order was maintained by Christian Klopper and his wife, a renowned strongwoman who challenged all visiting males to wrestle with her and almost invariably threw them over her shoulder.

The Utrecht republic was absorbed into the Transvaal in 1858 and at the end of the Anglo-Boer War it was returned to Natal.

Utrecht lies in a cattle farming and coal mining region.

Valley of a Thousand Hills

The river known to Africans as the

The Bhaca have some of the most colourful of the costumes of Africa.

1. An engaged girl, coyly concealing her face and standing in an attitude of respect to her elders.
2. The ornate costume of a young married woman — hair ochred and decorated with beadwork, a goatskin skirt with individual bead designs. The beaded knob over the forehead indicates marriage.
3. Another young Bhaca married woman. The cap of beadwork on her ochred hair is always worn when she is away from her home kraal.
4. A novitiate doctor kneels in respect before his teacher.
5. A Bhaca doctor in full regalia with goatskin shoulder-straps and switches. Her headdress reveals that she is a married woman.

4

5

Land of cannibals and a thousand hills

Mngeni ('the place of acacia trees') and to Europeans as the Mgeni has its source on the slopes of the 2 146-metre Spioenkop in the midlands of Natal and from there flows eastwards to the sea at Durban.

The river feeds the Midmar Dam, drives a hydro-electric plant at Howick, and then tumbles over the Howick and the Albert falls. Finally, between Pietermaritzburg and Durban, it flows for 64 kilometres through the spectacular Valley of a Thousand Hills.

This huge valley is the home of the Debe. During the early years of the 19th century these people were so ruined by Zulu raids that many of them turned cannibal and, assisted by packs of vicious dogs, hunted man for food. The cannibals gave the valley an evil reputation. Some of the region's inhabitants survived the attentions of the Zulus and the cannibals by taking refuge on the 959-metre Natal Table Mountain, known to the Zulus as emKhambathini ('place of giraffe acacia trees').

This massive, flat-topped mountain dominates the western end of the valley. Geologically, it is a blood brother of Table Mountain in the

Flood diversion weir in the Valley of a Thousand Hills.

Cape. Composed of sandstone, it has precipitous, bush-covered slopes, and a plateau summit, reached by an easy path from the western side. From the summit there are panoramic views of the valley, eastwards for 50 kilometres to the coast, and westwards for 120 kilometres directly across the midlands of Natal to the Drakensberg.

Parts of the Valley of a Thousand Hills are densely populated. Other parts are wild and bushy. Summer

temperatures are oven-hot.

A tarred road winds to the floor of the valley from Cato Ridge alongside the main Pietermaritzburg-Durban road. This road terminates at the Nagle Dam, built on the Mgeni River to supply water to Durban. At the dam are picnic grounds, a tea-room, a curio shop, fishing facilities, and a village where dancing displays and traditional costumes can be seen.

The Valley of a Thousand Hills is

rich in flowering plants, including arum lilies, fire lilies, snake lilies, red-hot pokers, and many species of aloes.

The old road to Durban, which branches off at Cato Ridge from the modern trunk road, twists and turns through majestic scenery for 27 kilometres along the southern edge of the valley.

There are several hotels, holiday farms and caravan parks along the old Durban road. Most of them have dramatic views into the valley. Bead work and other curios are sold in shops or by traders in traditional clothes.

For many years an artist, the late Miss C. Cheeseman, had a studio overlooking the valley. Her paintings of the valley, including a panorama identifying most of the landmarks, are collectors' pieces.

Vryheid

When Cetshwayo died on 8 February 1884 there was disagreement over who should succeed to the Zulu throne. Cetshwayo's son, Dinuzulu, found himself opposed by dissidents, notably a resolute fighting chief, Zibebu, who had been granted independence by the British in their efforts to bring peace to what was then Zululand after

The steep slopes leading down into the Valley of a Thousand Hills.

Plantations, maize fields and rural villages in the hill country near Vryheid.

the Anglo-Zulu War. Dinuzulu's followers, the Suthu faction of the Zulus, were no match for Zibebu's fighting men, who also had the support of a number of European frontiersmen. These included Johan Colenbrander, who provided Zibebu with valuable military guidance.

Dinuzulu was approached by a group of Europeans — mainly cattlemen from the north of Natal — who guaranteed to establish him as king of Zululand if he would reward them with farms.

Dinuzulu accepted and about 800 European mercenaries rallied to his support. They crowned him king of Zululand and then, with the Suthu army, set out to defeat Zibebu, which they accomplished in the Battle of Ghost Mountain.

Dinuzulu then found himself in a predicament. If he rewarded each of the 800 mercenaries with farms of the size they expected, there would be nothing left of Zululand. A prolonged argument followed. The mercenaries were tough and the Zulus had been weakened by their defeat in the Anglo-Zulu War and by their civil war with Zibebu.

Eventually, 500 mercenaries each received a farm of 1 600 hectares. Another 300 men who had arrived late received smaller grants, known as 'half farms'.

Using a compass and a cross-bar, the mercenaries, called the Committee of Dinuzulu's Volunteers, set out to survey all the farms. They went across Zululand to the sea and there was not enough room for all the required farms. The survey was then repeated, allocating smaller farms.

However, at the end of the second survey there was still not much left for the Zulus.

On 5 August 1884 the mercenaries formed the 'Nieuwe Republiek' (New Republic) with a capital named Vryheid ('liberty'), situated in northern Natal. German agents also arrived, with plans to develop a port at Lake St. Lucia as an outlet for the republic.

At this point the British government intervened to keep out the Germans and to ensure that some part of the country was left for the Zulu people. This fragment was proclaimed a British protectorate in 1887 and in July

Strange shapes and harsh erosion in the country near Vryheid in northern Natal. Flash floods cause such damage.

1888 the New Republic joined Paul Kruger's South African Republic.

At the end of the Anglo-Boer War the territory of the New Republic was transferred to Natal.

Vryheid has now grown into a large town, and is a centre for coal mining and ranching. A small museum containing relics from the days of the New Republic is housed in the building once used as the republic's council chamber. A fort stands behind the museum.

Weenen

The thorn-bush landscape through which the Bushman River flows on its way to join the Tugela is cattle country. The river also irrigates fields of vegetables, lucerne, groundnuts and citrus fruit.

In 1838 a town was laid out here by the Voortrekkers and named Weenen ('weeping') in memory of the massacres of trekkers by Zulus (see feature, pages 310-313). The town retains much of the atmosphere of the early days. There is a museum containing Voortrekker relics in a building erected by the Voortrekker leader, Andries Pretorius. In the garden of the museum is a restored watermill.

A narrow-gauge railway was built in 1907 to connect Weenen to Estcourt,

46,5 kilometres to the west, but the line is now closed.

Westville

In 1847 two Germans, H. Jaraal and P. Jung, bought 6 000 hectares of ground 6 kilometres west of Durban. They named the farm Westville in honour of Martin West, the British lieutenant-governor of Natal, and tried to grow cotton and coffee there, without much success.

Today Westville is a residential area for people working in Durban. The Durban-Westville University for Indians has its 200-hectare campus here.

NATAL'S EXOTIC CANE COUNTRY

THE NORTH COAST of Natal — the 100-kilometre stretch from Durban to the Tugela River — is sugar country. Its climate ranges from warm to hot and humid, and the Mocambique Current flowing down the coast is seldom cooler than 25 °C. The sands are golden-brown and the shores are lined with casuarinas, palms, and vivid flowering exotics such as hibiscus and bougainvillea.

Most of the rivers end in lagoons. Holiday resorts have sprung up, with luxury hotels looking out over swimming pools to the blue Indian Ocean. There are also tidal pools and bays with shark-protected beaches.

The northern coastal belt is about 50 kilometres wide — some 30 kilometres wider than the belt on the south coast. It was once a dense coastal forest inhabited by vervet monkeys, wild pigs and a large population of snakes, especially black and green mambas, pythons and adders. This green belt has numerous rivers, rich soil, and a setting ideal for the cultivation of tropical fruits and crops.

A few groups of Lala people settled along the north coast, but they were not numerous and the growth of the Zulu nation at the beginning of the 19th century made their existence precarious. Most of the Lala people fled. Those who remained made no effort to prosper — the possession of valuables would simply have attracted the attentions of a raiding Zulu regiment. In these primitive societies, poverty and docility were often the best defences in the struggle for survival.

The trade path from Durban to what was then Zululand led up the north coast. It was the route followed by the ivory hunters, traders, and also the Zulu army on its periodic raids into Natal and the Pondo country. Shaka liked the area so much that he built his last capital there — kwaDukuza, on the site of the present town of Stanger. His successor Dingane also had a substantial garrison post there — kwaHlomendlini ('place of the home guard') — although he preferred the more northerly parts of Zululand for his own residence.

Europeans noticed the potential of the area as they travelled through it on their journeys to trade with the Zulus. Pioneers observed that a species of wild sugar cane, called mpha by the Zulus, grew in the area. This cane was chewed with relish by African and European alike. It was juicy and sweet but its sugar content was not high enough to make it commercially valuable.

In the 1840s Mauritians settled on the north coast. The climate was so similar to that of their fair island in the Indian Ocean that they felt completely at home. They introduced the lovely casuarina (filaos) tree, which originates from Madagascar, and flowering shrubs and trees such as the poinciana and the flame tree. Litchi trees from Mauritius were also planted, together with pawpaws, bananas, and the richly flavoured, smooth-textured mango known as maison rouge.

In 1847 a Durban firm, the Milner Brothers, who traded with Mauritius, imported seeds and cuttings of crops from Mauritius and Reunion. Included in this experimental cargo were 40 000 tops of the inferior variety of sugar cane known as Mauritius red cane. This cargo was auctioned in Durban and purchased by settlers from various parts of Natal, who planted the tops on their lands.

Natal was in a state of economic doldrums at that time. Everybody admired the beauty of the countryside but nobody had been able to find a profitable crop for the area. The experimental shipment brought in by Milner Brothers was regarded with keen interest.

In 1848 a new settler arrived from Mauritius — Ephraim Rathbone. He travelled up the north coast to become overseer of an experimental cotton estate, managed by Edmund Morewood, on the Mdloti River. Cotton did not flourish in the area, but on his way there Rathbone noticed a patch of Mauritius red cane growing on a farm on the banks of the Mgeni River. Rathbone obtained a few samples of the cane from the farmer and he induced Morewood to plant them on a spare piece of ground on the cotton estate. This was the beginning of an industry that today produces more than 2 million tons of sugar a year — enough to supply the whole of South Africa and furnish a huge surplus for export. The original inferior variety of cane has long been replaced by cultivars of better quality, quick to grow and yielding more sugar.

Ballito

A popular holiday resort 50 kilometres north of Durban, Ballito has a shark-protected beach, tidal pools, a hotel, several restaurants and numerous holiday flats.

Compensation

Edmund Morewood was the manager of a cotton estate on the Mdloti River. His overseer, Ephraim Rathbone, planted an experimental patch of sugar cane. The cane grew well, but the company that owned the estate was primarily interested in cotton and was on the verge of bankruptcy.

In 1849 Morewood left the company and settled on a farm of his own, named Compensation, lying between the Tongati and Mhlali rivers. He took the sugar cane with him. His resources were limited, but he had become convinced that sugar was the crop for the north coast of Natal.

While the cotton company went out of business the sugar cane grew, and at the end of 1850 Morewood built a crude little mill. In this mill, early in 1851, he crushed his first crop of cane — the first sugar to be produced in Natal.

There was a sensation in Natal when people sampled Morewood's sugar. His mill and plantation became a place of pilgrimage for many other farmers who wanted to look, learn, and purchase some cane tops to plant on their own estates. There was a rush to buy land on the north coast and the

The estuaries of the north coast rivers are the homes of crabs and prawns.

THINGS TO DO AND SEE

Angling Winter and spring are the best seasons for angling in this area. During summer the rivers stain the sea with their muddy flood waters and fish tend to keep away. Barracuda and shad may be caught in winter and spring. Salmon, kingfish, stumpnose and grunter are present in summer. Sharks are numerous and fight stubbornly when caught. Especially vigorous are the shovelnose (sandshark), the greys, blackfins and ragged tooths.

Camping and caravanning There are camping and caravan grounds at many spots along this coast, such as Ballito, Salt Rock, Shakas Rock, Umhlanga Rocks and Sinkwazi Beach. All the parks are shady, and the weather is warm to hot throughout the year, with high humidity and rain being the only discomforts.

Fruit Tropical fruits on the north coast are superb, and include litchis, mangoes, avocados, pawpaws, guavas and bananas.

Sightseeing The trunk road along the coast — Shaka's Way — provides a scenic drive from Durban to the frontier of old Zululand on the Tugela River. The old north coast road, several kilometres inland, runs parallel to the trunk road. The old road serves the sugar estates, mills and 'sugar towns'. Traffic is often heavy, with trucks laden with cane. The estates and mills can be visited; tourists should apply to the offices at the mills.

Swimming Hotels and resorts have swimming baths and tidal pools. Sharks here can be particularly dangerous, especially in summer, and it is inadvisable to venture into the sea unless the bathing area is protected by nets.

A giant fruit-eating beetle feeding on sap oozing from a north coast tree.

entire economic situation in Natal suddenly brightened.

A replica of Morewood's pioneer sugar mill has been built in a garden on the site of the original mill in the midst of a vast sea of sugar cane. It can be reached via a signposted turn-off from the old north coast road 43 kilometres from Durban.

ekuPhakameni

One of the largest of the African Christian sects was founded in 1911 by a prophet named Isaiah Shembe of the Ngwaneni people. He named his movement the Nazarite Church. In the Inanda district he bought land and founded a village called ekuPhakameni ('place of spiritual uplift'). Before his death in 1935 Shembe had attracted a large number of followers. His son Galilee replaced him as prophet and the church continued to grow.

Shembe's grave at ekuPhakameni is regarded as a shrine, and in January, April, July and September of every year, festivals are held here. These are large gatherings, with the faithful dressed in elaborate costume. Dancing, singing, and feasting take place, and the scene is spectacular and animated. Visitors are welcome.

Inanda

Some 24 kilometres from Durban, along a road that climbs steeply into the high hills, lies the small administrative, magisterial and trading centre of Inanda ('the pleasant place'). The road passes through an area densely inhabited by African people and ends at one of the most magnificent viewing sites in Africa, with a panorama of the Valley of a Thousand Hills.

This area was once famous for its prolific wildlife as well as its scenery. The scenery will always remain, but unfortunately the area's wildlife has largely been driven away. There is still a reasonable and varied birdlife, with crowned and martial eagles, Knysna and purple-crested loeries, and the Narina trogon.

The former Inanda Game Park preserved some of this wildlife, and its beneficial influence remains.

Mhlali River

The Mhlali River is noted for the number of monkey orange trees that

Sugar-cane fields cover the hills of the north coast like a huge green blanket.

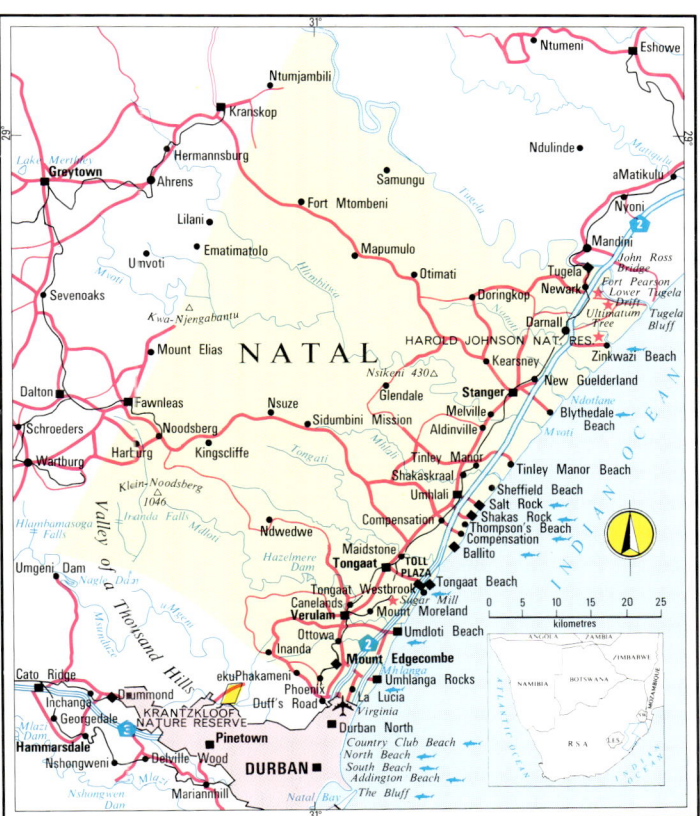

Where the greatest of the Zulus was murdered

grow along its banks. They are known in Zulu as mhlali trees. On opposite sides of the mouth of the river are two holiday resorts — Salt Rock and Umhlali. Both have hotels and caravan parks.

Higher up the river stands the Shakas Kraal sugar mill, with a small town next to it housing the workers.

Mount Edgecombe

The seat of the Earl of Mount Edgcumbe in Cornwall, England, is the source of the name of this sugar town. It lies in a tropical garden setting of flowering creepers and tall trees. A handsome Hindu temple graces the town's northern border.

William Campbell, the renowned sugar pioneer, settled in the area in 1850 on an estate he named Muckleneuk.

Mount Moreland

John Moreland surveyed this area, which is named after him.

It was here, in the 1860s, that Liege Hulett began a farming industry that eventually made the name of his family synonymous with sugar throughout South Africa. His first sugar mill at Tinley Manor was the start of a large industry.

New Guelderland

In 1859 a Dutch immigrant, Theodorus Colenbrander, founded a settle-

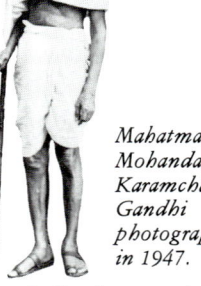

GANDHI IN NATAL

Mahatma Mohandas Karamchand Gandhi photographed in 1947.

A young Indian lawyer arrived in Durban in 1893 to take part in a lawsuit in the Transvaal. He booked a first-class train ticket to Johannesburg — and was ordered off the train because of his colour. He spent a cold night in the non-European waiting-room at Pietermaritzburg railway station.

The lawyer's name was Mahatma Gandhi. His experience made him decide to remain in Natal and help the growing community of Indians imported to work on the sugar plantations.

He stayed for 21 years and it was here that he formulated his famous doctrine of passive resistance. He founded the Phoenix Settlement in the Inanda district — a communal farm where all workers drew the same wage, and in their spare time wrote, edited and published the *Indian Opinion*, a newspaper that still exerts influence on Indian affairs.

Gandhi returned to India in 1914, but his name is still deeply revered by the Indian community in South Africa. Today a trust runs the Phoenix Settlement.

The elaborate facade of a Hindu temple. Such temples are the scene of many colourful ceremonies.

Sugar country near Stanger. Climate and soil are both ideal.

The flowers of the Natal bottlebrush.

ment which he named after his home town in Holland.

He brought a party of 80 Dutch immigrants to his settlement and housed them in a large building next to a sugar mill. The settlement did not prosper, but New Guelderland remains a nostalgic small village.

Shakas Rock

A rocky promontory of the north coast, believed to have been used as a lookout by the great Zulu chief, Shaka, is known as Shakas Rock.

The name is shared by the resort at its foot which has a hotel, several holiday cottages and flats, beautiful beaches and a tidal pool.

Stanger

During the last few years of his life, Shaka built a new capital for his Zulu nation in the warmth of the north coast. He named it kwaDukuza ('the place of the lost person') because of the capital's complex labyrinth of huts. It was here, in a small kraal attached to the capital, that Shaka was assassinated by two half-brothers, Dingane and Mhlangane, on 24 September 1828, and his body buried in a grain pit. The site, in a small garden in the centre of Stanger, is marked by a simple memorial erected in his honour by the Zulu nation.

Shaka's successor, Dingane, burnt kwaDukuza to the ground. In 1873 a European town was planned on the site and named after William Stanger, the surveyor-general of Natal. The town is now the commercial, magisterial and communications centre for a major sugar-producing district.

Stanger has a small but interesting local history museum.

Tongaat

The Tongati River is named after the Zulu word for the *Strychnos mackenii* trees that flourish on its banks. Europeans have corrupted this name to Tongaat and have applied it to a straggling sugar town.

Tongaat has an English-looking village green where cricket is played. Streets are shaded by jacarandas, poincianas and bamboos, and are lined with stalls selling tropical fruits, including exceptionally luscious litchis grown in the district.

FROM WILD GRASS CAME FORTH SWEETNESS...

Sugar cane belongs to the *Saccharum* genus of grass. Wild species grow in many warm, well-watered parts of the world, but the cultivated species came from New Guinea.

From there the cane was carried by man to Asia and it was a commercial crop in India as far back as 400 B.C. The Sanskrit word for the crop, sarkara, gave us the name 'sugar', and the Sanskrit name for the sweetmeat made from the juice, khanda, became the English 'candy'.

The cane is cultivated from cuttings — short pieces of stalk producing new plants which mature in about 12 months. After the cane is cut, new plants called ratoons grow. The process can be repeated until the fertility of the ground is exhausted and it must be ploughed and planted with new cuttings.

In the sugar plantations of Natal the cane grows up to 6 metres in height and in autumn it produces flowers in the form of a plume-like tassel containing minute seeds.

The cane is harvested by manual or mechanical cutting and transported to mills by truck or narrow-gauge plantation railways, several of which are still worked by delightful little steam locomotives.

At the mill the cane is crushed and the raw juice containing about 95 per cent of the sugar in the cane, is drawn off. The residual fibre, known as bagasse, is used for fuel, or in the manufacture of products such as paper or wallboard.

The juice is purified by the addition of lime and by boiling. The lime reacts on the various impurities and causes them to settle. The juice is decanted, leaving the solids behind. The clear liquid is then evaporated to produce a rich syrup.

Further evaporation results in the formation of sugar crystals. These pass into centrifugal machines that separate the molasses from the crystals. The molasses can be used as cattle feed, fermented into alcohol, made into a high-octane petrol, or processed to yield organic chemicals and yeast.

The raw sugar is shipped in bulk to a refinery. Here it is subjected to a number of mechanical and chemical processes which loosen the re-

Sugar cane ready for cutting.

maining film of molasses from the sugar crystals.

Filtration through granulated particles of bone, known as bone char, produces several grades of sugar, ranging from coarse to superfine, and from white to dark brown.

Morewood's Mill, a sugar mill established in 1850.

The first public sale of sugar in Durban, 23 June 1855.

The Tugela River at its most awesome

The lighthouse at the holiday resort of Umhlanga Rocks, a beacon for ships working along the north coast of Natal.

The town is the centre for the Tongaat Sugar Estates. The Moreland Molasses Company also has its home in this area. There is a golf course and a holiday resort at the mouth of the Tongati River.

Tugela River

The Tugela River marks the end of the north coast of Natal, with Kwazulu on its northern side. This is the principal river of Natal and Kwazulu, flowing through a prodigious valley set beneath towering cliffs. The river is known to the Zulus as Thukela ('something that startles').

As the frontier river between Natal and Kwazulu, the Tugela has played an important role in history. For many years it was a serious obstacle to travellers. What was known as the Lower Tugela Drift provided a hazardous crossing point, but only if the river was low. During floods the Tugela was impassable and travellers could be delayed for days.

Today the river is spanned by a bridge, 450 metres long, and named after John Ross, a 15-year-old boy who, in 1827, walked the 900-kilometre return journey from Durban to Lourenco Marques and back to obtain medicines needed by traders and hunters. The round trip, across wild country, took 40 days. When Ross visited Shaka to pay respects, the Zulu king provided him with an armed escort, and throughout the journey the youth was under the protection of the king.

Five kilometres before the John Ross Bridge is a turn-off from the trunk road leading east down the south bank of the Tugela River to its mouth. On its way, after 1,5 kilometres, is the original Lower Tugela Drift. Overlooking this is the ruin of a small fort, Fort Pearson, built in 1878 by the British when they were preparing for the invasion of what was then Zululand. It was named after Colonel Charles Knight Pearson, commander of the invasion force that had to cross the Tugela at this point.

One and a half kilometres from the fort the road passes a wild fig tree known as the Ultimatum Tree. In its shade, on 11 December 1878, the British presented an ultimatum to a Zulu delegation (see box page 356).

The country between Greytown and Stanger, with its huts and maize.

The Tugela River, traditional frontier between Kwazulu and Natal.

The terms of this ultimatum made the Anglo-Zulu War inevitable. From this old tree the road continues for another 7 kilometres, passing through a belt of coastal forest, and then reaches a shallow bay at the mouth of the river. There is a camping ground beneath the trees.

Umdloti Beach
The Mdloti River takes its name from a species of wild tobacco that grows on its banks. At the river mouth is a spacious lagoon and the holiday resort of Umdloti Beach, with hotels and bungalows overlooking a beach and a rock-enclosed tidal pool.

Umhlanga Rocks
The coastal trunk road to Kwazulu — Shaka's Way — provides a scenic drive up the coast, crossing the Umgeni River and leading through the suburb of Durban North. After 20 kilometres the road reaches the popular holiday resort of Umhlanga Rocks, with its impressive cluster of luxury hotels, caravan parks, boarding houses and bungalows. There is a protected beach here, fishing vantage points on the rocks, and swimming pools on the hotel terraces. Many sports facilities are available.

The name comes from the small Mhlanga ('reedy') River, which reaches the sea 3 kilometres north of the resort.

In 1972 the municipality of Umhlanga was established with the amalgamation of the resort of Umhlanga Rocks and the residential township of La Lucia.

Verulam
The middle reaches of the river known as the Mdloti, from the wild tobacco plants of that name that grow on its banks, flow through an area almost completely covered by sugar cane.

In 1850 a party of 400 Methodists immigrated to this area from a depressed Britain. They were under the patronage of the Earl of Verulam, and the party was well organized, bringing seeds, agricultural implements, a large marquee tent to serve as a meeting place, and a blue banner inscribed in gold with the name Verulam.

From Durban the settlers were taken in ox-wagons to the valley of the Mdloti, where they were allocated farms, and there they founded the attractive town of Verulam. The town is now inhabited mainly by Indians, and the original small farms have been swallowed by an ocean of sugar cane.

Elegant homesteads, gardens and cemeteries remain as reminders of the days of the first settlement.

Feeding holiday-makers is a major industry on the Natal north coast.

Cabana Beach, a modern holiday resort looking out over the blue Indian Ocean.

ENDLESS HILLS OF KWAZULU

KWAZULU IS A PLACE of hills, valleys and battlefields. A coastal terrace, sandy, flat and bushy, stretches inland, covering the lower slopes and choking up the valleys, but the overwhelming picture is of seemingly endless hills.

The climate is hot and humid on the coastal belt, but where the land is raised on the shoulders of the hills, the sea breezes sweep in, cooling the air and carrying misty rains which keep the vegetation green and luxuriant and fill the rivers, often to the point of flooding.

These conditions are ideal for wildlife. The continent of Africa is the home of the world's greatest variety of game, and no part of it offers more favourable conditions than Kwazulu. There is sweet grass, and also trees and shrubs with nutritious leaves and bark. Long before the advent of man this region was densely populated with birds, mammals, reptiles, insects and fish.

Most of the people who occupy Kwazulu today arrived at the beginning of the 17th century. They called themselves the Nguni, from the leader who had led them southwards on a migration from a forgotten origin in central East Africa. Behind these people came an even larger group, speaking the same language as the Nguni, but with a rather peculiar lisp, and acknowledging as their leader a man named Dlamini.

Both groups were delighted with this bountiful new land. They dispersed into numerous independent clans and built homes, cared for their livestock, hunted, and planted the few crops that they had brought with them. These newcomers found only a handful of San living in the area, and minor elements of a people known as the Lala, who were related to the Karanga of Zimbabwe.

The total number of people in those early days in what is now Kwazulu was little more than 5 000 — compared with 2 100 000 today. Some of the clans consisted of only a single family with its retainers and dependants. The clans feuded and fought with one another, but there was no rival ethnic group to challenge their possession of the new homeland. They flourished, their herds increased and few problems plagued them other than malaria — endemic on the coastal flats — and bilharzia. Each clan was independent and they acknowledged no overlord or king.

The cultural life of these people was primitive but rich. They believed in a rather vague Nkulunkulu ('great great one'), or omnipotent god, but had few fixed religious rituals. Of more significance to them was the supernatural world, which they believed to be densely populated by ghosts and weird creatures. Every pool, waterfall, prominent peak or rock was associated with a supernatural creature. Spirits of the ancestors also played an important role in the lives of these people.

Their clothes were simple, mostly skins and feathers. They had no cloth or beads until Swahili, Portuguese and other traders introduced these luxuries to them. Their huts, shaped like beehives, with frameworks of branches covered with plaited grass, were snug and dry in all seasons, and they harmonized with the surrounding hills.

The Nguni had a rich, expressive language, full of proverbs, metaphors and subtle meanings, but with no written form until recent times. The language adopted some clicks from the San, but these sounds were used more by southern groups than by those in the north, who adhered more rigidly to their original tongue.

These people were sturdily built rather than tall, burnt umber rather than black, courageous, resolute, making good friends and stubborn enemies. They were indulgent with their children, hospitable, conservative, intensely loyal to their chiefs, and superstitious. The Nguni were wonderful dancers and drummers, but produced no musical instruments other than drums.

Milk, mainly consumed as curds, was their principal diet. They seldom slaughtered their cattle — venison was the meat they ate mostly.

As with many African peoples, the women worked hard. They fetched water, cooked, cleaned, produced large numbers of infants, and farmed traditional crops — gourds and millet — as well as maize, introduced to them by the Portuguese and Tonga traders. The men and boys looked after the cattle. They liked to laze in the warm sun, and seldom worked hard. Their conversation was of fights, of the drinking of beer made from millet, of love and feuds and raids on other people's livestock and girls. The hills of their homeland were their entire world; they knew nothing and cared nothing about what lay beyond the sea to the east, or over the mountains far to the west — there lived the darkness of night and the unknown, and evil spirits lurking at the edge of a world that was flat.

Empangeni

In 1851 the Norwegian Missionary Society established a station in the valley of a stream named eMpangeni from the number of mpange trees (*Olinia cymosa*) that grow here. The mission was later moved to Eshowe, but in 1894 a magistracy named Empangeni was established in the valley and this was the beginning of the modern town.

Empangeni is a centre for sugar, cotton, cattle and timber. There is a large sugar mill near the town. The adjoining valley of the Mhlatuze River, as well as the surroundings of Empangeni, are covered by sugar plantations.

The first experimental timber plantation in this part of the country was created by the Natal government when eucalyptus trees were planted near Empangeni in 1905. The success of this plantation was the start of large-scale planting along the coastal belt.

Empangeni is a junction on the main railway line from Durban to Swaziland, Nkwaleni and Richards Bay.

Some 14 kilometres from the town lies the 295-hectare Enseleni Nature Reserve, established in 1948 on the banks of the Nseleni River. This is an area with a rich vegetation of mangroves, wild figs, papyrus and other water-loving plants. Aquatic birds,

On a country road in Kwazulu, oxen draw a sledge carrying a load of maize meal.

Kwazulu is a land of many hills. These are a few of them near Eshowe.

monitor lizards and several species of antelope such as nyala, impala, zebra and blue wildebeest also live in the reserve. There is a nature trail and a picnic site.

Eshowe

On the crest of a ridge of hills, 500 metres above sea level, is a forest known to the Zulus as Dlinza ('a gravelike place of meditation'). The town surrounding the forest is named Eshowe, which is said to be the sound of the wind sighing through the trees, but the name most likely comes from

the *xysmalobium* shrubs, called by the Zulus showe or shongwe. They are prolific in the area of the town.

The ridge is pleasantly relieved from the heat of the coast by sea breezes. 'It is always cool at Eshowe' say the Zulus — implying that there is always an escape from oppression somewhere — and Eshowe was a retreat for them during the height of summer.

In 1860 the Zulu prince Cetshwayo built himself a village on the heights, naming the place Eziqwaqweni ('the abode of robbers'). A mission station

was established nearby and acquired the name kwaMondi ('place of Mondi'), the Zulu name for the Reverend Ommund Oftefro, the Norwegian missionary in charge.

In January 1879, with the beginning of the Anglo-Zulu War, a British column under Colonel Charles Knight Pearson occupied the mission station, intending to use it as a base for an advance on the Zulu capital of Ulundi. Instead, to their surprise, they were besieged there for ten weeks by a Zulu force commanded by Dabulamanzi, a very determined war-

Syntomid moths (Euchromia formoca) *nestling on a leaf in Kwazulu.*

An African peach moth, its wings brilliantly coloured.

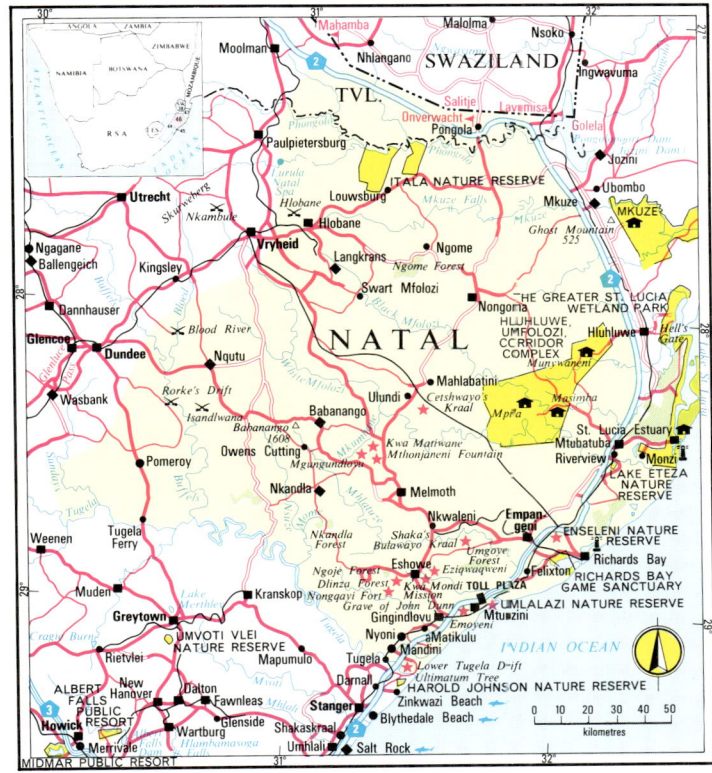

The place they named 'Gin, gin, I love you!'

rior. On 3 April 1879 the garrison was relieved by a British force sent from Natal. The mission was evacuated and promptly set on fire by the Zulus and destroyed.

At the end of the war, the British selected the area of Eshowe as the site for their administrative capital. A small fort was built, and some of the forest trees were cut down. In their place an attractive town grew up, with stores, offices and homes in a setting of natural parkland.

In 1887 Eshowe became the capital of the territory that was recognised as Zululand. It retains much of the atmosphere of its early days, when Zululand was the scene of incessant upheaval, feuding and fighting during the troubled period of its history after the Anglo-Zulu War.

The 'Beau Geste' type of fort built by the British administration now houses the Historical Museum, containing many relics of local events. This neat little fort was garrisoned by a Zulu force — the Reserve Territorial.Carbiniers, popularly known as the Nongqayi ('restrainers'). The fort was built with some difficulty, as there were no craftsmen in Zululand experienced in this type of construction. Two itinerant builders took on the contract, but the walls, when approaching a mere 3 metres in height, showed signs of collapsing under the pressure of the winds, and could obviously not have resisted any serious attack. These walls had to be pulled down, and new builders were found who did a better job, using sun-baked bricks cemented by a mixture of mud and cow dung known as daga.

The Dlinza Forest today provides a sanctuary for birds, vervet monkeys, wild pigs, blue and red duikers, bushbuck and other creatures. Paths and roads lead through the forest. In the centre is a clearing known as the Bishop's Seat. Occasional church services are held here and every three years a nativity play, written in 1953 by Selwyn Moberley, is presented in this lovely forest setting.

The municipal swimming pool and caravan park are on the fringes of the Dlinza Forest. The Municipality also maintains the Ocean View Game Park on the outskirts of the town. This sanctuary contains antelope, birds, warthogs and other wild creatures.

The annual Kwazulu Agricultural and Industrial Show, held in Eshowe in May or June, is the principal event of its kind in Kwazulu.

Gingindlovu

Cetshwayo, whose name meant 'the

DOCTORS' MEDICINE

In the African tradition there are two distinct types of 'doctor'. One is the Ngoma ('diviner'); the other is an Nyanga, who treats the sick. The doctor can be male or female and serves an apprenticeship with an established practitioner. The qualified doctor is regarded with considerable awe.

Diviners are consulted when an individual has some particular problem. Payment is agreed with the diviner and a consultation is held. The diviner consults the spirits in several ways, usually by 'throwing the bones'. For this ritual, the diviner has an assortment of items, each with a special significance.

The consultant explains his problem to the diviner who, after considerable preparatory ritual, scatters the bones onto a mat and interprets from their position the message of the spirits.

A diviner 'throwing the bones'.

A plantation of sisal trees against an afternoon thunderstorm. Sisal is used in the manufacture of fibres, string and rope.

slandered one', fought his brothers over the rights of succession to the Zulu throne. On 2 December 1856, at Ndondakusuka, he defeated his principal rival, his half-brother Mbulazi, who was supported by five other sons of the Zulu king, Mpande. Cetshwayo killed them all and from then was regarded as the undisputed heir to the throne. To commemorate his victory, Cetshwayo built a military stronghold 17 kilometres from the Ndondakusuka battlefield. This stronghold was named Gingindlovu ('the swallower of the elephant').

Near Gingindlovu the British force sent to relieve Eshowe fought with the Zulus in April 1879 (see box, page 356). The British soldiers nicknamed the place 'Gin, gin, I love you!' Today it is a railway junction on the main Kwazulu line, with a branch leading west to Eshowe.

Hluhluwe Game Reserve

The sheer beauty of the landscape alone would justify conservation of the area of the Hluhluwe Game Reserve and its companion, Umfolozi. Added to this is a wealth of plant life and animals, and an atmosphere of Kwazulu's ancient past. The beautiful Hluhluwe River, named from the Zulu word for the thorny monkey

Early morning in the Hluhluwe Game Reserve with the mists still lying on the floor.

A BOY CALLED 'HEAVEN' FINDS A HOME FOR THE PEOPLE DESTINED TO BECOME A GREAT NATION

One of the fragments of the Nguni migration which dispersed into what is now Kwazulu about 300 years ago was a small group led by a man named Malandela. His little group settled in the hot and fertile valley of the Mhlanthuze River.

When Malandela died, his elder son Qwaba stayed on, but a younger son, with his mother and a few dependants, left home and set off to find a place in the sun for himself. The son's name was Zulu, which in the language of his people meant 'Heaven'.

Zulu wandered westwards until he reached a shallow valley, watered by a stream known as the Mkhumbane ('river of the hollow'), and overlooked in the east by a high ridge, Mthonjaneni ('place of the little fountain') and to the north by the flat-topped Nhlazatsho ('mountain of green stones'), a landmark 1 437 metres high. Zulu settled in this valley and eventually died here. The site of his grave is revered as kwaNkosinkulu ('place of the great chief') and is marked by a euphorbia tree.

Zulu was succeeded by his son Phunga, then came Mageba, Ndaba and Jama. Each generation saw an increase in the numbers of the people until Jama's son, Senzangakhona, found himself at the head of a considerable group whose members knew themselves as the abakwaZulu ('people of Zulu').

Senzangakhona was a young man when he became chief in about 1785. The entire world of his people was the hollow in the hills. They lived in beehive-shaped huts, grazed cattle, goats and sheep, and grew sorghum, gourds, sweet potatoes and other crops. Life was lazy and quiet — a lull before the storm of change which was to make the peaceful little clan of the Zulus the most feared nation of warriors in Africa.

A Zulu warrior in traditional dancing dress, with ornamental shield and sticks.

Head-dress of a married woman.

Large earrings are very popular.

Head-dresses are dramatic and varied.

A bride at the Shembe festival.

'Luck heaps' of stones to ward off evil

ropes (*Dalbergia armata*) that grow in the riverine forest, flows through high hills. The river here is about 85 metres above sea level, and the hill summits approach 600 metres. Dense bush chokes up the valleys of the river and its tributaries, while patches of high forest and thick open grass grow on the hill slopes.

The entire region has long been a haunt of game. Rich grazing and a variety of habitats made the valleys and slopes attractive to wild creatures, and the presence of tsetse fly kept out the human hunters, especially the destructive white man with his guns.

By the 1890s the vast herds of free-ranging wild animals that had once roamed over the whole area of Kwazulu had been largely destroyed by hunters. Only in the valleys of the Hluhluwe and Mfolozi rivers were the wild animals undisturbed, and in 1897 these two areas were proclaimed game reserves.

In modern times the tsetse fly has been totally eradicated from both areas by chemical controls. Accommodation has been built for visitors, roads and trails have been made, and observation hides have been erected at various water-holes.

Hluhluwe, 25 000 hectares in area, contains white and black rhino, lion, elephant, giraffe, buffalo, nyala, zebra, blue wildebeest, kudu, impala, bushbuck, waterbuck, warthog, bush pig, leopard, baboon and cheetah.

Crocodiles, monitor lizards

THE WHITE CHIEF

One of the most extraordinary characters in the history of southern Africa was John Dunn (*above*) — the man who became a white chief of the Zulus.

Dunn was born in Port Alfred in 1833 and was three years old when his parents moved to Durban. His father was trampled to death by an elephant and his mother died a few years later. Young John earned a living working for transport riders and hunters.

During his expedition into the country of the Zulus he befriended the Zulu king, Cetshwayo, who invited him to become his adviser.

Dunn settled near the Ongoye Forest and married Catherine Pierce, the daughter of a renegade father and a Coloured mother. Later, with Catherine as head wife, he married 49 Zulu wives.

At the end of the Anglo-Zulu War the British divided the territory known as Zululand into 13 separate states, each under its own ruler. Dunn was given one of these areas — all the land along the coast from the Tugela to the Mhlatuze River. He built a village named Emoyeni ('windy place') as his administrative centre.

Dunn employed a European tutor to educate his 117 children. He ended up with so many dependants that after his death in 1895 a government commission allocated to them a 4 000-hectare reserve near the Tugela River.

Tropical vegetation growing at Charter's Creek on the shores of Lake St. Lucia. In the foreground are wild banana palms.

Pelicans in Lake St. Lucia, an ideal home for them with its rich fish life.

Fishing near the estuary of Lake St. Lucia.

(iguanas) and hippos live in the rivers. Snakes are varied, and this is good country to see black and green mambas, and pythons.

Bird life includes the maribou stork, white-backed vulture, bateleur, crested guinea-fowl, emerald cuckoo, narina trogon, ground hornbill, blue quail and Delegorgue's pigeon.

Animals in great variety and numbers can be seen from the game-viewing hide at Munywaneni, especially during the dry winter months, when this is one of the largest of the area's permanent water-holes.

The tourist camp is on the brow of one of the hills, with a view over the reserve and to the Indian Ocean 50 kilometres to the east. Where the road from the camp descends the hill slope on the way to Mtubatuba there is a vivane ('luck heap') of pebbles deposited by African travellers who, walking along the path through areas inhabited by wild game, hoped to ensure their own safety by placing on the heap these little offerings to the spirits.

The reserve is open throughout the year. Visitors bring their own food, which can be cooked for them by the resident staff. There is a curio shop, and there are caravan parks at the two entrances to the reserve (from Mtubatuba in the south and from Hluhluwe railway station in the east).

Lake St. Lucia

About 60 million years ago the sea receded and what was formerly part of its bed emerged as the sandy coastal terrace of Kwazulu. The terrace was covered with shallow depressions which filled up with sea and fresh water to form lagoons, lakes and estuary systems. This was the origin of Lake St. Lucia, a combined estuary and lagoon system formed roughly in the

ADVENTURES IN THE COUNTRY OF WHITE RHINOS

Kwazulu has always been rhino country and records of old hunters are filled with accounts of adventures with these great beasts.

Both white and black rhinos flourish here, though in fact the two species are the same colour — a rather dirty grey — and the origin of their popular names is obscure.

The white rhino is the larger of the two, weighing up to 5 tons. Despite its massive appearance and the formidable length of its horn (the South African record is 158,75 centimetres) it is an inoffensive animal, extremely short-sighted and inclined to lumber off rather than charge.

White rhinos live in groups and when threatened they form a circle, with their young in the centre and their horns all facing outwards.

A white, or square-lipped, rhinoceros.

Black rhinos are more lightly built than the white, but far more aggressive. The Zulus call them uBejane ('the vicious one').

The horn of the rhino is composed of tightly packed fibre growing from the skin and resting on a slightly hollowed base in the skull. The horns are often knocked off in fights or accidents.

Newly hatched loggerhead turtles head for the sea on the Kwazulu coast.

A grey-headed gull on the lookout for visitors at St. Lucia estuary.

Two white rhinoceros bulls testing their strength during the breeding season.

Lagoon paradise for hosts of game

shape of the letter H. The left (western) limb of the H is False Bay, 25 kilometres long, 3 kilometres wide and about 2 metres deep; the cross bar of the H is called Hell's Gate; the right (eastern) limb is Lake St. Lucia and is 40 kilometres long, 10 kilometres wide at one point, and between 1 and 2 metres deep. This is a world of reed-covered islets, sand banks and chan-

nels. The water ranges from the normal salinity of the sea (35 parts per 1 000) to high salinity in False Bay (up to 85 parts per 1 000).

The climate is warm to hot and humid, and the continual evaporation of fresh water leaves behind a steady concentration of residual salts, unless exceptional floods occur and the lake system is flushed out with fresh water

from rivers flowing into it.

Hippos, crocodiles, aquatic birds and fish abound in the area of Lake St. Lucia. Salmon, grunter, mud bream and other fish feed and breed in the waters. Numerous big game fish and sharks prowl the estuary.

About 600 hippos graze on the reeds, while on the verges of the lake many antelope are found — nyala,

bushbuck, reedbuck, grey and red duiker, suni and steenbuck. Bush pigs live in the thickets.

Bird life is prolific. There are flamingoes, pelicans, goliath herons, saddlebills, spoonbills, white-bellied korhaan, jacana, avocets, Caspian terns, green coucals, Knysna loerie, pink-throated longclaw and many other species.

A BRITISH ULTIMATUM BEGINS NINE MONTHS OF BLUNDERS AND BLOODSHED

War between the British and the Zulus was inevitable from the moment on 11 December 1878 when the British government presented an ultimatum. This demanded that the Zulus abandon their traditional military system, that missionaries be allowed to work in what was then Zululand and that a British resident be appointed to live with the Zulu king, Cetshwayo, to supervise relations between Zulus and Europeans.

The Zulus rejected the ultimatum and on 12 January 1879 the British launched a three-pronged invasion of Zululand.

One British column, known as the right-hand column, crossed the lower Tugela and marched on Eshowe, where they were besieged by a Zulu force. A second column, the left-hand column, invaded the north of Zululand, while the main British force, accompanied by Lord Chelmsford, the British commander-in-chief, invaded the centre of Zululand. This central column crossed the Buffels River at Rorke's Drift and on 20 January camped on a plain dominated by the hill known as Isandlwana.

The British were unaware that the main Zulu army of about 14 000 men was hiding nearby.

At about noon on 22 January the Zulu commander Ntshingwayo sent Cetshwayo's brother, Dabulamanzi, with about 3 600 men, to cut the road from Rorke's Drift. The main Zulu army headed for the British camp. The British were so ill-prepared that most of their ammunition was still secure in boxes. They faced the Zulus with fixed bayonets.

By two in the afternoon the fight was over and the camp was a gory

Isandlwana, a strangely shaped hillock dominating the battlefield at its foot.

mess. The British had lost 858 soldiers and 470 African allies. About 1 000 Zulus lay dead.

Lord Chelmsford withdrew the remnants of his central column to the safety of Natal.

Meanwhile the right-hand column remained in a state of siege in Eshowe. Only the left-hand column was active. It was confronted by a powerful Zulu force led by a Swazi renegade prince named Mbilini, whose stronghold was a flat-topped mountain named Hlobane.

On 28 March Colonel Wood, commander of the British left-hand column, attacked this stronghold and managed to reach the mountain summit. His men were busy rounding up

cattle when, looking down to the south-east, they saw the Zulu army approaching. The British retreated down the mountain, but 111 soldiers were killed. The rest of Colonel Wood's men reached a fortified camp on the slopes of Nkambule hill.

On 29 March 17 000 Zulus attacked the Nkambule camp. Five hours later the Zulus retreated with 2 000 warriors killed. The British had lost only 18 soldiers. It was the turning point of the war.

On 29 March 1879, at the head of more than 5 500 men, Lord Chelmsford set out from the Lower Tugela Drift. On 2 April Dabulamanzi led 10 000 Zulus against him at Gingindlovu, but in the face of withering fire

The cemetery containing casualties of the Nkambule battle near Vryheid in northern Natal. Such sad reminders of the Anglo-Zulu War may be found in many parts of Kwazulu.

some 700-1 200 Zulus were killed against only 13 British losses. The day after this victory — the battle of 'Gin, gin, I love you!', as the British nicknamed the place — Eshowe was relieved.

Chelmsford then led an invasion into central Zululand. Cautiously building little forts to guard his route, he advanced on the Zulu capital of Ulundi. There was no serious resistance and Cetshwayo sent a succession of pleas for peace. Chelmsford brushed them aside.

On 4 July his force of 5 000 men overran Ulundi and burned it down. Cetshwayo fled to northern Zululand. He was captured on 26 August 1879 and banished to Cape Town. The Anglo-Zulu War was over.

Memorial on the site of the battle.

The lake and its verges — 55 000 hectares — have been proclaimed a game reserve. There is hutted accommodation at Charter's Creek, and campsites at Fanies Island, False Bay and St. Lucia Estuary. Boats can be hired, and there are launch trips and wilderness trails.

Crocodiles are plentiful, especially at the mouths of rivers such as the Mkuze, which flows into the lake. There is no swimming in the lake, but fishing, boating and nature observation are particularly rewarding. Beware of sudden storms.

Winter is the most comfortable time to visit the lake. Mosquitoes are a menace in summer and the temperature is oppressive.

Mahlabatini

In the process of establishing control over what was then Zululand, the British founded several magistracies. One of these was Mahlabatini ('place of white sands') which dates from 1898.

The village lies on the summit of a ridge looking out over the hills and valleys of north-western Kwazulu.

Melmoth

A magistrate was stationed in April 1887 to administer a district named Mthonjaneni in the mist belt. The village was named Melmoth, after Melmoth Osborn, the British resident commissioner and chief magistrate.

Large plantations of wattle trees were created around Melmoth and in 1926 a wattle bark factory was established here. The village is now a centre of sugar cane, timber and wattle production.

Mgungundlovu

After the assassination of the Zulu king, Shaka, in 1828 (see box, page 358) Dingane consolidated his own position as successor by killing off any of the grandees of the nation whom he suspected of hostility. He then abandoned Shaka's capital of kwaDukuza (Stanger) and moved all the way back to the traditional home of the Zulu people — the valley of the Mkumbane stream in the north-west.

Here Dingane erected a new capital which he named uMgungundlovu ('the secret plot of the elephant'), referring to his intrigue against Shaka,

Zulu huts, thatched and carefully built on frameworks of wattle poles. They are warm in winter, dry and cool in summer.

A Zulu woman grinding maize near a cattle kraal.

A Zulu woman sewing a traditional goat-skin skirt.

Hill of execution once scavenged by vultures

THE CHIEF WHO MADE THE ZULUS SUPREME

At the beginning of each winter the all-conquering Zulu regiments would gather in their ancestral lands to pledge themselves to new conquests with the salute: 'Ngathi impi' — 'Because of us, war.'

The man who ruled over the Zulus at this time of their greatest glories, who had led their growth from a small clan into the dominant power on the coast of south-east Africa, was called Shaka.

He was the result of a meeting between the youthful chief of the Zulu clan, Senzangakhona, and a pretty girl called Nandi from the neighbouring Langeni clan. Three months after their alliance, word reached Senzangakhona that the girl was pregnant.

The young chief tried to talk himself out of the situation: 'Perhaps she is simply harbouring iShaka (an intestinal beetle). Six months later the 'beetle' arrived in the shape of a lusty son, who was promptly named Shaka.

The boy was taunted for his illegitimacy, but he soon proved himself a courageous warrior. When still young he invented a broad-bladed stabbing spear which proved to be a potent weapon.

Shaka became chief of the Zulus in 1816 when he was about 30. He mustered all the men of the Zulu clan below the age of 40.

Over the next few years he system-

Shaka, the renowned chief of the Zulus.

atically attacked every independent group in the vicinity, either driving them away or absorbing them into the Zulu nation.

By 1823 Shaka was triumphant. His army was supreme, his followers delirious with success. Cattle, loot and women simply poured into their hands, and the once peaceful little valley was too small to contain them all.

In the winter of 1823 Shaka began to build a new capital on a site overlooking the valley of the Mhlatuze River. He named it kwaBulawayo ('the place of the persecuted man').

In the hot summers his people tilled the fields and armourers made spears and shields. Each winter was a time for war, and raids were launched wherever people could be found still in possession of cattle or other forms of wealth.

In 1826 Shaka built another hut city further south on the site of what is now the town of Stanger. This place he named kwaDukuza ('the place of the lost person') because it was easy to get lost in the labyrinth of huts.

It was at kwaBulawayo in 1827 that his mother, Nandi, died. Henry Fynn and several British ivory hunters were with Shaka then, hunting elephants in the Mhlatuze Valley. They have left a description of the incredible sequence of events when Shaka heard of his mother's death. In an explosion of grief, about 7 000 local people were massacred.

In 1828 Shaka led his army on a great raid down the south coast of Natal and into the Pondo country of the Transkei. He returned to spend the summer at kwaDukuza. It was here, in a small outlying kraal towards sunset on 22 September, that Shaka was waiting to receive tribute from a visiting party of Tswanas. Two of his half brothers, Mhlangana and Dingane, suddenly strode into the cattle enclosure where Shaka was sitting and stabbed him to death. The next day the corpse was bundled into ox-hide and buried, with a few belongings, in an empty corn pit.

Zulu handicrafts exhibited in a roadside market near Mtunzini.

The monument to Piet Retief and the Voortrekkers at Mgungundlovu.

Zulu pots for sale on a roadside.

and the fact that he himself was often known as the elephant.

In 1837, when Piet Retief and his Voortrekkers visited the place, it was at the peak of its development. It was a labyrinth of huts, the scene of continuous bustle with women carrying water in pots, grinding maize, cooking food, and brewing beer. Herds of cattle were continually being driven into the central kraal for inspection by Dingane. Regiments were constantly coming in from outlying garrison duties or raids, led by officers reporting to the king or the army commander-in-chief, Ndela.

Dingane lived in a magnificent hut in the centre of this maze of dwellings. He held court in the shade of a large tree in one of the cattle kraals. Here he judged cases, imposing fines or sentencing to death those found guilty of serious crimes.

A hill slope overlooking the hut city was the place of execution. Known as kwaMatiwane ('place of Matiwane'), it was named after the chief of the Ngwaneni, who had been killed there. Hyenas, jackals and vultures scavenged the hill of execution and the hut city.

European visitors were always well received, provided they brought presents and acknowledged Dingane as king. They camped on a height overlooking the city, and all found the spectacle and experience of Mgungundlovu somewhat overwhelming. It was the culmination of an African primitive state — barbaric and utterly remote from the European concept of a civilized state and culture. Here the Zulu people were at the peak of their power. There were huge herds of

The chores of a married woman — a Zulu housewife, washing clothes in the Tugela.

Sugar cane, green and sweet, covering the hills to a sugar mill in the distance.

cattle. The women were beautifully dressed in skins and beads, and the regiments distinctive in their uniforms of feathers and skins, with coloured and patterned shields. Great dances were held, when the singing, stamping and pounding of drums continued well into the night.

Mgungundlovu was destroyed by fire when the Voortrekkers approached it after the Battle of Blood River in December 1838, but the core of the original hut city has now been rebuilt on its old foundations, and has been restored to what it used to be in Dingane's day. The graves of the early Zulu chiefs still remain, and also a large Dutch Reformed Church mission built on the site where the Reverend Francis Owen made his camp in 1837 and began teaching Christianity to the Zulu people.

Mtubatuba

When the railway was built along the coastal belt to Golela on the Swazi border, a siding was laid out at a place named Mtubatuba. Development was stimulated by large-scale planting of sugar cane in the area, and the construction in 1916 of a crushing mill at nearby Riverview.

The name Mtubatuba comes from the chief of the local section of the Zulu nation. He was given the name, which means 'he who was pummelled out', on account of the difficulty the midwives experienced at his birth.

This village is a colourful little trading centre, with much bustle in the streets on Friday afternoons and Saturdays, when rural people come to do their shopping.

There are large plantations of eucalyptus trees in the area and roads branch off east to Lake St. Lucia and west to Hluhluwe Game Reserve, Umfolozi Game Reserve, and Nongoma.

Mtunzini

Kwazulu is not an area for coastal resorts. The beaches shelve steeply and there is little protection against sharks. At Mtunzini ('the shady place') there is one pleasant, protected resort on a fine beach with a backdrop of coastal forest. John Dunn, the famous white chief (see box, page 354) had his holiday home at Mtunzini.

Here are forest-covered dunes with

Last resting place of a great Zulu chief

bush trails, small lakelets, and a spacious lagoon at the mouth of the Mlalazi River. In 1948 some 900 hectares of this coastal area were proclaimed a nature reserve. The reserve contains bush pig, reedbuck, blue and grey duiker and crocodiles. Birds and plant life are prolific, and the rare palmnut vulture breeds here.

There is a hotel at Mtunzini and a caravan park and camping ground in the Umlalazi Nature Reserve. Chalets may also be hired.

Nkandla

On the northern (Kwazulu) side of the valley of the Tugela River a dense forest grows along the sides of the precipice. To the Zulus it is known as Nkandla ('a place of exhaustion'). Even the modern road penetrates this

Sunset over the sanctuary area of the Richards Bay Harbour.

forest with difficulty, for its topography is extremely rugged and the vegetation dense.

Leopards, bushbuck, blue and grey duikers, monkeys and birds inhabit the forest, and its plant life is spectacular, with ferns, creepers, lianas, orchids and tall trees.

In the centre of the forest is a deep gorge hemmed in by cliff faces more than 600 metres high. A stream, the Mome ('the drainer'), tumbles into this gorge in a long waterfall, and then flows beneath the trees to join the Tugela. In this remote valley, Cetshwayo found refuge during the incessant fighting after the Anglo-Zulu War. He died on 23 April 1884 and was buried here. His grave is much revered by the Zulus.

In 1906 the Mome gorge became

THE SWEET NOTHINGS WHISPERED IN THE ZULU LANGUAGE OF BEADS

The Nguni groups living along the south-east coast, especially the Zulu, love beads. The women are experts in the subtle art of weaving beads into intricate patterns.

The San and early Bantu made beads from ivory, bone, clay, seeds, stones, sea-shells, egg-shells, plants, aromatic wood, gold and copper.

Arab and later European traders introduced beads as trade goods. Some of these early beads are so revered by Africans today that they are regarded as personifications of ancestral spirits.

One of the most fascinating manifestations of the art of beadwork is their use as a language. A girl will send her man an incwadi — a love letter made of beads.

Each colour has a different meaning: a white bead is called ithambo ('bone') and represents love and purity; a black bead is called isitimane ('shadow') and means grief, loneliness and disappointment; a pink bead is isiphofu ('poor one') and signifies poverty; a green bead is uluhlaza ('new grass') and implies lovesickness or jealousy; a blue bead is called ijuba ('dove'), symbolizing faithfulness; a red bead is igazi ('blood') and means tears and longing; a yellow bead is incombo ('young corn') and represents wealth; and a striped bead is intothoviyane ('the striped grasshopper') and implies doubt.

Using beads of different colours, girls create gentle reminders which they send to their men in the form of strings — with the message to be read from one end to the other — or in ornamental squares, with the message to be read from the outer edges towards the centre. Many expressions of feeling can be conveyed in this way, and the man can wear the beadwork if he is proud of it, or hide it if the message is angry.

A Zulu elder in full ceremonial dress.

Typical Zulu beadwork and wooden knives for sale in an open-air market place.

Hairstyle of a Zulu diviner.

A typical Zulu farmyard with its cluster of huts and rondavels, surrounded by maize fields and grazing lands.

the stronghold of Bambatha, chief of the small Zondi group, who led a revolt against European government, especially objecting to the payment of taxes. Many other dissidents joined him in this revolt, and the Nkandla Forest was the scene of a bitter little war.

Government forces tried to pin down the rebels, but Bambatha's men proved elusive.

After several vicious struggles, the government force trapped Bambatha and his men in the deep valley on 10 June 1906. Bambatha's men fought in the stream, hid in pools and scrambled up rapids, but he and 500 of his followers were killed.

The village of Nkandla lies at the edge of the forest. It is a small administrative and trading centre.

Nongoma

In 1887 the administrative centre of Nongoma was established high in the hills of north-western Zululand (now Kwazulu). The site of this place was known to the Zulus as kwaNongoma ('place of the diviner'), the name of the royal homestead of King Zwide, chief of the Ndwandwe.

Nongoma lay between the territories of the two great rival factions of the Zulus — the uSuthu and the Mandlakazi — and the government hoped that the establishment of the centre would put an end to the interminable fights and outrages of the period. In June 1888 Nongoma was destroyed by the uSuthu, but later rebuilt. Today it is a busy trading village serving a large part of Kwazulu.

Richards Bay

The Mhlatuze ('forceful') River received its name because of the power of its floods, which sweep down in summer with destructive strength. The river reaches the sea in a spacious, deep lagoon which is the home of hippos and aquatic birds. The lagoon covers 3 000 hectares and has a channel leading to the sea.

During the Anglo-Zulu War (1879) the British navy had to land stores on the coast and there was a search for suitable sites. Among the places surveyed was the lagoon of the Mhlatuze. The entrance was named Richards Bay after Admiral Sir F. W. Richards, the

A lone fig tree, remnant of a former forest, in the highlands near Nongoma.

Close-up of the wall of a Zulu hut, made of mud and poles.

A Zulu rondavel being re-thatched in preparation for another rainy season.

361

Spent bullets litter an ancient battlefield

In the Umfolozi Game Reserve, sunset after a long, hot day.

officer in command of the West Africa station of the Royal Navy.

No development took place at the time, but on several occasions in later years there were new surveys and plans for the building of a harbour. Meanwhile a holiday resort grew up on the northern side of the lagoon, offering good fishing and boating.

Huberta the wandering hippo began her adventures from the Mhlatuze lagoon in 1928 (see box, page 159). The largest recorded South African crocodile was shot in the lagoon by John Dunn in 1891. It was 6,7 metres long.

In 1935 the Richards Bay Game Sanctuary was created to protect the wildlife in and around the lagoon, and in 1943 the Richards Bay Park was established on 400 hectares of the shores to conserve the plant life.

After World War II, the development of South Africa made the creation of a new deep-water harbour essential for the export of metal ores on large bulk carriers and to provide services for supertankers. Durban harbour was already congested with cargo and could not offer the deep water needed for mammoth vessels.

The Richards Bay harbour was opened in 1976. An electric railway was constructed to link the new harbour with the mines of the interior. An oil pipeline links the tanker terminal with the Witwatersrand. An aluminium smelter and a fertilizer plant have been erected at the harbour, and large deposits of titanium are being mined in the sands close to the bay.

A village, established on the shores of the lagoon in 1954, became a town in 1969. Today Richards Bay is a fast growing municipality, with all the facilities and amenities of a growing town.

Ulundi

When Cetshwayo became king of the Zulus on 1 September 1873 he created, as was customary, a new capital for the nation. He decided to name this new capital uluNdi ('the high place'), usually called Ulundi by Europeans.

On 4 July 1879 the British army captured Ulundi and burned it down. This was the final battle of the Anglo-Zulu War (see box, page 356) and the plain on which it was fought is still littered with cartridge cases, spent bullets and other relics. A memorial has been erected on the site.

Modern Ulundi and Pietermaritzburg are contenders for the status of capital city of KwaZulu/Natal.

Umfolozi Game Reserve

The Mfolozi ('zigzag') River is so named because of its complex course through the hills of central Kwazulu. In its middle reaches the river divides into two: the Mfolozi emnyama ('Black Mfolozi') to the north and the Mfolozi emhlophe ('White Mfolozi') to the south. The colour differences are due to the soils through which the two rivers flow before they unite.

Where the rivers converge there is a tongue of land 50 000 hectares in extent, which is among the loveliest bush country in Kwazulu, backed in the north by a high ridge of hills.

This area between the two rivers has always been frequented by wild animals. It is classic savanna country. The grazing is rich, the climate — warm to hot, with ample water — suited to most African mammals. Hunters were for long kept out of the region by tsetse flies. Rhinos in particular liked the area and long after they had been hunted almost to the point of extinction in the rest of Africa, this area remained a sanctuary for both the black and the white species.

The Zulu people have always made great use of skins, feathers and beads in their dress. Their homeland is still an area of big game.

1. A Zulu chief, with headdress of feathers of the bishop bird. His cloak is a leopard skin.
2. A young girl playing the musical instrument known as the makwelane.
3. A maiden of the Tugela Valley in her finery of beads and metal bangles.
4. The costume of a young Zulu girl, a tasteful arrangement of beadwork.
5. A Zulu girl dressed in her brother's clothes during the Nomkhubulwane ritual held to propitiate the ancestral spirits at times of drought.
6. Zizwe zonke Mthethwa, one of the principal diviners of the Zulu people in his ceremonial dress, carefully designed 'to please the snakes'.
7. A Zulu youth herding cattle, dressed in customary skins and beads.

*The monument on the site of the batt-
lefield of Ulundi.*

In 1897 the Umfolozi Game Reserve was proclaimed. This and the
Hluhluwe reserve were to be permanent game sanctuaries, particularly for
white rhino, then on the list of endangered species. Unfortunately, however, a serious problem arose.
Zululand, as it was then called, was
becoming settled by European farmers. They acquired land cheaply
around the game reserves of Umfolozi
and Hluhluwe, but when they introduced livestock into the area they
suffered heavy losses owing to the dis-

ease of nagana, carried by the tsetse
fly. A campaign began to have all
game animals destroyed — by killing
the game, it was argued, the tsetse
would be deprived of nourishment,
and it would be eliminated. Thus
large, desirable areas would be open
to human settlement.

Conservationists found themselves
very much on the defensive. Farmers,
politicians and veterinary experts were
determined to destroy the remaining
wild animals in Zululand. The reserves
had never been opened to tourists and
scorn was poured on any suggestions
that future generations would take a
dismal view of their wanton destruction, or that more profit and pleasure
would come from them as game
reserves than from the establishment
of a few additional cattle ranches.

Umfolozi was regarded as an experimental area in the war against the
tsetse fly. A research station was established here in 1921 and a long and
controversial struggle began to eradicate the fly (see box, page 367). The
story of this anti-tsetse campaign
makes sad reading. About 100 000
animals were slaughtered in the
reserve before the lunacy of the campaign became apparent and the introduction of DDT spraying in 1945
effectively eradicated the fly.

Even at the height of the slaughter,

Zebras in the Umfolozi Game Reserve, a pattern of colour and design.

however, white rhinos were preserved,
and today a population of about 1 000
is maintained. The surplus — beyond
the carrying capacity of Umfolozi and
Hluhluwe — is distributed annually
to other reserves and zoos throughout
the world. There are also many black
rhino, as well as lion, giraffe, buffalo,
leopard, bushbuck, zebra, blue wildebeest, waterbuck, red and grey duiker,
steenbuck, mountain reedbuck, klipspringer, impala, kudu, nyala, warthog, spotted hyena and black-backed
jackal. Cheetah have also been re-
established in the Umfolozi Reserve.

The lions of Umfolozi have a
unique story. By the beginning of the
20th century it was thought that they
had been totally eradicated from this
region. Then in 1958 a solitary male
lion wandered south from Mocambique into the bush of Tongaland.
What motivated its travels is
unknown. It continued on its way
south for 350 kilometres, crossing
well-populated farming country,
slaughtering a few head of cattle for

food, and being tracked and hunted
by the usual band of trophy hunters
who sought the questionable honour
of shooting 'the last lion of Zululand'.

The lion outmanoeuvred all pursuers and, by a miracle, found itself
safe in the Umfolozi Game Reserve,
stocked with fat antelope which had
not seen a lion for generations. After
a few years of celibacy the lion was
joined by a bevy of females under mysterious circumstances and about 40
lions now keep the population explosion of game animals in Umfolozi under control.

The reserve is open throughout the
year. There is a hutted camp, a game-
viewing hide at one of the main drinking pools, a network of roads and
24 000 hectares of wilderness area
where parties are escorted on three-day
walks, camping at night in the bush.

Bird life includes night heron,
wood stork, Wahlberg's eagle, Shel-
ley's francolin, black-bellied korhaan,
Temminck's courser, Klaas's cuckoo,
little bee-eater and crested barbet.

5   6   7

LAND OF THE ALCOHOLIC PALMS

ABOUT 1550, IT IS SAID, there lived a man by the name of Tembe, whose home was on the shores of the bay of Lourenco Marques (Maputo). His people had long ago wandered into this area from Zimbabwe. On the shore where the waves of the Indian Ocean surge into the great bay they had settled to grow crops and to fish. With the arrival of Arab and Portuguese seafarers they then learned to be travelling traders. They carried beads and cloth into the interior of southern Africa, along with other novelties such as maize and the domestic cat, and they bartered these goods for ivory, gold, copper, horns and hides.

As the years passed, the people of Tembe prospered and increased in number. They also quarrelled and divided into two sections: one group retained the name of Tembe, and the second called themselves after a chief named Mabudu (misspelled Maputo by Europeans, which is the name applied to the lower reaches of the Usutu River and nowadays to the city formerly known as Lourenco Marques).

Mabudu's people migrated south from the bay and made their way into the flat, sandy, tree-covered region known as Tongaland. The Zulu had always casually referred to all people living in Mocambique as Tongas, meaning a ruled race. For want of a better name, the people of Mabudu and Tembe also became known as Tongas, and the southern part of their homeland as Tongaland. In modern times the name Maputaland has been applied to this area of 9 000 square kilometres. During the Cretaceous Period, 60 million years ago, all of Maputaland was beneath the sea. This accounts for the salty, sandy soil, which is full of shells. There is a heavy rainfall and the area is hot in summer, warm in winter.

Water collects in hollows in the sandy plains, forming lakelets and pans. In some of these the water is crystal clear, while others are fed by the muddy overflow from rivers. Rivers such as the Pongolo have complex courses over the sandy flats. The slope of the land is almost imperceptible, and the rivers dawdle and meander. The only incentive to flow at all is pressure of water from behind. When this pressure mounts during floods, the rivers spill over their low banks and water flows into adjacent hollows, where it slowly seeps away into the sand. The lakelets are a valuable asset to Tongaland. They are shallow and the water is always warm. Barbel and tiger-fish live in the lakelets; crocodiles feed on the fish and the occasional mammal; hippos sleep in the waters and feed on the dense vegetation covering the surrounding land. Aquatic birds are abundant — flamingoes, pelicans, wild duck and geese, kingfishers, fish eagles, reed cormorants, ospreys and the magnificent palmnut vultures all feed on the fish, frogs and other small creatures that live in the water. A part of the special magic of these shores has been the slow return, over many years, of marine turtles that come to the beaches to lay their eggs in burrows that the females scoop in the sand with their flippers.

The vegetation of this region resembles the collections of tropical plants seen in the hothouses of botanical gardens. More than 175 species of tree have been recorded here. The rivers tunnel beneath these trees, and there are long stretches where sunlight seldom penetrates through the canopy.

The wild fig trees are notable. These forest giants line the banks of all the rivers, but are specially plentiful along the Pongolo, where their boughs meet overhead or arch over to touch the water. Monkeys use the branches to cross the river, a multitude of birds build their nests in them, and the fruit provides nutrition for many wild creatures.

Nearer the coast, the forest thins and palms replace the trees. Lala palms grow in abundance, providing so generous a supply of free alcohol that many men and a few ingenious animals have seldom known what it is to be sober. To procure a drink, all one needs to do is cut a groove into the stem of a lala palm, fix a leaf into the groove to act as a spout, and tie a calabash to the trunk in such a way that the sap will drip from the leaf into the container. Fresh, the sap is a delicious soft drink; when 24 hours old it has fermented into a powerful alcoholic drink.

In this warm environment of water, trees, alcoholic palms, fish, elephants and numerous other game animals, the Tembe and Mabudu peoples lead carefree lives.

Unfortunately, other inhabitants of the area include some of the most aggressive of all mosquitoes, and summer nights can really hum. During winter the mosquitoes are more subdued, but they are always present. It is said that a slightly higher pitch to their song is discernible in the areas with lala palms.

Cape Vidal

Several of the coastal place names of Tongaland originated in 1822 when Captain W. F. Owen was instructed by the British admiralty to survey the coast of south-east Africa. One of his officers was Lieutenant Alexander Vidal, whose name was given to the rather stumpy cape — really a ledge of rock — on the isthmus separating Lake St. Lucia from the sea.

The cape was the scene of one of the most extraordinary shipwrecks along the coast of Africa. On the night of 31 January 1898 an old, leaky barque, the Dorothea, was abandoned at sea, 8 kilometres east of Cape Vidal. The weather was reported by contemporary newspapers as being calm, and the crew, in two boats, were picked up by passing steamers. The Dorothea simply drifted onto the shore at the cape and sank. There was no explanation as to why the ship had been abandoned.

The story put about in public was that the Dorothea, after a chequered career as a trader named the Ernestein, had been damaged on a reef as it entered the bay of Lourenco Marques. The barque had then been unloaded, and after lying on the beach for some time, was sold for £75 to a speculator named Pitt.

A striped reed frog (Hyperolius semidiscus), common in Tongaland.

The Usutu River flowing lazily through the forest country of Tongaland, a paradise for hippos and crocodiles.

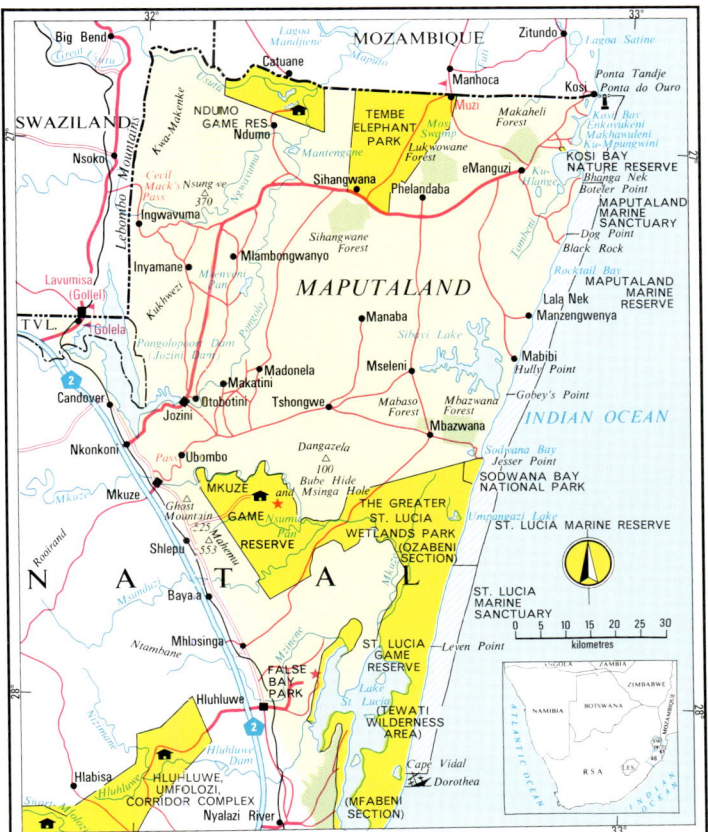

THINGS TO DO AND SEE

Angling Tiger-fish abound in the rivers and lakes. Armed with formidable teeth, they will attack anything that moves when they are feeding. Once on the hook they will fight to the end.

Barbel, or catfish, grow to more than 25 kilograms in the pans and rivers, and specimens 2 metres long are common. Mud fish and tilapia are also numerous.

Most of the coast of Tongaland is inaccessible by road, but fishermen can drive along the beach in four-wheel-drive vehicles, provided they have obtained the necessary access permits. Kingfish are the main sporting fish here; queen fish and garfish can also be taken.

Boating The adventurous use flat-bottomed boats or canoes to ride rivers such as the Pongolo. There are rapids, many hippos and crocodiles, and good fishing. The lakes at Kosi Bay and other places offer fine waters for boating and fishing.

Camping and caravanning There are no hotels in Tongaland. The two game reserves, Ndumu and Mkuzi, offer bungalow accommodation, and there is a camping area at Mkuzi. There are also camping grounds in several other areas including Sodwana and Kosi Bay.

Touring There is a gravel road as far as the Ndumu Game Reserve. Most of the other roads are sandy, demanding a powerful vehicle and careful driving. A tour in Tongaland is, however, a worthwhile and exciting experience.

After another year mouldering on the beach, the hulk had been sold by Pitt to a mysterious Johannesburg syndicate headed by a Doctor Kelly. Apparently the syndicate planned to use the ship for fishing.

Roughly patched up, put under the American flag and renamed the *Dorothea*, the ship then sailed for Durban under a Captain Harold Mathisson — ostensibly to be repaired properly.

However, the dockside gossips had a different and more sensational account. At this time the theft of gold

The trunk of a giant wild fig tree growing on the banks of the Mkuze River.

Death thwarts the searchers for sunken gold

bullion and the illicit buying of stolen gold on the Witwatersrand had reached astonishing proportions, and the mysterious Johannesburg syndicate was said to be heavily involved in the racket. It was said they bought the hulk to smuggle their loot out of South Africa, and that at least 120 000 ounces of gold were concealed among the ballast in the empty holds of the *Dorothea* — at current gold values worth about R50 million.

It was a peculiar story, full of evasions and contradictions.

Nevertheless, the rumours were enough to bring about many extraordinary attempts to salvage the lost treasure. Three months after the *Dorothea* had been wrecked, the salvage ship *Alfred Nobel*, under Captain Charles Gardiner, was sent from Durban by the Natal government to investigate. They located the *Dorothea* with its masts still above water, but constant bad weather prevented salvage. The wreck was in the surf, too close to land to be reached safely from the sea, and yet too awkward to reach from land in bad weather.

The *Alfred Nobel* returned to Durban. Then, in June 1899, the Johannesburg syndicate financed an expedition, using a small steam fishing boat, the *Nidaros*, an auxiliary surf boat, a diver and a salvage crew.

The weather was calm and the wreck was quickly located. The diver went down and soon found bars of yellow metal lying between the timbers. Wild with excitement he was hauled up, but the bars were found to be copper. Nobody could explain how they came to be in the wreck.

The surf boat was then anchored directly over the wreck. While the salvage men were working in the surf boat, a sudden killer wave capsized it, drowned the captain in command of the operation, two members of the crew, and the diver who was working below.

The next month the tug *Hansa*, commanded by Captain George Vibert, was sent up the coast by the syndicate. An overland expedition was also sent up to form a shore party.

The *Hansa* also carried a surf boat. This was lowered but it capsized over the wreck and was lost. The *Hansa* was forced to return to Durban for another

boat. By the time it got back to the wreck, seasonal bad weather had set in. After some abortive efforts to reach the wreck, the salvage was abandoned until the next winter season when the seas would be calmer.

The Anglo-Boer War broke out and this hindered further expeditions. In December 1899, however, the *Countess of Caernarvon* was chartered by another syndicate. Divers worked on the wreck, then returned to Durban claiming that they had recovered nothing save a few 'curios'.

In July 1901 Captain Vibert was once again on the scene, this time in a salvage steamer, the *Fenella*. Nothing was reported to have been recovered. In 1903 the steam tug *Ulundi* was sent here by the Natal government. After much work, the tug returned to Durban and reported that nothing had been found. In August 1904 the *Penguin* was despatched from Durban with a well-equipped party. Off the Zululand coast the ship encountered a violent storm. Eleven crew members were drowned; the rest abandoned the ship and it sank with all the salvage gear. The survivors had a grim 40-hour battle in an open boat without food and water before they reached the beach.

The promoters of the *Penguin* expedition hastily organized a second venture with the salvage ship *Good Hope* and a shore party. There were surf boats and two professional divers. While they were working here a company called the Dorothea Treasure Trove Syndicate was organized in the Transvaal, in December 1904. With Sir Edward Murray as chairman, this company published an elaborate prospectus stating that the 120 000 ounces of gold were packed in 12 large boxes and three leather bags, all covered with 15 centimetres of cement at the foot of the foremast.

However, still no report was lodged of any significant finds by this salvage company.

In 1906 the South African Salvage Company was organized to find the gold and in 1908 the Dorothea Barque Treasure Trove Syndicate searched the area of the wreck for six weeks. They claimed to have found nothing except wood and anchor chains. The anchor had been recovered by one of the earli-

An Imperial dragon-fly, with a wing span of 120 millimetres.

er companies, and left lying on the shore to mark the exact position of the wreck.

There is no record of any other company attempting to find the treasure. All that remains are rumours and whispers of surreptitious doings on this wild and lonely stretch of coast.

Ghost Mountain

Where the Mkuze River passes through the Lebombo Mountains in a precipitous, bush-covered pass stands

The formidably thorned Euphorbia grandiflora *in full flower.*

a peak, 529 metres high, known to the Zulus as Tshaneni ('the place of the small stone') and to Europeans as Ghost Mountain.

This mountain has a peculiar reputation. At irregular intervals over the years, strange lights and flickering fires are seen among the fissures and cliffs of the summit. Weird noises and strange calls are also heard.

The section of the Ndwandwe people headed by the Gasa family had their homes beneath this mountain

Ghost Mountain looms eerily through the mists on the banks of the Mkuze River.

CONQUEST OF MALARIA

There was a time when a new settler in areas such as the northern Transvaal and Tongaland was not regarded as 'naturalized' until he had caught malaria.

Every summer the hum of mosquitoes was the dominant sound in the quiet nights. All people could do was dose themselves with quinine and hope for the best. If cerebral malaria or the virulent blackwater fever was contracted, the victim generally died. Otherwise it was a matter of days of delirium and high fever.

In 1930-31 Professor N. H. Swellengrebel, a malaria expert from the League of Nations, visited South Africa to study the problem. He initiated research into malaria carriers, and subsequently Dr Botha de Meillon disclosed that of the many species of mosquito in South Africa, only two were malaria carriers. Both were essentially house-dwelling, biting at night and indoors.

A campaign of chemical spraying and the screening of houses achieved considerable success.

Today anti-malaria drugs have virtually ended the menace.

A driftwood tree at Cape Vidal standing like a monument to forgotten disaster.

TOLL OF THE TSETSE

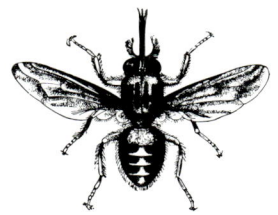

A tsetse, shown about 2½ times larger than natural size.

Probably the greatest single factor in giving Africa its name of the Dark Continent was the tsetse fly. For the deadly diseases that its bite passed into the blood — sleeping sickness in man and nagana in domestic livestock — made much of central Africa almost uninhabitable.

For many years it was thought that the only way to eradicate the tsetse was to destroy the animal life on which it fed.

From May 1929 to November 1930 the territories of Zululand and Tongaland took on the appearance of an abattoir.

Over a period of about ten years the numbers of tsetse flies dramatically dropped. It was jubilantly claimed that the menace had been overcome. But in 1940 there was an outbreak of nagana. It became apparent that the tsetse was simply subject to cycles.

As the flies increased once again, tens of thousands of wild animals were shot in the game reserves. The result of this action was that the tsetse fly moved out of the reserves in search of food, and between 1945 and 1946 more than 60 000 head of domestic livestock died of nagana in the neighbouring regions.

Finally, in 1945, experiments began with aerial spraying of D.D.T. The fly population dropped sensationally. By May 1953 not a single disease-carrying tsetse fly could be found in the area that had been treated. The tsetse fly had been vanquished and people were able to settle in the area without fear of the old diseases.

---

until they were conquered by Shaka in 1819 and the head of the family, Soshangane, fled with his followers into Mocambique. There he founded a group that became known after him as the Shanganes.

From early times it had been customary to bury the bodies of heads of the family on Ghost Mountain. High on its slopes there is a taboo cave, used as a tomb by generations of the Gasa family. Before burial, members of the family, together with their personal possessions, are wrapped in the skin of a black bull.

Soshangane and his descendants, although they lived 1 000 kilometres away in Mocambique, were also carried back to Ghost Mountain when they died. Their bodies, mummified and wrapped in black bull skins, had to be transported by bearers who travelled by night and hid during the day to avoid detection by the Zulus. Guardians were posted in the vicinity of the mountain to protect the tomb from wreckers and robbers. Descendants of these guardians still keep watch over the mountain.

Ghost Mountain will always be associated with one particularly melancholy event. After the Anglo-Zulu war in 1879, when the British tried to rule what was then Zululand by dividing it into 13 separate states, each with its own ruler, there was a period of chaotic rivalry, feuding and fighting.

The two principal rivals were Dinuzulu, son of the deposed Zulu king Cetshwayo, and Zibebu, head of the powerful Mandlakazi section of the Zulu nation.

In a series of bloody fights, Zibebu had the upper hand. Dinuzulu, in desperation, enlisted 800 European frontiersmen, who were promised rewards of farms for their help.

In June 1884 Dinuzulu's army of Europeans and Zulus invaded Zibebu's territory.

Zibebu was a strong and resolute leader and his Mandlakazi section was considered to be made up of the finest Zulu warriors. Nevertheless, although he also had a handful of European supporters, including the celebrated frontiersman, Johan Colenbrander (see box, page 508), he had very little

chance against the enemy.

Zibebu made a fighting retreat to the Mkuze River pass through the Lebombo.

On 5 June, in this rugged gorge beneath Ghost Mountain, there was a vicious struggle known as the Battle of Ghost Mountain. The Mandlakazi fought stubbornly but heavy rifle fire from the Europeans mowed them down. The battle continued in the bush, on the slopes of the mountain, and down the course of the river.

Eventually the Mandlakazi broke ranks, fleeing through the gorge and off into the dense forest country of Tongaland. The battlefield was littered with thousands of bodies, and even today the occasional human bone is sometimes found in the gorge.

Golela

On the western slopes of the Lebombo range, where the Pongolo River cuts through a narrow pass, there is a dense thicket known as Golela ('a gathering place of animals'). This was the personal hunting ground of the Nyawo chiefs. When the railway was

Where sea-shells are found on mountain slopes

Sand dunes and coastal forest separate the Kosi lakes from the sea.

built from Mtubatuba in 1926 across the coastal belt of what was then Zululand, the terminus on the Swazi border was named after this thicket.

Ingwavuma

The river known as the Ingwavuma is named after a species of tree — the Ngwavuma tree (*Pseudocassine transvaalensis*) — which is common on its banks.

The river makes its way through the Lebombo range by way of a spectacular pass. On the relatively cool plateau above this pass an administrative centre was established in 1895 at a place known to the local residents as Mthombeni ('place of the wild fig tree'). As the magisterial and commercial centre for the area watered by the Ingwavuma River, the village has adopted the name of the river.

Ingwavuma is a remote and quiet place with dramatic views, east over Tongaland, and west over Kwazulu and Swaziland, and the large expanse of water formed by the J. G. Strijdom Dam on the Pongolo River.

Kosi Bay

Among the most peculiar of the many mistakes Europeans have made with African place names was the naming of Kosi Bay. In 1822 the British navy sent Captain W. F. Owen with two ships to survey the coast of south-east Africa. The time allowed for this complex task was short, so some areas were surveyed only sketchily.

While anchored in what was then the bay of Lourenco Marques (where half his crew died of fever) Owen questioned the Africans about the country to the south. They told him of the Mkuze River, which he insisted on spelling 'Kosi'. When the survey started, the mouth of this 'Kosi' River was sought, but it was never found because the Mkuze flows into Lake St. Lucia.

On the coast, however, the surveyors located the estuary of a chain of lakes. This estuary was suspected of being the mouth of the missing Mkuze River, and was accordingly marked on the maps as 'Kosi Bay'. The biggest lake is Nhlange ('place of reeds') which covers an area of 37

THE UNLOVED CROCODILE — STILL LURKING AROUND AFTER 175 MILLION YEARS

A crocodile about to hatch . . .

. . . now inspects the world . . .

. . . and lazes in the sun.

The Zulus call the crocodile iNgwenya ('the lawless criminal'), but its principal victim is fish. The horror of being devoured by a crocodile, however, is very deep-seated in man. The very name, from the ancient Greek *krokodrilos* ('pebbleworms'), conjures up unpleasant images. Crocodile fossils have been found dating back 175 million years.

The only South African species — the common, or Nile, crocodile — is found in all the warmer African rivers. Adult specimens average about 4 metres in length, but they can grow to 6 metres or more.

The females lay about 40 eggs each year and bury them in sand, where they incubate in the warmth of the sun. Hyenas and birds eat many of the eggs. Those that survive hatch after 13 weeks and the young crocodiles come into the world fully capable of looking after themselves.

The crocodile plays its part in maintaining the balance of nature, but it is not much loved for the admittedly valuable work it does.

A mature crocodile on the banks of the Pongolo in the Ndumu Game Reserve.

THE RIVER HORSE

Hippos on the Pongolo banks.

The hippopotamus — the Greek word for river horse — was given its name because of the appearance of its head above water.

When intently watching an intruder, its odd little eyes filled with curiosity, small stubby ears twitching back and forth, nostrils flaring, the animal does bear some resemblance to a horse. But the rest of the creature is pure hippo — quiveringly obese, unwieldy and clumsy on land, and yet moving underwater with surprising ease, rising and descending at will by controlling the air in its stomach, and bouncing along the beds of lakes and rivers.

Although hippos are widely distributed all over Africa, there are only two species: the large, common variety; and a pigmy species found only in West Africa, which is not much bigger than a pig.

The common hippo is notably unaggressive, though a cow with a calf can become quite vicious, and a hippo surprised on land will trample or bite anything between it and the water.

The hippo spends most days dozing in the water with only the top of its head exposed. At the slightest disturbance it will sink down to the bed of the river or pool, remaining submerged for up to five minutes before rising to the surface for a quick gulp of air.

At night it leaves the water to feed on grass and other vegetation on the banks.

The hippo's movements in the water keep open channels which would otherwise become blocked by vegetation. In rivers where hippos have been exterminated masses of dead vegetation impede the water flow, sometimes choking it off entirely.

A *dead tree shrouded in spider web makes a weird and spectral sight in a strangely primeval land.*

square kilometres. Connected to Nhlange is a smaller lake, Mpungwini ('place of firewood'). Mpungwini is linked to a still smaller lake called Makhawulani. From Makhawulani an estuary known as Enkovukeni ('rise and fall') reaches the sea.

The chain of lakes is rich in fish. Sea pike, grunter, bream and many other fish find a congenial home in these waters. Bird life is also abundant, and includes several breeding pairs of fish eagles.

Nearby is the 20-hectare Kosi Bay nature reserve, which has a beautiful camping site.

The Tongaland coast of this region is a breeding ground for the world's largest marine turtle, the leatherback, as well as the smaller loggerhead. The leatherback can exceed a weight of 500 kilograms and a length of 2 metres.

Lebombo Mountains

Rising abruptly from the savanna plains of northern Kwazulu, the Lebombo range extends for 600 kilometres northwards until it loses itself in the valley of the Limpopo. Lebombo means 'a ridge'. To the eye, Lebombo resembles a long wall about 600 metres above the plains, with an almost level plateau summit and few outstanding peaks.

The ridge acts as the divide between the coastlands of Mocambique and the savanna plains of the eastern Transvaal and Swaziland. The plateau summit, about 5 kilometres wide, is a relatively cool and humidity-free haven for several small communities. In the past it was also home to many European renegades, bandits and escapists from civilization.

The ridge is geologically related to

the Drakensberg, and composed of the same rock material, basalt, which covered the entire surface of Natal about 150 million years ago. Massive natural erosion has destroyed most of this basalt covering, leaving only the Drakensberg and the Lebombo.

During Cretaceous times (60 million years ago) the sea flooded in over the plains of Tongaland and Mocambique, and the eastern cliffs of the Lebombo lay along the shoreline. Seashells can still be found on the lower slopes.

Mkuze River

It is not certain how this river acquired its name. It could be 'the river of warnings', or it may have taken its name from the mkuze trees (*Heteropyxis natalensis*) that grow along its banks. This river is harnessed for the irrigation

The rich animal life of crocodile country

of sugar cane and cotton. After passing through the Lebombo range it meanders across the sandy plains of Tongaland towards the sea, then swings southwards and flows into the northern end of Lake St. Lucia.

The mouth of the river is inhabited by many crocodiles.

Mkuzi Game Reserve

From the small trading centre and railway station of Mkuze there is a beautiful 18-kilometre drive through the Lebombo Mountains to the entrance of the Mkuzi Game Reserve. The reserve is now 30 500 hectares in extent and consists of a superb tract of natural parkland.

The reserve is the home of a large population of impala, black rhinoceros, hippo, giraffe, blue wildebeest, nyala, kudu, reedbuck, red and grey duiker, zebra, steenbuck, suni, bush pig, warthog, black-backed and side-striped jackal, and leopard. The Mkuze River and the Nsumu Pan contain many crocodiles, and there is a wealth of waterfowl.

Bird life includes the white-backed vulture, crested guinea fowl, Natal francolin, stilt, green-spotted wood dove, black cuckoo, white-fronted bee-eater and greater honeyguide.

The reserve has three game-viewing hides; at Bube, Msinga and Malibali.

There are wilderness trails and a hutted camp with cooks and helpers. Visitors must bring their own food. At the entrance is a caravan park.

Mkuzi is a small gem of a reserve, and botanists find the area rewarding. It was proclaimed a game reserve as early as 1912.

Ndumu Game Reserve

In 1924 a 10 000-hectare area of riverine forest country on the southern bank of the Usutu River was proclaimed the Ndumu Game Reserve. The name comes from that of a Tonga chief who once lived in the area.

Antelope such as nyala, bush-buck, impala, red and grey duiker, reedbuck and suni are numerous here and there are both black and white rhino. The primary feature of the reserve, however, is the astonishing wealth of life in the rivers and shallow pans. Hippos, crocodiles and aquatic birds

A herd of impala drinking at a water-hole in the Mkuzi Game Reserve on the eastern side of the Lebombo Mountains.

Two nyala bulls drinking at the Msinga water-hole in the Mkuzi Game Reserve.

A pair of hadeda ibises perform their ritual mating dance.

A lily trotter determinedly hunting for food at its water-hole.

A long cool drink for a thirsty warthog in the Mkuzi Game Reserve.

An impala rarz at an afternoon watering spot in the Mkuzi Game Reserve.

A group of thirsty baboons take refreshment in the Mkuzi Game Reserve.

A spotted hyena, powerful and aggressive, always hungry and alert.

A waterbuck ram, with powerful neck and fine horns, on the prowl.

Blue wildebeest and impala at a water-hole surrounded by thorn bush.

At ease against a fallen tree, a young cheetah lazes in the sunshine.

Mystery of the lake on a sandy coastal plain

A complex spider's web, almost a castle of intricately woven silk.

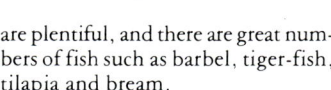

The fruit of Momordica involucrata, *common east of the Lebombo.*

Crocodiles basking on the banks of the Nyamiti Pan, lined by fever trees, in Tongaland's Ndumu Game Reserve.

are plentiful, and there are great numbers of fish such as barbel, tiger-fish, tilapia and bream.

There are at least 390 different bird species in the reserve, and approximately 200 species of trees. The forest is so dense in some places that the roads seem to vanish into long tunnels of greenery, trunks and shadows.

The broad Usutu River is a majestic sight, its banks lined with giant wild fig trees.

Over the years many crocodiles have been shot by professional hunters and poachers in search of skins, and the balance of life in the water systems of Tongaland has been disturbed. As the population of crocodiles diminished, barbel became so numerous that they endangered other fish species, such as tilapia and bream.

To re-create the original conditions, crocodiles are now bred in hatcheries and then released into Tongaland's water systems — in an effort to restore the balance of nature.

There is a hutted camp in the reserve with a communal kitchen, but visitors must bring their own food.

Ouro Point
The frontier line on the coast between Mocambique and South Africa is marked by a small lighthouse, erected on what is known as Ouro Point. In 1575 the Portuguese naval surveyor, Manuel Perestrello, explored the coast of Tongaland. From the rich colour of the sands he gave the name Rio de Medaos do Ouro ('the river of the sands of gold') to the mouth of the estuary at Kosi Bay. This name has been ab-

breviated to Ouro Point, which refers to the border lighthouse.

The area is popular with fishermen.

Pongolo River
The principal river of Tongaland is named the Pongolo, meaning 'the trough', because of its long, deep pools with steep sides. This river plays a major economic role in the area, filling the pans with water in the flood season and supporting a dense population of fish, crocodiles, hippos, aquatic brids — and people, who make use of the water for irrigation, and conduct large fishing industries in the pans.

The Tongas have always depended on fish as their principal source of protein because the tsetse fly, and the nagana disease it carries, was an ever-

present menace to livestock.

At the point where the Pongolo River passes through the Lebombo Mountains, at a place named Jozini after a headman who formerly lived here, the river has been harnessed by the J. G. Strijdom Dam (also known as the Jozini Dam) designed to irrigate 80 000 hectares of farmland suitable for the cultivation of sugar, rice, coffee, fibre crops, and various sub-tropical fruits.

Sibaya
The intensely blue lake known to the Tongas as Sibaya, meaning 'something enclosed', is a singular example of water entrapped in a deep hollow in a sandy coastal plain. The lake is 28 metres deep and nearly 50 square kilometres in extent. The water is fresh

and crystal clear, presumably fed by underground streams, for no river or stream flows into it but the level remains constant.

The bed and shores of the lake are made of fine white sand. There is no hill overlooking the area, but viewed from an aircraft the creatures of the lake — hippos, crocodiles and fish — can be seen quite clearly moving about beneath the surface. The hippos, rising and sinking from top to bottom and back again, and walking about on the floor of the lake, are particularly fascinating to watch.

Sodwana Bay National Park
On the coast of Tongaland, 90 kilometres east of Ubombo, there is a cluster of small lakes and marshes connected to the sea by a stream known as Sodwana ('little one on its own'). A drowsy coastal high forest grows around the lakes, providing shady camping sites for fishermen.

Birds are plentiful, and they include the Zulu batis and Rudd's apalis. Tonga red squirrels and several species of mongoose live in the forest, as well as suni, red and grey duiker, steenbuck, reedbuck and some exceptionally fat bush pigs.

In 1888 there was a plan to convert the area into a harbour, but the project proved to be impracticable.

Ubombo
In 1890, when the British annexed the territories of the Nyawo and Mngomezulu people who lived on the plateau summit of the Lebombo Mountains, they established a post named Ubombo. This isolated little post is perched on the summit, with wide panoramic views to the east, west and south, and is connected to the outside world by two passes, both steep enough to discourage casual visitors.

Ubombo is now a small village in a setting of tall trees. In early years there was a famous convenience here: a sign indicated 'Toilets' and directed people from the magisterial building down a path that diverged into two, signposted 'his' and 'hers'. Both branches ended at thickets of bush.

Services have improved in modern times, but there is no accommodation for visitors.

The eastern shores of Lake Sibaya. On the left stands the sand dune that separates the freshwater lake from the sea.

A rough suspension bridge crossing the crocodile-infested Pongolo River.

The wall of the J. G. Strijdom Dam built across the Pongolo River at Jozini.

ON THE ROOF OF SOUTHERN AFRICA

IN THE NEVER-ENDING process of the world's creation, the principal tools of nature have been fire, water, and to a lesser extent the winds. In the Drakensberg the combined efforts of the elements are clearly in evidence and even today this gigantic mass of rock is still in the throes of construction. The Drakensberg came into existence as a result of an astonishing change in the mood of nature. For more than 100 million years southern Africa had been a great swamp, with forests dripping rain — a haunt of weird reptilian monsters. Then, about 180 million years ago, there began a drastic change towards a new world.

Probably by altering the direction of the prevailing winds, nature swept away the rain. Swamps dried, forests died, and the monsters became fossilized, buried in mud that later turned to shales and sand as it dried and was compressed. This sand was rich in colour, oxidized by iron into shades of yellow, orange and red. Nature played with the sand, using winds to pile it up above the level of the former swamps, thus creating one of the most majestically beautiful of all geological rock systems — Clarens sandstone, about 300 metres thick.

Once again, some 25 million years later, a profound change occurred. Wind was abandoned as the major tool, and replaced by fire. Through great fissures in the mantle of the earth a huge mass of basaltic lava surged out, covering much of the surface to a depth of more than 1 000 metres, with a solid block of dark rock reaching up to 4 000 metres above sea level — the roof of southern Africa.

On to this roof fell the rains. This tool of creation now formed rivers that eroded deep valleys into the basalt. Much of the rain originated from the warm waters of the Indian Ocean. The mass of basalt began to dwindle, leaving a myriad unusual shapes and features, sculpted on a landscape of balancing rocks, pinnacles, cliffs, overhangs and deep caves.

On the eastern side the lava retreated before the onslaught of the weather, eroding backwards at a rate of about one metre every thousand years, leaving exposed beneath it an undulating, fertile scar 150 kilometres wide — the present sandstone landscape of Natal.

The remnant of the original mass of basalt still forms the roof of southern Africa. This is the high country of Lesotho. Viewed from the east, the basalt mass resembles a high wall, irregular along its summit, but with no gaps. The summit is a high-lying moorland, cut by gorges and valleys, but generally maintaining its altitude for 200 kilometres westwards until the entire basalt mass falls away abruptly to the central plains, with a precipitous edge almost as sheer as on the eastern side.

The Zulu-speaking people in the east called the edge of the basalt mass uKhahlamba ('a barrier') and they say that it resembles a row of spears. The summit they know simply as uluNdi or oNdini ('the heights'). The Sotho people who live on these heights call the eastern edge Dilomo tsa Natala ('the cliffs of Natal').

The basalt is crumbly and the run-off water from the summit has eroded deep gorges into its edge. Many rockfalls have etched even sharper precipices. Streams now cascade into these gorges. There are deep pools, dark caves, and many places so remote from the outside world that they can easily be imagined to be the abodes of spirits or legendary monsters.

Europeans named the southern part of the basalt massif the Drakensberg ('dragon mountain') because it seemed to be a natural home for such dramatic creatures. In former years several reports were made of sightings of dragons in the heights, and of mysterious tracks discovered in isolated places seldom visited by man.

Here too are the hideaways of rustlers and renegades, and caves with paintings by long-vanished peoples. All this makes up the intriguing setting and atmosphere of the legendary abode of the dragon.

Ngwane huts in the foothills of the Drakensberg near Bergville. The huts are built of thatched grass attached to a framework of wood.

A climber's view of the great basalt cliffs of the Drakensberg. The Mnweni area is in the centre of the picture.

Drakensberg. The river valley and the courses of the various headwater streams provide access to a superb concentration of mountains, including some of the best-known peaks in the Drakensberg. The 3 004-metre Cathedral Peak gives the area its name.

Cathedral Peak lies on the eastern

THINGS TO DO AND SEE

Angling Trout abound in the Drakensberg streams. The Giant's Castle, Himeville and Underberg areas are particularly renowned for their trout streams.

Camping and caravanning The Drakensberg is dream country for campers and caravanners. The Royal Natal National Park has a caravan ground amid trees and towering sandstone hills.

The forestry department maintains a camp at the approaches to Cathedral Peak.

The Dragon Peaks caravan park is at the approaches to Cathkin Peak and is part of the estate that is the home of the famous Drakensberg Boys' Choir

Giant's Castle Game Reserve has a park in a setting of mountains and trout waters.

There are several parks in the southern Drakensberg.

Climbing For 400 kilometres the Drakensberg of Natal and the Cape presents a continuous line of cliffs and peaks. Climbs range from easy to formidable. The Natal section of the Mountain Club of South Africa, in Durban, keeps records of first climbs and details of routes, and arranges meetings.

Riding The full length of the Drakensberg is negotiable on horseback. The Royal Natal National Park is enchanting riding country — one unforgettable bridle path leads to the summit of Mont-aux-Sources 23 kilometres away.

Cathedral Peak, the Cathkin Peak Valley, Giant's Castle, Drakensberg Garden, Bushman's Nek and other resorts and parks maintained by the Natal Parks Board all offer horses for hire.

Walking The summit ridge of the Drakensberg, the passes to the summit, the foothills, valleys and San caves with rock paintings offer memorable walking tours. There are hundreds of kilometres of paths.

Bergville

Only 50 kilometres from the towering cliffs of the Drakensberg and on the upper Tugela River is the town of Bergville.

This is the terminus of a branch railway line from Estcourt, a dairy centre, and also the nearest town to Mont-aux-Sources and Mnweni.

A blockhouse in the town, built by the British during the Anglo-Boer War, is a monument and museum. The Municipality maintains a holiday resort on the banks of the river.

Cathedral Peak

The Mlambonja ('river of the dog') has its headwaters in a series of gorges eroded deep into the main wall of the

Two severe Drakensberg climbs, the Amphlett (left) and the Tower (centre).

Peaks to test the nerve of any climber

Ngwane huts and maize fields in the valley of the Mlambonja River in the foothills of the Cathedral Peak area. Cathedral Peak is in the centre of the picture.

end of a spur of mountains branching off from the main wall, and is so jagged that the Zulus call it abaMponjwana ('the place of little horns'). The peaks on this spur include the 2 930-metre Bell, the 3 006-metre Outer Horn and the 3 005-metre Inner Horn. Lesser peaks are known by names such as the Mitre and the Chessmen. The Bell stands next to Cathedral Peak and offers a moderately difficult climb.

Of all the Drakensberg summits,

Cathedral Peak is the easiest to climb, with a path that leads from near the resort at its base to its summit. The main wall of the Drakensberg in the Cathedral Peak area maintains a height of more than 3 000 metres above sea level. Here are notable summits such as Indumeni ('place of thunder'), 3 200 metres high; Cleft peak, 3 281 metres high; Ndedema ('place of reverberations'), 3 078 metres high; and Qolo la maSoja ('bridge of the soldiers'), known to Europeans as the

Organ Pipes. Detached from the main wall are two jagged peaks, both famous among climbers — the 2 914-metre-high Pyramid, and the 2 926-metre-high Column.

The entire Cathedral Peak area is fine walking country. A network of paths covers the foothills and lower slopes of the mountains. A contour path leads along the slopes of the Drakensberg from Cathedral Peak to Cathkin Peak. The route is complex and about 60 kilometres long.

The upper valley of the Mlambonja and the valleys of its tributaries, the Inhlonhlo and the Ndumeni, can all be explored along footpaths. There are forests of trees and ferns, natural swimming pools, waterfalls, and many caves containing galleries of San rock art. The Ndedema Gorge, with its series of caves, is in this area. With a permit from the forestry office at Cathedral Peak, tourists can drive up Mike's Pass to the forestry areas. H. M. ('Mike') de Villiers was the forestry officer appointed in 1938 to establish a research station in the Cathedral Peak area. The war delayed the project, but it was resumed in 1945 and the pass was built to provide access to what is known as the 'Little Berg'. From the summit of the pass (1 500 metres) forestry roads and paths lead to research areas.

The first forestry research conducted in this area was to determine the consequences of planting pines in a water-catchment area. By 1972 it was proved that pine plantations used far more water than natural grassland, and were detrimental to streams. The water the Drakensberg supplies from its vast catchment area is highly valued, and the knowledge that plantations reduced water run-off brought an end to afforestation in the area. No farming or any other kind of development is now permitted, the Drakensberg today is preserved as a recreational wilderness area.

The preservation of such a natural wilderness, however, breeds problems. A grassland that is totally protected from grazing or other agricultural uses becomes, almost inevitably, a potential bonfire on a gigantic scale. Nature would shed the dead grass by means of a fire — which, for man, could be a major disaster.

Total protection also encourages secondary growth, such as shrubs and trees, to encroach on the grassland. Research in the Cathedral Peak area is now directed towards the management of a grassland wilderness by judiciously controlled burning. Different areas of the Little Berg are being studied for the effects of fires on grassland. The entire area is thus a field research laboratory. Visitors are welcome, but are expected to exercise caution to avoid any risk of fires.

There is a magnificent resort at the foot of Cathedral Peak, with a hotel, stables, shop, recreational areas, gardens and all the conveniences for mountaineers, hikers and riders. The forestry department has a caravan park in the shade of a wood on the banks of the Mlambonja River.

Cathkin Peak

One of the great corner-stones of the main wall of the Drakensberg, Cathkin Peak stands out so prominently

The Outer Horn and Inner Horn, part of the Cathedral ridge, in a stormy setting in the valley of the Mlambonja River.

A bottlebrush, one of the many flowers of the Drakensberg.

Sunset beyond the main wall of the Drakensberg.

THE CHIEF WHO FOUND LOVE AND A HOMELAND FOR HIS PEOPLE

The happy-ever-after love affair of the Ngwane chief Zikhali and a Swazi princess brought them not only contentment — it brought Zikhali's people to their present homeland in the foothills of the Drakensberg.

The Ngwane people are closely related to the original Zulu clan and resemble them closely in their customs and dress.

When the Zulu chief Shaka began his bloody process of nation-building early last century the Ngwane fled to the central plains. Under their chief, Matiwane, they lived as a robber band, trying to replace livestock taken from them by the Zulus. They looted the Sotho, but then found that their accumulated booty made them an even more attractive target for Zulu raids.

In 1828 they fled to the Transkei and began looting the Thembu people. The British garrison in Grahamstown mistook the newcomers for Zulus, sallied out and routed them.

Already decimated in numbers by clashes with the Zulu army, the Ngwane suffered further drastic losses and now faced the threat of virtual extinction.

With the remnants of his people, Matiwane made his way back to Zululand, intending to place himself at the mercy of Shaka. Meanwhile, Dingane had replaced Shaka, and he allocated to the Ngwane an area where they could settle.

Dingane formed a friendship with one of Matiwane's sons, Hlathi. When Hlathi died in circumstances suggestive of witchcraft, Dingane had Matiwane executed for the supposed crime.

The last of Matiwane's followers fled with his heir, Zikhali, to Swaziland. There Zikhali had a love affair with a Swazi princess called Nomlalati. The Swazi king, Sobhuza, opposed the affair and Zikhali was forced to flee back to Zululand.

Dingane listened to the young man's tale of blighted romance and was compassionate. He allocated to the Ngwane their present homeland in the afternoon shadow of the Drakensberg.

Here the remnants of the Ngwane gathered from many distant parts of the country. Zikhali's Swazi lover also slipped away from her father and joined them in their new home.

She and Zikhali lived happily without further misadventure. Their son, Ncwadi, succeeded his father as chief when Zikhali died in 1863.

On most early maps of the Drakensberg, Cathedral Peak is marked as Zikhali's Horn — the name first given to this peak in honour of the Ngwane chief.

The eerie realm of the one-eyed giant

Cathkin Peak, 3 148 metres high, stands on the extreme left, with Mount Memory to the right.

and dominates the entire range so completely that the Zulus have named it Mdedelele ('make room for him'), the name they give to a bully.

Cathkin Peak, 3 148 metres high, is detached from the main wall of the Drakensberg and offers mountaineers a long and moderately challenging climb. It was named in 1858 by a settler, David Gray, who farmed at its foot and called it after Cathkin Braes, near his home town of Paisley, in Scotland. Behind Cathkin Peak, between it and the main wall of the Drakensberg, there is a jagged pinnacle known from its shape as Monk's Cowl. This peak, 3 234 metres high, offers another moderately difficult climb.

On the main wall of the mountain is a massive, table-topped height, 3 348 metres, called Champagne Castle. This name was given to Cathkin Peak in the 1860s, when David Gray escorted a British army surveyor, Captain Grantham, on a climb. They carried a haversack which contained, among other things, a bottle of champagne to drink on the summit. They never reached the summit. At the point where they gave up the climb they decided to drink the champagne, but found that the bottle was half empty. Neither of the climbers would admit to having sneaked a drink, so they decided to blame the mountain and accordingly renamed it Champagne Castle. The two names were used until it was decided that Champagne Castle would refer only to the rock massif on the main wall.

North of Champagne Castle is a weirdly shaped ridge of spines and pinnacles known as the Dragon's Back. This ridge projects from the main wall and ends with a particularly strange-looking peak known to the Zulus as Ntunja ('the eye') and to Europeans as Gatberg ('hole mountain'). The peak is 2 408 metres high and the name arises from a huge hole beneath its summit that leads through the solid rock, giving the mountain the appearance of a petrified, one-eyed giant.

Cathkin Peak and the mountains around it are approached through the valley of the Sterkspruit ('strong stream'), which has it headwaters nearby. In its lower reaches the valley is broad and fertile with farmlands,

Cathkin Peak, with its head buried in the clouds on the left of the picture, dominates a rugged mass of mountains and foothills in the highest part of the Drakensberg.

meadows, and resorts, hotels, caravan parks and holiday homes.

One of the farms, Dragon Peaks, was bought in 1954 by a Durban journalist, Ronnie Tungay. In 1967 his son John opened a school on the farm for boys with musical talent. Today this school houses about 120 boarders, all members of the Drakensberg Boys' Choir, which is well-known internationally, having toured in countries as far away as Britain and Israel.

The Sterkspruit valley and the foothills of the Drakensberg make exciting riding country and most of the resorts have stables.

For trail riders and hikers there are hundreds of kilometres of paths, and it would take months to explore this rugged area. The Sterkspruit waterfall is a beautiful feature of the landscape. Wild flowers, San caves and patches of forest provide scenic interest. The ex-servicemen's M.O.T.H. organization

The Ngwane — a branch of the Nguni people, related to the Swazi — settled in the foothills of the Drakensberg as refugees during the Zulu troubles in the early 19th century.

The Ngwane costume is notable for its brilliant colour.

They are a conservative people and have tended to retain many of their original customs, especially their style of life and the architecture of their huts.

1. A recent bride clad in new beaded cloak and apron of marriage.
2. An engaged girl wearing a kilt of impending marriage.
3. A Sangoma, or diviner, in full ceremonial dress.
4. A Sangoma in the attitude of divining by 'smelling out'. She is in a trance.

1   2   3   4

379

At the end of a hard day's hiking — grilled trout

(Memorable Order of Tin Hats) maintains a sanctuary at the foot of Mount Memory (Sterkhorn). The sanctuary is dedicated to those who were killed in the two world wars.

The Monk's Cowl forest station, high on the slopes of Cathkin Peak, is the control centre for the 40 000-hectare Cathkin Peak Forest Reserve.

Coleford Nature Reserve

In the foothills of the Drakensberg, 27 kilometres from Underberg on the Bulwer-Swartberg road, lies the fishing resort and nature reserve known as Coleford. There is a camp with bungalows, each with its own kitchen. Guests bring their own food. The nature reserve is a sanctuary for black wildebeest, blesbok, red hartebeest and eland, which are bred here by the Natal Parks Board.

Horses can be hired, and the fishing for rainbow trout is outstanding — grilled trout is a standard evening meal in the camp.

Garden Castle

In 1835 the missionary Captain Allen Gardiner explored the southern Drakensberg. He recorded in his diary that on 17 October he was 'at one time, quite startled at the appearance of a rugged mountain which I have named the Giant's Castle. As seen over an intervening hill its resemblance to Edinburgh Castle, from one or two points, was so striking that, for the moment, I could almost fancy myself transported to Princes Street.'

In 1865 the surveyor Dr. Peter Sutherland transferred the name Giant's Castle to the mountain that is known by this name today. The peak formerly called Garden Castle he named after his second wife, Jane Garden Blaikie.

Garden Castle is a sandstone foothill of the main Drakensberg. It is only 1 400 metres high but its striking appearance makes it a prominent landmark. A resort at its foot is popular with riders, fishermen and walkers.

Giant's Castle Game Reserve

South of Cathkin Peak the main wall of the Drakensberg maintains a level of more than 3 000 metres for 35 kilometres, presenting a relentless wall of dark basalt rock which ends in a

The Drakensberg, looking down on the mountaineers' hut known as Bannerman.

huge corner-stone known to Europeans as Giant's Castle and to the Zulus as iNtabayikonjwa ('the mountain at which one must not point'). This name originates from a legend that the mountain dislikes being pointed at, or even being mentioned in conversation. It responds by bringing bad weather.

Giant's Castle, like Cathkin Peak, is an exposed, prominent massif, with the main Drakensberg swinging south-west behind it. Storms seem to gather around it — in winter there are heavy snowfalls and in summer violent thunderstorms. The mountain is 3 314 metres high and has some demanding climbs.

In 1903 a game reserve was proclaimed over 30 000 hectares of the foothills and slopes of the Giant's Castle area. The Bushman's River has its headwaters in this part of the Drakensberg and the foothills are thickly grassed, providing a natural home for

A pair of rock rats, untroubled by snow, high in the Drakensberg.

Black wildebeest (or Gnu) grazing on the rich, sweet grass that blankets the Drakensberg foothills.

LANGALIBALELE'S TRIAL

In 1873 the Natal government launched a campaign to disarm various groups who had acquired guns from gun-runners as inducements to work on the diamond fields at Kimberley.

Among the offending groups were the Hlubi of chief Langalibalele. He and his followers refused to surrender their guns and an expedition was sent to enforce the order. Langalibalele and the Hlubis fled up the Bushman's River.

With their pursuers close behind, the Hlubis made their way up the Drakensberg, following a route ever since known as Langalibalele's Pass.

During their flight the Hlubi left behind several thousand head of cattle. The government force were rounding these up when they were surprised by a group of Hlubi warriors. Three of the carbineers and two of their African allies were killed.

Langalibalele — whose name means 'the hot sun' — was eventually captured and handed over to the Cape authorities in chains.

Then followed one of the most celebrated wrangles in South Africa's legal history. Langalibalele was tried by a special court according to native law and banished for life to Robben Island in Table Bay. His people's possessions were confiscated.

The Bishop of Natal, J. W. Colenso, protested against the severity of the sentence. In London the trial was regarded as a travesty of justice because it was based on the legal fiction that Sir Benjamin Pine, the lieutenant-governor, was a native chief with arbitrary powers. It was also pointed out that the Cape government had acted outside its jurisdiction by enforcing a sentence outside the colony. Eventually the sentence was commuted and Langalibalele was set free.

Today, on the heights behind Giant's Castle, the graves of the five government men killed in the fight are marked by a mound of stones and a cross.

The Polela River, near Himeville — a well stocked trout stream flowing through the foothills of the Drakensberg.

eland, grey rhebuck, reedbuck, mountain reedbuck, oribi, red hartebeest, black wildebeest, blesbok, bushbuck, grey duiker and klipspringer. Black-backed jackals, baboons and many small predators are also plentiful.

Eland are the pride of the area, breeding here easily.

Bird life is varied and includes species such as black storks, black and martial eagles, lanner falcons, lammergeyers, orange-breasted rock jumpers, giant kingfishers, and Gurney's sugarbirds.

The Bushman's River is one of the most productive brown trout fisheries in South Africa and its upper gorge contains caves in which there are galleries of San paintings.

Many kilometres of paths and riding trails criss-cross the reserve. There is a stable at the Hillside camp and mountain trail rides two to four days long are organized.

There are two camps in the reserve. Visitors must bring their own food but cooks are available. There is a separate camping area and two mountaineers' huts on the heights of Giant's Castle. Climbing in the area is challenging, with some extremely severe routes. Notable peaks on the main wall include the 2 986-metre Old Woman Grinding Corn, and the 3 207-metre Njesuthi Twins at the headwaters of the quaintly named Njesuthi ('well-fed dog') River.

One of the rock faces, known as Bannerman, has a distinct resemblance to the profile of Sir Henry Campbell-Bannerman, Prime Minister of Britain from 1905-08.

Giant's Castle under heavy snow is a fine sight The summit can be reached fairly easily up a steep natural pass and from this high level the mountain roof of South Africa can be seen, stretching westwards in a panorama of boggy hollows and rocky peaks.

Himeville

The small rural centre and magistrate's seat of Himeville was founded in 1902 and named after Sir Albert Hime, the governor of Natal at that time. On the commonage is the Himeville Nature Reserve with two trout lakes in a well-grassed valley. Boats are available for hire and the reserve has a camping site. The lakes attract many wild fowl and there are a

A gallery of San paintings in a rock shelter below Giant's Castle.

The mountain where four great rivers are born

few resident antelope of various species. From Himeville a road leads up the Sani Pass to the top of the Drakensberg and into Lesotho.

Hodgson's Peak
During the middle years of the 19th century the San of the Drakensberg and the pastoralist settlers of Natal were involved in a long series of fights and bitter vendettas. The settlers had livestock, and they had steadily encroached on the San's ancient hunting grounds. The San withdrew to the remote highlands of Lesotho and from hide-outs in inaccessible valleys they raided into Natal, rustling livestock.

In 1862 the rustlers raided the farm Mount Park, owned by Charles Speirs. They escaped with 75 head of cattle and 15 horses, including a stud thoroughbred. Speirs roused his neighbours and chased the thieves into the wild country at the approaches to the southern Drakensberg of Natal.

The San were hard-pressed. They slaughtered the cattle and left the mutilated carcasses on the trail for the farmers to find. The chase continued in pouring rain. After eight days of hard riding the farmers caught up with a San rustler riding one of the stolen horses.

In the pursuit, one of the farmers, Thomas Hodgson, was fatally wounded by an accidental shot from one of his companions. He was buried on the slopes of this 3 257-metre peak, which is named after him.

The captured San was taken to one of the farms where, three years later, he died of tuberculosis.

The remainder of the San band escaped over the Drakensberg into Lesotho.

Kamberg Nature Reserve
In the heart of the trout fishing areas in the foothills of the Drakensberg lies the Kamberg Nature Reserve, 40 kilometres from the village of Rosetta. The reserve contains reedbuck, mountain reedbuck, grey rhebuck, eland, grey duiker and oribi.

There are 13 kilometres of excellent brown trout waters, and a camp with a central kitchen. Visitors must bring their own food but cooks are provided.

This is a delightfully peaceful resort for fishermen, photographers and nature lovers.

Loteni Nature Reserve
The Loteni River is a productive brown trout fishery. Some 12 kilometres of the river run through the Loteni Nature Reserve, 78 kilometres southwest of Nottingham Road.

This is one of the most scenically beautiful of the reserves in the foothills of the Drakensberg, a delight for walkers, riders, photographers, nature lovers and fishermen.

The camp has cooks but visitors must bring their own food. There is a small historical settlers' museum, and a good stable.

Wildlife includes reedbuck, mountain reedbuck, grey rhebuck, eland, grey duiker, oribi and bushbuck.

THE BEARDED VULTURE, HIGH-FLYING MONARCH OF THE MOUNTAINS

The monarch of the Drakensberg's high peaks is the bearded vulture — sometimes known as the lammergeyer. With a wing span of nearly 3 metres, these giant birds seem powerful enough to carry off a lamb, but their main food is carrion.

They are partial to bones and have a tongue adapted for extracting marrow. Small animals such as dassies also form part of their menu. The birds drop their food from a height and then swoop down to feed on the broken corpse.

At Giant's Castle there is an observation hide overlooking a bearded vulture nest in the mountains. Offal and other titbits are placed on a ledge in winter so that the birds can be viewed while feeding. Bearded vultures verge on the endangered list and are protected by law.

The white-backed and Cape vultures are more numerous, as are the lappet-faced vultures and the hooded vultures. One of the rare birds of southern Africa is the Egyptian vulture, which drops stones on ostrich eggs to break open the shells.

Another bird with a curious diet is the palm nut vulture. It eats the husks of palm trees as well as fish.

Black eagles, among the most audacious of all southern African birds of prey.

The indigenous species of southern African birds of prey include 8 vultures, 14 eagles, 7 falcons, 3 kestrels, 2 kites, a bat hawk, 2 buzzards, 9 goshawks and sparrow-hawks, 2 harriers — the gymnogene and the osprey — and the unique secretary bird. Another 12 migrants join them in summer.

Of the eagles, the black, the martial and the crowned are the most powerful; among the most daring are the blackbreasted and the brown snake eagles, which make no apparent distinction between venomous and harmless reptiles when they feed. They swoop down, seize the startled snake and fly off, dropping it to the ground to kill it and then eating it head first. Their thick feathers and scaly feet protect them from being bitten.

The sight of one of these birds flying upwards with a large, wriggling, enraged snake in its talons is a memorable experience.

The lammergeyer, largest of Africa's birds of prey.

The bateleur, devourer of many a dassie.

There are also many birds, especially kingfishers and storks.

Mont-aux-Sources

Two French Protestant missionaries, Thomas Arbousset and Francois Daumas, explored the mountainous highlands of Lesotho in 1830. After a difficult journey they reached the eastern edge of the great mass of basalt and found themselves on the plateau summit of a mountain known to the Sotho as Phofung ('place of eland'), but renamed by the missionaries Mont-aux-Sources ('mountain of sources') because on it they found the sources of many rivers and streams.

The plateau of Mont-aux-Sources is 3 048 metres high. The tremendous cliffs on the eastern edge form a massive curve known as the Amphitheatre. Set back westwards on the plateau is a hillock-like summit which crowns the whole mountain and reaches an altitude of 3 282 metres. On the slopes of this summit the Tugela River has its source. The infant river flows to the edge of the Amphitheatre and then plummets 2 000 metres in a series of sheer falls and cascades. This is the highest waterfall in South Africa. In winter the upper part of the waterfall freezes into a pinnacle of ice.

Close to the source of the Tugela is a second spring, which is the source of the Elands River. The two streams are separated by a low boggy ridge, which is the east-west watershed of southern Africa. The Elands veers north off this ridge, cascades from the summit in a series of falls for 1 200 metres, reaches the central plains and flows off to join the Vaal and through it the Orange. It reaches the Atlantic Ocean at a point on the west coast 1 400 kilometres away from the mouth of the Tugela River on the east coast.

Other rivers with their sources on the mountain are the Western Khubelu, a major tributary of the upper Orange; and the Eastern Khubelu, which once joined its western twin but was re-routed by the erosive retreat of the eastern wall of the Drakensberg. Most of its flow now tumbles over the Amphitheatre in the Ribbon Falls and joins the Tugela. Only a trickle flows westwards to join the Orange.

The Elands River tumbling down from the summit of Mont-aux-Sources.

On the northern side of Mont-aux-Sources, the northern end of the main Drakensberg is marked by the Sentinel, a great landmark 3 165 metres high.

The south-eastern end of the Amphitheatre is marked by the 3 009-metre Eastern Buttress. Between this buttress and the Amphitheatre is a jagged pinnacle known as the Devil's Tooth — one of the most dangerous climbs in the Drakensberg.

From the plateau summit of Mont-aux-Sources a path runs to the Royal Natal National Park (23 kilometres), and to the Witsieshoek Mountain Resort (9 kilometres). Two chain ladders, each with 100 rungs, help climbers to reach the summit.

The views from Mont-aux-Sources are superb — watching the dawn over Natal is an unforgettable experience.

In winter the summit is usually under heavy snow. Summer thunderstorms can be violent.

Mnweni

Between Mont-aux-Sources and Cathedral Peak there are no roads, but pathways lead to the rural villages of the Ngwane people, who live in the foothills of the mountain. The higher slopes can be reached only by climbers. In this rock wilderness are some

The view from the Sentinel across the Mont-aux-Sources Amphitheatre to the Eastern Buttress and the Devil's Tooth.

A summit crowned with minarets of rocks

The moody, mysterious Mont-aux-Sources Amphitheatre. The Sentinel is on the right and the eastern buttress on the left.

of the most beautiful of all the Drakensberg summits.

The Africans call the area Mnweni ('the place of fingers') because the spires of rock stand up like the fingers of a hand. Perhaps the loveliest of all the Drakensberg peaks is the Rockeries (also called Mnweni Castle). It is 3 117 metres high and its crown of minarets and towers of rock act as a mighty landmark behind which, on the western heights, the Orange River has its source.

Attached to the Rockeries are pinnacles such as Mponjawane ('the little horn') and the Inner and Outer Mnweni Needles. Immediately south of the Rockeries looms one of the largest single rock masses in the whole of the Drakensberg — the 3 145-metre Saddle, a huge lump of basalt shaped like the saddle of a horse.

Ndedema Gorge
The tributaries of the upper Mlambonja River flow through deep gorges, and in these are numerous caves and rock shelters formerly occupied by the San people. There are about 150 separate rock art galleries in the caves, which are largely concentrated in Ndedema Gorge.

The gorge takes its name from the river flowing through it, and the river takes its name from the Drakensberg peak on which it has its source. Ndedema is a corruption of Ndidima, which means 'a place of reverberation', and the name derives from the rumblings and tremors of powerful thunderstorms.

The gorge was a perfect home for the San from remote times. It is deep and well protected from harsh weather, and has ample fresh water in a clear river with a succession of pools for swimming. Tall forest trees grow all the way down the gorge, providing shade.

The grassy foothills of the Drakensberg attracted vast herds of antelope, notably eland, and the San hunters lived well. For a considerable period they were secure, without the threat of invasion by hostile peoples.

In the Ndedema Gorge there are 17 rock shelters and caves containing nearly 4 000 separate rock paintings.

The path to the summit of Mont-aux-Sources climbing around the Sentinel.

The San people had leisure and security, and their delight in art is evident in the humour and beauty of their work. The Ndedema Gorge is one of the world's finest treasures of rock art.

Among the caves, perhaps the most spectacular is the one called by the Ngwane people Sebayeni ('the kraal'), because it was used by herdsmen as a shelter for livestock.

In this cave there are 1 146 paintings and they reveal San art at its best. It was in the Ndedema Gorge that Harold and Shirley Ann Pager lived from 1965 to 1969 while studying the paintings and skilfully restoring in photographs their fading beauty by the ingenious but laborious technique of photographing them in black and white, making prints of the same size as the originals, and then colouring the prints in the original colours used by the artists. The result of this dedicated labour was the publication of the book *Ndedema*, now a standard work on the subject, reproducing the great majority of the paintings.

A path leads through the gorge from the Cathedral Peak forestry area to the valley of the Mhlwazini River. In this river valley is another cave, the Eland Cave, containing 1 639 paintings.

Oliviershoek
Adriaan Olivier, who farmed at the foot of the pass that bears his name, was a frontiersman known for his fights with rustlers in the 1850s. The pass was originally named Sungubala ('overcome a difficulty'), but in 1871, when the heavy traffic from the coast to the diamond fields made the construction of a more easily negotiated road essential, the pass was renamed Oliviershoek ('the glen of Olivier').

It is a spectacular pass with panoramic views of the northern Drakensberg, waterfalls, patches of forest and caves. The summit is 1 740 metres above sea level.

Royal Natal National Park
The Tugela River has its headwaters on the Mont-aux-Sources massif. The river hurtles down from the heights, dropping from more than 3 000 metres to 1 432 metres in a series of waterfalls (the highest of which is 614 metres), cascades and rapids.

WITH EARTH-COLOURS AND PRIMITIVE TOOLS, THE SAN ARTISTS MADE THE ROCKS LIVE

They took their colours from the earth. Their subject was the beauty and movement of the world around them. Their canvas was the whole of southern Africa. The San people were among the most prolific of the world's prehistoric artists.

Their paintings and engravings adorn thousands of rock shelters and caves, from the Cape Peninsula to Zimbabwe, from Swaziland to South West Africa.

It has been estimated that a total of approximately 15 000 decorated sites exist in southern Africa.

It is impossible to date most of the paintings. The oldest painting has been found in South West Africa and is about 27 000 years old; the most recent were probably produced during the late 1800s.

Many of the paintings have suffered damage from water, disintegration of the rock surface, and the carelessness of man. Modern herdsmen have sheltered their livestock in the caves and campers have made fires in them. Soot settling on the walls has done much harm. There has also been vandalism.

The San were among the first artists in the world to use the technique of foreshortening, which enabled them to depict their subjects realistically.

Inspection of the paintings reveals that the San were excellent draughtsmen. They knew exactly how to create the desired effect — the grace of an antelope, the power of a lion, the huge bulk of a rhino.

Part of the skill of the artists was in producing the paints. Most of the colours were produced by mineral ox-

San hunters setting off after venison, bows ready.

A rock art treasure, the White Lady of the Brandberg.

Part of the gallery of rock art at Sebayeni in the Ndedema Gorge.

Engraving produced by 'pecking' — hammering with a hard instrument.

ides found in the earth — iron oxides giving various shades of red, brown and yellow, manganese giving black, zinc oxides yielding white. It is thought that these materials were made into paint by mixing them with blood, milk, egg-white, urine or sap, and that the paint was applied with brushes made from animal hairs, plant fibres or feathers, or with the finger. Unfortunately there is no recorded description of a San artist at work.

A San who had been shot was found to be wearing a belt from which were suspended little horns containing pigment. It was assumed that he had been an artist.

The achievement of these artists is remarkable when it is remembered that there were never vast numbers of San people. They were scattered over the entire country, fragmented into hunting groups, families and small clans.

The dances, ceremonies, hunts, animals and supernatural creatures depicted on the cave walls and rock shelters reflect a rich and diverse society, pervaded by a profound appreciation of and sense of harmony with the world and all its wonders.

San rock paintings as they must have looked at the time of their original execution. This painting has been reproduced from a frieze in the Transkei.

Mule trains still follow the narrow trails

Numerous tributaries join the Tugela and it quickly swells to become a large river.

The 8 000-hectare area at the foot of Mont-aux-Sources was proclaimed a national park in 1906 and in 1950 the 794-hectare Rugged Glen Nature Reserve was added to it. The 'Royal' part of the name was tacked on in 1947 when the British royal family stayed here during their visit to South Africa.

The Royal Natal National Park is one of the great scenic show-pieces of southern Africa. Grey rhebuck, mountain reedbuck, grey duiker, bushbuck, blesbok, klipspringer and black wildebeest live here, as well as dassies and baboons.

The walking and riding paths of this national park are a delight. Thirty-one main paths lead to numerous beauty spots. Especially popular is the path leading for 11 kilometres up the Tugela Valley to its narrow gorge at the foot of the great waterfall. The path to the summit of Mont-aux-Sources, 23 kilometres long, takes the walker or rider to the very roof of southern Africa. The scenery is breathtaking.

Trout are found in the streams but the bed of the Tugela is filled with loose boulders and is too unstable for good fishing. There is a trout hatchery in the national park.

Accommodation in the park ranges from hotel to bungalows and caravan park and camping ground, all part of one of the world's most prestigious mountain resorts. There is also a stable here.

Climbing in the area is challenging. The Sentinel and the Devil's Tooth are two complex climbs, while the main wall of the Amphitheatre and the Eastern Buttress have precipitous rock faces.

Sani Pass

One of the traditional passes over the Drakensberg to the highlands of Lesotho follows the upper valley of the Mkomazana ('little Mkomazi') River. This is known as the Sani Pass, and it offers the visitor a singularly beautiful route into the mountains — primitive, rugged, and pervaded by an atmosphere from the past.

The river rushes through the gorge in a sequence of cascades. Caves and rock shelters are plentiful, and many of them contain San paintings on their walls.

The vegetation in this area is surprisingly luxuriant, and vultures nest in the high cliffs. The narrow track

High in the Sani Pass a Sotho transport rider gives his pack donkeys a short break.

Protea subvestita growing at 2 000 metres above sea level in the Sani Pass.

that climbs beside the river is still used by trains of pack mules and donkeys, escorted by Sotho riders on ponies — carrying sacks of meal and other trade goods into Lesotho, and bringing out wool, mohair and hides.

There is a hotel at the foot of the Sani Pass and a Mountaineers' Chalet on the summit, just inside the Lesotho border — at 2 865 metres, the highest licensed premises in southern Africa. In the pass itself there are several magnificent camping sites.

The track to the summit can only be used by four-wheel-drive vehicles. A police border post lies half way up the gorge, and beyond this the track continues for 56 kilometres over the mountain roof to Mokhotlong. The track passes on the way the highest point in southern Africa — the

The Tugela at the top of its fall from the Mont-aux-Sources plateau.

Summer mists covering the Drakensberg in the Royal Natal National Park.

Pack donkeys returning home high on the Sani Pass, principal gateway down the Drakensberg from Lesotho to Natal.

3 482-metre Thabana Ntlenyana ('nice little mountain') which has the appearance of a low hill on top of the high-lying moorlands.

On all sides of the pass there are mountains and cliffs to climb and explore.

Spioenkop Public Resort
The Natal Parks Board has created a large public resort and nature reserve at Spioenkop ('spy peak'). The game park is 400 hectares in area and is a sanctuary for black wildebeest, zebra, eland, impala, hartebeest and blesbok.

The dam at the resort is used for fishing and boating. The camp in the reserve is a good base from which to explore the central Drakensberg area and has a swimming pool. Visitors must take their own food.

Underberg
In 1917 the village of Underberg began as a terminus for the branch line from Pietermaritzburg. The berg ('mountain') under which the village lies is the 1 904-metre Hlogoma ('place of echoes'). The village is a centre for trout fishing. From here

The upper Mzimkulu River near Underberg, in the foothills of the Drakensberg.

roads lead to several resorts in the foothills of the Drakensberg. The view of the Drakensberg from Underberg is spectacular.

Van Reenens Pass
In the 1850s booming trade made essential the construction of a practical all-weather pass up the escarpment from Natal to the central plains of the Orange Free State.

Locating a route for such a pass was not easy, but Frans van Reenen, a farmer who lived at the foot of the escarpment, pointed out to the road engineers a route that he followed when driving livestock over the mountains to sell in the markets of the interior. The road engineers accepted this location and the Van Reenens Pass was opened in 1856. In 1891 a railway pass was also built.

The railway and road climb 681 metres between Ladysmith and the village of Van Reenen at the head of the pass. For both rail and road this is a fine pass with panoramic views. There is a look-out place known as Windy Corner on the summit of the road pass, 1 680 metres above sea level.

Vergelegen Nature Reserve
The headwaters of the Mkomazi (or Umkomaas) River contain large numbers of trout. The scenery here is breathtaking, with deep valleys leading up to the main wall of the Drakensberg. The Vergelegen Nature Reserve comprises 1 100 hectares of this secluded landscape, lying some 1 500 metres above sea level. There is a camp with cooks, but visitors must bring their own food.

This is primarily a fisherman's area, but the reserve is also a good base for exploring this part of the Drakensberg.

Winterton
In 1905 the Natal government built a weir across the Little Tugela River and founded an irrigation settlement later named Winterton in honour of the secretary for agriculture, H. D. Winter.

The village of Winterton is now a busy centre for farming in the foothills approaching the Cathedral Peak area of the Drakensberg.

Horrific legacy of 'The Last of the Gentleman's Wars'

'The Last of the Gentleman's Wars' later writers called it. Opposing generals addressed each other in the most courteous terms. The Boers, deeply religious, at times declined to attack on the Sabbath. British soldiers were trained more for ceremonial than war duties; their officers were more accustomed to the perfumes of sumptuous ballrooms than the stench of the battlefield. Yet this 'Last of the Gentleman's Wars' — the Anglo-Boer War — left the world a horrific legacy. The Boers, outnumbered but not outdone for ingenuity, inspired the art of trench warfare as used to such hideous effect on the Western Front during World War I.

In order to deprive the Boer forces of support, the British destroyed farm houses and good crops, placing non-combatants, women and children in bleak and unhygienic camps.

The war had its origin in a clash of interests between the expanding British Empire and the South African Republic in the Transvaal.

Discoveries of gold and other minerals in the Transvaal had transformed a quiet backwater into one of the most desirable countries on earth. The British government considered the republic inept and corrupt; the republic regarded the British as a land-grabbing threat to its independence.

There were constant rumours of war and the movement of troops. The republic used part of its new wealth to arm itself. The Republic of the Orange Free State was in alliance with the South African Republic and felt equally insecure.

On 9 October 1899 the Transvaal Republic presented the British government with an ultimatum. It demanded that Britain give up suzerainty over the Transvaal, withdraw troops from the Transvaal border, remove all reinforcements from South Africa, set up an arbitration committee to settle mutual differences, and give an assurance that British troops *en route* for the Cape would not be landed. If the conditions of the ultimatum were not complied with by 5 p.m. on 11 October, the republics would regard this as a declaration of war. The British did not respond. And so, on 11 October 1899 — at 'tea time', as *The Times* reported superciliously — war began.

The war was a struggle between two Davids and a Goliath. The republics had about 75 000 men, mainly drawn from a white population of 300 000. Britain had a population of 30 million, and a colonial empire, and at the peak of the war placed 250 000 men in the field, supported by vast resources of finance and material.

Republican forces, however, knew their home ground well — and how to use it in battle. They were righteous in the cause of independence, and were first class marksmen and horsemen.

Lord Dundonald's dash on Ladysmith — painted by Lucy Kemp-Welch.

The British were poorly trained and blindly confident.

The supreme republican commanders were Commandant-general Piet Joubert on the Natal front and General P. A. Cronjé on the western front. Both were elderly, courteous and well-liked — and utterly without the killer instinct of the ruthless conqueror. The British commander-in-chief was General Sir Redvers Buller, with General Sir George White on the Natal front.

Britain's forces in Natal were the primary threat to the Transvaal, and Joubert decided to strike them hard.

He launched his army across the border at the British units stationed at Dundee. The first battle on this part of the front took place on 20 October 1899 at Talana Hill. The next day a second republican force drove southwards to cut communications between Dundee and Ladysmith.

Both republican forces suffered setbacks but the British Goliath was sufficiently shaken by the onslaught to abandon Dundee and fall back on Ladysmith. The Transvaal forces pressed behind them, while a contingent from the Orange Free State rode down the escarpment from the west and the British found themselves compressed. They tried to shoulder the republican forces apart but on 24 October at Rietfontein and 30 October at Modderspruit and Nicholson's Nek, the British were defeated, driven into Ladysmith and besieged.

Joubert raided as far as Estcourt, but later withdrew to the hills overlooking the Tugela River and remained there in a strong position, defensively waiting for the British to attack.

On the western front the republican forces also struck quickly, but found themselves drawn into tedious, debilitating sieges. In the first action on this front, on 12 October at Kraaipan, a British armoured train was captured by General J. H. de la Rey, but the British forces in that part of the country fell back in separate groups to what was then Mafeking and Kimberley and held the republicans in two more dreary sieges, giving the British time to gather reinforcements.

General Sir Redvers Buller determined to relieve Ladysmith. He collided with the republican defensive line in the hills north of the Tugela. On 15 December 1899 Buller was halted at Colenso. He tried again at Spioenkop and at Vaalkrans, each time suffering defeat.

On the western front, General Lord

A military observation balloon used by the British during the Ladysmith siege.

Jan Christiaan Smuts in 1898 when he was state attorney of the Transvaal.

Lord Kitchener, the commander-in-chief during the later stages of the war.

Saving the guns at Colenso, *painted by Stanley Berkeley. This was one of the heroic episodes of the war. Lord Roberts lost his only son, Freddie, during the battle.*

A British armoured train with troops about to set off on a reconnaissance.

Methuen led a British force up the railway from the Cape in an attempt to lift the siege at Kimberley. On 22 November he drove the republican force back at Belmont, on 25 November he pushed them out of Graspan and on 28 November from Modder River.

The republicans retired to Magersfontein. They dug trenches at the foot of a koppie and waited. The British advanced to the koppie, expecting the enemy to be holding the highest ground. Suddenly the British marched into a barrage of gun-fire from the trenches. The advance was stopped on 11 December. The strategy of trench warfare had been born.

Other clashes took place in the Stormberg, south of the boundary of the Orange Free State. In this area of flat-topped hillocks and vast manoeuvring spaces, Major-general W. F. Gatacre suffered a defeat on 10 December 1899 and there was no further British advance from that direction for some time.

These defeats became known to the British as 'Black Week'. A new commander, the purposeful and effective Field-marshal Lord Roberts, was despatched from Britain to relieve General Buller. General Kitchener ac-

Piet Joubert (centre) and staff. He was the republican commander-in-chief.

General Louis Botha, General Joubert's successor.

Boer ammunition abandoned on the bank of a river at Paardeberg.

Trench warfare is born — then, concentration camps

'Long Cecil', a gun made in the De Beers workshop during the siege of Kimberley.

companied Roberts as chief of staff. They arrived in Cape Town in January 1900 and with reinforcements made their way to the western front, determined to relieve Kimberley, and hoping to knock the Orange Free State out of the war by capturing Bloemfontein.

On 15 February 1900 General John French led his cavalry through the republican siege lines around Kimberley. The siege was raised and Cronjé was forced to abandon his entrenched position at Magersfontein. Slowed by his wagon transport, he was moving back to defend Bloemfontein when he was caught at Paardeberg, surrounded, and after 12 days of resistance forced to surrender on 27 February.

On 13 March 1900, Roberts led his army into Bloemfontein. While he rested and marshalled his army, General C. R. de Wet manoeuvred over the eastern Orange Free State, defeating British forces at Sannaspos and Reddersburg, but was held when he tried to besiege Wepener.

In May 1900 Roberts marched out of Bloemfontein and headed northwards, brushing aside republican resistance on the Vet and Sand rivers. The outnumbered republican army could not risk a direct confrontation. On 28 May 1900 the British crossed the Vaal River and on 31 May entered Johannesburg — met by only token resistance. Pretoria was an open city and the British entered it on 5 June.

Roberts felt that the war was over apart from minor mopping-up. Kruger and his Transvaal government had abandoned Pretoria before its capture and, using a railway train, had withdrawn along the eastern line leading to the sea at the Portuguese port of Lourenco Marques (Maputo).

Expecting republican forces to surrender readily, the British set out to occupy the Transvaal and the Orange Free State. The republicans, meanwhile, were reorganizing.

Joubert, who had served his country valiantly, died on 27 March 1900. He was succeeded by the resolute General Louis Botha.

The British found the Orange Free State the easier republic to occupy. De Wet challenged them, but was defeated near Bethlehem and on 5 July 1900 Acting Chief Commandant M. Prinsloo, with 3 000 men, was forced to surrender near Fouriesburg. De Wet retreated into the Transvaal and the rest of the war consisted of Boer hit-and-run ambushes.

Charge of the Gordon Highlanders at Grobler's Kloof, 1899, by R. Simkin.

General Cronjé entertained by the British after his surrender at Paardeberg.

Boer sharpshooters in action holding the heights above Colenso.

Field-marshal Lord Roberts, the British commander-in-chief, a popular officer of great drive and courage. He was sent to South Africa at a time of considerable British despondency following disastrous setbacks on the Natal front.

General De la Rey, a resolute and expert republican leader.

A British column on the march to Colesberg across the hot and dusty veld.

Roberts had returned in triumph to Britain. Lord Kitchener took over command of the British army in South Africa and faced a complex task of trying to bring the war to an end. Meanwhile, in 1901, the British were compelled to raise even more substantial reinforcements.

Kitchener devised a 'scorched earth' policy, destroying farms suspected of sheltering republican forces, covering the country with barbed wire entanglements to impede the Boer horsemen, and building blockhouses at strategically important points.

Concentration camps were created — women and children whose homes were destroyed were placed here, where they could no longer help the republican forces and would be out of danger. These concentration camps were poorly managed. More than 26 000 women and children died in the camps, mostly from disease.

All through 1901 the guerrilla war raged unabated. On 9 April 1902 republican leaders met at Klerksdorp to discuss peace. A second meeting was held at Vereeniging on 15 May. Though undefeated, the Boers were heartsore at the deaths of many of their women and children.

A treaty was drawn up in Vereeniging and signed in Pretoria on 31 May 1902. Never again would the world see a 'Gentleman's War'.

The cost of the war to the British was 5 774 killed and 22 829 wounded. The Boers lost 4 000 men killed and an estimated 12 000 wounded.

All that was Left of Them, *painted by R. Caton-Woodville, which is among the National Army Museum collection.*

Boer sharpshooters behind a barricade await a British assault. The Boers used Mauser and Martini-Henry rifles with deadly effect.

A popular song sheet inspired by the defence of Mafeking (now Mafikeng).

Winston Churchill, prisoner-of-war, before his escape (see box, page 224).

Winston Churchill, prisoner-of-war, before his escape (see box, page 224).

Some of the defenders of Mafeking with a home-made gun.

TRANSKEI

TRANSKEI

FROM THE GREAT lakes of central Africa, all the way down the eastern side of the continent, the savannah stretches for 4 000 kilometres of bush-covered landscape. As it crosses Natal the savannah narrows and starts to peter out. South of the Mtamvuna River only fragments of it remain, with a belt of high forest lying along the coast. Inland there is rolling, undulating grassland, open and spacious, with scarcely a tree and only a few clumps of bush sheltering in the river valleys.

For 250 kilometres the rolling hills of grassland extend down the coast, and they reach some 150 kilometres inland. The Kei River marks the southern extent of this pleasant land 'across the Kei' which, for some 18 years until 1994, existed as an independent state.

The first human beings to live in the Transkei were the San and Khoikhoi groups who wandered over the grasslands, the San hunting for their food and the Khoikhoi grazing their livestock. Neither of these two peoples were numerous and in medieval times they were displaced by the ancestors of the people who live in Transkei today — the Xhosa, Pondo, Pondomise, Bomvana and other smaller groups.

The presence of these varied peoples is very apparent to any visitor to Transkei. Their rondavel homes of hardened mud, all uniform in size and design, are scattered over the grasslands like stars in a milky way set in a green coloured sky. With their walls painted white, their black-thatched roofs, the doorways all facing uniformly to the east — the side of the rising sun and of all good spirits — the anti-lightning charms on the roofs, the cattle kraals and pigsties, the homesteads of Transkei provide an enchanting spectacle that can be seen nowhere else in the world.

On the western side of the grassland the long wall of the Drakensberg provides a fortress-like barrier to the lands of the interior. To the east, the grassland falls away in lovely rolling slopes, divided by deep valleys through which sparkling rivers drain — to reach lagoons and sandy beaches where the Indian Ocean surges in with a restless murmur and an insistent pounding on rocky promontories and cliffs.

Herds of cattle graze on the slopes of the hills and herdboys while away the daylight hours in hunting birds and lizards, and by playing endless games. Girls go down to the streams to fill the pots with water and to wash the clothes. Women work in the fields and smoke their long pipes. Men sit in the sun, or go off to work in some distant mine or factory in the city.

Ox-drawn sledges, horses, and an occasional bus or truck make their way across the spacious landscape along bumpy tracks. White clouds drift lazily through a blue summer sky. In winter the smoke of innumerable fires clings to the ground around the huts like a fog, and the wind from the west brings with it the cold touch of the mountains sleeping beneath a blanket of snow.

Preceding page: Waves lap the shore of Coffee Bay with seductive gentleness, but the gathering storm clouds hint at the turmoil that nature often heaps upon Transkei's Wild Coast.

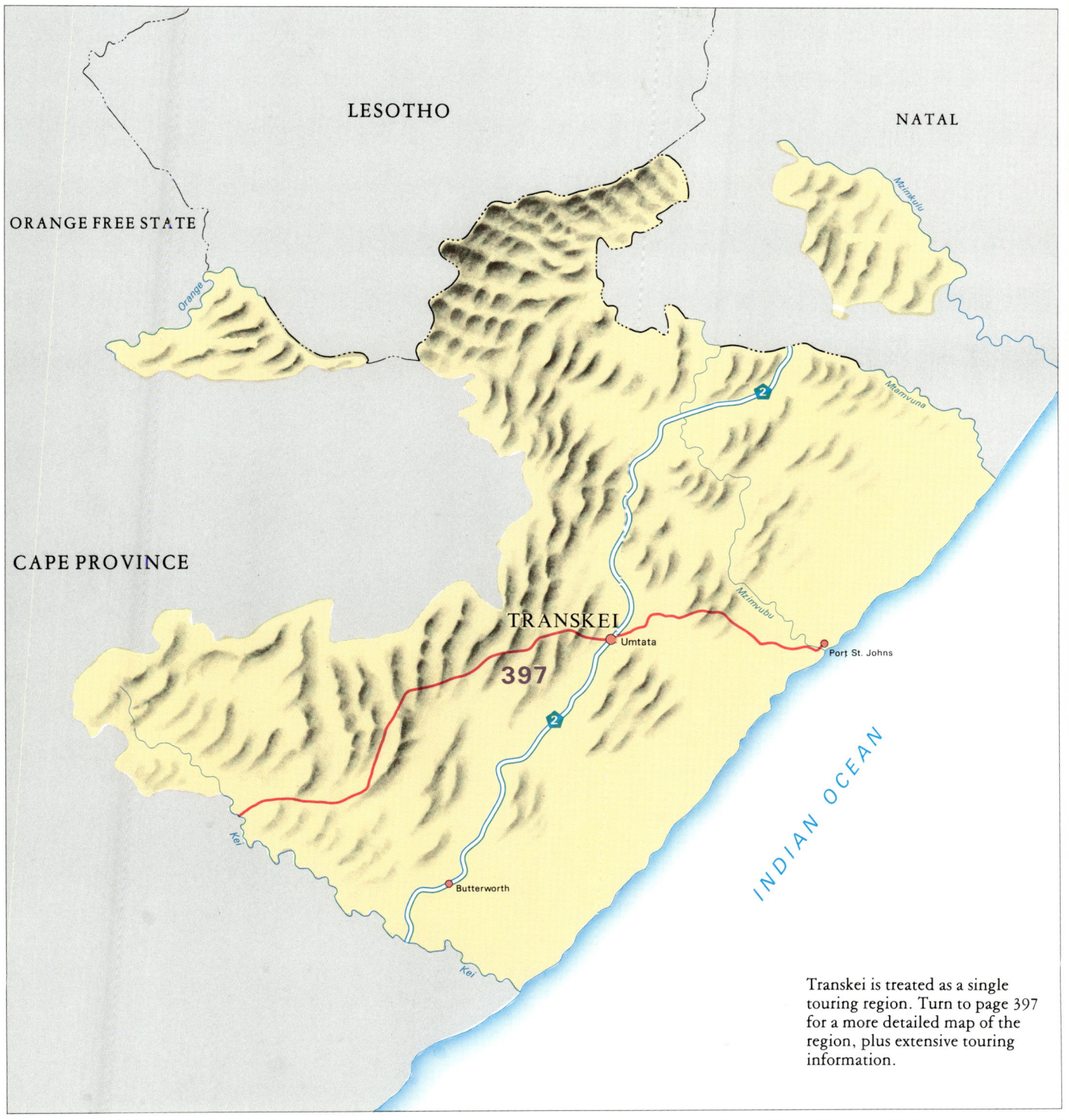

LESOTHO

NATAL

ORANGE FREE STATE

CAPE PROVINCE

TRANSKEI

397

Umtata

Port St. Johns

Butterworth

INDIAN OCEAN

Transkei is treated as a single
touring region. Turn to page 397
for a more detailed map of the
region, plus extensive touring
information.

ENTRANCING TRANSKEI

FROM THE KEI RIVER in the south to the Mtamvuna River in the north there is a rugged stretch of coast, 250 kilometres long, known as the Wild Coast. This is the coast of Transkei, the traditional home of several of the principal Bantu-speaking groups. It is a green and pleasant grassland stretching inland for about 150 kilometres to the foothills of the Drakensberg range. For many years the principal city of Transkei has been Umtata, seat of an Anglican bishopric. Living in the south of Transkei are the Gcaleka, in the middle the Tembu and Bomvana, and in the north the Pondo and Mpondomise groups. Smaller groups include the Cele and Xesibe, who live around Mount Ayliff, and the Fingo, who live in small communities mainly in the Gcaleka country.

Each group has its distinguishing costume, colours, beads and articles of clothing. Red and orange are the favourite colours of the Gcaleka, the Tembu and the Bomvana. A very light blue is the colour of the closely related Pondo and Mpondomise people. An especially notable feature of the countryside are the rondavel-type huts, all built with their doors facing east, an old convention of uncertain origin, possibly related to the Khoikhoi belief that the power of good lived in the east, and evil in the west.

In spring and summer the whole country is emerald green, with deep blue skies and glorious cloud formations. In autumn and winter the grass on the hills fades to a drab brown but the coastal belt remains green. Scenically, Transkei is at its best on the coast.

The Wild Coast is quite superb in its unspoilt beauty. There are lagoons, cliffs, palm trees, arum lilies, sandy bays, and rivers reaching the sea in deep valleys, many of them finding their way through the hills in incredibly involved convolutions. Exploring this coast is a delight for the nomad. There are pleasant hotels – relaxed places where formal dress is unknown – and many caravan and camping grounds in settings of great beauty.

The roads to the various coastal points lead through unforgettable scenery, offering innumerable interesting glimpses of the way of life of a people living in a manner totally different from that of Europe or Asia.

A calm summer day on the Wild Coast. Here the unspoilt bush-covered cliffs meet the surging waters of the Indian Ocean.

Such a pipe is a status symbol of a mature woman.

The downlands of Transkei — maize lands and pasturage.

THINGS TO DO AND SEE

Angling The Wild Coast is an angling area with many remote vantage points, often at the end of rough tracks, with accommodation in primitive camping grounds. In winter and spring there are game fish; in summer and autumn there are sharks and skates. Mazeppa Bay is famous for its hammerhead sharks.

In May the first sardine shoals of the season swim up the coast, followed by hordes of predator fish. This is when the angler catches bonito, barracuda, galjoen and bronze bream. At the fishermen's resorts such as Coffee Bay, Mazeppa Bay and Umngazi (Mngazi) Mouth, the talk in the camps and hotels is often of big catches.

The Pondoland section of the Wild Coast is perhaps the wildest part of all. Stormy, difficult of access, it offers magnificent sport for the big-game angler. In winter barracuda in countless thousands feed on the sardines, and huge sharks feed on everything. Prodigious flocks of seabirds hover overhead, diving and gorging themselves. The hammerhead sharks are gigantic and savage fighters. Shad, garrick, bream, musselcracker, mackerel and queenfish all provide fine eating.

Camping and caravanning Port St. Johns has a number of caravan parks with camping areas and bungalows. Several other places along the Wild Coast have camping grounds with simple facilities.

Hiking The forest-covered hills around Port St. Johns have paths leading to view sites and through many shadowy glades. The whole Wild Coast is ideal for walking with many caves, bays, remnants of shipwrecks, cliffs and capes to explore. For the hardy there is a fine walk down the coast from the Natal border to places such as Waterfall Bluff, where a river tumbles over a high cliff straight into the sea.

Photography Apart from its scenery, the Transkei's rural lifestyle and the traditional costumes provide fine opportunities for photographers. Always ask permission before you photograph anybody. Presents are expected.

Shell collecting The Wild Coast has a great variety of shells. Indo-Pacific species as well as shells of the temperate southern coast are found here.

Butterworth

The oldest town in Transkei, Butterworth grew up around a Wesleyan mission school that was built in 1827, but which was burned down during the period of the Frontier wars. The town lies on the main railway line through Transkei.

From the western heights, the white building of the Transkei hospital overlooks the town. The surrounding countryside is grassland.

Near the town are the impressive Butterworth River Cascades, 85 metres high, and also the Bawa Falls, known as the High Executioner, with a dramatic sheer drop of 110 metres, over which criminals were once pushed to their deaths.

Coffee Bay

High hills and soaring cliffs make a spectacular setting for the beautiful holiday resort of Coffee Bay. It is said to have received its name from a ship carrying a cargo of coffee which was wrecked in the bay. Many of the beans were washed up on the beach and some took root and grew into coffee plants.

This is a good place for swimming and fishing, and there are several hotels and a caravan park.

Where the seas roar through the Hole in the Wall

A classic meander of the Tina River near Thabankulu, in Pondoland.

The broad valley of the Bashee River.

The waterfall of the Magwa River, a 142-metre leap into a narrow gorge.

Collywobbles

A complicated series of twists, meanders and turns of the Mbashe (or Bashee) River has produced the strange landscape known as the Collywobbles. The bizarre effect is best viewed from the heights of the Mpozolo trading station, especially in early spring when the coral trees in the valley blossom a vivid scarlet.

The river mouth is marked with a powerful lighthouse, and there is also a holiday resort with a hotel here.

Flagstaff

The trading centre of Flagstaff in the high hill country of Pondoland is a picturesque sight on Fridays and Saturdays when the streets are crowded with the local people in their traditional costumes, trading skins for maize meal, sugar and other goods.

The town was originally the site of a store whose owner believed in Sunday observance. The rural people could not understand the custom and persisted in turning up when the store was shut. The owner eventually set up a tall pole from which he flew a flag to let everyone for miles around know when he was open for business.

Near the town is the Holy Cross Mission, with a large hospital founded in 1911.

Hole in the Wall

One of the most extraordinary features on the whole of the Wild Coast is a high cliff standing out in the sea like an island through which the waves have bored a hole big enough for a double-decker bus. The heavy surf shoulders its way through the Hole in the Wall with a deep rumble, and the people living in the area know the cliff as esiKhaleni, meaning 'the place of the sound'.

The cliff is extremely difficult to climb and some people who have made it to the top have been unable to get down again and have had to be rescued. Others have attempted to swim through the hole and have been killed when the waves threw them against the jagged barnacles on the sides.

The people living near the Hole in the Wall, known as the Abelunga ('European people'), are partially descended from sailors shipwrecked on this part of the coast in years gone by. The area is excellent for fishing and swimming, with breathtaking scenery and a particularly rich variety of shells.

The village of Kentani, a shady main street of stores and government offices.

The sea roars in through the Hole in the Wall — a great cavern eroded through a detached cliff.

Idutywa

This busy trading and communications centre was founded in 1884 in the valley of the Mputi River on the site of an older military post. The town, which in its early days was the scene of much dissension and several upheavals, is now a prosperous farming centre with numerous trading stations and two hotels.

Kentani

A tragic battle was fought at Kentani on 7 February 1878, during the ninth Frontier War. A garrison of almost 1 000 European and Fingo soldiers was attacked by a force of about 5 000 Xhosa warriors.

The Xhosa had been told by Xito, one of the most famous of all African diviners, that the soldiers' bullets could not harm them.

Urged on by their two great chiefs, Kreli and Sandile, they charged into a hail of bullets and were mown down. More than 300 Xhosa were killed for the loss of only two government soldiers.

What was left of the Xhosa force fled south of the Kei River with Sandile. The other chief, Kreli, also sur-

vived the slaughter. He hid in the forests but finally surrendered and spent the rest of his life quietly near Willowvale.

Kentani is now a small but very charming trading centre.

A tortuous scenic road leads from the town to various points along the Wild Coast.

Libode

The market at Libode is a picturesque bustle on Fridays and Saturdays when Pondo and Mpondomise people come in to do their shopping. The town is famous for their beadwork.

Beyond Libode, the road to Port St. Johns leads down through the valley of the Umngazi (Mngazi). The scenery is dramatic, particularly the great tilted rock known as Mlengani, which means 'the hanging one'. This is

The traditional costume of the Xhosa people is warm (for the climate is temperate) but colourful.

1. An elder warmly clad and with his face daubed in white clay, which is considered good for the skin.
2. A girl of marriageable age, her charms well displayed and beauty enhanced with beadwork.
3. A jester, who amuses the guests at a wedding feast.
4. A girl of marriageable age carrying water during a ritual associated with the special viewing of eligible maidens.
5. A diviner dressed in full regalia and 'smelling out' an answer to some problem brought by a client.
6. A mature Xhosa family man on his way to a meeting with his chief.
7. A Xhosa matron in her braided skirt and long apron.
Pipe-smoking is the privilege of a married, but never a single, woman.

Shipwreck that lures the treasure-seekers

TOUGH TESTS AND STRANGE RITUALS OF THE KHWETHA CEREMONY THAT TURNS A BOY INTO A MAN

During the winter months travellers in the Transkei may pass teenage African boys with the white-painted bodies and bizarre costume of the Khwetha, or circumcision lodge.

Every African boy has to go through such a lodge before he is regarded as a man. If he does not, even in old age he will still be referred to among his people as a boy, and no self-respecting woman would consider marrying him.

The age of the youth entering the initiation lodge varies. They stay at the lodge from the end of autumn until early spring. During this time they live in a special hut, usually in an isolated spot, and are instructed in the conduct, discipline and ethnic loyalties that will be expected of them as adults. They live frugally, undergo endurance tests, and are taboo to females.

In modern times the conditions and disciplines of individual lodges are probably not as severe as in former times. Nevertheless, this depends very much on the master of the lodge. A conservative lodge master can still impose a regimen of privations and tests of stamina which occasionally result in death.

Whatever happens within the lodge is kept a close secret and any member confiding to the outside world would seriously jeopardize his chances of ever being accepted by his people as manly.

The youths whiten their bodies with sandstone to protect them from evil, and usually wear a white sheepskin coat or blanket. For ceremonial occasions they dress in a reed skirt which they put on by tying one end to a tree and then winding themselves into it. A conical reed cap and reed mask complete the costume.

In this outfit the boys perform special dances. They imitate a bull, pawing the ground, snorting and tossing their heads in the air. They lose themselves in the dance, drumming their heels without lifting their feet off the ground, flexing their muscles and perspiring.

The boys like to be admired and photographed. They visit neigh-

Boys in the costume of the Khwetha circumcision ceremony.

After the ceremony a Khwetha boy is ready for manhood.

bouring huts and show off their dancing skills. But on such visits they always remain masked and females keep their distance.

With the coming of spring, the circumcision operation is performed.

The hut, costumes and other items used in the rituals are then burned and the boys are driven to a river, with the initiators ceremonially thrashing them as they go. Under no circumstances are the boys permitted

The straw dancing costumes of the Khwetha circumcision ceremony.

to look behind. They plunge into the water, wash away the white paint and with it the last of their boyhood.

When they emerge on the opposite bank they are boys no longer and receive from their fathers the formal gift of a new blanket. The boys return home, where they are smeared with red ochre, which is not removed for three months. When at last they wash it off they are finally regarded as adults, with the prospect of marriage after a customary delay of about four years.

Throughout their lives, the members of the lodge have a bond that obligates them to mutual aid and friendship. Depending on the character and knowledge of their lodge master, the lodge members carry with them into adult life some idea of the traditions of their people, the line of descent of their families and chiefs, political obligations, social duties and taboos.

occasionally called Execution Rock, because of a mistaken belief that criminals were once pushed to their deaths from here. Such executions were in fact carried out at a nearby cliff overlooking the valley.

Lusikisiki

The wind whispering through the marsh reeds at dusk is said to make the sound 'lusikisiki' — and this is the name given to the village that has grown up near the marsh and which is now the capital of Pondoland. It is a pleasant little place with its single main street full of trading stores and government offices.

The only hotel has in its grounds a cannon from the famous wreck of the *Grosvenor*. The little pub here has long been a base for ventures to recover treasure from the *Grosvenor* and other wrecks that lie along the wildest part of the Wild Coast down the coast road from Lusikisiki. The road also leads to several great tea estates and to the Magwa Falls.

The life of the village has a picturesque quality, and nearby is Qawukeni, 'the elevated place', which is the seat of the paramount chief of the Pondo people. Not far from Lusikisiki is Mount Nelson, former home of Khotso Sethuntsa, a millionaire herbalist who in his 90 years had 20 wives and about 200 children. He ascribed his virility to a secret potion called 'umangalala'.

Mazeppa Bay

Hammerhead sharks weighing up to 450 kilograms bring adventurous anglers to Mazeppa Bay. Its three spacious beaches, fringed with sundu palms, are sheltered by a rocky island connected to the shore by a rope bridge. The hotel is well known for its seafood.

The road to Mazeppa Bay from Kentani is a real switchback, leading through the Manubi Forest with tremendous views of the valley of the Qora River.

Mount Ayliff

A busy day in Mount Ayliff is like a scene from the Wild West, for this is great horseman country. Outside each trading station, clusters of horses can be seen tethered to hitching posts

A Transkei valley — rich soil, dense population. Here is primitive cultivation and grazing land, with few trees left for fuel.

The landmark of Mlengane, on the road to Port St. Johns.

A tiger moth of the warm valley of the Mzimvubu River.

Haunt of Huberta the wandering hippo

THE NATION THAT COMMITTED SUICIDE

There is a pool in the Gxara River that is filled to overflowing with terrible memories. For it was here that the strange predictions of a 14-year-old girl called Nongqawuse virtually led her people to commit suicide.

One day in 1856 Nongqawuse was sitting on the rocks above the pool looking down into the water when she fancied she saw the faces of her ancestors.

Nongqawuse told her people — the Gcaleka — that the ancestors were prepared to return to earth to drive Europeans from their country. But first, as an act of faith to prove their belief in the world of the spirits, the Gcaleka would have to kill all their cattle and destroy all their crops. Those who refused would be turned into frogs, mice and ants, and would be blown into the sea by a mighty whirlwind.

For ten months a kind of madness possessed the Gcaleka. They killed their livestock and destroyed their crops until they had nothing left but their faith.

The day of their salvation was to be 18 February 1857. On that day, Nongqawuse predicted, a blood-red sun would rise, stand still in the sky, and then set again in the east.

As the great day dawned, the Gcaleka people sat waiting. The sun rose. It made its slow passage across the hot February sky. A breeze blew off the sea as the sun set in the west. Darkness fell on a ruined people.

About 25 000 died of starvation. Others survived only through the help of neighbouring communities and Europeans.

As for Nongqawuse, the deluded people would have torn her to pieces but she fled to the King William's Town area to find safety with the British. For her own protection she was kept for a while on Robben Island. She spent the rest of her life on a farm in the Eastern Province and died in 1898.

Nongqawuse, spirit medium of the Xhosa, and the magic Gxara River Pool.

A coaster in the mouth of the Mzimvubu River towards the end of the last century.

while their owners do business or gossip on the verandahs of the stores. A dash of colour is added by the local people, the Xesibe, in their traditional costumes.

Mount Frere
A busy centre on the trunk road, Mount Frere has several stores, two hotels, government buildings and fine countryside. South of the town the road drops down to the vast valley of the Mzimvubu River. Also in the district are the handsome Tina Falls.

Nxaxo River
The Nxaxo River reaches the sea in a broad lagoon ideal for boating and windsurfing. Crested cranes nest on the islets in the river, and monkeys are numerous. Shell collectors can find many specimens here, and oysters are harvested from the rocks in the bay.

Port Grosvenor
In 1885 two rival traders attempted to develop a port for Pondoland in a bay close to the wreck of the *Grosvenor*. One cargo was landed but then the two traders began arguing with each other and the project was abandoned. Little remains of Port Grosvenor today but the name.

Port St. Johns
Few people visit Port St. Johns without being captivated by its beauty. It stands where the Mzimvubu River reaches the sea between Mount Thesiger and Mount Sullivan in a majestic setting of tremendous cliffs densely covered in sub-tropical forest. The port takes its name from the Portuguese ship, *St. John*, which was tragically wrecked a short distance up the coast in 1552.

It is a drowsy, easy-going place, with three superb beaches, several rocky headlands, excellent boating up the river — which is navigable for 10 kilometres — and many paths leading through the forest to beauty spots. The climate is perfect for holidays throughout the year, with sea temperatures high enough for even mid-winter bathing. In the river valley grow bananas, pawpaws, mangoes, litchis and avocados.

Roadside stalls sell fruit and beautifully made mats, baskets and curios.

Port St. Johns is said to have many ghosts, including one that haunts a hotel. It has always been the home of outlandish characters, none more colourful than Huberta, the famous wandering hippopotamus. She stayed for six months and each night wandered through the streets, chewing up the local gardens. Hippos had not been seen in the area for almost 100 years and there was much regret when she eventually left to continue her journey southwards (see box, page 159).

The British maintained a garrison at Port St. Johns during the scramble for Africa and coasters were still using the port right up to 1944. There are several hotels, caravan parks and camping grounds in beautiful settings.

Qolora Mouth
The small resort at the mouth of the Qolora River has a beautiful beach with excellent swimming and fishing.

A short walk leads to the enchanted pool of Nongqawuse, the young prophetess who promised to the Xhosa the destruction of the white man (see box).

The wreck of the *Jacaranda*, which foundered on 18 September 1971, can still be seen on the rocks nearby.

There are three hotels and a camping ground at the mouth of the river, and another camping site at Kobonqaba Point.

Qora Mouth
The road to Qora Mouth leads from Willowvale through forest country with spectacular views of the river valley and its deep gorges. This is the homeland of the Gcaleka, and many of the trading stations sell the handicrafts, curios and beadwork of these people. There is a resort at the mouth of the river, with a fine lagoon for boating and swimming, and a good beach.

Umngazi River
So many fights broke out along the Umngazi (Mngazi) River that it was said to flow with blood — and that is what the name means.

The river reaches the sea in a

The Tsitsa River waterfall, with its high column of spray.

The path leading to Second Beach at Port St. Johns, a beautiful beach in a sub-tropical setting.

The gateway at the mouth of the Mzimvubu River.

lagoon, and it has a resort at its mouth that is a favourite haunt of anglers.

There are many fishing points along the coast and some big catches have been made. Hammerhead sharks are frequently landed.

The surrounding countryside is a superb balance of hills and river, and the Umngazi (Mngazi) Valley is home to about 130 species of birds.

Umtata

Administrative buildings dominate the centre of Umtata, capital city during Transkei's period of independence from 1976 to 1994. The city stands on the banks of the Mtata River — the name means 'the taker' and is derived from a phrase 'Take him, our Father' used in the river-burial ceremonies accorded to Pondo chiefs.

Umtata had its beginning in 1869 as a military buffer between the warring Pondo and Tembu peoples, and ten years later a village had grown up behind the walled enclosure.

It is now a staging post on the trunk road and the junction of several routes leading down to the Wild Coast. There are several hotels and a caravan park, as well as a museum.

Willowvale

The village of Willowvale takes its name from the wild willows growing in the valley in which it lies. It was built as an administrative centre for the Gcaleka people, and the seat of their paramount chief is nearby.

The road through Willowvale leads on to Qora Mouth and Nqabara Point on the Wild Coast.

1. 'A woman of many husbands', as she is described in the local idiom. The elaborate decorations are the gifts of many lovers.
2. A Pondo youth. There is a love potion in the animal horn at his waist.
3. A Pondo married woman in gala dress. The pale blue colour is known to the Pondo as white because they were taught by the Europeans that blue dye makes white dye much whiter, and to their reasoning, therefore, blue is whiter than white.
4. A young girl, attractive to the boys with her bangles, bracelets, necklaces, beads and richly dyed cloth.

1   2   3   4

Graveyard of countless ships and sunken treasures

Years ago, ships from the East following the route around the southern end of Madagascar inevitably reached the shores of Africa off the Wild Coast. If the night was dark and the crews' instincts for longitude faulty, then they simply carried straight on to the shore. Thus did this graveyard of ships entomb so many victims.

Great numbers of ships and seamen vanished without trace. Other vessels were wrecked on the shore, and a few survivors managed to live through gruelling walks up the coast to the Portuguese settlements in Mocambique, or down the coast to Cape Town. These survivors had to face the constant threat of attack from primitive peoples and wild animals.

Some seamen turned cannibal, others committed suicide, or murdered one another for food, or simply settled down at whatever point they became exhausted, if they were lucky enough to make terms with the indigenous people they encountered.

Several small communities living on the coast claim descent from shipwrecked ancestors of European and Asian origin.

The Portuguese had a particular horror of this coast. So many of their trading vessels, heavily loaded with the wealth of the East, were wrecked upon the Wild Coast that it was partly responsible for the bankruptcy of their empire.

One of the classic wrecks in these parts was that of the *St. John* in June 1552. The vessel was deeply laden with cargo and carried several prominent Portuguese citizens.

The ship ran into a storm as it approached Africa. Masts and rudder were lost and the hulk was eventually dumped unceremoniously onto the rocky shore. More than 100 people drowned; most of the 440 survivors were badly injured by the rocks.

After resting on the shore for some weeks, the survivors started on the 700-kilometre trek up the coast to Lourenco Marques, the nearest point where there was any chance of finding people of their own kind.

The aged and weak soon dropped out. A trail of personal belongings was jettisoned by people who had started off the journey clinging to their valuables but who had then gradually weakened under the loads.

Some of the wealthy were at first carried in hammocks by sailors, who were rewarded with small gifts. As the sailors tired, they demanded more rewards until they became heavily burdened, and, unable to get more from their patrons, abandoned them.

After three months some survivors reached Lourenco Marques but learned that the annual trading vessel had just left. Bitterly disappointed, they rested a little while and then, ignoring the warnings of friendly natives, continued their walk, and far from the scene of their first disaster they fell prey to bandits who robbed them of their arms, clothes and other belongings. The captain, a nobleman of Portugal, his wife and two chil-

Gold medallions thought to have come from the wreck of the Grosvenor.

On the site of the Grosvenor *wreck, a relic of a salvage company.*

dren were among those who were stripped naked. His wife and children died and the captain became demented.

Eventually eight Portuguese and 17 slaves reached safety on the island of Mocambique, 1 600 kilometres from the scene of the wreck.

Two years after the wreck of the *St. John* another richly laden Portuguese ship, the *Sao Bento*, was also wrecked on the Wild Coast, this time at the mouth of the Mtata River. About 150 people were drowned; 99 Portuguese and 224 slaves reached the shore. The survivors made shelters for themselves from carpets and silks washed onto the beach. Among those who reached the beach from the *Sao Bento* was Manuel de Castro, who had been wrecked on the *St. John*, had walked to safety in Mocambique, had been taken back to India, and was now at last returning to Portugal. Wrecked once again on the Wild Coast, and with the prospect of another punishing trudge up the shore, he died in despair.

The rest of the survivors set out on the long walk north to Lourenco Marques. Along the coast they encountered a small group of survivors from the *St. John*. Some of these were now encouraged to continue the attempt to Lourenco Marques, others stayed put and were joined by members of the *Sao Bento* party.

Nearly three months after the wreck, 56 Portuguese and 6 slaves reached the bay of Lourenco Marques where, after a wait of four months, a Portuguese trading vessel arrived and took them away to safety.

On 24 March 1593 the *Santo Alberto* was wrecked near the Hole in the Wall, with the loss of 28 Portuguese and 35 slaves; 125 Portuguese, including two women, and 160 slaves survived.

A vast treasure went down with the

Salvage work on the Grosvenor. *A diver checks his equipment. Several cannon were recovered during this operation.*

An old engraving depicting the wreck on the Wild Coast of the Portuguese galleon Santo Alberto, *published in 1597.*

ship, but among the wreckage cast up on the beach were many items of practical value to the survivors. This salvage included arms and ammunition in usable condition, foodstuffs, bales of cloth, metal and beads suitable for trading, an astrolabe, writing paper and medical supplies. The captain and his officers were a competent group of men, and maintained strict discipline after the wreck.

A bold decision was made to leave the coast and walk to Mocambique by an inland route. On 3 April 1593 the party set off on what will always be regarded as one of the epic journeys in the history of southern Africa.

Some of the slaves spoke both Portuguese and one of the indigenous languages of Mocambique. Using them as interpreters, the Portuguese were able to communicate with the local people, convincing them that they were people in transit, and not invaders. Furthermore, the discipline of the survivors proved to be disconcerting to any bandits or predators, human and wild animal.

The party kept a detailed diary recording their adventures. They travelled so far inland that they became the first Europeans to see the Drakensberg and to explore the midlands of Natal. They hunted venison, fished in the rivers, and lived well. In the course of the journey nine Portuguese and 95 slaves dropped out and joined local settlements. The two women, one a girl of 16, did the whole journey of more than 1 500 kilometres without mishap. They reached the bay of Lourenco Marques on 30 June 1593 after 88 days of travelling. To crown their heroic journey through completely wild and unknown country, they found in the bay a trading vessel about to return to base at Mocambique. On this ship the survivors sailed away.

The wrecks of ships of other nations also littered the Wild Coast. The most remarkable British shipwreck was that of the *Grosvenor* on 4 August 1782. The ship was homeward bound from India and its wreck on a dark night was the beginning of a most remarkable series of events.

The *Grosvenor* was a treasure ship. Her bills of lading showed that the ves-

An engraving showing the wreck on the Wild Coast of the Portuguese galleon Sao Bento *in the 16th century.*

The wreck of the ill-fated Grosvenor *on the treacherous Wild Coast as painted by Robert Smirke in 1884.*

sel carried a cargo of bullion — jewels, coins, plate and many other precious goods taken from India by the British East India Company, then at the height of its career.

There were also rumours that the ship carried a king's ransom in loot being taken to Britain by adventurers said to have been concerned with the disappearance of the celebrated peacock throne of Persia.

Faulty charts were responsible for the wreck. Notwithstanding the warning of a look-out that he saw breakers ahead, the captain sailed his ship full-

The wreck of the Jacaranda, *which foundered on 18 September 1971.*

tilt onto the rocky shores of a deep bay known as Lambasi. Of the 123 people on board the *Grosvenor* only 15 were drowned. The rest reached the shore. Little wreckage was salvaged and the survivors were left with no more than the clothes they were wearing. Without arms, food or any materials suitable for trade, and with a very fractious company, their doom was almost inevitable. Only 18 survivors eventually reached the safety of the Dutch Settlement at the Cape.

The rest disappeared and their fate became part of the so-called 'kaffir-coast mysteries'.

News of the wreck and its rich cargo soon attracted attention. The site of the wreck is a deep rocky bay which is exposed to winds and strong seas. It is a source of marvel to modern visitors.

At least four different salvage companies and many individuals have laboured to recover the treasure of the *Grosvenor* The most ingenious schemes have been tried. One group planned to build a great dyke around the bay, pump out all the water, and then walk in to salvage the treasure. Two dykes were built, but both were destroyed by storms.

Another company sought to reach the wreck by digging a tunnel underneath the bed of the sea and then up to the wreck. Air locks were planned to keep the sea from flooding the tunnels. The company joined its predecessors in bankruptcy.

Cranes, divers, cables scraping the bed of the bay — almost every imaginable technique has been tried.

An impressive number of valuables have been recovered. Many thousands of coins have been found, as well as cannons and other bric-a-brac. But the big prize remains elusive. Technical problems of recovery have defied the most determined attempts to reach the remnants of the ship, now buried deep beneath sand, too near the rocks to be reached from the sea, in water too deep and stormy to be easily reached from the land.

At Lambasi and all along the Wild Coast there is always a chance of finding coins, beads, fragments of crockery and other relics along the shore.

Beneath the waves lie the hulks of the wrecks, on the shore are legends and yarns of treasure, and fascinating tales of the strange mixture of people who have searched for it.

BOTSWANA

BOTSWANA

A CASUAL VISITOR could be excused for missing the real nature of Botswana. He will see kilometre upon kilometre of flat, desolate scrubland stretching away as far as the eye can see in every direction; poor roads, a sparse population, little or no surface water, a climate ranging from freezing winter nights to roasting summer days. A dead wasteland. Or is it? The visitor who stays in Botswana a little longer will find a young country determined to thrust its way to prosperity, a country full of intriguing mystery and fascinating contrasts.

In the north the magnificent Okavango waterway, with its green and fertile plains, flows straight into a sea of sand, the Kalahari (or Kgalagadi) Desert, and vanishes.

Part of the Kalahari is a wilderness, not a desert. Its sands are largely covered with grasses which, though sparse, are sweet, and Texas cattle ranchers have been known to eye the area enviously for it supports some of the largest herds of game on the continent of Africa, as well as a huge domestic cattle population.

For many years after independence was gained in 1966, Botswana was listed by the United Nations as one of the world's 25 poorest countries. This unfortunate tag has now disappeared, for Botswana has subsequently been found to possess mineral wealth on a large scale. There is copper, nickel, coal, iron ore, manganese, and at Orapa massive new diamond pipes. Another diamond pipe, perhaps nearly as large as Orapa, has been developed about 480 kilometres to the south in Jwaneng. There may be much more mineral wealth, for what has always hindered geologists in Botswana is the immensely thick layer of sand, up to 100 metres deep in places. If this could be laid bare, what treasures might be revealed?

Tourism is another new boom industry. In the 19th century trophy hunters from all over the world trekked into the region of Ngamiland in northern Botswana in search of elephants, crocodiles, lions and other big game.

Later, however, the country's rich animal life seems to have been forgotten, and it was not until the 1960s that Botswana was rediscovered by the hunters. Now they come from all corners of the globe, to hunt or simply to witness a wild side of Africa that is steadily disappearing in other parts of the continent.

Great efforts are now being made to conserve this wildlife heritage. A host of large parks and reserves have been established and provide superb game viewing. The Moremi, Chobe, Khutse, Central Kalahari and Gemsbok are the best known.

Visitors to Botswana find a country that is one of Africa's most peaceful and democratic states.

Botswana's unit of currency, the Pula, is on a par with the Rand. The Pula takes its name from a traditional greeting and, appropriately for a land of such thirst, literally means 'rain'.

Preceding page: In the flat sand country of Botswana, a farmer stands next to a rack of millet, the staple food of the indigenous people.

408

ANGOLA

ZAMBIA

ZIMBABWE

Chobe

Okavango Delta

NAMIBIA

○ Maun

Makgadikgadi Pans

Francistown ⊙

Shashe

Ghanzi ⊙

BOTSWANA
411

Limpopo

Botswana is treated as a single
touring region. Turn to page 411
for a more detailed map of the
region, plus extensive touring
information.

Marico

Gaborone ⊙

Lobatse ⊙

Nossob

Molopo

TRANSVAAL

CAPE PROVINCE

KALAHARI COUNTRY

BOTSWANA, WITH AN area of 500 000 square kilometres, is larger than France. Two-thirds of it is covered by the grassy, thornbush-covered sands of the Kgalagadi, or Kalahari. Most of the population lives in the more fertile eastern region in the Limpopo River catchment area.

Man has lived in Botswana for at least 500 000 years. More than 10 000 years ago the San came and had the plains to themselves until about the 4th century A.D., when Shona-speaking groups of the Kgalagadi people began filtering into Botswana from the area now known as Zimbabwe. They were herders of cattle and goats, and they gave the Kalahari its name.

In the 16th century the Tswana, under the legendary chief, Masilo, arrived in Botswana from the north-east, and began pushing further westward, absorbing the Shona-speakers. The three politically dominant groups of Botswana today are named after the grandchildren of Masilo — the Kwena, Ngwato and Ngwaketse.

The country was to become an important link between the Cape and what was Rhodesia, and in 1884 the southern half was declared a British protectorate. This was later extended to include the rest of the country. It was initially called Bechuanaland, and was administered from Mafeking, now Mafikeng.

In 1966 the independent Commonwealth state of Botswana was created, with Gaborone as the capital. After an overwhelming election triumph, Sir Seretse Khama, grandson of Khama III, became the first president.

Chobe National Park

Game animals in immense numbers roam the emerald green wilderness of the Chobe National Park, on Botswana's northern borders. The park, 11 600 square kilometres, has been established on the flood plains of the Chobe River, a major tributary of the Zambezi. The entrance and headquarters of the park, at the village of Kasane, are an hour's drive from the Victoria Falls along a good gravel road.

The park has Botswana's largest herds of elephant. Hundreds may be seen along the riverbank in the dry season. Tourists may also see buffalo, sable, roan, eland, kudu, waterbuck, zebra, tsessebe, lion, leopard, impala, reedbuck, lechwe and, if lucky, the rare Chobe bushbuck. The river has hippos and crocodiles, and teems with tiger-fish, bream and barbel. Further inland, giraffe, gemsbok and wildebeest populate the veld. The park has at least 80 species of birds.

From Kasane boats take sightseers 30 kilometres upriver, and of the 80 kilometres of good gravel roads nearly 50 kilometres are along the Chobe. In the dry season, game builds up to such an extent that thousands of animals can be seen on the banks of the river.

Away from the river the habitat changes startlingly from forest and grassland to scrub and thickets. In the south of the park are the pans, reedy marshes and fossil lake beds of the Mababe Depression. Water-holes in the area have specially constructed hides for game viewing. Giraffe are common here, and reports of visitors seeing up to 50 at a time are not unusual.

Wildebeest and impala grazing in the grasslands of the Chobe Park.

The leaves of the mopane tree hang downwards to avoid sun-rays.

The praying mantis, an insect regarded with awe by the San.

THINGS TO DO AND SEE

Angling The Shakawe camp is popular with anglers going after tiger-fish in the Okavango. This species is also caught in the Chobe River at Kasane and Serondela and in the Thamalakane River at Maun. The Mopipi and Gaborone dams are stocked with bream, barbel and carp.

Birdwatching There is a famous vultury near Lobatse. Makgadikgadi Pan is renowned for its flamingoes and Lake Ngami is a nesting place for white pelicans, flamingoes and quelea finches. Many birds visit Khutse Pan when there is water. Hundreds of species abound in the Okavango Delta.

Camping and caravanning Botswana is rough country for towing caravans, but there are sites with full facilities at Kasane and Serondela. There are camping grounds at Crocodile Camp near Maun, the Chobe National Park, Camp San-ta-Wani in the Moremi Reserve, and at Shakawe on the Okavango River.

Sightseeing Lion, elephant, rhino, buffalo, hippo and vast herds of game animals can be seen in the wildlife reserves. There are boat trips up the Chobe River to view big game in the Chobe National Park. Expeditions can also be made up the Thamalakane River from Maun. Khutse Pan is the big game viewing point nearest to Gaborone. There are San paintings at Kalakamati, Manyana and in the Tsodilo Hills. Kolobeng has the remains of Livingstone's mission station.

Sports There are golf courses at Gaborone, Francistown, Orapa and Selebi-Pikwe.

The seemingly boundless flood plains of the Chobe River — meandering lazily on its way to join the Zambezi.

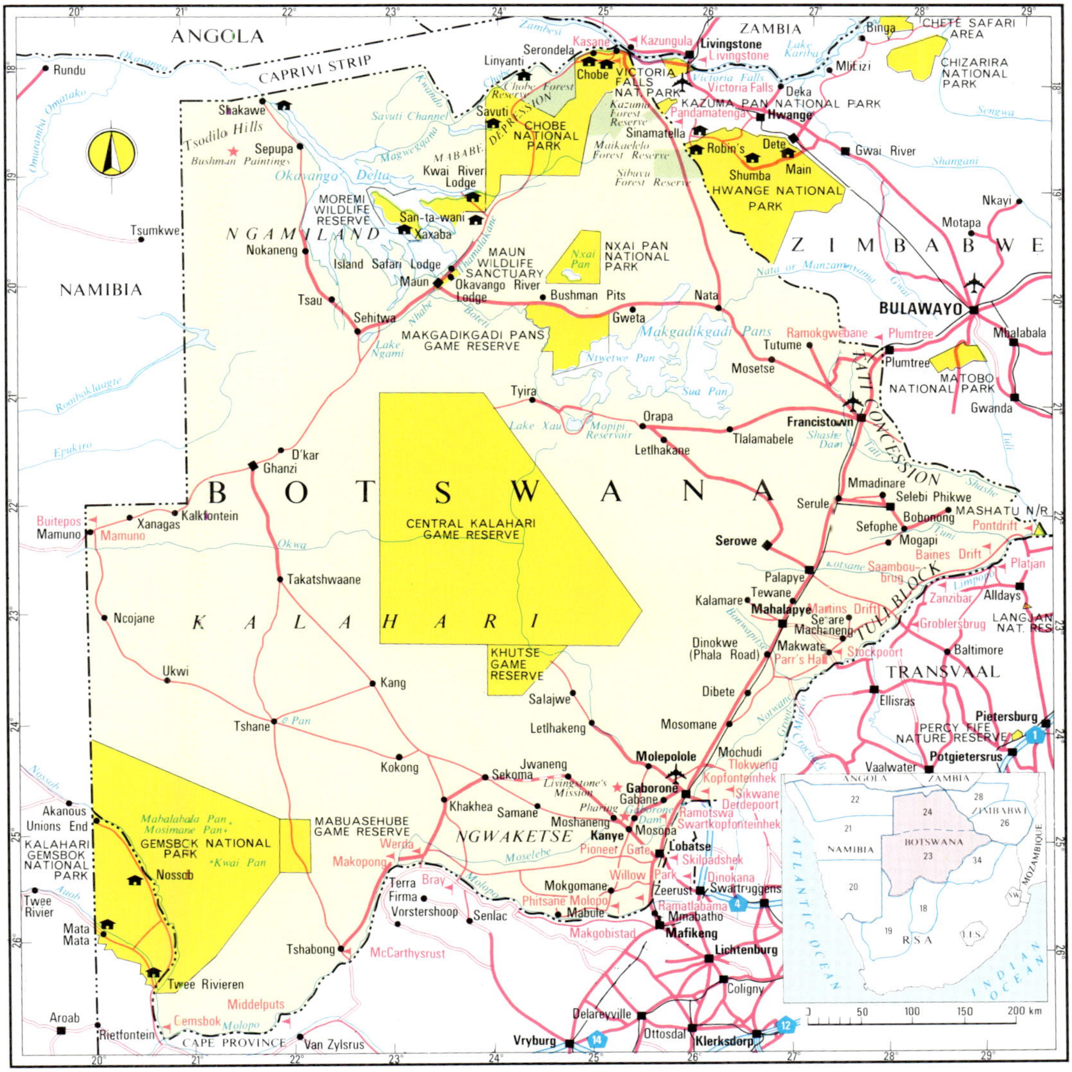

The park has two lodges for visitors, the Chobe Safari Lodge and the Chobe Game Lodge, both in Kasane.

Though the recommended road route is through Nata, there is an inferior road from Maun. The park is also served by an airstrip at Serondela.

Francistown

Africa's first modern gold rush took place in northern Botswana's Tati district, of which Francistown is the capital.

It is also the centre of mine workings thousands of years old.

The area's colourful modern history began in 1866, when an elephant shot by the hunter Henry Hartley fell dying next to a long-forgotten ancient mine. Hartley invited the German adventurer Karl Mauch to investigate and he found more workings along the Tati River.

Mauch travelled to Potchefstroom with a sample of gold-bearing rock — and the result was a wave of gold fever that brought in miners from England, Wales, New Zealand and Australia.

At the height of the rush, in 1869, the burgeoning settlement at the gold field was named Francistown after Daniel Francis, an English prospector and trader.

By the mid-1870s many of the mines had become uneconomic and were closed, although gold mining lingered on until 1964, when the last of the town's 45 mines was shut down. Wherever the modern miners

A game-viewing barge used by tourists visiting the Linyanti River.

Was this the site of gold mines of the past?

searched for gold they found evidence of a vanished people who were here many centuries before them. These people have been linked with the culture that built Zimbabwe in the north and worked other goldbearing outcrops in central Africa. Mining was stopped when they reached the level of the water-table. The miners had no means of pumping.

Today Francistown is surrounded by hundreds of old shafts, pit heads and mine dumps, grey and decaying in the sun. The town is one of Botswana's largest industrial centres, with engineering and textile works, and a game skin industry.

Recent mineral finds in northern Botswana have given new impetus to local industries.

Francistown has become a major staging point for the game parks in north and north-western Botswana.

One local industry, taxidermy, caters almost solely for tourists. Returning big-game hunters can have their catches stuffed and transported all over the world.

Gaborone
Almost overnight, the traditional African village of Gaborone was transformed into Botswana's thriving modern capital. It was originally the home of the Tlokwa and was named after their chief, Gaborone Matlapeng, who founded it in the 1890s. It remained a village until 1965, the year before Botswana's independence. Until then the country had been governed from outside its borders, in what was Mafeking, in the Cape Province. Partly because of the availability of adequate water supplies, Gaborone was chosen to be the new capital and a national assembly and administrative headquarters were built here.

Since independence the capital has acquired a national museum, a library and an art gallery. It has Roman Catholic and Anglican cathedrals and the University of Botswana has its campus here. The modern part of the town has been attractively planned amid a setting of trees. In the town centre there is a traffic-free shopping area. The national museum, a major tourist attraction, specializes in showing graphically how man has lived in Botswana from earliest times.

In the old part of the town Gaborone's first hotel still stands, although it is no longer in use. It was here that Cecil Rhodes lived for a time and where the abortive Jameson Raid on Johannesburg in 1895, inspired by Rhodes, is said to have been planned by Dr. Starr Jameson and his associates. Boer War remains — trenches, fortifications and camps — can be seen around the outskirts of the old town.

The Gaborone Dam is popular for boating and water-skiing.

Gemsbok National Park
The most remote of Botswana's game reserves takes its name from the magnificent gemsbok, also known as the oryx, an antelope with majestic slender horns, so sharp that they command the respect even of lions.

The Gemsbok National Park covers more than 11 000 square kilometres of desert in the extreme south-west of the country, an area where the yearly rainfall seldom rises above 125 millimetres. It is home to huge herds of gemsbok and other antelope, like the eland, which are capable of living for long periods without water, obtaining moisture from roots and succulent plants.

It is also the home of the famous black-maned lions, as well as smaller members of the cat family.

The park is the oldest in Botswana, having been established in the 1930s alongside the South African government's Kalahari Gemsbok National Park. It was created to assist government park officials in the control of game, and not as a tourist attraction in itself.

The park is administered by the warden of the South African Kalahari Gemsbok National Park, stationed at Twee Rivieren. There are no facilities for tourists. This arid area, which includes the fossil beds of the Auob and Nossob rivers and was once the home of *San* communities, is similar to the surrounding desert, with dunes of orange sand sparsely covered with thornscrub.

Kanye
In 1824 the missionary-explorer Robert Moffat came across the fortress town of Kanye, built by the Ngwaketse people on the plateau of a range of hills. Moffat wrote of it as a 'metropolis', for Kanye, the oldest village-town in Botswana, was already well established. Walls around the plateau had been built by Chief Makaba I in the 1790s to keep out marauders from the north. Kanye was ideal as a fortress for, apart from its hills, it had an adequate water supply

from a deep gorge in the nearby cliffs of Pharing.

The Ngwaketse built their huts around a kgotla (central meeting place), and as tradition and the seasons dictated, they would move out of the village at different times of the year to tend their lands and flocks.

Kanye did not become a permanent settlement until the 1850s, after it had been sacked by Boers. Since then it has grown steadily into a place of great charm. With a population of about 40 000 it is now the second largest town in Botswana. Serowe is the largest.

The town is split into two distinctive areas. On top of the hills is the

The road from Francistown to Maun crossing the flat country of the Kalahari.

traditional African village, with its kgotla and thatched rondavels. The houses have beautifully decorated courtyards of patterned clay. Although there is a modern water supply, young women are still to be seen carrying water jugs on their heads up the hill from the gorge.

At the foot of the hills are schools, the airport and government buildings, Kanye being the capital of the Ngwaketse district.

Asbestos is mined at nearby Moshaneng and manganese mines are also being developed in the area.

Kasane
The one claim to fame of Kasane is that here is the entrance and headquarters for the Chobe National Park. The Chobe River nearby is well stocked with bream and tigerfish and attracts abundant bird life.

Kolobeng
Once the home of David Livingstone in the 1840s while he planned his travels into the far interior, all that remains of the mission site of Kolobeng is the floor of his house and some graves. Nearby is a fig tree under which he preached.

Khutse and Central Kalahari Game Reserve
A visit to the Kalahari (or Kgalagadi) is like taking a step back in time. Huge migratory herds of game roam the arid, scrub-covered plains much as they have always done, hunted by a tiny population of San who still lead a Stone Age existence.

In dry months the vast tract of the Khutse and Central Kalahari Game Reserve, more than 16 000 square kilometres, is hostile and barren. But after the summer rains, animals migrate in great numbers across the veld in search of grass and water. A safari once reported seeing a herd of more than 40 000 hartebeest spread over many square miles. Elephant, springbok, zebra and wildebeest also move into the reserve.

Around Khutse Pan there are always gemsbok, kudu, steenbok, duikers, ostriches, black-backed jackals and bat-eared foxes. Eland and giraffe are spotted occasionally, while lion, leopard, hyena and wild dogs fre-

Excavations at the magnesium mine near Gaborone.

The dam at Gaborone that supplies the region's water.

Gemsbok in the Kalahari. They are thought to be the origin of the myth of the unicorn — their profile reveals only one horn.

Two springbok rams tussle in the Kalahari during the mating season.

A genet cat, one of the small predators of the Kalahari region.

Big-game safaris to 'the lake that burns'

A typical road through the dense thornbush country of the Kalahari.

quently visit the pan at night but are rarely seen in daylight. This is also a good spot to study the many species of desert birds, insects and reptiles.

There are many pans in the reserve, but not all are in areas open to the public. The Khutse Pan, however, is always open. It is the nearest point to the capital for viewing big game. The six-hour journey is over a fair gravel road through Molepolole, the last place where there are garage services. The sand track leading into the reserve is suitable only for four-wheel-drive vehicles. There is no water, petrol or accommodation in the reserve.

San guides at the Khutse Pan give visitors a unique insight into their homeland.

Lake Ngami

The broad expanse of Lake Ngami, on the fringe of the Kalahari, or Kgalagadi, can be a vast inland sea — or semi-desert. It is 65 kilometres long by 16 kilometres across. After most rainy seasons, water from the Okavango Delta spills into the lake along the Thamalakane River to the north. In droughts, Ngami has been known to dry up completely into a sea of reeds, as it did during the mid 1960s.

In the autumn of 1966, following a summer of better rains, the lake began to fill again. Fish that had lain dormant in the mud during the drought were soon plentiful again. Aquatic birds, for which the lake is famous, descended in huge flocks — white pelicans, flamingoes, marabou storks and countless waterfowl — and local fishermen once again had work to do. For Ngami, rich in plankton and well stocked with barbel, is the centre of Botswana's fishing industry.

In 1970 a fish processing plant was set up at Sehitwa, the largest village on the shores of the lake. About a ton of bream and barbel a day was caught for processing until the lake began to dry up in the mid-1970s. By 1977 Ngami was full again, and it was business as usual.

When first seen by explorer David Livingstone in 1849, Ngami teemed with game animals. Now it is the centre of large-scale livestock farming and this tends to keep away the game, although big herds of impala and tsessebe are still to be seen in the area.

Ngami is known as 'the lake that burns' because in some years lake dwellers burn reed beds to reclaim land needed for ploughing. The fires, fed by dry, mossy vegetation, often smoulder for months on end until rains extinguish them.

This is also a home of refugee communities. Tawana settled here long ago after a number of wars. Herero families who fled the Germans in the war of 1904-05 live here. Many local

The sands of the Kalahari are coloured red by iron oxides. Most of the Kalahari is flat, covered with thorn trees and long grass, but dunes such as this frequently occur.

Sycamore figs are found on the banks of most rivers of northern Botswana.

An Aptosimum *flower growing at Nxai Pan in Botswana.*

THE LOST CITY

Botswana is a land of mirages, where shimmering heat plays tricks with the senses. For nearly a hundred years men have argued about one great desert mystery — the Lost City of the Kalahari.

In 1885 an American showman, G. A. Farini, and his son, Lulu, claimed to have discovered the city during an expedition.

Farini reported that one day their wagon pulled up beside a 2-kilometre-long enclosure of stones. Inside this protective perimeter was what seemed to be a pavement of neatly laid-out squares forming a cross in the middle.

They spent several days in the area, digging and unearthing fragments, convinced this was a ruined city or a place of worship.

On their return from Africa the Farinis held an exhibition in London, showing sketches and maps of the lost city — but not a single photograph, although Lulu was known to be a keen photographer.

Many explorers have since tried to uncover proof of the city's existence. Aeroplanes and other modern devices have been used in these attempts — all to no avail. The question remains: was the Lost City of the Kalahari reality or mirage? History or hoax?

farmers are descended from Boers, known as the Thirstland Trekkers, who broke with President Thomas Burger's Transvaal government in the 1870s.

Safari companies run charter flights to the lake. Other visitors travel by road from Maun. Sometimes there have been tourist tent camps at the lake, but amenities like these tend to disappear with the periodic vanishing of the mysterious lake itself.

Lobatse

One of the longest cattle drives in the world begins at Ghanzi in the far west of Botswana. It crosses a vast tract of the Kalahari Desert and ends after 500 kilometres at Lobatse, in the country's south-eastern corner. For Lobatse is the centre of the flourishing cattle industry and has a large abattoir operated by the Botswana Meat Commission. Attached to the abattoir is one of the largest meat processing and canning plants in Africa. It handles all the considerable amount of beef now exported by Botswana.

Lobatse has become a bustling town, with cattle being driven in from all corners of Botswana for sale and slaughter. Cattle drovers, living it up in the manner of the Wild West, keep the shopkeepers, pubs — and the court — busy.

The town is set among low hills dotted with aloes. It still contains the remains of an old stone-walled fortress

village. It is the centre of one of the most fertile and productive districts in the country and has several industries, including a maize and malt mill.

Lobatse was regarded as the capital of Botswana before independence. The high court still sits here, and the legislative assembly met here for the first time. But lack of water hindered

development and Gaborone was made the capital. Lobatse's water problems have since been solved by the building of a pipeline from Gaborone Dam, and Lobatse remains the gateway to Botswana from South Africa.

It is linked to the Cape and the Transvaal by road and rail, and by air to Johannesburg.

The name Lobatse comes from the chief Molebatse. Two caves containing dripstone formations are found in the nearby hills. They are home to several small wild creatures.

Makgadikgadi and Nxai Pans

Two big fossil lake beds flank the main road from Francistown to Maun — the Makgadikgadi Pan on the southern side and the Nxai Pan to the north.

The hard, flat, soda-encrusted surface of the Makgadikgadi Pan.

A close-up of the surface of the Makgadikgadi Pan — a mixture of soda and mud.

By power-boat through the swamp-lands

Makgadikgadi is believed to be the largest salt pan in the world. When dry, which is most of the time, it is 6 500 square kilometres of glaring saline sand, white and absolutely flat. When the waters of the Okavango spill down the Boteti River after good summer rains, the whole area of the pan is flooded to a depth of a few centimetres, providing rich feeding for aquatic birds. Flamingoes and countless pelicans descend on Makgadikgadi.

Great herds of big game — wildebeest, zebra and springbok — water here and herds 10 000-strong can sometimes be seen on the plains beside the pan.

In the pan itself, animals stand out in startling fashion on the white salt, their legs shimmering and elongated through mirage caused by heatwaves and glare.

Both pans have been designated national game reserves. At Makgadikgadi the main road runs along the edge of the pan, which makes for easy viewing. At Nxai, a gravel road has been built leading from the main road over a high sand ridge.

Nxai is a much smaller depression than Makgadikgadi. Down in the pan small clumps of trees dominate a sea of grass cropped short by the game. There are almost always giraffe, springbok, bat-eared foxes and hartebeest in the area. In the rainy season migratory herds of gemsbok, wildebeest, buffalo, eland, zebra and elephant swell the numbers, and as many as 5 000 head of game have been seen in the pan at one time.

Near Nxai is another pan, Kgamakgama, where there are baobab trees and palms.

Maun

At the heart of Botswana's growing tourist industry is the small town of Maun, in the country's north-west. Maun is linked to Francistown in the east by a gravel road suitable for saloon cars, and also has a busy airfield. The town provides ready access to the Okavango Delta, the Moremi Wildlife Reserve, Lake Ngami, and the Makgadikgadi and Nxai salt pans, so it is the centre of much of the country's safari business.

Four-wheel-drive vehicles and power-boats can be hired at Maun.

Herding cattle on a dusty road in the ranching country near Maun.

The boats offer an ideal way to explore the Okavango swamp. It is possible to sail more than 600 kilometres through the swamp to Shakawe, near the Caprivi Strip border. Much more popular, however, are day cruises, which go only a few kilometres up the Thamalakane River from Maun.

The river life and bird life are exceptional. There is good barbel and bream fishing, and as there are no crocodiles in the area, swimming is popular.

Within 20 kilometres of Maun are the Island Safari Lodge, the Okavango River Lodge, and the Crocodile Camp, each of which is renowned for fishing, boating and waterskiing, as well as for popular truck trips into neighbouring wildlife areas.

A highlight of most river-based safaris is a boat trip at night on the Thamalakane. Guides use torches to show up the wonderfully varied fish life, including tiger-fish, and also to catch the glinting eyes of wild animals prowling the banks.

Maun is the chief town of the Tawana people, and also serves as the capital of the North West District. It is an attractive town of closely grouped rondavels. The population includes a sizeable Herero community descended from refugees who fled from the Germans in neighbouring South West Africa in 1904-05.

The town is served by Botswana Airways. There is a regular truck service to the cattle farming centre of Ghanzi in the western Kalahari.

A Herero woman, one of the diverse people of Botswana.

Melons growing on the roof of a hut, safe from livestock.

Moremi Wildlife Reserve

Many travellers regard the Moremi Wildlife Reserve as the most spectacular and beautiful game park in southern Africa. It covers more than 1 000 square kilometres of grassy flood plains in the north-eastern corner of the Okavango Delta. Apart from savanna, the terrain includes winding waterways with banks of reeds, palm-covered islands, thick forest, and lush, lily-covered lagoons where hippos bathe and sport.

With such a variety of vegetation comes an incredibly wide spectrum of wildlife. Huge herds of impala and tsessebe are always in the area, while in the dry season large herds of buffalo, wildebeest and zebra flock into the park from the Kalahari in search of food and water. The rare sitatunga and lechwe antelope live in the papyrus banks of the waterways. Lions, cheetahs and packs of wild dogs hunt in the open grassland. The reserve is home to an immense number of birds.

Red lechwe grazing in the swamplands of the Okavango River Delta.

FLAMINGOES BY THE MILLION DANCED IN A MAJESTIC CLOUD OF PINK AT A BIRD-WATCHERS' PARADISE

In July 1967, following good summer rains, the Makgadikgadi Pan in north-eastern Botswana was flooded for the first time in several years. Travellers on the road from Francistown to Maun were treated to an unforgettable sight. Millions of flamingoes, forming a vast cloud of pink, flapped and bobbed in the shallow water. Witnesses claimed that the flock of birds covered more than 20 square kilometres. Although huge flocks of flamingoes and pelicans often gather in the pan, this was the biggest flock ever recorded.

Botswana, generally, is a paradise for birds. Nowhere is this more evident than in the Chobe and Moremi wildlife sanctuaries, which are home to huge flocks of storks, ibis, herons, egrets, cranes, spurwing geese, Egyptian geese, ducks, guinea fowl and quail. Here too are the red bishop bird, the majestic bateleur eagle, and perhaps most beautiful of all, the carmine bee-eater.

Another bird of brilliant plumage to be found throughout the lagoons of the Okavango is the small malachite kingfisher, with blue feathers and a green crest. The lagoons sometimes echo to the eerie call of the fish eagle.

By contrast, at Otse mountain near Lobatse in southern Botswana, there is a fine vultury where more than 600 pairs of Cape vultures nest.

Lake Ngami has millions of redbilled quelea (finches) which fill the air with a constant whirring. Marabou storks are said to prey on the quelea by running up to a flock of watering birds, knocking several over with their huge wings, and then feeding at their leisure on the drowning victims.

A blue crane, the bird emblem of South Africa.

Wood storks nesting in fig trees in the Okavango Delta.

A golden bishop bird. Bird life in the Okavango Delta is very varied.

A nesting colony of carmine bee-eaters on the banks of the Chobe River.

A malachite kingfisher on an island in the Okavango River.

A marabou stork, grubby in appearance. These storks are scavengers.

Makgadikgadi Pan, during the rainy season, receives a covering of slushy water that attracts flamingoes by the thousand.

Town that could be the new Kimberley

Unlike most other game parks, the Moremi Wildlife Reserve allows visitors to approach game on foot. The park has been kept in as natural a state as possible by the Tawana people, who created it.

In 1961, worried about the increase in game hunting, the Tawana, under their regent, Mrs. Pulane Moremi, widow of Chief Moremi III, established the reserve on their own land. The project has been a great success, attracting many visitors every year. The Tawana have now handed over the management to the Department of Wildlife and National Parks.

Many of the visitors stay at the famous Khwai River Lodge, located on the northern edge of the reserve. On the south-eastern border of the reserve is Camp San-ta-Wani, named after a rare, small fox-like creature found in the area.

In the dry season, from May to early November, roads are passable to Land Rovers and trucks. In wet months, however, the reserve can be treacherous, with its roads flooded. Other dangers are always present. Malaria is endemic and tsetse fly infests the whole reserve.

Okavango Delta

Each summer, floods pour down from the highlands of Angola and the Okavango River and flow into a great network of narrow waterways, lagoons and lakelets in the Okavango Delta. The water courses through this huge, 10 000 square-kilometre expanse of flood plain and dissipates in the sands of the Kalahari. The Okavango region is frequently called a swamp, but the waters are generally beautifully clear. Most of the river's water is soaked up by the desert, or evaporates. In good years, a fraction may remain to flood Lake Ngami in the south and feed the Boteti River, which runs into Lake Xau in the west and eventually into the huge depression of the Makgadikgadi Pan.

The floods reach their peak in May, covering vast grass flats and making thousands of islands out of tree-covered ridges of land. The landscape is green as far as the eye can see. Thick papyrus grows everywhere, and in the northern parts of the delta it chokes the waterways so that they are impenetrable except by canoes.

This wilderness is uninhabited, except for the few river San who roam here. They still work iron with primitive bellows, making knives, axes and spears. Their canoes, called mokoros, are handhewn from logs.

In the parts of the delta where there is perennial water there are large numbers of crocodiles, hippos and buffaloes. Animals like the sitatunga, lechwe and Chobe bushbuck, which have adapted themselves to the conditions of reed and water, live on the islands.

The delta, generally, is hostile to visitors. They are warned to start taking anti-malaria tablets a week before arriving here. The town of Maun is the centre for safaris into this area.

Orapa

Large-scale diamond deposits are among the rarest of all mineral finds. Since World War II, geologists have searched the whole of Africa in the hope of finding another Kimberley — but until 1967 only three major pipes had been found. There was therefore great excitement in Botswana in that year when De Beers, the international diamond mining group, announced the find of a major diamond pipe at Orapa, on the eastern fringe of the Kalahari.

Mining could not start immediately. First a road had to be built from Francistown, then a power station, and most important of all, a pipeline had to be laid from Mopipi Pan to provide water for the mine and its community.

The mine was opened in 1971, and its development has been spectacular. In terms of output, although not of quality, it vies with the Mwadui pipe in Tanzania to be the most productive diamond mine in the world. More than 1 600 000 carats of mostly low-grade industrial diamonds, worth more than R20 million, are exported from here every year. A second major pipe has since been located at Jwaneng.

The new town of Orapa, one of the most modern in Botswana, has sprung up in the veld.

Financed by De Beers, this self-contained community has several

Part of the Okavango Delta in a setting of burnt, and burning, papyrus swamps.

A damsel fly in the Okavango Delta. Such insects flourish in the warmth.

A grasstop spider in its nest, another of the creatures of the Okavango country.

A shooting star streaks over a bush fire on an island in the Okavango Delta.

The placid surface of the Okavango swamps is covered with water-lilies.

schools, shops of all kinds, and medical services, and is an important new provider of employment. The town has a nine-hole golf course, tennis courts and two swimming pools.

Mopipi Pan has been transformed into a large reservoir, where there is boating and fishing.

Selebi-Pikwe
In only a few years the town of Selebi-Pikwe has grown from open veld into a community of about 30 000 people. The town is the centre of a large new copper-nickel mine and smelter complex.

Roads and a railway have been built to link the town with Botswana's main lines of communication. An airstrip has also been built nearby, and Air Botswana operates regular flights from Johannesburg.

The town, probably the fastest growing in Botswana, is not yet well equipped for visitors interested in sport. This is because priority has been given to developing the production of its much-needed mineral wealth.

Serowe
Large African village-towns are relatively common throughout Botswana. These are generally places where the kgotla (chief meeting place) has been sited, and around which the rondavels of the chief and the most important families have been built.

The dominant feature of the kgotla is a crescent-shaped windbreak of poles, in the shelter of which the daily business is carried out.

In Serowe, the chief town of the Ngwato people, there are many kgotlas. With a population numbering more than 40 000, Serowe ranks as Botswana's largest town.

It was first occupied by the Ngwato in 1902 when their chief, Khama III, decided to switch headquarters from nearby Palapye. The famous old chief, grandfather of Botswana's late President, Sir Seretse Khama, died in Serowe in 1923 at the age of 93. A statue of a duiker stands in the town centre in tribute to Khama III. It was unveiled in 1925 by the Prince of Wales.

Sir Seretse was born at Serowe in 1921. Serowe has several government offices to administer Ngwato affairs.

Tsodilo Hills
The honey and rose coloured granite cliffs of the Tsodilo Hills, on the north-western fringe of the Kalahari Desert, are world famous for their fascinating San paintings. They tower 385 metres above desolate flatlands to form a fortress-like ridge 20 kilometres long.

The hills were sacred to the San. Writer-explorer Laurens van der Post has called them the 'mountains of the gods', and they were certainly a focal point of dozens, perhaps even hundreds, of San migrations across the continent.

Stone Age tools, beads and pottery fragments are found throughout the area. But the most fascinating of Tsodilo's treasures are the cliff-face galleries of more than 2 000 San paintings.

The earliest paintings, thought to be at least 4 000 years old, depict individual animals in silhouette. Later works are of whole herds of game animals, while the most recent and sophisticated show men hunting the game. In only one place do the paint-

A fisherman of the Okavango. The canoe is his only means of navigating the delta.

ings overlap one another, which gives us some indication of the sense of order and purpose with which the San artists approached their work.

The San still live near Tsodilo — the only place known where they and their paintings can be found together. But today's San no longer paint the cliff faces, and they appear to know nothing of the techniques employed by their ancestors.

The Tsodilo Hills are extremely remote and difficult to reach. The journey from Maun, over a poor desert road, can take 14 hours or more. Water in the area is sparse and tourists are warned to take extra supplies. Despite all the hazards, however, every year sees more intrepid travellers journeying along the dusty roads to see the great heritage left behind by the desert painters of old.

San rock art in the Tsodilo Hills — a final phase of this art form.

The last home of the vanishing San

The barren, desolate wastes of the Kalahari Desert and parts of Namibia are the last home of the San, a race whose remarkable way of life has gone on virtually unchanged since the Stone Age. For more than 10 000 years these tiny people dominated the vast hinterland of southern Africa. But in the last few hundred years the advance of black and white races has driven the San out of one area after another until only the hostile, inaccessible wilderness remains. And although his existence is no longer under threat in such areas, it is possible that the San's hunter-gatherer life-style will disappear within the next ten years or so. Already, most of Botswana's 25 000 San live among other Africans as cattle herders. Only about 4 000 or 5 000 still live in the wilderness, surviving as they have always done by hunting and gathering wild plants for food.

The San knows only too well the value of water and this, say many experts, is what will ultimately change his way of life. For boreholes drilled in the Kalahari are attracting him out of the wilderness into a more settled existence. Meanwhile, scientists travel to the Kalahari to track down this elusive group and study their ways.

San live in small bands, each with a right of use over certain areas. They are careful not to trespass on their neighbours' land without permission.

The hallmark of their social attitudes is their utter belief in co-operation — within the family, the band, between bands, and with nature itself. Their customs are geared to exclude anything that might cause personal antagonism. There is, therefore, no ownership of property. Even the spoils of a hunt are divided according to customary allocation.

The San believes that if he misuses his environment he will incur the anger of the Supreme Being. So he never takes from the soil or from the herds of game around him any more than he needs to stay alive. In all his long history there is no evidence that he has ever needlessly exploited nature — and

A modern San family, wearing European clothes and using cooking utensils.

some experts have actually described the San as the world's greatest conservationists.

The size of the San bands varies from two or three families to groups numbering 120 or more. In the rainy season, when food is plentiful, much inter-band visiting goes on, and frequently the bands are united by marriages. The San believe that man is naturally gregarious and at his happiest when in company.

Dry seasons are a time of searches for food and moisture. Hunting is man's work, while women collect moisture-bearing plants and small animals. During periods of rain these people store all the water they can carry in ostrich-egg shells and calabashes, burying them in the earth or concealing them in the shade of a tree.

Desert San have names for every plant that grows in their area. Plant life, not meat, is their staple diet — a few square kilometres of desert might contain as many as 70 or 80 varieties of edible plants and roots.

From certain tasselled grasses they can tell where there is underground water. This is sucked up through hollowed-out reeds and stored in ostrich-egg containers.

One of the favourite foods of the Kalahari San is the tsamma melon, rather like a white-fleshed cross between a water melon and a gem squash. These moisture-laden plants frequently come to the rescue when there is no surface water. Sometimes a band will hold special ceremonies to mark the eating of tsamma melons.

The San are rightly regarded as great hunters. There are many tales of their prodigious stamina, outstanding eyesight and uncanny tracking abilities. In his book, *The Lost World of the Kalahari*, explorer Laurens van der Post tells of seeing San tracking game at a run for 30 kilometres non-stop and still being

A San hunter with primitive but deadly bow and poison-tipped arrow.

An encampment of San in the red sand dune country of the Kalahari.

A San woman and grandchild with ostrich-egg water containers.

strong enough at the end of the hunt to sprint full-tilt as they closed in on their quarry.

Their arrows are tipped with powerful poisons. This secret art of poison-making made them deadly adversaries of their black and white foes in the past. The poisons are blended from leaves, berries, spiders, caterpillars, grubs, crushed larvae, snake venom, poisonous ticks, and the pulp of a venomous worm.

It can be strong enough to kill the largest animal. A big buck may travel for 15 kilometres before collapsing from effects of the paralysing poison in its bloodstream. The San hunter will follow close behind, using all his wiles as a tracker to claim his prey. And behind him, very often, will come his entire band, ready to join in the feast.

The San's bow is small and light, and his arrows fragile — he relies on the poison to kill his prey rather than on any wound which is inflicted.

Nowadays metal arrowheads are often used. They are made from fencing wire taken from farms adjacent to San areas. The metal is not smelted — smelting is an art unknown to the San — but hammered with stone on a stone anvil.

A mere scratch with such an arrowhead is usually sufficient to enable the poison to penetrate an animal, but its effect is slow.

Water from grasses in the beast's stomach is sometimes drained off and drunk — perhaps the only real water the San will have for weeks. Then the band will feast until next to nothing is left, for it may be their last meal for many days.

Mostly about 1,5 metres tall, the San bear certain physical resemblances to the pygmies of the central African forests. Their mongoloid

A San hunter of the Kalahari, or Kgalagadi, with his bow, arrows and skin bag.

A San girl. The golden skin is characteristic of the Kung group.

San hunters in the Kalahari Gemsbok National Park. Lithe, lean and superb shots, they are in pursuit of gemsbok.

Forgotten skills of the San artists

A dance by a group of Kalahari San in celebration of plentiful food.

A typical San man of the central Kalahari, cheerful and proud.

Engravings, presumably the work of San people, who devised this form of art.

no longer practised.

One characteristic that the San certainly share with the ancient Egyptians is their talent for art. There are many excellent examples of San rock paintings in Botswana, from Kalakamati in the north to Tsodilo in the north-west and Manyana in the south.

Although the painting is now a forgotten art, the San still delight in telling ancient stories and legends in their staccato, clicking tongue.

They love to play music on hand-made instruments, and most of all, they love to dance. Dancing has deep religious significance for the San. Sometimes a dancer will fall into a trance, and he then believes himself to be in a supernatural state capable of seeing vast distances and of performing cures.

Another side of the San's artistic nature is seen in the making of karosses — blankets made from game hides. These are sold as sou-

eyes, high cheekbones and yellowish skin seem to indicate Asian origins. Some scientists say they may have been related to the earliest Egyptians.

Some San groups possess a characteristic known as steatopygia — excessively developed buttocks and fatty thighs, which act as a larder to be drawn on in lean times.

The men and women have parch-ment-like skin with many deep wrinkles which expands as enormous amounts of plants and meat are eaten.

In former centuries both the San and the Khoikhoi followed the unusual custom of cutting off the top joint of the little finger of the left hand of male babies. This custom was apparently connected with their ancient hunting mythology and it is

venirs and there is a good trade in them in Gaborone and Francistown.

In the 1930s it was feared that the San people were dying out, but today there is evidence that their numbers are actually increasing. Certainly, Africa's last hunter-gatherers are alive and well in Botswana's great wilderness area of the Kalahari or Kgalagadi Desert, and in the northern portion of Namibia.

San making a fire. Twirling a stick between the palms creates the necessary friction to set the tinder alight.

A San family at home in one of their typical primitive dwellings.

A San hunting group pitches camp on the site of a kill.

Rock engraving, presumably of San origin, at Twyfelfontein, in Damaraland.

A small San boy. These children are notable for their delicate bone structure.

The miniature set of bow and arrows carried by San men during courtship.

These rock engravings at Twyfelfontein date from the Stone Age.

LESOTHO

LESOTHO

MANY NAMES HAVE been used to describe the huge massif of volcanic basalt that crowns southern Africa with its highest mountains. This great highland comprises nine-tenths of the 30 500-square-kilometre state of Lesotho, home of the Basotho. They know the area simply as Maluting — meaning a place of mountain ranges. To Europeans it is the Switzerland of Africa, the rainy roof of southern Africa, and the principal watershed of the country where the Orange, Caledon and several other large rivers have their source.

The basalt highlands came into existence about 150 million years ago. At the end of the long period of deposition of the Karoo Sequence, nature suddenly switched her tools of creation, substituting fire for water.

The Karoo sediments had been laid down under water, and their final phase was a vast swamp inhabited by dinosaurs. The caprice of creation produced two totally different rock systems on part of the surface of this primeval bog: first was a layer of dry, wind-blown material which formed the brilliant, yellow-to-red Clarens sandstone; then above this sandstone, from the 2 000-metre level, a layer of material of entirely different composition was thrust forth by a large-scale eruption, and a mass of dark, molten basalt, nearly 1 500 metres thick, covered the Clarens sandstone in a fairly level, roof-like slab.

Onto this roof fell rain and snow. Basalt is crumbly and easily eroded by water, and the whole mass dwindled. Today only a tattered, but spectacularly beautiful, remnant is left. It is roughly triangular, with its apex in the north, on the summit of Mont-aux-Sources, where the borders of Lesotho, Natal and the Orange Free State meet. From the apex to the southern base of the triangle, where the Orange River drains to the west, are 250 kilometres of wild, eroded mountain landscape, laced with deep gorges through which streams find their way to rivers in still deeper gorges.

The eastern side of this basalt triangle is the Drakensberg; the western side is the Maluti ('the range'). The two sides of the basalt mass diverge and eventually are separated by more than 200 kilometres of valleys and mountain spurs such as the Thaba-Putsoa and the Central Range. In this mountain jumble are waterfalls, gorges, deep pools, long stretches of white-whipped water rich with trout, cattle posts, trading stations and missions — linked to one another by bridle paths.

In autumn these great heights and their tumbling hillsides are painted crimson by countless red-hot poker flowers. Winter then brings great blankets of snow, and the waterfalls turn to stalagmites and stalactites of ice. In spring the mountains ooze water and innumerable jewel-like springs glitter in the sunshine. Summer is the time of mighty electric thunderstorms, when great rumblings reverberate from one rock face to another and flashes of lightning stab down into the deep valleys.

Preceding page: The road to Lebono in the valley of the Little Caledon River, a world of sandstone foothills, willow-lined streams, rock shelters and caves.

Lesotho is treated as a single touring region. Turn to page 429 for a more detailed map of the region, plus extensive touring information.

ORANGE FREE STATE

NATAL

Caledon

Butha - Buthe

Senqu (Orange)

ORANGE FREE STATE

Maseru

Caledon

LESOTHO

429

Mafeteng

Semonkong

Mohale's Hoek

Senqu (Orange)

NATAL

CAPE PROVINCE

MAJESTIC LESOTHO

THE RIVER KNOWN to the Basotho as the Mohokare ('willow trees') from the wild willow trees that grow along its banks, and as the Caledon to Europeans, who named it in honour of the governor of the Cape, the Earl of Caledon, flows through a spacious valley. The grass-covered plains of the Free State lie to the west and the Maluti mountains to the east. Good soil, plentiful water and a moderate climate make this valley desirable to most forms of life.

In former years, great herds of plains game grazed in the valley. San hunting clans made their homes in the natural shelters of the Clarens sandstone and decorated them with superb multi-coloured paintings, attaining in this part of Africa the highest level of their unique culture.

Some time in the 18th century, offshoots of the same African people who had occupied Botswana found their way eastward across the central plains and discovered the delights of the valley of the Caledon. The San people and the game animals were forced out and the newcomers settled in their place. Each group had its own leader and was known by the name of a totem, or emblem, which was held taboo. All the groups spoke the same language but had no collective name. Until the beginning of the 19th century these immigrants prospered, but then came disaster. Political disturbances were stirring in the area now known as Kwazulu. Shaka was in the process of forming the Zulu nation, and refugee groups fled in every direction. Several found their way up the escarpment from Natal onto the central plains. They were destitute, and the sight of the Caledon Valley, with crops of sorghum and herds of cattle, all owned by a people who were not warlike or numerous, was very attractive.

The grim period of the Lifaqane ('migratory wars') began. The Caledon Valley became the scene of murder, raids and skirmishes. Many of the resident people lost everything. Remnants of them fled into the mountains and became cannibals. Others escaped from the once prosperous valley to join robber chiefs such as Mzilikazi, ending their lives in bloodshed, or eventually resettling as far away as the Zambezi River.

Those that remained did so because in the Caledon Valley there are many majestic sandstone hills — fragments of a higher plain eroded away by the river and its tributaries. These hills were the African equivalent of European feudal castles. The best of them had perhaps only one easily defended route to the summit. The sandstone cliffs were far too sheer for climbers, yet the summits provided enough grass and water for defenders and their livestock to survive a siege. Such natural fortresses saved the inhabitants of the valley from annihilation.

It was at this critical stage in their history that these people were called by the invaders the Suthu, because they had first been encountered in Swaziland, living on the banks of the Usutu River. The name means 'dark brown', and aptly describes the muddy water of the river. Descendants of this group are generally referred to now as Sotho, though those who live in Lesotho prefer to be known as Basotho ('Sotho people').

At the upper end of the Caledon Valley were the Kwena ('crocodile') people under a young chief named Lopoqo, nicknamed Moshoeshoe ('the shaver') owing to his skill in rustling the livestock of his neighbours. When Europeans encountered him they corrupted his nickname to Moshesh. This chief had a small stronghold on the flat-topped hill known as Butha-Buthe, but then heard of a remarkable hill some 100 kilometres down the valley. He determined to move to this stronghold. Accompanied by his following and their livestock, he made a hazardous journey, attacked on the way by cannibals.

Moshoeshoe reached the new stronghold late one afternoon in July 1824. At first sight he was disappointed with the place. It seemed too low and vulnerable. But as the shadows came and Moshoeshoe approached closer the hill seemed charged with strength and character, and loomed higher. Moshoeshoe climbed to the top and was delighted. It was spacious, richly grassed, with springs and pools and impregnable cliffs. There were only two possible routes to the summit, both easily defended, and the hill dominated one of the most fertile parts of the Caledon Valley. Moshoeshoe named it Thaba-Bosiu ('the mountain of the night') because it had appeared to gain power from the darkness. He built his village on the summit and never again left the place.

It was this stronghold that became the rallying point for the Basotho nation. Refugees coming from many other groups joined Moshoeshoe here, and from being the chief of the mountain he became paramount chief and king of the entire country. Moshoeshoe and Thaba-Bosiu form the basis of the modern history of Lesotho. Both the man and his stronghold remained invincible throughout the years of turmoil.

Butha-Buthe

South-west of a flat-topped natural fortress once used by the Basotho chief, Moshoeshoe, the British established an administrative post in the 1870s which they named Butha-Buthe — the original name of the fortress.

The village is an assembly of commercial and administrative buildings, a market place and a communal shop designed in the shape of a large straw sun hat where local handicrafts are sold. Trees shade the street. Nearby is the Caledon River and the border point of Caledonspoort.

The Butha-Buthe district has many caves containing San rock paintings. Sixteen kilometres from Butha-Buthe, near Sekubu Mission, is the colossal series of rock shelters named Sekubu ('place of the hippopotamus'). The shelters were occupied by San, cannibals, Basotho, and later used as stables.

A road leads from Butha-Buthe for 72 kilometres over the mountains to the Malibamatso ('dark pools') River, where there is a camp much used by fisher-

The old fort at Hlotse. It was attacked by the Basotho but never captured.

THINGS TO DO AND SEE

Angling The mountain streams of the highlands offer some of the best trout fishing in Africa. Rainbow trout were introduced to these streams in 1932. The fingerlings were carried in on pack mules and released in the streams, where they flourished in unpolluted water rich in natural foods. Yellowfish and barbel are found in lowland rivers such as the Caledon and the Orange.

Curios The Basotho are expert potters and weavers of baskets and mats. Their distinctive sun hats provide useful gifts and souvenirs. The national costume of the Basotho is a colourful and beautifully patterned blanket. Such blankets are specially made for the Basotho. Over the years fashion has produced many changes in design and colour. There are handicraft markets in all the towns. Maseru has a large display centre, managed by the village industries' development corporation.

Riding Trail-riding through the mountains of Lesotho is a favourite pastime. Organized companies provide horses, guides and camps.

Sightseeing The all-weather partly-tarred mountain road across the central highlands is sensational, but demands careful driving. The waterfalls of Lesotho, particularly Le Bihan Falls, are unforgettable. In summer, cloud formations above the Caledon Valley provide a dramatic backing to vividly coloured, oddly shaped mountains.

Skiing There are ski runs in the Butha-Buthe district, with lifts and cabins at the Oxbow lodge.

Walking The bridle paths through the highlands were made for pack animals and horses, but provide walkers with scenically exciting routes over the mountain ranges into the valleys — to pools, waterfalls, view sites and camping sites.

men, riders and winter skiers. The route is stunning, with signs warning drivers that they negotiate it at their own risk. From Malibamatso the road continues to the diamond mine at Letseng-la-Terae, and then to Mokhotlong and down the Drakensberg to Natal. This is the route of the annual Roof of Africa motor rally, staged in September.

Hlotse

In 1876 an Anglican mission was founded near the river named Hlotse ('dead meat'). The river is said to have been given this name because travellers habitually threw lumps of meat into it to distract the crocodiles and make the river safe to ford.

A magistracy and a small fort were built at the mission, and this was the core of the village which today is the administrative and trading centre for the Leribe district.

During the Gun War of 1880 between the government and the Basotho, several attacks were made on Hlotse.

The village was sacked but the fort held out. A famous visitor during these times was General 'Chinese' Gordon, who spent three days here on a fruitless attempt at a peace settlement.

Huts built of stones in a rock shelter in the foothills of the Maluti range.

The place of the fat, unmarried women

Mafeteng

This trading and administrative centre was somewhat invitingly named Mafeteng ('the place of the fat, unmarried women'). The local people have always admired plumpness in women, but it is jocularly said of the early women of this little town that they were on the verge of becoming hippos.

Mafeteng is a busy place for trade and its dusty streets are generally alive with a crowd of horsemen, whose blankets and straw sun hats make a colourful scene unique to this part of Africa.

The mountain scenery east of Mafeteng is spectacular. A rough road leads to a trading station named Masemouse in the valley of the Makhaleng River. Overlooking this valley is the 2 908-metre Thaba-Putsoa ('blue-grey mountain'), the highest peak in this part of Lesotho.

Maseru

In 1869 Maseru ('red sandstones') was founded as the seat of the British administration of the newly proclaimed Protectorate of Basutoland. The first British representative, Commandant James Bowker, made his camp here, and it became customary to refer to all trading and administrative centres of the country as 'camps'.

Huts in the village of Matsieng, dominated by a flat-topped hill.

Maseru lies in the valley of the Caledon, close to Maseru Bridge, the principal customs and immigration gateway into the Orange Free State. It is the capital of the modern state of Lesotho, with considerable development in industry and tourism. The village industries' development co-operative has a large store here, built in the shape of a sun hat. It offers for sale curios and handicrafts of the Basotho.

Mohale's Hoek

The chief Mohale presented ground to the British administration in 1884 for the establishment of a 'camp' as a centre for his district. The village of Mohale's Hoek, which occupies the site of the camp, has shady streets and an assortment of stores, offices and houses.

Overlooking the town golf course is a handsome sandstone hill, Castle Rock. South of the town is the cave of Motlejoa and his cannibal band, who used it as a stronghold in the 1820s.

Mokhotlong

On the eastern side of Lesotho, in the upper valley of the Senqu River, lies one of the remotest villages in southern Africa — the administrative centre of Mokhotlong ('the place of the bald-headed ibis'). A 56-kilometre track connects the village with the Sani Pass, leading down the Drakensberg to Natal. Only four-wheel-drive vehicles are permitted to use this track and much of the traffic consists of pack animals and horsemen. The summit of the Sani Pass is 2 860 metres high.

The highest mountain in southern Africa, Thabana-Ntlenyana (3 482 metres) is nearby. Riding, climbing and skiing are popular here.

Morija

South of Maseru, 43 kilometres down the valley of the Caledon, lies the principal mission founded in Lesotho by the French Protestants, and named Morija after Mount Moriah in the Holy

---

THE CANNIBALS' SONG

We are cannibals, we eat people.
We eat thee, we eat people.
We eat the brain of a dog,
and that of a little child.
We eat the fingers of people.
We eat the fat of mankind.

This is part of one of the blood-curdling songs that used to be sung when packs of cannibals roamed Lesotho, hunting down their fellow men like wild animals. One of the first French missionaries to reach Lesotho, Thomas Arbousset, estimated that between 1822 and 1828 about 30 000 human beings were eaten by cannibals. Originally the result of starvation, cannibalism later became a matter of preference.

Pits were dug and thongs stretched across the mountain paths to trip victims. They would be tied together and driven like cattle to the cannibals' mountain strongholds.

The usual method of execution was to place the victim in a pot overnight. His lips and little fingers would be cut off, and he would be left to bleed to death. The feast would be divided strictly according to rank, with choicer parts given to the leaders.

The Basotho favour a blanket as their national dress — their country is bitterly cold in the winter months when the high mountains are covered in snow. The blankets are brilliantly coloured and often have patterns especially devised for Basotho national celebrations.
1. A gallant of Lesotho in characteristic conical straw hat, wearing the blanket of independence, the crocodile totem of the ruling Kwena group and the torch of freedom.
2. A youth, a recent initiate from a circumcision school. He is now a dandy in decorated loin cloth.
3. A little girl in a fibre skirt and blanket, with a doll on her back.
4. A mature woman in dress, blanket and woollen cap.
5. A diviner in beaded skirt, tunic and cape, with rattles on her ankles and medicine horn on her breast.

The nimble fingers of a royal tapestry weaver at work in Maseru.

Goldsmithing at Royal Crown — unique jewellery in the process of creation.

Tapestry weaving is an art much practised by Basotho women. The royal tapestry weavers create special designs.

5

Selling handicraft work at the craft centre, Maseru — an animated, colourful and cheerful scene.

Maseru, capital of Lesotho, in its setting in the valley of the Caledon River on the western side of the country.

Mountain retreat once littered by corpses

Land. From its founding in 1833 it has been a centre for teaching, printing, Bible study and mission work.

The seat of the paramount chief, now the king of Lesotho, is close to the mission at Matsieng, where Moshoeshoe's son Letsie, heir to his father's kingdom, was educated.

Mount Moorosi

For a natural fortress and a rustlers' lair, it would be difficult to find a finer location than Mount Moorosi (2 356 metres). This mountain, 45 kilometres up the valley of the Orange from the village of Moyeni, completely dominates a rugged landscape.

Moorosi was chief of the Baphuthi people, who migrated here from Natal about 1850. Moorosi was bold and enterprising, and attracted to his leadership a mixed crowd of San and Basotho, as well as his own people. With the mountain as their stronghold, they raided the Orange Free State and the Cape and accumulated a rich booty of livestock, which they traded for gunpowder, weapons, liquor and other items.

In 1877 the British established an administrative post at Moyeni and tried to impose law and order on this unruly part of the world. Trouble with the rustlers was inevitable. The British arrested Moorosi's son, Doda. Moorosi's men attacked the gaol, rescued Doda and fled to the mountain. All demands for the surrender of Doda were rejected with insults and threats.

The British marshalled 250 men of the Cape Mounted Rifles — a tough, foreign-legion-type professional force — and, supported by yeomanry, sent it to subdue the rustlers. On 8 April 1879 the British force attacked the mountain stronghold but were driven back, with 34 men killed and many wounded. Two Victoria Crosses were awarded after the attack.

For months there was continuous fighting in the district. On 29 May the rustlers surprised a small outpost and shot 21 of the sleeping soldiers. One yeoman was captured in another skirmish, taken to the top of the mountain and decapitated in view of the soldiers below. The man's head was impaled on a pole and his body thrown over the precipice.

On 5 June the British attacked again. They were once more beaten back, leaving 14 casualties on the slopes. A Victoria Cross was awarded to Surgeon-major E. B. Hartley, who risked his life crawling to aid the wounded.

Attempts were made to settle the conflict by negotiation. The Prime Minister of the Cape, Sir Gordon Sprigg, met Moorosi half way up the slopes of the mountain, but nothing came of their discussion.

A bitterly cold winter passed, with the mountain covered in snow, and the fighting dragged on. The rustlers continued their raids and remained as truculent as ever. The British bided their time, preparing for a decisive attack. They assembled 400 men of the Cape Mounted Rifles and offered a reward of £200 for Moorosi or Doda, dead or alive, and £25 for the first man to reach the top of the mountain.

At midnight on 19 November the attack began. For four days previously artillery had shelled the mountain. The soldiers had blackened their faces and dressed in soot-covered clothes. They fought their way up the mountain for five hours. Ladders were dragged up and used to scale the topmost cliffs. As dawn came, the first soldier, Lieutenant C. J. Sprenger, reached the top. One of

---

THE MOUNTAIN ROAD — A SCENIC SWITCHBACK ON THE GRAND SCALE

The road that penetrates the high mountain massif of Lesotho starts 18 kilometres south of Maseru and leads eastwards directly towards the mountain wall of the Maluti, climbing to the summit of a plateau at the foot of the mountains.

There are many caves in this area and one of them, Ha Baroana ('home of the little San'), has a superb gallery of rock art.

Overlooking this area is the 2 885-metre Machache. The road climbs the range by means of the Lekhalo la Baroa ('pass of the San'). The summit of the pass is 2 260 metres high and the view westwards is superb. Eastwards, the road descends steeply into the gaunt valley of the river known as the Makhaleng ('place of aloes'). There is a hard, half-day return walk up the river's tributary, the Ligala, to the cascades and waterfall of Qiloane.

The road twists across the valley, climbs to the 2 331-metre summit of the pass known as Molimo Nthuse ('God help me') and continues until it reaches the summit of the Blue Mountain Pass, named after the 2 902-metre Thaba-Putsoa ('blue-grey mountain').

Crossing the deep valleys of the Likalaneng and Senqunyane rivers, the route passes fishing camps where the smell of trout grilling often lingers in the cool night air.

After reaching the summit of Cheche's Pass (2 560 metres) the road descends to the valley of the Mantsonyane ('small black') River, reaches the new administrative centre of Thaba-Tseka, crosses the Senqu valley, and is joined at Taung by a track from Mokhotlong.

A stream fed by heavy rain.

The mountain wall of the Maluti.

Sheep grazing near Molimo Nthuse.

San paintings in a rock shelter at Ha Kotso, in the foothills of the Maluti.

A GLUTTON'S FATE

The Basotho have a proverb: 'The rock of Raboshabane is slippery' — implying that life is full of pitfalls.

And so it proved for Raboshabane, a greedy character who thrived for a while during the period of the migratory wars.

His rock is a 200-metre-high pinnacle in the upper valley of the Koro-Koro River. Raboshabane established himself on the summit and informed the people living in the valley that, for a very moderate commission, he would undertake to store their harvests on the rock, guaranteeing absolute safety.

The Koro-Koro Valley was fertile and subject to frequent raiding. The idea of a safe store for their crops was attractive to the peasants. Soon Raboshabane had eight large storage huts on the summit of his rock, all filled with millet. He began to demand extortionate prices from the trusting peasants for meagre portions of their own crops.

Raboshabane's prosperity was great, but his success ran to fat — very dangerous at a time when cannibalism was rife.

One of the exploited peasants was an ill-nourished, scraggy fellow. He made his way to the stronghold of a cannibal brotherhood, relying on his unappetizing appearance to give him immunity from the man-eaters. He gave them a mouth-watering description of the fat glutton who lived on top of the rock.

A few nights later, 27 dark figures crept silently up the face of Raboshabane's rock, carrying clubs, spears and a large cooking pot. They stormed into the huts, dragged out Raboshabane and examined him. He was as advertised.

At this point the plot went awry, for after Raboshabane had been eaten, the cannibals chased the millet-owners away and presented the millet instead to Moshoeshoe in order to gain his favour. He gave it to other cannibals as part of his plan to convert his people from their flesh-eating habits.

The decorated walls of a hut, the traditional blanket, and a beer pot.

the rustlers looked down into his face.

'Don't come up here', he said considerately. 'I'll shoot you.'

'You go to hell', replied Sprenger, and shot the man dead. Sprenger then clambered onto the summit, followed by the rest of the soldiers. There was a hand-to-hand struggle. The summit was covered with the bodies of 200 of Moorosi's men, about 200 women and children killed by gunfire, and 43 soldiers. Another 84 soldiers were wounded. Moorosi's body was found among those of his men. His head was cut off and planted on the pole which had been used to exhibit the head of the captured yeoman. Doda and some of the rustlers had escaped by jumping over the precipices. A few survived, but others, including Doda, were so badly injured in their desperate escape bid that they died later.

The mountain slopes and summit are today a shrine of the Baphuthi and the burial site of leading chiefs.

Moyeni

In 1877 the British government established a centre for the administration of the south-western part of Lesotho, known as Quthing ('at the great river'). The village, or camp, was called Moyeni ('the place of wind'). In the Gun War of 1880 the place was hurriedly abandoned and later rebuilt on its present site. The original buildings of the village were occupied by the Paris Evangelical Mission and converted into an industrial school.

The modern village is noted for its trees and views. The surrounding region is rugged. It was a favourite resort of San and the many rock shelters in the area are decorated with a variety of paintings.

There are caves in the Ratlali

A stream cascades down to join the Orange River.

The Orange, twisting through mountains near Quthing.

Majestic waterfall at 'the place of smoke'

gorge, 8 kilometres from Moyeni, and in the grounds of the Masitise Mission on the outskirts of the village.

Qacha's Nek
The south-eastern portion of Lesotho, where the Senqu River makes a huge bend, changing the direction of its flow from south to west, is a wilderness of mountains and valleys, traditionally a rustlers' roost and the lair of many adventurous characters. Qacha is a corruption of the name of the celebrated chieftain Ncatya who had his eyrie on the high saddle that today carries his

The twin summits of Thabana-li-'Mele, meaning 'the teats of a woman'.

name and provides the only practical route from the Transkei to Lesotho.

The village of Qacha's Nek is the centre for a district where the Basotho grow wheat and corn in the valley of the Senqu, and run cattle and goats on the mountain slopes.

Blanketed horsemen come in to trade with storekeepers, and transport trucks make a difficult way along a steep road to reach Matatiele, in the Griqualand East district.

There are several missions in the Qacha's Nek district and there is superb riding along the bridle paths, which provide the sole links to many outlying trading stations, schools and administrative points.

Roma
The headquarters of the Roman Catholic mission in Lesotho is at Roma.

The mission was opened in 1862 when the Basotho chief Moshoeshoe granted a site to Bishop J. S. Allard and Father Joseph Gerard. They named the place Motse-oa-'Ma-Jesu ('village of the mother of Jesus'). They were joined by sisters of the Holy Family of Bordeaux.

In 1870 Father Francois Le Bihan, the discoverer of the Le Bihan Falls, built a burnt brick chapel and a double-storey building at the mission, which are still standing.

There are primary and secondary schools here, seminaries, a library and a hospital. There is also a cathedral and the University of Lesotho, which began in April 1945 as the Catholic University College, at first linked to the University of South Africa. When the Catholic University College opened there were six students under Father Paul Beaule, but its growth was rapid. It is now the National University of Lesotho.

The 193-metre plunge of the Maletsunyane Falls.

Qaba, with its eroded potholes and strangely shaped rocks.

Semonkong
In the 1870s the missionary Father Francois Le Bihan explored the mountain highlands, then completely wild and inhabited only by a few renegades and rustlers. At Semonkong ('the place of smoke') he discovered the colossal ravine into which the Maletsunyane River tumbles in a 193-metre-high waterfall. This great waterfall, often known as the Le Bihan Falls, is the highest in southern Africa. (The 614-metre Tugela Falls are really a cascade.)

Semonkong is named for the mist arising from the waterfall. The village is a small trading centre and is linked to the outside world by a bridle path and an airstrip.

Teyateyaneng
The village of Teyateyaneng ('shifting sands') takes its name from a river that was given the name because of the quicksands in its bed. In 1886 a camp was established by the British as a centre for the administration of the region. An Anglican mission was also founded and the well-known missionary Father William Wrenford worked

Near Semonkong, a winter wonderland of crisp white snow and ice.

A patrol of the Lesotho Mounted Police in the Caledon valley near Thaba-Bosiu. Lesotho's force is the world's only rival to the 'mounties' of Canada.

THE BASOTHO OF LESOTHO

The land is Lesotho, the language is Sesotho, an individual is a Mosotho and the people are Basotho. The nation was born in a welter of bloodshed, strife, starvation, cannibalism, and the stubborn courage of the founder-chief Moshoeshoe.

Moshoeshoe's first clash with Europeans came when, against his wishes, his men, angered by redrawn boundaries, began to rustle livestock from the settlers on the central plains.

These activities inevitably provoked reprisals. In 1852 the British, who were then controlling the Orange River Sovereignty, sent an army of 2 500 soldiers to subdue Moshoeshoe. Nothing was achieved. Moshoeshoe's men continued raiding into what became the Orange Free State when the British abandoned the central plains.

In 1858 the Orange Free State went to war against the Basotho in an effort to stop the raids. The Free State army reached the slopes of Thaba-Bosiu, but withdrew without attempting to attack so formidable an obstacle.

Open warfare broke out again in

The ruins of Moshoeshoe's residence.

June 1865. The Basotho were driven from their outlying mountains and on 3 August the Free State army arrived at Thaba-Bosiu, determined to launch an attack. About 3 000 men in the Free State force faced 20 000 Basotho — and the formidable mountain. Both sides used artillery. Moshoeshoe had attracted a few deserters from various British army units, and they formed a small artillery force on the mountain.

On 8 August the Free Staters tried to storm Thaba-Bosiu. Their commander, Louw Wepener, and ten other men, were killed, and the rest of the attackers driven back.

Moshoeshoe, however, also had his troubles. The mountain was hopelessly overcrowded with people and livestock. At least 16 000 head of cattle were killed by falling over the cliffs while another 40 000 are estimated to have died of thirst and hunger. The war dragged on until March 1868 when the British declared Basutoland a protectorate.

Moshoeshoe died on 11 March 1870 at the age of 84. He was buried on Thaba-Bosiu.

The British maintained their protectorate over the country, which they called Basutoland, for almost 100 years. The descendants of Moshoeshoe remained the heads of state but a British resident commissioner administered the country.

Lesotho became an independent state on 4 October 1966.

Moshoeshoe, founder of the Basotho nation, a man of courage and intelligence.

The isolated peak of Qiloane, and the sandstone cliffs of Thaba-Bosiu.

here for nearly 50 years. His thatched home still stands in the village.

The local people are known for their weaving. Riding is popular and there are numerous specimens of San art in the rock shelters of the area.

Thaba-Bosiu

Among the world's most remarkable natural fortresses, Thaba-Bosiu is unique. It is the classic example of the flat-topped hill-fortress used by the Basotho in times of war.

Thaba-Bosiu lies in the valley of the Phuthiatsana River. Massive natural erosion by the river has borne away most of the original level of the valley and left isolated segments resembling pieces of a jig-saw scattered on a floor. Each piece is detached, irregular in shape but flat-topped. Steep precipices make these hills almost impregnable.

Thaba-Bosiu is one of these hills. Its highest point is 1 769 metres above sea level and about 200 metres above the level of the river valley. The summit is grassy and several square kilometres in extent. During the rainy season numerous hollows fill with water. A few springs also surface here but tend to dwindle during the dry winters.

A notable and curious feature of the summit is a large dune of fine red sand. It is said that the spirit of the Basotho chief Moshoeshoe lingers on in this dune — and just as he, during his lifetime, would never leave the mountain top, so this dune is permanently attached to it. Wind causes the dune to wander about the summit, but if it approaches the edge, updraughts force it back. It is even said that samples of the sand, carried away as souvenirs by visitors, will somehow contrive to return to Thaba-Bosiu from all corners of the earth. The ruins of various residences, including Moshoeshoe's house, stand on top of the mountain. There are also cannons and other mementoes from the past.

Nobody lives on the summit today, but the village of Ha Rafutho lies at the foot of the path that climbs the mountain up the Khubela Pass. Guides escort visitors to the summit from this road. Where the path reaches the summit there is a vivane ('luck heap') of pebbles. Such piles of pebbles can be seen at the approaches to many former residences of great chiefs, and at strategic 'points of no return' where pathways cross borders into the areas of other groups. The pebbles are deposited by travellers, who mutter a plea to ancestral spirits for protection against confrontations with chiefs, trials, accusations, enemy attacks and unexpected dangers.

A poignant memorial on the mountain is the outline of a human foot that can be seen on a projecting ledge facing the isolated pinnacle of Qiloane. This is said to be the outline of the foot of Mateleka, a son of Moshoeshoe.

Mateleka was forbidden to marry the girl of his choice. The next day he climbed down to the ledge and carved out the footprint. Other people saw him in this precarious position and called to him to return to the summit. He climbed up, but the next morning he descended to the ledge, placed his foot in the carving and leaped over the precipice to his death.

The atmosphere of Thaba-Bosiu is pervaded by a sense of great strength and serenity. Moshoeshoe and several leading personalities of his following are buried on the summit, and the mountain is the great national shrine of the people of Lesotho. Memorial lectures are given here by scholars annually on 12 March — Moshoeshoe's Day.

SWAZILAND

SWAZILAND

THE KINGDOM OF Swaziland, though only 17 000 square kilometres in area, has an extraordinary diversity of scenery. On its western border stands a jumble of mountains — the northern end of the highveld of central South Africa. Well watered by rain and mist, the mountains are thickly grassed and are today densely planted with trees.

In these green highlands gold, asbestos and iron are found. Mining and timber make this region the most economically important part of Swaziland. The road from Mbabane to Piggs Peak and past the Havelock Mine to Barberton is an adventure into a world of deep valleys, steep gradients, beautiful views, and rivers cascading through narrow gorges in many waterfalls.

The highest peak in these mountains is Bulembu ('place of the spider') whose dome-like summit is 1 862 metres above sea level. The road from Piggs Peak to Barberton twists around the mountain slopes and winds down into that place of ugly memories — the sinister Valley of Death at Barberton. Before the road was built, prospectors blazed a bridle path into Swaziland which climbs near to the summit of Bulembu and crosses a great cleft by means of the Devil's Bridge, a natural stone causeway. This old path can still be followed and the climb is worth the effort. From the summit, almost the whole of this African kingdom can be seen.

The mountainous area is known to the Swazis as the Nkhangala ('treeless country'). To the east it gives way in easy stages to the lowveld — called by the Swazis the Hlanzeni ('place of trees') — stretching away to end in what resembles a garden wall. This is a long, level-topped range known as the Lebombo ('ridge') which serves as the border with Mocambique.

The entire width of Swaziland, facing eastwards from the heights of Bulembu, is 120 kilometres. North to south the country is 180 kilometres long, and on a clear day distant peaks, even those on the furthest borders, can be seen. In any direction, in any season, the view is awe-inspiring.

The lowveld is the sub-tropical garden of Swaziland. In it the soil is deep and rich with the humus of countless trees. The climate is warm and the rainfall heavy, with rivers and streams providing large quantities of water for irrigation. Sub-tropical fruits and nuts grow to perfection. Sugar cane flourishes while cattle fatten on the sweet grazing and the nutritious leaves and seed pods of the acacia trees.

East and west from the lowveld, the impression is very much that of a gigantic garden contained within high walls. The mountain range of the Lebombo in the east and the massive jumble of peaks of the Kobolondo, Makonjwa and Ngwena ranges in the west hold the country in their rocky arms. The deep blue sky seems to rest on these heights like the mighty dome of a fairy palace.

Preceding page: Young Swazi gallants, with stick and club, all set to go courting in their best finery. Each man spends many hours of preparation for such occasions.

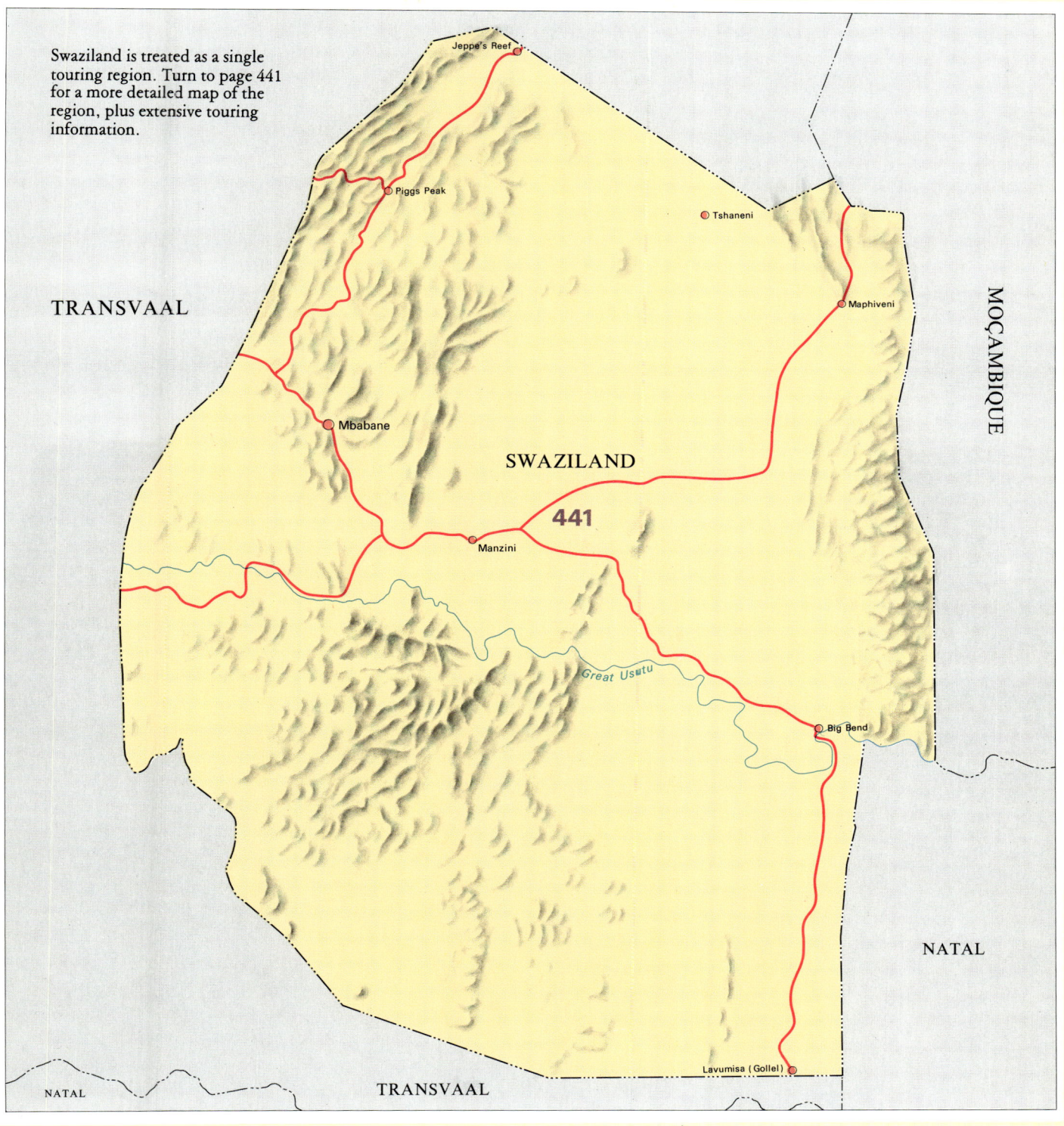

Swaziland is treated as a single touring region. Turn to page 441 for a more detailed map of the region, plus extensive touring information.

TRANSVAAL

MOÇAMBIQUE

Jeppe's Reef

Piggs Peak

Tshaneni

Maphiveni

Mbabane

SWAZILAND

441

Manzini

Great Usutu

Big Bend

NATAL

Lavumisa (Gollel)

NATAL

TRANSVAAL

THE SWAZI LEGACY

THE PEOPLE WHO became known as the Swazis were part of a large migratory mass which moved down the east coast of Africa about 1750. These people, led by a chief named Dlamini, called themselves the Nguni, and became fragmented into separate groups. One of these groups, under Ngwane III, migrated into Swaziland.

These first few families settled somewhere in the hills overlooking the Pongolo River. There Ngwane died and was buried in a taboo forest ever since known as eMbilaneni ('the hallowed place'). One family, that of Ngolotsheni, was appointed as guardians of the grave — descendants still carry out this task.

The settlers increased in numbers and called themselves the Ngwane, after their first leader. Ngwane's grandson, Sobhuza, gradually became ambitious. It was the time of nation-building among the other sections of the original migratory stream. The Zulus, Pondos, Xhosas and other Nguni people were expanding their territories and absorbing weaker neighbours. Sobhuza had no difficulty in securing control of the southern half of Swaziland, if only because there was hardly anybody living in the area. A few San hunted game in the lowveld, while in the valley of the Usutu River lived fragments of the groups inhabiting the highveld of central South Africa. These people spoke a different language from that of Sobhuza's followers. Sobhuza's people named them the Suthu because they first encountered them in the valley of the Usutu ('dark brown') river. The Suthu were either absorbed into Sobhuza's following or driven away. The name Sobhuza's people had given them was later applied to all similar groups in the interior of South Africa. In their language it took the form of Basotho.

Sobhuza was a particularly active nation-builder. His pocket army steadily brought every independent group in the future Swaziland under the control of their chief. The developing nation, however, also had troubles. It was frequently attacked by the Zulus. At one stage Sobhuza had to beg support from Portuguese traders in Lourenco Marques. These allies aided him in suppressing a rebellion among his conquered people, and also proved to be great benefactors for they presented Sobhuza with the first seeds of maize. This quickly became the staple crop of all the indigenous South African peoples.

Sobhuza's successor, his son Mswazi, became chief in 1836. By that time European missionaries and traders were already making their way into the country, which they called Swaziland after its chief.

For 32 years Mswazi guided his people through difficult times. When he became chief the Zulus were at the peak of their power and for many winter seasons their raiding armies swept northwards.

Mswazi died in 1868 and was succeeded by a seventeen-year-old son named Ludvonga, whose capital was built close to the Mdimba mountains at Nkanini ('the place of perversity'). The age of the Zulu raids was over. The Voortrekkers had broken their power and Ludvonga's short reign was a time of peace. He was succeeded by Mbandzeni during whose reign occurred the bizarre 'concession rush' (see box, page 448).

Mbandzeni's grandson, Sobhuza II, ruled Swaziland for 62 years — the monarch of an independent and increasingly modern state. Today a great number of tourists visit the country.

A Swazi farmyard, with a background of granite hills. Such a place is typical of a family home but the land always remains the communal property of the nation.

THINGS TO DO AND SEE

Angling The rivers of Swaziland are well stocked with scalies, yellowfish, barbel, bream, eels, and — in lower reaches where the water is warm — tiger-fish.

Camping and caravanning There are caravan and camping sites at Timbali, in the Ezulwini Valley, and near the hot springs at Siphofaneni, on the Usutu River.

Curios Swaziland is one of the richest sources of curios in Africa. There are markets at Manzini, Mbabane, Piggs Peak and the border post at Oshoek.

Carvings, pottery, mats, beadwork and many other items are made by the Swazis. Their work is original, and they are highly skilled.

Hot springs There are hot springs at the Royal Swazi Hotel and Spa and at Siphofaneni.

Sightseeing The Mlilwane Wildlife Sanctuary has walks and trail rides, and the Shiselweni district has beautiful mountains and valleys.

Rural life The Swazis are a handsome and proud people, and their costume is brilliantly coloured. Permission must always be requested before a photograph is taken. The annual ceremonies of the Incwala (around the first new moon of the year) and the reed dance in August/September are two impressive and spectacular rituals. They are held in the royal kraal of Lobamba. Visitors are welcome.

The valley of the Usutu River in central Swaziland, densely populated and the site of the royal villages.

Big Bend

The first sugar to be produced in Swaziland was manufactured in 1958 in a small mill brought from Natal to Big Bend — at the great bend of the Great Usutu River. A larger mill came into production in 1960 and now the village produces about 80 000 tons of sugar every year, most of which is exported. The cane is grown under irrigation from the Great Usutu River.

The village of Big Bend is the centre for the cane producers and mill workers.

Ezulwini

The Ezulwini ('place of heaven') Valley was named after one of the early Swazi royal kraals. The main east-west tarred road of Swaziland descends into the valley down a steep pass from Mbabane.

On the eastern side stand the Mdimba Mountains, riddled with caves and a traditional retreat of the Swazis during times of trouble. Several of their former kings are buried here in taboo caves.

On the floor of the valley stands a cluster of hotels and a caravan park. This valley is the principal playground for tourists in Swaziland. There is a casino, hot springs, the Mlilwane Wildlife Sanctuary, the Mantenga Falls in the Little Usutu River, the Swazi royal residence of Lobamba, the national stadium and the parliament building.

Overlooking the valley is the

The Usutu River making its great curve at Big Bend in the lowlands.

A miracle of engineering amid the wilderness

mountain named Nyonyane ('place of birds'). On the summit are ruins of a prehistoric fort built by members of a long-vanished Suthu people.

Maize, citrus and sub-tropical fruits and nuts grow in the valley.

Havelock Mine
The Havelock Swaziland Asbestos Mine is in such a mountainous and isolated region that it is astonishing to discover this massive complex of mining buildings, self-contained village and sports fields.

The mine goes back to December 1886, when a group of Natal men formed the Havelock Swaziland Prospecting Syndicate, named after Sir Arthur Havelock, governor of Natal.

Many traces of minerals were found, but the inaccessibility of the area made it unprofitable to mine anything other than gold. The syndicate vanished, but prospectors continued to search the area.

In 1923 Gowran Fitzpatrick,

A Swazi maiden in a dress specially made for the local market.

A Swazi diviner. Her people believe she has communion with spirits.

caretaker of the Piggs Peak Mine, which had closed down, employed Swazi prospectors in the area and one of them found asbestos in the valley of the stream known as the Duduzi ('loamy soil').

Fitzpatrick pegged 40 claims and offered the discovery to the Canadian firm of Turner and Newall, one of the principal asbestos mining houses in the world. The company investigated the find, but were uncertain whether the deposit was extensive enough to warrant the vast financial outlay necessary to establish a mine in such a remote area.

Five years later another prospector, Izaak Holthausen, also found asbestos in the bed of the Duduzi stream. He and his partner, Herbert Castle, worked for months to determine the extent of the discovery, then approached Turner and Newall and gave them details of the find.

The company spent eight months checking the outcrop before they became convinced of its potential profitability.

They eventually paid £240 000 for the 100 claims held by various prospectors — which at that time was the largest amount ever paid for a base mineral prospect in South Africa.

A miracle of engineering overcame

The cableway from the Havelock mine to Barberton in the Transvaal.

A moon moth, newly emerged from its cocoon, prepares for its first flight.

The Havelock asbestos mine. A huge deposit of white asbestos is being worked in the valley of the Duduzi stream.

Despite its small area, Swaziland has wide variations in vegetation and climate, making it excellent bird country. At least 462 species make their homes somewhere in the hills and bush of the country. In addition to the permanently resident species, there is a considerable influx of migrants from Europe and North Africa in summer.

The red-chested cuckoo, noted for the punctuality of its arrival every year (within a few days of 20 September), is one of the best-known of the migrants. Its call of 'piet-my-vrou' is so distinctive that the sound is always regarded a sure proof of the start of spring.

Lilac-breasted rollers — sometimes called blue jays — and the lovely red bishop birds add colour to the scenery, and their feathers feature in the personal decorations of Swaziland's warriors and princesses.

Long-tailed widow birds flutter over the grasslands. The tails of the males make them ponderous in flight, but the relatively drab little females bustle about, building nests for their mates in tufts of grass.

Chorister robins sing their splendid songs in the woods and undergrowth; cattle egrets cluster around grazing livestock, feeding on the grasshoppers and other insects disturbed by the moving beasts; hadedas fly down the river valleys, calling out in raucous tones until the cliffs echo to their sounds.

A visitor does not need to be an expert to appreciate the abundant bird life of Swaziland. One of the joys of travelling through this compact country is to observe the bird life in each successive zone. A handbook on bird identification, a pair of binoculars and a camera make excellent companions in Swaziland.

The golden-breasted bunting, a delightful and exquisitely coloured bird, small, agile and shyly inquisitive.

The wattled starling, a cheeky, enterprising bird, easy to tame.

The Natal francolin, a ground bird, always ready to hide itself.

The sand plover, ever ready to defend vigorously its territorial claims.

A giant kingfisher making a meal of a freshly captured fish.

The violet-eared waxbill, brilliantly coloured, graceful and constantly alert.

A sensational drive through the mountains

the problems of the remoteness of the region. An aerial cableway was built, running for 20 kilometres over the mountains and valleys to Barberton.

Fifty-two pylons carry the two cables of the cableway. In places the cableway is 188 metres above the ground, and its longest span is 1 220 metres across a deep valley.

At a steady speed of 9,5 kilometres an hour, 224 carriers ride the cableway at a time, each carrying 170 kilograms of asbestos or general freight.

Since the opening of the mine in June 1939, its entire output and all its requirements — stores and equipment — have been carried over the mountains by this spectacular, efficient cableway.

Today a road also connects the mine to Barberton and to Piggs Peak. This is a true scenic switchback of a road, with tremendous gradients and drops. Although it should be avoided in wet weather, in sunny conditions it offers the visitor a sensational drive.

Hhohho

The extraordinary name of Hhohho is applied to the north-western division of Swaziland. Originally it was the name of the royal residence of the Swazi chief Mswazi, who settled here in 1850 in order to be as far away as possible from the Zulus, who persistently raided the southerly parts of Swaziland. The name Hhohho is said to be derived from the barking of the numerous baboons that live here.

The royal kraal was in the natural parkland of the lowveld on the west bank of the swiftly flowing Lomati River, which has its many headwaters and springs in the mass of mountains that form the Makonjwa Range and the Kobolondo Heights. Makonjwa means 'that which is pointed at' — the name reflects a belief held in many parts of southern Africa that certain mountains, if pointed at, unerringly produce rain; Kobolondo is a European corruption of Gubolodhlo ('precipitous heights'), and aptly

The approach to the Swazi Houses of Parliament at Lobamba.

A typical Swazi hut of the old-time beehive shape — cool, snug and dry.

Time for bathing, always a welcome, cool relaxation on a hot afternoon.

THE MIGHTY USUTU, HEART OF THE NATION

The heart of Swaziland is the valley of the Usutu River and its tributaries. In this broad, warm, alluvial valley, overlooked by high mountains, live the majority of the Swazi people. Here too is the royal residence of Lobamba, the buildings of the Swazi parliament, the great assembly area where the nation gathers for ceremonies, and a cluster of hotels, caravan parks, hot springs, casino and game reserve.

At the point where the Little Usutu tributary joins the main stream stand the voluptuously shaped twin peaks known as Sheba's Breasts. Yet another tributary flows to reach the main stream through Ezulwini ('the place of heaven') Valley. The main road climbs steeply up the northern side of this valley to reach the capital of Mbabane.

Further down the valley, also on

The Nkomati near Piggs Peak.

its northern side, the rocky mass of the Mdimba Mountains looms — a taboo area, whose caves are used by the Swazis as a burial ground for their kings. Fields of maize and sorghum, groves of oranges and tung nuts cover the valley floor.

As the river loses altitude, the bush of the lowveld first infiltrates and then overwhelms the arable lands. Ranches replace farms and herds of cattle move through the bush.

Sugar cane grows where man has driven back the trees and used the river to irrigate the land.

The Little Usutu on its way through the Ezulwini Valley near Mbabane.

---

describes one of the most complex mountain massifs in southern Africa.

Yellowfish, scalies and bream are caught in the Lomati River.

Lebombo

The mountain range of Lebombo ('ridge') forms the full 150-kilometre eastern border of Swaziland.

With a plateau summit averaging 600 metres above sea level, this ridge provides a cool residential area, contrasting with the warm lowveld west and east of it. The soil is fertile, rainfall is high, and there are several villages along its length. The best known among these are Siteki, Lomahasha and Mhlumeni.

The Mantenga Falls, where the Little Usutu River joins the Usutu.

Swazi maidens at the reed dance, when they pay respects to the Queen Mother.

Swazi warriors at the Incwala, held at the time of the first new moon of the year.

Deep in the great plantations that cover the mist belt of Swaziland.

Malkerns

The centre of a citrus-growing region, Malkerns is also a major producer of pineapples, avocados and tomatoes. Golden Ranch has 365 hectares of pineapples under cultivation, and the international canning company of Libby's has a cannery here. Potatoes are also grown in this region.

Manzini

A trader named Bob Rogers set up a store in a tent on the banks of the Mzimneni River in 1885. The place became known to the Swazis as Manzini, after the local chief. The following year, Rogers was bought out by Albert Bremer, who built a hotel and a store. A town named after him,

Town that survived years of conflict

Bremersdorp, started to grow around the trading centre. In 1890 a British, Boer and Swazi triumvirate was formed to control the increasing European interests in the country, with Bremersdorp as its capital.

It was all but destroyed during the Anglo-Boer War, when it was first occupied by Lieutenant-colonel Ludwig von Steinacker and his extraordinary 'Steinacker's Horse' command of the British Army (see box, page 269), and then, on 23 July 1901, the Ermelo commander of the Transvaal army attacked the town, looted it and set it on fire.

At the end of the war Mbabane replaced Bremersdorp as the capital. However, the town was rebuilt, renamed Manzini, and became the main commercial centre of Swaziland.

Manzini is a pleasant little town with streets shaded by flowering trees.

There is a curio market where handicrafts are sold: mats, pots, carvings, spears, shields and many other novelties.

There is also an airport and an industrial township with several substantial factories. The climate is warm to hot, and Manzini has a relaxed way of life.

Manzini, the seat of the Roman Catholic bishop of Swaziland, has a cathedral completed in 1961.

Mbabane, sheltered in a green and pleasant valley.

Trees in great variety give Mbabane a park-like setting.

The colourful curio market of Mbabane.

The Swazi people favour cloth of lavish colour and design in their costume. Feathers are also important and some skins are used.

1. A Swazi girl in dancing dress with head streamers and ornamental dancing shield. This is the costume of puberty observances.
2. A Swazi bride, her hair built up and ochred to display her married status. In a workaday skirt she is ready for a life of chores.
3. A young warrior in the full dress of the Swazi army, characteristic stick in right hand, shield and spear in the left hand.
4. A new bride wearing her apron under the armpits in token of respect, a small mirror in her left hand as she surveys her new headdress.
5. A princess of the royal family, her hair bleached blond. She wears the feathers of the bishop bird.
6. The full ceremonial regalia of the Swazi army worn for dancing at the annual Incwala festival.
7. A young girl in everyday dress.
8. A slightly less formal military dress worn during the festival of the Incwala.

SWAZILAND

STRANGE RITUALS OF THE SECRET INCWALA

One of the most spectacular ceremonies to be seen in Africa is the Incwala, performed in Swaziland at the time of the first new moon of the year.

What is known as the Little Incwala starts at the preceding new moon. Priests are sent to each of the principal rivers of Swaziland, and to the sea, to obtain samples of water. When they return with these samples to the royal residence at Lobamba a season of ceremonies and songs continues until the moon is full.

Then the six days of the Incwala rituals begin. First the youths of the nation gather at the king's residence to sing songs in his praise and ask him to test them. Towards evening the king orders the youths to march 40 kilometres to a place named Egundwini.

The march has to be completed before midnight. Then, in the light of the full moon, each boy must cut from a lusekwane tree the largest branch he thinks he can carry. With these branches on their shoulders the youths march, singing, back to the royal residence. They deposit the boughs in the great cattle kraal of Lobamba and only then can they rest and refresh themselves.

The branches are used to construct a bower where the secret parts of the Incwala will be performed. The full strength of the Swazi army is mustered for the ceremony, and all the principal officials of the nation are present. They dress in special Incwala costumes of skins, and sing songs — full of sibilants and sounding like the sighing of the sea — which are taboo for the rest of the year and may not be recorded.

The climax comes when a pitch-black ox is driven into the bower and subjected to various ceremonies. Outside, the youths have gathered in the kraal and there is great excitement. The black ox is suddenly driven out from the bower. In a surging mass the youths overpower it and carry the inert body above their heads back into the bower where parts of the expiring animal are used in the ritual.

A second black ox is caught by the youths and taken into the bower, but this one is eventually released.

On the fourth day of the Incwala the king joins the warriors in a great dance, with the women of the royal family and court joining in.

The fifth day is reserved for seclusion and meditation. No work is done. On the last day of the Incwala a huge bonfire is lit and the warriors beg the ancestral spirits to show their acceptance of the Incwala by bringing rain. On nearly every last day of the Incwala rain does fall and the ceremony ends in feasting and rejoicing.

The Incwala is a complex ceremony of great significance to the Swazis. Visitors are welcome to watch but must leave during taboo sections, and they must always obey instructions from officials.

No attempt must be made to photograph or sound-record taboo parts of the ritual. The penalty is to have equipment broken.

The upper reaches of the Usutu River flowing past a pulp-producing mill.

Mbabane

A former British Army gunner, Bombardier Michael Wells, opened a pub and a store in 1888 at a fording place across the Mbabane ('bitter') River.

The pub flourished, for it was on a pathway followed by many fortune-hunters lured by gold discoveries.

A village sprang up around the store and at the end of the Anglo-Boer War the British chose it as the seat of their administration in Swaziland.

Mbabane lies at the edge of the highveld of Swaziland. Cool, healthy and well-watered, it is surrounded by luxuriantly grassed hills.

The main street, Miller Street, named after one of the earliest Swazilanders, Allister Miller, is lined with commercial and government buildings.

At its southern end stands the lively Swazi market, one of the principal markets for curios in Africa.

Mhlambanyati

The Colonial Development Corporation planted 50 000 hectares of pines

4   5   6   7   8

Where iron was mined 28 000 years ago

in 1949 in the Usutu Forest, on the northern side of the Great Usutu River. A pulp mill jointly owned by the corporation and Courtaulds was built on the river at Bhunya.

The village of Mhlambanyati ('where the buffaloes swim'), on the banks of the stream of the same name, is the commercial and residential centre for the forestry workers.

Mlilwane Wildlife Sanctuary
More than 1 000 head of large game animals live in the Mlilwane Wildlife Sanctuary.

There is a camp with chalets and a caravan park; there are many sites from which to view game and birds; and trail riding and walking are particularly rewarding.

The sanctuary was founded in July 1964. It covers 4 450 hectares of middleveld and highveld. King Sobhuza II supported the establishment of the sanctuary by becoming its first patron. The sanctuary is open from dawn to dusk every day.

Ngwenya
One of the oldest mines in the world was sited in the Ngwenya ('crocodile') Hills. Scientific tests of ash deposits indicate that the iron-rich bedrock of a cave on Lion Peak was mined, astonishingly, in 26 000 B.C.

The presence of iron in this border area was discovered, therefore, during the Middle Stone Age. In 1946 the Swaziland Geological Survey proved the large extent of the deposits and the Colonial Development Corporation,

---

THE KING WHO SOLD HIS NATION AND STARTED THE CRAZY SCRAMBLE OF THE SWAZILAND CONCESSION RUSH

In 1880 two prospectors, Tom McLachlan and Walter Carter, negotiated a concession with the Swazi king, Mbandzeni, giving them exclusive rights to prospect the mountains north of the Komati River. Two other prospectors, James and David Forbes, obtained rights to the area south of the Komati. Both groups struck it rich — and started the crazy free-for-all known as the Swaziland Concession Rush.

As news of the gold strikes spread, a flood of Europeans poured into Swaziland. Mbandzeni's capital, Mbekelweni, was besieged by fortune-seekers pleading for exclusive rights to various pieces of land.

By the time he died in 1889 Mbandzeni had granted more than 500 concessions covering practically every activity imaginable, and nearly every hectare of his country.

In return for these monopolies, the prospectors paid him an annual rent. But many of the concessions were absurd.

One held by a Mrs. Parr claimed exclusive rights to the running of refreshment rooms on railway stations. Somebody else had, in fact, secured a concession to build a railway. Another ingenious character had a concession covering the generation of steam, which would block any railway construction unless he was bought out, naturally at vast cost. Adventurers, swindlers and a few individuals who genuinely loved the country and wanted it to prosper took part in this scramble.

One speculator even had a concession for a mint. There were other concessions covering lotteries, pawn-broking, patent medicines, banking

and countless activities which, almost 100 years later, have still not commenced in Swaziland.

Mbandzeni was succeeded by his son, Bhunu, and then, on 12 November 1899, by Bhunu's baby son, Sobhuza II, who was destined to be one of the wisest of all the leaders of any African state.

With his mother, Ngolotsheni, the infant king lived at Lobamba, where the Swazi councillors and his grandmother, Labotsibeni, a woman renowned for her wisdom, ruled the nation. While the king grew up, this council of regents had to contend with considerable changes following the Anglo-Boer War.

A British special commissioner arrived and established his head-quarters at Mbabane, which rapidly grew into the principal administrative centre of what became the British protectorate of Swaziland.

For two-and-half years a British-appointed commission had the nightmarish task of endeavouring to clear up the concession tangle. Some concessionaires had vanished, others reappeared with the coming of peace, and lawyers were having a glorious time lodging claims, seeking damages and compounding the entire fiasco with their own greed.

The mess was partly resolved with the expropriation, at considerable cost, of all monopoly concessions interfering in the proper administration of the country.

However, this still left the Swazis as a nation of squatters living on private property, for every hectare of the country was claimed by one concessionaire or another. In 1907 one third of Swaziland was expropriated from the concessionaires, and this

area became the home of the Swazis. The British ran the country, leaving the Swazis to control their own affairs.

In this rather peculiar setting, Sobhuza grew up. In 1916 he went to Lovedale College in the Cape for two years. He then returned to Swaziland and began his final training for his role as head of state.

In 1921 Sobhuza was installed as the Swazi king and his first major task was to lead a delegation to London to challenge the legality of the concession situation, and especially the allocation of only a third of his country to his people. The petition failed and Sobhuza, then 21 years old, returned to Swaziland determined to fight the concessions in any possible way.

The principal land concession — a notorious piece of manoeuvring known as the Unallotted Land Concession — had been carefully devised by a shrewd concessionaire named John Thorburn. This secured ownership not only of all land not already allocated to concessionaires, but also of all land which became available in the future, when existing concessions lapsed. Through this iniquitous document, Thorburn planned to own, eventually, the entire country.

Sobhuza tested the validity of this concession by a legal action, but he lost. For the next 15 years he concentrated on strengthening his own position and gaining experience. Then, in 1940, he once again petitioned the British Crown and achieved some success. The British government bought land from various concessionaires and added it to that already owned by the Swazis. By this means, the Swazis secured half of

their country.

Sobhuza then organized a national fund to raise money by contributions from the Swazi people. This fund purchases land as it becomes available from concessionaires, and restores it to the Swazi nation.

With the coming of World War II the Swazis fought with the allies in North Africa and Italy, distinguishing themselves as courageous soldiers.

It was during the war — in 1940 — that the Colonial Development and Welfare Act was passed in Britain, and Swaziland was granted its first substantial infusion of capital. Altogether £6 million was allocated to develop the country.

At the end of the war, Swaziland surged forward into an era of economic development, with large-scale afforestation under the colonial development scheme as well as by private enterprise. Sawmills and factories were opened and holiday resorts established.

In 1967 the British granted the country full independence. Sobhuza led his nation into the new era with a minimum of disturbance, and without the corruption and exploitation common in so many newly independent states. Swaziland was fortunate in having this kindly, strong and intelligent leader.

In elections his supporters secured an overwhelming majority in parliament. The European residents of the country, known as Swazilanders, had an affection for Sobhuza which was equal to that of the Swazis themselves. Sobhuza II died in 1983.

On the troubled continent of Africa, Swaziland is a pleasing example of a country at peace with itself and the world.

in association with the Anglo-American Corporation, financed an iron-ore mine and a railway to convey ore to Lourenco Marques for export.

Before modern mining destroyed the ancient workings, they were explored by archaeologists. The early workers, using primitive tools, had excavated substantial quarries — one was 100 metres long, 25 metres wide and 13 metres deep.

They extracted haematite, the red iron ore that they used to decorate their bodies. Specularite, a sparkling black iron ore used in ancient rituals and for cosmetics, was also mined.

The 1 828-metre summit of the Ngwenya Hills is Swaziland's second highest peak after Bulembu (1 862 metres).

South of the mine is the railway terminus, Ka Dake, the Oshoek immigration and customs post on the Transvaal border, and a curio market.

Piggs Peak

High in the mountain country of north-western Swaziland lies the administrative, forestry and former mining centre of Piggs Peak.

Immediately to its west loom the mountains along the border with the Transvaal; southwards is the deep valley of the Komati River; northwards is the edge of the escarpment, with the lovely Pamponyane Falls; and in the east, the countryside falls away more gently to the lowveld.

The birth of Piggs Peak goes back to January 1884, when William Pigg discovered gold in what he called the Devil's Reef.

Mining continued on this reef for over 60 years, despite the extreme difficulty of transporting stores and

The Pamponyane waterfall, where the Lomati sweeps down to the lowveld.

THE RIETBOK RAM

The Lebombo ridge near Siteki was the stronghold of a colourful renegade — Bob MacNab (*above*), known to his friends, the Swazis, as the Rietbok Ram.

MacNab was born in Ayrshire and came to South Africa under the New Scotland land settlement scheme in the eastern Transvaal.

But his instincts were those of a cattle raider rather than a settler and he was soon carrying out rustling sorties from Swaziland into the Transvaal, Natal and Mocambique.

In 1871 he was caught in Newcastle, Natal, and ordered to be deported. He was sent under guard to Durban and placed on board the R.M.S. *Natal,* due to sail for Britain. Just before the ship sailed MacNab dived overboard, swam ashore and stole a horse to take him back to Swaziland.

The Swazis adored him and Mbandzeni, their king, was his personal friend. Farmers in neighbouring states would have lynched him, but once across the Swaziland border MacNab was inviolate and his behaviour impeccable.

One celebrated episode in MacNab's life was his confrontation with a ruffian named Charlie Dupont, who had stolen from a local widow. She appealed to MacNab for help.

When MacNab arrived at Dupont's house Dupont ran inside and refused to see him. But after some argument he appeared to relent.

He opened the door slightly and the trusting MacNab walked in.

Dupont promptly shot him in the chest.

MacNab was badly wounded and it was Dupont's mother who nursed him back to health. From the grateful MacNab she extracted a promise to forgive and forget — which he honoured.

Plantations of gum and pine trees in the Piggs Peak district.

machinery into what was a particularly inaccessible region.

Modern road building has made Piggs Peak the centre of some famed scenic drives.

The area around the village is now densely wooded by the plantations of Peak Forest and Swaziland Plantations.

In the village is a market offering handicrafts and curios, and a remarkable weaving industry started in 1958 by Mrs. Coral Stephens. This weavery has produced hand-woven curtains for theatres and private homes in many parts of the world.

Textiles and carpets in exquisite colours and unique patterns are also produced.

Shiselweni

The name Shiselweni ('place of burning') was originally applied to the capital of the 19th century Swazi king, Sobhuza I, built on the hills on the southern border of Swaziland.

Today Shiselweni is a citrus and cattle district with several small towns and villages, such as Nhlangano, Hlatikulu, Mahamba, Mhlosheni and Hluti.

The roads through the area are rough, but the scenery makes an

exploration worthwhile.

There are hotels at Nhlangano and Hlatikulu.

Siteki

The small administrative centre of Siteki takes its name from the Swazi isiTeki ('the place of marrying'). Mbandzeni, the Swazi king, granted veteran status to one of his regiments stationed here, thus giving the warriors the right to marry. The village is on the plateau summit of the Lebombo ridge, and is noted for its cool, healthy climate.

In the 1880s the area was used as a hideaway by many professional rustlers and hold-up men such as Bob MacNab and Charlie Dupont (see box).

Tshaneni

The largest project carried out in Swaziland by the Colonial Development Corporation is the Swaziland irrigation scheme at Tshaneni. A 65-kilometre irrigation canal directs water to 11 000 hectares of land on which sugar cane is grown. The Mhlume mill produces more than 88 000 tons of refined sugar every year.

Tshaneni ('the small stone') is the commercial and residential centre for this irrigation project.

NAMIBIA

NAMIBIA

Contents:

THE NAME Namibia means a place of great arid plains. It is an apt name for this vast country, which stretches far beyond the horizon, sun-bronzed and untamed. The northern part of the territory is more of a grassy, tree-covered savanna wilderness than a desert. Nevertheless, for most visitors to Namibia, the lasting impression of this extraordinary land is of its harshness, its lack of surface water, the almost overwhelming flood of sunshine, the bronze-coloured mountains and rocks and the strange vegetation.

This vast land remains one of the most sparsely populated on earth, with a population of 1 300 000 in its 823 145 square kilometres — over half a square kilometre of land for each human being.

The land discourages a dense human population. It is as though this region was under the spell of a sorcerer. The evil genius is the cold Benguela Current sweeping up the full length of the 1 400-kilometre coast. The temperature of the water, 12°C in winter and 22°C in summer, is too cold to allow much evaporation. This cold current, meeting hot, dry winds, causes fog to move in over the desert sustaining life in an otherwise arid area. Nevertheless, the inescapable fact is that, while Namibia's soil is excellent, its scenery spectacular, its minerals rich, for most of its area it is under the curse of drought.

The first Europeans who ventured into the interior of Namibia were explorers, and later came gun-runners and liquor dealers attracted by the readiness of local peoples to trade their livestock for these goods. In 1878 the British annexed the guano islands along the coast and the harbour of Walvis Bay, which was considered to be a convenient place from which to exercise discipline and extract taxes.

Further south, in the bay known to the Portuguese as Angra Pequena, a German trader, F.A.E. Luderitz, outmanoeuvred the British in 1883 by acquiring from the Nama people rights to the area around the bay. In 1884 the German Government placed the area under their protection. By 1884 they had imposed their government over the entire region, except for the awkward little British enclave of Walvis Bay and the guano islands.

The Germans remained until World War I, when South African troops invaded the territory from the south. At the end of the war, what was then called German South West Africa was put under the administrative control of South Africa by the League of Nations.

Following considerable controversy and a long period of civil unrest, elections were held under United Nations supervision in 1989 and Namibia gained independence from South Africa in March 1990. Four years later — in 1994 — South Africa ceded the territory of Walvis Bay to Namibia. This most interesting and scenically dramatic country, endowed with great natural wealth, has taken its place proudly among the sovereign nations of the world.

Preceding page: The face of the wilderness. Tufts of grass growing in open areas between the sand dunes of the Namib Desert.

ANGOLA

ZAMBIA

Kunene

Okavango

Etosha Pan

Tsumeb

1

469

NAMIBIA

BOTSWANA

2

Swakopmund

Windhoek

Walvis Bay

A T L A N T I C   O C E A N

1

455

Fish

Lüderitz

4

Keetmanshoop

1

Orange

CAPE PROVINCE

Namibia has been divided into
two touring regions, the south
and the north, with the purple
line indicating the division
between them. Turn to the page
indicated (large purple
numbers) for a detailed map of
each region, plus extensive
touring information.

LAND OF UNRELENTING SUN

NORTH OF THE Orange River lies what hunters and traders of the 19th century called Trans-Orangia, then a no-man's-land of arid plains shimmering in the heat and sun-bronzed rocky hills baked by relentless sunshine. Here the colours are the purples, reds, oranges and strange blues of the bricks of a disused furnace.

Vegetation is scanty and those plants that grow in this harsh setting are the toughest of all the grasses, shrubs and trees found in nature's garden. In this wilderness every plant is said to be thorny. This is not quite true; some of them seek protection by being unpalatable, others keep below the surface of the ground, with little exposed save a few gnarled-looking leaves or boughs.

Animal life has to be resourceful, stubborn and frugal in its requirements. The few watering places that exist here have always been the rarest and most desirable of treasures, and men who made their homes in the area fought over them with the frightening brutality of battles for survival.

San hunters, Khoikhoi, European renegades fleeing from justice in the Cape — these were the human pioneers of the area. Wild and restless, they lived free of control by any government. Only in 1884 was this no-man's-land brought under the control of the German Empire, and it became part of the colony of German South West Africa. Even then the men of the wilderness area remained unruly and stubborn, obsessed with feuds and personal hatreds.

Travelling through this area is made easy today by tarred roads and signposts. Even with these comforts, however, the traveller is aware of the essential wildness of a land so unfamiliar to the visitor from the outside world that he might almost have landed on another planet. Nearly everything is new: scenes and objects are strange, the perfumes of the night and the aromas of the hot winds of the day are exotic, wild, and untouched by any intrusions from the world of industry and pollution. The immensity of this wilderness is emphasized by the presence of the canyon of the Fish River. For 161 kilometres this gigantic scar stretches across the face of the land. Countless vicious storms have raged over this landscape in past ages and the result of their fury is this wound, as sharp and cruel as the weal from a lash.

The jagged ravine cuts deep into an arid surface of almost frightening harshness. Succulents and stunted, drought-resistant vegetation provide an occasional patch of green. Heat waves shimmer, mirages taunt the eye with deceptive lakes of glittering water, and dust devils spiral to the sky with snake-like sinuosity. From one horizon to the other, the silence is complete — even the wind seems to be hushed.

Where the Fish River joins the Orange, in the extreme south of the country, the landscape is especially harsh and inhospitable. It obviously wishes to be left alone. San and prospectors are the only humans who, undaunted even by such hostile conditions, have found their way into this area.

Fred Cornel, one of the classic old-time prospectors, claimed to have been taken by a San to a lost valley there, with a floor covered in diamonds. Sunstroke had made the prospector half delirious and he could never find the place again. Perhaps it was just a mirage or a dream which lost itself in nightmare. Other prospectors have found zinc, copper and gem-stones in this area, as well as strange minerals as yet of little value to man. All of them are held in the iron gauntlet of this great wilderness, beyond the reach of profitable exploitation.

The desolation, solitude and silence remain inviolate, as they have for countless millions of years. Man still hears a siren voice luring him there to search and find, but the price of intrusion is often death or ruin, and seldom a treasure more tangible than a phantom.

Ai-Ais

On the floor of the Fish River Canyon, in an extraordinary setting of high, forbidding cliffs, where the temperature can reach 48°C. at noon and is seldom lower than 35°C. even at night, a hot spring reaches the surface. The Khoikhoi and San were the first discoverers of the spring and they named it Ai-Ais, meaning 'very hot' — its temperature is 60°C. These early people believed that the mud and water of the spring, which is rich in fluoride, sulphur and chloride, had medicinal value. Occasionally they would visit the spring, but the oppressive heat and the absence of grazing

The face of a parched land. The grass seems to beg the heavens for rain.

The mission at Bethanien, oldest European building in Namibia.

The extraordinary rock formation known as Bogenfels, on the Skeleton Coast. It is in the prohibited area.

made the floor of the Fish River Canyon unsuitable for permanent human habitation.

Today the government maintains a modern resort at the spring, with flats, caravans and camping grounds. There are private baths, a restaurant, shop, and a large open-air swimming bath.

Ai-Ais is closed to the public from 1 November until mid-March — the hot months when life can be unbearable on the floor of the valley.

Brukkaros

One of the most distinctive landmarks on the main road from Keetmanshoop to Windhoek is the extinct volcano known unromantically by the name of Brukkaros ('trouser apron'), from a costume worn by a Khoikhoi clan who lived nearby.

The crater is about 2 kilometres in diameter, with a flat, rock-littered floor. In 1930 the Smithsonian Institution used this crater as an observation point for a detailed study of the surface of the sun. Bare of vegetation, hot and inhospitable, this mountain of dark-coloured lava looms steeply from a sun-scorched plain.

Fish River Canyon

Second in size only to the Grand Canyon of America, the Fish River Canyon is one of the natural wonders of Africa. The canyon is 161 kilometres long, up to 27 kilometres broad, and 549 metres deep, with sheer, precipitous sides.

THINGS TO DO AND SEE

Angling There are many good angling spots along the coast. Rock lobsters are numerous. The rivers are too erratic in their flow to contain many fresh-water fish, but the Fish River's connection as a tributary to the Orange allows yellowfish, barbel, mud mullet and other river fish to enter it during flood times, thus replenishing the fish population in its pools.

The dam in the Fish River at Hardap is well stocked with many types of southern African fresh-water fish.

Antiquities There are museums in Windhoek, Swakopmund, Keetmanshoop and Lüderitz. A narrow-gauge railway train has been preserved at the Windhoek museum. A weird locomotive preserved outside Windhoek station consists of two narrow-gauge locomotives welded back to back.

Boating Lüderitz Bay has protected water for all kinds of boating; Hardap Dam has amenities for all types of pleasure craft.

Camping and caravanning Namibia is a rewarding place to explore. Caravanners and campers are well served. There are sites and facilities at such places as Ai-Ais, the Daan Viljoen Game Reserve, Hardap Recreation Resort, Lüderitz, Swakopmund and Windhoek.

Game viewing The Daan Viljoen Game Reserve at Windhoek, the Namib-Naukluft Park and other nature sanctuaries protect many different species of wildlife.

Sightseeing Once considered to be accessible only to four-wheel-drive vehicles, Namibia now has tarred roads leading to most places of interest. The Fish River Canyon has a well-made gravel road running along the eastern verge of the canyon and leading to several viewing sites.

Swimming Swakopmund is the principal coastal resort of Namibia. There are also good beaches at Lüderitz. Sea water from the Benguela Current is often cold but the air is generally hot. There is usually more sunbathing than swimming at these beaches and care should always be taken to avoid excessive burning in the hot sun.

There is a public resort at the hot mineral springs at Ai-Ais and a swimming pool at the Hardap Dam.

Suddenly, eternity lies spread out at your feet

The Fish River meandering through its gigantic canyon nearly 550 metres below the plains. The river dries up during periods of drought.

It is set in a harsh, stony plain scantily covered with drought-resistant vegetation such as succulents and kokerbooms. The edge of the canyon is reached with startling suddenness. There is absolutely nothing to warn of the scenic drama ahead and the unwary could step straight into eternity. A road running for 58 kilometres along the eastern side of the canyon leads to a series of viewing sites. Paths wind to the floor of the canyon, where the Fish River flows through a succession of deep pools that dry up during periods of drought. There is a hot spring called Sulphur Spring on the banks of the river, and at its lower end there is the resort of Ai-Ais, built at another large hot spring. Hiking through the canyon is a popular endurance test for the hardy. Permits for these excursions must be obtained from the Department of Agriculture and Nature Conservation or the Directorate of Nature Conservation in Windhoek.

A medical examination is recommended and hikers are only permitted to do the trip in the relatively cool months from 1 May to 30 August.

Hikers generally cover the 80-kilometre stretch to Ai-Ais starting from the most northerly viewing sites. Food must be carried.

Yellowfish and barbel are plentiful in the pools of the canyon. Baboon, klipspringer, mountain zebra, leopard, snakes and monitor lizards live in the canyon, but not people. During World War II two Germans evaded detention as enemy aliens by hiding in the canyon. They were not found for the duration of the war, and date pips which they left on the ground grew into the palms that surround Sulphur Spring today.

Sunsets and dawns in the canyon can be sensational, and the experience of camping overnight next to one of the pools is eerie.

Gobabis

To the east of Windhoek, close to the border of Botswana, lies the little cattle ranching town of Gobabis, named from the Khoikhoi word Hoantabis, meaning 'a place where elephants drink'. This sun-baked town is the centre for a spread of ranches, while across the border lies the principal cattle country of Botswana. From the ranches cattle are taken by truck to abattoirs at Swakopmund or Cape Town.

Gobabis started as a Rhenish mission station in 1856 and in 1894 a military post was established here. The Swartnossob River, close to the town, flows erratically, but its pools retain water even during the dry season. These pools, and a spring of fresh water, attracted both men and animals to the area. The Hereros call the town ePako ('the pool').

The opening of the branch railway to Windhoek in 1930 transformed Gobabis from a rough little cattle outpost into a busy railhead. It became a municipality in 1944.

Hardap Dam

In its upper reaches, before descending into its great canyon, the Fish River is harnessed by a wall 32,2 metres

GHOST TOWNS SHROUDED IN THE DESERT SAND

The Namib Desert ghost towns of Elizabeth Bay and Kolmanskop — currently being restored — are haunted by wind and shrouded in shifting sand. Frayed strands of electric wire hang from the walls of derelict houses; dusty globes on skeletal cords swing from the ceilings in the desert wind; refrigerators, stoves and geysers lean at crooked angles; the water taps have run dry.

In the early 1900s Kolmanskop was inhabited by about 700 families. Each morning the ice-vendor came down the streets, which were even then smothered with sand, to deliver the daily ration of ice-blocks and cold drinks to each household.

Large metal screens around the gardens and corners of the houses helped to keep the sand at bay and a sand-clearing squad cleared the streets every day.

Until the beginning of World War I Kolmanskop was the headquarters of the country's diamond industry. Wages were good and virtually everything was free, including company houses, milk deliveries, and other fringe benefits.

The end of the railway at Kolmanskop, a ghost town near Lüderitz.

But eventually the diamond diggings around Kolmanskop — like those of Elizabeth Bay — yielded less and less. Families started to move away. One day Kolmanskop's sand-clearing squad failed to turn up, the ice-man stayed away, the school bell rang no more.

Undisturbed, the wind gusted along the deserted streets as it had since time began. Soon the metal screens collapsed and the pretty gardens and tidy streets were buried under the sand. Doors and windows creaked on their hinges, cracked window panes stared sightlessly across the desert. A new ghost town had been born.

Tours of Kolmanskop may be arranged through Consolidated Diamond Mines. Tourists cannot visit Elizabeth Bay.

Abandoned cart lies rusting at Elizabeth Bay.

The shrouded kitchen of Kolmanskop's club house.

Inside the ruined recreation hall in Elizabeth Bay.

Sand smothers what was once a Kolmanskop home.

A town steeped in the colonial past

Hardap Dam, in the Fish River near Mariental — a popular recreational area.

high, creating the largest dam in Namibia – a total of 25 square kilometres in area.

On the north-eastern shores of the Hardap Dam a resort has been developed with a caravan park, bungalows and a restaurant. There is swimming, boating, and fishing for large- and small-mouth yellowfish, blue kurper, carp, barbel, mud mullet and mudfish. An aquarium in the resort exhibits fish from this region.

A small game reserve shelters wildlife such as kudu, springbok, eland, hartebeest, mountain zebra, gemsbok, and more than 100 different bird species, including ostrich and fish eagle. Rock rabbits (hyraxes, or. dassies) are common.

Karasburg

The town of Karasburg is a road and rail staging post which serves as a gateway between Namibia and South Africa.

It is the trading and administrative centre for a region producing karakul sheep pelts.

Keetmanshoop

In 1866 the wealthy German industrialist, Johan Keetman, provided funds for a mission station to serve the Nama Khoikhoi in the southern portion of South West Africa. It was built on the banks of the Swartmodder ('black mud') River, which is usually a dry watercourse, but occasionally short, violent floods occur when freak rainstorms deluge the watershed.

The mission was named Keetmanshoop ('the hope of Keetman') and in

COOL KOKERBOOM

A solitary kokerboom precariously growing on the lip of a canyon.

In the arid areas along the coast of Namibia the most striking single piece of vegetation is the kokerboom (*Aloe dichotoma*).

It is a slow-growing and elegantly shaped aloe. Like all succulents it has developed specialized ways of living in areas of erratic and little rainfall. The kokerboom soaks up water and stores it in its succulent leaves.

Growing to a height of up to 7 metres, it is a smooth-barked tree with branches forming a rounded crown. The leaves are greyish-green and the flowers are bright yellow. Like other aloes, the kokerboom has fibrous wood.

The popular name 'kokerboom' — meaning 'quiver tree' — comes from the San's practice of using the branches as quivers for their poisoned arrows. Cutting a branch of suitable thickness, they scooped out the fibrous innards, leaving the bark to form a strong container.

The kokerboom grows in the most inhospitable country, without surface water and usually in a setting of sun-baked rocks.

It is often encountered growing in precarious positions, such as on the edges of canyons, possibly relishing the cool updrafts of wind. There is a kokerboom forest on the farm Gariganus, roughly 14 kilometres north-east of Keetmanshoop. They may also be seen growing on platforms of the disused railway line leading from Nababeep to Port Nolloth.

a region that was marked by local conflict, raids, rustling, and bloody vendettas, the place still managed to flourish. A substantial stone church built in 1895 dominates the town of Keetmanshoop which grew around the mission.

Keetmanshoop retains much of its original German atmosphere. Many of the buildings were designed in the German colonial style, with thick walls and ceilings to fend off the baking heat. After the Germans annexed South West Africa in 1884 a garrison was stationed here, first in a small fort and later in a castle-like building which now houses a police station and government offices. The environment of Keetmanshoop is harsh to the eye and relentlessly hot, but provides excellent grazing for karakul sheep,

and the production of karakul skins is the principal industry.

By 1908 the railway from Lüderitz on the coast to Keetmanshoop was completed. The railway station built by the Germans still exists as a fine example of their colonial style of architecture.

Keetmanshoop is today a major road and railway centre for southern Namibia. There are shops, churches, hotels and a caravan park. Drinking water comes from the Nauté Dam in the Löwen River 50 kilometres away. It rains occasionally, but sunshine is in generous supply.

Fourteen kilometres north-east of Keetmanshoop, on the farm Gariganus, there is a forest of about 300 kokerbome, or quiver trees (see box). The forest is a national monument.

The bronze colours of the wilderness at Nauté Dam near Keetmanshoop.

Lüderitz and the bay of Angra Pequena, a perfectly sheltered harbour.

The memorial to Bartholomew Dias overlooking Angra Pequena Bay.

A solidly built German colonial structure, the magistracy in Lüderitz.

Lüderitz

On the desert coast of Namibia there is a superb, land-locked natural harbour. It was discovered by the Portuguese explorer Bartholomew Dias in 1487 and named Angra dos Ilheos ('bay of the islets'), and later Angra Pequena ('little bay'). The hinterland of this harbour, unfortunately, was so arid, and drinking water so scarce, that no development took place in the area for many years. There was only fishing, sealing and the collection of guano from the islets.

In 1883 a wealthy merchant from Bremen, Adolf Lüderitz, motivated by a desire to expand the German empire, established a trading station on the shores of the bay. The coastal belt was purchased from the Khoikhoi chief of Bethanien, who owned it, and a settlement grew up. Drinking water was obtained by condensing sea water.

In 1884, at Lüderitz's request, Chancellor Bismarck put the settlement of Lüderitzbucht ('Lüderitz Bay') under the protection of the German government. This was the beginning of German control of the whole of South West Africa, except for the British enclaves of Walvis Bay and the guano islets.

Adolf Lüderitz had little personal satisfaction from his empire building. In 1886 he went prospecting to the Orange River and, together with his companion, drowned at sea.

The town of Lüderitz became a municipality in 1909. It flourished as a fishing centre, especially for the catching of pilchards. Rock lobsters are also found in large quantities, and the harbour is an established port for the

BIRDS THAT FLY A MAMMOTH ROUND TRIP EVERY DAY FOR A DRINK

A crimson-breasted shrike, feeding its young in a kameeldoring tree.

A nest of social weaver birds, shared with predatory reptiles.

A white-browed sparrow weaver, a perky creature of the arid areas.

The search for water is a major pre-occupation with all forms of life in arid areas. Some species of birds — the sand grouse for example — fly round trips of up to 32 kilometres each day just for a drink.

Other birds, with more limited powers of flight, are confined to the immediate vicinity of permanent water. For them, a pool that dries up represents a total disaster.

Heat is another problem for birds. Nests are generally built in whatever shade is available. The sociable weaver birds build extraordinary communal nests. These are huge, permanent structures where several hundred birds live together – each pair having their own chamber, with a tunnel leading to the shady underside of the nest.

Such structures are cool, but vulnerable to attack by predators. Snakes occasionally join the community, feeding on eggs and chicks. Honey badgers also raid the nests, tearing their way into the structure,

feeding on birds and eggs and often destroying the entire nest.

Namaqua and spotted sand grouse fetch water for their young in an ingenious way. The males wade into the water and soak their feathers, splashing and bobbing up and down in the water. They then fly off to their nests where the thirsty chicks drink

A scimitar-bill hoopoe using its specialized beak to feed on grubs.

the drops falling from the parent's body.

Larks of several species live in the arid areas, but the king of all the birds of these parts is the ostrich. Essentially birds of great, dry, open plains, their feathers reach perfection in a setting of dry heat, completely free of humidity.

A capped wheatear, easily distinguished by its black front.

The battle to keep the sand at bay

export of karakul skins and the import of stores for the mines of the interior.

The sea is cold but there are splendid, uncrowded beaches and excellent vantage points for fishermen.

The town has some interesting examples of colonial architecture. Buildings that remain from the days of the German empire include the railway station, old post office, hospital, turnhalle, residency, Lutheran church and old gaol.

There is a museum, and at Dias Point there is a replica of the stone cross originally erected there by Bartholomew Dias in 1487-88.

Exploring the coast around the bay is fascinating. Some places, such as Angra Point, can be reached only by four-wheel-drive vehicles, but many bathing and fishing areas are more accessible, such as Agate Beach, Radford Bay, Big Bay, the Fjord, Bone Bay and Esse Bay.

Bird life in Lüderitz Bay is spectacular, with flamingoes, cormorants, penguins, gannets, gulls and pelicans.

Huge sand dunes of the Namib Desert separate the harbour from the interior, and the road and railway frequently have to be cleared of drifting

THE BIZARRE AND WONDERFUL PLANT LIFE OF THE DESERT REGIONS

In the arid areas of southern Africa and America nature has evolved the remarkable form of plant life known as succulents, from the Latin *succus,* meaning sappy.

Succulents store their water in several ingenious ways. They coat themselves with wax, shade themselves with hairs or thorns, or grow thick cuticles, or stomata that are deep-seated, close to, or even under the ground.

For such plants leaves are something of a luxury, for they are too exposed to sunshine and the consequent loss of precious moisture.

Other succulents grow fleshy leaves with surfaces that are resistant to transpiration and so crowded that they shelter one another.

In southern Africa the principal

Hoodia gordonii, *known as the Queen of the Namib.*

succulent areas are the southern portion of Namibia, Namaqualand and the Little Karoo. Some succulents have adapted to areas of heavier rainfall, and are found in other parts but in limited numbers.

Many of the dwarf succulents are

great mimics. A characteristic of the Little Karoo and part of Namaqualand are the pebbles and rock fragments covering the surface. The dwarf succulents of several species have taken on the colours and shapes of the rocks. Popularly known as 'stone plants', these little plants seem intent on remaining inconspicuous for most of their lives, but once a year they flower for a brief period. As though they are enjoying their festive season, they shun all mimicry and drabness and turn the rocky surface into a magic garden.

The stapelias form another remarkable group of succulents. Known as carrion flowers, or star-fish flowers, they are found in several parts of the Cape. Their flowers are almost reptilian in appearance and

feel. They emit an offensive odour, which attracts the insects that fertilize the flowers.

A peculiarity of one of the larger succulents, the strange-looking *Pachypodium namaquanum* of the lower Orange River, is that its trunk always inclines towards the north. Because of this, these plants are sometimes called 'north poles'.

The mesembryanthemum family, popularly known as 'ice plants' or 'vygies', produce some of the plant world's most brilliantly coloured masses of flowers.

Aloes grow even on the snow-covered heights of Lesotho, and in the eastern Cape their flowering season in winter seems to set the mountain slopes on fire with orange and red flowers.

Lithops schwantesii, *camouflaged against quartz and calcrete stones.*

Stapelia flavopurpurea, *set amid stones, attracts pollinating insects.*

Huernia zebrina var. magniflora *in the shade of an acacia tree.*

Lapidaria margaretae, *a beautifully camouflaged stone plant.*

Huernia oculata, *exotic flowers close to the base of the plant.*

Adromischus maculatus, *a member of the Crassulaceae.*

Lithops bella, *a camouflaged stone plant, common in arid areas.*

The colourful Stapelia pulvinata, *which grows in salty granite soil.*

sand. The desert here is home to more than 50 species of succulent, and for the gem-stone collector there are agates and quartz.

The diamond area lies 10 kilometres inland.

Lüderitz has a tourist camp with bungalows, a caravan site, and camping grounds at fishing areas.

Mariental

The district around Mariental is one of the principal karakul-producing areas of Namibia.

Mariental itself is a railway and road centre, and the nearest town to the tourist resort at the Hardap Dam, 24 kilometres west. The town lies in a spacious grassy plain on the verge of the densely wooded area in the northern part of the territory.

Oranjemund

The remarkable town of Oranjemund, which is not open to the public without permission, is one of the world's principal diamond-producing centres.

This is a company town, created in 1936 to house workers in the diamond areas along the coast north of the Orange River mouth.

Vegetables and flowers are grown here because of the adequate water provided by the Orange River.

There are sporting, entertainment and educational amenities, and the town is flooded with sunshine. The prevailing south-west wind lowers the temperature and the climate is generally pleasant.

No services for tourists exist. Permission to visit Oranjemund must be obtained from the Consolidated Diamond Mines of South West Africa.

An old house in Mariental — a reminder of the German colonial era.

The rock formation known as the Finger of God before it fell down.

Rehoboth

The group known as the Basters ('half-breeds') originate from some 30 different European trek farmers who, about the end of the 18th century, found refuge in the wild country on the southern side of the valley of the Orange River. These men, an unruly lot, married Khoikhoi girls, and their children stayed together, forming their own clan.

In 1868 about 90 Baster families moved north to a wooded area in the central part of South West Africa.

At this place, known as Goregura-as ('the place where the zebras drink'), a mission station named Rehoboth had been established, but had been abandoned in 1864.

The Basters had far better luck. Their settlement, also named Rehoboth, flourished, and a village grew up among the trees, with a tall church watching over it.

The main north-south trunk road passes the outskirts of the village and travellers from the south — after the 400 kilometres in searing heat from Keetmanshoop across a bleached landscape — find Rehoboth a pleasant oasis on their journey to Windhoek, 84 kilometres to the north.

Rosh Pinah

The zinc mine at Rosh Pinah will always be associated with Mose Eli Kahan, one of the most courageous and persevering of all the prospectors of Namibia.

Born in Prussia on 25 June 1896, Mose Eli Kahan came to South West Africa in 1924 and became a pros-

pector. In the wilderness of the lower Orange he discovered a copper deposit which he named Lorelei. Despite enormous transport difficulties, he worked this deposit until the price of copper plummeted in 1930. He then began looking for diamonds and made several discoveries in the Namib Desert and along the Skeleton Coast, where he worked rich finds in marine terraces.

The zinc mine was his most spectacular find. He named it Rosh Pinah ('corner stone') because he considered it the most important of all his interests. The mine, now worked by the South African Iron and Steel Corporation (Iscor), lies in rugged, hot and barren country, and a gravel road had to be made at great expense to provide

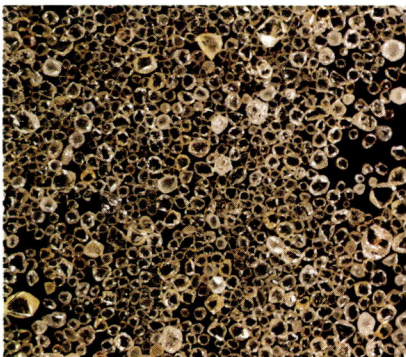

Part of one day's diamond production near the mouth of the Orange River.

an outlet to the railway station of Aus on the Lüderitz line, 160 kilometres to the north.

Swakopmund

The port of Swakopmund, at the mouth of the Swakop River, was founded in 1892 when the Germans tried to develop an alternative entry port to their colony — avoiding the British-held enclave of Walvis Bay. Swakopmund could only offer ships an exposed roadstead, and is no longer used as a port, but it has been developed as a holiday resort.

The water is cold but the beaches are spacious. Surfing is good and the pier is much used by fishermen.

The original German customs house is now a museum. The resort has

---

KARAKUL COUNTRY

In 1902 a German fur trader, Paul Thorer, made a business trip to Uzbekistan. The particular area he visited produced skins of Persian sheep known as karakul ('black lake'). Thorer purchased a quantity of skins and, as an experiment, 36 karakul sheep, which he shipped to Germany.

The damp, temperate conditions of Europe did not suit the karakuls; they flourish in semi-desert areas, and in Germany they showed signs of a decline.

The karakuls were shipped to the German colony of South West Africa, and adapted well to their new home.

After World War I, the South African administration stimulated the fur industry by building a breeding and experimental centre at Neudamm, near Windhoek. In 1919 the S.W.A. Karakul Breeders' Association was formed.

Karakul skins are taken from lambs that are slaughtered within 24 hours of their birth. Only the pelts of new-born lambs are valuable, as the fur hardens rapidly.

The industry has expanded dramatically. In 1937 more than one million pelts were exported for the first time; by 1976 the figure had reached 2,8 million, valued at R50 million.

Buildings scoured by the desert winds

The German-built railway station at Swakopmund. This was the coast terminal of the narrow-gauge railway system.

bungalows, a caravan park, swimming bath, golf course, and other recreational and sporting facilities.

Swakopmund is a convenient base for exploring the Skeleton Coast and the Namib Desert. The town is sometimes nearly overwhelmed by the desert. When the hot east wind blows and sandstorms sweep through the town, the experience is unforgettable.

Outside the town a steam tractor is preserved, known as 'Martin Luther'. The origin of the name was Martin Luther's famous statement: 'Here I stand; God help me, I cannot do otherwise'. The tractor was bought to haul goods to the interior but developed boiler problems and became stuck in the sand outside Swakopmund. It was abandoned where it had come to a standstill.

Usakos
On the banks of the Khan River, on the eastern edge of the Namib Desert, railway engineers created a watering place for locomotives and passengers.

Called Usakos, it grew into a village with a lime works, a few shops, a hotel, and relentless heat.

Walvis Bay
The harbour of Walvis ('whale') Bay is a well-protected anchorage and port with berths 12 metres deep. It is the principal entry port for Namibia and has developed into a busy town, with six pilchard factories and four whitefish factories.

The chief glory of the place is the bay, which slants from deep water into a shallow lagoon separated from the

The lighthouse and German administrator's residence at Swakopmund.

The steam tractor named Martin Luther, abandoned in the Namib.

A German-fortified residence overlooking the Swakop River.

The Lutheran Church in Swakopmund, a relic of German colonial days.

THE FABULOUS DIAMOND FIELDS OF THE DESERT

A one-carat diamond on a beach of garnet pebbles in the Namib.

Mystery surrounds the fabulous diamond fields of the south-western part of Africa. How did the diamonds get there? Why did it take so long for man to discover them, although they lay exposed on the surface?

In 1907 August Stauch, a German railway worker and amateur geologist, was handed a stone that one of his labourers had found in the sand of an embankment on the new line being built from Lüderitz to Aus. Stauch rubbed it against the glass of his wrist-watch. To his great excitement it scratched the glass. It was a diamond.

Two directors of the railway company provided Stauch with backing and he began prospecting. Within ten months he had found so many diamonds that an exhibition was staged in Swakopmund. By 1914 diamonds worth R17 million

Diamond crystals of the Namib.

had been found in the sands of the Namib Desert and along the coast. The diamonds were scattered erratically, but generally in the loose stones and earth.

Diamond production was restricted during the depressed times of the early 1920s. Prospecting continued, however, and many diamonds were found along the coast and in marine terraces immediately north of the mouth of the Orange River.

In the early 1920s Consolidated Diamond Mines of South West Africa was formed. It bought the interests of all the independent companies and secured exclusive rights for 50 years (since extended) over the entire area now known as Diamond Area No. 1. This consists of a belt of land 96 kilometres wide and 352 kilometres long running along the coast from the mouth of the Orange River to Hottentots Bay, north of Lüderitz.

Diamond Area No. 2 — the coastal belt from Hottentots Bay to south of Walvis Bay — was also opened to mining, and further fields were developed up the Skeleton Coast.

Today diamond production is the principal industry of Namibia. Output is maintained at about R150 million a year.

outer ocean by a spit of sand. The latter's northern tip, Pelican Point, is guarded by an automatic lighthouse.

The lagoon is the home of great numbers of aquatic birds, including flamingoes and pelicans. A total of 76 species of bird are found in the municipal bird park.

The lagoon is accessible to small boats, although there are many sandbanks.

The spectacle at sunset, when the birds are settling down for the night, is almost dreamlike. Brilliant colours and reflections float through the night as it echoes to the weird sounds of countless thousands of birds calling and crying, squawking, clucking or mewing.

A sandy track leads for 52 kilometres south to fishing resorts such as Sandwich Harbour. Bird lovers as well as fishermen find this track rewarding, but a four-wheel-drive

The Lutheran Church in the oven-hot little railway town of Usakos.

vehicle and a permit from the tourist authority are essential.

Bearing down on Walvis Bay from the east is the Namib Desert. The giant dunes always seem about to over-

The Sesriem Canyon, with the Namib waiting to absorb the flow of water.

Namibia's historic capital

whelm the town, and when the furnace-hot east wind blows, the desert blankets Walvis Bay with a layer of sand.

A road leads for 142 kilometres eastwards from Walvis Bay into the Namib to the desert research station in the Namib-Naukluft Park.

Another road leads eastwards to Maltahöhe, passing through the Kuiseb Canyon, 156 kilometres from Walvis Bay. This is a remarkable journey, but extremely hot in summer.

A tarred coastal road connects Walvis Bay to Swakopmund. It is 32 kilometres long and offers an easy drive along the verge of the Namib. A journey along this road in a sandstorm can be an alarming experience; daylight is obscured by clouds of dust and the road is invaded by drift sand.

Warmbad

The Khoikhoi people known as the Gami-nun ('dark bundle') or, in Afrikaans, the Bondelswarts, discovered the hot springs of Warmbad in the early 19th century. The land here was arid prairie country, but it could support a limited number of sheep and the hot springs yielded drinkable water.

The Bondelswarts made their home at the springs and today it is a village and trading centre for a scantily populated district where karakul sheep are the most valuable asset.

Windhoek

The capital of Namibia has had several different names. The Khoikhoi people called it Aigams ('hot water')

Preparing nets in the busy harbour of Walvis Bay.

A fishing boat about to leave the shelter of the harbour.

from the hot springs that surfaced here; in 1836 Sir James Alexander, the British prospector and explorer, visited the place and called it Queen Adelaide's Bath, in honour of the British queen; then Jonker Afrikaner, the Khoikhoi chieftain, renamed it Winterhoek after the farm in the Cape where he was born; finally, when the Germans came in 1890 they called it Windhoek ('windy corner'). It was officially spelled Windhuk in 1903, but the South Africans reverted to the use of Windhoek in 1920.

The city lies in a glen formed by one of the upper headwaters of the Swakop River. The glen, in a setting of high, rocky hills, is well covered with grass and trees — mainly species of acacia. Built on the undulating floor and sides of the glen, the city has a variety of levels with good viewing sites.

The Germans founded Windhoek on 18 October 1890, when Major Kurt von Francois took possession of the area on behalf of the German government. He built Francois Fort on a commanding height, and this romantic little stronghold is now a museum.

The fort was for some time the principal building on the site of the city, and the headquarters of the German administration of the whole of South West Africa. Trading stations and other buildings were built on the slopes below the fort and the town began to grow, particularly after June 1902, when a narrow-gauge railway was built, connecting it to the coast at Swakopmund.

Several buildings survive from the period of the German administration. These include the Evangelical Church, the administration building known jocularly as the Tintenpalast ('palace of ink'), several commercial buildings and some attractive private residences, including three handsome castles — Heinitzburg, Schwerinburg and Sanderburg — all built in the early 1900s on viewing sites in the hills above Leutwein Street.

The modern Assembly chambers contain decorative panelling and

A portrait of Crown Prince Wilhelm hanging in Schloss Duwisib.

Schloss Duwisib, a German castle built in 1908 on a farm near Maltahöhe.

THE 'KING'S' VISION

The 'vision' of Hendrik Witbooi was to cost South West Africa dearly in blood. In 1880, when war broke out between the Nama and Herero people, Witbooi was the leader of a Coloured group, known as the Witboois, who had migrated across the Orange River and settled with the Namas.

Inspired by his vision, he declared himself the 'king of Great Namaland' and announced that God had chosen him to lead the Namas against the Hereros. He aimed at destroying the Hereros and scorned the growth of German colonial power, showing obedience only to God and his vision.

The Germans surprised Witbooi at his stronghold at Horn Krams in April 1893. Although he escaped, he was compelled to surrender the following year at Naukluft. He lived under German supervision until 1904, when he rebelled, killing many German and Boer settlers in what was called the Witbooi War.

On 29 October 1905, Witbooi was wounded in an action against German troops. The wound was slight but blood poisoning set in and he died shortly afterwards.

murals carved with local timber. The Tintenpalast, with modern additions, is still used. Behind it is a small game sanctuary and below it is a superbly stocked garden of flowering trees.

Windhoek has a limited water supply, drawing on 41 boreholes and three dams — Avis, Goreangab and Sartorius von Bach — and water is recycled. Private gardens suffer from the shortage of water, especially in summer.

Windhoek is north of the Tropic of Capricorn and although its altitude — 1 686 metres above sea level — preserves it from some of the blistering heat of the lower areas, the sunshine can be dazzling. Precautions against sunburn are necessary.

There are some notable memorials in the city. The equestrian bronze statue to the memory of the troops and civilians who died in the Herero and Khoikhoi uprisings, and the memorial to Major Kurt von Francois are both fine examples.

The principal thoroughfare in Windhoek, Independence Avenue, is lined with imposing buildings, and the cosmopolitan nature of the population is clearly evident. German children in lederhosen, Herero women in their colourful Victorian 'mission' dress, sun-bronzed farmers, occasionally a San, yellow-skinned Khoikhoi, dark Bergdamas — all bustle along the pavements of Independence Avenue on a busy day.

A good time to see the crowds of Independence Avenue is in the last week of April and early May.

This is the time of one of the two annual carnivals, when there is an all-night masked ball. Although this is the coolest time of year, the people of Windhoek are always thirsty, and good beer is often preferred to the rather hard water.

The second annual carnival is in 'suicide' month — towards the end of October — when the air is electric dry and the heat before the rains oppressive enough to drive a few to suicide and a lot more to drink.

Apart from beer and oompah bands, Windhoek has many other sources of recreation.

In the city centre, facing on to Independence Avenue, is an attractive park, with paths, children's play area,

The ruins of Francois Fort in the Khomas Hochland of central Namibia.

The Tintenpalast, originally the German colonial headquarters in Windhoek.

A storm-laden sky frames the statue of Kurt von Francois, founder of Windhoek.

A narrow-gauge puffer used to draw trains to and from Swakopmund across the dunes of the Namib Desert.

open-air theatre, meteorites, the fossil skeleton of a primeval elephant, and a memorial which was erected in honour of the men who died in the Witbooi uprising.

The Goreangab Dam has amenities for water sports, and in the Khomas Hochland, 24 kilometres west of Windhoek, there is a game reserve, proclaimed in 1962 and named after the then administrator, Daan Viljoen. The reserve is a sanctuary for gemsbok, kudu, mountain zebra, hartebeest, eland, springbok, baboon and ostrich.

A dam in the Augeigas River attracts wild duck, geese and coot — over 200 different bird species altogether. Tilapia, black bass and barbel live in the waters. Around the dam are bungalows, caravan and camping grounds, a swimming pool and a restaurant.

There are wilderness trails in the game reserve. Horses can be hired in Windhoek.

Liebig House, a strange example of colonial architecture near Windhoek.

465

Gem-stones gleaming with all the colours of the rainbow

Namibia is blessed with an extraordinary assembly of rocks, gems and semi-precious stones. It is pleasant to imagine that the power of creation, remembering too late that water had been forgotten in this part of the world, compensated by a rich endowment of beautiful minerals.

Aquamarine, bluish-green or sea-green in colour, is found at Rössing near Swakopmund; tourmaline, mainly green and blue, is found near Usakos; amethyst, deep violet in colour, is widespread, but especially prevalent in the Otjiwarongo and Omaruru districts; agates lie on the beaches at Lüderitz; rose quartz – pink and red – is found in the Rössing Mountains; heliodor, a golden variety of beryl, is found only in Namibia.

A boulder of rose quartz, lying in the approaches to the Fish River Canyon.

Also found in this region are crystal varieties of feldspar known as amazonite (green), sunstone (golden), moonstone (white) and labradorite (purple).

The oxidized and silicified variety of crocidolite asbestos known as tiger's eye is found in the southern part of the country.

Jasper and topaz are common in many exquisite shades — brown, green, scarlet and yellow; also found here are blood-red pyrope garnets, the rarely found lustrous blue lapis lazuli, opals, and more than 100 different types of malachite sulphides and arsenites.

The rock of the Tsumeb region is particularly famous for its almost incredible variety of copper ores. Both sulphides and arsenites as well as pure native copper are found in the rock here.

The road to Ai-Ais, descending the side of the Fish River Canyon, passes huge outcrops of rose quartz. In some places, where rock- and landslides have removed the topsoil, the underlying rose quartz is revealed as though a graceful waterfall down the precipice had been magically transformed into pink crystal.

Apart from gem-stones, the rock-hunter finds Namibia a productive area for the discovery of meteorites. Of the thousands of meteorites that enter the earth's atmosphere each day, very few are found. The majority burn up before reaching the surface and most of the others crash into the sea or fall in regions where they are concealed by dense vegetation.

On the bare surfaces of Namibia meteorites are relatively easy to find. And a meteorite makes a treasure in any rock collection.

Fossils are also of great interest to collectors. Here again the bareness of the Namibian landscape makes them relatively easy to find.

There are fossil plants, petrified forests, and many molluscs, fish, remnants of prehistoric reptiles and mammals, and also of man, who lived in the area many thousands of years before the beginning of history.

To remove or possess fossils or meteorites a permit is needed from the National Monuments Council — but the hunter of semi-precious stones in this extraordinary country needs only patience and a keen eye. The casual rock-hunter is sure to be fortunate enough to find specimens. Even an inspection of a roadside ditch or a rubble dump at a gravel pit is generally rewarding.

The serious collector, however, has a scientifically determined field of search. Many organized parties of gem-stone enthusiasts visit Namibia in caravans.

For such collectors, finding the specimens in the field is only the beginning of the matter. What follows is the polishing, cutting, transforming into jewellery, or exhibitions of prize

Chalcopyrite with its gorgeous mixture of gold and peacock-blue colours.

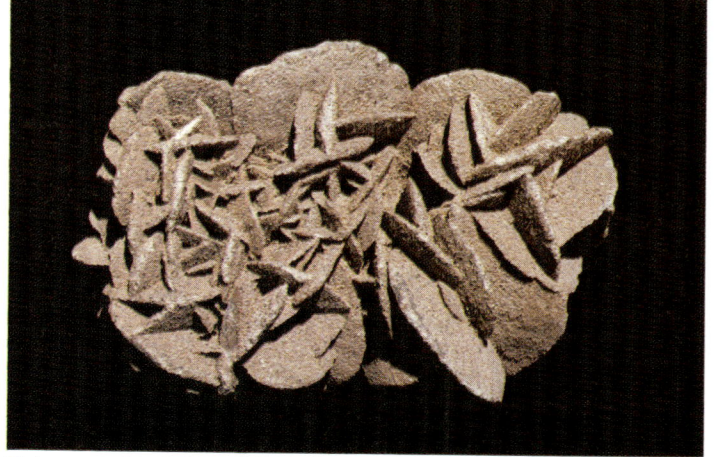

Gypsum or desert rose, a bizarre-looking rock found in the Namib Desert.

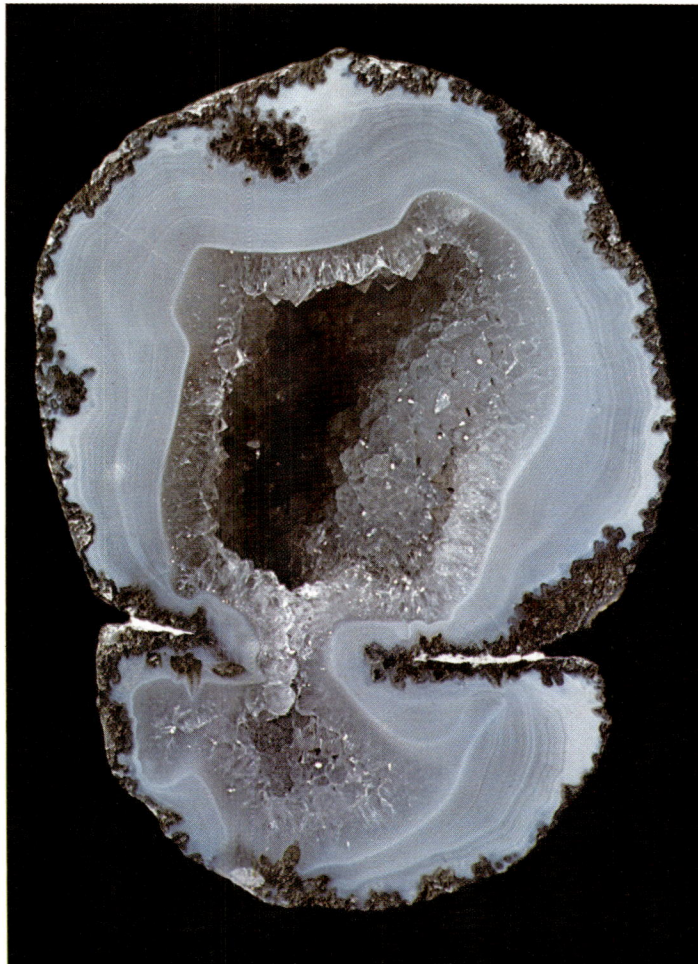

Agate, with a miniature fairy cavern contained in the centre.

Dioptase, with blancheite contained in the pointed end of the ore.

Stitchtite, a brilliantly hued stone found in asbestos country.

Seams of serpentine chrysotile asbestos contained in a bed of stitchtite.

Apophyllite, a lovely crystal rock, sharp and brittle to the touch.

Amethyst, a crystal notable for its delicate colour and complex form.

specimens in shows and displays around the world.

In most towns of Namibia – notably Windhoek, Walvis Bay, Swakopmund and Lüderitz – there are many dealers who hold considerable stocks of gem-stones.

Such specimens may be bought in the rough state or polished, or incorporated into necklaces, rings and other items of jewellery which are popular both here and overseas.

Beryl, source of the metal beryllium and a handsome gem-stone.

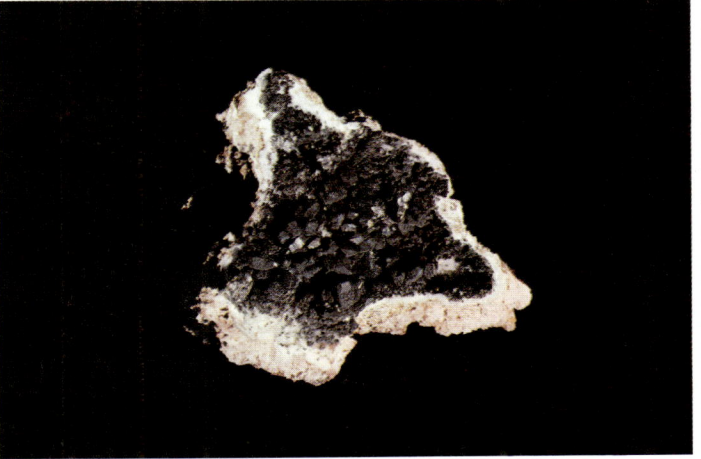

Descloizite crystals set as though nature had devised a brooch.

WHERE THE DESERT MEETS THE SEA

IT IS DIFFICULT to visualise a greater contrast than a desert alongside an ocean. Such a meeting of opposites occurs in Namibia where the edge of the Namib pushes a sea of hot sand into the frigid waters of the South Atlantic.

Portuguese seafarers called this wilderness of white sand 'the coast of hell'. Later it became better known as the Skeleton Coast, because of the dismal fate of castaways from ships that were wrecked here through the centuries, doomed to endure searing heat, clammy mists, total solitude and little drinking water or shelter.

The whole of the south-western side of Africa is a world of remarkable contrasts, packed with natural marvels and weird, almost unbelievable scenes. There are seemingly endless plains rippling with distant mirages; sharply etched peaks such as the granite Spitzkoppe — a dangerous 1 759-metre climb and a landmark not easily forgotten.

Green is a rare colour in this land, but in its place are brilliant shades of deep orange, red, and the purple of malachite-stained rock. The Verbrande Berg (Burnt Mountain) near Twyfelfontein appears black like the burnt-out embers in a stove. On a rocky slope close by, there is an astonishing and fascinating concentration of over a thousand rock paintings and engravings of game animals and their tracks.

The Brandberg range has among its heights the Königstein, at 2 586 metres the highest peak of Namibia, and also, in the Tsisab Gorge, the famous rock painting known as the White Lady of the Brandberg. (Despite its name, the figure in this painting is now believed to be neither white nor female.)

There are tracks of dinosaurs, believed to be 150 million years old, still clearly visible in the flat sedimentary rock near Kalkfeld, and 18 kilometres from Grootfontein, at Hoba, lies the world's biggest meteorite. It weighs over 54 000 kilograms and consists of 82 per cent iron and 16 per cent nickel. Its impact on the face of the earth must have been colossal, but when precisely this occurred has yet to be established.

Etosha, a 120-kilometre-by-50-kilometre shallow depression in the ground — a dried-out lake — is another of the region's remarkable natural phenomena. How it came to be there is debatable. One theory claims that the Kunene River, in former years, flowed into an inland sea or large lake before it changed its course to reach the Atlantic Ocean.

In exceptionally rainy periods parts of the Etosha Pan fill to a depth of approximately one metre, and then large flocks of graceful flamingoes and other waterbirds gather on these shallow sheets of water, to feed on algae and other aquatic organisms.

For the remaining nine months of the year Etosha is a place of mirages. Its dry, flat, white salt-encrusted surface shimmers in the heat, and sporadic dust-devils spiral up into the sky. Mirages can be seen of dream-like pools, trees, mountains, and hills beckoning on the horizon, but all vanish with cruel abruptness to disappoint any living creatures seeking refuge.

Diamonds are found in the desert sands along the coast, an inexhaustible jewellery box of gem-stones, both buried and lying on the surface. Why are they found here and not in areas with more water? Did nature suddenly have compassion for this sun-baked land?

Whatever the reason, a land was created which is so entirely different from anywhere else that comparisons are invalid. Namibia is a country that really must be seen to be believed.

Etosha Pan

In 1851 the explorers Sir Francis Galton and Charles Andersson were the first Europeans to visit the great pan known as Etosha ('the place of mirages'). The area around it teemed with game animals and the spectacle during the rainy season of December to March, with the pan filled with mud more than a metre deep and countless flamingoes resting here, made this one of the most exciting wildlife areas in Africa.

Fifty years later the German government built a fort at the eastern end of the pan, at Namutoni. In 1904 this fort was attacked by the Wambo. Only seven German policemen were stationed at the place at the time and they were short of ammunition. After seven hours of fighting they slipped away in the night and made their way southwards until they encountered a German column coming to their relief. The combined party returned to Etosha and recaptured the fort,

An aerial view of flood-season water flowing towards the Etosha Pan.

A model of the original Namutoni Fort, besieged by the Wambo in 1904.

Fort Namutoni as it is today, perfectly preserved, an elegant guardian of the northern wilderness and a great tourist resort.

are scattered over a vast grazing area, congregating in large numbers on the plains west of the pan where the grazing is good. At this time, bird life in the pan is varied, but Etosha National Park is unfortunately closed, except for Namutoni, which is open throughout the year. The 400 millimetres of rain that falls creates muddy roads and

which had been looted and largely destroyed by the Wambo warriors.

A new fort was built — a glistening, white, 'Beau Geste' stronghold which today, in a perfect state of preservation, is a romantic and unexpected piece of architecture to find in the wilderness of Africa. The new fort has never been under attack, and was a police post until the 1950s.

In 1907 the German government proclaimed Etosha Pan and its surroundings a game reserve. No tourist amenities were built, however, until 1952, when the construction of rest camps and roads began, particularly along the southern edge of the pan, where there are perennial waterholes that attract a concentration of wild animals.

During the rainy season, animals

THINGS TO DO AND SEE

Angling The cold waters of the Namibian coast teem with pilchards and anchovies although heavy commercial fishing in recent years has reduced their numbers. There are also large fish – galjoen, kabeljou, steenbras and stompneus, as well as sharks and rock lobsters.

Antiquities San paintings and rock engravings can be found in the northern mountains, notably in the Brandberg and at Twyfelfontein.

Boating The Sartorius von Bach Dam is used for water sports and picnics.

Camping and caravanning There is a resort and caravan park at Gross Barmen, which has an indoor thermal pool and an outdoor swimming pool. There are caravan and camping grounds in the Etosha National Park, and at Khorixas, Okahandja, Omaruru and Outjo. There are camping areas along the west coast.

Game viewing The Etosha National Park is one of the major sanctuaries for wild animals in Africa. There are three camps in the park.

Gem-stones The entire area of Namibia is rich in gem-stones. This is also one of the world's principal diamond areas. Restrictions on diamond prospecting are severe. Such restrictions do not apply to prospecting for the masses of semi-precious stones found here. However, some outcrops are worked commercially and permission from claim-holders or owners of private land is necessary to search such areas.

Sightseeing The Etosha Pan, the Namib-Naukluft Park, and the wild country around the Verbrande Berg (Burnt Mountain) and the Brandberg range offer beautiful scenery. The extraordinary Spitzkoppe lies on the road past Usakos to Hentiesbaai. The Petrified Forest, 24 kilometres west of Khorixas, is spectacular. The world's largest meteorite is at Hoba, near Grootfontein.

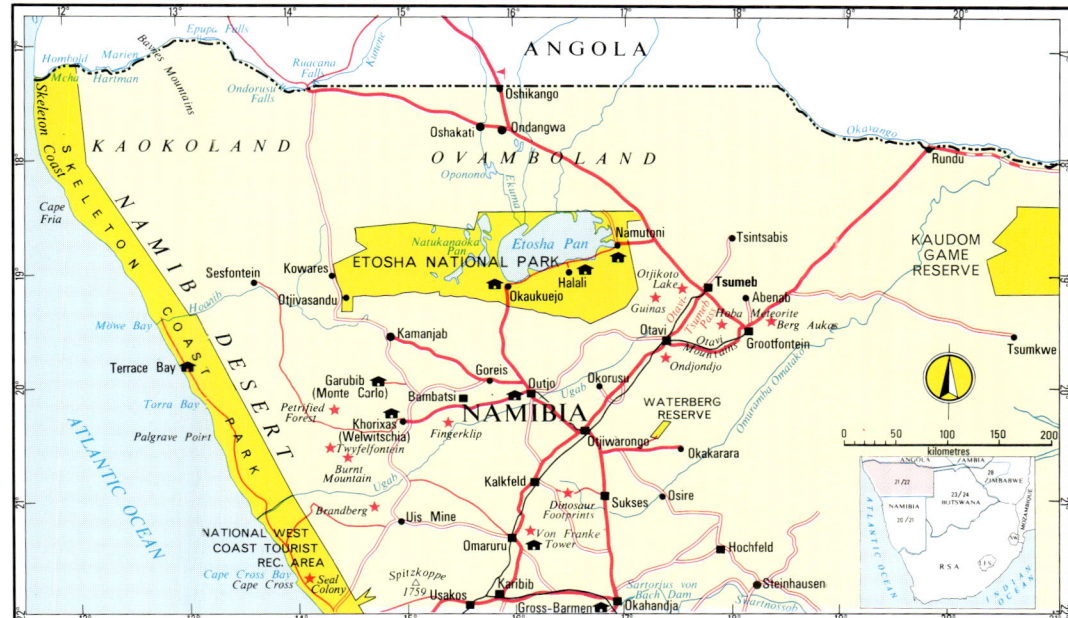

A haven for a marvellous variety of birds and beasts

excellent conditions for malaria-carrying mosquitoes. Temperatures are high — around 38°C. — and life is not very comfortable.

In the winter the temperature drops to below 30°C.

The vegetation of the park is typical mopane woodland, with grassy plains. There are tamboti trees, wild figs and dates, marula, makalani palms and several species of acacia thorn trees.

On the west side of the pan there is the so-called 'haunted forest' of moringa trees; these are the 'upside down' trees which the San say were thrown out of the garden of paradise and landed upside down on the ground. This is the largest forest of moringas in Namibia – the only part of the world where they are known to grow.

Bird life includes ostriches, kori bustards, black korhaan, guinea fowl, francolin, vultures, crows, hawks, eagles, doves, plovers, clapper larks, quelea, the crimson-breasted shrike (the bird emblem of Namibia), lilac-breasted rollers, flamingoes, Egyptian geese, spoonbills, avocets, ducks and storks.

The animal population is large and varied. There are elephant, zebra,

A watering hole in the Etosha National Park with a gathering of zebra, kudu, springbok, giraffe and guinea fowl.

A ground squirrel enjoying a meal dug out on the verges of Etosha Pan.

A relatively rare black-maned lion of the Etosha National Park.

A leopard on the prowl just before nightfall, after a lazy day spent sleeping. He is now ready for action and food.

The powerfully built gemsbok, watering in the Etosha National Park.

Zebra drink at a waterhole as a larger customer approaches.

The tower at the Okaukuejo entrance to the Etosha National Park.

Inside the walls of Fort Namutoni, a well-kept oasis and resting place.

The dainty Damara dik-dik, one of the most fragile and elusive of all African game animals, relying on speed for safety.

A chameleon making a jerky promenade in search of insects at Etosha Pan.

A lynx, or caracal, also known in South Africa as a rooikat.

A zebra mare and her foal, well conditioned and plump.

Where a giant from outer space came to earth

wildebeest, springbok, giraffe, eland, hartebeest, oryx, black-faced impala, kudu and Damara dik-dik. Among the predators are lion, leopard, cheetah and several species of wild cat. Hyena and jackal are the scavengers.

There are tourist camps at Namutoni, Halali and Okaukuejo, which is the main administrative camp.

Grootfontein
The San were the first to discover the watering place they named Gei-oub ('big fountain'). Europeans settled in the area in the 1880s and translated the name into Grootfontein. A town was created in 1907 as the centre for a prosperous ranching and agricultural area. The town is shady and colourful with jacarandas and other flowering trees.

For a short time during the 1880s the 'thirstland trekkers' (see box) planned to settle here.

To the west of the town, 18 kilometres away on the farm Hoba, lies the world's largest meteorite, discovered in 1920. Some 20 kilometres to the north there is the vanadium mine of Berg Aukas, one of the largest base metal producers in the world.

The Germans built a narrow-gauge railway to Grootfontein from Usakos in 1908, and the town is the railhead and forwarding point for road transport to Kavango.

Karibib
Usakos has won from Karibib its former importance as a communications centre, but Karibib remains a vital marketing town.

The railway track running through the centre of the town has helped it

A store at Karibib that dates back to the days of German control.

An old German hotel, once a place of much revelry, in Karibib.

Marble of fine quality and great thickness being quarried at a site near Karibib.

The meteorite discovered on the farm Hoba, near Grootfontein, in 1920.

VANISHED DREAMS OF THE THIRSTLAND TREKKERS
The so-called 'thirstland trekkers' were a deeply religious group, known as doppers, meaning 'dampers', because of their reputation for trying to discourage so-called social progress. When the Reverend Thomas Burgers was elected president of the Transvaal in 1872, this group rejected his teachings.

Absurd arguments developed over claims by the doppers that the building of railways was the work of Satan.

The doppers started to dream of leaving the Transvaal and trekking off in search of what they called *Beulah* (after the biblical land of rest). In 1874 these groups of people abandoned their homes in the Transvaal, loaded their goods onto wagons, and set out westwards across the Kalahari without any advance reconnaissance.

Livestock, women and children became victims of fever, dysentery and heat. Disputes arose.

In February 1878 the trekkers re-grouped at Olifantspan in South West Africa and attempted to patch up their differences, but were only partly successful. Then in 1881, fighting amongst the local inhabitants forced them to travel on to Humpata, in Angola.

There they quarrelled and fragmented, some remaining in Angola, a few returning to the Transvaal, others moving back to South West Africa where they tried to establish a republic near Grootfontein.

Yet more fights and feuds finally killed the dreams of Beulah.

retain much of its pioneering atmosphere.

Kunene River
The north-western frontier between Namibia and Angola is the Kunene River. This river has its watershed in the highlands of Angola. It streams southwards, enters the sand basin of the Kalahari and flows slowly through this level area, spreading out during floods and forming pans and swamps in the region.

At Olushandja the river swings westwards and tumbles 123 metres over the Ruacana Falls, then 32 metres over the Epupa Falls. For 150 kilometres it finds a way through the Baynes Mountains, and runs for another 100 kilometres across the Namib, finally reaching the Atlantic Ocean at what the Portuguese called the Sands of Hell, and what is now

ELEPHANTS OF THE BUSH AND FOREST, THE MONARCHS FOR WHOM EVEN THE LORDLY LION STANDS ASIDE

The elephants of Africa are of two groups: the bush, or savanna, elephant, *Loxodonta africana africana;* and the forest elephant, *Loxodonta africana cyclotis,* which is confined to the humid, equatorial forests of central Africa. The bush elephant ranges over a vast part of Africa and is common throughout East Africa and parts of southern Africa, despite having been systematically hunted by man.

Man is the only real enemy of the elephant. Occasionally a lion may succeed in killing a young elephant if it has strayed from the protection of its mother, but such occurrences are rare.

Elephants have a keen sense of social responsibility and members of a herd will adopt or protect orphaned, ailing or injured members of their community.

The average adult African bull elephant stands 3,2 metres at the shoulder. The largest-known elephant was shot in Damaraland, Namibia, on 5 April 1978. The animal, an old bull known affectionately as Bismarck, was 4,42 metres high. His tusks, however, were relatively small.

Elephants have a life span of about 80 years.

A legendary elephant of southern Africa was Dhlulamithi ('taller than the trees'). He lived in Mocambique and the south-eastern part of what is now Zimbabwe, and was regarded with great awe by the Shanganes. He was hunted but spared by the master poacher, S. C. Barnard, who was known as BveKenya ('the swaggerer') to the Shanganes. He too has become a legend in that part of Africa. Dhlulamithi was shot in 1933. His tusks weighed 73,5 and 73 kilograms.

The elephants of southern Africa do not usually carry exceptional tusks. The average mass is 30 to 45 kilograms. The world record pair was obtained in 1897 from an old bull elephant who lived on the slopes of Kilimanjaro. One tusk was 3,11 metres long and weighed 107 kilograms; the other was 3,18 metres long and weighed 102 kilograms, giving a combined mass of 209 kilograms.

Ivory hunting has been a profitable occupation in Africa since the dawn of history. Thousands of elephants have been killed and their tusks exported to markets in Asia, Europe and America, where they are

A young elephant with the small tusks usual in Namibia, where chemical deficiency inhibits the growth of ivory.

used for carving, and for the making of piano keys, jewellery and curios. The breed of professional ivory hunters included men whose names have become synonymous with adventure, and their activities provided the history of Africa with some colourful and exciting tales.

Henry Hartley was one of the most famous of the hunters of the Transvaal and Zimbabwe. His records show that he shot 1 200 bull elephants between 1845 and 1870.

His record bull carried a 55,3-kilogram tusk on one side and a broken tusk of 45,3 kilograms on the other side. From the whole tusk, a magnificent holy font was carved for St. Peter's in Rome.

During the Belgian occupation of the Congo (now Zaïre) the colonial administration domesticated the African elephant and found the animal a good worker. Circuses occasionally train African elephants and they perform well, but seem to be more excitable and unpredictable than their docile Asiatic relatives.

Large numbers of the African elephant are killed for food in Africa, and some are killed by poachers in search of ivory. Their range extends over huge areas of pure unadulterated wilderness where man seldom penetrates.

In these areas they are monarchs of the savanna and the forest, and even the lordly lion stands aside to let them pass.

A medium-sized herd of elephants on their way to a water-hole in the western Caprivi Strip of Namibia.

Pitiless land of mirages and shimmering heat

known as the Skeleton Coast.

The name Kunene was given to the river by the Hereros of Namibia. Kunene in the Herero language means 'right-hand side', and the name refers to the country north of the river. The country south of the river is known as the Kaokoland ('land on the left-hand side'). The Wambo people of the north simply call the river Omulongo ('the stream').

Namib Desert

Of all deserts, the Namib is the most accessible. It occupies the full length of the south-western coast of Africa, starting in the Cape Province at the mouth of the Olifants River and continuing across the Kunene River into Angola. More than 2 000 kilometres long, the Namib ranges from only 80 kilometres to 160 kilometres wide.

Several roads cross the desert, including the tarred road from Windhoek to Swakopmund, and two railway lines — Keetmanshoop to Lüderitz, and Windhoek to Swakopmund. A traveller can therefore view the Namib in comfort: he can pause awhile and walk on the sands, or he can follow one of the gravel roads or tracks which lead to surprising scenes.

In the Khoikhoi language the name Namib means a large, arid plain. The desert's colossal sand dunes, approximately 300 metres high in some places, are the highest of any desert. They are notable also for their elegantly sweeping shapes and endless curves. Mirages and heat waves shimmer and dance and the patterns on the sand are in constant movement.

The incongruousness of a desert lying next to the abundant water of an ocean is always apparent. The super-

In the blazing heat of the Kaokoland a herdboy drives his goats back to the kraal where they will shelter for the night.

The Kunene River, swollen with flood-waters.

Epupa Falls, where the Kunene tumbles into a canyon.

WEIRD WELWITSCHIA

In April 1852 an Austrian naturalist, Dr. Friedrich Martin Welwitsch, was appointed by the Portuguese government to research the plant life of what was then their colony of Angola. Dr. Welwitsch discovered many new botanical species, but none more extraordinary than the plant that bears his name, *Welwitschia mirabilis*, pictured above.

This is a modified tree that grows in areas of low rainfall where moisture is provided by mist.

The plant produces a turnip-like stem that can be more than a metre thick and may project up to 1,5 metres above the ground. From opposite sides of this stem two adult leaves develop. They are the same width as the stem and grow about 3 metres long, withering at the tips where they touch the ground.

The leaves split lengthwise, fraying into long ribbons and giving the impression of being several leaves constantly growing outwards.

The plant sends a taproot down as deep as 20 metres. When it is about 20 years of age, the welwitschia will produce its first flower. The life span of the plant is at least 1 000 years.

heated air of the desert is in constant collision with cold air creeping inland with the prevailing westerly winds. Fog results — clammy, salty and often impenetrable.

During the night, when the desert is cool, the fog probes inland and settles on the ground. With the dawn the daily struggle begins. Heat and ultra-violet light permeate the fog without difficulty, and the surface of the desert rapidly warms. Hot air starts to rise and lifts the fog, shattering it into clouds which drift in disarray and then disperse, leaving the sun to flood the desert with heat and light. But as the sun sets, the fog reappears, rolling in from the sea.

The unique Namib-Naukluft Park is the most accessible part of the desert for the tourist, and it contains many interesting features, as well as reliable gravel roads and camping sites. Food, water and bedding must be brought by visitors.

In the park are gigantic dunes, the strange *Welwitschia mirabilis* plants (see box), euphorbias, lithops, koker-booms and other aloes, and many other species of succulents.

Beetles, fishtails, termites and other insects feed on desiccated vegetation blown into the desert or deposited by the few plants that grow in the sand. These insects create their own water by oxidization. Feeding on them are spiders, scorpions, crickets, flies, wasps, shovel-nosed lizards, palmato geckos, sidewinder snakes and golden

The intermittently flowing Kuiseb River dividing the sand-dune country from the gravel-plain area of the Namib Desert.

Tsamma melons growing on the bed of a dry watercourse in the Namib Desert.

A narra plant relished by the San, which grows in the Namib Desert.

Sacred burial ground of the Herero chiefs

A sand dune looming over the bed of a dry watercourse in the Namib. These are among the highest dunes in the world.

The wilderness of Namibia at sunset, as the scorching sun begins to fade.

moles. Birds such as large bustards, ostriches and larks eat the bigger insects and the reptiles. In the water-courses — dry for most of the time but occasionally the scene of flash floods from the interior — oryx (gemsbok) and springbok live, and on the slopes there are numerous mountain zebra. Beneath the beds of river courses water is captured, and vegetation flourishes along the banks and in the beds themselves.

Living in the valley of the Kuiseb River are the Topnaar Khoikhoi. They keep goats, which live mainly on the seed pods dropped by species of acacia trees such as the ana, on the melons of the hardy narra plants, and on wild cucumbers — the *Cucumis africanus*

— whose seeds are believed by some to have aphrodisiac qualities.

Visitors to the Namib Desert should beware of sunburn.

Okahandja

The traditional home of the Herero, where most of their chiefs are buried, lies on the banks of the river known as the oKahandja ('small broad river'), so called because of its broad beds of white sand. In 1850 the Rhenish Missionary Society established a station amid the tall camelthorn trees growing in the river valley, and this was the beginning of a town, nowadays a ranching and dairy centre with a creamery and a meat-packing plant nearby.

Okahandja is a shady little town. The mission house and church still stand, and the graves of the Herero chiefs are now surrounded by a public park. In August each year, the Hereros gather in the park to hold a memorial service for their past leaders.

South of Okahandja is the Sartorius von Bach Dam recreation resort, with amenities for angling, water sports and picnics.

Okahandja is a rail and road centre on the main route from Windhoek to Walvis Bay. It is surrounded by high hills and mountains.

Omaruru

In an area shaded by tall trees growing around a spring known as oMaruru (bitter tasting), the Germans established a military station in 1894.

In the 1904 war with the Hereros this outpost, by then a small village, was besieged. The garrison had a

The acacia-shaded tomb of the great chief Maherero, near Okahandja.

The Franke Tower at Omaruru, where the Germans survived a Herero siege.

A MEETING PLACE OF STRANGE TONGUES AND FASCINATING CUSTOMS

Namibia is the home of a remarkably diverse population. The largest group – 46,3 per cent of the population – is the Wambo, whose homeland is in the northern part of the country along the border with Angola.

These people are made up of several formerly independent groups now united into one nation. According to tradition they entered Namibia from the east about the middle of the 16th century.

It is said that they originate from Mbo — a place that traditionally is also the origin of the Zulus.

After settling in the sand country of the north the Wambo occupied themselves mainly with growing millet, groundnuts, melons, beans and pumpkins. Their homes were clusters of family dwellings set in mazes of pallisaded passages walled with palm leaves.

There was almost no stone in this region of Namibia and a solitary outcrop of rock situated at Nehula became a national treasure where they ground their axes and sharpened their knives.

In the early years the Wambo were notorious for their brutal chiefs, and their unpleasant beliefs and burial rites.

The second largest ethnic group in Namibia consists of people of European origin, principally Afrikaans and English-speaking South Africans, and Germans.

Next in numbers are the group who call themselves the Nu-Khoin ('black people'). They are generally known as Damas ('Blacks'), the name given to them by the yellow-skinned Nama people. Europeans call them Bergdamas because they also live in the mountains.

They were traditionally scorned by most other people they encountered and many became slaves. They lived very primitively, and recognised no chief. Noted for their docility and industry, they made excellent blacksmiths, and were great dancers and musicians.

The Bergdamas have not the slightest idea of their origins and even their original language has been almost forgotten. They speak the languages of their various masters.

The Herero people are cattle-men and celebrated warriors. Their

Ovahimba women at a trading post in the Kaokoland.

women are renowned for their ultra-conservative but extremely attractive habit of wearing the full, ankle-length dresses introduced into the country in the last century by the wives of missionaries.

The Herero, like the Wambo, claim to have entered the country from the east, also about the middle of the 16th century. One of their distinctive customs is to maintain a sacred fire, which is never allowed to go out, in the centre of each settlement. This fire is the pivotal point of all important ceremonies. When a family moves to a new home, the sacred fire is carefully carried with them.

If it goes out, it must be rekindled immediately by means of ritual fire sticks, which are regarded as representatives of the ancestors.

The fifth largest group, the Nama Khoikhoi, are sheep-men who live in the arid areas south of the Swakop River. They have always been a fractious collection of separate groups, incessantly fighting one another, and the Herero, over grazing rights and water-holes.

The Nama are nomadic, living in portable huts made of reed mats and skins. Traditionally they had no interest in agriculture; the only plant they cultivated was dagga, which they smoked habitually. They lived on milk, meat, and wild roots and bulbs gathered by the women.

The Nama have no accurate concept of their origin, or when or how they came to Namibia. They are related to the Khoikhoi clans of the Cape, and several groups entered Namibia from the South during the last 200 years.

The sixth ethnic group, the San, are divided into sections and are among the most fascinating of people. Light yellow in colouring, averaging about 1,5 metres in height, they have delicately formed hands and feet and big bellies and buttocks.

They are nomadic hunters and have never grown crops. Waterholes, rock shelters and hunting grounds have always been their main concerns. The women collect bulbs, roots and wild fruits. The men hunt with bows and poisoned arrows for meat, mostly antelope.

The San live in family groups, recognizing no overall chiefs. They live close to nature, wear skins, and make ornaments from ostrich shells. They have a rich folk-lore and a certainty that they have always been in southern Africa, wandering at will after the herds of game, feuding with other clans over favoured areas or stolen women, but never knowing what it was to contend with an aggressive rival ethnic group until the advent, in the last 300 years, of Bantu people and Europeans.

Herero women in traditional costume based on the dress of missionary women.

A Herero woman scorns the heat in traditional missionary-style costume.

Bold and elegant — an Ovahimba man of the Kaokoland wilderness.

A Wambo elder at his cooking pot in the kraal of his homestead.

The spring from which grew a shady town

difficult time defending the place and 123 German civilians and soldiers were killed before the uprising was suppressed. A monument, built in 1907 and known as the Franke Tower, still stands. It is named after Captain Victor Franke, leader of the force who broke the siege.

The town of Omaruru grew in the shade of the trees and under the protection of the garrison. It became a municipality in 1909 and today is a centre for ranching and dairy farming. A large creamery was opened here in 1928 — the first in South West Africa. There is a large swimming bath and a caravan park in woodland settings.

Otavi

The Hereros were the first to settle in the well-watered area they named oTavi ('the gushing spring') after a

The Waterberg range near Otjiwarongo. Well watered, the mountains dominate a green and pleasant parkland.

THE BIZARRE MERRY-GO-ROUND OF FAMILY LIFE IN THE ROOKERY OF THE CAPE CROSS SEALS

In 1486 the Portuguese explorer Diego Cao erected a stone cross at the most southerly point reached in his exploration of the west coast of Africa. One of his most vivid impressions of the place that came to be known as Cape Cross must have been the huge seal colony.

Today about 60 000 seals use the area as a rookery, and their large numbers are proof of the richness of the fishing along the coast of Namibia.

The Cape fur seal roams the full length of the south-western coast of

Replica of the Diego Cao cross.

Africa and up the east coast to Algoa Bay. North of this the water becomes too warm and the number of seals dwindles. The cold water of the Benguela Current suits them best, and along the south-western coast of Africa there are numerous islets and isolated parts of the shore which they use as nurseries.

The cows produce a pup each year and it is the pups' pelts that yield the best fur. The earliest commercial exploitation of any part of Namibia was by the sealers from Europe and America who killed thousands of

Seal skins have remained consistently in demand. Pelts, salted and graded according to size and quality, are shipped overseas in large barrels. The carcasses are processed into bone-meal, liver oil, meat-meal and fat. The fat is used in perfume and for making margarine.

The breeding season is during November and December. At this time the bulls, weighing up to 300 kilograms, fight for territories in the nurseries. After many bloody battles a bull in his prime will have a substantial harem of cows, but the day he weakens, either through ill-health, injury or the onset of old age, a younger bull will invade his territory and take over his cows.

The diet of seals consists of fish, squid, octopus and crustaceans. An adult seal consumes about 5 kilograms of food a day. They hunt singly. There is no evidence of concerted planning by groups of seals. They frequent the shallows, searching the kelp beds for octopus, crab or crayfish, but they can also dive to depths of 80 metres.

An unexplained habit of seals is their swallowing of stones. It has been suggested that these stones act as ballast and as many as 70 have been found in the stomach of a seal.

Young seals seem to swallow more stones than adults.

Despite wild accusations against seals by fishermen, who regard them as voracious competitors, the presence of seals signifies the existence of ample fish and, owing to their wide range of tastes, only a portion of their diet brings them into competition with man.

Sleek and beautiful, seals are playful and friendly to swimmers and there is no record of a seal having attacked a human being.

The huge rookery at Cape Cross can be visited from 15 December to 15 January on Wednesdays and Saturdays only. Permits must be obtained from the magistrate at Swakopmund.

A male and female seal on the breeding grounds at Cape Cross.

A tombstone in an old German cemetery near Otjiwarongo.

powerful spring of fresh water that surfaces here. The 2 148-metre-high Otavi Mountains dominate the area. Well-wooded, the plains beneath them are fertile, and below the surface are deposits of cadmium, germanium, lead and zinc.

San and Hereros squabbled over the area for many years, and a pile of stones at Ondjondjo is said to be the grave of the Herero chief Nandayetu, who was killed by a San's poisoned arrow.

The town, which had its beginning with the establishment of a military station in 1896, became a municipality in 1958. Today, shaded by flowering trees, it is an attractive mining and agricultural centre.

Otjiwarongo

In 1904 a military station was established here on a gentle, grassy slope in the middle of an undulating plain. The name oTjiwarongo means 'the pleasant place', and the town that grew here in 1907, when the narrow-gauge railway was built, is a relaxed agricultural centre and staging post on the tourist route from Windhoek to Etosha Pan.

Tall trees grow in the area and give a welcome degree of shade to the town. There is a park — Paresis Park — with sports fields, a swimming bath and a caravan park.

Outjo

A cluster of low hillocks, known to the

A fascinating tourist road leads west from Outjo for 412 kilometres to the Skeleton Coast at Torra Bay.

On the way, the road passes a turn-off south to the strange rock landmark known as Fingerklip ('finger rock'). The rock, 35 metres high, has been worn into its distinctive shape by erosion.

Forty kilometres further along the main road is the tourist camp at Khorixas, a corruption of the Damara word 'gorigas' — a water bush that grows in the area.

This camp is situated in a park-like setting frequented by giraffe, oryx, kudu, zebra, black-nosed impala and springbok. There is a shop, a caravan and camping ground, a swimming bath and bungalows.

West of the camp, the road to the coast passes a petrified 'forest' consisting of the fossilized remains of several different species of trees. The indications are that these trees never grew in the area but were driftwood, dumped here when the sea penetrated far inland. Growing among the petrified trees are welwitschia plants (see box, page 474) and other species of drought-resistant vegetation.

Another 50 kilometres west along the road is Twyfelfontein, known in the Damara language as Uais ('one spring'). In this complex jumble of rock there is a great collection of primitive rock engravings dating back perhaps 5 000 years. There is no clue as to which people were responsible for these works, though it is conjectured that they were Khoikhoi. San artists later added paintings to the engravings.

East of Twyfelfontein is the weird landscape of the Verbrande Berg

Fingerklip looming above the wilderness and dwarfing a human figure.

('burnt mountain'). Here, assorted shales and basalt have been baked by the heat into vivid shades of almost every colour except green. The scene is unlike anything else on earth. In ages past the area was blasted with an eruption of basalt. It cooled and left these lovely colours and strange rock shapes.

Beyond the turn-off to the Verbrande Berg and Twyfelfontein the main road crosses the Namib Desert and after 212 kilometres it reaches the fishing resort of Torra Bay. A reliable car and a good driver are needed for this remarkable journey to the Skeleton Coast.

The name Twyfelfontein ('doubtful spring') was given in former years when wandering cattlemen, always searching for grazing for their herds, found the area good but the water supply unreliable. The spring lies in a valley hemmed in by arid, table-topped mountains, their slopes littered with giant red-coloured sandstone rocks. The 'doubtful' spring attracted game animals to the bush-covered floor of the valley, and the game brought primitive hunters who whiled away their time engraving on the rocks.

The trunk of a petrified tree near Khorixas.

The Organ Pipes — a rock formation near Verbrande Berg.

Fish teem in the clear waters of a sunken lake

THE BEETLE THAT BASKS IN FOG TO TAKE A DRINK

The arid dune country of the Namib Desert offers a classic example of how a living creature can adapt to an environment of the utmost severity.

In the early mornings and late afternoons the flightless, black beetle, *Onymacris unguicularis,* forages the dunes, feeding on plant matter carried by the winds. In a landscape that seems at first glance to offer nothing to eat the beetle bustles about, snatching up odd seeds and other food brought by the wind.

As evening comes, the beetle buries itself in the loose sand of a dune. There it sleeps snugly through the cold desert night, emerging either with the new day or, if it is thirsty, when the fog rolls in from the sea. For with the coming of the fog, the beetle begins to perform a strange ritual.

It climbs to the crest of a dune and stands facing the wind with its head down, almost in an attitude of prayer. Scientists call this 'fog basking'.

Fog condenses on the body of the beetle and trickles along narrow grooves in its shell. These grooves direct drops of water into the mouth of the beetle. With its thirst quenched, the beetle is then ready to withstand the intense heat and the dehydrating winds of the desert.

Other species of beetle, fishmoths and ants also live in the Namib, although none of them has adopted the ingenious fog-basking life-style. Most produce their own water through internal chemical processes.

These creatures eat fragments of desiccated vegetable matter that collect in the hollows between the dunes. This dry material would seem to be pretty poor fare for the sustenance of life, but it seems to be considered tasty by a surprising number of little creatures. The withered fragments are food and drink to them — and they themselves are food and drink for slightly larger forms of life.

Spiders, scorpions, crickets and wasps feed on the tiny vegetable-eaters. Moles and various reptiles, including the side-winder snake, feed in their turn on these intermediate life forms. Jackals and birds feed on the larger life forms, and the desert supports in this multiple-tiered manner a population far more numerous than would be suggested by a casual inspection.

Most of these desert creatures show an appreciation of the temperature levels of a sand dune. To suit their own preferences they burrow into a level where the temperature is to their liking. A cross-section of a Namib sand dune, awesome in its sheer mass and appalling sterility, would reveal many levels of occupied 'flats', each sheltering tenants who find them snug and secure.

The ranching town of Outjo, on the way to the Etosha National Park.

An old-time 'puffing Billy' locomotive, now in retirement at Outjo.

Hereros as oHutjo ('little huts'), has given Outjo its European name. It is the terminus of a branch railway from Otjiwarongo and a staging post for tourists driving north to the Etosha National Park. The town is the centre

A red velvet mite, one of the small creatures able to survive in the desert.

A breeding pair of Namib Desert beetles of the fog-basking family.

A Meloidae beetle — one of the Namib Desert's occasional visitors.

Tok-tokkie beetles, so named from the knocking noise they make.

An Odontopus sexpunctatus, *which feeds on the* Welwitschia mirabilis.

A Buprestid beetle, another of the Namib Desert's occasional visitors.

The original German-built Roman Catholic church at Tsumeb.

for a ranching and dairy industry, with a large creamery. There is a municipal tourist resort with bungalows and a caravan park in a shady setting.

Tsumeb

Centuries ago, an African prospector discovered a 12-metre high hill of vividly coloured malachite ore, composed of many different oxides, looming from the savanna parkland near the sunken lake of Otjikoto. The early prospectors had no way of knowing that the hill lay on top of a prodigious ore body. Modern investigation shows that this ore is contained in a pipe-like throat or crater, 185 metres by 75 metres in area, and reaching a depth of at least 1 500 metres.

How much metal was recovered from this remarkable mine by prehistoric workers is unknown, but since Europeans have worked the deposit they have recovered more than 700 000 tons of copper, 2 million tons of lead, 800 000 tons of zinc, and substantial quantities of cadmium, germanium and silver.

The mineral deposit is astonishing in its variety. There are more than 200 minerals contained in the pipe, including several different sulphides of copper ranging from yellow to blue. Native copper is a beautiful red, and there are also many oxidized forms in peacock blue and green, with red cuprite and yellow-green arsenates.

The Hereros called the place oTjisume. This name was corrupted by the Khoikhoi to Tsomsoub, and then by Europeans to Tsumeb.

Eighteen kilometres north of the town lies the sunken lake of Otjikoto. Formed by the collapse of the ceiling over a sinkhole, the lake is about 70-80 metres deep and filled with clear water containing many fish, including two rare species that hatch their fertilized eggs in their mouths.

There is another sunken lake, Guinas, 8 kilometres away, which also teems with fish. Presumably left in these isolated lakes by receding floodwaters, these fish have developed their own characteristics in the course of many generations.

Tsumeb is a mining town with a park in its centre. The mine ranks as the world's largest lead producer and the fifth largest copper producer.

The extraordinary granite rock mass known as Spitzkoppe. This is a severe test for any mountaineer.

Prehistoric rock engravings at Twyfelfontein.

The slag of a tin mine at Uis in the southern wilderness.

ZIMBABWE

ZIMBABWE

BETWEEN THE ZAMBEZI and the Limpopo rivers lies a parkland of 375 830 square kilometres endowed with an astonishing variety of trees. There is no part of this land where trees do not grow — generally so densely that only a few granite outcrops emerge as islands in a sea of green.

Beneath its rich covering of trees, this is a land dominated by the valleys of two majestic rivers. In the south, the Limpopo flows eastwards down a shallow, sultry valley. The northern side of this valley rises towards a long, narrow, arched watershed which provides a backbone to the landscape, a grass-covered plateau lying approximately 1 250 metres above sea level. North of this watershed ridge, which is seldom more than 50 kilometres wide, the land falls away again to the mighty Zambezi River, which flows through a relentlessly hot valley and forms the frontier with Zambia.

This parkland between the two great river valleys is dominated by a remarkable geological feature: huge outcrops of granite, some of the oldest datable rock so far found on earth, surge up from the depths, forming giant domes, whalebacks and shattered castles. Scientists estimate that these great masses of primeval granite have been in existence for approximately 3 000 million years.

It seems that, as molten matter surged upwards from the depths of the earth, shattering what was then the fragile outer skin of a cooling surface, it carried with it minerals and metals. While still in a liquid state, these metals and minerals flowed into crevices and cracks that had been scored in the surface of the earth by the emergence of the granites, turning the landscape into a treasure chest — bequeathing to its future inhabitants a fortune in gold, copper, chrome and asbestos.

A second remarkable feature of this landscape is what is known to geologists as the Great Dyke. Geological history records stupendous happenings in the story of creation, and one of the most spectacular of these took place in Africa about 650 million years ago.

Owing to a subterranean disturbance of unknown origin, the entire area of Africa was almost torn in half. In east Africa the Great Rift Valley was formed. Reaching southwards the tear narrowed, forming a trough running for approximately 650 kilometres north to south across the full width of this parkland lying between the Zambezi and the Limpopo, and then continuing still farther southwards into the Transvaal. To geologists this narrow southern part of the rift is known as the Great Dyke.

From the time man first wandered into this area between the rivers, the richness of minerals on the surface and the granite outcrops profoundly influenced his culture and history. All that was needed to convert the parkland into one of the pleasantest and most prosperous of all the political entities of Africa was an intelligent appreciation of its worth.

Preceding page: The lovely rush and bustle of the white water cascades in the Nyangombe ('the river of the oxen') near Nyanga in the eastern highlands of Zimbabwe, a place of trout and deep pools.

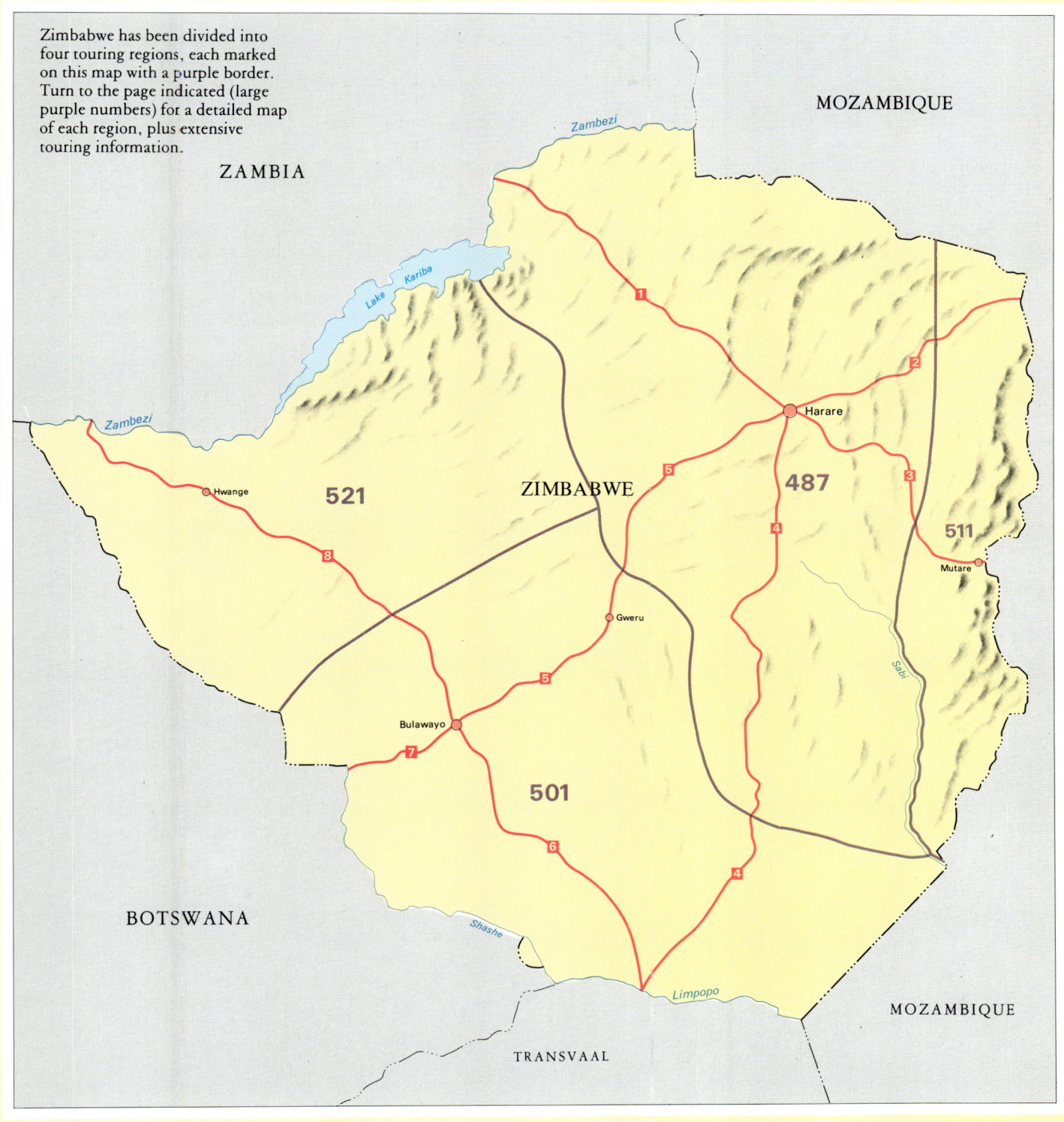

Zimbabwe has been divided into four touring regions, each marked on this map with a purple border. Turn to the page indicated (large purple numbers) for a detailed map of each region, plus extensive touring information.

ZAMBIA

MOZAMBIQUE

Zambezi

Lake Kariba

Zambezi

1

2

Harare

ZIMBABWE

487

3

Hwange

521

5

4

511

8

Mutare

Sabi

Gweru

5

501

Bulawayo

7

6

4

BOTSWANA

Shashe

Limpopo

MOZAMBIQUE

TRANSVAAL

MASHONALAND'S ANCIENT MARVELS

WHEN MZILIKAZI AND his Ndebele people invaded the parkland between the Limpopo and the Zambezi rivers they found it inhabited by a dismayed and unhappy people. Successive raiding armies from Zululand and Mocambique had brought almost total ruin to a once-flourishing African state. The resident people, mainly clans of the Karanga-Rozvi group, were politically shattered and economically ruined. What little they had left was now taken by the Ndebele. In exchange, all they received from the Ndebele was the name Shona, a contemptuous nickname, meaning a people on the way down, bankrupt and of no further account.

The relentless rhythm of human history had brought these people prosperity, then hurled them to their knees. Their only consolation was that their state had endured for more than 1 000 years, and in the primitive setting of Africa this was remarkable. In addition, they had attained a cultural level superior to that of any other people native to southern Africa.

It was about 500 A.D. that the ancestors of these people found their way south of the Zambezi. From the north they brought with them herds of cattle — a cross between the indigenous long-horned sanga and the hump-backed zebus introduced to East Africa by the Arabs — and a few crops such as millet, peas, roots and cucurbits.

They employed the simple agricultural technique of burning patches of forest, cultivating to exhaustion the topsoil of humus and ashes, and then moving on to repeat the process.

At that time, Africa was big and empty enough for this so-called shifting cultivation, and the San people who were already resident in the country were simply pushed away by a people superior in numbers and military strength.

Soon surface outcrops of metals were discovered. This discovery was made by migrants who probably were already familiar with metals, and who also knew how to mine them and how to fashion them into useful and valuable items. There was no other area in the continent of Africa where surface outcrops of iron, copper and gold were so numerous and so easy to work. The deposits were right on the surface, the rock containing them was reasonably soft to work, and the tree-rich parkland of Zimbabwe provided an inexhaustible supply of fuel for the essential smelting and blacksmithing.

According to the records of the Arabs on the east coast, by 1000 A.D. there was a steady trade in copper and gold with the people south of the Zambezi. It was never as profitable a trade as the ivory and slave trade further up the east coast. The Arabs never developed settlements as large as Kilwa or Mombasa further north, but there were several smaller trading bases such as Sofala and the islet that gave its name to Mocambique.

By this time the immigrants had established themselves as sole owners of what is now Zimbabwe. They called themselves the Karanga and lived under a monarch, or mambo, known as Mwene Mutapa ('the lord conqueror').

Long before the Portuguese discovered the route around the southern tip of Africa, rumours of this African state had reached Europe, where it was known as the Monomotapa Empire (from Mwene Mutapa) and was reputed to be the fabulous El Dorado, the land of gold of the ancients.

The mining industry flourished, and the Karanga people also built strange and unique stone walls around their settlements. There are thousands of ruins of these settlements, the largest of which was the capital and seat of the mambo — the ruin now known as Great Zimbabwe.

Sometime during the 15th century there was an upheaval, and the great Karanga people split in half. The mambo moved north to the Zambezi valley and the people who followed him became known as the Kore Kore, or 'locusts'. Those who remained behind called themselves the Rozvi, or 'spoilers', and they lived on at Great Zimbabwe and in the central parts of the country.

Both sections of the Karanga continued mining and building stone-walled settlements. Once the process of fragmentation had started, the Karanga people gradually lost their original strength, splitting into several independent and rival groups such as the Zezuru and the Tawara. All, however, retained the same language, life-style and belief in their god, Mwari.

It was these people who, after more than 1 000 years of isolation, suddenly found themselves under vicious attack from Zulu-speaking invaders. Their rulers were killed, their property looted, the men slaughtered, the women ill-treated, their walled settlements sacked and the survivors driven into the wilderness in search of sanctuary.

In this way the old empire of the Monomotapa ended, but in the part of Zimbabwe known as Mashonaland the descendants of the Karanga still live under their various tribal names. Their homeland of trees, granite domes, and the ruins of about 2 000 of their settlements, is a land rich in legends of a vanished civilization.

This land includes some of the most varied and spectacular scenery in Zimbabwe. Here are the flat, sparse lands on the banks of the Sabi River, and the towering red cliffs of the Gona-re-Zhou game reserve tucked into the most south-easterly point of the land. In the east are the mountains — Nyanga, Vumba and Chimanimani.

Take the north-west road from Harare and you will drive through tobacco and cattle country, past Chinhoyi Caves, whose untold depths have secrets of their own, to Kariba — one of the mightiest lakes built by man. Here too is a wildlife wonderland, where elephant and lion still roam free, unhindered by fences and civilization.

Shona huts and storage bins built on solid granite as a protection against termites.

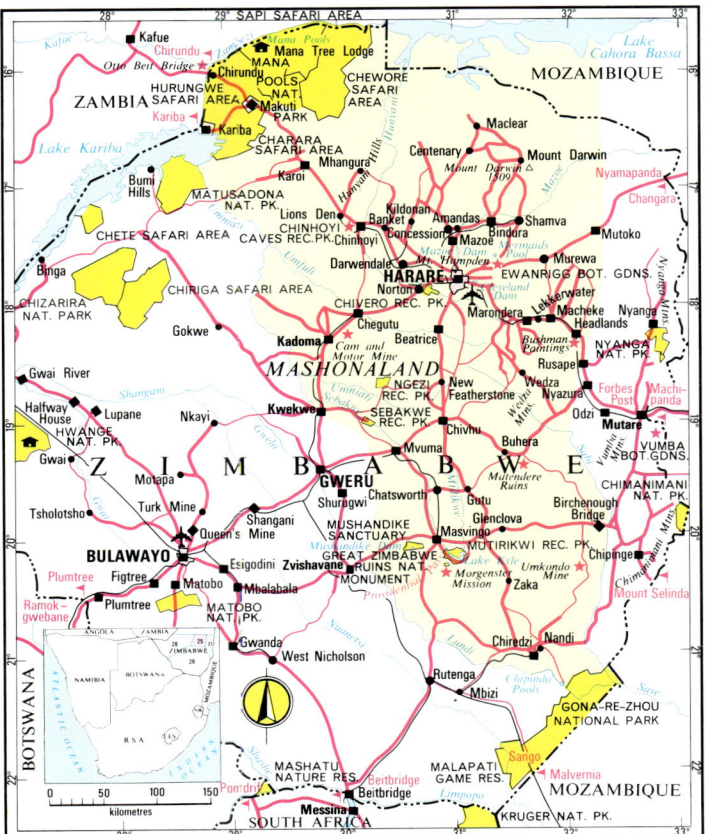

Banket

The village of Banket takes its name from a kind of gold-bearing rock, called 'banket' by the early prospectors because it resembled a Dutch sweetmeat of that name. The village of Banket grew as a small mining centre for a number of claims pegged out on a reef of this type.

Tobacco and maize farming are now the principal industries of the district.

Beatrice

The small agricultural centre of Beatrice, 55 kilometres south of Harare, was named after Beatrice Borrow, sister of H. J. Borrow, who held mining claims in the area.

The original mines are no longer worked but this is now a rich farming area noted for its excellent soil.

Bindura

The Kore Kore people who originally inhabited this region periodically burned the bush in their valley, but took great care to leave an overlooking hill untouched. The game animals in the area would flee to this hill for grazing and there, each spring, the Kore Kore hunted them. Because of this regular trapping of game the hill came to be known as Bindura ('a place of trapping').

In 1890 European prospectors found gold at several ancient workings

A disused gold-stamping mill of one of the small working mines.

THINGS TO DO AND SEE

Angling Although Zimbabwe is far from the sea, no angler can complain of lack of sporting opportunity. There are some 500 species of fish in the river systems of Zimbabwe. Even some salt-water species find their way up such rivers as the Sabi and Limpopo. Exotic fish such as carp and largemouth black bass have been introduced to lakes such as Cleveland, Kyle and Mushandike.

Many of the fish make excellent eating. Bream and hunyani salmon are delicious table fish. The largest fish are tiger-fish, which can reach up to 14 kilograms, and the Vundu, which reaches 36 kilograms. An angler feeling anything heavier on his line has caught a crocodile or hippo — and is advised to cut and run.

Antiquities The ruins of the old Karanga settlements in Zimbabwe are very photogenic and most of them are in beautiful settings.

Boating Power-boats and sailing boats are used on most of the lakes and conditions on the inland sea of Kariba are ideal for cruising. For the canoeist the river systems of the Zambezi and the Limpopo offer a thrilling challenge.

Botany The spring spectacle of the musasa trees (*Brachystegia*) undergoing their annual colour change is one of the world's most glorious botanical scenes. In winter the aloes are in flower at such places as the Ewanrigg National Park and Great Zimbabwe. There are innumerable species of trees here, some with brilliantly coloured flowers.

Camping and caravanning Zimbabwe is superb country for the outdoor lover and its caravan and camping grounds are among the best in Africa. There could be no more romantic a setting for a caravan park than the ruins at Great Zimbabwe. Harare, Masvingo, Chinhoyi, Kariba and the national parks all have camping grounds in park-like settings.

Riding The central plateau of Zimbabwe is ideal riding country. There are stables in Harare and the large towns.

Sports All towns in Zimbabwe have sports clubs for activities such as bowls, tennis, cricket, rugby, hockey, soccer, athletics and swimming. Polo is popular and horses can be hired.

Rocks piled up like a giant's playthings

in the valley below the hill. Mines were started and a village named Bindura grew as a trading centre.

Near the village is a large rock on which the Kore Kore chief, Mukozeko, sacrificed cattle to appease the ancestral spirits, in the belief that this would ensure good rains and crops.

Chegutu

This town was established in 1891 on a site about 29 kilometres east of the present location. It was moved in 1901 to the healthier and better-watered site of today.

Chegutu was originally called Hartley, after Henry Hartley, one of the most notable of the professional hunters of the last century.

From his home in the Magaliesberg range of the Transvaal, Hartley generally spent each winter season hunting in what are now Botswana and Zimbabwe.

In the course of his wanderings he observed the numerous ancient mine workings, shafts and adits sunk by various African peoples, especially the Karanga-Rozvi groups, into surface outcrops of metals such as gold, iron and copper.

In 1866 and 1867 Hartley brought the young German geologist, Karl Mauch, with him on two trips to examine these primitive workings and it was Mauch's enthusiastic report of the mining area which spread the notion around the world that in Zimbabwe lay the Ophir of the Bible and the El Dorado of the ancients.

Several factories and a large cotton mill are close to the town. There is a 16-hectare park in the town and boating and fishing in the Umfuli River.

On the early site of the town is the ruin of an earth fort which sheltered local residents during the uprising of 1896. There are also several graves dating from the same period.

Chinhoyi

In the dolomite at the foot of the Hunyani hills, the action of water over a long period of time has created a vast sinkhole filled with absolutely clear water 90 metres deep.

Viewed from the edge of the sinkhole, this water is a lovely blue colour, and the pool is home to a considerable number of goldfish released here by some unknown person.

A passageway leads down to the edge of this so-called 'Sleeping Pool', and there is also a complex series of tunnels and chambers containing dripstone formations.

An outlaw named Nyamakwere used these caves as a stronghold in the early years of the last century and legend has it that the pool is haunted by the spirits of travellers captured, robbed and killed by being thrown into the water. A large serpent is said to live in the caves.

A Zezuru headman named Tshinoyi eventually settled near the caves and his name, in the form of Sinoia, was given to them by European settlers. This name was recently respelled as Chinhoyi, as was that of the small town in the vicinity which serves as a centre for tobacco, maize farming and mining, particularly for copper and chrome.

The Chinhoyi Caves National Park has been created to preserve the caves. It offers a garden, picnic ground and restaurant.

Chirundu

Where the great north road reaches the Zambezi River, the customs and immigration posts of Zimbabwe and

Near Epworth Mission on the east side of Harare . . .

. . . there are strange balancing rocks. The area . . .

. . . might almost be a playground for a family . . .

. . .of giant children, their toys scattered over the floor.

The Chinhoyi Caves, a spectacular place of bizarre limestone formations.

Zambia swelter in the heat on either side of the river, overlooked by a bush-covered hill known as Chirundu from Tshivundu, a Tonka chief who once lived here.

The graceful 320-metre-long silver suspension arch of the Otto Beit Bridge carries the road over the river. Opened in 1939, this is one of the several bridges constructed from finance provided by the Otto Beit Trust.

Near Chirundu there is a fossil forest, and a Stone-Age site with numerous old implements. This site is preserved as a national monument.

Chivhu

In 1891 Hendrik Bekker pegged a farm on the road between Masvingo and Harare. He named it Enkeldoorn after a species of *Acacia robusta* tree growing here. (In Afrikaans these trees are known as enkeldoorns.)

Bekker later abandoned this farm and Enkeldoorn became a village, the centre of a prosperous agricultural community consisting largely of Afrikaans-speaking settlers. The village was recently renamed Chivhu.

Nearby, the missionary poet, Arthur Shearly Cripps, built his Church of the Five Wounds. His extensive journeys on foot around his vast parish are legendary odysseys.

Chizarira Game Reserve

Covering 1 910 square kilometres on the southern side of Lake Kariba, the Chizarira Game Reserve is a sanctuary for the game animals displaced from the Zambezi Valley by the waters of the man-made lake. There are numerous elephant, buffalo, rhino, various antelope species, lion and leopard. The reserve lies on the thickly bushed slopes and southern verges of the Zambezi Valley, and is intensely hot.

Concession

Henry Clay Moore, an American, secured from Lobengula, the Ndebele king, a concession to establish mines in his territory.

Cecil Rhodes took over this concession in 1893 and in exchange gave Moore rights to peg claims in Mashonaland.

Moore's claims were pegged in the Mazowe Valley and the village that grew next to his mine was named Concession. It is now an agricultural centre.

Near this village is Amandas, the original home of the celebrated spirit medium, Nehanda, one of the leaders of the 1896 uprising.

Epworth Mission

The area of the Epworth Mission, on the eastern outskirts of Harare, is known for its extraordinary rock formations.

These granite fragments are arranged in such strange shapes that the area leads one to think of a playground for a very untidy family of giant children who, packed off to bed, have left their toys scattered over the nursery floor.

A spirit medium named Tshiremba, or Chiremba, once lived in this weird area and in due course his name was given to it.

Among the rocks is Nhurikwa ('the piled-up one') and Dombo rwa Mwari ('the rock of God'), which was once used as an oracle. It was here that the voice of Mwari would answer the prayers of his numerous supplicants.

Ewanrigg Botanical Gardens

Basil Christian, an enthusiastic gardener and plant collector, especially of aloes, named his farm Ewanrigg after his brother, Ewan, who was killed in World War I. (Rigg is the Welsh word for a ridge.)

On his death, Basil Christian bequeathed his farm to the nation. The aloe collection here is the largest in southern Africa. There are also cycads and many aquatic and marsh plants. Winter is the most colourful time to visit this garden.

Gona-re-Zhou Game Reserve

The game reserve named Gona-re-Zhou ('refuge of the elephant') was proclaimed in 1967, largely as the result of the enthusiasm of the late Allan Wright, district commissioner of the area.

The reserve covers 4 964 square kilometres of wild country along the border of Zimbabwe and Mocambique. It was an area used as a hunting ground by Stephanus Cecil Barnard, the renowned ivory poacher known as BveKenya ('the swaggerer').

A giant elephant called Dhlulamithi ('taller than the trees') by the Shanganes was shot here in August 1967 by a hunter from South Africa. The left tusk weighed 62 kilograms and the right tusk 48 kilograms. The tusks are now displayed in the Pretoria Country Club and are listed in the standard Rowland Ward's *Records of Big Game* as the largest tusks obtained south of the Zambezi.

The reserve is now a sanctuary for many game animals. The extremely localized nyala antelope are found here, as well as the king or striped cheetah, an animal so rare as to be almost mythical. These cheetahs are slightly larger than normal and have distinctive striped markings. There are probably not more than 25 king cheetah in existence and very little is

Spring in Ewanrigg Botanical Gardens on the eastern outskirts of Harare.

Harare — the city where flowering trees are always in bloom

known about them.

The Lundi River, from Runde, meaning 'a river subject to great floods', flows through the reserve, and there are many hippos and crocodiles. The huge pools named Chipinda after a renowned chief, Tshipinda, are in the lower reaches of the river. Though extremely hot in summer, the area is pleasant in winter.

Harare

The 'city of flowering trees' is the name often given to Harare, the capital of Zimbabwe. There is considerable justification for this name, for throughout the year some trees or shrubs will be blooming along the city's broad avenues.

Spring — September, October and November — is the most colourful season. The hazy mauve jacarandas, bauhinias in two-colour varieties (pink and white, and white and purple), red Australian flame trees, spectacular yellow cassias, and scarlet flamboyants (or poincianas) are all in full bloom. African flame trees flower in summer, while bougainvillea in many different shades and poinsettias in red, yellow, white and pink seem to be perpetually in bloom.

Harare, formerly known as Salisbury, lies 1 500 metres above sea level on a fertile, well-watered plain with deep soil so red in colour that the Zezuru people who once lived in the area knew it as Gova, meaning 'red soil'. A low, rocky hillock, Harare Kopje, dominates the site. The Zezuru called it Neharare Chikomo ('the hillock of Neharare'), the name of a chief who is said to be buried there and after whom the city is now named.

It was from the top of this hillock, on 12 September 1890, that Frank Johnson, leader of the Pioneer Column, looked out over the surrounding countryside to survey the route to Mount Hampden, where a fort was to be built. From the hillock, Johnson could see Mount Hampden, 16 kilometres to the north-west, but he liked the appearance of the plain around the hillock on which he was standing. This area was an open parkland covered in elegant musasa trees, with leaves brilliant in spring colours. In his imagination, the young commander could easily visualize a garden

city growing in this verdant setting.

He rode back to the camp of the Pioneer Column and asked Sir Leander Starr Jameson, the personal representative of Cecil Rhodes, to join him on the hillock. Jameson immediately agreed that this was indeed a fine site for a fort and future capital of the country. Together they rode over the plain assessing its advantages and disadvantages.

With their minds made up, they returned to camp. At dawn the next day, 13 September 1890 an order was issued to the column:

1. *It is notified for general information that the Column, having arrived at its destination, will halt.*
2. *The name of this place will be Fort Salisbury.*

A camp was then made on the site of the present Anglican Cathedral and on 13 September the Union Jack was run up a musasa pole on what is now Cecil Square, a royal salute of 21 guns was fired and three cheers given for the Queen, and for Lord Salisbury, the prime minister of Great Britain after whom the place was named. This was the beginning of the modern city.

An earthen-work fort was built on the square. Close to the fort the British South Africa Company erected its headquarters and this was the foundation of the commercial centre.

Huts and shacks were soon built on sites favoured by individual pioneers and the infant city took on the appearance of a romantic, casual little frontier place with its fort and a constant coming and going of transport vehicles, horsemen and walkers.

The new township quickly began to attract settlers from the south. During the first 15 months of its existence, women were not permitted in the town, but once this ban was lifted, the place lost much of its frontier atmosphere and the community became more civilized.

In 1893 the defeat of the Ndebele chief, Lobengula, allowed the British South Africa Company's troops to occupy Bulawayo and Harare was suddenly confronted by a rival claiming to be the capital of the country. Houses in Harare were deserted and the streets became overgrown.

Those who remained, however, gradually halted the decay, sinking

wells, building the first two-storey houses, a market hall, and they even built a stock exchange.

At the outbreak of the Mashona uprising in 1896, settlers in the Mazowe Valley decided to take refuge in Harare, but they were cut off at the Alice Mine, 43 kilometres from the town.

From the telegraph office near the mine a dramatic unfinished message came through to Harare:

'We are surrounded.
Dickenson, Cass, Faull killed. For God's sake . . .'

Reinforcements from Harare reached the settlers on 19 June 1896 and escorted the survivors back to the town, fighting a running battle against the Mashona on the way. Harare itself was under siege for almost six weeks and many of the citizens sought refuge in the town gaol.

The railway from Beira, in Mocambique, reached Harare in 1899. Schools were built, small industries began to appear, and roads and gardens were laid out. The marshy ground alongside the Makabusi stream — which had been a problem for years — was drained, and buildings sprang up where they could not have been built before.

Plots were chosen for government buildings and the kopje area began to decline in popularity as people moved their homes to the residential area north of the old causeway built across this marshy ground. The name of Makabusi must surely be one of the most corrupted place names in Zimbabwe; it originates from the Mutyisambizi, meaning 'the river where the zebra is frightened'.

There were severe food shortages and considerable hardship in Harare during the Angola-Boer War, when supplies from the south were cut off. When the war ended, however, public works were begun to ease unemployment. Roads were made, trees planted and a library built.

As more of the area around the town came under cultivation, with cattle-breeding and maize and tobacco farming, Harare developed as a market town. The growth in population led to a water shortage and in 1913 the Cleveland Dam was built on the headwaters of the Makabusi River.

This dam not only supplied water

but also made electricity available for the first time.

In 1923 self-government was granted to the country with Harare as the capital. The town became a city in 1935. With the development of the automobile and later, air travel, the country and its capital were finally brought out of their isolation in the middle of Africa.

During the Second World War, Harare was surrounded by airfields of the Empire Training Scheme, under which thousands of allied pilots learned to fly. The end of the war brought an influx of immigrants from Europe and in 1954 Harare became the capital of the Federation of Rhodesia and Nyasaland.

The federation was dissolved in 1963 and Harare reverted to being the capital of Southern Rhodesia. Tall, modern buildings were erected, giving a dramatic new look to the Harare skyline, and hotels were built to cater for tourists and businessmen who came to the city in ever-increasing numbers.

Harare's position on the air-route between Europe and South Africa led to the construction of a new airport, capable of handling the largest aircraft, on the southern outskirts of the city.

Harare's climate is temperate, with sunny days and cool nights for seven months of the year. Although subtropical in summer it is rarely too hot for comfort. The rainfall of 760 millimetres a year makes Harare a garden city, with an atmosphere of restfulness and beauty. Almost every sport is catered for and cultural societies flourish.

In the heart of the city is the bold architecture of the National Gallery, one of the largest art galleries in southern Africa. The gallery is the home of a Shona stone-carving workshop. Exhibitions of Zimbabwean art are held regularly.

The Anglican Cathedral of St. Mary and All Saints stands on the site of the first church, built in 1890 by Canon Balfour from mud and poles. The original altar cross, made of cigar boxes, is now in the cathedral's St. George's Chapel. The ten bells in the tower were cast in London and each bears an English rose and a Zimbab-

The old Meikle's Hotel, Harare, demolished but not forgotten.

Sculptures of odd creatures inspecting the visitors at the Zimbabwe Museum.

The National Archives, housed in a vermin-proof building.

The lounge of the old Meikle's Hotel, a place of rendezvous, schemes and projects.

The city centre of Harare as seen from the summit of Harare Kopje. Modern buildings and crowded streets now cover the once tree-covered plain.

wean flame lily in its casting.

The cathedral was started in 1913 and completed in 1964.

A bronze flagstaff in Cecil Square marks the spot where the Union Jack was hoisted by the Pioneer Column on 13 September 1890.

There is an illuminated fountain with constantly changing patterns and colours in the square. It was built in 1950 at the time of the Diamond Jubilee.

Plants from Rhodes's cottage at Muizenberg in the Cape were originally planted here.

Ballantyne Park, in the suburb of Highlands, has a lake which is the home of many kinds of waterfowl, in-cluding migratory teal and other wild duck. The lake is stocked with bream and is a popular haunt of anglers.

On the summit of Harare Kopje there is a toposcope, presented to the city by the British South Africa Company in 1953 to mark the centenary of the births of Cecil Rhodes, Sir Leander Starr Jameson and Alfred Beit, all of whom were born in the same year and became great figures in the country's history. From the kopje there are magnificent views over the city and its surroundings, with the bronze plaques of the toposcope indicating the direction of numerous points of interest. An Eternal Flame is maintained at the summit as a memorial to all who died in the recent war of independence.

The Zimbabwe Museum in the civic centre contains a collection of the country's freshwater fish, also rock art exhibits, displays of extinct animals, tribal people of the regions, Iron-Age archaeology and pioneer history.

The MacGregor Geological Museum is in Fourth Street. It displays samples of the minerals and metals found in Zimbabwe.

The House of Assembly, where Parliament meets, was built in 1895 and was intended to be a hotel. The public is admitted to the Strangers' Gallery, and visitors may be shown around the building when parliament is not sitting.

At Alexandra Park, 4 kilometres north of the city centre, is the national botanic garden. Plants here include 5 000 trees representing 750 of Zimbabwe's species. There is also a herbarium and a collection of exotic shrubs.

The city's main park, Harare Gardens, covers 15 hectares and contains a working model of Victoria Falls, complete with rainbow. A band plays in the park on Sunday afternoons.

The gardens are famous for the spring displays of sweet peas, stocks, zinnias and marigolds.

The national archives in the city contain many documents from the country's past, and paintings of the pioneer days by Thomas Baines. Also in the archives are the diaries of David Livingstone.

There is a large municipal caravan and camping ground on the eastern outskirts, and several hotels and other places of accommodation in the city.

Headlands

Once a posting station on the road from Harare to Mutare, Headlands is today a small rural centre. Nearby are rock shelters containing galleries of San paintings.

Kadoma

This town is named after a Tonka chief who once lived in the area.

It originated in 1906 as a railway siding on the Bulawayo-Harare line and was until recently spelled as Gatooma. The town developed as a centre for mining, and the Cam and Motor

Poinciana (or flamboyant trees) in full bloom in a Harare street.

How the mighty Zambezi was harnessed

Virginia tobacco, one of the principal crops of Zimbabwe.

Karanga huts built of thatch and mud, cool in summer, warm in winter.

Mine, 5 kilometres to the east, was the largest gold mine in Zimbabwe.

Chrome, nickel, magnesite and iron are also found in the area.

Cotton is grown in the district and the David Whitehead Spinning Mill is situated in the town. There is a recreational area around Claw Dam, 15 kilometres away, with picnic sites, camping and fishing.

Kariba

One of the largest man-made lakes in the world was completed in 1959 when the Zambezi River was dammed at what the Tonka people call Kariba, meaning 'a little trap'. The building of the wall was a formidable feat of engineering and many men died during its construction. The Zambezi is a major river subject to colossal floods and harnessing it for electric power was a problem.

The dam wall is a double-curvature concrete arch with a crest length of 618 metres and a height of 128 metres. A 12-metre-wide road runs along the top. There are six flood-gates, each 9,1 metres by 9,4 metres.

The dam has created a lake 281 kilometres long and with a maximum width of 32 kilometres.

There are six turbo-generators in use and provision was made in the design of the dam wall for the eventual installation of a second set of turbo-generators.

The lake lies in an area of stifling summer heat.

The Zambezi Valley was originally occupied by the Tonka people, who were displaced by the waters of the lake and resettled on higher ground. Game animals were also rescued from the waters and released in the overlooking hills on the south side of the lake.

A holiday resort has been created on the verges of the lake. Boating and fishing attract many visitors, especially during winter months, from April to September, when the temperature is pleasant. October and November are 'suicide' months of extreme heat and December to April are also very hot. Such extreme temperatures — occasionally in excess of 49°C — must be taken into account by visitors. Precautions against excessive sunburn are necessary.

Bilharzia and crocodiles in the Zambezi make swimming foolhardy, but most places of accommodation have swimming pools.

Fishing is good, especially for tigerfish and bream.

In the town of Kariba there is a church built to the memory of those who died building the dam.

Accommodation at Kariba includes hotels, boatels and motels.

Karoi

Mica mining and tobacco farming are the principal industries of this part of Zimbabwe, which is crossed by the main road from Harare to Chirundu. It is said that in former years a muroyi, or witch, was executed by drowning in the river known after the event as the Karoyi. The village of Karoi takes its name from the river.

Lake Kyle

The dam at the junction of the Mtilikwe and Shagashi rivers was built in 1961 to provide water for the irrigation of sugar and citrus estates in the lowveld of Zimbabwe. A farm, named Kyle — a Scots word meaning 'a channel of water' — was inundated by the rising waters of the dam.

The Lake Kyle dam is 35 kilometres from Masvingo. Its wall is 311 metres long and 62 metres high, built across a gorge between granite hills. The dam is popular for boating and fishing. A 76-square-kilometre game reserve has been created on a peninsula jutting into the northern end of the lake and this is a sanctuary for kudu, waterbuck, giraffe, sable, zebra, eland, and white rhinos which were brought here from Zululand. There are daily pony trails, giving visitors the opportunity to do their game-viewing on horseback.

There is a fish research centre, a crocodile information centre, and an aquarium in the reserve. Lake Kyle is surrounded by granite hills and handsome parkland. Several rock shelters contain galleries of San paintings.

There are caravan and camping grounds, chalets and cottages.

Lake McIlwaine

A principal recreational area for the

The dam wall of Kariba with the flood gates open at the height of the flood season.

The church at Kariba, commemorating workers killed building the dam.

Tourists sailing Lake Kariba in the ferry Sealion.

Tourist accommodation at Kariba is designed to be cool and attractive.

The man-made inland sea of Lake Kariba. The lake is 281 kilometres long by 32 kilometres wide.

citizens of Harare is Lake McIlwaine, 42 kilometres from the city. In 1952 an earthen wall 85 metres long, 37 metres high and 274 metres wide was built to block the Hunyani River where it passed through a narrow gap in the hills. The resultant lake was named after Sir Robert McIlwaine, first chairman of the natural resources board.

Lake McIlwaine is surrounded by parkland. The northern shore has been developed into a recreational area with tea-rooms, yachting, aquaplaning and boating. There are picnic sites, caravan and camping sites, an aquarium and a restaurant. Fishing is good, with numerous tiger-fish, bream, yellowfish, barbel and Hunyani salmon.

The southern shores of the lake have been preserved as a game park occupying 1 600 hectares. White rhino, tsessebe, zebra, wildebeest and kudu have their homes in the area. There are several galleries of San paintings in rock shelters in the park.

Swimming in the lake is not advisable owing to the presence of bilharzia.

Macheke

The small rural centre of Macheke is situated in a natural rockery of granite boulders and rock fragments, many of them having particularly weird shapes. There are San paintings in rock shelters near the railway station. The name Macheke comes from an African term meaning 'a place of cultivated fields and gardens'.

Mana Pools National Park

In the flood plain of the Zambezi, downriver from Chirundu, lies a cluster of lakelets known as the Mana Pools. The lakelets are the remnants of old river channels, and they are fed by occasional floodwaters. They attract vast numbers of aquatic birds and are rich in fish. Large numbers of game animals frequent the area, especially elephant, buffalo, hippo, rhino, crocodile, various antelope, lion, leopard and wild dog.

The Mana Pools National Park is 2 196 square kilometres in extent. Visitors can explore the area on foot at their own risk. Summer temperatures are extremely hot, and precautions must be taken against mosquitoes and tsetse fly.

There is a large camping and caravan site, and National Park lodges. The game reserve is open from 1 May to 31 October.

Marondera

On the main road to Mutare, 72 kilometres from Harare, lies the pretty little agricultural centre of Marondera, named after a chief of the Zezuru people who once lived here. The town, which until recently was called Marandellas, is built around a large central square and is notable for its trees and pleasant climate.

Timber, cattle, wine, dairy products, grain and tobacco are produced in the district. The Borradaile Trust has cottages for the aged here, built in a garden setting. Marondera is also an important educational centre.

Anglers on the misty waters of the well-stocked Lake McIlwaine.

Lake Kyle near Masvingo explodes in a breathtaking sunset.

A peak honouring an English novelist

At nearby Lekkerwater are ruins of a Karanga settlement occupied between the 14th and 16th centuries.

Masvingo

The Pioneer Column sent by Rhodes to occupy Mashonaland made its way up Providential Pass to the middleveld of Zimbabwe. On 13 August 1890 the column reached a site where the men relaxed for six days, enjoying themselves and building an earthwork fort which was named Fort Victoria in honour of Queen Victoria.

This stronghold became a major staging post on the route from South Africa to Harare and the north. Fort Victoria — recently renamed Masvingo — grew as a centre for agriculture, ranching, mining and tourism. The celebrated ruins of Great Zimbabwe, Lake Kyle, Lake Kyle National Park and Game Park, and the Mushandike National Park (see separate entries) are in the vicinity.

Part of the original fort can still be visited, including the bell tower. In spring, Masvingo is brilliant with the flowers of poinsettias, jacarandas and bougainvillaea. There is a caravan park, hotels and a motel.

Matendere Ruins

These beautiful ruins crown the summit of a low exposure of granite in the Buhera district of Zimbabwe. This district contains the ruins of many other walled settlements of the Karanga-

Black and white ivory, the great African exports in the days of slavery.

Rozvi people but Matendere, meaning 'enclosures', is the largest.

Baobab trees grow in the ruins and the atmosphere is romantic and eerie, the surrounding country wild and densely covered in trees.

Mazowe

The valley of the river known as Mazowe ('the place of elephants') is one of the loveliest and most fertile in Zimbabwe. The ruins of many walled settlements, relics of ancient mining, signs of former Portuguese missions and trading posts, groves of lemon and olive trees still growing wild in the bush — all are proof of a long-established human settlement which was disrupted in the 19th century by the influx of raiding bands from Zululand and Mocambique, and the collapse of the Karanga state.

A decorated wall of the Matendere Ruins, near a giant euphorbia tree.

Today the valley is densely cultivated with citrus groves, and orchards of avocados, mangoes, litchis, various nuts such as pecans, granadilla vines and other tropical fruits.

Mazowe Dam, completed in 1920, irrigates a large area. The Mazowe Citrus Estate alone covers 21 000 hectares. Commercial trout breeding has been established and the dam is well known for the size of the carp caught in its waters.

The village of Mazowe is the principal centre for the valley.

Mermaids Pool

A popular resort for Harare residents is Mermaids Pool, 42 kilometres from the city. The pool, at the foot of a natural slide in a perennial stream, is 46 metres across and 5 metres deep. There is a restaurant and a variety of accommodation.

Morgenster Mission

The Reverend Andries Adriaan Louw, of the Dutch Reformed Church, established the mission of Morgenster ('morning star') in 1891. The mission, within sight of Great Zimbabwe, has a natural landmark in the form of two pinnacles of rock known as the

The summit of Mount Darwin with the wall built by vanished people.

Finger Rocks in its grounds.

On one rock there is a bronze plaque, unveiled in 1941 by the governor of the former Southern Rhodesia, Sir Herbert Stanley, to mark the jubilee of the mission.

At the same time, the Reverend Louw unveiled a 3-metre high snow-white concrete 'candle' powered by electricity, its candle commemorating the translation of the Bible into the Shona language.

The mission is well known for its school for the deaf, said to be the oldest in the country.

Tourists are asked to visit on a weekday unless they wish to attend the church service.

Mount Darwin

One of the most celebrated landmarks in the northern part of Zimbabwe is the 1 509-metre-high mountain known to the Kore Kore people as Pfura, meaning 'the one that surpasses'.

It was an important centre of religious worship and the summit is covered with the ruins of stone walls.

The Portuguese, deluded by the similarity of the name Pfura, regarded this as the Ophir of the Bible and the gold mining centre of the ancients. In 1889 the hunter, Frederick Selous, renamed the mountain in honour of Charles Darwin, while another peak close by received from him the name of Mount Thackeray, in honour of the English novelist.

North of the mountain is a small administrative village also named Mount Darwin. The country around it is undeveloped, with the ruins of many stone-walled settlements and the signs of primitive mining.

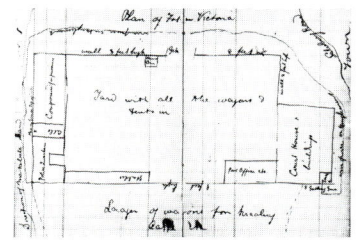

A modern reproduction (above) of the original plan of Fort Victoria (right), which was created by the Pioneer Column.

[Plan of Fort Victoria — diagram labels:]
Plan of Fort Victoria
Wire fence entanglement
Wall 8 feet high — Gate — 8 feet high
Maxim gun
Compound for prisoners
Maxim gun on top of cells
Cells
Yard with all the wagons and tents in
Wall 8 feet high
Salisbury Road — Town
Police Quarters
Stables
8 feet high
Court House and buildings
Post Office, etc
Tower
Wire fence entanglement
Gatling gun
Direction of Matabele Land
Laager of wagons for kraaling cattle, etc
Our tents

A selection of the many butterfly species found in Zimbabwe.

Mount Hampden

In 1880 Frederick Selous was hunting and exploring the north-eastern part of Zimbabwe when he reached an open plain with deep, red-coloured soil. Dominating this plain were several hillocks, the most notable of which rose about 150 metres above the plain, and was called Musitkwe, meaning 'the immovable'. Selous renamed it Mount Hampden in honour of John Hampden, the great opponent of Charles I of England.

The hill is covered with the ruins of stone walls believed to have been built in the 15th century. It was towards this hill that Selous guided the Pioneer Column sent by Rhodes in 1890 to occupy Mashonaland. The intention was to establish a town close to Mount Hampden, as Selous considered its situation to be the most suitable he had seen in the area for a settlement. However, the leader of the Pioneer Column, Frank Johnson, preferred the site of Harare, 15 kilometres south, and Mount Hampden was consequently left in peace.

Citrus estates in the Mazowe Valley, an area of gold mining and agriculture.

The Finger Rocks stand like sentries.

Mushandike National Park

The 12 900-hectare Mushandike National Park was opened in 1954 around the shores of the Mushandike Lake, 32 kilometres west of Masvingo. The lake is a popular fishing area, particularly for large-mouth bass, bream and barbel. The park is a sanctuary for sable, kudu, waterbuck and several species of smaller antelope. Leopards are present and the bird life includes flocks of flamingoes.

A rare geological feature of the park is the existence of stromatolites. These are rocks made up of fossil algae that date back 2 500 million years.

The park has an active research programme to domesticate eland and Cape buffalo, and is the home of the Natural Resources College, offering courses in Game Ranger work.

San rock shelters with paintings on the walls are also preserved in the park.

There is a caravan and camping ground.

Mvuma

One of the landmarks on the main road from Beitbridge across Zimbabwe to Chirundu is the tall smokestack of the old Falcon (later the Athens) gold mine. This mine flourished for many years. The smokestack was built on top of a hill to a height that would facilitate the dispersal of noxious chemical vapours.

Mvuma is now an agricultural centre. The name comes from the sounds of singing, drumming and the lowing of cattle which are said to be heard from a taboo pool here.

Norton

The small industrial township of Norton, 40 kilometres west of Harare, is named after Joseph Norton, owner of the farm on which the place was founded. He and his family were murdered here on 15 June 1896 at the outbreak of the Mashona uprising.

Providential Pass

When Frederick Selous was guiding the Pioneer Column on its journey to occupy Mashonaland in 1890, by pure chance he found an easy natural pass in a well-forested escarpment leading from the lowveld to the middleveld of Zimbabwe. On 13 August 1890, the Pioneer Column made its way up this pass, and the name Providential Pass was given to it.

Ten kilometres north of the summit, the pioneers founded Masvingo, which was to become an important staging post on the route from South Africa to Harare.

Shamva

One of the most fascinating of the mining centres of the northern part of Zimbabwe is the gold mining village of Shamva, named after the tsamvi species of wild fig trees which grow here. The gold mine situated just south of the village has created spectacular scars from its open cast workings and these will remain engraved on the hill summit for millenia.

A large rubble dump, a cluster of houses, the terminus of a branch railway from Harare and the buildings of the grain marketing board make up this centre.

Wedza

A section of the Karanga people known as the Mbire settled close to the range of mountains known from their richness in iron as Wedza, meaning 'a place of wealth'. The Mbire and other inhabitants mined this iron, making spearheads and agricultural tools.

The town of Wedza is the administrative headquarters of the area.

There are several caves and rock shelters in the district containing San paintings. Sealed up in the walls of the Markwe Cave are the remains of one of the former chiefs who had the hereditary title of Soswe.

Hills of historic importance are the Mtukwa and Mushwawo, which were used for shelter by early inhabitants during Ndebele raids.

Myths and mysteries of Great Zimbabwe

The complex of ruins known as Great Zimbabwe lies 30 kilometres southeast of Masvingo. The name is derived from the Shona maDzimbabwe, or dzimbahwe, meaning 'a great stone building', and this ruin is one of the best-known in the world.

Great Zimbabwe is beautifully situated in a fertile and well-watered valley at the head of the Mutirikwi River. Archaeological investigations indicate that this valley, as well as the hill dominating it where the bulk of the ruin stands, were inhabited by human beings of several different races from an early age.

Early man sheltered in the caves here, and by the 4th century A.D. the first Iron-Age people, apparently the Gokomere group, found their way to the area and discovered the desirability of the Mutirikwi Valley.

It was a place suitable for a king, an oasis of fertility in the wilderness of Africa, with pleasant breezes blowing up the valley to produce a mild and healthy climate.

The hill seems to have attracted the first Iron Age settlers. It was a natural stronghold, easy to defend, dominating the valley and containing several features which made it unique. One of these features was a cave in a natural acoustic shape. The voice of Mwari, the Karanga-Rozvi god, is said to emit from the cave.

Over the years so many people settled on the hill that it became overcrowded. Additional building sites were obtained by creating platforms made of piled-up granite rocks forming walls whose insides were filled with rubble; the conventional African mud-walled huts were then erected on the level surface.

Others settled in the valley at the foot of the hill. It appears that the king, the warriors and the priests of Mwari remained on the hill, while the queen, with the bulk of the people, lived down in the valley. The residence of the king was surrounded by a particularly large, well-built and impressive stone wall.

Considerable archaeological research has not revealed signs of the presence of any people foreign to Africa in these ruins other than a few traders or visitors. The evidence indicates that these vast ruins were built by substantially the same people as those living in Zimbabwe today.

Essentially, the ruins consist of walls made of fragments of granite piled one on top of the other. In the valley at the foot of the hill, more than 900 000 granite fragments were used in the construction of the Imba huru (Great Enclosure). The walls of this impressive structure — which early European explorers originally designated the Temple — are decorated with chevron patterns of black and white granite fragments.

The ruins on the hill, the Nharira ya

A view over the Valley of Ruins, as seen from high on the hill at Great Zimbabwe.

Mambo (Place of the King) — which the early European explorers called the Acropolis — originally surrounded the huts of the king, the warriors and the priests.

The builders of the ruins never erected any roofing. Their stonework walls always either enclosed living space, or supported platforms.

There are no ruins like these anywhere else in the world. The small-stone construction gives them immense power in the vast setting of Africa.

An imposing passageway leading towards the royal residence.

The beautifully built walls of the Great Enclosure.

Large building blocks, curiously, would be dwarfed by the setting, but the cumulative effect of thousands of small, piled fragments is of concentrated human effort.

Great Zimbabwe was probably inhabited from the earliest centuries A.D., though the massive structures of the Great Enclosure were probably built around 1200 A.D.

Digs in the western enclosure of the Hill Ruins have revealed evidence of five eras of occupation. The first ended during the 4th century, and it was at this time that the second began. The third — which is probably when the stone walls were built — began in about 1000 A.D. The fourth and richest period commenced during the 15th century. There is no evidence of economic or building activities after the 15th century.

Glass beads and china found in the ruins are proof of trade with the East. This probably came to an end with the decline in gold production, increasing internal population problems and invasions.

In the past a number of rather farfetched theories have been proposed concerning the builders of these nowruined settlements. They have been attributed variously to Indians, Phoenicians, King Solomon and the Queen of Sheba. Professional historians and archaeologists have never given much credence to such ideas.

Roger Summers, later the curator of Great Zimbabwe and author of the standard *Ancient Ruins and Vanished Civilizations of Southern Africa* (now keeper of antiquities at the National Museum in Bulawayo), was involved in the 1958 dig that uncovered the five epochs of Zimbabwe. He proved that the Shona people were fully capable of work of the quality of Zimbabwe before their power was broken by the invasion of warlike peoples from the south. 'That the native peoples . . . should have once been capable of building on so monumental a scale is perhaps the most exciting

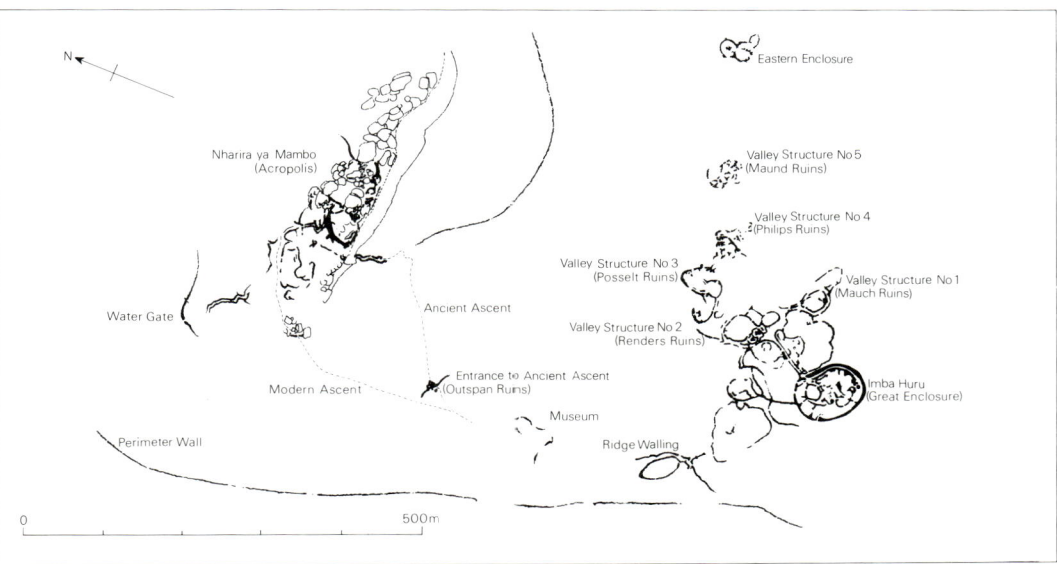

Within the walls of the Great Enclosure. The conical tower is thought to have represented fertility, in the form of a giant grainbasket.

discovery ever made by archaeologists in southern Africa,' says Summers.

Many gold ornaments, jewellery and artefacts were plundered from the ruins soon after they were discovered, seriously hampering the detective work of the archaeologists.

The high walls of the Imba Huru (Great Enclosure).

N

Eastern Enclosure

Nharira ya Mambo (Acropolis)

Valley Structure No 5 (Maund Ruins)

Valley Structure No 4 (Philips Ruins)

Valley Structure No 3 (Posselt Ruins)

Valley Structure No 1 (Mauch Ruins)

Valley Structure No 2 (Renders Ruins)

Water Gate

Ancient Ascent

Entrance to Ancient Ascent (Outspan Ruins)

Modern Ascent

Museum

Imba Huru (Great Enclosure)

Ridge Walling

Perimeter Wall

0   500m

The ruins of Great Zimbabwe. The hill complex covers the overlooking hill while the other ruins lie in the valley.

Sacred haunt of the Zimbabwe eagle

A platform in the Great Zimbabwe Hill Ruins, probably the site of a hut.

An entrance to the Great Enclosure, where the queen lived.

The first of the Zimbabwe eagles to be discovered, found by Posselt in 1889.

Lichen covers the granite blocks forming the Great Enclosure.

Two types of Zimbabwe building — later work (left), middle period (right).

The high wall of the Great Enclosure dwarfs a spectator.

The famous soapstone sculptures of Zimbabwe — a stylized fish eagle — were found in the Hill Ruins, indicating that this was possibly a sacred place. The fish eagle was the totem of the Hungwe section of the Karanga people. Replicas of the bird can be seen on the country's coins and the coat of arms.

A hunter, Willie Posselt, found the first Zimbabwe bird in the eastern enclosure of the Hill Ruins in 1889. He could not carry away the bird as it stood, so he hacked it from its pedestal and offered to sell it to President Paul Kruger of the Transvaal. But Cecil Rhodes, then prime minister of the Cape, made a bid for the bird and bought it.

Since Posselt's discovery, seven similar birds have been found, making a total of eight known to exist. Five complete birds and the upper half of a sixth are now in the site museum at Great Zimbabwe. The lower half of the sixth bird was 'lost' in Berlin during World War II. A seventh bird is now kept in the Bulawayo museum, and the eighth is in Cape Town at Groote Schuur.

In 1898, when the ruins were first discovered by German-born Adam Renders, they were overgrown with trees, bushes and creepers. Most of these have been cleared away but the huge *Mimusops zeyheri* trees, said to be several hundred years old, remain. These trees have edible fruits about the size and texture of olives.

Flame-red aloes stand sentinel throughout the complex. The Zimbabwe Valley is always green and often shrouded in mist, which adds an air of quiet mystery to the ruins. To visit the ruins by moonlight is a memorable experience.

There are beautiful trees here, and a rich variety of flowering creepers. The aloes are in flower during June and July.

Sunset bathes the Hill Ruins in a golden colour. These ruins, formerly known as the Acropolis, have a singular atmosphere of enchantment.

The Great Enclosure in its natural parkland setting.

The wall enclosing the king's residence in the Hill Ruins.

KINGDOM OF THE OUTCASTS

THE WESTERN DIVISION of Zimbabwe was named Matabeleland by European explorers. The original inhabitants had no such general name for the area. The San, who were the first to dwell in this region, and the Rozvi people who displaced them, left a rich legacy of place names on the rivers, mountains and other topographical features, but they had no need for any name describing a political division.

For many years, these Rozvi and San pioneers could scarcely have been aware that there were any other people in the world apart from themselves. They hunted, farmed, bred cattle, mined for iron and gold, made items of jewellery and various implements, and developed the architectural tradition of surrounding the habitations of their rulers with elaborate stone walls.

By the 17th century the San had gone, and the Rozvi and the related Karanga people had their first encounters with foreign interlopers. Portuguese traders and missionaries from the east coast penetrated the area. Relics found in ruins of walled settlements are conclusive proof that the Portuguese worked and lived here.

In the first quarter of the 19th century there came a drastic series of changes. Far south, in what is now Kwazulu, Shaka was welding a number of independent clans and peoples into a nation. In 1818 he defeated his principal rival, Zwide of the Ndwandwe people. The Ndwandwes were routed. Their chief fled into the Transvaal while three groups of his former followers fled northwards in search of sanctuary.

These Ndwandwe groups were led by Nxaba, Soshangane and Zwangendaba. The first two groups reached Mocambique, subdued the earlier inhabitants, joined together and formed the Shangane people.

Zwangendaba and his followers found their way into Zimbabwe and attacked the Rozvi people, sacked the walled settlements, and destroyed an African kingdom and a culture that had survived in isolation for about 1 000 years. With this destruction completed, Zwangendaba, in about 1835, led his men northwards on a spectacular career of looting, until eventually they entered what is now Tanzania, where their descendants live today.

The remnants of the Rozvi were not left to recover in peace. A grandson of the defeated Zwide, chief of the Ndwandwe people, was named Mzilikazi. He threw in his lot with Shaka for a while but then quarrelled, embezzled loot for himself, and was forced to flee from the wrath of the Zulus. It was these people, named maTebele ('the runaways', or 'disappearers') by the Sotho of the Transvaal, who in 1838 entered the western side of Zimbabwe. Here they discovered the central ridge with its cool and healthy climate, its excellent grazing, and the easy loot to be taken from the remaining Rozvi people.

In their own language, the followers of Mzilikazi called themselves the amaNdebele, the Zulu version of the Sotho maTebele. European hunters and missionaries, however, picked the Sotho form of the name, misspelt it Matabele, and called the Ndebele homeland in Zimbabwe Matabeleland. Despite widespread use of the term Matabele, the people themselves favour the use of Ndebele.

The kingdom created in the old Rozvi lands by Mzilikazi and his son, Lobengula, was a wild and primitive but singularly romantic state — perfectly suited to the rugged grandeur of a part of the world whose landscape is ancient and primeval, still not completely tamed, hauntingly beautiful in its massed granite domes and outcrops, rich in minerals and metals, drenched in sunshine, a haunt of big game, a natural garden of countless trees and flowering plants.

Beitbridge

The Cape to Cairo road crosses the Limpopo River boundary between South Africa and Zimbabwe by means of a road and rail bridge, 473 metres long, in 14 spans. The bridge was built by funds provided by Alfred Beit, the mining financier and colleague of Cecil Rhodes. It was opened in 1929.

On the Zimbabwean side of the river there is a village with hotels, caravan park and customs and immigration offices.

Bembesi

In 1838 Mzilikazi, the founder of the Ndebele people, was a real wanderer of the wastelands. In the previous year he had been defeated in the Transvaal, first by the Zulus and then by the Voortrekkers. The Ndebele fled northwards, dividing into two sections. Mzilikazi, with one section of his people, travelled north-west and reached the area of the Nambya people, living under a chief known as Hwange Rusumbami, called Wankie by Europeans.

After subduing these people, Mzilikazi made his way up the valley of the river the Ndebele named Bembesi, meaning 'something unpleasant'. This valley led them onto the central plateau where Mzilikazi found the second half of his followers settled in a fine new homeland, the Matabeleland of today.

On 1 November 1893, when the army of Cecil Rhodes's British South Africa Company invaded Matabele-land, the Ndebele army tried to halt them in the Bembesi Valley. The Matabele were armed with rifles, but the Europeans had the recently invented Maxim machine-guns. About 500 Ndebele were killed or wounded; only three Europeans were killed and six wounded. The Ndebele withdrew and, on 4 November 1893, the Europeans occupied Bulawayo without resistance. A small granite memorial marks the site of the Bembesi battle.

Bulawayo

When Mzilikazi, the Ndebele people's founder, died in 1868, there was much quarrelling and killing over the question of succession. His son Lobengula eventually became the new king and in 1872 he founded a capital which he named kwaBulawayo ('the place of the persecuted man'). In 1816, in Zululand, Shaka had also named his first capital kwaBulawayo for the same reason — he considered that he had been ill-used by rivals, 'killed by his enemies' as the Zulus say. The parallel was obvious to Lobengula, who was well aware of Zulu history.

Bulawayo (the prefix kwa- not being much used by Europeans) was built on the summit of the central plateau, 1 356 metres above sea level. It is sunny, warm to hot in summer, cool to cold in winter. Rain falls mainly in summer, and there are frequent violent thunderstorms. The city lies on an undulating plateau covered in savanna parkland and dominated by acacia trees.

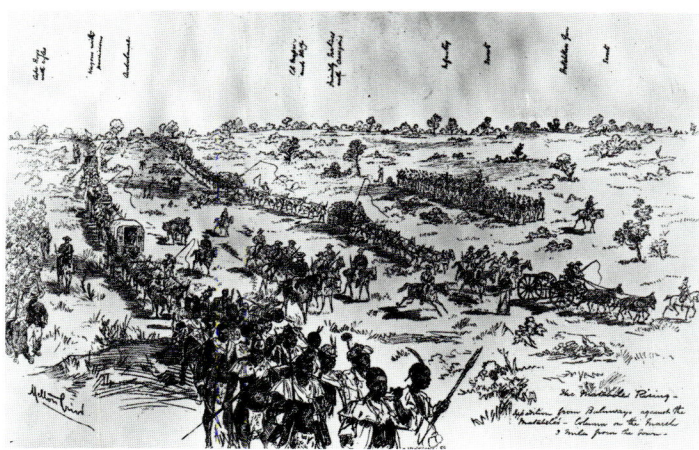

A sketch from the Illustrated London News *of the 1896 Ndebele uprising.*

Bulawayo with its high-rise buildings looming out of the central plateau.

On 1 November 1893, the Ndebele were defeated by the advancing army of the British South Africa Company. Lobengula fled to the north and his capital was set on fire and all but destroyed. Nothing of it remains except for the Indaba thorn tree still standing outside State House. Under this tree Lobengula used to hold court.

The new Bulawayo grew rapidly on the ruins of the old capital. The European founders of the town fondly imagined that it would grow to rival Johannesburg. There were rumours of vast gold fields in the vicinity and fortune-seekers rushed to the area.

Some gold was found — enough to see the start of a mining industry — while the ranching possibilities of the savanna and the strategic situation of the town (on the crossroads of the routes from the Cape to Cairo and from Botswana to Mocambique) made its growth inevitable.

In 1896 the Shona people in the east, and then the Ndebele in the west, rose against the government of the British South Africa Company. The market square of Bulawayo was converted into a fortified area, and a well dug to provide emergency water supplies. The town was packed with

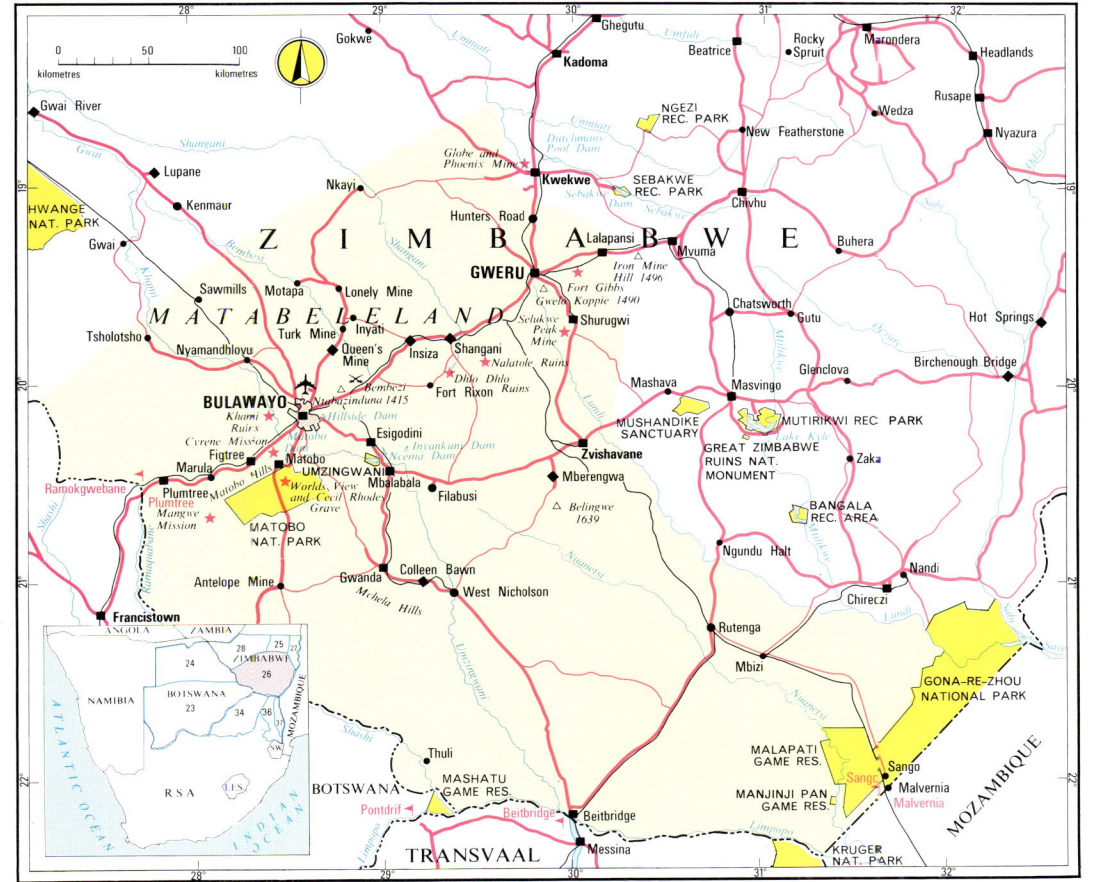

THINGS TO DO AND SEE

Angling Dams such as the Matobo, Ncema, Inyankuni, and Dutchman's Pool, and rivers such as the Khami and the Sebakwe, are stocked with about 500 species of fish, including barbel, bass, bream and carp. Tigerfish are found in the Limpopo and the lower Nuanetsi River. Beware of crocodiles and bilharzia.

Camping and caravanning There are many caravan parks and camping grounds in Matabeleland. The parks in Bulawayo, and in the Matobo National Park, are outstanding.

Musasa trees One of the great botanical spectacles of the world is the musasa trees of Zimbabwe going through their range of spring colours. The new leaves range from brilliant scarlet to plum and then to green. During September and October the massed effect is dazzling.

Sightseeing The Matobo National Park is a unique area for tourists. Scenery, plants and animals contribute to the spectacle of a most majestic part of the world. The drive from Gweru to Sebakwe, beautiful at all seasons, is exquisite in spring.

Sport Most sports are well served with playing fields, clubs, courts and tracks. Visitors are always welcome at the various clubs.

Swimming There are swimming baths in all the towns listed.

Streets wide enough to turn a wagon and oxen

The broad sweep of Bulawayo's Selborne Avenue.

The Zimbabwe International Trade Fair.

refugees and there were many battles in the vicinity (but never in the town itself). Casualties were heavy on both sides. The bloodshed ended only after Rhodes met the leaders of the Ndebele in four indabas, or conferences, held in the Matobo Hills.

With the coming of peace, Bulawayo made considerable progress. The railway from South Africa reached the town on 19 October 1897 and was extended north to the Victoria Falls and east to Harare. Mining flourished and Bulawayo became a substantial industrial centre. It was made a city in 1943.

When Bulawayo was planned, Rhodes ordered that the streets should be wide enough to allow a wagon with a full span of oxen to turn. Today the city is still noted for its unusually wide, straight streets.

The modern civic centre has been

A potter in the Mzilikazi Art and Craft Centre of Bulawayo.

A replica of underground workings displayed in the National Museum.

The Doddieburn elephant and some giraffe in the National Museum.

Bulawayo's Central Park, a retreat in the midst of the city.

The saddle-tank steam locomotive named Jack Tar, one of the earliest to work on the country's railways and now exhibited in the Railway Museum.

Cecil Rhodes presiding at one of the famous peace indabas with the Ndebele. Rhodes is seated on top of the rock. On his right is the renowned frontiersman Johan Colenbrander. On his left is Doctor Hans Sauer. In the rear is a reporter.

Here the city maintains a caravan park in a wooded setting.

There is also a spectacular illuminated fountain, built in 1968 to mark the 75th anniversary of the founding of Bulawayo. At night the fountain is a constantly changing pattern of water and colour.

The Railways Museum is in the suburb of Raylton. The rondavel used by Rhodes on his visits to Bulawayo, before Sir Herbert Baker designed the official residence, still stands.

Hillside Dam, 6 kilometres south of the city, is much used by anglers and boating enthusiasts. Alongside the dam are picnic sites, an aviary and a nature reserve. Near the grounds of the Zimbabwe International Trade Fair there is a 2-hectare ornamental lake called Table Bay in the Matsheumhlope ('white stone') River.

built as part of the original market square, with the well dug to provide water during the 1896 uprising preserved in a garden in front of the centre.

The only statue of Cecil Rhodes to be modelled from life stood at the intersection of Eighth Avenue and Main Street. The statue is now in the museum.

Bulawayo has two parks, Centenary and Central. Centenary Park, where the Rhodes Centenary Exhibition was held in 1953, contains a theatre, a miniature railway, a children's playground, a small game park and an aviary.

The impressive National Museum of Zimbabwe is also situated here.

The museum exhibits many articles recovered from the ancient ruins, especially from Great Zimbabwe. The geological department contains an extensive collection of minerals from Zimbabwe and all parts of the world. Among many other exhibits is a huge fossilized egg laid more than 2 000 years ago by the extinct *Aepyornis maximus* of Madagascar, the bird that inspired the story of the Roc in the legend of Sindbad the Sailor.

Also to be seen in the museum is the world's second largest mounted elephant, shot on Doddieburn ranch near the town of Gwanda.

Central Park has a superlative rose garden, a host of stately palms, and many other magnificent trees.

HOW LOBENGULA SOLD HIS KINGDOM FOR THE WHITE MAN'S FRIENDSHIP

Lobengula, son of Mzilikazi, the founder of the Ndebele people, succeeded his father as paramount chief in 1870 — and inherited a kingdom on the verge of revolt.

The rightful heir, Nkulumane, had disappeared, and the Zulu aristocracy of the people, ageing but proud, did not like Lobengula. His name was originally Nombengula, meaning 'the impetuous one', but he had been brought up by the Sotho section of the people and the Ndebele resented his preference for the Sotho version of his name. Lobengula earned further displeasure by naming his new capital Gibixhegu ('where the old men are discarded') — the name the Zulu king Shaka had given to his first capital, where a slaughter of dissidents took place.

Four months after he took power, Lobengula settled accounts with his enemies. In a violent battle, about 350 aristocrats were killed. From then on Lobengula was secure, but the real power of his people had been permanently weakened.

The aristocrats who had accompanied Mzilikazi on his excursion from Zululand had been the nation's military strength.

Lobengula, however, proved to be an intelligent and generally well-liked ruler once his first troubles had

The text of the so-called concession negotiated by Rhodes with Lobengula.

been resolved. He showed favour to Europeans — it was said that he had grown up with a young European girl who had been seized as a child when the Ndebele army had overrun Voortrekker camps along the Vaal River. When they were in their early teens the girl, at the cost of her own life, had saved Lobengula from the bite of a black mamba.

Lobengula made a diplomatic marriage with Xwalile, daughter of the Shangane ruler, Mzila. She walked all the way to his capital from Moçambique with 8 maids-of-

honour. Lobengula also married his bride's companions, but none of them ever produced a child and there was never an official heir to the Ndebele throne.

In 1872 Lobengula built a new capital and this became his permanent home. He named the place kwaBulawayo ('the place of the persecuted man'). Again the name was taken from one of the capitals of Shaka and referred to the fact that both leaders had confronted resistance to their accession to power, and therefore they had been persecuted or, symbolically, 'killed by their enemies'.

In 1888, Cecil Rhodes sent three men to negotiate a concession with Lobengula.

On 30 October of that year Lobengula was cajoled, confused and persuaded to sign a concession giving Rhodes complete and exclusive rights to all minerals found in his kingdom. In exchange he received £100 payable on the first day of every lunar month, 1 000 Martini-Henry rifles, 100 000 rounds of cartridges and a steam gunboat to patrol the Zambezi River. The gunboat was never delivered.

The era of Lobengula as a great king — who had always been a friend of the Europeans — was at an end.

Fragments of Chinese porcelain found in the Dhlo Dhlo ruins

Colleen Bawn

The mineral-rich area south of Bulawayo contains, amongst its mines, the limestone deposits pegged by a prospector named John Daly in 1895 and named Colleen Bawn from the Gaelic for 'fair girl'. The mine and mills produce cement and the village and its surroundings are covered in grey-white limestone dust in the dry season.

Cyrene Mission

West of Bulawayo, 32 kilometres along the road to Botswana, is the Anglican Cyrene Mission, notable for

The dam at Hillside Park, a pleasure resort popular with the people of Bulawayo.

its unique school of art, founded in 1939 by Canon Edward Paterson.

The walls of many of the buildings are elaborately decorated and the work of the artists, mainly Ndebele, is sought by collectors in Zimbabwe and from overseas.

Dhlo Dhlo

The stone walls at Dhlo Dhlo are among the most dramatic of the ruins of the Rozvi people. These ruins were built in the late 17th century and tradition has it that this place was formerly a favourite residence of the Rozvi king, or 'mambo'.

THE FOOLHARDY VENTURE THAT ENDED IN THE TRAGEDY OF 'WILSON'S LAST STAND'

One of the most poignant and unnecessary tragedies to occur in the history of southern Africa was the pursuit of the defeated Ndebele King Lobengula — and the killing of his pursuers by warriors of his army.

On 4 November 1893 the British South Africa Company of Cecil Rhodes occupied Bulawayo with little resistance from the Ndebele.

Lobengula had fled from his capital, leaving it in flames. Sir Leander Starr Jameson — leader of the ill-fated Jameson raid (see Rhodes box, page 37) — was in command of the company's force and decided that Lobengula should be captured.

A message was sent to Lobengula telling him of the occupation of his capital and demanding his surrender. Lobengula replied that he was prepared to surrender, but asked where he was to live. Nothing further was heard from him.

Major P. Forbes and 300 men were sent to find Lobengula. It was the start of the rainy season and the further the column advanced north on the trail of the Ndebele king, the thicker the mud became. On 27 November Forbes sent half of his men back to Bulawayo with the wagons, which were becoming useless in the mud. About 150 men continued the pursuit.

Clear tracks indicated the presence of a substantial number of Ndebele warriors, but the small company force disregarded these signs. On 3 December the company

The last stand of Major Allan Wilson, depicted in a painting by Allan Stewart.

force was close to the Shangani River, where they found a small village. They were told that Lobengula had slept there the previous night. It was evening, and Forbes decided to camp for the night but he ordered Major Allan Wilson to take a small party and reconnoitre ahead for not more than two hours.

Night fell and there was no sign of Wilson. Suddenly two of his men returned to camp. They brought a message from Wilson saying that he was certain he was close to Lobengula and would bivouac in the bush, await reinforcements, then capture the king at dawn. Soon three more men rejoined the main force with the news that Wilson had heard Lobengula's voice shouting something which sounded like: 'Why did you take my money if you still want to fight?' Wilson had then retreated

half a kilometre.

Forbes immediately sent 20 men to boost Wilson's meagre force.

Before dawn Forbes and the rest of the men set out to reach Wilson. They heard the sound of a violent struggle about 6 kilometres away. As they made their way towards the noise, a mass of Ndebele warriors ap-

The Wilson Memorial, World's View.

peared through the bush. There was a fierce skirmish. Forbes was forced to retire. As his men retreated, three of Wilson's men rode through the bush and tersely informed him that they were the sole survivors of Wilson's party.

Forbes decided to retreat. All the way the Ndebele harried his force, recovering livestock which the Europeans had seized, ambushing and sniping at the former attackers.

The nightmare only ended on 13 December when Forbes and his men met a relief force led by Rhodes.

There were many bitter recriminations about the fiasco of Lobengula's pursuit. In February 1894 James Dawson and James Reilly volunteered to ride north from Bulawayo to see if they could find Lobengula and learn the fate of Wilson and his men. They found an Ndebele commander who led them to the site of Wilson's last stand. Corpses littered the area.

The commander told the two Europeans that the dispirited and heartsore Lobengula had not wanted to fight. He had sent two of his headmen to find the Europeans and give them a thousand gold sovereigns as a token of his surrender. The messengers had encountered two members of the Bechuanaland Border Police, who were with the pursuers.

They accepted the sovereigns, telling no-one else, and thereby sent Wilson and his men to their death.

The unique style of the Cyrene artists.

Wall paintings decorate the buildings of the Cyrene Mission west of Bulawayo.

Excavation of the ruins has produced fragments of Chinese Ming porcelain, Dutch gin bottles, brass plate and candlesticks, two cannons, glass beads, a bronze censer, a bell, priest's seal, gold chain, a wealth of gold ornaments, embossed silver plate and various items indicating the presence here of an early Portuguese mission station.

Signs of destruction by fire suggest that Dhlo Dhlo was attacked, sacked and destroyed, probably in the early 19th century. Who the attackers were is not known, but they were possibly raiders from Zululand, such as Zwangendaba's warriors.

More damage was done to the ruins in the 1890s by vandals styling themselves the Ancient Ruins Company, formed with the purpose of digging into all the ruins in the hope of finding buried treasure. Many gold coins and items of jewellery were found by this company but much damage was done.

The original name of the Dhlo Dhlo ruins is not known. Dhlo Dhlo is simply a European corruption of the Ndebele word 'dlodlo', meaning a 'headring'. This name merely describes the circular shape of the ruins, which are positioned on the brow of a low granite dome.

Esigodini
The main road from Bulawayo to Beitbridge descends the escarpment of the central plateau of Zimbabwe, losing 250 metres of altitude and reaching the 1 100-metre level of the middleveld.

The rural centre of Esigodini (formerly Essexvale) lies in this area. Near Esigodini are the Ncema Dam — the headquarters of the Bulawayo Power Boat Club — and the popular picnic area of the Inyankuni Dam.

Figtree
Beneath the wild fig that still grows in the village of Figtree, early hunters and traders had to wait for permission from the king of the Ndebele before proceeding further.

There is an old saying that wherever you find a fig tree there is gold nearby. This may derive from an ancient practice of planting a fig tree on the site of gold finds. So far no gold has been found at Figtree.

Fort Rixon
Theodore Rixon was the owner of a farm 80 kilometres east of Bulawayo. During the 1896 war with the Ndebele a small fort was built on the farm for the protection of local farmers and miners.

South of the village of Fort Rixon, at the site of the now ruined fort, is a memorial to settlers killed during battles with the Ndebele.

Gwanda
The ranching and mining centre of Gwanda is named after a grassy shrub growing here. Gold, asbestos and scheelite are mined in the area.

There are several caves in the hills south of the town. One of these, found in 1955, contains San paintings, stone implements and pottery 2 000-3 000 years old.

Gweru
The administrative capital of the central province of Zimbabwe is Gweru (formerly Gwelo), founded in 1894 and proclaimed a city in 1971. Ranching, farming and industrial development have contributed to the prosperity of the city.

The Gweru district is rich in gold, chrome, iron, asbestos, limestone, coal, barytes, lithium and tungsten, and there are some diamonds. Numerous ancient workings show that early miners — Rozvi, Karanga and other peoples — worked in this area.

The name Gweru comes from the Shona name for the river which flows intermittently through the city — Gweru, meaning 'dry'.

Gweru has grown in a park-like setting and its streets are shaded by many flowering trees. In September and October jacarandas reach perfection while the gardens are full of roses and bougainvillea. In November the poinciana (flamboyant) trees are in full bloom. In May the poinsettias

One of the finest examples in Zimbabwe of the decorative skill of the builders of the stone walls. This is at Dhlo Dhlo.

The staggering view back through 3 000 million years

produce a lovely variety of shades and colours. The garden of roses in front of the municipal offices is a magnificent sight in spring.

The city is laid out around a long, low hill known as Gweru Kopje. There are army and air force training centres on the outskirts. Gweru is also the home of the showground of the Midlands Agricultural Society. The city's industrial base includes a major railway junction and an extensive marshalling complex.

Intaba Zika Mambo Ruins
The massive fortress-like ruins of Intaba Zika Mambo are historically amongst the most important in Zimbabwe.

Many relics of gold smelting have been recovered from the ruins.

According to tradition, the last reigning mambo, or king, of the Rozvi people, Tshirisamuru, lived in this fortress in 1831 when it was attacked by a raiding band from Zululand, led by Zwangendaba. The Rozvi mambo was caught and skinned alive, and the fortress sacked.

The name Intaba Zika Mambo means 'the hill of the king'. There are several other similar but smaller ruins of stone-walled settlements in the area.

Inyati
In 1859 Mzilikazi, the Ndebele king, granted permission to the London Missionary Society to establish a mission station in the area north of Bulawayo that was garrisoned by the nyathi ('buffalo') regiment of his army. The missionaries who arrived corrupted the name to Inyati.

This station was the beginning of their efforts to convert the Ndebele to Christianity.

The city hall of Gweru at night. In the front is a rose garden.

The difficulties the missionaries encountered must have been severe. The Reverend William Sykes, who worked in the mission from its founding until his death in 1887, never baptized a single convert.

Inyati was the first permanent European settlement in the area between the Limpopo and Zambezi rivers after the last Portuguese missionaries left Zimbabwe at the beginning of the 19th century.

The first known white birth in Zimbabwe was at Inyati — Livingstone Moffat, son of the Reverend John Moffat and his wife Emily, was born here on 15 April 1860.

Khami Ruins
In a setting of trees on the banks of the Khami River lie the extensive Khami Ruins, considered to be one of the last important stone-walled settlements created by the Rozvi people. The ruins consist of a succession of walled terraces. Many of the walls are patterned in black and grey stones, and a passageway leads through the ruins to the summit of a low hill overlooking a great pool in the river. On this summit stand the remains of a large, mud-walled building.

Many relics have been recovered from these ruins, including European-made items such as plates and agricultural tools, which suggest that the place was the site of a Portuguese mission station. A Dominican cross made of granite can still be seen on a small hill in the vicinity.

According to tradition, the last Rozvi king to live at Khami was Djiri Mutinhima, who fled when Mzilikazi arrived with his Ndebele people in 1838.

The Khami Ruins remain as a most atmospheric and impressive relic of a vanished African civilization. The name Khami, given to the river, means 'slow flowing'.

Kwekwe
In 1890 an African guide showed an old gold working to a prospector, E. T. Pearson. He pegged the site and named the outcrop the Phoenix Reef. A second outcrop, about 150 metres away, was named the Globe Reef.

The two claims were combined in 1894 to become one of the best known and most profitable of the gold mines of Zimbabwe, the Globe and Phoenix Mine.

Other gold mines, such as the Gaika, were also started in the vicinity, and a town grew up. It was originally called Que Que but recently the spelling was changed to Kwekwe. The name comes from the river Kwekwe which flows nearby, and the river derived this name from the African term for the noise the frogs make at night.

On the Sebakwe River, close to the Kwekwe, is the Dutchman's Pool Dam, a popular recreational area with its own camping ground.

Also nearby are the pretty Sebakwe Poort, where the river passes through a ridge of hills, and the Sebakwe National Park, with boating, fishing, bungalows and a caravan and camping ground. The park is a sanctuary for small antelope and other wild creatures.

The Paper House, Zimbabwe's oldest colonial building and now a national monument, now houses the National Museum of Gold Mining History.

There is a caravan park in the town itself.

Lalapanzi
A marsh in this region was much cursed during the pioneer days. Oxen

The grave of the great chief Mzilikazi at Entumbane in the Matobo.

Khami Ruins outside Bulawayo. The site is relaxing, the atmosphere almost tangible, the history mysterious.

would often sink to their bellies in the mud, giving the impression of lying down, hence the name of Lalapanzi ('lying down').

This is predominantly a chrome-mining and farming community. Two forts dating from pioneer days still remain in the vicinity — Fort Gibbs and Iron Mine Hill.

Limpopo River

The frontier between Zimbabwe and South Africa lies along the Limpopo River. The river, the main drainage channel of the northern Transvaal and southern Zimbabwe, is known by a variety of names.

In the upper reaches, Europeans know it as the Crocodile. The Tswana people call it Noka e Udi, meaning 'a river of steep banks'; the Venda people call it Vhembe, meaning 'the gatherer'; while the Shanganes of Mocambique call it Mete, meaning

The dam in the Maleme River, surrounded by lush bush-covered hills.

'the swallower'. The Ndebele call it Ngulukudela ('the river that floods'), and also iliMphopho ('the river of the waterfall'). Europeans have corrupted this name into Limpopo.

The river has its headwaters on the Witwatersrand. Fed by many tributaries it flows northwards, is dammed at Hartbeespoort, and then swings eastwards to become the boundary between Botswana and South Africa.

After 300 kilometres, the Limpopo is joined by the Shashi, and for 250 kilometres forms the boundary between Zimbabwe and South Africa. It then enters Mocambique, and reaches the Indian Ocean after crossing 400 kilometres of sandy lowlands.

Marula

The small railway and agricultural centre of Marula is named after the marula trees which are common in the area. Their plum-like fruit, with a mango taste, is relished by wild creatures and man. The fermented fruit makes a powerful alcoholic drink.

The original trail from the south followed by the first missionaries, hunters and traders travelling to visit the Ndebele came through the Matobo Hills by means of the Mangwe Pass, 31 kilometres south of Marula.

This road is still in use. There is a memorial at the pass to the pioneer travellers who made use of it.

Matobo National Park

Tradition tells that when Mzilikazi, the renowned Ndebele king, first saw the vast assembly of granite domes exposed on the south-western escarpment of the Zimbabwean central plateau, he remarked with humour that the scene was like an assembly of the elders of his people. He gave the area the name of amaTobo, meaning 'the bald heads'.

The name, corrupted by Europeans to Matopos, is remarkably apt. This is indeed a gathering of the ancients. The 80-kilometre-long concentration of granite consists of the oldest rocks known to man. Their age is estimated at more than 3 000 million years. In all that time they have changed little.

The atmosphere and appearance of the granite outcrop is extraordinary. Few visitors fail to sense that they are in the presence of the primeval force

Curse of the massacre's lone survivor

of creation as it was near to the time of the beginning of the earth. The great masses of weirdly shaped rocks — domes, whale-backs, castles — the caves painted by the San, the sacred mountains of the Karanga, the oracles from which came the voice of Mwari ('God'), all contribute to this atmosphere.

The Matobo was used as a stronghold by the Ndebele in the 1896 uprising. It was here that Cecil Rhodes met the Ndebele leaders in the four indabas, or conferences, that ended the fighting.

Rhodes was captivated by the sheer power and beauty of the rock wilderness. When riding in the area he found one colossal dome known to the Karanga as Marindidzimu ('the haunt of the ancestral spirits'). On the summit there is a crown of giant boulders.

'The peacefulness of it', Rhodes observed to companions, 'the chaotic grandeur of it all! I call this one of the views of the world. It brings home to me how very small we all are.'

Sitting in the cool shadow of a boulder, he added: 'I shall be buried here, looking in that direction.' He pointed north.

Rhodes died in his seaside cottage at Muizenberg in 1902. His body was conveyed by train to Bulawayo, and then to the Matobo Hills, where he was buried as he had desired on the summit of the granite dome, known as World's View.

Sir Leander Starr Jameson, Rhodes's friend and colleague, and Sir Charles Coghlan, the first prime minister, are also buried on top of World's View.

The remains of Major Allan Wilson and the men of his patrol who lost their lives in the pursuit of Lobengula are contained in a monument erected on the summit (see box, page 504).

Rhodes bequeathed to the people of the country his holdings on the verges of the Matobo Hills. His company, the British South Africa Company, added to his bequest and the Rhodes Matobo National Park was created to preserve the area.

Animal life here includes giraffe, leopard, sable antelope, kudu, baboon, monkey, rhino, and numerous small antelopes.

Vegetation is rich, with many tall

Kudu-coloured dome of Mbalabala, Ndebele name of the greater kudu.

trees. In spring the musasas are brilliantly coloured and the coral trees are aflame with orange and scarlet flowers.

There are caravan and camping sites in the park.

Mbalabala

The main road from Beitbridge to Bulawayo passes a cluster of granite domes on the verge of the central plateau. One of the most massive of these domes is 65 kilometres south of Bulawayo. It has a colour so similar to that of the greater kudu — fawn grey with white stripes — that the Ndebele call it Mbalabala, their name for that species of kudu.

There is a railway whistle-stop and a small trading centre for the ranching district at the foot of the dome.

Mberengwa

The 1 639-metre-high mountain known to the Shona as Mberengwa ('the notable one') is a landmark believed by local people to have supernatural powers. It is said to emit a roaring sound and to set itself alight. Until recently it was called Belingwe.

There is a small administrative and trading centre close to the mountain. Gold and emeralds are mined here.

Nalatale Ruins

Among the most beautiful of the walled settlements built by the Rozvi people in Zimbabwe are the Nalatale Ruins. As with most of these ruins, the original name has been forgotten. In the Ndebele language Nalatale simply means 'the walls'.

The ruins stand on the summit of a low bluff of the Insiza range of granite hills. The structure consists of a massive raised platform which sup-

WHITE WHIRLWIND

In an age of adventures and frontiersmen, Johan Colenbrander, known as 'The White Whirlwind,' was a prince of his kind.

Colenbrander, born in Pinetown, Natal, in 1856, served in the Anglo-Zulu War of 1879. During the protracted disturbances in Zululand brought about by the post-war division of the country into 13 principalities, he was an ally of the chief Zibebu until the latter's defeat at the Battle of Ghost Mountain in 1884.

Colenbrander then moved to Swaziland and participated in the so-called concessions rush (see box, page 448).

Later still, in Johannesburg, he was offered employment as an interpreter to one of the concession-seeking parties travelling to Bulawayo to see Lobengula in 1888.

From Bulawayo, Colenbrander escorted a party of Ndebele chiefs to London to see Queen Victoria and the British government and plead in vain for a protectorate over Lobengula's country.

Colenbrander returned to Bulawayo and worked for Rhodes throughout a period of intrigue and change.

At the end of the 1896 uprising of the Ndebele and Shona people, Colenbrander was Rhodes's right-hand man in negotiating a peace. During the Anglo-Boer War, Colenbrander was colonel of Kitchener's Fighting Scouts.

Colenbrander died tragically on 10 February 1918 while leading a cavalry charge during the filming of *The Symbol of Sacrifice*. His horse tripped while fording the Klip River and Colenbrander drowned.

ported the residence of the king.

Ntabazinduna

When Mzilikazi, in 1838, united his followers who had become separated after their defeat by the Voortrekkers in the Transvaal, he found that during the separation of the two sections his heir, Nkulumana, had practically taken over the king's power. It is al-

leged that Mzilikazi had the young man assassinated.

The six leading advisers of Nkulumana were ordered to the top of a hill 16 kilometres east of Bulawayo, ostensibly to take part in a cleansing ceremony, with oxen slaughtered as atonement for the suspected disloyalty of the men. Mzilikazi, however, ordered his executioners to kill the advisers. Tradition has it that one man, Dambisamahubo, escaped. He fled to the east, cursing Mzilikazi. It is said that when the dry east wind blows, withering the crops, this is the curse of Dambisamahubo.

The hill has since been known as Ntabazinduna, meaning 'the hill of the headmen'.

Nyamandhlovu

An Ndebele regiment named the Nyamayendlovu ('flesh of the elephant') once garrisoned this savanna country north of Bulawayo. Members of the regiment acted as game warders of Mzilikazi's private hunting preserve. In the centre of the area there was a small, dried-out lakelet called by the San Tshololo Njowe ('the head of an elephant'). This is now known as Tjolotjo. The village of Nyamandhlovu, named after the regiment, is a centre for a timber and ranching district.

In 1959 the bones of a dinosaur, 180 million years old, were found near the village. The site is a national monument. The bones are in the national museum in Bulawayo.

Plumtree

The small centre of Plumtree had its

A gallery of rock art in Nswatugi Cave in the Matobo National Park.

Like a ruined castle, a pile of rocks on an outcrop in the Matobo Hills.

The grave of Cecil John Rhodes on the summit of World's View.

A tame rock lizard on the summit of World's View.

An elephant shrew, lively resident of the Matobo Hills.

beginning in 1897, when the railway was built from South Africa to Bulawayo and on to Victoria Falls.

A large marula tree, with its plum-like fruit, grew on the site and gave the station its name.

Shurugwe

Lying in thickly wooded country, the mining centre of Shurugwe (formerly Selukwe) is one of the most attractive of the small towns of Zimbabwe. It was established in 1899 to serve the district's mining industry.

In spring the area is aflame with the scarlet and plum colours of the musasa trees and hazy mauve colours of the jacarandas that are planted along many of the town's streets.

The Rozvi-Karanga people mined iron and other metals in this area from about 1 000 years ago, and there are numerous ancient workings.

The modern mines around Shurugwe concentrate largely on high-grade chrome deposits.

The village lies on the edge of the escarpment of the Zimbabwean central plateau and the views south and east are magnificent.

West Nicholson

Andrew Nicholson was a prospector of the early 20th century who worked several small mines in the area named West Nicholson after him.

The boom mining years — the age of the so-called 'small worker' in Zimbabwe — were in the 1920s. Several of the mines still work, but the railhead of West Nicholson is today dominated by the packing plant of a meat factory.

The district is now best known for its

Zinjanja Ruins, near Fort Rixon, among the last to be built in Zimbabwe.

large-scale cattle ranching operations.

Zinjanja Ruins

In 1894 a mining financier, Hans Sauer, while prospecting with two mining engineers, was led to the ruins of a former Rozvi settlement. That day was Queen Victoria's birthday, so he named the site Fort Regina in her honour.

The site was known to the Ndebele as Zinjanja. The ruins consisted of a circular terrace covering the summit of a low hill.

The walls supporting the terrace were well built and the structure was remarkable for what seemed to be a number of shafts, each going down about 6 metres and about 30 centimetres in diameter. Modern research shows that they were dug for sanitation purposes.

The idea of searching for treasure intrigued the three men. They moved on to the nearby Dhlo Dhlo ruins, where they found gold beads, ornaments, cannons and other items in such quantity as to stimulate them to launch the Ancient Ruins Company with the purpose of scouring the numerous ruins of the country. Only the intervention of Cecil Rhodes prevented the mass destruction of many architectural treasures.

The Zinjanja, or Regina, Ruins are in the Fort Rixon area and are of notable beauty and elegance.

Zvishavane

The savanna lowland between Bulawayo and Masvingo is rich in minerals, especially iron and asbestos.

Zvishavane is one of several places in this area with names based on the Rozvi word shava, meaning the red-brown of iron oxides. The asbestos mine here is the largest in Africa.

MAGIC MOUNTAINS OF THE EAST

FEW FRONTIERS ARE more spectacular than that between Mocambique and Zimbabwe. This is a 350-kilometre range of mountains and ridges of great scenic drama. For the people of both countries, the mountains are the wall of a garden, awe-inspiring yet gentle to behold.

The highest point of this mountain wall is Nyangani, 2 593 metres above sea level. The summit line of the rest of the wall is around the 2 000-metre level, and the contrast in climate between the heights and the lowlands to the east and west is extreme. Mocambique is hot and humid, Zimbabwe warm and dry for eight months of the year. The mountain summits are boggy sponges, cold and crisp, free of the bilharzia and mosquitoes of the lowlands.

Groups of the Karanga-Rozvi people made their homes in these frontier mountains. They lived on the warmer slopes and in the valleys and only retreated to the heights to avoid attack. The Nyika settled in the central section of the mountains about 500 years ago, and from them Europeans have named this area Manicaland.

The Nyika refer to the mountains as Mutarandanda, meaning 'an undulating, rugged country'. Individual peaks have their own names and legends. There is Dangamvuru ('the starter of the rains') — it is said that the rains first reveal their seasonal approach by clouds on this mountain. From Nyangui ('the place of shouting'), legend says, sound the voices of spirits calling out to man. Tshinyakweremba ('the place of tired feet') gets its name from scars caused by landslides.

Legend has it that once there was a village beneath Tshinyakweremba. To it one day came a stranger who was old, tired and poor. He asked for hospitality, but the villagers were drinking beer and jeered at him, so he withdrew to the bush.

One woman pitied the stranger and took beer and food to him. He told her that he was a spirit sent by the ancestors. They had heard that the villagers were degenerate. His visit was to test them. Their reception had confirmed the stories of their decay. He had determined, therefore, to destroy the village.

The woman carried the tale to the villagers, but they derided her. She fled as the sun set. Looking to the mountain summit, she saw the stranger calling on nature to destroy the village. As she watched there was a crash of thunder and a flash of lightning. The face of the mountain collapsed over the village and buried it beneath a pile of rocks.

Even today the area has a mysterious quality. A forest grows over the rocks. Monkeys conceal themselves in the trees. Many birds and butterflies flutter through the shadows. On quiet nights the sound of revelry and drumming is said to be heard coming from the buried village, whose inhabitants, entombed for ever, are still irrepressibly jolly but now share their beer more liberally with all the other sirens, ghosts, spirits and goblins who have their homes in these magic mountains of the eastern districts of Zimbabwe.

THINGS TO DO AND SEE

Angling Trout are abundant in the streams and lakes of Nyanga, the Nyanga Downs and Troutbeck.

The angling season lasts from November to the end of May, but certain lakes in the area may be fished all year round.

Antiquities The extensive ruins at Ziwa and those at Nyanga rank among the world's major archaeological attractions.

Camping and caravanning The caravan and camping parks in the Nyanga National Park, at Mutare, in the Vumba National Park and in the Chimanimani National Park are all shaded by lush woodland.

Climbing and hiking The national parks of Chimanimani and Nyanga contain many trails and climbs.

Riding Most hotels provide horses for riding. All will advise where stables are to be found.

Swimming The mountain streams are free from bilharzia.

A party of hikers on a natural history excursion in the Chimanimani Mountains of the eastern districts of Zimbabwe.

The old road from Chimanimani to Mutare, winding through the bush-covered hills below the Chimanimani Mountains.

Birchenough Bridge.

The Beit Trust, founded by Alfred Beit, multi-millionaire partner of Cecil Rhodes, provided money for the building of many bridges and culverts and other improvements to roads and railways of the country. The bridge over the Save River, the Birchenough Bridge, is one of the Trust's finest gifts to the country. This bridge is a single-span arch 329 metres long and carries the road 18 metres above the river.

It was designed by Ralph Freeman, the designer of Australia's Sydney Harbour Bridge, and named after Sir Henry Birchenough, a chairman of the Beit Trust. The ashes of Sir Henry and his wife, Mabel, are contained in one of the pillars of the bridge, which was completed in 1935.

Cashel

Lying in a deep valley on the tourist route between Mutare and Chimanimani, the village of Cashel is the centre of an agricultural industry producing fruit and vegetables, mainly for canning. The village is named after an officer of the British South Africa Police who retired here after the First World War.

Chikore

A giant wild fig tree grows on a hill known as Chikore ('the place of the little cloud'). Beneath this tree the chief of the Dondo section of the Shona performed his rain-making ritual, and the cloud which so often condenses over the hilltop is said to be proof of his powers.

There is a small ruin of an old walled settlement built on a site with a handsome view, especially east and south over the low-lying savanna country.

Chimanimani

When settlers from the Orange Free State arrived in 1892 to take up grants of land in the eastern mountains of the country, they founded a village called Melsetter — after their leader's former family home in the Orkneys.

This village, now named Chimanimani, lies 1 800 metres above sea level on the plateau of the ridge of the eastern mountains. To the east lie the Chimanimani Mountains.

Chimanimani is the entry point for the Chimanimani National Park.

The village is a straggling little place, shaded by trees planted by the pioneers. Several of the buildings, including the church, date back to the coming of the settlers.

Around the village the scenery is cloaked with green. The old road from Mutare reaches the village through Cashel by means of a scenic route. The new road is more direct, but also a scenic drive.

The graceful steel girders of the Birchenough Bridge.

The Save River in the dry season.

511

Waterfall whipped into a gigantic bridal veil

The Bridal Veil Falls near Chimanimani. The pool is said to be haunted.

Near Chimanimani are the Bridal Veil Falls, where a stream falls down a cliff, the water being caught by the winds and converted into a spray resembling the veil of a bride.

The Pork Pie Mountain, named from its shape, is also very close to Chimanimani. On its slopes there is a 2 000-hectare nature sanctuary containing eland, zebra, bushbuck, grey duiker, klipspringer, and a great variety of other wild creatures.

Chimanimani Mountains

Part of the eastern border of Zimbabwe consists of the mountain range known as the Mawhenge ('rocky place'). The range is only 45 kilometres long but is of remarkable beauty. While the rest of the mountains of the eastern districts are made of grey-blue granite, the Mawhenge consists of sugary-white quartzite, a geological system deposited by water about 1 000 million years ago and known to geologists as the Frontier System. This range sparkles in the sunshine and its peaks, up to 2 399 metres high, are dramatically jagged.

The Musapa River flows through a narrow pass in the range. The pass is known to the Ndawu people as Tshimanimani, meaning 'to be squeezed together'. The name Chimanimani Mountains derives from that of the pass.

A national park was created in part of the Chimanimani Mountains in 1951. It is reached from the village of Chimanimani. A pathway, used for hundreds of years by pedlars bringing in trade goods from Mocambique and by Rozvi and Karanga people carrying gold dust to the coast ports, climbs the western slopes of the mountains and crosses an inner valley, then descends the eastern slopes through Skeleton Pass into Mocambique.

The plant life of the park is varied and similar to that of the south-western Cape. The soil of the park is decomposed quartzite, whereas that of the Cape is decomposed sandstone, but both are sedimentary. To the eye they seem unlikely looking bases for the favourable growth of plants, but they are rich in chemical foods. In the Chimanimani Mountains grow half-a-dozen varieties of protea, as well as everlastings, erica and pin-cushions. Cedar and yellowwood trees grow to perfection. Mixed with these temperate south-western Cape types of plant life are tropical ferns and orchids similar to those of Madagascar, which is on the same line of latitude — 20° south.

Sable, eland and other antelope roam through the mountains. Leopards hunt baboons on the high slopes while the Bundi River, which flows through the central valley, is well populated with trout.

The Chimanimani National Park is ideal country for hiking and climbing. There is a well-built hut in the central valley which visitors use as a base for exploring the park.

Chipinge

A buttress in the eastern mountains of Zimbabwe is called by the Tsanga people Tshipinga, meaning 'something that impedes a traveller'. The village of Chipinge takes its name from this buttress.

Chipinge consists of a few streets lined with shops, government offices and residences. There are flowering trees, colourful gardens, and the climate is warm, with a moderate rainfall.

The village is the centre of a prosperous farming industry producing tea, coffee, sugar, cereal crops, tropical fruit, pecan and macadamia nuts, wattle, vegetables and dairy produce. Cheddar cheese from Chipinge is renowned in southern Africa.

Europeans first settled in this area in 1892, when Thomas Moodie led a trek of 68 adults, children and servants from Bethlehem in the Orange Free State to the eastern mountains of Zimbabwe, where Cecil Rhodes had offered grants of land to attract settlers.

Chirinda

On the southern end of the eastern mountains is a 550-hectare forest known to the Shanganes as Tshirinda ('a refuge'). This is a high forest of ironwoods, wild figs and red mahogany trees. One of the red mahogany trees is 66 metres high and has a girth of 16 metres. This particular tree is still growing and, with the rest of its species in the Chirinda forest, comes into bloom each November with in-

The forest of ironwood and mahogany at Chirinda, in the eastern mountains.

numerable small white flowers.

Ferns and mosses in great profusion cover the floor of the forest while creepers and lianas hang from the trees. Parasitic figs, *Ficus natalensis*, strangle many of the forest giants by growing like pythons around their trunks.

The Chirinda forest is notable for the butterflies and moths which feed on the rotting vegetation.

In the forest stands the Mount Selinda mission station, while close to it is the Gungunyana plantation of the Zimbabwean government forestry department.

There is a border gate opening into Moçambique, with a road leading to the small town known as Espungabera ('the wood of the rock rabbits'), about 5 kilometres to the east.

Christmas Pass

When F. W. Bruce surveyed the road from Harare to Mutare he found himself camped on Christmas Day 1891 on the summit of the pass and named it Christmas Pass. From this summit there is a panoramic view down to the town of Mutare and far away along the southern reaches of the eastern mountains of Zimbabwe.

CHAMELEON MAGIC

Chameleon — camouflage expert.

To many of the indigenous peoples of southern Africa the chameleon is a creature of superstition. The folklore of the San and the Khoikhoi contains many stories of this harmless little reptile and the awe in which it is held is a tribute to its strange appearance, with gaping, toothless mouth, peculiar eyes moving quite independently of each other, and its slow, jerky walk.

Africa is the principal home of chameleons. In Zimbabwe and the northern Transvaal, the East African chameleon, *Chamaeleo dilepsis*, is found, reaching a length of 30 centimetres.

In most other parts of southern Africa, members of the *Microsaura* genera are common.

These are all small chameleons, some only 5 centimetres in length.

The ability of the chameleon to blend in with its environment by changing colour is its best known characteristic and principal means of defence.

Himalaya

From the Vumba mountains there is a magnificent view across the Burma Valley to a 2 212-metre-high mountain ridge known as Himalaya. The summit of this ridge can be reached by a gravel road which branches off from the main Mutare-Chimanimani road 44 kilometres south of Mutare. The drive is dangerous in wet weather, but the scenery is on the grand scale.

Yellow arum lilies, everlastings and proteas grow on the slopes and musasa trees are brilliant in spring colours. Seed potatoes are grown in the valleys and Romney Marsh sheep flourish in the cold, wet climate.

After 48 kilometres of stiff climbing the road reaches the summit plateau and the border gate with Moçambique at a place known to the Shanganes as Tsetsserra ('Hurry on'), for the cold at this altitude has caused the deaths of many travellers.

Honde Valley

One of the great views of Zimbabwe is from the main road from Mutare to Nyanga, looking east into the valley of the Muhonde ('river of euphorbia trees'). On the bush-covered floor of the valley stands a strangely shaped cluster of rocks known as Masimiki ('rocks that stand upright'). They resemble a giant Stonehenge.

A dassie (rock-rabbit) family basking in the valley of the Sabi River.

The poisonous Amanita muscaria *toadstool growing in granite soil.*

The city that moved to catch the trains

The valley leads into the flat coastal terrace of Mocambique.

Hot Springs
In the valley of the Sabi River and its tributary, the Odzi, south of Mutare, there are two hot springs. Wild bee-keeping is a profitable occupation for the farmers here, and log hives can be seen wedged in the dusty trees.

Mutare
When Cecil Rhodes made his first visit to the country he journeyed inland from Beira and, following the only track then in use, crossed the mountain divide and descended into the valley of the Mutare River. His heart must have been gladdened at the sight of more than 160 mines in the early stages of development. To Rhodes this was proof of the immense riches of the country which he fondly imagined to be the El Dorado of the Ancients and the Ophir of the Bible. Even the Nyika name of the river, Mutare ('the river of ore'), was an indication of early mining and the recovery of precious metals.

This rowdy little mining area was given the name of Umtali, which was the Shangane form of Mutare.

The original settlement had a short life. Less than five years after it was established its inhabitants were informed that the narrow-gauge railway being built from Beira would not be able to cross the mountains into the Mutare Valley. The surveyors had found an easier way through a natural gap 18 kilometres to the south, and the town would be separated from the railway by a spur of mountains.

Cecil Rhodes offered a radical solution to the problem. As the railway could not come to the town, he suggested that the town move to the railway. He offered to lay out a new town and allocate stands to everybody who moved from the old settlement, and also pay them compensation towards the cost of removal. In 1896 Mutare (known until recently as Umtali) was recreated on its present site and the old town abandoned to the bush.

The site of the new town is in the valley of the stream known as the Sakubva, from the shrubs of that name which grow on its banks. The setting of granite mountains is so

The granite peaks of the eastern mountains looking down on the Honde Valley.

awesome that Mutare ranks as one of the most beautifully situated cities in southern Africa.

Its surveyor, Rhys Fairbridge, laid wide streets, a spacious park and, to Rhodes's desires, a site for a stock exchange and a race track.

The valley is warm and fertile. Vegetation is luxuriant, gardens colourful, and the streets shaded by flowering trees such as jacaranda and flame trees.

Mutare became a city on 1 October 1971. It has a theatre, concert hall, civic centre and first-class sporting facilities, including an Olympic-size swimming bath.

The Mutare Museum, in Victoria Avenue, has displays of the plant and animal life of Manicaland, the district of Mutare. There are exhibits of live reptiles, antique firearms, tractors, locomotives, Cecil Rhodes's private coach, and wagons. A pre-historic sec-

---

IMPORTED PLANTS TURNED THE PEOPLE OF SOUTHERN AFRICA INTO TEA-DRINKERS

Picking tea in the eastern highlands plantations in the Pungwe Valley.

Tea is not indigenous to Africa, but from at least the time of the opening by the Portuguese of the sea route around the Cape from Asia to Europe, it was shipped from China and Ceylon and became a common drink in the coastal settlements of Mocambique and the Cape. Carried into the interior by hunters, traders and missionaries, tea was introduced to the indigenous peoples. At first a novelty, tea-drinking became an amiable habit. Nowadays more than 10 000 million cups of tea are drunk

each year in southern Africa, an average of 500 cups a year for each member of the population.

The first known attempt to cultivate tea in southern Africa was in Natal. About 1850 Robert Plant introduced tea plants from Kew Gardens in England. A few years later, others imported plants from Assam and China, but the experiments did not prove profitable and were abandoned.

In 1877 the Natal government imported more plants and seed and

Liege Hulett, among others, made an experimental plantation on his Kearsney estate on the north coast of Natal. This plantation, covering 1 800 hectares of land, was continued until 1946 before being finally replanted with sugar cane, which was the general crop in that part of the country.

In its natural Asian home tea grows in areas of high rainfall, at least 1 500 millimetres a year, and few parts of southern Africa are ideal for the crop. The most suitable are parts of Pondoland, the north-eastern Transvaal and the eastern districts of Zimbabwe. In 1925 two tea-planters from Assam, Arthur Wood and Grafton Phillips, migrated to Zimbabwe and started a nursery of tea-plants in the valley of the Tanganda stream near Chipinge. They soon discovered that there was insufficient rain. They decided to irrigate from the stream. Such artificial watering was unique in tea-growing, but to their delight it worked. In 1929 the first crop of Tanganda tea was harvested, only 517 kg, but the flavour was excellent. Within 20 years they were harvesting over 500 000 kg a year.

The waterfall at the head of the Pungwe Gorge, looking north-west. The lowlands of Moçambique lie to the right.

tion displays pottery, skeletons and other relics of early man. An aloe garden contains most species indigenous to Zimbabwe.

On the outskirts of the city stands La Rochelle, a magnificent house bequeathed to the country by Lady Courtauld, wife of the textile magnate. It stands in 150 hectares of landscaped gardens, woods and parkland. The house is open to the public.

Overlooking the city from the north-west is a granite dome, named Murahwa's Hill after a Nyika subchief who once lived there. On its summit is the ruin of a defensive wall, and caves on its western side contain San paintings and storage bins where Nyika people stored grain in case of attack. Near the summit is a rock which was struck to warn the local people of impending trouble — its sound resembles that of a gong.

A restoration of an old-time sunken cattle kraal in the Nyanga Mountains.

The flora of Nyanga is reminiscent of the Cape. This is Protea asymmetrica.

The lovely, shady woodlands of the Nyanga National Park.

Ingenious alarm system of a vanished people

The hill is a nature reserve, rich in birds, butterflies and several small species of wild animals such as rock rabbits.

On the floor of the valley stands Cross Kopje, which has on its summit a 10-metre-high stone cross, dedicated to Zimbabweans who died during the First World War.

Around the city are view sites such as Chace's View and the mountain drive, both reached from the top of Christmas Pass.

In a small garden at the top of Christmas Pass stands a bronze statue to Kingsley Fairbridge — son of Mutare's first surveyor — Fairbridge's pet dog and their constant Nyika companion, Jack. Fairbridge founded an organization to bring children from British orphanages to train as farmers in the country and other British territories.

A municipal caravan park is on the heights near the summit of Christmas Pass.

Nyanga National Park

In the first half of the 19th century a celebrated spirit medium, Sanyanga, held sway over the plateau summit of the mountain known after him as Nyanga. It is an area of granite mountains and lush green plateaus. Rainfall is heavy and this area is a sponge and watershed, containing the sources of many streams which tumble to the east and west in waterfalls and rapids.

The Nyangani (2 790 metres) is

Cross Kopje — the cross is a monument to troops killed in World War I.

the highest mountain of Zimbabwe.

Cecil Rhodes heard of the beauty of this mountain area in 1896, while visiting Mutare. He secured a block of farms here and on one of them, Fruitfield, he built a stone farmhouse which became his private mountain retreat.

On his death in 1902, Rhodes bequeathed 28 900 hectares of these fruit farms to the nation and this area became the Rhodes Nyanga National Park. The farmhouse Rhodes built became the Rhodes Nyanga Hotel, which is still in use and carefully preserved.

In the original stables, with their 650-millimetre-thick walls, there is a museum containing furniture used by Rhodes and photographs tracing his life.

Apart from its scenery, the Nyanga National Park contains some of the most remarkable ruins in Zimbabwe. These ruins are peculiar to the moun-

tain area and their nature and history has created considerable controversy. The ruins, scattered over 6 250 square kilometres of mountain land, are an assortment of stone walls, enclosures, irrigation furrows, terraces, platforms and what are known to Europeans as slave pits, but to the Nyika as matanga epasi, or underground cattle enclosures. Researchers are sometimes puzzled by the smallness of the enclosures, but they would have been adequate for the dwarf cattle or other small livestock then kept by the people of Zimbabwe.

The people responsible for these ruins seem to have abandoned the area more than 100 years ago. They were probably the Nyika people, or another section of the Karanga-Rozvi group.

Wars and raids from the south probably forced these people to flee from the warm lowlands and find sanctuary in the heights, and the

peculiar nature of the ruins was probably influenced by the cold, damp conditions of the mountain area. To plant crops the inhabitants were forced to construct terraces and irrigate them with canals. To protect their livestock from the weather, they built the underground enclosures. Their own huts were built above the underground pits and an ingenious alarm system was included in the design. A wooden pole was planted in the middle of the tunnel exits. Any livestock attempting to leave would push against the pole. The pole projected up through the roof of the tunnel, through the floor of the residential hut, and was connected to the primitive bed used by the owner.

MAGNIFICENT MUSASA

The graceful musasa trees.

One of the most gorgeous of the world's botanical spectacles takes place in Zimbabwe each spring when the musasa trees produce their new leaves.

Musasa trees are numerous throughout Zimbabwe and although they grow elsewhere in Africa — in Zambia, Malawi and the north-eastern Transvaal — it is between the Limpopo and Zambezi rivers that they reach perfection.

The trees reach a height of 30 metres, with trunk diameters of a metre. They have a complex and extremely graceful network of boughs. They lose their leaves in winter. The young leaves emerge in spring brilliantly coloured pink, red, plum and fawn.

These colours seem especially vivid and varied on escarpments.

Musasa seeds mature in pods. When the pods are ripe they suddenly burst open, the halves spiral and scatter the seeds sometimes 10 metres from the tree.

African huts near Mutare in the eastern mountains.

Bauhinia galpinii *flowering in the granite sandveld.*

The view from St. Swithins. The peaks and bush-covered plateau are a sponge for the springs of many rivers.

The 2 495-hectare Mtarazi Falls National Park, formerly a separate entity, has now been incorporated in the Nyanga National Park. Rainfall is high here, and many streams have their source in this area of rugged mountain moorland. These streams include the Mtarazi, so named from the sound of its water falling over a sheer cliff in a 600-metre leap into the Honde Valley. Long before the water of the stream reaches the bottom of this fall it has been converted into mist and spray which moistens a beautiful rain forest growing immediately beneath it. The rare blue duiker is sometimes seen here.

Vegetation in this part of the park includes patches of high forest and several species of flowering erica.

Nyanga National Park contains many streams stocked with rainbow trout, from hatcheries in the park near the Mare Dam. Every stream contains rapids or falls. Especially notable are the Mtarazi, Honde and Nyangombe falls. The plant life is rich, with proteas, everlastings and erica of the area similar to those of the south-western Cape.

There are drives, walks, climbs and view sites into such valleys as the Honde and the Pungwe. The summit of Nyangani can be reached along the circular drive which takes motorists on a tour of the entire park. In and around the park are caravan parks, camping grounds, lodges, cottages and hotels.

Across the northern border of the park lies the small village of Nyanga, the administrative and communications centre for the area.

Penhalonga

Between 1890 and 1925 more than 160 gold mines were worked in the valley of the Mutare River. Long before the establishment of these mines people such as the Nyika obtained considerable quantities of gold from the gravels of the river, whose name means 'the river of ore'.

In 1889 a prospector from Barberton, J. H. Jeffreys, working with the Mocambique Company of Portugal, pegged two groups of ancient workings on a visibly rich outcrop of ore. He named the claim groups the Penhalonga Mine and the Rezende Mine, after officials of the Mocambique company. Both mines were brought into production early in the 1890s and before they were exhausted they rewarded their owners with a fortune in gold, silver, lead and copper.

The village of Penhalonga grew as a centre for the mines. Today the village is almost deserted, its buildings dilapidated, and most of the shops stand deserted along the one street of the village.

THE MYSTERIOUS RUINS ONCE THOUGHT TO BE THE OPHIR OF THE BIBLE

Throughout southern Africa are more than 18 000 relics of the curious, ancient stone-walled settlements known to the Shona-speaking people as maDzimbabwe.

Most of these ruins are in Zimbabwe and the northern Transvaal, in country where there are large exposures of granite. Granite, although hard, weathers naturally into fragments of suitable size for building, and most of the granite country of southern Africa occurs in the area of summer thunderstorms.

A scorching hot morning is often followed by a weather change of devastating contrast. Suddenly the shadow of a thundercloud sweeps over the rock exposure. Icy rain and hailstones fall on the heated rock. The stresses of so abrupt a cooling are too much for the rock. It cracks and flakes. In the cracks rain collects. The cloud passes as suddenly as it came. The sun reheats the rock, the water in the cracks expands and turns to steam, the pressure in the cracks becomes overwhelming and the granite flakes into segments.

The ancestors of the Shona-speaking people of Zimbabwe built sturdy walls by simply piling granite fragments on top of one another.

The granite fragments were never used for building anything other than walls. The homes of the builders remained the conventional mud-walled, thatched huts usual in Africa.

From the second half of the 19th century, when such ruined settlements were first seen by hunters from the south, many curious travellers' tales were spun.

Theories were commonplace that these ruins were somehow part of the Ophir of the Bible, the El Dorado of the ancients.

Nothing in these ruins proves that they were ever built by any other than the self-same African people who live in the area today, but the older stories with their suggestion of great mystery have a way of surviving despite their total lack of scientific support.

The ruins of the mysterious fort of Nyangwe.

Entrance to an underground cattle kraal or 'slave pit'

The ancient trails of the gold traders

The Save River flowing southwards before its big bend into Mocambique.

From the village a road leads up the slopes of the divide between Zimbabwe and Mocambique, passing on the way many abandoned mine workings. On the summit there is a border gate, a small Mocambique frontier post, and a plaque marking the place where Cecil Rhodes, in 1891, first entered the land which was, until recently, to bear his name.

In that same year three nurses, Rose Blennerhasset, Lucy Sleeman and Beryl Welby, walked here from Beira, 360 kilometres away, to establish a hospital. They crossed the eastern mountains above Penhalonga, and 2 kilometres south of the village there is a memorial garden containing a plaque commemorating their foundation of nursing services in the country. Also in this same garden stands a wild fig tree, under which the chiefs of the Nyika people used to gather in order to hold court.

Lake Alexander, 35 kilometres north from Penhalonga, supplies water to Mutare. There is a cascade in the Mutare River within view of Penhalonga.

Rusape

The town of Rusape ('sparing of its waters') takes its name from the erratic flow of the Lesape river west of the town. There are galleries of San paintings in various caves in the vicinity. One of these painting sites, known as Diana's Vow, contains a series of pictures showing the burial rites of a chief.

On the old scenic road to Nyanga is the St. Faith Mission, home of a workshop and training school run by the African sculptor Job Kekana.

A white-collared crow looks out over the eastern highlands.

Here, too, are the graves of three soldiers killed in a battle with Chief Makoni of the Hungwe people on 3 August 1896. Makoni was defeated in the battle and his capital burned, but he later rebuilt his settlement and harassed local farmers. A small force was sent out from Mutare with orders to take Makoni prisoner. He retreated to a nearby cave with about 100 of his men. Dynamite charges were placed at the entrance to the cave. A man named Jenkins climbed down a sheer cliff face on a rope to light the fuse and then scrambled hand-over-hand back up the cliff before the dynamite was detonated. The explosion forced Makoni to surrender.

Lake Rusape is popular for fishing, sailing and water ski-ing.

Save River

There is a romantic legend about the beginning of the great river that drains the western side of the eastern mountains of Zimbabwe. The Duma section of the Shona people say that when they first settled in their present homeland there was a drought. The sister of their leader was a woman of great compassion. She wept at the hardships of the people and died of a broken heart. From her grave came a spring, the Mutsave — the perennial flow of fresh water which is the source of the Save River.

The Save River is a major river of Zimbabwe and Mocambique.

When Europeans came to Zimbabwe, they confused the name of Save with that of the Sabi River in the Eastern Transvaal.

Tradition has it that Arab dhows used to sail up the river from the small port of Nshava at its mouth. The dhows could navigate as high as the junction of the Sabi and the Lundi rivers. Above this point porters carried goods to the markets of the interior of the country and the northern Transvaal.

The valley of the river is fertile and the climate extremely hot. Many thousands of baobab trees grow here, and among the many other plant species to be found in the valley is the beautifully flowered Star of the Sabi (*Adenium multiflorum*).

There are hot springs at Rupisi, in the Save Valley, and in the valley of

The flowers of the Star of the Sabi. The plant thrives in baking heat.

The flower of the baobab. The fruit has a rich Vitamin C content.

its tributary, the Odzi. In the middle reaches of the Save Valley is an agricultural experimental station.

Tanganda

The valley of the Tanganda ('flooding river') is one of the principal tea-producing areas of the eastern districts of Zimbabwe.

In 1925 two tea planters from Assam, Arthur Wood and Grafton Phillips, settled in this valley and established an experimental nursery of tea plants. They soon discovered that the rainfall in the valley was inadequate and they decided to irrigate the tea plants, although such a practice was unconventional in the traditional production of tea.

The Tanganda provided ample water for the project and it was successful.

In 1929 the first crop was picked and Tanganda tea now makes a major contribution to the economy of southern Africa.

Troutbeck

Major Alfred McIlwaine, a renowned trout fisherman and rugby player, settled in the country in 1926. The depression of the '20s practically

The Ziwa Ruins, the most extensive of the ruined walled settlements, covering 125 square kilometres.

ruined him, but in 1933 he was offered an allotment of cheap land on the Nyanga Downs in exchange for developing the area as a trout fishing resort.

McIlwaine accepted and named his new home Troutbeck. The trout were introduced in 1934 from the Cape. Dams were built and trout waters made available to fishermen.

The Nyanga, Nyanga Downs and Troutbeck areas combine into one of the finest trout-fishing areas of southern Africa.

Umvumvumvu

The river known as the Umvumvumvu ('river of plenty') flows through a warm and fertile valley which produces maize, fruit and other foodstuffs.

Vumba

South-east of Mutare lies a bulky granite ridge known to the Nyika people as mubvumbi ('the mountains of drizzle').

Europeans call the area the Vumba, and the road that reaches it from Mutare provides one of the most spectacular drives in southern Africa, climbing steeply to 1 585 metres above sea level within a mere 10 kilometres of the city.

The slopes of the Vumba are densely forested and the musasa trees growing here provide a brilliant spectacle each spring, with their new leaves blood-red in colour.

The highest point in the Vumba is Castle Beacon (1 911 metres), a giant granite dome topped by a telecommunications tower.

After 24 kilometres the road passes through a small forest called the Bunga ('dense forest'), which is notable for the fact that it contains 250 species of fern. Eventually the road reaches a turn-off to the Vumba National Park, a 200-hectare botanical garden that has been created around the shores of a small lake.

The park is one of the show pieces of Zimbabwe. Its gardens are notable for azaleas, begonias, proteas, ferns, gladioli, hydrangeas and flame lilies. There is a swimming pool, an artificial lake, and a camping and caravan park

The misty forested slopes of the Vumba ('drizzle', mountains.

covering 3 hectares.

The farm Cloudlands, obtained in 1891 by Lionel Cripps, who became first speaker in the House of Assembly, was bequeathed by him to the people of the country. Cripps also presented the Bunga Forest to the nation.

Hosts of butterflies and moths live in the Vumba forest. Samango monkeys, leopards, duikers of various species and bushbuck are common in the area, and a unique species of dwarf chameleon is found here.

Ziwa Ruins

Dominated by the 1 744-metre-high granite mountain of Ziwa is an extraordinary complex of ruins covering about 125 square kilometres of countryside. The ruins, formerly known as the Van Niekerk Ruins after the local farmer who guided the first archaeologist through the area, consist of low stone walls, passages, enclosures and terraces.

The builders appear to have been a section of the Rwe people, and it seems that the peak period of building was in the 17th century. What motivated the Rwe people in this activity is unknown. The stonework is primitive, but of such an extent that it must have taken several generations of labourers to complete.

Students of African history believe that the carrying of the stones and the placing of them in position was almost certainly the work of women and children.

The ruins centre around Ziwa Mountain and two minor adjoining peaks, one named Hamba. The politico-religious head of the community probably had his residence on the slopes of Hamba Mountain.

The walls provided scant military defence. In the early years of the 19th century, when Zimbabwe was invaded by Zulu-speaking groups, the Rwe people were almost annihilated and only fragments of this population group remain in existence today.

Many of the ruins contain grinding stones which were used by the women for making flour, and also stone seats. On the slopes of Hamba Mountain there is a six-metre-tall phallic rock, and a cave thought to have been regarded as the residence of an oracle.

TO THE MIGHTY ZAMBEZI

ON ITS NORTH-WESTERN side the central plateau of Zimbabwe slopes gently down into the flat, forest-covered sea of sand of the Kalahari, overlapping eastwards across the border from Botswana. For 480 kilometres the road from Bulawayo finds a way across this tangled wilderness as if it followed some invisible guiding star. There are few natural landmarks save occasionally the crossing of some stream, or the passing of some outstanding tree. Apart from the coal mining centre of Hwange there are no towns, only a few small trading stations built in clearings made like islands in the vast green sea of trees.

The forest is rich in its number and variety of trees. The Zimbabwe teak (mgusi) trees produce fine timber and sleepers made from them carry much of southern Africa's rail system. Bloodwood (mukwa) trees, and mahogany (mkuthlu) also yield timber, while in the watercourses grow waterbooms (mdoni) and ebony (mutshenje).

Acacia species, known as singa trees to the Ndebele, perfume the forest with their white and yellow blossoms. Mopane trees seem to drowse through the hot hours of sunshine, their leaves drooping to allow the sun's rays to pass harmlessly to the ground. Musasa trees, their branches a delicate tracery against the sky, beautify the forest with the brilliance of the colour of their spring leaves.

The forest has always been a haunt of big game. Elephants and giraffes feed on the fresh leaves on the tree tops, the elephants pushing the trees over if the tender shoots are beyond reach. Buffalo, sable antelope, zebra, wildebeest, roan antelope, impala, eland, gemsbok, waterbuck and other antelope species find ample food, browsing, grazing, licking the outcrops of lime which occur in many areas, and being incessantly hunted by lion, leopard, cheetah, wild dog and other predators.

To any visitor, this wild garden is immensely exciting. For many kilometres the forest is almost impenetrable. The traveller feels imprisoned in a tangle of shrubs and trees. Then suddenly there is an open glade or watercourse with an entrancing vista, grassy slopes, and a herd of game animals grazing in the distance or scampering away from the intruder. There are 1,4 million hectares of this forest country preserved as the Hwange National Park, one of Africa's principal nature sanctuaries.

At the end of the long run north from Bulawayo there is a climax to this forested, sandy plain which is shattering in its visual impact. It is as though nature has lulled the traveller into acceptance as a fact that the entire world is really flat, and there is no end to trees, and no horizon ever broken by mountains. In this mood, the traveller, with no warning of gentle slope or dwindling forest, reaches the banks of the Zambezi and is confronted by an instant transition of scenery.

The Zambezi River is one of the major rivers of the world and is a majestic spectacle. The surging flow of water, the riverine forest, the rich aquatic life, the birds and game animals, the unpredictable moods of a river so vast are awe-inspiring. The Lozi ferrymen have a song which they sing as they paddle its waters:

'The mighty Zambezi,
Nobody knows
Where it comes from,
Or where it goes.
I only know
It is born in the skies
And flows to far places
Before it dies.'

It is this river that has as its greatest glory one of the natural wonders of the world, the Victoria Falls of David Livingstone, the Mosi o a Tunya or 'smoke that rises' of the Kololo people, the Manza Thunqayo or 'water that rises like smoke' of the Ndebele, a place of wonder to all, and of great religious veneration to the Tonka people who saw in its rainbow a sure sign of the presence there of God. To the Tonka only the spirit of nature, the all-powerful creator, could live in a place so beautiful and awesome.

Binga

Many Tonka people, displaced from their original homes by the flooding of the Zambezi Valley during the creation of Lake Kariba, were resettled on the higher slopes at the outpost of Binga, named from the thick forest country which encloses it.

Binga is a popular resort for fishermen. There are chalets, caravan and camping sites, boats for hire, and many fishing spots in the upper reaches of Lake Kariba.

Chete Game Reserve

This reserve, 1 250 square kilometres in extent, is not open to the public. It is used for research by the University in Harare.

Densely forested, it lies on the southern slopes of the Zambezi Valley. Wildlife includes buffalo, elephant, black rhino and numerous antelope such as tsessebe, roan, sable, bushbuck, eland, impala, kudu and waterbuck. Hippo and crocodile are also abundant, and lion, leopard, cheetah and wild dog are present.

Dete

The river known as the Dete ('reedy river') has given its name to this village on the main railway line from Bulawayo to Victoria Falls. It is the nearest railway station for the Hwange National Park main entrance and camp, 27 kilometres away. Built from Bulawayo in 1903, the railway runs straight for 116 kilometres between Gwai and Dete — the longest straight section of rail in southern Africa.

Hwange

Hwange takes its name from Hwange Rusumbani, one time chief of the Nambiya section of the Rozvi people who live in the area.

When the Ndebele entered Zimbabwe in 1838 they conquered the Nambiya, and their homeland became the hunting preserve of the Ndebele chief, Mzilikazi.

When the Ndebele were defeated by the British South Africa Company forces in 1893, prospectors entered the area to investigate mineral deposits. A German prospector, Albert Giese, was told by the local people of 'stones that burned'. He investigated, and pegged one of the largest coal outcrops in Africa. Six years later, in 1899, the Wankie Coal, Railway and Exploration Company was formed to work the coal deposits. This was the start

The Zambezi River, a vegetable ivory palm, and the sun sinking after a long day.

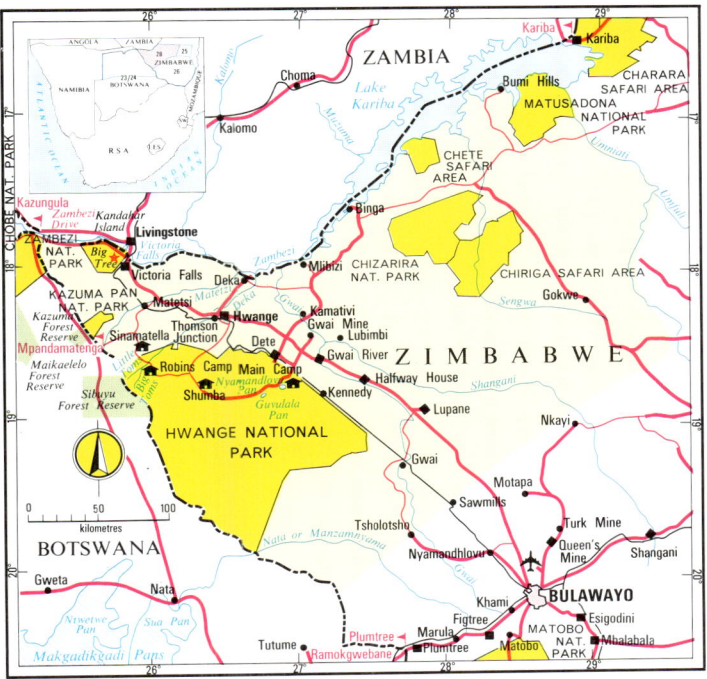

of the town Wankie, recently respelt as Hwange.

Hwange is a baking-hot little place, permeated with the odour of coal. There is some ranching in the district, but coal mining dominates local life.

In June 1972 there was a disastrous series of underground explosions in one of the workings, killing 427 men, most of whom are still buried in their coal-black tomb.

Hwange National Park

In 1928 the Legislative Assembly proclaimed 13 000 square kilometres of north-western Zimbabwe a game reserve. This was the beginning of one of the largest of all nature sanctuaries in Africa.

Edward Davison, a 22-year-old official in the tsetse control department, was appointed warden of the reserve, and held the post for the next 33 years. His name will always be honoured as that of one of the champions of conservation in southern Africa.

At the time of its proclamation the reserve was a huge parkland with no roads or human settlement. In former years, before the Ndebele subdued the local Rozvi people, there were a few stone-walled settlements among clusters of low, granite hills at places such as Bumbusi, Matowa and Shangano. San once hunted in this area and on the rocks are strange engravings of the tracks of game animals and human beings.

The area of the reserve was mainly the level projection eastwards of the Kalahari sand country, covered in trees, with very few hills or outcrops of rock.

In a not-too-distant geological period there had been a drainage system southwards into the Nata River.

One of Africa's greatest wildlife sanctuaries

This system had fallen into disuse owing to a change in the weather or level of the land, leaving behind marshes, shallow lakes and pans, and, in the south, a strange series of parallel sand dunes, each almost exactly 1,5 kilometres from the next, with teak trees growing on the crests and mopane trees in the dips. The reason for the regularity of these dunes is obscure. The pans, a major influence on the wild animal population, are perhaps the most remarkable physical features of the national park. They are mainly 20 metres to 30 metres in diameter and seldom more than 1 metre deep at their fullest, after the summer rainy season. By the end of the winter, many are completely empty.

During the summer, heavy rains cause the wild animals to disperse. Although the park is then at its best, green and beautiful, the animals are spread over so large an area that they are not easily seen.

The coming of the dry season brings a profound change. Animals gather near the pans, where they are assured of water, natural salts, and sodium and lime dissolved in the water.

Some of the pans were once natural hollows in the sand, where rain collected. The majority, however, owe their existence to the presence of salt on or near the surface. Ants or other burrowing creatures conveyed these salts to the surface in antheaps. Wild animals gathering at such places over a considerable time consumed enough of the salt-impregnated sand to create hollows. During the rains, water collected in these hollows, dissolving lime and sodium from the sand, which made it palatable to game.

Pans are steadily enlarged by animals drinking the water and wallowing in the mud.

A herd of buffalo or elephant carry away a considerable amount of mud on their bodies. The surface drainage of rain into the pans, and wind-blown dust, replaces only some of the material.

The largest pans are in the areas of the richest lime and sodium deposits. These are some of the principal watering places for wild animals in Africa, and rank among the great natural spectacles of the world.

Edward Davison reached the new

A warthog, daubed with sticky mud after a bath, full of curiosity.

THE TIMBER GIANTS OF THE ZIMBABWE PARKLAND

A forest of acacia and teak.

In the vast parkland of Zimbabwe are a great many species of trees of exceptional beauty and economic value. The sand country between Bulawayo and Victoria Falls is particularly productive of timber. In this densely forested area grows the Zimbabwe teak (*Baikiaea plurijuga*), known to the Ndebele as the mgusi. A magnificent tree, it grows to nearly 18 metres and more in height, and has a trunk up to a metre in diameter.

Wood from the mgusi tree has provided flooring for houses in many parts of the world. Smooth and hard-wearing, the wood is handsome in appearance and not prone to splintering. Railway sleepers, window frames, furniture and dug-out canoes are all made from this timber.

The bloodwood tree (*Pterocarpus angolensis*), known to the Karanga as the mukwa, grows up to 20 metres, with a trunk of 3,5 metres in diameter. Widespread in central Africa, it is greatly valued for its durable timber, ideal for furniture. In the past this wood was used to make spear shafts, paddles and canoes. The roots, bark, leaves and flowers are also used for a variety of medicinal purposes. The sap of the tree, red and sticky to the touch, gives the bloodwood tree its name.

The red mahogany (*Khaya nyasica*) is a true forest giant. The famed 'Big Tree' in the forest at Mount Selinda is of this species. It is about 60 metres high with a trunk 5 metres in diameter.

The white (or Natal) mahogany reaches a height of 20 metres with a trunk 1,5 metres in diameter. This is the *Trichilia emetica* tree, which favours the hot areas of central Africa. It shelters beneath its boughs a host of smaller trees, and supports many creepers and lianas. The timber is soft and is used by carvers to make masks, ladles and curios. The seeds, resembling the eyes of dolls, yield an oil which is used in the making of soap. The bark yields a purgative, while the leaves are said to be a cure for insomnia if placed in the sufferer's bed.

Other trees of the region are the waterbooms and the African ebony.

game reserve on a dark night in September 1928, leaving the Bulawayo-Victoria Falls train at Kennedy siding. He was welcomed by John Lundin, a professional game-catcher who worked in the area and had promised to guide the young warden on his first explorations. A few other Europeans lived along the railway, trading or hunting for a living.

West of the railway, however, there was only wilderness, occasionally visited by San hunters from Botswana. On the north-western border, where the country becomes more hilly, studded with granite and other types of rock, there lived an extraordinary recluse named Herbert Robins, a gnome-like man who owned two farms, Big Toms and Little Toms, on two tributaries of the Deka River. The farms were named after a hunter, Tom Saddler, who used to hunt in the area in the 1870s.

Robins had built a comfortable house equipped with an upstairs observatory, for he was keen on astronomy and had a powerful telescope. He spent most of his nights watching the stars and slept during the hot hours of daylight. People visiting him in daylight found him irritable on being awakened, invariably dressed in pyjamas and a knitted jelly-bag cap of the type worn by old-time sailors.

He regarded the young warden as an interloper in his private preserve, and when a track was made from the reserve to his property he dug a pit in

Herbert Robins, the strange recluse of Big Toms and Little Toms farms.

the centre to prevent Davison from making visits. Despite this, Robins was an intelligent, well-read man, and a member of several learned societies. On his death in 1939 his farms became part of the game reserve. His farmhouse and observatory are now the centre for Robins Camp, one of the three tourist camps of the Hwange National Park. The other two are Main Camp (the headquarters near Dete railway station) and Sinamatela. All three camps are spacious and have well-equipped caravan parks, chalets, lodges and bungalows.

On 27 January 1950 the Hwange Game Reserve (at the time it was spelt Wankie Game Reserve) was proclaimed a national park, and by the time of his transfer in 1961 to an administrative position in Harare, Davison could look back on the creation of a natural sanctuary for one of the most varied populations of wild animals to be found in any of the game reserves or national parks of Africa. This population varies seasonally, but in winter Hwange National Park is so full of game that it is a tourist spectacle unexcelled by any other national park in Africa.

Elephants are particularly numerous, with about 14 000 in the area during the winter months. Probably owing to a dietetic or mineral deficiency, the elephants of this part of Africa have never been notable for large tusks, and this has tended to protect them from ivory hunters.

Buffalo herds of more than 1 000 animals are common. Eland, zebra, giraffe, wildebeest, kudu, roan, sable, impala, gemsbok, tsessebe, and many other antelope are plentiful.

Warthog, baboon and monkeys abound, and the principal predators are lion, leopard, cheetah, wild dog, hyena (spotted and brown) and jackal. There are also smaller creatures such as porcupine, ratel, lynx, antbear and various species of wild cat.

About 400 kilometres of game viewing roads have been built in the park, but only about one-third of the area is open to tourists.

At pans such as Nyamandlovu and Guvulala there are observation platforms that afford the visitor an excellent vantage point from which to see and photograph game. On moon-

A cheetah, superbly built for speed. This is the fastest of all animals, reaching a speed of 120 kilometres an hour.

A winter wonderland teeming with big game

lit nights visitors are allowed to sit here and watch the constant comings and goings of the animals.

Kazungula

The Pandamatenga road, the pioneer trail blazed from South Africa to the Zambezi River, reached the Zambezi at a point marked by a huge muzun-guru (*Kigelia pinnata*) tree. At this place, named Kazungula after the tree, a pont was provided to carry passengers and goods across the river and into Zambia. The old tree still stands and a modern pont makes regular crossings across the river.

Pandamatenga

On the border between Botswana and Zimbabwe is the village of Pandama-tenga, which takes its name from a man of the Mlilima people, Mutenga, an ivory hunter in the early 19th century. He had a hunting camp in a grove of mpanda trees (*Lonchocarpus capassa*, or rain trees) near the source of the Matetzi River.

The camp was a staging post on the first trail blazed from Tati, in the south, to the Victoria Falls. This trail became known to Europeans as the Pandamatenga trail. When surveyors located the boundary between Zimbabwe and Botswana, they found it convenient simply to follow the trail, and the centre of the road was regarded as the boundary line.

Mutenga and his family were killed

by the Ndebele. A European trader and hunter, George Westbeech, then established a store here, and the place has remained a trading centre.

After World War II the British Government attempted to promote cattle farming in what was then Bechuanaland, and a village was built at Pandamatenga. However, this settlement was abandoned when the scheme collapsed, and the well-built modern houses, club, offices and swimming bath fell into ruin.

STRIP-ROAD SAFARIS

The strip road leading to Victoria Falls.

In parts of Zimbabwe are a few remaining stretches of a remarkable type of road: strip roads, created in the 1930s when the country urgently required better tracks but lacked money for proper road construction.

Such roads are simply two parallel surfaced strips. Providing traffic is not heavy, this construction is infinitely preferable to a mud or gravel surface. If two vehicles come from opposite directions, or one wants to pass the other, one vehicle has to move to one side, but each still has two wheels on a secure strip.

In 1930 the first concrete strip road in Zimbabwe was built on a section of the Gweru to Shurugwi route. The strips were each 61 centimetres wide and 84 centimetres apart, to suit the standard motor vehicle. These strips were considered suitable for traffic densities of up to 400 vehicles a day at maximum speeds of 65 kilometres an hour.

Fearsomely horned sable antelope at a water-hole in the Hwange National Park.

A warning in the Hwange park — a grim reminder that 'eat or be eaten' is the law of life in the wilds.

A giraffe, heading for a water-hole in the acacia thornbush country of Hwange.

Roan antelope, seldom numerous but always present in thornbush country.

A look-out platform at the famed Nyamandlovu Pan water-hole.

A herd of buffalo, more than 1 000 strong, watering and wallowing in a shallow pan in the Hwange park.

Tourist bungalows in the warm setting of the Hwange park's Robins Camp.

A herd of impala on their way to drink, with two warthogs having already arrived.

The unrivalled majesty of Victoria Falls

To the Tonka people, such an awesome spectacle could only mean that this was the domain of God. To David Livingstone, a scene 'so lovely must have been gazed upon by angels in their flight'. To modern man, that scenic phenomenon is one of the world's greatest miracles: the majestic, unrivalled Victoria Falls.

In its upper reaches, the infant Zambezi gives no hint of the dramatics to come. It has its source in a lonely grove of trees on the watershed between Zambia and Zaïre. Joined by many tributary streams, the river soon grows, and for 1 200 kilometres it flows rather lazily over the surface of the vast sheet of lava which forms the plateau of Central Africa. The Aluyi people who live along this stretch of the river know it as the Lwambayi ('great river'), and each flood season they move to the higher-lying verges.

In the season of floods — March to June — the river swells greatly, but the shallow valley contains it and the movement of the water is still slow. Only a few minor rapids high up the valley, and the small Gonye Falls, give it a flurry of speed.

Suddenly the river experiences a great change. It reaches a series of cracks in the sheet of lava which lie directly across the course of the river, so placed that it seems as though nature decided to play a prank on the lazy river giant. The lava sheet is 300 metres thick. The cracks in it are narrow and filled with soft earth and broken rock. The river, leisurely scouring out its course, found the lowest (most south-easterly) of the cracks and began carrying away the soft filling. The effect of this was the excavation of a deep trench cutting across the flow of the river.

Into this trench tumbled the water, and immediately it had to find a way out again. For a time there was a chaotic rising and falling of water. Then, on the lower edge of the trench, the river found a weak spot. This could have been the dislodgement of a single boulder. The river flow was then concentrated at this point, for it offered the easiest escape route from the trench. The weak spot was steadily lowered and widened until a remarkable waterfall had been created.

Along the full width of its course the river tumbled into a deep trench only about 200 metres wide. At the bottom of this trench the water rushed about in wild disorder and then shouldered its way out of the trench through the narrow gorge which formed from the original weak spot. At the entrance to the gorge a surging mass of water was caught in a series of whirlpools resembling a boiling pot. The view from the lower opposite edge of the trench must have been breathtaking.

After a time the river found another weak spot in the upper edge of the trench. This weak spot also grew to

The 'smoke that rises' — the great columns of spray rising from Victoria Falls.

become a gorge through which the river forced its way, abandoning the fall over the remaining upper edge of the trench.

At this stage in its development, the spectacle had changed. The river now poured into the trench through one deep gorge, raced along the bottom of the trench and then out through the gap in the lower side.

So far, this remarkable series of erosions has been repeated in eight successive parallel cracks. Each crack went through a similar process of transformation in a series of vast erosions spread over the last 500 000 years. The present crack is just past the most spectacular stage of its develop-

ment. Most of the river flow still falls over the full width of the crack, but a weak spot is already being deepened on the western end. This is the Devil's Cataract.

Eventually the present waterfall will disappear and the river will flow into the trench through this deepening gorge. At least two more faults lie across the course of the river, immediately above the present fall, and there are possibly even more concealed further up the course. Future visitors, therefore, may be rewarded with a spectacle even more astonishing than that of today.

The Kololo people living along the upper reaches of the river named the waterfall Mosi o a Tunya ('the smoke that rises'). The Ndebele called it aManza Thunqayo ('water that rises like smoke'). When David Livingstone became the first-known European to see the falls on 16 November 1855, he named them the Victoria Falls, in honour of Queen Victoria.

Livingstone reached the falls by canoe. He first saw the clouds of thundering spray from about 10 kilometres upstream. Immediately above the falls he changed into a lighter canoe and was paddled to the island that seems

David Livingstone, the first known European to see Victoria Falls.

The Zambezi River tumbling headlong into the deep trench across its bed.

The edge of the Victoria Falls at the season of medium flow.

to be on the verge of toppling into the thrashing waters below. From this island, Kazeruka, or Livingstone Island, he peered down into the spray and got his first glimpse of the magnitude of the falls.

His guides told him that at three spots near the falls the Tonka chiefs offered sacrifices to ancestors. These spots are within sight of a rainbow usually arching the spray, which to the Tonka marked the presence of God.

When Livingstone re-visited the falls the next day he planted peach,

Victoria Falls at near-peak flow. The rainbow is present during all sunny hours, and at times of bright moonlight.

apricot and coffee seeds and carved his name on a tree.

'This was the only instance in which I indulged in this weakness', he later told William Baldwin, the second white man known to have seen the falls. The two met during Livingtone's third visit to the falls.

The Victoria Falls are 1 700 metres wide and 100 metres high. They are one-and-a-half times as wide and twice as high as the Niagara Falls. The Victoria Falls are divided into the Devil's Cataract (27 metres wide and 60 metres high); the Main Falls, which in turn are divided by a project-

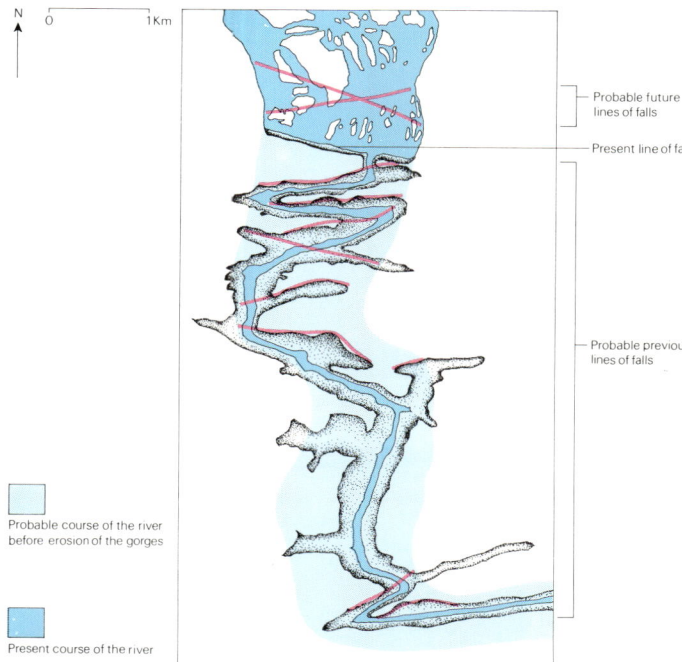

The Victoria Falls, showing the zigzag series of gorges created by the river eroding the contents of cracks across its course.

The edge of Victoria Falls, the successive gorges, and the rail-road bridge.

INDEX

The alphabetical sequence is arranged word-by-word, the hyphenated entries being treated as separate words. Page numbers in bold type indicate references accompanied by illustrations.

538

Acknowledgments

Many people and organizations assisted in the preparation of this book. The publishers wish to thank all of them, particularly the following.

Gunter Brozel; C. Dickson; John Comrie Greig; Richard Isemonger; Major George Iwanowsky; Pete Jurgens; Dr Dennis Madide; John Martin; Victor Millard; Penny Miller; Margot Murray; Dr C Pama; F. A. Shillington; Patrick Smith; Barbara Tyrrell; H. G. Zimmerman.

Anglo American Corporation of South Africa; Benoni Publicity Association; Bloemfontein Visitors Information Bureau; Bophuthatswana, Directorate of Tourism; Botswana, Department of Wildlife and National Parks; Botswana, Ministry of Commerce and Industry, Tourism Division; Cango Caves, Oudtshoorn; Cape of Good Hope Nature Reserve; Captour; Chamber of Mines Public Relations Office; Council for Scientific and Industrial Research; De Beers Consolidated Mines; Diamond Board for South West Africa; Divisional Councils: Caledon, Calvinia, Cape Town, Langeberg, Outeniqua; Durban Local History Museum; Durban Publicity Association; East London Publicity Association; Electricity Supply Commission; Graaff-Reinet Publicity Association; Greylingstad Village Council; Impala Platinum Ltd; Johannesburg Publicity Association; Killie Campbell Africana Library; Kirstenbosch Botanic Gardens; Krugersdorp Publicity Association; Kwazulu Government Offices; Lesotho National Tourist Office; Mountain Club of South Africa, Natal Section; Municipalities: Belfast, Boksburg, Brakpan, Cornelia, East London, Ermelo, Heidelberg (C.P.), Kimberley, Middelburg (Tvl), Oudtshoorn, Piet Retief, Pretoria, Roodepoort, Springs, Vanderbijlpark, Vereeniging, Westonaria; Natal Anti-Shark Measures Board; Natal Parks, Game and Fish Preservation Board; National Parks Board; National Tourist Bureaux: Bloemfontein, Cape Town, Kimberley, Pretoria; Port Elizabeth Publicity Association; Pretoria Publicity Association; S.A. Department of Agriculture; S.A. Department of Environment Affairs; S.A. Department of Health and Welfare; S.W.A. Department of Nature Conservation; S.W.A. Government Archives; Simmer and Jack Mine; South African Coal, Oil and Gas Corporation; South African Defence Force Documents Section; South African Institute for Medical Research; South African Library, Cape Town; South African Museum, Cape Town; State Herald, Government Archives, Pretoria; Stellenbosch Publicity Association; Sun International; Swaziland, Ministry of Commerce, Industry, Mines and Tourism; Table Mountain Preservation Board; Transkei, Department of Commerce, Industry and Tourism; Transkei, Tourist Liaison Officer; University of Botswana; University of Cape Town; University of Port Elizabeth; University of Stellenbosch; University of Swaziland; University of the Witwatersrand; Voortrekker Monument Museum Board of Control; Waterval-Boven Health Committee; Wine and Spirit Board; Zimbabwe National Tourist Board.

The publishers acknowledge their indebtedness to the following books which were used for reference.

Abantu: An Introduction to the Black People of Southern Africa by Martin West and Jean Morris (Struik); *An African Aristocracy* by Hilda Kuper (Oxford University Press); *The African Elephant* by Rennie Bere (Golden Press); *The African Elephant and its Hunters* by Denis Lyell (Health Cranton); *The Anglo-Boer War* by Johannes Meintjies (Struik); *Baanbrekers en Jagters van Suid-Afrika* by S. le Roux (Nasionale Pers); *Barrier of Spears* by Reginald Pearse (Timmins); *Beads. South Africa* by Margaret Ford (J. R. Ivy); *Birds of South Africa* by Austin Roberts (Central News Agency); *Bird Safari* by Peter Ginn (Longman Rhodesia); *The Black Wattle* by S. P. Sherry (University of Natal Press); *Bophuthatswana at Independence* by Bureau for Economic Research Re Bantu Development (Bureau for the Bophuthatswana Government); *The Cape of Adventure* by Ian Colvin (Maskew Miller); *A Checklist of the Birds of the Bechuanaland Protectorate and the Caprivi Strip* by R. Smithers (Trustees of the National Museums of Southern Rhodesia); *Churchills in Africa* by Brian Roberts (Hamilton); *A Cradle of Rivers* by David Dodds (Purnell); *Designs on Life* by Ernest Ullman (Timmins); *Dictionary of South African Biography Volume 1 and 2* (Nasionale Boekhandel); *The Distribution and Abundance of Tsetse* by John Glasgow (Pergamon); *Encyclopaedia Americana* (Americana Incorporated); *Encyclopaedia Britannica* (Encyclopaedia Britannica Incorporated); *Encyclopaedia Rhodesia* (College Press); *English/Zulu Dictionary* by Rev. C. Roberts (Kegan Paul); *Forest Succession and Ecology in the Knysna Region* by John Phillips (Government Printer); *Genealogy of the Rex Family* by Arthur Beddy (Balkema); *George Rex: Death of a Legend* by Patricia Storrar (Macmillan South Africa); *George Rex of Knysna* by Susan Metelerkamp (Timmins); *Gold in South Africa* (Chamber of Mines of South Africa); *The Gold Miners* by Alan Cartwright (Purnell); *The Great Hunters* by Geoffrey Haresnape (Purnell); *Great Shipwrecks* by Jose Burman (Struik); *The Great Trek* by Eric Walker (A. & C. Black); *The Guardians* by Joy MacLean (Books of Rhodesia); *The Guide to Botswana* by Guy Winchester-Gould (Winchester Press); *The Guide to Lesotho* by David Ambrose (Winchester Press); *Historical Dictionary of Swaziland* by John Grotpeter (Scarecrow Press); *The Historical Monuments of South Africa* by Jacobus Oberholster (Rembrandt van Rijn Foundation for Culture for the National Monuments Council); *Historic Rhodesia* by Oliver Ransford and Peter Steyn (Longman Rhodesia); *History of the Basuto. Ancient and Modern* by David Ellenberger (Basutoland Government); *A History of Southern Africa* by Eric Walker (Longmans); *A History of Swaziland* by James Matsebula (Longman Penguin Southern Africa); *Huberta Goes South* by Hedley Chilvers (Central News Agency); *Huisgenoot* (30 July 1956); *The Hunter and His Art* by Ione and Jalmer Rudner (Struik); *An Illustrated World History of the Sheep and Wool Industry* (South African Wool Board); *The Indigenous Livestock of Eastern and Southern Africa* by I. Mason and J. Maule (Commonwealth Agricultural Bureaux); *Kingdom of the Elephant* by E.A. Temple-Perkins (Melrose); *Lesotho* by Dick and Colleen Schwager (D. Schwager); *Lions and Virgins* by Cornelis Pama (Human & Rousseau); *Man Against Tsetse* by John McKelvey (Cornell University Press); *The Migratory Springbucks of South Africa* by Samuel Cronwright-Schreiner (T. Fisher Unwin); *My Early Life* by Winston Churchill (Macmillan); *No More the Tusker* by G. G. Rushby (Allen); *Northern Rhodesian Journal 1964* (Northern Rhodesia Society); *Notes on Tea Estates in Africa* by Wilson Smithett and Company (Thomas Skinner); *Our Green Heritage* by Willem Immelman (Tafelberg); *Outspan* (January 1953); *The Oxford English Dictionary* (Clarendon Press); *The Oxford History of South Africa* by Monica Wilson and Leonard Thompson (Clarendon Press); *The Pace of the Ox: A Life of Paul Kruger* by Marjorie Juta (Human & Rousseau); *Personality* (November 1971); *Portuguese in South-East Africa, 1600-1700* by Eric Axelson (Witwatersrand University Press); *President Paul Kruger* by Johannes Meintjies (Cassell); *Remarkable Voyages and Shipwrecks* by George Barrington (Simpkin, Marshall & Company); *Republic of Bophuthatswana* (Chris van Rensburg Publications); *Rider Haggard, His Life and Works* by Morton Cohen (Hutchinson); *Road Atlas and Touring Guide of Southern Africa* (The Automobile Association of South Africa); *Rock Art of Southern Africa* by Cranmer Cooke (Books of Africa); *Roget's Thesaurus* (Penguin); *The Role of Trypanosomiases in African Ecology* by John Ford (Clarendon Press); *Rule of Fear* by Peter Becker (Longmans); *Shaka's Heirs* by John Selby (Allen & Unwin); *Shipwreck and Empire* by James Duffy (Harvard University Press); *The Social System of the Zulus* by Eileen Krige (Longmans); *South Africa 1976* (Department of Information); *South African Geographical Journal December 1936* (South African Geographical Society); *South African Journal of Science Volume 41* (South African Association for the Advancement of Science); *South African Panorama* (October 1973 and October 1975); *Southern Cape Forests and Trees* by Friedrich von Breitenbach (Government Printer); *South West Africa: Land of Extremes* by Hans Jenny (South West African Scientific Society); *Springbok Management* by R. Bigalke, R. Liversidge and J. Schijf (Northern Cape Branch of the Wildlife Society of South Africa); *Standard Encyclopaedia of Southern Africa* (Nasou Limited); *The Story of Sugar* (South African Sugar Association); *The Story of the British Settlers of 1820 in South Africa* by Harold Hockly (Juta); *The Story of Wool* (South African Wool Board); *Swaziland* by Dudley Barker (H.M.S.O.); *Tea in Natal: Past, Present and Future* by J. L. Hulett (Natal Mercury); *Tea in Our Land Through Three Centuries* by Eric Rosenthal (Tea Bureau); *A Time to Die* by Robert Cary (Timmins); *To the Banks of the Zambezi* by Tom Bulpin (Nelson); *Trail of the Copper King* by Tom Bulpin (Timmins); *Trees of Southern Africa* by Eve Palmer and Norah Pitman (Balkema); *Trees of Southern Africa* by K. C. Palgrave (Struik); *Tribal Peoples of Southern Africa* by Barbara Tyrrell (Books of Africa); *The True Story of the Grosvenor East Indiaman* by Percival Kirby (Oxford University Press); *The Tswana* by Isaan Schapera (International African Institute); *The Warrior People* by Charles Binns (R. Hale); *The Warriors* by R. Summers and C. Pagden (Books of Africa); *The Washing of the Spears* by Donald Morris (Simon & Schuster); *White Gold: The Story of African Ivory* by Derek Wilson and Peter Ayerst (Heinemann); *Winston Churchill Volume 1: Youth, 1874-1900* by Randolph Churchill (Heinemann); *Who's Who in Southern Africa* (Argus Printing and Publishing Company); *Wilde Roeping: Die Verhaal van Beroemde Wildjagters in Suider-Afrika* by Christiaan Strydom (Tafelberg); *Young Winston's Wars* ed. Frederick Wood (L. Cooper); *Zulu/English Dictionary* by C. Doke and B. Vilakazi (Witwatersrand University Press); *500 Years: A History of South Africa* by C. F. J. Muller (Academica).

Use was also made of pamphlets in the South African Library Pamphlet File.

Photographers and illustrators

John Shapley; Cloete Breytenbach; John Shapley; Wool Board. 85 R W Robertson; Denoon Sieg; R W Robertson. 86 T V Bulpin; Anthony Bannister; Department of Tourism; Department of Tourism. 87 August Sycholt; Dirk Schwager. 88 T V Bulpin; T V Bulpin; Gerald Cubitt. 89 Anthony Bannister; Richard Boycott; V C Carruthers; V C Carruthers; Gerald Cubitt. 90 Gerald Cubitt; Alice Mertens. 91 Top right, John Meek; remainder, supplied by the Bureau of Heraldry, by kind permission of the registered owners. 92 Top left, centre left, supplied by the Government Printer, by kind permission of the Prime Minister's office; bottom centre right, Carl Meek, by kind permission of the South African Reserve Bank; bottom extreme right, George Proper, by kind permission of the South African Railways; remainder, supplied by the Bureau of Heraldry, by kind permission of the registered owners. 93 Top left, John Meek; top right, Carl Meek, by kind permission of the South African Reserve Bank; centre right, John Meek; bottom extreme left, Reader's Digest; bottom centre left, centre right, Carl Meek; remainder, supplied by the Bureau of Heraldry, by kind permission of the registered owners. 95 Gerald Cubitt; T V Bulpin. 96 T V Bulpin; T V Bulpin; Gerald Cubitt; Diagram, John Meek. 97 Penny Miller; Gerald Cubitt; Gerald Cubitt. 98 Gordon Douglas; Gordon Douglas; Gordon Douglas; Gordon Douglas; T V Bulpin. 99 Gordon Douglas. 100 Anthony Bannister; Brian Rees; Brian Rees; Robin Brown; Robin Brown; Robin Brown; Robin Brown; Brian Rees. 101 Anthony Bannister; Robin Brown; Anthony Bannister; Anthony Bannister. 103 Will Till; Gordon Douglas. 104 T V Bulpin; Gordon Douglas; Gordon Douglas. 105 Gordon Douglas; Alan Roberts. 106 Gerald Cubitt; Gerald Cubitt; Gordon Douglas. 107 Denoon Sieg; T V Bulpin; T V Bulpin; Gerald Cubitt. 108 Gordon Douglas; Gordon Douglas; Gerald Cubitt; Gordon Douglas; Gordon Douglas. 109 Anthony Bannister. 110 Anthony Bannister; Anthony Bannister; Gerald Cubitt. 111 Anthony Bannister; Anthony Bannister; Gerald Cubitt; Gerald Cubitt; Anthony Bannister; Anthony Bannister. 113 T V Bulpin; T V Bulpin; Diagram, John Meek. 114 Dirk Schwager. 115 All, Satour. 116 T V Bulpin; T V Bulpin. 117 T V Bulpin; T V Bulpin; Gordon Douglas. 118 Herman Potgieter; Gordon Douglas; Gordon Douglas; Gordon Douglas. 119 August Sycholt; T V Bulpin; Satour; Elliot Collection, Cape Archives. 120 T V Bulpin; Gordon Douglas; Gordon Douglas; Gordon Douglas; T V Bulpin. 121 Both, Gordon Douglas. 122 Gerald Cubitt; R W Robertson. 123 Gordon Douglas. 124 Gordon Douglas; KWV Publicity; Will Till; Will Till. 125 T V Bulpin; Gordon Douglas; Illustration, Michael Woods. 126 T V Bulpin; T V Bulpin; Jean Morris; Will Till. 127 Both, Gerald Cubitt. 128 A A Jorgensen; South African Railways. 129 A A Jorgensen; South African Railways; South African Railways. 130 South African Railways; A A Jorgensen; Diagram, John Meek. 131 South African Railways; A A Jorgensen; A A Jorgen-

sen; South African Railways. 133 T V Bulpin; T V Bulpin; Gordon Douglas. 134 David Steele; David Steele. 135 Port Elizabeth Publicity Association; D F Larsson; Gerald Cubitt. 137 Gerald Cubitt; Herman Potgieter; Gordon Douglas; T V Bulpin; Gerald Cubitt. 138 Nielen Schaefer; J Weimann; J Weimann; J Weimann; J Weimann; Nielen Schaefer; J Weimann. 139 All, T V Bulpin. 140 Fineline Action Photography; Diagram, John Meek; Robin Ford. 141 Fineline Action Photography; other two Trevor Gotsman. 142 Gordon Douglas; August Sycholt; August Sycholt. 143 Gordon Douglas. 144 Mary Evans Picture Library; Gordon Douglas; Irene Tongue; Irene Tongue. 145 Both, Gordon Douglas. 146 Gordon Douglas; T M Chaplin; Irene Tongue; Irene Tongue; Mary Evans Picture Library. 147 Irene Tongue; J R Freeman; T V Bulpin. 148 T V Bulpin; T V Bulpin; Jean Morris. 149 Gordon Douglas. 150 Diagrams, John Meek; T V Bulpin; Reader's Digest. 151 T V Bulpin; Reader's Digest; T V Bulpin; T V Bulpin. 153 T V Bulpin; Department of Tourism; Department of Tourism; Gordon Douglas. 154 T V Bulpin; East London Publicity Association; Color Library. 155 East London Publicity Association; J B Poulter; Gerald Cubitt; Satour; East London Publicity Association; J B Poulter. 157 Both, Irene Tongue. 158 Gordon Douglas; Irene Tongue; Irene Tongue; Gordon Douglas. 159 T V Bulpin; Illustration, Tony Linsell/Linden Artists. 160 Gerald Cubitt; H G Zimmermann. 161 All, Gordon Douglas. 162 Satour. 163 Anthony Bannister. 164 Gerald Cubitt; Gordon Douglas; Colin Campbell. 165 Bottom right, Penny Miller; remainder, T V Bulpin. 166 Cloete Breytenbach. 167 Cloete Breytenbach; T V Bulpin; Anthony Bannister; Department of Tourism. 168 Gordon Douglas; Colin Campbell. 169 South African Library, by kind permission of Howard Timmins Publishers from 'A Fortune Through My Fingers' by Jack Carstens; Gerald Cubitt; Gordon Douglas. 171 Gordon Douglas. 172 Gordon Douglas; Gerald Cubitt. 173 De Beers; Satour; Department of Tourism; De Beers. 174 Gordon Douglas; De Beers; De Beers. 175 Diagram, John Meek; Satour; De Beers; Illustrated London News; De Beers; De Beers. 176 Department of Tourism; De Beers. 177 Gerald Cubitt; Gordon Douglas; De Beers; Gordon Douglas; Gordon Douglas; Will Till. 178 Gordon Douglas. 179 Gordon Douglas; Reader's Digest; Reader's Digest; Reader's Digest; Gordon Douglas. 180 Gordon Douglas. 181 T V Bulpin/Scott-Hayward; T V Bulpin. 182 Gerald Cubitt. 183 T V Bulpin; Gordon Douglas; T V Bulpin. 184 T V Bulpin; South African Library. 185 Gordon Douglas; Gordon Douglas; Anthony Bannister. 186-7 Ralph King. 190 Gordon Douglas; T V Bulpin. 191 The Barnett Collection, The Star, Johannesburg; A A Jorgensen; Gerald Cubitt. 193 Satour; A A Jorgensen; Satour; Illustration, Charles Pickard/Reader's Digest. 194 John Meek; The Barnett Collection, The Star, Johannesburg; T M Chaplin. 195 John Meek; John Meek; A A Jorgensen; The Star, Johannesburg. 196 T M Chaplin; T M Chaplin; John Meek; Denoon Sieg. 197 John Meek; Gerald Cubitt; Satour;

T V Bulpin. 198 Satour; Ralph King. 199 John Meek; John Meek; Gerald Cubitt; John Meek; Gerald Cubitt; Africana Museum/Satour, Johannesburg. 200 John Meek; The Barnett Collection, The Star, Johannesburg; Anthony Bannister; Jean Morris. 201 The Barnett Collection, The Star, Johannesburg; Satour. 202-3 All, The Barnett Collection, The Star, Johannesburg. 204 T V Bulpin. 205 A A Jorgensen; Benoni Municipality. 206 T V Bulpin; Chamber of Mines; Chamber of Mines. 207 R W Robertson; T V Bulpin; Mary Evans Picture Library. 208 Gordon Douglas; T V Bulpin. 209 T V Bulpin; Pat Smith; Pat Smith; Pat Smith. 210 Satour; Optima; Africana Museum/Satour; Optima. 211 Chamber of Mines; Color Library; Ralph King; Gerald Cubitt; Illustration, Michael Woods; T V Bulpin. 212 Africana Museum/Satour; Africana Museum/Satour; Satour; Chamber of Mines; Illustration, Michael Woods; Satour. 213 Jean Morris; Chamber of Mines; Satour; Chamber of Mines. 215 Eli Weinberg, Johannesburg; T V Bulpin. 216 Gordon Douglas; T V Bulpin. 217 T V Bulpin; T V Bulpin; Anthony Bannister; T V Bulpin. 218 T V Bulpin; Color Library; A A Jorgensen; Gordon Douglas. 219 R W Robertson; Gordon Douglas; Gordon Douglas; T V Bulpin 220 Both, T V Bulpin. 221 Jean Morris. 222 Gordon Douglas; T V Bulpin; Gerald Cubitt. 223 T V Bulpin; T V Bulpin; Anthony Bannister; T V Bulpin. 224 T V Bulpin; Anthony Bannister; Gerald Cubitt; Gordon Douglas. 225 Denoon Sieg; Gordon Douglas. 226 D C H Plowes; Anthony Bannister; Anthony Bannister. 227 All, Anthony Bannister. 228 Pretoria City Council. 229 Gerald Cubitt; Pretoria City Council; Pretoria City Council; T V Bulpin. 231 Pretoria City Council; F W Robertson; Pretoria City Council; Pretoria City Council; Ralph King. 232 Pretoria City Council; Pretoria City Council; Gordon Douglas; Gordon Douglas. 233 Gerald Cubitt; Gordon Douglas; Gordon Douglas; T V Bulpin. 234 Jean Morris; Dirk Schwager; Ralph King; Jean Morris; Martin Mauve, by kind permission of Fort Klapperkop Military Museum, Pretoria. 235 Pretoria City Council; Pretoria City Council; Jean Morris; Diagram, John Meek. 236 Satour; Illustration, Barbara Tyrrell. 237 Pretoria City Council; Illustrated London News; Pretoria City Council; Illustration, Barbara Tyrrell. 238 Gordon Douglas. Voortrekker Monument Museum; R W Robertson. 239 Satour; Color Library. 241 Both, Gordon Douglas. 242 T V Bulpin; Anthony Bannister; Department of Tourism; Illustration, Barbara Tyrrell. 243 T V Bulpin; Illustration, Barbara Tyrrell. 244 Illustration, Barbara Tyrrell. 245 Will Till; Department of Tourism; T V Bulpin; Will Till; Ralph King; Gordon Douglas. 246 Ralph King; Gerald Cubitt. 247 Gerald Cubitt; Anthony Bannister; T V Bulpin; T V Bulpin. 248 T V Bulpin. 249 Both, Gerald Cubitt. 250 Gordon Douglas. 251 Gerald Cubitt; John Cook/Household Manual/Reader's Digest. 252 Gordon Douglas; Satour. 253 Gerald Cubitt. 254 Both, T V Bulpin. 255 T V Bulpin; Gordon Douglas; Gerald Cubitt. 256 Satour; Gerald Cubitt;

Gerald Cubitt; Gerald Cubitt. 257 T V Bulpin; Gordon Douglas; Gerald Cubitt. 258 A A Jorgensen; Gerald Cubitt. 259 A A Jorgensen; Gordon Douglas; Gordon Douglas. 260 Ralph King; T M Chaplin; Rhodesia Tourist Board. 261 Ralph King; Chris McBride/Ernest Stanton Publishers; Ralph King. 262 T V Bulpin. 263 Gordon Douglas. 264 Gerald Cubitt; Gordon Douglas; Gordon Douglas; T V Bulpin; T V Bulpin. 265 T V Bulpin; Gordon Douglas; Mary Evans Picture Library; T V Bulpin; Color Library; T V Bulpin; T V Bulpin. 267 Gordon Douglas; T V Bulpin; T V Bulpin; Gordon Douglas; T V Bulpin. 268 Both, T V Bulpin. 269 T V Bulpin; T V Bulpin; Gerald Cubitt. 270 Both, Gerald Cubitt. 271 Both, T V Bulpin. 272 Gerald Cubitt. 273 Satour; Gordon Douglas; T M Chaplin. 274 D C H Plowes; T V Bulpin; Satour. 275 D C H Plowes; Gerald Cubitt; Ralph King; Gerald Cubitt. 276 Gerald Cubitt. 277 Gerald Cubitt; Gerald Cubitt; Peter Barichievy; Ralph King; Peter Barichievy; Peter Barichievy; Gerald Cubitt; Gerald Cubitt; Peter Barichievy. 278 D C H Plowes; T V Bulpin. 279 Herman Potgieter; Ralph King; Herman Potgieter; Herman Potgieter; Satour. 280 Satour. 281 Satour; T V Bulpin. 282 Gordon Douglas. 283 Both, Sun International. 284-5 Gordon Douglas. 288 A A Jorgensen; Gordon Douglas; T V Bulpin. 289 August Sycholt. 291 Gerald Cubitt; Mary Evans Picture Library; Color Library. 292 Gordon Douglas; Gordon Douglas; Jean Morris; A A Jorgensen. 293 Gordon Douglas. 294 Color Library; August Sycholt; August Sycholt. 295 A A Jorgensen; Gerald Cubitt; A A Jorgensen; Gerald Cubitt. 296 A A Jorgensen; Peter Barichievy; D C H Plowes; Peter Barichievy; D C H Plowes. 297 Gordon Douglas; Gordon Douglas; Gerald Cubitt; Gordon Douglas; Gordon Douglas. 298 T V Bulpin. 299 Gordon Douglas; Gordon Douglas; T V Bulpin. 300 Gordon Douglas; Ralph King; Gordon Douglas. 301 Gerald Cubitt; Mary Evans Picture Library; T V Bulpin; Gerald Cubitt; Anthony Bannister. 302 Department of Tourism; T M Chaplin; Gordon Douglas. 303 Both, Gordon Douglas. 304 Ralph King; R W Robertson; Penny Miller. 305 Gerald Cubitt; Gordon Douglas; T V Bulpin; Gordon Douglas. 306 Satour; Color Library; Gordon Douglas. 307 Department of Tourism; Pretoria City Council; T V Bulpin; Gerald Cubitt; R W Robertson. 308 Both, T V Bulpin. 309 Gordon Douglas; T V Bulpin; Gerald Cubitt; T V Bulpin. 310 Satour; National Cultural History and Open-Air Museum; National Cultural History and Open-Air Museum. 311 T V Bulpin; T V Bulpin; Diagram, John Meek. 312 National Cultural History and Open-Air Museum; Pretoria City Council. 313 Illustration, David Wray; Gordon Douglas; Pretoria City Council. 314-5 Gordon Douglas. 319 T V Bulpin; Durban Publicity Association. 321 Department of Tourism; Herman Potgieter; Killie Campbell Africana Library; Killie Campbell Africana Library; Durban Publicity Association. 322 Gerald Cubitt; Gerald Cubitt; Herman Potgieter; Roger van der Molen; Herman Potgieter; Herman Potgieter.

323 Neville Poulter; Neville Poulter; Herman Potgieter. 324 Gerald Cubitt; Durban Publicity Association; Durban Publicity Association. 325 Herman Potgieter; Gerald Cubitt; Jean Morris; Jean Morris. 326 Durban Publicity Association; T V Bulpin; Gerald Cubitt. 327 Neville Poulter; Natal Anti-Shark Measures Board; Natal Anti-Shark Measures Board; Illustration, Michael Woods. 328 Department of Tourism. 329 Both, Gerald Cubitt. 330 T V Bulpin; Peter Steyn; Peter Steyn; T V Bulpin. 331 Jean Morris; T V Bulpin; T V Bulpin; T V Bulpin. 332 Both, T V Bulpin. 333 T V Bulpin; Illustration, Michael Woods. 335 Gerald Cubitt; Department of Tourism; Gordon Douglas. 336 T V Bulpin; Herman Potgieter; Gerald Cubitt. 337 Gordon Douglas; Will Till; Department of Tourism. 338 Gerald Cubitt. 339 Gerald Cubitt; Color Library; Simon van der Stel Foundation; Color Library. 340 T V Bulpin; Illustration, Barbara Tyrrell. 341 Satour; Illustration, Barbara Tyrrell. 342 T V Bulpin; Gerald Cubitt; Gerald Cubitt. 343 Gerald Cubitt. 344 Anthony Bannister. 345 Gerald Cubitt; Anthony Bannister. 346 Jean Morris; Popperfoto. 347 Gerald Cubitt; D C H Plowes; British Sugar Bureau; Huletts; Huletts. 348 Gerald Cubitt. 349 Gerald Cubitt; Gerald Cubitt; Jean Morris; Cabana Beach Hotel. 351 Gerald Cubitt; A A Jorgensen; Anthony Bannister; Anthony Bannister. 352 Gerald Cubitt; Jean Morris. 353 Gerald Cubitt; Gerald Cubitt; Gerald Cubitt; Jean Morris; Jean Morris; Jean Morris. 354 Local History Museum/Durban; Gerald Cubitt. 355 Gerald Cubitt; Gerald Cubitt; Gerald Cubitt; Anthony Bannister; Anthony Bannister; Peter Johnson. 356 Gordon Douglas; Gerald Cubitt; Gerald Cubitt. 357 Color Library; Jean Morris; Gerald Cubitt. 358 Jean Morris; Gordon Douglas; Local History Museum/Durban. 359 Gerald Cubitt; Jean Morris; Gerald Cubitt. 360 Gerald Cubitt; Gerald Cubitt; Jean Morris; Herman Potgieter. 361 Gordon Douglas; Gerald Cubitt; A A Jorgensen; A A Jorgensen. 362 Ralph King; Illustration, Barbara Tyrrell. 363 Gerald Cubitt; Gordon Douglas; Illustration, Barbara Tyrrell. 364 Anthony Bannister. 365 Gerald Cubitt; Linda Vergnani (Spencer-Smith). 366 Anthony Bannister; Gerald Cubitt; Gerald Cubitt. 367 Herman Potgieter; Mary Evans Picture Library. 368 Anthony Bannister; Natal Parks, Game and Fish Preservation Board; Gerald Cubitt; Natal Parks, Game and Fish Preservation Board; Natal Parks, Game and Fish Preservation Board. 369 Gerald Cubitt; Ralph King. 370 Jean Morris; Gerald Cubitt; Gerald Cubitt; Gerald Cubitt. 371 All, Gerald Cubitt. 372 All, Gerald

Cubitt. 373 Anthony Bannister; Gerald Cubitt; Color Library. 374 Gordon Douglas. 375 Pete Jurgens; August Sycholt. 376 Gordon Douglas. 377 Herman Potgieter; Herman Potgieter; August Sycholt. 378 Herman Potgieter. 379 Gordon Douglas; Illustration, Barbara Tyrrell. 380 Pete Jurgens; August Sycholt; D C H Plowes. 381 Gordon Douglas; Jean Morris. 382 D C H Plowes; P R Barnes; Peter Barichievy. 383 T V Bulpin; Gerald Cubitt. 384 Both, Gordon Douglas. 385 Harald Pager; Harald Pager; T V Bulpin; National Cultural History and Open-Air Museum; Harald Pager. 386 August Sycholt; D C H Plowes; Ralph King; A A Jorgensen. 387 Satour; Gordon Douglas. 388 Royal Albert Memorial Museum/Exeter; Cape Archives; Pretoria City Council; Pretoria City Council. 389 National Army Museum/Chelsea; Cape Archives; Cape Archives; Pretoria City Council; Cape Archives. 390 Cape Archives; National Army Museum/Chelsea; National Army Museum/Chelsea; Cape Archives; Pretoria City Council; Pretoria City Council; Cape Archives. 391 National Army Museum/Chelsea; Cape Archives; National Army Museum/Chelsea; Pretoria City Council; Cape Archives. 392-3 Herman Potgieter. 396 Alice Mertens. 397 Alice Mertens; Herman Potgieter. 398 Alice Mertens; Satour; T V Bulpin; Illustration, Barbara Tyrrell. 399 Herman Potgieter; T V Bulpin; Illustration, Barbara Tyrrell. 400 Herman Potgieter; August Sycholt; Alice Mertens. 401 Alice Mertens; Ralph King; Anthony Bannister. 402 T V Bulpin; with kind permission of C. Struik Publishers from 'Disaster Struck'; T V Bulpin. 403 T V Bulpin; T V Bulpin; T V Bulpin; Illustration, Barbara Tyrrell. 404 Both, August Sycholt. 405 T V Bulpin; Line illustrations, with kind permission of C. Struik Publishers from 'Shipwrecks off the Coast of Southern Africa'; Local History Museum/Durban; T V Bulpin. 406-7 A A Jorgensen. 410 All, Anthony Bannister. 411 Both, Anthony Bannister. 412 A A Jorgensen. 413 Dirk Schwager; Dirk Schwager; Gerald Cubitt; Gerald Cubitt; Satour. 414 A A Jorgensen; Gerald Cubitt. 415 Anthony Bannister; Gerald Cubitt; A A Jorgensen; A A Jorgensen. 416 Ralph King; A A Jorgensen; A A Jorgensen; Anthony Bannister. 417 Gerald Cubitt; Anthony Bannister; Peter Barichievy; Anthony Bannister; Peter Barichievy; Anthony Bannister; Gerald Cubitt. 418 Anthony Bannister; Gerald Cubitt; Anthony Bannister; A A Jorgensen. 419 A A Jorgensen; A A Jorgensen; Anthony Bannister. 420 All, Gerald Cubitt. 421 Satour; T V Bulpin; Gerald Cubitt. 422 Gordon

Douglas; remainder, Gerald Cubitt. 423 Anthony Bannister; Gerald Cubitt; Gerald Cubitt; Anthony Bannister. 424-5 Gordon Douglas. 429 Gordon Douglas; Dirk Schwager; Dirk Schwager; Dirk Schwager; Illustration, Barbara Tyrrell. 431 Dirk Schwager; Dirk Schwager; Dirk Schwager; Illustration, Barbara Tyrrell; Dirk Schwager; T V Bulpin. 436-7 Jean Morris; Dirk Schwager; August Sycholt; Dirk Schwager. 432 All, Dirk Schwager. 433 Dirk Schwager; August Sycholt; Dirk Schwager. 434 All, Dirk Schwager. 435 Gordon Douglas; Dirk Schwager; T V Bulpin. 436-7 Jean Morris. 440 Jean Morris. 441 Jean Morris; Sartoc. 442 Jean Morris; Jean Morris; Denoon Sieg; Gerald Cubitt; Anthony Bannister. 443 All, Peter Barichievy. 444 T V Bulpin; T M Chaplin; Jean Morris; Jean Morris; Dirk Schwager. 445 Dirk Schwager; Dirk Schwager; Dirk Schwager; A A Jorgensen. 446 Jean Morris; Dirk Schwager; Herman Potgieter; Illustration, Barbara Tyrrell. 447 Jean Morris; Illustration, Barbara Tyrrell. 449 T V Bulpin; Jean Morris; Sartoc. 450-1 Anthony Bannister. 454 H Vergnani; Gerald Cubitt. 455 Gerald Cubitt. 456 Gerald Cubitt. 457 Anthony Bannister; Gerald Cubitt, August Sycholt; Gerald Cubitt; August Sycholt. 458 Gerald Cubitt; T V Bulpin; Gerald Cubitt. 459 Gerald Cubitt; Gordon Douglas; Gerald Cubitt; Peter Barichievy; H Vergnani; Peter Barichievy; Peter Barichievy; Peter Barichievy. 460 Gerald Cubitt; remainder, D C H Plowes. 461 All, Gerald Cubitt. 462 Gerald Cubitt; Gordon Douglas; August Sycholt; H Vergnani; Gerald Cubitt. 463 Anthony Bannister; Gerald Cubitt; Anthony Bannister; Anthony Bannister. 464 All, Gerald Cubitt. 465 Gerald Cubitt; Ralph King; Gerald Cubitt; R W Robertson; Gerald Cubitt. 466 Gordon Douglas; T V Bulpin; T V Bulpin. 467 Nielen Shaefer; remainder, T V Bulpin. 468 Both, Gerald Cubitt. 469 Satour. 470 Satour; Anthony Bannister; Satour; Gerald Cubitt. 471 Anthony Bannister; Gerald Cubitt; Gerald Cubitt; Gordon Douglas; A A Jorgensen; Satour; H Vergnani; H Vergnani. 472 A A Jorgensen; Gerald Cubitt; A A Jorgensen; Nielen Shaefer. 473 Zimbabwe Tourist Board; Gerald Cubitt. 474 All, Gerald Cubitt. 475 Anthony Bannister; H Vergnani; Anthony Bannister. 476 Nielen Shaefer; A A Jorgensen, Gerald Cubitt; Gerald Cubitt. 477 Gerald Cubitt; Gerald Cubitt; Jean Morris; Gerald Cubitt; Gerald Cubitt. 478 Gerald Cubitt; August Sycholt. 479 Gerald Cubitt; Gerald Cubitt; Gerald Cubitt; Anthony Bannister. 480 Gerald Cubitt; Gerald Cubitt; Anthony Bannister; Gerald Cubitt; Gerald Cubitt; Gerald Cubitt; Anthony Bannister; Gerald Cubitt; Anthony Bannister. 481

Gerald Cubitt; D C H Plowes; Gerald Cubitt. 482-3 Zimbabwe Tourist Board. 487 Both, Color Library. 488 All, Will Till. 489 D C H Plowes; National Archives of Zimbabwe; Zimbabwe Tourist Board. 491 National Archives of Zimbabwe; remainder, Zimbabwe Tourist Board. 492 Jean Morris; Zimbabwe Tourist Board; T M Chaplin; Will Till; Zimbabwe Tourist Board; Zimbabwe Tourist Board. 493 Gordon Douglas; Anglo-American; Zimbabwe Tourist Board. 494 National Archives of Zimbabwe; T V Bulpin; T V Bulpin; Diagram, John Meek; National Archives of Zimbabwe. 495 T V Bulpin; Gordon Douglas; Anglo-American. 496 T V Bulpin; Will Till. 497 Gordon Douglas; Diagram, John Meek; T V Bulpin. 498 Color Library; T V Bulpin; Gordon Douglas; Diagram, John Meek; Zimbabwe Tourist Board; Zimbabwe Tourist Board. 499 T V Bulpin; Gordon Douglas; Zimbabwe Tourist Board. 501 Zimbabwe Tourist Board; National Archives of Zimbabwe. 502 Bulawayo Publicity Association; Bulawayo Publicity Association; remainder, Zimbabwe Tourist Board. 503 Both, National Archives of Zimbabwe. 504 Gordon Douglas; National Archives of Zimbabwe; Will Till. 505 Zimbabwe Tourist Board; Zimbabwe Tourist Board; T V Bulpin. 506 Ralph King; T V Bulpin. 507 Both, Zimbabwe Tourist Board. 508 D C H Plowes; D C H Plowes. 509 Zimbabwe Tourist Board; Ralph King; Will Till; T M Chaplin; D C H Plowes. 510 D C H Plowes. 511 Gordon Douglas; Zimbabwe Tourist Board/Ian Murphy; Zimbabwe Tourist Board. 512 D C H Plowes. 513 Zimbabwe Tourist Board; Gerald Cubitt; D C H Plowes; D C H Plowes. 514 Both, D C H Plowes. 515 Zimbabwe Tourist Board; August Sycholt; Zimbabwe Tourist Board; D C H Plowes. 516 D C H Plowes; T V Bulpin; Gerald Cubitt; D C H Plowes. 517 D C H Plowes; Zimbabwe Tourist Board; Zimbabwe Tourist Board. 518 Zimbabwe Tourist Board; D C H Plowes; D C H Plowes; August Sycholt. 519 Both, Zimbabwe Tourist Board. 521 Ralph King; T V Bulpin. 522 Zimbabwe Tourist Board; T V Bulpin; National Archives of Zimbabwe. 523 Zimbabwe Tourist Board. 524 Peter Johnson; T V Bulpin; Zimbabwe Tourist Board; Jean Morris. 525 Gordon Douglas; remainder, Zimbabwe Tourist Board. 526 Zimbabwe Tourist Board; Mary Evans Picture Library; T M Chaplin. 527 Will Till; Gordon Douglas; Diagram, John Meek; Zimbabwe Tourist Board. 528 Ralph King; Zimbabwe Tourist Board; Zimbabwe Tourist Board; Zimbabwe Tourist Board; National Archives of Zimbabwe. 529 Gordon Douglas.

Colour Separations by Hirt & Carter